W9-BBX-546

McDougal Littell

SENIOR AUTHORS Rick Billstein
Jim Williamson

McDougal Littell
Evanston, Illinois • Boston • Dallas

AUTHORS

SENIOR AUTHORS

Rick Billstein Department of Mathematical Sciences, University of Montana, Missoula, Montana

Jim Williamson Department of Mathematical Sciences, University of Montana, Missoula, Montana

CONSULTING AUTHORS

Perry Montoya Teacher, Mesa Public Schools, Mesa, Arizona

Jacqueline Lowery Teacher, Indian Queen Elementary School, Fort Washington, Maryland

Dianne Williams Teacher, Booker T. Washington Middle School for International Studies, Tampa, Florida

THE STEM PROJECT

Middle Grades Math Thematics® is based on the field-test versions of The STEM Project curriculum. The STEM Project was supported in part by the

under Grant No. ESI-9150114. Opinions expressed in *Middle Grades Math Thematics®* are those of the authors and not necessarily those of the National Science Foundation.

STEM WRITERS

Mary Buck, Clay Burkett, Lynn Churchill, Chris Clouse, Roslyn Denny, William Derrick, Sue Dolezal, Doug Galarus, Paul Kennedy, Pat Lamphere, Nancy Merrill, Perry Montoya, Sallie Morse, Marjorie Petit, Patrick Runkel, Thomas Sanders-Garrett, Richard T. Seitz, Bonnie Spence, Becky Sowders, Chris Tuckerman, Ken Wenger, Joanne Wilkie, Cheryl Wilson, Bente Winston

STEM TEACHER CONSULTANTS

Polly Fite, Jean Howard, Paul Sowden, Linda Tetley, Patricia Zepp

ABOUT THE COVER

The students shown on the back cover are from John Glenn Middle School in Maplewood, Minnesota.

ISBN 0-618-50170-3 3456789–VJM– 09 08 07 06

MIDDLE GRADES

MATH*Thematics*

WELCOME

COURSE GOALS

This course will help you:

- Learn all the important middle grades mathematics concepts and skills that prepare you for high school and beyond.
- Develop the reasoning, problem solving, and communication skills that enable you to apply mathematics to real-life activities.
- Value mathematics and become confident in using it to make decisions in daily life.

SUCCESS THROUGH EXPLORING MATHEMATICS

Theme Approach

You will be learning through thematic modules that connect mathematical concepts to real-world applications.

Active Learning

The lessons in this course will get you actively involved in exploring, modeling, and communicating mathematics using a variety of tools, including technology when appropriate.

Varied Practice and Assessment

The variety of types of practice and assessment will help reinforce and extend your understanding. You will learn to assess your own progress as you go along.

MAKING CHOICES

Connecting the Theme *Many real-world situations require people to make choices and decisions. You'll see how mathematics can help you analyze situations in your daily life and make wise decisions.*

Module Features

Assessment Options

SEARCH and RESCUE

74

Connecting the Theme *When a hiker is lost, a plane goes down, or a boat is missing, a Search and Rescue team is called in to find them. You'll investigate some of the mathematics related to search and rescue operations.*

Module Features

Assessment Options

A UNIVERSAL LANGUAGE

Connecting the Theme *By exploring how mathematics has been used in other countries and in other times, you'll see why it is called "a universal language."*

Module Features

Assessment Options

The ART of MOTION

230

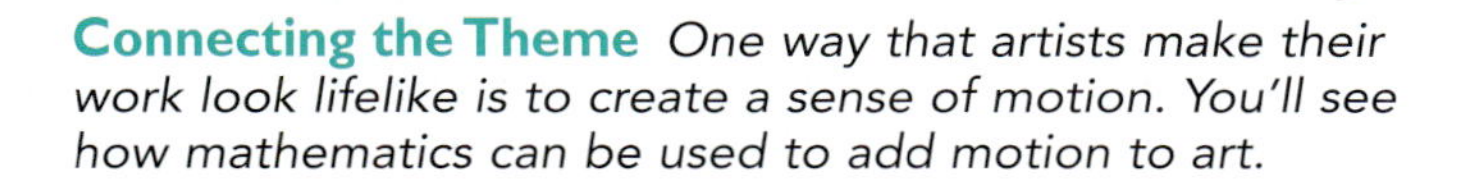

Connecting the Theme *One way that artists make their work look lifelike is to create a sense of motion. You'll see how mathematics can be used to add motion to art.*

Module Features

Assessment Options

RECREATION

Connecting the Theme *People relax in many different ways, such as running, attending movies, and playing sports. You'll investigate some of the mathematics related to recreational activities.*

Module Features

Assessment Options

FLIGHTS of FANCY

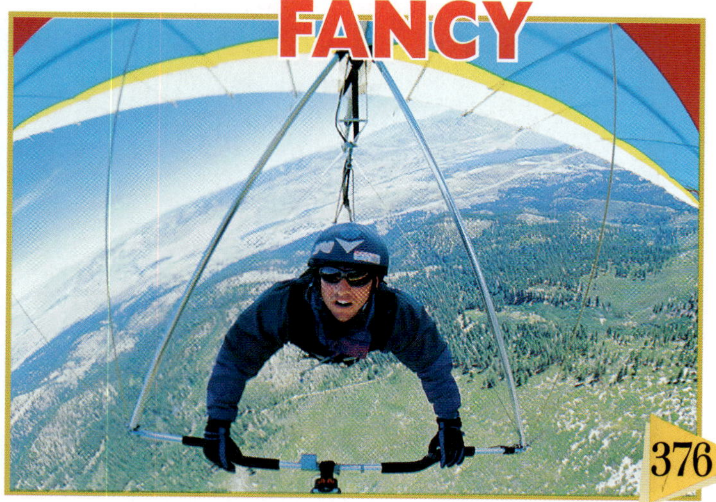

376

Connecting the Theme *In this module, you will explore the flight of humans, birds, kites, and even a whale! You'll construct models to interpret and solve problems.*

Module Features

Assessment Options

HEALTH and FITNESS

Module Features

Assessment Options

Connecting the Theme *People must make decisions about health issues every day. You'll learn how mathematics can help you make good health choices about nutrition, exercise, and adequate rest.*

HEART of the CITY

MODULE 8

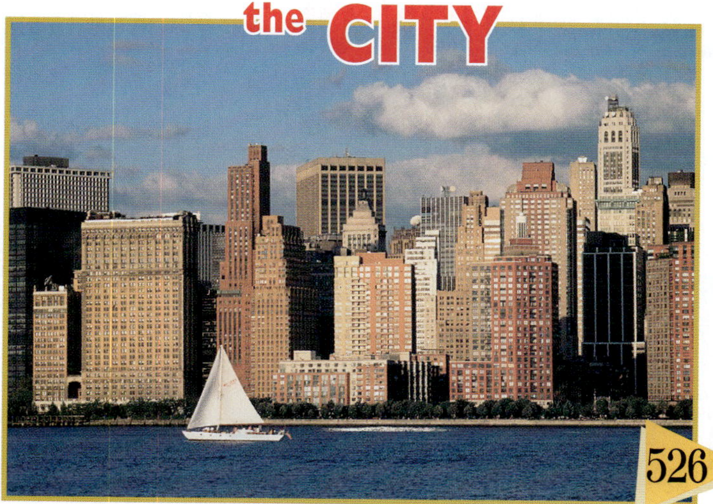

526

Connecting the Theme *Managing traffic, constructing sky-scrapers, and designing plazas all depend on mathematics. You'll see how mathematics can be used as a tool to help organize many aspects of city life.*

Module Features

Assessment Options

STUDENT RESOURCES

ORGANIZATION OF THE BOOK

This book contains eight modules. To get an overview of the modules and their themes, look at the Table of Contents starting on p. iv.

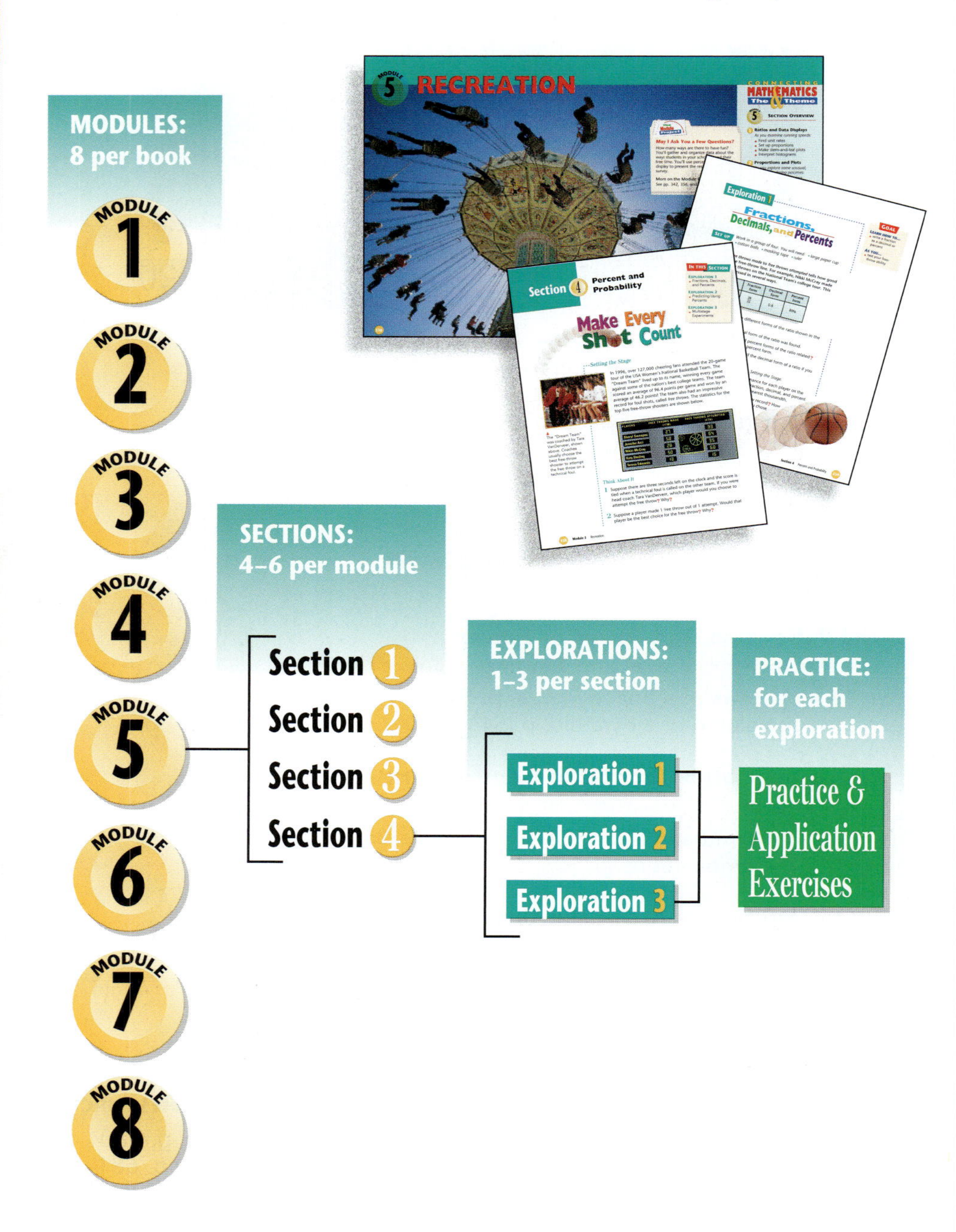

Module Theme & Project

Each module's theme connects the mathematics you are learning to the real world. *Recreation* is the theme of Module 5. The Module Project that you'll work on is introduced at the beginning of the module.

Connecting Mathematics and the Theme
The math topics you'll be learning and the settings in which you'll be learning them.

MODULE 5 RECREATION

The Module Project

May I Ask You a Few Questions?

How many ways are there to have fun? You'll gather and organize data about the ways students in your school spend their free time. You'll use percents and a visual display to present the results of your survey.

More on the Module Project
See pp. 342, 356, and 373.

CONNECTING MATHEMATICS & The Theme

MODULE 5 SECTION OVERVIEW

1 **Ratios and Data Displays**
As you examine running speeds:
- Find unit rates
- Set up proportions
- Make stem-and-leaf plots
- Interpret histograms

2 **Proportions and Plots**
As you explore some unusual, thrilling, or daring pastimes:
- Solve proportions using cross products
- Make a scatter plot
- Fit a line to a scatter plot
- Interpret box-and-whisker plots

3 **Percent**
As you analyze movie ratings:
- Estimate and find percents
- Find a missing part or whole

4 **Percent and Probability**
As you study sports statistics:
- Write a fraction as a decimal or a percent
- Use percents to make

310

The Module Project
As you learn new math skills, you can apply them to your work on the Module Project. By the end of the module, you'll be able to complete the project and to present your results.

Completing the Module Project

May I Ask You a Few Questions?

You have gathered and organized data about the free time of students in your school. In order for your survey to be useful, you must now share your findings. In this module you have learned several ways to present data.

Choosing a Data Display Many magazines and newspapers display survey results in bar graphs, line plots, histograms, or tables. Often the data is in percent form. But no matter the form, the visual display of the data must be clear and informative.

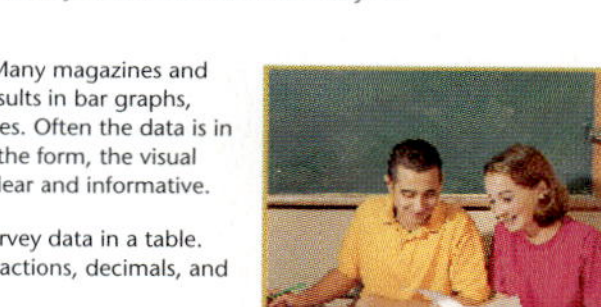

7. Summarize your class survey data in a table. Present the data using fractions, decimals, and percents.

8. Make a general statement about the results shown in the table that you made in Project Question 7. Does the statement answer the topic question? Explain.

9. Decide what type of visual display, other than a table, would best organize your data. Create your display. Be sure to include a title.

10. Explain your choice of visual display in Project Question 9. Why do you think your choice is a good way to show the data? Does it answer the topic question as well as the table you created in Project Question 7? Why or why not?

11. If you were to organize another survey, what topic would you research? What would you do differently?

Section 4 Completing the Module Project  373

SECTION OVERVIEW

SECTION ORGANIZATION

The diagram below illustrates the organization of a section:

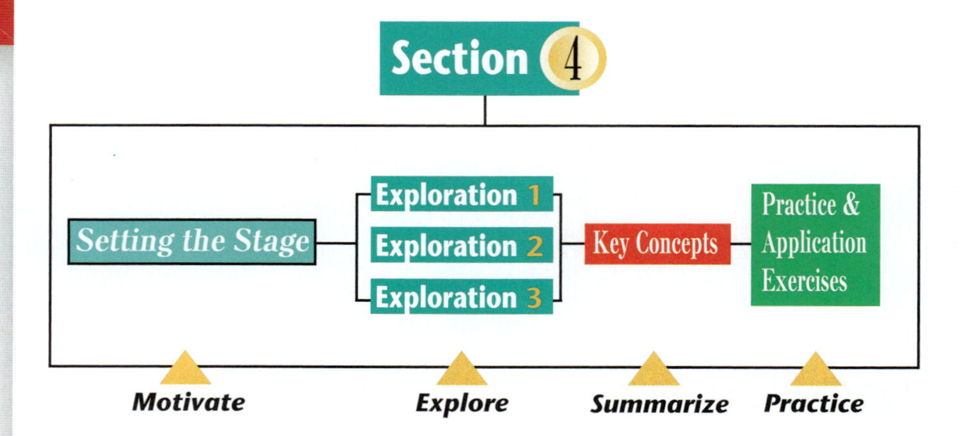

Section 4 **Percent and Probability**

IN THIS SECTION
- **EXPLORATION 1** Fractions, Decimals, and Percents
- **EXPLORATION 2** Predicting Using Percents
- **EXPLORATION 3** Multi-stage Experiments

Section Title and Math Focus
The title of Section 4 is *Make Every Shot Count*. Its math focus is *Percent and Probability*.

Setting the Stage

Setting the Stage begins with a reading, graph, activity, or game to introduce the section.

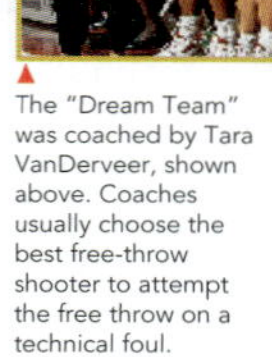

The "Dream Team" was coached by Tara VanDerveer, shown above. Coaches usually choose the best free-throw shooter to attempt the free throw on a technical foul.

In 1996, over 127,000 cheerir... tour of the USA Women's Nat... "Dream Team" lived up to its ... against some of the nation's b... scored an average of 96.4 poi... average of 46.2 points! The te... record for foul shots, called *fr*... top five free-throw shooters are shown below.

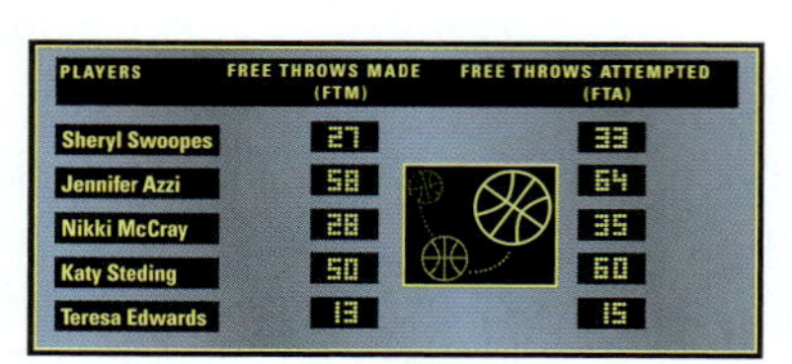

PLAYERS	FREE THROWS MADE (FTM)	FREE THROWS ATTEMPTED (FTA)
Sheryl Swoopes	27	33
Jennifer Azzi	58	64
Nikki McCray	28	35
Katy Steding	50	60
Teresa Edwards	13	15

Think About It

1 Suppose there are three seconds left on the clock and the score is tied when a technical foul is called on the other team. If you were head coach Tara VanDerveer, which player would you choose to attempt the free throw? Why?

2 Suppose a player made 1 free throw out of 1 attempt. Would that player be the best choice for the free throw? Why?

EXPLORATIONS & KEY CONCEPTS

In the explorations you'll be actively involved in investigating math concepts, learning math skills, and solving problems.

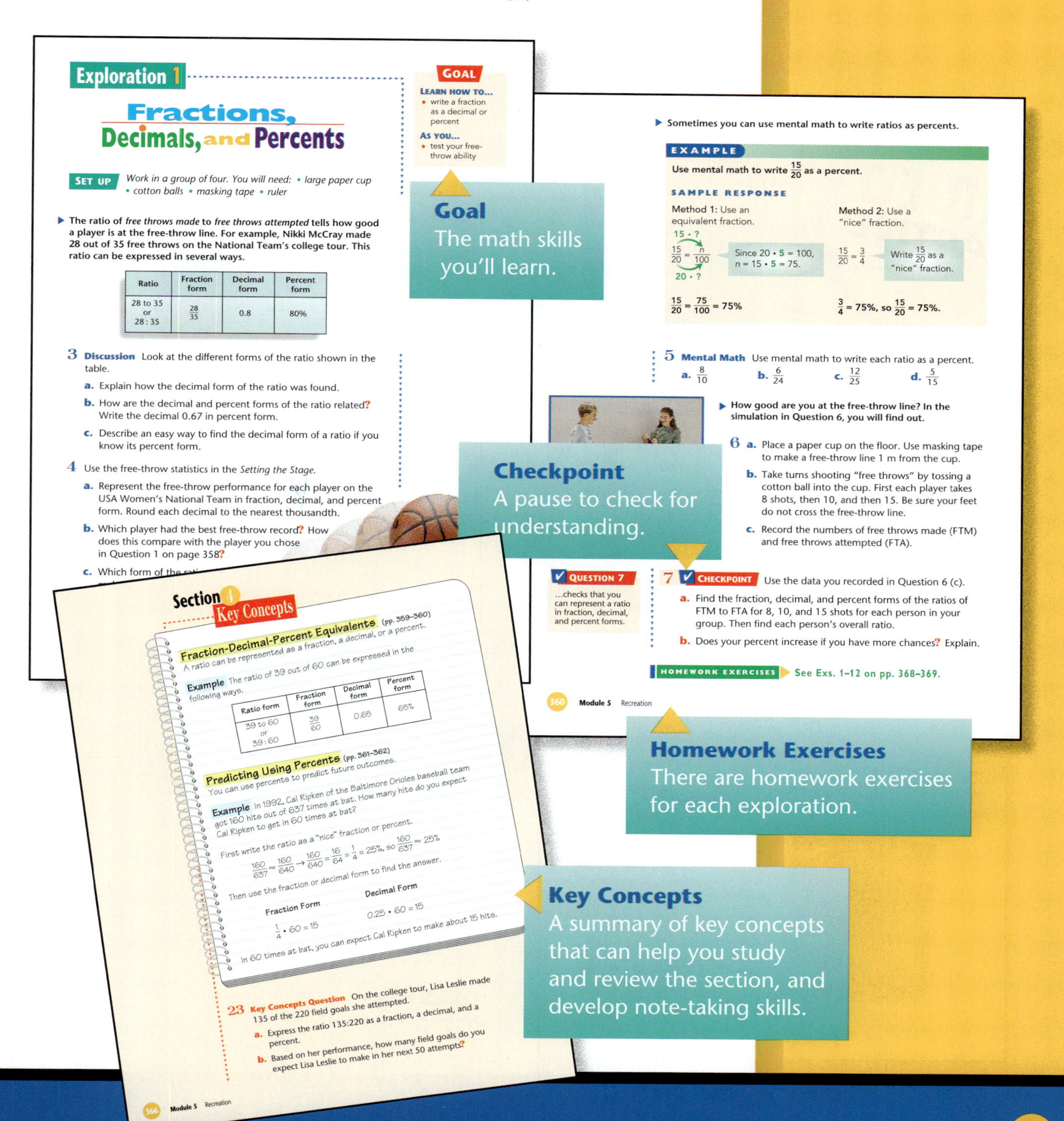

Exploration 1

Fractions, Decimals, and Percents

GOAL

LEARN HOW TO...
- write a fraction as a decimal or percent

AS YOU...
- test your free-throw ability

SET UP *Work in a group of four. You will need:* • *large paper cup* • *cotton balls* • *masking tape* • *ruler*

▶ **The ratio of** ***free throws made*** **to** ***free throws attempted*** **tells how good a player is at the free-throw line. For example, Nikki McCray made 28 out of 35 free throws on the National Team's college tour. This ratio can be expressed in several ways.**

Ratio	Fraction form	Decimal form	Percent form
28 to 35 or 28 : 35	$\frac{28}{35}$	0.8	80%

3 Discussion Look at the different forms of the ratio shown in the table.

a. Explain how the decimal form of the ratio was found.

b. How are the decimal and percent forms of the ratio related? Write the decimal 0.67 in percent form.

c. Describe an easy way to find the decimal form of a ratio if you know its percent form.

4 Use the free-throw statistics in the *Setting the Stage*.

a. Represent the free-throw performance for each player on the USA Women's National Team in fraction, decimal, and percent form. Round each decimal to the nearest thousandth.

b. Which player had the best free-throw record? How does this compare with the player you chose in Question 1 on page 358?

c. Which form of the ra...

▶ **Sometimes you can use mental math to write ratios as percents.**

EXAMPLE

Use mental math to write $\frac{15}{20}$ as a percent.

SAMPLE RESPONSE

Method 1: Use an equivalent fraction.

$\frac{15}{20} = \frac{n}{100}$ (15 • ? ; 20 • ?)

Since 20 • 5 = 100, n = 15 • 5 = 75.

$\frac{15}{20} = \frac{75}{100} = 75\%$

Method 2: Use a "nice" fraction.

$\frac{15}{20} = \frac{3}{4}$ Write $\frac{15}{20}$ as a "nice" fraction.

$\frac{3}{4} = 75\%$, so $\frac{15}{20} = 75\%$.

5 Mental Math Use mental math to write each ratio as a percent.

a. $\frac{8}{10}$ b. $\frac{6}{24}$ c. $\frac{12}{25}$ d. $\frac{5}{15}$

▶ **How good are you at the free-throw line? In the simulation in Question 6, you will find out.**

6 a. Place a paper cup on the floor. Use masking tape to make a free-throw line 1 m from the cup.

b. Take turns shooting "free throws" by tossing a cotton ball into the cup. First each player takes 8 shots, then 10, and then 15. Be sure your feet do not cross the free-throw line.

c. Record the numbers of free throws made (FTM) and free throws attempted (FTA).

QUESTION 7 ...checks that you can represent a ratio in fraction, decimal, and percent forms.

7 CHECKPOINT Use the data you recorded in Question 6 (c).

a. Find the fraction, decimal, and percent forms of the ratios of FTM to FTA for 8, 10, and 15 shots for each person in your group. Then find each person's overall ratio.

b. Does your percent increase if you have more chances? Explain.

HOMEWORK EXERCISES ▶ See Exs. 1–12 on pp. 368–369.

360 Module 5 Recreation

Section 1 Key Concepts

Fraction-Decimal-Percent Equivalents (pp. 359–360)

A ratio can be represented as a fraction, a decimal, or a percent.

Example The ratio of 39 out of 60 can be expressed in the following ways.

Ratio form	Fraction form	Decimal form	Percent form
39 to 60 or 39 : 60	$\frac{39}{60}$	0.65	65%

Predicting Using Percents (pp. 361–362)

You can use percents to predict future outcomes.

Example In 1992, Cal Ripken of the Baltimore Orioles baseball team got 160 hits out of 637 times at bat. How many hits do you expect Cal Ripken to get in 60 times at bat?

First write the ratio as a "nice" fraction or percent.

$\frac{160}{637} \approx \frac{160}{640} \rightarrow \frac{160}{640} = \frac{16}{64} = \frac{1}{4} = 25\%$, so $\frac{160}{637} \approx 25\%$

Then use the fraction or decimal form to find the answer.

Fraction Form: $\frac{1}{4} \cdot 60 = 15$

Decimal Form: $0.25 \cdot 60 = 15$

In 60 times at bat, you can expect Cal Ripken to make about 15 hits.

23 Key Concepts Question On the college tour, Lisa Leslie made 135 of the 220 field goals she attempted.

a. Express the ratio 135:220 as a fraction, a decimal, and a percent.

b. Based on her performance, how many field goals do you expect Lisa Leslie to make in her next 50 attempts?

366 Module 5 Recreation

SECTION OVERVIEW

PRACTICE & APPLICATION

Practice and Application Exercises will give you a chance to practice the skills and concepts in the explorations and apply them in solving many types of problems.

Balanced Practice
These exercises develop numerical and problem solving skills, and the ability to write about and discuss mathematics.

Section 4 Practice & Application Exercises

1. **Basketball** In the 1996 NCAA women's college basketball championship game, Tennessee beat Georgia 83 to 65. The table shows some of the field-goal statistics for four Tennessee players from that game. Represent each player's field-goal performance in fraction, decimal, and percent forms. Round each decimal to the nearest thousandth.

Player	Field goals made	Field goals attempted
Goldsclaw	6	16
Conklin	5	8
Marciniak	5	13
T. Johnson	7	10

Baseball A player's batting average is the decimal form of the ratio of *number of hits* to *times at bat* rounded to the nearest thousandth.

Find the 1992 batting average for each player.

2. David Justice (Braves): 124 for 484
3. Barry Larkin (Reds): 162 for 533
4. Frank Thomas (White Sox): 185 for 573
5. Bip Roberts of the Cincinnati Reds and Jon Kruk of the Philadelphia Phillies both had .323 batting averages in 1992, which were high enough for third and fourth place in the National League batting average race. Roberts had 172 hits in 532 times at bat. Kruk had 164 hits in 507 times at bat. Which player was in third place? How did you find your answer?

Luis Ulacia is shown rounding third base after hitting a home run in the first inning of the game against the United States.

6. **Olympics** On July 28, 1996, the United States Olympic baseball team lost to the defending Olympic championship team from Cuba by a sco of 10–8. Find the batting average for each player the game whose batting results are shown in the table. Represent each average in fraction, decima and percent form.

Player	Hits	Times at bat
Ulacia (Cuba)	2	5
Paret (Cuba)	1	3
Lee (U.S.A.)	3	4
Glaus (U.S.A.)	1	4

368 Module 5 Recreation

Consider the experiment of flipping a coin and rolling an 8-sided die. Shade a grid to find the probability of each event.

18. heads and the number 6
19. tails and a number less than 4
20. tails and an odd number
21. heads and a number greater than 2
22. Suppose this spinner is spun twice.
   a. **Writing** Which of the grids below could you shade to find the probability that the first spin will be red and the second spin will be blue? Explain.

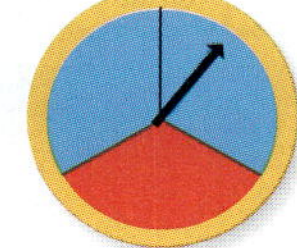

A. 10×10 grid B. 3×3 grid C. 3×6 grid

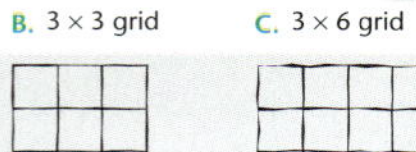

   b. Copy the grid you chose in part (a). Shade it to find the probability that the first spin is red and the second is blue.
23. A box contains two red and three blue marbles. Three marbles are removed from the box one after another without looking. After each marble is removed, its color is recorded and the marble is put back into the box before the next marble is removed.
   a. Copy and complete this tree diagram to show the outcomes of this experiment. Label each branch of the tree with the probability.
   b. Use the tree diagram to find the probability of each event.
   • removing three red marbles

first marble
R
B

Reflecting on the Section
helps you pull together what you've learned in the form of an oral report, journal writing, visual thinking, research, or a discussion.

24. **Challenge** Suppose three marbles are removed from the box in Exercise 23 one after another, but each marble is not replaced before the next marble is removed. Repeat parts (a) and (b) of Exercise 23 for this experiment.

Reflecting on the Section

25. During her previous basketball games this season, Alyssa made 20 free throws in 40 attempts. She calculated her free-throw percent to be 50%. In today's game, she made 10 free throws out of 10 attempts, or 100%. Alyssa thinks her free-throw percent is now 75%. Is she correct? Explain.

Journal
Exercise 25 checks that you understand how to use percent to make predictions

Spiral Review

Solve each proportion. (Module 5, p. 352)

26. $\frac{18}{12} = \frac{24}{x}$ 27. $\frac{3}{13} = \frac{x}{325}$ 28. $\frac{x}{100} = \frac{4}{5}$ 29. $\frac{5}{x} = \frac{2}{20}$

ADDITIONAL PRACTICE

At the end of every section, you'll find Extra Skill Practice. You can use these exercises to check that you understand important skills before starting the next section.

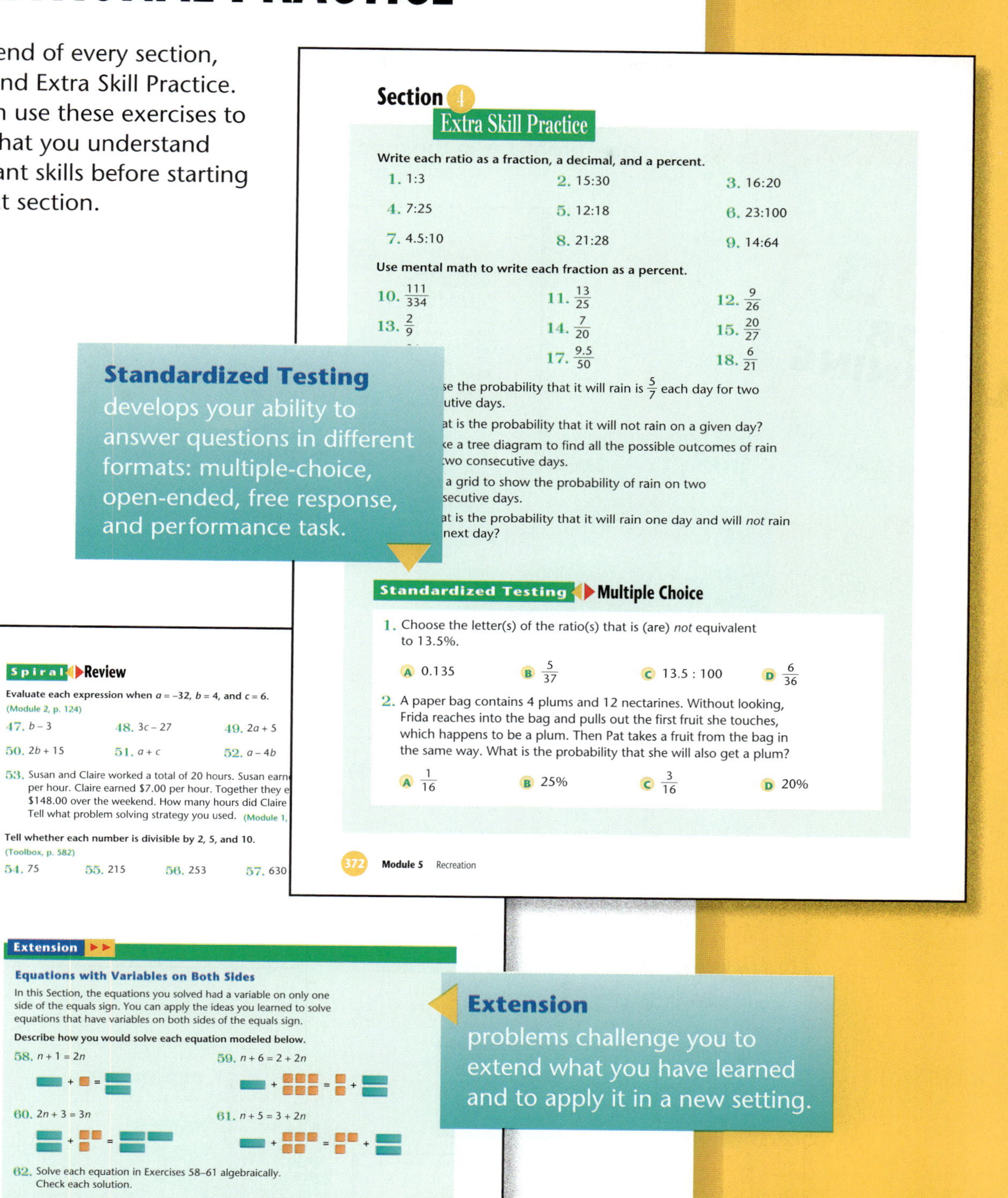

Section 4 Extra Skill Practice

Write each ratio as a fraction, a decimal, and a percent.

1. 1:3
2. 15:30
3. 16:20
4. 7:25
5. 12:18
6. 23:100
7. 4.5:10
8. 21:28
9. 14:64

Use mental math to write each fraction as a percent.

10. $\frac{111}{334}$
11. $\frac{13}{25}$
12. $\frac{9}{26}$
13. $\frac{2}{9}$
14. $\frac{7}{20}$
15. $\frac{20}{27}$
17. $\frac{9.5}{50}$
18. $\frac{6}{21}$

...se the probability that it will rain is $\frac{5}{7}$ each day for two ...utive days.

...at is the probability that it will not rain on a given day?

...ke a tree diagram to find all the possible outcomes of rain ...two consecutive days.

... a grid to show the probability of rain on two ...secutive days.

...at is the probability that it will rain one day and will *not* rain ...next day?

Standardized Testing ▸ Multiple Choice

1. Choose the letter(s) of the ratio(s) that is (are) *not* equivalent to 13.5%.

   A 0.135 B $\frac{5}{37}$ C 13.5 : 100 D $\frac{6}{36}$

2. A paper bag contains 4 plums and 12 nectarines. Without looking, Frida reaches into the bag and pulls out the first fruit she touches, which happens to be a plum. Then Pat takes a fruit from the bag in the same way. What is the probability that she will also get a plum?

   A $\frac{1}{16}$ B 25% C $\frac{3}{16}$ D 20%

372 Module 5 Recreation

Spiral ▸ Review

Evaluate each expression when $a = -32$, $b = 4$, and $c = 6$. (Module 2, p. 124)

47. $b - 3$
48. $3c - 27$
49. $2a + 5$
50. $2b + 15$
51. $a + c$
52. $a - 4b$

53. Susan and Claire worked a total of 20 hours. Susan earn... per hour. Claire earned $7.00 per hour. Together they e... $148.00 over the weekend. How many hours did Claire... Tell what problem solving strategy you used. (Module 1,...

Tell whether each number is divisible by 2, 5, and 10. (Toolbox, p. 582)

54. 75
55. 215
56. 253
57. 630

Extension ▸▸

Equations with Variables on Both Sides

In this Section, the equations you solved had a variable on only one side of the equals sign. You can apply the ideas you learned to solve equations that have variables on both sides of the equals sign.

Describe how you would solve each equation modeled below.

58. $n + 1 = 2n$
59. $n + 6 = 2 + 2n$
60. $2n + 3 = 3n$
61. $n + 5 = 3 + 2n$

62. Solve each equation in Exercises 58–61 algebraically. Check each solution.

63. a. Does the equation $x + 35 = x + 13$ have a solution? Explain.
    b. Does the equation $x + 4 = 4 + x$ have a solution? Explain.

Standardized Testing develops your ability to answer questions in different formats: multiple-choice, open-ended, free response, and performance task.

Extension problems challenge you to extend what you have learned and to apply it in a new setting.

TECHNOLOGY OVERVIEW

CALCULATORS & COMPUTERS

There are many opportunities to use calculators, as well as mental-math and paper-and-pencil methods. Special Technology pages show you how to use computer programs to explore concepts and solve problems in the module.

GOAL

LEARN HOW TO...
- multiply and divide decimals by powers of 10
- write numbers in scientific notation

AS YOU...
- look at calculator displays

KEY TERM
- scientific notation

Exploration 3

Scientific Notation

SET UP *You will need:* • *Labsheet 4B* • *calculator*

▶ **The number of digits a calculator can display is limited, but calculations with large (or small) numbers are still possible. A universal method is used to represent large and small numbers.**

23 **Try This as a Class** For parts (a) and (b), describe how the results are displayed on a calculator as the steps are carried out.

a. Clear the calculator and then enter 10. Multiply by 10 and look at the result. Continue multiplying by 10 and looking at the result at least 20 times.

b. Clear the calculator and then enter 10. Divide by 10 and look at the result. Continue dividing by 10 and looking at the result at least 20 times.

c. What did the calculator display after completing part (a)? part (b)? Why does this happen?

24 **Discussion** Most calculators have a special way to display large and small numbers. Three displays for the same number are shown.

1E15 1e+15 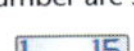

hat number is represented by the displays?

rite this number in standard form.

hy is the number not displayed in standard form?

nd Quotients with Powers of 10 Suppose a calculator 3456e+13. This is the same as 1.23456 • 10^{13}, a decimal ltiplied by a power of ten.

et 4B for Questions 25 and 26.

the directions on Labsheet 4B to complete the *Product Table.*

Using Calculators

Calculators can be especially useful as a problem solving tool. The questions on this page help make calculator use meaningful.

TECHNOLOGY **Using Spreadsheet Software**

You can use most spreadsheets to create a bar graph for Question 16(a).

Step 1 Enter the data for the graph into the spreadsheet. The categories for the bars (the amounts of time in hours) should be entered in column A as text. The data for the lengths of the bars (the average mathematics proficiencies) should be entered in column B.

File Edit Format Calculate Options View

AVERAGE MATH PROFICIENCY

B6 × ✓ 245

	A	B	C	D	E	F
1	Time (hours)	Average math proficiency				
2	1 or less	269				
3	2	268				
4	3	265				
5	4 or 5	260				
6	6 or more	245				

Step 2 To make a graph, highlight the data you entered and select the option that lets you make a chart. Then select the type of graph you want to make.

Options
Make Chart...
Protect Cells
Unprotect Cells
Add Page Break
Remove Page Break
Lock Title Position
Print Range...
Go To Cell...

Chart Options
Modify: Axis, Series, Labels, General
Gallery: Bar, Line, Scatter, Pie, Stacked Bar, X–Y Line, X–Y Scatter, Pictogram

Step 3 Experiment with the labels, grid lines, and scale until the graph appears the way you want it to.

Eighth Grade Students' Television Viewing and Math Proficiency
Average math proficiency: 270, 260, 250, 240, 230
1 or less, 2, 3, 4 to 5, 6 or more
Time (hours)

64 **Module 1** Making Choices

Using Computers

Technology pages illustrate the use of spreadsheet, graphing, statistical, probability, and drawing software.

ASSESSMENT & PORTFOLIOS

In each module there are a number of questions and projects that help you check your progress and reflect on what you have learned. These pages are listed under *Assessment Options* in the Table of Contents.

E^2 stands for Extended Exploration — a problem solving project that you'll want to add to your portfolio.

Wrap It Up

SET UP *You will need:* • *paper bag* • *scissors* • *tape or glue* • *ruler*

The Situation

Many of the products we buy in stores come in boxes. The shapes of boxes are chosen for various reasons, such as shelf size or ease of handling. Package designers must also think about the amount of material used to create them. Reducing the total area of the outside surface of the box is a major factor in any package design.

The Problem

What is the biggest box that can be wrapped using a paper bag?

Something to Think About

- What kind of space figure is a box?
- How can making a net help you solve the problem?
- What measure(s) do you need to maximize in order to produce the biggest box?
- Is there any other information you need to obtain before you can begin working on this problem? If so, what is it?

Present Your Results

Give an oral report describing how you created your box design. Include the volume and the surface area of the box. Be sure to display your net and the b

Student Self-Assessment

Student Resource

If your score is in the shaded area, explain why on the back of this sheet and stop.

The star indicates that you excelled in some way.

Problem Solving

1 I did not understand the problem well enough to get started or I did not show any work.
2
3 I understood the problem well enough to make a plan and to work toward a solution.
4
5 I made a plan, I used it to solve the problem, and I verified my solution.

Mathematical Language

1 I did not use any mathematical vocabulary or symbols, or I did not use them correctly, or my use was not appropriate.
2
3 I used appropriate mathematical language, but the way it was used was not always correct or other terms and symbols were needed.
4
5 I used mathematical language that was correct and appropriate to make my meaning clear.

Representations

5 I used appropriate and correct representations to solve the problem or explain my solution.

5 I extended the ideas in the solution to the general case, or I showed how this problem relates to other problems, mathematical ideas, or applications.

5 The presentation of my solution and reasoning is clear and can be understood by others.

Module 1 Extended Exploration 49

Assessing Problem Solving

For each E^2, you can use the Student Self-Assessment Scales. They will help you become a better problem solver.

MODULE 5 Review and Assessment

Write each rate as a unit rate. (Sec. 1, Explor. 1)

1. $\frac{95 \text{ min}}{11 \text{ mi}}$
2. $\frac{\$15}{4 \text{ lb}}$
3. $\frac{86 \text{ mi}}{3 \text{ gal}}$
4. $\frac{250 \text{ km}}{16 \text{ L}}$

Use the table for Exercises 5–7. (Sec. 1, Explor. 2)

5. Make a stem-and-leaf plot of the data. Be sure to include a key and a title.
6. Find the range, the mean, the median, and the mode for the data.
7. Colorado has about 160,000 acres of state parkland. Suppose you include Colorado in the list. How would your stem-and-leaf plot change?

Use the histogram for Exercises 8–10. (Sec. 1, Explor. 3)

Areas of State Parks in 10 States (in thousands)

State	Acres (in thousands)
Alabama	48
Arkansas	45
Georgia	60
Hawaii	25
Idaho	44
Kansas	37
Maine	72
Montana	47
Rhode Island	8
Virginia	50

Module Review and Assessment

Each module ends with exercises to help you review and assess what you've learned.

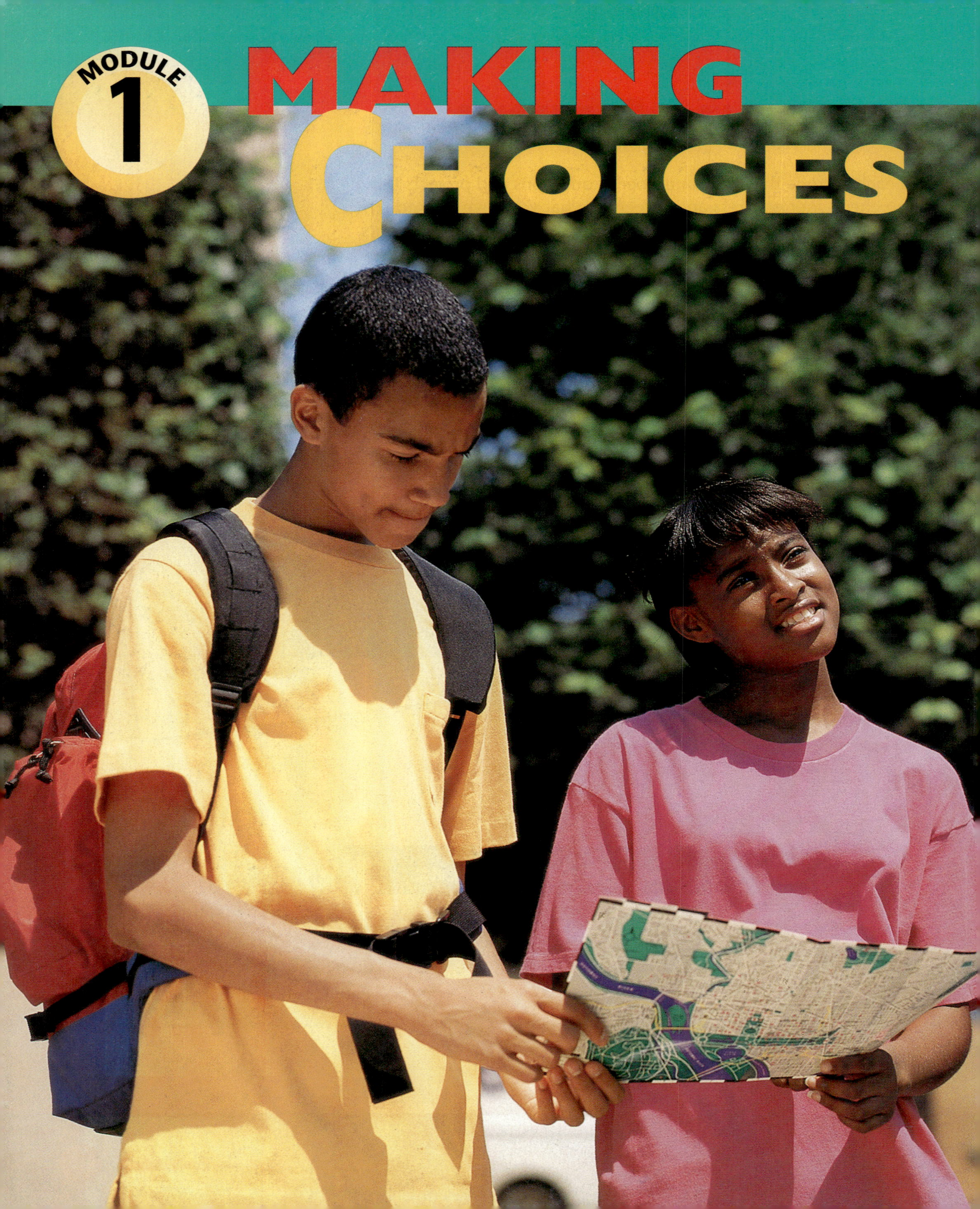
MODULE
1
MAKING
CHOICES

CONNECTING MATHEMATICS & The Theme

MODULE 1 SECTION OVERVIEW

1 Data Displays

As you consider Olympic athletes' decisions:

- Interpret bar and line graphs
- Make frequency tables

2 Sequences and Exponents

As you find patterns and use them to make predictions:

- Represent sequences with graphs and equations
- Predict terms of sequences
- Use exponents in expressions
- Find the volume of a cube

3 Probability

As you decide on a game strategy:

- Find theoretical and experimental probabilities of events

4 Problem Solving

As you predict the effect of lifestyle changes on health:

- Solve problems using a 4-step approach

5 Assessing Problem Solving

As you explore how to become a more creative problem solver:

- Evaluate solutions and make connections to other problems

6 Expressions and Representations

As you think about ways to improve your mathematical language skills:

- Use the order of operations to evaluate expressions
- Choose a bar or a line graph

The Module Project: Tune In to Data

How do television advertisers try to influence your choice? You'll collect data to research this question. For a presentation of what you have learned, you'll choose appropriate representations for your data.

More on the Module Project

See pp. 11, 38, 46, 69, and 71.

INTERNET
To learn more about the theme:
http://www.mlmath.com

Section 1 Data Displays

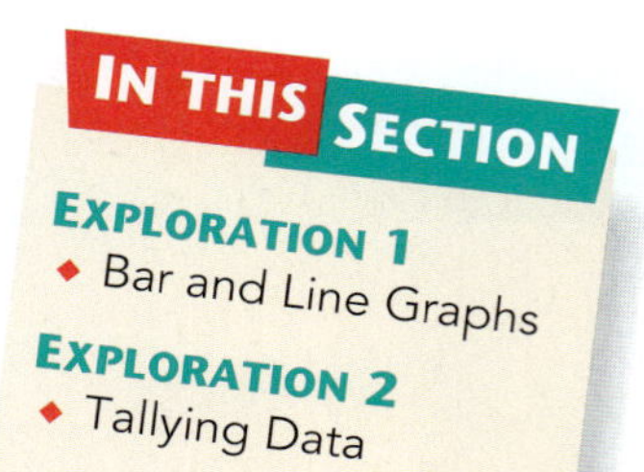

Going for the GOLD

Setting the Stage

Did you ever dream of winning an Olympic gold medal? Earning a spot on an Olympic team requires more than skill and a love of the sport.

A newspaper surveyed the 1994 United States Winter Olympics team about what they gave up for their sport. The graph shows the results.

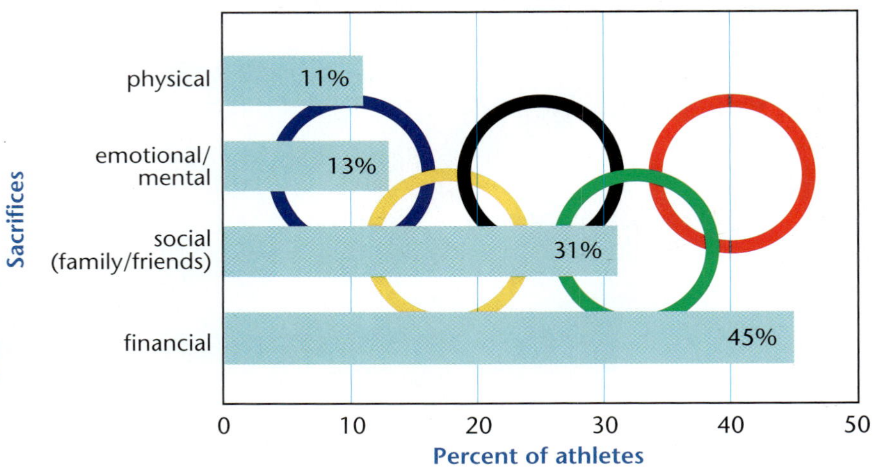

"What's vacation? Between skiing and school, I don't get too much time for it."
—Nikki Stone, freestyle skier

Think About It

1 What did most athletes feel was their greatest sacrifice?

2 The bar for athletes whose sacrifice was financial is about how many times as long as the bar for those who said it was physical?

Like athletes, you must make choices in situations you meet every day. In this module, you'll learn skills to help you make wise decisions.

Exploration 1

BAR and Line GRAPHS

GOAL

LEARN HOW TO...
- interpret data in percent form
- interpret bar and line graphs

AS YOU...
- explore data about the Olympics and education

KEY TERMS
- bar graph
- vertical axis
- percent
- horizontal axis
- line graph
- interval

Some of the choices you have in life are minor ones: *What should I wear today?* Others will be more important: *What classes should I take?* And some will even affect your well-being: *Is it okay for me to smoke?*

▶ **When you make a decision, you need information about the choices. Sometimes this information comes in the form of a bar graph, which displays data that fall into distinct categories.**

Use the bar graph on page 2 for Questions 3–7.

3 Every graph should have a title.

a. Who was surveyed?

b. What information is displayed in the graph?

4 Graphs should be clearly labeled. The categories for this bar graph appear along the **vertical axis**. What does the label "Financial" mean?

▶ **The symbol % on the bar graph stands for *percent*. Percent means "per hundred" or "out of 100."**

45%

45 percent

45 per 100

45 out of 100

FOR ▶ HELP with *percent*, see **TOOLBOX, p. 588**

5 The **horizontal axis** of the bar graph is labeled with a scale of numbers. What do the numbers on this graph represent?

6 **Try This as a Class** Use the concept of percent.

a. How many athletes responded to the survey?

b. Does 45% mean 45 athletes in this survey? Explain.

c. In this survey, is 31% of the athletes *more than* or *less than* 31 athletes? Explain.

7 ✔ **CHECKPOINT** Compare the bars for two categories of the graph that you did not already compare. What does your comparison tell you about sacrifices made by the athletes surveyed?

...checks that you can interpret a bar graph with data in percent form.

▶ **Interpreting Line Graphs** **A line graph is often used to display data that change over time. A double line graph can help you compare two sets of data. For Questions 8–12, use the graph below, which shows one result of a choice about education.**

8 What information is displayed in the double line graph?

▶ **Each step between grid lines on a scale is an interval. The horizontal and vertical axes are marked with different scales.**

9 What is represented by each interval on the vertical scale?

10 **a.** In about what year was the average salary of workers with a bachelor's degree $25,000?

b. Estimate the average salary of workers with a high school diploma in 1990.

11 What decisions might someone studying this graph be trying to make?

...checks that you can interpret a line graph.

12 ✓ **CHECKPOINT** Think about the two groups of people represented in the graph.

a. How have annual salaries changed over time for each group?

b. How has the difference in average salaries between these two groups changed over time?

HOMEWORK EXERCISES ▶ See Exs. 1–15 on pp. 8–9.

Exploration 2

Tallying DATA

GOAL

LEARN HOW TO...
- make a frequency table

AS YOU...
- gather and analyze data about time spent on homework

KEY TERMS
- frequency table
- frequency

SET UP *You will need:* • *Labsheet 1A* • *ruler*

▶ **To "go for the gold" in school as well as in sports requires time for practice. An important decision you'll make this year is how much time to spend on homework each day.**

13 Choose the letter of the phrase that best represents the amount of time you spent doing homework each day last year for all subjects.

A. did not usually have homework

B. did not do assignments

C. one half hour or less

D. one hour

E. two hours

F. more than two hours

▶ **You can use a frequency table like the one shown below to collect your classmates' answers to Question 13.**

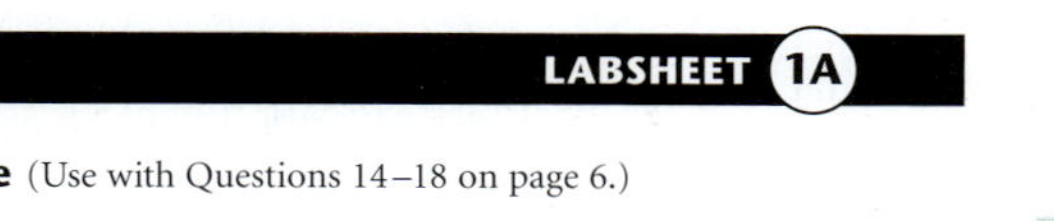

Name ______________________ Date __________

MODULE 1 **LABSHEET 1A**

Homework Frequency Table (Use with Questions 14–18 on page 6.)

Directions

- Make a tally mark (|) in the *Tally* column to represent each of your classmates' answers to Question 13. Include your own answer.
- Count the tally marks in each category and write the total in the *Frequency* column.

Time spent on homework	Tally	Frequency
did not usually have homework		
did not do assignments		
one half hour or less		
one hour		
two hours		
more than two hours		

The total number of tally marks in each category is the **frequency** for that category.

Use Labsheet 1A for Questions 14–18.

✓ QUESTION 14

...checks that you can complete a frequency table.

14 **✓ CHECKPOINT** Record each of your classmates' answers to Question 13 in the *Homework Frequency Table*.

15 Use the data in the *Homework Frequency Table* to complete the *Homework Bar Graph*.

16 How did you choose the scale for the horizontal axis of the *Homework Bar Graph*?

17 How can you find the most frequent answer to Question 13 from the *Homework Frequency Table*? from the *Homework Bar Graph*?

FOR ▶ HELP with *making a bar graph*, see **TOOLBOX, p. 594**

▶ **Comparing Bar Graphs** **Before you decide how much time to spend on homework, it might help to compare the bar graph you made in Question 15 with a graph based on a national survey.**

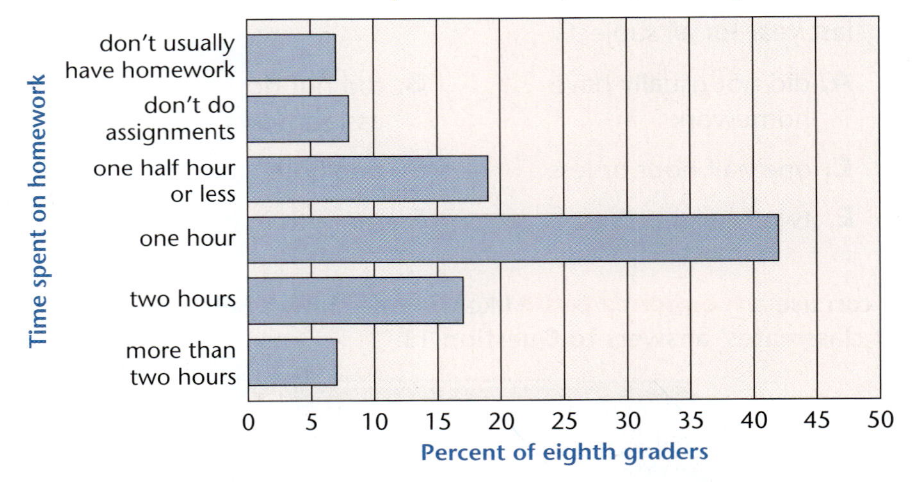

18 **Use Labsheet 1A.** How is the bar graph above like your class's *Homework Bar Graph*? How is it different?

19 Would it be better to compare the time you spent on homework each day last year with the information in the bar graph above or with your class's data? Explain your choice.

20 **Discussion** What other information would you want to have to help you decide how much time you should spend on homework? Why?

HOMEWORK EXERCISES ▶ **See Exs. 16–21 on pp. 9–10.**

Section 1 Key Concepts

Analyzing Bar and Line Graphs (pp. 2–4)

To make good choices, you need information. A bar graph displays data that fall into distinct categories. A line graph can show how data change over time.

Example

The graph shows the percent of U.S. residents (the number of people per 100) who were 10 to 14 years old as of April 1 of each year.

Every graph should have a title.

The scale along the vertical axis goes from 0% to 12%.

The horizontal axis is divided into 10-year intervals.

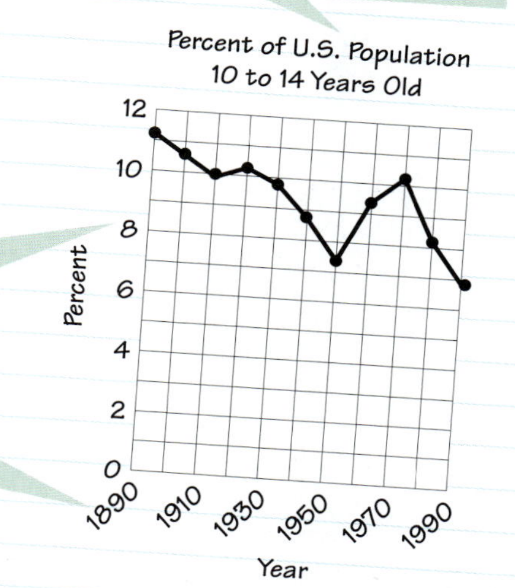

Using Frequency Tables (pp. 5–6)

Frequency tables show how often each data item occurs.

Example

The frequency table and the bar graph show participation in the Vermont Youth Conservation Corps in 1992.

Age	Tally	Frequency
17	III	3
18	~~IIII~~ II	7
19	~~IIII~~ ~~IIII~~	10
20	~~IIII~~ I	6
21	II	2

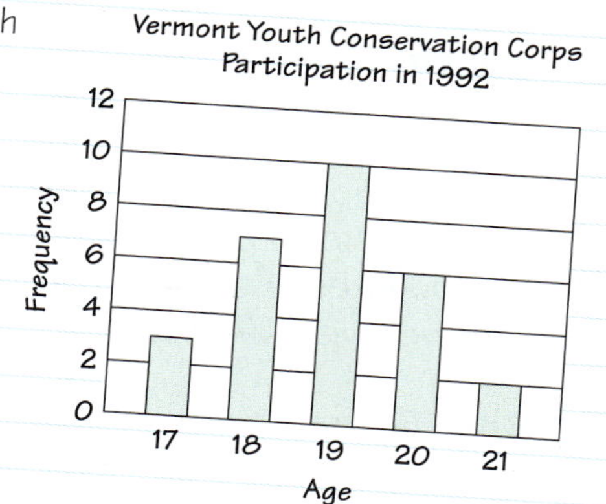

Key Terms

- bar graph
- line graph
- percent
- vertical axis
- horizontal axis
- interval
- frequency
- frequency table

21 Key Concepts Question For each graph above, state one fact that you can learn from the graph.

Section 1 Practice & Application Exercises

YOU WILL NEED

For Exs. 28–30:
- graph paper

Baseball Cards **Use the line graph below for Exercises 1–5.**

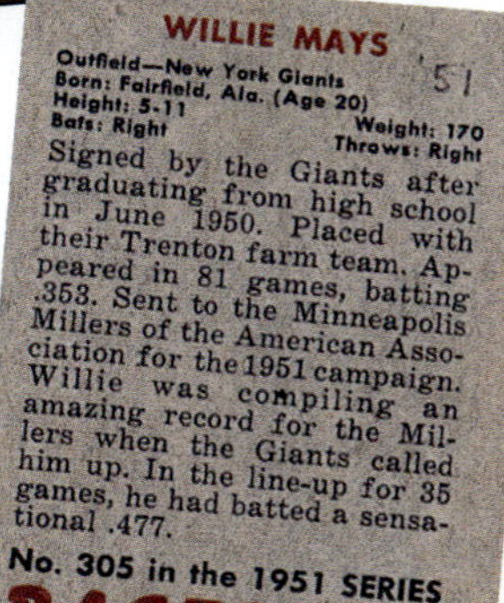

Willie Mays excelled at all aspects of baseball. He hit 660 home runs, set stolen base records, and made a spectacular catch in the 1954 World Series.

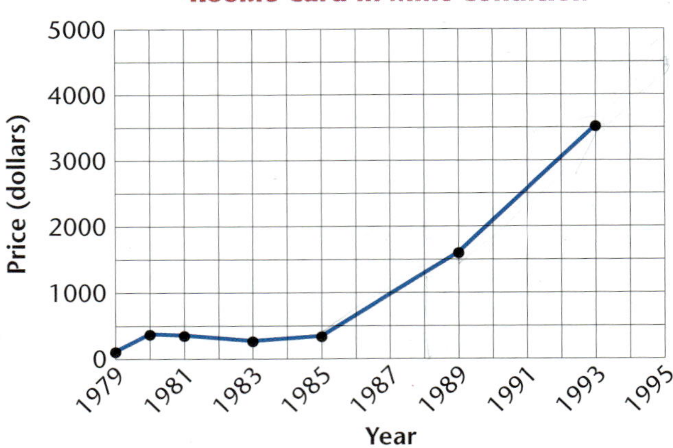

1. Estimate the price of a Willie Mays card in 1988.

2. In which year do you think the price of a Willie Mays card was about $2500?

3. Estimate the price of a Willie Mays card in 1995. Explain how you arrived at your answer.

4. **Open-ended** Write a question of your own that can be answered by the information in the graph.

5. **Writing** Suppose an investor is deciding whether to buy a Willie Mays 1951 Bowman rookie card in mint condition. What are two facts about the history of its price from 1979 to 1993 that may affect the investor's decision?

Estimation **For each group of people surveyed, tell whether 23% of the group is *more than, less than,* or *equal to* 23 people.**

6. 200 students
7. 75 pilots
8. 84 moviegoers
9. 570 dancers
10. 100 runners
11. 23 writers

Job Changes **The double bar graph displays some results of a survey that included 1053 people in Japan and 1002 people in the United States. Use the graph for Exercises 12–15.**

Job Changes among 18 to 24 year olds in Japan and in the United States

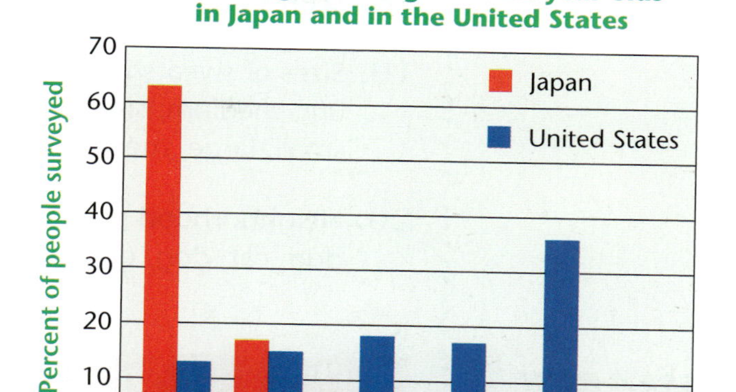

12. What information is displayed in the graph?

13. In which country have more than 60% of the young adults surveyed never changed jobs?

14. Compare the percent of young adults in Japan who changed jobs twice to the percent of young adults in the United States who changed jobs twice.

15. **Challenge** About how many young adults surveyed in the United States have changed jobs only once?

16. The frequency table shows participation in the *Vermont Youth Conservation Corps* in 1995. This organization trains teenagers and young adults to carry out conservation and park management projects on public lands in Vermont.

Age	Tally	Frequency
16	HHT HHT HHT HHT HHT IIII	29
17	HHT HHT HHT HHT HHT HHT HHT	35
18	HHT HHT HHT HHT HHT HHT II	32
19	HHT HHT HHT HHT HHT II	27
20	HHT HHT HHT	15
21	I	1

In 1995, Youth Corps crews completed 53,447 hours of work. They worked to clear trails, seed riverbanks, organize tourist information, install bat houses, and build tables and benches.

a. Make a bar graph of the data.

b. How is your graph from part (a) like the bar graph on page 7? How is it different?

c. Make a double bar graph of the 1992 data and the 1995 data.

d. Use your graph from part (c) to describe how participation in the organization has changed over time.

Make a frequency table for each set of data.

17. Pieces of mail received each day for a month: 5, 6, 5, 10, 6, 8, 7, 8, 8, 5, 9, 7, 7, 8, 6, 7, 5, 9, 6, 7, 8, 6, 9, 6, 6, 5, 5

18. Scores on a five-point quiz: 5, 5, 4, 3, 4, 4, 2, 4, 4, 5, 3, 3, 4, 4, 3

19. Sizes of sweatshirts for a softball team: small, large, large, medium, medium, small, extra large, large, medium, large, medium, small, large, medium, large

20. Neighborhood pets: dog, dog, cat, none, none, dog, fish, horse, dog, cat, dog, gerbil, snake, none, cat, cat, cat, dog, fish, none

RESEARCH

Exercise 21 checks that you can interpret a bar graph.

Reflecting on the Section

21. **a.** Find an example of a bar graph in a newspaper or a magazine.

b. What is the title of the graph?

c. Are the axes clearly labeled? Explain.

d. What decision can the bar graph help a person make? State two facts shown by the graph that may affect the decision.

Spiral Review

Find the area of each rectangle. (Toolbox, p. 593)

22. 8 in. by 5 in.

23. 6 yd by 9 yd

24. 4 ft by 5 ft

Find the fraction of each set that is shaded. (Toolbox, p. 584)

25. △ △ △ △ △

26. ○ ○ ○ ○ ○ ○

27. □ □ □ □ □ □ □ □

Draw each percent on a 100 grid on graph paper. (Toolbox, p. 588)

28. 20%

29. 38%

30. 75%

Tune In to Data

SET UP *Work in a group.*

How do you feel about television commercials? Do you watch too many? Over the next few weeks your group will research television commercials: how often they air, the types of products they advertise, how advertisers use them to influence you, and so on. For your project, your group will present the data you collect and what you learn from the data.

Frequency Tables You can use a frequency table to collect data about how often commercials air and the products they advertise.

1 Decide the following with your group.

a. Which two half-hour time slots will you observe each day? Example: 7:00 P.M. to 7:30 P.M. and 8:00 P.M. to 8:30 P.M.

b. Pick one or two channels to track for five days (Monday–Friday). You'll track each channel during the same time slot each day.

c. Who will observe the channels during the time slots each day?

2 Create a frequency table for your observation periods.

3 Collect the data for your observation period(s). Write down what you thought of the commercials you watched. Were they better or worse than the show they interrupted? Explain.

Observer: Lionel
Day of week: Tuesday
Time Slot: 7–7:30 pm Channel: 8
Program: Star Trek
Notes:

Product advertised	Tally	Frequency
Cars	||||	4
Food	||	2
Restaurants	|	1
Medicine	||||	4
Cosmetics	|	1

Total number of commercials = 12

The products advertised may be different for your time slot.

Use the bar graph for Exercises 1–3.

1. About how many Internet hosts (or machine addresses) were there in January of 1994?
2. Compare the number of Internet hosts in January of 1995 with the number in January of 1996.
3. Do you think the data in the bar graph can be displayed in a line graph? Explain.

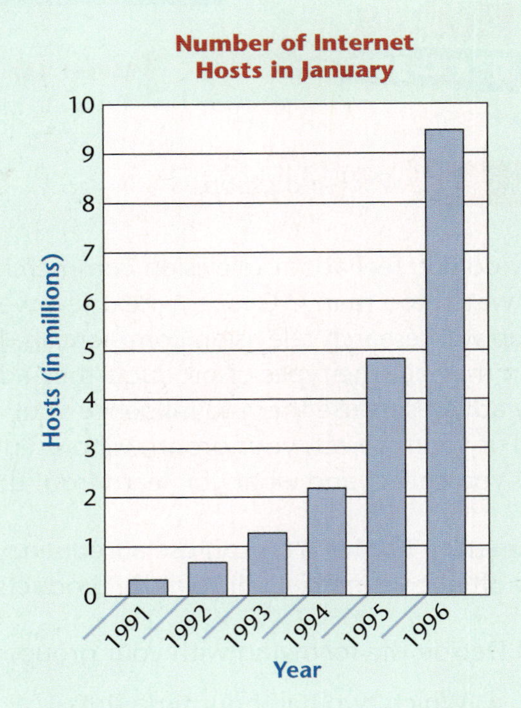

Estimation **For each group of people surveyed, tell whether 51% of the group is *more than, less than,* or *equal to* 51 people.**

4. 25 artists
5. 51 musicians
6. 100 athletes
7. 300 actors

Make a frequency table for each set of data.

8. The number of phone calls listed for each day on a month's bill: 2, 1, 3, 2, 4, 2, 1, 4, 5, 2, 5, 3, 2, 1, 2, 3, 6, 4, 5, 3, 2, 0, 2, 4, 1, 3, 4, 3, 1, 2
9. The ages of a team of students cleaning up a neighborhood playground: 12, 11, 15, 12, 12, 13, 15, 14, 10, 11, 14, 15, 15, 12, 12, 13, 14, 10, 15, 12, 14, 14, 13, 11

Study Skills Taking Notes

Taking notes allows you to keep a record of what you are learning. Be sure to take notes that make sense to you and that you will be able to understand later.

1. a. Look at your notes for this section. What ideas did you record?
   b. What changes can you make to your notes so they are easier to use? Rewrite your notes for this section with these changes.

Section 2 Sequences and Exponents

IN THIS SECTION

EXPLORATION 1
- Modeling Sequences

EXPLORATION 2
- Exponents, Squares, and Cubes

PATTERNS and PREDICTIONS

Setting the Stage

Read the poem by Shel Silverstein and think about whether the boy is making "Smart" choices.

SMART

My dad gave me one dollar bill
'Cause I'm his smartest son,
And I swapped it for two shiny quarters
'Cause two is more than one!

And then I took the quarters
And traded them to Lou
For three dimes—I guess he don't know
That three is more than two!

Just then, along came old blind Bates
And just 'cause he can't see
He gave me four nickels for my three dimes,
And four is more than three!

And I took the nickels to Hiram Coombs
Down at the seed-feed store,
And the fool gave me five pennies for them,
And five is more than four!

And then I went and showed my dad,
And he got red in the cheeks
And closed his eyes and shook his head—
Too proud of me to speak!

Think About It

1. a. What was the boy trying to do?

   b. Explain the pattern he followed to make each trade.

2. a. How much money did the boy lose altogether?

   b. For which trade did he lose the most money?

3. What other trading choices might the boy have made?

4. Follow the boy's pattern to list the trades he might make if his dad gives him a $20 bill. Answer Question 2 for these trades.

Finding and using patterns to make predictions is an important problem-solving strategy. It can help you make good choices in a variety of decision-making situations.

GOAL

LEARN HOW TO...

- model sequences
- make predictions

AS YOU...

- explore visual patterns

KEY TERMS

- sequence
- term
- term number
- equation
- variable

Exploration 1

Modeling Sequences

SET UP *You will need:* • *Labsheets 2A and 2B* • *25 square tiles or graph paper*

▶ **The boy in the poem followed a pattern to make his trades. You can follow a pattern to find numbers in a *sequence*. A sequence is an ordered list of numbers or objects, called terms.**

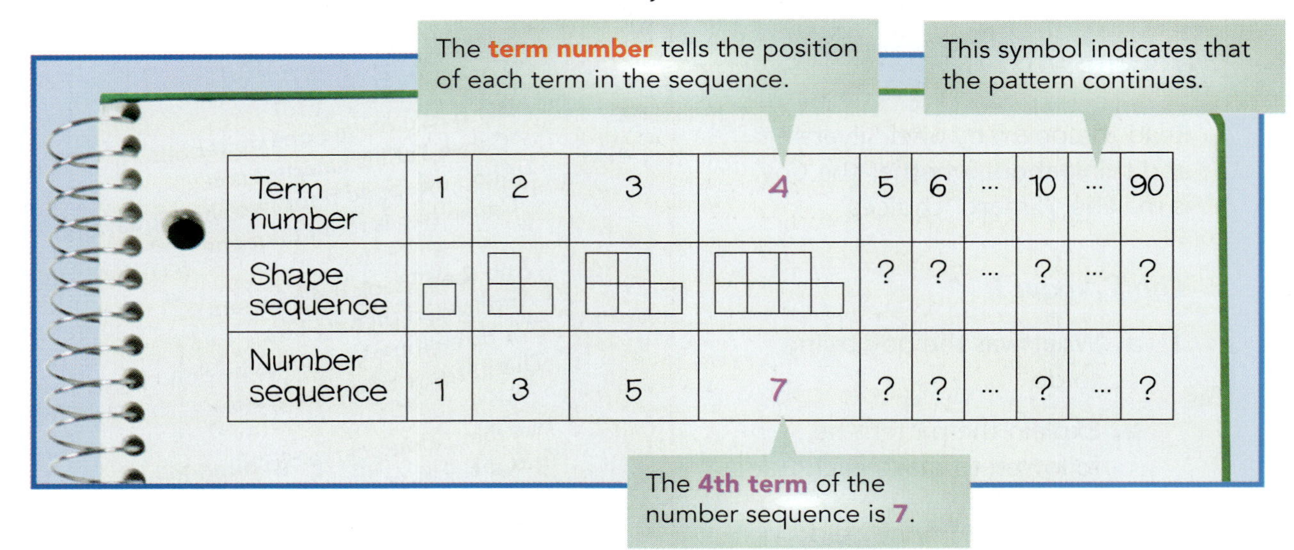

Term number	1	2	3	4	5	6	...	10	...	90
Shape sequence					?	?	...	?	...	?
Number sequence	1	3	5	7	?	?	...	?	...	?

5 How are the number sequence and the shape sequence in the table related?

6 **a.** Use square tiles (or draw a picture) to model the 5th term of the shape sequence.

b. What is the 5th term of the number sequence?

7 **a.** What pattern can you use to predict the 6th term of the shape sequence?

b. Predict what the 6th term of the number sequence will be.

8 **Discussion** Share your patterns from Question 7(a). Predict the 10th and 90th terms of the number sequence. Present your method(s) to the class.

▶ **Graphing Sequences** **Another way to explore a sequence is to set up a table of values and graph the values on a coordinate plane.**

Sequence Table

Term number	Term
1	1
2	3
3	5
4	7
5	9

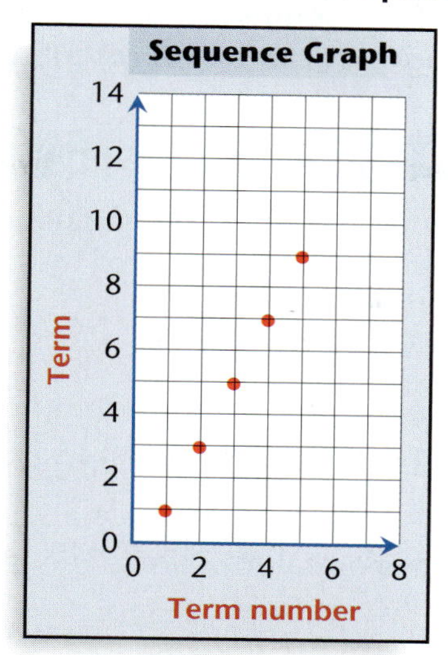

9 **a.** Describe how the points are arranged on the graph.

b. If the number sequence continues, how could your answer to part (a) help you predict the 6th and 7th terms?

10 ✔ **CHECKPOINT** **Use Labsheets 2A and 2B.** You'll build models with square tiles (or draw pictures) and complete a table, make a graph, and write a word sentence for three *Building Patterns*.

...checks that you can model a sequence with a table, a graph, and a word sentence.

▶ **In Question 7 you used a pattern to predict a term of the sequence 1, 3, 5, 7, ... You may have noticed that the number of squares in each term of the shape sequence is equal to 2 times the term number minus 1. For example:**

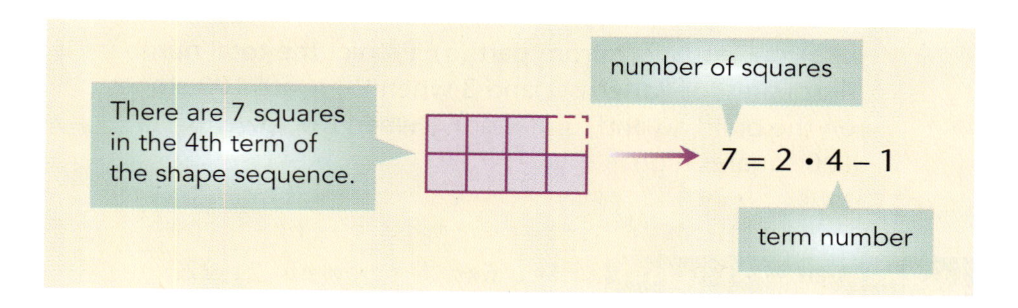

▶ An **equation** such as $7 = 2 \cdot 4 - 1$ is a mathematical sentence stating that two quantities are equal. You can use *variables* to write an equation for a sequence. A **variable** is a quantity that is unknown or that changes. It can be represented by a letter or a symbol.

EXAMPLE

Write an equation for the sequence 1, 3, 5, 7, ... Use the equation to predict the 100th term of the sequence.

SAMPLE RESPONSE

Since the terms and the term numbers change, you can use variables to represent them. Let t = the term. Let n = the term number.

The term is equal to 2 times the term number minus 1.

$$t = 2 \cdot n - 1$$
or
$$t = 2n - 1$$

"2 times n" can be written $2 \cdot n$ or $2n$.

Use this equation to predict the 100th term of the sequence.

$$\begin{aligned} t &= 2n - 1 \\ &= 2 \cdot 100 - 1 \\ &= 200 - 1 \\ &= 199 \end{aligned}$$

For the **100th** term, the term number n is **100**.

The 100th term in the sequence 1, 3, 5, 7, ... is 199.

11 How many squares are there in the 100th term of the shape sequence in the table on page 14?

✓ QUESTION 12

...checks that you can write an equation for a sequence and use it to make predictions.

12 **✓ CHECKPOINT** **Use Labsheets 2A and 2B.**

a. Use your word sentences to write an equation for each *Building Pattern*. Be sure to identify what each variable represents.

b. Use your equations from part (a). Predict the total number of squares for Patterns 1 and 3 when there are 100 stories on the building and for Pattern 2 when the tower is 100 squares high.

HOMEWORK EXERCISES ▶ See Exs. 1–11 on pp. 21–22.

Exploration 2

EXPONENTS, SQUARES, and CUBES

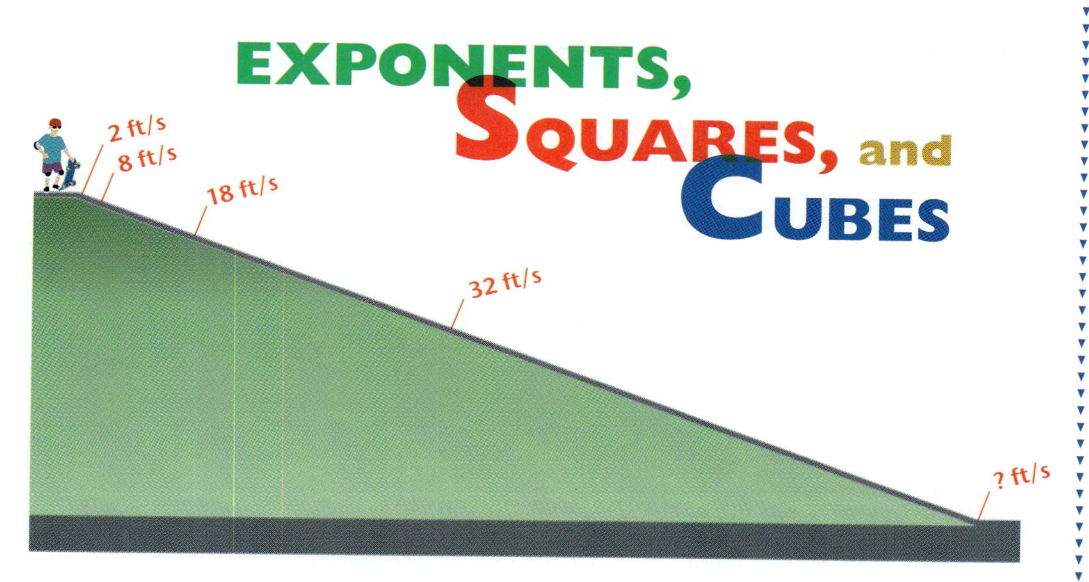

GOAL

LEARN HOW TO...
- use exponents
- find the volume of a cube

AS YOU...
- explore speeds of a skateboarder

KEY TERMS
- exponent
- base
- exponential form
- standard form
- power
- cube
- volume
- face
- edge
- vertex

13 The boy is deciding whether to skateboard down the hill. The numbers show the speed he would be going at each distance from the hilltop. Would you skate down the hill? Why?

▶ **In Exploration 1, you saw patterns involving addition, subtraction, and multiplication. In this Exploration you'll learn how to use exponents to find the skateboarder's speed at the bottom of the hill. Exponents can show a pattern of repeated multiplication.**

base **exponent**

exponential form → $3^4 = 3 \cdot 3 \cdot 3 \cdot 3 = 81$ ← **standard form**

3 is used as a factor 4 times.

You read 3^4 as "3 to the 4th **power**."

14 **a.** Copy and complete the table.

Term number	1	2	3	4	5	6
Exponential form of sequence	3^1	3^2	3^3	3^4	?	?
Standard form of sequence	3	9	27	?	?	?

b. If the sequence in part (a) continues, how could you use exponents to predict the 10th term?

▶ **Area Patterns** **The squares in the shape sequence below are made up of small squares. Each side of a small square is 1 unit long. You can find a related number sequence for the area of each shape.**

15 **a.** Sketch the next two shapes in the sequence.

b. How can you find the area of a square from the length of a side?

c. If the sequence in the table continues, what are the first five terms of the number sequence for the area of each shape?

Term number	Shape sequence
1	□
2	⊞
3	▦
4	?
5	?

…checks that you can use exponents to write an equation for a sequence.

16 **CHECKPOINT** The following sequence is another way to represent the area pattern in the shape sequence above.

$1^2, 2^2, 3^2, \ldots$

You read 3^2 as "3 to the 2nd power" or as "3 squared."

a. How is this sequence related to the shape sequence above and to the number sequence you wrote in Question 15(c)?

b. Write an equation for the area of a square. Let s = the length of a side of a square. Let A = the area of the square.

c. Use your equation from part (b) to find the area of a square that has sides of length 10 cm.

▶ **Volume Patterns** **A cube is a space figure with six square surfaces. The sequence of cubes below has a related number sequence that gives the *volume* of each cube. The volume is the number of *unit cubes* that fill the figure.**

Term number	1	2	3	…
Shape sequence				…

A unit cube is 1 unit long, 1 unit wide, and 1 unit high.

17 How many unit cubes make up each term in the shape sequence?

a. 1st term **b.** 2nd term **c.** 3rd term

▶ **There are 1000 centimeter cubes in the large cube below, so its volume is 1000 cm^3. (You read cm^3 as "cubic centimeters.") Another way to find the volume of a cube besides counting unit cubes is to use an equation.**

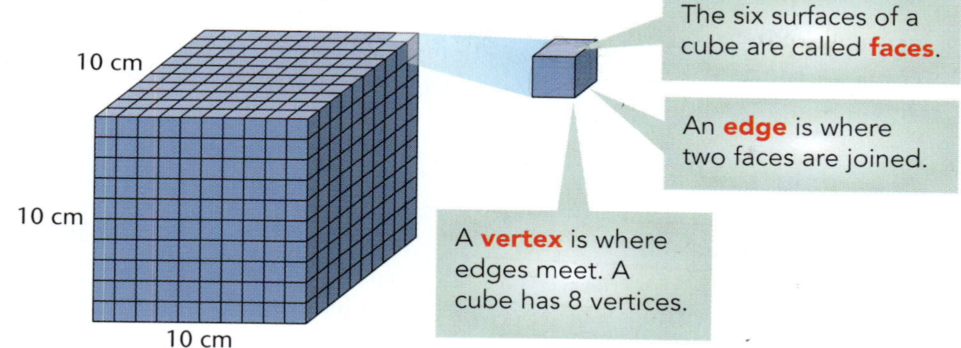

18 **Discussion** Explain how the lengths of the edges of the large cube above can be used to find its volume.

19 **a.** Write an equation for the volume of a cube. Let s = the length of an edge of a cube. Let V = the volume of the cube.

b. Use your equation from part (a) to find the volume of the first three cubes in the shape sequence at the bottom of page 18.

c. Describe how your answers in part (b) compare with those in Question 17.

20 ✓ **CHECKPOINT** Find the volume of a cube with edges of each length.

a. 1 cm **b.** 5 in. **c.** 50 m **d.** 300 ft

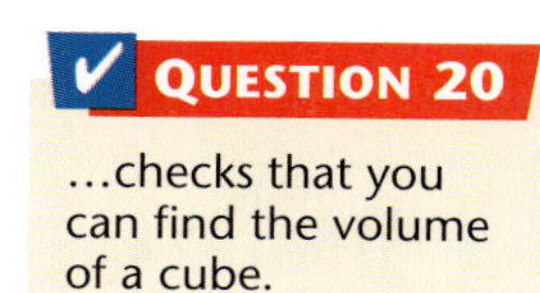

21 The fifth term in the table below is the speed that the skateboarder on page 17 will reach at the bottom of the hill.

Speed (feet per second)	2	8	18	32	?
Exponential form	$1^2 \cdot 2$	$2^2 \cdot 2$	$3^2 \cdot 2$	?	?

a. Study the pattern in the table. Then write the 4th and 5th terms of the sequence in exponential form.

b. What will the skateboarder's speed be in feet per second when he reaches the bottom of the hill? What will his speed be in miles per hour? (*Hint:* 5280 ft = 1 mi)

c. What advice would you give this skateboarder?

HOMEWORK EXERCISES ▶ See Exs. 12–32 on pp. 23–24.

Section 2 Key Concepts

Key Terms

sequence

term

term number

Sequences (pp. 14 and 15)

A sequence is an ordered list of numbers or objects, called terms. Each term has a term number that tells the term's position in the sequence.

Example Make a table and a graph for the sequence 5, 10, 15, 20, ...

Sequence Table

Term number	Term
1	5
2	10
3	15
4	20

The 4th term of the sequence is 20.

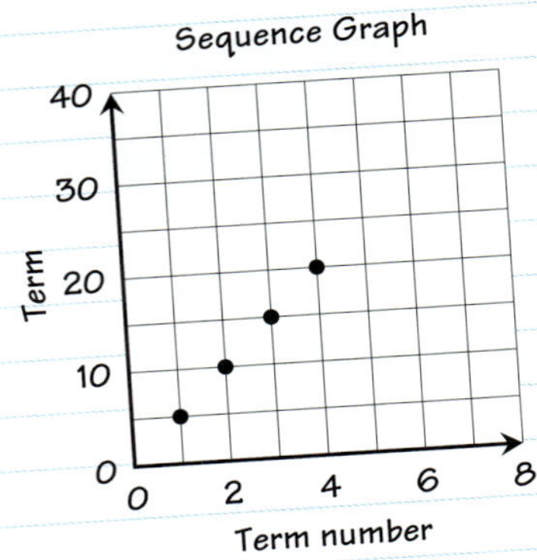

equation

variable

Equations and Variables (p. 16)

You can use variables to write an equation that shows how a term in a sequence is related to its term number. A variable is a letter or a symbol used to represent unknown quantities or quantities that change.

Example Write an equation for the sequence 5, 10, 15, 20, ...

The term t is 5 times the term number n.

$$t = 5 \cdot n$$

$$t = 5n$$

exponent

base

power

Exponents (p. 17)

An exponent tells you how many times a base is used as a factor. The value of any number to the 1st power is that number.

$$10^5 = 10 \cdot 10 \cdot 10 \cdot 10 \cdot 10 = 100{,}000$$

100,000 is the 5th power of 10.

base (10) — exponent (5)

22 Key Concepts Question Find the 20th term of the sequence represented by the equation $t = 5n$, where t is the term and n is the term number.

Section 2 Key Concepts

Key Terms

volume

cube
- **face**
- **edge**
- **vertex**

exponential form

standard form

Squares and Cubes (pp. 18–19)

The formulas for the area of a square and the volume of a cube can be written using exponents.

Area of a Square

$A = s \cdot s = s^2$

You read s^2 as "s squared."

Volume of a Cube

$V = s \cdot s \cdot s = s^3$

You read s^3 as "s cubed."

Example Find the volume of a cube when the length of an edge is 8 ft.

$V = s^3$

$= 8^3$ ← exponential form

$= 8 \cdot 8 \cdot 8$

$= 512$ ← standard form

The volume is 512 ft^3.

23 Key Concepts Question The length of an edge of a cube is 4 in. Find the volume of the cube and the area of one of its faces.

Section 2 Practice & Application Exercises

Suppose the boy in the poem on page 13 begins with 2 bills. Then he trades them for 4 of the next lesser bill or coin, and so on, according to the pattern 2, 4, 6, 8, 10, ... (*Note:* He can trade for half dollars.) For each starting amount, how much will he lose altogether?

1. 2 one-dollar bills
2. 2 two-dollar bills
3. **Challenge** Assume that the boy in the poem finds someone to agree to any trade. Describe a pattern he can use so that he will not lose money overall on his trades although each trade is for the next lesser bill or coin.

4. Use the shape sequence in the table.

a. Draw pictures of the 5th and 6th terms of the sequence.

b. Write the number sequence that matches the first six terms of the shape sequence.

c. Write a word sentence to describe a pattern you could use to predict the 7th term of the number sequence.

d. Make a table of values for the first 10 terms of the number sequence. Use it to make a graph of the sequence.

e. Use your graph to predict the 15th term of the number sequence.

Term number	Shape sequence
1	
2	
3	
4	
⋮	⋮

Write an equation for each word sentence. Use *t* for the term and *n* for the term number.

5. The term is six times the term number.

6. The term is one less than the term number.

7. The term is five more than the term number.

8. The term is half the term number.

For each sequence, make a table, draw a graph, and write an equation. Then predict the 100th term.

9. 7, 14, 21, 28, ...

10. 199, 198, 197, 196, ...

11. **Social Studies** Arizona and Oregon became states on the same day, February 14, but in different years. Arizona's first year as a state was Oregon's 54th year.

Arizona's years of statehood	1	2	3	4	...
Oregon's years of statehood	54	55	56	57	...

a. Arizona became a state in 1912. When did Oregon become a state?

b. When Arizona celebrates 100 years of statehood, how many years will Oregon have been a state?

Write each product in exponential form.

12. 2 • 2 • 2
13. 3 • 3
14. 7 • 7 • 7 • 7 • 7

Write each power in standard form.

15. 5^2
16. 4^3
17. 11^4
18. 6^5
19. 10^6
20. 0^{15}
21. 1^{50}
22. 1592^1

23. Predict the 100th term of the sequence $2^3, 4^3, 6^3, 8^3, \ldots$.

Find the volume of a cube with edges of each length.

24. 7 mm
25. 11 ft
26. 80 cm
27. 25 in.

Chinese Noodles To make dragon's beard noodles, a chef takes noodle dough, stretches it, and then folds it in half. The chef repeats this process, making more noodles with each fold. An experienced noodle maker can stretch and fold the dough 8 times.

Number of folds	Number of noodles
1	2
2	4
3	8
⋮	⋮

28. Suppose a chef folds the dough 8 times. How many noodles will there be?

29. How many folds are required to make about 500 noodles?

30. a. Copy and complete the table. Then graph the values.

Side length (cm)	10	20	30	40
Area of a square (cm^2)	?	?	?	?

b. How does the area of a square change when you multiply the length of each side by 2? by 3? by 4?

c. Copy and complete the table. Then graph the values.

Edge length (cm)	10	20	30	40
Volume of a cube (cm^3)	?	?	?	?

d. How does the volume of a cube change when you multiply the length of each edge by 2? by 3? by 4?

e. **Writing** Compare your answers to parts (b) and (d). Is the effect on area of doubling a side length the same as the effect on volume of doubling an edge length? Explain.

31. **Challenge** The volume of a cube is 700 cm^3. Estimate the length of an edge. Explain your method.

Visual THINKING

Exercise 32 checks that you can predict terms in a sequence and find the volume of a space figure.

Reflecting on the Section

32. Find the volume of the 5th shape in the sequence. The edge of each small cube is 5 cm long.

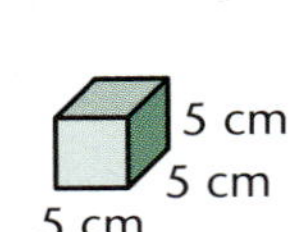

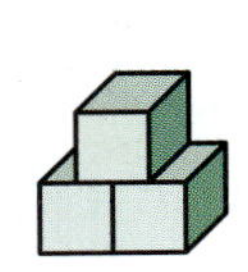

Spiral Review

Use the bar graph at the right. (Module 1, pp. 2–3)

33. About what fraction of the votes did Rosa get?

34. Which person got about one third of the votes?

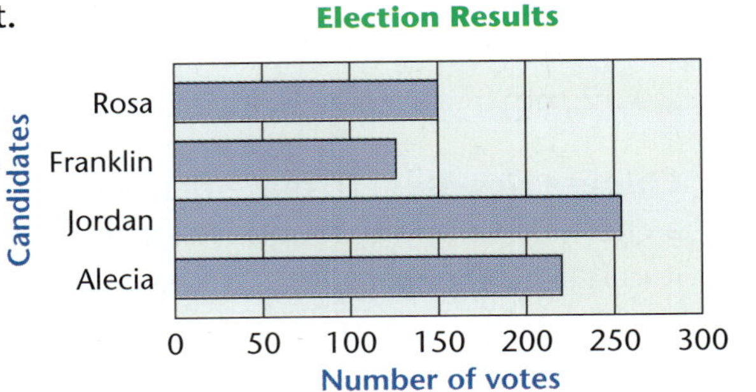

Write an equivalent fraction for each fraction below. (Toolbox, p. 585)

35. $\frac{1}{2}$ **36.** $\frac{20}{25}$ **37.** $\frac{3}{7}$

Career Connection

Trader: David Lei

David Lei is the president of a trading company that buys and sells goods around the world. To get the best price, he must try to keep shipping costs low.

38. Shipping costs can be based on the number of cubic meters of goods shipped. The table shows shipping costs determined this way.

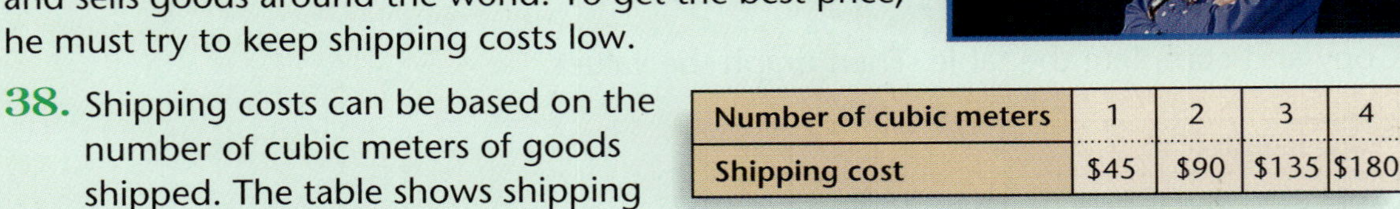

Number of cubic meters	1	2	3	4
Shipping cost	$45	$90	$135	$180

a. Write an equation for the cost c of shipping based on the number n of cubic meters of goods.

b. Extend the table to include the next 6 terms of the sequence.

c. Graph the data in your table.

39. Suppose it costs $1000 to ship a 57 m^3 cargo container from Hong Kong to San Francisco. Use the graph you made in part (c) of Question 38. Predict when it becomes less expensive to pay for shipping by container rather than by the cubic meter.

Think About It

1 The *Difference Game* involves both *choice* and *chance*. What part involves choice? What part involves chance?

2 Did you use the same arrangement of chips for every game? Why or why not?

3 What can you do to help decide where to place your chips on the *Game Board*?

Exploration 1

What Are the CHANCES?

GOAL

LEARN HOW TO...
- list the outcomes for an event
- find and compare experimental probabilities

AS YOU...
- analyze the *Difference Game*

KEY TERMS
- experiment
- outcome
- event
- probability
- experimental probability

SET UP *Work with a partner. You will need:* • *Labsheets 3A and 3B* • *18 chips* • *2 number cubes or dice*

▶ **In the *Difference Game*, you had to choose where to place your chips.**

4 **a.** Should you place any chips on the 6? Why or why not?

b. Suppose a difference does not occur very often. Should you put many of your chips on that number? Explain.

▶ **To make good choices about where to put the chips, it helps to know your chances of getting a particular difference on a roll.**

5 **Use Labsheet 3B.**

a. Roll the number cubes 18 times. Record how often each difference occurs in the *Results of 18 Rolls* table.

b. What differences seem to occur most often? least often?

c. What fraction of the 18 rolls resulted in a difference of 2? Record your answer in the last column of the table.

d. Repeat part (c) for the other differences from 0 through 6.

The difference is 6 – 2 = 4.

▶ **When you rolled the number cubes and found each difference in Question 5(a), you were conducting an experiment. The result of an experiment is an outcome. For the roll shown, the outcome is a difference of 4. An event is any set of outcomes.**

✓ QUESTION 6

...checks that you can list the outcomes for an event.

6 **✓ CHECKPOINT** Suppose the experiment is to roll the number cubes and record the difference.

a. What are all the possible outcomes of the experiment?

b. Which outcomes make up the event the *difference is even*?

▶ **A probability is a number from 0 through 1 that tells how likely it is that an event will happen. Each of the fractions you wrote for Question 5 is an experimental probability because each was found by doing an experiment.**

EXAMPLE

Suppose, that when you roll two number cubes 18 times you get a difference of 4 on 3 rolls. What is the experimental probability of getting a difference of 4?

SAMPLE RESPONSE

Since the difference is 4 on $\frac{3}{18}$ of the rolls, the experimental probability of a difference of 4 is $\frac{3}{18} = \frac{1}{6}$.

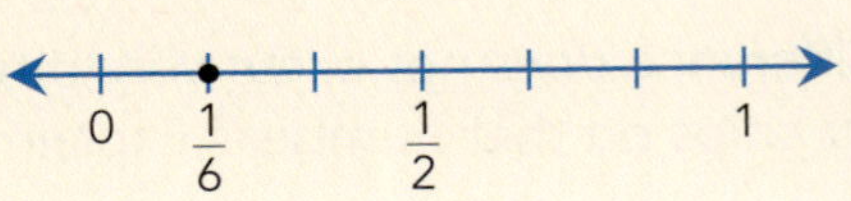

FOR ▶ HELP

with *writing fractions in lowest terms*, see

TOOLBOX, p. 585

7 **Discussion** **Use Labsheet 3B**. Look at the experimental probabilities in the last column of the *Results of 18 Rolls* table.

a. In the *Difference Game*, what does it mean to say the experimental probability of a 1 is $\frac{5}{18}$?

b. Which, if any, of the differences have a probability of 0?

c. What does a probability of 0 mean?

d. What is the probability that the difference is less than 7? Why?

e. What do you think a probability of 1 means?

f. Is an event more likely to occur when its probability is *greater than* one half or *less than* one half?

▶ **Use Labsheet 3B for Questions 8–10.** **The *Results of 72 Rolls* frequency table is reproduced below.**

8 **a.** Record the frequencies from the *Results of 18 Rolls* table in the column labeled *My Group* of the *Results of 72 Rolls* table. Then do the same with the frequencies of three other groups.

b. Complete the *Total frequency* column.

c. Complete the *Experimental probability* column.

Results of 72 Rolls (Use with Questions 8–10 on page 29.)

Difference	Group frequencies				Total frequency	Experimental probability
	My group	Group 1	Group 2	Group 3		
0						
1						
2						
3						
4						
5						
6						
			Total number of rolls →		72	

Add the frequencies for the four groups.

The total frequency is what fraction of the 72 rolls?

9 **Discussion** Use both the *Results of 72 Rolls* table and the *Results of 18 Rolls* table.

a. Compare the experimental probabilities in the two tables. How are the probabilities alike? How are they different?

b. Which set of probabilities do you think gives a better indication of how likely it is for each difference to occur? Why?

FOR ▶ HELP with *comparing fractions*, see **TOOLBOX, p. 586**

10 **Try This as a Class** Use the probabilities in the *Results of 72 Rolls* table to predict how many times each difference 0 through 6 will occur in 18 rolls of the number cubes.

11 **a. Discussion** How can your answer to Question 10 help you decide where to place your chips in the *Difference Game*?

b. Use Labsheet 3A. Use the answers to Question 10 to place the 18 chips on a *Game Board*. Roll the number cubes until all the chips have been removed. How many times did you roll the number cubes? Compare the number of rolls with those in the *Frequency Table*.

HOMEWORK EXERCISES ▶ See Exs. 1–12 on pp. 34–35.

GOAL

LEARN HOW TO...
- find theoretical probabilities

AS YOU...
- explore outcomes when rolling one or two number cubes

KEY TERMS
- theoretical probability
- equally likely

Exploration 2

Theoretical PROBABILITY

SET UP *Work with a partner. You will need:* • *Labsheets 3C and 3D* • *2 number cubes or dice (red and blue)*

Sometimes probabilities can be determined without actually doing an experiment. Such probabilities are called theoretical probabilities.

12 **a.** What are all the possible outcomes when a number cube is rolled once?

b. Discussion The theoretical probability of rolling a 4 is $\frac{1}{6}$. Why do you think $\frac{1}{6}$ is the theoretical probability for this event?

✓ QUESTION 13

...checks that you can find and compare probabilities.

13 **✓ CHECKPOINT** **Use Labsheet 3C.**

a. Follow the directions for *Rolling One Number Cube* and completing the table. You'll be finding both experimental and theoretical probabilities.

b. How does the experimental probability of each outcome in the table compare with its theoretical probability?

When the probability of two or more outcomes is the same, the outcomes are equally likely.

14 **Discussion** Are all six possible outcomes equally likely when you roll one number cube? when you play the *Difference Game*? Why or why not?

15 **Discussion** Suppose that one of the number cubes used in the *Difference Game* is red and the other one is blue. You roll a red 1 and a blue 5 to get a difference of 4.

a. What other rolls result in a difference of 4?

b. Do you think the rolls that result in a difference of 4 are equally likely? Why or why not?

TECHNOLOGY Using Probability Software

You can use probability software to conduct experiments, such as rolling a die or number cube, tossing a coin, or spinning a spinner. The steps below show you how to gather data for 150 rolls of a die. You can use the results to answer Question 13 on page 30 without ever rolling a number cube or die.

Step 1 Select the type of experiment to run.

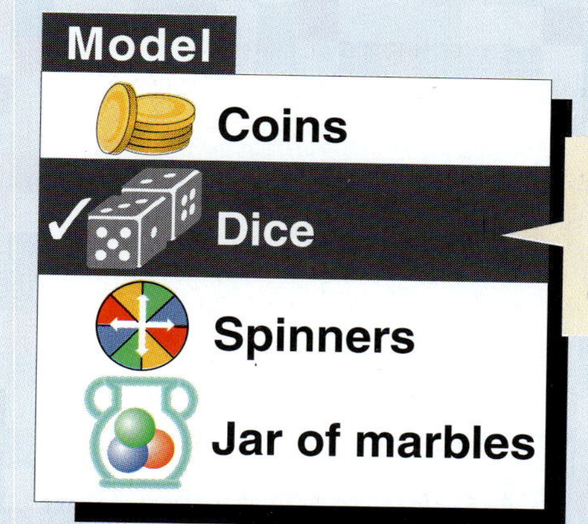

Choose the dice as the model for your experiment.

Step 2 Enter how many times to conduct the experiment. Then select how you would like to display the results.

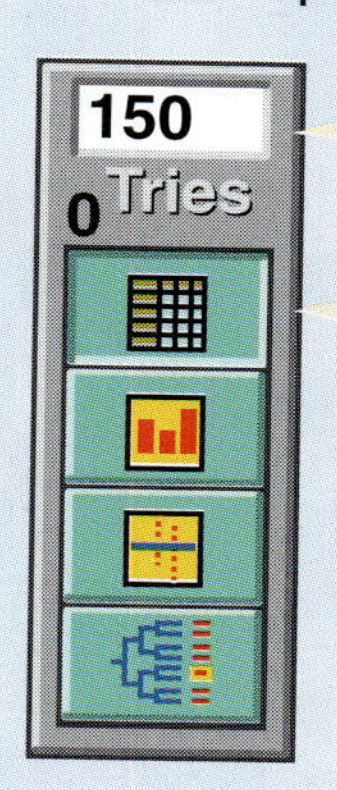

Enter 150 rolls.

Choose a table display.

Step 3 Run the experiment.

The *theoretical probability* is the probability, before the experiment, that each outcome will occur.

Frequency is the number of times the outcome occurred.

Values	A Theor. Prob.	B Freq.	C Rel. Freq.
⚀	16.7%	28	18.7%
⚁	16.7%	27	18.0%
⚂	16.7%	23	15.3%
⚃	16.7%	23	15.3%
⚄	16.7%	23	15.3%
⚅	16.7%	26	17.3%
Sum:	100%	150	100%

Experimental probability is also called *relative frequency*. It can be shown as a fraction, a decimal, or a percent.

Your table will show you data for 150 rolls of a die. You can choose to have it record the theoretical probability, the frequency, the experimental probability, or all three.

Use Labsheet 3D for Questions 16–18.

16 Suppose you roll a red number cube and a blue number cube. Record all the possible differences in the *Difference Chart*. Then answer parts (a)–(f) on the labsheet.

Based on the results in the chart, the probability of rolling a difference of 4 is $\frac{4}{36}$, since there are a total of 36 possible outcomes and 4 of them, or $\frac{4}{36}$ of all the possible outcomes, are "4." This can be written as shown.

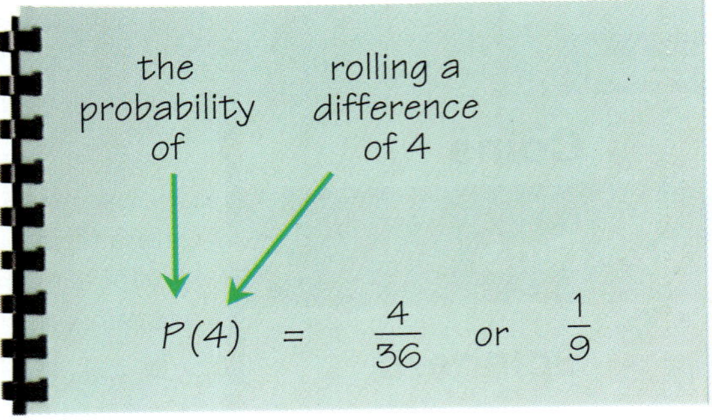

Name ____________________ Date ____________________

MODULE 1 — **LABSHEET 3D**

Difference Chart (Use with Questions 16–18 on page 32.)

Directions Suppose you roll a red number cube and a blue number cube. Complete the *Difference Chart* below to show what difference results from each roll. An example is shown. Then answer the questions below.

a. Which difference occurs most often in the chart? Which occurs least often?

b. How many boxes are there to fill in on the chart (including the ones filled in for you)?

c. What fraction of the boxes contain a difference of 4?

d. What is the theoretical probability of rolling a difference of 4?

e. What fraction of the boxes contain a difference of 6?

f. What is the theoretical probability of rolling a difference of 6?

Red \ Blue	1	2	3	4	5	6
1					(5 − 1) 4	
2	1					
3						
4			(4 − 3) 1			
5						
6						

***Difference Game* Theoretical Probability Table** (Use with Questions 17 and 18 on page 32.)

Directions Complete the table at the right by finding the theoretical probability of each difference shown in the *Difference Chart* above. Then find the sum of the theoretical probabilities.

Theoretical Probabilities for the *Difference Game*
P(0) =
P(1) =
P(2) =
P(3) =
P(4) = $\frac{4}{36}$, or $\frac{1}{9}$
P(5) =
P(6) =
Sum =

17 Use the *Difference Chart* to complete the *Difference Game Theoretical Probability Table* that appears on Labsheet 3D.

18 Think back to the experimental probabilities for the *Difference Game* that you found in Question 8 on page 29.

How do those experimental probabilities compare with the theoretical probabilities you found in Question 17**?**

19 Explain how knowing the theoretical probability of rolling a particular difference can help you make good choices in the *Difference Game*.

HOMEWORK EXERCISES ▶ See Exs. 13–30 on pp. 35–37.

Section 3 Key Concepts

Key Terms

probability

impossible event

certain event

experiment

experimental probability

outcome

event

theoretical probability

equally likely

Probability and Experimental Probability (pp. 27–29)

A probability is a number from 0 through 1 that tells how likely it is that an event will happen. An impossible event has a probability of 0. A certain event has a probability of 1.

Probabilities determined by repeating an experiment a number of times and observing the results are called experimental probabilities.

Example Suppose the spinner below was spun 60 times with the results shown in the table.

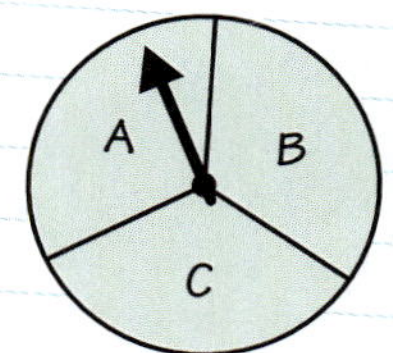

Outcome	Frequency
A	17
B	25
C	18

Since $\frac{17}{60}$ of the spins landed on A, the experimental probability of spinning an A is $\frac{17}{60}$. This can also be written as $P(A) = \frac{17}{60}$.

Theoretical Probability (pp. 30–32)

Probabilities that are determined without actually doing an experiment are theoretical probabilities.

Outcomes are equally likely if they have the same chance of occurring.

Example Since the spinner above is divided into 3 equal-sized sectors, all three possible outcomes A, B, and C on the spinner have the same chance of occurring, so they are equally likely.

The theoretical probability of spinning an A is $\frac{1}{3}$, or $P(A) = \frac{1}{3}$.

20 Key Concepts Question Use the spinner and the frequency table from the first Example. For each indicated event, find the experimental probability and the theoretical probability.

a. $P(B)$ **b.** $P(A \text{ or } C)$ **c.** $P(\text{not } A)$

Section 3 Practice & Application Exercises

YOU WILL NEED

For Ex. 6:
- coin

For Ex. 26:
- 25 toothpicks or drinking straws

For Ex. 38:
- bag and 8 cubes using 3 different colors

Estimation **Tell whether you think the probability of each event is 0, 1, or between 0 and 1. If the probability is between 0 and 1, do you think it is *greater than* or *less than* $\frac{1}{2}$? Give a reason.**

1. The snow in your area will be great for snowboarding this weekend.

2. Someone in your household will make a long-distance phone call in the next week.

3. You'll go on a field trip during this school year.

4. You'll move in the next year.

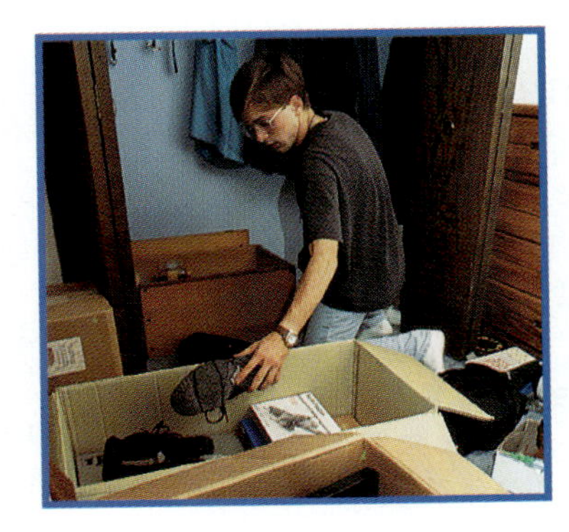

5. Marta spun the spinner shown 26 times. She got an even number on 10 spins.

   a. Based on Marta's results, what is the experimental probability of getting an even number on a spin?

   b. Describe an event that has a probability of 1 and an event that has a probability of 0.

6. a. One method for deciding between two choices is to toss a coin. What are all the possible outcomes when you toss a coin?

b. Toss a coin 50 times. Record your results in a frequency table. Then find the experimental probability of getting heads and the experimental probability of getting tails.

Suppose you roll two number cubes. List at least three outcomes that will produce each event.

7. a difference of 3

8. a difference of 0

9. a sum of 6

10. an even sum

11. a difference of 2 or more

12. a sum of 9 or more

13. Suppose a coin is tossed once.

a. Find the theoretical probabilities *P*(heads) and *P*(tails).

b. How do the results of part (a) compare with the experimental probabilities you found in Exercise 6(b)?

14. **Football** Football teams toss a coin before each game. The team that wins the toss chooses whether to kick or receive the ball at the start of the game. The article shown describes a high school football team's unfortunate win/loss record both on the field and in the opening coin toss.

a. The article mentions an "improbable pair of losing streaks" with which a high school football team opened its 1983 season. Which of these losing streaks was more improbable in your opinion? Why?

b. The article says that ". . . . it's a whole lot easier to change one's luck than one's skill." Do you agree? Explain.

There's a Moral Here, Cougar Fans

. . . an improbable pair of losing streaks: The Cougars had lost not only 21 straight games but also, amazingly, every pregame coin toss over the same span. [The team] proceeded to lose its 22nd straight game, 58–0, the worst defeat in the school's history, but not before finally winning a coin flip. Which goes to show, we suppose, that it's a whole lot easier to change one's luck than one's skill.

Sports Illustrated, September 5, 1983

Complete Exercise 15. Then for Exercises 16–24, find the theoretical probability of each event.

Outcome for blue cube	Outcome for red cube 1	2	3	4	5	6
6	?	?	?	?	11	?
5	?	?	?	?	?	?
4	5	?	?	?	?	?
3	?	?	?	?	?	?
2	?	?	?	?	?	?
1	?	?	?	?	?	?

15. Suppose you roll a red cube and a blue cube. Copy and complete the table to show the sums (outcomes) that can occur.

16. *P*(2) **17.** *P*(6) **18.** *P*(1) **19.** *P*(8)

20. *P*(3) **21.** *P*(7) **22.** *P*(4 or 5) **23.** *P*(even)

24. *P*(sum is even and greater than 6)

Native American Games **Use the information below for Exercises 25 and 26.**

Many Native American peoples developed games that involved probability. In several types of Native American stick games, one player separated an odd number of sticks into two bundles and a second player tried to guess, without counting, which bundle had an *even* number of sticks. A correct guess counted as a win.

25. Suppose you use 25 sticks to play a stick game like the ones described above.

a. If there are 12 sticks in the bundle chosen by the second player, then he or she wins. List all possible outcomes that produce a win. Then list all possible outcomes that produce a loss.

b. Find the theoretical probability of the second player's winning the stick game.

26. **Home Involvement** Work with a partner.

a. Play the stick game from Exercise 25 forty times. Use 25 straws or toothpicks for sticks. Use a table like the one shown to keep track of each game's results.

Event	Tally	Frequency
win	?	?
loss	?	?

b. Use your results from part (a) to find the experimental probability of the second player's winning the stick game.

c. How does your answer to part (b) compare with your answer to Exercise 25(b)?

27. Suppose an experiment involves spinning the spinner once.

a. What are all the possible outcomes of the experiment?

b. Are landing on green and landing on blue equally likely events? Why or why not?

c. What fraction of the spins do you expect to land on green? on blue? Give a reason for your answer.

d. **Writing** Suppose you repeat the experiment 40 times. What results do you expect? Do you think the results will always match your expectations? Why or why not?

Challenge Sketch a spinner for each situation.

28. The possible outcomes are X and Y. The probability of spinning an X is two times the probability of spinning a Y.

29. The possible outcomes are E, F, and G. The probability of spinning an E is $\frac{3}{4}$. The probability of spinning an F is $\frac{1}{8}$.

Reflecting on the Section

Be prepared to discuss your response to Exercise 30 in class.

30. Suppose that the weather forecaster on television predicts that the chance of rain tomorrow is 70%. (Remember, $70\% = \frac{7}{10}$.)

a. Is tomorrow a good day to have a cookout? Explain.

b. What is the probability it will not rain tomorrow?

Discussion

Exercise 30 checks that you understand the meaning of probability.

Spiral Review

For each sequence, make a table, draw a graph, and write an equation. Then predict the 100th term. (Module 1, p. 20)

31. 10, 20, 30, 40, ...

32. 16, 17, 18, 19, ...

For Exercises 33–35, find each sum or difference. (Toolbox, p. 581)

33. 25.47 + 12.16

34. 2.45 + 9 + 3.1

35. 10 – 4.983

36. Find the mean of these travel times, in minutes, to get to school: 10, 18, 25, 36, 40, 15, 22, 34, 32, 18, 21, 29. (Toolbox, p. 595)

Extension

Predicting from a Sample

37. Suppose a bag contains 6 cubes: 3 red, 2 green, and 1 yellow. Suppose you pick a cube without looking in the bag.
    a. Find the theoretical probability of picking each color.
    b. Find the sum of the three probabilities you found in part (a).
    c. Suppose you add more yellow cubes to the bag. How many should you add so that $P(\text{yellow}) = \frac{1}{2}$? Explain.

38. **Home Involvement** Work with a partner. One person should fill a bag with 8 cubes of 3 colors, without showing the other person. The second person should pick a cube, record the color, and put it back in the bag.

    After repeating this experiment 20 times, the second person should use experimental probabilities to guess how many cubes of each color are in the bag.

Tune In to Data

SET UP *Work in a group. You will need your data from Project Question 3.*

Making Predictions from Data During the past week, you collected data about television commercials. Now you'll examine the data.

4 Gather together all the data your group has collected.

5 Study your group's data. Then discuss each question.
   a. Was the number of commercials about the same for each time slot?
   b. What types of products were advertised? Were the same products advertised during each time slot?
   c. How do advertisers try to influence your choices?
   d. Can you make any predictions about the number of commercials and the products you might see advertised during your favorite program? Explain.

Section 3 Extra Skill Practice

For Exercises 1–19, use the table and information below.

Suppose a bag contains 8 marbles, with 2 each of the colors red, yellow, blue, and green. An experiment involves picking a marble from the bag, recording its color, and putting it back in the bag. The table shows the results after the experiment has been repeated 100 times.

Outcome	Frequency
red	40
yellow	20
blue	28
green	12

Find the experimental probability of each event.

1. *P*(red)
2. *P*(yellow)
3. *P*(blue)
4. *P*(green)
5. *P*(not red)
6. *P*(red or yellow)
7. *P*(not green)
8. *P*(brown)
9. *P*(not yellow)

Find the theoretical probability of each event.

10. *P*(red)
11. *P*(yellow)
12. *P*(blue)
13. *P*(green)
14. *P*(not blue)
15. *P*(blue or red)
16. *P*(not yellow)
17. *P*(brown)
18. *P*(not red)
19. How many red marbles do you expect to get if you repeat the experiment 500 times? Did you use *experimental probability* or *theoretical probability* to find your answer? Explain.

Standardized Testing ▶ Performance Task

Suppose a coin bank contains only 8 quarters. One quarter is dated 1955, 1 quarter is dated 1975, 3 quarters are dated 1985, and 3 quarters are dated 1997. Shaking the coin bank causes one coin at a time to come out randomly.

1. What is the probability that the first coin to come out is dated 1975? Explain.
2. Suppose the first coin to come out is *not* dated 1985. What is the probability that the second coin to come out is dated 1985? Explain.
3. What is the probability that the last coin to come out is a quarter? Explain.

Problem Solving

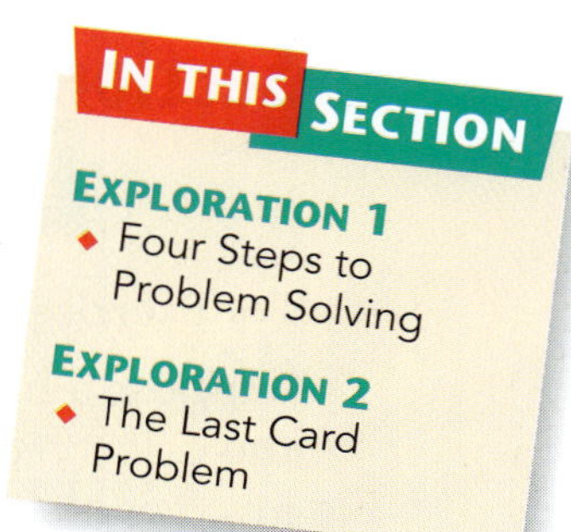

Setting the Stage

When you make a choice that affects your health or well-being, you may have to interpret information and analyze claims made by others.

The table displays data from a study. It shows how changing to an active lifestyle could lengthen a man's life span. In the study, an active lifestyle involves using 2000 or more Calories (Cal) per week on exercise.

Effects on Men of a Change to an Active Lifestyle

Age when active lifestyle began	Estimated increase in life span (years)
35–39	2.51
40–44	2.34
45–49	2.10
50–54	2.11
55–59	2.02
60–64	1.75
65–69	1.35
70–74	0.72
75–79	0.42

Think About It

1 **a.** How many years could a man who begins an active lifestyle at age 67 expect to gain?

b. Suppose a man begins exercising on his 67th birthday and wants to gain the additional years stated in the table above. What is the least number of total calories he will have to use on exercise by age 80?

2 What do you notice about the estimated number of years gained as you read the table from top to bottom?

3 The study shows how the choice to change from an inactive to an active lifestyle could affect the length of a man's life.

   a. What choices, other than amount of exercise, can people make that might affect the length of their lives?

   b. What are some factors that they might not be able to change?

4 What does the table suggest to you about the effects of exercise?

Exploration 1

Four Steps to PROBLEM SOLVING

GOAL

LEARN HOW TO...
- recognize the steps of the 4-step approach to problem solving

AS YOU...
- solve a problem about exercise

SET UP *Work in a group of three.*

In response to the study, two doctors questioned whether the number of years gained would justify the time and effort needed to burn 2000 Cal per week. They explored the study's claim about years gained for a man beginning exercise at age 35 and continuing until age 80.

To investigate the claim, the doctors focused on stair-stepping. They found that it takes one second to climb 2 stairs, and that climbing 70 stairs burns 28 Cal.

▶ **How did these doctors know how to evaluate the study's claim? Problem solving has been described as "what you do when you don't know what to do." Some people use a 4-step approach to solve problems, as you will do in Questions 5–8.**

5 **a.** Discuss what the two doctors were trying to do. In your own words, state the problem the doctors tried to solve.

b. Make a list of information needed to solve this problem. Check off information you already have, and circle information you'll need to calculate or find.

6 Discuss how you would go about solving the problem.

7 Solve the problem individually.

8 Look back over your solution.

a. Check all your computations.

b. Does your solution answer the question your group asked**?** Explain.

c. Explain another way you could have solved the same problem.

d. The two doctors were interested in whether the gain in years is worth the time spent exercising. What do you think**?** Write a brief letter expressing your thoughts. Be sure to include your solution to the problem and how you found it.

9 **Try This as a Class** Questions 5–8 illustrate the steps in the 4-step approach to problem solving. Describe each step by writing a short phrase about what you did for each question.

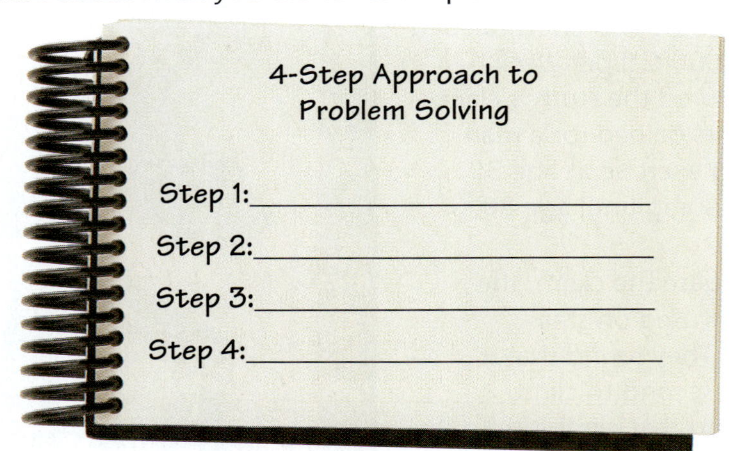

HOMEWORK EXERCISES ▶ **See Exs. 1–3 on p. 45.**

Exploration 2

GOAL

LEARN HOW TO...
- apply the 4-step approach to problem solving

AS YOU...
- predict outcomes in a card problem

SET UP *Work in a group. You will need 15 index cards numbered from 1 to 15.*

One of the steps in the 4-step approach is to make a plan to solve the problem. Making a plan often involves choosing a problem solving strategy such as *look for a pattern* or *use a model*. You might use one of these strategies as you explore the Last Card Problem.

▶ **The Last Card Problem** **Start with a stack of cards in numerical order from top to bottom. Then do as follows:**

Put the top card face up on the table.

Put the next card on the bottom of the stack.

Continue until all the cards are face up.

▶ **Can you predict what the last card will be if you know how many cards you start with?**

10 Suppose you start the Last Card Problem with six cards.

a. Which card do you think will be last?

b. Try the experiment with your cards. Were you right?

11 Suppose you start the Last Card Problem with nine cards. What will be the number on the last card?

12 Suppose you start with 16 cards or 20 cards. What will be the number on the last card in each case? Explain your answers.

HOMEWORK EXERCISES See Exs. 4–7 on pp. 45–46.

4-Step Approach to Problem Solving (p. 42)

Step 1: Understand the Problem

- Read the problem carefully, probably several times.
- Identify what the question is.
- Restate the problem in your own words.
- Identify the information needed to solve the problem, and determine if any of it is missing.

Step 2: Make a Plan

You may have to choose several problem solving strategies such as:

- try a simpler problem
- make an organized list
- act it out
- use logical reasoning
- make a picture or diagram
- make a table
- look for a pattern
- guess and check
- work backward
- use an equation

Step 3: Carry Out the Plan

- Solve the problem using the strategies you selected.
- You may need to change strategies.

Step 4: Look Back

- Check that you answered the question being asked.
- Check that your solution seems reasonable.
- Check that your work is accurate.
- Try to find another method to solve the problem and compare the results.
- Study the solution to see if the method can be generalized or extended to other situations or to solve other problems.

Key Concepts Questions

13 **a.** Which strategies did you use when you solved the card problems in Question 12?

b. Why would you want to use more than one strategy?

14 Why is looking back an important step in problem solving?

Section 4 Practice & Application Exercises

1. Calculator Assume a person jogging 1 mi at a rate of 5 mi/h will burn 100 Cal.

a. At this rate, how many minutes does it take to jog 1 mi?

b. At this rate, how many minutes per week must a person jog to burn 2000 Cal?

c. At age 35, a man changes to an active lifestyle. If he jogs regularly until age 80, how many minutes of his lifetime will he have to spend jogging to burn 2000 Cal per week?

d. **Writing** Is jogging as efficient as stair-stepping for increasing the number of years you live? Explain.

2. **Geometry Connection**
Three rhombuses with sides 1 in. long can be placed side by side as shown to form a figure with a perimeter of 8 in. If another figure is formed in the same way using 20 rhombuses, what will its perimeter be?

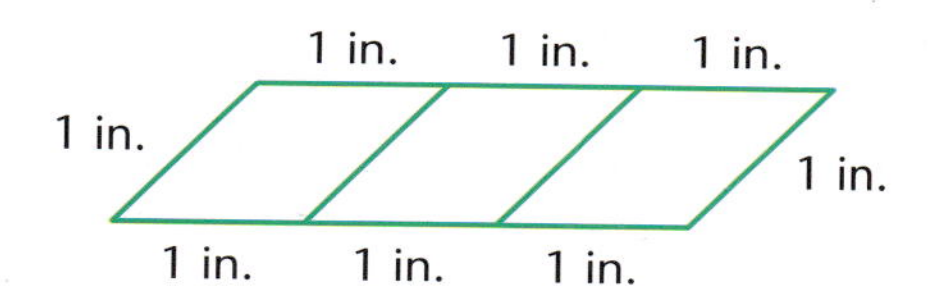

3. A pet shop has 12 dogs and cats. Each dog is fed 5 oz of pet chow per meal and each cat is fed 3 oz. It takes 42 oz of pet chow to feed all 12 animals one meal. How many dogs are there?

4. Two cards are on a table. A 12 is written on one of the cards and a 9 on the other. Each card also has a number written on its back. By turning over one or both or neither of the cards and adding the two numbers showing, you can get each of these sums: 15, 16, 20, and 21. What number is written on the back of each card?

5. Natasha's scores on her first three quizzes were 88, 72, and 80. She reasons that if she scores high enough on the next quiz, then the mean of her quiz scores will be at least 90. Do you think Natasha's solution is reasonable? Why or why not?

6. **Challenge** Suppose you buy lunch for the drama club. You have enough money to buy 20 salads or 15 sandwiches. The members want 12 sandwiches. How many salads can you buy?

Oral Report

Exercise 7 checks that you recognize the 4-step approach to problem solving.

Reflecting on the Section

Be prepared to report on the following topic in class.

7. Describe a situation in daily life when you have had to solve a problem. How was the process you used similar to the 4-step approach?

Spiral Review

8. The spinner shown is spun once and the color of the section that the spinner lands on is recorded. (Module 1, p. 33)

   a. What are all the possible outcomes of the experiment?

   b. What is the theoretical probability of each outcome?

   c. Suppose the spinner is spun 30 times. How many times would you expect to get red?

Use compatible numbers to estimate each quotient. (Toolbox, p.583)

9. $19\overline{)101}$ 10. $83\overline{)164}$ 11. $148\overline{)612}$

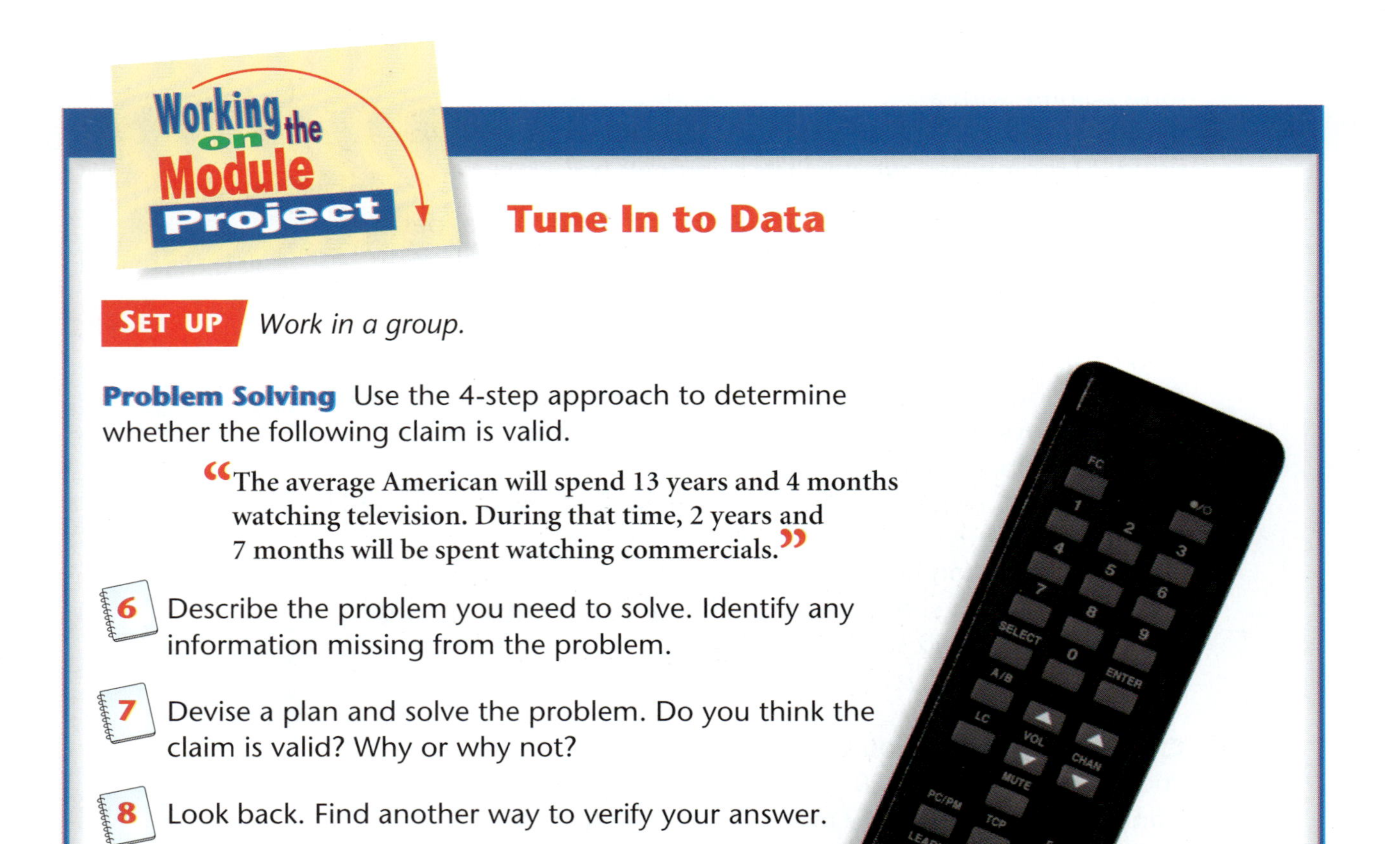

Working on the Module Project

Tune In to Data

SET UP *Work in a group.*

Problem Solving Use the 4-step approach to determine whether the following claim is valid.

> "The average American will spend 13 years and 4 months watching television. During that time, 2 years and 7 months will be spent watching commercials."

6 Describe the problem you need to solve. Identify any information missing from the problem.

7 Devise a plan and solve the problem. Do you think the claim is valid? Why or why not?

8 Look back. Find another way to verify your answer.

1. David earns $6.00 per hour plus $9.00 for every extra hour he works over 40 h per week. If David earned $285.00 last week, how many extra hours did he work?

2. Cynthia needs $1500 to buy a computer. The table shows how much money she had in October, November, and December. If this pattern continues, in what month will she be able to buy the computer?

Month	Amount of money
October	$600
November	$750
December	$900

3. Jermaine sent a message to four friends. Two of the friends each sent the message to three other people and the other two friends each sent the message to five other people. Each of these other people then sent the message to one other person. How many people in all were sent the message?

4. Jenna and Elizabeth play soccer at a local playground. They are both on the soccer field today, but they have different schedules. Jenna plays every 2 days and Elizabeth plays every 4 days. How many times will they both be on the soccer field on the same day during the next eight weeks?

Standardized Testing Free Response

Suppose Jana plans on doing five events (Events A–E) at an athletic competition. The judges require that Event C be performed either first or last. In how many different orders can Jana perform her five events?

FOR ASSESSMENT AND PORTFOLIOS

THE Painted CUBE

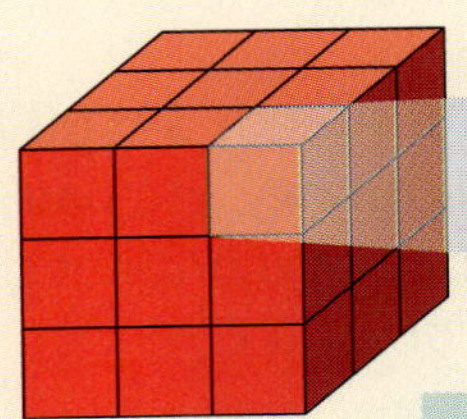

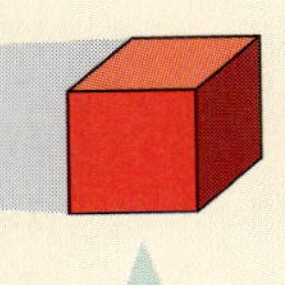

A unit cube has edges 1 unit long.

The Situation

Katie, a student at the world's first orbiting middle school, noticed that unit cubes float in zero gravity. If she was careful, she could even build floating geometric shapes with the unit cubes.

One day Katie used the unit cubes to build a larger floating cube that was three units long on each edge. She then painted all the exposed faces of the unit cubes bright red. Unfortunately, just after she finished, she sneezed, scattering the unit cubes. No cubes remained attached to each other.

The Problem

When Katie gathers the cubes, how many cubes will she find that have exactly 6 faces painted red? 5 faces painted red? 4 faces painted red? 3 faces painted red? 2 faces painted red? 1 face painted red? 0 faces painted red?

Something to Think About

- How many unit cubes should she have in all?
- Does each unit cube have the same number of painted faces?

Present your Results

Write a summary that clearly explains how you solved the problem. Include any drawings or other representations that will help make your explanation clear to others.

The Assessment Scales on page 49 will help you and your teacher think about your work on this and other Extended Explorations (E^2). The presentation scale will help you assess how well you present your results: Remember, a solution should always include an explanation of your work as well as your answer. In Sections 5 and 6, you will learn to use the other scales.

Student Self-Assessment

Student Resource

If your score is in the shaded area, explain why on the back of this sheet and stop.

The star indicates that you excelled in some way.

Problem Solving

1 2 3 4 5

1 — I did not understand the problem well enough to get started or I did not show any work.

3 — I understood the problem well enough to make a plan and to work toward a solution.

5 — I made a plan, I used it to solve the problem, and I verified my solution.

Mathematical Language

1 2 3 4 5

1 — I did not use any mathematical vocabulary or symbols, or I did not use them correctly, or my use was not appropriate.

3 — I used appropriate mathematical language, but the way it was used was not always correct or other terms and symbols were needed.

5 — I used mathematical language that was correct and appropriate to make my meaning clear.

Representations

1 2 3 4 5

1 — I did not use any representations such as equations, tables, graphs, or diagrams to help solve the problem or explain my solution.

3 — I made appropriate representations to help solve the problem or help me explain my solution, but they were not always correct or other representations were needed.

5 — I used appropriate and correct representations to solve the problem or explain my solution.

Connections

1 2 3 4 5

1 — I attempted or solved the problem and then stopped.

3 — I found patterns and used them to extend the solution to other cases, or I recognized that this problem relates to other problems, mathematical ideas, or applications.

5 — I extended the ideas in the solution to the general case, or I showed how this problem relates to other problems, mathematical ideas, or applications.

Presentation

1 2 3 4 5

1 — The presentation of my solution and reasoning is unclear to others.

3 — The presentation of my solution and reasoning is clear in most places, but others may have trouble understanding parts of it.

5 — The presentation of my solution and reasoning is clear and can be understood by others.

Section 5 Assessing Problem Solving

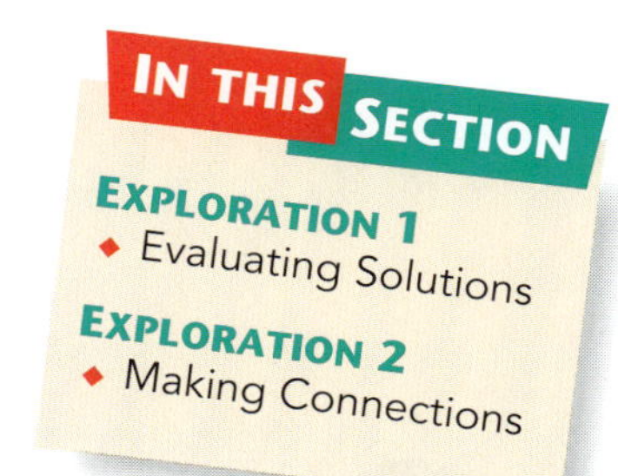

Creative Solutions

Setting the Stage

The reading below describes how Alesia Revis and her friend Sylvester solved a problem.

ALESIA

by Eloise Greenfield and Alesia Revis

A friend of mine named Sylvester came down to my office to have lunch with me today. When we left the cafeteria, we had to go through this corridor where the floor slopes uphill. It wasn't easy in our wheelchairs. My arms gave out, and then Sylvester said, "Hold on to my chair," and he pulled both of us. I should have held on with my left hand because my right arm is stronger and I could have helped roll my chair, but by the time I thought of it, we were halfway up the hill, and I was afraid that if I tried to switch hands I would roll backward and get hurt. Anyway, we made it. We got through it with nobody else's help and I was so proud of us.

Think About It

1 What problem did Alesia and Sylvester face?

2 Describe how their approach to the problem was like the 4-step approach to problem solving.

▶ **Alesia faced a special challenge related to getting around in a wheelchair. Having good problem solving skills can help you make good choices when you face your own challenges.**

Exploration 1

Evaluating SOLUTIONS

GOAL

LEARN HOW TO...
- use the problem solving scale

AS YOU...
- evaluate solutions to the Last Card Problem

▶ **One way to improve your problem solving skills is to evaluate or assess your past experiences. You can use the Assessment Scales on page 49 to assess your work in mathematics. In this Section you'll evaluate solutions to the Last Card Problem from Section 4.**

The problem solving scale helps you evaluate your approach to solving a problem.

A marker is used to draw a segment along the scale. This student scored at level 4 on this scale.

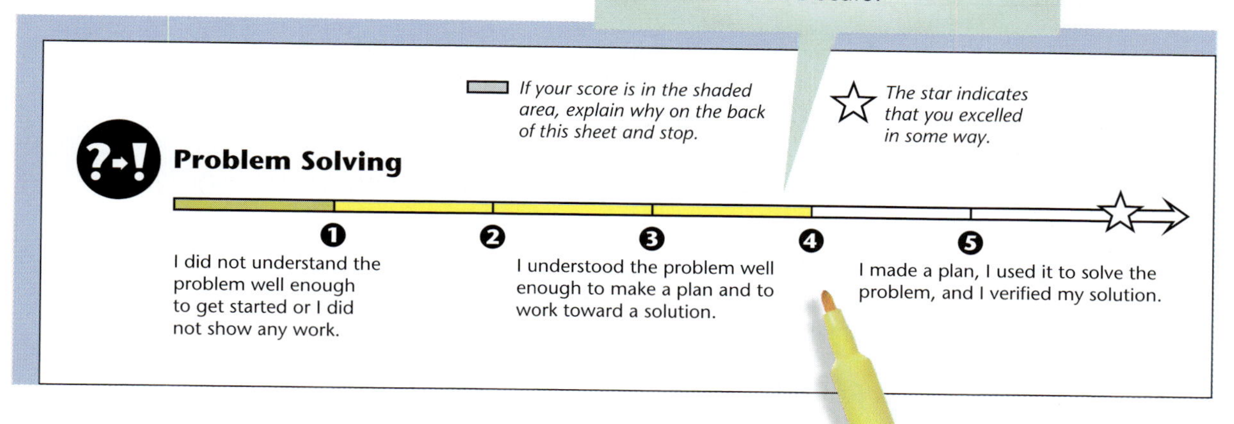

▶ **When you assess your work using the problem solving scale, think about whether you:**
- **understood the problem**
- **made a plan**
- **carried out the plan to solve the problem**
- **looked back to verify your solution**

3 **Try This as a Class** Discuss how the problem solving scale is related to the 4-step approach to problem solving you used in Section 4.

4 In Question 12 on page 43 of Section 4, you were asked to solve the Last Card Problem for 16 cards and for 20 cards. Suppose a group found the last card in each case but did not show any work. How would the group score on the problem solving scale? Why?

▶ **Here is how Kim's group approached the Last Card Problem.**

First we used the strategy "try a simpler problem." We found that with 3 cards the number on the last card was 2.

Next we decided to try the strategies "make a table" and "look for a pattern" to see if we could predict the last card for 16 and 20 cards.

Number of cards	1	2	3	4	5	6	7	8	9	10	11	12	13	14	15
Number on last card	1	2	2	4	2	4	6	8	2	4	6	8	10	12	14

We used our 15 numbered cards to complete our table, but we could not find a pattern.

5 **Discussion** If Kim's group stops without finding a solution, how should they score their work on the problem solving scale? Why?

6 Describe any patterns you see in the table made by Kim's group.

▶ **When your approach to a problem does not help you find a solution, you may need to try a different method. As a new approach, Kim's group modeled each move for 6 cards.**

Why are **1**, **3**, and **5** crossed out?

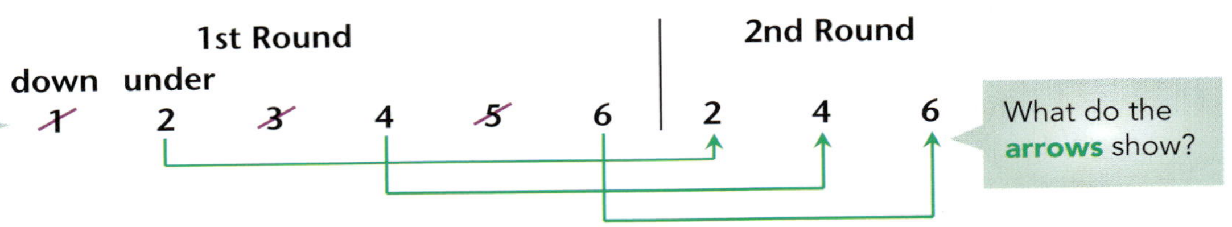

7 **a.** Copy and complete the model. What number is crossed out next? What will be the last card?

b. Use this method to solve the Last Card Problem for 16 cards and for 20 cards.

...checks that you can assess a solution using the problem solving scale.

8 ✓ **CHECKPOINT** Suppose Kim's group uses the method above and finds the last card for 16 cards and for 20 cards. How should they score their work on the problem solving scale? Why?

HOMEWORK EXERCISES ▶ See Exs. 1–3 on p. 56.

Exploration 2

MAKING Connections

GOAL

LEARN HOW TO...
- use the connections scale

AS YOU...
- find ways to extend your solution to the Last Card Problem

SET UP *You will need:* • *Labsheet 5A* • *marker for highlighting* • *your group's solution to Question 12 on page 43*

▶ **When you solve problems, you sometimes see familiar patterns. The table shows patterns that Greg's group recognized while working on the Last Card Problem.**

Number of cards	1	②	3	④	5	6	7	⑧	9	10	11	12	13	14	15
Number on last card	1	2	2	4	2	4	6	8	2	4	6	8	10	12	14

9 **a.** Why do you think an X was drawn over the data for 1 card?

b. Why do you think brackets were drawn under the table?

c. Why do you think circles were drawn around 2, 4, and 8?

d. Suppose you continue the table. What do you think the next circled number will be? Why? How would you describe the circled numbers?

▶ **Greg's group connected another mathematical topic, the powers of 2, to the Last Card Problem. You can use the connections scale to assess how well you make mathematical connections.**

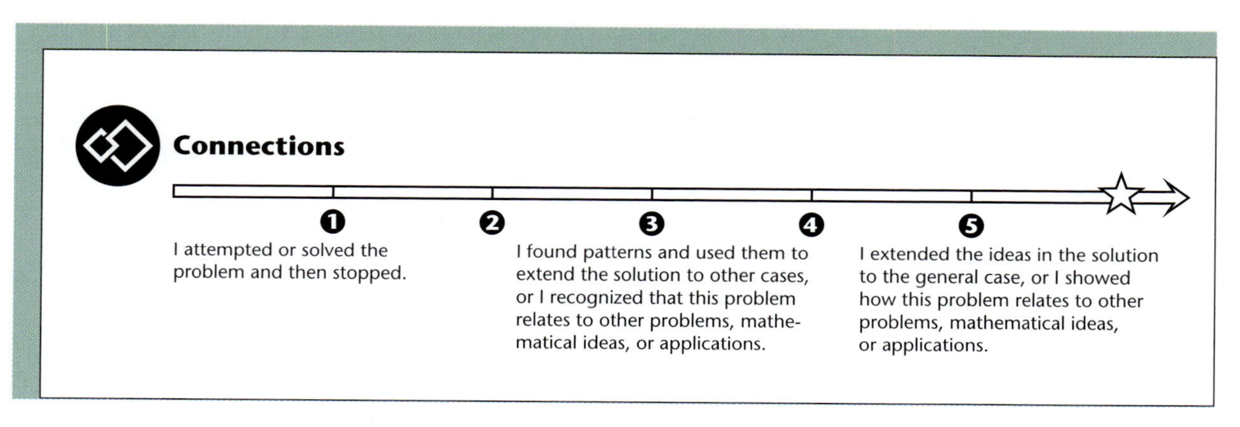

You might score a 3 on the connections scale if you:
- recognize how the problem is related to other problems
- recognize connections to other mathematical topics
- extend the solution beyond the original problem

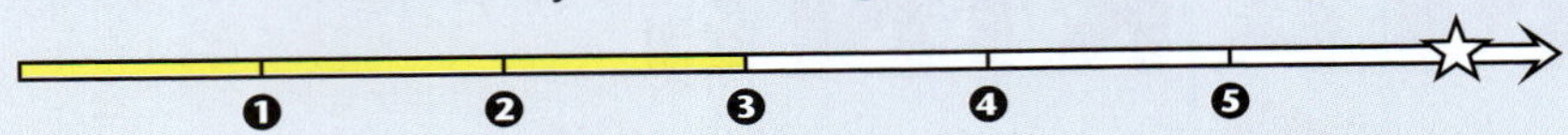

You might score a 5 on the connections scale if you:
- show how the problem or mathematics can be applied elsewhere
- extend the problem to the general case

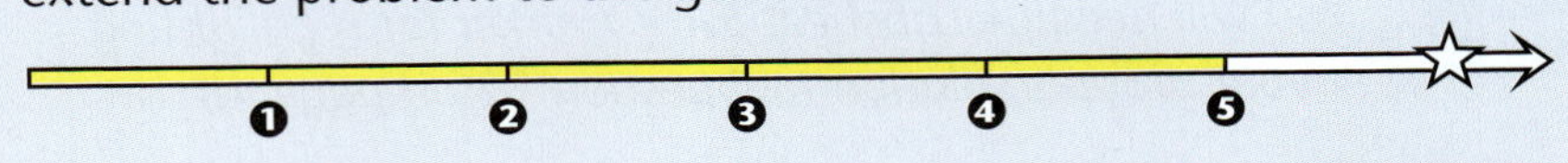

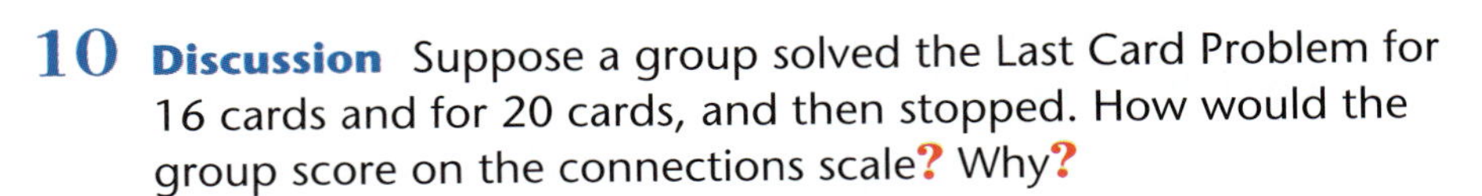

10 **Discussion** Suppose a group solved the Last Card Problem for 16 cards and for 20 cards, and then stopped. How would the group score on the connections scale? Why?

✓ QUESTION 11

...checks that you can assess a solution using the connections scale.

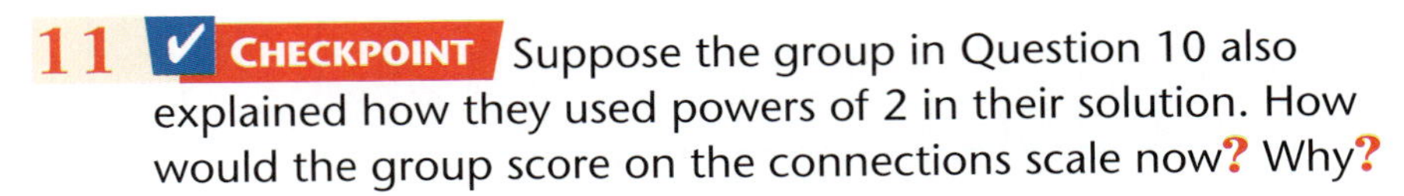

11 **✓ CHECKPOINT** Suppose the group in Question 10 also explained how they used powers of 2 in their solution. How would the group score on the connections scale now? Why?

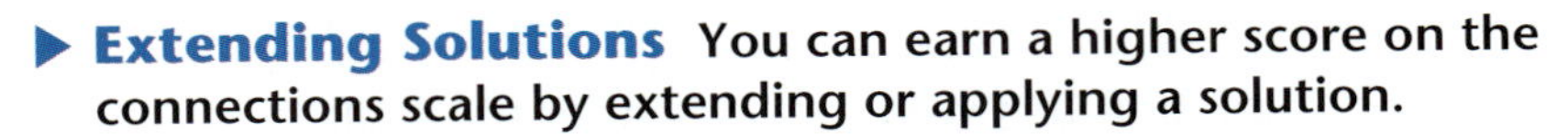

▶ Extending Solutions **You can earn a higher score on the connections scale by extending or applying a solution.**

12 **a.** What is the next power of 2 after 16?

b. Look at the table on page 53. What pattern do you see? Does it continue for 17 cards, 18 cards, and so on?

Use Labsheet 5A for Questions 13 and 14.

13 **a.** Complete the *Last-Card Table* through 20 cards.

b. How could you verify (check) your answers?

14 **a.** Without extending the table any more, predict the last card for a stack of 33 cards.

b. Complete the *Last-Card Table* through 33 cards. Compare your prediction in part (a) with your answer in the table.

15 **Discussion** For each situation, tell how you would assess a student's solution to Questions 12–14 on the connections scale.

a. The student's work includes everything in Questions 12–14.

b. The student's work identifies a pattern and shows how to use it with *any number* of cards (the general case).

16 Use Labsheet 5A.

a. Use the *Two Assessment Scales* to assess your group's solution to Question 12 on page 43 of Section 4.

b. Explain why you rated your group as you did on each scale.

17 Discussion When would you shade a scale as far as the ☆?

HOMEWORK EXERCISES ▶ See Exs. 4–7 on pp. 56–57.

Section 5 Key Concepts

The purpose of the Assessment Scales is to help you evaluate your solutions to problems and increase your problem solving ability.

Problem Solving Scale (pp. 51–52)
The problem solving scale is used to assess how well you apply the 4-step approach to problem solving.

Connections Scale (pp. 53–55)
The connections scale helps assess the connections you make to other problems, mathematical concepts, or applications.

Example Here are two ways Greg's group could have scored at level 5 on the connections scale:

- The group extended the Last Card Problem to determine the number on the last card no matter how many cards they used (general case).
- The group explained why the last card drawn equals the number of cards in the stack only when the number of cards is a power of 2.

18 Key Concepts Question What problem solving strategies were used in this Section to solve the Last Card Problem?

Section 5

Practice & Application Exercises

YOU WILL NEED

For Exs. 3 and 5:
- Labsheet 5B, marker

For Ex. 4:
- 10 cards numbered 1–10

For Ex. 6:
- Labsheet 5A

1. **Visual Thinking** Choose the letter(s) of the pattern(s) that can be folded into a cube. Then draw two other patterns that will work.

   A.

   B.

   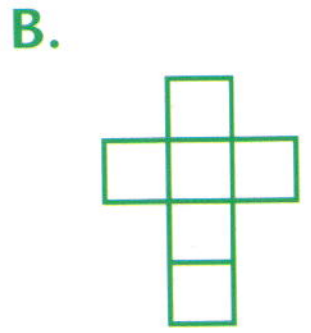

   C.

   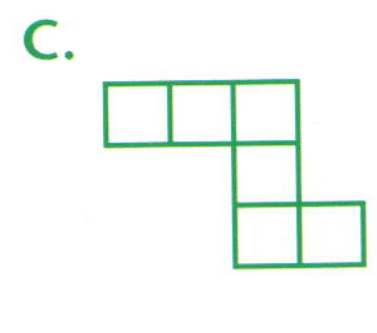

2. Suppose next semester you want to take music, advanced science, creative writing, and basketball. Music is held periods 1, 2, and 4 only. Advanced science is offered periods 2, 3, and 4. Creative writing meets periods 1, 2, and 3, while basketball is offered periods 1, 3, and 4. List all the possible ways you could take these four classes.

3. **Use Labsheet 5B.** Assess your work in Exercises 1 and 2 using the problem solving scale.

4. Suppose you have 10 cards numbered from 1 to 10. How would you order the cards so that when you follow the procedure below, the cards are in numerical order in a pile on a table, with the 1 at the bottom and the 10 at the top? (*Note:* Your solution should explain what you did and why you did it.)

   - Place the top card face up on a table.
   - Put the second card on the bottom of the stack.
   - Place the third card face up on the table.
   - Put the fourth card on the bottom of the stack, and so on, until all cards are on the table.

5. **Use Labsheet 5B**. Assess your work in Exercise 4 using the *Two Assessment Scales*. Give reasons why you rated your work the way you did, and describe what you could do to improve your solution.

6. **Challenge Use Labsheet 5A.** How could you use the patterns in the *Last-Card Table* to determine the number on the last card no matter how many cards you started with?

Reflecting on the Section

Write your response to Exercise 7 in your Journal.

7. The problem solving scale used in this section can be used to assess activities other than mathematics. Explain how the problem solving scale can be used to assess your performance in one activity you perform regularly. Activities to consider are science homework, chores, sports, or music.

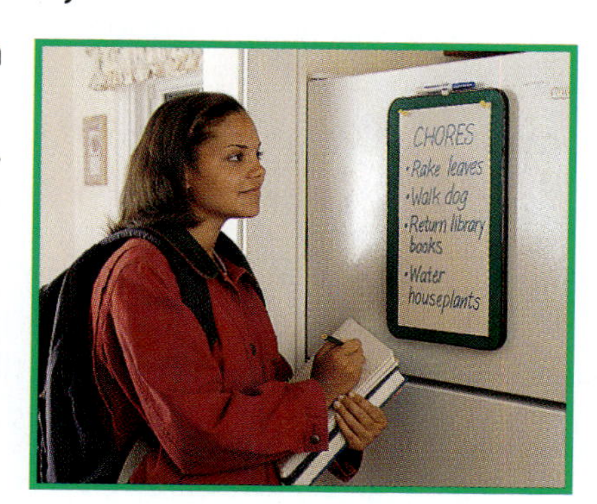

Journal

Exercise 7 checks that you can use the problem solving scale to assess your work.

Spiral Review

8. Juanita was taking archery. One day she shot 6 arrows at the target shown. Each arrow hit the target. Which of the following numbers could have been her score: 5, 32, 19, 56, 47? Explain your reasoning. (Module 1, p. 44)

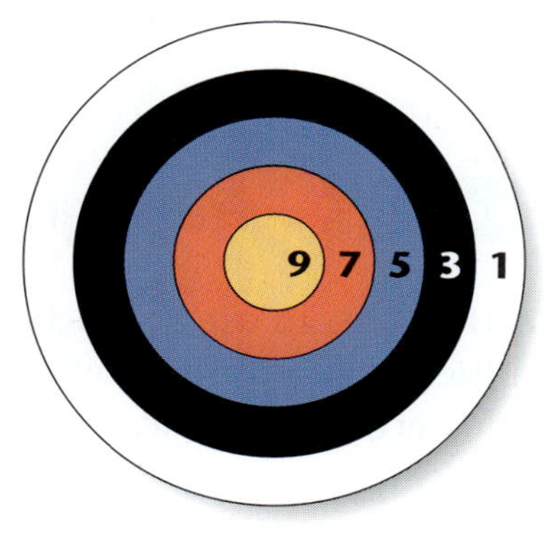

Replace each __?__ with the correct measure. (Toolbox, p. 592; Table of Measures, p. 597)

9. 9 h = __?__ min
10. 4 yd = __?__ in.
11. 48 oz = __?__ lb
12. 60 ft = __?__ yd
13. 5 lb = __?__ oz
14. 3600 s = __?__ h

Estimation Estimate the value of each expression. Explain how you made each estimate. (Toolbox, pp. 582–583)

15. $236 \cdot 18$
16. $2683 \div 91$
17. $236 + 481 + 352$
18. $1917 - 398$
19. $51 \cdot 122$
20. $104 + 92 + 113$

Section 5 Extra Skill Practice

1. a. Suppose you have quarters, dimes, and pennies with a total value of \$1.19. How many of each coin can you have without being able to make change for a dollar?
   b. Show that the combination of coins that you found in part (a) is the largest amount of money in these 3 coins that you can have without being able to make change for a dollar.
   c. What score would you give your work in parts (a) and (b) on the problem solving scale on page 51?

2. a. **Visual Thinking** Find the total number of triangles in the diagram.
   b. What score would you give your solution in part (a) on the problem solving scale on page 51?

3. a. A book states that the average person in the United States will spend 1091 h in movie theaters in his or her lifetime. Do you think this claim is correct? Explain. (Assume the average life-span of a person living in the United States is 74.9 years.)
   b. What score would you give your solution in part (a) on the problem solving and connections scales on pages 51 and 53?

Standardized Testing ▶ Free Response

Suppose Alex has \$12. He wants to use as much of the \$12 as possible to treat some friends to a picnic lunch. Each person will get a sandwich, a dessert, and a drink.

a. Explain how Alex could find the number of friends he can invite and the combination of menu items to serve.

b. Is there a different way to solve this problem? Explain.

c. Alex wants to treat 4 friends to the same menu next month, and 5 friends the month after that. Can he use the solution from part (a) to help him find out how much money he needs each time? Explain.

Pine Point Specials

Item	Price
Sandwich	
regular	\$1.89
deluxe	\$2.33
Dessert	
Cookie	\$.89
Apple	\$.67
Drink	\$.75

(no charge for water)

Section 6 Expressions and Representations

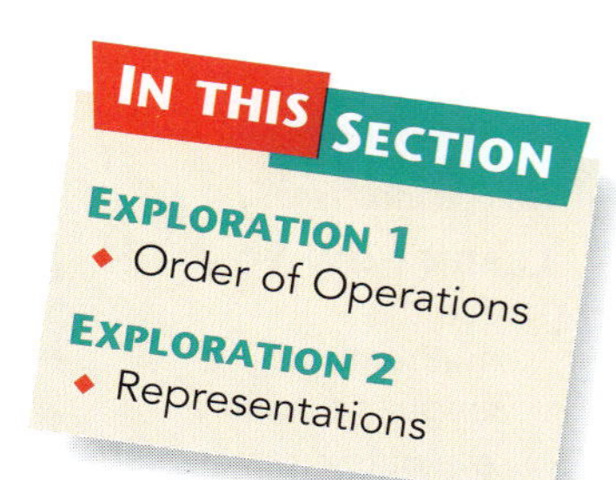

The Clear CHOICE

Setting the Stage

Communicating your ideas and decisions clearly and correctly is an important skill. When you solve a problem and explain your solution, you should choose the words, symbols, and pictures you use carefully. The cartoon shows how important this can be.

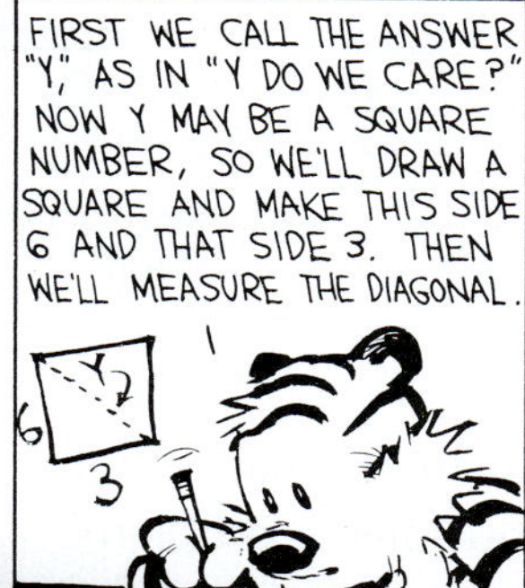

Think About It

1 What mathematical terms and picture does Hobbes (the tiger) use? Are they accurate and appropriate? Explain.

2 **a.** Write an explanation telling Calvin how to solve his problem.

b. What choices did you make when deciding how to present your explanation? Did you use pictures? words? symbols?

c. Was your explanation clear and appropriate? Explain.

▶ **In this Section, you will examine ways to assess and improve your mathematical communication skills.**

GOAL

LEARN HOW TO...
- use the mathematical language scale
- evaluate expressions using the order of operations

AS YOU...
- solve problems

KEY TERMS
- expression
- evaluate
- order of operations

Exploration 1

ORDER of OPERATIONS

▶ **Mathematics has its own language of words and symbols. You probably used mathematical language to explain how to solve Calvin's problem. You can use the mathematical language scale from the Assessment Scales on page 49 to assess how well you use mathematical vocabulary and symbols.**

Mathematical Language

❶ I did not use any mathematical vocabulary or symbols, or I did not use them correctly, or my use was not appropriate.

❷

❸ I used appropriate mathematical language, but the way it was used was not always correct or other terms and symbols were needed.

❹

❺ I used mathematical language that was correct and appropriate to make my meaning clear.

3 Why is it important that mathematical symbols, words, and rules be used correctly when you solve a problem?

4 **a.** What score do you think Hobbes should give himself for his explanation of how to find 6 + 3? Why?

b. What score would you give your explanation and why?

▶ **In Calvin's problem, 6 + 3 is a numerical *expression*. An expression is a mathematical phrase that can be formed using numbers, variables, and operation symbols.**

5 **Discussion** For parts (a) and (b), in what order must you do the operations to get the answers given?

a. $5 + 2 \cdot 25 = 175$

b. $5 + 2 \cdot 25 = 55$

c. The expression $5 + 2 \cdot 25$ can be used to represent the total value (in cents) of a nickel and two quarters. Which of the answers from parts (a) and (b) gives the correct value?

▶ To **evaluate** a numerical expression, you carry out the mathematical operations in the correct order. This order is known as the **order of operations.**

6 **Discussion** Discuss the order in which the operations were performed in each case to get the correct answer.

a. $3 \cdot 6 + 27 = 45$

b. $36 - 24 \div 4 = 30$

c. $12 \div 3 + 10 = 14$

d. $15 + 12 \cdot 6 = 87$

e. $12 \div 6 \cdot 2 = 4$

f. $36 - 15 + 5 = 26$

g. $3 \cdot 4 - 54 \div 6 = 3$

h. $48 \div 4 - 6 \cdot 2 = 0$

7 Use correct and appropriate language to state a rule that describes the order of operations for an expression containing addition, subtraction, multiplication, and division.

▶ **Grouping Symbols** **Operations within grouping symbols such as parentheses and brackets are carried out first. A fraction bar indicates that you carry out operations in the numerator separately from those in the denominator. Then you divide numerator by denominator.**

8 For each expression, in what order were the operations carried out to get 35?

a. $[15 - (6 + 4)] \cdot 7 = 35$

b. $\frac{(8 + 6) \cdot 5}{8 - 6} = 35$

9 **Try This as a Class** Discuss where grouping symbols and exponents fit into the order of operations to get the correct answers shown.

a. $3 \cdot (6 + 4) = 30$

b. $2 \cdot 3^2 = 18$

c. $(2 \cdot 3)^2 = 36$

d. $2 \cdot (3 + 4)^2 = 98$

e. $[(5 - 4)^6 + 2] \cdot 8 = 24$

f. $\frac{48 \div (7 - 3)}{24 - 18} = 2$

10 Use parentheses to rewrite $54 \div 6 - 3 \cdot 2$ so the result is 12.

11 ✓ **CHECKPOINT** Evaluate each expression.

a. $9 + 2 \cdot 4$

b. $10 \div 2 + 16 \div 8$

c. $\frac{(12 - 5) \cdot 6}{6 + 1}$

d. $[(5 - 3)^3 \div (7 - 5)] \cdot 5^2$

... checks that you can follow the order of operations to evaluate expressions.

HOMEWORK EXERCISES ▶ See Exs. 1–17 on p. 66.

GOAL

LEARN HOW TO...
- use the representations scale
- decide when a line graph is appropriate

AS YOU...
- explore television viewing habits

Exploration 2

Representations

▶ **Equations, tables, graphs, and diagrams are representations that can be used to help explain solutions. You can use the representations scale to assess how well you use representations.**

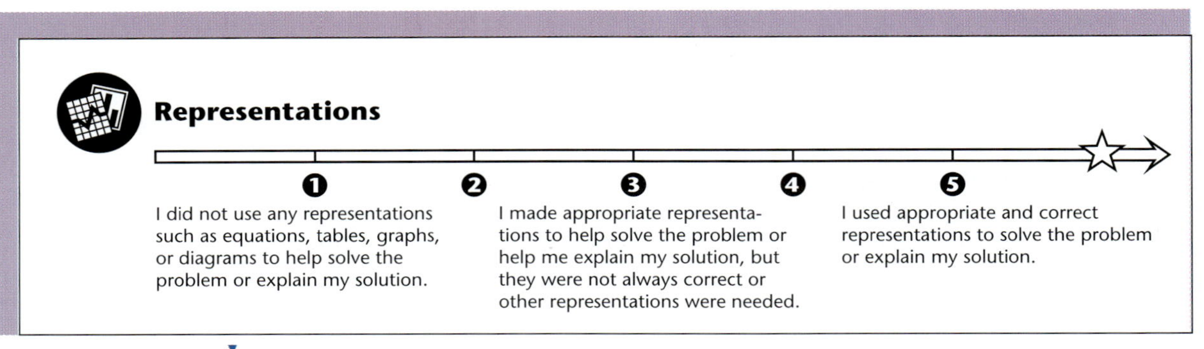

12 In the cartoon on page 59, Hobbes used a picture in his explanation to Calvin. What score do you think Hobbes should give himself on the representations scale? Why?

▶ **George is in the seventh grade. He thinks this table he saw in a newspaper can help him decide whether to change his television viewing habits to improve his mathematics proficiency next year.**

Eighth Grade Students' Reports on Amount of Time Spent Watching Television Each Day (1990)

Amount of time (hours)	Percent of students	Average mathematics proficiency
1 or less	12%	269
2	21%	268
3	22%	265
4 to 5	28%	260
6 or more	16%	245

Percents are rounded to the nearest whole percent.

The highest possible score is 500.

13 **Discussion** George thinks that on average he watches 3.5 h of television each day. Does he fit into any of the categories for "Amount of time"? Explain.

▶ **George made a line graph to compare his television viewing habits with those of eighth graders. On the graph he plotted data from the table and a point *G* to represent himself.**

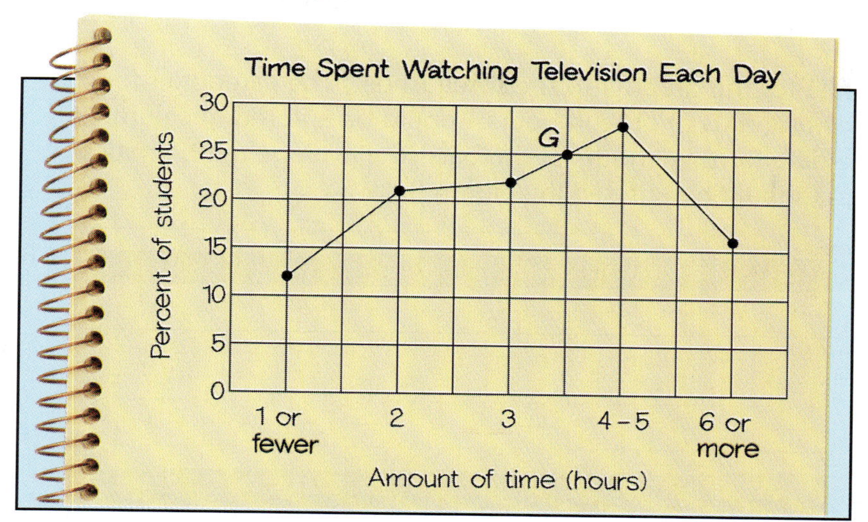

14 **Try This as a Class** Using his graph, George made the following observation. "I watch 3.5 h of TV per day. From my graph, I can see that 25% of eighth graders watch the same amount of TV."

a. How did George get 25%? Is his observation correct? Explain.

b. Does George's graph accurately represent the data from the table? Explain.

c. Is a line graph an appropriate way to represent this data? Explain.

d. Is there a better way to represent the data? Explain.

15 ✓ **CHECKPOINT** If the graph above is the only representation George used to explore the situation, how do you think he should score himself on the representations scale? Why?

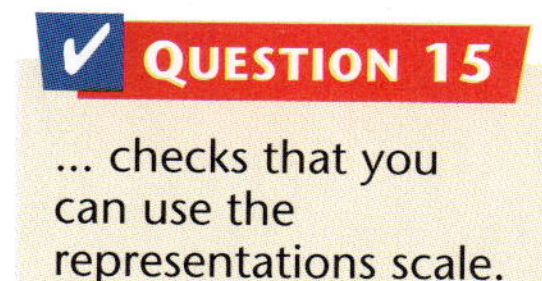

16 George also wants to investigate whether the amount of time spent watching television is related to the average mathematics proficiency.

a. Make a bar graph of the mathematics proficiency data. Include a title for the graph and label the axes.

b. What observation(s) might George make using your bar graph?

c. Why is a bar graph more appropriate than a line graph for these data?

 TECHNOLOGY **Using Spreadsheet Software**

You can use most spreadsheets to create a bar graph for Question 16(a).

Step 1 Enter the data for the graph into the spreadsheet. The categories for the bars (the amounts of time in hours) should be entered in column A as text. The data for the lengths of the bars (the average mathematics proficiencies) should be entered in column B.

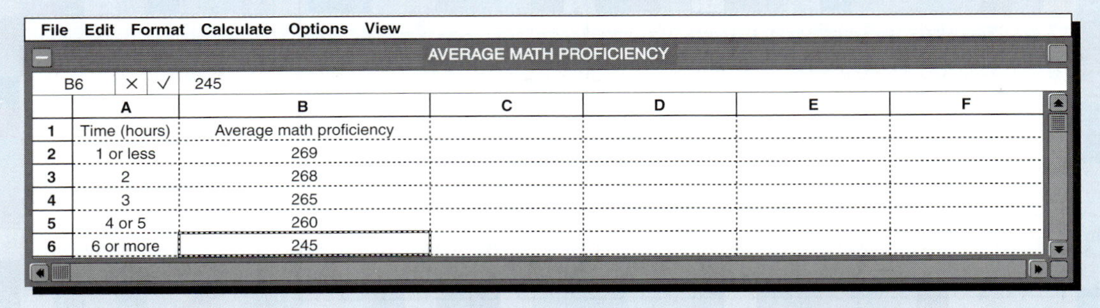
File Edit Format Calculate Options View

AVERAGE MATH PROFICIENCY

B6 × √ 245

	A	B	C	D	E	F
1	Time (hours)	Average math proficiency				
2	1 or less	269				
3	2	268				
4	3	265				
5	4 or 5	260				
6	6 or more	245				

Step 2 To make a graph, highlight the data you entered and select the option that lets you make a chart. Then select the type of graph you want to make.

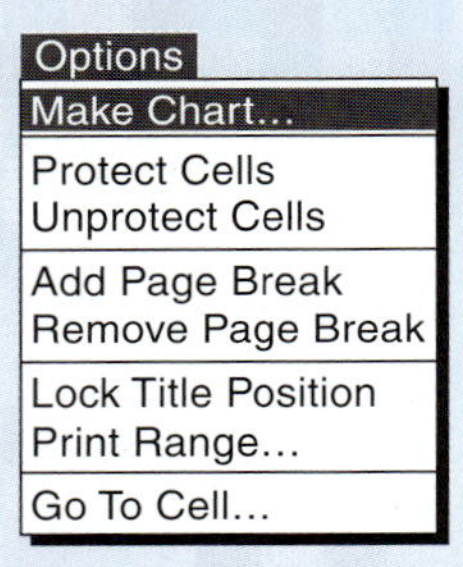

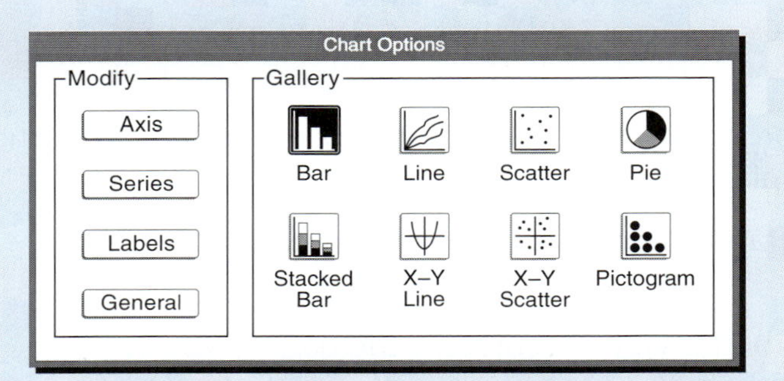

Step 3 Experiment with the labels, grid lines, and scale until the graph appears the way you want it to.

Eighth Grade Students' Television Viewing and Math Proficiency

Average math proficiency: 230, 240, 250, 260, 270

Time (hours): 1 or less, 2, 3, 4 to 5, 6 or more

17 a. Nationwide, about half of the eighth graders who took the mathematics proficiency test in 1990 scored above 262, and about half scored below. George watches 3.5 h of TV each day. Based on these facts and the bar graph you made in Question 16(a), do you think George should change how much TV he watches? Why?

b. Suppose George decides to watch less TV. Can he be certain that his mathematics proficiency will change? Explain.

See Exs. 18–26 on pp. 67–68.

Section 6 Key Concepts

Mathematical Language Scale (p. 60)

The mathematical language scale assesses how well you use mathematical vocabulary and symbols.

Order of Operations (pp. 60–61)

It is important to use the correct order of operations when evaluating expressions.

- First, evaluate expressions set apart by grouping symbols. Start with the innermost pair of symbols.
- Next evaluate all powers.
- Then do all multiplication and division in order from left to right.
- Finally, do all addition and subtraction in order from left to right.

Example

$3 + [11 + (7 - 4)]^2 \div 7$

$3 + [11 + 3]^2 \div 7$

$3 + 14^2 \div 7$

$3 + 196 \div 7$

$3 + 28$

31

Representations Scale (pp. 62–63)

The representations scale assesses how well you use equations, tables, graphs, and diagrams to help solve a problem or explain your solution.

Key Terms

expression

order of operations

evaluate

18 Key Concepts Question Describe the steps you follow to evaluate $3 + 5 \cdot (6 - 3)^2$.

YOU WILL NEED

For Ex. 18(b):
- Labsheet 6A

For Exs. 31–34:
- ruler

Section 6 Practice & Application Exercises

Evaluate each expression using the order of operations.

1. $48 - 6 \cdot 7$ **2.** $9 \cdot (6 + 5) - 9$ **3.** $9 \cdot 8 - 64 \div 8$

4. $12 + 16 \div 2^2 - 2$ **5.** $27 \div (12 - 9) \cdot 9$ **6.** $(6 - 4)^2 \cdot (12 + 3)$

7. $\frac{(10 - 8) \cdot 9}{5 + 1}$ **8.** $\frac{70 \div (12 - 5)}{15 \div 3}$ **9.** $3^3 \div [6^2 - (16 + 8)]$

10. Write and evaluate an expression to represent the value (in cents) of 2 half-dollars, 5 quarters, 6 nickels, 3 dimes, and 3 pennies.

Use grouping symbols to make each statement true.

11. $28 - 9 \cdot 2 = 38$ **12.** $6 + 5 \cdot 3 - 2 = 11$

13. $6 + 6 \div 2 \cdot 6 - 1 = 30$ **14.** $4 \cdot 5 - 4^2 + 3 = 1$

15. Challenge Use grouping symbols to make the statement $2 + 7^2 - 3^2 \div 3^2 - 1 \cdot 5 = 35$ true.

16. *Pizza by the Inch* sells square pizza. The smallest pizzas are 5 in. on each side and sell for \$1.99. The next size is a 10 in. by 10 in. for \$4.99. The largest pizza costs \$19.99 and has 20 in. sides.

a. Which size is the best buy? Justify the operations you used to make your decision.

b. Use the mathematical language scale on page 60. What score would you give your solution to part (a)?

17. Geometry Connection Read these instructions:

> "Draw a closed, four-sided flat figure that has sides that are segments that are all the same length and that has corners that are all the same shape."

a. Write instructions for the same task using fewer words.

b. Compare your instructions with the given ones in terms of correctness and appropriateness.

18. A circus has unicycles and tricycles. There are 25 cycles, with a total of 51 wheels.

a. How many of each type of cycle does the circus have?

b. **Use Labsheet 6A.** Use the *Three Assessment Scales* to assess your solution to part (a).

Use the line graph for Exercises 19–21.

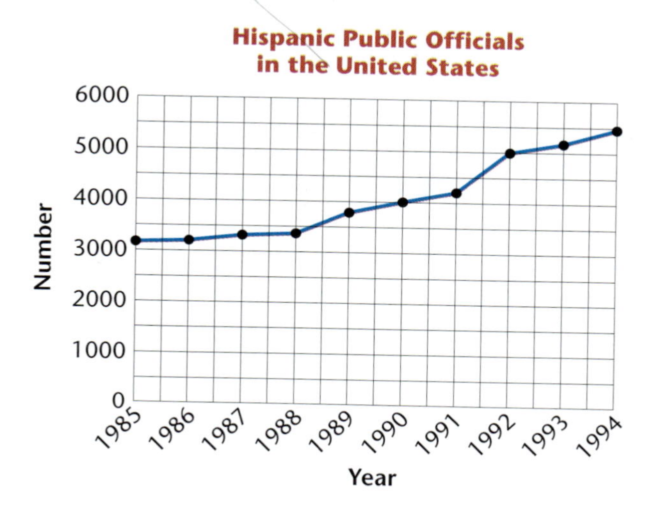

19. What was the approximate number of Hispanic public officials in the year 1990?

20. In what year was the number of Hispanic public officials about 5000?

21. **Interpreting Data** Describe any trends in the data that the line graph helps you see.

22. **Choosing a Data Display** Decide whether a double bar graph or a double line graph is the most appropriate representation of the data in the table. Explain.

Teens' Weekly Spending, 1994

Goods or services	Boys	Girls
Food, snacks	$10.10	$6.50
Clothing	$6.19	$10.65
Entertainment	$4.35	$3.45
Records, tapes, CDs	$1.55	$1.80
Grooming/cosmetics	$1.10	$3.35

23. A student used the diagram below to show that

$$2(3 + 4) = 2 \cdot 3 + 2 \cdot 4.$$

Use the representations scale on page 62 to assess the student's diagram. What do you think the student's score should be? Why?

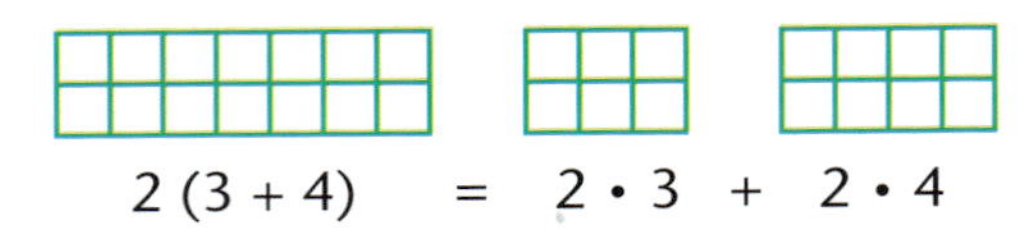

24. A student was trying to choose the most accurate and appropriate diagram from the following to show that $\frac{2}{3}$ of 6 is 4. Which should the student choose and why?

A. 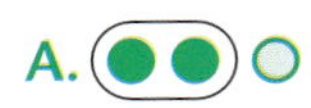 B.  C.   

25. **Create Your Own** Make a diagram to show that $2 \cdot 3 = 3 \cdot 2$. Then use the representations scale on page 62 to assess your diagram.

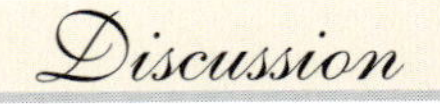

Exercise 26 checks that you can use correct and appropriate words and representations.

Reflecting on the Section

Be prepared to discuss your response to Exercise 26 in class.

26. It is not always easy to give walking or driving directions to help someone find a certain location.

a. Write instructions and draw a corresponding map to explain to someone how to get from your school to another location. Choose a location that requires at least five steps in your instructions.

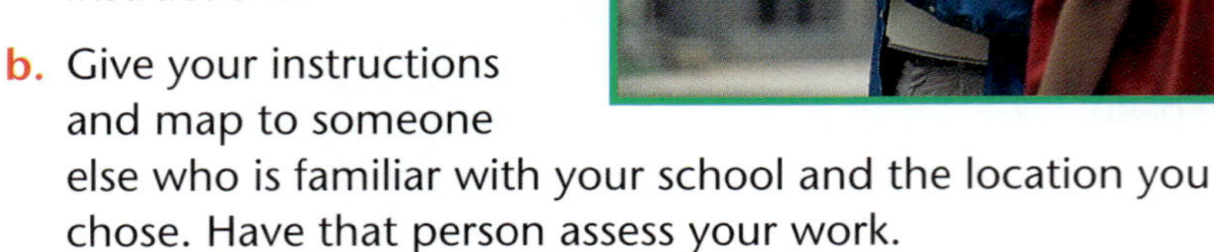

b. Give your instructions and map to someone else who is familiar with your school and the location you chose. Have that person assess your work.

c. Did the person find that your instructions and map were correct and appropriate? that your meaning was clear? Make adjustments if needed. How did the assessment help you improve?

Spiral Review

For Exercises 27–30, suppose each face of a cube was painted either red, white, or blue. The cube was rolled 60 times and the results were recorded in the table. Find each experimental probability.
(Module 1, p. 33)

Outcome	Frequency
red	20
white	33
blue	7
total	60

27. P(red)

28. P(white)

29. P(blue)

30. How many faces do you think were painted each color? Explain your thinking. (Module 1, pp. 44 and 55)

Use a ruler to draw a segment of each length. (Toolbox, p. 591)

31. $1\frac{1}{2}$ in.

32. $5\frac{3}{4}$ in.

33. $6\frac{7}{8}$ in.

34. $3\frac{5}{16}$ in.

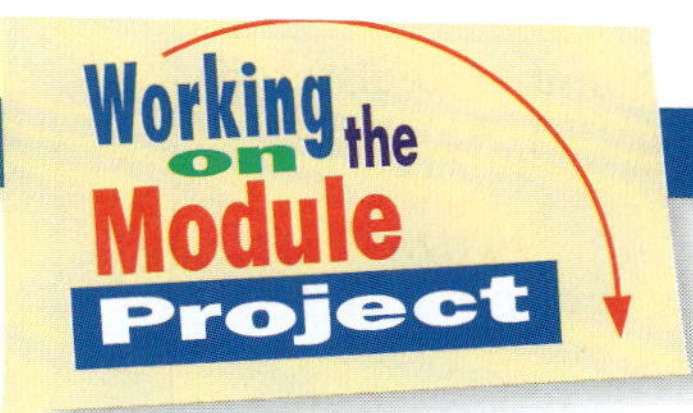

Tune In to Data

SET UP

- *Work in a group.*
- *You will need your group's data from Module Project Question 4.*

Displaying Data A visual display of the data you gathered about television commercials can help people quickly understand what you have learned from the data.

9 Look over the data from Module Project Question 4. What patterns or trends, if any, do you notice in the data?

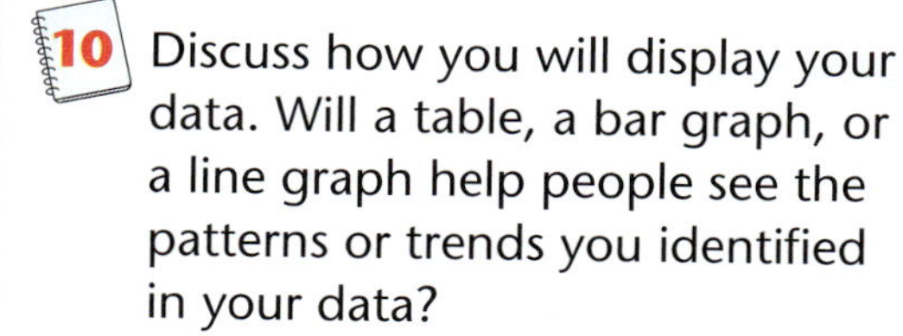

10 Discuss how you will display your data. Will a table, a bar graph, or a line graph help people see the patterns or trends you identified in your data?

11 Create representations that accurately display the patterns or trends you identified in two different sets of your data.

Section 6 Extra Skill Practice

Evaluate each expression using the correct order of operations.

1. $32 - 2 \cdot 10$
2. $4 \cdot (7 - 5) + 6$
3. $6 \cdot 3 - 30 \div 5$
4. $9 + 50 \div 5^2 \cdot 4$
5. $26 - (2^3 + 12) + 4^2$
6. $(3 + 7)^2 \cdot (8 - 5)^2$
7. $\frac{16 \div (2 + 6)}{3 - 2}$
8. $\frac{17 + (9 - 4)}{18 \div 9}$
9. $\frac{(40 + 8) \div 8}{7 - 4}$
10. $2 + [(8 + 7) \div 5] + 8 - 4$
11. $8 + [(4^2 - 1^2) - 12] \cdot 10$

Use grouping symbols to make each statement true.

12. $30 - 10 \div 5 = 4$
13. $3 + 12 \cdot 6 = 90$
14. $24 \div 2 + 2 = 6$
15. $3^2 + 5^2 \div 2 = 17$

16. a. Make a graph of the data in the table.

    b. Does the graph help you quickly understand the relationships among the data in the table? Explain.

1996 AKC Registrations	
Breed of Dog	**Number Registered**
Pomeranian	39,712
German shepherd	79,076
beagle	56,946
dachshund	48,426
poodle	56,803

Standardized Testing ▶ Multiple Choice

1. Which expression has the same value as $3 \cdot 4^3$?

   A $12 \cdot 12 \cdot 12$ B $3 \cdot 4 \cdot 4 \cdot 4$ C $3 \cdot 3 \cdot 3 \cdot 4 \cdot 4 \cdot 4$

2. A rectangular planter is 6 in. high, 20 in. long, and 9 in. wide. Suppose a gardener fills the planter $\frac{1}{4}$ full of potting soil. Which expression could be used to find the amount of soil needed?

   A $4(20 + 9 + 6)$ B $20 \cdot 9 \cdot \frac{6}{4}$ C $20 + 9 + \frac{6}{4}$ D $4(20 \cdot 9 \cdot 6)$

Tune In to Data

In this module, you have collected and analyzed data about television commercials. To complete the project, your group will present the data you collected and what you have learned from it.

SET UP

- *Work in a group.*
- *You will need your group's data and tables or graphs from Module Project Questions 4 and 11.*

12 With your group, discuss what you learned from the data you collected. Be sure to discuss the following topics:

- the number of commercials shown at various times
- the types of products commercials advertise
- how advertisers use commercials to influence your decisions
- the "average lifetime" claim about television viewing

13 How might you communicate this information to the class? Brainstorm with your group on ways to present your data and what you learned from it.

14 What other ideas do you have for preparing a group presentation that you would add to the list on the notebook?

Ideas for Preparing a Group Presentation

1. Everyone should participate in the presentation.
2. Presentation
   - possible types:
     - lecture
     - news show
     - panel discussion
     - skit
     - song
     - commercial
   - use representations (tables, graphs, diagrams, and so on)

15 Work as a team to prepare a presentation of the information you gathered on television commercials.

16 Present your facts about commercials to the class.

MODULE 1 Review and Assessment

You will need: • *graph paper* (Ex. 8)

Use the line graph for Exercises 1–5.
(Sec. 1, Explor. 1)

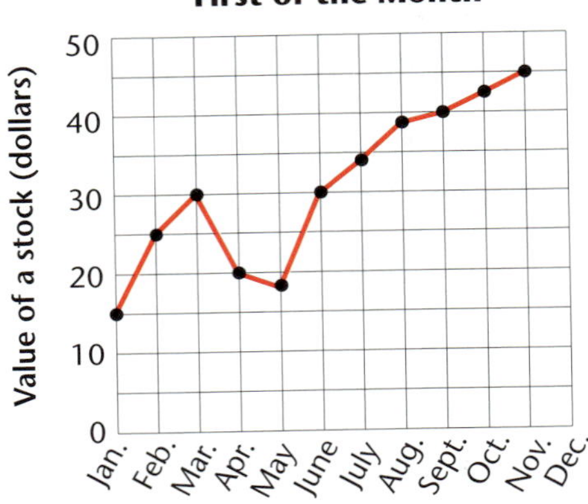

1. What was the value on January 1?
2. When was the value $30?
3. During what months did the value decrease?
4. During what month did the value increase the most?
5. What do you think the value of the stock will be on December 1? Why?
6. Make a frequency table for the following set of data. (Sec. 1, Explor. 2)

   Amounts withdrawn in one hour from an automatic teller machine: $20, $50, $20, $10, $30, $40, $100, $30, $50, $30

7. Look at the sequences below. (Sec. 2, Explors. 1 and 2)

   1 , 4 , 9 , ...

   a. How is the number sequence related to the shape sequence?

   b. Make a table for the number sequence. Extend it to include the fourth term.

   c. There is a pattern in the first four terms of the sequence that is related to exponents. Add another row to your table. Write the first four terms in exponential form. Describe the pattern.

   d. Use the pattern you identified in part (c) to find the fifth term. Write it in both exponential form and standard form.

   e. Predict the 50th term in the number sequence.

8. Make a table, draw a graph, and write an equation for the sequence 6, 12, 18, 24, ... Then predict the 100th term. (Sec. 2, Explor. 1)
9. Find the volume of a cube when the length of an edge is 9 cm. (Sec. 2, Explor. 2)

Use the spinner for Exercises 10–13.

10. George spun the spinner 50 times. His results are shown in the table. Find the experimental probability for each outcome. **(Sec. 3, Explor. 1)**

Outcome	Tally	Frequency
red	卌 卌 ||||	14
blue	卌 卌	10
green	卌 卌 卌 卌 卌 |	26

Suppose an experiment consists of spinning the spinner once and recording the color the spinner lands on. (Sec. 3, Explor. 2)

11. List the possible outcomes of the experiment.

12. Find the theoretical probability of each outcome.

13. Suppose you spin the spinner 60 times. About how many times would you expect it to stop on red?

14. Use the 4-step approach to solving problems to find the total number of triangles of any size in the shape shown at the right. Explain your solution. **(Sec. 4, Explor. 1)**

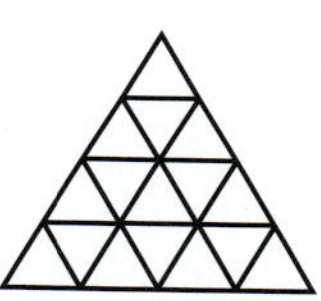

15. Assess your work in Exercise 14 using the problem solving scale on page 49. **(Sec. 5. Explor. 1)**

Evaluate each expression without using a calculator. (Sec. 6, Explor. 1)

16. $20 - 4 \cdot 5$

17. $3 \cdot (4 + 5) \cdot 6$

18. $2 + 54 \div 3^2 - 2$

19. Suppose a group of hikers are walking west. To avoid a steep slope, they walked 3 km north, 2 km west, 2 km north, 4 km west, and 5 km south. How many fewer kilometers would the hikers have walked if they did not have to avoid the steep slope? **(Sec. 6, Explor. 2)**

Reflecting on the Module

20. Writing Write a letter to an adult member of your family describing what you have done in this module. Discuss the mathematics you learned. You may also want to talk about what you liked most and least about the module.

MODULE 2
SEARCH and RESCUE

CONNECTING
MATHEMATICS & The Theme

SECTION OVERVIEW

1 Looking at Angles

As you learn a rescue skill:
- Name and measure angles
- Classify angles
- Use supplementary and complementary angles

2 Integers and Coordinates

As you study elevation:
- Compare integers
- Find opposites and absolute values of integers
- Identify and plot points in a coordinate plane

3 Integer Addition and Subtraction

As you explore wind-chill temperatures:
- Use a model to work with integers
- Add and subtract integers

4 Function Models

As you compare rescue options:
- Model a function with a table, an equation, or a graph
- Evaluate expressions with variables

5 Addition and Subtraction Equations

As you explore backpack weights:
- Write addition and subtraction equations
- Solve equations using models and inverse operations

The Module Project

Planning a Search

You'll imagine that you are a member of a search and rescue team and develop a search strategy for finding a lost person. You'll write a newspaper article about planning your search.

More on the Module Project

See pp. 86, 99, 114, and 143.

INTERNET
To learn more about the theme:
http://www.mlmath.com

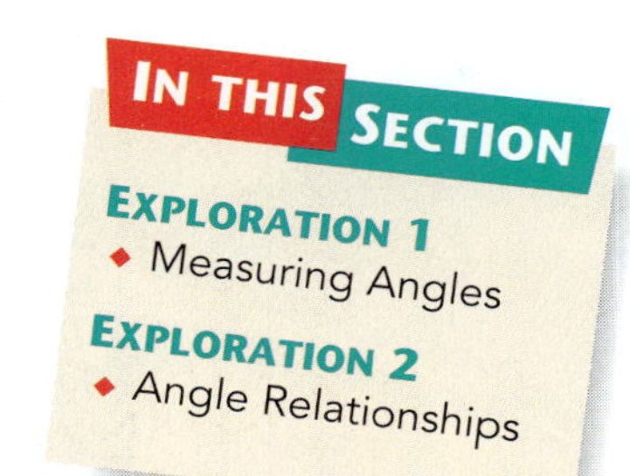

HEADING OUT

Setting the Stage

In the book *Hatchet* by Gary Paulsen, Brian Robeson is going to visit his father in northern Canada. The 13-year-old is a passenger in a two-person plane when suddenly the pilot has a heart attack.

HATCHET *by Gary Paulsen*

[Brian] looked at the dashboard of the plane, studied the dials and hoped to get some help, hoped to find a compass, but it was all so confusing, a jumble of numbers and lights.

. . .

He tried to figure out the dials. . . . He thought he might know which was speed—it was a lighted number that read 160—but he didn't know if that was actual miles an hour, or kilometers, or if it just meant how fast the plane was moving through the air and not over the ground.

. . .

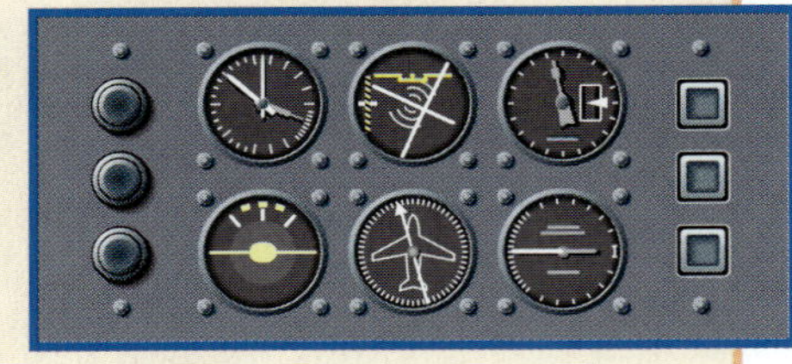

When the pilot had jerked he had moved the plane, but Brian could not remember how much or if it had come back to its original course. Since he did not know the original course anyway and could only guess at which display might be the compass—the one reading 342—he did not know where he had been or where he was going. . . .

▶ **When a plane goes down or a hiker is lost in the wilderness, search and rescue (SAR) teams are called in to search for and rescue survivors. Some of the tools and the strategies that SAR teams use involve mathematics.**

Think About It

1 **a.** Brian thinks the speed of the plane might be 160 miles per hour or 160 kilometers per hour. Which is faster?

b. How could Brian use the plane's speed to estimate its location?

2 Why do you think Brian "hoped to find a compass"?

3 What would you do in this situation if you were Brian? What information would help you?

Exploration 1

MEASURING ANGLES

GOAL

LEARN HOW TO...
- name and measure angles
- classify angles

AS YOU...
- learn a skill SAR team members need

KEY TERMS
- ray
- angle
- vertex
- degree
- right angle
- straight angle
- acute angle
- obtuse angle

SET UP *You will need:* • *Labsheet 1A* • *protractor* • *ruler*

To find their way through unfamiliar territory, SAR team members may need to use a navigational compass. Knowing about *rays* and *angles* can help you understand how to read a compass.

A **ray** is part of a line. It starts at an endpoint and goes on forever in one direction.

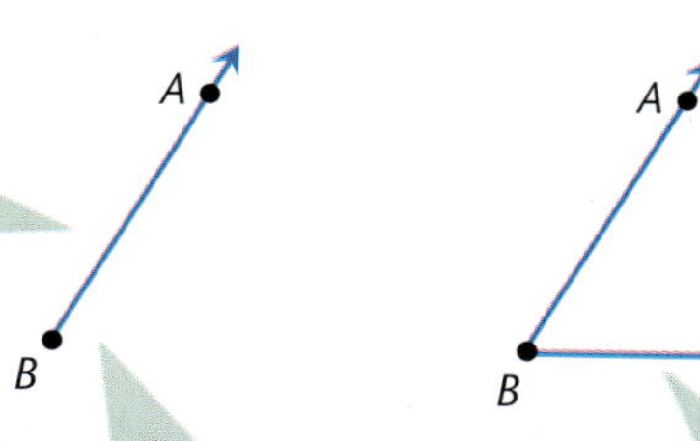

Ray *BA* is written $\overrightarrow{BA}$. Always write the endpoint first.

This angle is formed by $\overrightarrow{BA}$ and $\overrightarrow{BC}$.

4 **Discussion** Use the angles shown above and at the right.

a. Point *B* is the *vertex* of the angle shown above. Point *E* is the vertex of the angle at the right. What do you think *vertex of an angle* means?

b. Which rays form the angle at the right?

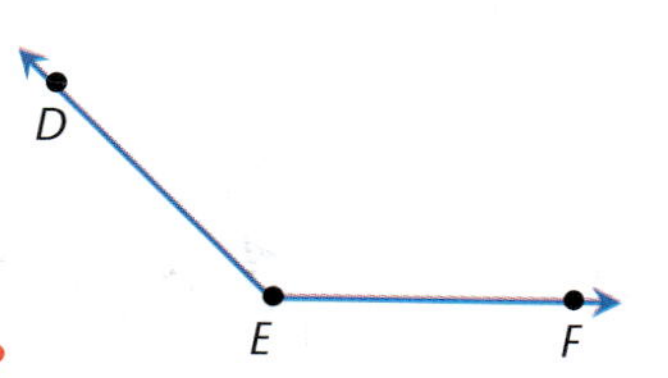

Naming Angles An **angle** is formed by two rays with a common endpoint called the **vertex** of the angle. You can name an angle using labeled points and the angle symbol, $\angle$.

EXAMPLE

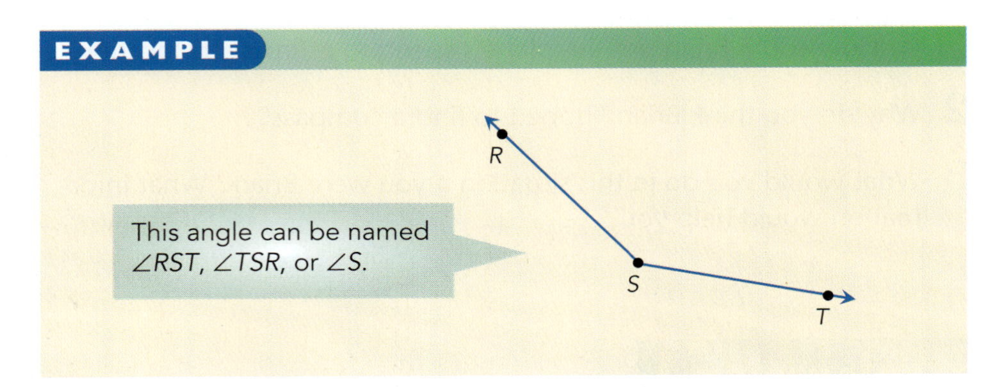

5 **a.** Which rays form the angle in the Example? Which point is the vertex?

b. The angle in the Example cannot be named $\angle SRT$. Why not? (*Hint*: Think about the points in the order in which they appear.)

QUESTION 6 ...checks that you know how to name angles.

6 **CHECKPOINT** Look back at the angles on page 77. Name each angle in three different ways.

Measuring Angles Imagine one ray of an angle rotating around the vertex while the other ray is fixed in place. You can measure the angle by measuring the amount of rotation. An angle is measured in units called *degrees*.

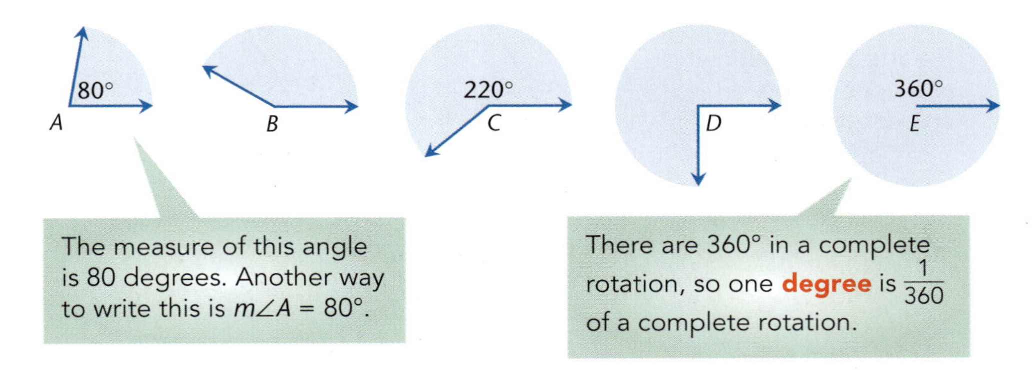

7 What is the measure of half of a complete rotation? What do you think an angle with that measure looks like?

8 **Estimation** Estimate the measure of each angle.

a. $\angle B$ **b.** $\angle D$

Using a Protractor

Student Resource

You can use a protractor to measure and draw angles. To draw an angle whose measure is 45°, follow these steps:

Step 1 Create one side of the angle by drawing a ray. The endpoint will be the vertex of the angle.

Step 2 Place the center of the protractor on the vertex. Line up the ray with the base line of the protractor, at 0°.

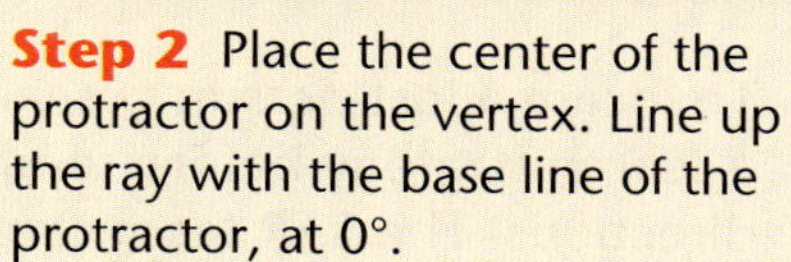

Step 3 Follow the numbers as they increase from 0°. Mark a point at 45°.

Step 4 Draw a second ray from the vertex through the point.

9 **Try This as a Class** The ray drawn in Step 4 above passes through the number 135. Why is the measure of the angle not 135°? Why do you think there are two sets of numbers on the protractor?

10 **Use Labsheet 1A.** Measure each angle on the Labsheet. Use your results to answer parts (a)–(d) below about *Types of Angles.*

a. What is a **right angle?** **b.** What is a **straight angle?**

c. What is an **acute angle?** **d.** What is an **obtuse angle?**

11 ✓ **CHECKPOINT** Draw a right angle, an acute angle, an obtuse angle, and a straight angle. Find the measure of each angle.

✓ **QUESTION 11**

...checks that you can draw and measure different types of angles.

HOMEWORK EXERCISES ▶ See Exs. 1–14 on p. 84.

GOAL

LEARN HOW TO...
- use supplementary angles and complementary angles

AS YOU...
- find compass headings

KEY TERMS
- supplementary angles
- complementary angles

Exploration 2

ANGLE RELATIONSHIPS

SET UP *Work with a partner. You will need:*
- *Labsheets 1B and 1C*
- *protractor*
- *ruler*

▶ **To locate a lost person, a search and rescue team needs to first develop a search strategy before sending out search parties in different directions. The SAR team can use a *compass heading* to describe each direction. Like angles, headings are measured in degrees.**

The needle on a magnetic compass points to the *north magnetic pole*, which is determined by Earth's magnetic field. Throughout this module, north (N) always refers to magnetic north.

Headings are always measured in a clockwise direction starting from north, which is at 0°. This compass diagram shows a heading of 53°.

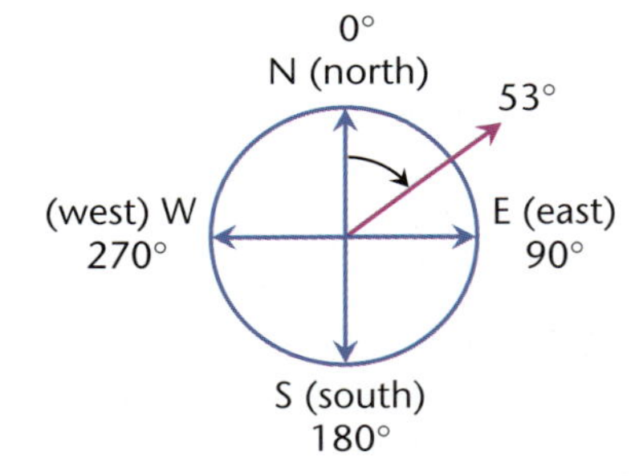

12 **Discussion** Use the compass diagram above.

a. How is the degree scale on a magnetic compass like the scale on a protractor? How is it different?

b. North (N) has a heading of 0°. What heading is used for east? for south? for west?

c. What heading, other than 0°, could you use for north?

▶ **North, south, east, and west are the *principal directions*. Knowing their headings can help you estimate other headings.**

13 **Use Labsheet 1B.** For each of the *Heading Diagrams*, estimate the heading by drawing a ray. Compare methods with your partner.

▶ **You can use principal directions to plot actual headings on a map. Two methods to plot a heading of 220° are shown below.**

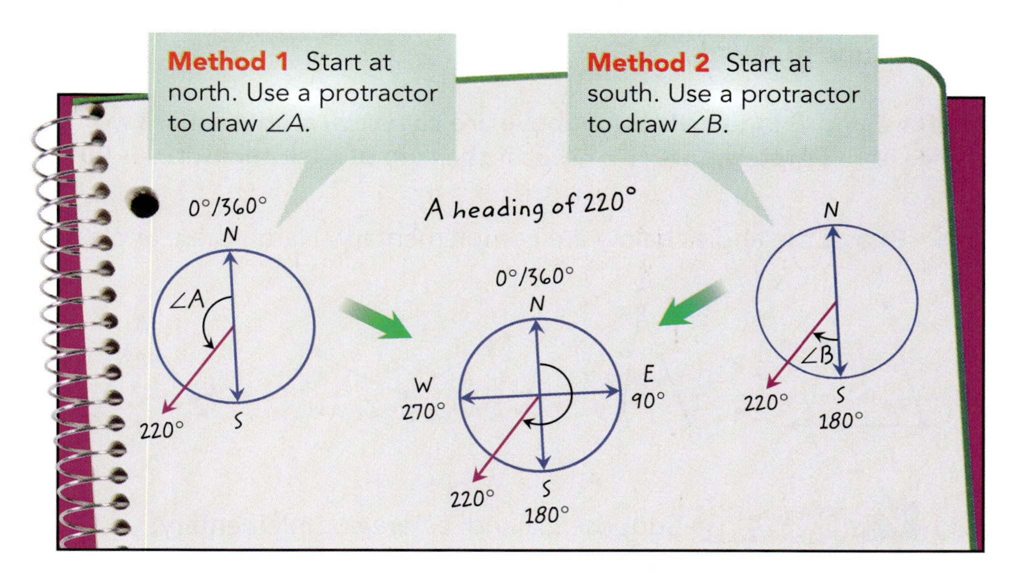

14 **a.** Use the compass diagrams above. Without using a protractor, find $m\angle A$ and $m\angle B$. Explain how you found each measure.

b. What is the sum of $m\angle A$ and $m\angle B$**?** Explain.

▶ **Angles *A* and *B* in the diagrams above are *supplementary angles*. Two angles are supplementary angles if the sum of their measures is 180°.**

15 Two of the angles below are supplementary. Name these angles.

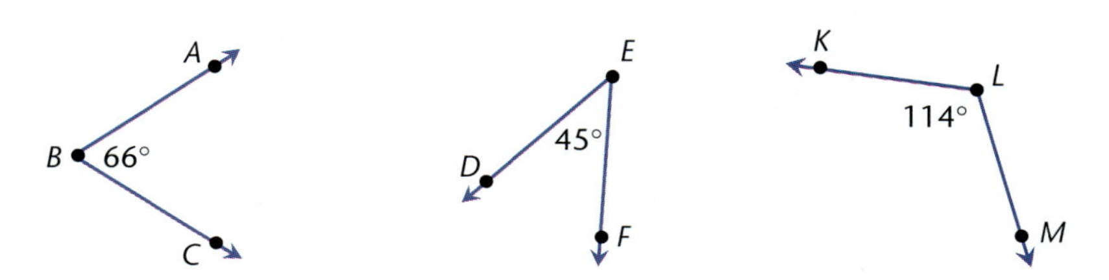

16 **✓ CHECKPOINT** Suppose $\angle W$ and $\angle Y$ are supplementary. Find $m\angle Y$ if $m\angle W = 75°$.

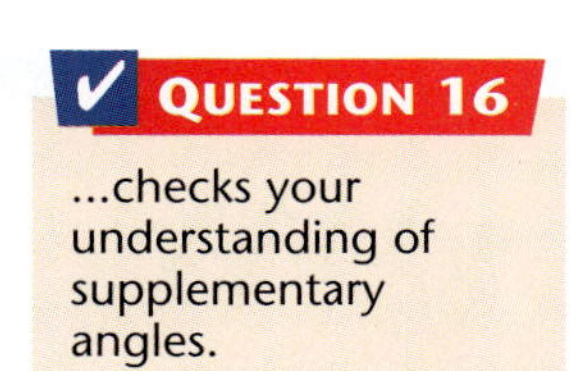

▶ **You can also use the principal directions east and west to plot actual headings. For example, a 310° heading is between 270° and 360°.**

17 **a.** Use the compass diagram. Without using a protractor, find $m\angle C$ and $m\angle D$. Explain how you found each angle measure.

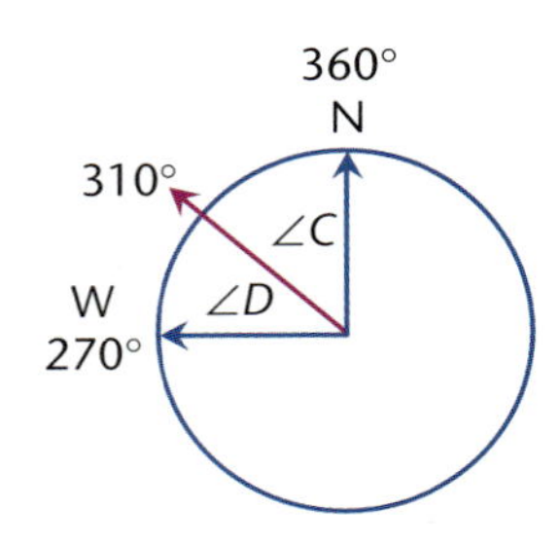

b. What is the sum of $m\angle C$ and $m\angle D$?

▶ **Angles *C* and *D* in the diagram above are *complementary angles*. Two angles are complementary angles if the sum of their measures is 90°.**

18 Two of the angles below are complementary. Name these angles.

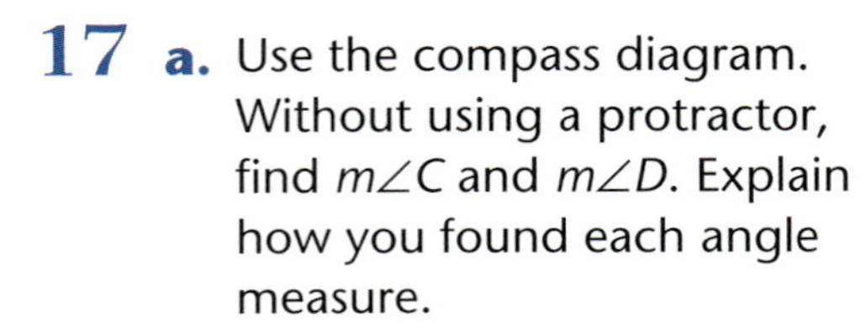
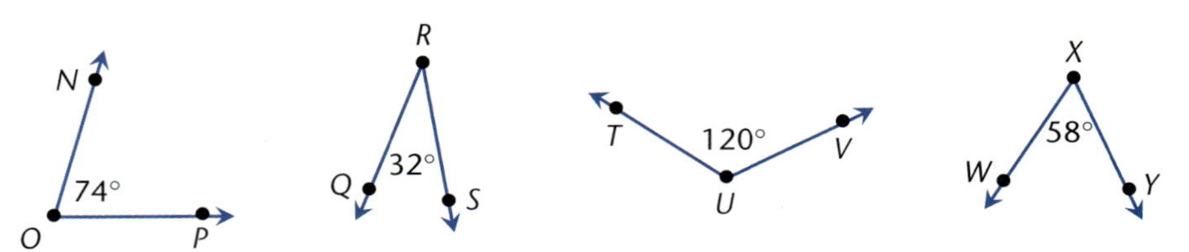

QUESTION 19

...checks your understanding of complementary angles.

19 **CHECKPOINT** Suppose $\angle S$ and $\angle T$ are complementary. Find $m\angle T$ if $m\angle S = 15°$.

20 **Use Labsheet 1B.** For each of the *Heading Diagrams*, use a protractor to draw a ray for the heading.

21 **Use Labsheet 1C.** In the reading from *Hatchet* on page 76, Brian guesses that the 342 on the display might be a compass heading. Follow the directions on Labsheet 1C for *Plotting a Heading* on a map of northern Canada like the one shown.

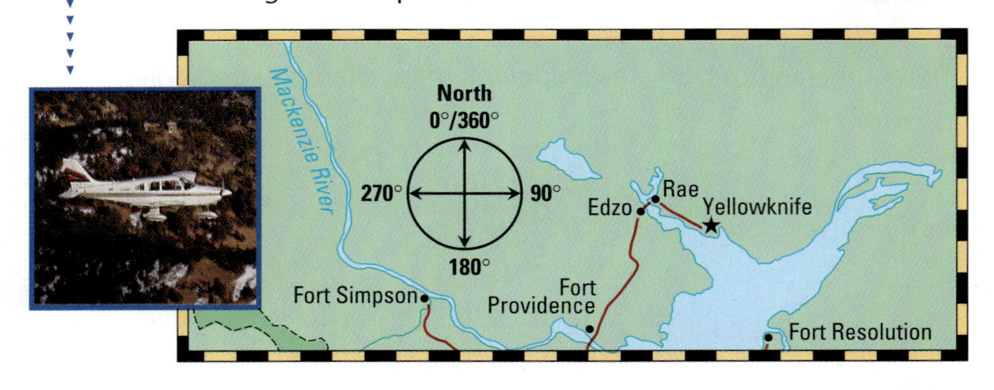

HOMEWORK EXERCISES ▶ See Exs. 15–30 on pp. 84–85.

Section 1 Key Concepts

Rays and Angles (pp. 77–78)

An angle is formed by two rays that have a common endpoint. The common endpoint of the rays is the vertex of the angle. ∠QRS is formed by $\overrightarrow{RQ}$ and $\overrightarrow{RS}$.

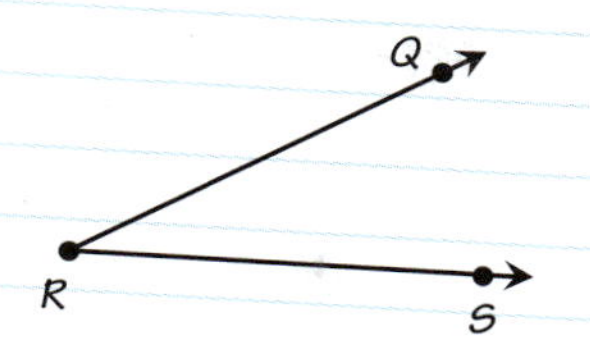

Measuring and Classifying Angles (pp. 78–79)

Angles are measured in degrees. A complete rotation is 360 degrees, or 360°. An angle can be classified by its measure.

Example

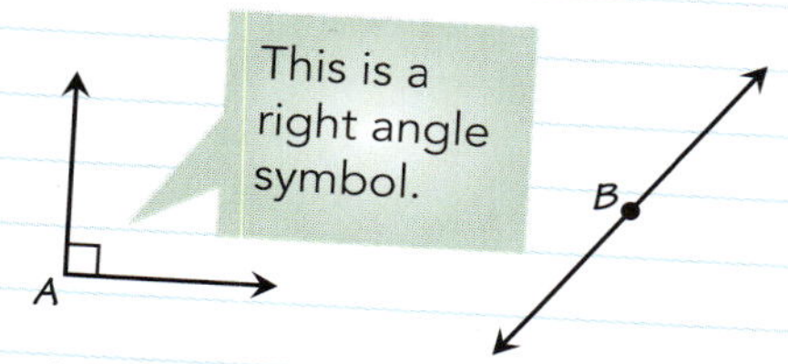

B

m∠C = 30°

C

m∠D = 110°

D

right angle
Its measure is 90°.

straight angle
Its measure is 180°.

acute angle
Its measure is greater than 0° but less than 90°.

obtuse angle
Its measure is greater than 90° but less than 180°.

Supplementary and Complementary (pp. 80–82)

Two angles are supplementary angles if the sum of the measures of the angles is 180°.

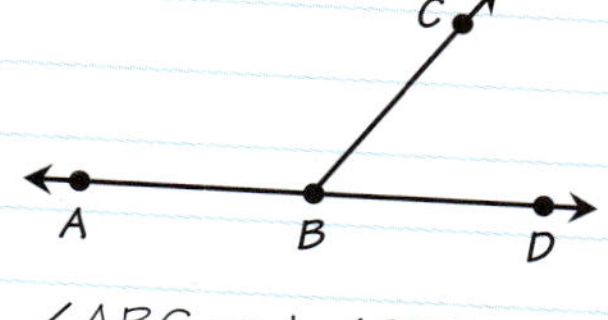

∠ABC and ∠CBD are supplementary.

Two angles are complementary angles if the sum of the measures of the angles is 90°.

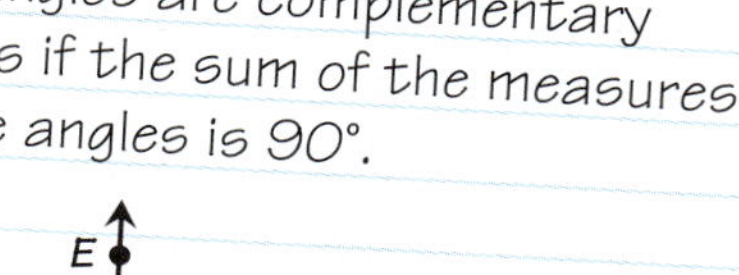

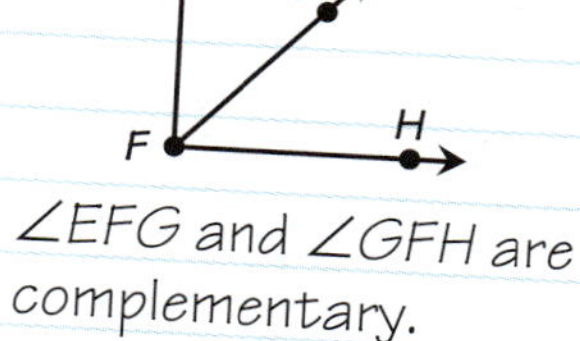

∠EFG and ∠GFH are complementary.

Key Terms

angle

ray

vertex

degree

right angle

straight angle

acute angle

obtuse angle

supplementary angles

complementary angles

22 Key Concepts Question For each situation, classify the angles as *acute*, *obtuse*, or *right*. Explain.

a. ∠M and ∠N are supplementary angles and m∠M = m∠N.

b. ∠X and ∠Y are complementary angles.

Section 1 Practice & Application Exercises

YOU WILL NEED

For Exs. 5–14:
- protractor

For Exercises 1–6, use the diagram.

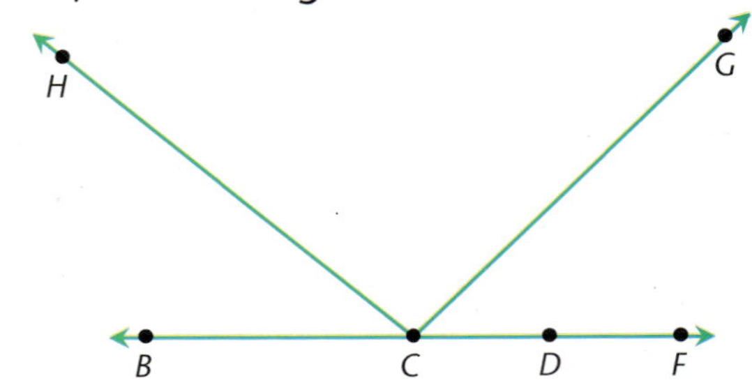

1. Name the ray that passes through point *H*.
2. Name two rays that have point *D* as an endpoint.
3. Name three angles that have $\overrightarrow{CH}$ as a side.
4. Name all the angles that have vertex *C*.
5. Name an acute angle and find its measure.
6. Name an obtuse angle and find its measure.

Draw an angle with each measure. Then classify each angle as *acute, obtuse, right,* or *straight*.

7. 90°
8. 85°
9. 138°
10. 150°
11. 53°
12. 180°
13. 100°
14. 30°

Estimation For Exercises 15 and 16, estimate the heading on each compass diagram.

15.

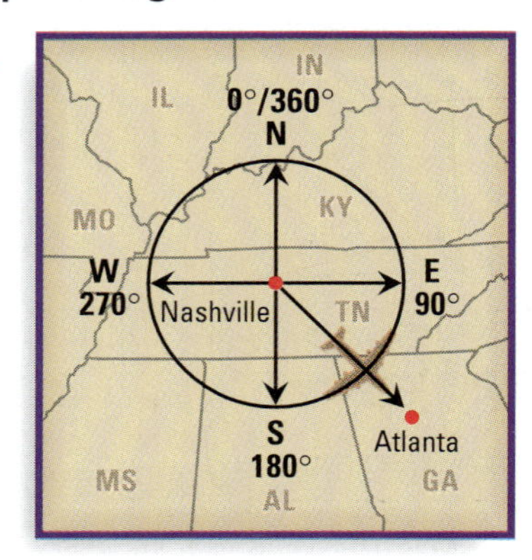

16.

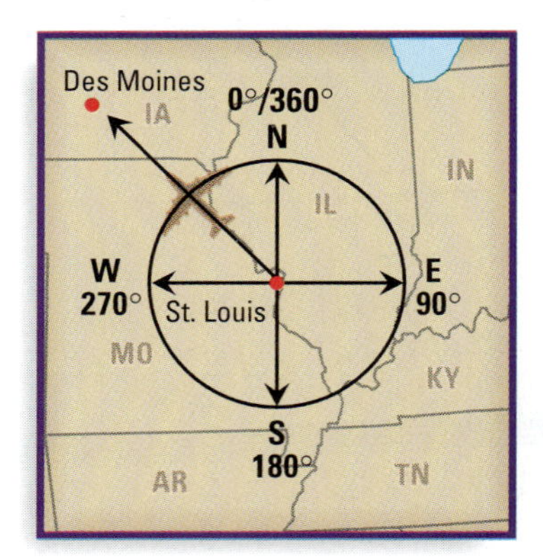

17. **Writing** A plane flies from point *Q* with a heading of 158°. Another plane flies from point *Q* in the opposite direction. Find the heading of the second plane. Explain your thinking.

Use the diagram on the photo.

18. Name three pairs of supplementary angles.

19. Name two pairs of complementary angles.

20. Estimate the measure of the angle between the minute hand and the hour hand.

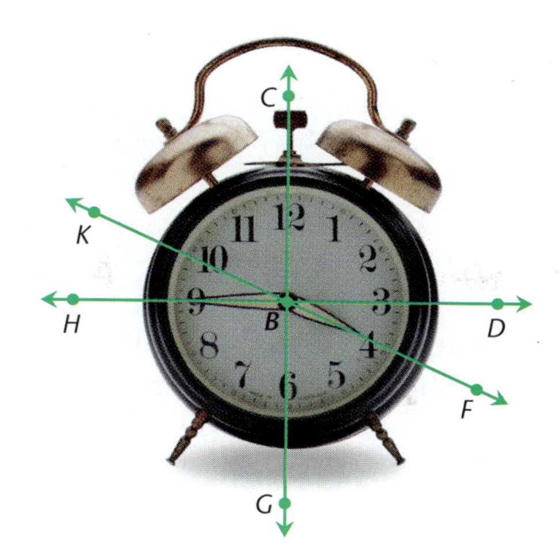

For each angle measure:
a. Find the measure of a supplementary angle.
b. Find the measure of a complementary angle, if possible.

21. 15° 22. 63° 23. 45° 24. 38°

25. 87° 26. 125° 27. 95° 28. 115°

29. **Challenge** $\angle F$ and $\angle G$ are complementary angles. Suppose the measure of $\angle F$ is 10° more than the measure of $\angle G$. Find $m\angle F$.

Reflecting on the Section

Be prepared to report on the following topic in class.

30. Describe two ways to locate a 290° heading. Use these methods to estimate headings of 290° on two separate compass diagrams.

Oral Report

Exercise 30 checks your understanding of angle measures.

Spiral Review

Evaluate each expression. (Module 1, p. 65)

31. 48 – 32 ÷ 8 32. 30 ÷ (6 – 4) 33. $6 + 4^2$

34. **Displaying Data** Make a bar graph of the data. (Toolbox, p. 594)

The Most Common Names of Places in the United States				
Name	Midway	Fairview	Oak Grove	Five Points
Number	207	192	150	145

Find the perimeter of a rectangle with the given dimensions.
(Toolbox, p. 593)

35. length = 5 ft, width = 2 ft 36. length = 16 in., width = 7 in.

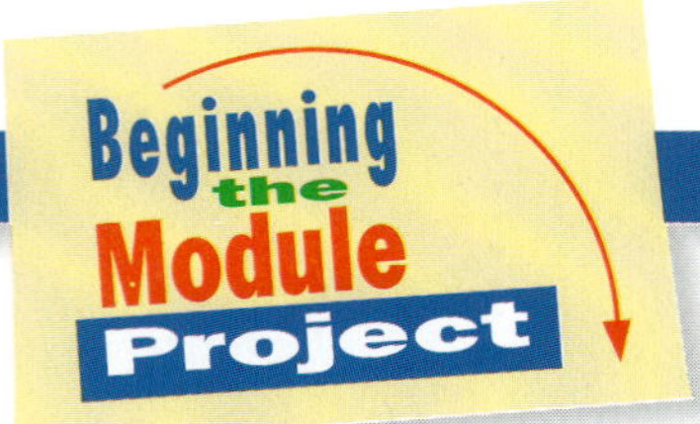

Planning a Search

Gina Roberts is a pilot who lives in Laverton, a small town in the outback of western Australia. She has flown solo before, but now she is ready for her longest flight ever—440 mi to visit a friend in Nullagine.

Only 1.5 hours after Gina's takeoff, the Laverton airport tower receives a distress call. Gina is experiencing engine trouble. She gives her location as 185 mi from Laverton at a heading of 344°. Then communication is lost.

For your module project, you'll imagine that you are a member of a search and rescue (SAR) team and use your new mathematical skills to develop a search strategy for finding Gina.

SET UP

You will need:

- *Project Labsheet A*
- *protractor*

Using Headings A storm is approaching, and Gina's chances of survival depend on a quick and well-planned search. You can use her last known heading to begin planning a search strategy.

Use Project Labsheet A. Use the *Regional Map* to answer Questions 1–4.

1 On the *Regional Map*, find Gina's location when radio communication was lost. Mark this spot with an X.

2 A search plane will be sent out from Wiluna. Find the distance and heading it must fly to reach location X.

3 The search plane holds enough fuel to travel 560 mi and must return to Wiluna. Use the *Regional Map* to plan a search pattern to find the missing plane. Be sure to include headings and distances for each leg of the search.

4 For each heading, tell which city a plane leaving Wiluna will fly over.

a. 265° b. 135° c. 355°

Section 1 Extra Skill Practice

You will need: • *protractor* (Exs. 4–8)

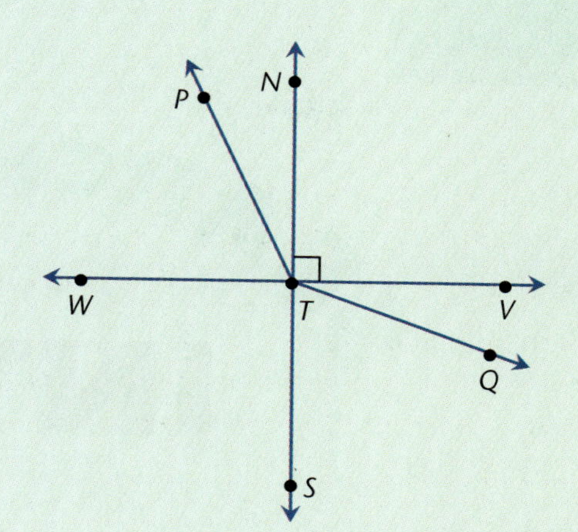

For Exercises 1–4, use the diagram.

1. Name two rays that pass through point W.
2. Name the endpoint of ray $\overrightarrow{NS}$.
3. Name all the acute angles that have $\overrightarrow{TQ}$ as a side.
4. Name an obtuse angle and find its measure.

Draw an angle with each measure. Then classify the angle as *acute, obtuse, right,* or *straight*.

5. 180°
6. 28°
7. 65°
8. 155°

9. Name a complementary angle and a supplementary angle to $\angle NTP$ in the diagram above.

For each angle measure:
a. Find the measure of a supplementary angle.
b. Find the measure of a complementary angle, if possible.

10. 72°
11. 163°
12. 35°
13. 56°

Study Skills ▶ Determining Your Learning Style

There are many ways to learn—by listening, reading, looking at pictures, writing, watching, doing, and so on—with others or on your own. The way you learn best is your *learning style*.

1. List several activities that you do well. Tell how you learned to do each one. Based on your answers, describe your learning style.

This book contains activities and questions that fit different learning styles. Find an example of each in Module 1.

2. hands-on activity
3. group activity
4. reading selection
5. Discussion question
6. Writing exercise
7. Visual Thinking exercise

Section 2 Integers and Coordinates

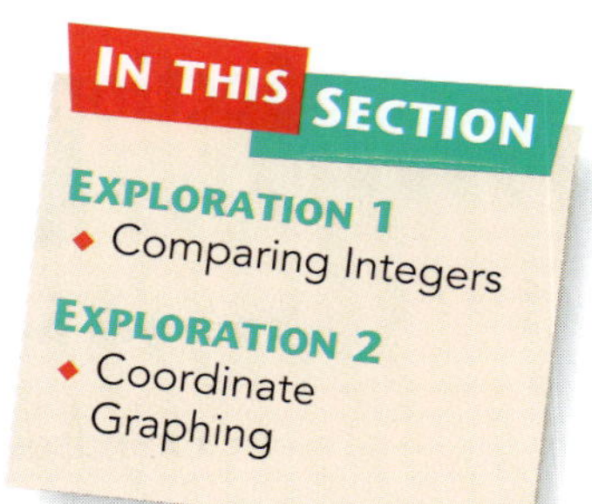

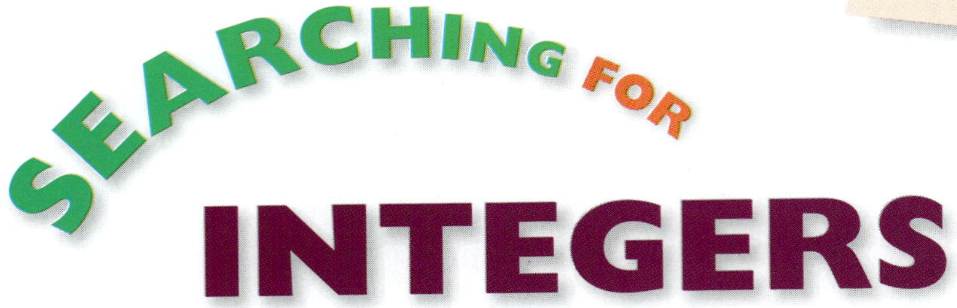

INTEGERS

Setting the Stage

One tool that search and rescue teams use to plan a search is a *contour map*. A contour map shows the elevation and the steepness of a land area. These factors are important because they affect the walking or hiking conditions of an area. In the map below, the change in elevation between contour lines is 10 ft.

This is a peak.

The elevation along this contour line is 50 ft above sea level.

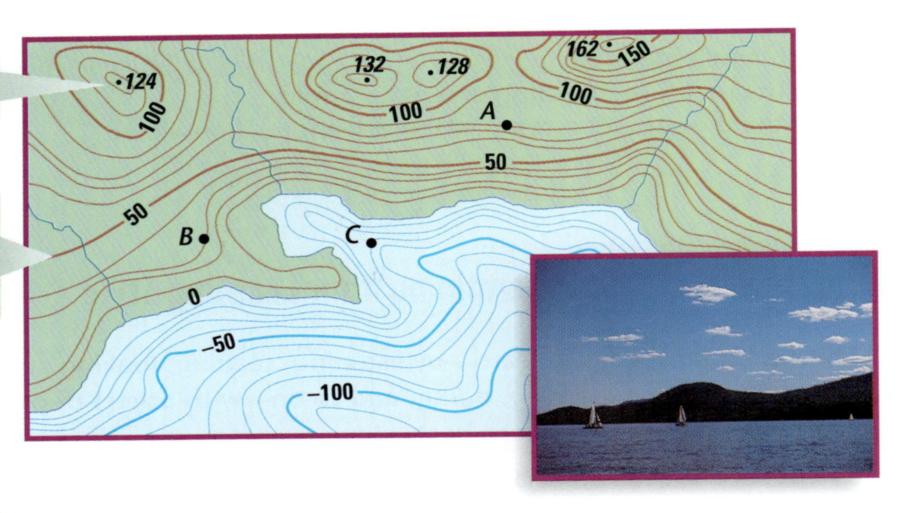

Think About It

1 What is the elevation at point *A*? How did you determine it?

2 How can you use a contour map to tell if a region is relatively flat?

3 What is the highest elevation shown on the map?

4 What symbol sets an elevation below sea level apart from an elevation above sea level?

Exploration 1

COMPARING INTEGERS

GOAL

LEARN HOW TO...
- compare integers
- find opposites and absolute values of integers

AS YOU...
- learn about elevation

KEY TERMS
- positive
- negative
- integer
- inequality
- opposite
- absolute value

▶ **One way to think about elevations above and below sea level is to say that those above sea level are greater than 0 or positive, and that those below sea level are less than 0 or negative.**

200 ft above sea level. The elevation is 200 ft or "positive 200."

200 ft below sea level. The elevation is –200 ft or "negative 200."

5 Rewrite each elevation using symbols instead of words.

a. Mount Rainier, Washington: 14,410 ft above sea level

b. Venice Beach, California: at sea level

c. Makaweli Reef, Hawaii: 116 ft below sea level

▶ **The numbers you have been using are *integers*. The integers are the numbers ... , –3, –2, –1, 0, 1, 2, 3, ... You can also show the integers on a number line.**

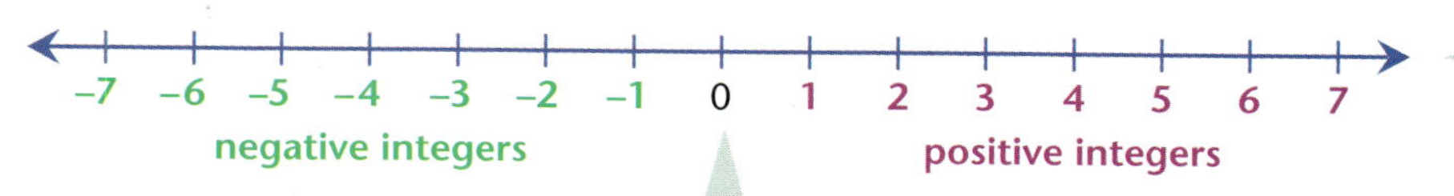

The arrowheads mean the integers go on forever in both directions.

0 is neither positive nor negative.

6 Use the number line shown above.

a. List the next five integers on the right side of the number line.

b. List the next five integers on the left side of the number line.

▶ **Comparing Integers** The highest elevation in Africa is 19,340 ft at the peak of Mount Kilimanjaro. The lowest elevation in Africa is –512 ft at the surface of Lake Assal. These two elevations can be compared with an **inequality**, which is a mathematical sentence stating that one quantity is greater than or less than another.

The elevation of Mt. Kilimanjaro	**is greater than**	the elevation of Lake Assal.
	$19{,}340 > -512$	
The elevation of Lake Assal	**is less than**	the elevation of Mt. Kilimanjaro.
	$-512 < 19{,}340$	

▶ **You can use a number line to help compare two integers.**

EXAMPLE

Write two inequalities to compare –7 and –3.

The integers increase as you go from left to right on a number line.

SAMPLE RESPONSE

Graph the numbers on a number line.

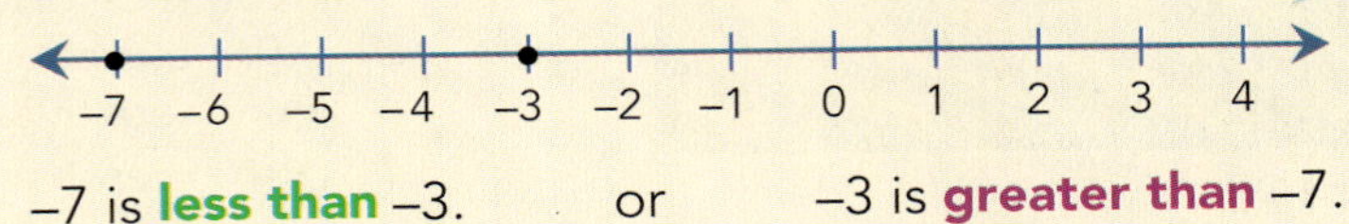

–7 is **less than** –3. or –3 is **greater than** –7.

$-7 < -3$ or $-3 > -7$

7 **a.** Where on a number line are the integers less than –7? List four integers less than –7 in increasing order.

b. Where on a number line are the negative integers greater than –7? Give an example of a negative integer greater than –7.

8 Write two inequalities to compare the numbers in each pair.

a. 25 and 26 **b.** –76 and 123 **c.** –22 and –23

✓ QUESTION 9

...checks that you can compare two integers.

9 **✓ CHECKPOINT** Replace each __?__ with > or <. You may want to use a number line.

a. 6 __?__ –8 **b.** –1 __?__ –2 **c.** 3 __?__ 9

d. –5 __?__ 0 **e.** –9 __?__ –5 **f.** 3 __?__ –3

10 Look back at the elevations on the map on page 88.

a. What do you notice about the distances of points *B* and *C* from sea level?

b. Where would these elevations be located on a number line?

▶ **Two numbers that are the same distance from 0 but on opposite sides of 0 on a number line are opposites. The opposite of 0 is 0.**

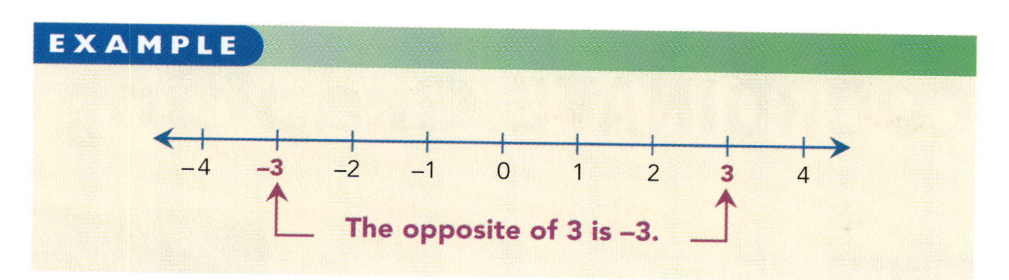

11 7 and –7 are opposites but 2 and –1 are not. Why not?

12 ✓ **CHECKPOINT** Find the opposite of each integer.

a. 10 **b.** 0 **c.** –8

d. –235 **e.** 51 **f.** –103

✓ **QUESTION 12**

...checks that you can find the opposite of an integer.

▶ **The absolute value of a number is the distance from the number to 0 on a number line.**

EXAMPLE

You read $|-4|$ as "the absolute value of negative four."

$|-4| = 4$ and $|4| = 4$

4 units 4 units

–4 –3 –2 –1 0 1 2 3 4

13 What is the absolute value of –100? of 100? How do they compare?

14 ✓ **CHECKPOINT** Find each absolute value.

a. $|-5|$ **b.** $|-9|$ **c.** $|12|$

d. $|0|$ **e.** $|-12|$ **f.** $|17|$

✓ **QUESTION 14**

...checks that you can find the absolute value of an integer.

15 The elevations of two points both have an absolute value of 150. What can you say about the elevations?

16 Can the absolute value of a number be negative? Explain.

HOMEWORK EXERCISES ▶ See Exs. 1–50 on pp. 95–97.

GOAL

LEARN HOW TO...
- identify and plot points in a coordinate plane

AS YOU...
- work with parallel and perpendicular lines

KEY TERMS
- plane
- intersect
- parallel
- perpendicular
- coordinate plane
- origin
- ordered pair
- coordinate

Exploration 2

COORDINATE Graphing

SET UP *You will need graph paper.*

In 1912, the giant passenger ship *Titanic* struck an iceberg and sank. The wreck was found in 1985 after searchers combed the waters with a sonar device. The searchers used latitude and longitude lines to mark the location of the *Titanic* so they could find it again.

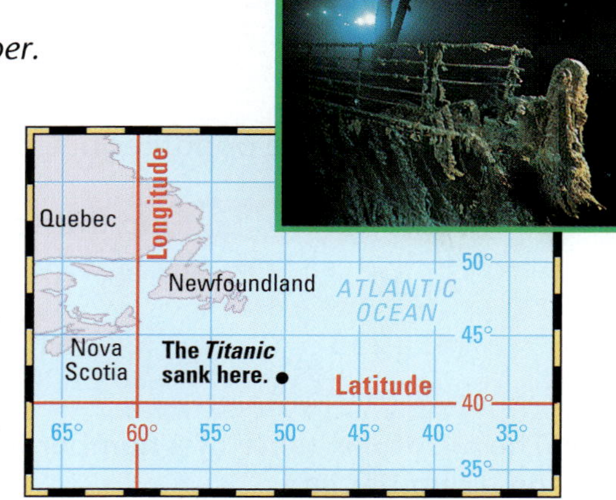

▶ **For small areas, searchers often lay a grid over a map of the search area. The grid is made up of *parallel* and *perpendicular* lines.**

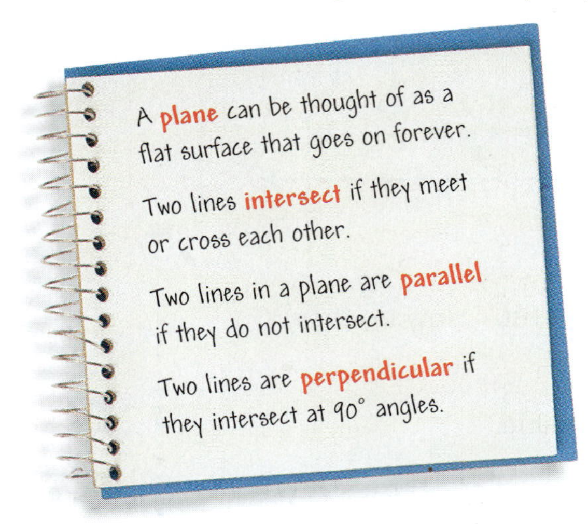

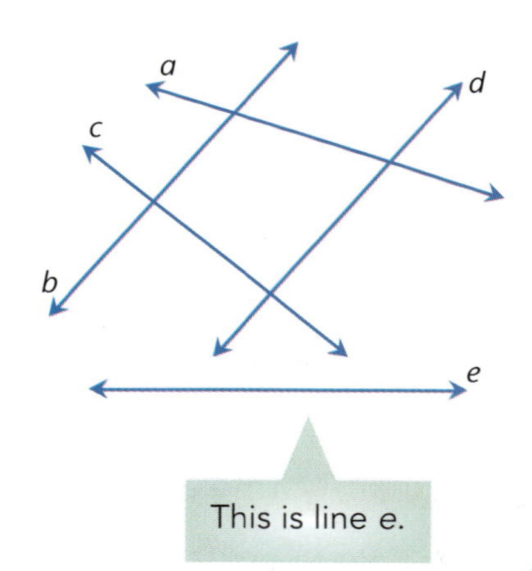

17 Which lettered pairs of lines above appear to be parallel to each other? perpendicular to each other?

18 The drawings of lines *d* and *e* above do not intersect. Are lines *d* and *e* parallel to each other? Explain.

19 In the paragraph about the *Titanic*, what type of paths does the phrase "combed the waters" suggest?

▶ **Searchers can use a *coordinate system* based on a grid to give directions and report their findings.**

EXAMPLE

A **coordinate plane** is a grid with a horizontal axis and a vertical axis that intersect at the **origin**. An **ordered pair** of numbers, called **coordinates**, can be used to identify and plot points in a coordinate plane. Point *P* has coordinates (**3**, **−2**).

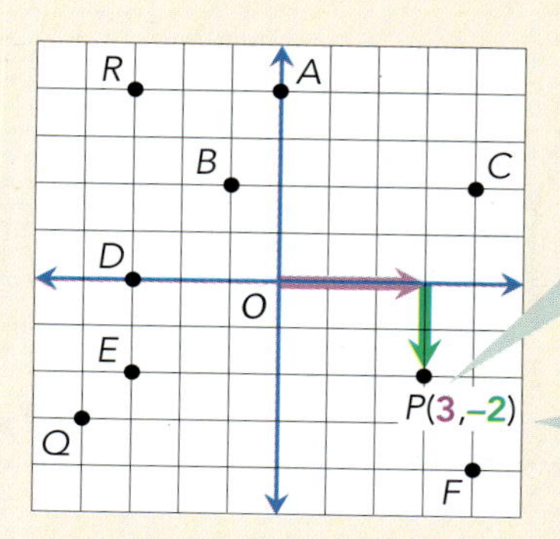

The **first coordinate** in an ordered pair gives a point's location left or right of the vertical axis.

The **second coordinate** gives the location up or down from the horizontal axis.

Use the coordinate plane in the Example for Questions 20–25.

20 Describe how the grid lines in a coordinate plane are related to each other.

21 The coordinates of point *R* are (−3, 4). Describe what the coordinates tell you about point *R*.

22 What are the coordinates of point *Q*?

23 Do the coordinates (2, 5) and (5, 2) describe the location of the same point? Explain.

24 What are the coordinates of the origin? Why do you think it is called the origin?

25 ✓ **CHECKPOINT** Give the coordinates of points *A* through *F*.

26 Plot each point in a coordinate plane.

a. *W*(4, −1) **b.** *X*(−1, 4) **c.** *Y*(−3, −3)

d. *Z*(5, 4) **e.** *S*(−2, 2) **f.** *T*(2, −1)

✓ **QUESTION 25**

...checks that you can identify the coordinates of a point.

HOMEWORK EXERCISES See Exs. 51–59 on pp. 97–98.

Section 2 Key Concepts

Key Terms

integer

negative

positive

inequality

opposite

absolute value

plane

intersect

parallel

perpendicular

Integers (pp. 89–91)

The integers are the numbers:

negative integers	zero	positive integers
..., −4, −3, −2, −1	0	1, 2, 3, 4, ...
The opposites of the counting numbers.		The counting numbers.

You can write inequalities to compare integers. (p. 90)

Example $-5 < 1$ or $1 > -5$

1 is greater than −5 because 1 is farther to the right.

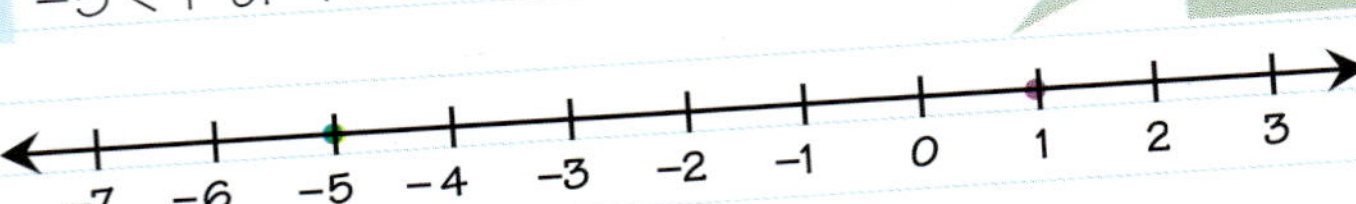

Opposites are the same distance from 0 but on opposite sides of 0 on a number line. The opposite of 5 is −5. The opposite of 0 is 0. (p. 91)

The absolute value of a number is the distance between the number and 0 on a number line. The absolute value of 0 is 0. (p. 91)

Example The absolute value of −3 is written $|-3|$. Because −3 and 3 are both 3 units from 0 on a number line, $|-3| = |3| = 3$.

Line Relationships (p. 92)

Two different lines in a plane either intersect or are parallel. When they intersect at a 90° angle, the lines are perpendicular.

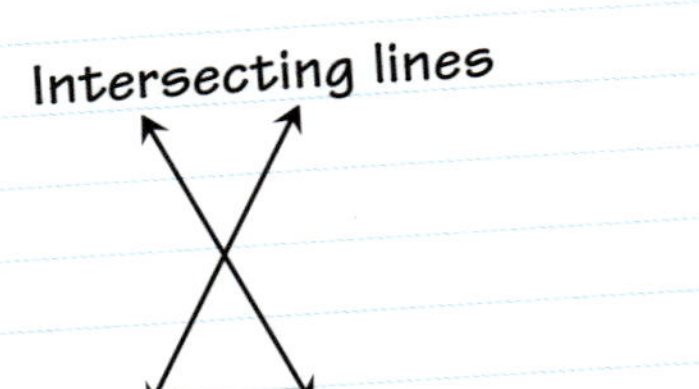

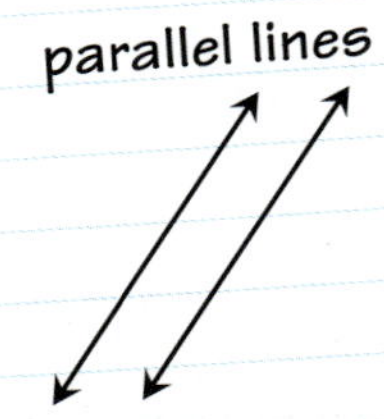

perpendicular lines

27 Key Concepts Question Explain the difference between the opposite of an integer and the absolute value of an integer.

Section 2 Key Concepts

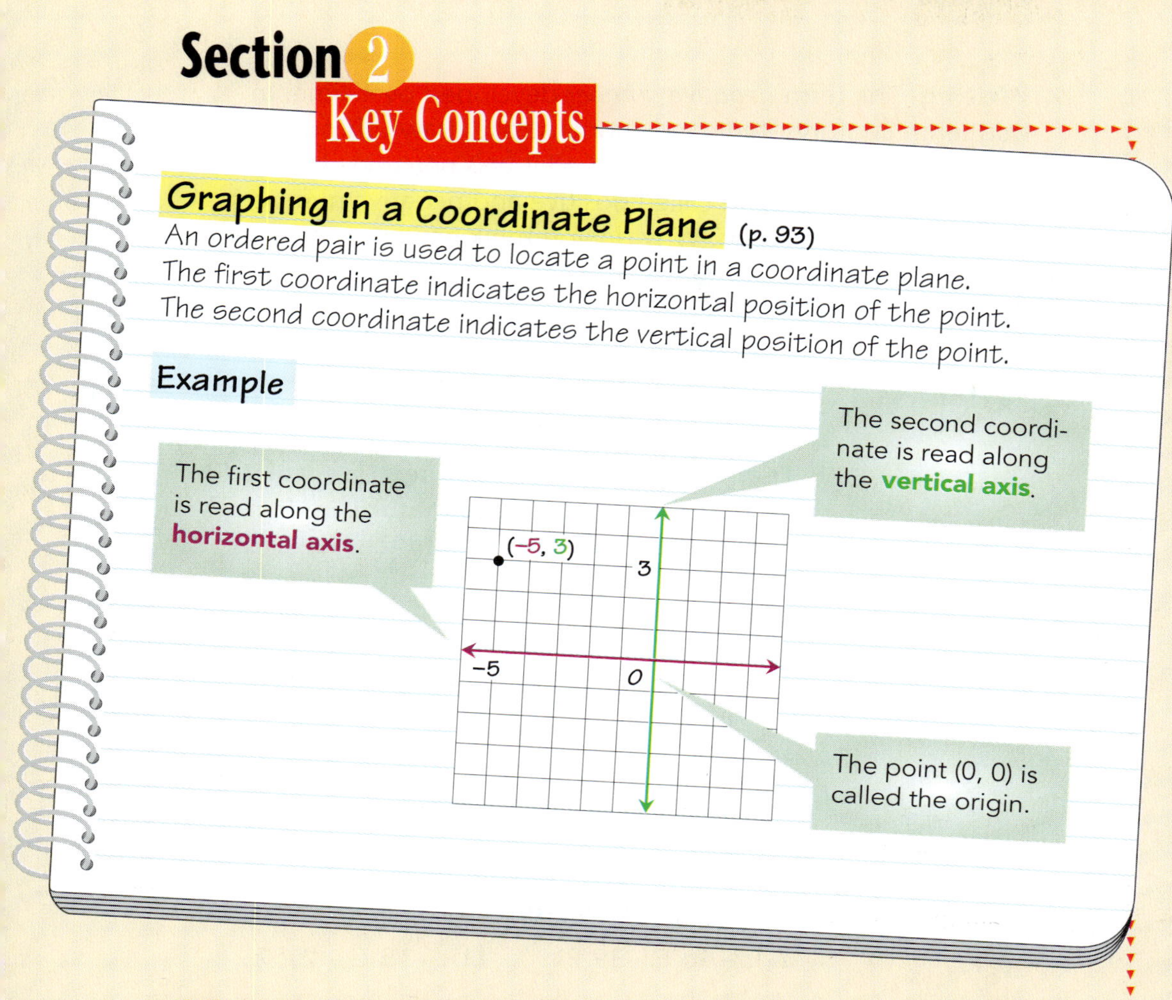

Key Terms

ordered pair

coordinate plane

coordinate

origin

28 Key Concepts Question Describe how to locate the point with coordinates (–5, –3). How are the points (–5, 3) and (–5, –3) related?

Section 2 Practice & Application Exercises

YOU WILL NEED

For Exs. 56 and 59:
- graph paper

For each description in words, represent the change using an integer and an appropriate unit of measure.

1. You add $25 to your savings.
2. The speed of a car decreases 15 mi/h.
3. The stock market drops five points.
4. Water in a swimming pool rises 6 in.

5. Writing The term *negative number* developed over time. In thirteenth century China, a diagonal stroke drawn through the right-hand digit of a number showed it was negative. In 1600, John Napier of Scotland called positive and negative numbers *abundantes* and *defectivi*. Why do you think he chose these terms?

Replace each __?__ with > or <.

6. 7 __?__ 0
7. 0 __?__ –4
8. 29 __?__ 35
9. –8 __?__ 13
10. 4 __?__ –21
11. –50 __?__ –75

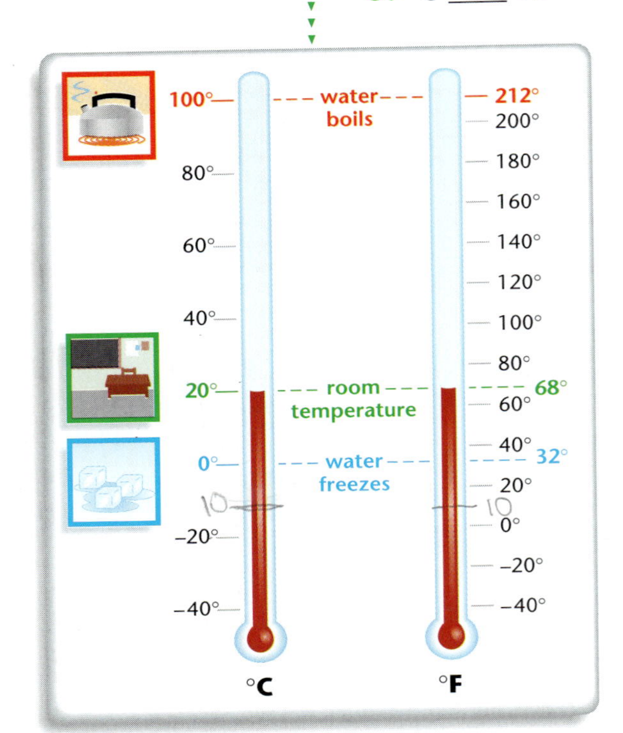

Temperature **Use the temperature scales to give an approximate temperature, in degrees Celsius and in degrees Fahrenheit, for each situation.**

12. the outside temperature today
13. the temperature of a slightly cool room
14. the temperature on a very cold day in your city or town

For each pair of temperatures below, identify the colder temperature.

15. –40°F, –39°F
16. –18°C, –21°C
17. 33°F, 0°C
18. 80°F, 40°C
19. 50°F, 5°C
20. –10°C, 10°F

Find the next three terms of each sequence.

21. 8, 6, 4, 2, ...
22. –15, –23, –31, –39, ...
23. –250, –200, –150, –100, ...

24. Copy and complete the table by describing each opposite situation. Then describe each situation and its opposite using integers and appropriate labels.

Situation	Opposite situation
1000 ft above sea level	1000 ft below sea level
20 min in the past	?
50 mi north	?
10 yd gain in football	?

Find the opposite of each integer.

25. 6 **26.** −4 **27.** −9 **28.** 18

29. −24 **30.** 76 **31.** 0 **32.** −306

Algebra Connection You read $-x$ as "the opposite of x." Find the value of $-x$ for each value of x.

33. $x = 4$ **34.** $x = -8$ **35.** $x = -100$ **36.** $x = 42$

Find the absolute value of each integer.

37. −8 **38.** 5 **39.** 0 **40.** 19

41. −62 **42.** 96 **43.** 514 **44.** −1025

Replace each ? with > or <.

45. $|-7|$? $|5|$ **46.** −5 ? 10 **47.** $|-9|$? $|-2|$

48. $|3|$? $|-8|$ **49.** 16 ? −16 **50.** −9 ? −10

Map Reading Use this map of Puerto Barrios, Guatemala.

51. Name two streets that are parallel.

52. Name two streets that are perpendicular.

53. Name two streets that intersect but are not perpendicular.

54. **Writing** Why do you think streets are laid out in a grid in some cities?

55.

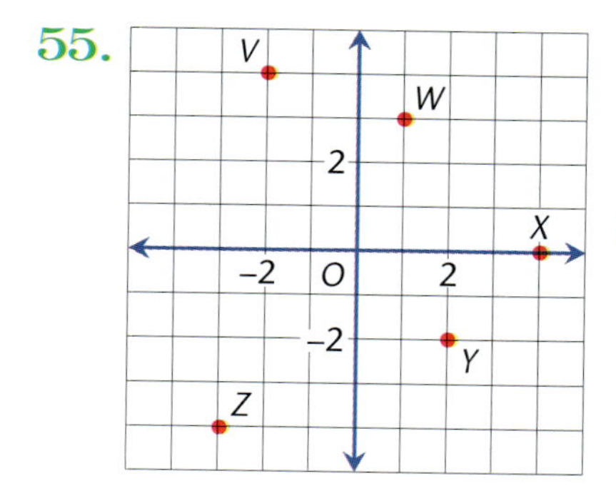

a. Identify the coordinates of the points V through Z in the coordinate plane.

b. Which two points in the plane have first coordinates that are opposites? second coordinates that are opposites?

56. Graph each ordered pair in a coordinate plane. Draw segments to connect the points in alphabetical order. Then connect point N back to point A to form a closed figure.

$A(6, 6)$ $B(8, 0)$ $C(6, 0)$ $D(8, -2)$

$E(6, -4)$ $F(-4, -4)$ $G(-6, 0)$ $H(-10, -4)$

$K(-10, 6)$ $L(-6, 2)$ $M(-2, 6)$ $N(2, 6)$

Challenge Three different lines, *x*, *y*, and *z*, lie in a plane. For each situation, make a sketch and decide how line *x* is related to line *z*.

57. Line x is parallel to line y. Line y is parallel to line z.

58. Line x is perpendicular to line y. Line y is perpendicular to line z.

Visual THINKING

Exercise 59 checks your understanding of ordered pairs.

Reflecting on the Section

59. In a coordinate plane, the points (2, 1), (2, –2), and (–5, –2) are three corners of a rectangle. Without plotting the points, determine the coordinates of the fourth corner. Then plot the points on graph paper. Were you correct?

Spiral Review

For each angle measure, find the measure of a complementary angle. (Module 2, p. 83)

60. 43° 61. 82° 62. 26°

63. **Displaying Data** Make a line graph of the data. (Toolbox, p. 595)

Average Monthly Temperatures in Aswan, Egypt			
January	60°F	July	93°F
February	65°F	August	92°F
March	72°F	September	89°F
April	80°F	October	82°F
May	88°F	November	72°F
June	91°F	December	64°F

Find each sum or difference. (Toolbox, p. 587)

64. $\frac{2}{5} + \frac{1}{5}$ 65. $\frac{1}{4} + \frac{2}{4}$ 66. $\frac{7}{9} - \frac{2}{9}$ 67. $\frac{5}{6} - \frac{4}{6}$

Planning a Search

SET UP *You will need Project Labsheet B.*

Elevation and Search Areas When the search and rescue (SAR) team finds the plane, there is no sign of Gina, and her backpack is missing. To narrow down the search area, the team uses data organized into *Probability Zones* to predict where Gina will be found in relation to the *Point Last Seen* (PLS). The data are based on what other people in similar situations have done, and on the elevation of the area.

Use Project Labsheet B. Use the *Probability Zones* and the *Map of Point Last Seen* to answer Questions 5–8. The location of the plane is the PLS.

5 The search plane locates Gina's downed plane at the X on the *Map of Point Last Seen*. Would the search pattern you developed on page 86 of Section 1 have located Gina's plane?

6 **a.** What is the probability of finding a lost person between 2 and 3 mi downhill from the PLS?

b. What is the probability of finding a lost person within 4 mi of the PLS?

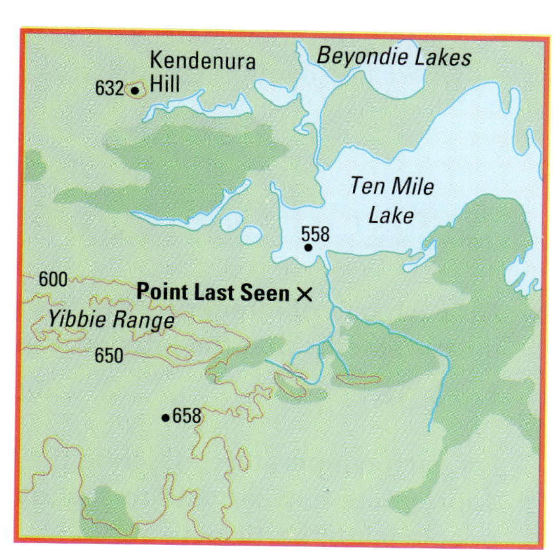

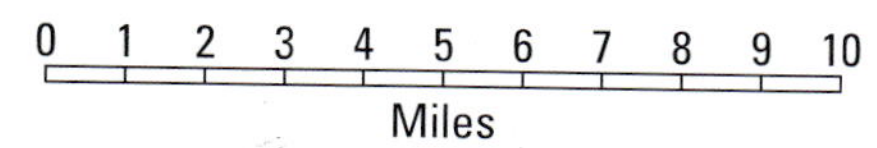

7 Create and describe a search plan for an 8 person SAR team. Be sure to think about:

- how you would divide your team
- the amount of area that can be covered on foot
- the short amount of time available (4 hours until dark)
- areas that you will not bother to search and why

8 On the *Map of Point Last Seen*, shade the areas covered by your search plan.

Rewrite each value using symbols instead of words.

1. Elevation of Salton Sea Airport, California: 85 ft below sea level
2. Lowest recorded temperature, Vostok, Antarctica: 89°C below zero

Replace each __?__ with $>$ or $<$.

3. 4 __?__ 7
4. –9 __?__ –17
5. 7 __?__ –7
6. 29 __?__ 0
7. –65 __?__ 0
8. –40 __?__ –1
9. –50 __?__ 11
10. –6 __?__ –18
11. –14 __?__ 14
12. –31 __?__ –23
13. 0 __?__ –40
14. –87 __?__ 87

For each integer:
a. Find its opposite.
b. Find its absolute value.

15. 8
16. –1
17. –16
18. 85
19. –2001
20. 461
21. –93
22. 5
23. –72
24. 55

For Exercises 25–28, use the diagram.

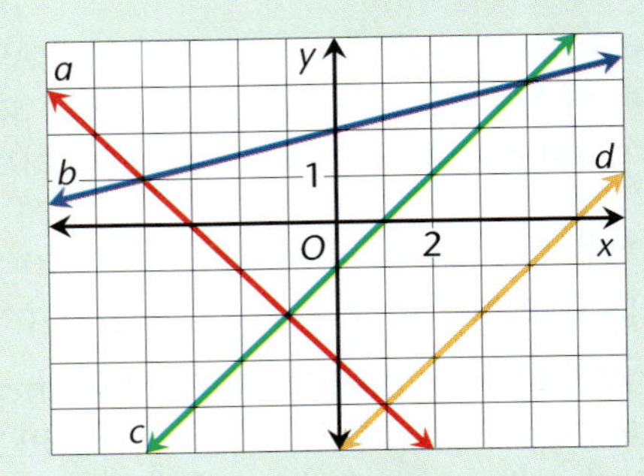

25. Which line is parallel to line *c*? perpendicular to line *c*?
26. Are lines *b* and *d* parallel? Explain.
27. Identify the coordinates of four points where pairs of lines intersect.
28. Identify the coordinates of the point where line *d* intersects each axis.

Standardized Testing ▶ Open-Ended

For each pair of integers, write a word problem that contains measurements that the integers can represent.

1. –5, 18
2. –206, 157

For each temperature, describe the type of clothing that would be appropriate to wear outdoors, and name two outdoor activities that people might participate in.

3. 30°C
4. –1°C
5. –10°F

Section 3 Integer Addition and Subtraction

EXPLORATION 1
- Modeling Integer Operations

EXPLORATION 2
- Adding Integers

EXPLORATION 3
- Subtracting Integers

Setting the Stage

A hiker is injured and a passerby on the same trail uses a cellular phone to call for help.

"Help! A hiker is injured along Emerson trail, about 5 miles from Crystal Falls."

Think About It

1. Can rescue workers tell where the caller is from the information given? If not, what else would the caller need to tell them?

2. Moves along a number line can be used to model a hiker hiking along a trail.

   a. How is describing the location of a hiker on a trail like describing the position of a point on a number line?

   b. Describe another travel situation you can model by moving on a number line. What point would you use as 0? What would be the positive and negative directions?

Search and rescue work can involve life-threatening situations. The ability to clearly communicate information, such as location, is very important. Rescuers must give instructions to those in danger and follow directions to avoid becoming lost themselves.

▶ **Rescuers use integers when they work with wind-chill charts. In this section, you will learn to add and subtract integers as you use your skill at following directions.**

GOAL

LEARN HOW TO...
- use a model to work with integers

AS YOU...
- take hikes along a number line

Exploration 1

Modeling INTEGER Operations

SET UP *Work in a group of four. You will need:*
- *Labsheets 3A, 3B, and 3C*
- *scissors*
- *three paper clips*

▶ **In this activity, you'll explore what happens when you move in different ways along a number line.**

3 **Use Labsheets 3A and 3B.** Follow the directions on Labsheets 3A and 3B to set up a number line and build three spinners. Then follow the steps below to practice hiking on the number line. Each group member should have a turn as the hiker.

First Three members of the group spin the spinners and give the directions to the hiker in the following order.

1 Start at the number shown on the START spinner.

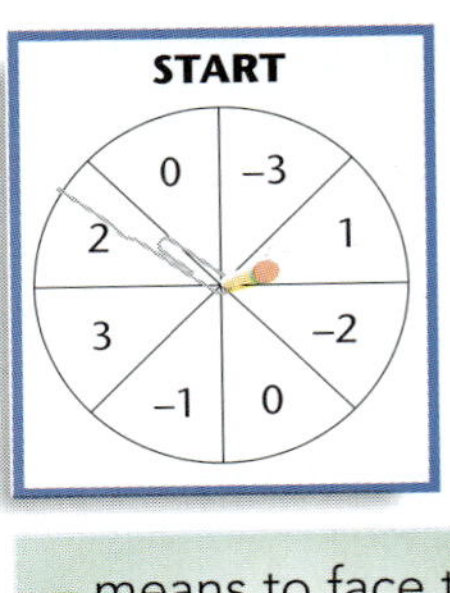

– means to face the negative direction.

2 Face the direction shown on the DIRECTION spinner.

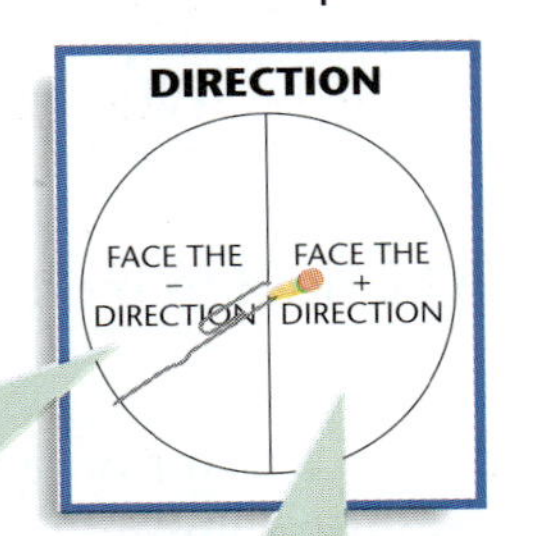

+ means to face the positive direction.

3 Move in the way described on the MOVE spinner.

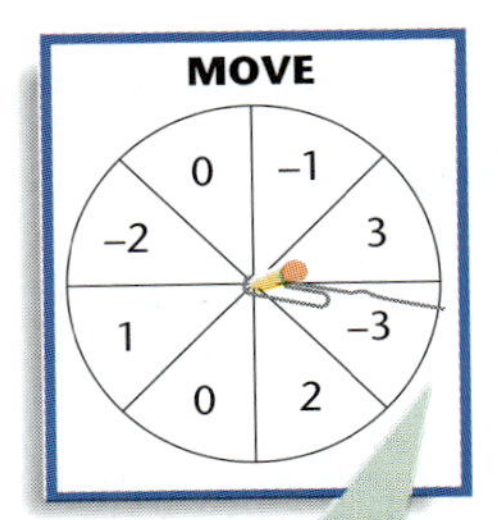

3 means move forward 3 units. –3 means move backward 3 units.

Then The hiker follows the instructions and calls out the number he or she finishes at on the number line.

4 **Use Labsheet 3C.** Continue taking turns hiking on the number line. Record each hike and the finishing position until you complete the *Table of Hikes*.

5 **Discussion** Why is it not necessary to label one of the 0's on the MOVE spinner as −0?

HOMEWORK EXERCISES ▶ See Exs. 1–5 on pp. 110.

Exploration 2

Adding INTEGERS

GOAL

LEARN HOW TO...
- add integers
- use properties of addition

AS YOU...
- analyze hikes along a number line

KEY TERMS
- commutative property of addition
- associative property of addition

SET UP *You will need Labsheet 3C with data from Question 4.*

▶ **Adding Integers with the Same Sign** The "hikes" you took in Exploration 1 can help you think about adding integers. Addition of integers can be modeled on a number line with an arrow.

EXAMPLE

Find the sum −3 + (−5).

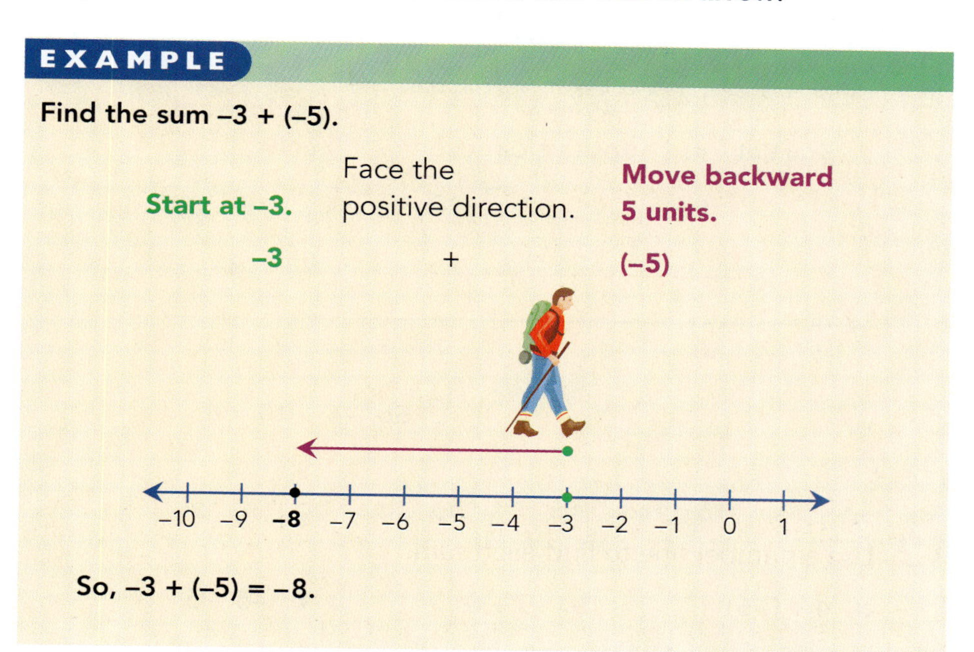

So, −3 + (−5) = −8.

6 **Use Labsheet 3C.** In the *Table of Hikes*, can you find a hike that models the addition of two negative integers? If so, write the addition problem and the sum.

7 Draw a number line and an arrow to find each sum.

a. 2 + 9 **b.** –7 + (–2)

8 **Try This as a Class** Think about adding two integers with the same sign.

a. Is the sum of two positive integers *positive* or *negative*?

b. Is the sum of two negative integers *positive* or *negative*?

c. Explain how to add two negative integers.

9 Suppose a student recorded a hike as –6 + 0. What did the student do on that turn?

10 Find each sum. Use a number line if necessary.

a. 5 + 0 **b.** 0 + (–2) **c.** –3 + 0 **d.** 0 + 0

✓ QUESTION 11

...checks that you understand what happens when you add 0 and a number.

11 **✓ CHECKPOINT** What is the sum of 0 and a number?

▶ **Adding Integers with Different Signs** **You can also model addition of a positive integer and a negative integer on a number line.**

EXAMPLE

Find the sum –4 + 10.

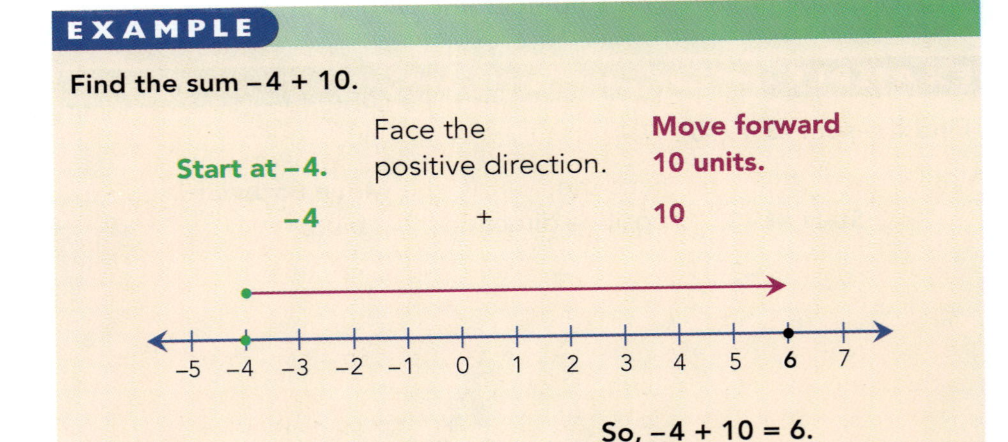

So, –4 + 10 = 6.

12 Use a number line to find each sum.

a. 4 + (–6) **b.** –3 + 6 **c.** –5 + 5

13 **Try This as a Class** Think about adding two integers with different signs.

a. When is the sum positive? negative?

b. Explain how to add any two integers with different signs.

14 Give MOVE instructions so that the hiker stops at 0. Write each answer in words and as a number.

a. Start at 5. Face the positive direction.

b. Start at -3. Face the positive direction.

15 **a.** How is each answer in Question 14 related to the starting point?

b. When is the sum of two integers zero?

16 ✓ **CHECKPOINT** Find each sum.

a. $22 + (-13)$ **b.** $-18 + (-17)$ **c.** $-19 + 7$

d. $31 + (-40)$ **e.** $-16 + 16$ **f.** $-7 + (-7)$

✓ **QUESTION 16**

...checks that you know how to add integers.

17 Use a number line to find the sum $10 + (-4)$. How does this compare with the sum in the Example on page 104?

18 Find each sum.

a. $-3 + 2$ **b.** $2 + (-3)$

c. $(-2 + 8) + 15$ **d.** $-2 + (8 + 15)$

19 How do the expressions in parts (a) and (b) of Question 18 compare? How do the sums compare?

20 How do the expressions in parts (c) and (d) of Question 18 compare? How do the sums compare?

▶ **Properties of Addition** **The commutative property of addition says that you can change the order of numbers in an addition problem and still get the same sum. The associative property of addition says that you can change the grouping when you add numbers and still get the same sum.**

21 **Discussion** Use properties of addition and mental math to find the value of the expression $-4 + 3 + 6 + 4 + (-6)$.

HOMEWORK EXERCISES ▶ See Exs. 6–23 on pp. 110–111.

GOAL

LEARN HOW TO...
- subtract integers

AS YOU...
- explore wind-chill temperatures

Exploration 3

Subtracting INTEGERS

When rescuers respond to a call for help, they must be prepared for the weather conditions. On cold and windy days, they might refer to a wind-chill chart like the one shown below. The difference between the thermometer reading and the temperature felt by the body can be great enough to endanger victims and rescuers.

22 **a.** The wind-chill temperature for a thermometer reading of 30°F and a 20 mi/h wind speed is shown on the wind-chill chart below. Find the wind-chill for 20°F and a 15 mi/h wind.

b. To find out how much colder it feels with the wind blowing, write a subtraction expression to represent the difference between the thermometer reading and the wind-chill temperature you found in part (a).

Step 1 Find the thermometer reading.

Estimated wind speed	Actual thermometer reading (°F) 40	30	20	10	0	–10	–20	–30	–40
Calm	40	30	20	10	0	–10	–20	–30	–40
5 mi/h	37	27	16	6	–5	–15	–26	–36	–47
10 mi/h	28	16	4	–9	–21	–33	–46	–58	–70
15 mi/h	22	9	–5	–18	–36	–45	–58	–72	–85
20 mi/h	18	4	–10	–25	–39	–53	–67	–82	–96
25 mi/h	16	0	–15	–29	–44	–59	–74	–88	–104

Wind-chill Temperature (°F)

Step 2 Read down the column to find the wind speed.

Step 3 Where the row and the column meet, you'll find the wind-chill temperature that you would feel.

Little danger if properly clothed

Increasing danger

Great danger

▶ To find the difference between thermometer readings and wind-chill temperatures, you may need to subtract integers. You have already done this in some of your "hikes" in Exploration 2.

23 **a.** Give START, DIRECTION, and MOVE instructions for a hike on a number line that would be recorded as the subtraction expression you wrote for part (b) of Question 22. Where would the hike end?

b. How can you change the instructions you gave in part (a) so the hiker starts at the same place, but faces the positive direction, and still ends up at the same finishing position?

c. Write an expression to represent the hike in part (b).

d. Look at your answer to part (c). How can 20 – (–5) be rewritten as an addition problem? What is the sum?

e. How much colder is the wind-chill temperature of –5°F than the thermometer reading of 20°F?

▶ Subtracting Integers on a Number Line **The number line can help you see that every subtraction problem has a related addition problem with the same answer.**

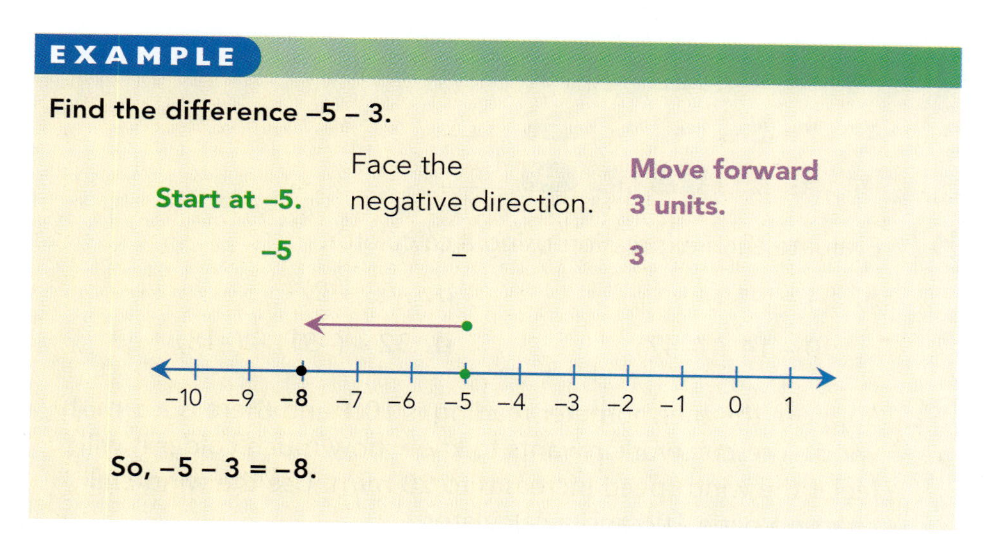
EXAMPLE

Find the difference –5 – 3.

So, –5 – 3 = –8.

24 **Discussion** What addition problem can be shown with the same diagram as in the Example? Describe how your answer can be interpreted as adding the opposite.

25 Draw a number line to find the difference 2 – 4. What addition problem can be shown with the same diagram?

26 **a.** Think about the START, DIRECTION, and MOVE commands for the problem $-5 - (-3)$. Draw a number line diagram showing the subtraction.

b. What is the result of $-5 - (-3)$?

c. Write the related addition problem that has the same result as $-5 - (-3)$.

27 What related addition problem has the same result as $2 - (-8)$?

✓ QUESTION 28

...checks that you know how to subtract integers.

28 **✓ CHECKPOINT** Find each difference.

a. $1 - 5$ **b.** $4 - (-6)$ **c.** $-3 - 2$

d. $2 - 3$ **e.** $-3 - (-6)$ **f.** $4 - (-1)$

▶ Calculator **You can use a calculator to add and subtract integers. For example, to find the sum $3 + (-8)$, you can use the following key sequence.**

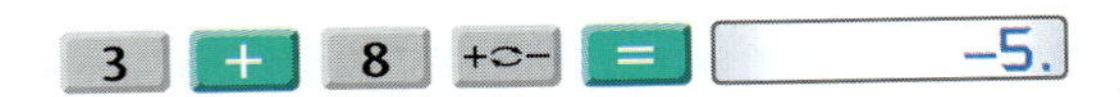

29 What does the [+⊂−] key do?

30 Replace each ___?___ with the correct number.

a. [9] [−] [2] [+⊂−] [=] ___?___

b. [4] [+⊂−] [+] [5] [=] ___?___

31 Evaluate each expression using a calculator.

a. $84 - (-19)$ **b.** $-63 + 27$

c. $90 - 14 + (-47)$ **d.** $32 + (-51) - (-18)$

32 Suppose the thermometer reading is 10°F and there is a 5 mi/h wind. A rescue worker wants to know how much colder it will feel if the wind speed increases to 20 mi/h. Use the wind-chill chart on page 106 and a calculator.

a. Find the wind-chill temperature for the wind speed of 5 mi/h.

b. Find the wind-chill temperature for the wind speed of 20 mi/h.

c. Find the difference between your answer to part (a) and your answer to part (b).

d. Interpret your answer to part (c) in relation to the situation.

HOMEWORK EXERCISES ▶ See Exs. 24–47 on pp. 111–113.

Section 3 Key Concepts

Key Terms

Number-Line Models (pp. 102–108)

You can think of addition and subtraction as hikes on a number line.

Example $2 + (-6) = -4$ $2 - 6 = -4$

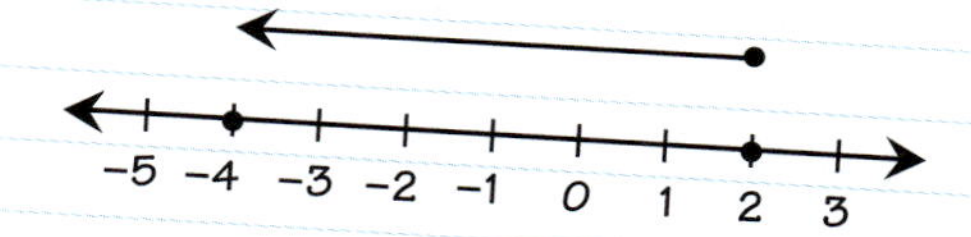

Adding Integers (pp. 103–105)

To add two integers with the same sign, add the absolute values of the integers. The sum has the same sign as the integers you are adding.

Examples $8 + 5 = 13$ and $-3 + (-7) = -10$

To add two integers that have different signs, subtract the smaller absolute value from the greater one. The sum has the same sign as the integer with the greater absolute value.

Examples $9 + (-6) = 3$ and $4 + (-5) = -1$

The answer is negative because $|4| < |-5|$.

The sum of **0 and a number** is that number. The sum of **a number and its opposite** is 0. Reordering and regrouping can help you find sums of more than two numbers using mental math. **(pp. 104–105)**

properties of addition

commutative

associative

Subtracting Integers (pp. 106–108)

You can rewrite a subtraction problem as an addition problem. To subtract an integer, add its opposite.

Examples $6 - (-9) = 6 + 9 = 15$ and $5 - 7 = 5 + (-7) = -2$

33 Key Concepts Question Find a possible value of x in each case.

a. $3 + x$ is positive. **b.** $3 + x$ is 0. **c.** $3 + x$ is negative.

d. $3 - x$ is positive. **e.** $3 - x$ is 0. **f.** $3 - x$ is negative.

YOU WILL NEED

For Ex. 48:
- graph paper

Section 3 Practice & Application Exercises

A hiker on a number line follows each set of directions. Determine where the hiker will finish. Record the moves as an addition problem with its sum or as a subtraction problem with its difference.

1. Start at –4. Face the positive direction. Move backward 2 units.
2. Start at 5. Face the positive direction. Move forward 6 units.
3. Start at 0. Face the negative direction. Move forward 8 units.
4. Start at –3. Face the negative direction. Move backward 7 units.
5. Suppose the hiker shown below is given the instructions "Start at 2, face the negative direction, and move forward 3."

   a. Where does the hiker stop after following the instructions?
   b. If the hiker starts at 2, what other set of instructions can be given so the hiker finishes at the same location?
   c. What set of instructions can be given so the hiker remains at 2?

Find each sum.

6. $-2 + (-5)$
7. $0 + (-17)$
8. $12 + 3$
9. $-18 + (-3)$
10. $19 + 36$
11. $-11 + 0$
12. $-9 + (-10) + 8$
13. $-13 + 8 + (-4)$
14. $6 + 0 + (-6)$

For a correct answer on a TV game show, a positive dollar amount is added to a player's score. For an incorrect answer, a negative dollar amount is added. For Exercises 15–17, suppose the players have the scores shown.

15. If Danessa answers a $600 question correctly, what will be her new score?

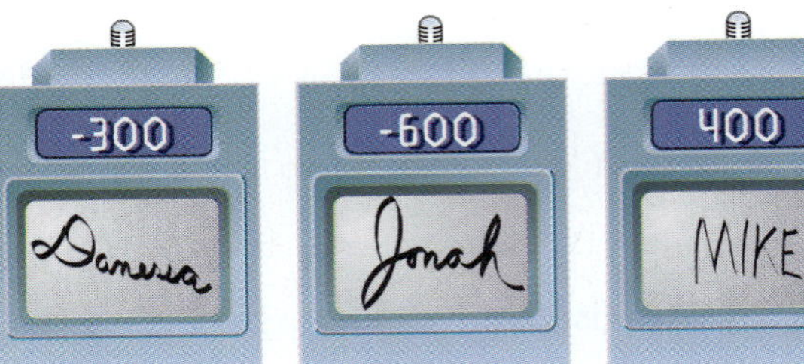

16. Use the scores on page 110. If Mike answers a \$600 question incorrectly, what amount is added to his score? What is his new score?

17. Suppose both Jonah and Mike answer the last question, worth \$300, incorrectly, but Danessa gives the correct answer. Use the scores on page 110. Who wins? What is each player's final score?

For Exercises 18 and 19, write and evaluate an addition expression to model each situation.

18. A team loses 8 yd on one play of a football game and gains 3 yd on the next. Find the total number of yards gained or lost.

19. A company loses \$30,000 in the first quarter of a year, then gains \$43,000 in the second quarter. Find the total amount of money gained or lost in that time.

Mental Math **Find each sum mentally. Use properties of addition.**

20. $-2 + 0 + (-9) + 9$

21. $-13 + 8 + (-2) + (-8)$

22. $-9 + 7 + 12 + (-7) + 9$

23. $5 + (-12) + (3 + 12)$

Rewrite each subtraction problem as the related addition problem that has the same answer.

24. $7 - 2$

25. $-10 - (-2)$

26. $0 - 6$

27. $9 - (-17)$

28. **Wind Chill** Refer to the wind-chill chart on page 106 to determine the difference between the thermometer reading and the wind-chill temperature for each condition in the chart below.

Estimated wind speed	Actual thermometer reading	Wind-chill temperature
10 mi/h	−30°F	?
25 mi/h	40°F	?

29. **Estimation** Estimate the wind-chill temperature for a thermometer reading of 15°F and a wind speed of 20 mi/h.

Find each difference.

30. $9 - (-13)$

31. $-12 - 5$

32. $-7 - 13$

33. $-7 - (-13)$

34. $12 - 7$

35. $12 - (-7)$

The highest point in the United States is Mount McKinley, in Alaska. It has an elevation of 20,320 ft.

The deepest lake in the world is Lake Baikal in central Siberia, Russia. It has a depth of 5712 ft.

The lowest point in the United States is in Death Valley, California. It has an elevation of –282 ft.

Geography **Use the information above for Exercises 36 and 37.**

36. What is the difference in elevation between Mount McKinley and Death Valley?

37. The deepest point of Lake Baikal is 4219 ft below sea level. How high above sea level is the surface of the lake?

38. **Weather** The most unusual temperature rise ever recorded occurred in Spearfish, South Dakota, on January 22, 1943. The temperature was –4°F at 7:30 A.M. and 45°F at 7:32 A.M. How many degrees did the temperature rise during those 2 minutes?

Evaluate each expression.

39. 7 – (–10) + 8
40. –13 + 4 – 9
41. 19 + (–5) – 3
42. (5 – 16) – (–2)
43. (16 – 5) – (–2)
44. 16 – [5 – (–2)]

45. Look back at the expressions in Exercises 42–44 and their values. Tell whether there are commutative and associative properties of subtraction.

46. **Challenge** Find a path through Integer Woods for the hiker. The hiker can move only horizontally or vertically from integer to integer. The sum of the numbers in a path must equal the exit number.

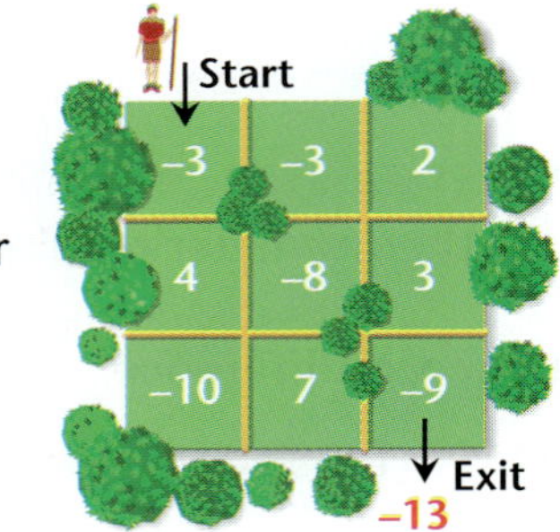

Reflecting on the Section

Write your response to Exercise 47 in your journal.

47. a. Suppose you started at 4 on a number line and wanted to move in the positive direction. What numbers could you add? What numbers could you subtract?

b. Suppose you started at 4 on a number line and wanted to move in the negative direction. What numbers could you add? What numbers could you subtract?

c. Using a number line, explain why subtracting an integer is like adding its opposite.

Journal

Exercise 47 checks your understanding of integer addition and subtraction.

Spiral Review

48. Graph these ordered pairs in a coordinate plane: $A(-3, 1)$, $B(4, 1)$, $C(4, -2)$, and $D(-3, -2)$. (Module 2, p. 95)

Mental Math Find each sum or difference mentally. (Toolbox, p. 581)

49. 2.36 + 0.98 50. 87.41 – 19.95 51. 14.32 – 7.75

Find the next three terms of each sequence. (Module 1, p. 20)

52. 31, 27, 23, 19, ... 53. 25, 36, 49, 64, ...

Extension

Consecutive Integers

If you count by ones beginning with any integer, you get a set of consecutive integers.

Example:

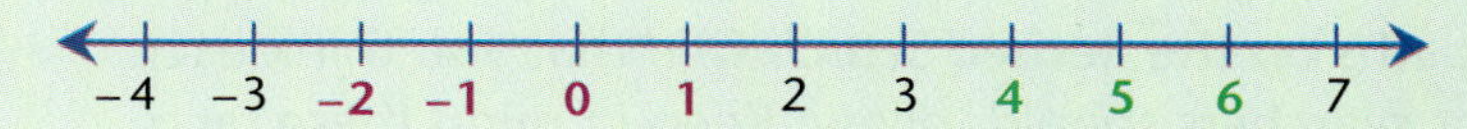

–2, –1, 0, 1 are consecutive integers.

4, 5, 6 are consecutive integers.

54. The sum of three consecutive integers is –57. What are the three integers?

55. The sum of eight consecutive integers is 12. What are the eight integers?

Planning a Search

SET UP *You will need Project Labsheet C.*

Hiking on a Coordinate Grid When a searcher finds a clue, the search and rescue team organizes a new phase of the search. The team sets up a coordinate grid with the location of the clue as its origin. Then team members hike at a steady pace along the grid lines, hoping to find the person they are searching for, or another clue.

Use Project Labsheet C. A searcher found an empty juice box at point *C* on the map. Use the *Search Grid* and the *Revised Search Grid* to answer Questions 9 and 10.

9 Eight searchers, S1 through S8, hiked along the lines of the *Search Grid* at a steady rate of 2 mi/h, and searcher S4 found footprints in the mud at point *F*. How long did it take searcher S4 to reach this point?

Kendenura Hill
632
Beyondie Lakes
Ten Mile Lake
558
600
Point Last Seen ×
Yibbie Range
650
658
C
0 1 2 3 4 5 6 7 8 9 10
Miles

10 The team established a *Revised Search Grid*. This square region is 1 mi on a side and point *F* is the origin.

a. Plot point *F* at the center of the *Revised Search Grid*.

b. Draw the paths on the *Revised Search Grid* that you think each of the eight searchers should follow. Keep in mind these facts.

- The searchers walk at the same rate (2 mi/h).
- The searchers walk along grid lines only.
- There are about 1.5 hours of daylight remaining.
- The searchers will begin at point *F* and return to point *F* after 1 hour to revise the plan, if necessary.

A hiker on a number line follows each set of directions. Determine where the hiker will finish. Record the moves as an addition problem with its sum or as a subtraction problem with its difference.

1. Start at -2. Face the positive direction. Move forward 5 units.
2. Start at 4. Face the negative direction. Move backward 2 units.
3. Start at -1. Face the negative direction. Move forward 3 units.

Find each sum.

4. $5 + 7$
5. $-6 + (-3)$
6. $0 + (-5)$
7. $-12 + 9$
8. $28 + (-37)$
9. $-13 + 18$
10. $-58 + 58$
11. $-52 + (-48)$
12. $45 + (-37)$
13. $-78 + 68$
14. $-84 + (-96)$
15. $49 + (-49)$

Mental Math **Find each sum using mental math. Use properties of addition.**

16. $-25 + 6 + 0 + (-6)$
17. $14 + (-9) + (26 + 9)$
18. $3 + 14 + (-3) + (-4)$
19. $-2 + 12 + (-8) + (-2)$
20. $-6 + (-14) + 21 + 9$
21. $17 + (-8) + (-12) + (-17)$

Evaluate each expression.

22. $3 - 7$
23. $0 - (-6)$
24. $-5 - 3$
25. $13 - (-8)$
26. $-22 - 6$
27. $-2 - (-18)$
28. $29 - 33$
29. $-15 - (-5)$
30. $9 - (-6) - 7$
31. $-8 - 4 + (-18)$
32. $29 + (-17) - (-3)$
33. $-6 + 7 - (-5)$
34. $9 - 12 - 11$
35. $-16 + (-7) - (-14)$

Standardized Testing ▶ Multiple Choice

1. Point B lies halfway between points A and C. What is the coordinate of point C?

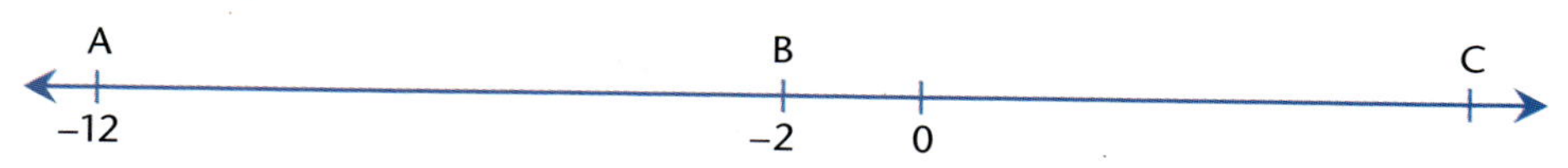

Ⓐ 6 Ⓑ 8 Ⓒ 10 Ⓓ 14

2. Evaluate $-14 + 3 - (-17) + (-4) - 11$.

Ⓐ -12 Ⓑ 8 Ⓒ -9 Ⓓ -5

FOR ASSESSMENT AND PORTFOLIOS

A PHONE CHAIN

The Situation

When a search and rescue team is needed, all members of the search and rescue team must be notified as quickly as possible. This is often accomplished through a phone chain. In a phone chain, the first person calls two people. Each of those people call two more people. Each of those people call two more people and so on, until everyone in the search and rescue team is notified of the emergency.

The Problem

Estimate the least amount of time it would take using a phone chain like the one described above to notify all the members in a 55-person search and rescue team.

Something to Think About

- How might a table or drawing help you solve this problem?
- Could you modify the procedure to shorten the total amount of time involved? If so, how?
- What are some assumptions you might need to make about phone calls?

Present Your Results

Describe what you did to solve the problem. Explain why you solved it this way. Show any drawings, diagrams, charts, or tables that you used to solve the problem. Why do you think your solution is accurate?

Section 4 Function Models

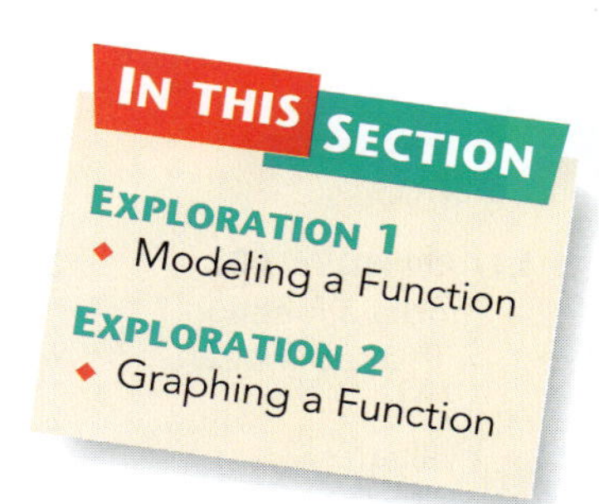

URBAN RESCUE

Setting the Stage

A bus is caught in raging flood waters ... people are trapped on top of a burning skyscraper... a plane crashes into an icy river...

These are just some of the emergency situations in urban areas requiring the skills of helicopter rescue personnel.

▲ A helicopter transports someone to a hospital.

▲ Police practice their helicopter-rescue skills.

Think About It

1 What kinds of skills do you think are important for members of a rescue team to have?

2 What factors do you think affect the response time of emergency vehicles in urban rescue situations?

3 What are some advantages and disadvantages of using helicopters instead of other emergency vehicles for urban rescues?

▶ **In this section you'll explore how tables, equations, and graphs are used to understand search and rescue situations and to make decisions.**

GOAL

LEARN HOW TO...
- model a function with a table or an equation
- evaluate expressions with variables

AS YOU...
- explore distance, rate, and time

KEY TERMS
- evaluate
- equation
- function

Exploration 1

Modeling a FUNCTION

Travel time is critical in emergency situations. During medical emergencies, helicopters travel 2 miles per minute (mi/min). Ambulances travel at whatever speed (rate) the traffic will allow.

4 **a.** Suppose an ambulance travels 55 miles per hour (mi/h). How far will it go in 1 hour? in 2 hours? in 3 hours?

b. What method did you use to answer part (a)?

The table shows the distances traveled by a helicopter going 2 mi/min for different travel times.

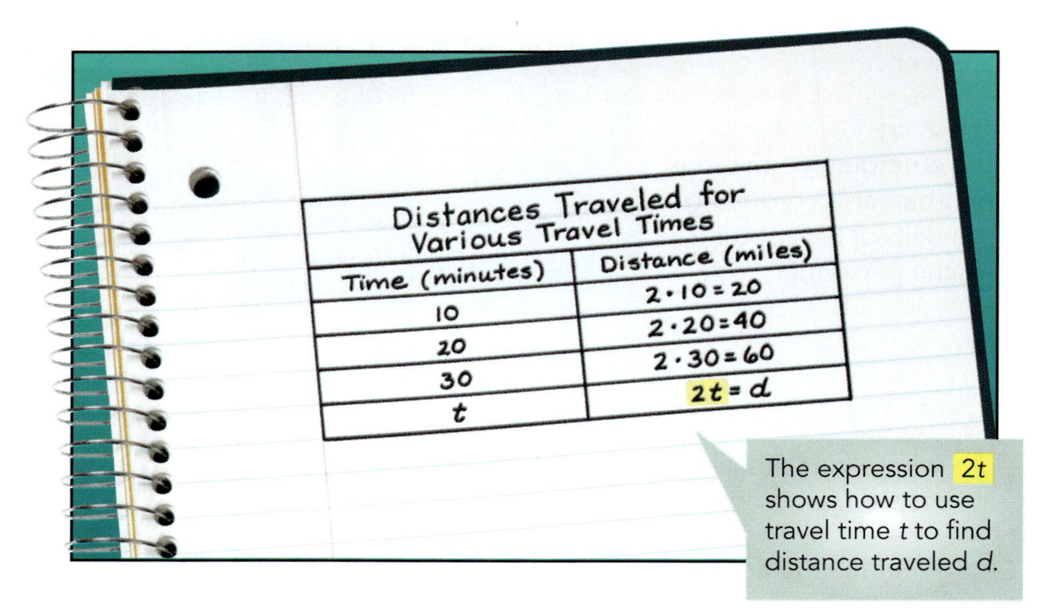

Distances Traveled for Various Travel Times

Time (minutes)	Distance (miles)
10	$2 \cdot 10 = 20$
20	$2 \cdot 20 = 40$
30	$2 \cdot 30 = 60$
t	$2t = d$

5 An expression can be formed using variables as well as numbers and operation symbols.

a. What operation is used in the expression $2t$ in the table?

b. What does the expression $2t$ tell you about how to use the rate 2 mi/min and a travel time to find the distance traveled?

▶ You can **evaluate** an expression that has a variable by substituting a value for the variable and performing the operations.

EXAMPLE

Evaluate $2t$ when $t = 40$ to find the distance traveled in 40 min by a helicopter going 2 mi/min.

SAMPLE RESPONSE

$$2t = 2(40)$$
$$= 80$$

Substitute 40 for t and then multiply.

A helicopter going 2 mi/min will travel 80 mi in 40 min.

▶ **When two expressions are equal, you can write an equation to express the relationship. For example:**

Distance traveled is rate × time.

$$d = rt$$

6 Use an ambulance's rate of 55 mi/h for parts (a) and (b).

a. Make a table of the distances traveled in 4, 5, 6, and t hours.

b. Write an equation relating distance traveled and travel time.

▶ **A function is a relationship between input and output. For each input, there is exactly one output. Output depends on input. For example, the distance traveled depends on the travel time.**

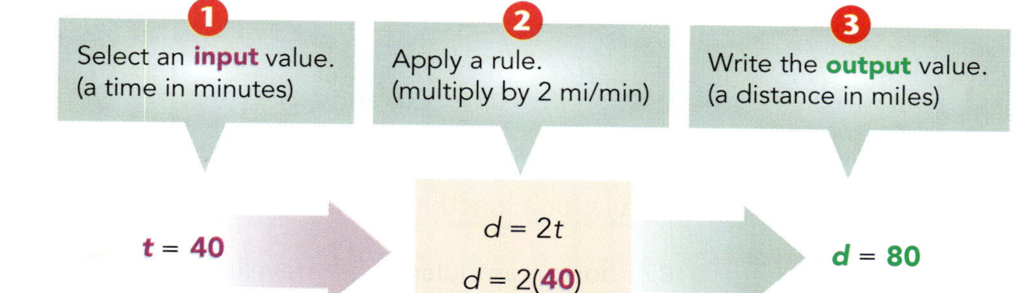

7 **Discussion** Use the function in the diagram.

a. What input values make sense for this function when t represents a time and d represents a distance?

b. Explain why the output will always be 80 when $t = 40$.

8 **Try This as a Class** Suppose a group of s searchers includes four relatives of a lost boy along with m members of an SAR team.

a. In words, describe the relationship between m and s.

b. What type of numbers make sense as values for m and s?

✓ QUESTION 9

...checks that you can model a function with a table or an equation.

9 **✓ CHECKPOINT** Make a table using three possible input values for m to model the situation in Question 8. Then write an equation relating m and s.

▶ **Expressions with Two Operations** **Some situations can be modeled using expressions that involve two operations.**

10 Suppose a helicopter starts 50 mi from its destination and travels 2 mi/min. Let t = the number of minutes the helicopter travels.

a. What does the expression $2t$ model?

b. What does the expression $50 - 2t$ model?

c. Which two operations are involved in the expression $50 - 2t$?

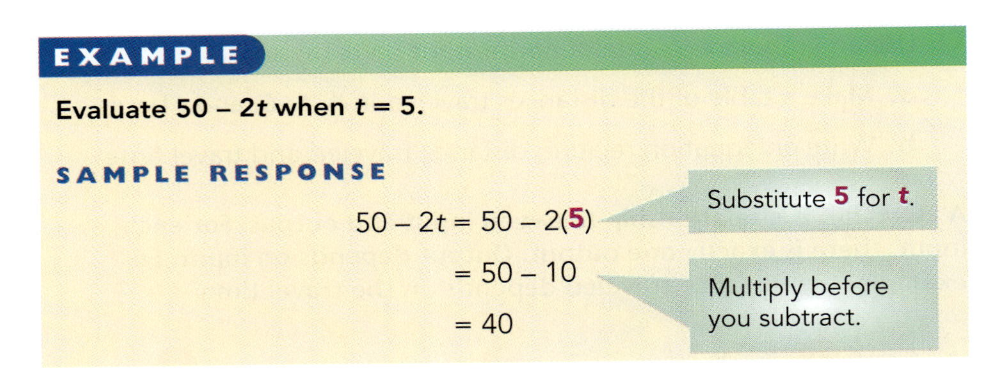

EXAMPLE

Evaluate $50 - 2t$ when $t = 5$.

SAMPLE RESPONSE

$$50 - 2t = 50 - 2(5)$$
$$= 50 - 10$$
$$= 40$$

Substitute **5** for **t**.

Multiply before you subtract.

11 **a.** Evaluate $50 - 2t$ when $t = 10$, $t = 20$, and $t = 30$.

b. What values of t make sense in the situation in Question 10?

c. Can $50 - 2t$ be a rule for a function? Why or why not?

✓ QUESTION 12

... checks that you can write and evaluate an expression to model a situation.

12 **✓ CHECKPOINT** By noon an ambulance has traveled 40 mi from its starting point and continues to travel at 55 mi/h.

a. Let t = the travel time since noon. Write an expression to model the total distance the ambulance has traveled.

b. Use the expression to find the distance traveled by 2:00 P.M.

HOMEWORK EXERCISES ▶ See Exs. 1–24 on pp. 125–126.

Exploration 2

Graphing a FUNCTION

SET UP *You will need:* • *Labsheet 4A* • *a ruler*

GOAL

LEARN HOW TO...
- model a function with a graph

AS YOU...
- choose between emergency vehicles

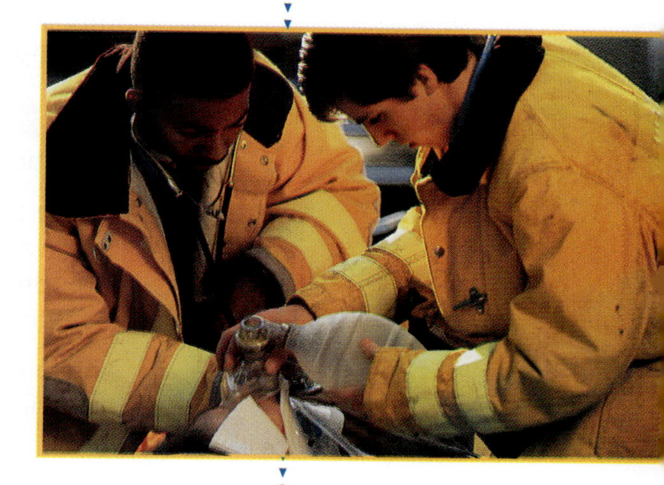

Emergency medical technicians (EMTs) at an accident scene must decide how to transport someone to a hospital that provides the right care.

The diagram below gives information about a highway accident scene. The ambulance at the scene and a medical helicopter nearby can both handle the emergency. In this exploration you'll see which vehicle will get to the hospital sooner.

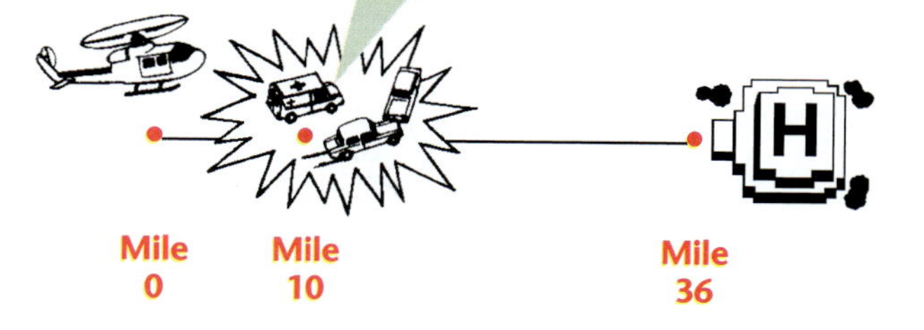

13 **Use Labsheet 4A.** Use the *Location Table*.

a. Complete the *Location Table* to show the ambulance's location after various travel times.

b. Write an equation that relates the variables m and t in the table.

14 **Discussion** How long will it take the ambulance to reach the hospital? Explain how you got your answer.

15 **Use Labsheet 4A.** Plot the values from the *Location Table* on the *Location Grid*. Draw a line through the points to the edge of the grid.

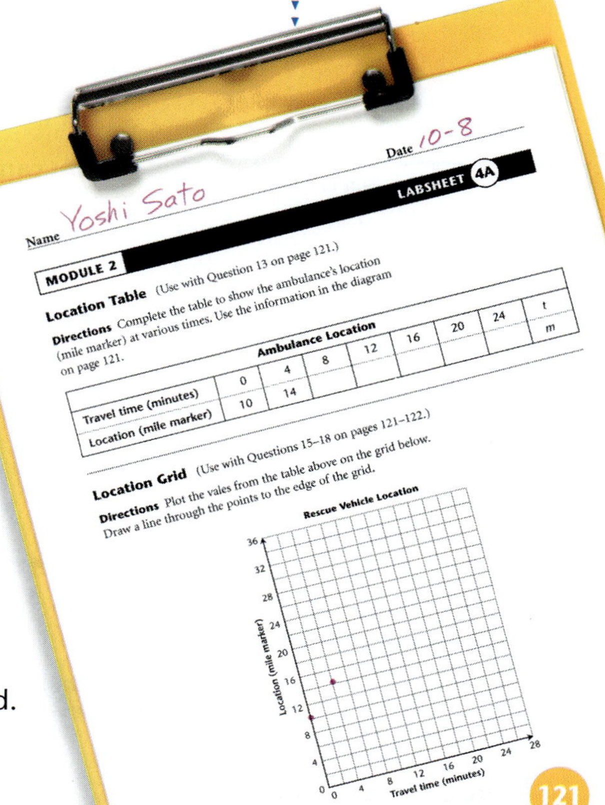

Name Yoshi Sato Date 10-8

LABSHEET 4A

MODULE 2

Location Table (Use with Question 13 on page 121.)

Directions Complete the table to show the ambulance's location (mile marker) at various times. Use the information in the diagram on page 121.

Ambulance Location								
Travel time (minutes)	0	4	8	12	16	20	24	t
Location (mile marker)	10	14						m

Location Grid (Use with Questions 15–18 on pages 121–122.)

Directions Plot the vales from the table above on the grid below. Draw a line through the points to the edge of the grid.

Use the *Location Grid* from Labsheet 4A for Questions 16–18.

16 **a.** The values on the vertical axis of the *Location Grid* range from 0 to 36 mi. Why do you think these values were chosen?

b. Why do you think the values used on the horizontal axis were chosen?

c. What mile marker will the ambulance be at in 10 min?

d. In Question 14 you figured out how long it would take the ambulance to reach the hospital. Does your answer match what is shown on your graph? Explain.

✓ QUESTION 17

...checks that you can model a function with a graph

17 **✓ CHECKPOINT** Suppose the helicopter in the diagram below is chosen for the trip to the hospital.

a. Make a table of values like the one for the ambulance to show the helicopter's location m at various travel times t.

b. Write an equation that relates the variables m and t.

c. Plot the values from your table on the Location Grid. Draw a line through the points.

The helicopter can travel an average of 2 mi/min.

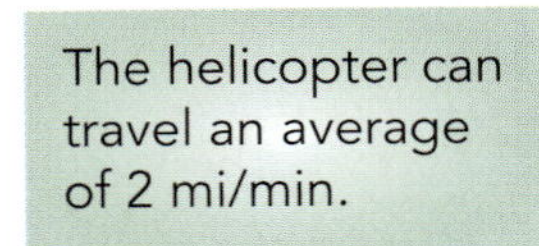

▶ You can compare functions by graphing them on the same grid. The lines on your *Location Grid* can help you decide which vehicle will get to the hospital sooner.

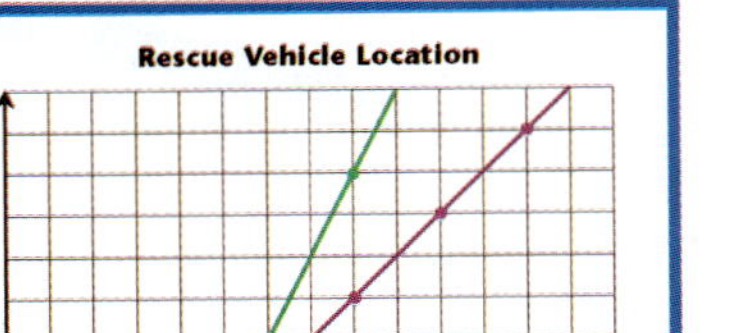

18 **a.** The rescue vehicles start at different locations. How is this shown on your *Location Grid*?

b. The two lines on your graph *intersect* (cross). What are the coordinates of the point where the lines intersect? What do the coordinates tell you about the situation?

c. Which vehicle will get to the hospital sooner? How much sooner? Explain how you got your answers.

HOMEWORK EXERCISES ▶ See Exs. 25–36 on pp. 126–128.

You can also use a graphing calculator or graphing software to make and analyze the graphs in this exploration.

Step 1 To graph a function, you enter its equation, using X for the input variable and Y for the output variable.

The equations you wrote for Questions 13(b) and 17(b) can be entered where the screen shows Y1 and Y2.

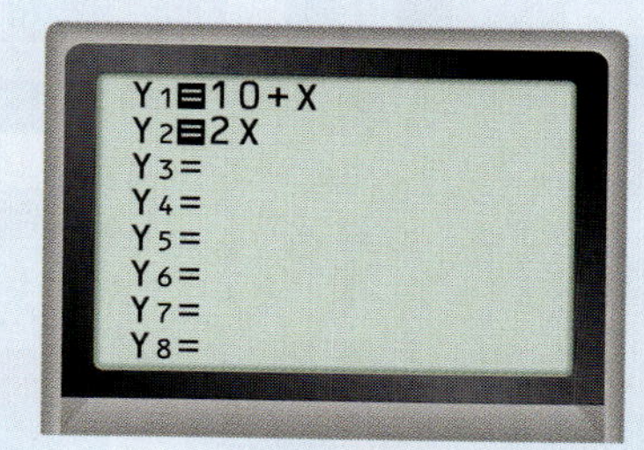

Step 2 To set the *viewing window* for your graph, enter the values you want shown along each axis. Then graph.

Enter the minimum, maximum, and scale values for X and Y.

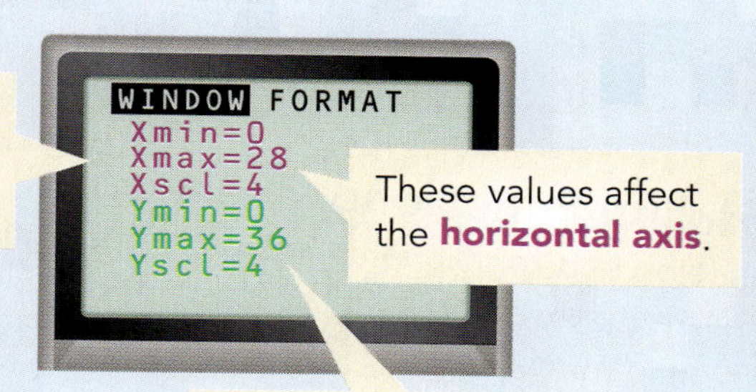

These values affect the **horizontal axis**.

These values affect the **vertical axis**.

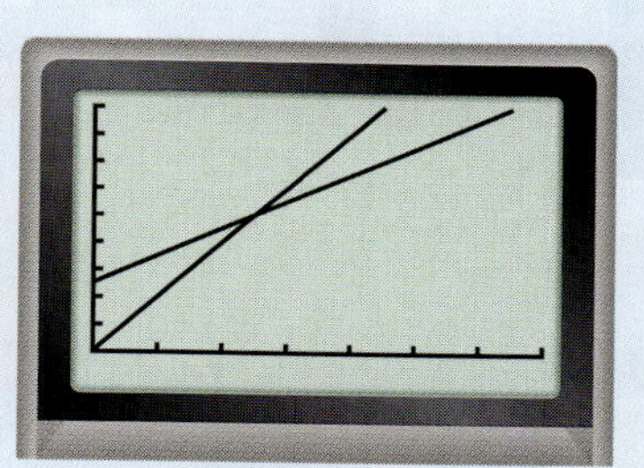

Step 3 Use the TRACE feature to estimate values for the function in Questions 16(c) and 18(b), or use the INTERSECTION or the TABLE feature to find exact values.

Use the arrow keys to trace along a line and see coordinates of points.

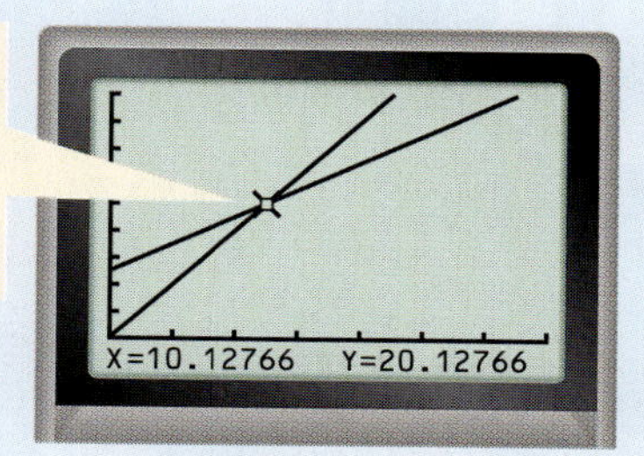

X	Y1	Y2
0	10	0
2	12	4
4	14	8
6	16	12
8	18	16
10	20	20
12	22	24

X=10

A minimum value of 0 and an increase of 2 in each step were chosen for this table.

Section 4 Key Concepts

Key Terms

evaluate

Evaluating Expressions (pp. 118–120)

To evaluate an expression that has a variable, substitute a value for the variable and perform the operations.

Example A family on a 1200-mile road trip has traveled for t hours at r miles per hour. This expression represents the distance left to travel:

$$1200 - rt$$

distance traveled = rate × time

To find the distance left to travel after 9 h at an average rate of 45 mi/h, evaluate $1200 - rt$ when $r = 45$ and $t = 9$.

$$\begin{aligned} 1200 - rt &= 1200 - 45 \cdot 9 \\ &= 1200 - 405 \\ &= 795 \text{ (mi)} \end{aligned}$$

Substitute 45 for r and 9 for t. Then simplify.

function

equation

Modeling Functions (pp. 118–122)

A function is a relationship between input and output. For each input, there is exactly one output. Output depends on input. You can model a function in many ways.

Example A number y is one less than twice another number x.

Table (p. 118)

input x	0	1	2
output y	−1	1	3

This table shows only a few of the possible values for x and y.

Equation (p. 119)

$$y = 2x - 1$$

Graph (pp. 121–122)

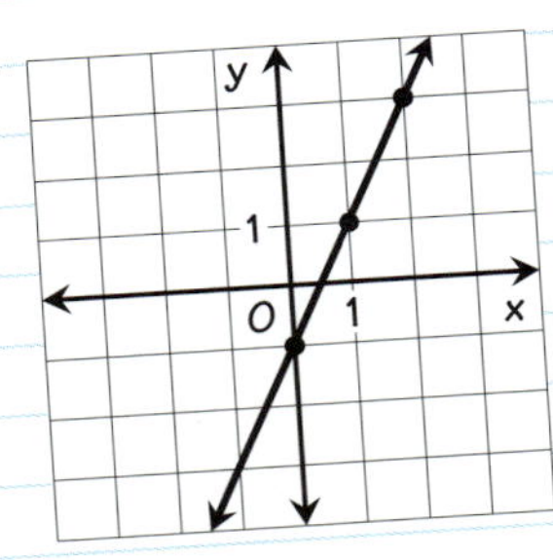

19 Key Concepts Question The equation $d = 1200 - 45t$ models the situation in the first example, when d is the distance left to travel at an average rate of 45 mi/h. Graph the equation using reasonable values.

Section 4 Practice & Application Exercises

YOU WILL NEED

For Exs. 25–27, 29–31, 34, 43, and 44:
- graph paper

For Ex. 35:
- graphing calculator

Choose the letter of the expression that models each situation.

1. At a box office, the price of a ticket is p dollars. What is the price at a ticket outlet that charges an extra \$2 per ticket?

A. $2p$ **B.** $p - 2$ **C.** $p + 2$

2. A *fathom* is equal to 6 ft. How many feet are there in n fathoms?

A. $6n$ **B.** $n \div 6$ **C.** $6 \div n$

Write an expression that models each situation.

3. The price of a compact disk is p dollars. What is the price after a \$3 increase?

4. Geometry Connection The measure of an angle is x degrees. What is the measure of a complementary angle?

Evaluate each expression when $a = 3$, $b = 5$, and $c = -7$.

5. $40a$ **6.** $25b$ **7.** $120 \div b$

8. $75 \div a$ **9.** $a + 18$ **10.** $b - 9$

11. $c + 14$ **12.** $b + c$ **13.** $c - b$

14. Recreation The *Texas Folklife Festival* celebrates cultural diversity with music, dance, crafts, costumes, and food.

TEXAS FOLKLIFE FESTIVAL

The table models the relationship between the number of tickets sold n and the amount of money collected c.

a. Copy and extend the table to include the amounts collected for these values of n: 25, 30, 35, and 40.

Tickets sold	Amount collected (\$)
0	0
5	40
10	80
15	120
20	160
n	c

b. Write an equation to model the relationship between the number of tickets sold and the amount collected.

c. How much money is collected when 23 tickets are sold?

d. What type of numbers make sense as values for n?

Evaluate each expression when $x = 10$, $y = -4$, and $z = 2$.

15. $2z + 4$

16. $5x - 22$

17. $3z - x$

18. $2z + y$

19. $4x + y$

20. $x - 9z$

21. $y + 8z$

22. $y - 3x$

23. $xz - y$

24. **Travel** It costs $10 for a person up to 17 years of age to join American Youth Hostels, and $15 to buy a required sleeping sack. Worldwide, the average cost to stay in a hostel is $9 per night.

   a. Make a table that shows the costs for 1, 2, 3, 4, and 5 nights.

   b. Write an equation to model the relationship between the number of nights n spent in a hostel and the total cost c.

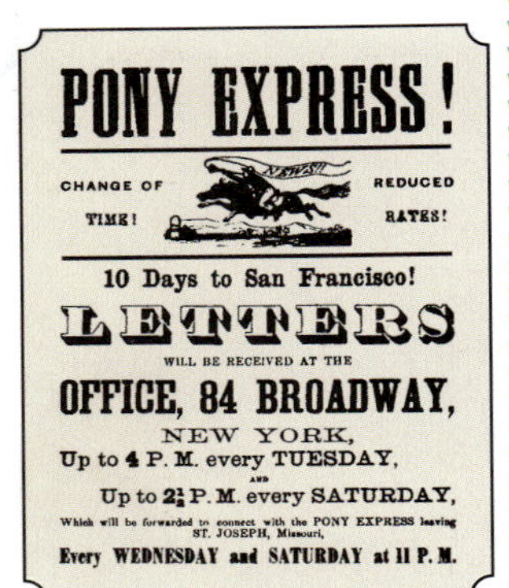
PONY EXPRESS!
CHANGE OF TIME! REDUCED RATES!
10 Days to San Francisco!
LETTERS
WILL BE RECEIVED AT THE
OFFICE, 84 BROADWAY,
NEW YORK,
Up to 4 P. M. every TUESDAY,
AND
Up to 2½ P. M. every SATURDAY,
Which will be forwarded to connect with the PONY EXPRESS leaving ST. JOSEPH, Missouri,
Every WEDNESDAY and SATURDAY at 11 P. M.

The Pony Express delivered mail for only 18 months. In 1861, a telegraph line to California made the service unnecessary.

25. **Social Studies** The table shows ways that mail traveled across the United States in the early to late 1860s.

   a. Choose one of the rates given above. Make a table showing the distances traveled for travel times of 0, 1, 2, 3, 4, 5, and 6 hours.

   b. Use the rate you chose in part (a). Write an equation to model the distance traveled d in relation to travel time t.

   c. Graph the data from your table in part (a) on graph paper. Label each axis with reasonable values. Include axis titles and a graph title.

   d. Use coordinates to label the point on your graph that shows the distance traveled in 4.5 hours.

Copy and complete the table of values for each equation. Then graph each equation in a coordinate plane.

26. $y = x + 2$

x	−2	−1	0	1	2
y	?	?	?	?	?

27. $y = 2x - 5$

x	0	2	4	6	8
y	?	?	?	?	?

28. Open-ended Describe a situation that can be modeled by one of the equations in Exercises 26 and 27. Tell what values make sense for the variables in that situation.

Make a table of values for each equation when $x = -1$, $x = 0$, and $x = 1$. Then graph each equation in a coordinate plane.

29. $y = x + 3$

30. $y = x - 4$

31. $y = 2 - x$

32. Interpreting Data The graph models two mountain bike trips. Riders with equal skills are riding on different trails.

a. **Writing** Who is traveling on the easier trail? Explain your thinking.

b. How far does each rider travel in 2 hours? Is this consistent with your answer to part (a)?

c. Make a table of values for each trip.

d. Write an equation for each trip.

33. Challenge Describe how you can use the graph in Exercise 32 to find the rate at which each rider is traveling.

34. Bowling Costs Some bowling alleys charge by the hour. Rashida compared the costs per hour for two people to bowl together at two different bowling alleys.

Bowling Alley A:	Bowling Alley B:
\$4 for 2 pairs of shoes plus \$17 per hour	\$2 for 2 pairs of shoes plus \$18 per hour

a. Let x = the bowling time (in hours). Let y = the total charge (in dollars). Use them to model each option with an equation.

b. Graph your equations from part (a) on one coordinate grid.

c. When is Bowling Alley A less expensive?

d. When are the charges the same for both bowling alleys?

35. Graphing Calculator Repeat Exercise 34 for the following situation: the hourly rate for Bowling Alley B is \$18.50, but all other conditions stay the same.

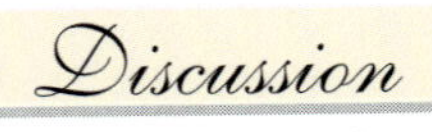

Exercise 36 checks that you understand some ways to model a function.

Reflecting on the Section

Be prepared to discuss your response to Exercise 36 in class.

36. In this section, you've seen functions modeled with tables, equations, and graphs. Describe the advantages and disadvantages of each type of model.

Spiral Review

Find each sum or difference. (Module 2, p. 109)

37. –18 + (–42)

38. –6 – (–13)

39. –10 – 7

Suppose you roll an eight-sided die with faces labeled 1 to 8 and all outcomes are equally likely. Find the theoretical probability of each event. (Module 1, p. 33)

40. *P*(3)

41. *P*(9)

42. *P*(odd number)

43. Make a table, draw a graph, and write an equation for the sequence 6, 7, 8, 9, … . Then predict the 100th term. (Module 1, p. 20)

Career Connection

Paramedic: Scott Rosenfeld

One of the greatest challenges paramedic Scott Rosenfeld faces is treating an injured child. To find out whether the injury has resulted in shock, he can measure the injured child's blood pressure to see whether it's too low.

44. Scott Rosenfeld can use a formula to estimate whether a child's *systolic* blood pressure is below a "safe" limit. The formula applies to children over two years old through their early teens:

Lower limit for systolic blood pressure = 70 + (2 × child's age)

a. Make a table of values and a graph to show the relationship between systolic blood pressure and age.

b. What are reasonable input and output values for the situation?

You will need: • *graph paper* (Exs. 18–21)

Write an expression that models each situation.

1. Luisa is 5 cm taller than Ruth. Ruth is n centimeters tall. How tall is Luisa?
2. Brian drove for 3 hours at r miles per hour. How far did he drive?

Evaluate each expression when $x = 2$, $y = 4$, and $z = -3$.

3. $25x$
4. $64 \div y$
5. $z + 3$
6. $x - 12$
7. $y \div x$
8. $2 + z$
9. $9y$
10. $-5 - y$
11. $2y + 5$
12. $15x - 7$
13. $z - xy$
14. $3x + y$

Model each relationship between x and y with a table and an equation. For the table, use three input values that make sense.

15. A house number y is 2 less than a nearby house number x.
16. The distance to the mall is y miles. The distance to the library is x miles. The distance to the mall is twice the distance to the library.
17. A number y is 6 more than twice another number x.

Make a table of values for each equation when $x = -1$, $x = 0$, and $x = 1$. Then graph each equation in a coordinate plane.

18. $y = x$
19. $y = x + 1$
20. $y = 1 - x$
21. $y = x + 4$

Standardized Testing ▶ Free Response

The Kartanel family took a 4-hour car trip from Praitis to Veloysha.

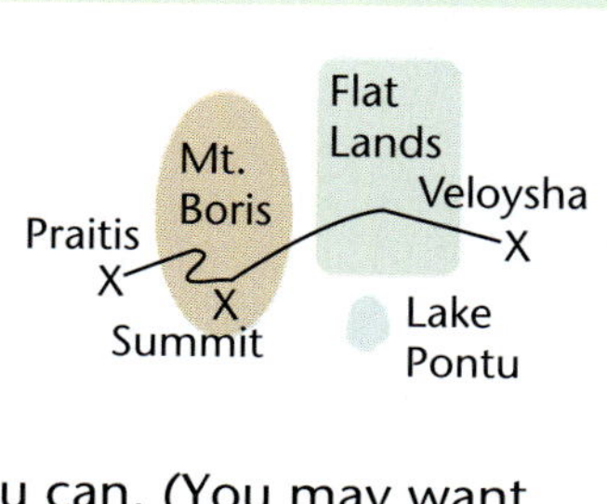

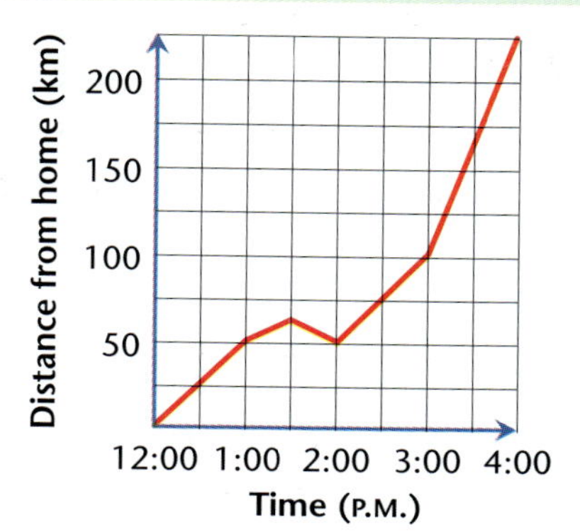

Use the map and the graph to describe the Kartanels' trip during each hour. Tell as much about the trip as you can. (You may want to think about their average speed for each hour and why they slowed down or sped up.)

Addition and Subtraction Equations

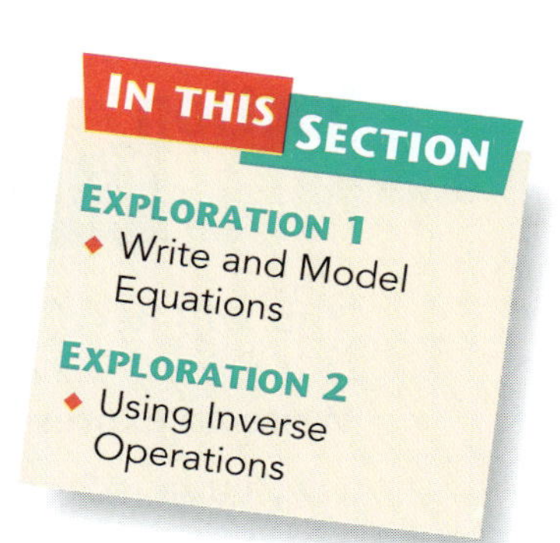

Setting the Stage

Have you ever felt as if your arms would break if you had to carry your books another minute? Just how much extra weight do you carry at school? Students at Monte Cassino Middle School in Tulsa, Oklahoma, weighed their backpacks and discovered that they carry anywhere from 11 lb to 26 lb.

Search and rescue (SAR) teams find creative ways to keep the contents of their backpacks as light as possible. Backpack weights for SAR team members vary according to each member's fitness, the search area, and the time of year.

Think About It

1 How have the items shown above been made lighter?

2 About how many of your math books would it take to reach a weight of 26 lb?

3 What are some ways that you could reduce the weight of the materials that you carry with you during the day?

4 Estimate how many pounds of school materials you carry home with you on a typical day. Explain how you made your estimate.

Exploration 1

WRITE AND MODEL EQUATIONS

SET UP *You will need algebra tiles.*

GOAL

LEARN HOW TO...
- write addition and subtraction equations
- solve addition equations using models

AS YOU...
- examine the contents of a backpack

KEY TERMS
- solution of an equation
- solve an equation

Weather conditions affect what an SAR team member must carry. In a cold climate, a team member may need to carry 6 lb of warm clothing. In a hot climate, the 6 lb of clothing might be traded for 5 lb of extra water and 1 lb of sunscreen and insect repellent.

This trade can be modeled in several ways.

Verbal statement	Weight of extra water	plus	weight of sunscreen and insect repellent	equals	weight of warm clothing
Equation	5 lb	+	1 lb	=	6 lb
Balance model					

The water, sunscreen, and insect repellent can replace the warm clothing.

5 **Try This as a Class** Use the balance model above.

a. Why can the rescuer exchange the warm clothing for water, sunscreen, and insect repellent?

b. Why does the balance scale work as a model for an equation?

▶ **Equations Involving Variables** Suppose a rescuer can carry 25 lb. The rescuer has a 6 lb tent, a 4 lb sleeping bag, a 5 lb backpack, plus other items. Here are two ways to model the situation, where x represents the weight of the other items.

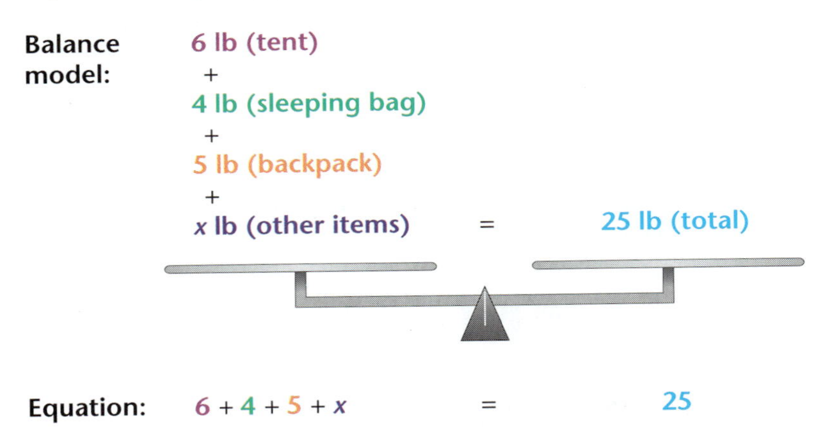

Equation: $6 + 4 + 5 + x = 25$

6 **a.** What is the unknown weight x the rescuer could carry?

b. Explain how you found the value of x in part (a).

▶ **Balance models can help you visualize an equation and remember that both sides represent the same amount. Equations can be used to model a variety of situations.**

EXAMPLE

Suppose an SAR team with 30 members includes 14 men. Let w = the number of women on the team. Write an equation to model the total number of SAR team members.

SAMPLE RESPONSE

Number of women	plus	number of men	equals	total number on SAR team
w	+	14	=	30

7 **a.** Why is 20 not a reasonable value for w in the Example?

b. What is the unknown number of women on the team in the Example?

8 Suppose an SAR team with 30 members includes 12 women. Choose a variable to represent the number of men on the team and write an equation to model the situation.

▶ **Sometimes equations that model a situation involve subtraction.**

EXAMPLE

Between midnight and 2:00 A.M., the temperature dropped 4°F. At 2:00 A.M. the temperature was –1°F. Write an equation to model the situation.

SAMPLE RESPONSE

Temperature at midnight (°F)	minus	drop in temperature (°F)	equals	temperature at 2:00 A.M. (°F)
t	$-$	4	$=$	-1

9 Find the temperature at midnight for the situation in the Example.

10 ✓ **CHECKPOINT** An SAR team ate 56 meals. They had 6 meals left over. Write a subtraction equation to model the situation. Use one variable and tell what it represents.

...checks that you can use equations to model situations.

11 Describe a situation that each equation could model.

a. $w + 3 = 8$ **b.** $15 - c = 4$

▶ **Algebra Tiles** **You can use algebra tiles to model equations. The tile represents the variable. The tile represents 1.**

EXAMPLE

You model the equation $x + 5 = 8$ with algebra tiles as follows:

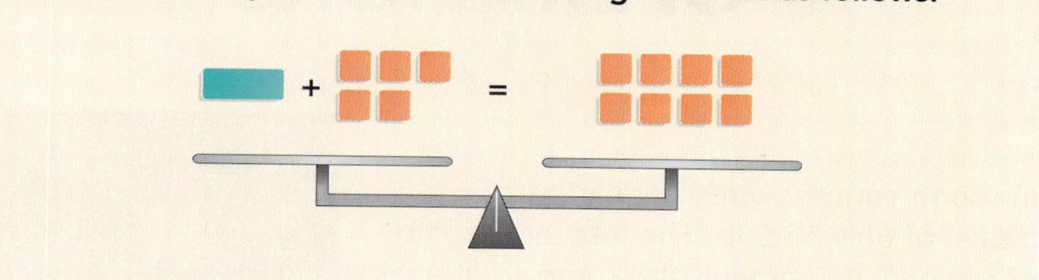

12 **a.** Use algebra tiles to model the Example above. Remove two tiles from the side of the equation with the . What must you do to the other side to keep the equation balanced?

b. How many tiles must represent in the Example above for the equation to be balanced? How did you get your answer?

A value of a variable that makes an equation true is a **solution of the equation**. The process of finding solutions is called **solving an equation**.

13 **a.** Write an equation represented by the algebra tile model.

b. Using algebra tiles, get the [tile] tile for the model in part (a) alone on one side of the equation while keeping the two sides balanced. Describe your method.

c. Solve the equation you wrote in part (a).

QUESTION 14

...checks that you can use a model to solve an addition equation.

14 **CHECKPOINT** Repeat Question 13 for this algebra tile model.

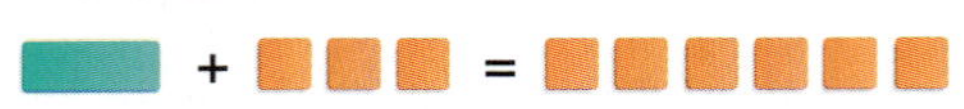

HOMEWORK EXERCISES See Exs. 1–17 on pp. 138–139.

GOAL

LEARN HOW TO...
- use inverse operations to solve addition and subtraction equations
- check solutions

AS YOU...
- explore weight limits for a backpack

KEY TERMS
- inverse operations

Exploration 2

USING INVERSE OPERATIONS

In rough country, a rescuer can carry a total of only 18.5 lb. The rescuer has 7 lb of essential equipment plus some additional equipment. Let x = the number of pounds of additional equipment.

15 **a.** Write an addition equation that represents the situation above.

b. What can you do to both sides of the equation to get x alone?

c. Why is it difficult to represent this situation with a model?

▶ **Addition and subtraction are inverse operations. They "undo" each other. Inverse operations are helpful in solving equations.**

Here are keys to solving an equation:

- Use inverse operations to get the variable alone on one side.
- Keep the equation balanced by keeping both sides equal.

▶ **When you use symbols and variables to solve an equation, you are solving the equation *algebraically*.**

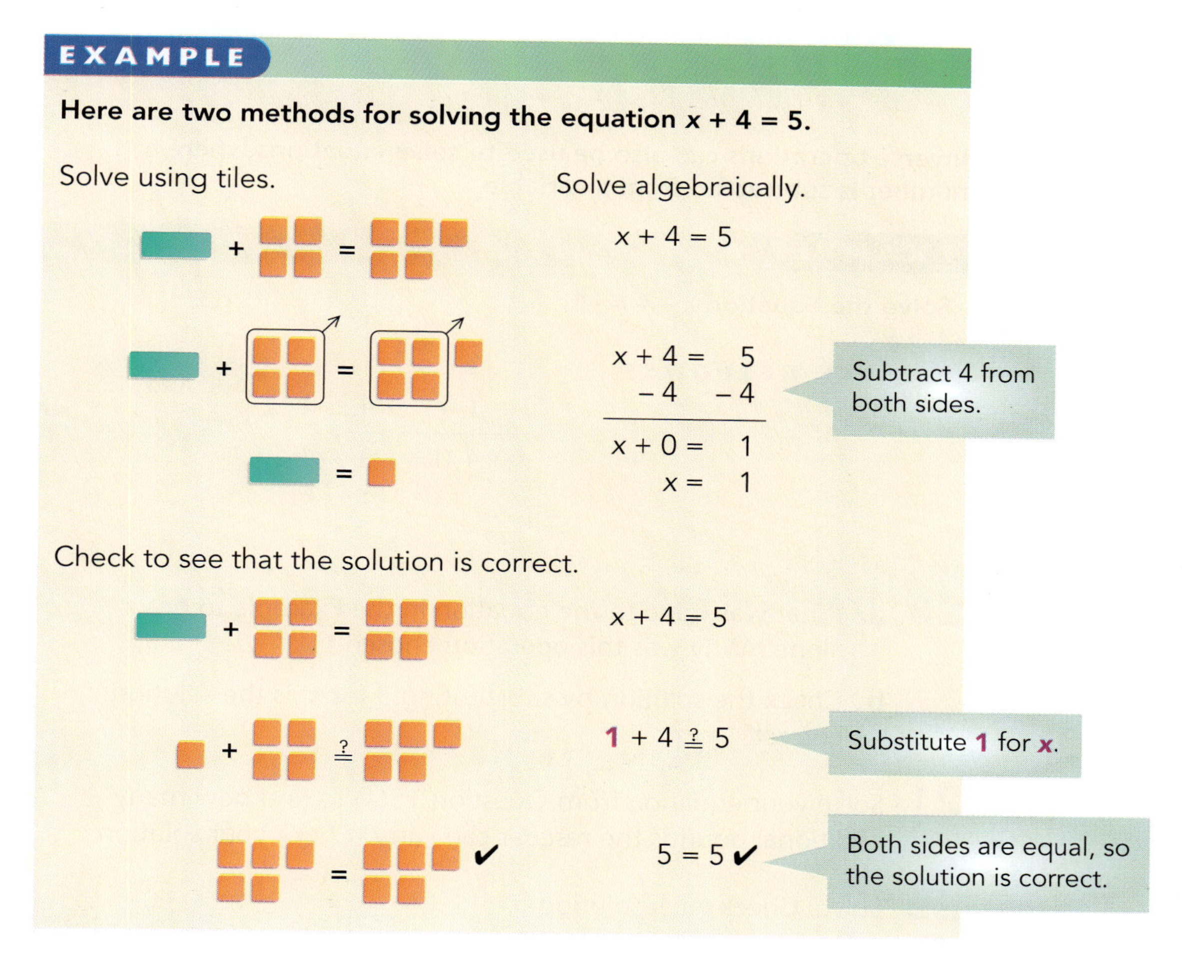

16 **a.** In the Example, what was done to the equation to get x alone?

b. Describe the steps in checking the solution. Why is a question mark included in the check process?

c. Why is it important to check the solution?

17 Tim solved the equation $x + 47 = 65$ as shown at the right. Check to see whether Tim's solution is correct.

✓ QUESTION 18

...checks that you understand how inverse operations can help you solve equations.

18 **✓ CHECKPOINT** Solve. Check each solution.

a. $n + 18 = 102$ **b.** $-2 = a + 5$

19 **Try This as a Class** Use the equation $h + (-3) = 5$.

a. What would you do to both sides of the equation to "undo" the addition to get h alone?

b. How could you use addition to solve this equation?

c. Use your method from part (b) to solve the equation $y + (-8) = 16$.

▶ **Inverse operations can also be used to solve equations where a number is subtracted from a variable.**

EXAMPLE

Solve the equation $x - 4 = -1$.

SAMPLE RESPONSE

$$\begin{array}{rr} x - 4 = & -1 \\ +4 & +4 \\ \hline x + 0 = & 3 \\ x = & 3 \end{array}$$

Add 4 to both sides.

20 **a.** What was done to the equation in the Example to get x alone? Why was this operation chosen?

b. Check the solution by substituting 3 for x. Is the solution correct?

21 Solve your equation from Question 15(a) to find how many additional pounds the rescuer can carry. Check your solution.

22 Solve. Check each solution.

a. $n - 3 = 6$ **b.** $z - 1 = -4$ **c.** $-6 = k - 7$ **d.** $p - (-2) = 4$

✓ QUESTION 23

...checks that you understand how to verify a solution.

23 **✓ CHECKPOINT** A student's solution of the equation $x - 7 = -2$ is 9. A check of this solution is shown. What does the check tell you? What is the solution of the equation?

check

$x - 7 = -2$

$9 - 7 \stackrel{?}{=} -2$

$2 \stackrel{?}{=} -2$

HOMEWORK EXERCISES ▶ See Exs. 18–46 on pp. 139–140.

Section 5 Key Concepts

Key Terms

Modeling Equations (pp. 131–134)

Balance models can help you visualize an equation and remember that the expressions on either side of an equation must be equal. Algebra tile models can help you solve (find a solution of) an equation.

solve an equation

solution of an equation

Using Inverse Operations to Solve (pp. 134–136)

The goal when you solve an equation is to get the variable alone on one side of the equation.

One method that can help you reach the goal is to use inverse operations. Inverse operations "undo" one another. Addition and subtraction are inverse operations.

inverse operations

Remember that any operation done on one side of an equation must also be done on the other side to keep the equation balanced.

Example Subtraction "undoes" addition when you solve an equation.

Solve $n + 3 = 8$.

$$\begin{aligned} n + 3 &= 8 \\ -3 &\quad -3 \\ n + 0 &= 5 \\ n &= 5 \end{aligned}$$

Subtract 3 from both sides.

Check that $n = 5$.

$$\begin{aligned} n + 3 &= 8 \\ 5 + 3 &\stackrel{?}{=} 8 \\ 8 &= 8 \checkmark \end{aligned}$$

Substitute your solution in the equation.

Example Addition "undoes" subtraction when you solve an equation.

Solve $n - 6 = -2$.

$$\begin{aligned} n - 6 &= -2 \\ +6 &\quad +6 \\ n + 0 &= 4 \\ n &= 4 \end{aligned}$$

Add 6 to both sides.

Check that $n = 4$.

$$\begin{aligned} n - 6 &= -2 \\ 4 - 6 &\stackrel{?}{=} -2 \\ -2 &= -2 \checkmark \end{aligned}$$

24 Key Concepts Question Explain how the steps in the Examples keep each equation "balanced" and help to solve each equation.

Section 5 Practice & Application Exercises

YOU WILL NEED

For Exs. 5–7 and 31:
- algebra tiles

Write an equation that each model represents.

1. [variable tile] + [4 unit tiles] = [8 unit tiles]

2. [variable tile] + [3 unit tiles] = [4 unit tiles]

3. **Open-ended** Describe a situation that can be modeled by the equation $n + 4 = 6$. Be sure to tell what the variable represents.

4. **Open-ended** Describe a situation that can be represented using a subtraction equation. Write an equation to model the situation. Use one variable and tell what it represents.

Make an algebra tile model that represents each equation. Then use the model to help you find each solution.

5. $x + 2 = 4$
6. $3 + x = 4$
7. $10 = x + 2$

Social Studies **In 1933, the 20th Amendment to the Constitution set January 20 as the inauguration date for the President, and January 3 as the inauguration date for members of Congress. Write an addition equation to model each situation. Let y = the number of years served.**

8. Dwight D. Eisenhower, the first President limited to two terms by a later amendment to the Constitution, served from 1953 to 1961.

9. Barbara Jordan, the first African-American woman from a Southern state elected to the House of Representatives, served from 1973 to 1979.

10. Dalip Singh Saund, the first Asian-American elected to the House of Representatives, served from 1957 to 1963.

11. **Geometry Connection** Use the diagram below.

a. Write an addition equation that describes the relationship between the angles.

b. Write a subtraction equation that describes the relationship between the angles.

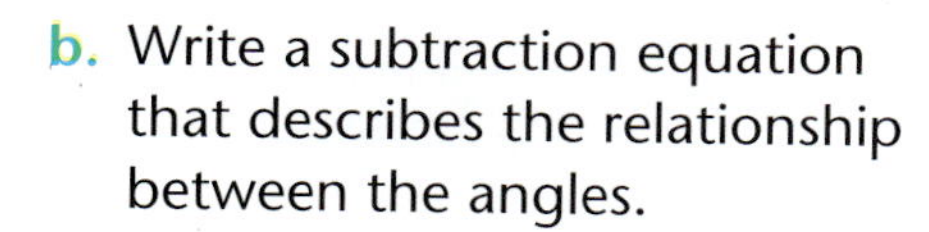

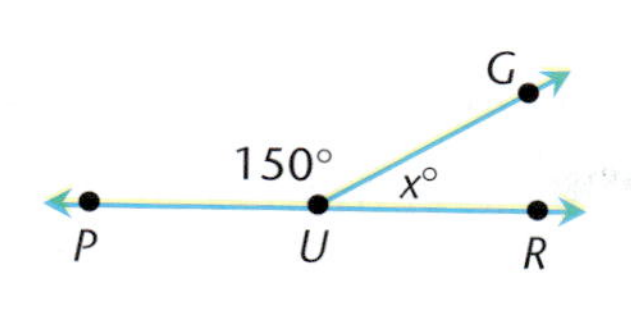

Write an addition equation to model each situation. Use one variable and tell what it represents.

12. The track team gets 2 new members, raising the membership to 20.

13. Of the 12 people in the 200 yd dash, 5 of them set a new "personal best."

14. Alicia won 3 medals. She now has 17.

Write a subtraction equation to model each situation. Use one variable and tell what it represents.

15. Anna sold 70 prints. She had 8 left over.

16. After paying $5.75 for lunch, John received $4.25 in change.

17. The number of customers on a paper route drops to 28 after 4 people cancel their subscriptions to the newspaper.

Solve. Check each solution.

18. $a + 19 = 47$

19. $8 + w = 110$

20. $q - 26 = 37$

21. $53 = v - 19$

22. $b + 27 = -16$

23. $z - 25 = -2$

24. $-15 = n + 32$

25. $-16 + d = 24$

26. $y - 18 = -66$

27. $74 = -8 + h$

28. $c - (-6) = -7$

29. $1 = k - (-1)$

30. Is 6 a solution of the equation $-8 + n = 2$? Explain.

31. **Challenge** Write an equation that the model below represents. Then use algebra tiles to solve the equation. Use symbols to record what you do at each step.

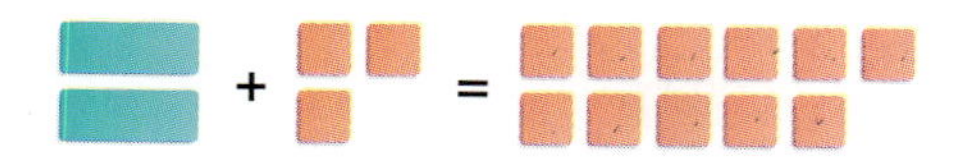

FOR ▶ HELP with *adding and subtracting decimals*, see **TOOLBOX, p. 581**

Banking For Exercises 32–34, write an equation to model each banking situation. Identify the variable you use. Solve each equation and check your solution.

32. Shellie withdrew money from her bank account to buy a used mountain bike. What was the balance in her account before the withdrawal?

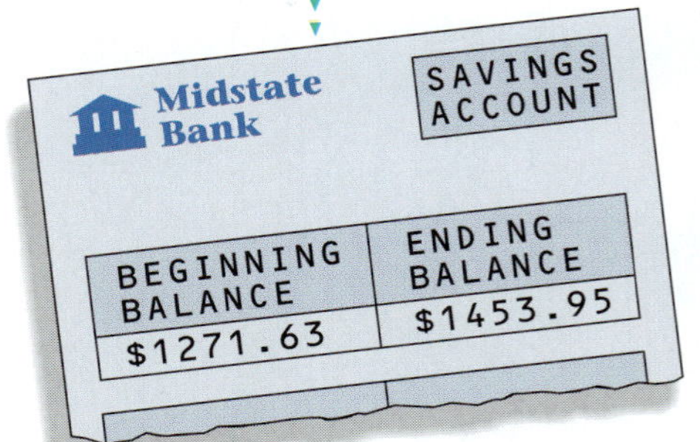

33. Darius is saving money for a trip with the Spanish club. What was the increase in his savings this month?

34. Darius expected his ending balance to be $1450.24. What was the amount of interest he forgot to include?

35. **Writing** Describe how you would solve the equation $n - 49.75 = 682.94$ using a calculator.

Choosing a Method Tell whether you would use mental math, paper-and-pencil, or a calculator to solve each equation. Then solve.

36. $17.3 + a = 62.1$
37. $b - 11 = 4$
38. $c + 95 = 88$
39. $x + 8 = -2$
40. $y - 237 = 54$
41. $12 = z - 8.1$
42. $-10 + r = 13$
43. $11 = 6 + s$
44. $t - 8 = -20.5$

45. **Geometry Connection** Two angles are complementary. One angle has a measure of 37°. Let a = the measure of the other angle.
    a. Write an addition equation to represent the situation.
    b. Solve your equation from part (a). Check your solution.

RESEARCH

Exercise 46 checks that you understand how to write and solve equations.

Reflecting on the Section

46. Research the terms of three former members of Congress from your own state who were elected after 1933 and who served full terms. Let y = the number of years served. Write and solve both an addition equation and a subtraction equation to model each situation. Check each solution.

Spiral Review

Evaluate each expression when $a = -32$, $b = 4$, and $c = 6$.
(Module 2, p. 124)

47. $b - 3$

48. $3c - 27$

49. $2a + 5$

50. $2b + 15$

51. $a + c$

52. $a - 4b$

53. Susan and Claire worked a total of 20 hours. Susan earned \$8.00 per hour. Claire earned \$7.00 per hour. Together they earned \$148.00 over the weekend. How many hours did Claire work? Tell what problem solving strategy you used. (Module 1, p. 44)

Tell whether each number is divisible by 2, 5, and 10.
(Toolbox, p. 582)

54. 75

55. 215

56. 253

57. 630

Extension

Equations with Variables on Both Sides

In this Section, the equations you solved had a variable on only one side of the equals sign. You can apply the ideas you learned to solve equations that have variables on both sides of the equals sign.

Describe how you would solve each equation modeled below.

58. $n + 1 = 2n$

59. $n + 6 = 2 + 2n$

60. $2n + 3 = 3n$

61. $n + 5 = 3 + 2n$

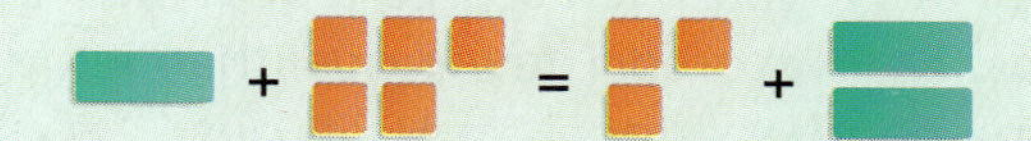

62. Solve each equation in Exercises 58–61 algebraically. Check each solution.

63. a. Does the equation $x + 35 = x + 13$ have a solution? Explain.

b. Does the equation $x + 4 = 4 + x$ have a solution? Explain.

Write an equation that each model represents.

1.

2.

3.

Write an addition or subtraction equation to model each situation. Use one variable and tell what it represents.

4. Alexis blew out 11 candles, but 2 remained lit.
5. Jill picked 53 apples. She and her brother together had 85 apples.
6. Oscar spent \$5 and has \$14 remaining.
7. Jenn needs 8 points in her last turn of bowling to tie the high score of 121.

Solve. Check each solution.

8. $a + 14 = 32$
9. $q - 21 = 29$
10. $y - 5 = -6$
11. $b + 28 = -15$
12. $6 + f = 24$
13. $43 = v - 13$
14. $z - 60 = -12$
15. $-12 = n + 43$
16. $-10 + d = 17$
17. $54 = -18 + h$
18. $c - (-5) = -9$
19. $3 = k - (-3)$
20. $46 + m = -23$
21. $-19 = -14 + t$
22. $s - (-12) = 25$
23. $11 = -7 + p$

Standardized Testing ▸ Performance Task

At soccer practice one day, Heidi, Jen, and Sheila together took a total of 36 shots. Heidi took 3 more shots than Jen did. Sheila took 3 fewer shots than Jen did.

During the same practice, Heidi, Jen, and Sheila combined for a total of 10 goals. Jen scored a goal on 1 out of every 3 shots she took. Heidi scored 1 fewer goal than Jen did. Sheila scored the same number of goals as Heidi did.

Sue, who is the goalie, says that based on their performance during practice, Jen is the most likely to score during the game. Do you agree with Sue? Present a convincing argument to support your answer.

Planning a Search

Throughout this module, you have used mathematics to help searchers locate a lost person. When someone is lost, searchers throughout the world use these and other techniques in their race against time. Did you know that victims are found alive more than 95% of the time? Careful planning and the good use of mathematics make this possible.

Now you'll learn where Gina was found and decide whether your search plan would have located her. To complete your module project, you'll write a newspaper article about planning a search.

11 The point F on the grid at the right is the spot where searchers found footprints in the mud. A searcher found Gina resting at point $(2, -4)$ on this grid.

a. Did you include the point where Gina was found in the last part of your search plan in Question 10 on page 114?

b. If your answer to part (a) was *No*, what adjustments to your search plan would have located Gina?

4
2
F
−4 −2 0 2 4
−2
−4

0 0.1 0.2 0.3 0.4 0.5 0.6 0.7 0.8 0.9 1
Miles

12 Write a newspaper article about the search and rescue of Gina. Describe the search procedures. Be sure to include a description of how mathematics was used in the search.

MODULE 2 Review and Assessment

You will need: • *protractor* (Ex. 4) • *graph paper* (Exs. 12–15 and 30)

For Exercises 1–4, use the diagram at the right.

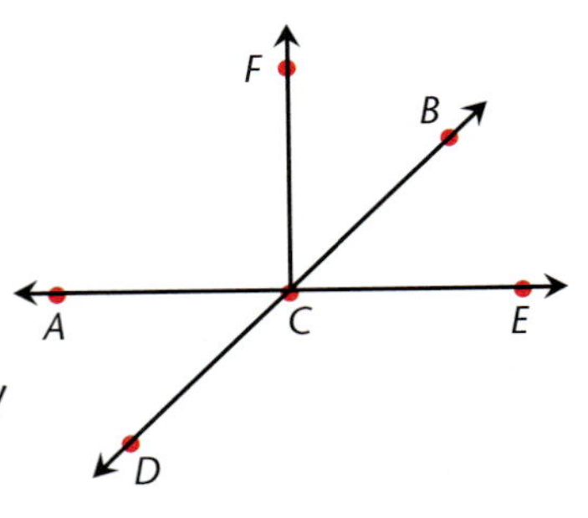

1. Name two acute angles. (Sec. 1, Explor. 1)
2. Name two obtuse angles. (Sec. 1, Explor. 1)
3. Name two straight angles. (Sec. 1, Explor. 1)
4. a. Find the measure of $\angle BCE$. (Sec. 1, Explor. 1)

   b. Name and find the measure of a complementary angle and a supplementary angle to $\angle BCE$. (Sec. 1, Explor. 2)

5. During the 1994 Winter Olympics, athletes competed underground in an ice hockey stadium. Parts of the stadium are 50 m below ground level. The stadium was built inside Norway's newly-created Gjøvik cavern.

   How can you use integers to describe this situation? Be sure to indicate what positive integers, negative integers, and zero represent. (Sec. 2, Explor. 1)

6. List the following integers in order from least to greatest: –2, 8, 14, 0, –5, –10, 6. (Sec. 2, Explor. 1)

Find the opposite and the absolute value of each integer. (Sec. 2, Explor. 1)

7. 5
8. –1
9. 72
10. –303

11. Ski jumpers practice creating an ideal body position to maximize the length of their jumps, as shown in the drawing. (Sec. 2, Explor. 2)

    a. What does it mean to say that the jumper's upper body is almost parallel to the skis?

    b. How would the skier look if his or her body were perpendicular to the skis?

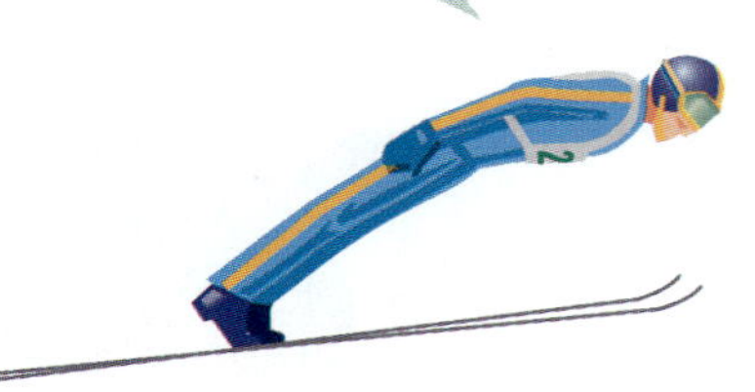

The skier's upper body is almost parallel to the skis.

Graph each ordered pair in the same coordinate plane. (Sec. 2, Explor. 2)

12. (3, 2)
13. (–1, 4)
14. (–5, –5)
15. (–4, 1)

Evaluate each expression. (Sec. 3, Explors. 2 and 3)

16. $-3 + 7$
17. $-8 + (-4)$
18. $6 + (-10)$
19. $4 - 15$
20. $-15 - (-12)$
21. $2 - (-5)$
22. $-8 + 13 - 2$
23. $-8 - 7 - 4$

Evaluate each expression when $x = 3$, $a = 6$, $b = -3$, and $y = 1$.
(Sec. 4, Explor. 1)

24. $10x$
25. $a - b$
26. $3 \div y$
27. $2x - 23$
28. $3a + b$
29. $4x + 2y$

30. The average speed of a recreational skier is 15 mi/h, or 22 ft/s. The fastest speed of a speed skier is 139 mi/h, or approximately 204 ft/s.
(Sec. 4, Explor. 2)

Time (seconds)	Distance traveled (feet)	
	Recreational skier	Speed skier
10	?	?
20	?	?
30	?	?
40	?	?

a. Copy and complete the table to show the distance traveled in feet by each skier in 10 s, 20 s, 30 s, and 40 s.

b. Write an equation that shows the relationship between d, the distance traveled in feet, and t, the time in seconds for each skier.

c. Graph your equations from part (b) on the same coordinate grid. Draw lines connecting the points for each skier.

d. Use your graph to find out which skier will travel farthest in 45 s. How much farther will the skier go?

31. Julian bought 45 baseball cards. He now has 315. Write an equation to model the situation. Identify the variable you use.
(Sec. 5, Explor. 1)

Solve. Check each solution. (Sec. 5, Explors. 1 and 2)

32. $d - 33 = 18$
33. $25 + f = 17$
34. $-2 + k = -7$
35. $s - (-4) = 10$
36. $-1 + x = -8$
37. $15 = w - 6$

Reflecting on the Module

38. **Writing** Write a letter to one of your other teachers describing what you have done in this module. Discuss how the mathematics you learned might be used in that teacher's class. You may also want to talk about what you liked most and least about the module.

MODULE 3

A Universal Language

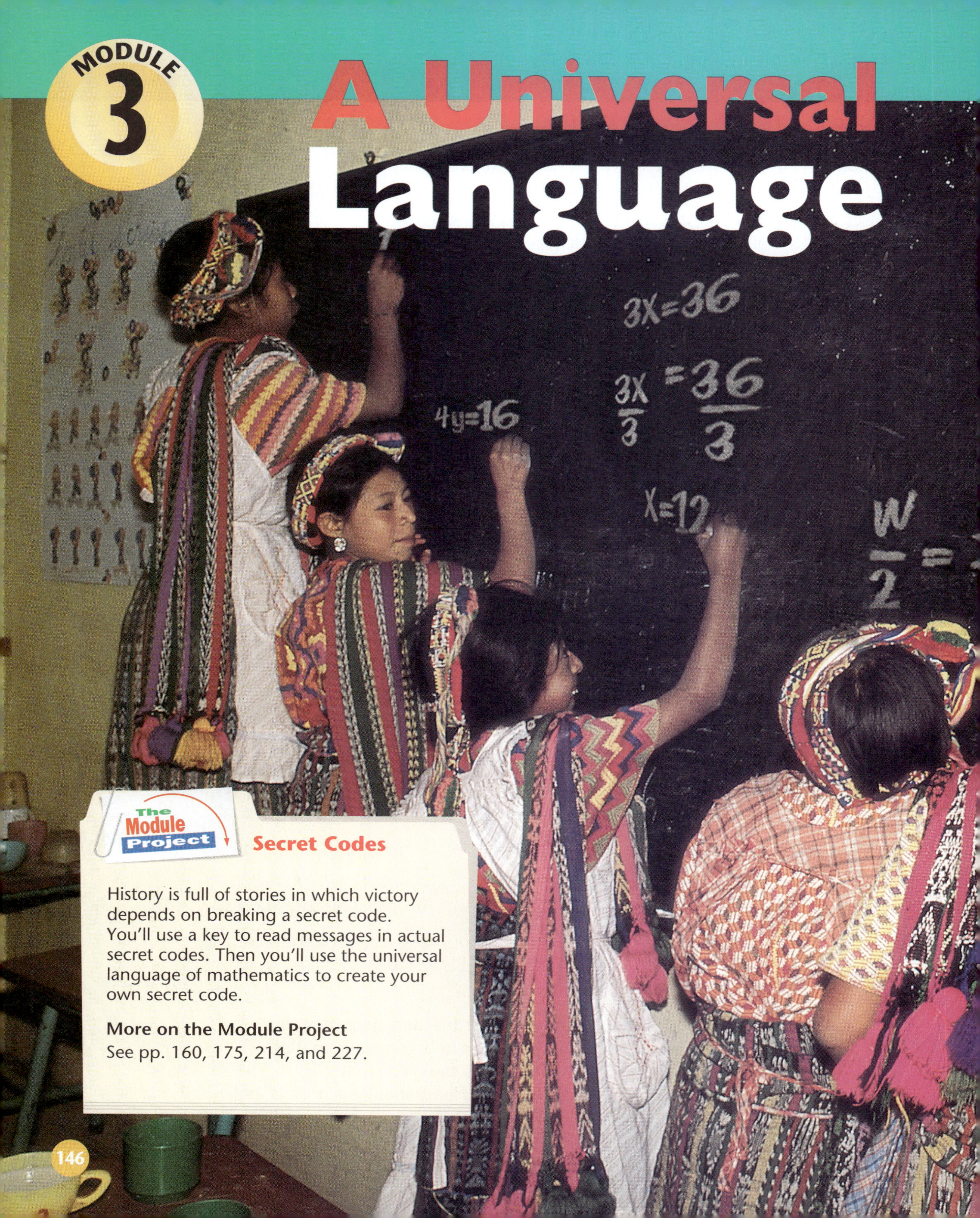

The Module Project

Secret Codes

History is full of stories in which victory depends on breaking a secret code. You'll use a key to read messages in actual secret codes. Then you'll use the universal language of mathematics to create your own secret code.

More on the Module Project

See pp. 160, 175, 214, and 227.

CONNECTING

MATHEMATICS & The Theme

SECTION OVERVIEW

1 Factors, Divisibility, and Multiples
As you explore numbering patterns on clocks and calendars:
- Find prime factorizations
- Find common factors and multiples

2 Fractions and Tree Diagrams
As you compare mathematics lessons from around the world:
- Add and subtract fractions
- Use tree diagrams to find probabilities

3 Fractions and Mixed Numbers
As you work with a monetary system used in colonial America:
- Add and subtract mixed numbers

4 Decimals and Exponents
As you learn about people who invented new ways to write decimals and powers:
- Write a decimal as a fraction
- Use integer exponents to write numbers in scientific notation

5 Metric Units of Length
As you explore a universal system of measurement:
- Convert metric lengths

6 Triangles and Equations
As you examine the use of symbols on national flags:
- Construct triangles
- Solve equations that involve multiplication and division

INTERNET
To learn more about the theme:
http://www.mlmath.com

Section 1 Factors, Divisibility, and Multiples

IN THIS SECTION

EXPLORATION 1
- Prime Factorization

EXPLORATION 2
- Common Factors

EXPLORATION 3
- Common Multiples

The movement of shadows cast by the sun as it moved across the sky was used to indicate the passing hours.

Setting the Stage

Throughout history, people have watched and recorded the natural signs all around them. The Konso of central Africa described certain parts of the day by the activity that took place at that time. Their name for the period between 5:00 P.M. and 6:00 P.M., *kakalseema*, means "when the cattle return home."

The system of dividing the day into 24 hours came from the ancient Egyptians. They divided night into 12 hours, numbered the daytime hours 1–10, and assigned dawn and dusk 1 hour each.

Stone structures such as the 4000 year old Stonehenge in England were some of the earliest clocks.

Often called the "universal language," mathematics provides a way to communicate in a clear and precise way about time, money, measurements, shapes, and many other things.

Think About It

1 What daily activities divide your day? Do these activities fall in one-hour intervals (8:00 to 9:00 A.M., 9:00 to 10:00 A.M., etc.)?

2 The Egyptian hours were not all the same. The summer daytime hours lasted longer than the winter daytime hours. Why do you think the hours were not equal?

Exploration 1

Prime Factorization

GOAL

LEARN HOW TO...
- find factors
- find the prime factorization of a number

AS YOU...
- explore different clock faces

KEY TERMS
- factor
- divisible
- prime
- composite
- prime factorization

SET UP *You will need Labsheet 1A.*

▶ **Although our day is divided into 24 hours, the faces of many clocks show only 12 hours. In this exploration you'll explore different possibilities for clock faces and decide which one is best.**

3 **Use Labsheet 1A.**

a. On the clock face below, 4 jumps were made to get back to the START position. How large is each jump?

b. Follow the directions on Labsheet 1A to complete the *Dot Jumping Table*.

c. Discussion Look at your results. How are the number of jumps, the jump size, and the number of dots related?

d. If you made jumps of 7 dots on a circle with 24 dots, would you land on START after one time around the circle? Why or why not?

4 **Use Labsheet 1A.**

a. Use your table to find all the ways of dividing the 12 months of the year into groups with the same number of months.

b. Which method of dividing the months most closely follows the way the year is divided into seasons?

▶ **In the dot-jumping activity, you found the *factors* of 12, 13, 14, and 15 by determining the number and the size of the jumps needed to land on START. For example, on a circle with 12 dots, you return to START after 6 jumps of size 2. This shows that 6 and 2 are factors of 12.**

When one whole number divides another whole number with no remainder, the first number is a factor of the second. This also means that the second number is divisible by the first.

EXAMPLE

You can make an organized list to find all the factors of 36.

Start a list with 1 and the number.

Then, think of the next pair of factors.

$1 \cdot 36 \Rightarrow$ **1**, **36**

$2 \cdot 18 \Rightarrow$ 1, **2**, **18**, 36

$3 \cdot 12 \Rightarrow$ 1, 2, **3**, **12**, 18, 36

$4 \cdot 9 \Rightarrow$ 1, 2, 3, **4**, **9**, 12, 18, 36

$6 \cdot 6 \Rightarrow$ 1, 2, 3, 4, **6**, 9, 12, 18, 36

5 **a.** How do you know when you have found all the factors?

b. Why is the factor 6 not listed twice?

▶ **In the dot-jumping activity, you found that 13 had only two factors, 1 and 13. If a number has only two factors, 1 and itself, then it is prime. If a number has more than two factors, then it is composite. The numbers 0 and 1 are neither prime nor composite.**

6 Tell whether each number is *prime* or *composite*.

a. 2 **b.** 20 **c.** 23 **d.** 32

7 Find all the factors of each number. Tell which factors are prime.

a. 20 **b.** 35 **c.** 78 **d.** 120

▶ **When you write a number as a product of prime factors, you are writing the prime factorization of the number.**

8 Discussion Jorge used a factor tree to help him write the prime factorization of 36. Look at Jorge's factor tree below.

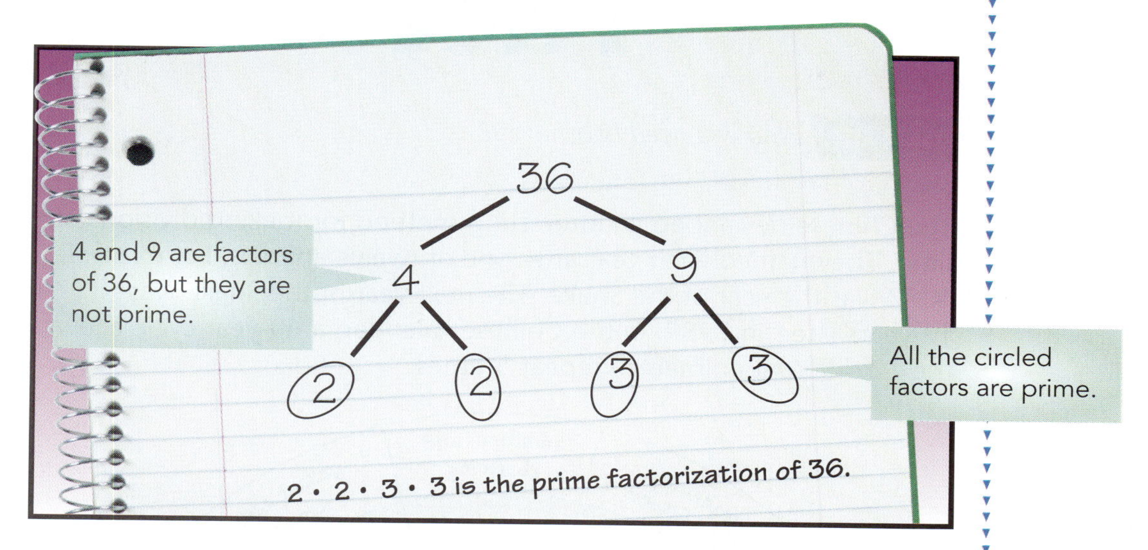

a. Why do you think another row was added after 4 and 9?

b. Suppose you drew a factor tree for 36 starting with the factors 2 and 18. Would you get the same prime factorization as Jorge? Explain.

c. How can you write the prime factorization of 36 using exponents?

d. How can you use the prime factorization of 36 to find other factors of 36?

FOR ◀ HELP with *exponents*, see **MODULE 1, p. 20**

9 ✓ CHECKPOINT Find all the factors of each number. Then write the prime factorization of each number.

a. 18 **b.** 30 **c.** 64 **d.** 100

✓ QUESTION 9

...checks that you can find factors and write prime factorizations.

10 a. Many clock faces show only 12 hours, and the hours are repeated to make a 24-hour day. What other clock faces could be used to keep time? Give the number of hours on each clock face and how many times the hours would have to be repeated to make a 24-hour day.

b. Which clock face do you think would be best to use? Why?

HOMEWORK EXERCISES ▶ See Exs. 1–34 on pp. 157–158.

GOAL

LEARN HOW TO...
- use divisibility rules to find factors
- find the greatest common factor of two or more numbers

AS YOU...
- explore the Chinese calendar

KEY TERM
- greatest common factor (GCF)

Exploration 2

Common Factors

SET UP *You will need Labsheet 1B.*

The Chinese developed an interesting method for making divisions of time. They named each year after one of twelve animals. For example, 1977 was the year of the Snake. The next year of the Snake was 12 years later, in 1989. In the Chinese calendar, a 60-year cycle allows the 12 different animals to repeat 5 times.

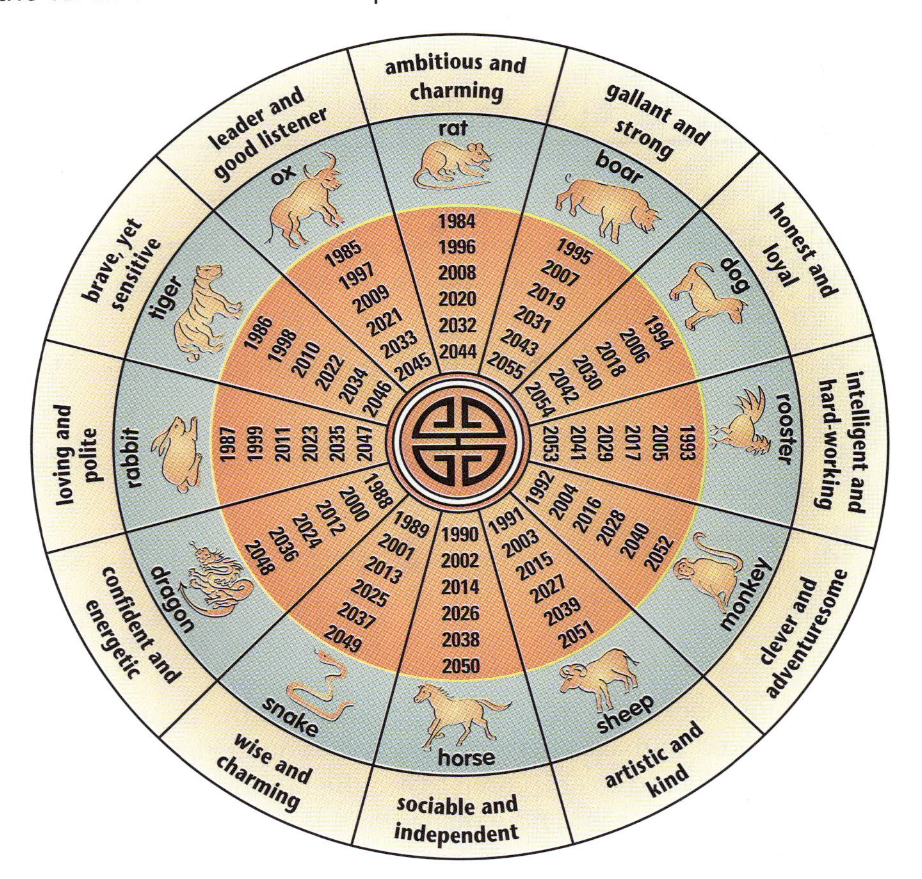

11 According to the Chinese calendar, when is the next year of the Snake after 1989?

12 For which animal is the year of your birth named?

▶ **Divisibility Rules** **To determine some factors of a number, you can use divisibility rules. For example, a number divisible by 10 has a 0 in the ones place.**

13 **Discussion** Without dividing, how can you tell that a number is divisible by 2? by 5?

14 **Use Labsheet 1B.**

a. Complete the *Divisibility-by-Nine Table* and look for a pattern involving the sum of the digits.

b. Write a rule for telling whether a number is divisible by 9.

c. Use your calculator to try the rule you wrote in part (a) with other numbers.

d. Write a rule for telling whether a number is divisible by 3. (*Hint:* The rule is similar to the rule for 9.)

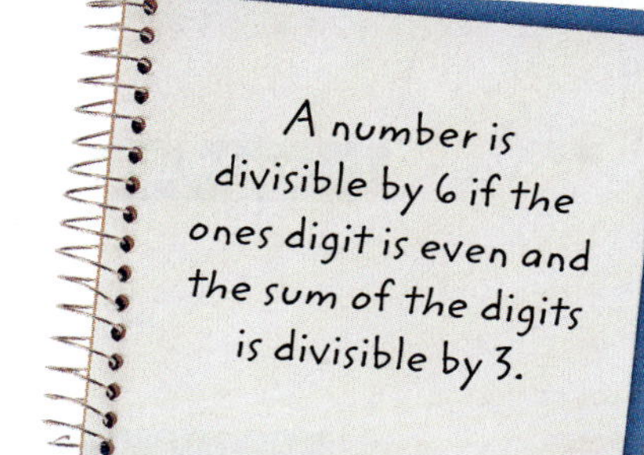

15 On the notebook at the right, a student wrote a divisibility rule for 6. Is this rule correct? Why or why not?

16 The responses in the second column of the table indicate whether the numbers in the first column are divisible by 4.

a. Copy the table and use a calculator to tell whether the numbers in the third column are divisible by 4.

b. How are the numbers in the third column related to the numbers in the first column?

c. Write a rule for telling whether a number is divisible by 4.

d. List some 3-digit and 4-digit numbers and test your rule. Does it work?

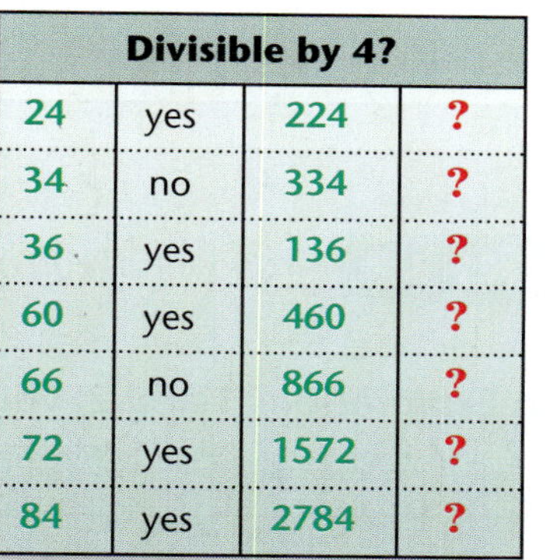

Divisible by 4?			
24	yes	224	?
34	no	334	?
36	yes	136	?
60	yes	460	?
66	no	866	?
72	yes	1572	?
84	yes	2784	?

17 ✓ **CHECKPOINT** Use divisibility rules to tell whether each number is divisible by 2, 3, 4, 5, 6, 9, and 10.

a. 1362 **b.** 5220 **c.** 1268 **d.** 375

...checks that you can tell whether a number is divisible by 2, 3, 4, 5, 6, 9, and 10.

18 Write a rule for divisibility by 12 and test your rule with some 3-digit and 4-digit numbers. (*Hint:* Think about the divisibility rule for 6.)

▶ Numbers often have some factors in common. The **greatest common factor (GCF)** of two or more numbers is the greatest factor that is common to those numbers.

19 **a.** Use divisibility rules to help list all the factors of 42 and 56.

b. What factors do 42 and 56 have in common?

c. Which is the greatest common factor you found in part (b)?

...checks that you can find the GCF of two or more numbers.

20 ✓ **CHECKPOINT** Find the GCF of each group of numbers.

a. 24, 4 **b.** 7, 12 **c.** 28, 32, 36

21 What other numbers of animals could the Chinese have used to complete the 60-year cycle? (*Hint:* Use the factors of 60.)

HOMEWORK EXERCISES ▶ See Exs. 35–55 on p. 158.

GOAL

LEARN HOW TO...
- find the least common multiple of two or more numbers

AS YOU...
- work with a January calendar

KEY TERMS
- multiple
- least common multiple (LCM)

Exploration 3

Common Multiples

SET UP *You will need Labsheet 1C.*

▶ In Explorations 1 and 2, you found factors of numbers. For example, $12 = 2 \cdot 6$, so 2 and 6 are factors of 12. A **multiple** of a whole number is the product of that number and any nonzero whole number. For example, 12 is a multiple of 2 and a multiple of 6.

EXAMPLE

You can make a partial list of the multiples of 6.

$$1 \cdot 6 = 6$$
$$2 \cdot 6 = 12$$
$$3 \cdot 6 = 18$$
$$4 \cdot 6 = 24$$
$$\vdots$$

The multiples of 6 are 6, 12, 18, 24, ...

Use Labsheet 1C for Questions 22–25.

22 **a.** Follow the directions on Labsheet 1C to find the multiples of 1, 2, and 3.

b. Which spaces on the *Calendar of Multiples* have both a ② and a ③?

▶ **Each of the numbers you listed in Question 22(b) is a multiple of 2 and a multiple of 3. The least number that is a multiple of two or more numbers is the least common multiple (LCM) of those numbers.**

23 Use the *Calendar of Multiples* to find the LCM of 2 and 3.

24 Complete the calendar by placing a ④ in the spaces containing multiples of 4, a ⑤ in the spaces with multiples of 5, and so on. Continue until you have marked the calendar with the multiples of all the numbers up to and including 31.

25 **a.** List the common multiples of 3, 4, and 6 shown on the calendar.

b. What is the least common multiple of 3, 4, and 6?

26 ✓ **CHECKPOINT** Find the LCM of 10 and 15. Then explain how you found it.

✓ **QUESTION 26**

...checks that you can find the LCM of two numbers.

27 **a.** Write the prime factorization of 10 and of 15.

b. List the prime numbers that are factors of 10, of 15, or of both. Do not list any factor more than once. Find the product of these factors.

c. How does your answer to part (b) compare with the LCM of 10 and 15 you found in Question 26?

28 **a.** The LCM of 6 and 18 is 18. Find another pair of numbers whose LCM is one of the original numbers.

b. The LCM of 6 and 5 is 30. Find another pair of numbers whose LCM is the product of the numbers.

29 The Dogon people of West Africa used astronomical observations to mark the passage of time. For example, they chose their leader when Jupiter (about a 12-year orbit) and Saturn (about a 30-year orbit) completed an orbit around the sun together. How often did they choose a leader?

A Dogon man stands on the Bandiagara Cliffs in Mali, Africa.

HOMEWORK EXERCISES ▶ See Exs. 56–68 on p. 159.

Section 1 Key Concepts

Key Terms

factor

prime

prime factorization

composite

divisible

greatest common factor (GCF)

multiple

least common multiple (LCM)

Prime Factorization (pp. 149–151)

Every whole number other than 0 or 1 is either prime or composite.

The prime factorization of a number is the product of its prime factors.

Example

24 is a composite number. $24 = 2 \cdot 2 \cdot 2 \cdot 3$ 2 and 3 are prime numbers.

Divisibility and Common Factors (pp. 152–154)

A number is divisible by...	
3	if the sum of the digits is divisible by 3.
4	if the number formed by the tens and ones digits is divisible by 4.
6	if it is divisible by both 2 and 3.
9	if the sum of the digits is divisible by 9.

The GCF of two or more numbers can be found by listing their factors.

Example The factors of 48: **1**, **2**, **3**, **4**, **6**, 8, **12**, 16, 24, 48
The factors of 36: **1**, **2**, **3**, **4**, **6**, 9, **12**, 18, 36
The GCF of 48 and 36 is 12.

Multiples (pp. 154–155)

The LCM of two or more numbers can be found by listing their multiples.

Example Multiples of 8: 8, 16, **24**, 32, 40, **48**, ...
Multiples of 12: 12, **24**, 36, **48**, ...
The LCM of 8 and 12 is 24.

30 Key Concepts Question Replace each __?__ with 2, 4, or 8 to make each statement true.

a. __?__ and __?__ are factors of __?__.

b. __?__ and __?__ are multiples of __?__.

c. The LCM of __?__ and __?__ is __?__.

d. __?__ is prime; __?__ and __?__ are composite.

Section 1 Practice & Application Exercises

YOU WILL NEED

For Exs. 72–74:
- protractor

Find all the factors of each number.

1. 12
2. 27
3. 45
4. 53
5. 64
6. 71
7. 100
8. 124
9. 121
10. 144
11. 150
12. 225

13. The number 25 has an odd number of factors. Find five other numbers that have an odd number of factors. What pattern do you notice?

Tell whether each number is *prime* or *composite*.

14. 3
15. 8
16. 12
17. 19
18. 21
19. 31
20. 33
21. 47

Find the prime factorization of each number.

22. 16
23. 28
24. 30
25. 36
26. 46
27. 50
28. 75
29. 170

30. **Cheerleading** Two guidelines for high school cheerleading are listed. Suppose a 32-person squad is planning pyramids with backward dismounts. What is the greatest possible number of backward dismounts the squad can perform at the same time?

Cheerleading Guidelines
- All pyramids are limited to two persons high.
- All backward dismounts from pyramids must use three catchers.

dismount

catchers

31. **Challenge** Ann Chang's class has 24 students and Mark McKay's class has 36 students. The two classes are going to a museum together. At the museum the students will be divided into smaller groups. Each group must contain students from both classes, and the students from each class must be divided evenly among the groups. List all the possible ways the groups can be set up.

Geometry Connection For each rectangle:

a. Find the area and the perimeter.

b. Find the length and width of a rectangle with the same area and a smaller perimeter.

c. Find the length and width of a rectangle with the same area and a greater perimeter.

32. 6 in. by 2 in.

33. 10 m by 3 m

34. 9 ft by 4 ft

Tell whether each number in Exercises 35–42 is divisible by each of the numbers 2, 3, 4, 5, 6, 9, and 10.

35. 77 **36.** 96 **37.** 112 **38.** 275

39. 300 **40.** 414 **41.** 780 **42.** 1075

43. Make and test a rule for divisibility by 8. (*Hint:* Think about the divisibility rule for 4.)

44. List five numbers that are divisible by 25. Then list five numbers that are divisible by 100. Use your results to write divisibility rules for 25 and for 100.

Find the greatest common factor of each group of numbers.

45. 9, 12 **46.** 14, 21 **47.** 15, 30

48. 64, 48 **49.** 53, 71 **50.** 48, 120

51. 60, 75, 90 **52.** 96, 180, 192 **53.** 78, 104, 117

54. a. Can two even numbers have a GCF of 1? Explain.

b. Can two odd numbers have a GCF of 1? Explain.

55. Create Your Own Jupiter has short days and long years. Using our time, a Jupiter day is only 9 h 55 min long. One Jupiter year is about 4333 Earth days.

a. Design a calendar for a year that contains 4333 Earth days. Tell the numbers of days in a month and months in a year.

b. **Writing** Explain why you designed your calendar as you did.

Find the least common multiple of each group of numbers.

56. 2, 4
57. 4, 6
58. 6, 8
59. 8, 10
60. 12, 15
61. 20, 25
62. 5, 7, 10
63. 9, 18, 36
64. 8, 14, 28

65. Lucinda made just one list to find the LCM of 14, 36, and 63. Describe how she can find the LCM by listing the numbers 63, 126, 189, and 252.

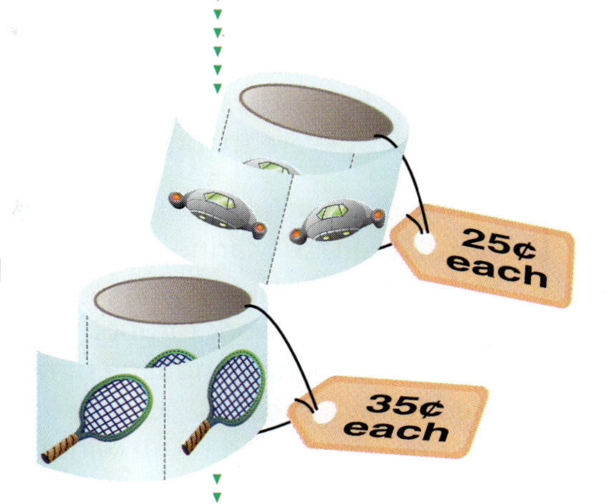

66. The price for one type of sticker is 25¢ each. Another type costs 35¢ per sticker. Suppose the same amount of money is spent on each type. What is the least total amount that can be spent?

67. a. Antonio asks if there is such a thing as a greatest common multiple. What would you tell him?

b. Is there a least common divisor? Explain.

Reflecting on the Section

68. Explain how the problem of finding the number of ways to arrange desks in rows with the same number of desks in each row is related to factors, divisibility, and multiples.

Visual THINKING

Exercise 68 checks that you can apply ideas about factors, divisibility, and multiples.

Spiral Review

Solve. Check each answer. (Module 2, p. 137)

69. $x + 38 = 90$
70. $z - 53 = 798$
71. $-102 = y - 47$

Find the measure of each angle. Then classify each angle as *acute, obtuse, right,* or *straight*. (Module 2, p. 83)

72. 

73. 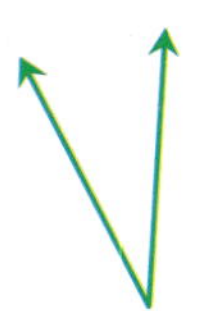

74. 

Find each sum or difference. (Toolbox, p. 587)

75. $\frac{1}{5} + \frac{2}{5}$
76. $\frac{5}{8} - \frac{3}{8}$
77. $\frac{10}{23} - \frac{7}{23}$
78. $\frac{12}{35} + \frac{8}{35}$

Secret Codes

Have you ever learned sign language? Do you understand Russian? There are over 6500 languages used throughout the world and no one can possibly understand them all. This can be an advantage when people are trying to keep communications secret.

Using the Language of Mathematics During World War II, the U.S. Marine Corps used the Navajo language as a code, since it was known only to the Navajo people. As you work through this module, you'll see how the universal language of mathematics can be used to design codes. For your project, you'll create your own code and test it with members of your class.

Code	Translation	Meaning
lo-tso	whale	Battleship
besh-lo	iron fish	Submarine
lo-tso-yazzie	small whale	Cruiser

▲ Two Marines using the Navajo code during the battle for Bougainville in 1943

The Roman Emperor Julius Caesar created a code in which each letter was replaced by another letter that was three places farther on in the alphabet. Applying the Caesar shift code to the English alphabet results in the code key below.

Original letter	A	B	C	D	E	F	G	H	I	J	K	L	M	N	O	P	Q	R	S	T	U	V	W	X	Y	Z
Code letter	D	E	F	G	H	I	J	K	L	M	N	O	P	Q	R	S	T	U	V	W	X	Y	Z	A	B	C

1 Use the code key to decode each message.

a. XQGHUVWDQG WKH SUREOHP **b.** GHYLVH D SODQ

c. FDUUB RXW WKH SODQ **d.** ORRN EDFN

2 A different shift code was used for the following message. Decode the message. Then describe any strategies you used.
DRO MKOCKB MYNO SC OKCI DY ECO

3 How many possible shift codes are there for our alphabet?

Section 1 Extra Skill Practice

Find all the factors of each number.

1. 18
2. 24
3. 51
4. 180
5. 72
6. 169
7. 84
8. 75
9. 108
10. 125
11. 91
12. 56

Find the prime factorization of each number.

13. 24
14. 35
15. 81
16. 88
17. 90
18. 105
19. 120
20. 128
21. 54
22. 80
23. 48
24. 60

Tell whether each number is divisible by each of the numbers 2, 3, 4, 5, 6, 9, and 10.

25. 42
26. 56
27. 87
28. 96
29. 124
30. 1585
31. 1620
32. 2560

Find the greatest common factor of each group of numbers.

33. 9, 27
34. 12, 36
35. 15, 20
36. 72, 90
37. 64, 96, 144
38. 88, 110, 143
39. 98, 105, 112
40. 45, 135, 225

Find the least common multiple of each group of numbers.

41. 6, 9
42. 8, 12
43. 9, 15
44. 16, 20
45. 2, 5, 8
46. 4, 6, 9
47. 6, 10, 12
48. 8, 12, 16

Study Skills Using Mathematical Language

Some words have similar meanings in everyday language and in mathematics. Some have quite different meanings.

1. Look at the list of words below. Tell the meaning of each word in everyday language.
   a. axes
   b. factor
   c. negative
   d. mean
   e. origin
   f. variable
2. Explain how the meaning of each word in Exercise 1 is either similar to or different from its meaning in mathematics. (*Hint:* Use the Glossary.)

Section 2 Fractions and Tree Diagrams

IN THIS SECTION

EXPLORATION 1
- Comparing Fractions

EXPLORATION 2
- Adding and Subtracting Fractions

EXPLORATION 3
- Tree Diagrams and Probability

Mathematically Speaking

Setting the Stage

Sprechen Sie Deutsch? (Can you speak German?) Maybe not, but see how much you can understand of this page from a German mathematics book.

13.2. Der Bruch als Teil mehrerer Ganzen

1. Mutter hat 3 Pfannkuchen gebacken und in Viertel geteilt. Heike und Thomas dürfen sich jeder $\frac{3}{4}$ Pfannkuchen nehmen. Heike will sich von den obersten Kuchen $\frac{3}{4}$ abnehmen. Thomas kann es einfacher. Er nimmt sich 3 übereinanderliegende Viertel, von jedem Kuchen also $\frac{1}{4}$, das sind auch $\frac{3}{4}$ Pfannkuchen.

2. Der Bruch $\frac{3}{4}$ kann also auf zwei verschiedene Arten entstehen:

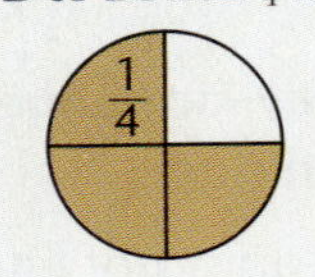

a. Ein Pfannkuchen wird in vier gleiche Teile geteilt. 3 Teile davon werden zu einem Bruch zusammengefaßt: $\frac{3}{4}$ **Pfannkuchen**.

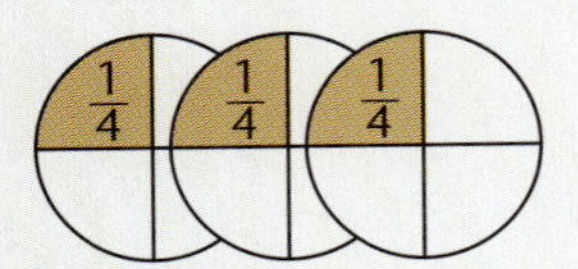

b. Drei Pfannkuchen werden aufeinandergelegt und geviertelt. Es liegen dann jeweils 3 Viertelstücke aufeinander, das sind: $\frac{3}{4}$ **Pfannkuchen**.

Think About It

1 What mathematics concept is presented in the German text? How do you know?

2 Tell a story that could go with the pictures.

Exploration 1

Comparing Fractions

GOAL

LEARN HOW TO...
- write fractions in lowest terms
- compare fractions using least common denominators

AS YOU...
- read a flow chart

KEY TERMS
- equivalent fractions
- lowest terms
- least common denominator

▶ **As you saw from the page of the German book, mathematical ideas can be communicated without language. Many of the same numerals, diagrams, and symbols are used in different countries. Students all over the world use >, <, and = to compare numbers.**

3 Use the circle diagrams to compare the fractions. Replace each __?__ with >, <, or =.

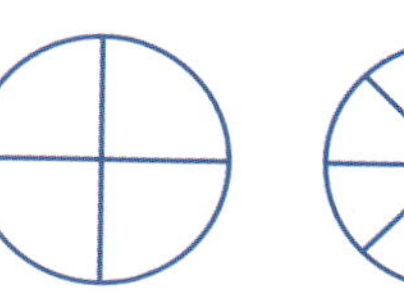

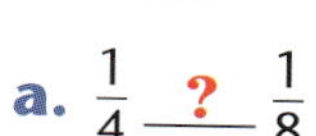

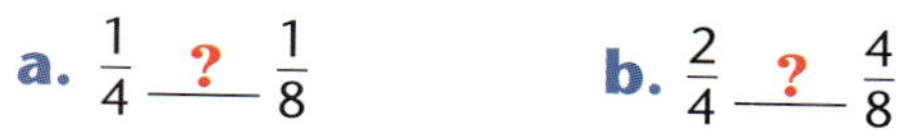

a. $\frac{1}{4}$ __?__ $\frac{1}{8}$ **b.** $\frac{2}{4}$ __?__ $\frac{4}{8}$ **c.** $\frac{3}{4}$ __?__ $\frac{7}{8}$

▶ **Fractions that represent the same amount are equivalent fractions. To write a fraction in lowest terms, you need to find an equivalent fraction where the greatest common factor of the numerator and denominator is 1.**

FOR ▶ HELP
with *equivalent fractions*, see
TOOLBOX, p. 585

4 Which fractions in Question 3 are equivalent fractions? Are they in lowest terms? Explain.

5 Use this example from a German mathematics lesson.

Beispiel means "example."

a. Find the GCF of 36 and 84.

b. Is $\frac{36}{84}$ in lowest terms? How do you know?

c. Find the GCF of 3 and 7.

d. Is $\frac{3}{7}$ in lowest terms? How do you know?

6 Discussion Use the German example: $\frac{36}{84} \underset{12}{=} \frac{3}{7}$.

a. Although fraction concepts are universal, sometimes a slightly different notation is used. Why do you think the number 12 is printed underneath the equals sign in the example?

b. How can the idea of greatest common factor be used to find an equivalent fraction in lowest terms?

✓ QUESTION 7

...checks that you can write a fraction in lowest terms.

7 ✓ CHECKPOINT Write each fraction in lowest terms.

a. $\frac{10}{18}$ **b.** $\frac{12}{27}$

8 How can you use your answers to Question 7 to compare $\frac{10}{18}$ and $\frac{12}{27}$?

▶ Comparing Fractions

The *flow chart* below appears in a Bulgarian mathematics book in a lesson about comparing fractions.

9 Try This as a Class Look at the examples shown along the left and right sides of the flow chart.

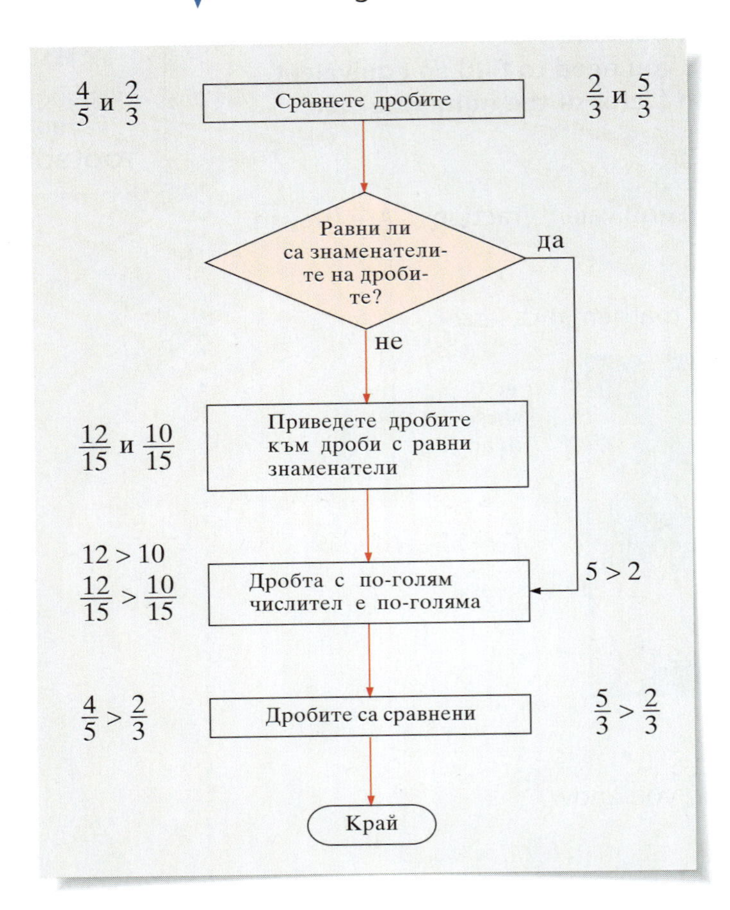

a. What do you think the question in the shaded box is asking?

b. For the example on the right, why do you think the third box of the flow chart is skipped? What do you think are the instructions in the third box?

c. Why are fifteenths used to compare the two fractions on the left side?

d. In the fourth box, what parts of the fractions are compared to find the greater fraction? Why?

▶ One way to compare fractions is by finding the *least common denominator*. The **least common denominator** of two fractions is the least common multiple of the denominators.

EXAMPLE

Compare $\frac{5}{8}$ and $\frac{7}{12}$.

SAMPLE RESPONSE

24 is the LCM of 8 and 12.

First Find a common denominator.

The least common denominator of $\frac{5}{8}$ and $\frac{7}{12}$ is 24.

Next Rename each fraction as an equivalent fraction with the common denominator.

$$\frac{5}{8} = \frac{5 \cdot 3}{8 \cdot 3} = \frac{15}{24} \quad \text{and} \quad \frac{7}{12} = \frac{7 \cdot 2}{12 \cdot 2} = \frac{14}{24}$$

Then Compare the fractions that have the same denominator.

$$\frac{15}{24} > \frac{14}{24}, \text{ so } \frac{5}{8} > \frac{7}{12}$$

10 In the Example, two fractions are renamed using the least common denominator. How does this method compare with the Bulgarian method?

11 **Create Your Own** Create a flow chart of your own for comparing fractions. Include two examples that show how to use your flow chart. In one example, use fractions that have a common denominator. In the other example, use fractions that do not have a common denominator.

12 ✓ **CHECKPOINT** Compare each pair of fractions.

Replace each __?__ with >, <, or =.

a. $\frac{3}{5}$ __?__ $\frac{3}{4}$ **b.** $\frac{2}{5}$ __?__ $\frac{1}{5}$ **c.** $\frac{2}{3}$ __?__ $\frac{11}{15}$

d. $\frac{19}{20}$ __?__ $\frac{54}{60}$ **e.** $\frac{7}{18}$ __?__ $\frac{5}{12}$ **f.** $\frac{55}{90}$ __?__ $\frac{11}{18}$

✓ **QUESTION 12**

...checks that you can compare fractions.

HOMEWORK EXERCISES ▶ See Exs. 1–30 on pp. 171–173.

GOAL

LEARN HOW TO...
- add and subtract fractions with unlike denominators

AS YOU...
- explore fraction models from other countries

Exploration 2

Adding and Subtracting Fractions

SET UP *You will need Labsheet 2A.*

▶ **Models for adding and subtracting fractions are also universal. See the examples below from an Australian textbook and a Japanese textbook.**

Australian textbook:

For example, for $\frac{3}{8} + \frac{2}{8}$

Japanese textbook:

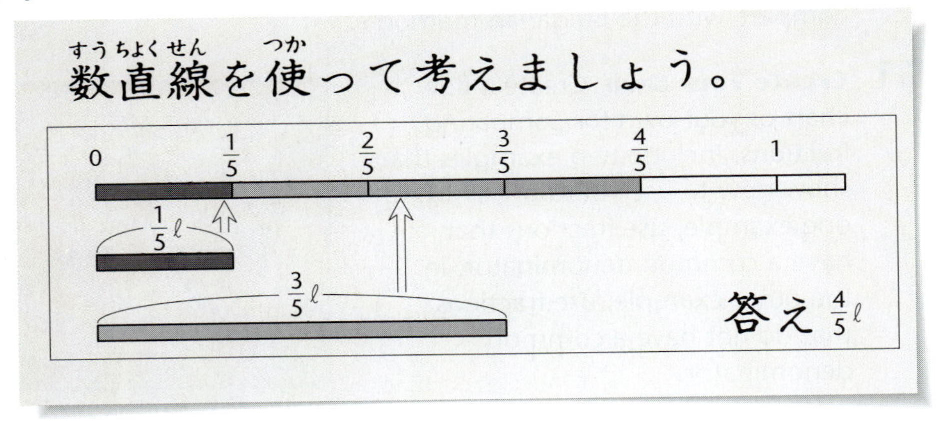

13 **a.** Explain what the examples are trying to show.

b. What makes these examples universal?

c. Write the equation each example represents.

14 **a.** Explain how to add two fractions that have the same denominator without using a diagram.

b. Explain how to subtract two fractions that have the same denominator without using a diagram.

FOR ▶ HELP with *adding and subtracting like fractions, see* **TOOLBOX, p. 587**

15 Find each sum or difference. Write each answer in lowest terms.

a. $\frac{3}{10} + \frac{5}{10}$ **b.** $\frac{1}{4} + \frac{1}{4}$ **c.** $\frac{5}{8} - \frac{3}{8}$ **d.** $\frac{11}{12} - \frac{7}{12}$

16 Why is it difficult to use models to find each answer?

a. $\frac{1}{2} + \frac{1}{5} = \underline{\ ?\ }$

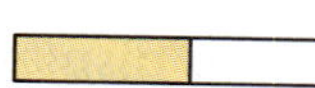 + 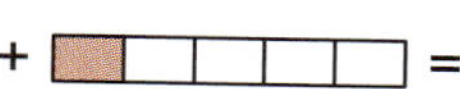 = 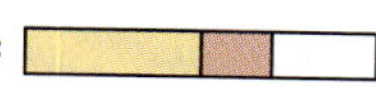

b. $\frac{2}{3} - \frac{1}{4} = \underline{\ ?\ }$

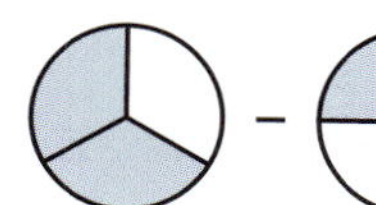 − 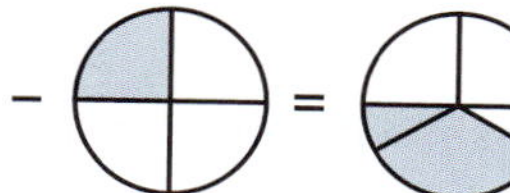 =

c. $\frac{1}{3} + \frac{1}{8} = \underline{\ ?\ }$

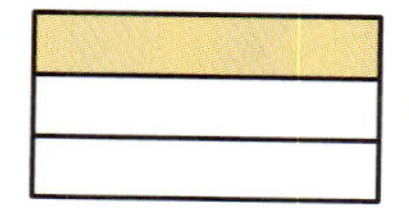 +  = 

17 **Estimation** Use the models in Question 16. Which of the following choices is closest to the sum in part (a)? the difference in part (b)? the sum in part (c)?

A. less than $\frac{1}{4}$

B. greater than $\frac{1}{4}$ but less than $\frac{1}{2}$

C. greater than $\frac{3}{4}$

D. greater than $\frac{1}{2}$ but less than $\frac{3}{4}$

18 **Use Labsheet 2A.** Use the *Equivalent Fraction Models* to find exact answers to the problems in Question 16.

19 **Estimation** Estimate whether each sum or difference is *greater than, less than,* or *equal to* $\frac{1}{2}$.

a. $\frac{1}{5} + \frac{7}{10}$ **b.** $\frac{1}{3} + \frac{1}{6}$ **c.** $\frac{15}{16} - \frac{1}{8}$ **d.** $\frac{2}{3} - \frac{1}{4}$

20 **Discussion** How can equivalent fractions be used to find the exact sum or difference of two fractions?

21 ✓ **CHECKPOINT** Find the exact sum or difference for each expression in Question 19.

✓ **QUESTION 21** ...checks that you can add and subtract fractions with unlike denominators.

HOMEWORK EXERCISES ▶ See Exs. 31–43 on p. 173.

GOAL

LEARN HOW TO...

- use a tree diagram to find outcomes and probabilities

AS YOU...

- think about choosing marbles from a jar

KEY TERM

- tree diagram

Exploration 3

TREE Diagrams and Probability

▶ The example below is written in Spanish, but the *tree diagram* is universal. **Tree diagrams** can be used to display the possible outcomes of an experiment.

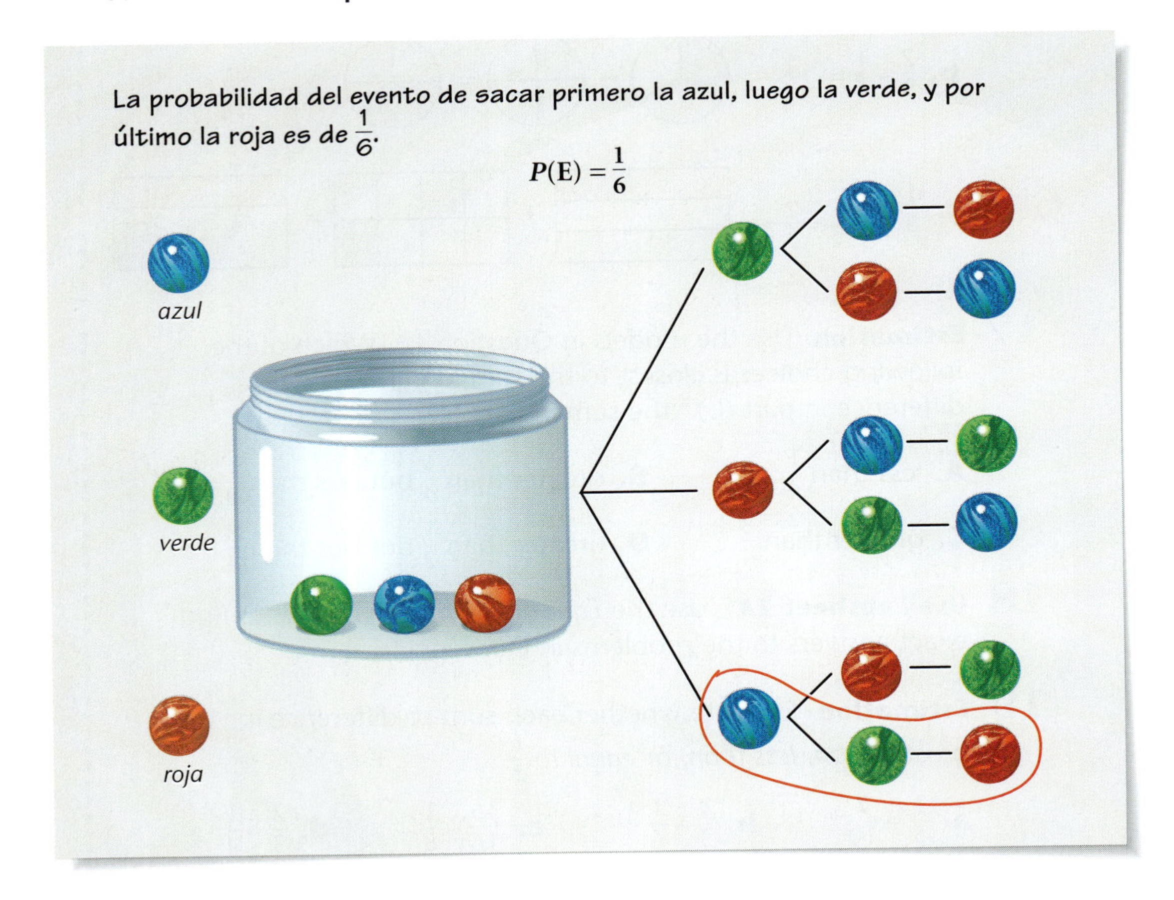

22 **a.** What experiment does the tree diagram above represent?

b. How many possible outcomes are there?

c. Why is the probability of the circled combination of marbles equal to $\frac{1}{6}$?

d. What event does the E in $P(E) = \frac{1}{6}$ describe?

23 **Try This as a Class** Look at the branches in the tree diagram on page 168.

a. Why are there three branches coming from the jar of marbles?

b. Why does each of the three marbles in the first column have two branches extending to the right?

c. Why does each of the marbles in the second column have only one branch extending to the right?

d. Is a marble replaced after it is chosen? How can you tell?

Some events for the experiment on page 168 are listed below. Use these events for Questions 24–27.

Event J: taking an *azul* marble out of the jar first, then a *roja* marble, then a *verde* marble

Event K: taking out a *roja* marble first

Event L: not taking out a *verde* marble last

Event M: taking out any combination of three marbles that includes an *azul* marble

24 Use the tree diagram to find each theoretical probability.

a. $P(J)$ **b.** $P(K)$ **c.** $P(L)$ **d.** $P(M)$

25 ✓ **CHECKPOINT** Suppose three marbles are taken out of the jar one at a time and each marble is *replaced* in the jar before the next one is taken out.

a. Draw a tree diagram to list all the possible outcomes. Use a *verde*, an *azul*, and a *roja* marble.

b. How does this tree diagram differ from the one on page 168?

c. Use the tree diagram you drew for part (a) to find the theoretical probabilities of events J, K, L, and M.

✓ **QUESTION 25**

...checks that you can use a tree diagram to list outcomes and find probabilities.

26 When a marble is *not replaced* after it is taken out of the jar, $P(azul, azul, azul) = 0$. What is the probability of this event when a marble *is replaced* after it is taken out?

27 **Discussion** Compare the probabilities of events J, K, L, and M in Question 24 with those in Question 25(c). Are there any events for which the probabilities did not change? Explain.

HOMEWORK EXERCISES See Exs. 44–48 on p. 174.

Section 2 Key Concepts

Key Terms

equivalent fractions

lowest terms

least common denominator

Equivalent Fractions (pp. 163–164)

Equivalent fractions can be found by multiplying or dividing the numerator and denominator of a fraction by the same number.

Example To write the fraction $\frac{27}{36}$ in lowest terms, find an equivalent fraction where the GCF of the numerator and denominator is 1.

The GCF of 27 and 36 is 9.

$$\frac{27}{36} = \frac{27 \div 9}{36 \div 9} = \frac{3}{4}$$

The GCF of 3 and 4 is 1.

Comparing Fractions (pp. 164–165)

Fractions can be compared by renaming them as equivalent fractions using the least common denominator.

Example

$$\frac{5}{8} = \frac{25}{40} \text{ and } \frac{13}{20} = \frac{26}{40}$$

$$\frac{25}{40} < \frac{26}{40}, \text{ so } \frac{5}{8} < \frac{13}{20}$$

The least common denominator of $\frac{5}{8}$ and $\frac{13}{20}$ is 40.

Adding and Subtracting Fractions (pp. 166–167)

One way to add or subtract fractions is to rename them using a common denominator.

Example

$$\frac{2}{7} + \frac{3}{14} = \frac{2 \cdot 2}{7 \cdot 2} + \frac{3}{14}$$

$$= \frac{4}{14} + \frac{3}{14}$$

$$= \frac{7}{14}$$

$$= \frac{1}{2}$$

The least common denominator is 14.

28 Key Concepts Question Refer to the last Example above. How is a method for finding $\frac{2}{7} - \frac{3}{14}$ like the method shown for finding $\frac{2}{7} + \frac{3}{14}$? How is it different?

Section 2

Key Concepts

Key Terms

tree diagram

Tree Diagrams (pp. 168–169)

A tree diagram can be used to find the outcomes of an experiment and to find probabilities.

Example Suppose event A is choosing a pink ball first and choosing a green ball second.

Experiment 1
First ball chosen is replaced.

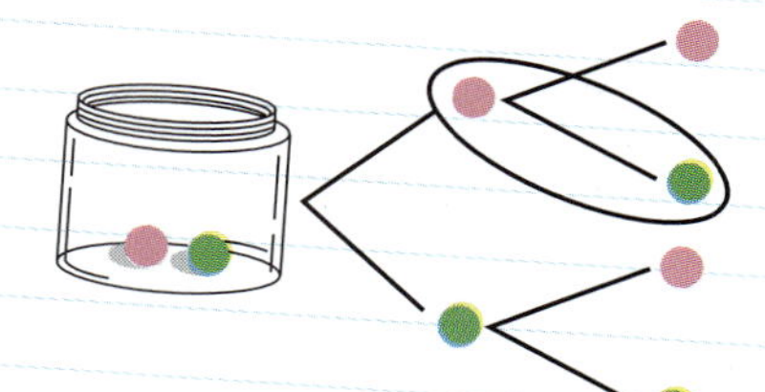

$P(A) = \frac{1}{4}$

Experiment 2
First ball chosen is not replaced.

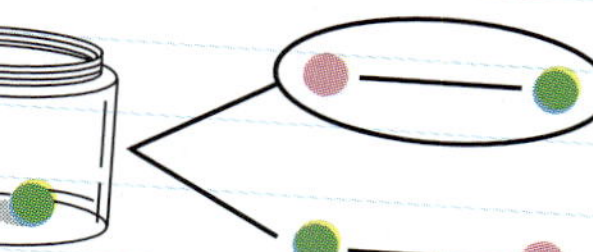

$P(A) = \frac{1}{2}$

29 Key Concepts Question In Experiment 1 above, find the probability that a green ball will be chosen second.

Section 2

Practice & Application Exercises

Write each fraction in lowest terms.

1. $\frac{3}{15}$
2. $\frac{14}{21}$
3. $\frac{6}{8}$
4. $\frac{9}{15}$
5. $\frac{18}{42}$
6. $\frac{34}{119}$
7. $\frac{150}{390}$
8. $\frac{160}{256}$
9. **Challenge** Suppose a fraction has a numerator that is 28 less than its denominator. The fraction written in lowest terms is $\frac{2}{3}$. What is the fraction?

History **For Exercises 10–12, use the data in the table. Write each fraction in lowest terms.**

10. the fraction of rulers who reigned more than 40 years

11. the fraction of rulers who reigned 45 years

12. the fraction of rulers who reigned less than 47 years

Salote Tupou III became Queen of Tonga at age 18. Tonga consists of three main island groups in the Pacific Ocean east of Fiji.

Long Reigning Woman Rulers

Ruler	Country	Years reigned (as of 1996)
Victoria (1837–1901)	United Kingdom	64
Wilhelmina (1890–1948)	Netherlands	58
Afua Koba (1834–1884)	Asante Empire	50
Salote Tupou III (1918–1965)	Tonga	47
Elizabeth II (1952–present)	United Kingdom	45
Elizabeth I (1558–1603)	England	45
Maria Theresa (1740–1780)	Habsburg Empire	40
Maria I (1777–1816)	Portugal	39

Mental Math **For Exercises 13–15, you'll use mental math to compare special pairs of fractions.**

13. a. The fractions $\frac{3}{16}$ and $\frac{3}{14}$ have the same numerator. How can you tell which fraction is greater without finding a common denominator?

b. If two fractions have the same numerator, how can you tell which fraction is greater?

c. Use your answer to part (b) to find a fraction that is greater than $\frac{5}{25}$ but less than $\frac{5}{19}$.

14. a. **Visual Thinking** Explain how the diagram shows that $\frac{11}{12} > \frac{7}{8}$.

b. Make a diagram to compare $\frac{2}{3}$ and $\frac{3}{4}$.

c. Suppose the difference between the numerator and the denominator of each fraction you are comparing is 1, as in parts (a) and (b). How can you tell which fraction is greater?

d. Use part (c) to find three fractions greater than $\frac{15}{16}$ but less than 1.

15. a. Tell whether each of the fractions $\frac{10}{18}$, $\frac{12}{25}$, and $\frac{59}{100}$ is *greater than* or *less than* $\frac{1}{2}$.

b. Describe a general method for comparing a fraction with $\frac{1}{2}$.

Estimation Tell whether each fraction is closer to 0, $\frac{1}{2}$, or 1.

16. $\frac{1}{15}$ 17. $\frac{3}{8}$ 18. $\frac{11}{12}$ 19. $\frac{2}{5}$

Choosing a Method Tell whether you would use *mental math*, *estimation*, or *paper-and-pencil* to compare each pair of fractions. Then replace each __?__ with >, <, or =.

20. $\frac{5}{7}$ __?__ $\frac{5}{9}$ 21. $\frac{15}{16}$ __?__ $\frac{13}{16}$ 22. $\frac{3}{7}$ __?__ $\frac{6}{11}$

23. $\frac{24}{32}$ __?__ $\frac{3}{4}$ 24. $\frac{7}{10}$ __?__ $\frac{5}{8}$ 25. $\frac{3}{8}$ __?__ $\frac{1}{3}$

26. $\frac{5}{18}$ __?__ $\frac{7}{16}$ 27. $\frac{5}{6}$ __?__ $\frac{6}{7}$ 28. $\frac{10}{21}$ __?__ $\frac{15}{28}$

Graph each set of numbers on a number line. Then list them in numerical order.

29. $\frac{1}{2}, \frac{1}{8}, \frac{3}{4}, \frac{5}{8}$ 30. $\frac{1}{3}, \frac{1}{2}, \frac{1}{6}, \frac{5}{6}, \frac{2}{3}$

Find each sum or difference. Write each answer in lowest terms.

31. $\frac{1}{3} + \frac{1}{8}$ 32. $\frac{3}{5} + \frac{4}{15}$ 33. $\frac{3}{4} - \frac{7}{10}$ 34. $\frac{6}{7} - \frac{3}{4}$

35. $\frac{1}{9} + \frac{2}{3}$ 36. $\frac{3}{7} - \frac{1}{21}$ 37. $\frac{5}{12} - \frac{7}{18}$ 38. $\frac{3}{22} + \frac{1}{11}$

39. $\frac{1}{2} + \frac{1}{3} + \frac{1}{2} + \frac{2}{3}$ 40. $\frac{1}{15} + \frac{1}{10} + \frac{2}{15} + \frac{3}{10}$

41. **Writing** Two students added the fractions $\frac{1}{4}$ and $\frac{5}{12}$ incorrectly. Look at their solutions. Describe the errors that were made and explain how to correctly add the fractions.

Bill	Janell
$\frac{1}{4} + \frac{5}{12} = \frac{6}{16}$	$\frac{1}{4} + \frac{5}{12} = \frac{6}{12}$

42. A student spent half an hour walking and a quarter of an hour jogging. What part of an hour did the student spend on these two activities?

43. Town officials reported that $\frac{3}{4}$ of the eligible voters voted *Yes* on a proposed addition to the middle school, $\frac{1}{20}$ voted *No*, and $\frac{1}{5}$ did not vote. Does this report cover all of the eligible voters? Explain.

For Exercises 44–47, use the tree diagram. A magician's hat holds three items. You take them out, one at a time.

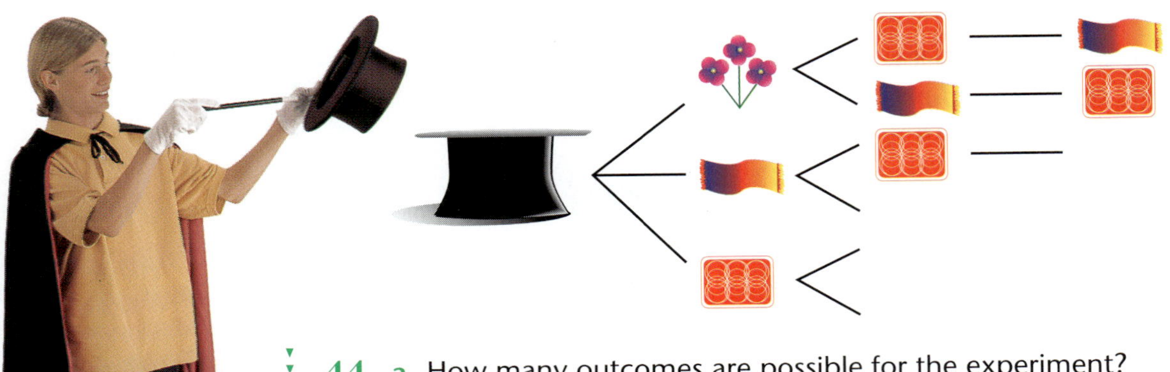

44. **a.** How many outcomes are possible for the experiment?

b. Does this experiment involve replacement? Explain.

45. Suppose you add a fourth object to the hat. Then you take out two objects, one at a time, without replacing the first object taken.

a. Draw a tree diagram to show the possible outcomes. How many outcomes are possible?

b. Describe two events that have different probabilities of occurring. Give the probability of each event.

46. In Exercise 45(a), how many outcomes would there be if the first object was put back into the hat before the second object was taken out? Would this affect the events you described in Exercise 45(b) or their probabilities? Why or why not?

47. Look at your tree diagram for Exercise 45(a). Event A is taking a card out first and taking a scarf out second. Event B is taking flowers out first and taking a card out second. Find the probability of each event.

a. $P(\text{A})$ **b.** $P(\text{B})$ **c.** $P(\text{A or B})$

Reflecting on the Section

Be prepared to report on the following topic in class.

Oral Report

Exercise 48 checks that you understand and can apply models to add and subtract fractions.

48. An exchange student arrives in your math class.

a. Draw a model to show the student how $\frac{1}{2} + \frac{1}{3}$ can be rewritten using a common denominator.

b. Use your model to show the student how to find $\frac{1}{2} + \frac{1}{3}$.

c. Explain how the model can also be used to find $\frac{1}{2} - \frac{1}{3}$.

Spiral Review

Find the GCF of each pair of numbers. (Module 3, p. 156)

49. 10, 12 **50.** 36, 90 **51.** 19, 50

Write each power in standard form. (Module 1, p. 21)

52. 10^2 **53.** 2^5 **54.** 1^{99}

Find each sum or difference. (Toolbox, p. 587)

55. $5\frac{1}{3} + 7\frac{1}{3}$ **56.** $2\frac{3}{7} + 8\frac{1}{7}$ **57.** $8\frac{4}{5} - 5\frac{1}{5}$

Secret Codes

SET UP

Work with a partner.

Using Tree Diagrams The numeral "10000" may mean "ten thousand" to you, but it can also represent one or more letters of a coded word. In the Huffman code, a series of 0s and 1s, along with a code tree, is used to create a code.

Each digit of a code number, either a 0 or a 1, tells you which branch to follow at each fork on the tree. In the code tree below, 1 means "follow the right branch" and 0 means "follow the left branch." The path for T is highlighted on the tree.

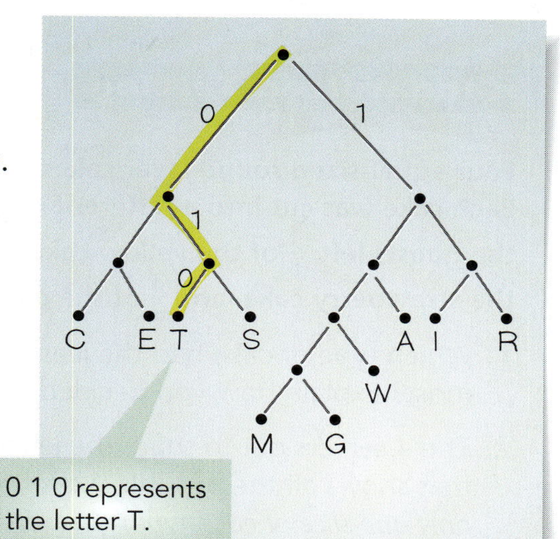

0 1 0 represents the letter T.

4 a. What letter does 10000 represent?

b. Would splitting 10000 into 100 and 00 produce two letters? Why?

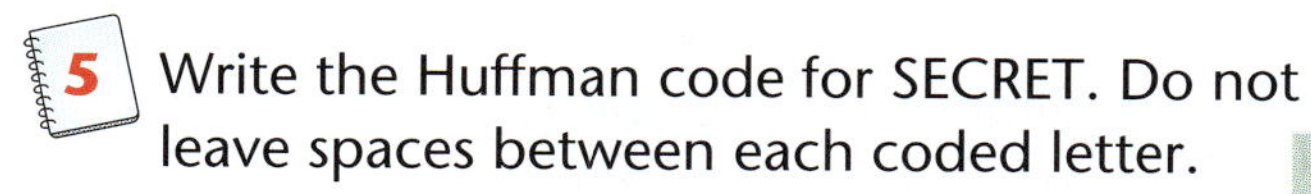

5 Write the Huffman code for SECRET. Do not leave spaces between each coded letter.

A code tree must contain the letters in the message, but it can have other letters, too.

6 Create your own code tree and encode a message to your partner. Then decode your partner's message using his or her code tree.

Section 2 Extra Skill Practice

Write each fraction in lowest terms.

1. $\frac{9}{12}$
2. $\frac{2}{22}$
3. $\frac{46}{69}$
4. $\frac{10}{35}$
5. $\frac{27}{243}$
6. $\frac{25}{125}$
7. $\frac{15}{31}$
8. $\frac{12}{28}$
9. $\frac{36}{52}$
10. $\frac{5}{100}$

Replace each ? with >, <, or =.

11. $\frac{5}{11}$? $\frac{9}{22}$
12. $\frac{8}{10}$? $\frac{7}{8}$
13. $\frac{2}{3}$? $\frac{2}{18}$
14. $\frac{3}{5}$? $\frac{5}{9}$
15. $\frac{2}{7}$? $\frac{1}{3}$
16. $\frac{7}{9}$? $\frac{3}{4}$
17. $\frac{10}{16}$? $\frac{6}{10}$
18. $\frac{6}{15}$? $\frac{8}{20}$

Find each sum or difference. Write each answer in lowest terms.

19. $\frac{3}{8} + \frac{9}{16}$
20. $\frac{1}{12} + \frac{2}{3}$
21. $\frac{11}{18} - \frac{1}{3}$
22. $\frac{4}{5} + \frac{1}{6}$
23. $\frac{3}{4} - \frac{1}{12}$
24. $\frac{4}{5} - \frac{2}{7}$
25. $\frac{7}{15} + \frac{3}{10}$
26. $\frac{20}{33} + \frac{5}{22}$
27. Suppose you are taking the numbers 1, 2, 3, and 4 out of a hat to pick the order for members of a relay team.
    a. Would it make sense to put each number back in the hat before taking out the next number? Why or why not?
    b. Draw a tree diagram to show all the possible outcomes.
    c. What is the probability that runner 2 goes first and runner 4 goes second?

Standardized Testing ▶ Performance Task

Four equal-sized round layer cakes were served at a special event. Each cake was cut into a different number of equal-sized slices. After the guests left, $\frac{1}{8}$ of the yellow cake, $\frac{3}{16}$ of the chocolate cake, $\frac{1}{6}$ of the strawberry cake, and $\frac{3}{9}$ of the pineapple cake remained.

1. Which type of cake had the least amount left over? Which had the most? Explain how you decided.
2. The 4 servers get to share the leftover cake. Draw a tree diagram that shows all the possible ways they can share the cakes *if there is only one slice of each type left* and *they do not cut up the slices.* How would your solution change if the two assumptions in italic type were not stated?

Section 3 Fractions and Mixed Numbers

IN THIS SECTION

EXPLORATION 1
- Renaming Fractions and Mixed Numbers

EXPLORATION 2
- Adding and Subtracting Mixed Numbers

Two Bits for your Thoughts

Setting the Stage

SET UP *Work in a group. You will need:* • *Labsheet 3A* • *shopping list and coins from Labsheet 3B*

Imagine buying a shirt with a basket of carrots. This method of exchange, called *bartering*, does not always work well. What one person may want to use for barter, another person may not need. Instead, coins and bills with agreed-on values have become the "universal language" of trade.

The picture shows a Spanish dollar. This was the main money used for trade in colonial America. Often these coins were cut into 2, 4, or 8 equal-sized pieces to make change.

$\frac{1}{8}$ of a Spanish dollar was called 1 *bit*.

Use Labsheets 3A and 3B. What was it like to shop in colonial America? Follow the directions on the labsheets and use your *Shopping Lists and Coins* (Spanish dollars and bits) to purchase items from the *Colonial Price List*.

Think About It

1 How much money did you have when you began shopping? How much did you have after you made your purchases?

2 Did you have enough money to buy everything on your list? If not, which items did you decide not to buy and why?

3 Did you always have the correct change? If not, describe how you paid for the item(s).

GOAL

LEARN HOW TO...
- write fractions as mixed numbers
- write mixed numbers as fractions

AS YOU...
- exchange colonial money

KEY TERM
- mixed number

Exploration 1

Renaming Fractions and Mixed Numbers

If you had lived in colonial America, a knowledge of fractions and *mixed numbers* would have helped you when you made purchases with Spanish dollars.

4 Suppose a colonial merchant had 11 bits.

a. If the merchant combined bits to make Spanish dollars, how many Spanish dollars and how many leftover bits did the merchant have?

b. What fraction represents the leftover bits?

▶ **Fractions as Mixed Numbers** **You can use the same thinking as in Question 4 to write fractions as *mixed numbers*. A mixed number is the sum of a nonzero whole number and a fraction between 0 and 1.**

EXAMPLE

Suppose you have 21 bits and you want to exchange the bits for whole Spanish dollars and bits.

21 bits is the same as 21 eighths of a Spanish dollar.

$$\frac{21}{8} = \frac{8}{8} + \frac{8}{8} + \frac{5}{8}$$
$$= 2 + \frac{5}{8}$$
$$= 2\frac{5}{8}$$

Think: How many eighths make a **whole**? How many eighths are left?

5 What mixed number is equal to $\frac{15}{4}$? If necessary, use the coins or make a sketch.

6 Discussion Explain how to find each part when you write a fraction as a mixed number.

a. the whole number

b. the numerator of the fraction

c. the denominator of the fraction

7 ✓ CHECKPOINT Write each fraction as a whole number or as a mixed number in lowest terms.

a. $\frac{13}{8}$ **b.** $\frac{18}{4}$ **c.** $\frac{34}{5}$ **d.** $\frac{16}{2}$

...checks that you can write a fraction as a mixed number.

▶ **Mixed Numbers as Fractions** **Suppose a colonist has 3 Spanish dollars and 7 bits and wants to buy an item that costs 27 bits. Does the colonist have enough money? One way to find out is to look at the total number of bits.**

3 Spanish dollars and 7 bits = __?__ bits

8 a. How many total bits does the colonist have?

b. Explain how to find the number of eighths in $3\frac{7}{8}$ dollars without counting the individual bits.

9 The diagram shows $8\frac{2}{3}$. Use your method from Question 8(b) to write $8\frac{2}{3}$ as a fraction: $8\frac{2}{3} = \frac{?}{3}$.

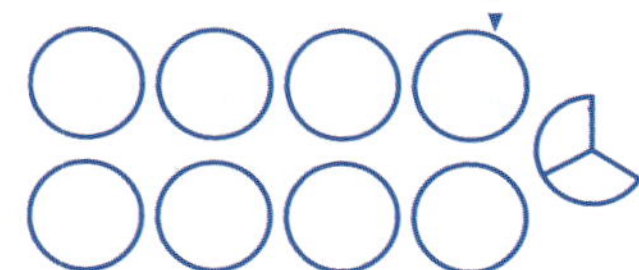

10 Discussion Explain how to find each part when you write a mixed number as a fraction.

a. the denominator **b.** the numerator

11 ✓ CHECKPOINT Write each mixed number as a fraction.

a. $2\frac{3}{4}$ **b.** $3\frac{5}{6}$ **c.** $10\frac{1}{2}$ **d.** $14\frac{2}{3}$

...checks that you can write a mixed number as a fraction.

HOMEWORK EXERCISES ▶ See Exs. 1–26 on pp. 184–185.

GOAL

LEARN HOW TO...
- add and subtract mixed numbers

AS YOU...
- think about buying and selling using Spanish dollars and bits

Exploration 2

Adding and Subtracting Mixed Numbers

12 Suppose you are a colonial merchant and have sold some food for $3\frac{1}{2}$ Spanish dollars and some other goods for 2 dollars and 5 bits.

a. How many whole dollars do you have?

b. Can you combine the broken pieces to equal another dollar? If so, describe how. (*Hint:* How many bits equal $\frac{1}{2}$ of a dollar?)

c. How many total dollars and leftover bits do you have? Write your answer as a mixed number of dollars.

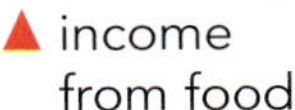

▲ income from food

▲ income from other goods

American colonists buying and selling goods at an outdoor marketplace ▶

▶ **Adding Mixed Numbers** **Tatiana found the answer to Question 12(c) by adding mixed numbers.**

13 **Discussion** Study Tatiana's work.

a. Based on what you know about adding fractions, explain why $3\frac{1}{2}$ is rewritten as $3\frac{4}{8}$.

b. Explain why $5\frac{9}{8} = 6\frac{1}{8}$.

c. How does your answer to Question 12(c) compare with Tatiana's answer?

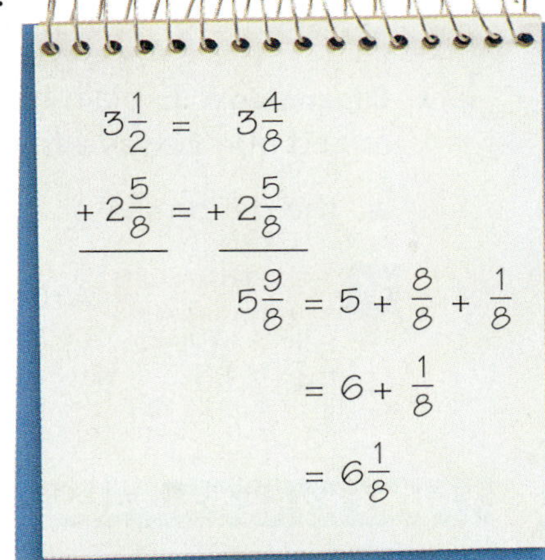

14 ✓ **CHECKPOINT** Find each sum.

a. $7\frac{1}{8} + 8\frac{2}{3}$ **b.** $4\frac{3}{4} + 1\frac{5}{12}$ **c.** $3\frac{4}{5} + 12\frac{1}{2}$

✓ **QUESTION 14**

...checks that you can add mixed numbers.

▶ **Subtracting Mixed Numbers** **When subtracting mixed numbers, you may have to rewrite the fraction part.**

15 Suppose you have $4\frac{5}{8}$ Spanish dollars and you buy a fiddle for $3\frac{1}{4}$ dollars.

cost of a fiddle

$4\frac{5}{8}$ **dollars** – $3\frac{1}{4}$ **dollars**

a. How many whole dollars do you have left?

b. How many bits do the remaining pieces equal? (*Hint*: How many bits equal $\frac{1}{4}$ of a Spanish dollar?)

c. How much money will you have left altogether? Write your answer as a mixed number of Spanish dollars.

16 ✓ **CHECKPOINT** Find each difference.

a. $7\frac{1}{2} - 2\frac{3}{8}$ **b.** $10\frac{2}{3} - 6\frac{2}{5}$ **c.** $24\frac{1}{2} - 20\frac{1}{3}$

✓ **QUESTION 16**

...checks that you can subtract mixed numbers.

17 **Discussion** Suppose a colonist has $4\frac{1}{2}$ Spanish dollars and wants to buy an item for 2 Spanish dollars and 5 bits.

a. How many dollars and bits will the colonist have left after buying the item? (*Hint:* Think about how a Spanish dollar can be traded for bits.)

b. Write your answer to part (a) as a mixed number.

▶ **Subtracting with Regrouping** Mixed number subtraction problems may involve *regrouping*, where one whole is written as a fraction.

EXAMPLE

You can use a model to help you find the difference $3\frac{1}{4} - 1\frac{3}{4}$.

Not enough fourths to subtract $\frac{3}{4}$.

Trade one whole for $\frac{4}{4}$.

Regroup wholes and fourths.

18 **a.** Write an explanation of each step.

		Step 1		Step 2		Step 3
$4\frac{1}{2}$	=	$4\frac{4}{8}$	=	$3 + \frac{8}{8} + \frac{4}{8}$	=	$3\frac{12}{8}$
$-2\frac{5}{8}$	=				=	$-2\frac{5}{8}$

b. Find the difference $4\frac{1}{2} - 2\frac{5}{8}$. Compare it with your answer to Question 17(b).

19 **Try This as a Class** Think about subtracting mixed numbers.

a. Write a sequence of steps for subtracting mixed numbers.

b. Follow the steps you wrote in part (a) to find $3\frac{3}{4} - 1\frac{1}{8}$ and $4 - 1\frac{3}{4}$. Revise the steps if necessary.

✓ QUESTION 20

...checks that you can subtract any mixed numbers.

20 **✓ CHECKPOINT** Find each difference.

a. $4\frac{1}{8} - 2\frac{3}{8}$ **b.** $13 - 2\frac{3}{4}$ **c.** $25\frac{4}{9} - 8\frac{1}{3}$ **d.** $10\frac{3}{4} - 7\frac{4}{5}$

HOMEWORK EXERCISES ▶ See Exs. 27–43 on pp. 185–187.

Section 3 Key Concepts

Key Term

mixed number

Renaming Fractions and Mixed Numbers (pp. 178–179)

Example Write $\frac{11}{3}$ as a mixed number.

$\frac{11}{3} = \frac{3}{3} + \frac{3}{3} + \frac{3}{3} + \frac{2}{3}$

$= 1 + 1 + 1 + \frac{2}{3}$

$= 3\frac{2}{3}$

Example Write $2\frac{1}{4}$ as a fraction.

$2\frac{1}{4} = 1 + 1 + \frac{1}{4}$

$= \frac{4}{4} + \frac{4}{4} + \frac{1}{4}$

$= \frac{9}{4}$

Adding and Subtracting Mixed Numbers (pp. 180–182)

Example Find $7\frac{2}{3} + 2\frac{1}{2}$.

$7\frac{2}{3} = 7\frac{4}{6}$

$+\,2\frac{1}{2} = +\,2\frac{3}{6}$

$9\frac{7}{6} = 9 + \frac{6}{6} + \frac{1}{6}$

$= 9 + 1 + \frac{1}{6}$

$= 10\frac{1}{6}$

Write the fraction as the sum of two fractions between 0 and 1.

Example Find $5\frac{2}{9} - 2\frac{5}{9}$.

$5\frac{2}{9} = 4\frac{11}{9}$

$-\,2\frac{5}{9} = -\,2\frac{5}{9}$

$2\frac{6}{9}$ or $2\frac{2}{3}$

Regroup so there are enough ninths to subtract $\frac{5}{9}$.

21 Key Concepts Question Matt uses the method shown at the right to subtract mixed numbers.

$5\frac{1}{3} = \frac{16}{3}$

$-\,1\frac{2}{3} = -\,\frac{5}{3}$

$\frac{11}{3} = 3\frac{2}{3}$

a. Explain Matt's method.

b. Compare this method with the method shown in this section.

c. Which method would you use to find $25\frac{3}{8} - 19\frac{7}{8}$? Why?

Section 3
Practice & Application Exercises

Write each fraction as a mixed number.

1. $\frac{23}{5}$
2. $\frac{22}{7}$
3. $\frac{42}{10}$
4. $\frac{47}{15}$

Describe the error that was made when each fraction was written as a mixed number. Give the correct mixed number.

5. $\frac{8}{3} = 1\frac{5}{3}$
6. $\frac{11}{4} = 3\frac{1}{4}$
7. $\frac{31}{2} = 15$
8. $\frac{27}{5} = 5\frac{5}{2}$

Write each mixed number as a fraction.

9. $1\frac{1}{8}$
10. $2\frac{2}{5}$
11. $4\frac{4}{9}$
12. $8\frac{5}{6}$
13. $9\frac{2}{5}$
14. $12\frac{1}{4}$
15. $14\frac{1}{2}$
16. $17\frac{2}{3}$

Replace each __?__ with the correct mixed number or fraction.

17. A 66 in. tall gorilla stands __?__ ft tall.

The gorilla is the largest living primate. ▶

18. A 992 lb polar bear weighs __?__ tons.

◀ The greatest weight recorded for a polar bear in the wild was an amazing 2210 lb!

19. A 270 lb ostrich weighs __?__ tons.

The ostrich is the largest living bird. ▶

FOR▶HELP with *conversions,* see **TABLE OF MEASURES, p. 596**

20. A 126 in. tall African elephant stands __?__ ft tall.

◀ The African bush elephant is the largest living land animal.

Choose a Method Tell whether you would use *mental math*, *estimation*, or *paper-and-pencil* to compare each fraction and mixed number. Then replace each __?__ with >, <, or =.

21. $2\frac{4}{5}$ __?__ $\frac{7}{3}$

22. $\frac{17}{2}$ __?__ $8\frac{3}{4}$

23. $3\frac{1}{4}$ __?__ $\frac{13}{2}$

24. $\frac{31}{6}$ __?__ $5\frac{1}{6}$

25. $\frac{32}{3}$ __?__ $10\frac{5}{7}$

26. $4\frac{1}{2}$ __?__ $\frac{5}{2}$

Use the ruler to help you evaluate each expression.

FOR ▶ HELP with *reading a ruler*, see **TOOLBOX, p. 591**

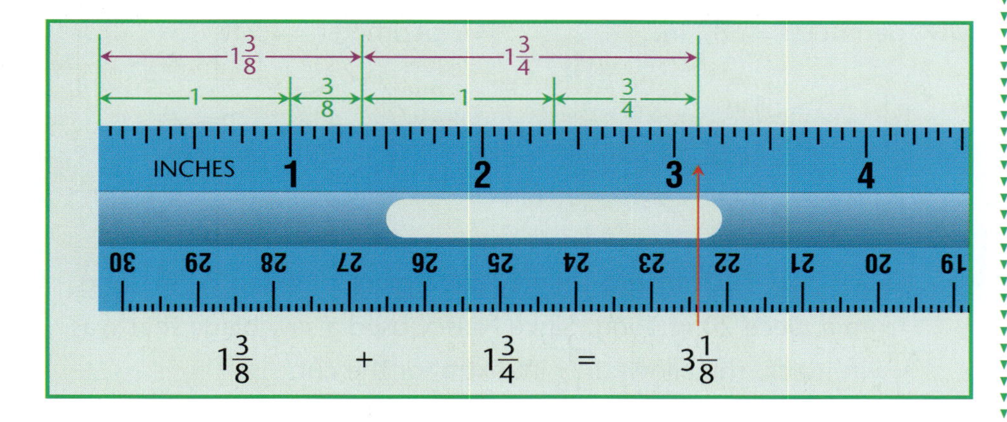

27. $1\frac{1}{2} + 1\frac{1}{4}$

28. $2\frac{1}{8} - 1\frac{1}{4}$

29. $4 - 2\frac{1}{4} - \frac{1}{8}$

Find each sum or difference.

30. $15 + 4\frac{7}{12}$

31. $12 - 1\frac{1}{3}$

32. $10\frac{3}{4} + 23\frac{1}{16}$

33. $5\frac{1}{3} - 2\frac{1}{4}$

34. $\frac{7}{8} + 3\frac{1}{2}$

35. $9\frac{9}{11} + 13\frac{5}{22}$

36. Giant bamboo can grow up to $1\frac{1}{2}$ ft in a day.

   a. Suppose a 3 ft giant bamboo plant grew $1\frac{1}{2}$ ft one day, $1\frac{1}{3}$ ft the next day, and $\frac{3}{4}$ ft on each of the next 2 days. How tall would the plant be then?

   b. Suppose a $5\frac{1}{2}$ ft giant bamboo plant grew $1\frac{1}{4}$ ft one day, 1 ft the next day, and $\frac{7}{8}$ ft on each of the next 3 days. How tall would the plant be then?

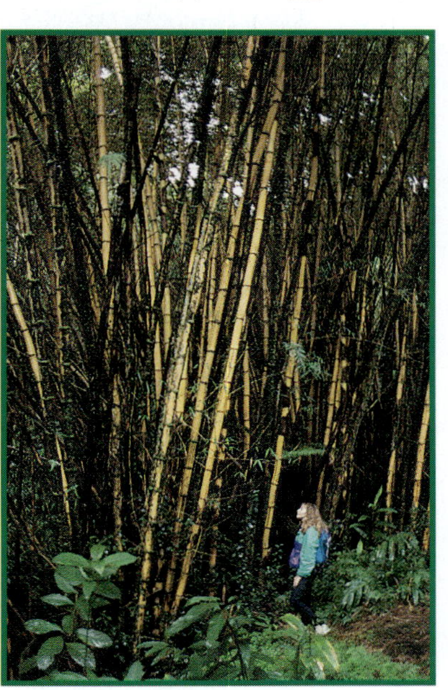

◀ There are more than 1000 kinds of bamboos. Some bamboos can reach 100 ft in height.

FOR ▶ HELP with *perimeter*, see **TOOLBOX, p. 591**

Algebra Connection **For each figure, write an equation relating the perimeter and the lengths of the sides. Then solve to find *x*.**

37. perimeter = 8 in.

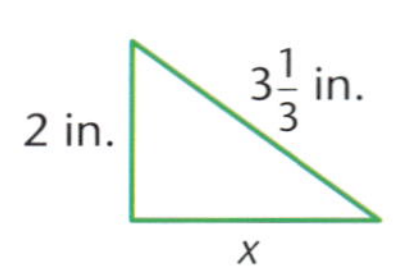

38. perimeter = 14 ft

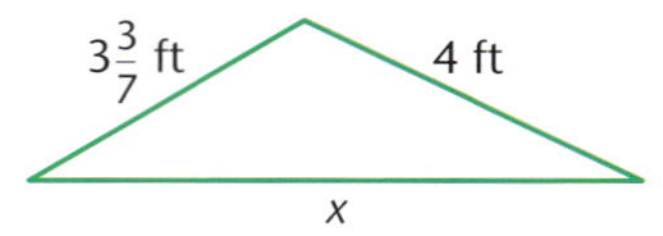

39. perimeter = $18\frac{1}{2}$ in.

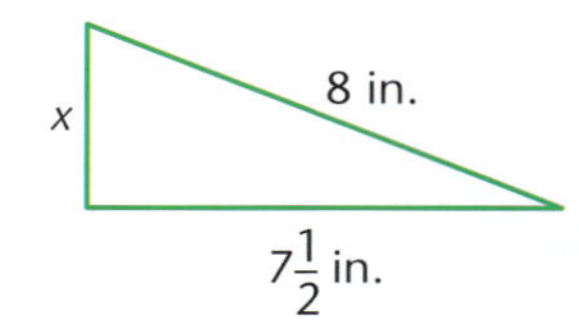

40. perimeter = 15 ft

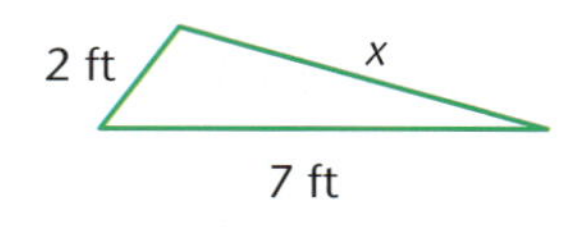

41. **Industrial Technology** Nancy cut a piece of wood $8\frac{3}{8}$ in. long from a piece 20 in. long. Since Nancy used a saw blade that was $\frac{1}{16}$ in. thick, she allowed $\frac{1}{16}$ in. extra for the cut.

a. How much wood is left over?

b. If Nancy had started with a piece of wood $10\frac{1}{2}$ in. long, how much wood would be left over?

c. Why is it important to know the thickness of the saw blade?

42. **Open-ended** Write a problem that can be solved using the equation $3\frac{1}{4} + x = 10\frac{3}{8}$. Then solve the equation.

Reflecting on the Section

Write your response to Exercise 43 in your journal.

43. The Spanish dollar is no longer used as a form of money, but fractions are still important in many monetary systems.

   a. What fractional parts of a United States dollar are represented by the value of the coins we use today?

   b. For which coin does the coin's name tell its value? Explain.

Journal

Exercise 43 checks that you understand and can apply fractions.

Spiral Review

Find each sum or difference. (Module 3, p. 170)

44. $\frac{1}{4}+\frac{2}{3}$ **45.** $\frac{5}{9}-\frac{1}{6}$ **46.** $\frac{4}{5}-\frac{2}{15}$ **47.** $\frac{7}{12}+\frac{11}{18}$

Find each sum or difference. (Toolbox, p. 581)

48. 0.249 + 1.806 **49.** 2.35 – 1.7 **50.** 3.0102 – 0.098

51. What is the measure of each angle formed when a Spanish dollar is cut into 4 equal-sized pieces? into 8 bits? (Module 2, p. 83)

Career Connection

Composer: Maia

One of Maia's compositions, *Key Vibrations, Symphony #1*, contains several music styles. Composers like Maia need to count beats and measures in music. A $\frac{4}{4}$ *time signature* means there are 4 beats in a *measure*. A whole note (𝅝) is a complete measure in $\frac{4}{4}$ time. A half note (𝅗𝅥) is half a measure in $\frac{4}{4}$ time, and so on, for quarter notes (♩), eighth notes (♪), and sixteenth notes (𝅘𝅥𝅯).

52. Using a $\frac{4}{4}$ time signature, write the number of measures represented by each set of notes.

   a. 1𝅗𝅥 + 2♩'s **b.** 1𝅝 + 6♪'s + 4𝅘𝅥𝅯's **c.** 3♩'s + 6♪'s + 3𝅗𝅥's

Section 3

Extra Skill Practice

Write each fraction as a mixed number.

1. $\frac{8}{5}$
2. $\frac{7}{3}$
3. $\frac{7}{4}$
4. $\frac{11}{2}$
5. $\frac{23}{3}$
6. $\frac{15}{2}$
7. $\frac{66}{5}$
8. $\frac{92}{9}$
9. $\frac{30}{7}$
10. $\frac{45}{8}$
11. $\frac{51}{5}$
12. $\frac{31}{25}$

Write each mixed number as a fraction.

13. $2\frac{4}{5}$
14. $5\frac{1}{2}$
15. $9\frac{3}{7}$
16. $4\frac{2}{3}$
17. $8\frac{1}{4}$
18. $12\frac{2}{5}$
19. $20\frac{1}{6}$
20. $2\frac{5}{8}$
21. $30\frac{4}{5}$
22. $45\frac{1}{2}$
23. $64\frac{1}{3}$
24. $100\frac{7}{9}$

Find each sum or difference and write the answer in lowest terms.

25. $1\frac{1}{3} + 2\frac{3}{4}$
26. $2\frac{2}{5} + 3\frac{1}{8}$
27. $4\frac{1}{2} - 4\frac{1}{4}$
28. $5\frac{5}{7} + 6\frac{3}{7}$
29. $4\frac{5}{9} - 2\frac{2}{3}$
30. $10\frac{1}{4} - 8\frac{1}{6}$
31. $9 + 2\frac{1}{5}$
32. $10\frac{7}{8} - 9\frac{5}{6}$
33. $4\frac{2}{5} - 3\frac{4}{7}$
34. $3\frac{3}{4} + 8\frac{11}{12}$
35. $10\frac{7}{8} + 12\frac{1}{6}$
36. $15\frac{6}{13} - 12\frac{17}{26}$
37. An artist is putting cord around the edge of a rectangular picture frame. The dimensions are $7\frac{3}{8}$ in. by $5\frac{1}{4}$ in. Find the perimeter.

Standardized Testing ▶ Multiple Choice

1. Which fraction is equal to $9\frac{8}{17}$?

   (A) $\frac{89}{17}$ (B) $\frac{72}{17}$ (C) $\frac{8}{153}$ (D) $\frac{161}{17}$

2. Find $11\frac{1}{12} - 2\frac{1}{3}$. Which is (are) the correct difference(s)?

   (A) $8\frac{3}{4}$ (B) $9\frac{1}{12}$ (C) $\frac{109}{12}$ (D) $\frac{35}{4}$

EXTENDED E2 EXPLORATION

FOR ASSESSMENT AND PORTFOLIOS

Colonial Curren¢y

The Situation

Before the American Revolution, the Spanish dollar was the principal coin used in colonial America. At the same time, merchants used the British money system of *pounds* (£), *shillings* (s), and *pence* (d)—the plural of *penny*—for keeping financial records in the colonies.

1£ = 20s   1s = 12d

Since *all* coins were in short supply, many colonies printed their own paper money as well, like the Massachusetts Bay note shown. Each bill usually represented some fraction of a Spanish dollar that was easy to convert to British shillings and pence.

The Problem

Design a system of colonial paper money.
Each bill should be less than or equal to a Spanish dollar.

Something to Think About

- Use the Massachusetts Bay note to find the value of a Spanish dollar in pence.
- In colonial times a pair of shoes cost \$1, a pen cost 2 bits, a turkey cost $\$\frac{1}{4}$, and a chair cost $\$5\frac{7}{8}$ in Spanish coins.

  What is a reasonable number of paper bills to use to buy these items, if they were also priced in British money?
- What information should you print on each of your paper bills?

Present Your Results

Write a letter to a colonial governor explaining why your system of paper money should be used in the colony. You may want to make a sketch showing your design of the paper money.

Decimals and Exponents

EXPLORATION 1
- Decimal Place Values

EXPLORATION 2
- Integer Exponents

EXPLORATION 3
- Scientific Notation

Bright Ideas

Setting the Stage

Some people think that adding and subtracting fractions is difficult. The mathematician Simon Stevin certainly felt this way! In 1585, he published *De Thiende* ("The Tenth"), a book designed to teach everyone "how to perform with an ease, unheard of, all computations . . . by integers without fractions."

Stevin might have used an example like the one at the right to explain his method. Can you decode it?

12⓪ 6① 8②
1⓪ 5① 9②
13⓪ 11① 17②
13⓪ 12① 7②
14⓪ 2① 7②

Think About It

1 Look at the example shown above.

a. What problem is solved? How would you write the problem?

b. Explain what happens at each step in Stevin's solution. How would you show these steps?

2 How would Stevin have written the number 29.587?

3 Use Stevin's method to find each sum or difference.

a. 2⓪ 7① 8② + 5⓪ 4① 2② **b.** 5⓪ 4① 2② − 2⓪ 7① 8②

Exploration 1

Decimal Place Values

GOAL

LEARN HOW TO...
- compare numbers using the decimal place value system
- write a decimal as a fraction

AS YOU...
- play a game with number squares

KEY TERM
- decimal place

SET UP *Work in a group. You will need 10 cards numbered 0 through 9.*

▶ **Simon Stevin's ideas for writing decimal fractions and calculating with them helped inspire the universal *decimal place value system*. In the decimal system, the value of a number is expressed by writing digits in certain positions called decimal places.**

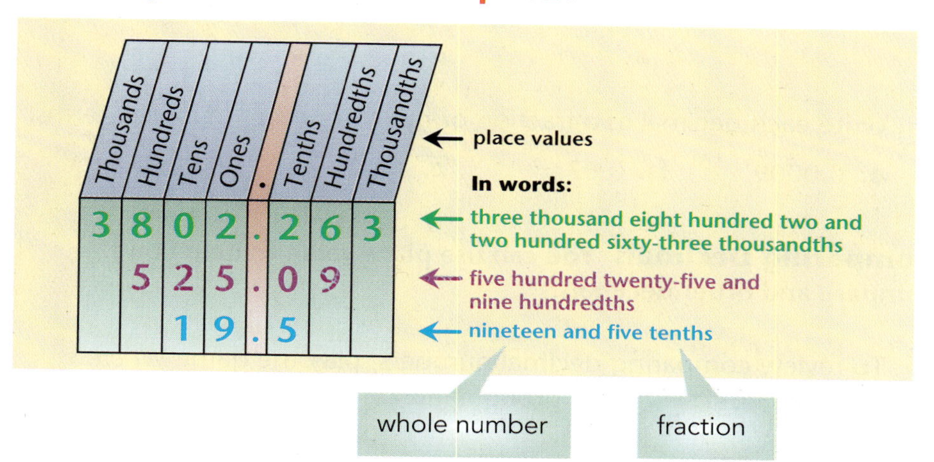

4 Try This as a Class Look at the chart above.

a. What is the purpose of the decimal point?

b. What happens to the value of each place as you move one place to its left? two places to its left?

c. What is the place value of the seventh decimal place to the left of the decimal point?

d. What happens to the value of each place as you move one place to its right?

e. What is the place value of the sixth decimal place to the right of the decimal point?

5 In 32.67159, the 7 is in the hundredths place, so its value is $7 \cdot 0.01$ or 0.07. In words, its value is "seven hundredths." Write the value of each digit in 32.67159 as a decimal and in words.

...checks that you can read and write decimal numbers.

6 ✓ **CHECKPOINT** For each number written in words, write the decimal form. For each number written in decimal form, write its value in words.

a. six and fifty-eight hundredths **b.** 12.056

c. one hundred and three tenths **d.** 0.1037

▶ Writing Decimals as Fractions

To write a decimal as a fraction, you may want to first identify the decimal's value in words.

EXAMPLE

1.25 means one and twenty-five hundredths.

$$1.25 = 1\frac{25}{100} = 1\frac{1}{4}$$

Hundredths means the denominator is 100.

7 Write each decimal as a fraction or mixed number in lowest terms.

a. 0.0009 **b.** 0.67 **c.** 56.2 **d.** 1.375

▶ Comparing Decimals

You can use place value to help you compare and order decimals.

8 To review comparing decimal numbers, play the game *Where's the Best Place?* with your group a few times.

Where's the Best Place?

The object of the game is to build the greatest number possible.

- Each player makes a number chart as shown.

Game 1	0	.				

- Use ten cards numbered 0 through 9. Shuffle the cards and place them face down in a pile.
- One player draws a digit from the pile. Each player must decide where to write that digit in his or her number chart.
- After a digit is written, it cannot be erased. Once a digit is drawn, it cannot be used again in that game.
- The game is over when all places on each number chart are filled. The player with the greatest number wins the game.

9 Answer the questions relating to the game *Where's the Best Place?*

a. Suppose 9 is chosen first. Where is the best place to put the 9? Explain your choice.

b. Suppose 0 is chosen first. Where is the best place to put the 0? Explain your choice.

c. How would your game strategy in parts (a) and (b) be different if 0 were not always in the ones place?

10 The number charts of four students playing *Where's the Best Place?* are shown.

Christine | 0 | . | 5 | 6 | ? | 4 |

Julius | 0 | . | 5 | 4 | ? | 6 |

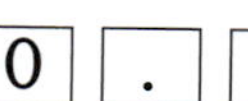

Marcus | 0 | . | 5 | 6 | 4 | ? |

Delia | 0 | . | 5 | 4 | 6 | ? |

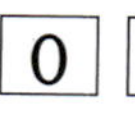
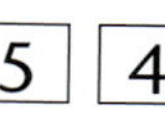

a. Can Delia win the game? Explain.

b. Can Christine win the game? Explain.

c. Suppose "3" is chosen next. Who will win the game? Explain.

EXAMPLE

You can compare two decimals by comparing digits with the same place value, beginning at the left.

The **ones digits** are equal.

5.7 _?_ 5.69

Compare the **tenths digits: 7 > 6**.

So, 5.7 > 5.69.

11 Marcus argues that 5.69 > 5.7 because 69 > 7. Explain to Marcus why this is not correct.

12 ✓ **CHECKPOINT** Replace each _?_ with >, <, or =.

a. 0.663 _?_ 0.671 **b.** 1.37 _?_ 1.365 **c.** 15.3 _?_ 2.68

d. 0.96 _?_ 0.960 **e.** 0.509 _?_ 0.51 **f.** 19.6 _?_ 1.96

✓ **QUESTION 12**

...checks that you can compare decimals.

HOMEWORK EXERCISES ▶ See Exs. 1–30 on pp. 199–200.

GOAL

LEARN HOW TO...
- use integer exponents to read and write numbers

AS YOU...
- explore powers of 10

KEY TERM
- power

Exploration 2

INTEGER Exponents

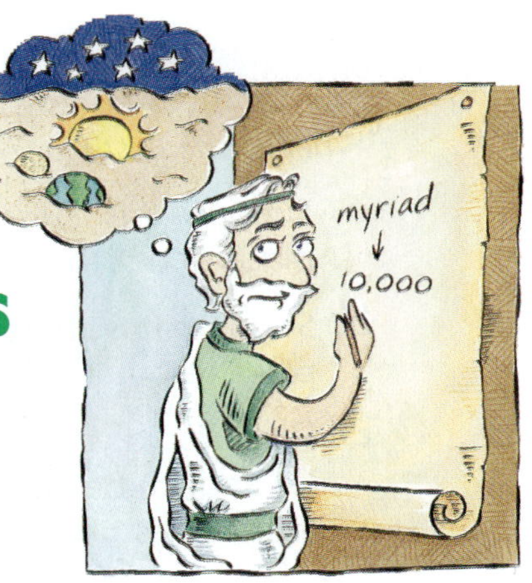

SET UP *You will need:* • *Labsheet 4A* • *calculator*

Archimedes, a Greek scientist and mathematician (287–212 B.C.), loved a challenge. One day he decided to find out the number of grains of sand it would take to fill the known universe! Unfortunately, the largest number the ancient Greeks had a name for was a *myriad* or 10,000. Archimedes knew this was not large enough.

13 **Discussion** We have names for numbers greater than 10,000— million, billion, trillion. Why do you think the ancient Greeks did not?

▶ **Archimedes had the idea to name a number greater than a myriad by multiplying a myriad by a myriad — a *myriad of myriads*. He developed the idea of exponents by continuing this pattern.**

FOR ◀ HELP with *exponents*, see **MODULE 1, p. 20**

14 In exponential form, 10,000 is written as 10^4. Name the base and the exponent.

15 Archimedes used a myriad of myriads, or 10,000 • 10,000, to name numbers. Write the value of 10,000 • 10,000 in each form.

a. exponential form using 10,000 as the base

b. standard form

c. exponential form using 10 as the base

According to some accounts, Archimedes may have worked out problems in the sand. ▶

Use Labsheet 4A for Questions 16–19.

16 **Discussion** A number that can be written using an exponent and a base is a **power**. For example, $1000 = 10 \cdot 10 \cdot 10 = 10^3$, so 1000 is "the third power of 10" or "10 to the third power."

a. Describe how multiplication can be used to complete the *Positive Powers of 10 Table* on Labsheet 4A. Complete the table.

b. What is the relationship between the exponent and the standard form of a positive power of 10?

17 Describe how division can be used to complete the *Integer Powers of 10 Table*. Then complete the table.

18 Look at the fraction forms of 10^{-1}, 10^{-2}, and 10^{-3} in the *Integer Powers of 10 Table*.

$$10^{-4} = \frac{1}{10{,}000} = \frac{1}{10^4} \text{ since } 10{,}000 = 10^4$$

a. Rewrite the fraction forms of 10^{-1}, 10^{-2}, and 10^{-3} so that the denominators are powers of 10.

b. How are the exponents in the denominators related to the original exponents?

c. Write 10^{-5} as a decimal, as a fraction, and as a fraction with its denominator in exponential form.

19 Calculator You can use a calculator to evaluate powers. For example, to find 7^4 you can use this key sequence:

a. Complete the *Powers of 2 Table* on Labsheet 4A.

b. How are the exponents in the denominators of the fractions related to the original exponents?

20 **Try This as a Class** Think about your work with powers.

a. Explain how to find the value of an expression where the base is a positive integer and the exponent is a negative integer. Give an example.

b. What is the value of 2^0? of 10^0? of any nonzero base to the 0 power?

21 **Discussion** Archimedes calculated 10^{63} grains of sand would fill the universe, but he knew there were greater numbers.

a. Describe how numbers greater than 10^{63} can be written. Is there a greatest positive number? Explain.

b. How can exponents be used to write very small positive numbers? Is there a least positive number? Explain.

22  Write each number as a fraction with its denominator in exponential form.

a. 10^{-1} **b.** 5^{-3} **c.** 10^{-6}

...checks that you can rewrite expressions with negative exponents.

HOMEWORK EXERCISES See Exs. 31–55 on pp. 200–201.

GOAL

LEARN HOW TO...
- multiply and divide decimals by powers of 10
- write numbers in scientific notation

AS YOU...
- look at calculator displays

KEY TERM
- scientific notation

Exploration 3

Scientific Notation

SET UP *You will need:* • *Labsheet 4B* • *calculator*

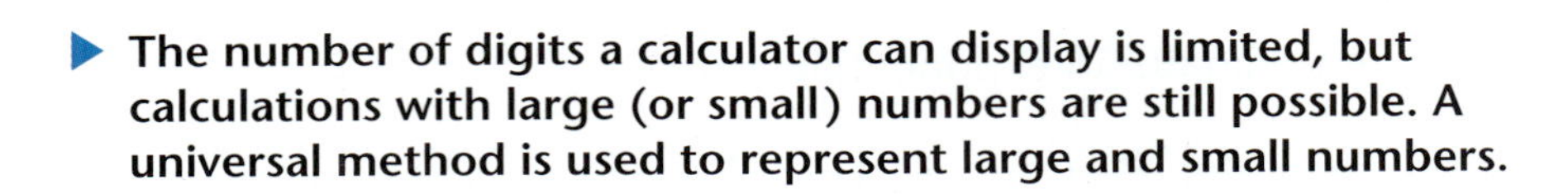

▶ **The number of digits a calculator can display is limited, but calculations with large (or small) numbers are still possible. A universal method is used to represent large and small numbers.**

23 **Try This as a Class** For parts (a) and (b), describe how the results are displayed on a calculator as the steps are carried out.

a. Clear the calculator and then enter 10. Multiply by 10 and look at the result. Continue multiplying by 10 and looking at the result at least 20 times.

b. Clear the calculator and then enter 10. Divide by 10 and look at the result. Continue dividing by 10 and looking at the result at least 20 times.

c. What did the calculator display after completing part (a)? part (b)? Why does this happen?

24 **Discussion** Most calculators have a special way to display large and small numbers. Three displays for the same number are shown.

1E15   1e+15   

a. What number is represented by the displays?

b. Write this number in standard form.

c. Why is the number not displayed in standard form?

▶ **Products and Quotients with Powers of 10** **Suppose a calculator displays 1.23456e+13. This is the same as 1.23456 • 10^{13}, a decimal number multiplied by a power of ten.**

Use Labsheet 4B for Questions 25 and 26.

25 Follow the directions on Labsheet 4B to complete the *Product Table.*

26 **Discussion** Look at your completed *Product Table*. Describe how to multiply a decimal by a positive power of 10. Then describe how to multiply a decimal by a negative power of 10.

Use Labsheet 4B for Questions 27 and 28.

27 Follow the directions on Labsheet 4B to complete the *Quotient Table*.

28 **Discussion** Look at your completed *Quotient Table*. Describe how to divide a decimal by a positive power of 10. Then describe how to divide a decimal by a negative power of 10.

29 **✓ CHECKPOINT** Find each product or quotient without using a calculator.

a. $11.634 \cdot 10^3$ **b.** $11.634 \cdot 10^0$ **c.** $11.634 \cdot 10^{-1}$

d. $9.75 \div 10^3$ **e.** $9.75 \div 10^0$ **f.** $9.75 \div 10^{-1}$

✓ QUESTION 29

...checks that you can multiply or divide a decimal by a power of 10.

30 If 1.23456e+13 represents $1.23456 \cdot 10^{13}$, write the number represented by 2.376e–8 in standard form.

31 **Discussion** Find each missing exponent. Explain your method.

a. $0.00036 = 3.6 \cdot 10^?$ **b.** $3{,}600{,}000 = 3.6 \cdot 10^?$

▶ **When a calculator displays a number as the product of a decimal and a power of 10, the decimal number is greater than or equal to 1 and less than 10. Numbers written this way are written in scientific notation.**

EXAMPLE

standard form		scientific notation
$12{,}345{,}000 = 1.2345 \cdot 10{,}000{,}000$	=	$1.2345 \cdot 10^7$
$0.0058 = 5.8 \cdot 0.001$	=	$5.8 \cdot 10^{-3}$

32 **✓ CHECKPOINT** Write each number in scientific notation.

a. 257,034 **b.** 0.0000727 **c.** 126.935

...checks that you can write numbers in scientific notation.

HOMEWORK EXERCISES ▶ See Exs. 56–79 on pp. 201–202.

Section 4 Key Concepts

Key Terms

Decimal Place Values (pp. 191–193)

decimal place

In the decimal place value system, the positions of the digits in a number determine their values. To compare decimals, you need to compare place values.

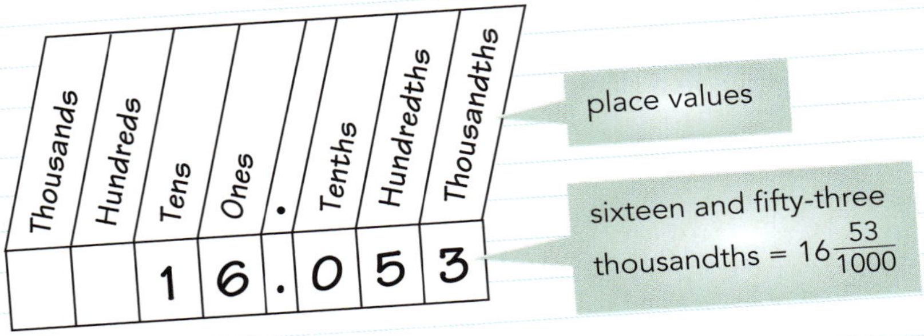

Thousands	Hundreds	Tens	Ones	.	Tenths	Hundredths	Thousandths
		1	6	.	0	5	3

place values

sixteen and fifty-three thousandths = $16\frac{53}{1000}$

Example Compare 2.335 and 2.34.

2.335
2.34

The **ones** and **tenths** digits are equal. Compare the **hundredths** digits: **3 < 4**.

So, 2.335 < 2.34.

Integer Exponents (pp. 194–195)

power

Positive and negative integers and zero can be used as exponents. A number that can be written in exponential form is a power of the base.

Examples

the 4th power of 5

$5^4 = 5 \cdot 5 \cdot 5 \cdot 5 = 625$

$4^{-3} = \frac{1}{4^3} = \frac{1}{4 \cdot 4 \cdot 4} = \frac{1}{64}$

4 to the negative third power

The 0 power of any nonzero number is 1.

$36^0 = 1$

33 Key Concepts Question Write each expression in standard form.

a. 10^{-8} **b.** 12^0 **c.** $3.98 \cdot 10^4$ **d.** $0.04 \div 0.1$

Section 4 Key Concepts

Key Terms

Multiplying and Dividing by Powers of Ten (pp. 196–197)

When multiplying and dividing by powers of ten, the exponent can help you decide where to place the decimal point.

Examples

$25.34 \cdot 10^3 = 25{,}340$ The decimal point **moves right 3** places.
$25.34 \div 10^4 = 0.002534$ The decimal point **moves left 4** places.
$25.34 \cdot 10^{-2} = 0.2534$ The decimal point **moves left 2** places.
$25.34 \div 10^{-1} = 253.4$ The decimal point **moves right 1** place.

Scientific notation is a method for writing large and small numbers.

scientific notation

Examples Write 5261 and 0.013 in scientific notation.

a number between 1 and 10

$5261 = 5.261 \cdot 1000 = 5.261 \cdot 10^3$ ← a power of 10
$0.013 = 1.3 \cdot 0.01 = 1.3 \cdot 10^{-2}$

34 Key Concepts Question Find each product.

a. $213.24 \cdot 10^{-4}$ **b.** $149.7 \cdot 10^{-5}$

c. $0.0049 \cdot 10^{-3}$ **d.** $0.01735 \cdot 10^6$

Section 4 Practice & Application Exercises

Write each number in words.

1. 2523.12 **2.** 0.987 **3.** 43.065 **4.** 1.00198

Write each number as a fraction or a mixed number.

5. 0.98 **6.** 23.7 **7.** 0.208 **8.** 0.0059

9. 1.0019 **10.** 3.24054 **11.** 10.085421 **12.** 15.06005

▲ Barbara Sampson used her knowledge of telecommunications to start her own business in 1986.

13. In 1992 women-owned businesses in the United States numbered 6.4 million and employed 13.2 million people. Why do you think these values are written this way? Write each value in standard form.

Replace each ? with >, <, or =.

14. 0.24 __?__ 0.240

15. 1.873 __?__ 1.875

16. 12.64 __?__ 11.65

17. 0.13 __?__ 0.126

18. 28.1 __?__ 2.81

19. 0.004 __?__ 0.040

Match each number with a point on the number line below.

20. 0.666 **21.** 1.0 **22.** 0.6 **23.** 0.9059

24. 0.95 **25.** 0.09 **26.** 0.500 **27.** 0.0075

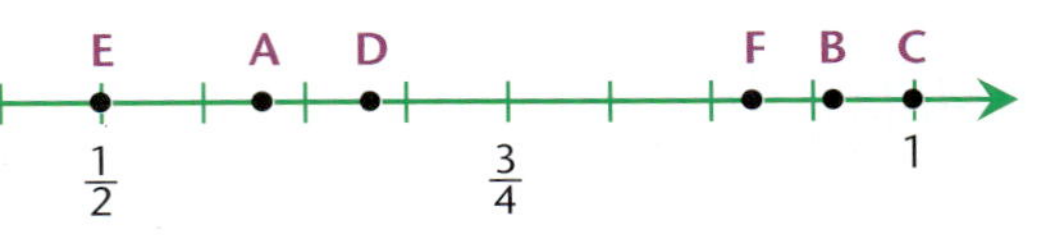

28. Open-ended Write three decimal numbers with corresponding points located between points *E* and *F* on the number line above.

29. History The Chinese used decimal fractions and place values as early as the third century A.D. A measurement of 3.142 *tshun* (Chinese inches) would have been expressed as 3 *tshun*, 1 *fen*, 4 *li*, 2 *hao*. What do you think the words *fen*, *li*, and *hao* mean?

30. Library Science Books are arranged on shelves in some libraries according to the *Dewey Decimal System*. List these Dewey decimal numbers in order from least to greatest: 513.01, 510.006, 510.42, 500.95, 510.4, 510.024, 513.52, 500.522, 510, 510.78.

Write each power of ten in standard form.

31. 10^2 **32.** 10^7 **33.** 10^1 **34.** 10^0

35. 10^{-1} **36.** 10^{-3} **37.** 10^{-4} **38.** 10^{-6}

Write each power as a fraction with its denominator in standard form.

39. 2^{-4} **40.** 3^{-2} **41.** 6^{-3} **42.** 2^{-8}

43. 5^{-4} **44.** 8^{-3} **45.** 12^{-2} **46.** 20^{-3}

Write each number in exponential form with base 10.

47. 1,000,000 **48.** 0.01 **49.** 10

50. 0.0001 **51.** 0.000001 **52.** 1

Atoms **Use the information below for Exercises 53–55.**

The hydrogen atom is the lightest atom. It has a diameter of 0.00000001 cm and a mass of $17 \cdot 10^{-25}$ g. It is so small that a drop of water contains 10^{21} hydrogen atoms.

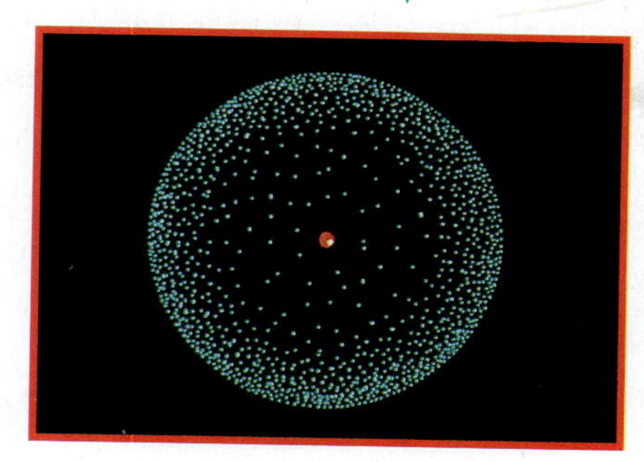

▲ Computer-generated image of hydrogen atom

53. Write the diameter in exponential form with base 10.

54. Write the mass as a fraction with its denominator in exponential form.

55. Write 10^{21} in standard form.

Write each product or quotient in standard form.

56. $3.6 \cdot 10^5$

57. $12.25 \cdot 10^{-3}$

58. $15.3612 \cdot 10^2$

59. $13.024 \cdot 10^4$

60. $101.397 \cdot 10^{-1}$

61. $0.139 \cdot 0.0001$

62. $0.2385 \cdot 1000$

63. $436 \div 10{,}000$

64. $58 \div 0.00001$

65. $5437 \div 10^3$

66. $0.0138 \div 10^{-4}$

67. $1.205 \div 10^2$

Write each number in scientific notation.

68. 32,405

69. 120,684

70. 98.335

71. 229.0098

72. 0.0052

73. 0.000075

Challenge **Write each product or quotient as a decimal.**

74. $\frac{2.8 \cdot 10^4}{7 \cdot 10^5}$

75. $(6 \cdot 10^3)(9 \cdot 10^{-5})$

Astronomy **Use the table.**

76. Write the distance of each moon from the planet it orbits. Use scientific notation.

77. Write the mass of each moon in standard form.

78. List the moons by mass from least to greatest.

Five Moons in the Solar System

Moon	Planet	Distance from planet (km)	Mass (kg)
Deimos	Mars	23,000	$2.00 \cdot 10^{15}$
Phobos	Mars	9,000	$1.08 \cdot 10^{16}$
Adrastea	Jupiter	129,000	$1.91 \cdot 10^{16}$
Leda	Jupiter	11,094,000	$5.68 \cdot 10^{15}$
Ananke	Jupiter	21,200,000	$3.82 \cdot 10^{16}$

Jupiter

Journal

Exercise 79 checks that you can relate place values and exponents.

Reflecting on the Section

Write your response to Exercise 79 in your journal.

79. Simon Stevin would have written 12.368 as 12⓪3①6②8③. Explain how the circled numbers he used in his notation are related to place values and exponents.

Spiral Review

Find each sum or difference. (Module 3, p. 183)

80. $2\frac{1}{4} + \frac{1}{8}$ **81.** $3\frac{2}{3} - 1\frac{1}{9}$ **82.** $\frac{1}{8} + 1\frac{2}{5}$ **83.** $4\frac{3}{5} - 2\frac{2}{15}$

Find the volume of a cube with each side length. (Module 1, p. 21)

84. 5 in. **85.** 10 ft **86.** 1 m **87.** 5 cm

Estimate each length or height using the unit in parentheses. (Toolbox, pp. 582–583)

88. a bed (feet) **89.** a door (inches) **90.** a flag pole (yards)

Extension

Products and Quotients of Powers

When two numbers in exponential form have the same base, the exponents can help you find their product or quotient.

91. Find each product or quotient. Then find the missing exponent.

a. $10^3 \cdot 10^1 = 10^?$ b. $2^5 \cdot 2^3 = 2^?$ c. $4^0 \cdot 4^3 = 4^?$

d. $2^{-5} \cdot 2^{-3} = 2^?$ e. $10^{-5} \cdot 10^2 = 10^?$ f. $9^3 \cdot 9^{-2} = 9^?$

g. $10^3 \div 10^1 = 10^?$ h. $2^5 \div 2^3 = 2^?$ i. $5^2 \div 5^3 = 5^?$

j. $4^0 \div 4^3 = 4^?$ k. $10^{-5} \div 10^2 = 10^?$ l. $9^3 \div 9^{-2} = 9^?$

92. Compare the exponents in each multiplication or division problem in Exercise 91 with the exponent in its answer. What pattern do you notice for the multiplication problems? for the division problems?

93. Write rules for multiplying and dividing powers with the same base.

Write each number as a fraction or mixed number in lowest terms.

1. 0.005
2. 0.14
3. 12.8
4. 1.225

Replace each ? with $>$, $<$, or $=$.

5. 0.342 ? 0.345
6. 1.84 ? 1.837
7. 12.2 ? 10.29
8. 0.091 ? 0.0910
9. 0.18 ? 0.175
10. 13.6 ? 1.36

Write each power of ten in standard form.

11. 10^3
12. 10^{-2}
13. 10^0
14. 10^4
15. 10^6
16. 10^{-7}
17. 10^5
18. 10^{-5}
19. 10^8
20. 10^1

Write each power as a fraction with its denominator in standard form.

21. 2^{-3}
22. 4^{-2}
23. 2^{-5}
24. 6^{-2}
25. 8^{-4}
26. 7^{-2}
27. 3^{-4}
28. 5^{-1}
29. 1^{-7}
30. 2^{-6}

Write each product or quotient in standard form.

31. $2.45 \cdot 0.001$
32. $10^2 \cdot 0.0488$
33. $129{,}723 \cdot 10^{-5}$
34. $10^{-3} \cdot 98.05$
35. $104.6 \div 10^2$
36. $6825 \div 10^{-4}$
37. $305.908 \div 10^{-3}$
38. $0.004 \div 10^{-6}$
39. $0.312 \div 10^2$

Write each number in scientific notation.

40. 1255
41. 0.0061
42. 36,040
43. 184,536
44. 0.00089
45. 1017.70
46. 0.836271
47. 905.33
48. 0.061

Standardized Testing ▶ Multiple Choice

1. Which is the greatest number?

   A. $\frac{127}{4}$ B. 40^{-3} C. 31.75 D. $3.18 \cdot 10^1$

2. Which number is the quotient $6.3 \div 10^2$?

   A. 630 B. 0.063 C. 10^{-2} D. 0.21

Section 5 Metric Units of Length

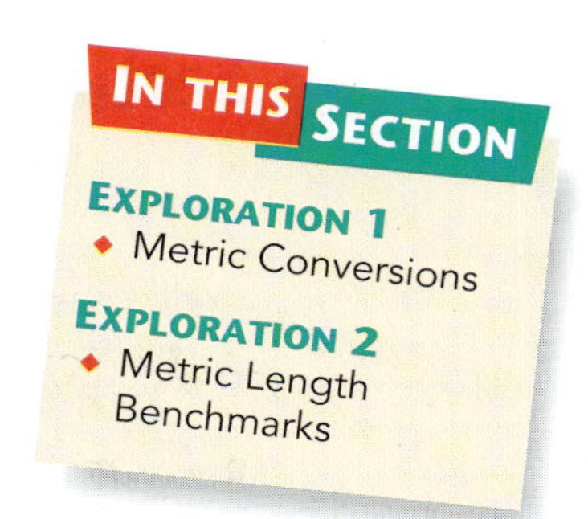

A Winning Measure

Setting the Stage

SET UP *Work in a group. You will need:* • *string* • *chalk or masking tape* • *scissors*

In the past, measurements were not universal. Many old systems of measure were based on lengths of parts of the body.

A span was the distance between the tips of the thumb and the little finger when the hand was spread open. What would happen in an Olympic competition if the lengths of standing jumps were measured using spans?

Make a starting line with tape or chalk. Take turns jumping as far as you can from a standing position. Have someone mark your ending position. Cut a piece of string the length of your jump.

Think About It

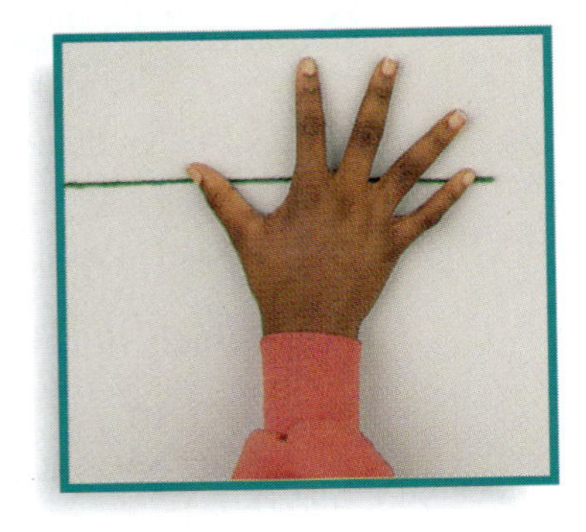

1. Look at the span of your own hand. Estimate the length of your jump in spans.

2. Measure the string using your span and compare it with your estimate. Make a table with two columns labeled *Student's name* and *Length of jump (in spans)*. In your table, record your name and the length of your jump in spans.

3. In your table, record the measures for your group.

4 Were all the jump measures in your group a whole number of spans? If not, how were parts of a span recorded?

5 Using only the results in your table, can you determine the longest jump in your group? Explain.

6 How many different spans do you think were used to measure the jumps of students in your class?

Exploration 1

GOAL

LEARN HOW TO...
- convert from one metric unit to another

AS YOU...
- look at long jump results

KEY TERMS
- meter (m)
- millimeter (mm)
- centimeter (cm)
- kilometer (km)

SET UP *Work in a group. You will need:* • *strings from the* Setting the Stage • *meter stick or metric measuring tape*

▶ **The creation of the metric system ended the confusion caused by using many different local systems of measure. Metric measures of length are based on the meter (m). The ruler below shows some parts of a meter.**

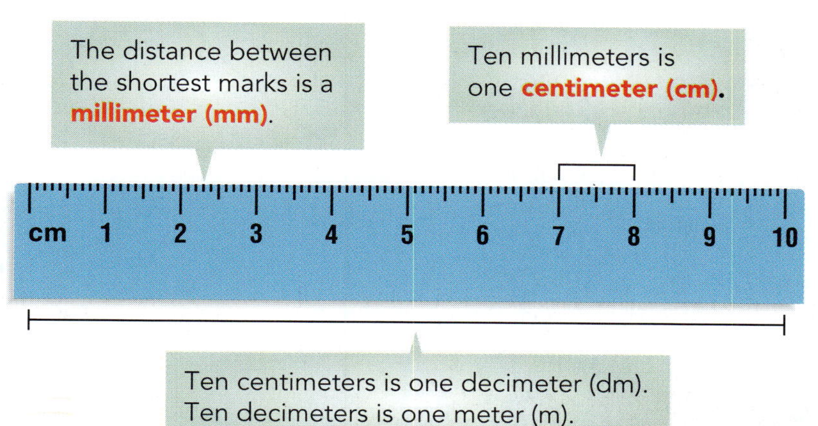

7 Use the diagram.

a. How many centimeters are in a meter?

b. How many millimeters are in a meter?

▶ **Longer units of length are also based on the meter.**

10 meters = 1 dekameter (dam)
10 dam = 1 hectometer (hm)
10 hm = 1 kilometer (km)

8 A **kilometer (km)** is a metric unit used to measure longer distances, such as highway distances. How many meters are in one kilometer?

9 **a.** How many kilometers are there in 1345 m? Explain.

b. How many centimeters are there in 9 km? Explain.

▶ **Converting Units** **The conversion chart shows the relationship between metric units of length.**

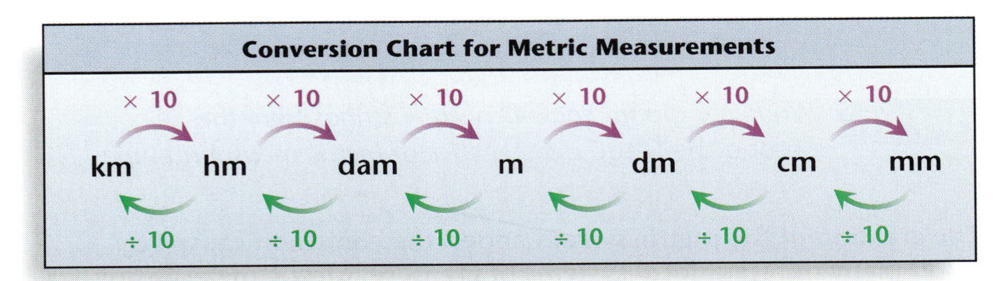

▶ **Metric measurements can be changed from one unit of measure to another by multiplying or dividing by powers of ten.**

EXAMPLE

4.5 m = __?__ cm

× 100

4.5 m = 450 cm

__?__ m = 500 cm

5 m = 500 cm

÷ 100

...checks that you know which operations to use when converting metric units.

10 **CHECKPOINT** Use the conversion chart to decide whether you multiply or divide by a power of ten in each case.

a. to convert from a longer unit of measure, such as kilometers, to a shorter unit of measure, such as centimeters

b. to convert from a shorter unit of measure, such as millimeters, to a longer unit of measure, such as meters

▶ **The most commonly used units of measure for metric length are the kilometer, meter, centimeter, and millimeter.**

11 What power of ten is used to convert between the given units?

a. millimeters and centimeters **b.** centimeters and meters

c. millimeters and meters **d.** meters and kilometers

12 ✓ **CHECKPOINT** Replace each _?_ with the correct measure.

a. 3.1 km = _?_ m **b.** 0.9 cm = _?_ m

c. 1.28 cm = _?_ mm **d.** 0.62 m = _?_ mm

✓ **QUESTION 12**

...checks that you can convert metric units of length.

13 **a.** Measure, to the nearest half of a centimeter, the string that represents the length of the jump you made in the *Setting the Stage.*

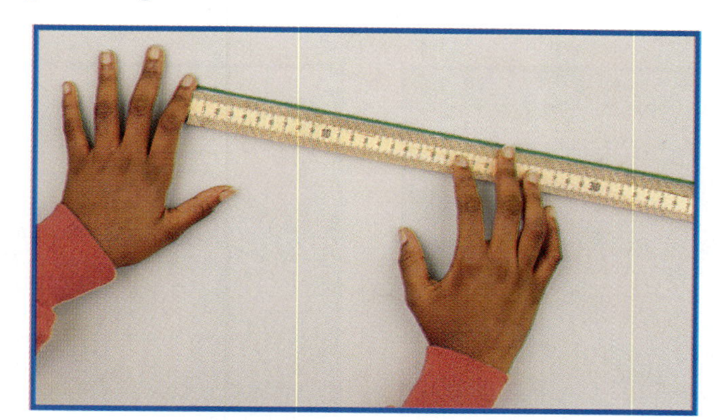

b. Make a table with four columns, labeled *Student's name*, *Centimeters*, *Millimeters*, *Meters*. Record your name and the length of your jump in centimeters.

c. Collect the results of part (a) from the other members in your group. Record their results in your table.

d. Use powers of ten to complete the *Millimeters* and *Meters* columns in your table.

14 Which member(s) of your group jumped farther than 0.5 m, but less than 175 cm?

15 Besides ending the confusion caused by using many different systems of measurement, what are some other advantages of the metric system?

HOMEWORK EXERCISES ▶ See Exs. 1–20 on pp. 211–212.

GOAL

LEARN HOW TO...
- recognize metric benchmarks
- use benchmarks to estimate lengths in metric units

AS YOU...
- estimate and measure lengths in your classroom

KEY TERM
- benchmark

Exploration 2

Metric Length Benchmarks

SET UP *You will need:* • *meter stick or metric tape measure* • *metric ruler*

You can use something whose measure you know as a benchmark to estimate lengths. The best benchmarks are ones that can be easily used in a variety of situations. Below are some items that could be used as benchmarks.

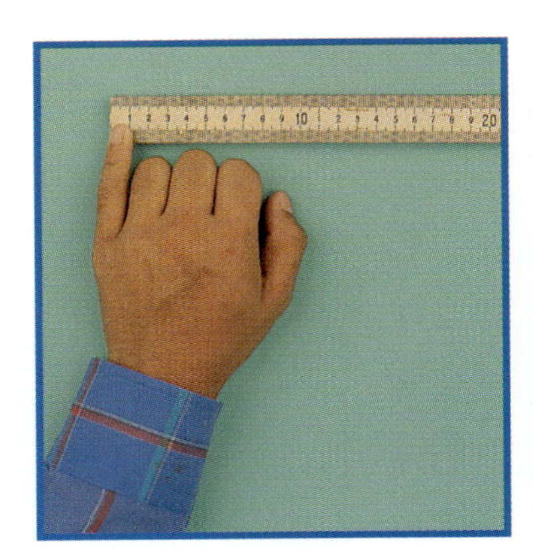

16 **Discussion** Look at the benchmarks.

a. What is an advantage of using your arm length as a benchmark? What is a disadvantage?

b. Is the width of a little finger a good benchmark for everyone to use for 1 cm? Explain.

17 Use a meter stick or a metric tape measure.

a. Hold the meter stick alongside you with one end touching the floor. About how far up does it reach?

b. The measurement in part (a) can serve as a benchmark for 1 m. Find examples of objects or distances in your classroom that represent about 1 m in length.

c. Explain why each item you found in part (b) would or would not make a good benchmark.

18 ✔ **CHECKPOINT** Estimate each measurement in the table in meters. Then measure the length in meters, record the measure, and compare your estimate with the actual measure.

...checks that you can use benchmarks to estimate lengths.

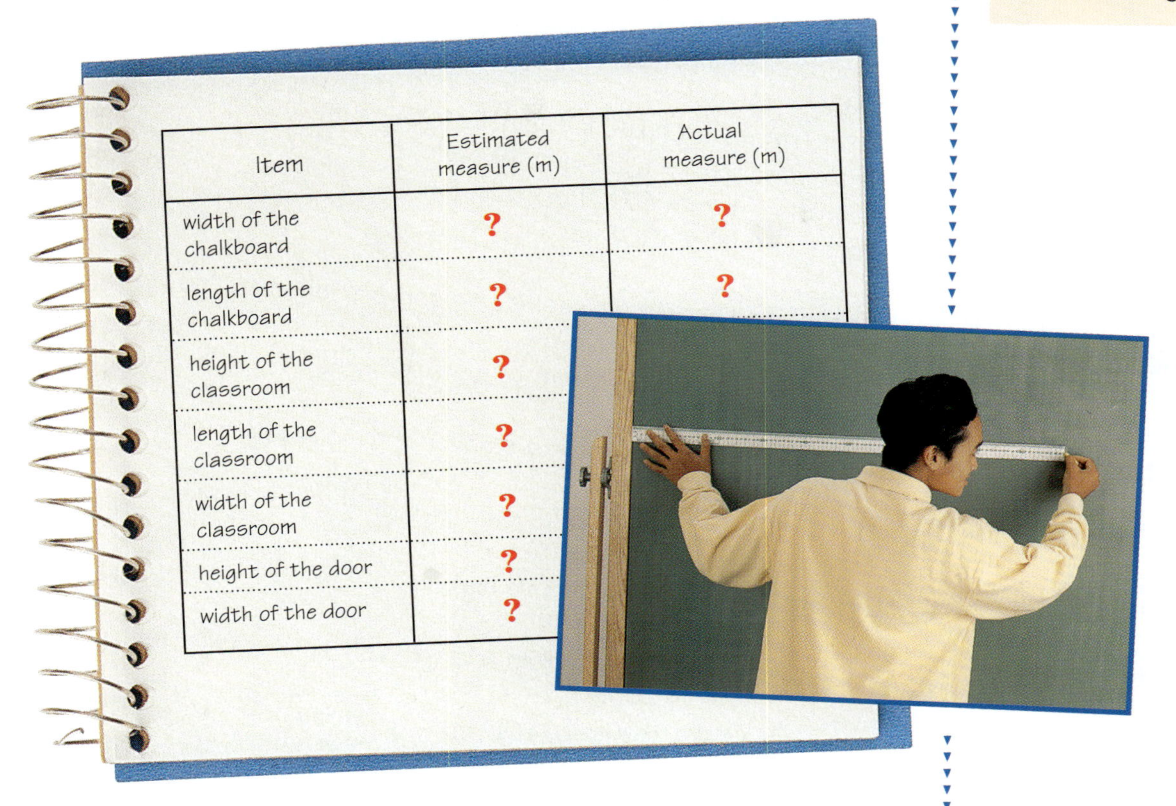

Item	Estimated measure (m)	Actual measure (m)
width of the chalkboard	?	?
length of the chalkboard	?	?
height of the classroom	?	
length of the classroom	?	
width of the classroom	?	
height of the door	?	
width of the door	?	

19 Find a convenient benchmark for each length.

a. 1 cm **b.** 5 cm **c.** 10 cm **d.** 20 cm

20 **a.** Use your benchmarks from Question 19 to estimate the length of each segment in centimeters.

A ____ *B*

C ________________________________ *D*

E ________________ *F*

G ____ *H*

b. Measure each segment to the nearest tenth of a centimeter. Compare the measurement with your estimates in part (a).

HOMEWORK EXERCISES ▶ **See Exs. 21–40 on pp. 212–213.**

Section 5 Key Concepts

Key Terms

Metric System (pp. 205–207)

The most commonly used metric units of length are related as follows:

meter (m)

1 meter (m) = 0.001 km, 100 cm, or 1000 mm

centimeter (cm)

1 centimeter (cm) = 0.01 m or 10 mm

millimeter (mm)

1 millimeter (mm) = 0.001 m or 0.1 cm

kilometer (km)

1 kilometer (km) = 1000 m

You can use these relationships to convert among units.

Example Convert 378 mm to centimeters.

You **divide** to convert from a smaller unit to a larger unit.

378 mm ÷ 10 = 37.8 cm

10 mm = 1 cm

Example Convert 2.4 km to meters.

You **multiply** to convert from a larger unit to a smaller unit.

2.4 km • 1000 = 2400 m

1000 m = 1 km

Benchmarks (pp. 208–209)

benchmark

The best benchmarks are ones that can be easily and conveniently used in a variety of situations.

Example Suzanne uses the length of her shoe as a benchmark for a measure of 25 cm. She estimates the width of a doorway as 4 shoe lengths, which is about 100 cm or 1 m.

21 Key Concepts Question Explain how you can use the relationships between the metric units of length to find out how many millimeters there are in a kilometer.

Section 5 Practice & Application Exercises

YOU WILL NEED

For Exs. 21–28, 40:
- metric ruler

For Ex. 40:
- customary ruler

1. Running competitions may use a course that is 3 km, 5 km, or 10 km long.
   a. Write the length, in meters, of each course.
   b. For an average person, 1 m is about two walking steps. About how many steps would it take an average person to walk each course?
   c. Suppose k represents a distance in kilometers and d represents the same distance in meters. Write a formula for converting from kilometers to meters.

Replace each ? with the correct measure.

2. 200 cm = __?__ m
3. 1.8 km = __?__ m
4. 8.75 cm = __?__ mm
5. 400 m = __?__ km
6. 3.2 km = __?__ cm
7. 68.04 mm = __?__ m
8. 5.06 cm = __?__ km
9. 600 km = __?__ mm

Replace each ? with $>$, $<$, or $=$.

10. 0.023 km __?__ 2.3 m
11. 4050 mm __?__ 4.05 m
12. 8 cm __?__ 10 mm
13. 12.4 cm __?__ 56.2 m
14. 9.05 cm __?__ 12 km
15. 3.8 mm __?__ 38 km

Animal Jump Records **The world record jumps of several animals are described using an inappropriate metric unit. Change the metric unit to one that gives a better idea of the distance each animal jumped.**

16. A dog named Bang jumped 914 cm while chasing a hare.
17. A South African sharp-nosed frog averaged 3400 mm for each jump in a triple-jump competition.
18. In an experiment done in 1910, a common flea jumped 0.00033 km.
19. In Australia, a female red kangaroo jumped 12,800 mm in the midst of a chase.

20. Challenge A decimeter is equal to ten centimeters and a hectometer is equal to ten thousand centimeters. What is the relationship between a decimeter and a hectometer? How many decimeters are in a hectometer?

Estimation **Use benchmarks to estimate and draw a segment with each length. Then check your estimates with a metric ruler.**

21. 3 cm **22.** 15 cm **23.** 21 cm **24.** 40 mm

25. 4 cm **26.** 105 mm **27.** 0.15 m **28.** 0.2 m

29. Writing Look at your answers to Exercises 24 and 25. Which measurement is more accurate? Explain.

Copy each measure. Then place a decimal point in the number so that the measure is reasonable for the object or animal shown.

30. length: 170 cm

31. height: 0.9 mm

32. width: 250 mm

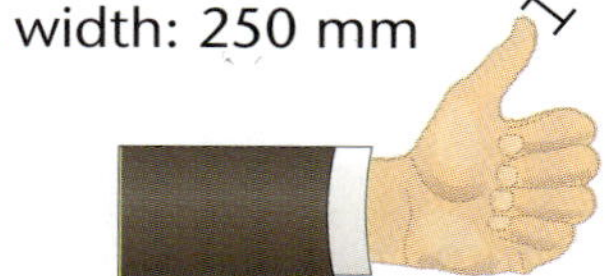

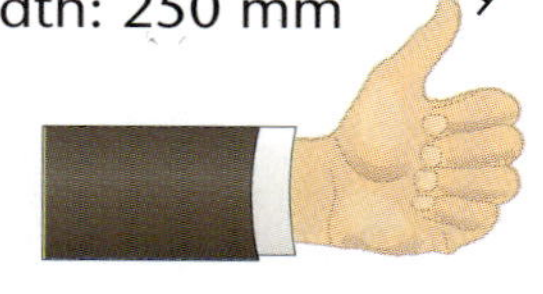

33. height: 125 m

34. length: 0.03 cm

Writing **Tell if each measure is *reasonable* or *unreasonable*. Compare the measures with others you have already estimated to support your answers. If a measure is unreasonable, give a better estimate.**

Example: length of a bed: 1 m — Unreasonable. Since most adults are between 1 m and 2 m tall, the length of a bed is about 2 m.

35. distance from floor to door knob: 2 m

36. length of a car: 5 m

37. distance from kitchen to living room: 90 m

38. height of a backyard fence: 9 m

39. length of a city swimming pool: 15 m

Reflecting on the Section

Be prepared to discuss your response to Exercise 40 in class.

40. The United States uses the inch, foot, yard, and mile as its customary units of length.

    a. Use a customary ruler and a meter stick to compare the length of a yard with that of a meter. Which is longer? Can you use the same benchmark for both a meter and a yard? Explain.

    b. Suppose the length of a race is 5 mi, or about 8 km, and you want to express that distance in smaller units. Using mental math, is it easier to convert the length of the race from miles to yards or from kilometers to meters? (1760 yd = 1 mi) Why?

> *Discussion*
>
> Exercise 40 checks that you can apply and compare measurements.

Write each number in exponential form with base 10. (Module 3, p. 198)

41. 1000 42. 0.001 43. 10 44. 1

Interpreting Data **In 1994 Alvin Straight, a 73-year-old man from Laurens, Iowa, rode his lawn mower to southwestern Wisconsin to visit his brother. Use the graph to answer the questions.** (Module 1, p. 7)

45. About how long did it take Alvin Straight to travel 25 mi? 10 mi?

46. About how far did Alvin Straight travel in $1\frac{1}{2}$ h? in $3\frac{1}{2}$ h?

Alvin Straight's Lawn Mower Trip

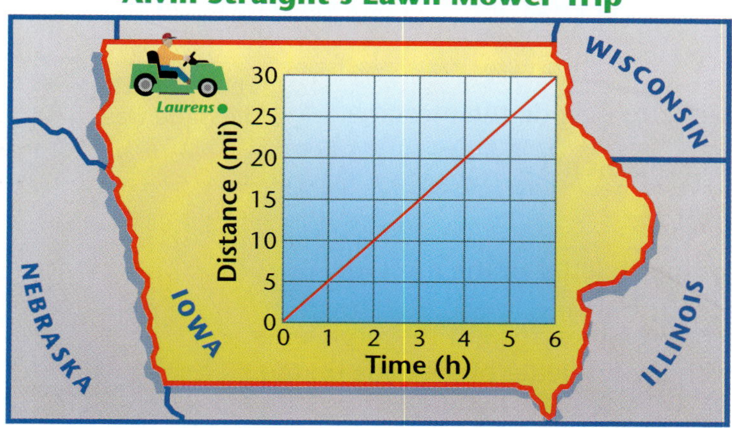

Solve each equation. Then check each solution. (Module 2, p. 137)

47. $20 = n - 5$ 48. $n + 17 = 44$ 49. $n - 11 = 35$

50. $-8 + n = 22$ 51. $5 + n = -7$ 52. $49 = n - 100$

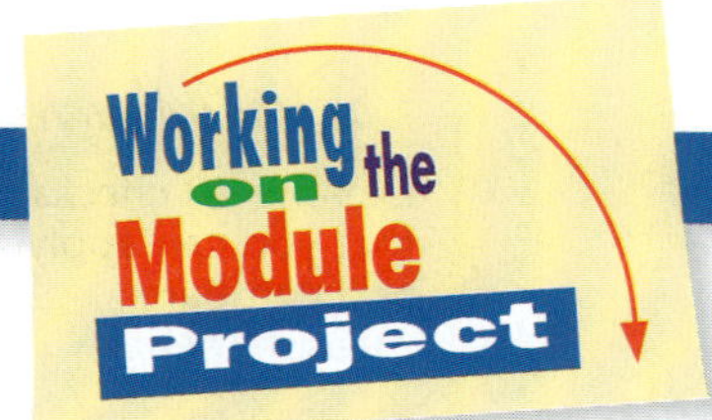

Secret Codes

Understanding the Problem Suppose you came across a cash register receipt like the one shown below. You probably would not think it was a secret message, but it is! Each of the numbers 23 23 5 19 30 26 33 26 26 29 15 represents a letter.

 **7** Describe strategies that you can use to try to break the code.

The code used on the receipt is similar to the Caesar shift code described on page 160, but each letter of the message is shifted by a different amount, and different numbers can represent the same letter.

The code phrase THANK YOU determines how much each letter is shifted. Each letter in THANK YOU is given a number based on the letter's position in the alphabet (A = 1, B = 2, and so on).

8 The table shows how the message can be decoded. Copy the table and complete the first two columns by writing the numbers on the receipt and the letters of the code phrase THANK YOU.

Code number	Code letter	Code letter's position in the alphabet	Decoded letter's position in the alphabet	Decoded letter
23	T	20	3	C
23	H	8	15	O
5	A	1	4	D

Thank You!
$23.23
5.19
30.26
33.26
26.29
15.00

The third letter of the message was shifted 1 place. 4 + 1 = 5

 **9** The equation $c - s = p$ can be used to decode the message.

a. What do you think c, s, and p represent?

b. How can you find the value of s?

c. Use the equation to find the fourth letter of the message.

10 **a.** Complete the table and decode the message. (At the ninth letter of the message, start over with the first letter of the code phrase.)

b. What was used to end the message?

 **11** **a.** Use a code word or phrase to write a message to a partner.

b. Can you decode your partner's secret message without the code word or phrase?

Section 5 Extra Skill Practice

Replace each __?__ with the correct measure.

1. 482 m = __?__ cm
2. 125 mm = __?__ cm
3. 5 km = __?__ mm
4. 300 m = __?__ km
5. 32 mm = __?__ m
6. 7.01 cm = __?__ m
7. 39.6 km = __?__ cm
8. 1.85 m = __?__ mm
9. 500.8 mm = __?__ m
10. 3.24 km = __?__ mm

Replace each __?__ with >, <, or =.

11. 43 mm __?__ 12 cm
12. 2.4 km __?__ 2400 mm
13. 88,000 m __?__ 88 km
14. 14 cm __?__ 8 km
15. 75 cm __?__ 0.3 m
16. 13 mm __?__ 1300 m
17. 5.1 cm __?__ 634 mm
18. 33 m __?__ 3300 cm
19. 427.99 km __?__ 500,000 cm
20. 654.2 cm __?__ 70,000 m

Copy each measure. Then place a decimal point in the number so that the measure is reasonable.

21. thickness of a dictionary: 600 mm
22. height of a table: 70 m
23. length of a pen: 1450 cm
24. length of a school bus: 115 m
25. width of a door: 0.8 cm
26. length of an eraser (not on a pencil): 5000 mm

Standardized Testing ▶ Open-ended

Think of something that would make a good benchmark for estimating each measure. Explain how you would use each benchmark and why it is convenient in that situation.

a. the width of a bedroom
b. the length of a goldfish
c. the height of a tree
d. the length of a street
e. the height of a cat
f. the distance around a finger

a. Could the receiver decode the message correctly?
b. Could the eavesdroppers break your code?

Section 6 Extra Skill Practice

Tell whether each set of side lengths *can* or *cannot* form a triangle. If they can, tell whether the triangle is *isosceles, equilateral,* or *scalene*.

1. 8 cm, 9 cm, 14 cm
2. 23 in., 23 in., 16 in.
3. 7 km, 16 km, 25 km
4. 16 in., 16 in., 20 in.

MODULE 3 Review and Assessment

Find the prime factorization of each number. (Sec. 1, Explor. 1)

1. 12
2. 21
3. 24
4. 42
5. 68

Find the greatest common factor (GCF) and the least common multiple (LCM) of each group of numbers. (Sec. 1, Explors. 2–3)

6. 6, 8
7. 36, 90
8. 25, 30, 75
9. 20, 42, 280

Replace each __?__ with >, <, or =. (Sec. 2, Explor. 1)

10. $\frac{3}{20}$ __?__ $\frac{4}{25}$
11. $\frac{2}{9}$ __?__ $\frac{1}{4}$
12. $\frac{5}{7}$ __?__ $\frac{3}{5}$
13. $\frac{4}{21}$ __?__ $\frac{12}{63}$

14. Suppose a coin is tossed 3 times in a row and the results of the tosses are recorded in order. (Sec. 2, Explor. 3)
    a. Draw a tree diagram to represent all the possible outcomes.
    b. What is the probability that the second toss is a head?

Find each sum or difference. (Sec. 2, Explor. 2; and Sec. 3, Explors. 1 and 2)

15. $2\frac{4}{9} + 3\frac{1}{3}$
16. $1\frac{7}{8} - 1\frac{1}{6}$
17. $8\frac{3}{5} - 4\frac{9}{10}$
18. $14 + 3\frac{12}{25}$

Write each number as a fraction or a mixed number in lowest terms. (Sec. 4, Explor. 1)

19. 0.075
20. 12.25
21. 87.00340
22. 0.100005
23. 3.00528

24. Write two decimal numbers that are between 2.815 and 2.82. (Sec. 4, Explor. 1)

Replace each __?__ with >, <, or =. (Sec. 4, Explor. 1)

25. 0.87 __?__ 0.8695
26. 3.05 __?__ 3.10
27. 6.8 __?__ 6.800

Write each number as a fraction with its denominator in standard form. (Sec. 4, Explor. 2)

28. 10^{-5}
29. 5^{-3}
30. 1^{-9}
31. 6^{-1}
32. 11^{-2}

Write each product or quotient in standard form. (Sec. 4, Explor. 3)

33. $25.32 \cdot 10^5$
34. $25.32 \cdot 0.001$
35. $25.32 \div 10{,}000$
36. $25.32 \div 0.01$

Write each number in scientific notation. (Sec. 4, Explor. 3)

37. 8,900,000,000
38. 342,000
39. 0.00038
40. 12.0056

Replace each ? with the correct measure. (Sec. 5, Explor. 1)

41. 35 cm = __?__ mm

42. 3 m = __?__ cm

43. 440 m = __?__ km

Tell whether each measure is *reasonable* or *unreasonable*. Explain your choice. (Sec. 5, Explor. 2)

44. the height of a desk from the floor to the desk top: 90 cm

45. the length of a jump rope: 0.002 km

Tell whether segments with the given side lengths *can* or *cannot* form a triangle. If they can, classify the triangle as *isosceles, equilateral,* or *scalene.* (Sec. 6, Explor. 1)

46. 3 km, 5 km, 4 km

47. 2 cm, 10 cm, 13 cm

48. 1 ft, 1 ft, 1 ft

Solve. Check each answer. (Sec. 6, Explor. 2)

49. $6x = 216$

50. $\frac{y}{2} = 14$

51. $51 = 3m$

52. $22 = \frac{n}{6}$

53. Look at the checkered flag. (Sec. 6, Explor. 2)

a. Write an equation that shows how the total area of the black squares in the flag is related to the area of the flag. Be sure to identify any variables you use.

b. Use your equation to find the total area of the black squares if the area of the flag is 60 in.^{2}.

c. Use your equation to find the area of the flag if the total area of the black squares is 24 in.^{2}.

Reflecting on the Module

54. Writing Explain how mathematics is a universal language. To make your point, give examples using at least two of the mathematical ideas you have learned in this module.

MODULE
4
THE ART OF
MOTION

Section 5 Extra Skill Practice

Replace each ? with the correct measure.

1. 482 m = ___?___ cm
2. 125 mm = ___?___ cm
3. 5 km = ___?___ mm
4. 300 m = ___?___ km
5. 32 mm = ___?___ m
6. 7.01 cm = ___?___ m
7. 39.6 km = ___?___ cm
8. 1.85 m = ___?___ mm
9. 500.8 mm = ___?___ m
10. 3.24 km = ___?___ mm

Replace each ? with > , < , or = .

11. 43 mm ___?___ 12 cm
12. 2.4 km ___?___ 2400 mm
13. 88,000 m ___?___ 88 km
14. 14 cm ___?___ 8 km
15. 75 cm ___?___ 0.3 m
16. 13 mm ___?___ 1300 m
17. 5.1 cm ___?___ 634 mm
18. 33 m ___?___ 3300 cm
19. 427.99 km ___?___ 500,000 cm
20. 654.2 cm ___?___ 70,000 m

Copy each measure. Then place a decimal point in the number so that the measure is reasonable.

21. thickness of a dictionary: 600 mm
22. height of a table: 70 m
23. length of a pen: 1450 cm
24. length of a school bus: 115 m
25. width of a door: 0.8 cm
26. length of an eraser (not on a pencil): 5000 mm

Standardized Testing  Open-ended

Think of something that would make a good benchmark for estimating each measure. Explain how you would use each benchmark and why it is convenient in that situation.

a. the width of a bedroom
b. the length of a goldfish
c. the height of a tree
d. the length of a street
e. the height of a cat
f. the distance around a finger

Section 6 Triangles and Equations

EXPLORATION 1
- Constructing Triangles

EXPLORATION 2
- Multiplication and Division Equations

Symbols of the People

Setting the Stage

People have been sending messages using shapes and symbols for hundreds of years. Flags and banners can express ideas and communicate information without words. The designs of many of these flags are based on geometric concepts.

Navigation

▲ This flag shows the *International Code of Signals* symbol for "person overboard."

Humanitarian Services

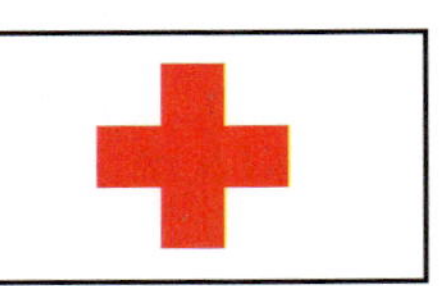

▲ In many countries of the world this *Flag of Healing* is the sign of emergency medical assistance.

Sports

▲ Flags such as this checkered flag are used in some sports to signal the referee or the participants.

Think About It

1 Find an example of each geometric figure on one of the flags.

a. a rectangle **b.** a triangle **c.** an acute angle **d.** a right angle

e. a pair of triangles that are the same size and shape

2 **a.** What is the checkered flag used for?

b. What fraction of the checkered flag is black?

Exploration 1

Constructing TRIANGLES

SET UP *You will need:* • *Labsheet 6A* • *metric ruler* • *compass*

GOAL

LEARN HOW TO...
- classify triangles by side length
- construct triangles and circles
- determine which side lengths will form a triangle

AS YOU...
- examine flags

KEY TERMS
- congruent
- isosceles
- equilateral
- scalene
- circle
- center
- radius
- chord
- diameter
- arc
- construction

Many nations around the world have a national flag to symbolize their country. Some of these flags contain triangles.

Use Labsheet 6A for Questions 3–5.

3 Follow the directions on the labsheet to measure and group the triangles on the *Flags with Triangles*.

4 **Discussion** One way to classify triangles is by the lengths of their sides. Two segments that are equal in length are **congruent**. Did anyone in your class group the triangles using 0, 2, and 3 congruent sides? What other groupings were used?

▶ **Some of the triangles you measured on Labsheet 6A had at least two congruent sides. These triangles are isosceles. Triangles with three congruent sides are equilateral. If all its sides are different lengths, a triangle is scalene.**

5 **a.** Classify each triangle you measured as *isosceles, equilateral*, or *scalene*.

b. Which triangles can be classified more than one way? Why?

6 **CHECKPOINT** Classify the triangle with each set of side lengths as *isosceles, equilateral*, or *scalene*. Be as specific as possible.

a. 7 in., 5 in., 3 in. **b.** 1 m, 1 m, 1 m **c.** 2 cm, 4 cm, 4 cm

...checks that you can classify triangles.

7 Use your ruler to draw each triangle and label the side lengths.

a. isosceles triangle that is not equilateral **b.** equilateral triangle

c. scalene triangle with 5 cm, 8 cm, and 9 cm sides

▶ **Some triangles are more difficult to draw than others. A compass is one tool that can make the job easier if you know how to use it.**

Student Resource

Compasses and Circles

You can use a compass to construct a *circle*.

To construct a circle, mark the *center C* of the circle. Place the tip of the compass on *C* and make a complete rotation.

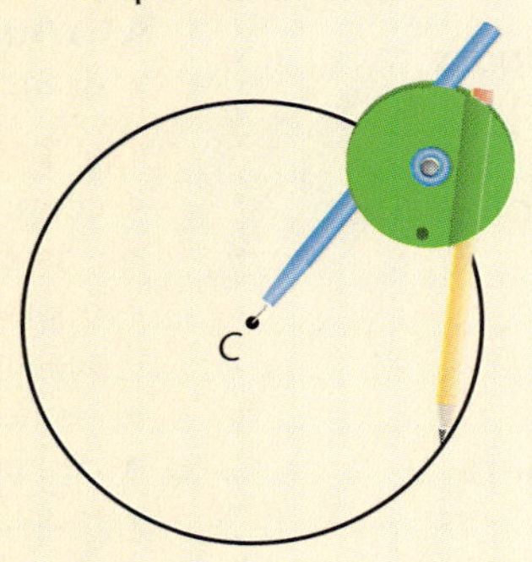

A **circle** is the set of all points in a plane that are the same distance from a given point called the **center**.

A segment such as $\overline{CD}$ whose endpoints are the center and any point on the circle is a **radius** of the circle. The length of any radius is called *the* radius.

A segment such as $\overline{AB}$ whose endpoints are both on the circle is a **chord**.

Any chord such as $\overline{EF}$ that passes through the center of a circle is a **diameter** of the circle. The length of any diameter is called *the* diameter.

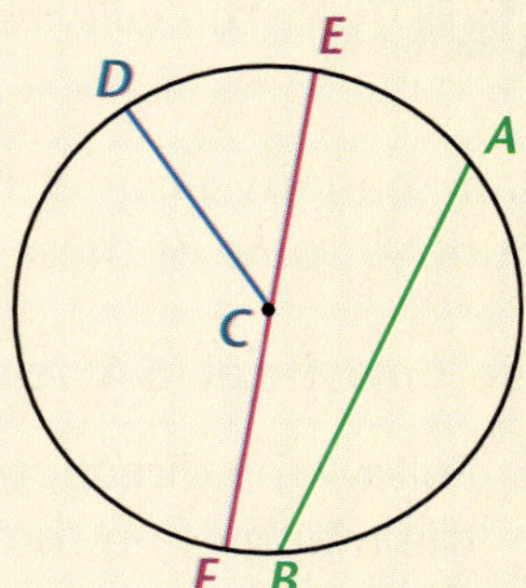

8 Construct a triangle with sides of length 4 cm, 6 cm, and 8 cm.

Step 1 Draw an 8 cm segment with endpoints *A* and *B*.

Step 2 Open your compass to a radius of 6 cm. Place the tip on *A*. Draw an *arc* below $\overline{AB}$.

An **arc** is part of a circle.

Step 3 Open your compass to a radius of 4 cm. Place the tip on *B*. Draw an arc that intersects the first arc.

Step 4 Label the intersection point *C*. Draw segments $\overline{AC}$ and $\overline{BC}$ to complete the triangle.

▶ **You can draw some figures using just a straightedge and a compass. Drawings made this way are called constructions.**

9 If possible, construct a triangle with the side lengths given. If not, explain why not. Label the sides with their lengths.

a. 1 cm, 3 cm, 6 cm **b.** 2 cm, 3 cm, 4 cm

10 **a.** **Try This as a Class** What relationship must exist among the lengths of three segments for them to form a triangle?

b. Change one side length in a set of three side lengths in Question 9 so that they will form a triangle.

11 ✓ **CHECKPOINT** Tell whether segments with the given lengths *can* or *cannot* form a triangle. If they can, construct the triangle.

a. 2 cm, 3 cm, 8 cm **b.** 5 cm, 7 cm, 9 cm

✓ **QUESTION 11**

...checks that you can tell whether 3 segments form a triangle, and that you can construct a triangle.

HOMEWORK EXERCISES ▶ See Exs. 1–10 on p. 224.

Exploration 2

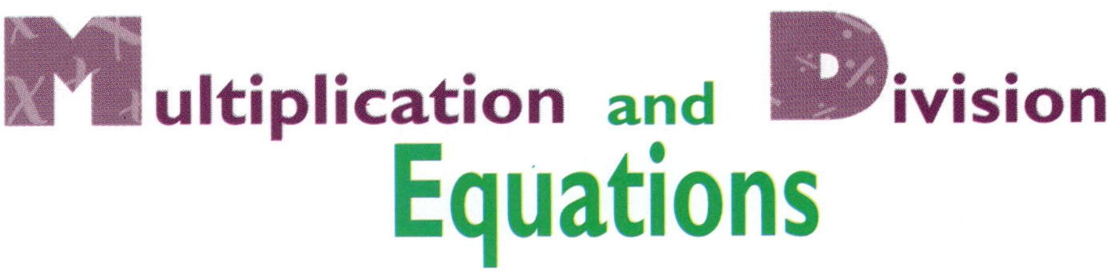

GOAL

LEARN HOW TO...
- write and solve multiplication and division equations

AS YOU...
- explore size relationships in flag designs

SET UP *You will need a metric ruler.*

A country's flag may come in different sizes, but the relationships between the shapes in the design must stay the same.

12 The state flag of Spain is shown.

a. Measure the widths of the stripes to the nearest centimeter.

b. Describe the relationship between the widths.

13 Copy the table. Use the relationship you described in Question 12(b) on page 219 to complete the table.

Spain's State Flag in Different Sizes						
Width of yellow stripe (cm)	10	14	?	18	?	15
Width of each red stripe (cm)	?	?	6	?	5.5	?

14 Sometimes a relationship can be described by different equations. In each equation, y is the width of the yellow stripe and r is the width of one red stripe on Spain's state flag. Choose the letters of the equations that correctly describe the relationship between y and r.

A. $2y = r$ **B.** $y = 2r$ **C.** $\frac{r}{2} = y$

D. $\frac{y}{2} = r$ **E.** $y = \frac{1}{2}r$ **F.** $r = \frac{1}{2}y$

▶ **Since flags come in different sizes, mathematical language is often used to describe the flags so the designs will be made with the correct dimensions. In *Flags of the World*, by E. M. C. Barraclough, a description of the flag of Denmark includes the following lines.**

"... the width of the cross is one seventh the hoist, the rectangles at the hoist are squares with sides three sevenths of the hoist, and the length of the rectangles in the fly is half as much again as that of the squares."

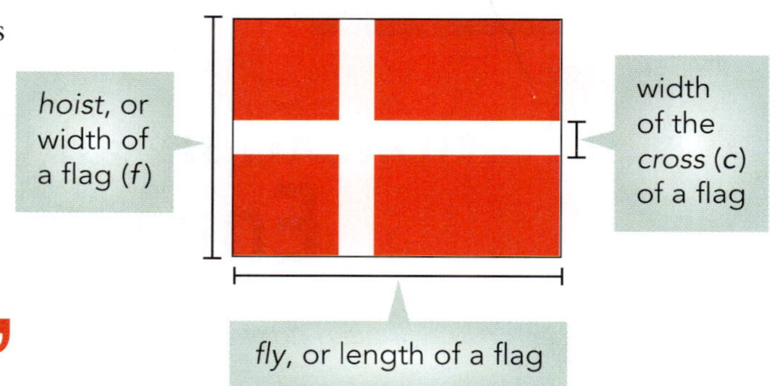

▶ **A verbal description can be used to write an equation.**

Description in Words	Equation
The width of the cross is one seventh the hoist.	$c = \frac{1}{7}f$, where c = width of cross, and f = width of flag (hoist).

15 Write an equation for this description of Denmark's flag. *The width of the flag is seven times the width of the cross.*

16 ✓ **CHECKPOINT** Write an equation to describe each relationship. Identify any variables you use.

a. The width of Jamaica's flag is half the length of the flag.

◀ Each color on Jamaica's flag is a symbol—green for hope, black for hardships, and gold for sunlight.

b. The width of India's flag is three times the width of one of the stripes.

◀ The wheel at the center of India's flag is the *Dharma Chakra*, or Wheel of Law.

...checks that you can write an equation to describe a relationship.

17 The relationship between the width of the cross on Denmark's flag and the width of the flag itself can be written in two ways.

Description in words	Equation
The width of the cross c is one seventh the width of the flag f.	$c = \frac{1}{7}f$
The width of the flag f is seven times the width of the cross c.	$7c = f$

a. Use one of the equations to find the width of the cross when the width of the flag is 21 in.

b. Which equation did you use? Why?

18 **Discussion** Inverse operations can help you see how the equations above are related.

$7c = f$

Step 1 $\frac{7c}{7} = \frac{f}{7}$

Step 2 $c = \frac{f}{7}$, or $c = \frac{1}{7}f$

Dividing by 7 is the same as multiplying by $\frac{1}{7}$.

a. In Step 1, what is the result of dividing $7c$ by 7? Why?

b. Why is f divided by 7 in Step 1?

▶ **You can use the method above to solve equations. Look at the example on the next page.**

EXAMPLE

Use the equation $7c = f$ to find the width of the cross (c) when the width of the flag (f) is 17.5 in.

$$7c = f$$

Substitute **17.5** for **f**.

$$7c = 17.5$$

$$\frac{7c}{7} = \frac{17.5}{7}$$

Divide both sides of the equation by **7**.

$$c = 2.5$$

Check: $7c = 17.5$

$7(2.5) \stackrel{?}{=} 17.5$

$17.5 = 17.5$ ✔

The width of the cross is 2.5 in.

✔ QUESTION 19

...checks that you can solve equations by dividing.

19 ✔ CHECKPOINT Solve. Check each solution.

a. $3x = 24$ **b.** $40 = 5x$ **c.** $4x = 72$

20 Try This as a Class Suppose the cross on a flag of Denmark is 4 in. wide. The equation $c = \frac{f}{7}$ can be used to find the width of the flag. Write an explanation to replace each ? in boxes (a) and (b). Then answer the questions in box (c).

$$c = \frac{f}{7}$$

a. ?

$$4 = \frac{f}{7}$$

$$7 \cdot 4 = 7 \cdot \frac{f}{7}$$

b. ?

$$28 = f$$

c. What is the result of multiplying $\frac{f}{7}$ by 7? Why?

Check: $c = \frac{f}{7}$

$4 \stackrel{?}{=} \frac{28}{7}$

$4 = 4$ ✔

✔ QUESTION 21

...checks that you can solve equations by multiplying.

21 ✔ CHECKPOINT Solve. Check each answer.

a. $\frac{y}{2} = 49$ **b.** $113 = \frac{1}{3}x$ **c.** $\frac{z}{5} = 2021$

22 Use the equations you wrote in Question 16.

a. If the width of a Jamaican flag is 24 in., what is the length?

b. If the width of an Indian flag is 27 in., what is the width of one of its stripes?

HOMEWORK EXERCISES ▶ See Exs. 11–24 on pp. 224–225.

Section 6 Key Concepts

Classifying and Constructing Triangles (pp. 217–219)

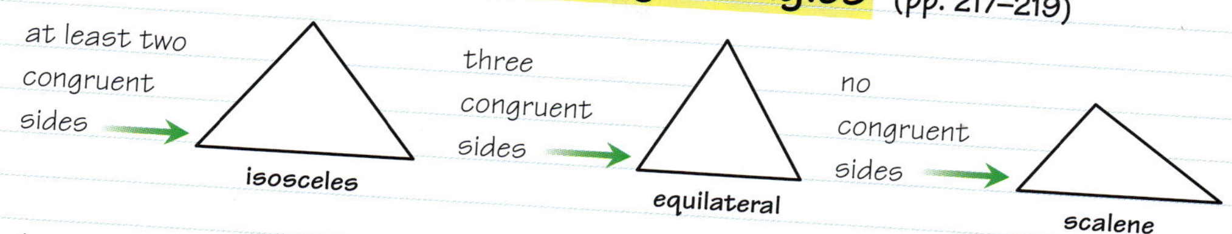

A triangle can be constructed if the sum of the lengths of any two sides is greater than the length of the third side.

Example A triangle cannot be formed since $2 + 1 < 4$.

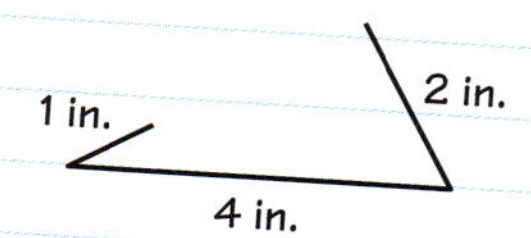

Multiplication and Division Equations (pp. 219–222)

Multiplication and division can be used to solve equations.

Example

Divide both sides by 3.

$3x = 54$

$\frac{3x}{3} = \frac{54}{3}$

$x = 18$

Check: $3x = 54$

$3 \cdot 18 \stackrel{?}{=} 54$

$54 = 54$ ✓

Example

Multiply both sides by 2.

$\frac{y}{2} = 37$

$2 \cdot \frac{y}{2} = 2 \cdot 37$

$y = 74$

Check: $\frac{y}{2} = 37$

$\frac{74}{2} \stackrel{?}{=} 37$

$37 = 37$ ✓

Key Terms

congruent

isosceles

equilateral

scalene

construction

circle
- **center**
- **radius**
- **chord**
- **diameter**
- **arc**

23 Key Concepts Question The lengths of two sides of a triangle are 3 in. and 7 in.

a. What whole-inch lengths will work for the third side?

b. Which lengths from part (a) will make the triangle isosceles? scalene?

c. Suppose that twice the length x of the third side is equal to the sum of the lengths of the other two sides. Find x.

Section 6

Practice & Application Exercises

YOU WILL NEED

For Exs. 1–3, 10:
- compass
- ruler

Use a compass and a ruler to construct each triangle. Label the sides with their lengths.

1. an isosceles triangle with sides of length 4 in., 4 in., and 5 in.

2. a scalene triangle with sides of length 2 in., 3 in., and 4 in.

3. an equilateral triangle with sides of length $3\frac{1}{2}$ in.

Tell whether each set of side lengths *can* or *cannot* form a triangle. If a triangle can be formed, tell whether the triangle is *isosceles, equilateral,* or *scalene.*

4. 3 in., 3 in., 5 in.
5. 2 km, 4 km, 6 km
6. 9 cm, 9 cm, 9 cm
7. 3.2 m, 4.1 m, 7 m
8. 7 m, 12 m, 23 m
9. $7\frac{1}{2}$ in., 8 in., 15 in.

10. **Create Your Own** Use a compass and a ruler.
    a. Design a rectangular flag. Include one or more triangles in your design.
    b. Give the side lengths of each triangle and classify each triangle as either *isosceles*, *equilateral*, or *scalene*.
    c. What are the dimensions of your flag? Find its area.
    d. What other geometric shapes are part of your flag design?

FOR ▶ HELP with finding the *area of a rectangle*, see **TOOLBOX, p. 593**

Solve. Check each answer.

11. $3w = 27$
12. $12y = 36$
13. $\frac{z}{3} = 6$
14. $5x = 25$
15. $15y = 300$
16. $9 = \frac{1}{3}x$
17. $\frac{r}{50} = 8$
18. $128 = 4z$

Write a multiplication equation to model each situation. Then solve each equation.

19. There are 3 times as many volunteers this year as last year. Last year there were 12 volunteers.

20. A population has doubled in 8 years. Eight years ago the population was 12,000.

21. A farm has 5 times as many chickens as pigs. The farm has 6 pigs.

22. The width of an enlarged photograph was 8 times its original size of 3 in. × 5 in.

23. Jen volunteers at the school store. This year she sold 4 times as many pens as last year.

a. Write an equation using two variables to describe the relationship between the numbers of pens sold this year and last year. Identify the variables you use.

b. Use the same variables as in part (a) to write a different equation describing the same relationship.

c. If Jen sold 76 pens this year, how many did she sell last year?

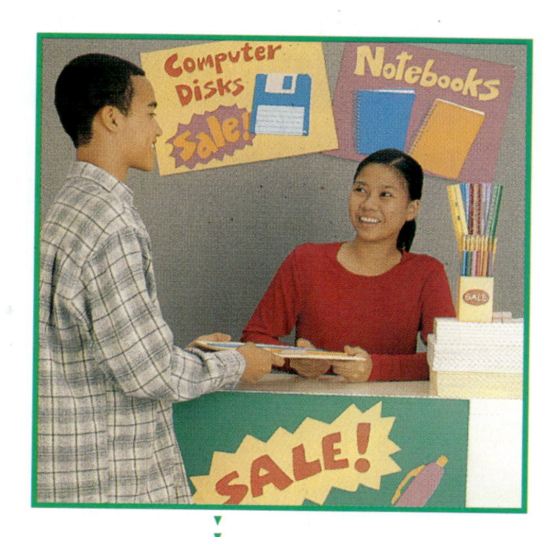

Reflecting on the Section

Be prepared to discuss your response to Exercise 24 in class.

24. **a.** The side lengths of three equilateral triangles are x, y, and z. Length y is three times length x and twice length z. Write an equation that shows the relationship between x and y.

b. Suppose the value of x is 4 in. Find the value of y.

c. What is the value of z when x is 4 in.? Explain.

Discussion

Exercise 24 checks that you can apply ideas about triangles.

Spiral Review

Replace each ? with the correct measure. (Module 3, p. 210)

25. 300 cm = __?__ m

26. 4.6 km = __?__ m

27. 9.75 cm = __?__ mm

28. 10.84 cm = __?__ km

29. The temperature is –28°F at 7 P.M. It falls 15°F that night, then rises x°F to a temperature of –34°F by noon the next day. (Module 2, p. 109)

a. Write an equation involving x to describe the situation.

b. Solve the equation to find the value of x.

Find the perimeter of a rectangle with each length l and width w. (Toolbox, p. 593)

30. $l = 4$ cm, $w = 6$ cm

31. $l = 2$ in., $w = 18$ in.

32. $l = 15$ m, $w = 20$ m

33. $l = 2$ ft, $w = 3\frac{1}{2}$ ft

Section 6 Extra Skill Practice

Tell whether each set of side lengths *can* or *cannot* form a triangle. If they can, tell whether the triangle is *isosceles, equilateral,* or *scalene.*

1. 8 cm, 9 cm, 14 cm
2. 23 in., 23 in., 16 in.
3. 7 km, 16 km, 25 km
4. 16 in., 16 in., 20 in.
5. 4.7 m, 4.7 m, 4.7 m
6. 7.2 in., 9.8 in., 17 in.
7. 32 ft, 42 ft, 52 ft
8. 3.2 ft, 3.4 ft, 4.2 ft
9. 12 mm, 12 mm, 28 mm
10. $8\frac{1}{2}$ yd, $11\frac{3}{4}$ yd, 3 yd

Solve. Check each answer.

11. $\frac{x}{4} = 9$
12. $7q = 56$
13. $2 = \frac{y}{5}$
14. $430 = 10k$
15. $11 = \frac{y}{9}$
16. $\frac{x}{3} = 60$
17. $8x = 120$
18. $12y = 60$
19. $\frac{z}{25} = 3$
20. $6h = 132$
21. $56 = 4y$
22. $1 = \frac{x}{12}$

Write a multiplication or division equation to model each situation. Then solve each equation.

23. There were twice as many students in the chorus this year as last year. Last year there were 39 students in the chorus.
24. John saved 5 times as much money for the trip as Steve did. John saved $60.

Standardized Testing ▸ Free Response

1. Use a compass and a metric ruler to draw an example of each type of triangle that has a 7 cm long side and a 3 cm long side. Label the side lengths.

   a. isosceles triangle

   b. scalene triangle

2. One banner is 3 times as long as a second banner. The first banner is $8\frac{1}{2}$ ft long. Write a multiplication equation to model the situation. Then solve the equation.

Secret Codes

SET UP *Work with a partner.*

In this module, you explored several types of secret codes and some of the techniques used to create them. Now you are ready to create your own.

Design a secret code. Your secret code must:

- include a code key
- represent every letter of the alphabet and include spaces between words
- be different in some way from the codes you have learned about in this module

To test your code, do the following:

- With your partner, choose who will be the sender and who will be the receiver. Have the sender write a short message without revealing it to the receiver and use the key to code the message. The receiver will have a copy of the code key.
- Work with another group, who will act as eavesdroppers. The sender will "transmit" the coded message. See whether the receiver can decode the message using the code key. Also see if the eavesdroppers are able to decode your message.

Write a short description of your test.

a. Could the receiver decode the message correctly?

b. Could the eavesdroppers break your code?

MODULE 3 Review and Assessment

Find the prime factorization of each number. (Sec. 1, Explor. 1)

1. 12 2. 21 3. 24 4. 42 5. 68

Find the greatest common factor (GCF) and the least common multiple (LCM) of each group of numbers. (Sec. 1, Explors. 2–3)

6. 6, 8 7. 36, 90 8. 25, 30, 75 9. 20, 42, 280

Replace each ? with >, <, or =. (Sec. 2, Explor. 1)

10. $\frac{3}{20}$? $\frac{4}{25}$ 11. $\frac{2}{9}$? $\frac{1}{4}$ 12. $\frac{5}{7}$? $\frac{3}{5}$ 13. $\frac{4}{21}$? $\frac{12}{63}$

14. Suppose a coin is tossed 3 times in a row and the results of the tosses are recorded in order. (Sec. 2, Explor. 3)
    a. Draw a tree diagram to represent all the possible outcomes.
    b. What is the probability that the second toss is a head?

Find each sum or difference. (Sec. 2, Explor. 2; and Sec. 3, Explors. 1 and 2)

15. $2\frac{4}{9} + 3\frac{1}{3}$ 16. $1\frac{7}{8} - 1\frac{1}{6}$ 17. $8\frac{3}{5} - 4\frac{9}{10}$ 18. $14 + 3\frac{12}{25}$

Write each number as a fraction or a mixed number in lowest terms. (Sec. 4, Explor. 1)

19. 0.075 20. 12.25 21. 87.00340 22. 0.100005 23. 3.00528

24. Write two decimal numbers that are between 2.815 and 2.82. (Sec. 4, Explor. 1)

Replace each ? with >, <, or =. (Sec. 4, Explor. 1)

25. 0.87 ? 0.8695 26. 3.05 ? 3.10 27. 6.8 ? 6.800

Write each number as a fraction with its denominator in standard form. (Sec. 4, Explor. 2)

28. 10^{-5} 29. 5^{-3} 30. 1^{-9} 31. 6^{-1} 32. 11^{-2}

Write each product or quotient in standard form. (Sec. 4, Explor. 3)

33. $25.32 \cdot 10^5$ 34. $25.32 \cdot 0.001$
35. $25.32 \div 10{,}000$ 36. $25.32 \div 0.01$

Write each number in scientific notation. (Sec. 4, Explor. 3)

37. 8,900,000,000 38. 342,000 39. 0.00038 40. 12.0056

Replace each ? with the correct measure. (Sec. 5, Explor. 1)

41. 35 cm = __?__ mm **42.** 3 m = __?__ cm **43.** 440 m = __?__ km

Tell whether each measure is *reasonable* or *unreasonable*. Explain your choice. (Sec. 5, Explor. 2)

44. the height of a desk from the floor to the desk top: 90 cm

45. the length of a jump rope: 0.002 km

Tell whether segments with the given side lengths *can* or *cannot* form a triangle. If they can, classify the triangle as *isosceles, equilateral,* or *scalene*. (Sec. 6, Explor. 1)

46. 3 km, 5 km, 4 km **47.** 2 cm, 10 cm, 13 cm **48.** 1 ft, 1 ft, 1 ft

Solve. Check each answer. (Sec. 6, Explor. 2)

49. $6x = 216$ **50.** $\frac{y}{2} = 14$ **51.** $51 = 3m$ **52.** $22 = \frac{n}{6}$

53. Look at the checkered flag. (Sec. 6, Explor. 2)

a. Write an equation that shows how the total area of the black squares in the flag is related to the area of the flag. Be sure to identify any variables you use.

b. Use your equation to find the total area of the black squares if the area of the flag is 60 in.^{2}.

c. Use your equation to find the area of the flag if the total area of the black squares is 24 in.^{2}.

Reflecting on the Module

54. Writing Explain how mathematics is a universal language. To make your point, give examples using at least two of the mathematical ideas you have learned in this module.

MODULE
4
THE ART OF
MOTION

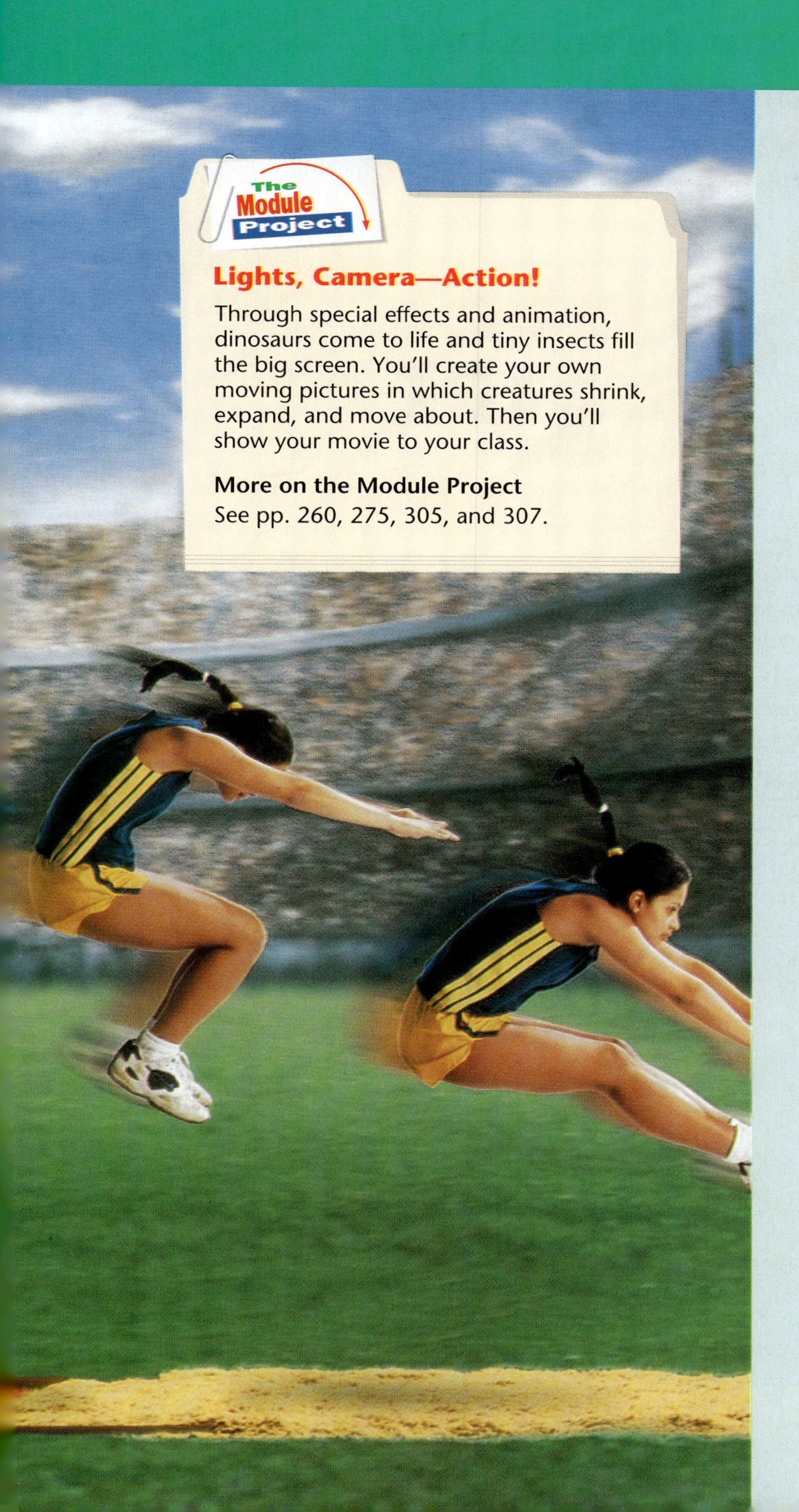

Lights, Camera—Action!

Through special effects and animation, dinosaurs come to life and tiny insects fill the big screen. You'll create your own moving pictures in which creatures shrink, expand, and move about. Then you'll show your movie to your class.

More on the Module Project
See pp. 260, 275, 305, and 307.

CONNECTING MATHEMATICS & The Theme

SECTION OVERVIEW

1 Circumference, and Multiplication and Division of Fractions

As you make and use a simple moving picture machine:

- Find the circumference of a circle
- Multiply and divide fractions

2 Decimal Multiplication and Division

As you examine photos of motion too fast for the eye to see:

- Multiply and divide decimals
- Write quotients as terminating and repeating decimals
- Interpret division with zero

3 Rotations and Reflections

As you explore patterns that create a sense of motion in art:

- Describe a rotation
- Identify a reflection and lines of symmetry

4 Multiplication and Division of Integers

As you learn about special effects in movies, such as reverse motion:

- Multiply and divide integers
- Evaluate expressions with fractions, decimals, or integers

5 Translations, Similarity, and Two-Step Equations

As you explore animation:

- Use coordinates to describe translations
- Identify similar figures
- Solve two-step equations

INTERNET
To learn more about the theme:
http://www.mlmath.com

Circumference, and Multiplication and Division of Fractions

EXPLORATION 1
- Circumference of a Zoetrope

EXPLORATION 2
- Multiplying Fractions

EXPLORATION 3
- Dividing Fractions

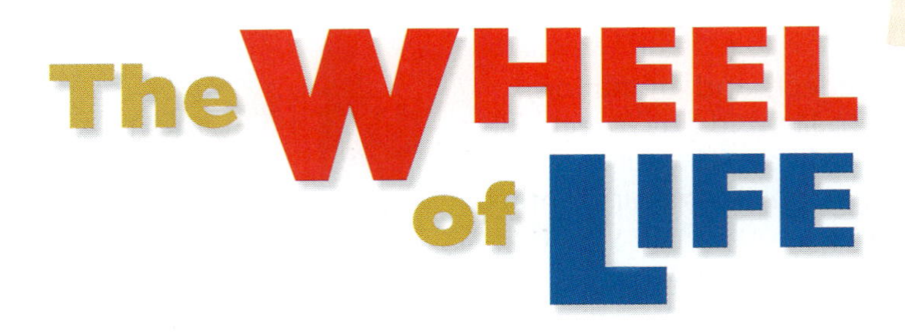

Setting the Stage

Life is always in motion. One way artists capture the feeling of life in their work is to create a sense of motion. In this module you'll explore how mathematics can be used to add motion to art.

One art form that captures the art of motion is motion pictures. One of the first moving picture machines was called a *zoetrope* (zō′ ē trōp′), which means "wheel of life" in Greek.

A zoetrope is a large open cylinder. To use a zoetrope, you place a long strip of paper inside it. The strip has a drawing that is repeated over and over, each time with a slight change. When the zoetrope is spun, the drawing appears to come to life.

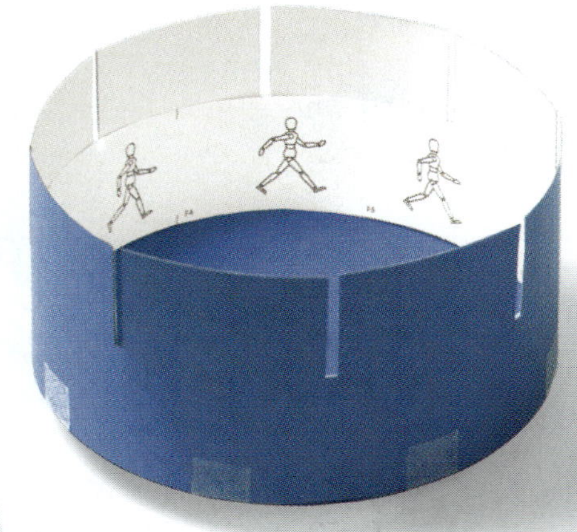

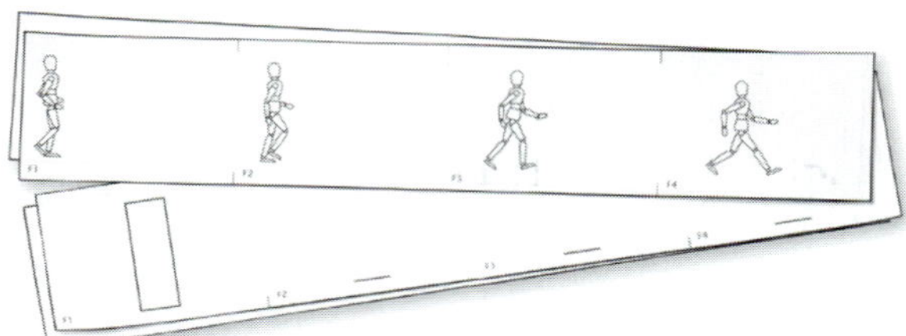

Think About It

1 What shapes are needed to build the base and the wall of a zoetrope?

2 Suppose you spin the zoetrope shown above. What do you think you will see?

Exploration 1

Circumference of a ZOETROPE

GOAL

LEARN HOW TO...
- find the circumference of a circle

AS YOU...
- build a zoetrope

KEY TERM
- circumference

SET UP *Work in a group. You will need:* • *2 copies of Labsheet 1A* • *Labsheet 1B* • *compass* • *ruler* • *sheet of white paper* • *large sheet of dark poster board* • *scissors* • *glue* • *several circular objects* • *string* • *calculator* • *push pin* • *tape* • *small cardboard box or eraser*

▶ **Your group will use geometry and measurement to build a zoetrope.**

3 Follow Steps 1 and 2 to make the base of the zoetrope.

Step 1 Use a compass and a ruler to draw a circle with a $3\frac{1}{2}$ in. radius on a sheet of white paper.

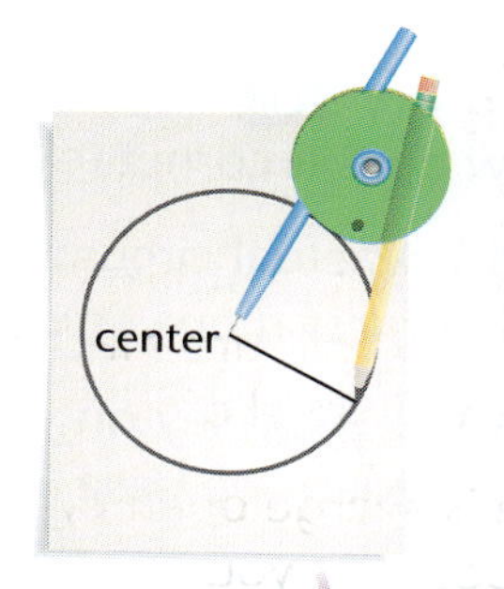

Step 2 Glue the sheet of paper onto a corner of the poster board. Then cut out the circle.

▶ **In Question 1, you may have noticed that the wall of the zoetrope can be made from a rectangle. The length of the rectangle must be equal to the distance around the zoetrope's circular base, or its circumference.**

4 Use your ruler to estimate the circumference of the zoetrope base to the nearest inch. Describe your method.

▶ **When you know the diameter of a circle, another way to find its circumference is to use the relationship between the circle's circumference and its diameter.**

5 **a.** Use string and a ruler to measure the circumference and the diameter of 3 or 4 circular objects. Record your results.

b. The circumference of each object is about how many times its diameter?

c. How can you estimate the circumference of a circle if you know its diameter? Estimate the circumference of your zoetrope base.

▶ **The exact relationship between the circumference (C) of a circle and its diameter (d) is given by the equation:**

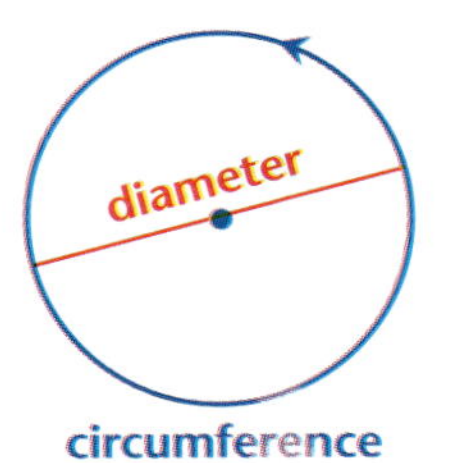

You read π as "pi."

$$\pi = \frac{C}{d} \quad \text{or} \quad C = \pi d$$

Calculator **Use a calculator to answer Question 6.**

6 **a.** Press the π key on your calculator. What value is displayed? How does it compare with your estimate in Question 5(b)?

b. Will the actual circumference of the zoetrope base be *greater than* or *less than* your estimate in Question 5(c)? Explain.

c. Use the π key on your calculator to find the circumference of the zoetrope base. Round your answer to the nearest inch.

d. You round decimals the same way you round whole numbers. Look at the value of π from part (a). Rounded to the nearest hundredth, π is 3.14. Explain why.

✓ QUESTION 7

...checks that you can find the circumference of a circle when you know its diameter.

7 **✓ CHECKPOINT** Use 3.14 or the π key to find the circumference of a circle with each measure. Round each answer to the nearest hundredth.

a. diameter = 6 in. **b.** diameter = 13 ft **c.** radius = 8 cm

8 **Use two copies of Labsheet 1A.** Follow Steps 3–5 to make the wall of the zoetrope.

Step 3 On poster board, draw a rectangle that has a width of $3\frac{1}{2}$ in. and a length equal to the circumference you found in Question 6(c). Cut out the rectangle.

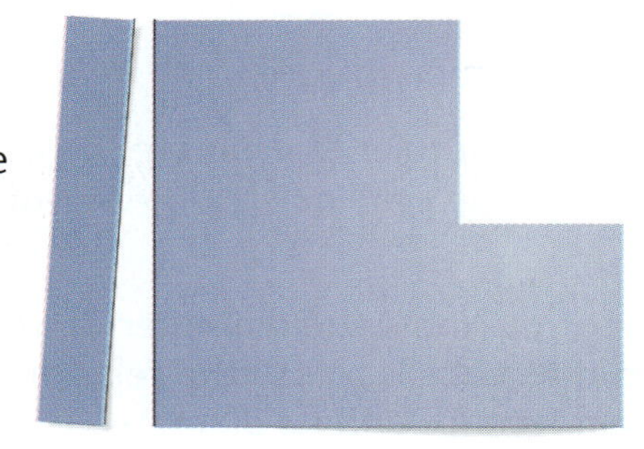

Step 4 Cut out the four *Zoetrope Side Strips* from two copies of Labsheet 1A. Glue the strips to the rectangle. Cut out the shaded slots.

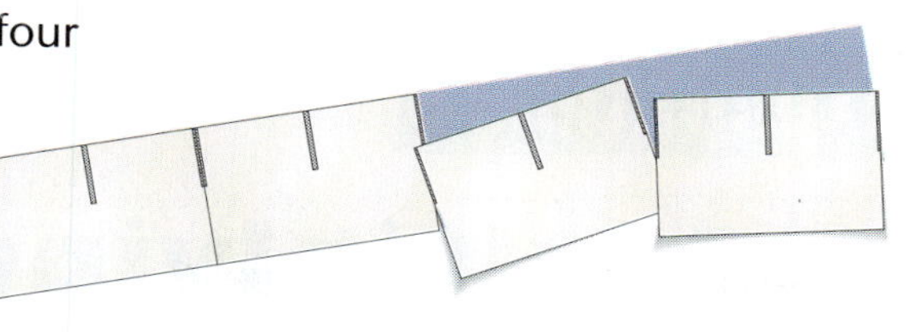

Step 5 Gently curve the wall until the ends meet. Tape the ends together.

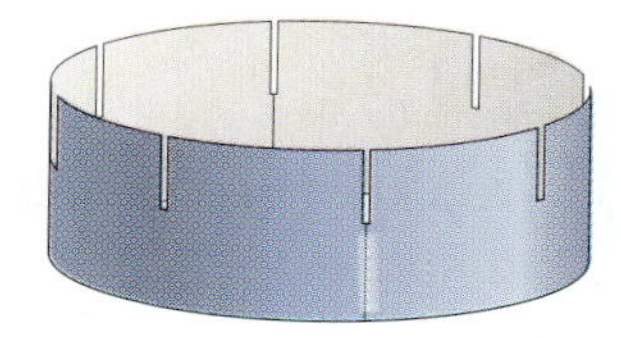

9 Follow Steps 6 and 7 to put together the zoetrope.

Step 6 Line up the unslotted edge of the wall with the base. Then tape them together.

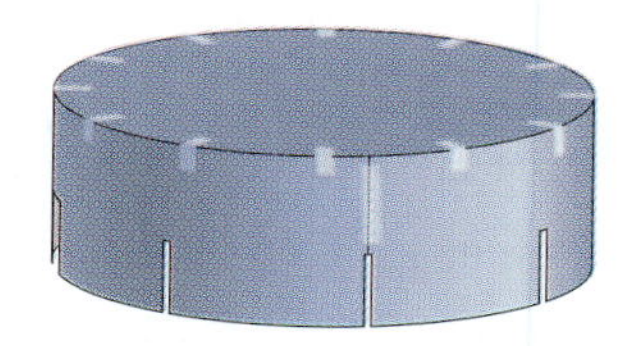

Step 7 Put a push pin through the center of the base and into the cardboard box or eraser.

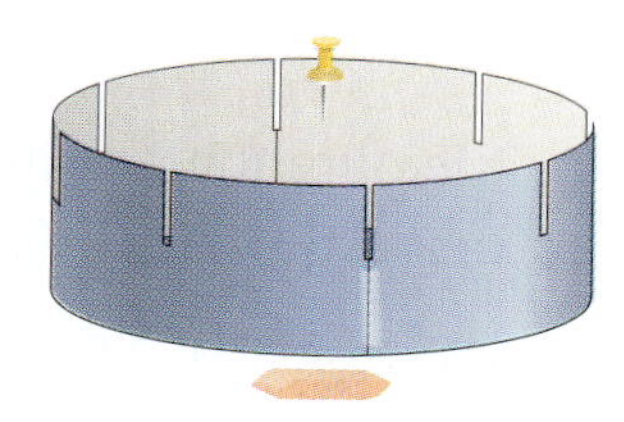

10 **Use Labsheet 1B.** Follow the directions below to make the *Animation Strip* and spin it in your zoetrope.

First Cut out the four sections of the *Animation Strip.* Tape them together in order, F1, F2, and so on, with no overlap.

Next Place the *Animation Strip* in your zoetrope so that each frame is centered under a cutout slot.

Then Hold the cardboard box or eraser on a level surface so the zoetrope is at eye level. You may need to kneel down. Spin the zoetrope and look through the slots.

11 Describe what you see when you spin the zoetrope forward (counterclockwise) and backward (clockwise).

12 **Discussion** Suppose you make the rectangular wall of a zoetrope before you make the circular base. Explain how you can use the length of the wall to find the diameter of the base.

HOMEWORK EXERCISES ▶ **See Exs. 1–5 on pp. 242–243.**

GOAL

LEARN HOW TO...
- multiply fractions and mixed numbers
- use the distributive property
- find reciprocals

AS YOU...
- begin to create a zoetrope strip

KEY TERMS
- distributive property
- reciprocals

Exploration 2

Multiplying FRACTIONS

SET UP *You will need:* • *Labsheet 1C* • *ruler* • *fraction calculator (optional)*

▶ **Use Labsheet 1C for Questions 13 and 15 as you begin to make an interesting animation strip that uses rectangles.**

13 For the first four frames of the *Animated Rectangle,* the height of each rectangle will be half the height of the rectangle in the previous frame. The length of the base of each rectangle will be the same.

a. Measure the height of the rectangle in Frame 1 (F1) to the nearest $\frac{1}{16}$ in.

b. Use paper-folding or your ruler to find half of the height of the rectangle in F1. This will be the height of the rectangle in Frame 2 (F2).

c. Draw the rectangle in F2. Use the segment in F2 for the base.

FOR ▶ HELP with *reading a customary ruler,* see **TOOLBOX, p. 591**

14 Fraction Calculator Because $\frac{1}{2}$ of $1\frac{1}{2}$ means $\frac{1}{2} \cdot 1\frac{1}{2}$, or $\frac{1}{2} \cdot \frac{3}{2}$, a fraction calculator can be used to find the product. Enter the key sequence below on your calculator. Does the calculator display agree with your answer in Question 13(b)?

15 **a.** Copy and complete the table to find the heights of the rectangles in F2, F3, and F4 of the *Animated Rectangle.*

b. Draw the rectangles in F3 and F4. Use the segment in each frame for the base of the rectangle.

Frame	Height of rectangle (in.)
F1	$1\frac{1}{2}$ or $\frac{3}{2}$
F2	$\frac{1}{2}$ of $\frac{3}{2}$ = ?
F3	$\frac{1}{2}$ of ? = ?
F4	$\frac{1}{2}$ of ? = ?

16 **Discussion** Look at the results in your table from Question 15.

a. Write multiplication equations that show how you found the heights of the rectangles in F2, F3, and F4.

b. Look for a pattern in the multiplication equations you wrote in part (a). How can you find the products without using a ruler, paper-folding, or a calculator?

c. What would be the height of the rectangle in F2 if the height of the rectangle in F1 were $1\frac{3}{4}$ in.? $\frac{5}{8}$ in.? Use a ruler to check.

▶ **Writing Products in Lowest Terms** **Sometimes it is easier to divide by common factors in the numerator and denominator before you multiply fractions.**

EXAMPLE

Find $\frac{6}{7} \cdot \frac{5}{18}$ in lowest terms.

Notice that a numerator and a denominator share the **common factor 6**.

$$\frac{\overset{1}{\cancel{6}}}{7} \cdot \frac{5}{\underset{3}{\cancel{18}}} = \frac{1}{7} \cdot \frac{5}{3} = \frac{5}{21}$$

Divide by 6.

Divide by 6.

17 **Discussion** In the Example, the numerator and the denominator also share the common factor 2. If you divide by the common factor 2, will you get a product in lowest terms? Explain.

18 Use the method in the Example to evaluate $\frac{9}{20} \cdot \frac{14}{27}$. Which common factor(s) did you divide by before you multiplied?

▶ **When you multiply a mixed number by a whole number or a fraction, it is sometimes easiest to use the distributive property to multiply each part of the mixed number separately.**

EXAMPLE

$$3 \cdot 2\frac{2}{3} = 3\left(2 + \frac{2}{3}\right) = (3 \cdot 2) + \left(3 \cdot \frac{2}{3}\right) = 6 + 2 = 8$$

19 Suppose the height of the rectangle in F1 of a zoetrope strip is $1\frac{3}{8}$ in. and you want to double its height from F1 to F2. Use the distributive property to find the height of the rectangle in F2.

20 How can you use the distributive property to evaluate $\frac{1}{2} \cdot 10\frac{2}{3}$?

...checks that you can multiply fractions and mixed numbers.

21 ✓ **CHECKPOINT** Find each product. Write each answer in lowest terms.

a. $\frac{5}{7} \cdot \frac{2}{3}$ **b.** $\frac{1}{6} \cdot 4$ **c.** $\frac{5}{6} \cdot \frac{18}{35}$

d. $10 \cdot 7\frac{2}{5}$ **e.** $\frac{5}{8} \cdot 2\frac{2}{5}$ **f.** $1\frac{1}{2} \cdot 2\frac{2}{3}$

22 The first two frames of two zoetrope strips are shown below. Replace each ? with the fraction you must multiply by to change the height in F1 to the height in F2.

a.

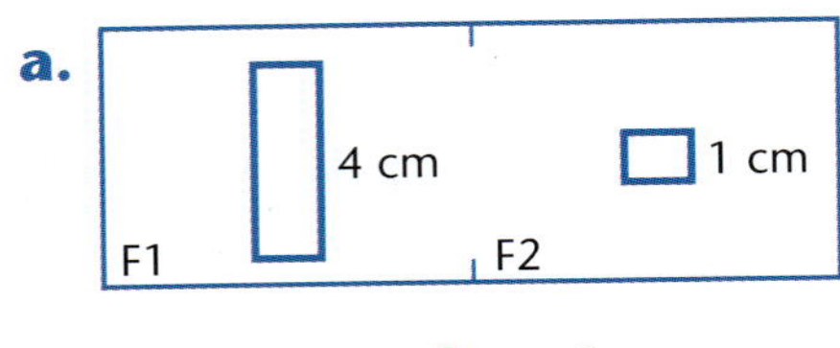

$4 \cdot$ ___?___ $= 1$

b.

F1 $\frac{3}{8}$ in. F2 1 in.

$\frac{3}{8} \cdot$ ___?___ $= 1$

▶ **The products in Question 22 were both 1. Two numbers whose product is 1 are reciprocals of each other.**

EXAMPLE

$\frac{4}{7} \cdot \frac{7}{4} = \frac{28}{28} = 1$

$\frac{4}{7}$ and $\frac{7}{4}$ are reciprocals.

$\frac{1}{3} \cdot 3 = \frac{1}{3} \cdot \frac{3}{1} = \frac{3}{3} = 1$

$\frac{1}{3}$ and 3 are reciprocals.

23 **Discussion** Look at the Examples and your answers to Question 22.

a. Describe a way to find the reciprocal of a fraction, a nonzero whole number, and a mixed number.

b. Does the number 0 have a reciprocal? Explain.

✓ **QUESTION 24**

...checks that you can find the reciprocal of a number.

24 ✓ **CHECKPOINT** Replace each ? with the number that makes the multiplication equation true.

a. $\frac{1}{2} \cdot$ ___?___ $= 1$ **b.** $5 \cdot$ ___?___ $= 1$ **c.** $3\frac{3}{4} \cdot$ ___?___ $= 1$

HOMEWORK EXERCISES ▶ See Exs. 6–27 on pp. 243–244.

Dividing FRACTIONS

GOAL

LEARN HOW TO...
- divide fractions and mixed numbers

AS YOU...
- finish your zoetrope strip

SET UP *You will need:* • *Labsheet 1C with completed Frames 1–4* • *ruler* • *scissors* • *tape* • *colored pencils* • *zoetrope*

▶ **To complete the last three frames of the *Animated Rectangle*, you'll divide the height of the rectangle in each previous frame by $\frac{1}{2}$. One way to divide is to separate into equal-sized parts.**

EXAMPLE

To find $4 \div \frac{1}{2}$, think about how many $\frac{1}{2}$-inch segments there are in 4 in.

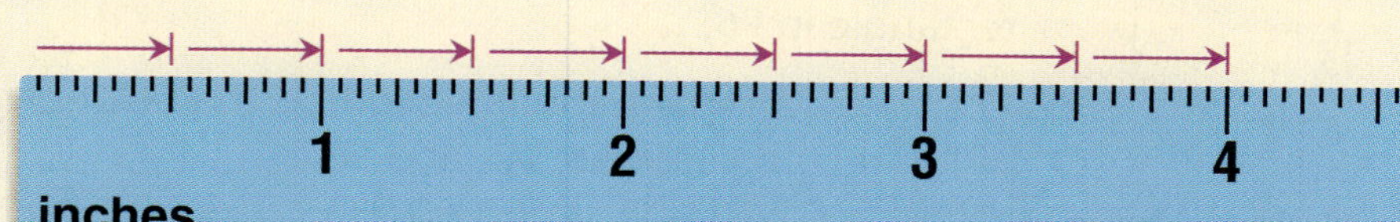

By looking at a ruler, you can see that there are eight $\frac{1}{2}$-inch segments in 4 in., so

$$4 \div \frac{1}{2} = 8$$

25 Use a ruler or draw a picture to find each quotient.

a. $3 \div \frac{1}{2}$ **b.** $3 \div \frac{1}{4}$ **c.** $3 \div 1\frac{1}{2}$ **d.** $3 \div \frac{3}{4}$

26 **a.** Look for a pattern in your answers to Question 25. For each expression, find the number you can multiply 3 by to get the same answer.

b. It is not always possible to find a quotient using a ruler. Why would $3 \div \frac{5}{6}$ be difficult to evaluate with a ruler? How can you use multiplication to find the quotient $3 \div \frac{5}{6}$?

27 **Discussion** Explain a method you can use to divide fractions without using a ruler.

28 Find each quotient using your method from Question 27. Then use a ruler to check your results. Does your method work? If not, how can you modify it so that it does work?

a. $\frac{7}{8} \div \frac{1}{16}$ **b.** $4 \div \frac{1}{4}$ **c.** $1\frac{1}{4} \div \frac{1}{8}$ **d.** $5\frac{1}{4} \div 1\frac{3}{4}$

✓ QUESTION 29

...checks that you can divide fractions and mixed numbers.

29 **✓ CHECKPOINT** Find each quotient.

a. $2 \div \frac{2}{3}$ **b.** $\frac{2}{3} \div 2$ **c.** $6\frac{7}{10} \div \frac{3}{10}$ **d.** $3\frac{1}{2} \div 1\frac{4}{5}$

▶ **Use Labsheet 1C for Questions 30 and 31. You should have completed Frames 1–4 in Exploration 2.**

30 You can find the height of each rectangle in Frames 6–8 of the *Animated Rectangle* by dividing the height of the previous rectangle by $\frac{1}{2}$.

Frame	Height of rectangle (in.)
F5	$\frac{3}{16}$
F6	? ÷ ? = ?
F7	? ÷ ? = ?
F8	? ÷ ? = ?

a. The height of the rectangle in Frame 5 (F5) is $\frac{3}{16}$ in. Write a division expression for the height of the rectangle in F6.

b. Copy and complete the table to find the heights of the rectangles in F6, F7, and F8.

c. Draw the rectangles in F6, F7, and F8. Use the segment in each frame for the base of the rectangle.

31 To view the *Animated Rectangle,* follow the directions below. Then describe what you see. You may want to add your own visual effects to make the animation more interesting.

First Cut out the four strips and tape them together so the frames are in order, with no overlap.

Next Use one color to shade the interior of the rectangles in Frames 1–8.

Then Place the completed strip in the zoetrope so the frames are centered under the slots. Spin the zoetrope.

HOMEWORK EXERCISES ▶ **See Exs. 28–43 on pp. 244–245.**

Key Terms

Circumference (pp. 233–235)

Circumference is the distance around a circle. The relationship between a circle's circumference (C) and its diameter (d) is given by:

π is about 3.14.

$$\pi = \frac{C}{d} \text{ or } C = \pi d$$

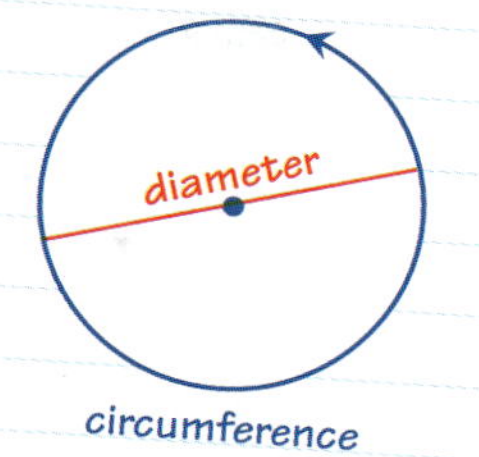

circumference

Rounding Decimals (p. 234)

You round decimals the same way you round whole numbers.

Example To the nearest hundredth, 0.23874 is 0.24.

hundredths place

$8 \geq 5$, so round the 3 up to 4.

Multiplying Fractions (pp. 236–238)

To multiply fractions, you first multiply the numerators. Then you multiply the denominators.

Sometimes it is easier to divide by all the common factors before you multiply to get a product in lowest terms.

Example

Divide by 8.

Divide by 3.

$$\frac{\overset{1}{\cancel{8}}}{\underset{3}{\cancel{9}}} \cdot \frac{\overset{5}{\cancel{15}}}{\underset{2}{\cancel{16}}} = \frac{1}{3} \cdot \frac{5}{2} = \frac{5}{6}$$

You can use the distributive property to multiply a mixed number. (p. 237)

Example $\frac{1}{3} \cdot 6\frac{1}{4} = \frac{1}{3}\left(6 + \frac{1}{4}\right) = \left(\frac{1}{3} \cdot 6\right) + \left(\frac{1}{3} \cdot \frac{1}{4}\right) = 2 + \frac{1}{12} = 2\frac{1}{12}$

distributive property

Reciprocals (p. 238)

Two numbers whose product is 1, such as 5 and $\frac{1}{5}$, are reciprocals.

reciprocals

Key Concepts Questions

32 Find the circumference of a circle with a diameter of 4 in.

33 Explain two ways to find $6 \cdot 2\frac{1}{9}$.

Continued on next page

Section 1 Key Concepts

Dividing Fractions (pp. 239–240)

To divide a number by a fraction, you multiply the number by the reciprocal of the fraction.

Example To find $3\frac{2}{3} \div \frac{5}{9}$, multiply $3\frac{2}{3}$ by $\frac{9}{5}$.

$$3\frac{2}{3} \div \frac{5}{9} = \frac{11}{3} \div \frac{5}{9} = \frac{11}{3} \cdot \frac{9}{5} = \frac{11}{\cancel{3}_1} \cdot \frac{\cancel{9}^3}{5} = \frac{11}{1} \cdot \frac{3}{5} = \frac{33}{5} = 6\frac{3}{5}$$

The **reciprocal** of $\frac{5}{9}$ is $\frac{9}{5}$.

34 Key Concepts Question Find $4\frac{1}{3} \div \frac{5}{6}$ in lowest terms.

Section 1 Practice & Application Exercises

Sequoias, or redwood trees, are among the largest and oldest living things. They may be over 300 ft tall, over 10 ft in diameter, and several thousand years old.

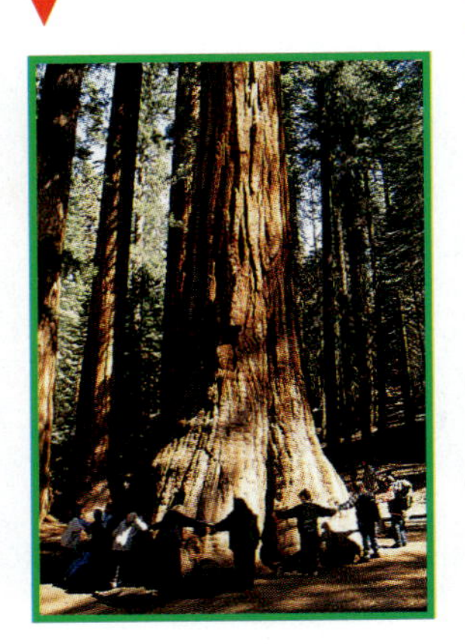

For Exercises 1–5, use 3.14 or the π key on a calculator. If necessary, round each answer to the nearest hundredth.

Find the circumference of each circle.

1. diameter = 19 ft
2. radius = 7 m
3. diameter = 1 in.

4. **Forestry** Suppose you want to estimate an uncut tree's diameter.

   a. How can you use the circumference of a tree's trunk to estimate its diameter?

   b. Use your method from part (a) to estimate each diameter.

Tree	giant sequoia	American elm	black willow	sugar maple
Circumference (ft)	83	26	33	19
Diameter (ft)	?	?	?	?

5. Native American Tepees Tepees made from poles covered with animal skin or tree bark served as homes for some tribes of the North American Great Plains. The poles used to build the frame of a tepee must be at least 4 ft longer than the diameter of the circular base of a tepee to allow for tying them together. Suppose a tepee has a base circumference of 35 ft. Estimate the height of its poles.

Find each product. Write each answer in lowest terms.

6. $\frac{5}{9} \cdot \frac{1}{6}$ **7.** $\frac{7}{8} \cdot 4$ **8.** $\frac{5}{9} \cdot \frac{3}{35}$

9. $4 \cdot 2\frac{3}{8}$ **10.** $2\frac{7}{15} \cdot \frac{5}{11}$ **11.** $2\frac{1}{4} \cdot 1\frac{1}{6}$

12. $\frac{4}{7} \cdot \frac{14}{15} \cdot \frac{5}{12}$ **13.** $\frac{7}{8} \cdot 6 \cdot 3\frac{1}{2}$ **14.** $4\frac{2}{3} \cdot 1\frac{5}{7} \cdot \frac{3}{4}$

15. How could you have used the distributive property to find some of the products in Exercises 6–14? Which ones?

16. Ikebana In the Sogetsu school of Japanese floral arranging, the heights of the main stems, called the *shin*, *soe*, and *hikae*, depend on the diameter and the height of the vase. For a large arrangement, the heights should be as follows.

- The height of the *shin* must be twice the sum of the diameter of the vase and the height of the vase.
- The height of the *soe* must be three-quarters the height of the *shin*.
- The height of the *hikae* must be half the height of the *soe*.

Suppose a florist uses a vase that has a $7\frac{1}{2}$ in. diameter and is 3 in. tall. How tall must each main stem be?

a. *shin* **b.** *soe* **c.** *hikae*

Estimation **Use compatible numbers to estimate each product.**

Example: $\frac{1}{4} \cdot 17 \longrightarrow \frac{1}{4} \cdot 16 = \frac{1}{4} \cdot \frac{16}{1} = 4$

$\frac{1}{4} \cdot 17$ is a little more than 4.

16 is close to 17 and it is divisible by 4.

17. $\frac{1}{3} \cdot 13$ **18.** $23 \cdot \frac{1}{6}$ **19.** $\frac{1}{5} \cdot 32$ **20.** $61 \cdot \frac{1}{4}$

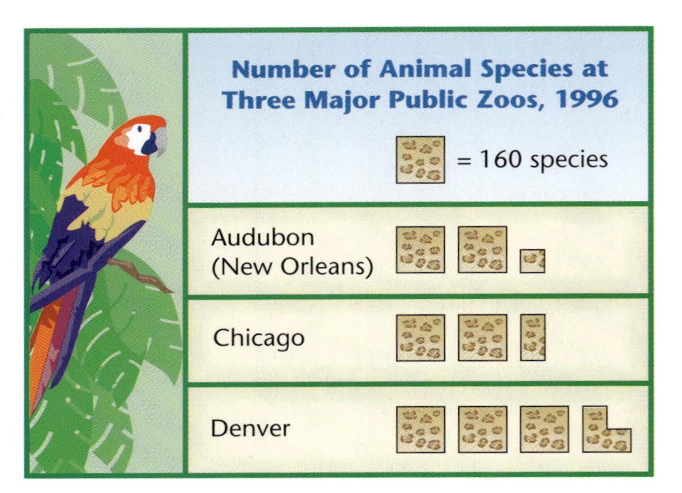

21. Interpreting Data Look at the graph.

a. How many symbols are used to represent the number of animal species at the Audubon Zoological Park?

b. Use your result from part (a) to find the number of animal species at the Audubon Zoological Park.

c. How many animal species are there at the Chicago Zoological Park? at the Denver Zoological Park?

22. Suppose you want to cover a floor that is $4\frac{1}{4}$ ft wide and $8\frac{1}{2}$ ft long with tiles that are 1 ft by 1 ft. How many tiles will you need?

Find the reciprocal of each number.

23. $\frac{3}{7}$ **24.** 12 **25.** $\frac{25}{8}$ **26.** $2\frac{4}{5}$

27. Challenge Replace each ? below with one of the digits 2, 4, 6, or 8 to create an expression for each product. Do not repeat digits.

$\frac{?}{?} \cdot \frac{?}{?}$

a. the greatest product

b. the least product

c. the product that is closest to 1

Find each quotient. Write each answer in lowest terms.

28. $\frac{2}{3} \div \frac{4}{9}$ **29.** $1 \div \frac{2}{7}$ **30.** $\frac{5}{8} \div \frac{5}{8}$ **31.** $4 \div 1\frac{1}{5}$

32. $\frac{7}{9} \div \frac{5}{12}$ **33.** $6 \div \frac{1}{8}$ **34.** $\frac{4}{5} \div \frac{3}{7}$ **35.** $\frac{6}{11} \div 4$

36. $2\frac{4}{7} \div \frac{2}{3}$ **37.** $1\frac{4}{5} \div 1\frac{1}{2}$ **38.** $\frac{5}{6} \div 7\frac{1}{3}$ **39.** $2\frac{5}{8} \div 1\frac{1}{6}$

40. Carpentry "Penny" is the unit used for the size of a nail. An 8-penny nail is twice the length of a 3-penny nail. An 8-penny nail is $2\frac{1}{2}$ in. long. What is the length of a 3-penny nail?

41. Writing Answer without actually doing the division. Do you expect the quotient $\frac{2}{3} \div \frac{4}{5}$ to be *greater than* or *less than* 1? *greater than* or *less than* $\frac{2}{3}$? Explain how you know.

42. Theater Northern Illinois University has a collection of scale models of stage sets for scenes from operas performed on campus. The models are built $\frac{1}{48}$ actual size. The model shown is a public square in nineteenth century Bohemia, a region of the Czech Republic.

a. A door on one of the buildings in the model is $\frac{11}{16}$ in. wide and $1\frac{3}{4}$ in. tall. Find the actual dimensions of the door.

b. The red-and-white striped pole in the model is $4\frac{5}{8}$ in. high. How many of these scale-model poles can be cut from a 1 ft long dowel?

c. **Open-ended** Use facts about the scale model. Write and solve a word problem that involves fraction multiplication. Then write and solve a word problem that involves fraction division.

Reflecting on the Section

Be prepared to discuss your response to Exercise 43 in class.

43. Suppose F1 of a zoetrope strip shows a person. To make the person appear taller, which of the following can be done to the person's height? Give an example to justify each choice.

A. multiply by $\frac{1}{2}$

B. divide by $\frac{1}{2}$

C. multiply by $\frac{4}{3}$

D. divide by $\frac{4}{3}$

Discussion

Exercise 43 checks that you understand the effects of multiplying and dividing by fractions.

Spiral Review

Tell whether each combination of side lengths can form a triangle. (Module 3, p. 223)

44. 15 cm, 6 cm, 7 cm

45. 20 in., 9 in., 12 in.

Evaluate each expression. (Module 1, p. 65)

46. $15 - 3 \cdot 2$

47. $26 + (14 - 8)$

48. $56 \div 7 \cdot 5$

Replace each __?__ with the correct power of 10. (Module 3, p. 199)

49. 2.7 • __?__ = 270

50. 0.043 ÷ __?__ = 4.3

51. 31 ÷ __?__ = 3100

52. 9.6 • __?__ = 0.0096

Section 1 Extra Skill Practice

For Exercises 1–5, use 3.14 or the π key on a calculator. Find the circumference of each circle with the given diameter. Round each answer to the nearest hundredth.

1. 5 m
2. 32 cm
3. 24 ft
4. 15 in.
5. 10.5 cm

Find each product. Write each answer in lowest terms.

6. $\frac{1}{7} \cdot \frac{2}{9}$
7. $\frac{5}{11} \cdot \frac{3}{10}$
8. $16 \cdot \frac{3}{8}$
9. $\frac{10}{13} \cdot 26$
10. $\frac{7}{12} \cdot \frac{2}{21}$
11. $18 \cdot \frac{7}{9}$
12. $\frac{5}{9} \cdot 2\frac{7}{10}$
13. $5\frac{1}{3} \cdot 1\frac{1}{8}$
14. $4\frac{1}{2} \cdot \frac{8}{9}$
15. $10 \cdot 7\frac{3}{5}$
16. $\frac{2}{3} \cdot \frac{18}{25} \cdot \frac{3}{8}$
17. $4 \cdot 2\frac{1}{2} \cdot \frac{6}{7}$

Find the reciprocal of each number.

18. 7
19. $\frac{8}{11}$
20. $\frac{19}{5}$
21. $4\frac{1}{3}$
22. 45

Find each quotient. Write each answer in lowest terms.

23. $\frac{5}{6} \div \frac{1}{12}$
24. $\frac{3}{7} \div \frac{6}{11}$
25. $\frac{2}{3} \div \frac{4}{9}$
26. $\frac{10}{13} \div \frac{25}{26}$
27. $8 \div \frac{4}{7}$
28. $\frac{5}{9} \div 10$
29. $2\frac{4}{7} \div \frac{3}{4}$
30. $5\frac{1}{4} \div 1\frac{2}{5}$
31. $5\frac{1}{2} \div 3\frac{1}{6}$
32. $\frac{5}{6} \div 7\frac{1}{2}$
33. $6 \div 2\frac{4}{5}$
34. $\frac{41}{84} \div 3$

Study Skills Listening

To become an active listener, you need to give your full attention to what is being said. While you are listening, ask yourself whether you understand everything, and make connections between ideas. Try to picture in your mind what the speaker is talking about.

1. Have a partner read aloud the *Setting the Stage* on page 232. Practice being an active listener while your partner is reading.
2. After you have listened to the reading, write down the ideas you remember. Include any questions you thought of while listening.

Section 2 Decimal Multiplication and Division

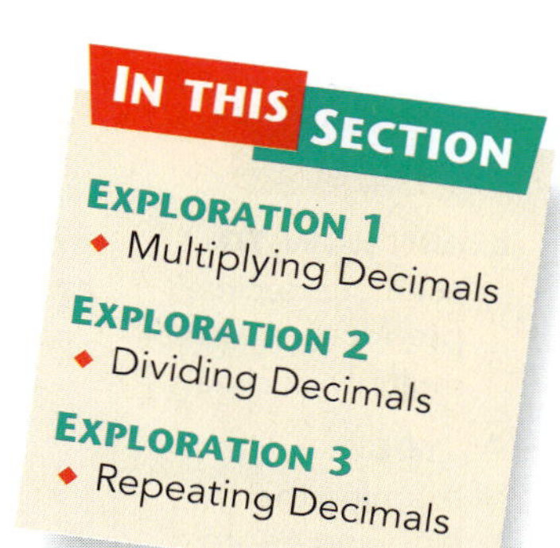

THROUGH THE CAMERA'S EYE

Setting the Stage

The world of things too small or too fast for the eye to see can be captured through the art of photography. A tiny flying insect called a *green lacewing* is shown here in the first stages of a backward loop.

The lacewing's movement has been made more visible by freezing the action for short time intervals and enlarging the size of the image.

Think About It

1 The actual body length of a green lacewing is only about 1.4 cm. Which phrase do you think describes the relationship between the size of the image in the photo and the insect's actual size? Explain.

A. 10^2 times actual size

B. 0.099 times actual size

C. 1.5 times actual size

D. 1.05 times actual size

E. 11.9 times actual size

F. $6\frac{1}{5}$ times actual size

GOAL

LEARN HOW TO...
- estimate decimal products
- multiply decimals

AS YOU...
- examine the lacewing photo

Exploration 1

Multiplying DECIMALS

SET UP *Work with a partner. You will need a calculator.*

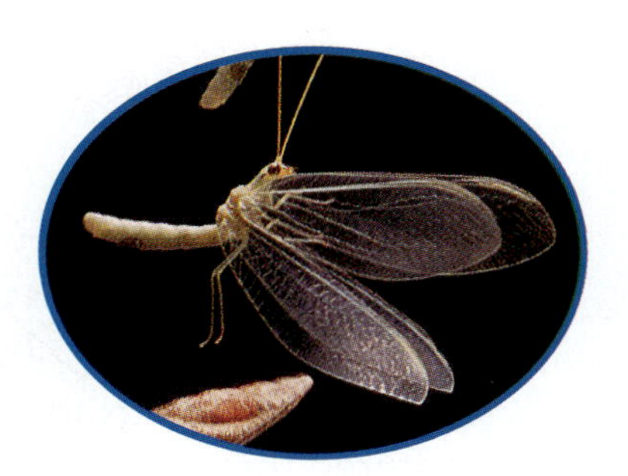

▶ **To find how much the image in the photo is enlarged, you can estimate the product of 1.4 and each choice in Question 1 on page 247. One way to estimate decimal products is to use powers of 10.**

FOR ◀ HELP with *multiplying by powers of 10,* see **MODULE 3, p. 199**

EXAMPLE

Suppose you guessed that the lacewing in the photo is 0.099 times its actual size. To check your guess, you can estimate the product (1.4)(0.099) by substituting a power of 10 for 0.099.

$$(1.4)(0.099) \approx (1.4)(0.1)$$
$$\approx 0.14$$

"is approximately equal to" ($\approx$)

0.099 is between 0.1 and 0.01, but is closer to 0.1.

2 **a.** Will the exact product (1.4)(0.099) be *greater than* or *less than* the estimate of 0.14 in the Example? How can you tell without multiplying 1.4 and 0.099?

b. If the guess in the Example is correct, then the image of the lacewing's body in the photo should be about 0.14 cm long. Do you think 0.14 cm is a reasonable estimate? Explain.

3 Suppose you guessed that the image in the photo is 11.9 times actual size. Estimate the product (1.4)(11.9) by substituting a power of 10 for 11.9. Is the guess reasonable? Explain.

✓ QUESTION 4

...checks that you can use powers of 10 to estimate decimal products.

4 **✓ CHECKPOINT** Copy each problem. Use estimation with powers of 10 to place the decimal point in each product.

a. (0.36)(9.6) = 3456

b. (348.7)(0.22) = 76714

c. (52.14)(0.89) = 464046

d. (0.092)(96.85) = 891020

5 **Try This as a Class** Look at your results from Question 4.

a. How were the digits in each product determined?

b. How is the number of decimal places in each product related to the number of decimal places in the two factors?

c. To find (0.12)(0.4), you must use a zero as a placeholder after you multiply the digits. Which is correct: *0.480* or *0.048*? Why?

6 ✓ **CHECKPOINT** Find each product.

a. (4.57)(0.9) **b.** (189.5)(6.4) **c.** (0.012)(7.75)

... checks that you can multiply decimals.

▶ **This game can help you find other strategies for estimating decimals.**

HIT THE TARGET

- The first player enters the starting number on a calculator.
- Then players alternate turns entering [×], a decimal number, and [=].
- The first player to get a number on the calculator display that is within the given target range (including the endpoints) is the winner.

Sample Starting number: 200 Target range: 114 to 124

		Display
Player 1 enters	[2] [0] [0] [×] [.] [5] [=]	100.
Player 2 enters	[×] [1] [.] [1] [=]	110.
Player 1 enters	[×] [1] [.] [0] [5] [=]	115.5

Since 115.5 is between 114 and 124, Player 1 wins!

7 Calculator Play the game *Hit the Target* with each number and range.

a. 350, range: 767 to 777 **b.** 475, range: 350 to 360

8 **Discussion** Predict whether each product will be *greater than*, *less than*, or *equal to* the number in red. Explain how you know.

a. (**3.6**)(1) **b.** (**4.75**)(0.92) **c.** (**57.97**)(1.007)

9 Describe the product when a positive number is multiplied by 0, by a number between 0 and 1, and by a number greater than 1.

10 Find the actual change in size in Question 1 on page 247. The body length of the image in the photo is 2.15 cm.

HOMEWORK EXERCISES ▶ See Exs. 1–12 on p. 257.

GOAL

LEARN HOW TO...
- estimate decimal quotients
- divide decimals

AS YOU...
- investigate the flight of a golf ball

Exploration 2

Dividing DECIMALS

The photo shows a golf club striking a golf ball. Each image of the club and the ball follows the previous one by 0.001 seconds.

FOR HELP with *dividing by powers of 10*, see **MODULE 3, p. 199**

11 **Try This as a Class** By looking at the printing on the ball, you can see that the ball spins. It spins about one half of a revolution in 0.004 s. Suppose it continues to spin at the same rate.

a. About how long does it take the ball to make one revolution?

b. The entire flight of the golf ball lasts about 6 s. Write a division problem that can be used to find how many revolutions the ball will make during its flight.

c. How can you use a power of 10 to estimate the quotient from part (b)? Estimate the quotient.

✓ QUESTION 12

... checks that you can use powers of 10 to estimate quotients of decimals.

12 **✓ CHECKPOINT** Use powers of 10 to estimate each quotient.

a. $9.62 \div 1.1$ b. $46.75 \div 0.091$ c. $0.5 \div 11.2$

13 Copy each problem. Use estimation to place the decimal point in each quotient.

a. $98\overline{)24.50}$ with quotient 25

b. $8\overline{)108.0}$ with quotient 135

c. $116\overline{)8386.8}$ with quotient 723

14 **Try This as a Class** Look at your results from Question 13.

a. How were the digits in each quotient determined?

b. How is the position of the decimal point in each quotient related to the position of the decimal point in the dividend?

c. Find the quotient $68\overline{)138.04}$.

15 **Discussion** Look at these division problems.

$8\overline{)72}$ $\quad$ $80\overline{)720}$ $\quad$ $88\overline{)792}$ $\quad$ $800\overline{)7200}$

a. How are the divisors and dividends in the last three problems related to the divisor and the dividend in the first problem?

b. Find all four quotients. What do you notice about them?

c. What happens to the quotient when you multiply the dividend and the divisor by the same number?

▶ **Dividing by a Decimal** **In Question 14, you explained how to divide a decimal by a whole number. You can use this skill and the pattern you found in Question 15 to divide by a decimal.**

16 In Question 11(c), you estimated the number of revolutions the golf ball makes in 6 s by using the quotient $0.008\overline{)6}$.

a. By what power of 10 can you multiply the divisor 0.008 to make it a whole number? What must you do to the dividend to keep the quotient the same?

b. Use part (a) to rewrite the problem $0.008\overline{)6}$. Then find the quotient and compare it with your estimate in Question 11(c).

17 Find the quotients $1.648 \div 0.8$ and $0.00578 \div 0.17$.

▶ **Remainders** **When division has a remainder, you have to write a zero at the end of the dividend to continue to divide.**

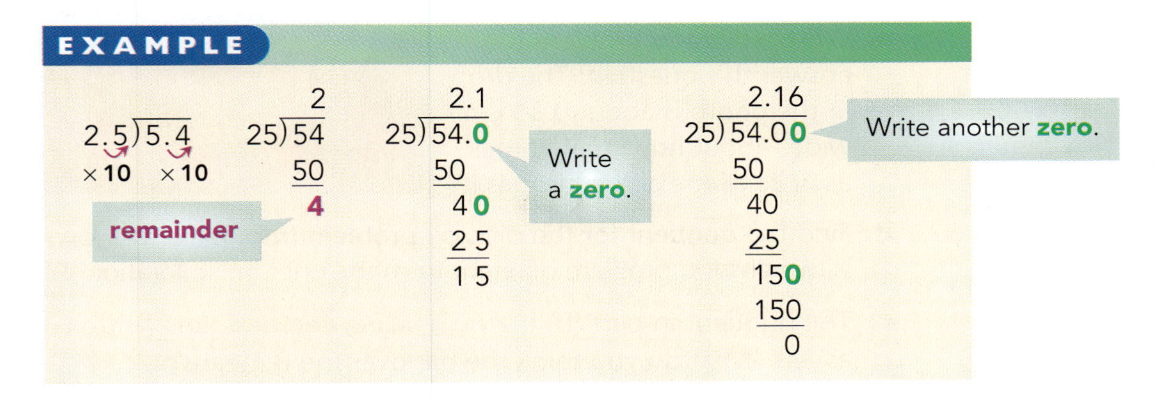

18 **Discussion** Look at the Example on page 251.

a. The dividend changed from 54 to 54.0 and then to 54.00. How is 54 related to 54.0 and 54.00?

b. How are the quotients in each stage of the division different?

c. How do you know when the division is complete?

19 Find the quotient $3.4\overline{)50.49}$.

✓ QUESTION 20

...checks that you can divide decimals.

20 **✓ CHECKPOINT** Find each quotient. Use estimation to check.

a. 48.6 ÷ 22.5 **b.** 0.315 ÷ 0.005 **c.** 14.7 ÷ 2.4

HOMEWORK EXERCISES ▶ See Exs. 13–26 on pp. 257–258.

GOAL

LEARN HOW TO...
- find quotients that repeat
- write a fraction as a decimal
- interpret division with zero

AS YOU...
- analyze a photo of a drop of milk

KEY TERMS
- repeating decimal
- terminating decimal

Exploration 3

Repeating DECIMALS

SET UP *You will need a calculator.*

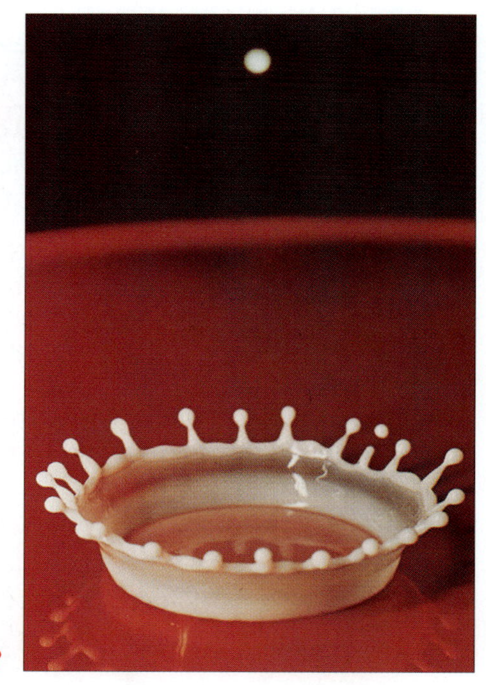

▶ **The photo shows a drop of milk falling onto a plate of milk.**

21 **Try This as a Class** The actual diameter of the drop is 0.09 cm.

a. Write a division problem to answer this question: The drop in the photo is about 0.35 cm wide. About how many times as wide as the actual drop is it?

b. Find the quotient for the division problem from part (a). How is this division problem different from the ones in Exploration 2?

c. The quotient in part (b) is a **repeating decimal**. It is written as $3.\overline{8}$. What do you think the bar over the 8 means?

▶ **When remainders begin to repeat in a division problem, you can tell that the quotient will be a repeating decimal.**

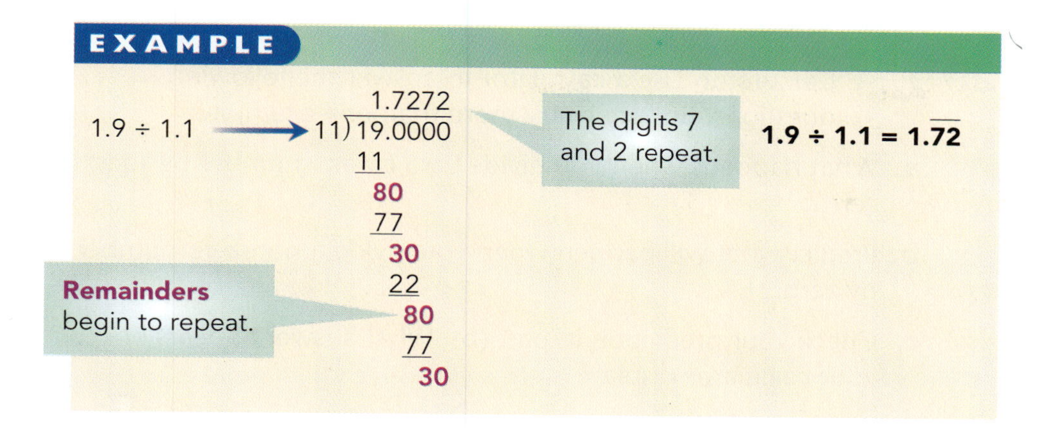

▶ **Writing a Fraction as a Decimal** **You can write the decimal equivalent of a fraction by dividing the numerator by the denominator. For example, $\frac{6}{11}$ = 6 ÷ 11 = 0.545454 ... = 0.$\overline{54}$.**

22 Write each decimal carried out to 6 decimal places.

a. 0.5$\overline{45}$ **b.** 0.5$\overline{4}$ **c.** 0.$\overline{545}$

23 Order 0.5$\overline{45}$, 0.5$\overline{4}$, and 0.$\overline{545}$ from least to greatest.

24 ✓ **CHECKPOINT** Find each quotient.

a. 0.9)12.1 **b.** 0.56 ÷ 3.3 **c.** 7.89 ÷ 1

d. $\frac{5}{6}$ **e.** 0.12)0.9456 **f.** 0.45 ÷ 2.7

25 The quotients in Question 24(c) and 24(e) are examples of **terminating decimals**. Why do you think they are called terminating decimals?

26 Suppose you want to round a quotient to the nearest hundredth. How far should you carry out the division? Why? Round the quotient 6.73 ÷ 0.49 to the nearest hundredth.

27 **Discussion** Look at your results from Question 24. What can you say about the quotient when a positive number is divided by 1? by a number greater than 1? by a number between 0 and 1?

28 Predict whether each quotient will be *greater than*, *less than*, or *equal to* the number in red. Explain how you know.

a. **8.7** ÷ 1 **b.** **13.12** ÷ 1.2 **c.** $\frac{69.3}{0.99}$

✓ **QUESTION 24**

...checks that you can find and write quotients that are repeating decimals.

▶ **Division and Zero** **You know that the product of any number and zero is always zero. Now you'll explore what happens when a division problem involves zero.**

29 Calculator Use a calculator to answer the following questions. Be sure to try more than one example.

a. What happens when you divide zero by any number besides zero?

b. Predict what will happen when you divide a non-zero number by zero.

c. Check your prediction in part (b). What answer appears on your calculator display?

▶ **Your calculator might have displayed an error message when you tried to divide a number by zero because division by zero is *undefined*. To understand why, you can explore some division equations involving zero.**

30 **Try This as a Class** One way to find a quotient is to solve a related multiplication equation, as in the first row of the table below.

a. Copy and complete the table. For each division equation, write a related multiplication equation. If possible, find the value of x that makes the equation true. Otherwise, write *undefined*.

Division equation	Related multiplication equation	Value of x
$12 \div 3 = x$	$3 \cdot x = 12$	4
$0 \div 3 = x$	$3 \cdot x = 0$	?
$12 \div 0 = x$	?	?
$0 \div 0 = x$	?	?

b. Does each division equation have a quotient? If not, which ones do not? Why?

c. Do the results in your table agree with your answers to Question 29?

d. Use your results from parts (a)–(c) to explain why division by zero is undefined.

HOMEWORK EXERCISES ▶ See Exs. 27–46 on pp. 258–259.

Section 2 Key Concepts

Multiplying Decimals (pp. 248–249)

To multiply decimal numbers, you first multiply them as whole numbers. Then the number of decimal places in the product is the sum of the numbers of decimal places in the factors.

You can use powers of 10 and estimation to check whether a product of decimals is reasonable.

Example

2 places, 2 places

(66.**25**)(0.**82**) = 54.**3250** ← 2 + 2 = 4 decimal places

Check: The factor 0.82 is a little less than 1, so the product will be a little less than 66.25. Therefore, 54.325 is a reasonable answer.

Dividing Decimals (pp. 250–251)

To divide decimal numbers, you first multiply the divisor and the dividend by a power of 10 that will make the divisor a whole number. Then you divide. You may have to write zeros at the end of the dividend.

Example 16.2 ÷ 7.5

7.5)16.2
× 10   × 10

```
     2.16
75)162.00
   150
    120
     75
     450
     450
       0
```

You place the decimal point in the quotient above the decimal point in the dividend.

Check: The quotient 2.16 is reasonable, because 16.2 ÷ 7.5 ≈ 16 ÷ 8 = 2.

31 Key Concepts Question Estimate each product or quotient. Tell whether your estimate is *greater than* or *less than* the exact answer. Then find the exact answer.

a. (7.8)(0.995) **b.** 720 ÷ 0.08 **c.** (6.05)(2.2)

Continued on next page

Section 2 Key Concepts

Key Terms

repeating decimal

terminating decimal

Repeating and Terminating Decimals (pp. 252–253)

A decimal in which a digit or a sequence of digits keeps repeating is a repeating decimal. The bar indicates which digits repeat. A decimal that stops is a terminating decimal.

You can write the decimal equivalent of a fraction by dividing the numerator by the denominator. (p. 253)

Examples

repeating decimal

terminating decimal

$\frac{4}{15} = 4 \div 15 = 0.2666\ldots = 0.2\overline{6}$

$\frac{7}{8} = 7 \div 8 = 0.875$

The digit 6 repeats.

Division with Zero (p. 254)

Zero divided by any non-zero number is always zero, because the product of zero and any non-zero number is always zero.

Example $0 \div 9 = 0$, because $0 \cdot 9 = 0$.

Division by zero is undefined, because there is no number by which you can multiply zero to produce a non-zero product.

Example $9 \div 0$ is undefined, because there is no number that makes $0 \cdot ? = 9$ a true statement.

32 Key Concepts Question Predict whether each quotient will be *greater than*, *less than*, or *equal to* the number in red. Then find the exact quotient to check each prediction.

a. $\mathbf{4.5} \div 1$ **b.** $\mathbf{0.64} \div 0.015$ **c.** $\frac{\mathbf{0.8}}{1.1}$

Practice & Application Exercises

YOU WILL NEED

For Exs. 54–57:
- protractor

Copy each problem. Use estimation to place the decimal point in each product.

1. (0.09)(7.2) = 648
2. (215.4)(0.3) = 6462
3. (4.78)(0.652) = 311656
4. (591.6)(3.87) = 2289492

Find each product. Show your work.

5. (25.9)(9.78)
6. (0.09)(3.6)
7. (102.1)(0.7)
8. (415.2)(0.89)
9. (32.76)(0.025)
10. (0.48)(0.15)

Estimation For Exercises 11 and 12, use estimation. Explain your method. Then tell whether the exact answer will be *greater than* or *less than* your estimate.

11. Carlos placed a bunch of grapes on a scale at a fruit stand. The bunch weighed 2.7 lb. Grapes are on sale for $1.59 per pound. Suppose Carlos has a $5 bill. Does he have enough money to buy the grapes? Explain.

12. Electricity usage is measured in kilowatt-hours (kW • h). The bill shows the amount of electricity used for the month of February, along with the price per kW • h. Estimate the cost of the electricity for February.

Electricity Bill

Dates: 2/1/97 through 2/28/97

Number of kW • h		Price per unit
244	×	$0.12647

Copy each problem. Use estimation with powers of 10 to place the decimal point in each quotient.

13. 23.4 ÷ 0.08 = 2925
14. 4.41 ÷ 0.12 = 3675
15. 115 ÷ 9.2 = 125
16. 49.7 ÷ 1.4 = 355
17. A student took the quiz shown. Without doing the problems, find two errors. Explain how you identified each error.

Exploration 2 Quiz

1. 92.4 ÷ 77 = 1.2
2. 1.3 ÷ 0.25 = 0.52
3. 344.1 ÷ 9.25 = 37.2
4. 57.5 ÷ 0.08 = 718.75
5. 39.6 ÷ 0.11 = 36

Find each quotient. Show your work.

18. $27 \div 4.5$ **19.** $0.34 \div 0.04$ **20.** $1.8\overline{)10.08}$

21. $1.74 \div 0.3$ **22.** $0.005\overline{)90}$ **23.** $0.87 \div 1.2$

24. **Geometry Connection** Suppose a circle has a circumference of 157 cm. Find the diameter of the circle. Use 3.14 for π. Do not use a calculator.

25. Carmen finds a picture of a grasshopper in a science magazine. The picture caption reads, "Picture is 0.8 of actual size."

a. Is the picture *larger* or *smaller* than the actual grasshopper?

b. Suppose the actual grasshopper is 5.2 cm long. How long is the picture?

c. Suppose the picture is 36 mm long. How long is the actual grasshopper?

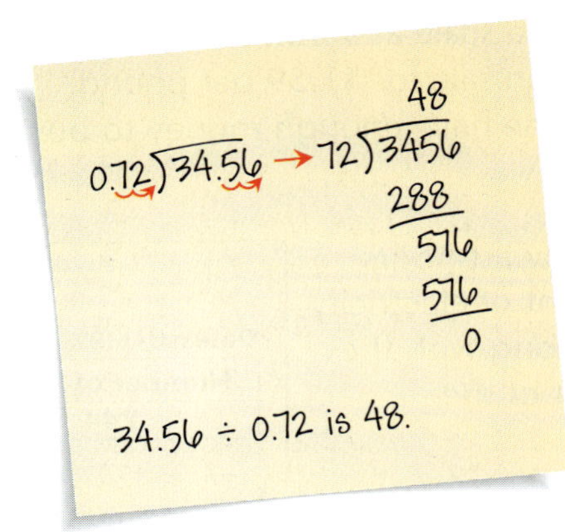

26. Brenda's solution to the problem $34.56 \div 0.72$ is shown. Is she correct? Do you think her method will always work? Explain.

Write each decimal carried out to six decimal places.

27. $0.\overline{315}$ **28.** $6.\overline{36}$ **29.** $0.02\overline{7}$ **30.** $101.\overline{81}$

Find each quotient. Show your work.

31. $0.47 \div 0.6$ **32.** $0.45\overline{)13.6}$ **33.** $1.4 \div 2.7$

34. $\frac{1.2}{9}$ **35.** $56.12 \div 0$ **36.** $0.11\overline{)67.5}$

Write each fraction as a decimal rounded to the nearest hundredth.

37. $\frac{5}{8}$ **38.** $\frac{2}{3}$ **39.** $\frac{7}{12}$ **40.** $\frac{3}{7}$

Predict whether each quotient will be *greater than, less than,* or *equal to* the number in red. Explain how you know.

41. **14.67** $\div$ 9.1 **42.** $\frac{\mathbf{30.1}}{0.86}$ **43.** **5.825** $\div \frac{102}{101}$

44. Graphic Design Graphic designers often need to reduce photos to fit in a small space. A graphic designer for an art book needs to include a photo of a sculpture in the book. In the photo, the sculpture is 18.7 cm high. In the book, the sculpture must be 5.5 cm high.

a. About how much does the designer need to reduce the photo?

b. Find the reduction that will make the photo fit perfectly into the book's space. Explain the method you used.

45. Challenge Replace each ? with one of the digits 1, 3, 5, or 9 to create an expression for each quotient. ? • ? ÷ ? • ?

a. the least quotient

b. the greatest quotient

Reflecting on the Section

Write your response to Exercise 46 in your journal.

46. Margo works part-time at a clothing store. She is paid monthly. Part of her earnings statement for the month of May is shown.

May Earnings		
Hourly rate	Hours worked	Gross earnings
$9.88	53.75	$351.05

a. Use estimation with powers of 10 to check whether Margo's earnings statement is accurate.

b. Write and solve an equation to find out whether the earnings statement is accurate.

c. Which method is better, part (a) or part (b)? Why?

Journal

Exercise 46 checks that you can estimate with decimals in real-life situations.

Spiral Review

Evaluate each expression. (Module 4, pp. 241–242)

47. $\frac{3}{8} \cdot \frac{4}{11}$

48. $4 \div \frac{2}{5}$

49. $2\frac{1}{4} \cdot 8$

50. $3\frac{1}{3} \div \frac{5}{6}$

51. $2\frac{1}{5} \cdot \frac{5}{12}$

52. $5\frac{2}{5} \div \frac{3}{10}$

53. Val lives 11 blocks due east of Cora. Cora lives 4 blocks due west of Amy. Where does Amy live in relation to Val? (Module 1, p. 44)

Draw an angle with each measure. Then classify each angle as *acute, obtuse, right,* or *straight*. (Module 2, p. 83)

54. 60°

55. 145°

56. 22°

57. 174°

Lights, Camera—Action!

You'll explore several mathematical concepts that can be used to create special animated effects to use in your zoetrope. To complete the project, you'll work as a group to create and set up a viewing station featuring several animation strips that use the special effects of your choice.

SET UP

You will need:

- *Project Labsheet A*
- *scissors*
- *tape*
- *compass*
- *ruler*
- *colored pencils or markers (optional)*

Estimation Use your estimation skills to create a shrinking effect.

1 You can use a copying machine to reduce the size of a figure that is too difficult to redraw. For example, a 75% reduction will result in a figure 0.75 times its actual size. Suppose you want to use a copying machine to shorten the figure in Frame 1 (F1) by about 6 mm in each frame from F2 to F4.

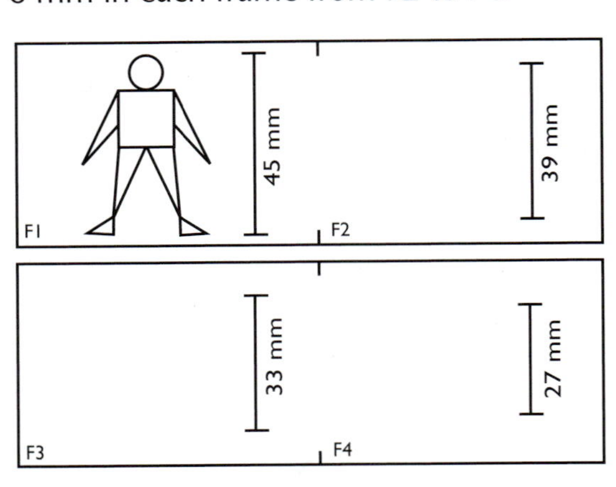

a. Estimate the height of the figure needed for F2 in relation to the height of the original figure in F1. What percent reduction should you use to create the figure for F2 on a copying machine?

b. Estimate the percent reduction you should use on the original figure in F1 to create the figures for F3 and F4.

2 **Use Project Labsheet A.**

a. Cut out the pieces of *Blank Zoetrope Strip A* and tape them together in order.

b. Draw a rectangle with a base length of 5 cm and a height of 1.5 cm in the center of F1. Complete F2–F8 by reducing each previous base length by 0.5 cm and increasing the height by 0.5 cm. Color the interior of each rectangle.

c. Place your strip in the zoetrope with the frames centered under the slots. Spin the zoetrope. Describe what happens.

Section 2 Extra Skill Practice

You will need: • graph paper or 150 pennies (optional) **(Exs. 37–40)**

Find each product. Estimate to check that answers are reasonable.

1. (5.3)(2.6)
2. (17)(3.9)
3. (6.32)(0.87)
4. (65)(0.12)
5. (4.58)(0.034)
6. (13.8)(9.5)
7. (0.009)(289.6)
8. (0.56)(0.7)
9. (237.1)(19.4)
10. (0.019)(0.27)
11. (48)(25.31)
12. (0.84)(0.39)

Predict whether each product will be *greater than*, *less than*, or *equal to* the number in red. Explain how you know.

13. (**45.8**)(0.23)
14. (1.76)(**931.2**)
15. (**642.9**)(1)
16. (0.089)(**0.51**)

Find each quotient. Estimate to check that answers are reasonable.

17. $72\overline{)0.216}$
18. 21.28 ÷ 0.56
19. $1.6\overline{)10.384}$
20. $\frac{9}{11}$
21. $0.35\overline{)2.1}$
22. 378.92 ÷ 0
23. $\frac{2.4}{21.6}$
24. 46.3 ÷ 0.09
25. $0.076\overline{)17.48}$
26. $\frac{15}{22}$
27. 48.02 ÷ 49
28. 0 ÷ 0.281

Predict whether each quotient will be *greater than*, *less than*, or *equal to* the number in red. Explain how you know.

29. **24.32** ÷ 0.38
30. $185\overline{)\mathbf{82.14}}$
31. **537.4** ÷ 1
32. **74.25** ÷ 0.99
33. **562** ÷ 3488
34. **87** ÷ 87.3
35. **484** ÷ 0.8
36. **0.732** ÷ 5

Visual Thinking **For Exercises 37–40, draw and shade 10 × 10 grids or use pennies to represent and find each product or quotient.**

37. (6)(0.15)
38. (12)(0.09)
39. 1.5 ÷ 6
40. 1.36 ÷ 4
41. **Open-ended** For each of Exercises 37–40, describe a real-world situation that can be represented using the given expression.

Standardized Testing ◀▶ Multiple Choice

1. Use estimation with powers of 10 to choose the product (0.033)(401.52).

   (A) 13.25016 (B) 132.5016 (C) 1.325016 (D) 1325.016

2. Which is the quotient 0.09 ÷ 1.1?

   (A) 0.082 (B) 0.081 (C) 0.81 (D) $0.0\overline{81}$

Section 3 Rotations and Reflections

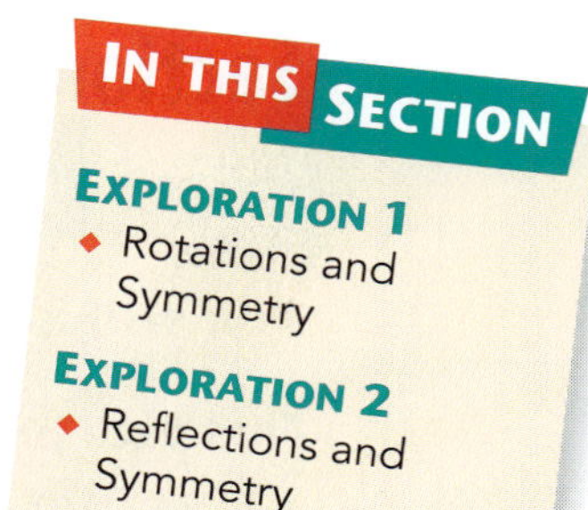

The MATH of MOTION

Setting the Stage

A sense of motion is sometimes created in artworks by the clever use of patterns, as in these Native American designs.

▲ This "whirlwind" design was woven into an Apache basket tray.

▲ A metalworker of the Fox tribe stamped and scribed this ornate pattern on a silver pin.

▲ Tiny colored beads were used to create this design for a Fox belt. The pattern combines the styles of both Plains and Woodlands tribes.

Think About It

1 Choose two of the artworks above. Explain how you think each design creates a sense of motion.

2 Look for designs on objects in your classroom such as clothing, backpacks, posters, and so on, that create a sense of motion. Explain how each design achieves this effect.

Exploration 1

Rotations and Symmetry

SET UP *You will need:* • *Labsheets 3A and 3B* • *scissors* • *tape* • *tracing paper* • *zoetrope* • *protractor*

GOAL

LEARN HOW TO...
- rotate a figure
- describe a rotation
- identify rotational symmetries

AS YOU...
- study designs used in artwork

KEY TERMS
- rotation
- center of rotation
- image
- rotational symmetry
- rotational symmetries

3 **Use Labsheet 3A.** Each frame of the *Jewelry Design Zoetrope Strip* contains part of the petal design used on the Fox silver pin shown on page 262.

a. Cut out the pieces of the zoetrope strip and tape them together. Place the strip in the zoetrope so that each frame is centered under a slot.

b. What do you think will happen when the zoetrope is spun?

c. Spin the zoetrope clockwise and observe what happens. Describe what you see.

d. Now spin the zoetrope counterclockwise. Is the result the same as in part (c)? Explain.

4 **Use Labsheet 3B.** Follow the directions on Labsheet 3B to investigate how the *Stick Figure* can be rotated from one position to another.

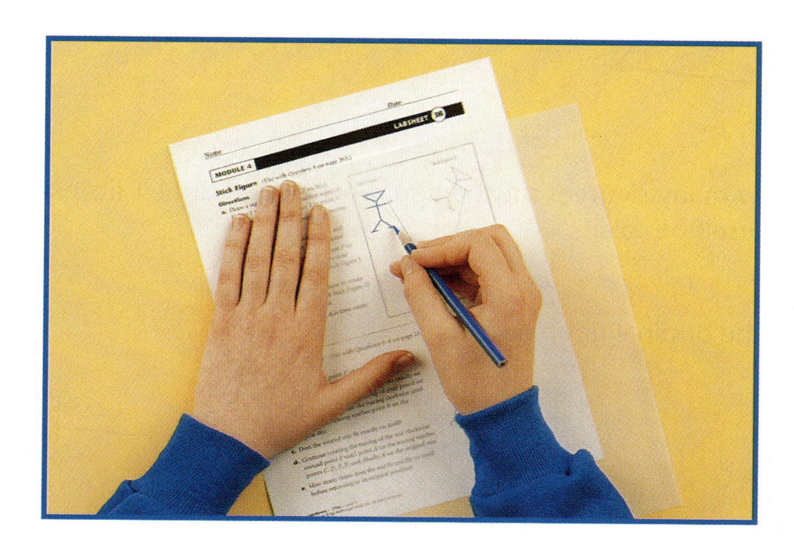

▶ A **rotation** turns a figure about a fixed point—the **center of rotation**—a certain amount in one direction, either clockwise or counterclockwise. The new figure is the **image** of the original figure. In this book, the image for any transformation is shown in red.

EXAMPLE

The rotation shown can be described in two ways.

Clockwise Rotation

The image is a **90° clockwise rotation** of the original figure about point *P*.

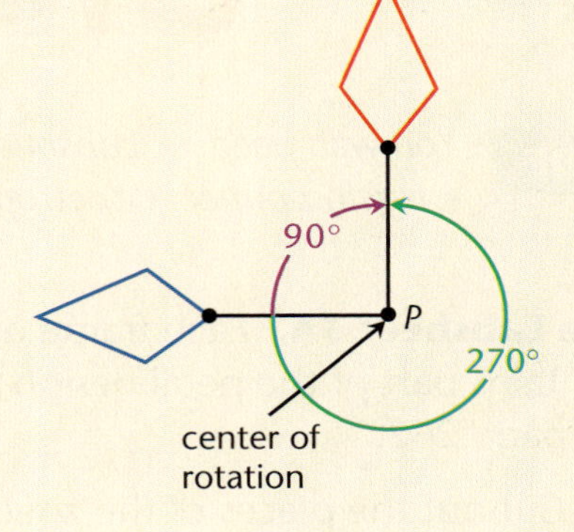

Counterclockwise Rotation

The image is a **270° counter-clockwise** rotation of the original figure about point *P*.

5 Find the number of degrees each figure must be rotated in the opposite direction to obtain the same result as each indicated rotation.

a. 180° clockwise rotation

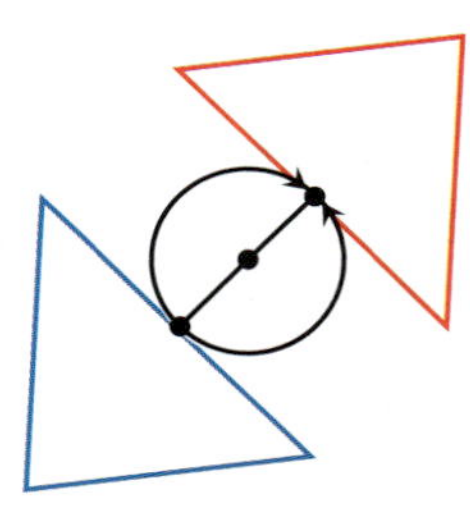

b. 135° counterclockwise rotation

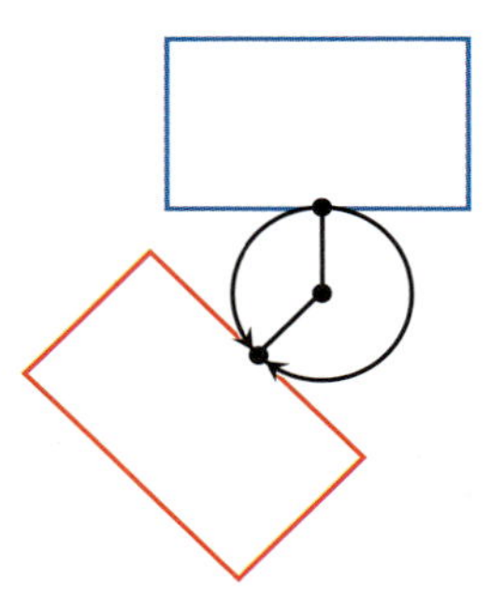

6 How many degrees must a figure be rotated until it fits exactly on itself**?** Explain.

QUESTION 7

...checks that you can describe a rotation.

7 **CHECKPOINT** Describe the rotation of the original figure in two ways.

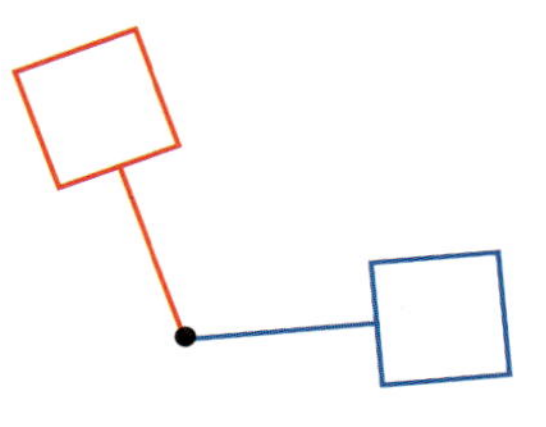

▶ **You have explored rotations about a point outside a figure. Now you'll investigate rotations about a point that is inside a figure.**

Use Labsheet 3B for Questions 8 and 9.

8 Follow the directions on Labsheet 3B to investigate what happens when you rotate the *Six-Pointed Star* about its center.

▶ **A figure that fits exactly on itself after a rotation of less than 360° about a point has rotational symmetry.**

A.

B.

These figures have rotational symmetry.

C.

D.

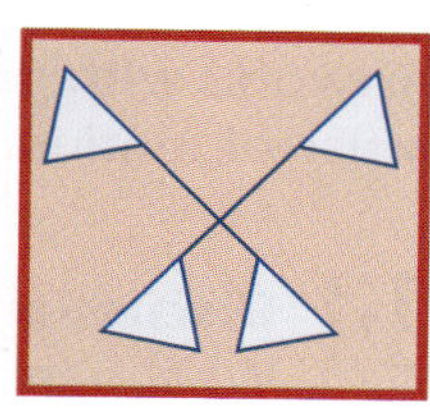

These figures do not have rotational symmetry.

▶ **The amounts of rotation that fit a figure exactly on itself are the rotational symmetries of the figure.**

9 **Discussion** *The Six-Pointed Star* on Labsheet 3B has rotational symmetries of 60°, 120°, 180°, 240°, and 300°. How do you think these angles were determined?

10 Look at figures A and B above that have rotational symmetry.

a. How many rotational symmetries does each figure have?

b. Describe all the rotational symmetries of each figure.

11 ✓ **CHECKPOINT** Find all rotational symmetries of each figure.

a.

b.

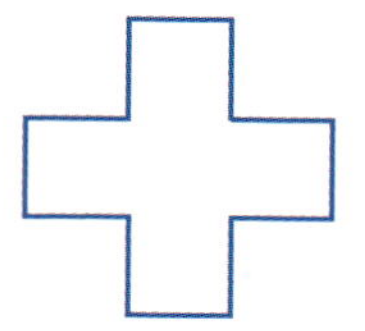

c.

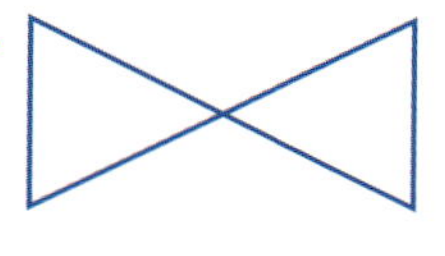

✓ **QUESTION 11**

...checks that you can identify all the rotational symmetries of a figure.

12 Look at the designs shown on page 262.

a. Which designs appear to have rotational symmetry?

b. Estimate the rotational symmetries for each design in part (a).

HOMEWORK EXERCISES ▶ See Exs. 1–13 on pp. 271–272.

GOAL

LEARN HOW TO...
- identify a reflection
- identify lines of symmetry

AS YOU...
- explore mirror images in art

KEY TERMS
- vertex of a triangle
- congruent
- reflection
- line of reflection
- line symmetry
- line of symmetry

Exploration 2

REFLECTIONS and SYMMETRY

SET UP *You will need:* • *Labsheet 3C* • *ruler* • *2 sheets of tracing paper* • *mirror, polyester film, or MIRA®*

▶ **Artworks with patterns that contain mirror images can also create a sense of motion.**

13 **Discussion** Imagine that you are looking at yourself in a mirror. What happens to your reflection when you raise your left hand? when you move closer to the mirror? when you move farther away from the mirror?

14 Follow Steps 1–3 to investigate mirror images.

Step 1

Fold a sheet of tracing paper in half. Then draw a triangle with a dark pencil or pen.

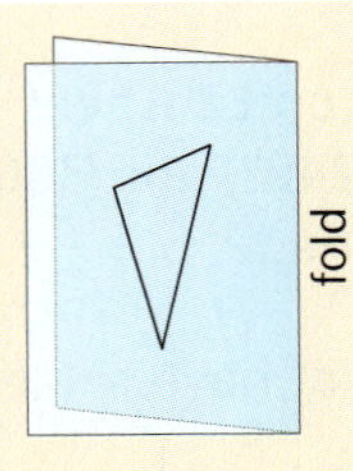

Step 2

Turn over your folded paper and trace the triangle you drew in Step 1.

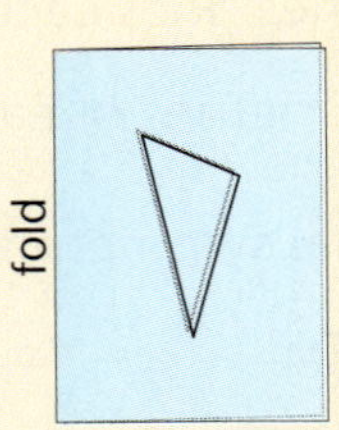

Step 3

Unfold your paper. Label the *vertices* of your original triangle *A*, *B*, and *C*.

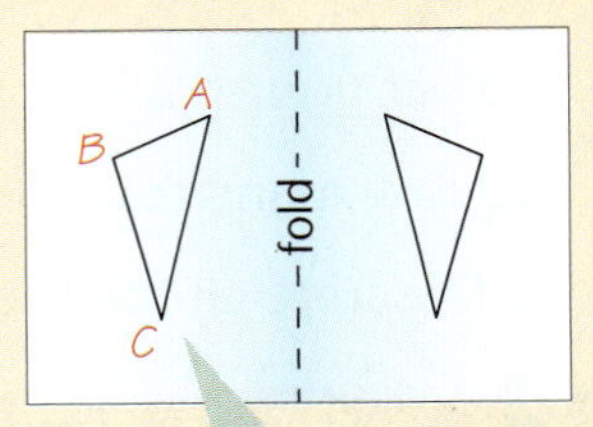

Each point where two sides of the triangle meet is a **vertex**.

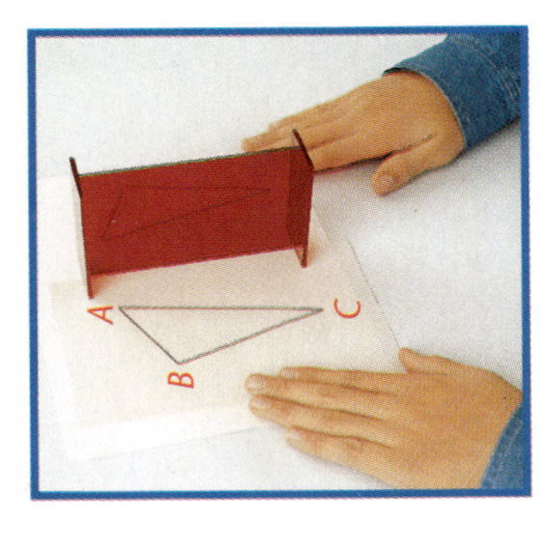

15 The triangle with vertices *A*, *B*, and *C* is called "triangle *ABC*" and written $\triangle ABC$. Place a MIRA® on the fold so you can see the reflection of $\triangle ABC$.

a. Describe the reflection of $\triangle ABC$. How is the reflection of $\triangle ABC$ related to the triangle on the right side of the fold?

b. What do you think will happen to the reflection of $\triangle ABC$ when the MIRA® is moved closer to $\triangle ABC$? farther away from $\triangle ABC$?

16 Place the MIRA® on the fold again. Use A', read as "A prime," to label the image of point A. Use B' and C' to label the images of points B and C.

▶ **Two figures that are the same shape and the same size are congruent.**

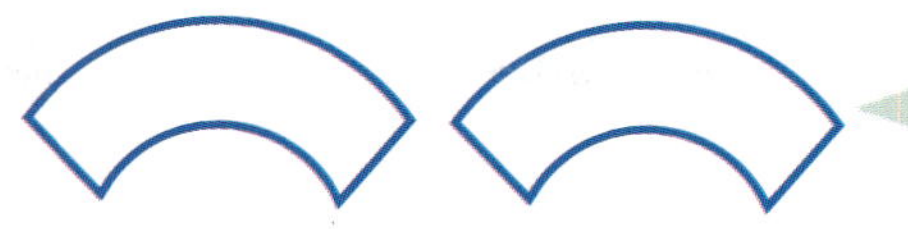

The figures are congruent.

17 Make another tracing of $\triangle ABC$. Use the tracing to show that $\triangle ABC$ and $\triangle A'B'C'$ are congruent. What did you have to do to the tracing in order to show that the triangles are congruent?

▶ **$\triangle A'B'C'$ is the *reflection* of $\triangle ABC$ across the fold. A reflection is a flip across a line. The line is the line of reflection. The result is a mirror image of the original figure.**

EXAMPLE

Each image is a reflection of the original figure across the line shown.

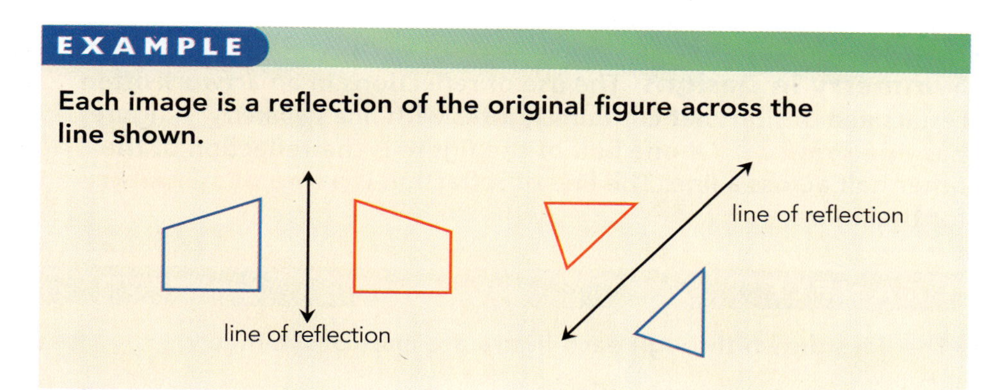

18 Use your drawing from Question 14 to investigate some of the properties of reflections.

a. Draw a segment along the fold to represent the line of reflection.

b. Draw a segment connecting A and its image, A'. This segment is written as $\overline{AA'}$. Now draw $\overline{BB'}$.

c. Use M to label the point of intersection of $\overline{AA'}$ and the line of reflection. Use N to label the point of intersection of $\overline{BB'}$ and the line of reflection.

d. Look at the four angles formed where $\overline{AA'}$ intersects the line of reflection. What do you notice?

e. Measure the distance from A to M and the distance from A' to M. How do the two distances compare?

f. Measure the distance from B to N. Without measuring, predict the distance from B' to N. Then check your prediction.

✓ QUESTION 19

...checks that you can identify a reflection.

19 ✓ CHECKPOINT Tell whether each image is a reflection of the original figure across the line between them. For any that are not reflections, explain why they are not.

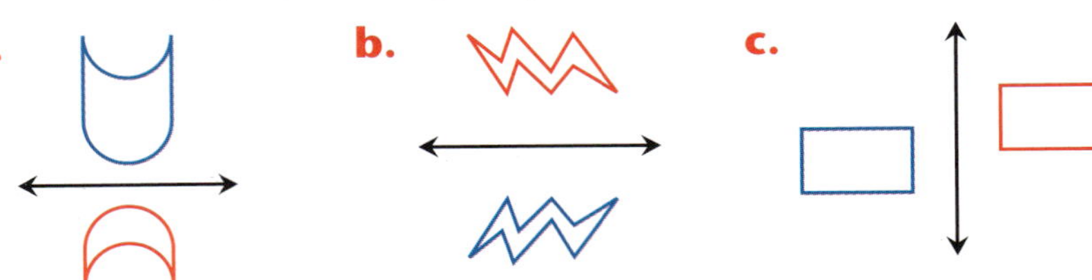

20 Use Labsheet 3C. Look at the *Congruent Butterflies*.

a. How can you find a line of reflection that will reflect the top butterfly so that it fits exactly on the bottom butterfly?

b. Use your method from part (a) to locate and draw the line of reflection.

▶ **Symmetry in Designs** **The use of reflections in an artwork often results in a design that contains figures with *line symmetry*. A figure has line symmetry if one half of the figure is the reflection of the other half across a line. The line of reflection is a line of symmetry for the figure.**

Line symmetry is common in nature. A black fly, shown here greatly enlarged, has a vertical line of symmetry.

EXAMPLE

The lines drawn through each figure are lines of symmetry.

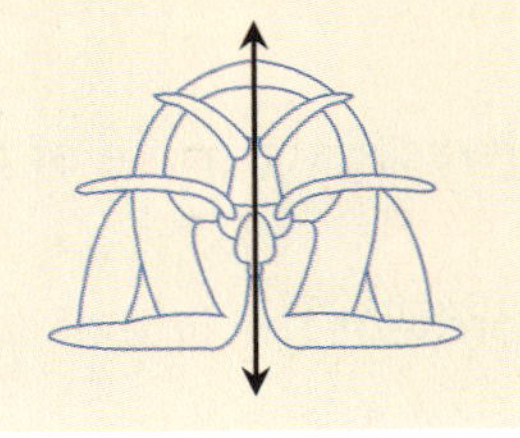

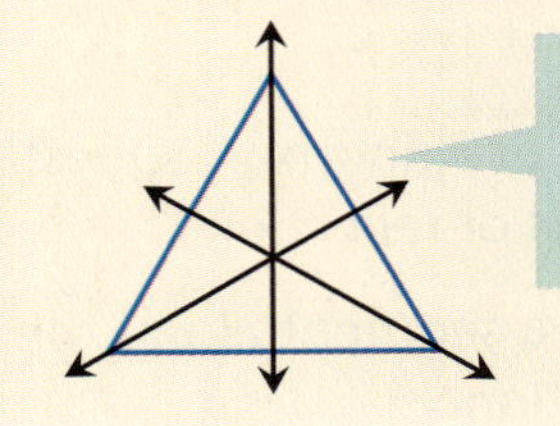

Some figures have more than one line of symmetry.

21 Use Labsheet 3C. Draw all the lines of symmetry on each portion of the *Fox Belt Design*.

22 Create Your Own Draw a shape that has at least two lines of symmetry.

✓ QUESTION 23

...checks that you can identify lines of symmetry.

23 ✓ CHECKPOINT Draw a square. Then draw all its lines of symmetry. How many lines of symmetry does a square have?

HOMEWORK EXERCISES ▶ See Exs. 14–31 on pp. 272–274.

TECHNOLOGY Using Computer Drawing Software

You can use computer drawing software to create a shape with two lines of symmetry for Question 22 on page 268.

Step 1 Choose the auto grid option to show a grid on your screen. From any point on a grid line, draw a continuous line or shape.

You can also draw intersecting horizontal and vertical lines.

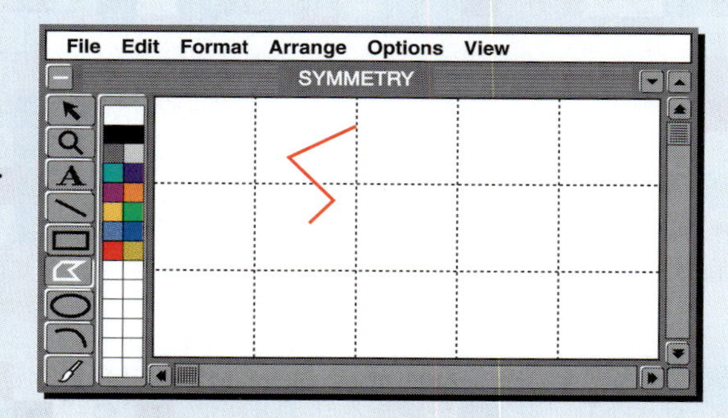

Step 2 Duplicate your figure. Then flip the copy horizontally or vertically. Drag the copy so that it meets the original figure.

The shape has one line of symmetry.

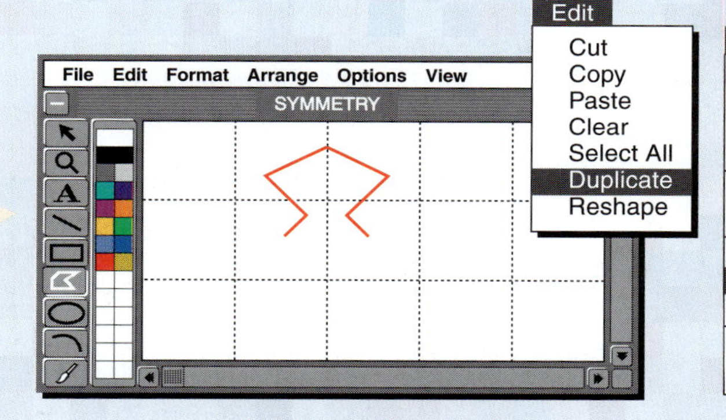

Step 3 To create a second line of symmetry, first group the two images to form one object. Next duplicate the object and flip the copy horizontally or vertically. Then drag the copy so that it meets the original object.

The shape has vertical and horizontal lines of symmetry.

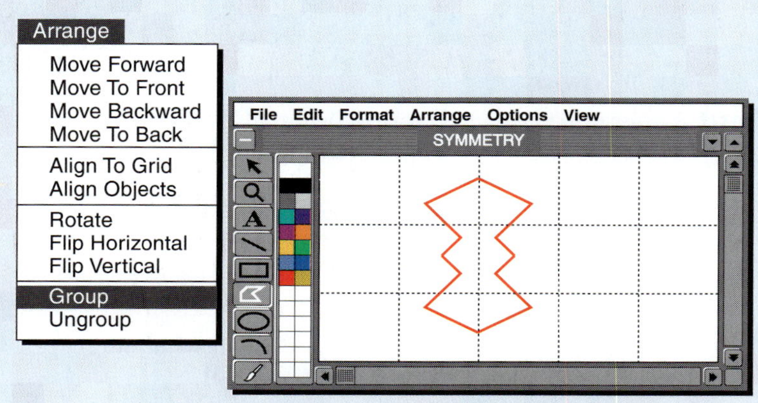

Section 3 Key Concepts

Key Terms

rotation

image

center of rotation

rotational symmetry

rotational symmetries

reflection

line of reflection

congruent

vertex of a triangle

Rotations (p. 264)

A rotation turns a figure about a point a certain number of degrees either clockwise or counterclockwise. The new figure is the image of the original figure.

Example The figure shows a 60° clockwise or 300° counterclockwise rotation around point *P*.

P is the center of rotation.

Rotational Symmetry (p. 265)

A figure that fits exactly on itself after being rotated less than 360° about a point has rotational symmetry.

Example This figure has rotational symmetries of 72°, 144°, 216°, and 288°.

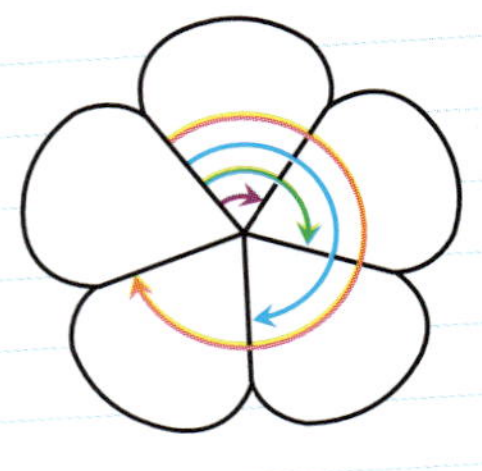

Reflections (p. 267)

A reflection flips a figure across a line.

Example

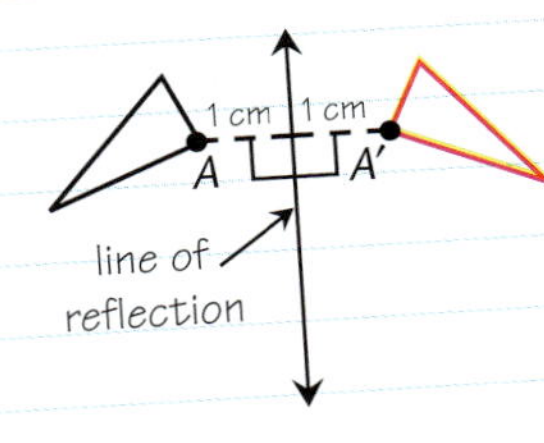

Each point on the original figure and its image are the same distance from the line of reflection.

If you connect a point and its image with a segment, the segment will intersect the line of reflection at a right angle.

The original figure and its image are congruent, since they are the same size and shape.

24 Key Concepts Question Tell whether each letter has rotational symmetry. If so, find all its rotational symmetries.

B O X E S

Section 3 Key Concepts

Key Terms

line symmetry

line of symmetry

Line Symmetry (p. 268)

If one half of a figure is a reflection of the other half, the figure has line symmetry.

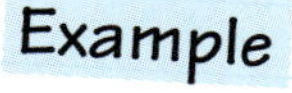

Example

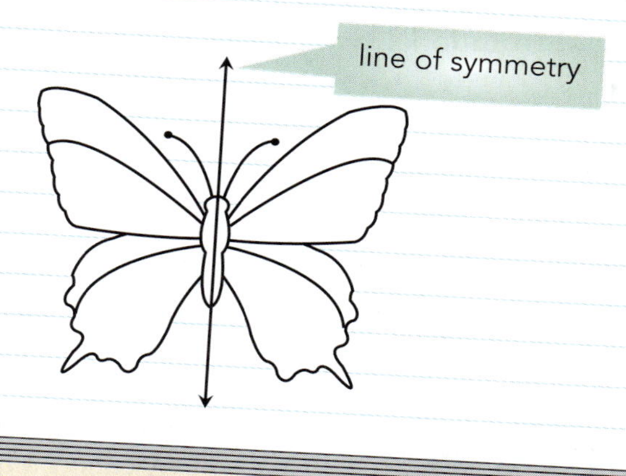

25 **Key Concepts Question** Tell whether each letter in Question 24 has line symmetry. If so, copy the letter and draw all its lines of symmetry.

Section 3 Practice & Application Exercises

YOU WILL NEED

For Exs. 1–2:
- protractor

For Exs. 4, 8–11, 28–30:
- protractor
- ruler

For Exs. 5–7:
- tracing paper

For Exs. 45–46:
- Labsheet 3D
- tracing paper
- ruler
- protractor

For each clockwise rotation of the original figure in Exercises 1 and 2:

a. **Estimation** Estimate the amount of rotation.

b. Find the actual amount of rotation.

c. Describe another rotation that results in the same image.

1.

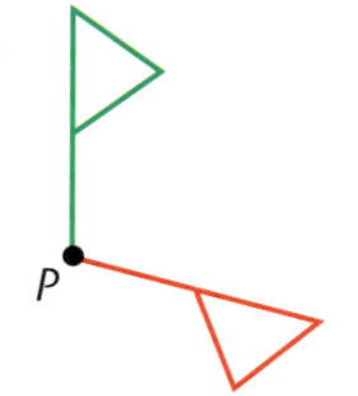

2.

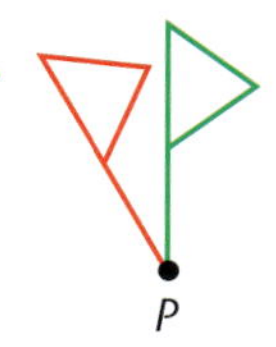

3. How many degrees does the minute hand of a clock rotate in 5 min? in 12 min?

4. **Open-ended** Draw a scalene triangle with a right angle. Mark and label a point below the triangle to use as the center of rotation. Then draw the image of the triangle after a 60° counterclockwise rotation.

Trace each shape below. Then use your tracing to determine whether the shape has rotational symmetry. For each shape that has rotational symmetry, find all its rotational symmetries.

5. 

6. 

7. 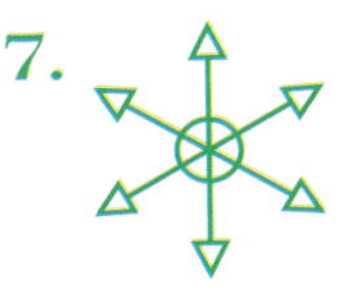

8. **Create Your Own** The Fox pin design shown on page 262 has rotational symmetry. Create your own pin design that has rotational symmetry.

Diatoms are one-celled or colonial algae that live under water. ▶

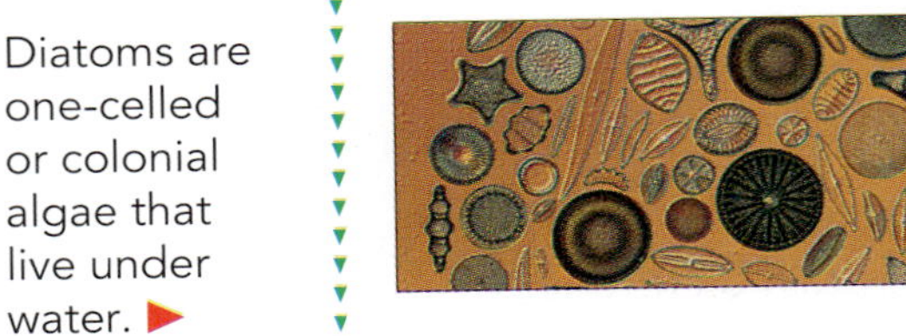

Biology The microscopic organisms shown below, called *diatoms*, have rotational symmetry. Find all the rotational symmetries of each diatom.

9. 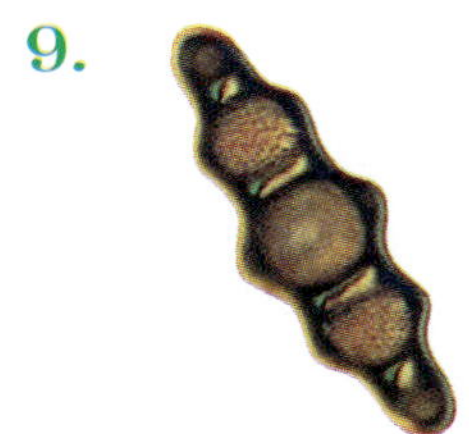

10. 

11. 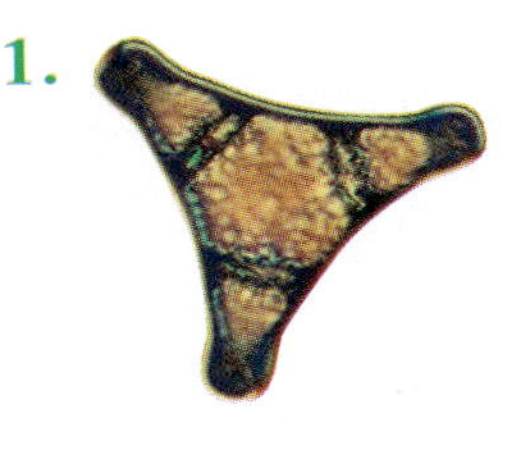

12. **Challenge** Draw a figure that has rotational symmetries of 90°, 180°, and 270°.

13. **Writing** Several angles of rotation can be used to create designs with rotational symmetry. How can you use the prime factorization of 360 to make a list of possible rotational symmetries?

Tell whether each diagram shows a reflection of the original figure across the given line. If not, explain why not.

14. 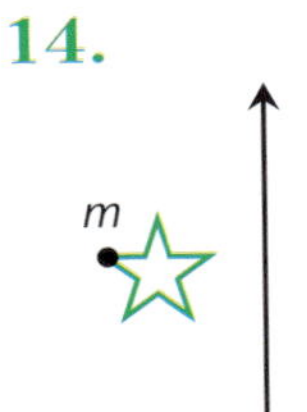

15. 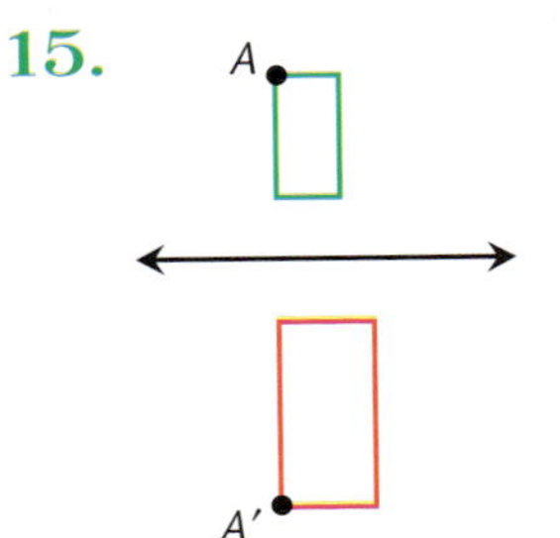

16. 
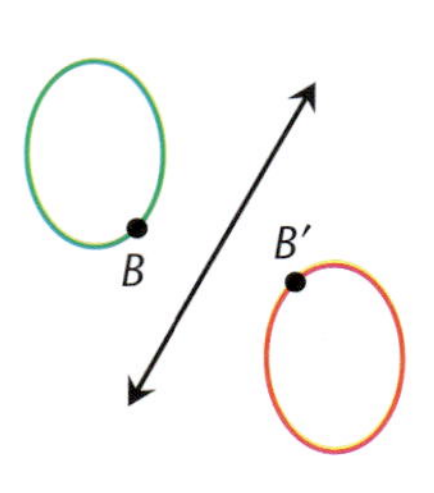

Tell whether the figures in each pair are congruent.

For each figure, tell whether the line shown is a line of symmetry. If it is not, explain why not.

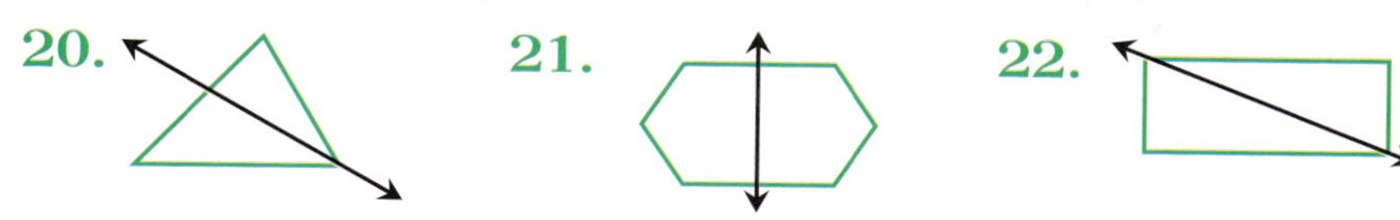

Native American Designs Many Native American peoples enhanced the beauty of everyday objects with elaborate decorations. The rug shown below was made by the Navajo people.

This Navajo rug was woven about 1940.

23. Tell whether the design on the rug shown above has rotational symmetry. Explain.

24. Tell whether the design shown above has line symmetry. Explain.

25. **Writing** Explain how reflections were used in the rug design.

26. *Palindromes* are words or numbers that look the same whether they are written from left to right or from right to left. For example, the name ANNA and the number 525 are both palindromes.

    a. Some palindromes have line symmetry. Identify the line of symmetry in the word MOM.

    b. Find two other examples of word or number palindromes that have line symmetry.

27. **Visual Thinking** Think of two objects in nature that have line symmetry. Make a sketch of each object.

Challenge For each description, draw a figure that fits the description.

28. has both line symmetry and rotational symmetry

29. has rotational symmetry but not line symmetry

30. has line symmetry but not rotational symmetry

Reflecting on the Section

RESEARCH

Exercise 31 checks that you can recognize rotations and reflections.

31. A logo is a symbol that identifies a company, a sports team, or some other organization. Look through newspapers, magazines, catalogs, and other sources to find logos that use a rotation, a reflection, or possibly both in their designs. Cut out or copy the logo to share with the class.

Spiral Review

Find each product or quotient. (Module 4, pp. 255–256)

32. (30.4)(0.07)

33. $0.3\overline{)97.56}$

34. (51.8)(2.3)

35. $\frac{4.8}{11}$

36. (0.089)(0.06)

37. 38.6 ÷ 0.4

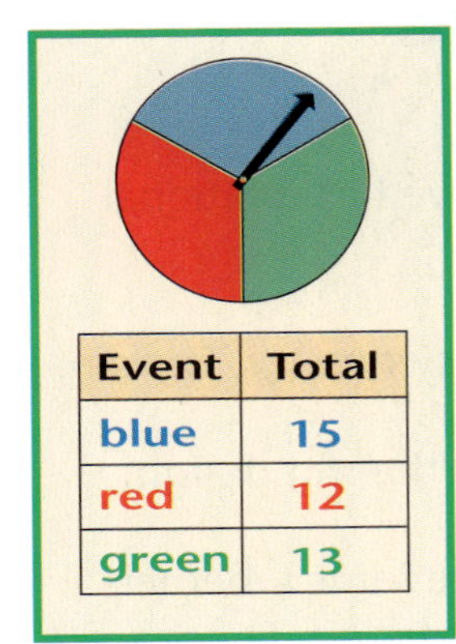

Event	Total
blue	15
red	12
green	13

38. Suppose the spinner was spun 40 times. Use the results in the table to answer parts (a) and (b). (Module 1, p. 33)

a. What is the experimental probability that the spinner stops on red? on blue?

b. Suppose the spinner is spun 120 times. About how many times do you expect the spinner to stop on red? on blue?

Find each sum or difference. (Module 2, p. 109)

39. –16 + 7

40. 26 – (–13)

41. –54 + 54

42. –38 – (–5)

43. –9 + (–25) + 6

44. –42 – 11 – (–7)

Extension

Finding the Center of Rotation

Use Labsheet 3D for Exercises 45 and 46.

45. Follow the directions to explore how to find the center of rotation for the *Rotated Stick Figure*.

46. Use the center of rotation you found in Exercise 45. Draw the image of the Stick Figure after a 50° counter-clockwise rotation.

Lights, Camera—Action!

SET UP *You will need:* • *Project Labsheet A* • *scissors* • *tape* • *protractor* • *zoetrope*

3 **Use another copy of Project Labsheet A.** Cut out the pieces of *Blank Zoetrope Strip A* and tape them together.

4 a. Mark a point in the center of each frame of the zoetrope strip to use as a center of rotation.

45° clockwise rotation of the figure in F1.

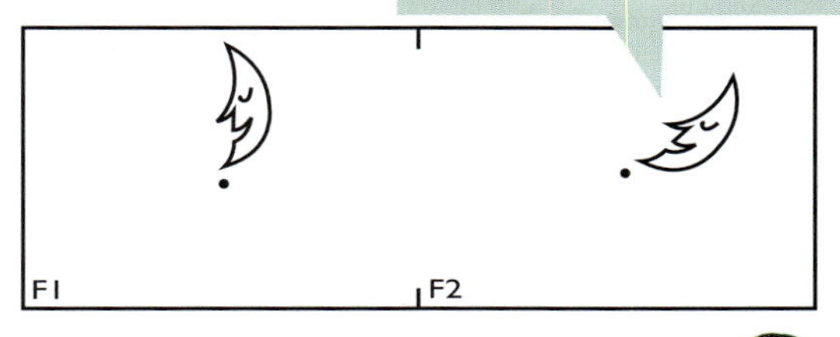

b. Draw a small figure centered in the upper half of Frame 1 (F1) above the point you marked in part (a). Then draw the image of the figure after the rotation of your choice in F2.

c. What angle of rotation did you use? Why?

d. Complete F3–F8 by rotating the image in the previous frame by the same number of degrees you used in part (b).

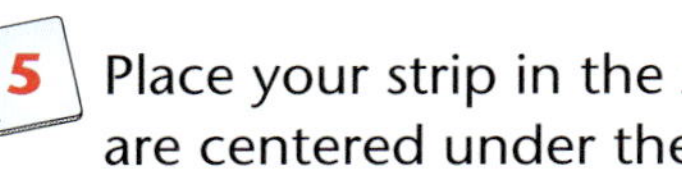

5 Place your strip in the zoetrope so the frames are centered under the slots. Then spin the zoetrope. Describe what you see.

Section 3
Extra Skill Practice

You will need: • *protractor* **(Ex. 1)** • *ruler* **(Ex. 1)**

1. Draw a triangle. Mark and label a point below the triangle to use as the center of rotation. Then draw the image of the triangle after a 130° clockwise rotation.

Determine whether each shape has rotational symmetry. For each shape that has rotational symmetry, find all its rotational symmetries.

2. 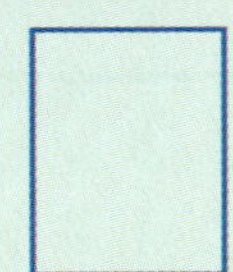

3. 

4. 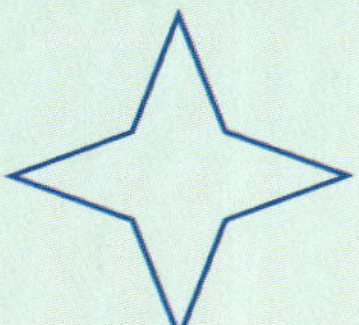

5. 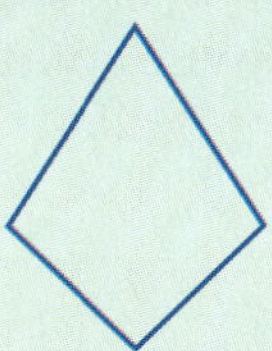

Tell whether each diagram shows a reflection of the original figure across the line.

6. 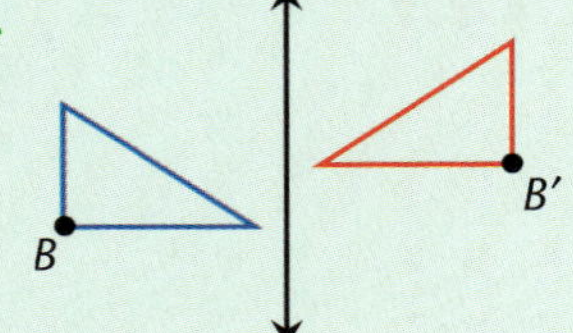

7. 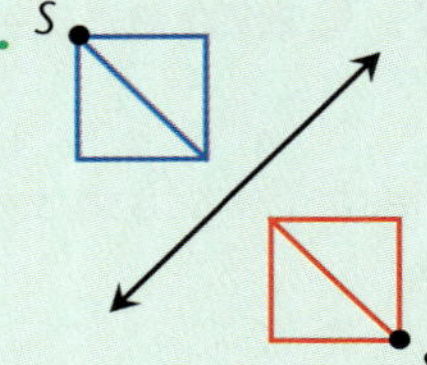

8. 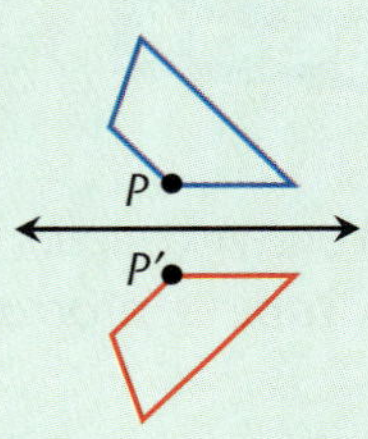

Tell whether the figures in each pair are congruent.

9. 

10. 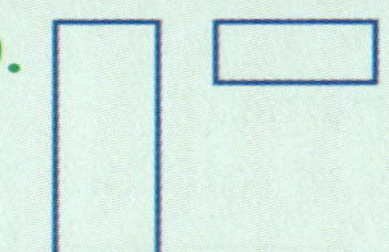

11. 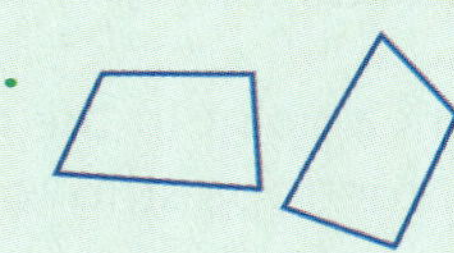

Standardized Testing ▶ Free Response

One figure in each pair is the image of the other after one or two transformations. Name the type(s) of transformation(s) that was (were) used to produce each image from the original figure.

1. 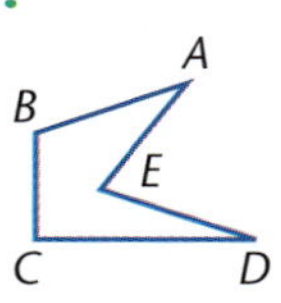

2. 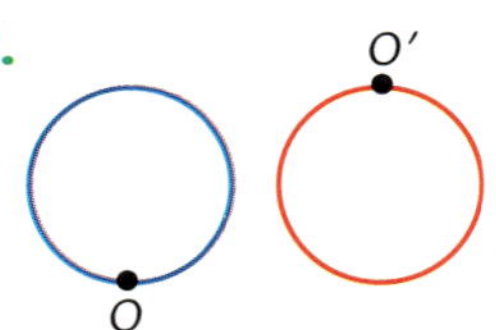

3. 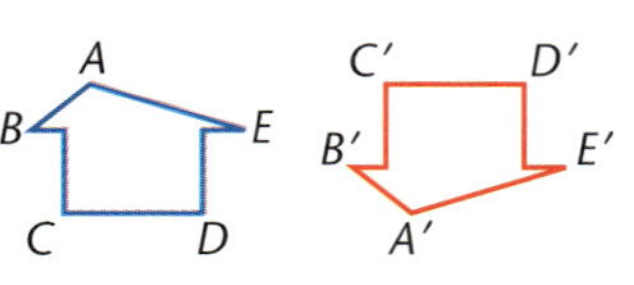

FOR ASSESSMENT AND PORTFOLIOS

Congruent Snowflakes

SET UP *You will need:* • *white paper* • *scissors*

The Situation

You can create snowflake designs by folding a piece of white paper and cutting out different shapes.

The Problem

Create the paper snowflake shown below.

Something to Think About

- How can you use rotational symmetry and line symmetry to help solve the problem?

Present Your Results

Write a summary that clearly explains how you solved the problem. Include any drawings or other representations that will help make your explanation clear to others.

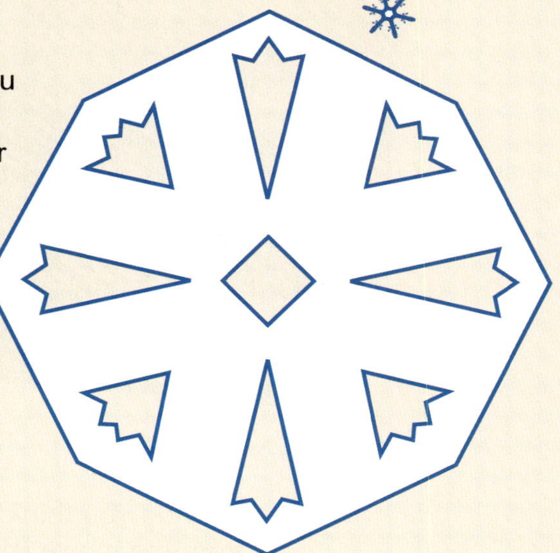

Section 4 Multiplication and Division of Integers

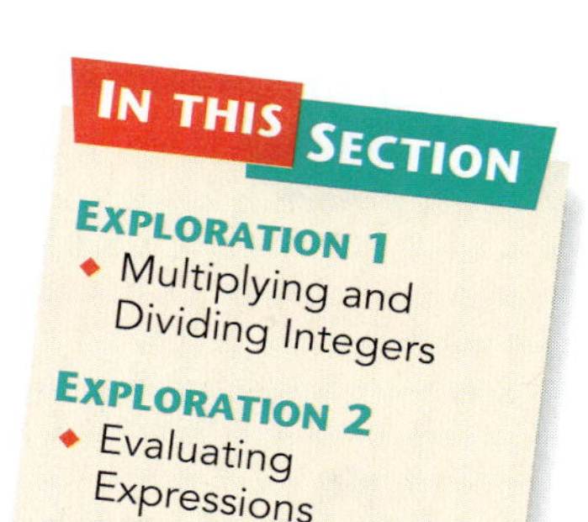

Special EFFECTS

Setting the Stage

One of the first special effects used by moviemakers was *reverse motion*, which was created by running film backward.

The 1922 silent film *Payday* contains a famous reverse motion scene. Charlie Chaplin plays a construction worker forced to catch bricks tossed up by co-workers on the ground.

Chaplin, standing on a high open framework, catches the bricks any way he can—with his feet, his chin, etc. Amazingly, he catches them all without falling!

Think About It

1 a. How do you think reverse motion was used to create the scene from the movie *Payday* shown above?

b. What are some other interesting visual effects that might be created using reverse motion?

Exploration 1

Multiplying and Dividing INTEGERS

GOAL

LEARN HOW TO...
- multiply and divide integers

AS YOU...
- experiment with reverse motion

KEY TERMS
- commutative property of multiplication
- associative property of multiplication

SET UP *Work in a group. You will need:* • *Labsheets 4A–4C* • *zoetrope* • *scissors* • *tape*

▶ **You can use your zoetrope to experiment with the effects created by reverse motion.**

Use Labsheets 4A–4C for Questions 2–4.

2 **a.** Cut out the pieces of the zoetrope strip of *A Person Walking Forward* and tape them together. Place the strip in your zoetrope so that each frame is centered under a slot.

b. Predict what will happen to the image when you spin the zoetrope forward (counterclockwise) and backward (clockwise). Record your predictions in the *Walking Person Table.*

c. Spin the zoetrope forward and backward and observe what happens to the image. Record your findings in the *Walking Person Table.*

3 Repeat parts (a)–(c) of Question 2 for the zoetrope strip of *A Person Walking Backward.* Record your predictions and results in the *Walking Person Table.*

4 Look at your completed *Walking Person Table.*

a. Which results were most surprising? Why?

b. What patterns do you see in the table? Explain.

▶ **You saw that there is a pattern in the different effects created by opposite motions in a zoetrope. In this exploration, you'll see how a similar pattern can be used to multiply and divide integers.**

▶ **Multiplication can be shown as movement on a number line, using repeated addition.**

EXAMPLE

Find the product 2 • (–3).

2 • (–3) means, "Add negative three 2 times."

Start at –3.	Face the positive direction.	**Move backward 3 units.**
–3	+	**(–3)**

–7 **–6** –5 –4 –3 –2 –1 0 1

So, 2 • (–3) = –6.

5 **Discussion** How can you show 3 • (–2) on a number line?

6 Find each product by writing the multiplication as a repeated addition and finding the sum.

a. 3 • 4 **b.** 3 • 0 **c.** 3 • (–4)

Use Labsheet 4C for Questions 7 and 8.

7 Follow the directions to complete the *Multiplication Table*.

8 **Discussion** You can use your results from Question 7 to help discover rules for multiplying integers.

a. Is the product of a positive integer and a negative integer *positive* or *negative*?

b. Is the product of two negative integers *positive* or *negative*?

c. How can you find the products in parts (a) and (b)?

✓ **QUESTION 9**

...checks that you can multiply integers.

9 ✓ **CHECKPOINT** Find each product. (*Note:* 3(–7) = 3 • (–7).)

a. 3(–7) **b.** (–4)(–12) **c.** –9(8) **d.** (–1)(–1)

10 How do the expressions (–5)(–9) and (–9)(–5) compare? How do their products compare?

11 How do the expressions (–2)(3 • 4) and (–2 • 3)4 compare? How do their products compare?

▶ Properties of Multiplication The **commutative property of multiplication** says that you can change the order of numbers in a multiplication problem and still get the same product. The **associative property of multiplication** says that you can change the grouping when you multiply numbers and still get the same product.

12 **Mental Math** Use the properties of multiplication and mental math to find the product (–5)(25)(–6)(–4).

▶ Dividing Integers You used patterns to help discover how to multiply integers. Now you'll use these patterns to divide integers.

13 **Try This as a Class** For every division problem, there is a related multiplication problem. For example, consider the division $12 \div 6 = 2$. The related multiplication is $6 \cdot 2 = 12$.

a. Think about the division equation $-20 \div 5 = x$. Write the related multiplication equation.

b. What number must x equal to make the multiplication equation you wrote in part (a) true?

c. What is the quotient $-20 \div 5$?

14 Write and solve a multiplication equation to find each quotient.

a. $30 \div (-6) = x$ **b.** $-14 \div 2 = x$ **c.** $-9 \div (-3) = x$

d. $-17 \div 17 = x$ **e.** $45 \div (-15) = x$ **f.** $-32 \div 4 = x$

15 **Discussion** Think about your results from Question 14.

a. Consider the division $180 \div (-5)$. Will the quotient be *positive* or *negative*? How do you know?

b. Write your own rule for dividing integers.

16 **✓ CHECKPOINT** Find each quotient.

a. $-18 \div (-3)$ **b.** $\frac{35}{-7}$ **c.** $-150 \div 5$ **d.** $\frac{-48}{-6}$

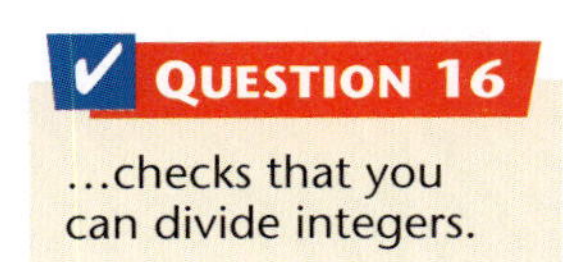
✓ QUESTION 16

...checks that you can divide integers.

17 Is division associative? commutative? Support each answer with examples.

18 **Discussion** Describe how the effects you saw in the zoetrope with the person walking forward and backward are related to the rules for multiplying and dividing integers.

HOMEWORK EXERCISES ▶ See Exs. 1–26 on pp. 285–286.

GOAL

LEARN HOW TO...
- evaluate expressions that contain decimals, fractions, or integers

AS YOU...
- explore how early moviemakers took close-up shots

Exploration 2

Evaluating Expressions

In the early days of moviemaking, a close-up was considered a special effect. Because the camera did not move, the actors had to walk toward the camera.

Have you ever taken a close-up photo of a friend that came out blurry? To get a sharp picture in a close-up, the distance between the lens and the film must be increased. To focus close-ups, early moviemakers used extension tubes.

EXAMPLE

Suppose a 12.5 mm extension tube was added to a 25 mm lens for a close-up shot. Use the formula below to find the amount the lens opening setting had to be decreased in this situation.

$$\text{decrease in setting} = \frac{\text{lens size (mm)} + \text{extension length (mm)}}{\text{lens size (mm)}}$$

$$= \frac{25 + 12.5}{25}$$

$$= \frac{37.5}{25}$$

$$= 1.5$$

Remember, you must follow the order of operations.

The lens opening setting must be decreased by 1.5.

FOR HELP with *order of operations*, see **MODULE 1, p. 65**

19 Why was the addition operation performed before the division operation in the Example above?

20 Suppose a 20.5 mm extension tube is added to the lens in the Example for a different close-up shot. Find the amount the lens opening setting must be decreased.

21 For each expression, choose the letter of the correct value.

a. $3 \cdot 5\frac{2}{3} - 7$

b. $-36 \div (-2 + 11)$

c. $\frac{21}{0.3 + 0.4}$

A. 30	**B.** –4
C. 10	**D.** –2

22 Copy each number sentence and add grouping symbols to make each a true statement.

a. $-5 - 2 \cdot 7 + (-3) = -13$ **b.** $\frac{2}{3} \cdot 1\frac{3}{4} + \frac{5}{8} = 1\frac{7}{12}$

23 ✓ CHECKPOINT Evaluate each expression.

a. $5\frac{3}{4} - 2\frac{1}{2} \cdot \frac{3}{8}$ **b.** $3.4 \cdot (7 - 2.9) + 11$ **c.** $-42 \div 8 + 5^2$

✓ QUESTION 23

...checks that you can evaluate expressions that contain fractions, decimals, or integers.

24 Suppose afternoon ticket prices at a movie theater are \$3 for children under 16 and \$5 for adults. Evening ticket prices are \$4.50 for children under 16 and \$7.75 for adults.

a. Choose variables for the number of children's tickets and the number of adults' tickets sold. Write an expression for the income in dollars from afternoon ticket sales each day.

b. Suppose 234 children's tickets and 127 adults' tickets were sold one afternoon. Use the expression you wrote in part (a) to find the income from afternoon ticket sales.

c. Write an expression for the income from evening ticket sales.

d. Look at the table. Use the expressions you wrote in parts (a) and (c) to determine whether the total income from ticket sales in dollars is correct. If not, find the correct total.

Motion Theater Ticket Sales			
Number of afternoon tickets sold		Number of evening tickets sold	
Children under 16	346	Children under 16	293
Adults	177	Adults	314
Total income from ticket sales in dollars			\$5657.25

25 Evaluate each expression when $x = -6$.

a. $18.2 - x \cdot 4$ **b.** $6x + \frac{1}{2}$ **c.** $54 \div (3 - x)$

d. $\frac{1}{2}x + 7.2$ **e.** $-12 - (x + 4)$ **f.** $\frac{2x + 1}{5}$

HOMEWORK EXERCISES ▶ See Exs. 27–52 on pp. 286–287.

Section 4 Key Concepts

Key Terms

properties of multiplication
commutative
associative

Multiplying and Dividing Integers (pp. 280–281)

The product or quotient of two integers:

- is positive when both integers are positive or both are negative.
- is negative when one integer is positive and the other is negative.

Examples $-3(-8) = -3 \cdot (-8) = 24$ $\quad -24 \div (-8) = 3$

$3(-8) = 3 \cdot (-8) = -24$ $\quad -24 \div 3 = -8$

Reordering or regrouping can help you find products of more than two numbers using mental math. (p. 281)

Evaluating Expressions (pp. 282–283)

You evaluate expressions containing fractions, decimals, or integers the same way you evaluate whole number expressions. Follow the order of operations and evaluate expressions inside grouping symbols first.

Example

$$\frac{(-7) \cdot 8^2 - 3}{-6 - (-1)} = \frac{(-7) \cdot 64 - 3}{-6 - (-1)}$$

$$= \frac{-448 - 3}{-6 - (-1)}$$

First evaluate the numerator.

$$= \frac{-451}{-6 - (-1)}$$

Then evaluate the denominator.

$$= \frac{-451}{-6 + 1} = \frac{-451}{-5} = 90\frac{1}{5}$$

Key Concepts Questions

26 What can you tell about two integers if their product is positive? if it is negative?

27 Evaluate each expression.

a. $-13 + 4 \div (-2)$ **b.** $2\frac{5}{6} - 1\frac{1}{3} \cdot \frac{1}{4}$

Section 4
Practice & Application Exercises

> **YOU WILL NEED**
>
> **For Ex. 60:**
> - graph paper
> - ruler
>
> **For Exs. 61–66:**
> - algebra tiles

Find each product.

1. $(-6)(5)$
2. $15(-4)$
3. $7(-6)$
4. $(-5)(-8)$
5. $(-9)(-4)$
6. $(22)(-11)$
7. $(-3)(12)$
8. $30(-9)$

Find each quotient.

9. $-24 \div 6$
10. $\frac{72}{-9}$
11. $-45 \div (-9)$
12. $\frac{-63}{9}$
13. $\frac{-77}{-7}$
14. $136 \div (-2)$
15. $\frac{200}{-4}$
16. $96 \div (-4)$

Find each product.

17. $(-2)(-3)(-8)$
18. $(3)(-10)(-1)4$
19. $3(3)(-2)(4)$
20. $(-5)(-7)(-2)(-8)$
21. $(-7)(-8)(3)$
22. $6(-25)(-2)(-4)(-5)$

23. Look at your answers to Exercises 17–22. Think about the number of positive and negative factors in each expression. When is the product of a set of integers positive? When is it negative?

24. **Golf** In golf, *par* is the number of strokes considered necessary to complete a hole in expert play. A *birdie* is a score of one stroke under par, and a *bogey* is a score of one stroke over par.

    a. Use integers to represent par, a birdie, and a bogey.

    b. Jamal and Craig finished a round of 18 holes with the given numbers of pars, birdies, and bogeys. What integer represents each golfer's final score as a number of strokes over, under, or at par?

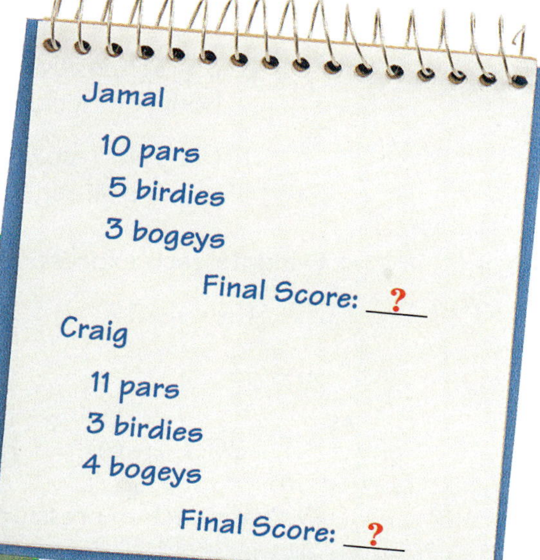

25. The chart shows the net gain or loss of a small company over the first three quarters of its start-up year. Suppose each quarter lasts 90 days.

Financial Report (in dollars)

	1st Quarter	2nd Quarter	3rd Quarter
Net sales			
Bicycles	$12,560	$18,944	$21,490
Parts	5,800	2,500	7,820
Service	788	651	560
	19,148	**22,095**	**29,870**
Costs and expenses			
Building operation	12,400	10,790	12,095
Employee wages	13,048	10,495	12,375
	25,448	21,285	24,470
Net gain (loss)	**(6,300)**	**810**	**5,400**

Parentheses indicate a loss, or negative amount.

a. Find the mean loss per day during the first quarter.

b. Find the mean gain per day during the second quarter.

c. Find the mean loss or gain per day over all three quarters.

26. Challenge Think about the expressions $(-5)^3$ and $(-5)^4$.

a. Write $(-5)^3$ and $(-5)^4$ as multiplication expressions.

b. Evaluate each multiplication expression you wrote in part (a). $(-5)^3 =$ __?__ and $(-5)^4 =$ __?__.

c. Is $(-5)^3$ *positive* or *negative*? Is $(-5)^4$ *positive* or *negative*? Explain how you decided.

d. Use your results from parts (a)–(c) to write a rule for evaluating powers of negative integers.

Evaluate each expression.

27. $4.5 \cdot 7 - 12$

28. $\left(\frac{2}{7} + \frac{4}{21}\right) \div 5$

29. $-11 + 2^3(-3)$

30. $2\frac{2}{5} \div 4 + \frac{2}{3}$

31. $-64 \div (-9 - 7)$

32. $26.79 - 0.31 \cdot 8$

33. $-2(13 - (-6))$

34. $0.49 \div 0.7 - 3$

35. $-18 \div 3^2 + 5(-6)$

Evaluate each expression when $e = 5$, $f = 7.2$, and $g = 0.4$.

36. $3g$

37. $\frac{f}{e}$

38. $21.8 - f$

39. $(e + f) \cdot g$

40. Telephone Rates Suppose a phone company charges \$2.30 for the first minute and \$.87 for each additional minute for a long-distance call from Los Angeles, California, to Sydney, Australia. The length of each call is rounded up to the nearest minute.

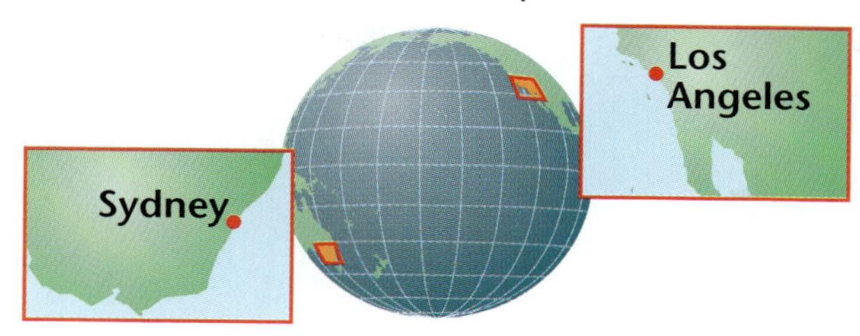

a. Let x = the number of additional minutes after the first minute. Write an expression that represents the total cost of the call for any number of minutes.

b. How much will a 12 min call cost?

Evaluate each expression when $a = -6$ and $b = -2$.

41. $15 - b$ **42.** $8b$ **43.** $\frac{42}{a}$ **44.** $3b + 7$

Evaluate each expression when $x = \frac{3}{4}$, $y = 6$, and $z = 1\frac{1}{3}$.

45. $5x$ **46.** $7 - z$ **47.** $y \div \frac{4}{5}$ **48.** $9z + y$

49. Open-ended Write a word problem that can be solved by evaluating the expression $4x + 10$ when $x = -6$. Then solve the problem.

50. Temperature To convert a Celsius temperature to the equivalent Fahrenheit temperature, you can use the expression $1.8C + 32$, where C is the temperature in °C. What is the Fahrenheit temperature equivalent to 14°C?

51. Snowy Tree Crickets You can use the expression $\frac{5}{9}(n + 8)$ to estimate the temperature in degrees Celsius, where n is the number of times a snowy tree cricket chirps in 15 seconds. Suppose a snowy tree cricket chirps 34 times in 15 seconds. Estimate the Celsius temperature to the nearest degree.

Reflecting on the Section

Write your response to Exercise 52 in your journal.

52. Can you tell whether the product or quotient of two integers is *greater than* or *less than* either integer when both are negative? when one is positive and one is negative? Explain.

Journal

Exercise 52 checks that you understand multiplication and division with integers.

Spiral Review

Tell whether each figure has *line symmetry, rotational symmetry,* or *both.* (Module 4, pp. 270–271)

53. 

54. 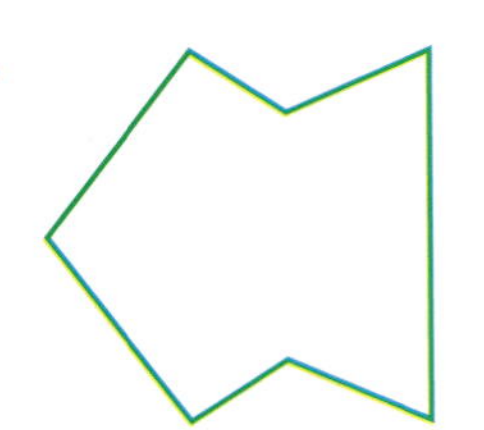

55. 

Solve each equation. Check each answer. (Module 3, p. 223)

56. $6x = 42$
57. $\frac{y}{4} = 36$
58. $9s = 81$
59. $\frac{r}{13} = 52$

60. a. Graph the ordered pairs (1, 4), (4, 1), (–6, 1), and (–4, 4) in a coordinate plane. (Module 2, p. 95)

b. Draw segments to connect the points in the order listed in part (a). Connect the last point to the first point. Name the polygon that is formed.

Extension

Simplifying Variable Expressions Using Algebra Tiles

Algebra tiles can help you see how to simplify an expression with more than one term.

Follow the steps below to simplify each expression. Let the  tile represent the variable x and the ▪ tile represent the number 1.

First
Model the expression using algebra tiles.

Then
Simplify the expression by grouping like tiles.

$\mathbf{2x + 3} \quad + \quad \mathbf{x + 1} \quad = \quad \mathbf{3x + 4}$

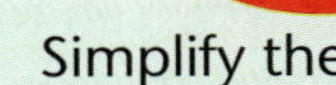

61. $3x + 1 + 2x$
62. $4x + 2x$
63. $5 + 3x + 4$
64. $2x + 7x + 5$
65. $6 + 3x + 4x$
66. $3x + 3x + 2x$

Section 4 Extra Skill Practice

Find each product or quotient.

1. $(-7)(4)$
2. $12(-4)$
3. $-27 \div (-3)$
4. $7(-6)$
5. $(-8)(-6)$
6. $-42 \div 6$
7. $\frac{-45}{-9}$
8. $(32)(-11)$
9. $98 \div (-7)$
10. $\frac{63}{-9}$
11. $(-4)(-8)(-2)$
12. $140 \div (-4)$

Evaluate each expression.

13. $-15 + 2^3(-7)$
14. $\left(\frac{1}{6} + \frac{7}{18}\right) \div \frac{5}{8}$
15. $(1.4)(8) - 3.6$
16. $4\frac{3}{4} \cdot \frac{5}{6} + 11$
17. $-124 \div (-2 - 6)$
18. $5^2 \cdot (37.9 - 4.31)$

Evaluate each expression when $a = \frac{3}{4}$, $b = 6$, and $c = 1\frac{1}{3}$.

19. $7 \div c$
20. ab
21. $2a + b$
22. $9 - ac$

Evaluate each expression when $q = 2.4$, $r = 0.7$, and $s = 8$.

23. $3r$
24. $q \div s$
25. $(q - r) \cdot s$
26. $9r + q$

Evaluate each expression when $x = -3$, $y = 9$, and $z = -5$.

27. $27 - z$
28. $12x$
29. $y + z \cdot x$
30. $(-42 - y) \div x$

Standardized Testing ◆ Performance Task

Roger Jones bought 16 pens priced at \$.23 each. As he was leaving the store, he noticed a sign that read, "All pens on sale for 2 cents off." So he went back to the checkout counter and explained that he did not receive the discount on his purchase. "You owe me the difference between \$.23 and \$.02, multiplied by 16," he explained. To which the cashier replied, "If that is true, then *you owe me* \$3.36!"

Explain to the cashier and Roger Jones what, if any, mistakes in mathematics each made and how to correct them. Use integers to represent the numbers in the problem.

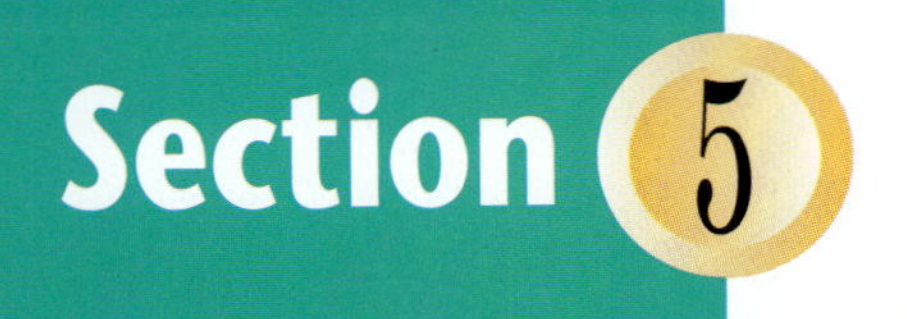

Translations, Similarity, and Two-Step Equations

ANIMATION

Setting the Stage

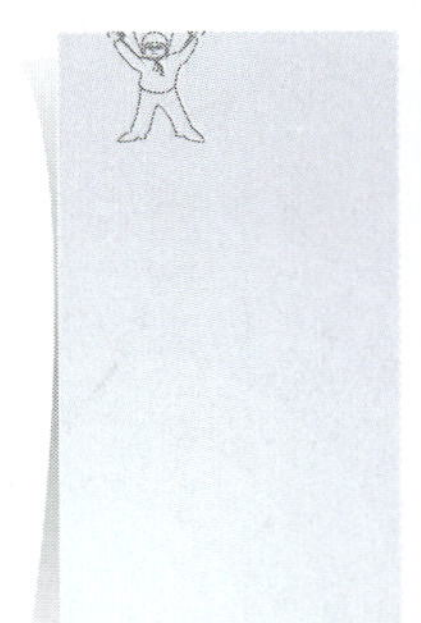
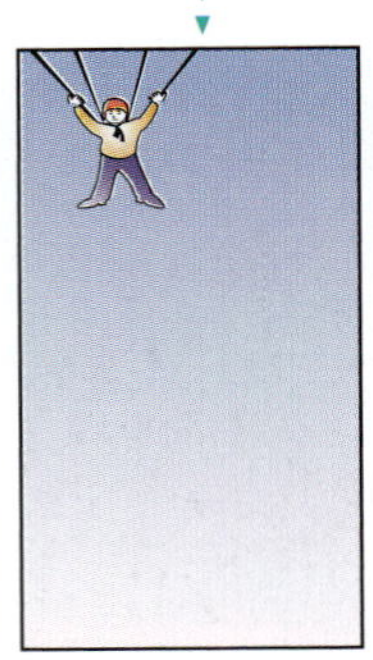

When animated cartoons first replaced the zoetrope, artists still had to draw every frame much as you have done in this module. Today, to use computer animation to show a character parachuting to the ground, artists need to draw only the first, middle, and last frames—a computer draws all the frames in between!

Think About It

1 Suppose you were shown only the hand-drawn sketches of the computer animation sequence above. Do you think you would be able to tell what was happening in the sequence? Explain.

2 Sketch the first, the middle, and the last drawing of a simple computer animation sequence of your own.

Exploration 1

TRANSlations

SET UP *You will need:* • *Labsheet 5A* • *tracing paper* • *graph paper*

GOAL

LEARN HOW TO...
- use coordinates to describe translations
- locate the image from a translation on a coordinate plane

AS YOU...
- explore ways to create animations

KEY TERMS
- transformation
- translation
- *x*-axis
- *y*-axis

▶ **Computer animators used *transformations* to parachute the character on page 290 to the ground. A transformation is a change in a figure's shape, position, or size. The reflections and rotations you learned about in Section 3 are two types of transformations.**

3 A **translation**, or slide, is another type of transformation. Each image below is a translation of the original figure.

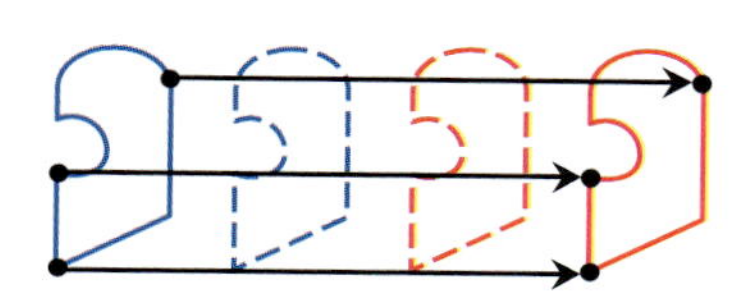

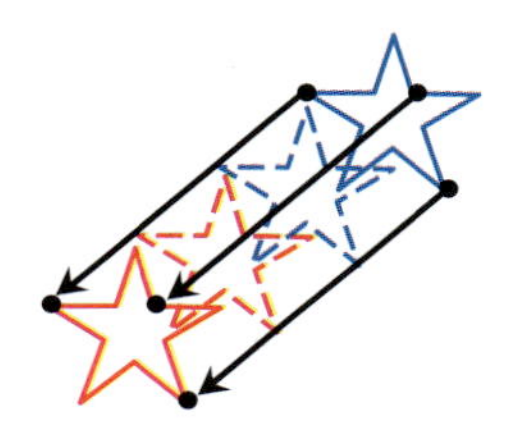

a. Trace one of the original figures shown. Then slide the tracing along the arrows until it fits exactly on the image.

b. Did you have to flip or turn the tracing in order to make it fit exactly on the image?

c. Are the original figure and its image congruent? Explain.

d. Use the directions *up* or *down* and *right* or *left* to describe the movement shown by each translation.

4 **Discussion** The transformations below are not translations.

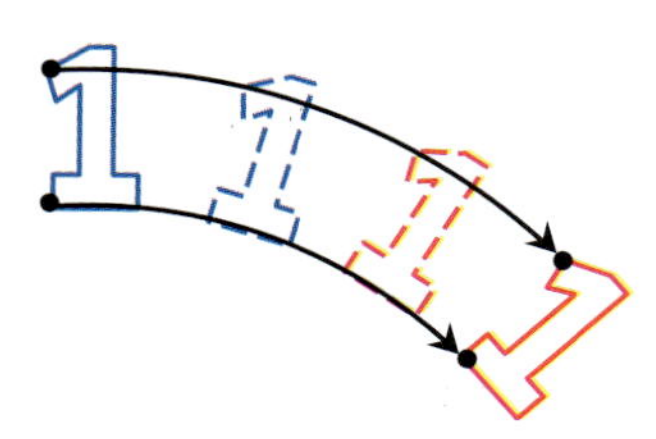

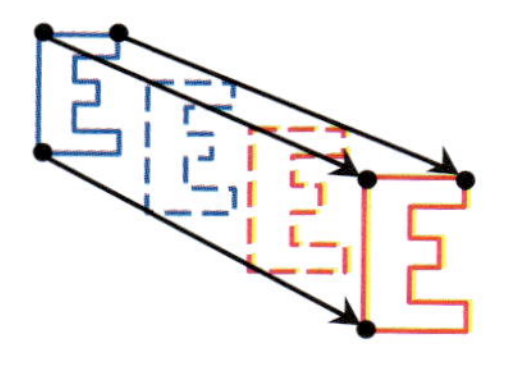

a. How does each transformation differ from the translations shown in Question 3?

b. How would you define a translation?

▶ **The transformations used to move figures on a computer screen are described using the coordinates of points on the figures. Image 1 and Image 2 below are the results of two different translations of △*ABC*.**

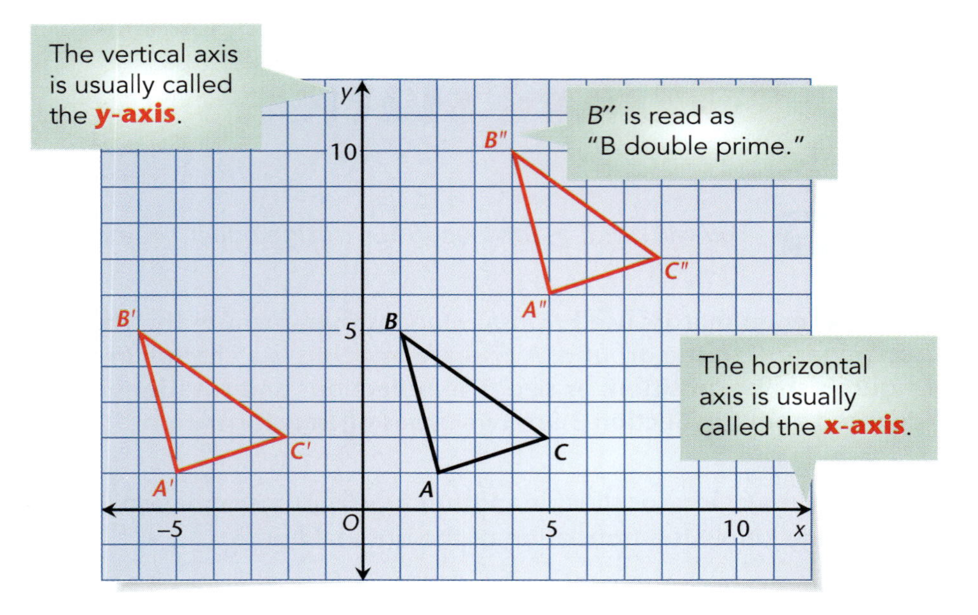

5 Describe the translation of △*ABC* that results in the image △*A′B′C′*.

6 Copy and complete the table. Record the coordinates of the vertices of △*ABC* and the vertices of its two images.

	Vertex	Coordinates	Vertex	Coordinates	Vertex	Coordinates
△*ABC*	*A*	(2,1)	*B*	?	*C*	?
△*A′B′C′*	*A′*	?	*B′*	?	*C′*	?
△*A″B″C″*	*A″*	?	*B″*	?	*C″*	?

7 **Discussion** Look at your completed table from Question 6.

a. How are the coordinates of the vertices of △*A′B′C′* related to the coordinates of the vertices of △*ABC*?

b. How does the relationship you found in part (a) describe the movement on the coordinate plane shown by the translation?

c. Repeat parts (a) and (b) for △*A″B″C″* and △*ABC*.

8 Suppose a third translation of △*ABC* subtracts 5 from the *y*-coordinate of each vertex of △*ABC*. Describe the location of the image of △*ABC* produced by this translation.

▶ **In Questions 6–8 on page 292, you saw that a translation can be defined by describing how the coordinates of the points of the original figure are changed. The notation $(x + 1, y - 2)$ means add 1 to each x-coordinate and subtract 2 from each y-coordinate.**

9 **Use Labsheet 5A.** Follow the directions on Labsheet 5A for *Translating a Figure* with the translation $(x + 1, y - 2)$.

10 Use coordinates to describe each translation.

a. 2 units to the right

b. 1 unit to the left, 3 units up

11 ✓ **CHECKPOINT** Suppose you want to translate a triangle 3 units to the left and 4 units down.

a. Use coordinates to describe the translation.

b. Draw a triangle with vertices (–2, 2), (3, 5), and (4, 1) on a coordinate plane. Then draw its image after the translation. Label the coordinates of the vertices of the image.

...checks that you can use coordinates to describe a translation and locate an image.

12 **Discussion** Help! The character shown has lost its image. Its image is the result of the translation $(x - 10, y + 1)$.

a. Use the directions *right* or *left* and *up* or *down* to describe how the translation moves a figure.

b. Use coordinates to describe the translation that will make the image move back so it fits exactly on the original figure.

c. Suppose the tip of the left foot of the image is at (11, 5). Find the coordinates of the tip of the left foot of the original figure.

HOMEWORK EXERCISES ▶ See Exs. 1–13 on pp. 300–301.

GOAL

LEARN HOW TO...
- stretch or squash a figure on a coordinate plane
- identify similar figures

AS YOU...
- explore ways to make animation more realistic

KEY TERM
- similar

Exploration 2

CHANGING SIZE and SHAPE

SET UP *Work in a group of three. You will need:* • *Labsheet 5B* • *graph paper* • *ruler*

To make movement appear smoother and more realistic, animators often use *stretch* and *squash* effects, as shown in this animation sequence of a bouncing ball.

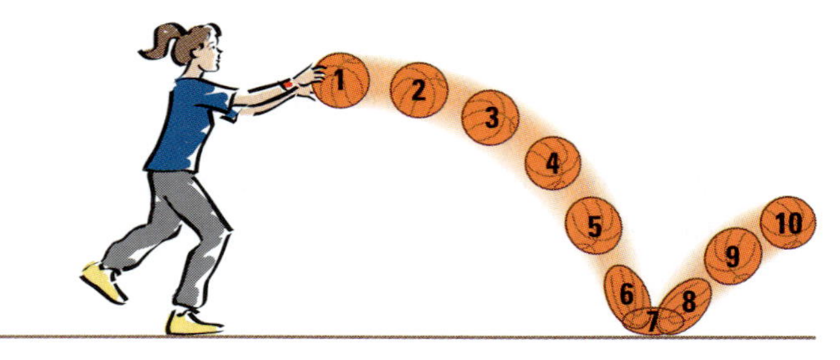

13 In which drawings is the ball squashed or stretched?

14 **a.** Which of the drawings are translations of drawing 1?

b. How can you tell that the other drawings are not translations of drawing 1?

Squashing and stretching transformations can be described with coordinates.

Use Labsheet 5B for Questions 15–17.

15 Follow the directions on Labsheet 5B to explore how different transformations can be used in *Stretching and Squashing a Figure.*

16 **Discussion** Use the image you drew on Labsheet 5B.

a. Find the height and the width of figure *ABCDE* and the height and the width of the image you drew.

b. Does the image you drew show a stretch in both the height and the width of the original figure? Explain.

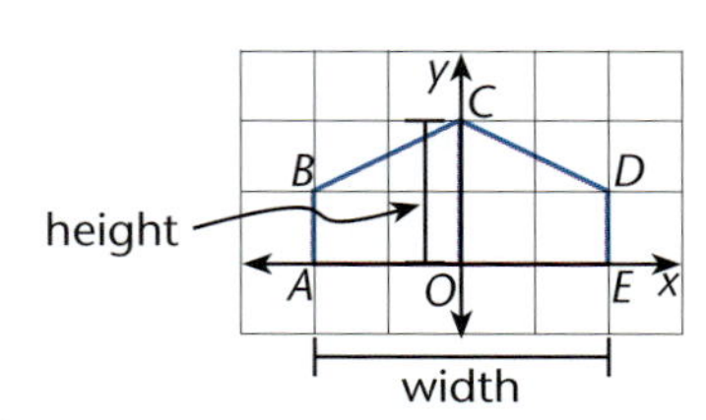

▶ **Figures are** **similar** **if they have the same shape, but not necessarily the same size.**

EXAMPLE

These are similar triangles.

Congruent figures are similar.

These are *not* similar triangles.

17 Look at the images the members of your group drew on Labsheet 5B.

a. Which images look similar to figure *ABCDE*? Why?

b. Find the lengths of the sides of each image you listed in part (a).

c. How do the lengths of the sides you found in part (b) compare with the lengths of the sides of figure *ABCDE*? How do your findings relate to the transformation?

18 **a.** Copy $\triangle EFG$ on graph paper.

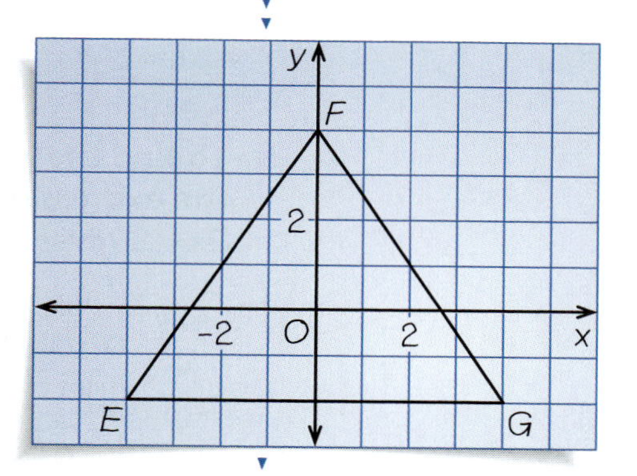

b. Predict whether each transformation below will result in an image that is similar to $\triangle EFG$.

A. $\left(\frac{1}{2}x, y\right)$ **B.** $\left(x, \frac{1}{2}y\right)$ **C.** $\left(\frac{1}{2}x, \frac{1}{2}y\right)$

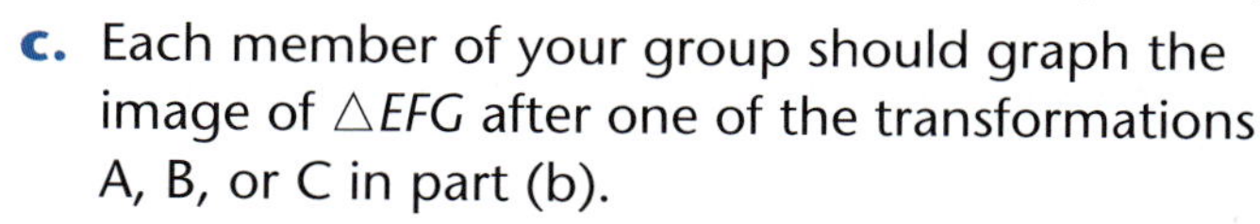

c. Each member of your group should graph the image of $\triangle EFG$ after one of the transformations A, B, or C in part (b).

d. Determine whether each image is similar to $\triangle EFG$. Explain your reasoning.

19 ✓ **CHECKPOINT** Tell whether each transformation will result in an image that is similar to the original figure. Explain.

a. $(x, 2y)$ **b.** $(3x, 3y)$ **c.** $\left(\frac{1}{4}x, \frac{1}{2}y\right)$

20 **Discussion** Suppose $\triangle Q'R'S'$ is the image of $\triangle QRS$ after the transformation $(x, 2y)$. The coordinates of R' are $(-3, 8)$. How can you use the coordinates of R' to find the coordinates of R?

✓ **QUESTION 19**

...checks that you can use coordinates to find whether a transformation produces a similar image.

HOMEWORK EXERCISES ▶ **See Exs. 14–21 on pp. 301–302.**

GOAL

LEARN HOW TO...
- solve two-step equations

AS YOU...
- explore how to change both the shape and the location of an animated figure

Exploration 3

Solving TWO-STEP EQUATIONS

SET UP *You will need Labsheet 5C.*

▶ **Sometimes computer animators need to change the shape of a figure *and* move it across the screen. For this type of transformation, they use multiplication and division with addition and subtraction.**

21 **Discussion** How do you think the transformation $(2x + 3, 3y - 4)$ will change the shape and the location of the flag shown?

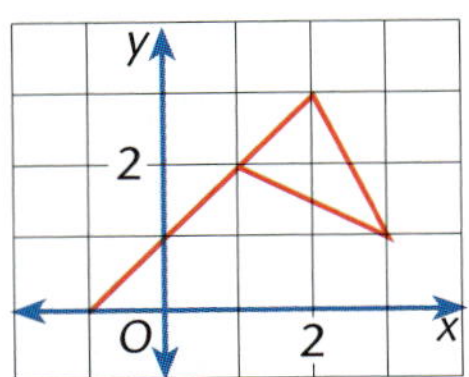

22 **Use Labsheet 5C.** Follow the directions to examine the effects of the transformation $(2x + 3, 3y - 4)$ on the flag.

▶ **To find the x-coordinate of point A' (the image of A), you evaluated the expression $2x + 3$ for $x = -1$. Substituting -1 for x in the expression $2x + 3$ gives $2(-1) + 3$.**

23 **Discussion** When you evaluate the expression $2(-1) + 3$, which operation do you perform first? Why?

▶ **The order of operations tells you how to evaluate an expression.**

FOR HELP with *order of operations*, see **MODULE 1, p. 65**

EXAMPLE

Evaluate the expression $2x + 3$ when $x = 4$.

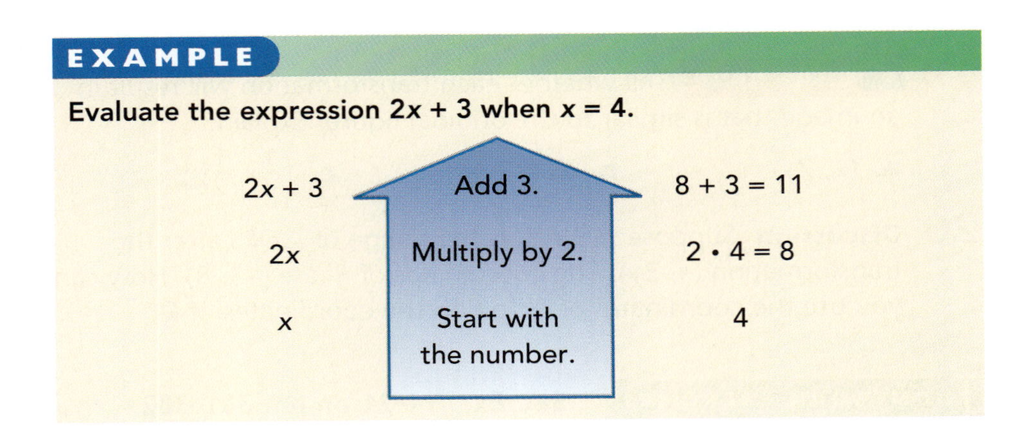

24 **Use Labsheet 5C.** Mark the point (7, 2) on the image you drew of the flag. Predict the coordinates of the point on the original figure that was transformed to (7, 2).

▶ **Sometimes you want to find the coordinates of a point when you know the coordinates of its image. To find the *x*-coordinate, first write an equation using the expressions for the *x*-coordinate from the transformation and from the image.**

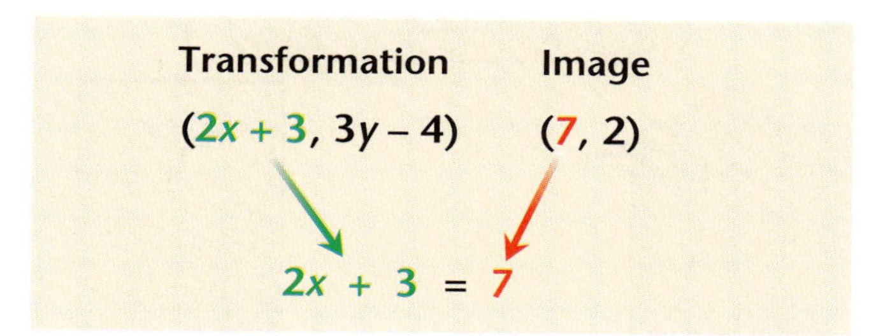

▶ **Then you need to find a value for *x* that makes the equation true.**

25 **Discussion** Examine the diagram below that shows the steps for solving the equation $2x + 3 = 7$.

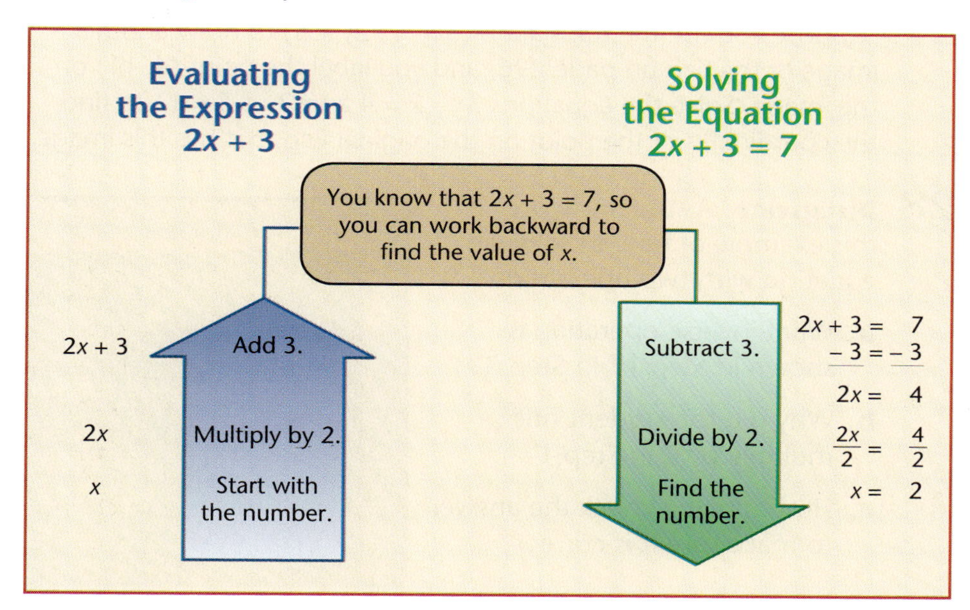

a. What inverse operation is used to undo the multiplication $2x$?

b. Why do you *subtract 3* before you *divide by 2*?

c. How do you know in what order to use the inverse operations to solve an equation?

26 **a.** To find the y-coordinate of the point whose image is (7, 2) after the transformation $(2x + 3, 3y - 4)$, use the diagram below to solve the equation $3y - 4 = 2$.

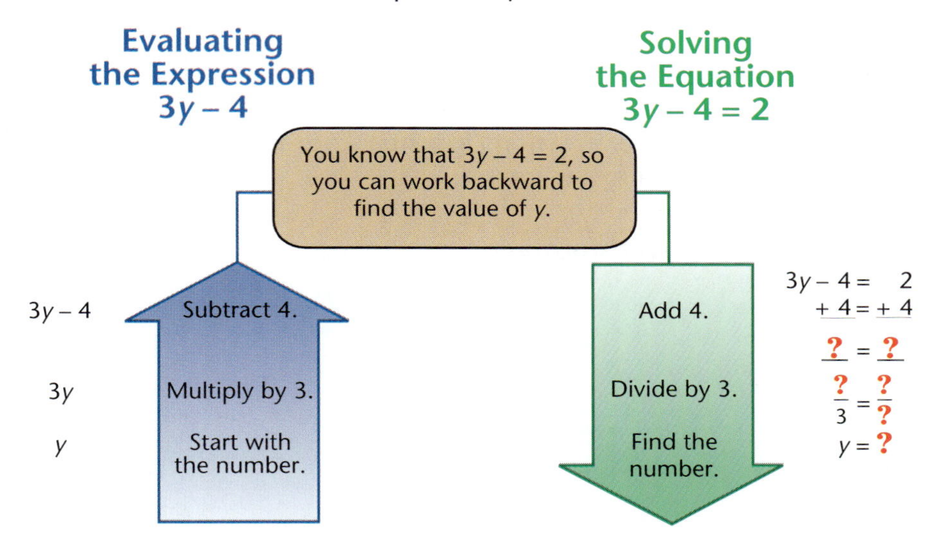

b. How do the coordinates you found in part (a) and in Question 25 compare with your prediction from Question 24?

27 Suppose you use the translation $(3x - 2, 2y + 5)$ to draw another image of the flag on page 296, and you label the point (4, 11) on the image. Solve the equations $3x - 2 = 4$ and $2y + 5 = 11$ to find the coordinates of the point on the original flag that has this image.

28 **Discussion** A student wrote this example of how to solve an equation with two operations.

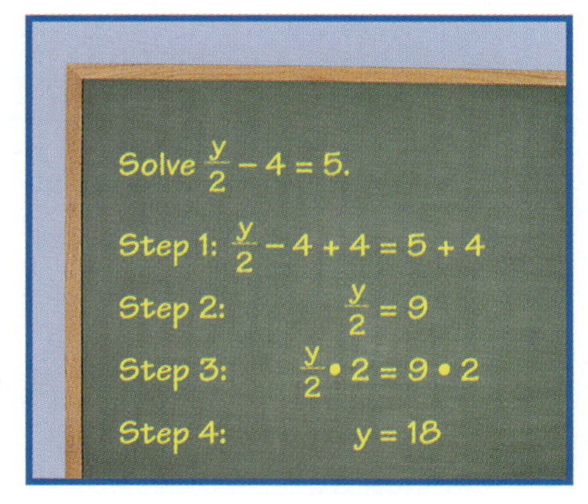

a. What inverse operation is shown in Step 1? in Step 3?

b. Why did the student not multiply by 2 in Step 1?

c. How can you check the answer to make sure it is correct?

✓ QUESTION 29

...checks that you can solve two-step equations.

29 **✓ CHECKPOINT** Solve each equation. Check each solution.

a. $9x - 6 = 21$ **b.** $\frac{y}{3} + 2 = 14$ **c.** $-2x + 7 = 15$

HOMEWORK EXERCISES ▶ See Exs. 22–39 on pp. 303–304.

Section 5 Key Concepts

Transformations and Translations (pp. 291–293)

A transformation is a change in a figure's shape, size, or location. Transformations can be described using coordinates.

A translation is a transformation that slides a figure to a new location. The image is congruent to the original figure.

Example The original trapezoid is translated 4 units to the right and 2 units up.

Original: (x, y)
Image: $(x + 4, y + 2)$

Transformations that Stretch or Squash (pp. 294–295)

You can stretch or squash a figure horizontally by multiplying the x-coordinates of all its points by the same factor, or vertically by multiplying the y-coordinates of all its points by the same factor. A factor greater than one stretches. A factor between zero and one squashes.

When you stretch or squash a figure horizontally and vertically by the same factor, the image is similar to the original figure. Figures are similar if they are the same shape, but not necessarily the same size.

Examples

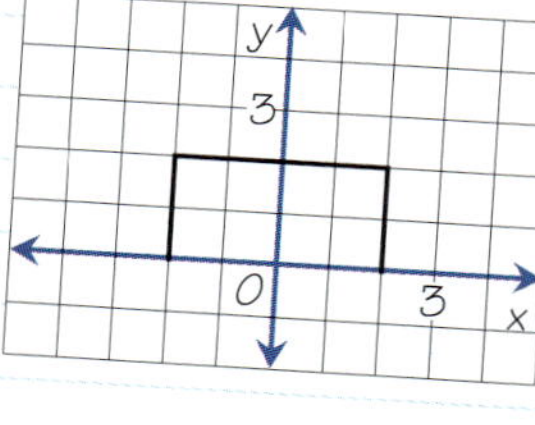

horizontal stretch   vertical squash

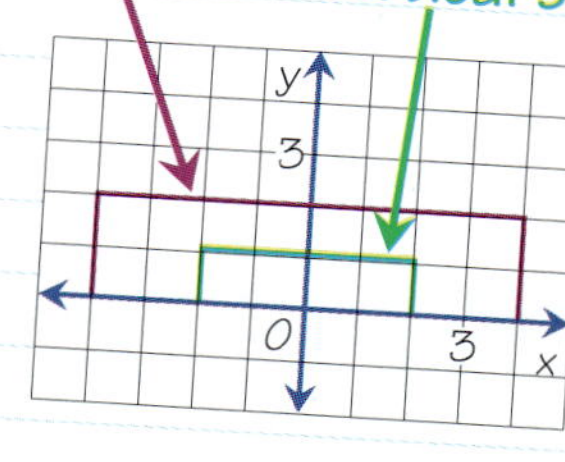

similar to original

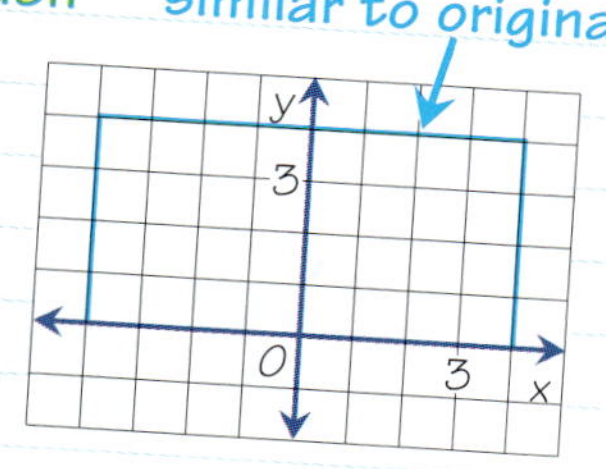

Key Terms

transformation

translation

***x*-axis**

***y*-axis**

similar

30 Key Concepts Question Choose the letters of the transformations that result in an image similar to the original figure. Explain.

A. $\left(\frac{1}{5}x, \frac{1}{5}y\right)$ **B.** $(x + 3, y - 1)$ **C.** $(4x, 3y)$

Continued on next page

Section 5 Key Concepts

Solving Two-Step Equations (pp. 297–298)

You solve two-step equations by working backward through the order of operations using inverse operations.

Example Solve the equation $3n - 8 = 13$ and check your solution.

$3n - 8 = 13$	
$3n - 8 + 8 = 13 + 8$	Step 1: Add 8 to both sides.
$3n = 21$	Step 2: Simplify.
$\frac{3n}{3} = \frac{21}{3}$	Step 3: Divide both sides by 3.
$n = 7$	Step 4: Simplify.

Check: $3(7) - 8 = 21 - 8 = 13$ ✔

31 Key Concepts Question The coordinates of the image of a point after the transformation $\left(2x + 17, \frac{y}{2} + 4\right)$ are (19, 9). Find the coordinates of the original point.

Section 5 Practice & Application Exercises

YOU WILL NEED

For Exs. 12–13 and 16:
- graph paper

For Ex. 37:
- calculator

Tell whether each diagram shows a translation of the original figure. If not, explain why not.

1.

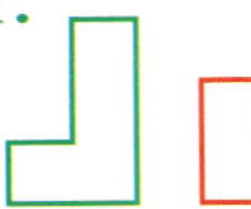

2.

3.

Describe each translation using coordinates.

4. 9 units to the left
5. 5 units down
6. 12 units up
7. 3 units to the right
8. 6 units to the right and 7 units up
9. 2 units to the left and 4 units down

10. **African Patterns** Many traditional African patterns were created by translating a design. Use coordinates to describe how the design shown was translated to create the pattern.

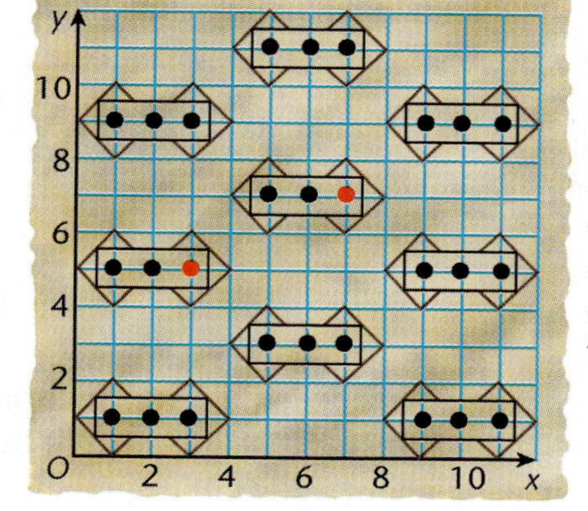

The *Namba*, or knot, fabric pattern was created by the Kuba people of the Congo. It has its origin in the knotting of string to make fishnets.

11. **Research** Look through clothing catalogs or newspapers to find two examples of patterns that were created by translating a figure. Cut them out to show in class.

Draw a rectangle on a coordinate plane. Then draw its image after each translation.

12. $(x + 3, y - 4)$
13. $(x - 2, y - 5)$

For Exercises 14 and 15, tell which figures in each set are similar.

14.

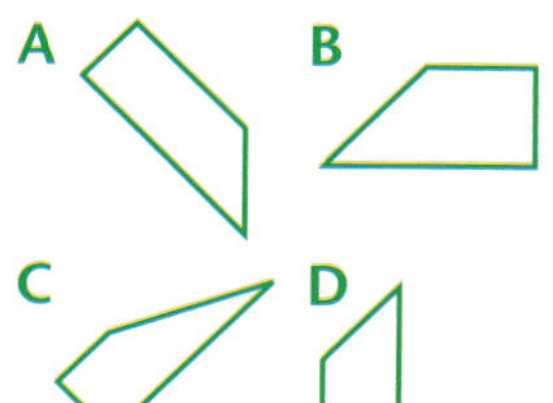

15.

16. a. Copy rectangle *WXYZ* on graph paper.

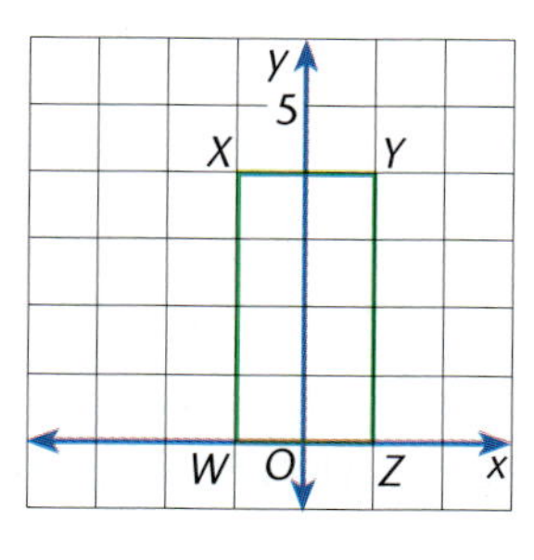

b. For each transformation, predict how the size, shape, or location of the image of rectangle *WXYZ* will differ from that of the original figure.

Transformation A: $(3x, y)$

Transformation B: $(x - 2, y)$

Transformation C: $\left(x, \frac{y}{4}\right)$

Transformation D: $(3x, 3y)$

c. Draw each image. Tell whether the image is similar to rectangle *WXYZ*. Explain your reasoning.

Computer Graphics With most computer drawing software, you can stretch or squash a graphic by dragging one of the *handles* of its *boundary box*. Choose the letter of the transformation that describes each stretched image of the graphic at the right.

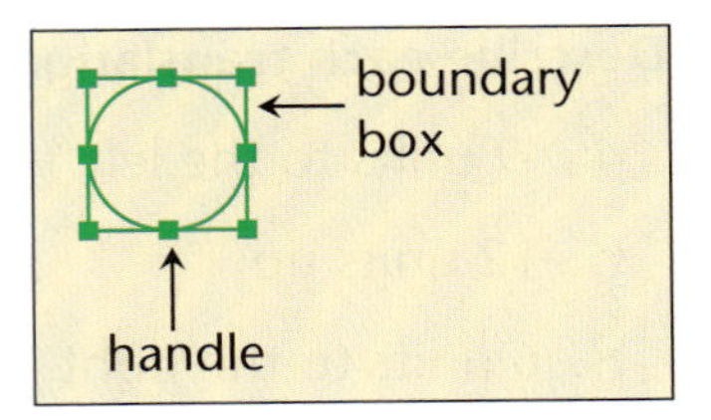

17. 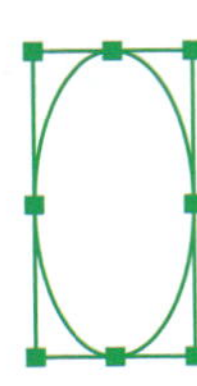

18. 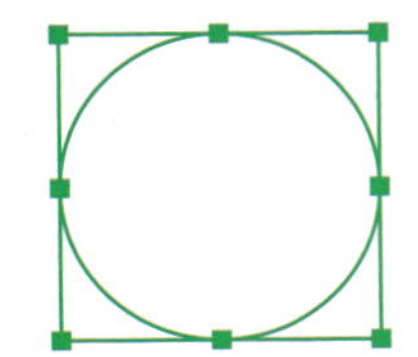

19. 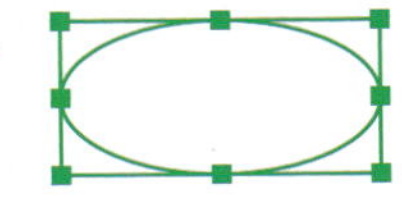

A. $(2x, 2y)$ B. $(2x, y)$ C. $(x, 2y)$

20. Suppose a computer animator wants to use the transformation $(5x, y)$ to stretch the figure shown.

a. Make a sketch of how you think the figure will look after the transformation.

b. What transformation of the image you drew in part (a) will undo the stretch and result in an image that is the same size and shape as the original figure?

21. a. The figure at the right shows the image of $\triangle ABC$ after a reflection across the y-axis. Write the coordinates of the vertices of $\triangle ABC$ and the vertices of its image.

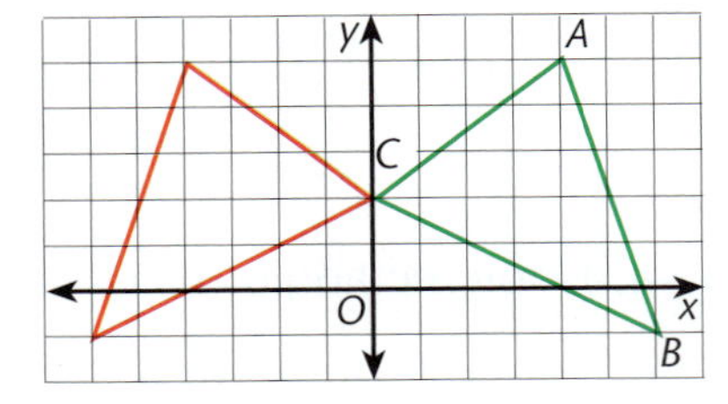

b. By what numbers can you multiply the coordinates of a point to reflect it across the x-axis? the y-axis?

c. Write the coordinates of the image of each point after a reflection across the indicated axis.

$Q(3, 7)$, x-axis

$R(4, 0)$, y-axis

$S(-5, -8)$, y-axis

$T(-4, 9)$, x-axis

Solve each equation. Check each solution.

22. $2t + 9 = 17$

23. $\frac{n}{3} - 6 = 4$

24. $12 + 4y = -32$

25. $5m - 4.5 = 7$

26. $2 + \frac{x}{4} = 2$

27. $-9b + 6 = 21$

28. $\frac{p}{6} - 11 = 37$

29. $12h + 45 = 72$

30. $\frac{k}{7} + 0.6 = 5.7$

For Exercises 31–33, write an equation to represent each statement. Then solve the equation and check your solution.

31. Seven more than twice a number is thirty-one.

32. A number divided by three and then decreased by eight is five.

33. Four increased by the product of a number and six is eighteen.

34. A bike rental store charges a flat fee of $15 plus $3 per day to rent a mountain bike.

a. Let x = the number of days a mountain bike is rented. Write an equation to show the cost of renting a mountain bike.

b. Suppose a person was charged $63 for renting a mountain bike. For how many days did the person rent the bike?

35. Open-ended Write a word problem that can be answered by solving the equation $4x - 15 = 33$. Then solve the problem.

36. Firefighting To calculate how far a water stream from a fire hose with a $\frac{3}{4}$ in. diameter nozzle will reach, firefighters use this formula:

$$S = \frac{n}{2} + 26$$

n = nozzle pressure in pounds per square inch

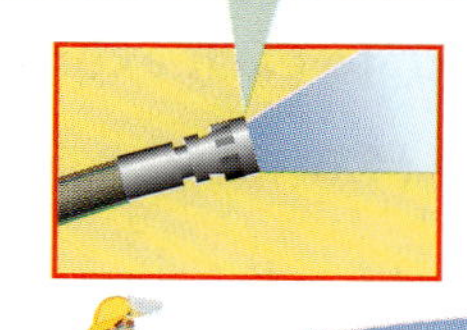

a. Suppose the end of a fire hose with a $\frac{3}{4}$ in. diameter nozzle is positioned about 60 ft from a fire for safety reasons. Use the formula to find the amount of nozzle pressure needed for the water stream to reach the fire.

b. **Challenge** For every $\frac{1}{8}$ in. increase in nozzle diameter, the water stream reaches another 5 ft. Suppose the nozzle of the fire hose used in part (a) had a 1 in. diameter. What nozzle pressure would be needed to reach the fire?

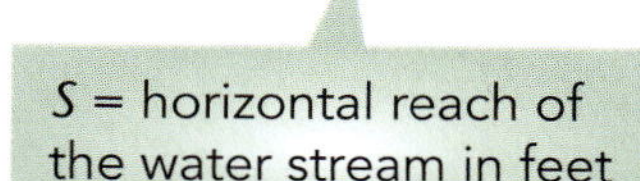

S = horizontal reach of the water stream in feet

37. Calculator Describe a key sequence that you can use to solve the equation $\frac{x}{7} - 12 = 5$ on a calculator. Then use your key sequence to solve the equation. Check your solution.

38. $\triangle R'S'T'$ is the image of $\triangle RST$ after the transformation $\left(3x - 2, \frac{y}{2}\right)$. The coordinates of the vertices of $\triangle R'S'T'$ are $R'(-5, 1)$, $S'(-2, 2)$, and $T'(1,1)$. Find the coordinates of the vertices of $\triangle RST$.

Journal

Exercise 39 checks that you can solve two-step equations.

Reflecting on the Section

Write your response to Exercise 39 in your journal.

39. Examine Owen's solution to the equation $2x + 7 = 18$ and his teacher's comment. Where did Owen make an error? What should he have done instead?

$2x + 7 = 18$

$\frac{2x}{2} + 7 = \frac{18}{2}$

$x + 7 = 9$

$x + 7 - 7 = 9 - 7$

$x = 2$

Owen, please review and redo your work. If $2x + 7 = 18$ and $x = 2$, then $2 \cdot 2 + 7$ should equal 18, but it does not.

Spiral Review

Evaluate each expression. (Module 4, p. 284)

40. $(4.6 + 7.2) \cdot 5$
41. $-9 - 28 \div 7$
42. $\frac{4}{9} \cdot (-12) + 3$
43. $11 + 6 \cdot 3\frac{3}{8}$
44. $0.32 \div 0.8 \cdot 1.2$
45. $-68 \div 2 + (-54)$

Replace each ? with the number that makes the statement true. (Table of Measures, p. 597)

46. 3 h = __?__ min
47. 25 min = __?__ s
48. 90 min = __?__ h

Replace each ? with >, <, or =. (Module 3, p. 170)

49. $\frac{7}{24}$ __?__ $\frac{5}{12}$
50. $\frac{3}{27}$ __?__ $\frac{2}{9}$
51. $\frac{4}{16}$ __?__ $\frac{7}{48}$

Career Connection

Animator: Karen Kiser

Frame	1	3	6	10
Size	1	0.3	1.4	1

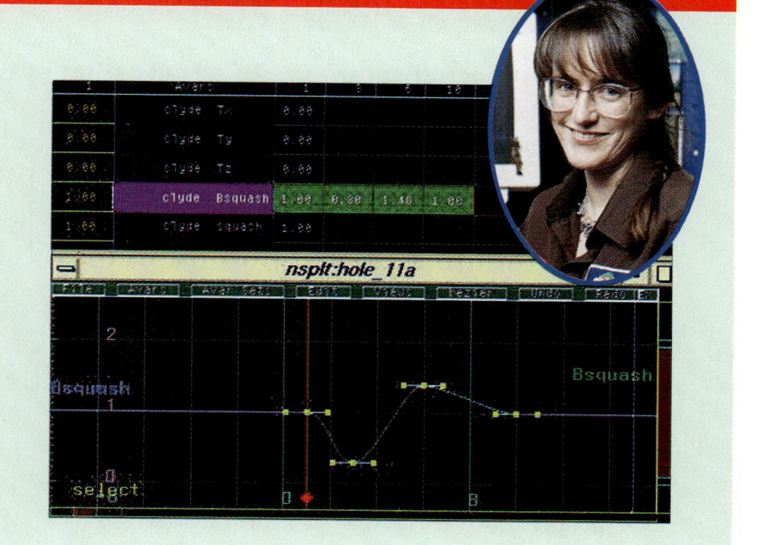

Karen Kiser uses a table like the one above to show computer commands that animate squashes and stretches. For example, a command of *size 2* multiplies the y-coordinate by 2 and divides the x-coordinate by 2.

52. Use coordinates to describe the change in size in each frame.

Lights, Camera—Action!

SET UP

You will need:
- *Project Labsheet B*
- *scissors*
- *tape*

Transformations **Use transformations to create your own animation strip.**

6 **Use Project Labsheet B.** Each frame of *Blank Zoetrope Strip B* represents the first quadrant of a coordinate plane.

a. Cut out the zoetrope strip pieces and tape them together.

b. Draw a simple figure in Frame 1 of the strip. Mark several points on the figure and record their coordinates.

c. Decide how to move the figure from frame to frame. Then use coordinates to describe your transformation.

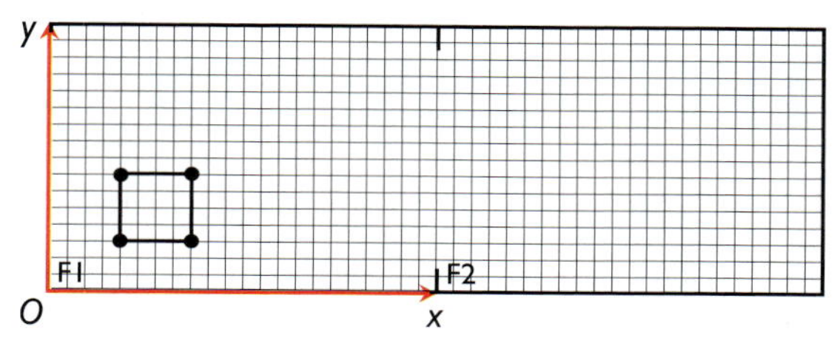

d. Complete F2–F3 by drawing the image of the figure in the previous frame after your transformation from part (c).

7 Place your animation strip in the zoetrope so the frames are centered under the slots. Spin the zoetrope. What do you see?

Section 5 Extra Skill Practice

Tell whether each diagram shows a translation of the original figure. If not, explain why not.

1. 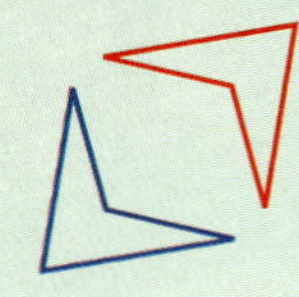

2. 

3. 

For Exercises 4–6, describe each translation using coordinates.

4. 3 units to the left and 6 units down
5. 1 unit to the left and 5 units up
6. 8 units to the right and 2 units down
7. Draw a triangle on a coordinate plane. Then draw its image after the translation $(x - 2, y + 3)$.

Tell whether each transformation will result in an image that is similar to the original figure. Explain your reasoning.

8. $\left(\frac{1}{2}x, 2y\right)$

9. $(4x, y)$

10. $\left(\frac{1}{5}x, \frac{1}{5}y\right)$

11. Suppose a computer animator wants to use the transformation $\left(x, \frac{1}{4}y\right)$ to squash the figure at the right. Make a sketch to show how the car will look after the transformation.

Solve each equation. Check each solution.

12. $2y + 8 = 42$
13. $9x - 17 = 19$
14. $\frac{s}{4} + 11 = 20$
15. $21n - 7 = 35$
16. $6z - 7 = 13$
17. $\frac{q}{8} - 5 = 7$
18. $35 + 4r = 15$
19. $\frac{f}{9} - 12 = 3$

Standardized Testing ▶ Open-ended

Sketch a small, simple design on a coordinate plane. Next, describe how the transformation $(2x + 2, \frac{3}{4}y)$ would change your design. Then, sketch the image of your design for that transformation. Locate a point on the image and find the coordinates of the corresponding point on the original figure.

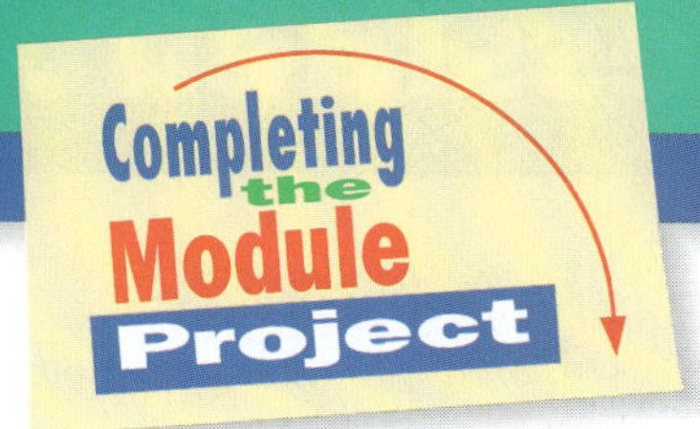

Lights, Camera—Action!

In this module you have been using mathematics to create special animated effects with your zoetrope strips. To complete the project, you'll work as a group to create and set up a viewing station featuring several animation strips that use the special effects of your choice.

SET UP

Work in a group.

You will need:

- *Project Labsheets A and B*
- *zoetrope*
- *poster paper*
- *scissors*
- *tape*
- *ruler*
- *protractor*

Choose your favorite animation strip from the ones you have already made, or create a new one by applying the techniques you have learned. Be sure that each group member contributes at least one strip for the viewing station.

Create a sign for your viewing station. Include the title of each animation strip, a brief description of the mathematical ideas that were used to create it, and the animator's name.

Some of the mathematical ideas you have explored are:

- fraction multiplication and division
- decimal estimation
- integer multiplication and division
- transformations: rotations, reflections, translations, stretches and squashes
- solving equations

Set up your viewing station. Be sure your sign is clearly visible.

Now it's showtime! With your group, visit each viewing station and view the animation strips.

MODULE 4 Review and Assessment

You will need: • *calculator* (Exs. 1–3) • *protractor* (Ex. 29) • *tracing paper* (Ex. 30) • *graph paper* (Ex. 42)

Use 3.14 or the π key on a calculator. Find the circumference of a circle with each measure. If necessary, round each answer to the nearest hundredth. (Sec. 1, Explor. 1)

1. diameter = 12 cm
2. radius = 4 ft
3. diameter = 23 ft

Find the reciprocal of each number. (Sec. 1, Explor. 2)

4. 1
5. $\frac{5}{8}$
6. $1\frac{1}{3}$
7. 9

Find each product or quotient. Write each answer in lowest terms. (Sec. 1, Explors. 2 and 3)

8. $\frac{5}{8} \cdot \frac{4}{9}$
9. $\frac{3}{10} \div \frac{2}{5}$
10. $7\frac{1}{2} \cdot 3$
11. $\frac{8}{9} \div \frac{2}{3}$
12. $3 \div \frac{5}{6}$
13. $4\frac{2}{5} \cdot 2\frac{5}{6}$
14. $8\frac{4}{7} \div \frac{1}{3}$
15. $\frac{8}{11} \cdot 2\frac{3}{4}$

Estimate each product or quotient. Tell whether each estimate will be *greater than* or *less than* the exact answer. Then find the exact answer. (Sec. 2, Explors. 1 and 2)

16. $(3.2)(0.09)$
17. $3.2 \div 0.9$
18. $(4)(0.103)$
19. $47 \div 0.011$
20. $2.5 \div 8$
21. $(7.9)(1.25)$
22. $(38)(0.07)$
23. $28.96 \div 0.24$

Write each fraction as a decimal. (Sec. 2, Explor. 3)

24. $\frac{3}{8}$
25. $\frac{5}{6}$
26. $\frac{2}{9}$
27. $\frac{8}{5}$

28. Which quotients in Exercises 24–27 are terminating? Which are repeating? (Sec. 2, Explor. 3)

29. Tell whether the top part of the windmill shown at the right has rotational symmetry. If so, find all its rotational symmetries. (Sec. 3, Explor. 1)

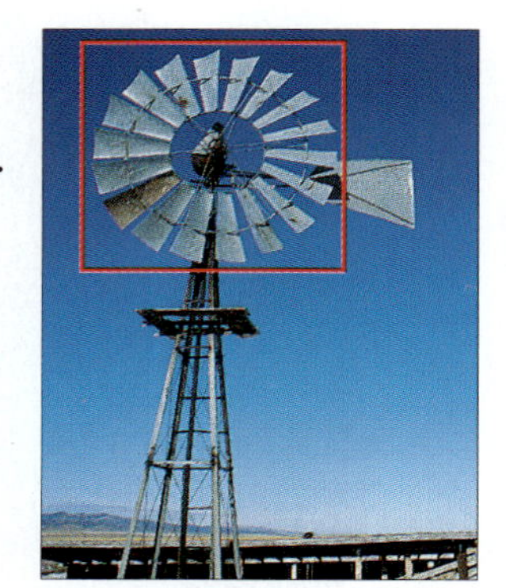

◄ This windmill is in Southern Utah.

30. Tell whether the diagram shows a reflection of the original figure across the given line. If not, explain why not. **(Sec. 3, Explor. 2)**

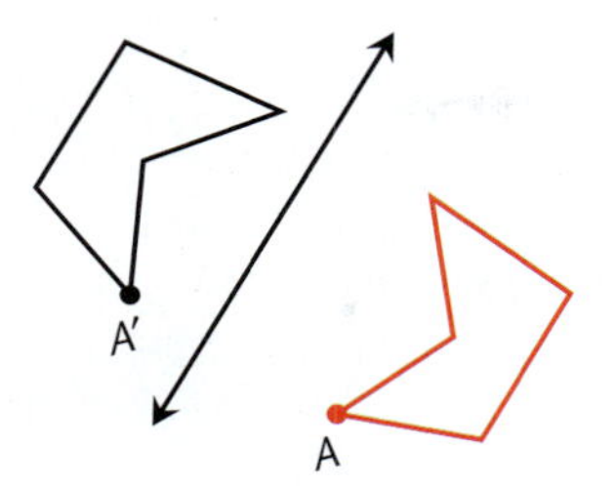

Find each product or quotient. (Sec. 4, Explor. 1)

31. $9(-7)$ **32.** $28 \div (-4)$ **33.** $(-12)(-6)$ **34.** $-36 \div 6$

35. $-104 \div (-8)$ **36.** $(-2)(-13)(-1)$ **37.** $-\frac{12}{3}$ **38.** $7(-4)(3)(-5)$

Evaluate each expression. (Sec. 4, Explor. 2)

39. $6.2 \div (2.1 + 1) \cdot 14.7$ **40.** $2\frac{5}{8} \cdot 1\frac{1}{2} - 3$ **41.** $\frac{3^3 + 5(-3)}{-7 - (-4)}$

For Exercises 42 and 43, use $\triangle ABC$ shown at the right.

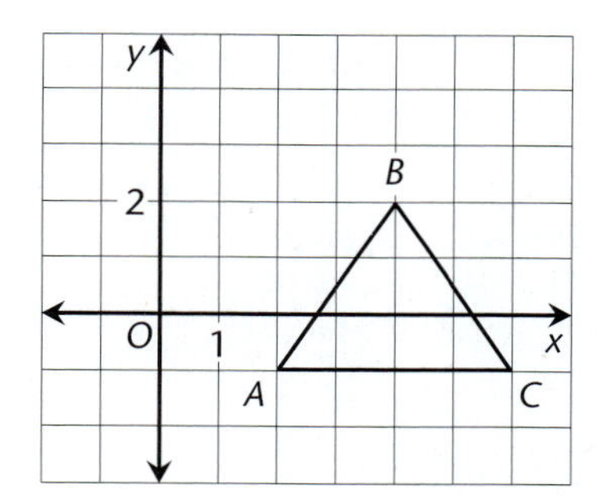

42. a. Suppose you want to move $\triangle ABC$ 3 units to the left and 1 unit down. Describe the transformation using coordinates. **(Sec. 5, Explor. 1)**

b. Draw $\triangle ABC$ on graph paper. Then draw its image after the translation in part (a).

43. Use transformations I, II, and III. **(Sec. 5, Explor. 2)**

I: $\left(2x, \frac{y}{2}\right)$ II: $\left(2x, 2y\right)$ III: $\left(\frac{x}{2}, y\right)$

a. For each transformation of $\triangle ABC$, predict how the size, the shape, or the location of the image of $\triangle ABC$ will be different from that of the original figure.

b. Draw each image and tell whether it is similar to $\triangle ABC$.

Solve each equation. Check each solution. (Sec. 5, Explor. 3)

44. $2x + 4 = 28$ **45.** $3n - 7 = 29$ **46.** $\frac{y}{4} + 15 = 17$

Reflecting on the Module

47. Writing Describe how rotations, reflections, and translations are alike and how they are different. Give examples and draw sketches to support your answer.

MODULE
5
RECREATION

CONNECTING MATHEMATICS & The Theme

MODULE 5 SECTION OVERVIEW

The Module Project

May I Ask You a Few Questions?

How many ways are there to have fun? You'll gather and organize data about the ways students in your school spend their free time. You'll use percents and a visual display to present the results of your survey.

More on the Module Project
See pp. 342, 356, and 373.

1 Ratios and Data Displays

As you examine running speeds:

- Find unit rates
- Set up proportions
- Make stem-and-leaf plots
- Interpret histograms

2 Proportions and Plots

As you explore some unusual, thrilling, or daring pastimes:

- Solve proportions using cross products
- Make a scatter plot
- Fit a line to a scatter plot
- Interpret box-and-whisker plots

3 Percent

As you analyze movie ratings:

- Estimate and find percents
- Find a missing part or whole

4 Percent and Probability

As you study sports statistics:

- Write a fraction as a decimal or a percent
- Use percents to make predictions
- Find theoretical probabilities when two or more events occur one after the other

INTERNET
To learn more about the theme:
http://www.mlmath.com

Ratios and Data Displays

Exploration 1
- Ratios and Proportions

Exploration 2
- Stem-and-Leaf Plots

Exploration 3
- Histograms

Setting the Stage

How do you spend your free time? In this module, you'll explore some of the ways young people enjoy their free time today.

One popular leisure activity is running. In the book *Zanboomer*, a high school student named Zan Hagen decides to take up cross-country running. Her coach, Rinehart, helps her train for a three-mile race.

Zanboomer by R.R. Knudson

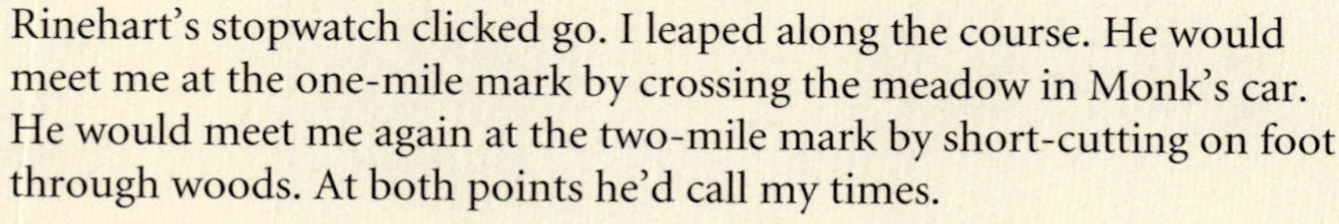
Rinehart's stopwatch clicked go. I leaped along the course. He would meet me at the one-mile mark by crossing the meadow in Monk's car. He would meet me again at the two-mile mark by short-cutting on foot through woods. At both points he'd call my times.

...

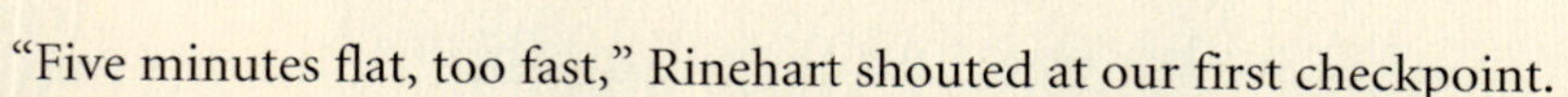
"Five minutes flat, too fast," Rinehart shouted at our first checkpoint.

The second mile I saved too much by tripping into a water hazard. "Meathead," I called myself.

"Ten minutes, fifty seconds," Rinehart blared. His math was right, my pace wrong.

Think About It

1 Zan's goal was to run each mile of the three-mile race in 5 minutes, 10 seconds. How did her times at the one-mile and two-mile marks compare with that goal?

2 Zan finished her three-mile training run in 16 minutes. How long did it take her to run the last mile?

Exploration 2

Stem-and-Leaf Plots

Every year there are hundreds of benefit races throughout the United States. The Seattle Pratt and Chew Classic is a 4 mi race that benefits an emergency feeding program for the homeless. The finishing times for the 16-and-under age group in the 1995 Classic are shown.

GOAL

LEARN HOW TO...
- interpret and make stem-and-leaf plots

AS YOU...
- examine race results

KEY TERMS
- median
- mode
- stem-and-leaf plot
- range

For Questions 12–13, use the results shown at the right.

Name	Time (min)
Dan	31
Alesa	42
Elizabeth	39
Eben	34
Stephanie	36
Fong	31
David	39
Megan	51
Ryan	37
David	42
Randy	39
Laura	31
Andrew	40

Name	Time (min)
Michael	24
Matthew	37
Loreen	57
Jacquie	81
Patrick	31
Garrett	25
Shannon	43
Shelby	39
Zachariah	33
Tyler	40
Ilsa	34
Graham	65
Greer	50

12 **Discussion** Suppose a middle school student finished the Pratt and Chew Classic with a time of 35 min. Based on the results shown at the right, do you think that time is *fast*, *slow*, or *average*? Explain.

▶ **One way to answer Question 12 is to find an average or typical finishing time.**

13 **a.** Find the mean of the finishing times for the 16-and-under age group. Round your answer to the nearest tenth.

b. The **median** is the middle item when you order a data set from least to greatest. When there are an even number of data items, the median is the mean of the two middle numbers. Find the median of the finishing times for the 16-and-under age group.

c. The **mode** is the item or the items that appear most often in a data set. Find the mode of the finishing times for the 16-and-under age group.

FOR ▶ HELP with *mean*, see TOOLBOX, p. 595

14 **a.** Suppose 81 had not been included in the data set. How would that affect each average you found in Question 13?

b. **Discussion** Which average in Question 13 do you think best represents the running data? Explain.

▶ **When data values are spread over a wide range, a graph may describe the data more effectively than an average value. One type of graph you can use is a stem-and-leaf plot. The stem-and-leaf plot below shows the finishing times from the table on page 315.**

title

Seattle Pratt and Chew Classic
16-and-under Age Group, 1995

Stem	Leaves
2	4 5
3	1 1 1 1 3 4 4 6 7 7 9 9 9 9
4	0 0 2 2 3
5	0 7 7
6	5
7	
8	1

6|5 represents 65 min

The stems are ordered vertically from least to greatest.

The leaves of a stem are ordered horizontally from least to greatest.

key

15 Compare the data in the table with the stem-and-leaf plot.

a. Why do you think the numbers 2 through 8 were chosen as the stems for the running data?

b. Why are there no leaves for the stem 7?

c. What do the stems represent?

d. What do the leaves represent?

e. What finishing time is represented by 4|3?

f. How are two or more identical finishing times shown in the stem-and-leaf plot? Give an example to support your answer.

16 **a.** The slowest finishing time for the 16-and-under age group was 81 min. What was the fastest finishing time?

b. The **range** of a data set is the difference between the greatest data value and the least data value. What is the range of the finishing times for the 16-and-under age group?

17 **Discussion** Use the stem-and-leaf plot shown above.

a. A *cluster* in a data set is a group of data values that are close in value. One cluster appears around the value 39. Where else do you see a cluster in the data?

b. A *gap* in a data set is a place where there is a "jump" between data values. One gap occurs between 57 and 65. Where else do you see a gap in the data set?

c. How could you use the stem-and-leaf plot to group the data values into fast, slow, and average times?

▶ **Suppose you wanted to find out how the finishing times of teachers compare with the finishing times of students 16-and-under who ran in the 1995 Seattle Pratt and Chew Classic.**

The finishing times of all the teachers who ran in the race are listed at the right. All times have been rounded to the nearest minute.

Name	Time (min)
Maxwell	26
Julie	44
Marcia	35
Charles	28
Candy	31
Debra	36
Ron	31
Wayne	25
Karen	28
Jeff	28
Erin	41
Eric	38
Brendan	23

Name	Time (min)
	30
	42
	35
	39
	26
	37
	25
	38
	38
	26
	28
	31
	29

18 **✓ CHECKPOINT** Complete parts (a)–(d) to make a stem-and-leaf plot of the teachers' finishing times in the 1995 Pratt and Chew Classic.

a. Use the running times to choose the stems. List each stem in a column from least to greatest. Draw a vertical segment to separate the stems from the leaves.

b. Use each data value to create a leaf to the right of a stem. Be sure the leaves are listed in order from least to greatest.

c. Include a key that identifies one of the values represented by the stem-and-leaf plot.

d. Write a title for your stem-and-leaf plot.

✓ QUESTION 18

...checks that you can make a stem-and-leaf plot.

19 **Discussion** Use the stem-and-leaf plot you made in Question 18 showing the teachers' race results.

a. Find the median, mode, and range of the running times.

b. Where do you see gaps or clusters in the data? Look back at Question 17.

c. Suppose a teacher finished the Pratt and Chew Classic with a time of 35 min. Explain whether you would consider that time *fast*, *slow*, or *average*.

d. How do your answers in parts (a)–(c) compare with the answers in Questions 13, 16, and 17 for the students?

HOMEWORK EXERCISES ▶ See Exs. 14–16 on pp. 322–323.

GOAL

LEARN HOW TO...
- interpret histograms

AS YOU...
- examine the results of a 5K race

KEY TERM
- histogram

Exploration 3

Histograms

In Exploration 2, you saw running times displayed with a stem-and-leaf plot. Sometimes another type of data display is more convenient.

The Schoolpower Laguna Beach Classic is run along the Pacific coast and through a scenic canyon. In 1996, runners aged 3–78 helped raise money to aid local schools.

20 **Discussion** Nearly 1000 people ran in the 5 km, or 5K, race of the 1996 Schoolpower Laguna Beach Classic. Their times ranged from the winning time of 15 min 36 s to times slightly over an hour.

a. Estimate the range of the running times in the 5K race.

b. Suppose you had a list of all the individual running times for the 5K race. Why would it be difficult to use a stem-and-leaf plot to display the data?

The frequency table below shows how many runners finished the 1996 Schoolpower 5K race in each of the time intervals listed. The *histogram* below displays the same data.

1996 Schoolpower Laguna Beach Classic Finishing Times

Interval (min:s)	Frequency
15:00–24:59	168
25:00–34:59	462
35:00–44:59	218
45:00–54:59	121
55:00–64:59	21

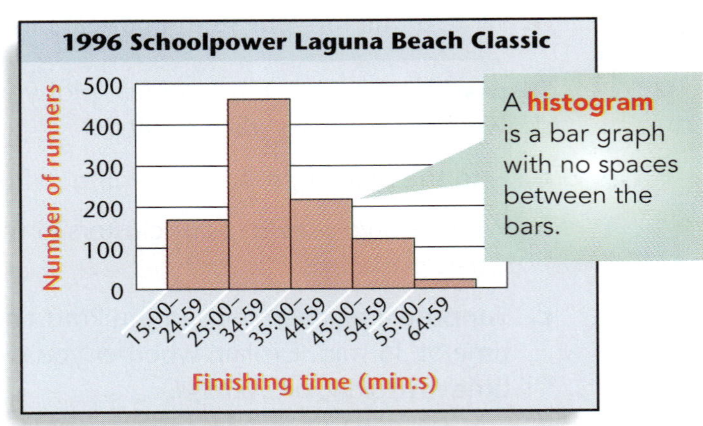

21 **a.** Why does the first time interval start at 15 rather than at 0?

b. In which time interval did most of the runners finish the race?

c. How many runners finished in the 45:00–54:59 time interval?

22 **Discussion** Can you use the frequency table or histogram to find the slowest finishing time? Explain.

23 Suppose a runner finishes a 5K race with a time of 35 min. Do you think this time is *fast*, *slow*, or *average*, based on the results in the histogram? Explain.

HOMEWORK EXERCISES See Exs. 17–18 on pp. 323–324.

Section 1 Key Concepts

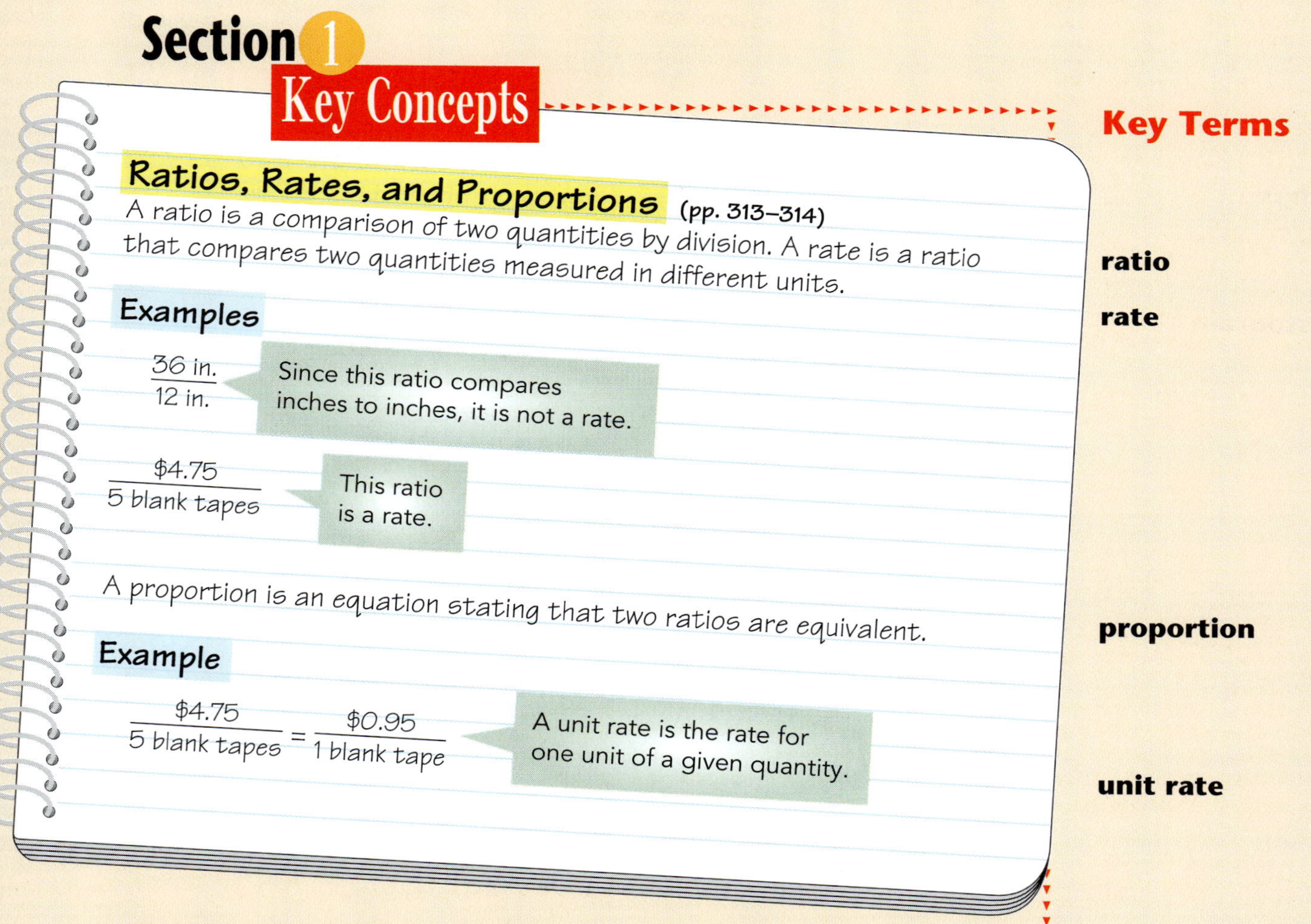

Key Terms

ratio

rate

proportion

unit rate

24 **Key Concepts Question** Suppose a female runner can run at a constant rate of 7 min/mi. Using this rate, determine how long it would take her to finish the Boston Marathon (26.2 mi).

Continued on next page

Section 1 Key Concepts

Key Terms

stem-and-leaf plot

median

mode

range

histogram

Displays of Data (pp. 315–319)

Stem-and-leaf plots, frequency tables, and histograms can be used to organize and display data. Stem-and-leaf plots show each data item.

1972–1996 Boston Marathon Women's Championship Times
(All times were rounded to the nearest minute.)

14 | 2 3 4 4 5 5 5 5 5 5 5 7 7 9
15 | 0 4 4 5
16 | 2 5 7 7 9
17 |
18 | 6 9

16|7 represents 167 min

The **mode** is the data item that appears most often.

The **median** is the middle data value of an ordered data set.

The range of a set of data is the difference between the greatest data value and the least data value. The range of the data set above is 189 min – 142 min = 47 min.

Frequency tables and histograms display frequencies in given intervals.

1972–1996 Boston Marathon Women's Championship Times

Time (min)	Frequency
140–149	14
150–159	4
160–169	5
170–179	0
180–189	2

A histogram is a special type of bar graph. The bars of a histogram touch each other.

25 Key Concepts Question Was the runner in Question 24 on page 319 fast enough to win the Boston Marathon in any year from 1972 to 1996? Use both graphs above to find how many marathons she would have won. Which graph was easier to use?

Practice & Application Exercises

YOU WILL NEED

For Ex. 13:
- graph paper
- ruler

Write each rate as a unit rate.

1. $\frac{39\text{ min}}{6\text{ mi}}$
2. $\frac{152\text{ mi}}{8\text{ gal}}$
3. $\frac{\$16.50}{3\text{ lb}}$
4. $\frac{24\text{ servings}}{4\text{ pans}}$
5. $\frac{18¢}{3\text{ min}}$
6. $\frac{\$1.89}{2\text{ bunches}}$

7. **Whales** A single blue whale may eat 4.5 tons of krill, a type of small shrimp, per day. Copy and complete the proportion below to show how many tons of krill a blue whale may eat in one week.

$$\frac{4.5\text{ tons}}{1\text{ day}} = \frac{?\text{ tons}}{7\text{ days}}$$

8. **Weather** For a rainstorm to be defined as a cloudburst, rain must fall at a rate of at least 4 in. per hour. Suppose it rains 5.7 in. in 1.5 h. Could that be described as a cloudburst?

9. **Ultra-Marathons** Helen Klein holds many of the records in the 65–69-year-old age group for ultra-marathoners, athletes who run races much longer than marathons. In 1991 she ran 100 mi in about 21 h. Represent Helen Klein's running pace as a unit rate. Round your answer to the nearest tenth.

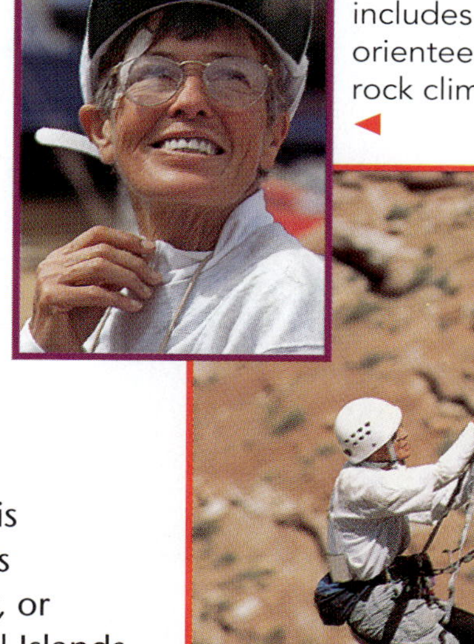

In 1995, at the age of 72, Helen Klein completed the Eco-Challenge competition in Utah. The Eco-Challenge includes hiking, orienteering, and rock climbing.

10. **Population** The total area of the Marshall Islands is 70 mi^2. The total population of the Marshall Islands is about 61,000 people. Find the *population density,* or unit rate of people per square mile, for the Marshall Islands.

11. **Race-Walking** To receive the Presidential Sports Award for race-walking, a person must race-walk a total of 200 mi at an average rate no slower than 12 min/mi.

    a. Copy and complete the table below to show the distance covered and race-walking times for a rate of 12 min/mi.

Time (min)	?	12	?	120	?
Distance (mi)	0.5	1	5	?	200

    b. How many hours would it take to race-walk a total of 200 mi at a rate of 12 min/mi?

12. Fuel Efficiency The cruise ship *Queen Elizabeth 2* moves only about 60 ft for each gallon of diesel fuel that it burns. About how many gallons of fuel are used when the ship travels one mile?

13. Suppose Toni walks at the rates shown in the table below.

Time (s)	1	5	20	30	50
Distance (ft)	5	25	100	150	250

a. How far would you expect Toni to walk in 25 s?

b. **Challenge** This data can be graphed to create a picture of Toni's walking rate. Draw a coordinate plane with seconds along the horizontal axis and feet along the vertical axis. Then use the numbers in the table to graph Toni's walking rate. Draw segments to connect the points in order.

c. Use the graph to find how far you would expect Toni to walk in 25 s. Compare this answer with your answer in part (a).

14. Skyscrapers The stem-and-leaf plot below shows the numbers of stories in the 20 tallest buildings in New York City.

▲ One Worldwide Plaza is on a former site of Madison Square Garden.

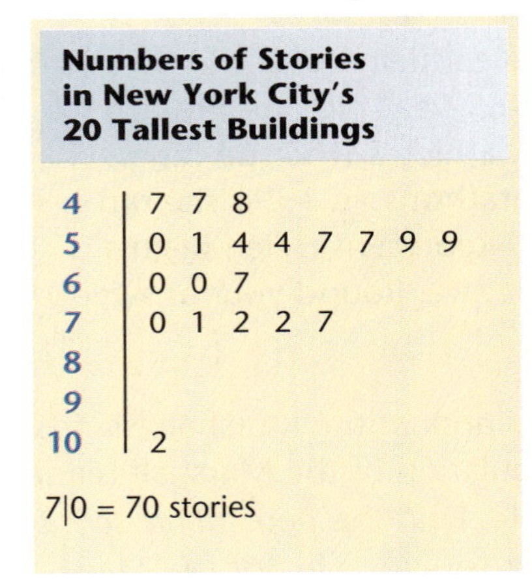

Numbers of Stories in New York City's 20 Tallest Buildings

Stem	Leaves
4	7 7 8
5	0 1 4 4 7 7 9 9
6	0 0 7
7	0 1 2 2 7
8	
9	
10	2

7|0 = 70 stories

▲ Carnegie Hall Tower towers over Carnegie Hall, a famous concert hall built in 1891.

a. Do you notice any gaps or clusters in the data? Explain.

b. What is the range of the data on the stem-and-leaf plot?

c. Based on the data in the stem-and-leaf plot, how many stories do you think the tallest building in New York City has?

d. **Writing** The 47-story *One Worldwide Plaza* in New York City is 778 ft tall, while the 60-story *Carnegie Hall Tower* in New York City is only 757 ft tall. Explain how this can be true.

15. **History** The stem-and-leaf plot at the right gives the approximate age at which each king or queen of England since 1154 was crowned.

Ages of English Monarchs when Crowned, since 1154

Stem	Leaves
0	1 9 9
1	0 2 4 7 8 8 8
2	1 2 3 4 5 5 5 6 8
3	0 1 1 3 3 6 7 7 8
4	0 1 3 4
5	1 4 7 9
6	4

3|0 = 30 years old

a. What is the range of the ages shown on the stem-and-leaf plot?

b. Find the median and the mode of the data.

c. Suppose the next English monarch is 60 years old when crowned. How does this number affect the median of the data set? the mode of the data set?

Top Ten Prize-Winning Horses, 1996

Horse	Wins	Earnings
Cigar	19	$9,999,815
Alysheba	11	$6,679,242
John Henry	39	$6,597,947
Best Pal	18	$5,129,645
Sunday Silence	9	$4,968,554
Easy Goer	14	$4,873,770
Unbridled	8	$4,489,475
Spend A Buck	10	$4,220,689
Creme Fraiche	17	$4,024,727
Devil His Due	11	$3,920,405

16. The table at the left shows the top 10 prize-winning horses as of 1996, and the number of races they won.

a. Make a stem-and-leaf plot to show the number of races won by each of the horses. Be sure to include a title and a key for your plot.

b. Use the stem-and-leaf plot to find the range, the mean, the median, and the mode of the number of wins.

c. What would you consider an average number of wins for this group of horses? Explain.

17. **Marathons** The histogram shows the number of women in each age group who completed the 1995 Seattle Marathon in a time of less than 3.5 h. Use the histogram to answer each question.

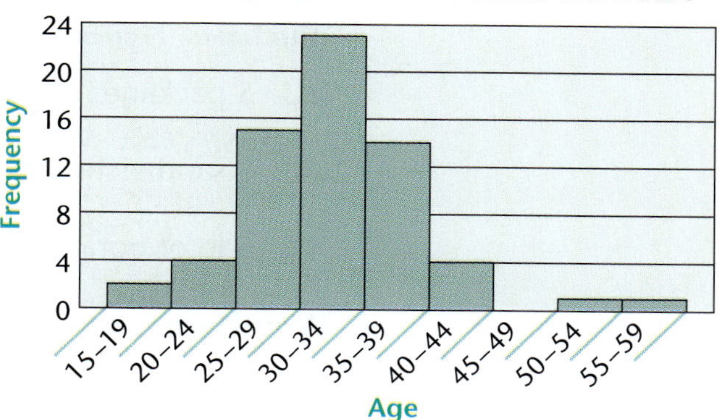

a. How many different ages are included in each interval?

b. About how many women aged 40 years and older finished the marathon in less than 3.5 h?

c. Why might the statement, "The oldest woman to finish the marathon in less than 3.5 hours was 59 years old," be incorrect?

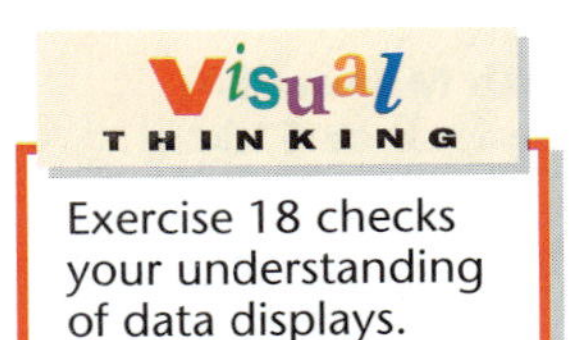

Exercise 18 checks your understanding of data displays.

Reflecting on the Section

18. Use the stem-and-leaf plot and the histogram showing the results of the 1995 Seattle Pratt and Chew Classic for students in the 16-and-under age group.

Seattle Pratt and Chew Classic 16-and-Under Age Group, 1995

Stem	Leaves
2	4 5
3	1 1 1 1 3 4 4 6 7 7 9 9 9 9
4	0 0 2 2 3
5	0 7 7
6	5
7	
8	1

6|5 represents 65 min

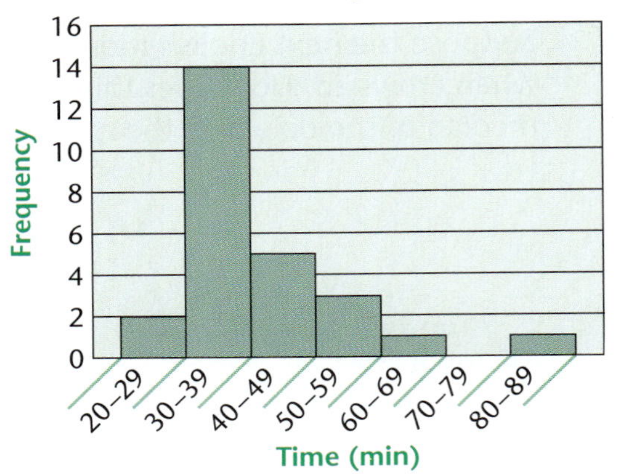

a. Copy the stem-and-leaf plot and turn it sideways. Compare it with the histogram. What do you notice about the shapes of the two displays? Why do you think this happens?

b. Will a histogram and a stem-and-leaf plot made from the same data set always show the same relationship that you saw in part (a)? Explain.

Spiral Review

Solve each equation. Check each solution. (Module 4, p. 300)

19. $4n + 17 = 50$ **20.** $\frac{y}{3} + 4 = 92$ **21.** $\frac{x}{4} - 3 = -15$

Use mental math to find a reasonable estimate for the cost of each purchase. (Toolbox, pp. 582–583)

22. 5 packages of gum at $0.39 per package

23. 3 sandwiches at $2.48 per sandwich

24. 5 lb of potatoes at $3.98 for 10 lb

Write each fraction in lowest terms. (Module 3, p. 170)

25. $\frac{11}{33}$ **26.** $\frac{12}{60}$ **27.** $\frac{19}{38}$

28. $\frac{30}{150}$ **29.** $\frac{8}{20}$ **30.** $\frac{40}{48}$

Section 1 Extra Skill Practice

Write each rate as a unit rate.

1. $\frac{\$43}{4\text{ h}}$
2. $\frac{127\text{ km}}{8\text{ L}}$
3. $\frac{672\text{ noodles}}{3\text{ boxes}}$
4. $\frac{40\text{ gal}}{9\text{ min}}$
5. Pamela begins a 24-question math quiz at 1:16 P.M., answers every question, and hands in her paper at 1:32 P.M. Represent the pace at which she answered the questions as a unit rate.
6. This list gives the heights, in inches, of the students in a seventh-grade math class: 64, 57, 62, 68, 54, 64, 59, 63, 64, 60, 59, 58, 65, 56, 58, 64, 60, 55, 66, 57, 61. Use these heights to make a stem-and-leaf plot, including a key and a title. State the range, the median, the mode, and the mean of the data. What would you consider to be an average height for this group of students? Explain your choice(s).
7. Use the histogram at the right. Is the number of students who read 6 or more books *greater than, equal to,* or *less than* the number of students who read fewer than 6 books?

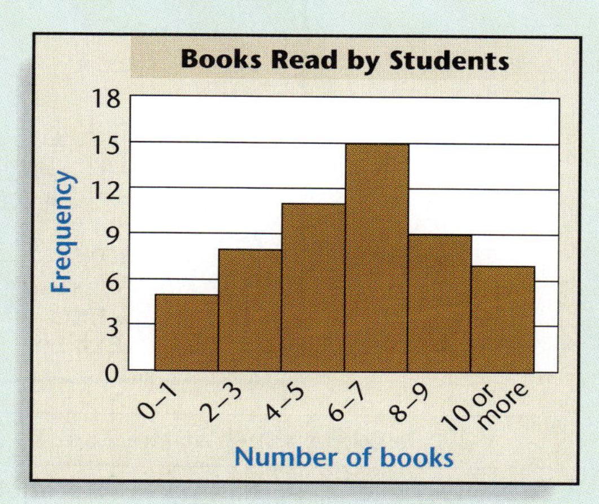

Study Skills Creating a Test

To reinforce what you have learned, it may be helpful to create your own test and then solve it. To create a test, you need to think about the important ideas taught and about which questions show how well you understand these ideas.

1. a. Look back through Section 1. Identify the important ideas.

   b. Create a test based on these ideas and then solve your test to make a solution key.

2. a. Ask a classmate to complete your test. Use your solution key to grade the test.

   b. Ask the student who took the test for suggestions about how the test could be improved. Revise the test and solution key based on these suggestions.

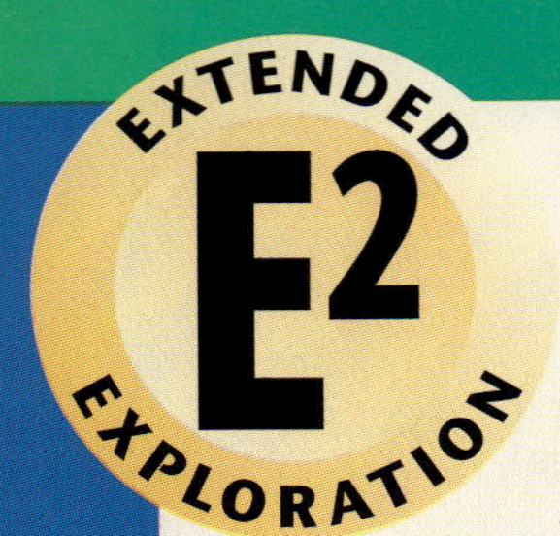

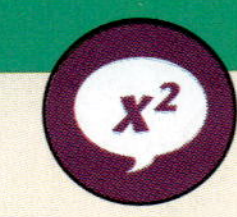

FOR ASSESSMENT AND PORTFOLIOS

What's for Lunch?

The Situation

You have been hired to lead tours at the zoo shown on the map below.

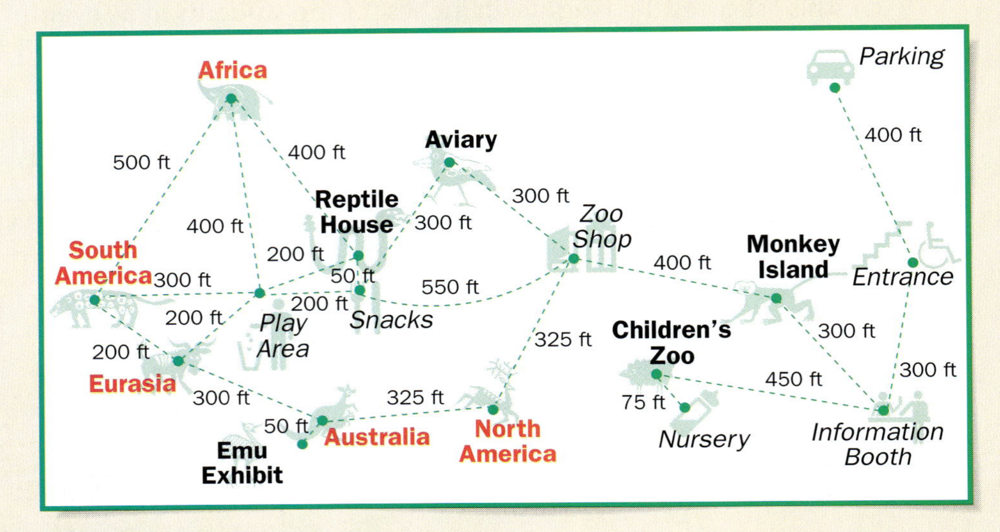

Feeding Times at the Zoo		
Animal	Starting time	Location in the zoo
chimpanzee	11:30 A.M.	Africa
hippopotamus	10:00 A.M.	Africa
kangaroo	9:30 A.M.	Australia
Japanese macaque	9:00 A.M.	Eurasia
Siberian tiger	11:00 A.M.	Eurasia
sea lion	10:00 A.M.	North America
polar bear	11:30 A.M.	North America
jaguar	11:00 A.M.	South America
llama	9:30 A.M.	South America

The Problem

Design a tour that starts at the Play Area and visits as many of the animal feedings and exhibits as possible while keeping walking distance to a minimum. (*Note:* Feedings last approximately 20 min.). Spend at least 30 min at each of the five major areas of the zoo, labeled in red on the map. The tour can start as early as 8:30 A.M. but must end by 12 noon.

Present Your Results

Describe your tour. Include data on the total time spent on the tour, the exhibits and animal feedings visited, and the total distance walked. Explain the decisions and assumptions you made to solve this problem.

Section  Proportions and Plots

EXPLORATION 1
- Cross Products

EXPLORATION 2
- Scatter Plots

EXPLORATION 3
- Box-and-Whisker Plots

Setting the Stage

For many of us, a great way to spend an afternoon might include going to the movies, playing a sport, or going for a bike ride. For Ashrita Furman, an afternoon off means time to ride on a pogo stick. For Eddy McDonald, it might be time to spend testing his yo-yo skills. And Richard Rodriguez could use the time to get ready for his next roller-coaster marathon.

Think About It

1 Record-holder Ashrita Furman covered a distance of 16 mi on a pogo stick in 6 h 40 min. Estimate his speed in miles per hour (mi/h).

2 Eddy McDonald completed 8437 yo-yo loops in 1 h and 21,663 yo-yo loops in 3 h. Which is the faster rate?

3 Richard Rodriguez set a world record by riding the Big Dipper roller coaster at Blackpool Pleasure Beach in England for 549 h! For how many days did he ride the Big Dipper?

GOAL

LEARN HOW TO...
- solve proportions using cross products

AS YOU...
- explore the riders' experience on a roller coaster

KEY TERM
- cross products

Exploration 1

Cross Products

Many people enjoy the thrill of riding a roller coaster. The feelings of being pulled out of your seat and of being pushed back into it are due to changes in speed and direction of motion. The sensations you feel on a roller coaster are related to your weight, which depends on Earth's gravity, or 1 G. The diagram below explains more about what happens when you ride a roller coaster.

If you weigh 100 lb and experience 2 G going up a hill on a roller coaster, you feel as if you weigh twice your weight, or 200 lb. You can use a proportion to show this relationship.

$$\frac{100 \text{ lb}}{1 \text{ G}} = \frac{200 \text{ lb}}{2 \text{ G}}$$

actual weight (100 lb); apparent weight at 2 G (200 lb)

4 Use a proportion like the one above to find each value.

a. the apparent weight at 0.5 G of a person who actually weighs 215 lb

b. the actual weight of a person who has an apparent weight of 520 lb at 4 G

5 **Discussion** Suppose at liftoff an astronaut has an apparent weight of 531 lb at 4.5 G. The proportion below can be used to find the astronaut's apparent weight at 12 G. Why might it be difficult to solve this proportion using your method from Question 4?

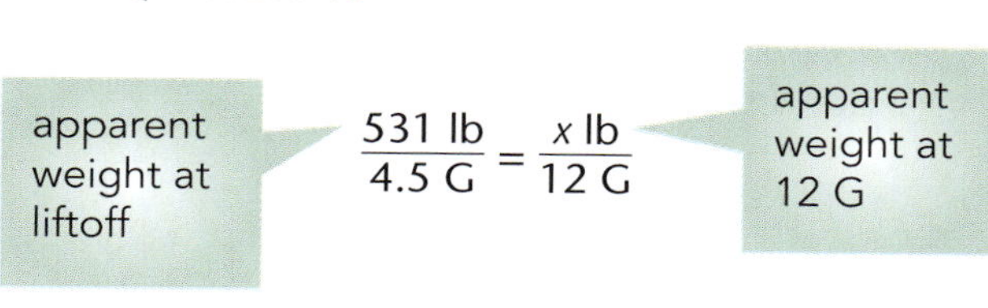

The first looping roller coaster in the United States, the Flip-Flap, opened in 1895 at Coney Island in Brooklyn, New York. Its riders experienced a whopping 12 G—more than twice what astronauts experience during liftoff!

▶ **Recall that a proportion is an equation stating that two ratios are equivalent. You can use this idea to discover another way of solving proportions.**

6 For each pair of ratios, determine whether the ratios are equivalent. Explain the method you used.

a. $\frac{2}{6} \stackrel{?}{=} \frac{3}{9}$ **b.** $\frac{6}{11} \stackrel{?}{=} \frac{4}{7}$ **c.** $\frac{6}{8} \stackrel{?}{=} \frac{12}{16}$

d. $\frac{6}{9} \stackrel{?}{=} \frac{9}{12}$ **e.** $\frac{3}{24} \stackrel{?}{=} \frac{4}{36}$ **f.** $\frac{10}{15} \stackrel{?}{=} \frac{12}{18}$

▶ **In the proportion below, the products $2 \cdot 9$ and $3 \cdot 6$ are cross products.**

EXAMPLE

$2 \cdot 9 = 18$ $\frac{2}{6} = \frac{3}{9}$ $3 \cdot 6 = 18$

7 Evaluate the cross products for each pair of ratios in Question 6. What do you notice about the cross products when the ratios are equivalent? What do you notice when they are not equivalent?

8 **Discussion** Look at your results from Question 7. How can you use cross products to determine whether two ratios are equivalent?

9 For each pair of ratios, use cross products to determine whether the ratios are equivalent.

a. $\frac{8}{15} \stackrel{?}{=} \frac{5}{9}$ **b.** $\frac{3}{12} \stackrel{?}{=} \frac{5}{20}$ **c.** $\frac{3}{25} \stackrel{?}{=} \frac{1}{8}$ **d.** $\frac{7}{21} \stackrel{?}{=} \frac{12}{39}$

▶ **In Question 10 you will explore why you can use cross products to find out whether two ratios are equivalent.**

10 **Try This as a Class** Use the proportion $\frac{4}{6} = \frac{6}{9}$.

a. Rewrite the ratios using a common denominator equal to the product of the two denominators.

Original ratios	Product of denominators	Equivalent ratios
$\frac{4}{6} = \frac{6}{9}$	$6 \cdot 9 = 54$	$\frac{4 \cdot ?}{54} = \frac{6 \cdot ?}{54}$

b. Compare the products in the numerators of the equivalent ratios you wrote in part (a) with the cross products for the ratio pair. What do you notice?

11 **a.** Choose one pair of equivalent ratios from Question 6 on page 329. Repeat parts (a) and (b) of Question 10 for the ratios you chose. What do you notice about the products in the numerators?

b. Choose a pair of ratios from Question 6 that are not equivalent. Repeat parts (a) and (b) of Question 10 for this ratio pair. What do you notice about the products in the numerators?

▶ **You can use cross products to solve proportions with an unknown.**

12 **Try This as a Class** In Question 5 on page 329 you examined this proportion.

$$\frac{531 \text{ lb}}{4.5 \text{ G}} = \frac{x \text{ lb}}{12 \text{ G}}$$

a. Use cross products to write an equation for the proportion.

b. How would you solve the equation you wrote in part (a)**?**

c. Solve the equation to find the rider's apparent weight at 12 G.

d. What is the rider's actual weight at 1 G**?**

✓ QUESTION 13

...checks that you can solve a proportion.

13 **✓ CHECKPOINT** Solve each proportion.

a. $\frac{68}{12} = \frac{51}{x}$ **b.** $\frac{3}{5} = \frac{n}{16}$ **c.** $\frac{5}{s} = \frac{8}{7}$ **d.** $\frac{x}{24} = \frac{15}{180}$

HOMEWORK EXERCISES ▶ See Exs. 1–11 on pp. 337–338.

Exploration 2

Scatter Plots

GOAL

LEARN HOW TO...
- make a scatter plot
- fit a line to a scatter plot

AS YOU...
- examine how much a rubber band stretches

KEY TERMS
- scatter plot
- fitted line

SET UP *Work in a group of four or five. You will need:* • *Labsheet 2A* • *rubber band* • *50 pennies* • *large paper clip* • *small paper clip* • *tape* • *lined paper* • *metric ruler* • *small plastic (sandwich) bag* • *strand of uncooked spaghetti*

A daredevil rides a hot air balloon 150 ft into the air and jumps out wearing a harness attached to 50 ft rubber bands called *bungee cords.* This is bungee jumping, an activity that is not for everyone. The greater the jumper's weight, the more bungee cords are needed to prevent the jumper from hitting the ground.

▶ **In this activity, you'll model bungee jumping and explore the relationship between weight and the stretch of a rubber band.**

14 **Use Labsheet 2A.** Follow the directions on Labsheet 2A to set up the *Rubber Band Stretch Experiment.*

15 **a.** Add 5 pennies to the plastic bag.

b. When the bag stops moving, mark the location of the bottom edge of the rubber band. Write the number of pennies in the bag next to your mark.

c. Repeat parts (a) and (b) seven times.

Number of pennies	Distance stretched (cm)
5	?
10	?
15	?
20	?
25	?
30	?
35	?
40	?

16 **a.** Take the pennies out of the bag, but do *not* remove the paper or rubber band apparatus from the wall.

b. Measure the distance from the top edge of the paper to each 5-penny mark.

c. Copy and complete the table at the left.

Use Labsheet 2A for Questions 17–19.

17 **a.** Plot the data points from your group's table and the other groups' tables on the *Rubber Band Stretch Graph*.

b. What do you notice about the points on the graph?

▶ **The graph you drew in Question 17(a) is a *scatter plot*. A scatter plot can be used to compare two sets of data. If the data points are close to a line, it may be possible to *fit a line* to the scatter plot to help make predictions.**

18 **a.** Place a piece of spaghetti on the scatter plot so that the data points are close to the spaghetti and there are about the same number of points on one side of the spaghetti as on the other side.

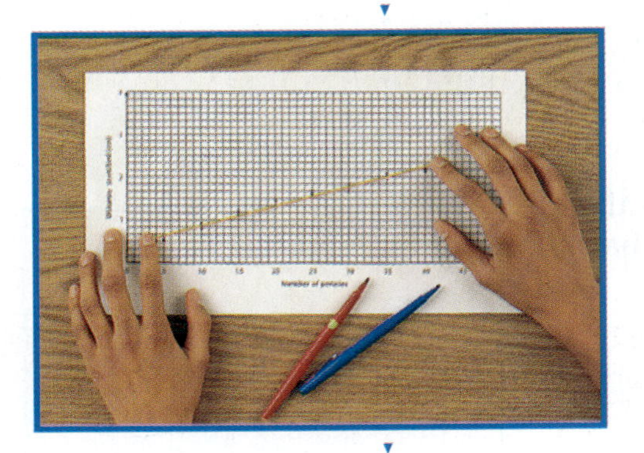

b. Draw a line segment along the piece of spaghetti. This is a **fitted line** for the scatter plot.

c. **Discussion** Do you think every person will draw the same line? Explain.

d. Use the fitted line to predict the distance the rubber band will stretch with 27 pennies in the bag. Then predict how far it will stretch with 50 pennies in the bag.

e. Place 27 pennies in the bag. Mark the point on the notebook paper that the bottom edge of the rubber band reaches. Then add enough pennies to the bag to total 50 and mark the paper.

f. Measure the two new distances. How close are these distances to the estimates you made in part (d)?

✓ QUESTION 19

...checks that you can use a fitted line to make predictions.

19 **✓ CHECKPOINT** Use the fitted line from Question 18(b) to predict the distance the rubber band will stretch with 32 pennies.

20 **Discussion** A 100 ft bungee cord with a $\frac{5}{8}$ in. diameter will stretch to a maximum of 150 ft with a 140 lb load. A 300 lb load can increase the stretch to 200 ft. How do you think the stretch length was determined for different weights?

HOMEWORK EXERCISES ▶ See Exs. 12–15 on pp. 338–339.

TECHNOLOGY Using Technology to Make Scatter Plots

You can use spreadsheet software or other graphing technology to make your scatter plot for Question 17 on page 332.

Step 1 Enter the data for the graph into the spreadsheet.

Enter the data for the horizontal axis in column A.

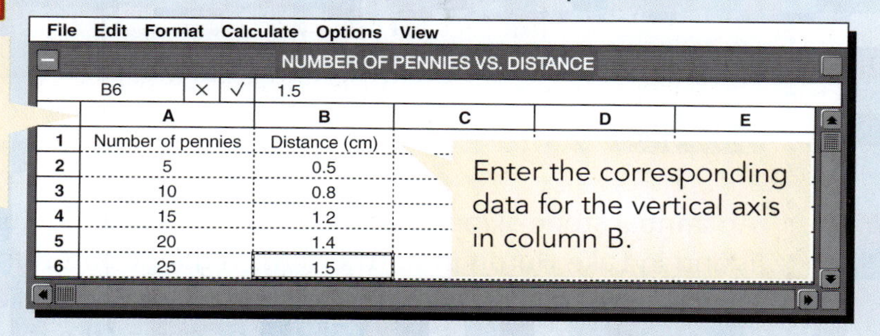

Step 2 To make a graph, highlight the data you entered and choose the option that makes a chart. Then select the type of graph you want to make.

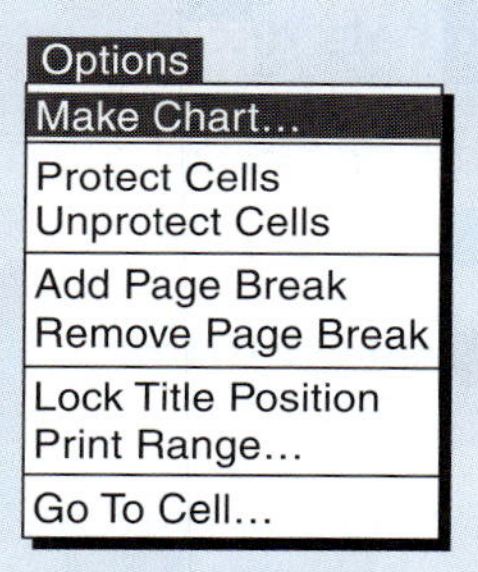

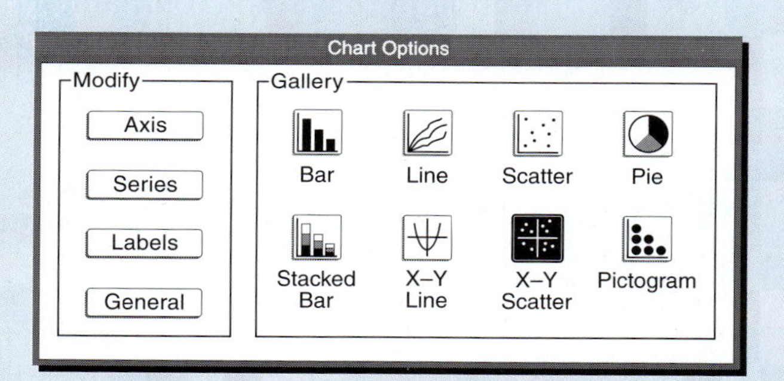

Step 3 Experiment with the labels, grid lines, and scale until the graph appears the way you want it to. Be sure to include a title.

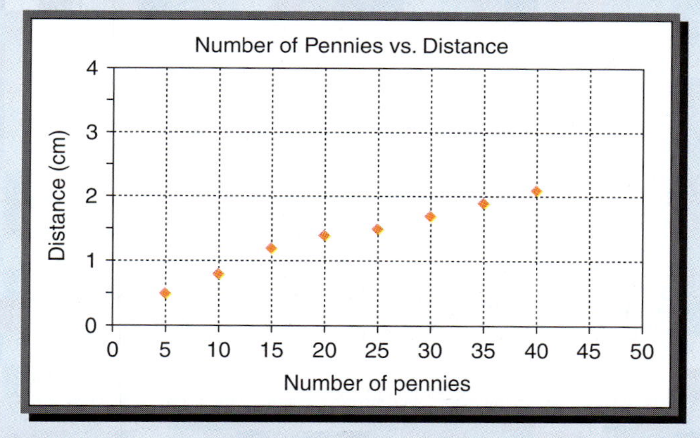

Step 4 You can print out the graph and draw a fitted line through your scatter plot as you did in Question 18 on page 332. Some graphing technology will also let you draw a fitted line or it will draw one for you.

GOAL

LEARN HOW TO...
- interpret box-and-whisker plots

AS YOU...
- examine stone-skipping data

KEY TERM
- box-and-whisker plot

Exploration 3

Box-and-Whisker Plots

SET UP *You will need Labsheet 2B.*

An annual stone-skipping tournament is held every July 4 on Mackinac Island in Lake Huron in northern Michigan. Contestants pitch stones over the water. The winner is the person who makes a stone *skip,* or bounce off the surface, the most times before the stone sinks.

▶ **Suppose you want to know whether your stone skipping is good enough to win the tournament. To help decide, you could use a box-and-whisker plot to analyze the winning numbers of skips in past tournaments.**

▲ In 1996, Sarah Marx won the Mackinac Island Stone Skipping Tournament in the 12-years-and-under division.

Winning Numbers of Skips: Mackinac Island Stone Skipping Tournament, 1969–1984*

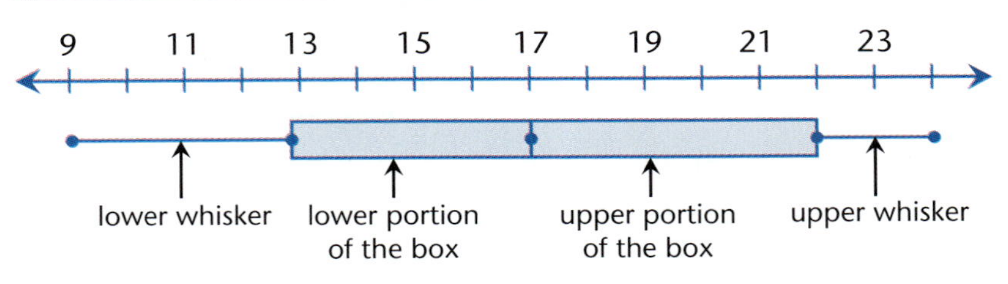

*except 1981

Use Labsheet 2B for Questions 21–25.

21 To find out how the *Box-and-Whisker Plot* displays a set of data, record each winning number of skips on a line plot.

22 **Discussion** In 1973 and 1975, records were set for the least and greatest numbers of skips. What were the record numbers? Where are they shown on the box-and-whisker plot?

23 **a.** On the box-and-whisker plot, how many data points are represented by each whisker, including the endpoints?

b. One whisker is longer than the other whisker. Does that mean that it represents more data points? Explain.

24 **a.** The vertical segment in the box is at 17. How many data points are greater than 17? less than 17? Do you think the vertical segment represents the *mean*, the *median*, or the *mode*?

b. A box-and-whisker plot divides a data set into four groups. About what percent of the total number of data values are in each of the four groups?

25 **Try This as a Class** The number of skips four people can make are given below. Use the box-and-whisker plot to find each person's chance of winning the tournament. Explain.

a. 8 skips **b.** 17 skips **c.** 22 skips **d.** 13 skips

▶ **Box-and-whisker plots are useful for comparing two or more sets of data. The box-and-whisker plots below show how two stone-skipping rivals have performed in competition from 1992–1995.**

Numbers of Skips: Mackinac Island Stone Skipping Tournament, 1992–1995

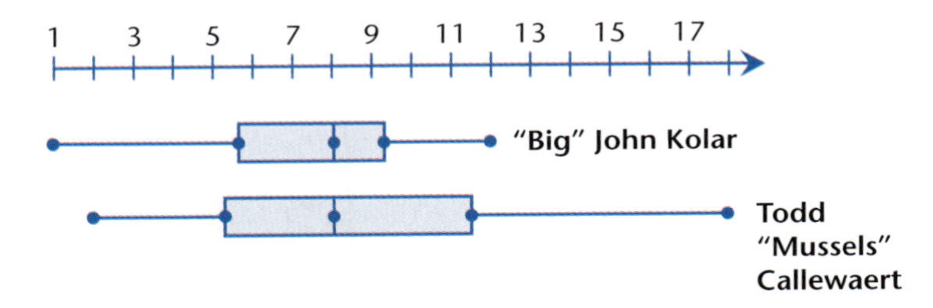

26 ✓ **CHECKPOINT** Use the box-and-whisker plots above.

...checks that you can interpret box-and-whisker plots.

a. Each year contestants make 6 throws. Each plot above shows 24 throws for the four years of competition. About how many data points are in each box? in each whisker?

b. Who had the most skips in 1992–1995 tournament play? Who had the fewest? How many skips was this for each?

c. Compare the median number of skips made by each stone skipper during the four years of tournament play.

d. The best 25% of Todd Callewaert's throws from 1992–1995 made 11.5 skips or more. How does this compare with John Kolar's throws?

e. Is it possible to tell who won most often in the years 1992–1995? Explain.

HOMEWORK EXERCISES ▶ See Exs. 16–18 on pp. 340–341.

Section 2 Key Concepts

Key Terms

cross products

Cross Products (pp. 328–330)

You can use cross products to solve a proportion.

Example Solve the proportion $\frac{3}{2} = \frac{x}{6}$.

$\frac{3}{2} \times \frac{x}{6}$

$3 \cdot 6 = 2x$

Use cross products to write an equation. Then solve the equation.

$\frac{18}{2} = \frac{2x}{2}$

Divide both sides by 2.

$x = 9$

scatter plot

fitted line

Scatter Plots and Fitted Lines (pp. 331–333)

You can use a scatter plot to explore how two data sets are related. If the points are close to a line, you can use a fitted line to make predictions.

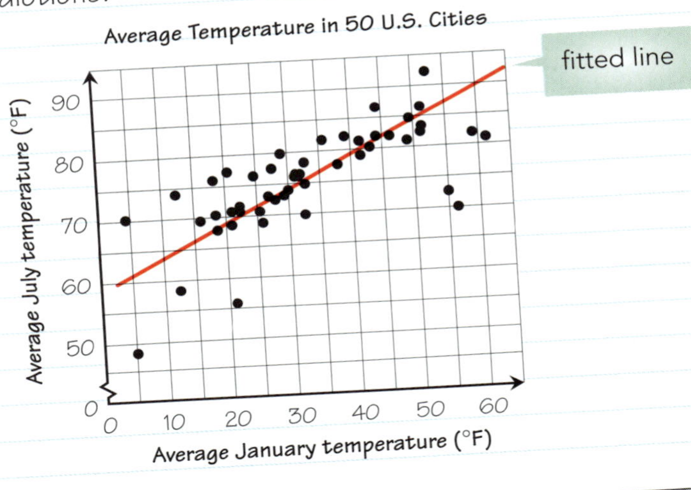

Key Concepts Questions

27 Solve each proportion.

a. $\frac{3}{4} = \frac{n}{18}$ **b.** $\frac{2}{11} = \frac{y}{88}$ **c.** $\frac{8}{70} = \frac{6}{t}$

28 Use the scatter plot above to predict the temperature in July for a city that has an average January temperature of 40°F.

Section 2 Key Concepts

Key Term

box-and-whisker plot

Box-and-Whisker Plots (pp. 334–335)

Sometimes you can use a box-and-whisker plot to display data.

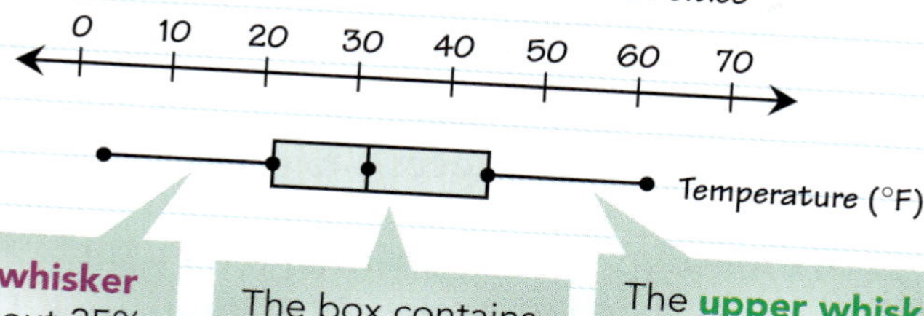

The **lower whisker** contains about 25% of the data values.

The box contains about 50% of the data values.

The **upper whisker** contains about 25% of the data values.

29 Key Concepts Question Use the box-and-whisker plot shown above.

a. Estimate the maximum data value recorded.

b. About how many of the 50 cities had average January temperatures below 22°F? Explain.

Section 2 Practice & Application Exercises

YOU WILL NEED

For Exs. 14–15:
- graph paper
- ruler

1. **Zoos** Nine apes at the National Zoological Park in Washington, D.C., eat a combined total of 12 lb of oranges per day. How many pounds of oranges are needed per day to feed 15 apes?

2. Japanese macaques (mə-kăks´) are short-tailed monkeys. Two Japanese macaques get 0.5 kg of biscuits each day. How much would seven macaques get each day?

3. How many grams of protein are contained in 510 g of tuna if 85 g of tuna contain 24 g of protein?

4. The morning menu for one orangutan is shown below. Write a morning menu that can be used to feed 10 orangutans.

Morning Menu for One Orangutan

1 apple	*1/4 lb boiled meat*
1/2 lb kale	*1/3 lb green beans*
1/2 orange	*1/3 lb monkey biscuits*
2 stalks celery	

5. A giant panda eats 150 lb of bamboo every 5 days. How many pounds of bamboo would you expect it to eat in 30 days?

6. **Currency Exchange** Suppose an American tourist in London exchanges 150 U.S. dollars and receives 100 British pounds. How many British pounds should the tourist receive for 600 U.S. dollars?

Solve each proportion.

7. $\frac{2}{x} = \frac{14}{28}$ 8. $\frac{7}{10} = \frac{x}{3}$ 9. $\frac{6}{x} = \frac{9}{10.5}$ 10. $\frac{10}{16} = \frac{x}{24}$

11. Calculator To solve the proportion $\frac{4.8}{2} = \frac{x}{5}$, Ang used the key sequence 4 . 8 ÷ 2 × 5 =.

a. Ang got an answer of 12. Is she correct?

b. Describe the method Ang used to solve the proportion.

c. Describe another key sequence to solve the proportion.

12. Choose the letter of the scatter plot that you think shows the better fitted line. Explain your choice.

A. Lorna's scatter plot B. Andrea's scatter plot

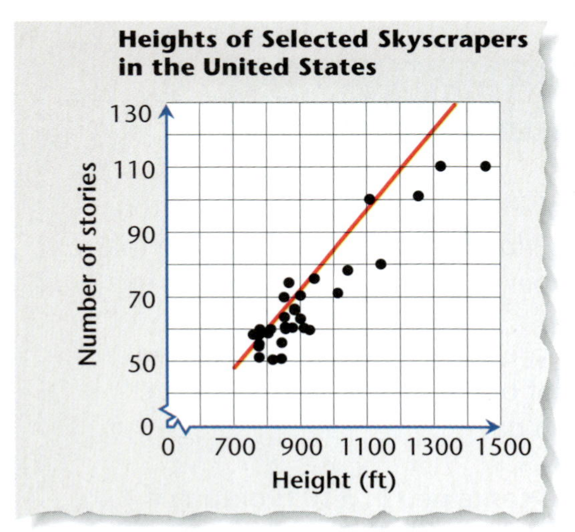

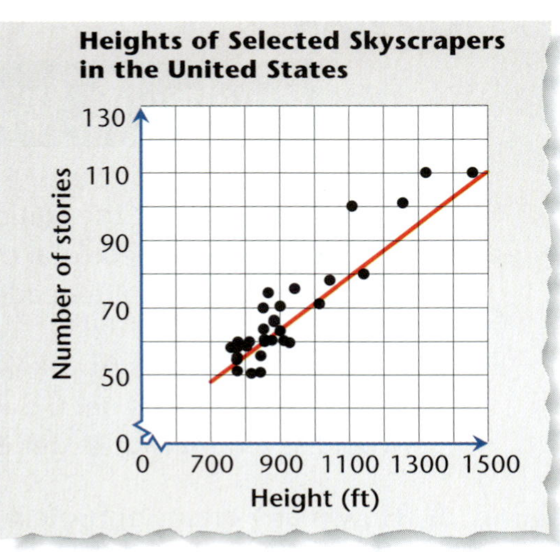

13. Use the scatter plot you chose in Exercise 12.

a. About how many stories would you expect a 1200 ft skyscraper to have?

b. **Writing** There are two skyscrapers with a height of 900 ft. One has 71 stories, while the other has 64 stories. Why do you think they have different numbers of stories?

c. **Challenge** About how many feet tall is an average story?

14. The first two columns of the table below show the floor sizes of different tents and the number of sleepers each tent can hold.

a. Use the data in the first two columns of the table to make a scatter plot.

b. Draw a fitted line for your scatter plot.

c. Using your graph, predict the floor size of a tent that can sleep 12 people.

Tent Sizes and Prices

Floor size (ft^2)	Number of sleepers	Price
135	4	$162.99
140	6	$289.99
160	8	$309.99
200	10	$299.99
108	5	$159.99
110	6	$184.99
64	4	$99.99
81	5	$139.99
100	6	$199.99
109	6	$229.99
49	3	$89.99
60	3	$109.99

15. The last column of the table above shows the price of each tent.

a. Use the data in the last two columns to make a scatter plot.

b. Draw a fitted line for your scatter plot.

c. Using your graph, predict the price of a tent that can sleep 12 people.

16. Automobile Racing The Indianapolis 500 is an annual 500 mi race for automobiles. The box-and-whisker plots below show the winning times for selected years. All times have been rounded to the nearest minute.

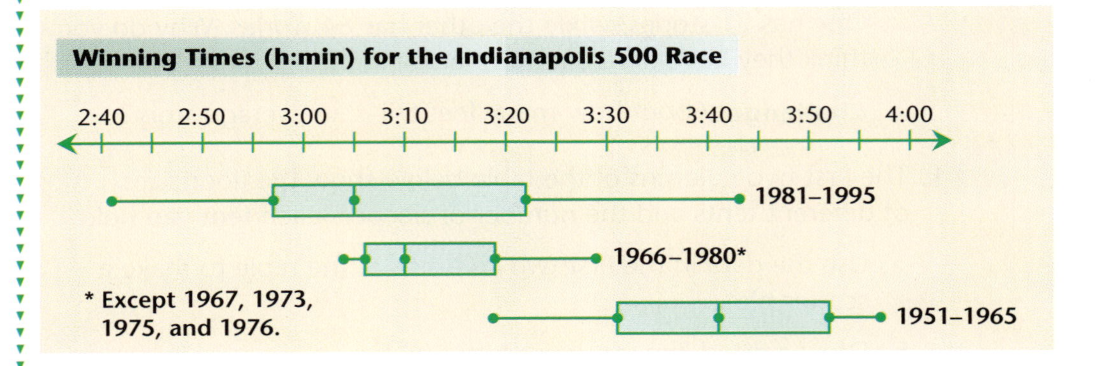

a. In the 1951–1965 box-and-whisker plot, the slowest time was 3 h 57 min. Estimate the fastest winning time for those years.

b. Estimate the median winning time in the period 1966–1980.

c. About 25% of the winning times from 1981–1995 were between 3 h 22 min and 3 h 44 min. How do these times compare with those in the years 1966–1980? 1951–1965?

d. **Open-ended** Make two statements based on the plots for the periods 1981–1995 and 1951–1965.

17. Chess In 1995, Garry Kasparov successfully defended his world championship chess title against Anand Viswanathan in an 18-game match. The stem-and-leaf plot shows the number of moves in each of the 18 games. Choose the letter of the box-and-whisker plot below that represents the data shown in the stem-and-leaf plot. Explain how you know.

1995 World Chess Championship

Number of Moves per Game

Stem	Leaves
1	2 6
2	0 1 2 5 5 7 7 8 9
3	1 5 6 8
4	1 3
5	
6	3

3|5 represents a game of 35 moves

Number of Moves per Game

0 10 20 30 40 50 60 70

Plot A

Plot B

Plot C

Reflecting on the Section

18. Both graphs show temperature data for the same 50 cities.

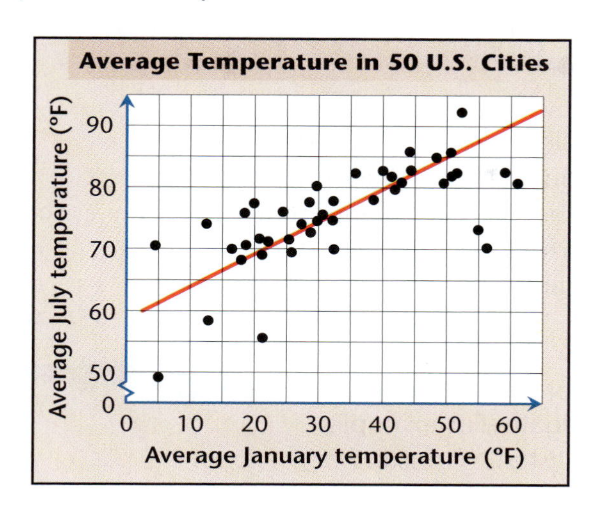

Average January Temperature in 50 United States Cities (°F)

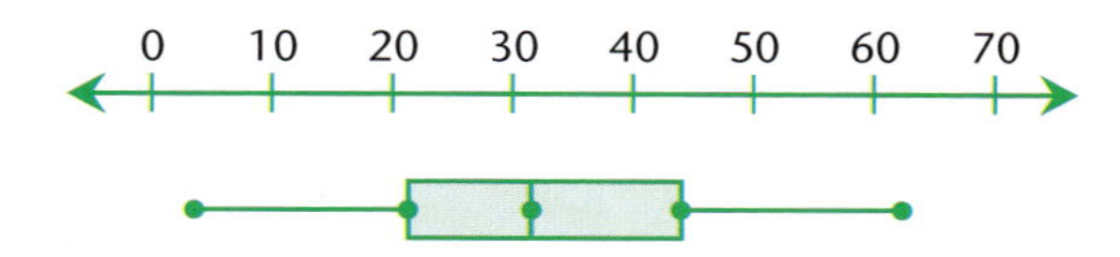

a. What was the lowest average temperature in January for the 50 cities? Which graph could you use to determine this?

b. About how many of the 50 cities are in the box portion of the box-and-whisker plot?

c. Estimate the range of the average temperatures in July for the cities that are in the box of the box-and-whisker plot.

Visual THINKING

Exercise 18 checks that you understand box-and-whisker and scatter plots.

Spiral Review

Write each rate as a unit rate. (Module 5, p. 319)

19. $\frac{\$290}{40 \text{ h}}$ 20. $\frac{45 \text{ min}}{5 \text{ mi}}$ 21. $\frac{\$13}{2 \text{ lb}}$

Write each product in exponential form. (Module 1, p. 20)

22. $5 \cdot 5$ 23. $4 \cdot 4 \cdot 4 \cdot 4$ 24. $3 \cdot 3 \cdot 3 \cdot 3 \cdot 3$

Write each fraction as a decimal. (Module 4, p. 256)

25. $\frac{2}{5}$ 26. $\frac{5}{15}$ 27. $\frac{9}{45}$

May I Ask You a Few Questions?

A survey or opinion poll is a way to collect information about a group of people. For your module project, your class will work together to create a survey that investigates how the students in your school spend their free time. Next, you and your partner will interview students and collect information. Then, you will organize the data and decide how to present your findings.

SET UP

You will need:

- *clipboard or other writing surface*

Creating a Survey As a class, decide what question about free time your survey will investigate. For example, "How often do students at our school listen to music?" or "What types of music do students listen to?" You may also pick a general topic, such as "How do students spend their free time?"

a. Write 5 to 10 survey questions about your topic. Be sure to include questions that ask the age, the grade level, and the gender of the person answering the survey form.

b. Review your questions. Will the people being surveyed understand each question? Do the questions provide enough information for your topic? Make any changes necessary.

Gathering Data In most schools it would be difficult to collect information from every student. It is easier to survey a *representative sample* of students. Because this sample must represent the entire school, you will survey people from each grade level. Your teacher will help you select an appropriate sample size.

Your sample must also be *random*. This means that each person in the population has an equal chance of being surveyed. For example, you could choose to survey every tenth person on a school roster.

Describe how your class will choose your random representative sample. Then conduct your survey.

Solve each proportion.

1. $\frac{8}{12} = \frac{r}{27}$
2. $\frac{6}{t} = \frac{3}{18}$
3. $\frac{24}{54} = \frac{20}{v}$
4. $\frac{32.5}{x} = \frac{5}{14}$

Use the data in the table.

5. Make a scatter plot of the data.
6. Fit a line to the data.
7. Using your fitted line, predict the average depth of a sea with an area of 500,000 mi^2.

Oceans and Seas		
Name	Area (mi^2)	Average depth (ft)
Okhotsk Sea	613,900	2818
Gulf of Mexico	595,800	4961
Bering Sea	889,600	5243
South China Sea	1,422,800	3478
Caribbean Sea	1,063,300	8173
Mediterranean Sea	971,400	4902
Japan Sea	377,600	5748
Andaman Sea	232,400	3596
Red Sea	173,700	1831

Use the box-and-whisker plot below.

8. Estimate the maximum and the minimum data values.
9. Of the 30 games played, about how many had scores below 65?
10. About how many games had scores above 78?

Women's National Basketball Association Team Scores, 1997

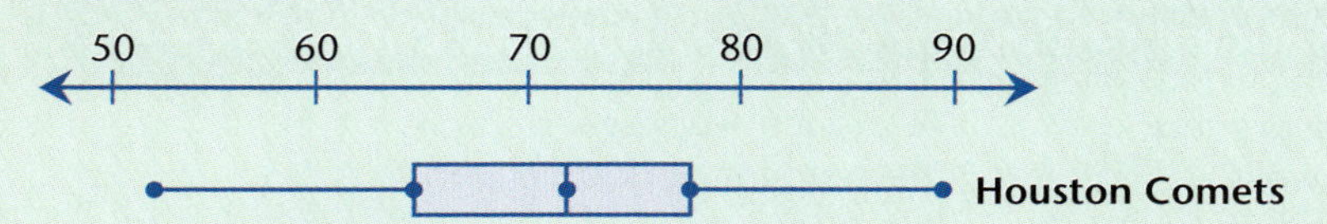

Standardized Testing ▸ Open-ended

Create a 20-item data set that can be represented by the box-and-whisker plot. Copy the plot and add a title.

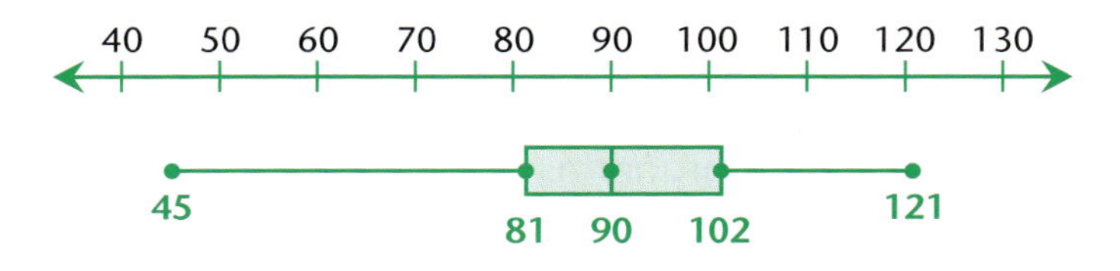

Section 3 Percent

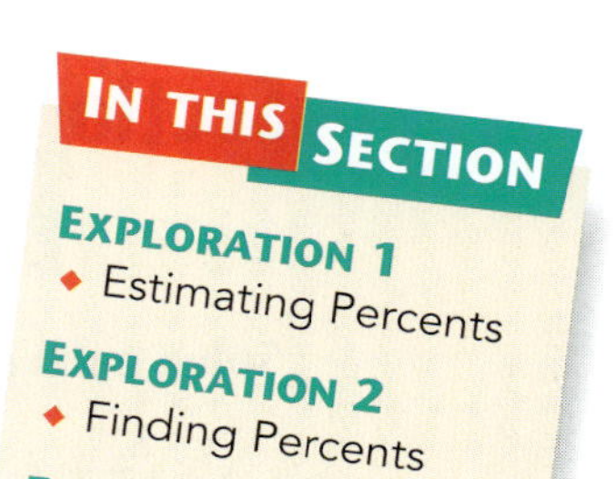

You Be the Critic

Setting the Stage

Going to the movies is a favorite pastime of many people. At any given time, many movies compete for your viewing attention. To decide which movies you want to see, you can use reviews and rating systems such as the one shown below.

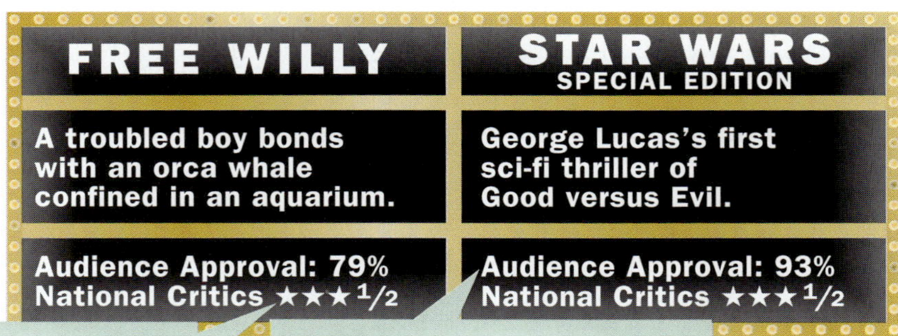

4 stars is the highest rating, and 1 star is the lowest. Half-stars may be given.

Audience Approval rating is the percent of people who gave the movie $3\frac{1}{2}$ or 4 stars.

Try This as a Class **Choose two movies or television programs. Using 1–4 stars, have each student in your class rate the two choices. Make a frequency table to show the results.**

Think About It

1 For each movie or program your class rated, write a ratio to compare the number of students who gave it $3\frac{1}{2}$ or 4 stars with the total number of students who rated the movie or television program.

2 Is your class's Audience Approval rating for each movie or program rated *greater than 25%*? *greater than 50%*? *greater than 75%*?

Exploration 1

Estimating Percents

GOAL

LEARN HOW TO...
- estimate percents

AS YOU...
- analyze movie ratings

SET UP *You will need:* • *Labsheet 3A* • *the table from the* Setting the Stage

Suppose that 17 of the 30 students who saw a movie gave it a rating of $3\frac{1}{2}$ or 4 stars. You can use *"nice" fractions* to estimate the percent equivalent of $\frac{17}{30}$.

"Nice" fractions are fractions such as $\frac{1}{5}$, $\frac{1}{2}$, $\frac{3}{4}$, and $\frac{7}{10}$ that can easily be converted to percents.

$\frac{1}{5} = 20\%$ $\frac{1}{2} = 50\%$

$\frac{3}{4} = 75\%$ $\frac{7}{10} = 70\%$

3 The ratio $\frac{17}{30}$ is close to the ratio $\frac{18}{30}$. Is $\frac{17}{30}$ *greater than* or *less than* $\frac{18}{30}$? How do you know?

4 **a.** What "nice" fraction is equivalent to $\frac{18}{30}$?

b. What is the percent equivalent of the fraction in part (a)?

c. Estimate the percent equivalent of $\frac{17}{30}$.

▶ **You can use a percent bar model to help visualize $\frac{17}{30}$ as a percent.**

5 **Use Labsheet 3A.** You can also estimate the percent represented by $\frac{17}{30}$ using a percent bar.

▶ **Some other "nice" fractions, and their percent equivalents, are given on page 346.**

Fraction-Decimal-Percent Relationships

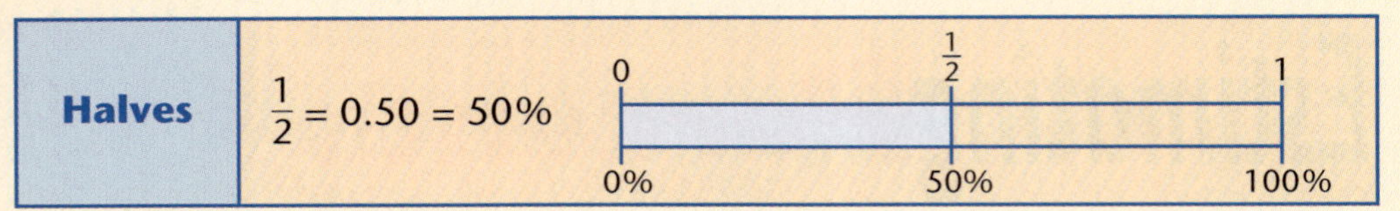

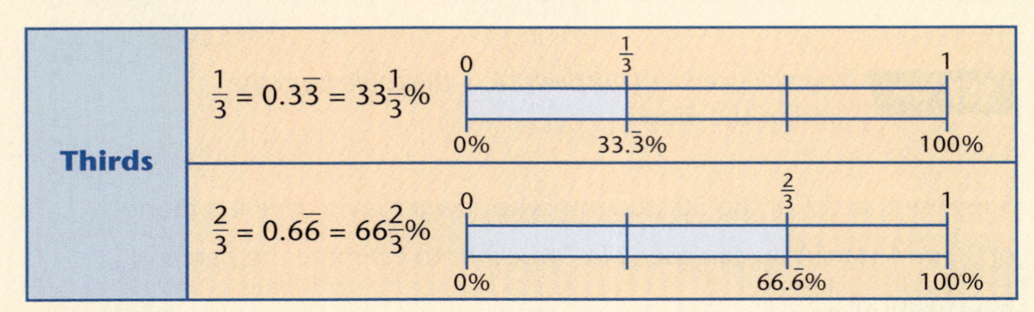

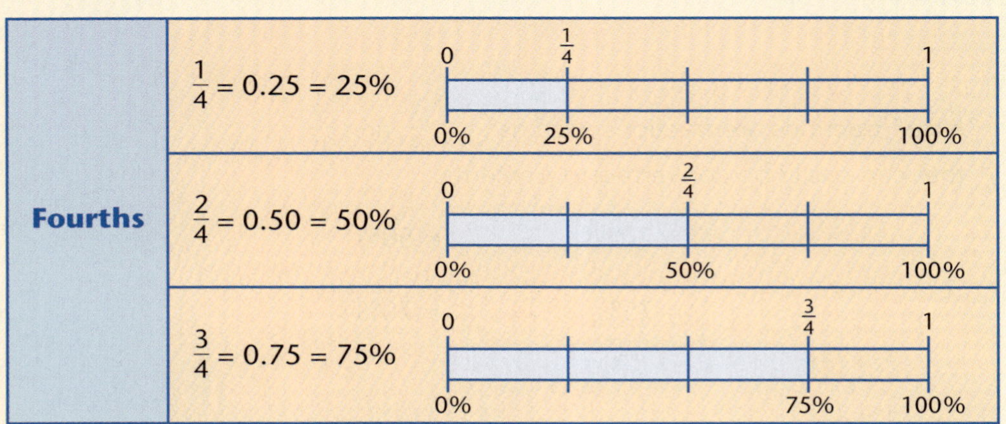

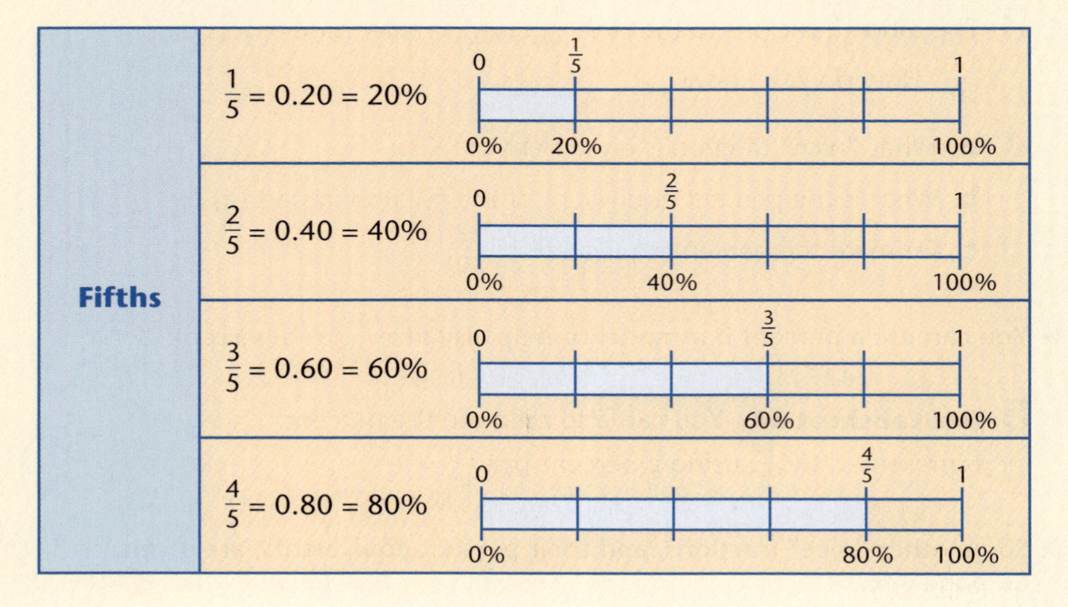

6 Suppose 22 out of 28 students gave a movie a rating of $3\frac{1}{2}$ or 4 stars.

a. What "nice" fraction would you use to estimate the percent equivalent of $\frac{22}{28}$?

b. Use the fraction from part (a) to estimate the Audience Approval rating for this movie.

c. Discussion What other "nice" fractions can you use to estimate the percent? Which gives the best estimate?

7 Suppose 9 out of 24 students gave a movie a rating of $3\frac{1}{2}$ or 4 stars. Estimate the Audience Approval rating as a percent. Explain your reasoning.

8 ✓ **CHECKPOINT** Estimate the percent equivalent of each fraction.

a. $\frac{13}{18}$ **b.** $\frac{8}{48}$ **c.** $\frac{29}{104}$

...checks that you can estimate percents.

9 **Try This as a Class** Julia estimates $\frac{5}{24}$ with the nice fraction $\frac{6}{24}$. Yvonne uses the "nice" fraction $\frac{5}{25}$.

a. The percent equivalent of $\frac{5}{24}$ is about 21%. Whose estimate is closer to the percent equivalent?

b. Which do you think changes a fraction more, adding 1 to the *numerator* or adding 1 to the *denominator*?

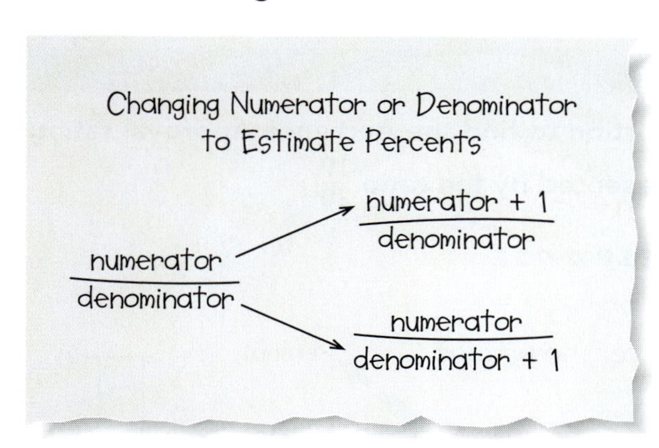

c. Is your answer to part (b) true when the numerator is greater than the denominator?

10 Estimate the Audience Approval rating for the two movies or programs rated by your class in the *Setting the Stage* on page 344.

HOMEWORK EXERCISES See Exs. 1–7 on p. 353.

GOAL

LEARN HOW TO...
- find percents

AS YOU...
- find Audience Approval ratings

Exploration 2

Finding Percents

SET UP *You will need the frequency table from the* Setting the Stage *on page 344.*

11 **Try This as a Class** Suppose a class gave two movies $3\frac{1}{2}$ or 4 stars as shown in the ratios below.

a. Estimate the Audience Approval rating for each movie. Explain the reasoning you used.

b. Using estimation, can you determine which movie had a higher Audience Approval rating? Explain.

▶ **A percent bar model can help you see how to set up a proportion to find the exact percent equivalent for a ratio.**

EXAMPLE

Set up a proportion to find the Audience Approval rating for Movie A, represented by the ratio $\frac{19}{30}$.

SAMPLE RESPONSE

Rotate the bar 90° so the parts are over the wholes.

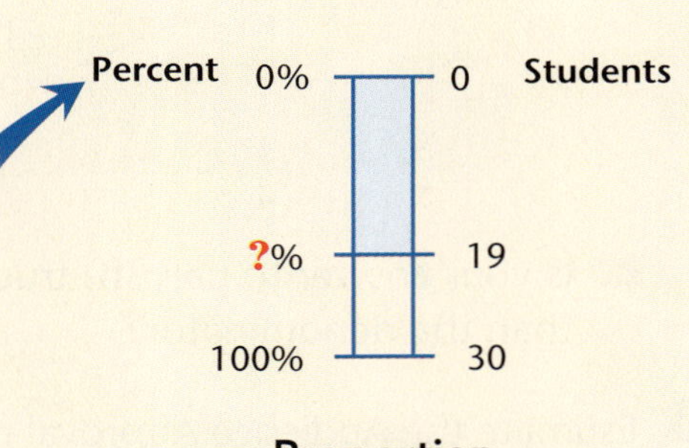

The shaded part represents the students who liked the movie.

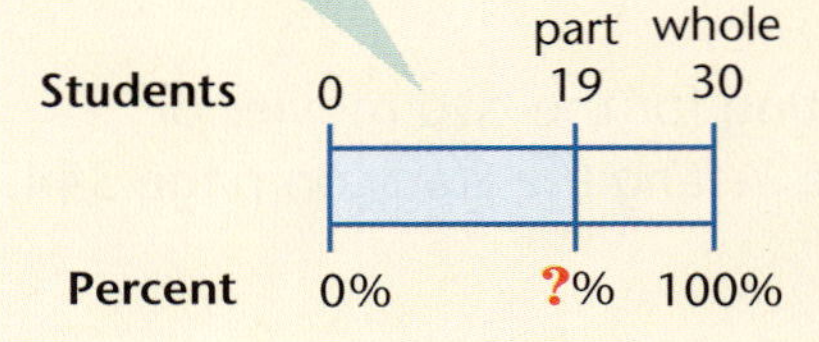

Proportion

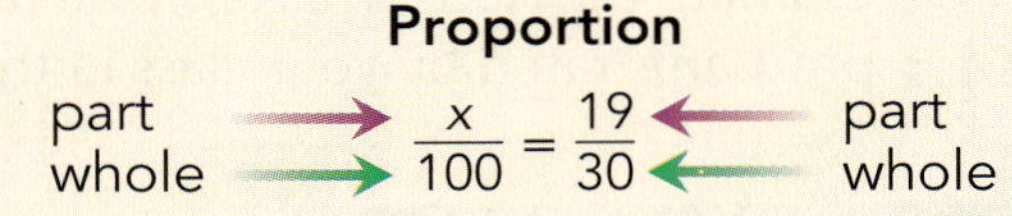

$$\frac{x}{100} = \frac{19}{30}$$

12 Solve the proportion in the Example on page 348 to find the Audience Approval rating for Movie A. Round your answer to the nearest whole percent. How does the answer compare with your estimate in Question 11?

13 ✓ **CHECKPOINT** Set up and solve a proportion to write each ratio as a percent.

a. $\frac{27}{90}$ **b.** 35 to 105 **c.** $\frac{18}{63}$

✓ **QUESTION 13**

...checks that you can set up and solve a proportion to find a percent.

14 **a.** Set up and solve a proportion to find the Audience Approval rating for Movie B to the nearest whole percent.

b. Which movie received a higher Audience Approval rating, Movie A or Movie B?

c. Is $\frac{19}{30} = \frac{15}{24}$? Explain why rounding to the nearest whole percent may be misleading.

15 **Discussion** Sometimes rounding to the nearest whole percent may not give the best answer.

a. Find the Audience Approval rating for Movie B to the nearest tenth of a percent.

b. Does your answer in part (a) change your answer to Question 14(b)? Explain.

Audience Approval rating for Movie A rounded to the nearest tenth of a percent

$$\frac{x}{100} = \frac{19}{30}$$

$$30x = 1900$$

$$x = \frac{1900}{30}$$

$$30 \overline{)1900.0} = 63.\overline{3}$$ ← about 63.3%

180
100
90
100

Write each ratio as a percent. Round to the nearest tenth.

16 $\frac{8}{35}$ and $\frac{22}{97}$ **17** $\frac{14}{29}$ and $\frac{15}{35}$ **18** $\frac{7}{35}$ and $\frac{8}{49}$

19 **Try This as a Class** Use your class's star ratings from page 344.

a. Set up and solve a proportion to find the Audience Approval rating for each movie or television program. Round each answer to the nearest tenth of a percent.

b. Which movie or program had a higher Audience Approval rating?

c. Find a fraction that has a percent equivalent within 0.5% of each class Audience Approval rating.

HOMEWORK EXERCISES ▶ See Exs. 8–14 on pp. 353–354.

GOAL

LEARN HOW TO...
- find a missing part or whole

AS YOU...
- find how many people rated a movie

Exploration 3

Finding Parts or Wholes

▶ **Audience Approval ratings are based on exit polls of at least 300 filmgoers per movie. If you know the total number of people surveyed, you can use "nice" fractions to estimate how many people gave a movie $3\frac{1}{2}$ or 4 stars.**

20 Suppose a survey of 300 people was used to determine the 79% Audience Approval rating for *Free Willy*. The percent bar below shows one way a "nice" fraction can be used to estimate how many people gave the movie $3\frac{1}{2}$ or 4 stars.

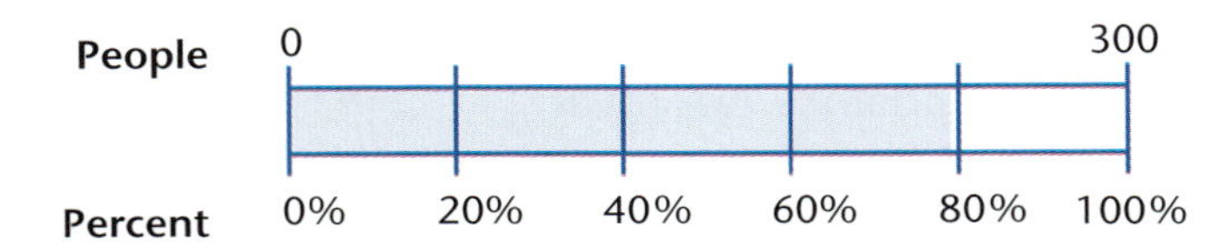

a. What "nice" fraction is equivalent to 20%?

b. Find 20% of 300.

c. What "nice" fraction is equivalent to 80%?

d. Use your answers from parts (a)–(c) to estimate 79% of 300.

▲ In the late 1960s, an audience at the Rivoli Theater in South Fallsburg, New York, viewed a "3-D" movie through special glasses.

21 **Discussion** Set up and solve a proportion to find 79% of 300. (*Hint:* Think of rotating the percent bar.) How does the exact answer compare with your estimate in Question 20?

$$\frac{\text{part}}{\text{whole}} \rightarrow \frac{79}{100} = \frac{?}{?} \leftarrow \frac{\text{part}}{\text{whole}}$$

✔ QUESTION 22

...checks that you can find a percent of a number.

22 **✔ CHECKPOINT** Suppose a survey of 400 people was used to determine the 76% Audience Approval rating for a movie.

a. Estimate 76% of 400 using a "nice" fraction.

b. Find 76% of 400.

23 Suppose 350 people rated the movie *Star Wars—Special Edition*, which had an Audience Approval rating of 93%.

a. Estimate the number of people who gave *Star Wars—Special Edition* $3\frac{1}{2}$ or 4 stars. Explain the method you used.

b. Set up and solve a proportion to find 93% of 350.

▶ **You just used proportions to find the part when you know the whole. Sometimes you know the part and need to find the whole.**

24 **Discussion** Suppose a movie has an Audience Approval rating of 45% because 162 people gave it a rating of $3\frac{1}{2}$ or 4 stars.

a. Is 162 the *part* or is it the *whole*? Explain.

b. Estimate how many people rated the movie. Explain the method you used.

▶ **You can use a proportion to find the whole.**

EXAMPLE

45% of a number is 162. Set up a proportion to find the whole.

SAMPLE RESPONSE

	Percent		**People**	
part → / whole →	$\frac{45}{100}$	=	$\frac{162}{x}$	← part / ← whole

25 Solve the proportion in the Example to find the total number of people who rated the movie in Question 24. How does your answer compare with your estimate in Question 24(b)?

26 Suppose 9 people give a movie a rating of $3\frac{1}{2}$ or 4 stars, resulting in an Audience Approval rating of 36%. Set up and solve a proportion to find how many people rated the movie.

27 ✓ **CHECKPOINT** Suppose 27% of a number is 135. What is the number? Explain the method you used.

✓ **QUESTION 27**

...checks that you can find the whole amount if you are given the percent.

HOMEWORK EXERCISES ▶ See Exs. 15–26 on pp. 354–355.

Section 3 Key Concepts

Percent Bar Model (pp. 345–347)

When solving problems involving percent, "nice" fractions can be used to help estimate solutions. "Nice" fractions can be converted to percents easily. The estimation can be shown on a percent bar model.

Example About what percent is 31 out of 40?

$\frac{31}{40}$ is close to the "nice" fraction $\frac{3}{4}$.

$\frac{3}{4} = 75\%$, so $\frac{31}{40}$ is a little more than 75%.

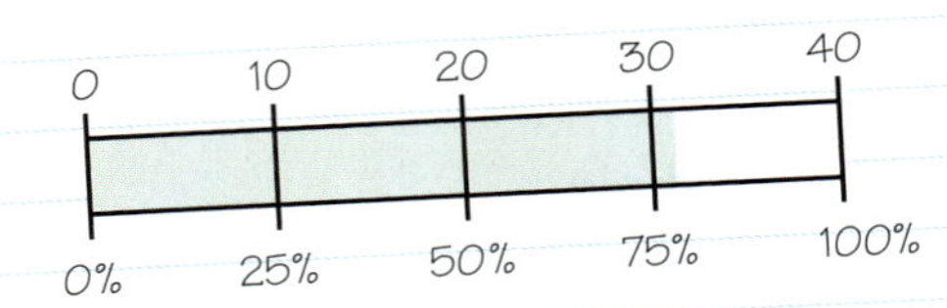

Proportions and Percents (pp. 348–351)

You can use proportions to find a missing part or whole.

Example

Suppose 65% of students surveyed say they prefer creamy peanut butter to chunky peanut butter. If 78 students preferred creamy, how many students were surveyed?

Since the total number of students surveyed is not known, the variable x represents the whole.

	Percent		Students	
part →	65	=	78	← part
whole →	100		x	← whole

$$\frac{65}{100} = \frac{78}{x}$$

Solving the proportion gives $x = 120$, so 120 students were surveyed.

28 Key Concepts Question Find each missing part or whole.

a. 11% of a number is 44.

b. 73% of 124 is a number.

Section 3

Practice & Application Exercises

1. Suppose that 7 out of 12 commercials during a certain TV show are about food. Draw a percent bar and use it to estimate the percent of commercials that advertise food.

2. It is estimated that 1 out of 11 employed Americans works in a shopping center or a shopping mall. Estimate the percent of Americans who work in a shopping center or a mall.

3. In a movie survey, 5 out of every 16 people who responded gave a movie a rating of 9 or 10 on a scale of 1 to 10.

   a. What "nice" fraction can you use to estimate the percent of people who gave the movie a rating of 9 or 10?

   b. Estimate the percent of people who gave a movie a rating of 9 or 10.

Estimate the percent equivalent of each ratio.

4. $\frac{7}{12}$ 5. $\frac{20}{24}$ 6. $\frac{9}{40}$ 7. $\frac{25}{33}$

8. Set up and solve a proportion to find the actual percent for Exercises 1 and 2. Round each answer to the nearest percent.

Write each ratio as a percent. Round each answer to the nearest tenth.

9. $\frac{4}{12}$ 10. $\frac{27}{135}$ 11. $\frac{51}{68}$ 12. $\frac{48}{750}$

13. **Entertainment Spending** In 1990, on average, each person under the age of 25 spent $833 on entertainment. Of that amount, $344 was spent on televisions, radios, and sound equipment. What percent of the entertainment money was spent on televisions, radios, and sound equipment?

14. **Publishing** Of the 46,738 new books published in 1990, 5172 were for juveniles. What percent of the books were for juveniles?

15. According to a Gallup poll, on any given day, 71% of the 250 million people in the United States read a newspaper and 36% read a magazine.

   a. Estimate the number of people in the United States who read a newspaper yesterday.

   b. Estimate the number of people in the United States who will read a magazine today.

16. Television Viewing The percent bar below shows 50% of the United States population.

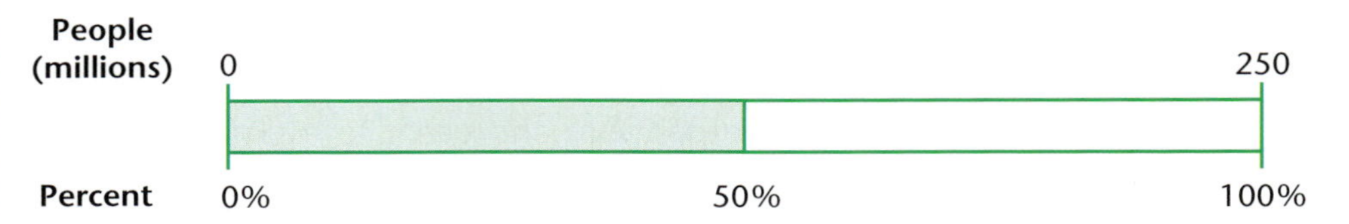

a. According to a survey in *TV Guide*, 46% of people in the United States said they would not stop watching television for anything less than $1 million. Estimate the number who would not stop watching television for anything less than $1 million.

b. In the same survey, 25% said they would not give up television even if they were given $1 million. Estimate the number of people in the United States who would not stop watching television even if they were given $1 million.

17. Suppose 68% of students at a school do not like the dress code. If 374 students do not like the dress code, how many students are there in the school? Explain your reasoning.

Find each unknown number.

18. 15% of a number is 13.5.

19. 12 is 30% of a number.

20. 82% of a number is 533.

21. 62% of 25 is a number.

22. Challenge Teenagers from three schools estimated how much time they spent viewing or listening to each medium on a school day. Here are their combined results.

Medium	Time spent (min)	
	Mean	Median
television	136	120
radio	101	60
records/tapes	87	60
MTV	29	0

a. The percent of the teenagers who did not watch MTV at all must be greater than what percent? How do you know?

b. Suppose teenagers spent a mean of 29% of their free time listening to the radio. How long is their total free time?

23. Suppose that when a math teacher eats in a restaurant, the teacher tips exactly 15% of the total bill. After enjoying a meal, the teacher leaves $2.40 on the table. How much did the meal cost?

24. a. Based on your own experience, estimate the number of minutes of free time a teenager has on a typical school day.

b. Use your answer to part (a) and the mean time spent on each medium listed in Exercise 22 to estimate the percent of free time teenagers spent on each of the various media.

c. Do you think the percents for students in your school would be *higher, lower,* or *the same as* the results you found in part (b)? Explain your answer.

25. Jo set up the proportion $\frac{100}{350} = \frac{x}{34}$ to find 34% of 350.

a. Is there anything wrong with Jo's proportion? Explain.

b. Set up a proportion that will give the correct answer, and solve it.

Reflecting on the Section

26. Find examples that show how percents are used in discounting prices. Describe the examples, and explain how you could use "nice" fractions to estimate or find the amount of each discount.

RESEARCH

Exercise 26 checks that you understand how to find a percent of a number.

Spiral Review

Solve each proportion. (Module 5, p. 336)

27. $\frac{3}{5} = \frac{x}{15}$ 28. $\frac{x}{9} = \frac{20}{180}$ 29. $\frac{8}{x} = \frac{32}{40}$

Find the absolute value of each integer. (Module 2, p. 94)

30. –121 31. 43 32. –1

Write each fraction in lowest terms. (Module 3, p. 170)

33. $\frac{25}{30}$ 34. $\frac{14}{49}$ 35. $\frac{27}{81}$

Extension 

The Interest Formula

To find the simple interest I paid on an amount, or *principal*, you can use this formula:

$$I = p \times r \times t$$

Find the simple interest in each situation.

36. $p = \$1200$
    $r = 5\%$
    $t = 1$ year

37. $p = \$1800$
    $r = 7\%$
    $t = 4$ years

38. $p = \$1000$
    $r = 5.5\%$
    $t = 8$ months

39. **Challenge** Suppose in Exercise 37 the interest earned each year were left in the account, so that the principal increased each year.

    a. Find the total interest earned in 4 years.

    b. Compare your answers for part (a) and Exercise 37.

May I Ask You a Few Questions?

Analyzing Data Each pair of students should report their results to the class. Then the class can organize and analyze all the data.

 3 How many students did you and your partner interview? Use fractions and percents to compare your sample size with that used by the entire class.

 4 Use fractions and percents to summarize the combined data. What did the survey reveal? Do the results vary by age? by grade level? by gender?

 5 How do the class results compare with the information you collected with your partner? Are the results what you expected? Did the different sample sizes affect your findings? Describe and explain any differences or similarities.

 6 Suppose you and your classmates surveyed only your friends. Why is this not a random sample? Why is it not a representative sample?

Section 3 Extra Skill Practice

Estimate the percent equivalent of each ratio.

1. $\frac{10}{18}$
2. $\frac{23}{45}$
3. $\frac{44}{198}$
4. $\frac{21}{34}$
5. $\frac{35}{125}$
6. $\frac{36}{81}$
7. $\frac{73}{90}$
8. $\frac{5}{18}$

Write each ratio as a percent. Round to the nearest tenth.

9. $\frac{30}{120}$
10. $\frac{42}{210}$
11. $\frac{24}{36}$
12. $\frac{18}{54}$
13. $\frac{55}{90}$
14. $\frac{13}{70}$
15. $\frac{14}{20}$
16. $\frac{15}{75}$

Solve for each unknown number.

17. 11% of a number is 17.6.
18. A number is 23% of 16.
19. 65% of a number is 455.
20. A number is 90% of 180.
21. A number is 40% of 27.
22. 25% of a number is 48.
23. 21% of a number is 126.
24. A number is 17% of 20.

Standardized Testing ▸ Performance Task

Copy and complete the table. If necessary, round to the nearest tenth of a percent. Write a paragraph explaining what the table shows, and describe at least one conclusion that you can draw from the table.

Day	Students surveyed*	Good	OK	Not good
Monday	28	21 (?%)	? (21.4%)	? (3.6%)
Tuesday	27	16 (?%)	7 (?%)	4 (?%)
Wednesday	25	? (32%)	? (52%)	4 (?%)
Thursday	24	6 (?%)	3 (?%)	? (?%)
Friday	?	4 (20%)	2 (?%)	? (?%)

* Students who were absent or brought lunches were not surveyed.

Section 4 Percent and Probability

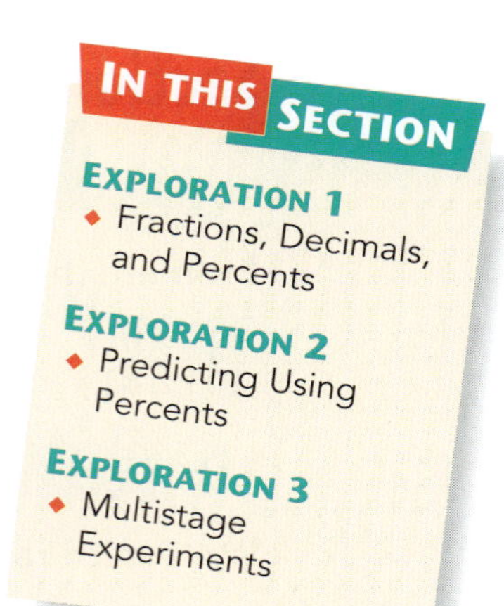

Make Every Shot Count

Setting the Stage

The "Dream Team" was coached by Tara VanDerveer, shown above. Coaches usually choose the best free-throw shooter to attempt the free throw on a technical foul.

In 1996, over 127,000 cheering fans attended the 20-game tour of the USA Women's National Basketball Team. The "Dream Team" lived up to its name, winning every game against some of the nation's best college teams. The team scored an average of 96.4 points per game and won by an average of 46.2 points! The team also had an impressive record for foul shots, called *free throws*. The statistics for the top five free-throw shooters are shown below.

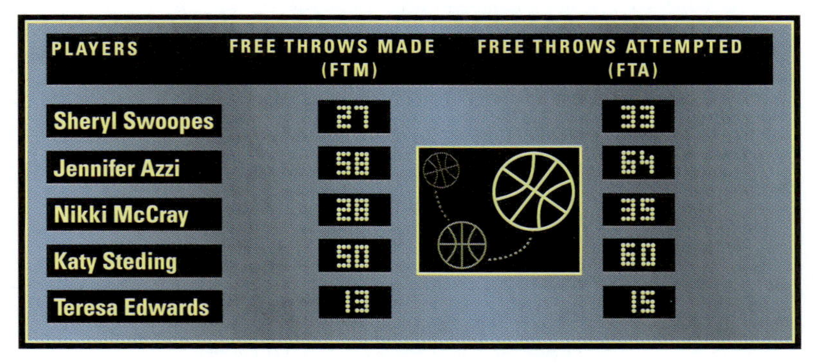

PLAYERS	FREE THROWS MADE (FTM)	FREE THROWS ATTEMPTED (FTA)
Sheryl Swoopes	27	33
Jennifer Azzi	58	64
Nikki McCray	28	35
Katy Steding	50	60
Teresa Edwards	13	15

Think About It

1 Suppose there are three seconds left on the clock and the score is tied when a technical foul is called on the other team. If you were head coach Tara VanDerveer, which player would you choose to attempt the free throw? Why?

2 Suppose a player made 1 free throw out of 1 attempt. Would that player be the best choice for the free throw? Why?

Exploration 1

Fractions, Decimals, and Percents

GOAL

LEARN HOW TO...
- write a fraction as a decimal or percent

AS YOU...
- test your free-throw ability

SET UP *Work in a group of four. You will need:* • *large paper cup* • *cotton balls* • *masking tape* • *ruler*

▶ **The ratio of *free throws made* to *free throws attempted* tells how good a player is at the free-throw line. For example, Nikki McCray made 28 out of 35 free throws on the National Team's college tour. This ratio can be expressed in several ways.**

Ratio	Fraction form	Decimal form	Percent form
28 to 35 or 28 : 35	$\frac{28}{35}$	0.8	80%

3 Discussion Look at the different forms of the ratio shown in the table.

a. Explain how the decimal form of the ratio was found.

b. How are the decimal and percent forms of the ratio related? Write the decimal 0.67 in percent form.

c. Describe an easy way to find the decimal form of a ratio if you know its percent form.

4 Use the free-throw statistics in the *Setting the Stage*.

a. Represent the free-throw performance for each player on the USA Women's National Team in fraction, decimal, and percent form. Round each decimal to the nearest thousandth.

b. Which player had the best free-throw record? How does this compare with the player you chose in Question 1 on page 358?

c. Which form of the ratio makes comparing the statistics easiest?

▶ Sometimes you can use mental math to write ratios as percents.

EXAMPLE

Use mental math to write $\frac{15}{20}$ as a percent.

SAMPLE RESPONSE

Method 1: Use an equivalent fraction.

$$\frac{15}{20} = \frac{n}{100}$$

(15 • ?, 20 • ?)

Since 20 • **5** = 100, n = 15 • **5** = 75.

$\frac{15}{20} = \frac{75}{100} = 75\%$

Method 2: Use a "nice" fraction.

$$\frac{15}{20} = \frac{3}{4}$$

Write $\frac{15}{20}$ as a "nice" fraction.

$\frac{3}{4} = 75\%$, so $\frac{15}{20} = 75\%$.

5 **Mental Math** Use mental math to write each ratio as a percent.

a. $\frac{8}{10}$ **b.** $\frac{6}{24}$ **c.** $\frac{12}{25}$ **d.** $\frac{5}{15}$

▶ **How good are you at the free-throw line? In the simulation in Question 6, you will find out.**

6 **a.** Place a paper cup on the floor. Use masking tape to make a free-throw line 1 m from the cup.

b. Take turns shooting "free throws" by tossing a cotton ball into the cup. First each player takes 8 shots, then 10, and then 15. Be sure your feet do not cross the free-throw line.

c. Record the numbers of free throws made (FTM) and free throws attempted (FTA).

✓ QUESTION 7

...checks that you can represent a ratio in fraction, decimal, and percent forms.

7 **✓ CHECKPOINT** Use the data you recorded in Question 6 (c).

a. Find the fraction, decimal, and percent forms of the ratios of FTM to FTA for 8, 10, and 15 shots for each person in your group. Then find each person's overall ratio.

b. Does your percent increase if you have more chances? Explain.

HOMEWORK EXERCISES See Exs. 1–12 on pp. 368–369.

Exploration 2

Predicting Using Percents

SET UP *You will need your results from Question 6 on page 360.*

GOAL

LEARN HOW TO...
- estimate percents using "nice" fractions and mental math
- use percents to make predictions

AS YOU...
- examine basketball statistics

▶ **On the team's college tour, the USA Women's National Team showed that they were great not only at free throws, but also at two- and three-point field goals from all over the court!**

8 Discussion On the college tour, the team's center, Rebecca Lobo, made 43 of the 99 field goals she attempted. How could you use mental math to estimate the percent of field goals she made?

▲ A 3-point field goal is made from behind the 3-point line.

▶ **Teresa Edwards made 11 out of the 23 three-point field goals she attempted during the tour. Two "nice" fractions that can be used to estimate her three-point percent are shown below.**

Original Fraction	"Nice" Fractions
$\frac{11}{23}$	$\frac{11}{22}$ and $\frac{12}{25}$

These fractions are approximations of the original fraction.

9 Discussion Think about the fractions $\frac{11}{23}$, $\frac{11}{22}$, and $\frac{12}{25}$.

a. The fraction $\frac{12}{25}$ is a "nice" fraction because the denominator is a factor of 100. Why is $\frac{11}{22}$ a "nice" fraction?

b. Use mental math to estimate Edwards's three-point percent using the "nice" fraction $\frac{11}{22}$. Is the estimate *higher* or *lower* than the actual percent?

c. Use mental math to estimate Edwards's three-point percent using the "nice" fraction $\frac{12}{25}$.

d. The percent form of $\frac{11}{23}$ is about 47.8%. Which "nice" fraction, $\frac{11}{22}$ or $\frac{12}{25}$, is a better estimate for $\frac{11}{23}$?

✔ QUESTION 10

...checks that you can estimate percents using mental math and "nice" fractions.

10 **✔ CHECKPOINT** Field goal statistics for individual players during the USA Women's National Team's 1996 college tour are shown below. Estimate the percent of field goals made by each player.

Player	Field goals made	Field goals attempted
Sheryl Swoopes	103	198
Dawn Staley	3	18
Katy Steding	47	125

▶ **Percents can be used to show the past performance of a basketball player. If you think of the percents as experimental probabilities, you can also predict a player's future performance.**

EXAMPLE

Nikki McCray made about 30% of her three-point field goals during the college tour. Estimate the number of three-point field goals she might make in her next 50 attempts.

SAMPLE RESPONSE

Method 1: Use fraction form.

$30\% \text{ of } 50 = \frac{3}{10} \cdot 50 = 15$

Method 2: Use decimal form.

$30\% \text{ of } 50 = 0.30 \cdot 50 = 15$

You can expect Nikki McCray to make about 15 of the next 50 three-point field goals that she attempts.

11 Ruthie Bolton made about 80% of the free-throws she attempted during the 20-game tour. About how many free throws would you expect her to make in her next 25 attempts?

✔ QUESTION 12

...checks that you can use percents to make predictions.

12 **✔ CHECKPOINT** On the tour, the USA Women's National Team made 112 of 336 three-point field goals attempted. Based on that record, tell how many three-point field goals you would expect the team to make in each number of attempts.

a. 60 **b.** 80 **c.** 45 **d.** 120

13 Use your results from Question 7 on page 360. Based on your free-throw results, find the number of free throws you would expect to make in 35 attempts. Explain your reasoning.

HOMEWORK EXERCISES ▶ See Exs. 13–17 on p. 369.

Exploration 3

Multistage Experiments

SET UP *You will need graph paper.*

GOAL

LEARN HOW TO...
- find theoretical probabilities for a multistage experiment

AS YOU...
- analyze repeated free throws

KEY TERM
- multistage experiment

▶ **A player fouled while shooting is allowed two free-throw attempts. You can use the player's past performance to find the theoretical probability that the player will make 2, 1, or 0 free throws.**

Suppose Nikki McCray had been fouled while shooting. Since she made 28 out of 35 free throws during the National Team's college tour, the probability that she will make a free throw is $\frac{28}{35}$ or 80%.

14 **a.** How many of the 35 attempted free throws did Nikki McCray miss during the college tour?

b. Find the probability that Nikki McCray will miss a free throw. Write your answer as a percent, a decimal, and a fraction.

▶ **The probabilities can be shown by a tree diagram.**

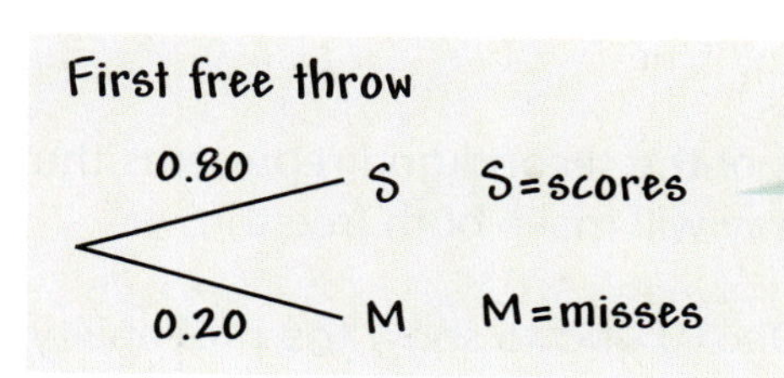

She makes the free throw and scores.

15 **a.** What outcomes are shown in the tree diagram?

b. How is the probability of each outcome shown?

▶ **Branches can be added to the tree to show all the possible outcomes when Nikki McCray attempts two free throws.**

Assume that her second outcome is not affected by the first one.

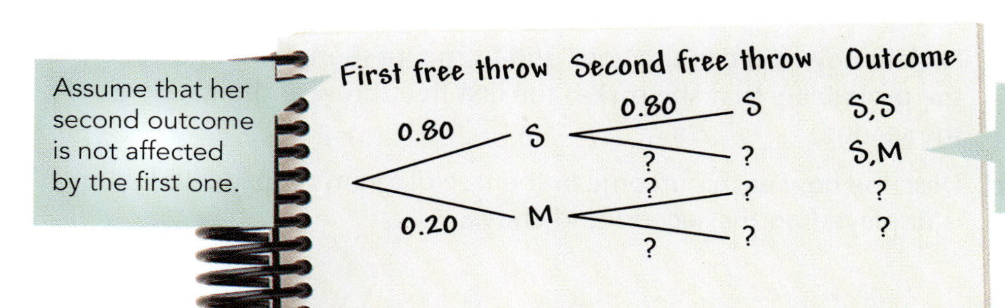

She makes the first, and misses the second.

16 **a.** Copy and complete the tree diagram on page 363 showing all the possible outcomes for Nikki McCray's two free throws. Replace each question mark with the appropriate probability or outcome.

b. What outcome does "M,S" represent?

c. Do you think the probability that Nikki McCray makes both free throws is *greater than, less than,* or *equal to* 0.80? Why?

▶ **You can use a 10×10 grid to determine the probability that Nikki McCray will make both.**

Start on the left and shade in complete **columns**.

Start at the top and shade in complete **rows**.

Shade 80% of the **columns** to show the probability that she makes her first free throw.

Shade 80% of the **rows** to show the probability that she makes her second free throw.

The part of the grid that is shaded twice represents the probability that she makes both free throws.

17 Which part of the second grid represents the probability that Nikki McCray will make both free throws?

18 Shade a 10×10 grid to show the probability that Nikki McCray will *miss* both free throws. What is that probability?

19 **Discussion** Think about the grid you shaded in Question 18 and the second grid shown above.

a. How are the two grids alike?

b. How could you have used the second shaded grid above to find the probability that she misses both free throws?

c. Explain how you can use your grid from Question 18 to find the probability that she makes the first free throw and misses the second.

d. Describe how each outcome in the tree diagram on page 363 is displayed on the second grid above.

20 **Try This as a Class** In Question 17, the probability that Nikki McCray will make both free throws is $0.8 \cdot 0.8 = 0.64$.

a. What do the factors 0.8 and 0.8 represent in this product?

b. How can these numbers be read from the tree diagram?

c. Explain how the probability that she makes the first free throw and she misses the second free throw can be computed without using a grid.

d. What is the probability that she makes at least one of the free throws attempted?

▶ **A situation like the repeated free throw attempts, which involves two or more events happening one after the other, is a multistage experiment.**

21 **✓ CHECKPOINT** Suppose Jennifer Azzi is fouled while shooting. Overall, she made 58 of the 64 free throws she attempted.

a. Make a tree diagram showing all possible outcomes for the free throws attempted. Label each branch with the probability.

b. What is the probability that she makes exactly one free throw?

c. What is the probability that she does not make either free throw?

d. What is the probability that she makes at least one free throw?

✓ QUESTION 21

...checks that you can use a tree diagram to find probabilities in multistage experiments.

22 If a player who is not shooting is fouled after the opposing team has committed six fouls, she is allowed one free throw attempt. If she makes the free throw, she is allowed one more attempt.

a. Draw a tree diagram showing all possible outcomes for Jennifer Azzi in this situation.

b. What is the probability that Jennifer Azzi makes exactly one free throw? How does this probability compare with the probability you found in Question 21(b)? Explain.

HOMEWORK EXERCISES ▶ See Exs. 18–25 on pp. 370–371.

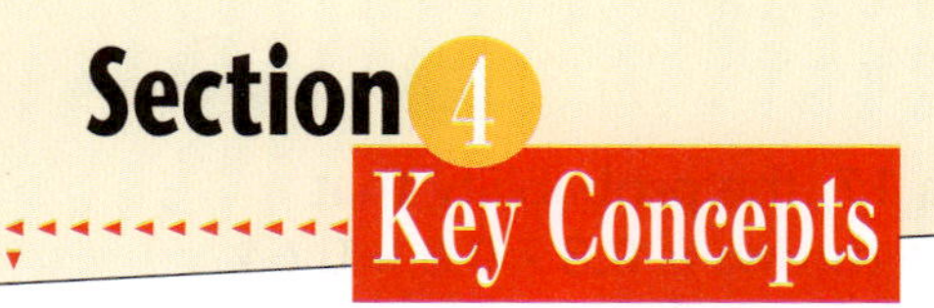

Fraction-Decimal-Percent Equivalents (pp. 359–360)

A ratio can be represented as a fraction, a decimal, or a percent.

Example The ratio of 39 out of 60 can be expressed in the following ways.

Ratio form	Fraction form	Decimal form	Percent form
39 to 60 or 39 : 60	$\frac{39}{60}$	0.65	65%

Predicting Using Percents (pp. 361–362)

You can use percents to predict future outcomes.

Example In 1992, Cal Ripken of the Baltimore Orioles baseball team got 160 hits out of 637 times at bat. How many hits do you expect Cal Ripken to get in 60 times at bat?

First write the ratio as a "nice" fraction or percent.

$$\frac{160}{637} \approx \frac{160}{640} \rightarrow \frac{160}{640} = \frac{16}{64} = \frac{1}{4} = 25\%, \text{ so } \frac{160}{637} \approx 25\%$$

Then use the fraction or decimal form to find the answer.

Fraction Form

$\frac{1}{4} \cdot 60 = 15$

Decimal Form

$0.25 \cdot 60 = 15$

In 60 times at bat, you can expect Cal Ripken to make about 15 hits.

23 Key Concepts Question On the college tour, Lisa Leslie made 135 of the 220 field goals she attempted.

a. Express the ratio 135:220 as a fraction, a decimal, and a percent.

b. Based on her performance, how many field goals do you expect Lisa Leslie to make in her next 50 attempts?

Probability and Multistage Experiments (pp. 363–365)

An experiment that consists of doing two or more things one after the other is a multistage experiment.

The probabilities of the outcomes of a multistage experiment can often be found by shading a grid or constructing a tree diagram.

Example A bag contains three yellow chips and one blue chip. A chip is drawn from the bag, the color is noted, and then the chip is put back in the bag.

If this experiment is done twice, what is the probability that the first chip is yellow and the second is blue?

Shaded Grid

Shade $\frac{3}{4}$ of the grid to show the probability that the first chip is yellow.

Shade $\frac{1}{4}$ of the grid to show the probability that the second chip is blue.

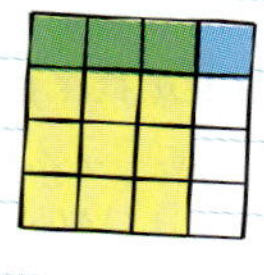

Tree Diagram

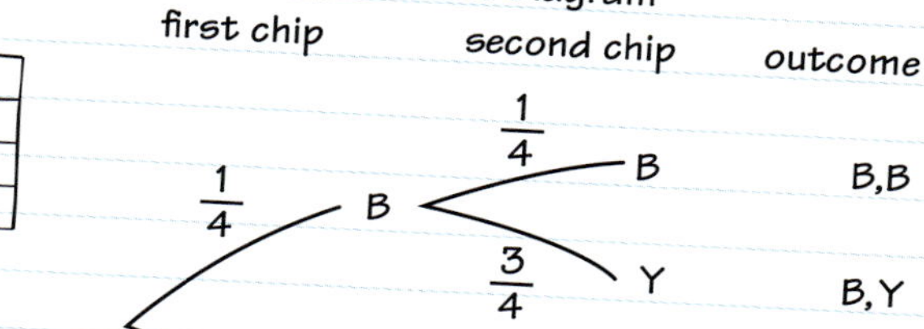

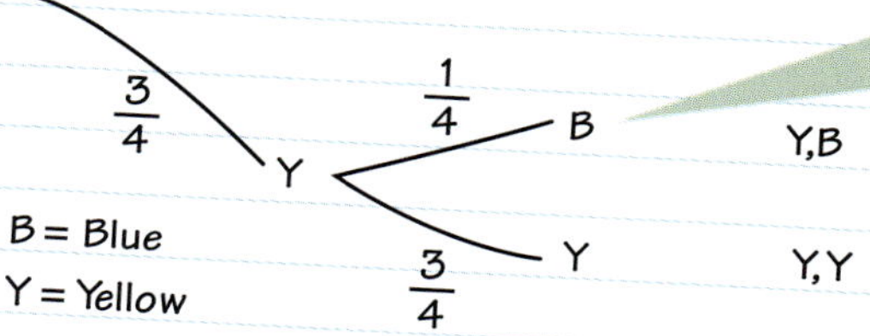

B = Blue
Y = Yellow

$P(\text{first Y, then B}) = \frac{3}{4} \cdot \frac{1}{4} = \frac{3}{16}$

The probability that the first chip is yellow and the second chip is blue is $\frac{3}{16}$.

Key Term

multistage experiment

24 Key Concepts Question Use the Example above.

a. What outcome is represented by each region on the grid—blue? yellow? white?

b. What is the probability of the outcome represented by each region described in part (a)?

Section 4

Practice & Application Exercises

1. Basketball In the 1996 NCAA women's college basketball championship game, Tennessee beat Georgia 83 to 65. The table shows some of the field-goal statistics for four Tennessee players from that game. Represent each player's field-goal performance in fraction, decimal, and percent forms. Round each decimal to the nearest thousandth.

Player	Field goals made	Field goals attempted
Holdsclaw	6	16
Conklin	5	8
Marciniak	5	13
T. Johnson	7	10

Baseball A player's batting average is the decimal form of the ratio of *number of hits* to *times at bat* rounded to the nearest thousandth. Find the 1992 batting average for each player.

2. David Justice (Braves): 124 for 484

3. Barry Larkin (Reds): 162 for 533

4. Frank Thomas (White Sox): 185 for 573

5. Bip Roberts of the Cincinnati Reds and Jon Kruk of the Philadelphia Phillies both had .323 batting averages in 1992, which were high enough for third and fourth place in the National League batting average race. Roberts had 172 hits in 532 times at bat. Kruk had 164 hits in 507 times at bat. Which player was in third place? How did you find your answer?

Luis Ulacia is shown rounding third base after hitting a home run in the first inning of the game against the United States. ▼

6. Olympics On July 28, 1996, the United States Olympic baseball team lost to the defending Olympic championship team from Cuba by a score of 10–8. Find the batting average for each player in the game whose batting results are shown in the table. Represent each average in fraction, decimal, and percent form.

Player	Hits	Times at bat
Ulacia (Cuba)	2	5
Paret (Cuba)	1	3
Lee (U.S.A.)	3	4
Glaus (U.S.A.)	1	4

Write each ratio in percent form.

7. 9 : 50
8. $\frac{1}{4}$
9. 0.1
10. 0.975
11. $\frac{50}{80}$
12. $\frac{162}{225}$

13. **Jewelry** Eighteen-karat gold is 75% pure gold. Suppose a piece of 18-karat gold jewelry weighs 2 oz. Use mental math to determine how many ounces of pure gold the jewelry contains.

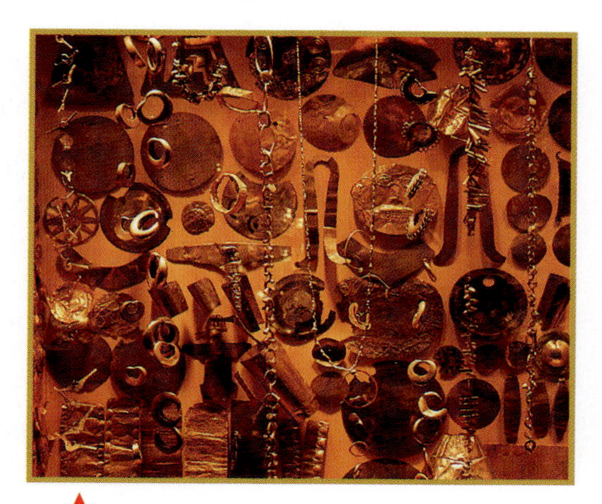

The *Museo del Oro* (Gold Museum) in Bogotá, Colombia, preserves over 33,000 gold objects made by the native cultures before the arrival of Europeans.

14. **Interpreting Data** If given the ability to travel through time, to become invisible, to fly, or to read minds, about 20% of 560 adults polled in a magazine would choose the ability to fly. Another 35% would choose the ability to travel through time. Suppose 2000 adults had been polled. How many of them would you expect to choose each ability listed below?

a. fly like a bird

b. travel through time

c. become invisible or read minds

15. **Challenge** Use the meaning of *batting average* given for Exercises 2–6. Brian Hunter of the Atlanta Braves had one hit in the 1992 World Series and had a .200 batting average. Sid Bream, also of the Braves, had the same average in 15 times at bat in the World Series.

a. How many times did Brian Hunter bat in the World Series?

b. How many hits did Sid Bream have in the World Series?

16. Suppose Charisse is studying sleep patterns. She records the total amount she sleeps each night for one year. At the end of the year, she finds she has slept 2628 h out of the total 8760 h in the year.

a. What percent of the year did Charisse spend sleeping?

b. Estimate how long you can expect Charisse to sleep tonight.

c. Is it likely that she will sleep exactly the number of hours you found in part (b)? Explain.

17. About 26 million people in the United States wear contact lenses. Of that total, about 21% are between the ages of 18 and 25. Estimate the number of people aged 18 to 25 in the United States who wear contact lenses.

Consider the experiment of flipping a coin and rolling an 8-sided die. Shade a grid to find the probability of each event.

18. heads and the number 6

19. tails and a number less than 4

20. tails and an odd number

21. heads and a number greater than 2

22. Suppose this spinner is spun twice.

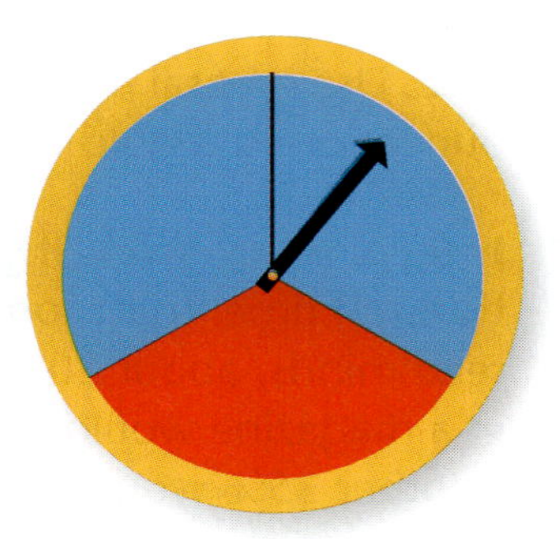

a. **Writing** Which of the grids below could you shade to find the probability that the first spin will be red and the second spin will be blue? Explain.

A. 10×10 grid

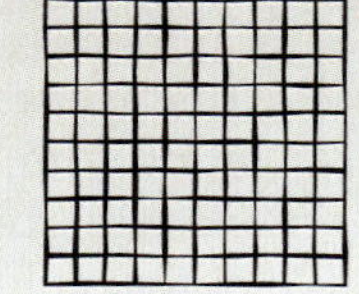

B. 3×3 grid

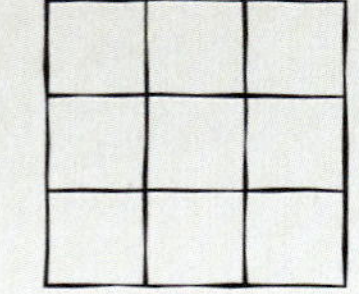

C. 3×6 grid

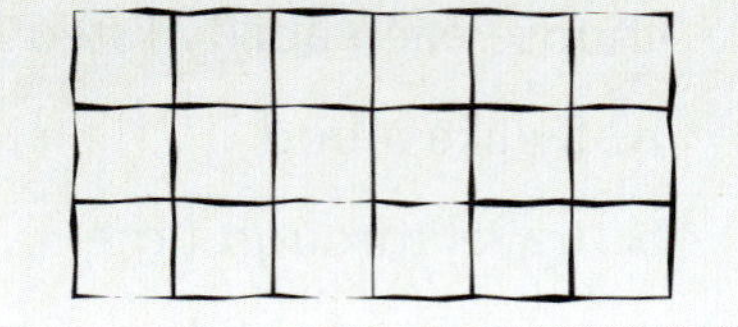

b. Copy the grid you chose in part (a). Shade it to find the probability that the first spin is red and the second is blue.

23. A box contains two red and three blue marbles. Three marbles are removed from the box one after another without looking. After each marble is removed, its color is recorded and the marble is put back into the box before the next marble is removed.

a. Copy and complete this tree diagram to show the outcomes of this experiment. Label each branch of the tree with the probability.

first marble

R

B

b. Use the tree diagram to find the probability of each event.

- removing three red marbles
- removing three blue marbles
- removing a blue, then a red, and then a blue marble
- removing a red, then a red, and then a blue marble
- removing exactly two red marbles
- removing at least one red marble

24. Challenge Suppose three marbles are removed from the box in Exercise 23 one after another, but each marble is not replaced before the next marble is removed. Repeat parts (a) and (b) of Exercise 23 for this experiment.

Reflecting on the Section

Write your response to Exercise 25 in your journal.

25. During her previous basketball games this season, Alyssa made 20 free throws in 40 attempts. She calculated her free-throw percent to be 50%. In today's game, she made 10 free throws out of 10 attempts, or 100%. Alyssa thinks her free-throw percent is now 75%. Is she correct? Explain.

Journal

Exercise 25 checks that you understand how to use percent to make predictions.

Spiral Review

Solve each proportion. (Module 5, p. 336)

26. $\frac{18}{12} = \frac{24}{x}$ **27.** $\frac{3}{13} = \frac{x}{325}$ **28.** $\frac{x}{100} = \frac{4}{5}$ **29.** $\frac{5}{x} = \frac{2}{20}$

Career Connection

Pharmacist: Kristi Melby

Kristi Melby's job as a pharmacist includes determining the proper amount, or dosage, of medicine, and mixing powdered medicine with a liquid to form a solution.

Kristi Melby serves Native American families on the Fond du Lac Reservation in Cloquet, Minnesota.

30. For children, the proper dosage of some medicines depends on body weight. For example, the children's dosage of penicillin is 15 milligrams (mg) for each kilogram of body weight. Write and solve a proportion to find how many milligrams of penicillin Kristi Melby should give a child who weighs 44 lb. (*Hint:* Use 5 kg as the equivalent of 11 lb.)

31. Every 5 milliliters (mL) of an oral solution of penicillin should contain 250 mg of penicillin powder.

a. Express this information as a unit rate.

b. Write and solve a proportion to find how many milliliters of solution Kristi Melby needs to make for 900 mg of penicillin.

Section 4 Extra Skill Practice

Write each ratio as a fraction, a decimal, and a percent.

1. 1:3
2. 15:30
3. 16:20
4. 7:25
5. 12:18
6. 23:100
7. 4.5:10
8. 21:28
9. 14:64

Write each fraction as a percent using estimation or mental math.

10. $\frac{111}{334}$
11. $\frac{13}{25}$
12. $\frac{9}{26}$
13. $\frac{2}{9}$
14. $\frac{7}{20}$
15. $\frac{20}{27}$
16. $\frac{24}{98}$
17. $\frac{9.5}{50}$
18. $\frac{6}{21}$
19. Suppose the probability that it will rain is $\frac{5}{7}$ each day for two consecutive days.
    a. What is the probability that it will not rain on a given day?
    b. Make a tree diagram to find all the possible outcomes of rain on two consecutive days.
    c. Use a grid to show the probability of rain on two consecutive days.
    d. What is the probability that it will rain one day and will *not* rain the next day?

Standardized Testing ▶ Multiple Choice

1. Choose the letter(s) of the ratio(s) that is (are) *not* equivalent to 13.5%.

   A 0.135　B $\frac{5}{37}$　C 13.5 : 100　D $\frac{6}{36}$

2. A paper bag contains 4 plums and 12 nectarines. Without looking, Frida reaches into the bag and pulls out the first fruit she touches, which happens to be a plum. Then Pat takes a fruit from the bag in the same way. What is the probability that she will also get a plum?

   A $\frac{1}{16}$　B 25%　C $\frac{3}{16}$　D 20%

May I Ask You a Few Questions?

You have gathered and organized data about the free time of students in your school. In order for your survey to be useful, you must now share your findings. In this module you have learned several ways to present data.

Choosing a Data Display Many magazines and newspapers display survey results in bar graphs, line plots, histograms, or tables. Often the data is in percent form. But no matter the form, the visual display of the data must be clear and informative.

Summarize your class survey data in a table. Present the data using fractions, decimals, and percents.

Make a general statement about the results shown in the table that you made in Project Question 7. Does the statement answer the topic question? Explain.

Decide what type of visual display, other than a table, would best organize your data. Create your display. Be sure to include a title.

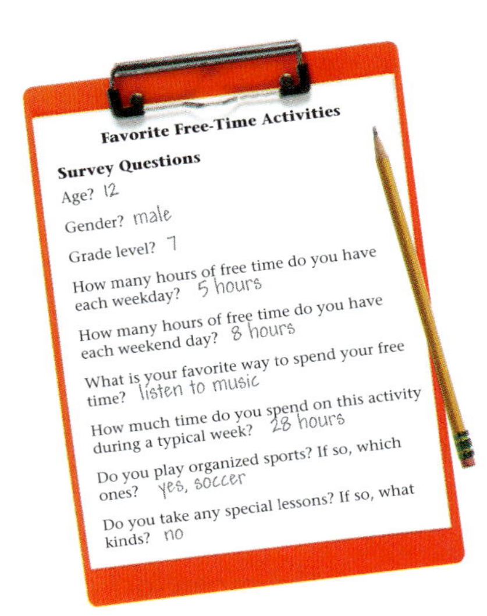

Favorite Free-Time Activities

Survey Questions

Age? 12

Gender? male

Grade level? 7

How many hours of free time do you have each weekday? 5 hours

How many hours of free time do you have each weekend day? 8 hours

What is your favorite way to spend your free time? listen to music

How much time do you spend on this activity during a typical week? 28 hours

Do you play organized sports? If so, which ones? yes, soccer

Do you take any special lessons? If so, what kinds? no

Explain your choice of visual display in Project Question 9. Why do you think your choice is a good way to show the data? Does it answer the topic question as well as the table in Project Question 7? Why or why not?

If you were to organize another survey, what topic would you research? What would you do differently?

MODULE 5 Review and Assessment

You will need: • *Review and Assessment Labsheet* (Ex. 15)

Write each rate as a unit rate. (Sec. 1, Explor. 1)

1. $\frac{95 \text{ min}}{11 \text{ mi}}$
2. $\frac{\$15}{4 \text{ lb}}$
3. $\frac{86 \text{ mi}}{3 \text{ gal}}$
4. $\frac{250 \text{ km}}{16 \text{ L}}$

Use the table for Exercises 5–7. (Sec. 1, Explor. 2)

Areas of State Parks in 9 States	
State	**Acres (in thousands)**
Alabama	50
Arkansas	47
Georgia	57
Hawaii	25
Idaho	42
Maine	75
Montana	41
Rhode Island	9
Virginia	66

5. Make a stem-and-leaf plot of the data. Be sure to include a key and a title.

6. Find the range, the mean, the median, and the mode for the data.

7. Colorado has about 340,000 acres of state parkland. Suppose you include Colorado in the list. How would your stem-and-leaf plot change?

Use the histogram for Exercises 8–10. (Sec. 1, Explor. 3)

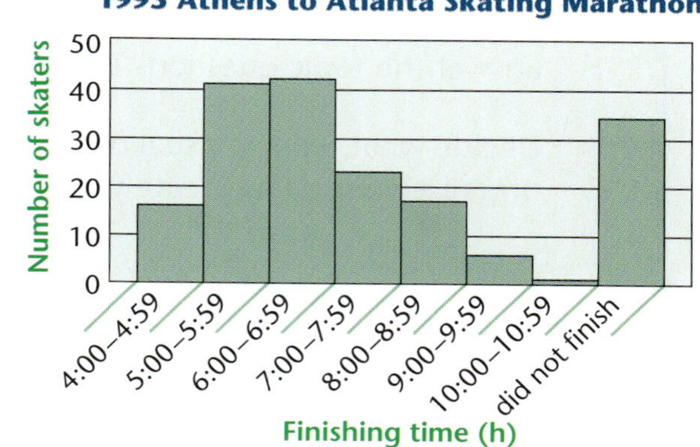

8. About how many skaters finished the marathon in less than 7 h?

9. Can you tell the winning time of the marathon? Explain.

10. For which two time intervals was the combined number of skaters about the same as the number of skaters who did not finish the race?

Solve each proportion. (Sec. 2, Explor. 1)

11. $\frac{20}{x} = \frac{10}{17}$
12. $\frac{8}{9} = \frac{12}{x}$
13. $\frac{x}{414} = \frac{31}{713}$

14. A theater that shows large-format 3-D movies uses special film that runs through the projector at a rate of 5.5 ft/s. (Sec. 2, Explor. 1)
    a. How long will it take 30 ft of film to run through the projector?
    b. How many miles long is a film that runs through the projector in 40 min?

15. Use the Review and Assessment Labsheet. Plot the points on the *Bridge Length Graph* and then answer the questions on the labsheet. (Sec. 2, Explor. 2)

Use the box-and-whisker plot shown below. (Sec. 2, Explor. 3)

16. Estimate the median time for each race.

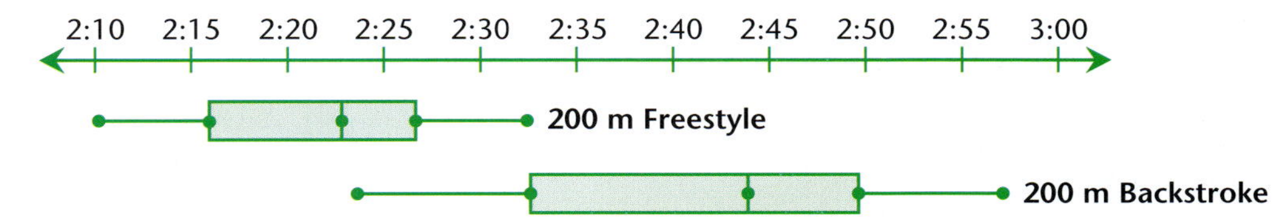

Estimate the percent equivalent of each ratio. (Sec. 3, Explor. 1)

17. $\frac{4}{19}$

18. $\frac{19}{26}$

19. $\frac{43}{66}$

20. $\frac{28}{70}$

Write each fraction as a percent. Tell which fraction is greater. (Sec. 3, Explor. 2)

21. $\frac{28}{56}$ and $\frac{32}{58}$

22. $\frac{7}{9}$ and $\frac{63}{78}$

Find each unknown number. (Sec. 3, Explor. 3)

23. 27% of 502 is a number.

24. 6% of a number is 70.

25. A bag contains 3 red marbles and 2 blue marbles. One marble is taken out of the bag without looking. The color is recorded and the marble is returned to the bag. Then the process is repeated once more. (Sec. 4, Explors. 1–3)

a. Draw a tree diagram that shows all the possible outcomes of the experiment. What is the theoretical probability of getting two red marbles? Write the answer as a fraction, a decimal, and a percent.

b. Suppose the experiment is done 300 times. About how many times would you expect to get two red marbles?

Reflecting on the Module

26. Journal Describe a situation in everyday life in which you could use one of the mathematical ideas from the module.

MODULE
6
FLIGHTS of FANCY

CONNECTING MATHEMATICS & The Theme

SECTION OVERVIEW

1 Inequalities, Polygons, and Probability

As you study wing design:

- Write and graph inequalities
- Find areas of polygons
- Find geometric probabilities

2 Square Roots, Surface Area, and Area of a Circle

As you examine a variety of kite designs:

- Find and estimate square roots
- Find surface areas of prisms
- Find areas of circles

3 Triangles and Similarity

As you investigate airplanes used by early barnstormers:

- Find unknown measures in similar polygons
- Find the scale of a drawing
- Classify triangles by their angles

4 Parallel Lines and Angles of Polygons

As you analyze early plane designs:

- Find angles formed by a transversal and parallel lines
- Find the sum of the angles of triangles and of quadrilaterals

5 Volume of a Prism and Metric Relationships

As you explore problems involved in shipping a whale:

- Find volumes of prisms
- Use relationships among metric units
- Use weighted networks

The Module Project

Wild Wings

How do designers of planes improve their designs? In this project, you'll test and analyze two designs for gliders. Then you'll use geometry and measurement ideas to compare the designs and suggest ways to improve them.

More on the Module Project

See pp. 408, 433, and 451.

INTERNET
To learn more about the theme:
http://www.mlmath.com

Inequalities, Polygons, and Probability

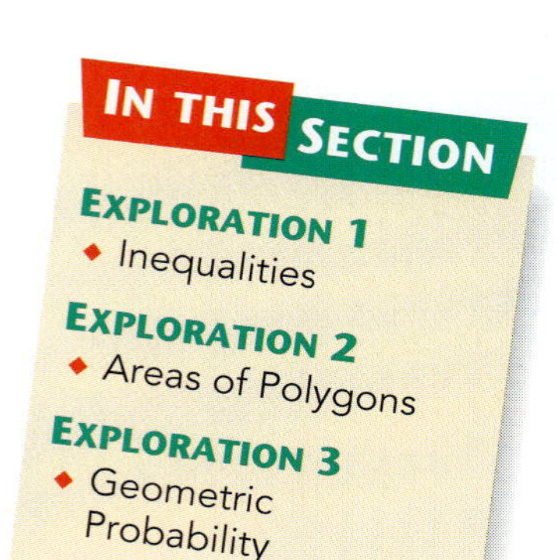

Setting the Stage

The history of flight is filled with daring and imaginative people, such as Otto Lilienthal.

MACHINES *by Robert O'Brien*

. . . Lilienthal became enthralled with flight while watching the storks of his native Pomerania soar over his house on their unwieldy wings. In 1891, at the age of 43, he began building and flying gliders—monoplanes with curved, ribbed batwings. In the next five years, he made more than 2,000 glides, many from a man-made hill shaped like a cone, so that he could take off downhill in any direction that the wind dictated.

Detailed drawing of a monoplane glider designed by Lilienthal in 1895 ▶

▲ Lilienthal also built biplane gliders.

Think About It

1 What do you think a monoplane is?

2 In the five years after he started building gliders, what was the average number of glides Lilienthal made each year?

Exploration 1

INEQUALITIES

SET UP *You will need a 3 in. by 11 in. strip of paper.*

GOAL

LEARN HOW TO...
- write and graph inequalities

AS YOU...
- investigate how wing design makes flight possible

KEY TERM
- inequality

Otto Lilienthal studied birds to try to learn the secrets of flight. Like many of the pioneers of flight, he noticed that a bird's wings are curved and streamlined, not flat.

As a wing moves through a stream of air, some of the air passes over the top and some goes underneath. The two airstreams meet again behind the wing.

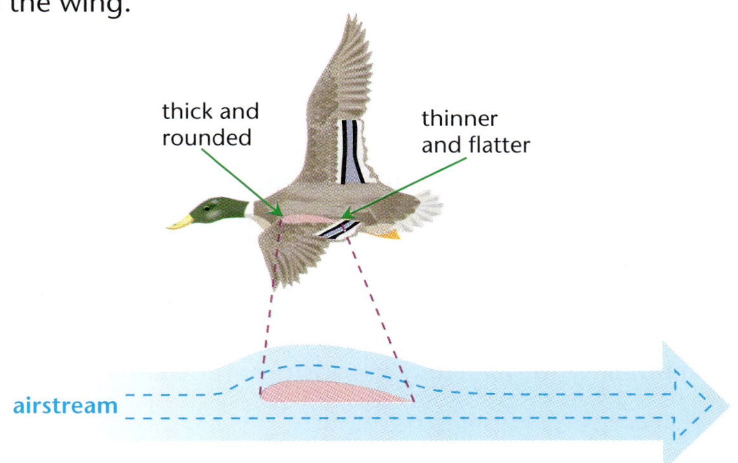

3 You can use a strip of paper to investigate the effect of air moving over a wing. Hold the strip of paper along a short side.

a. Air is pressing against all sides of the paper with equal force, so why does the paper droop?

b. Blow across the top of the paper. Describe what happens.

c. What happens if you blow harder, increasing the speed of the air?

d. What happens if the speed of the air is decreased?

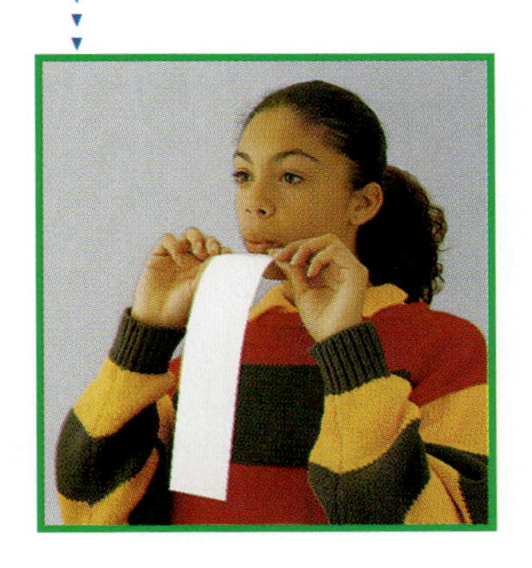

▶ **Daniel Bernoulli, an 18th century Swiss mathematician, discovered that when the speed of a liquid or gas such as air increases, the pressure that it exerts decreases. This is *Bernoulli's principle.***

4 **Discussion** When you blew across the paper in Question 3, the air above the paper moved faster than the air below it.

a. According to Bernoulli's principle, explained on page 379, was the air pressure pressing down on the top of the paper *greater than* or *less than* the air pressure pushing up on the bottom of the paper?

b. Use your answer to part (a) to explain why the paper rose when you blew across it.

Because a bird's or plane's wing is curved, the air passing over it moves faster than the air passing underneath it. The faster-moving air above the wing exerts less pressure on the wing than the air underneath. This difference in air pressure creates an upward force called *lift*.

5 **Try This as a Class** Birds must fly faster than 11 mi/h to create enough lift to overcome the downward pull of gravity.

a. List several speeds greater than 11 mi/h.

b. Draw a number line and plot the points that represent the speeds you listed in part (a).

▶ **There are many flying speeds that are greater than 11 mi/h. Instead of trying to list or plot them all, you can write an *inequality*. The symbols $>$, $<$, $\geq$, and $\leq$ are used to write inequalities.**

EXAMPLE

Write an inequality for all flying speeds greater than 11 mi/h.

Let f be flying speed in miles per hour.

Flying speed is greater than 11 mi/h.

The inequality is read, "f is greater than 11."

$$f > 11$$

Graph the inequality on a number line to show all the possible solutions, that is, all the values of f that make the inequality a true statement.

The open circle means 11 is not included.

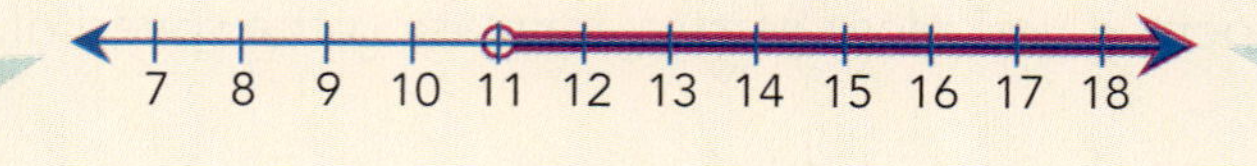

The shaded part of the number line shows the solutions.

6 **a.** Is 9.5 mi/h a solution of the inequality in the Example? Is 11.04 mi/h a solution? How does the graph show this?

b. What does the arrowhead on the right side of the graph mean?

7 The house sparrow is one of the slowest birds. Its flying speed is usually less than or equal to 19 mi/h.

a. Write an inequality to represent all flying speeds less than or equal to 19 mi/h.

b. The graph of the inequality from part (a) is shown below. Why do you think the circle is filled in**?**

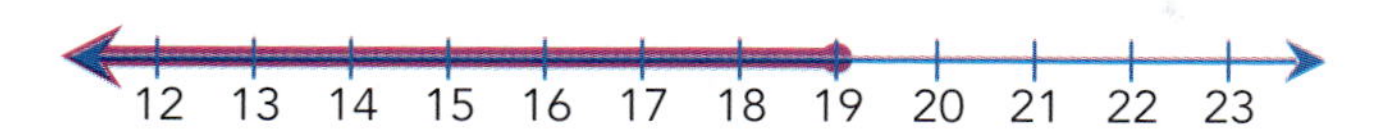

c. The house sparrow's flying speed is usually greater than or equal to 16 mi/h. Write an inequality for this fact. Then sketch a number line and graph the inequality.

▶ **Combining Inequalities** **The information about a house sparrow's flying speed can be combined into one inequality.**

EXAMPLE

Let s = house sparrow's flying speed in miles per hour.

s **is greater than or equal to** 16 and s **is less than or equal to** 19.

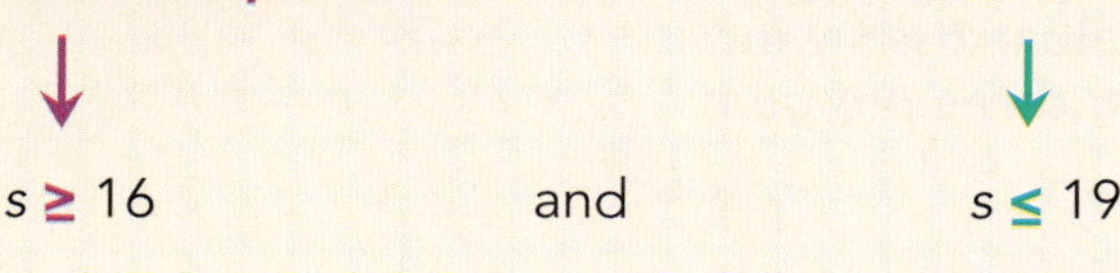

$s \geq 16$ and $s \leq 19$

$$16 \leq s \leq 19$$

This statement can be read as, "16 is less than or equal to s and s is less than or equal to 19."

8 **a. Discussion** How would you graph the inequality $16 \leq s \leq 19$**?**

b. Graph the inequality $16 \leq s \leq 19$.

9 ✓ **CHECKPOINT** Choose a variable to represent the speed of the bird or plane in each speed fact below. Use the variable to write an inequality for the fact, then graph the inequality.

a. Spine-tailed swifts are among the fastest birds in the world. They have been clocked at flying speeds of up to 218 mi/h.

b. The *Spirit of St. Louis*, the plane Charles Lindbergh flew on the first solo transatlantic flight in 1927, was designed to fly at speeds of at least 49 mi/h but below 125 mi/h.

✓ **QUESTION 9**

...checks that you can write and graph an inequality.

HOMEWORK EXERCISES ▶ **See Exs. 1–12 on pp. 389–390.**

AREAS of POLYGONS

GOAL

LEARN HOW TO...
- find the areas of polygons

AS YOU...
- study the wing of an albatross

KEY TERMS
- polygon
- concave
- convex
- regular polygon
- parallelogram
- quadrilateral

SET UP *Work with a partner. You will need:*
- *ruler*
- *6–10 ice-cream sticks*

One factor to consider when designing a glider is how much weight its wings must carry. This is called the *wing loading* and is measured by dividing the glider's total weight by its total wing area.

To help decide how large the wings of their "flying machines" had to be, some early fliers studied the wing loading of birds—especially large soaring birds such as vultures and albatrosses.

▲ The wandering albatross is a large sea bird that can soar above the ocean for an hour or more without ever flapping its wings!

▶ **How can you estimate the area of a bird's wing? One way is to use *polygons* to model its size and shape. In the drawing, an albatross's wing is modeled with three *polygons*.**

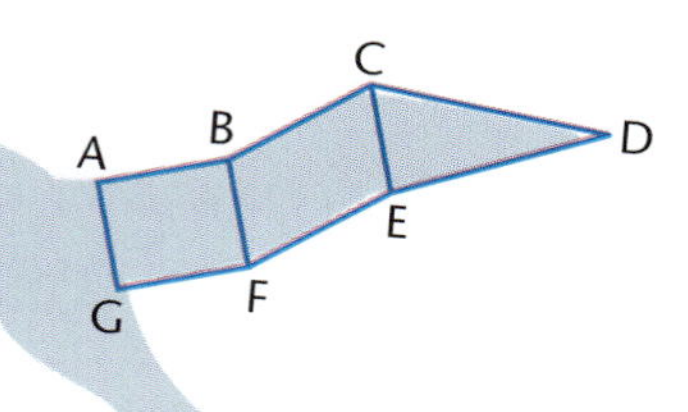

10 A **polygon** is a simple, flat closed figure formed by segments.

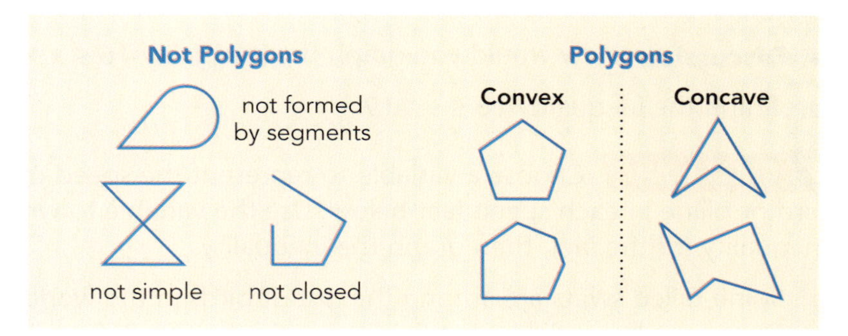

a. What does *simple* mean? What does *closed* mean?

b. How are **concave** and **convex** polygons different?

c. In a **regular polygon**, all the segments are the same length and all the angles are equal in measure. Is a square a regular polygon? Explain.

11 **a.** Tell whether each of the three polygons used to model the albatross wing is *concave* or *convex*.

b. Is polygon *ABCDEFG* in the model *concave* or *convex*? Explain.

▶ **You can estimate the area of one wing of the albatross in the drawing by finding the sum of the areas of the three polygons used to model it.**

12 Polygon *ABFG* at the right is a rectangle. Find its area and explain your method.

A B G F
1.1 ft
1.3 ft

FOR ▶ HELP with *finding the area of a rectangle*, see **TOOLBOX, p. 593**

▶ **Another type of polygon used in the wing model is a *parallelogram*. A parallelogram is a quadrilateral (a 4-sided polygon) in which both pairs of opposite sides are parallel.**

13 **Discussion** Which of the polygons used to model the albatross wing on page 382 appear to be parallelograms?

14 **Try This as a Class** Complete parts (a)–(d) to discover how to find the area of a parallelogram.

a. Follow these steps to make a parallelogram.

Form a rectangle with your ice-cream sticks. Measure the length and width of the rectangle.

Place a ruler along the left side of the rectangle. Rotate the ruler to form a parallelogram by making the left and right sides longer.

b. How does the area of the parallelogram you made in part (a) compare with the area of the original rectangle?

c. The length of the base *b* of a parallelogram and its height *h* are measured as shown on the notebook. How are the length of the base and the height of the ice-cream-stick parallelogram related to the length and width of the original rectangle?

h
b

d. Write a formula for finding the area *A* of a parallelogram if you know its height *h* and the length of its base *b*.

✓ QUESTION 15

...checks that you can find the area of a parallelogram.

15 **✓ CHECKPOINT** Quadrilateral *BCEF* in the model of the albatross wing on page 382 is a parallelogram. Its dimensions are shown at the right. What is its area**?**

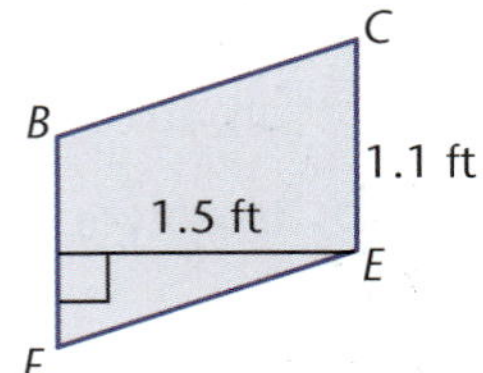

16 **Try This as a Class** The dimensions of $\triangle CDE$ in the model of the albatross wing are shown below. The figure shows how a triangle congruent to $\triangle CDE$ can be put together with $\triangle CDE$ to form a parallelogram.

a. How are the areas of the two triangles related**?**

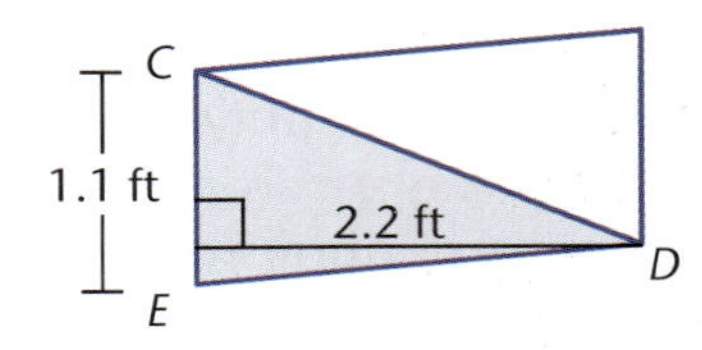

b. How are the length of the base and the height of $\triangle CDE$ related to the length of the base and the height of the parallelogram**?**

c. If you know the area of the parallelogram, how can you find the area of one of the triangles**?**

d. Write an expression that can be used to find the area A of a triangle if you know its height h and the length of its base b.

e. What is the area of $\triangle CDE$**?**

17 **a.** Use your results from Questions 12, 15, and 16(e) to find the area of one wing of the albatross shown on page 382.

b. Assume both wings of the albatross have the same area. What is the total wing area**?**

18 **a.** Suppose the albatross in the drawing on page 382 weighs 20 lb. Use the total wing area in Question 17(b) and the formula below to find the wing loading of the albatross in pounds per square foot. Round your answer to the nearest hundredth.

$$\text{wing loading} = \frac{\text{total weight}}{\text{total wing area}}$$

combined area of both wings

b. One of Otto Lilienthal's gliders had a total wing area of 150.7 ft^2. Without the pilot, the glider weighed 44 lb. Suppose the pilot weighed 170 lb. To the nearest hundredth, what was the wing loading of the glider**?** How does its wing loading compare with the wing loading of the albatross**?**

HOMEWORK EXERCISES ▶ See Exs. 13–18 on p. 391.

Exploration 3

GEOMETRIC PROBABILITY

SET UP *Work with a partner. You will need:* • *tape* • *ruler* • *3 in. by 5 in. index card* • *scissors* • *construction paper*

GOAL

LEARN HOW TO...
- use areas to find theoretical probabilities
- find the probabilities of complementary events

AS YOU...
- simulate a skydiving competition

KEY TERMS
- complementary events
- geometric probability

One of the first recorded attempts at human flight occurred in A.D. 852 in Cordoba, Spain. Someone leaped from a tower, but instead of flying, fell to earth. Fortunately, this foolhardy person's cloak caught enough air to prevent any serious injury, turning this impossible attempt at flight into a parachute jump!

▶ **Since that "flight," parachutes have become so advanced that skydivers compete to land in small target areas. You will simulate a skydiving competition by launching an autogyro over a landing area.**

19 Make an autogyro.

Step 1

Cut a $1\frac{1}{2}$ in. by 5 in. rectangle from the index card, and fold it into three $\frac{1}{2}$ in. by 5 in. rectangles.

Step 2

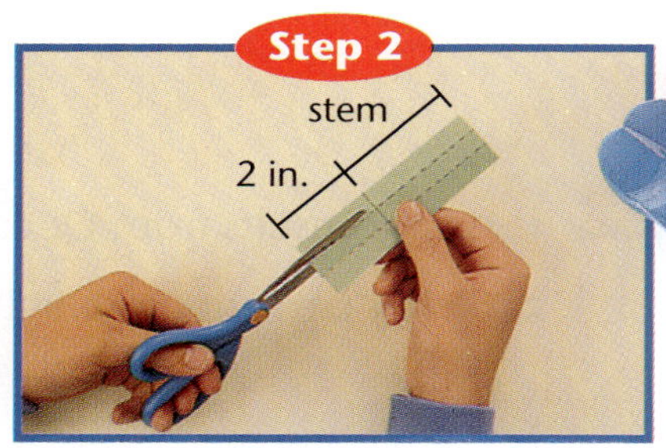

Make a 2 in. cut along each fold.

Step 3

Fold the rectangles together to form a triangular tube. Tape the edges of the stem together.

Step 4

Fold down the cut strips so they are perpendicular to the taped stem.

20 Make a landing area by taping four sheets of $8\frac{1}{2}$ in. by 11 in. paper together to form a 17 in. by 22 in. rectangle.

Cut out a square target with sides $8\frac{1}{2}$ in. long from a piece of construction paper, and tape it in the center of the rectangle.

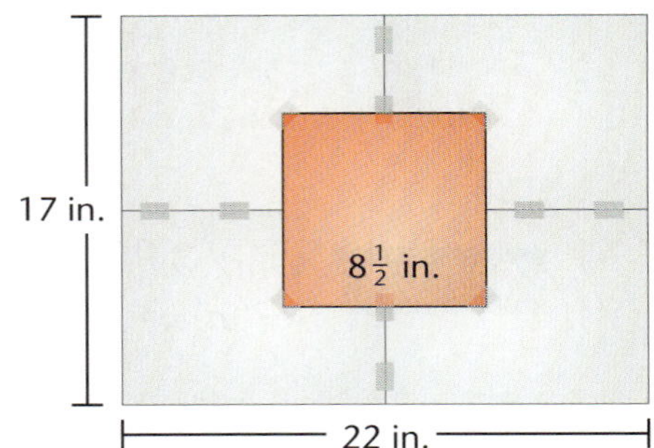

21 **a.** Place the landing area on the floor. Launch your autogyro as shown below. Repeat 10 times and record the number of times the stem end of the autogyro lands inside the square target. Redo any trials where the end of the autogyro lands off the paper landing area.

b. Repeat part (a), letting your partner make the launches.

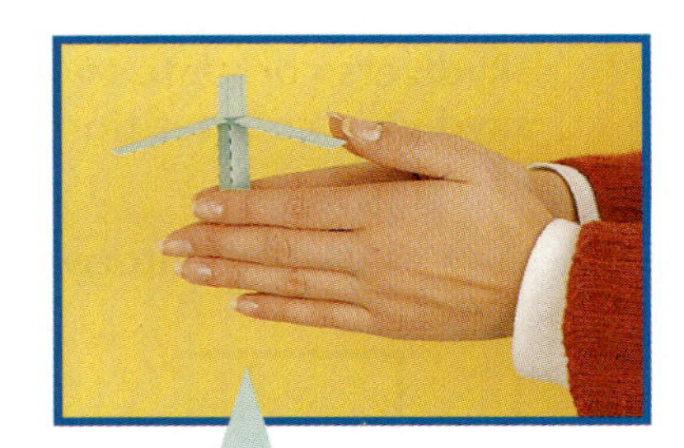

Twirl your autogyro between your hands and release it at shoulder level.

22 Use your results from Question 21.

a. What percent of your 10 "jumps" landed on the square target?

b. What percent of the 20 "jumps" made by you and your partner landed on the square target?

FOR HELP with *probability*, see **MODULE 1, p. 33**

23 **Try This as a Class** Use the jump data from the entire class.

a. What is the experimental probability that the autogyro lands on the target? that the autogyro does not land on the target?

b. What is the sum of the probabilities in part (a)?

▶ **Either the autogyro lands on the target or it does not. The events *the autogyro lands on the target* and *the autogyro does not land on the target* are *complementary events*. Two events are complementary events if one or the other must occur, but they cannot both happen at the same time.**

24 **Try This as a Class** If two events are complementary, what must be true about their probabilities?

▶ **The theoretical probability of landing on the target can be calculated by finding the ratio of the area of the target to the total landing area. This is a geometric probability.**

$$\text{probability of landing on the target} = \frac{\text{area of the target}}{\text{total landing area}}$$

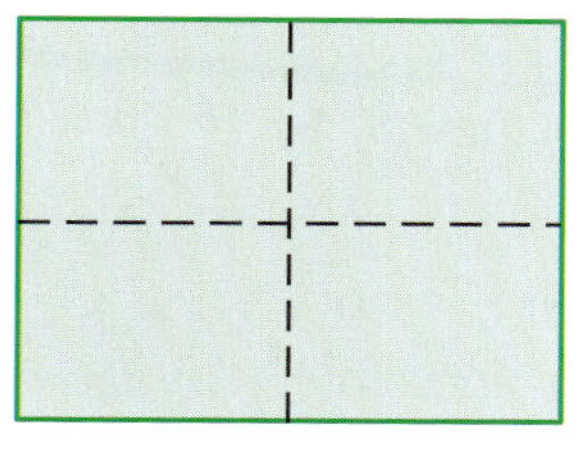

total landing area

area of the target

25 **a.** Find the theoretical probability of landing on the target. Write it as a fraction and as a percent rounded to the nearest tenth.

b. Why do you think this is called a *geometric probability*?

FOR HELP with *theoretical probability*, see **MODULE 1, p. 33**

26 **Discussion** Use your answers to Questions 22, 23(a), and 25(a).

a. How does the theoretical probability of landing on the target compare with the experimental probabilities?

b. Why might there be differences between the theoretical and the experimental probabilities?

27 **a.** Describe two ways you could find the theoretical probability of hitting the landing area but not landing on the target.

b. What is the theoretical probability of not landing on the target?

28 **CHECKPOINT** Use the figure.

a. Find the probability that a small object dropped on the figure will land on the shaded target.

b. Find the probability that a small object dropped on the figure will not land on the shaded target.

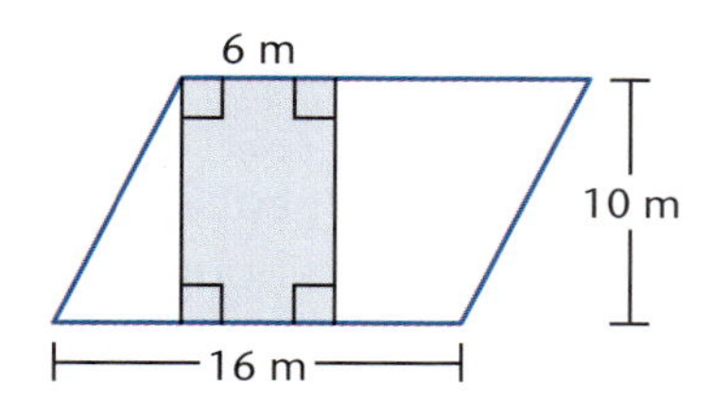

QUESTION 28

...checks that you can find a geometric probability and the probability of a complementary event.

HOMEWORK EXERCISES ▶ See Exs. 19–26 on pp. 391–392.

Section 1 Key Concepts

Key Terms

inequality

Inequalities (pp. 379–381)

The statements $t > 10$ and $13 < x \leq 19$ are examples of inequalities.

$t > 10$ is read "t is greater than 10."

$13 < x \leq 19$ is read "13 is less than x and x is less than or equal to 19."

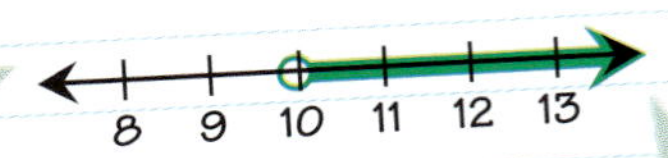

The open circle means 10 is not included.

The shading means all numbers to the right of 10 are included.

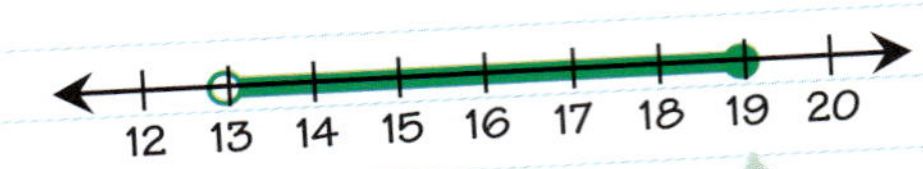

The filled-in circle means 19 is included.

polygon

convex

concave

quadrilateral

parallelogram

regular polygon

Polygons (pp. 382–384)

A polygon is a simple, closed flat figure made of segments. A polygon that has four sides is a quadrilateral. A parallelogram is a quadrilateral that has two pairs of parallel sides.

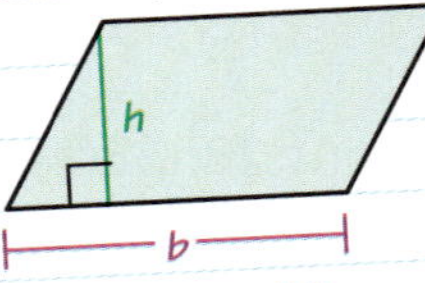

Area = bh

h

b

Area = $\frac{bh}{2}$, or Area = $\frac{1}{2}bh$

The area of a parallelogram is the product of the length of its **base** and its **height**.

The area of a triangle is half the length of its **base** times its **height**.

You can find the area of some polygons by separating them into triangles and parallelograms.

29 Key Concepts Question

Use the graph of flying speeds in miles per hour.

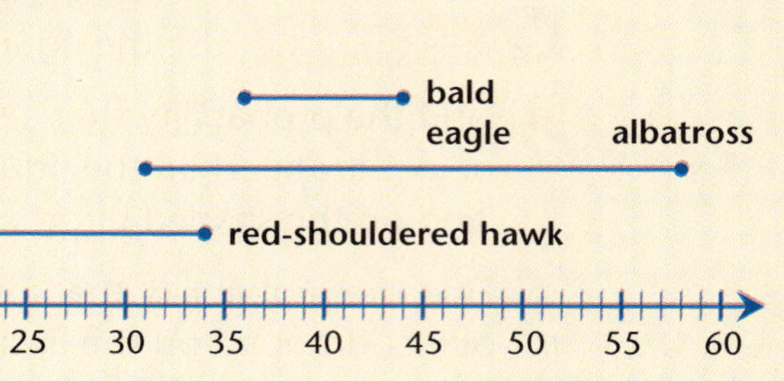

a. Write an inequality for the speed of a red-shouldered hawk.

b. Which bird has the greatest range of speeds?

c. Which birds can fly faster than 40 mi/h?

Section 1 Key Concepts

Key Terms

geometric probability

complementary events

Geometric Probability (pp. 385–387)

A probability that is based on lengths, areas, or volumes of figures is a geometric probability.

Example Suppose a point is selected at random on $\overline{RT}$.

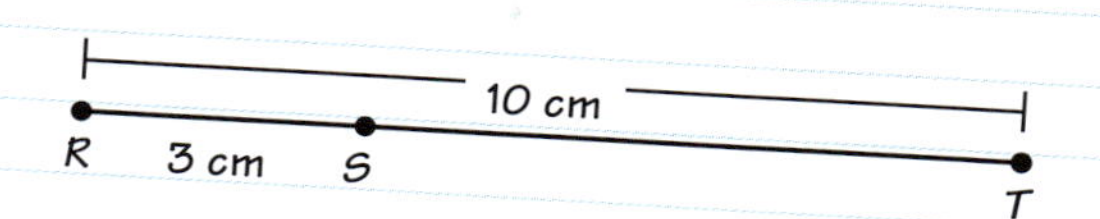

The probability that the point is on $\overline{RS}$ is $\frac{\text{length of } \overline{RS}}{\text{length of } \overline{RT}} = \frac{3}{10}$, or 30%.

Two events are complementary if one event or the other must occur, but they cannot both happen at the same time.

In the Example, the events "the distance between the point and point R is less than or equal to 3 cm" and "the distance between the point and point R is greater than 3 cm" are complementary.

The sum of the probabilities of two complementary events is 1.

30 Key Concepts Question An object is dropped onto the landing area shown. What is the probability that the object will land in the shaded region? in the unshaded region?

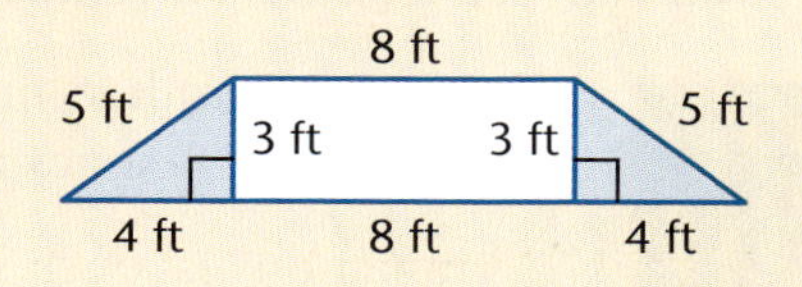

Section 1 Practice & Application Exercises

For Exercises 1–4, write an inequality to represent each statement. Then graph the inequality on a number line.

1. x is less than 8.
2. b is greater than or equal to 3.
3. h is greater than 5 and less than or equal to 11.
4. 4 is less than p, and p is less than 7.

5. History The Women's Auxiliary Ferrying Squadron (WAFS) was formed during World War II to train women to fly military aircraft. Initially, candidates were required to have not less than 500 hours of logged flight time. Write an inequality to represent this statement, and then graph the inequality.

Hummingbirds **For Exercises 6–9, use the graphs below.**

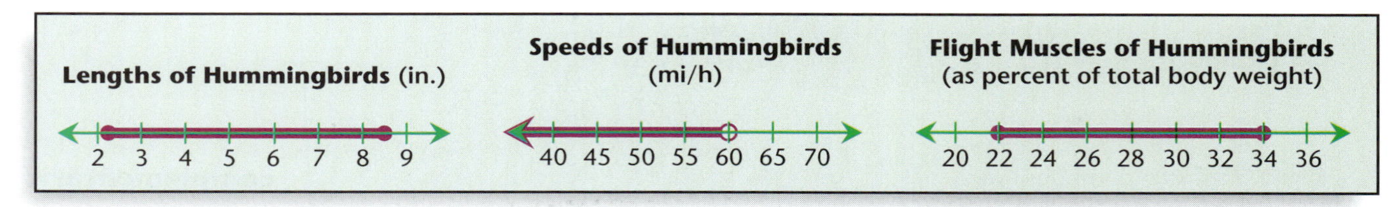

6. The smallest bird in the world is the Cuban bee hummingbird. Estimate its length.

7. Estimate the range of lengths of hummingbirds.

8. Write a statement describing the speeds hummingbirds fly.

9. What percent of a hummingbird's body weight is the weight of its flight muscles? Express your answer as an inequality.

Use the statements and graphs below for Exercises 10–12. An inequality that represents each statement is graphed on the number line below.

The original *Wright Flyer I* is on display in the National Air and Space Museum in Washington, D.C.

"The Wright brothers built the first successful airplane in 1903. The *Wright Flyer I* flew at speeds ranging from 30 mi/h through 35 mi/h."

"A cinnamon teal duck, clocked flying at 32 mi/h, was startled and raced away at 59 mi/h."

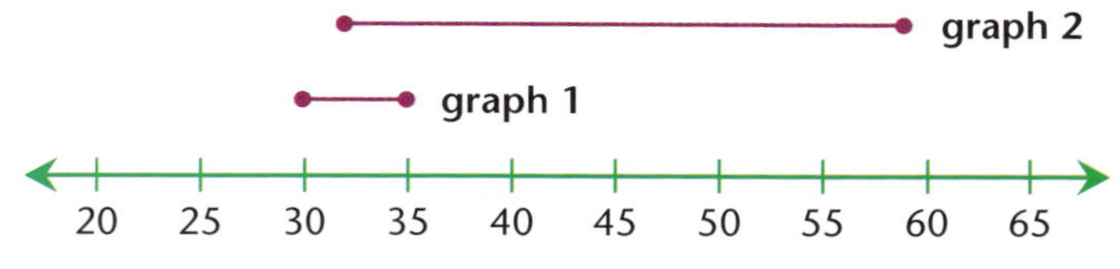

10. Which graph represents the speed of the *Wright Flyer I*?

11. How can you use the graphs to find the numbers that are solutions of both inequalities?

12. Write a statement that compares the speeds of the cinnamon teal duck and the Wright brothers' airplane.

13. Which of the quadrilaterals below are parallelograms? If a quadrilateral is not a parallelogram, explain why.

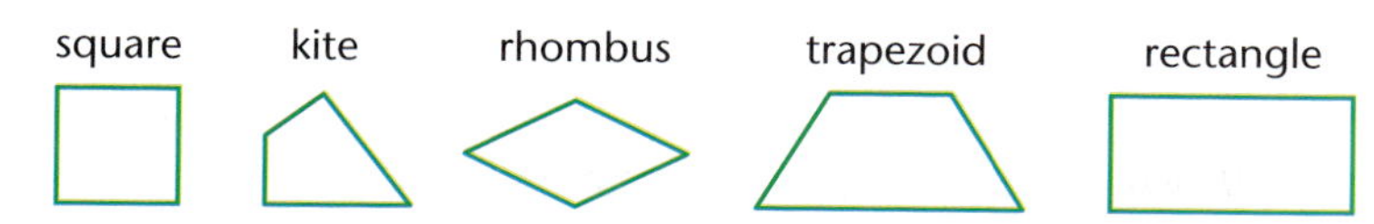

14. Open-ended Draw two 5-sided polygons, one that is convex and one that is concave.

15. Challenge Can a parallelogram be concave? Explain.

16. The figures below show three different heights h of $\triangle ABC$.

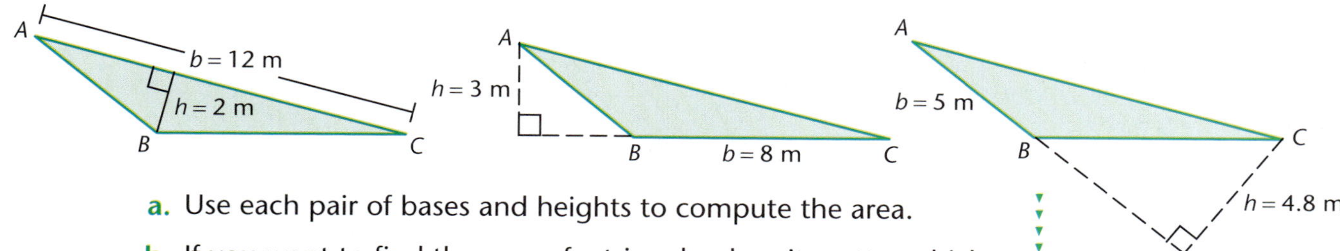

a. Use each pair of bases and heights to compute the area.

b. If you want to find the area of a triangle, does it matter which side you use as the base? Explain.

17. a. Which segment represents the height of parallelogram $EFGH$ — $\overline{EH}$, $\overline{FH}$, or $\overline{EY}$? Explain your choice.

b. Find the area of parallelogram $EFGH$.

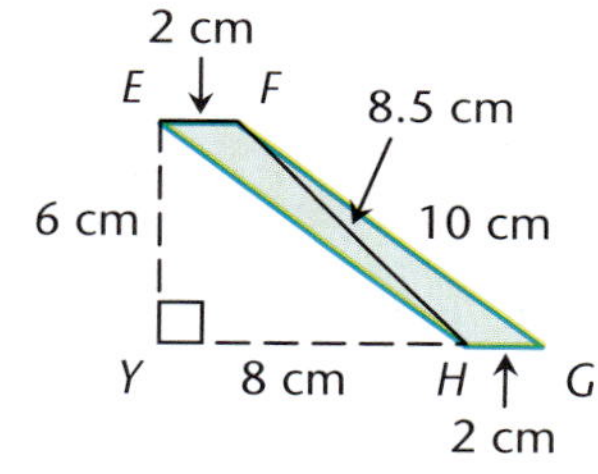

18. A rough sketch of a glider wing is shown below.

a. Find the area of the wing.

b. The glider has two identical wings. What is its total wing area?

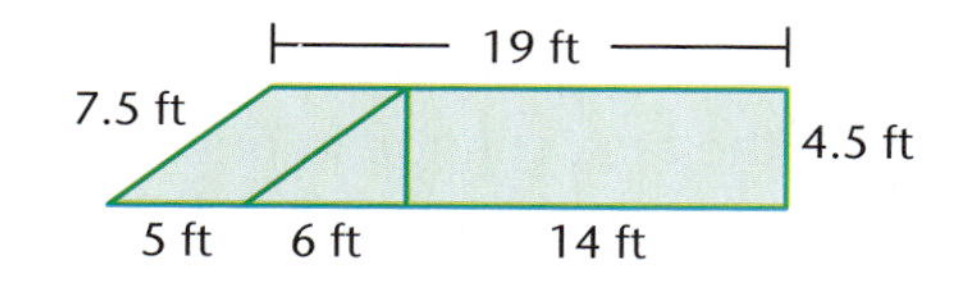

c. The glider's total weight is 920 lb. Use the formula

wing loading $= \dfrac{\text{total weight}}{\text{total wing area}}$ to find its wing loading.

Find the probability that an object dropped on each figure will land on the shaded target.

19. 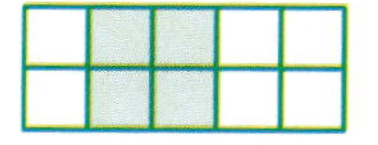

20. 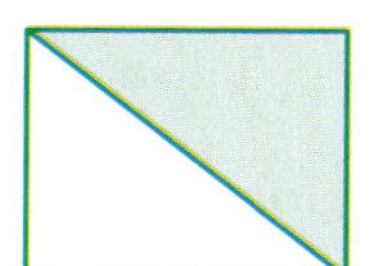

21. 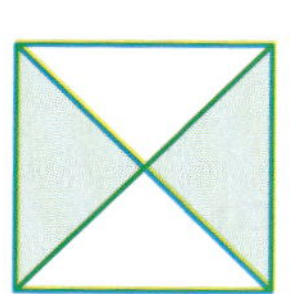

The probability that an object dropped onto the square region below will land inside the shaded circle is $\frac{3}{5}$.

10 m

10 m

22. What is the probability that the object will land in the unshaded region?

23. What is the area of the circle?

A coin is tossed onto a game board. If the center of the coin lands on the shaded region, player I wins. If not, player II wins.

24. Which game board below is fair to both players, that is, makes their chances of winning equal?

A.

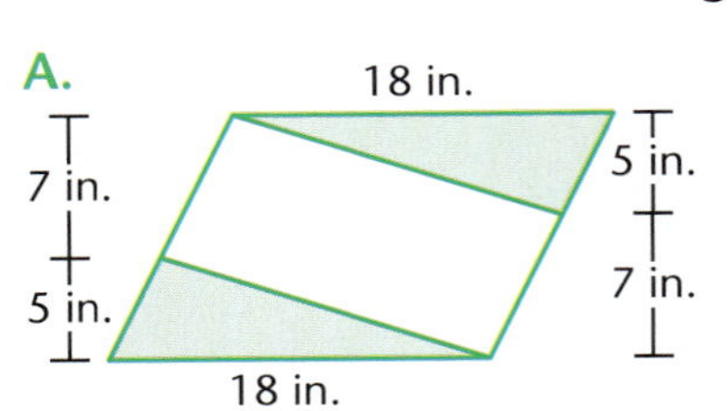

B.

14 in.

10 in.

6 in. 6 in.

C.

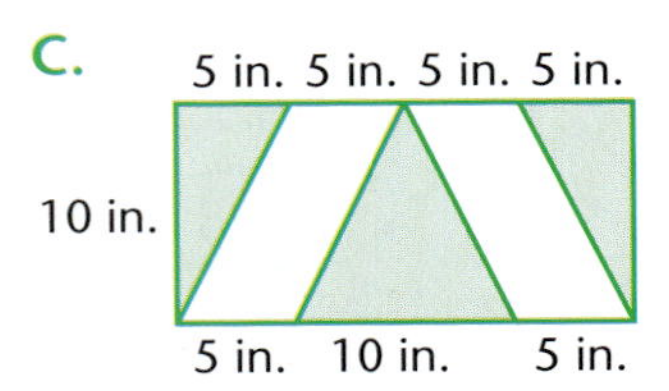

25. If you want player I to have a greater chance of winning, which game board in Exercise 24 should you choose? Explain.

Visual THINKING

Exercise 26 checks your understanding of the areas of parallelograms.

Reflecting on the Section

26. In Exploration 2, you made a rectangle from ice-cream sticks and slanted them to form a parallelogram with the same area. Now suppose you make a square from four ice-cream sticks as shown. When you slant the sticks, the parallelogram formed has an area *less than* the area of the square. Why does the area change in one case but not the other?

Spiral Review

Use mental math to write each fraction as a percent. (Module 5, p. 366)

27. $\frac{11}{23}$ 28. $\frac{16}{45}$ 29. $\frac{31}{122}$ 30. $\frac{49}{251}$

Find the prime factorization of each number. (Module 3, p. 156)

31. 12 32. 25 33. 48 34. 100

Write each power in standard form. (Module 1, p. 21)

35. 2^2 36. 5^2 37. 9^2 38. 10^2

Section 1 Extra Skill Practice

For Exercises 1–6, write an inequality to represent each statement. Then graph the inequality on a number line.

1. *a* is greater than 8.
2. *k* is less than or equal to 2.
3. *r* is greater than 4 and less than 7.
4. *s* is greater than 9 and less than 14.
5. 6 is less than *t*, and *t* is less than or equal to 13.
6. *b* is greater than 5 and less than or equal to 9.

Tell whether each figure is a parallelogram. If it is not, explain why.

7. 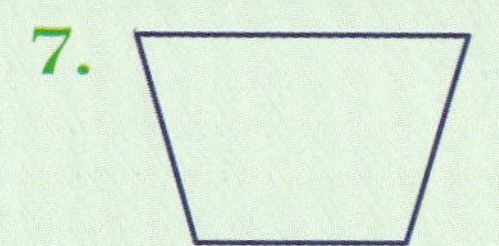
8. 
9. 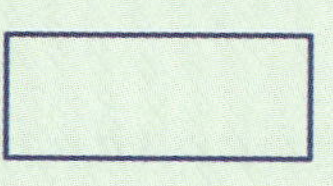
10. 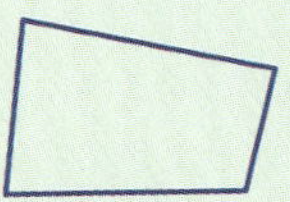

Classify each polygon as convex or concave.

11.
12. 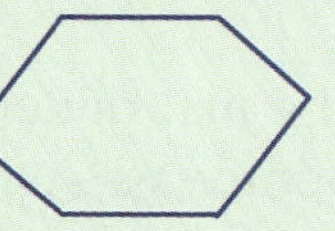
13. 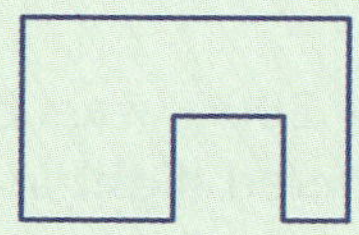
14. 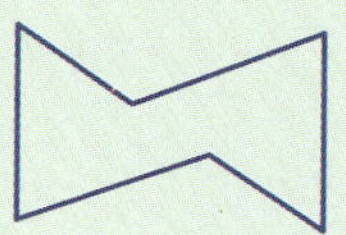

Find the probability that a small object dropped on each figure will land on the shaded target.

15. 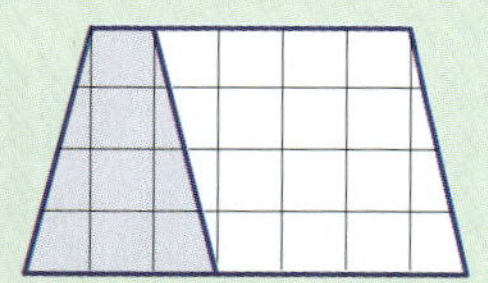
16. 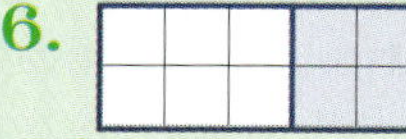
17.

Study Skills Making Connections

Previewing and reviewing can help you understand and remember the concepts in each section. Before studying a new topic, think about what you already know about it or about related topics. When you have completed the section, think about how the ideas that were new to you fit in with those you already had.

1. Preview the goals and topics of Section 2. Describe any ideas that seem familiar to you. List any terms that are unfamiliar to you.
2. When you have completed Section 2, review its goals and topics. Describe the new ideas that you have learned and, if possible, connect them with topics you already understand. Did you learn anything that caused you to change your thinking about something? If so, how did your ideas change?

Square Roots, Surface Area, and Area of a Circle

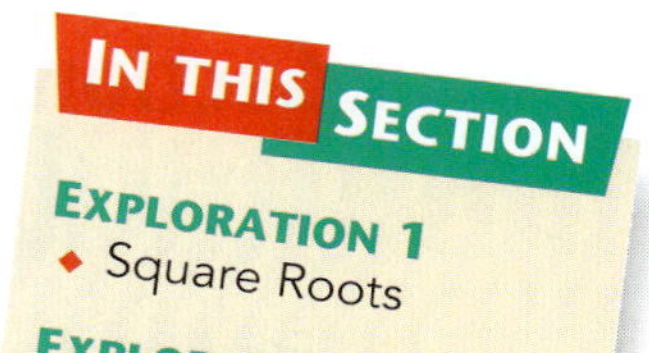

EXPLORATION 1
- Square Roots

EXPLORATION 2
- Surface Areas of Prisms

EXPLORATION 3
- Area of a Circle

Setting the Stage

SET UP *You will need a protractor.*

Over 2000 years before the first gliders were invented, the Chinese had mastered flight in a different way—with kites. In China and other Asian countries, kites were more than toys. They were tools for signaling, for lifting supplies, and even for flying people!

Centuries later, kite flying became a children's hobby in the United States. Francis M. Rogallo's childhood interest in kites inspired him to become an aeronautical engineer and, eventually, to combine a kite with a parachute to create the parawing.

▲ Today, Rogallo's idea is applied to the sport of hang gliding.

Think About It

1 The flying angle of a kite is the angle the kite string forms with the ground. The best flying angle of a kite in moderate winds is from 45° to 60°.

flying angle

ground

a. Write an inequality for the range of the best flying angles.

b. Draw a horizontal segment on a sheet of paper to represent the ground. Use a protractor to make a drawing that illustrates the range of the best flying angles of the kite in the air.

2 What shapes might you see if you look at a hang glider in flight?

Exploration 1

Square ROOTS

GOA

LEARN HOW TO...
- find square roo of perfect square
- estimate square roots to the nearest tenth

AS YOU...
- investigate the design of a parawing

KEY TERMS
- square root
- principal square root
- perfect square

SET UP *You will need a calculator.*

Francis Rogallo and his wife Gertrude Rogallo experimented with different parawing designs by making paper models and tossing them into the air. When one flew better than the others, they made a larger version out of cloth and went to the beach to test it. They tested model after model, making changes and throwing away the failures.

In kite flying, the ratio of the total weight of the kite to the area of the *sail*—the surface that catches the wind and moves the kite—is very important. This ratio is called *sail loading.*

3 Look back at the definition of *wing loading* on page 384 in Section 1. How is sail loading for kites like wing loading for birds and gliders?

4 In flight, a parawing appears to be triangular, but when flattened out, it turns out to be a square. The sail area of a parawing is the area of a square. Find the sail area of each parawing.

a.

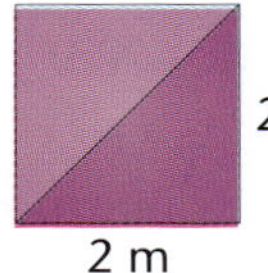

b.

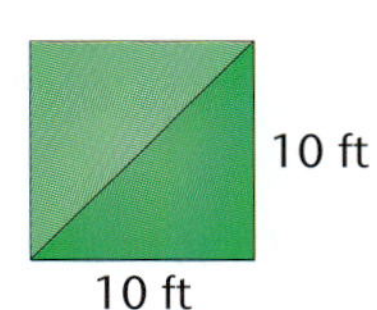

c.

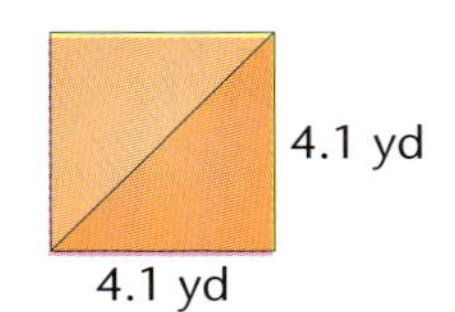

▶ **The area A of a square can be found by multiplying the length s of a side of the square by itself ($A = s \cdot s$), or by squaring s ($A = s^2$).**

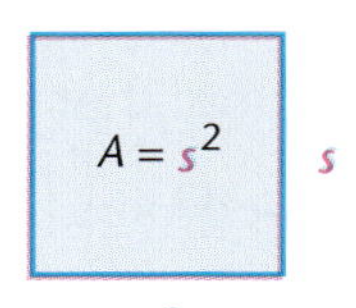

To find the length of a side of a square when the area is known, you can look for a number that when multiplied by itself equals the area.

EXAMPLE

Find the length of a side of a square that has an area of 49 cm^2.

SAMPLE RESPONSE

$s^2 = 49$

$s = 7$

Think: __?__ • __?__ = 49

7 • 7 = 49

The length of a side is 7 cm.

▶ **The solution, 7, of the equation in the Example is a square root of 49.**

5 Find the length of a side of a parawing with each area.

a. 16 ft^2 **b.** 36 m^2 **c.** 225 $in.^2$

6 **Discussion** Think about the square roots of 49.

a. Is −7 a square root of 49? Why or why not?

b. Would −7 be a reasonable solution for the length of a side of a parawing? Explain.

▶ **The positive solution of the equation $s^2 = 49$ is the principal square root of 49 and is written $\sqrt{49}$.**
The same symbol with a negative sign, $-\sqrt{49}$, is the negative of the principal square root.

$\sqrt{49} = 7$	$-\sqrt{49} = -7$
The principal square root of 49 is 7.	The negative of the principal square root of 49 is −7.

7 **Mental Math** Use mental math to find each square root.

a. $\sqrt{64}$ **b.** $-\sqrt{81}$ **c.** $\sqrt{1}$ **d.** $-\sqrt{0}$

▶ **A perfect square is a number that is the square of a whole number. For example, 25 is a perfect square since $25 = 5 \cdot 5 = 5^2$.**

8 Show that each number is a perfect square.

a. 81 **b.** 400 **c.** 121

…checks that you can find the principal square root of a perfect square.

9 **CHECKPOINT** Find each square root.

a. $\sqrt{121}$ **b.** $\sqrt{9}$ **c.** $-\sqrt{144}$ **d.** $\sqrt{100}$

10 **Try This as a Class** Since 52 is not a perfect square, its principal square root is not a whole number.

a. What two consecutive perfect squares is 52 between?

b. Find the principal square root of the perfect squares in part (a).

c. What two whole numbers is $\sqrt{52}$ between?

d. Use guess-and-check and a calculator to estimate $\sqrt{52}$ to the nearest tenth.

e. Calculator Use the $\sqrt{\ }$ key on a calculator to find $\sqrt{52}$. Compare it with your estimate in part (d).

11 **✓ CHECKPOINT** Give two consecutive whole numbers that each principal square root lies between. Then estimate each square root to the nearest tenth.

a. $\sqrt{12}$ **b.** $\sqrt{73}$ **c.** $\sqrt{150}$

✓ QUESTION 11

...checks that you can estimate the square root of a number to the nearest tenth.

HOMEWORK EXERCISES ▶ See Exs. 1–10 on pp. 405–406.

Exploration 2

Surface AREAS of PRISMS

GOAL

LEARN HOW TO...
- identify prisms and their parts
- draw a net for a prism
- find the surface area of a prism

AS YOU...
- investigate box kites

KEY TERMS
- prism
- face
- base
- vertex
- edge
- net
- surface area

SET UP *Work with a partner. You will need:* • *scissors* • *tape* • *centimeter grid paper* • *two centimeter cubes*

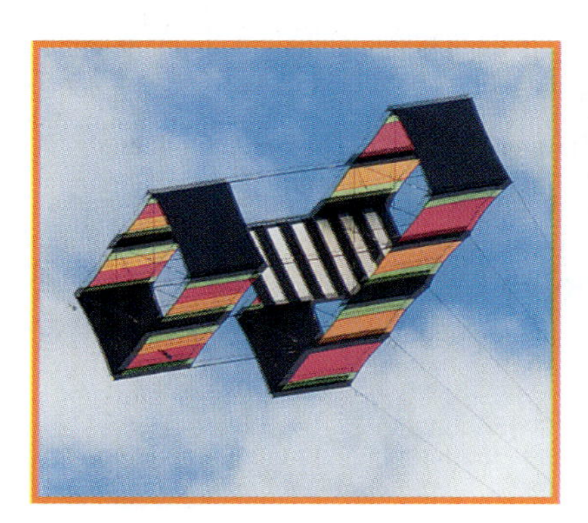

The parawing is not the only kite design based on a square. In 1893, Lawrence Hargrave, an Australian, designed a kite that became the basis for the *biplane*, the type of plane built by the Wright Brothers.

In the Hargrave box kite, squares and rectangles form open rectangular prisms or "boxes."

▶ A **prism** is a space figure that has flat surfaces or **faces** shaped like polygons. Two of the faces, the **bases**, are parallel and congruent. The other faces are parallelograms.

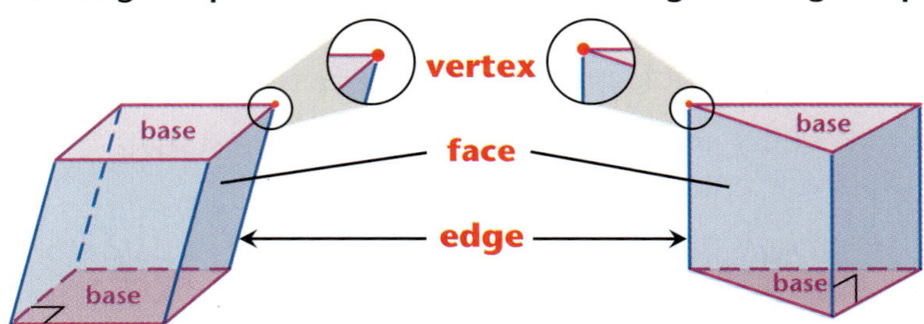

12 **Discussion** What do you think "the bases are parallel" means?

13 Replace each __?__ with a word or phrase that makes each a true statement.

a. Two faces of a prism meet at a(n) __?__.

b. Three edges of a prism meet at a(n) __?__.

c. Prisms are named by the __?__.

14 **Try This as a Class** Use the prisms shown above.

a. How many faces, vertices, and edges does the rectangular prism have?

b. Would the numbers of faces, vertices, and edges of another rectangular prism be the same as in part (a)? Explain.

c. Repeat parts (a) and (b) for a triangular prism.

15 **Discussion** Look at the right rectangular prism shown below.

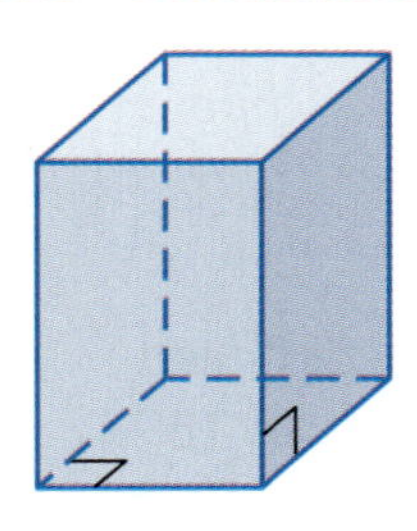

a. How is this prism different from the rectangular prism shown above? How is it like the right triangular prism?

b. Can a rectangular prism have more than one pair of bases? Explain.

c. What is the name for a rectangular prism for which all the faces are congruent?

✓ QUESTION 16

...checks that you can name prisms and identify their faces, vertices, and edges.

16 **✓ CHECKPOINT** Use the prism shown below.

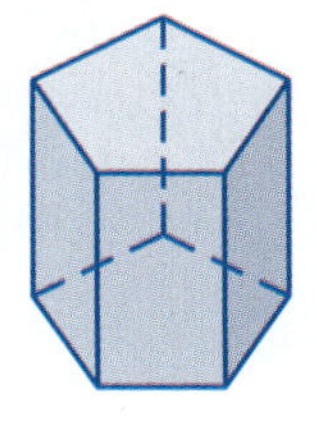

a. What kind of prism is this?

b. How many faces, vertices, and edges does this prism have?

▶ *Surface area* **is an important factor to consider in the design of a kite. As you answer Questions 17 and 18, you will find out what surface area is and how to calculate it.**

17 The figure shown in the photo below is a **net**, a flat pattern that can be cut out and folded to form a space figure without any gaps or overlap. You can use this net to cover a centimeter cube.

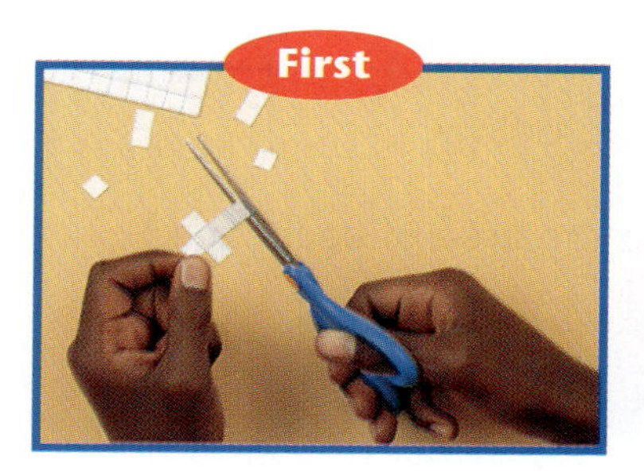

Cut a net like the one above out of centimeter grid paper.

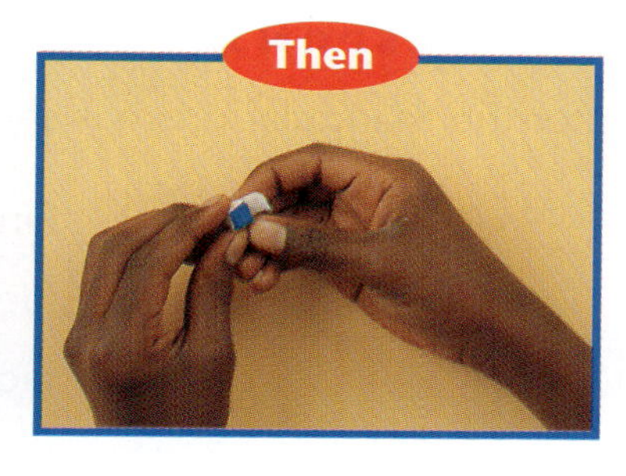

Fold the net along the segments, and use it to cover a centimeter cube.

18 **a.** Use centimeter grid paper to make as many different nets as possible to cover the cube. Try covering the cube to make sure each net actually works. Then tape each net to a piece of paper to keep a record of it.

b. What is the area of each net you made?

c. The number of square centimeters of paper used to make each net is the cube's **surface area**. What is the surface area of the cube?

19 Use two centimeter cubes to form a prism, as shown. Use centimeter grid paper to determine which of the nets made up of centimeter squares will cover the prism with no overlap. If a net will not cover the prism, explain why not.

A.

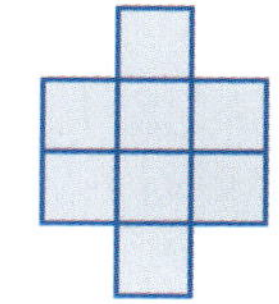

B.

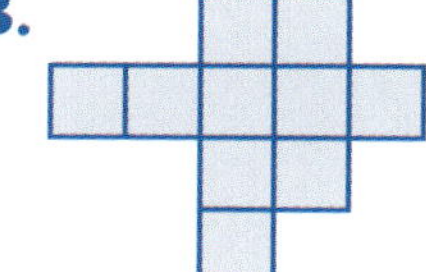

C.

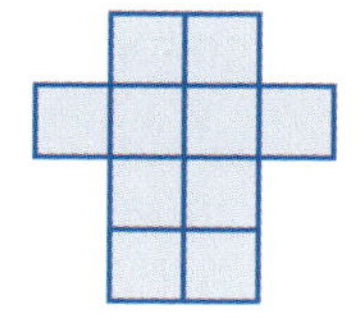

20 What is the surface area of the prism formed by the two centimeter cubes in Question 19?

▶ In Questions 17–20, you saw that the surface area of a prism is the sum of the areas of its faces.

EXAMPLE

Find the surface area of the right triangular prism.

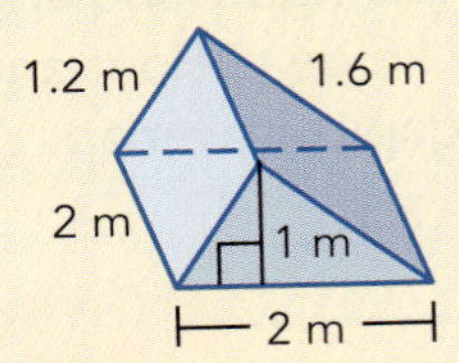

SAMPLE RESPONSE

A net for the triangular prism is shown below.

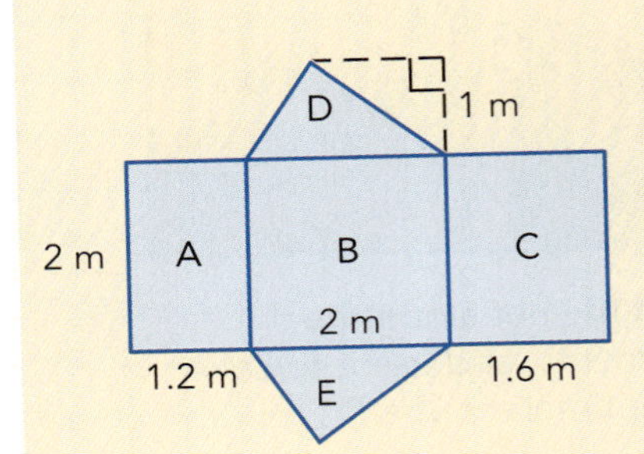

Find the area of each face.

face A: $1.2 \cdot 2 = 2.4$

face B: $2 \cdot 2 = 4$

face C: $1.6 \cdot 2 = 3.2$

face D: $\frac{1}{2} \cdot 2 \cdot 1 = 1$

face E: $\frac{1}{2} \cdot 2 \cdot 1 = 1$

The surface area is the sum of the areas of the five faces.

Surface Area = $2.4 + 4 + 3.2 + 1 + 1 = 11.6$

The surface area is 11.6 m^2.

✓ QUESTION 21

... checks that you can find the surface area of a prism.

21 ✓ CHECKPOINT Use the drawing below. The drawing shows a variation of Hargrave's box kite that is still flown today.

a. Sketch a net for the faces of a right rectangular prism with length 20 in., width 20 in., and height 36 in. Label the edges of each face with its dimensions.

b. Find the surface area of the prism.

c. Find the area of the material covering the boxes.

d. What fraction of the 20 in. × 20 in. × 36 in. prism is covered?

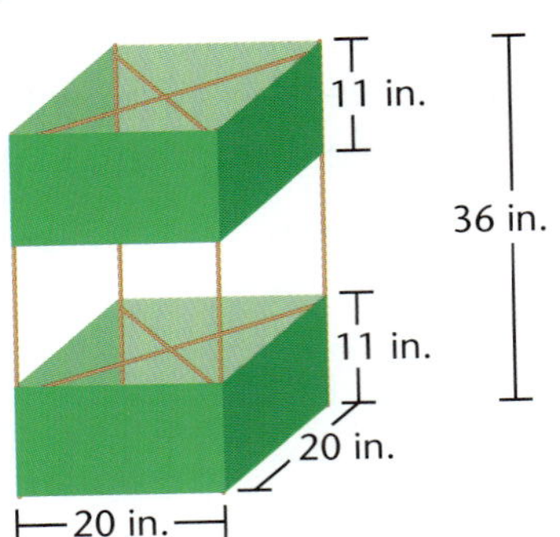

HOMEWORK EXERCISES ▶ See Exs. 11–15 on pp. 406–407.

Exploration 3

AREA OF A CIRCLE

GOAL

LEARN HOW TO...
- find the area of a circle

AS YOU...
- investigate kite designs

SET UP *You will need:* • *Labsheet 2A* • *scissors* • *tape* • *ruler*

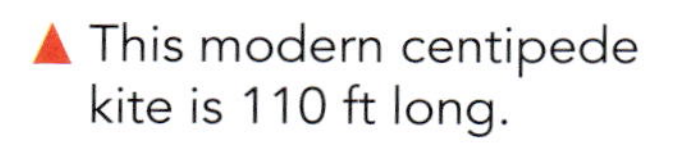

Probably nowhere in the world does enthusiasm for kites run as high as it does in Japan. In the early years of this century, tens of thousands of people flocked to kite-flying festivals held in open fields far from the cities' kite-destroying power lines.

In Japan there was also a strong drive to build ever bigger and better kites, such as the centipede kite shown at the right. The frame of a centipede kite is constructed with bamboo, and silk is used to cover the circles.

Centipede kites can be hundreds of feet long. Due to their length, centipede kites require great skill to fly. By adding circular sections after the kite was in the air, a kite enthusiast constructed a centipede kite that was over a quarter of a mile long!

▲ This modern centipede kite is 110 ft long.

▲ It took 30 people to fly this huge centipede kite during the annual kite flying festival held along the Edo river in Japan in 1964.

22 Sketch a circle. Draw and label each segment and indicate each measure.

a. a diameter **b.** a radius

c. the circumference **d.** the area

FOR ◀ HELP with *the parts of a circle* and *circumference*, see **MODULE 4, p. 241**

23 **Discussion** A centipede kite is made from circular pieces of silk. How can you estimate the amount of silk in a centipede kite?

▶ **In Section 1 you used rectangles to develop a formula for the area of a parallelogram. You can use the same idea to find the area of one of the circles in a centipede kite.**

24 **Use Labsheet 2A.** Follow the directions below.

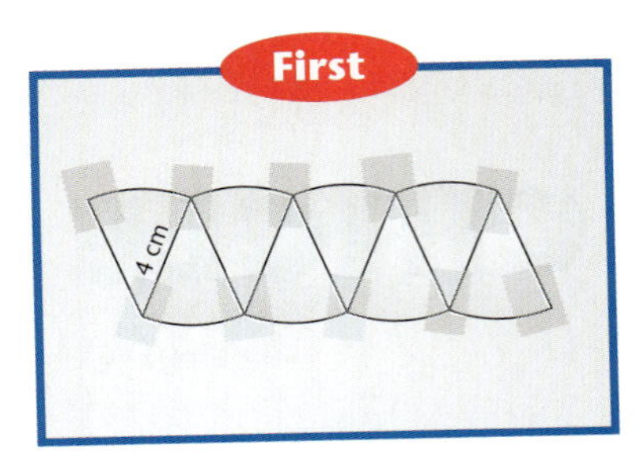

Cut out the *Circle.* Then cut apart the eight sectors and arrange them to form the figure shown. Tape the figure to a sheet of paper.

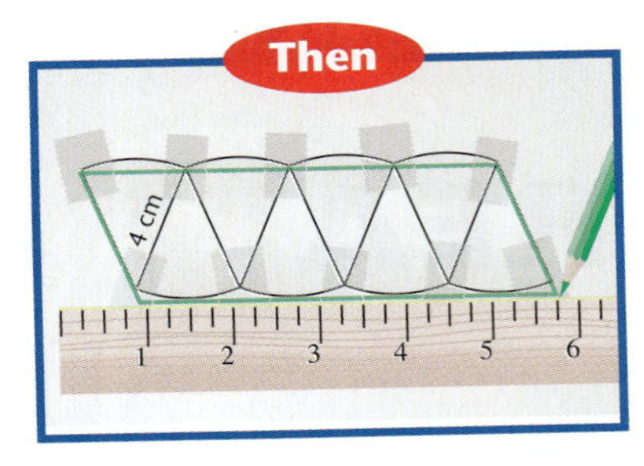

Use a ruler to draw segments across the top and bottom of your figure. Extend the sides of the figure to meet the bottom segment.

25 What kind of polygon is the new figure you drew in Question 24?

26 **Try This as a Class** Use the figure you made in Question 24.

a. **Estimation** Explain how you could use the new figure you drew to estimate the area of the circle. Then estimate the area. Do you think this is a good estimate? Why or why not?

b. How is the length of the base of the figure related to the circumference of the circle?

c. How is the height of the figure related to the radius of the circle?

27 **Discussion** Examine the drawings shown.

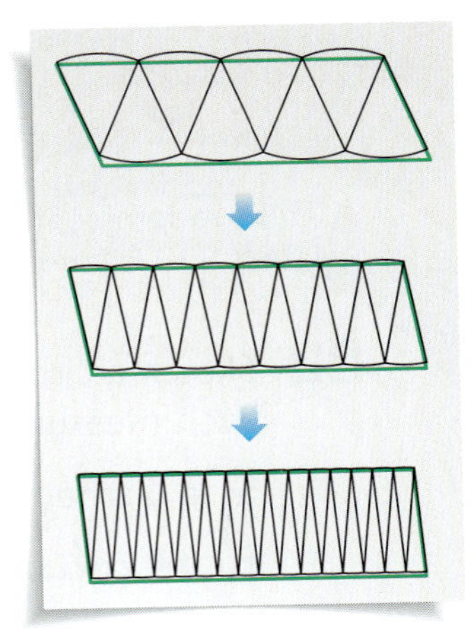

a. As a circle is cut into more and more sectors and put back together as shown, what begins to happen to its shape?

b. The area *A* of a parallelogram is found by multiplying the length of its base *b* by the height *h*, or $A = bh$. Use your figure to explain why this formula can be written as $A = \frac{1}{2}Cr$ to find the area of a circle, where *C* is the circumference and *r* is the length of the radius of the circle.

28 The circumference C of a circle is equal to $2\pi r$, where r is the length of the radius. Rewrite the formula $A = \frac{1}{2}Cr$ by substituting $2\pi r$ for C.

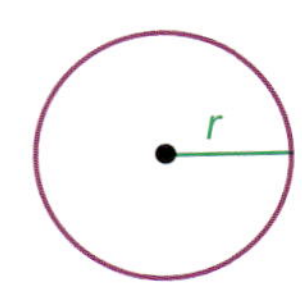

29 The area of a circle with radius r is $A = \pi r^2$. Compare πr^2 with the expression you wrote for Question 28. Do they have the same value? Explain.

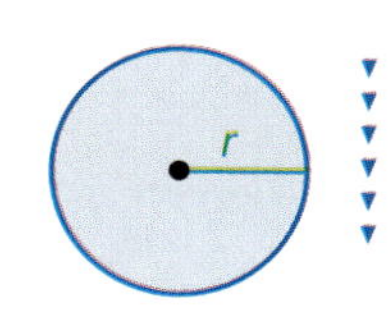

▶ **You can use the equation $A = \pi r^2$ to find the area of a circle when you know the length of its radius.**

EXAMPLE

Find the area of a circle with radius 3.2 cm. Use 3.14 for π to find the approximate area.

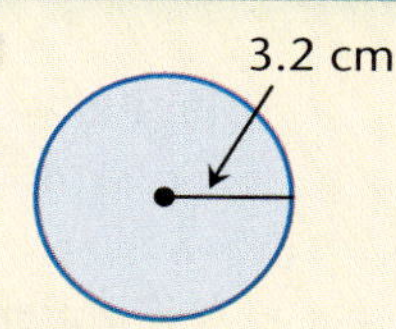

SAMPLE RESPONSE

Exact Area	Approximate Area
$A = \pi r^2$	$A = \pi r^2$
$= \pi(3.2)^2$	$= \pi(3.2)^2$
$= \pi(10.24)$	$\approx 3.14(10.24)$
$= 10.24\pi$	≈ 32.15
The exact area is 10.24π cm².	**The approximate area is 32.2 cm².**

This is an approximation because 3.14 is an approximation for π.

For Questions 30–31, use 3.14 or the π key on a calculator.

30 **Try This as a Class** Use your figure from Question 24.

a. Use $A = \pi r^2$ to write an expression that represents the exact area of the *Circle*.

b. Find the approximate area of the *Circle*.

c. If you were planning to make a circle kite with a 4 cm radius, would you use your answer from part (a) or from part (b) to order the material? Why?

d. How does the area of the circle from part (b) compare with the estimated area of the figure in Question 26(a)?

31 ✓ **CHECKPOINT** A centipede kite has 10 in. diameter circles.

a. Find the exact area of one circle.

b. Find the approximate area of one circle.

c. About how many square inches of silk were used to make all 11 circles of the kite?

...checks that you can find the area of a circle.

HOMEWORK EXERCISES See Exs. 16–23 on p. 407.

Section 2 Key Concepts

Key Terms

square root

Square Roots (pp. 395–397)

If $A = s^2$, then s is a square root of A.

Example Find the square roots of 900.

Since $(30)^2 = 900$ and $(-30)^2 = 900$, the square roots of 900 are 30 and -30.

principal square root

perfect square

Every positive number has two square roots. The principal square root of a positive number, indicated by $\sqrt{\ }$, is the positive square root. A number is a perfect square if its principal square root is a whole number.

Examples $\sqrt{256} = 16$, so 256 is a perfect square.
$\sqrt{14} \approx 3.74$, so 14 is not a perfect square.

Prisms and Surface Area (pp. 397–400)

prism

base

face

vertex

edge

net

A prism is a space figure that has flat surfaces shaped like polygons. Pairs of faces meet in segments called edges, and the edges meet in points called vertices.

The **bases** are congruent and parallel. The other **faces** are shaped like parallelograms. The prisms you see from this point on in the book will be right prisms.

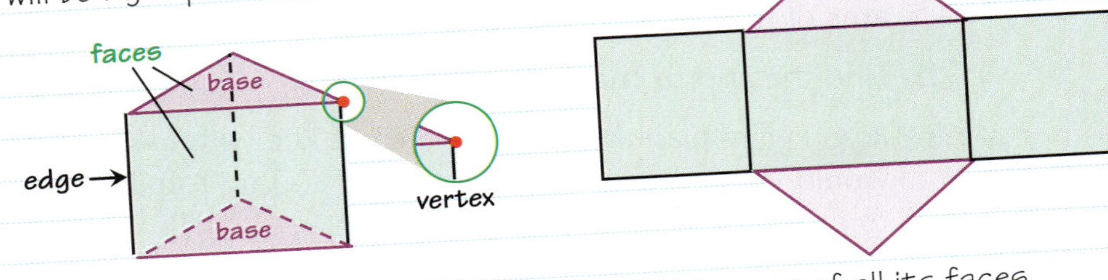

surface area

The surface area of a prism is the sum of the areas of all its faces. You can use a net to help find the surface area of a prism.

32 Key Concepts Question Use the rectangular prism below.

a. Draw a net showing the faces of the prism. Label the edges of each face with its dimensions.

b. What is the surface area of the prism?

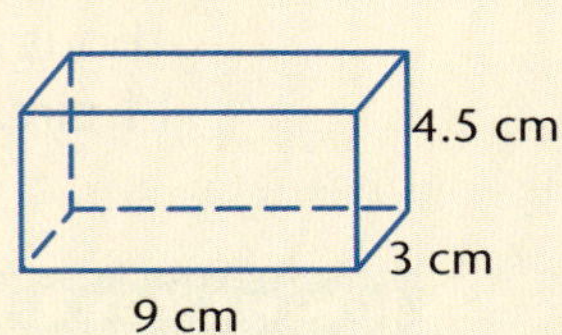

Section 2 Key Concepts

Area of a Circle (pp. 401–403)

The area of a circle A is equal to πr^2, where r is the **radius** of the circle.

Example Find the area of a circle with **radius 5.5 in.**

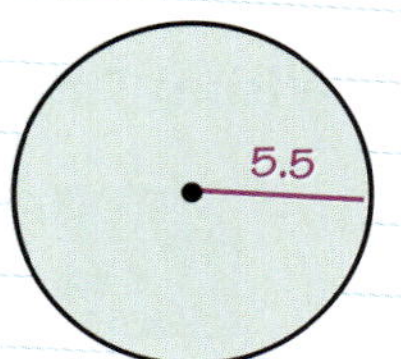

$A = \pi r^2 = \pi(5.5)^2 = \pi(30.25)$

The exact area of the circle is 30.25π in.^{2}.

$A \approx 3.14 \cdot 30.25 = 94.985$

The approximate area of the circle is 94.99 in.^{2}.

You can approximate the area by using 3.14 or the π key on a calculator.

33 Key Concepts Question Use the figure.

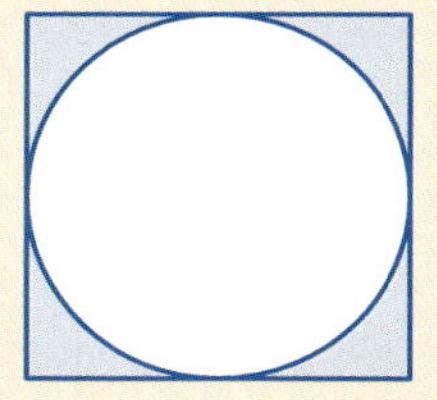

a. The square has an area of 169 in.^{2}. Find the length of a side.

b. What is the exact area of a circle with a diameter equal to the length in part (a)?

Section 2 Practice & Application Exercises

1. History In 1821, Captain Dansey of the British Royal Artillery designed a square kite for rescuing shipwreck victims. The kite had an area of 81 ft^2. Find the dimensions of the kite.

Find each square root. If the square root is not a whole number, find the two consecutive integers it is between.

2. $\sqrt{196}$ **3.** $-\sqrt{225}$ **4.** $-\sqrt{169}$ **5.** $\sqrt{2.56}$

Estimate each square root to the nearest tenth.

6. $\sqrt{93}$ **7.** $\sqrt{205}$ **8.** $\sqrt{17}$ **9.** $\sqrt{546}$

10. Kites You can use the formula $m = 7\sqrt{\frac{w}{A}}$, where m is the minimum wind speed, w is the weight in ounces, and A is the area in square feet of the surface used to lift the kite, to calculate the minimum wind speed in miles per hour required to fly a box kite. Find the minimum wind speed required to lift a box kite with a weight of 5.6 oz and an area of 8.71 ft^2.

11. Visual Thinking Four prisms were made from centimeter cubes.

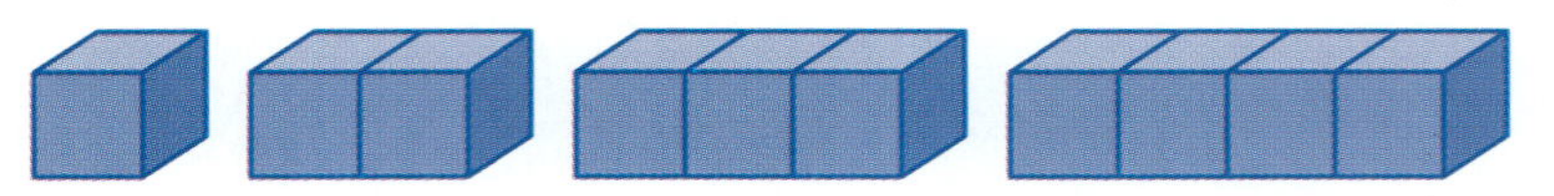

a. Find the surface area of each prism.

b. Look for a pattern in your answers for part (a). What would be the surface area of a prism made with 10 centimeter cubes arranged in the same way? How did you find your answer?

12. Visual Thinking A net for a cereal box is shown below. It was formed by cutting the box open and flattening it.

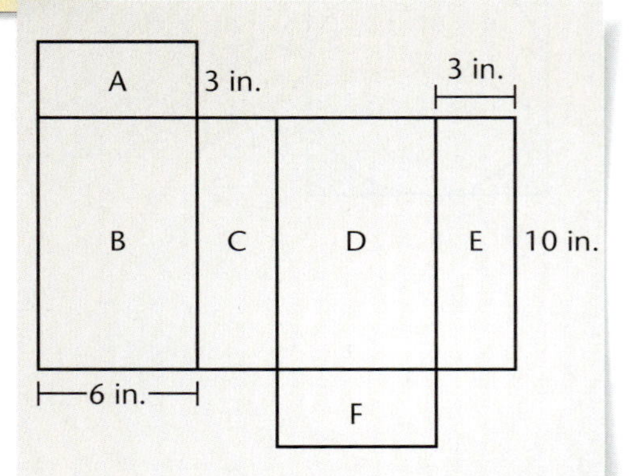

a. If the box were put back together, which faces do you think would be the top and the bottom?

b. The lengths of some edges of the box are labeled. Make a sketch of the net and label the dimensions of each face.

c. Find the surface area of the cereal box.

d. Suppose the cost of the cardboard to make a box is 0.3¢ per square inch. How much does the cardboard for one box cost?

e. If you had to make 1000 boxes, what would your cost be?

f. Why is surface area important in the design of a cereal box?

13. Use the rectangular prism shown.

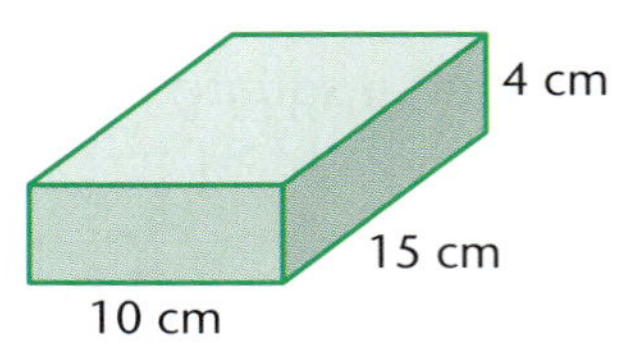

a. Sketch a net for the prism.

b. Find the area of each face.

c. Find the surface area of the prism.

14. Find the surface area of the right triangular prism shown. (*Hint:* Look carefully at the labels.)

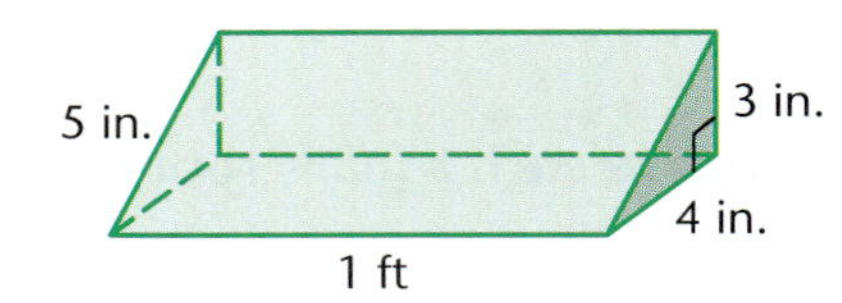

15. **Challenge** Suppose the boxes for a Hargrave kite like the one shown on page 400 are made with faces that are all congruent squares. Suppose 2500 in.^{2} of fabric is used to cover eight of the faces. How long is each edge of a box in the kite?

Use π to write an expression for the exact area of each circle. Then use 3.14 or the π key on a calculator to find the approximate area.

16. 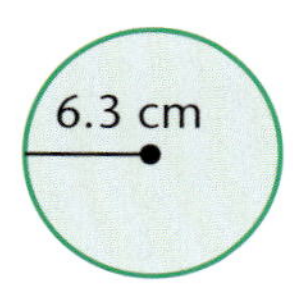

17. 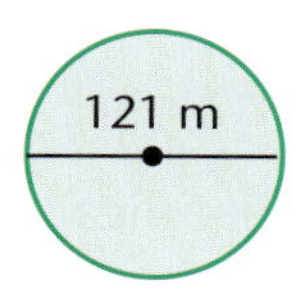

18. 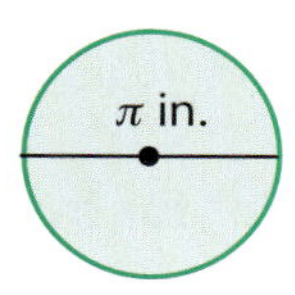

Find the radius of a circle with each area.

19. $A = 225\ ft^2$

20. $A = 0.49\ m^2$

21. $A = 16.81\ yd^2$

22. **Japanese Archery** In *kyudo,* a form of Japanese archery, archers aim at circular targets or *mato.*

   a. Find the areas of targets that have diameters of 36 cm, 18 cm, and 9 cm.

   b. Look at your answers from part (a). If the diameter of a circle is one half the diameter of another circle, will its area also be one half the area of the other circle? Explain.

The most common *kyudo* target is the 36 cm *mato* used for *kinteki* (regular close-range shooting).

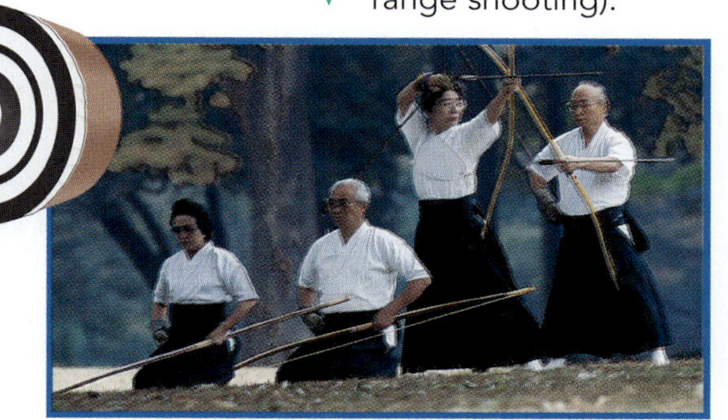

Reflecting on the Section

Be prepared to report on the following topic in class.

23. Describe a situation in which it would be helpful to know the surface area of a prism.

Oral Report

Exercise 23 checks that you understand the surface area of a prism.

Spiral Review

Write an inequality to represent each statement. (Module 6, p. 388)

24. t is greater than 11.

25. p is less than or equal to 6.

Use division to write each fraction as a decimal. (Module 4, p. 256)

26. $\frac{1}{8}$

27. $\frac{2}{5}$

28. $\frac{14}{23}$

29. $\frac{21}{31}$

Write each fraction in lowest terms. (Module 3, p. 170)

30. $\frac{2}{4}$

31. $\frac{3}{12}$

32. $\frac{15}{25}$

33. $\frac{18}{48}$

Wild Wings

SET UP *You will need:* • *Project Labsheet A* • *ruler* • *tape* • *balance scale (optional)*

Ideas for making a faster plane, or for making a glider that flies higher or farther, can come from many sources. In 1967, a magazine organized a paper airplane competition in the hope that the designs might lead to future jet designs. In this project, you will make gliders, analyze their designs, and suggest ways to improve their flying ability.

Surface Area of a Prism Follow the directions to make a Wild Wing, fly it, and find its sail loading, or weight divided by surface area.

1 **Use Project Labsheet A.**
Follow the steps to *Create a Wild Wing.*

2 Fly your Wild Wing by throwing it overhand as shown below.

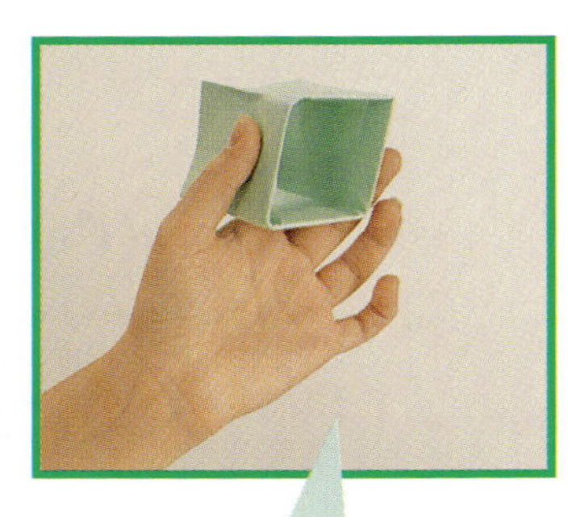

The folded edge should face forward.

3 **a.** Find the outside surface area of your Wild Wing in square feet.

b. Use a scale or the table to find your Wild Wing's weight.

c. What is the sail loading of your Wild Wing in ounces per square foot?

Type of paper	Weight of $8\frac{1}{2}$ in. × 11 in. sheet (oz)
copier	0.17
notebook	0.11
construction	0.18

Find each square root.

1. $\sqrt{64}$ 2. $\sqrt{256}$ 3. $\sqrt{49}$ 4. $\sqrt{289}$

Estimate each square root.

5. $\sqrt{79}$ 6. $\sqrt{90}$ 7. $\sqrt{30}$ 8. $\sqrt{249}$

For Exercises 9 and 10, use the prism shown.

9. What kind of prism is this?
10. How many faces, vertices, and edges does this prism have?

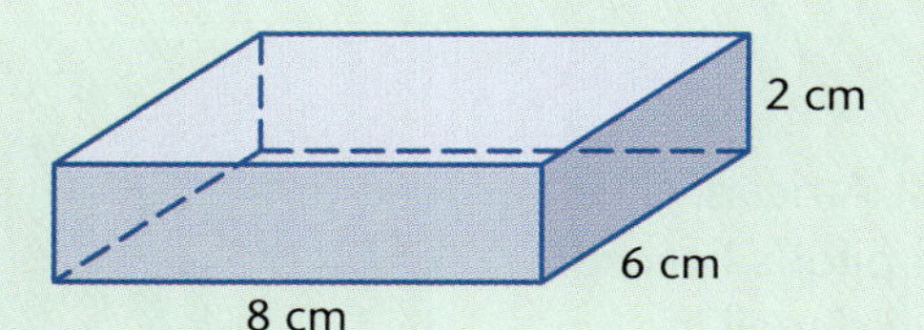

11. Use the rectangular prism shown at the left.
    a. Sketch a net for the prism.
    b. Find the surface area of the prism.

Use π to write an expression for the exact area of each circle. Then use 3.14 or the π key on a calculator to find the approximate area.

12.

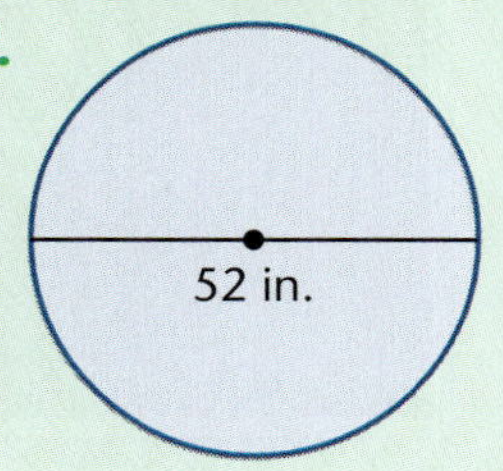

13.

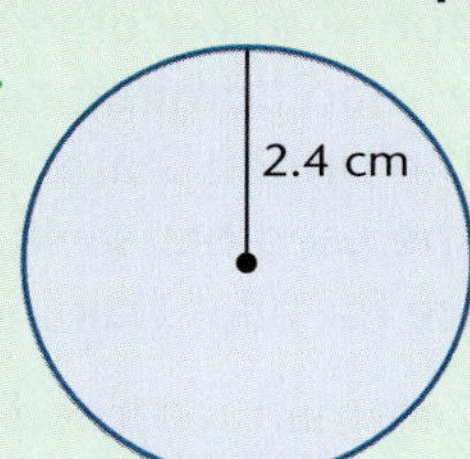

14.

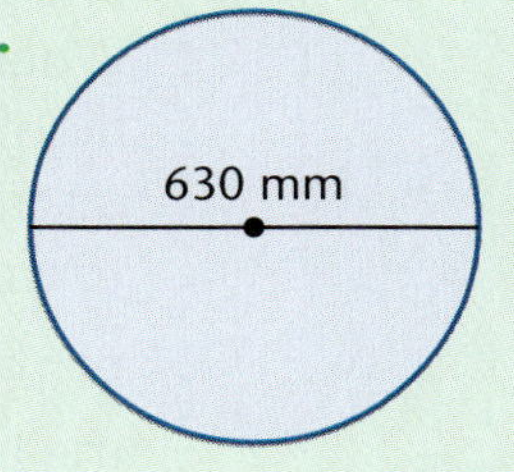

Standardized Testing ◀▶ Multiple Choice

1. Find the exact area of a circle whose radius is 3 cm long.

   A 3π cm^2 B 9π cm^2 C 6π cm^2 D 9 cm^2

2. Choose the greatest measure. Use 3.14 for π.

   A $\sqrt{420}$ cm^2 B Area of a circle with a diameter of 5 cm

   C Surface area of a cube with an edge of 2 cm

Section 3 Triangles and Similarity

EXPLORATION 1
- Scale Drawings and Similarity

EXPLORATION 2
- Unknown Measures in Similar Figures

Setting the Stage

Bessie Coleman was the first African-American woman to earn a pilot's license. Born in Texas in 1893, she did well in school, but could not afford to finish college. Eventually she moved to Chicago, where she opened a chili parlor and saved her money to become a pilot. When she was refused admittance to flight school in the United States due to discrimination, she used her savings to travel to France for pilot training.

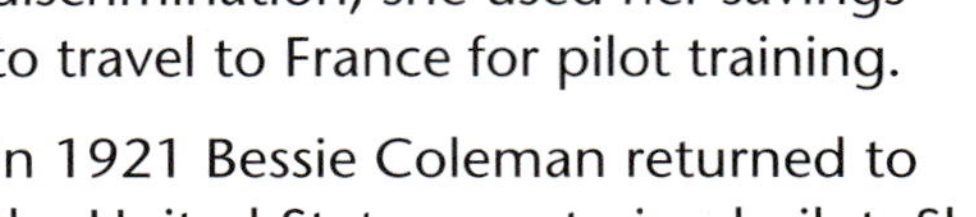

In 1921 Bessie Coleman returned to the United States as a trained pilot. She traveled around the country as a *barnstormer*, giving flying exhibitions. She thrilled thousands with her daring aerial feats. The money she earned was saved toward her dream of opening a flying school to train other African-American pilots.

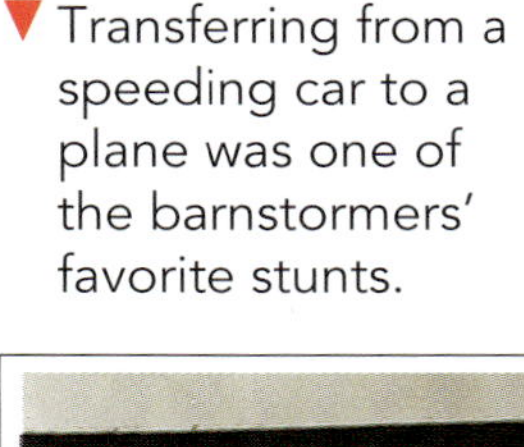

▼ Transferring from a speeding car to a plane was one of the barnstormers' favorite stunts.

Think About It

1 How long ago was Bessie Coleman born?

2 How old was Bessie Coleman when she returned to the United States?

3 What do you think a "barnstormer" is?

Exploration 1

SCALE DRAWINGS and SIMILARITY

GOAL

LEARN HOW TO...
- identify similar and congruent polygons
- find the scale of a drawing or model

AS YOU...
- learn about the Curtiss Jenny airplane used by barnstormers

KEY TERMS
- corresponding parts
- scale of a drawing

SET UP *Work with a partner. You will need:* • *Labsheet 3A* • *ruler* • *protractor*

In the book *Epic of Flight: Barnstormers & Speed Kings* by Paul O'Neil and the Editors of Time-Life Books, barnstormers are described this way:

> The barnstormers, as they called themselves, [wandered] from coast to coast to perform in rough pastures, at big-city air shows and, when fortune beckoned, in motion-picture melodramas.
>
> At first, these . . . fliers could keep their stomachs and fuel tanks full by merely offering rides—for five dollars and up—in their Curtiss Jennys. Then, as novelty wore thin, the barnstormers teamed up to develop repertoires of spectacular tricks.

The Curtiss JN-4, referred to as a *Jenny*, was a favorite airplane of barnstorming pilots such as Bessie Coleman.

Use Labsheet 3A for Questions 4–7.

4 **a.** Two *Curtiss Jennys* are shown on the labsheet. Follow the instructions to make cutouts of the planes.

b. Place the large plane 60 cm from and parallel to the edge of a table and tape it in place. Then, while viewing with one eye from the edge of the table, position the small plane so it *exactly* blocks out your view of the large plane.

c. How far is the small plane from the edge of the table?

d. Write the ratio of the distance in part (c) to 60 cm (the distance from the large plane to the edge of the table).

e. Which ratio is closest to your answer to part (d): *1 : 1, 1 : 2, 1 : 3,* or *1 : 4*? How did you determine this?

5 **a.** Measure the length of each plane to the nearest tenth of a centimeter.

b. What is the ratio of the length of the small plane to the length of the large plane?

c. How does this ratio compare with the one you found in Question 4(e)?

6 **a.** What do you think the ratio of the height of the small plane to the height of the large plane will be? Why?

b. Measure the height of each plane. What is the ratio of the height of the small plane to the height of the large plane?

7 **a.** Measure $\angle A$, the angle between the tail and the body, on the drawing of each plane. (You may need to extend the sides to measure the angle.) What do you notice about the measures of the angles?

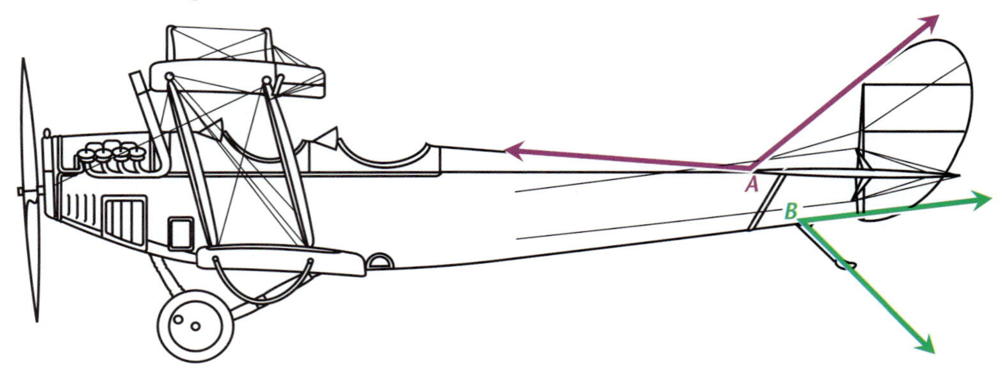

b. How do you think the measure of $\angle B$ on the small plane is related to the measure of $\angle B$ on the large plane?

c. Measure $\angle B$ on each drawing. Was your prediction in part (b) correct? Explain.

FOR HELP with *similar figures*, see **MODULE 4, p. 299**

► **The small drawing of the Jenny is similar to the large drawing of the Jenny. When two figures are similar, for each part of one figure there is a corresponding part on the other figure. For example, the diameter of the wheel on the large plane corresponds to the diameter of the wheel on the small plane.**

8 **Try This as a Class** Think about your results in Questions 5–7.

a. When two figures are similar, what do you think is true about their corresponding angles?

b. What do you think is true about the ratios of the lengths of their corresponding parts?

9 Try This as a Class $\triangle ABC$ below is similar to $\triangle GDF$. This is written $\triangle ABC \sim \triangle GDF$. How does the statement $\triangle ABC \sim \triangle GDF$ show which parts of the triangles are corresponding parts?

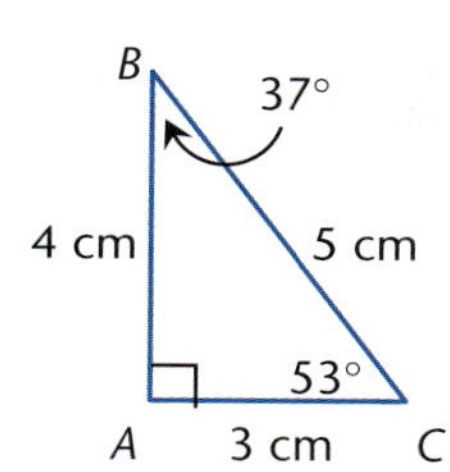

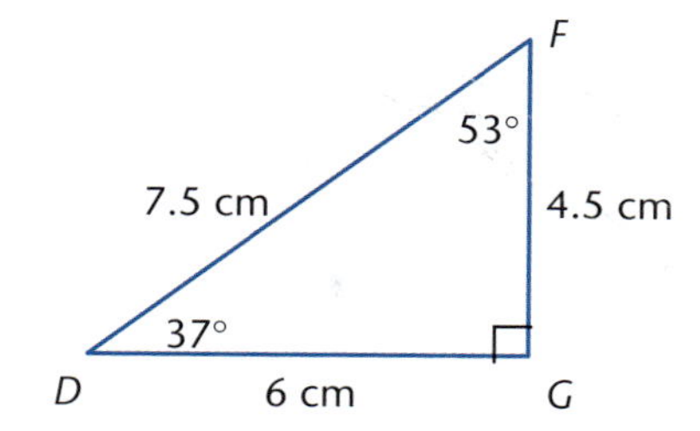

10 ✓ CHECKPOINT Use the measures of corresponding angles and the lengths of corresponding sides to show that $\triangle ABC \sim \triangle GDF$.

✓ QUESTION 10

...checks that you can use the measures of the sides and angles to show that two polygons are similar.

11 Discussion Recall from Module 4 that polygons are congruent if they have the same shape *and* the same size. For example, $\triangle PQR$ below is congruent to $\triangle WXV$. This is written $\triangle PQR \cong \triangle WXV$.

a. Identify the corresponding angles and the corresponding sides of the triangles.

b. Are congruent polygons always similar? Explain.

c. Are similar polygons always congruent? Explain.

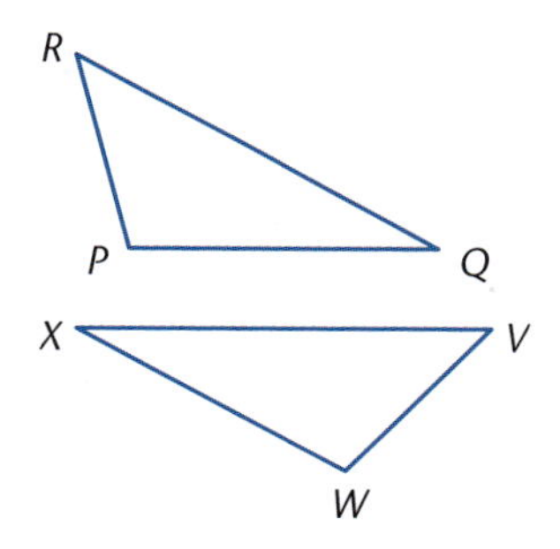

▶ **You have been working with *scale drawings* of a Curtiss Jenny. The drawings are similar to a "full size" drawing of the plane. The scale of a drawing is the ratio of a length measurement on the drawing to the measurement of the corresponding part on the object represented.**

12 ✓ CHECKPOINT A Curtiss Jenny has a length of about 8 m.

a. What is the length of a Curtiss Jenny in centimeters?

b. Choose one of the drawings. What is the length in centimeters of the Jenny in the drawing? What is the scale of the drawing?

c. Use the drawing and the scale to estimate the height of an actual Jenny in meters.

...checks that you can find the scale of a drawing and use it to find an unknown measurement.

HOMEWORK EXERCISES ▶ See Exs. 1–10 on p. 418.

GOAL

LEARN HOW TO...
- classify triangles by the measures of their angles
- find unknown measures of similar figures

AS YOU...
- use scale drawings of a Curtiss Jenny

KEY TERMS
- acute triangle
- obtuse triangle
- right triangle

Exploration 2

UNKNOWN MEASURES in SIMILAR FIGURES

SET UP *Work with a partner. You will need: • Jenny cutouts from Exploration 1 • ruler • protractor*

In Question 4 on page 411, you experimented with where to place the cutout of the small plane in order to exactly block your view of the large plane.

13 **a.** Suppose the large plane is 40 cm from the edge of the table. How far from the edge do you think the small plane must be placed in order to block the view of the large plane?

b. Tape the large plane 40 cm from the edge of the table. Then tape the small plane in the place you predicted in part (a).

c. Does the small plane block your view of the large plane? Explain.

You can use similar triangles to find where to place the small plane. But first you need to explore some properties of similar triangles.

14 **a.** Draw two different triangles that each contain a 30° and a 70° angle. Label one as Triangle A and the other as Triangle B.

b. What is the measure of the third angle of each triangle?

c. Measure the length of each side of the triangles to the nearest millimeter and write each ratio below in decimal form. Round each answer to the nearest hundredth.

- shortest side of Triangle A : shortest side of Triangle B
- longest side of Triangle A : longest side of Triangle B
- remaining side of Triangle A : remaining side of Triangle B

15 Repeat Question 14 using two triangles that each contain a 20° and a 50° angle.

16 **Discussion** Use the triangles you drew in Questions 14 and 15.

a. Are the triangles you drew in Question 14 similar? Are the ones you drew in Question 15 similar? Explain.

b. If the measures of two angles of one triangle are equal to the measures of two angles of another triangle, what seems to be true about the triangles?

17 **Try This as a Class** Use the triangles you drew in Questions 14 and 15.

a. The triangles you drew in Question 14 are **acute triangles**. How would you define an acute triangle?

b. The triangles you drew in Question 15 are **obtuse triangles**. How would you define an obtuse triangle?

c. How would you define a **right triangle?** Draw an example of a right triangle.

▶ **In similar polygons, the ratios of the lengths of the corresponding sides are equal, and the corresponding angles have equal measures. So, you can often use known measures of one polygon to find unknown measures of a similar polygon.**

EXAMPLE

$\triangle ABC \sim \triangle XYZ$. Find XZ.

XZ is read as, "the length of $\overline{XZ}$."

SAMPLE RESPONSE

$\overline{AB}$ and $\overline{XY}$ are corresponding sides.

$\overline{AC}$ and $\overline{XZ}$ are corresponding sides.

So, $\frac{AB}{XY} = \frac{AC}{XZ}$

$\frac{12}{9} = \frac{8}{XZ}$

$XZ = 6$

XZ is 6 cm.

18 **Discussion** Describe two ways to solve the proportion in the Example.

...checks that you can find unknown measures of similar figures.

19 ✓ **CHECKPOINT** $\triangle PQR \sim \triangle STV$.

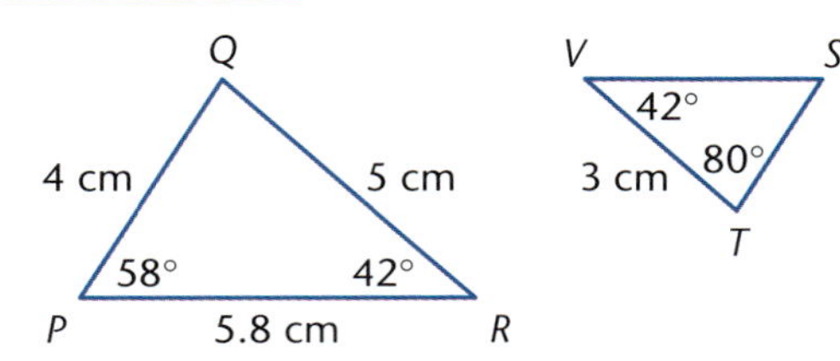

a. What is the measure of $\angle VST$? of $\angle PQR$?

b. Find VS and ST.

▶ **If the small plane exactly blocks the view of the large one, then when the cutouts are viewed from the side, you can imagine two right triangles—a small one, $\triangle ABE$, and a large one, $\triangle ACD$.**

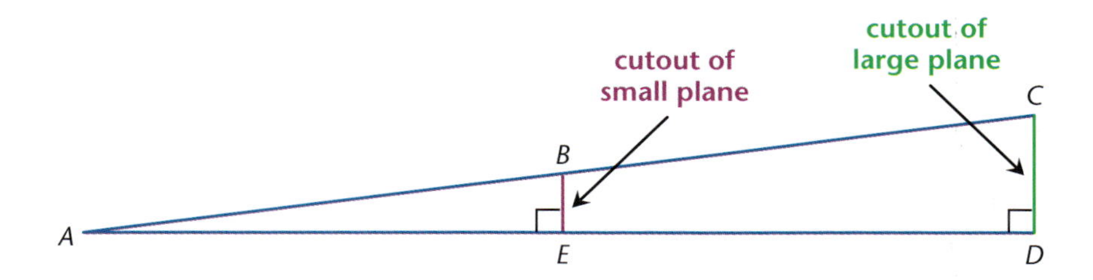

20 **Discussion** How do you know $\triangle ABE \sim \triangle ACD$?

21 **Try This as a Class** Use the Jenny cutouts and the diagram above.

a. Side $\overline{BE}$ in $\triangle ABE$ corresponds to side $\overline{CD}$ in $\triangle ACD$. What is the ratio of BE to CD?

b. Which side of $\triangle ABE$ corresponds to $\overline{AD}$ in $\triangle ACD$?

c. What is the ratio of AE to AD? How do you know?

d. If $\overline{AD}$ is 40 cm long, what is the length of $\overline{AE}$? Explain.

22 **a.** Where is the eye of the viewer located in the diagram?

b. Is $\overline{AD}$ 40 cm long? Explain.

23 **a.** Use your results from Questions 20–22 to improve your prediction of where to place the small plane when the large plane is 40 cm from the edge of the table.

b. Check your prediction.

HOMEWORK EXERCISES ▶ See Exs. 11–21 on p. 419.

Section 3 Key Concepts

Key Terms

Similar and Congruent Figures (pp. 411–416)

corresponding parts

Similar figures have the same shape but not necessarily the same size. In similar polygons, the measures of the corresponding angles are equal and the ratios of the lengths of the corresponding sides are equal.

Example Trapezoid *ABCD* is similar to trapezoid *MNQP*.

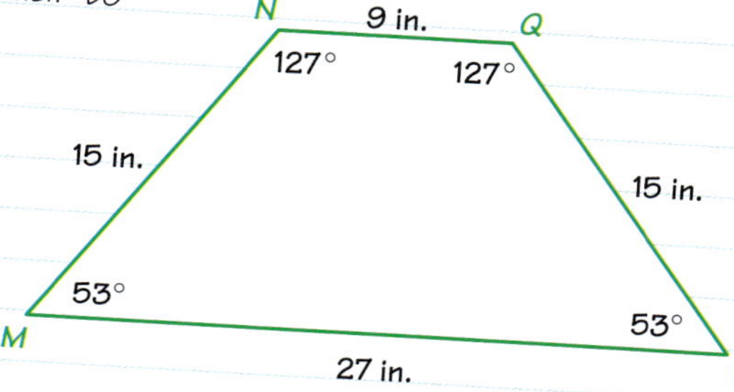

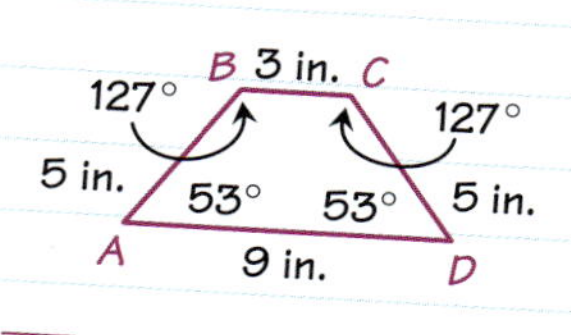

$\overline{NQ}$ and $\overline{BC}$ are corresponding sides. Since $\frac{NQ}{BC} = \frac{9}{3} = 3$, each side of trapezoid *MNQP* is three times as long as the corresponding side of trapezoid *ABCD*.

Similar figures that have the same shape and the same size are congruent. The lengths of corresponding sides and the measures of corresponding angles of congruent polygons are equal.

scale of a drawing

The scale of a model or drawing is the ratio of a length on the model or drawing to the length of the corresponding part on the actual object.

Classifying Triangles (p. 415)

Triangles can be classified by the measures of their angles.

An acute triangle has only acute angles.

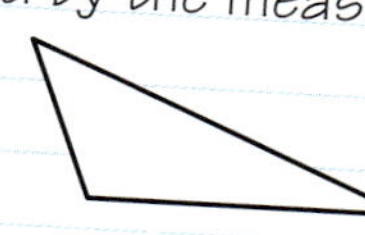

An obtuse triangle has one obtuse angle.

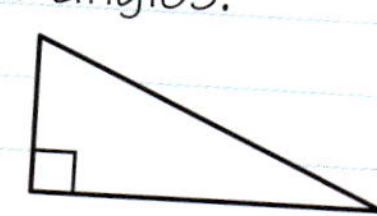

A right triangle has one right angle.

acute triangle

obtuse triangle

right triangle

Key Concepts Questions

24 The height of trapezoid *ABCD* in the Example above is 4 in. What is the height of trapezoid *MNQP*?

25 On a map, two cities are 1.5 in. apart. The scale of the map is 1 in. : 50 mi. What is the actual distance between the two cities?

You will need

For Exs. 1–4 and 20:
- protractor

For Exs. 1–7 and 20:
- ruler

Section 3 Practice & Application Exercises

Tell whether the polygons in each pair are *similar, congruent,* or *neither.* If the polygons are similar or congruent, write a statement that can be used to identify the corresponding parts.

1.
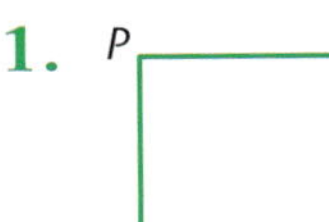

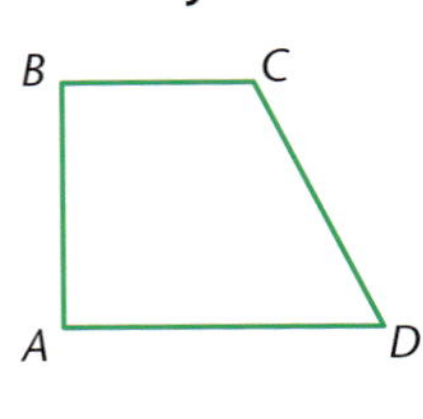

2.
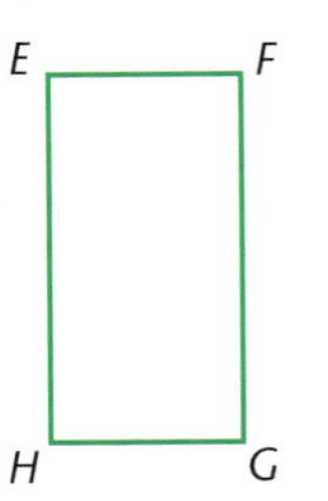

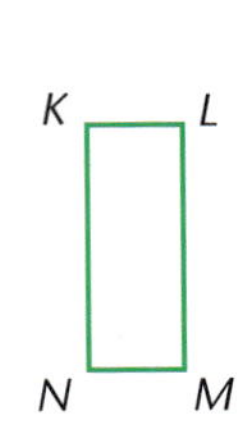

3.
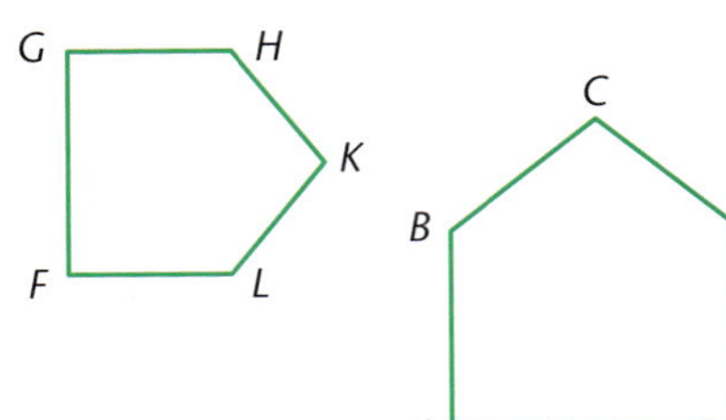

4.
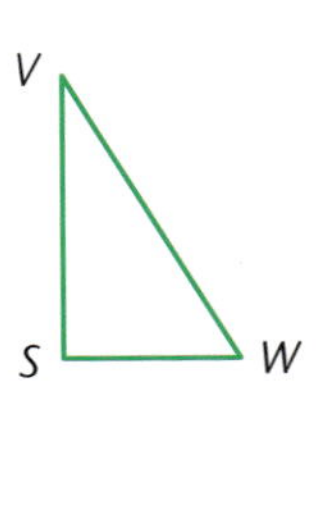

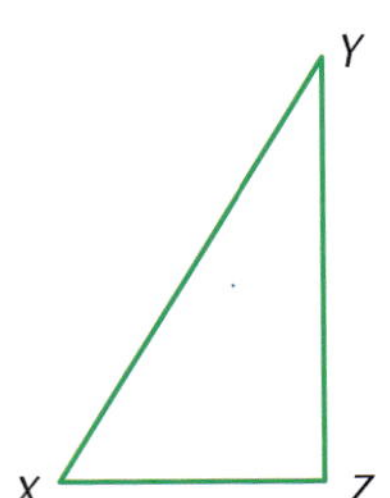

Aviation **A scale drawing of a passenger plane is shown below. Each centimeter on the drawing corresponds to 1200 cm on the plane. Estimate each measurement on the plane in meters.**

5. length
6. height
7. wingspan

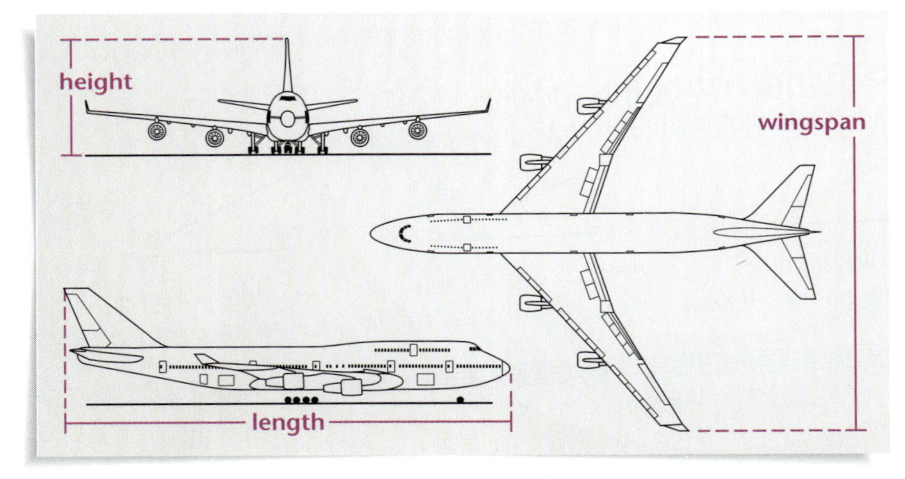

Microscopes **A microscope magnifies an object to make it appear larger. The amount of magnification can be described by using a scale. For each scale, how long does a 9 mm long housefly appear to be when seen through a microscope?**

8. 10 : 1
9. 20 : 1
10. 200 : 1

Classify each triangle as *acute, obtuse,* or *right.*

11. 7 in. 80° 7 in. 50° 50° 9 in.

12. 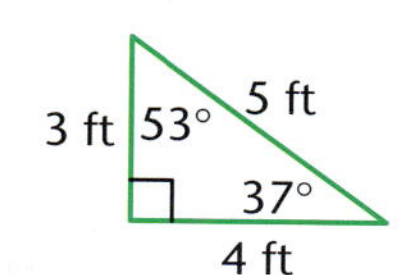

13. 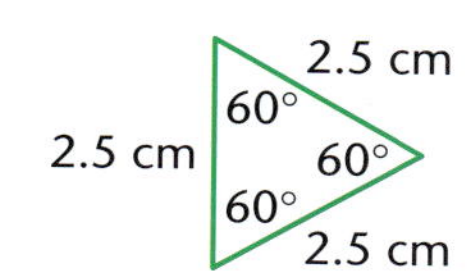

14. 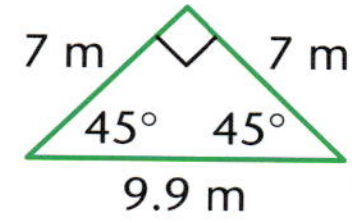

15. 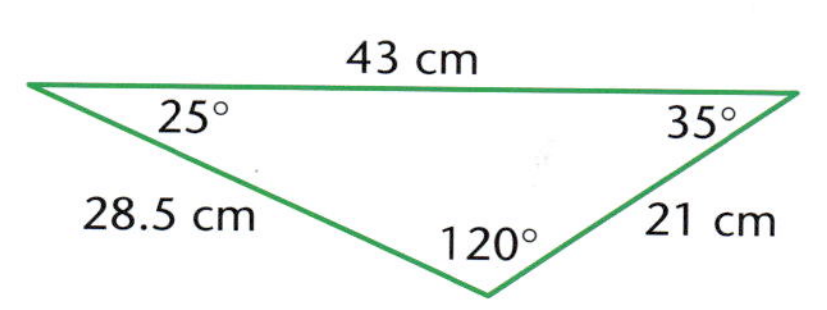

Use the similar polygons shown below for Exercises 16–19.

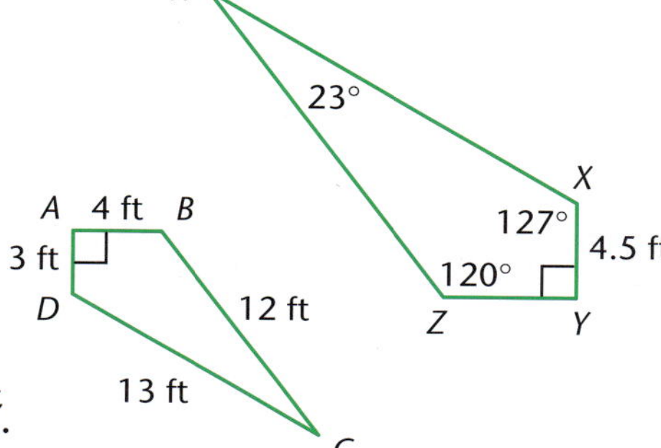

16. $\overline{XY}$ corresponds to $\overline{DA}$. What angle corresponds to $\angle XYZ$ and what is its measure?

17. Find the measures of $\angle ABC$, $\angle BCD$, and $\angle CDA$.

18. Which segment corresponds to $\overline{DC}$? What is its length?

19. Find the lengths of $\overline{WZ}$ and $\overline{YZ}$.

20. **Open-ended** Draw two similar triangles in which the ratio of the corresponding sides is 2.5 to 1. Explain how you know the two triangles are similar.

Reflecting on the Section

21. The polygons in each pair shown below are similar.

A. 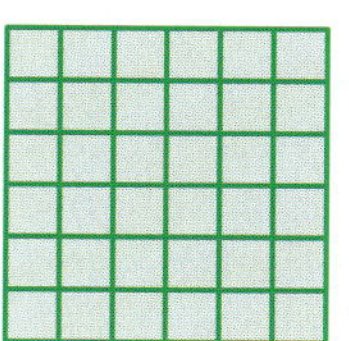

B. 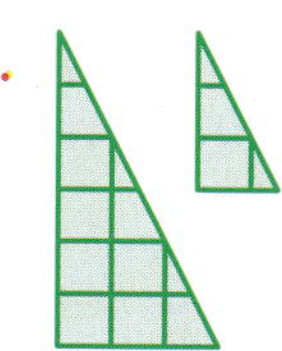

C. 

a. For each pair of polygons shown, write a ratio that compares the lengths of the sides.

b. For each pair of polygons shown, write the ratio of the area of the smaller polygon to the area of the larger polygon.

c. How are the ratios of the areas in part (b) related to the scale you found for each pair of polygons in part (a)?

Visual THINKING

Exercise 21 checks that you understand similar figures and scale drawings

Spiral Review

Find the surface area of each prism. (Module 6, p. 404)

22.

18 in.
10 in.
10 in.

23.

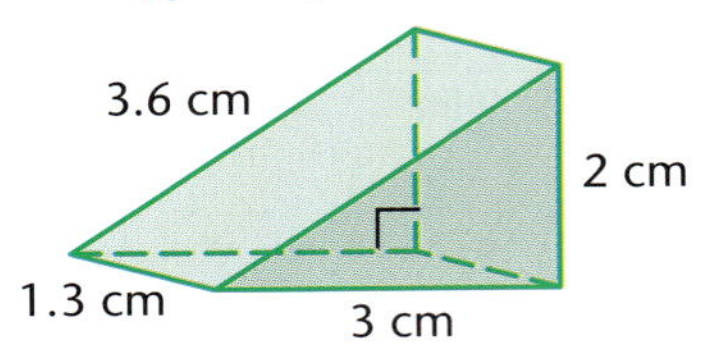

Find each difference. (Module 3, p. 183)

24. $3\frac{1}{8} - 2\frac{1}{4}$ **25.** $4\frac{1}{2} - 3\frac{1}{2}$ **26.** $5\frac{1}{2} - 2\frac{1}{2}$

For each angle, find the measure of a supplementary angle. (Module 2, p. 83)

27. 72° **28.** 90° **29.** 112° **30.** 155°

Career Connection

Artist: Jesse Treviño

Jesse Treviño paints the people and landmarks of San Antonio, Texas, in a realistic style. At first glance, you might mistake his paintings for photographs.

During combat in Vietnam, Jesse Treviño lost his right hand, the hand he used for painting. When he came home, he taught himself to paint with his left hand.

31. Jesse Treviño used one of his paintings, *The Spirit of Healing*, as the model for a hospital mural. The original painting is 4 ft across and about 8 ft 10 in. high.

a. The hospital mural is about 39 ft 7 in. across. About how high is it?

b. The painting shown is titled *La Raspa*. Suppose Jesse Treviño used this painting as the model for a mural. Using the same scale that was used for the *The Spirit of Healing* mural, what would be the dimensions of the *La Raspa* mural?

La Raspa is a Spanish phrase that translates as "Snow Cone."

Section 3

Extra Skill Practice

$\triangle XYZ$ is similar to $\triangle TUV$.

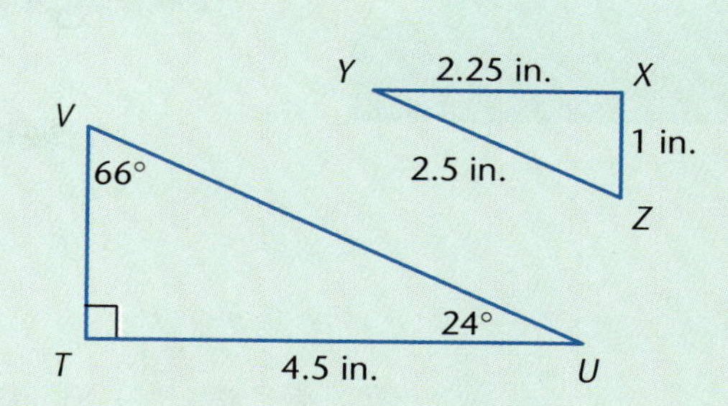

1. $\overline{XY}$ corresponds to $\overline{TU}$. What segments correspond to $\overline{ZX}$ and $\overline{YZ}$?
2. Find the measures of $\angle XYZ$, $\angle YZX$, and $\angle ZXY$.
3. Find the lengths of $\overline{UV}$ and $\overline{VT}$.

Classify each triangle as *acute, obtuse,* or *right*.

4. 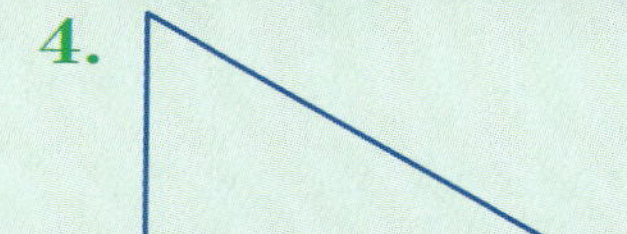

5. 85° 50° 45°

6. 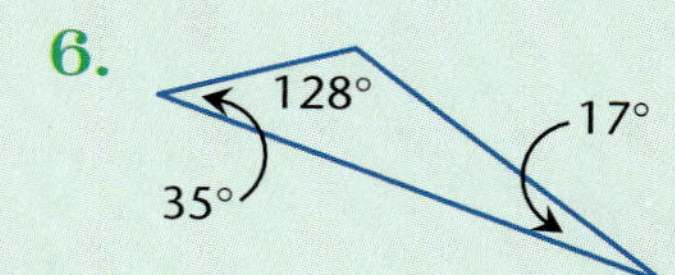

7. 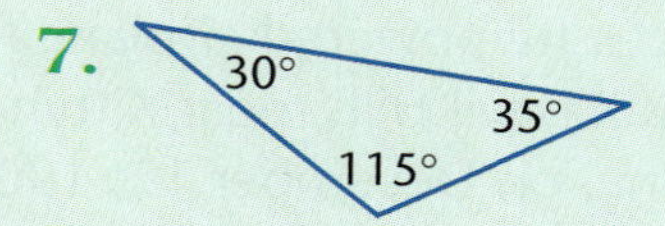

8. 47° 60° 73°

9. 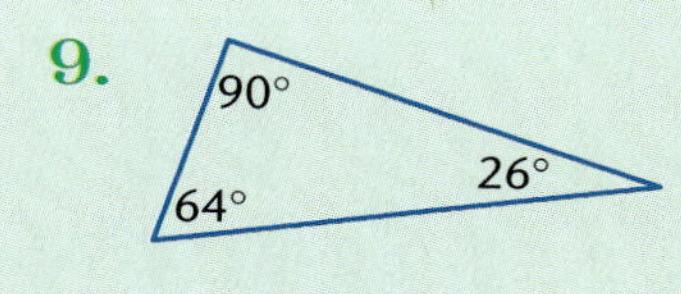

Trapezoid *EFGH* is similar to trapezoid *LMNK*.

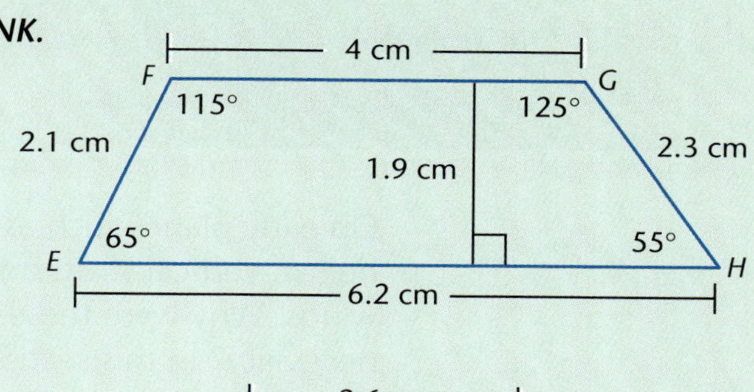

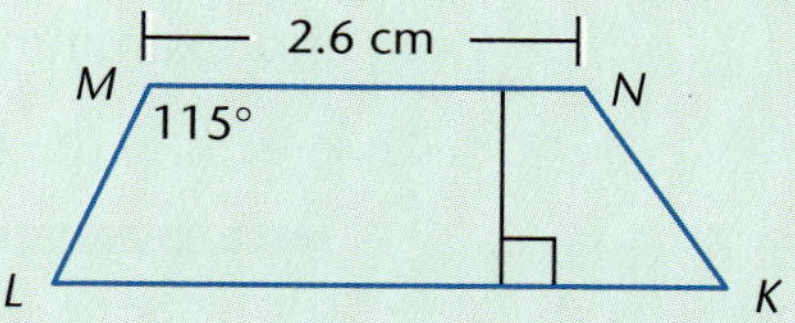

10. The height of trapezoid *EFGH* is 1.9 cm. What is the height of trapezoid *LMNK*?
11. Find the measures of $\angle MNK$, $\angle NKL$, and $\angle KLM$.
12. Find the lengths of $\overline{LM}$, $\overline{NK}$, and $\overline{KL}$.

Standardized Testing ▶ Free Response

1. Must two pentagons that have congruent angles be similar? Why or why not?
2. Must two pentagons that have congruent sides be similar? Why or why not?

Parallel Lines and Angles of Polygons

EXPLORATION 1
- Angles Formed by a Transversal

EXPLORATION 2
- Angles of Triangles and Quadrilaterals

WINGING IT!

Setting the Stage

The first successful powered airplane flight occurred at Kill Devil Hills, near Kittyhawk, North Carolina, on December 17, 1903. With Orville Wright at the controls, the *Wright Flyer I* lurched to an altitude of almost 10 ft and flew about 120 ft before returning to the ground. The whole flight, from liftoff to landing, lasted only about 12 seconds.

On early planes such as the *Wright Flyer III,* shown in the diagram below, vertical struts and diagonal wires helped support the airplane's wings. Why were these supports important? Were both types necessary? In this section, you will explore these questions by making and examining wings.

The *Wright Flyer I* was grounded by a gust of wind on its fourth flight. However, the Wright Brothers continued to improve on its design. Their *Wright Flyer III*, built in 1905, was the first practical plane.

Think About It

1 **a.** What was the speed in feet per second of the *Wright Flyer I* during its first flight?

b. Can you run this fast? Explain.

Exploration 1

ANGLES FORMED BY A TRANSVERSAL

SET UP *Work with a partner. You will need:*
- *Labsheets 4A and 4B* • *scissors* • *ruler* • *tape*
- *2 index cards (3 in. by 5 in.)* • *protractor*

GOAL

LEARN HOW TO...
- find relationships among angles formed by parallel lines and a transversal

AS YOU...
- make a model wing

KEY TERMS
- transversal
- exterior angles
- interior angles
- corresponding angles
- vertical angles
- alternate interior angles
- alternate exterior angles

2 **Use Labsheet 4A.** You can investigate the purpose of the vertical struts by creating Wing 1 from index cards. Follow the steps on the labsheet to *Build a Wing.*

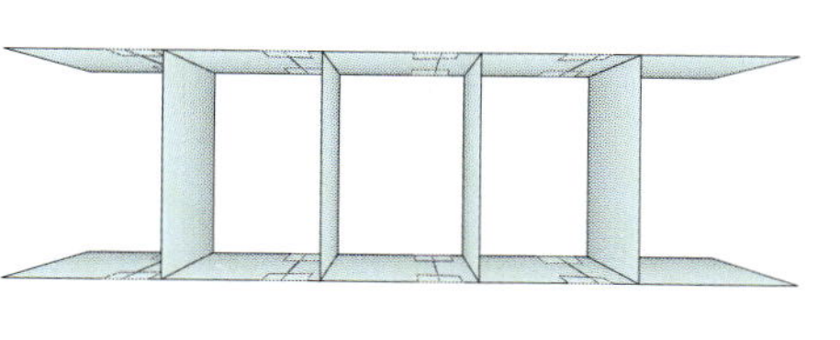

3 **a.** What is the purpose of the vertical struts?

b. Is your wing rigid? How could you make it stronger?

c. How are the bases of the wing related?

▶ **You can use segments to draw a simplified model of the wing design. In the drawing, two parallel lines are intersected by other lines called transversals.**

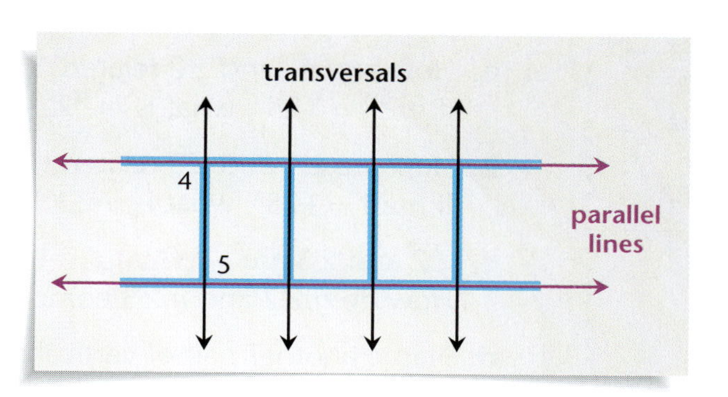

4 **a.** In the drawing above, what is true about $m\angle 4$ and $m\angle 5$?

b. Locate $\angle 4$ and $\angle 5$ from part (a) on your paper model of Wing 1. As you move the top base to the right, what happens to $m\angle 4$ and $m\angle 5$?

c. How do you think $m\angle 4$ and $m\angle 5$ compare?

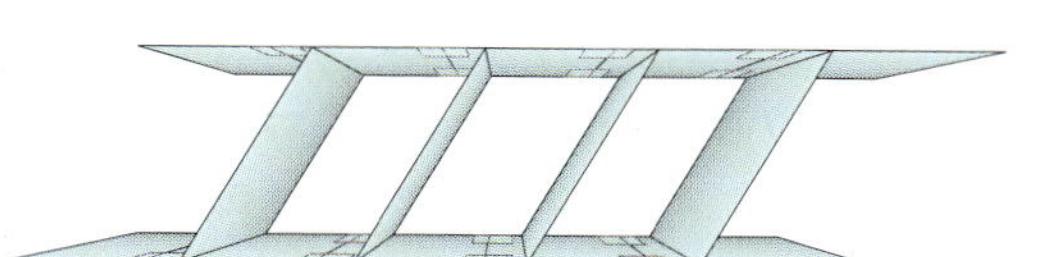

▶ **When a transversal intersects two parallel lines, eight angles are formed. These angles are related to each other.**

5 **a.** ∠1, ∠2, ∠7, and ∠8 are all **exterior angles**. Why do you think they are called exterior angles?

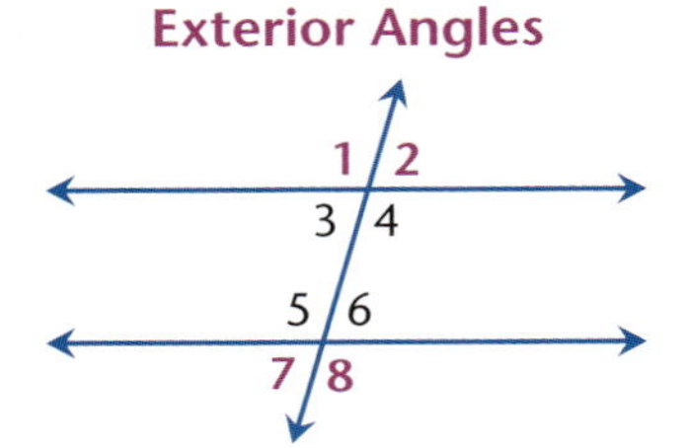

b. ∠3, ∠4, ∠5, and ∠6 are all **interior angles**. How does this name describe their location?

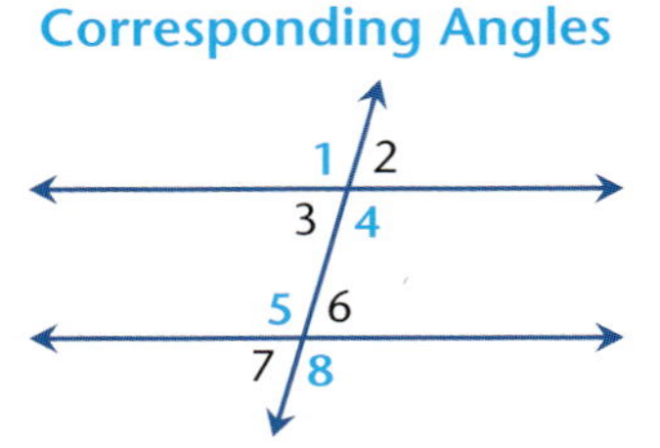

6 **Corresponding angles** come in pairs. ∠1 and ∠5 are corresponding angles, and so are ∠4 and ∠8.

a. Name two other pairs of corresponding angles.

b. How do you think the measures of corresponding angles compare?

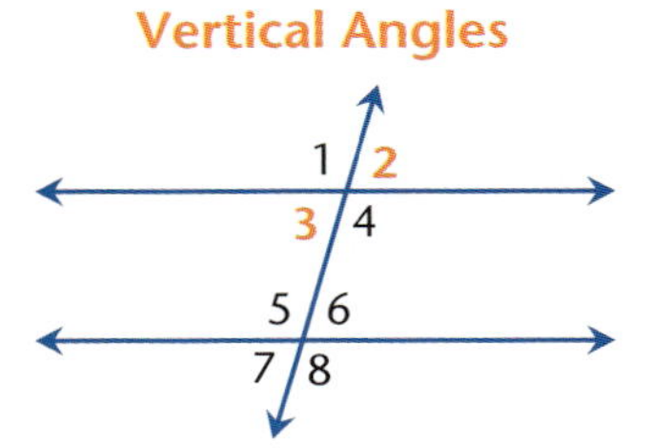

FOR ◀ HELP with *supplementary angles*, see **MODULE 2, p. 83**

7 **a.** How are ∠1 and ∠2 related? If $m\angle 1 = 125°$, what is $m\angle 2$?

b. How are ∠1 and ∠3 related? If $m\angle 1 = 125°$, what is $m\angle 3$?

c. ∠2 and ∠3 are **vertical angles**. How do $m\angle 2$ and $m\angle 3$ compare?

d. Name another pair of vertical angles.

Vertical Angles

8 ∠3 and ∠6 are **alternate interior angles**.

a. How does the term describe the location of these angles?

b. Name another pair of alternate interior angles.

c. How do you think the measures of alternate interior angles compare?

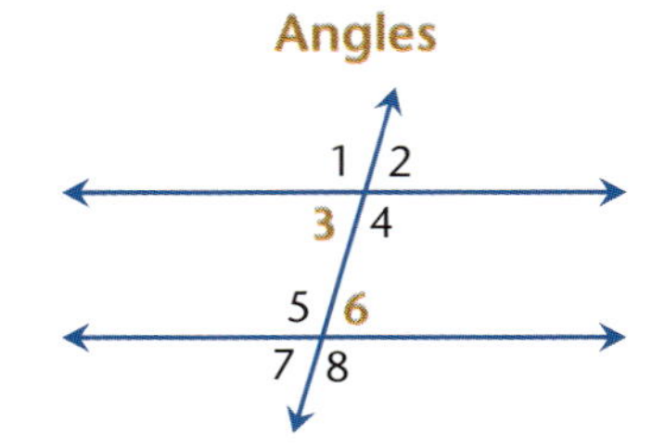

Alternate Interior Angles

▶ **In Question 9, you can check the observations you made in Questions 6–8 and find other relationships among the angles.**

Use Labsheet 4B for Questions 9 and 10.

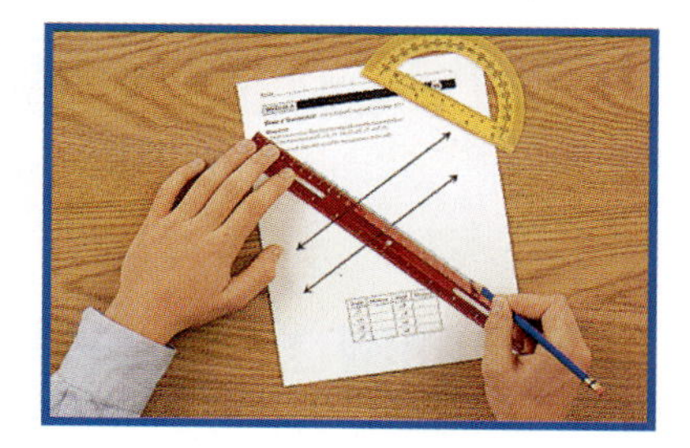

9 Use a ruler to *Draw a Transversal* through the parallel lines. Then use a protractor to find the measures of the eight angles formed.

10 **Try This as a Class** Use your answers to Question 9.

a. How do the measures of the corresponding angles compare?

b. How do the measures of the alternate interior angles compare?

c. How do the measures of the **alternate exterior angles** compare?

d. How do the measures of the vertical angles compare?

e. How do your answers in parts (a), (b), and (d) compare with your answers in Questions 6(b), 7(c), and 8(c)?

f. Compare your answers in parts (a)–(d) with your classmates'. Are the relationships in parts (a)–(d) true for any transversal drawn through parallel lines?

11 ✓ **CHECKPOINT** The figure below shows parallel lines $\overleftrightarrow{PS}$ and $\overleftrightarrow{LT}$ cut by transversal $\overleftrightarrow{MR}$. Without using a protractor, find the measure of each named angle.

a. $\angle PQM$ **b.** $\angle TNR$ **c.** $\angle MNT$

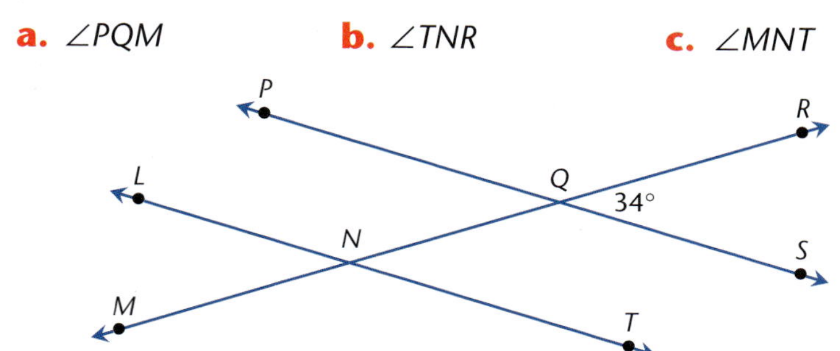

...checks that you can use the relationships among angles formed by a transversal and parallel lines.

12 **Discussion** How do you think the Wright brothers could have checked that the bases of their plane's wings were parallel?

HOMEWORK EXERCISES ▶ See Exs. 1–15 on pp. 430–431.

GOAL

LEARN HOW TO...

- find the sum of the measures of the angles of triangles and quadrilaterals

AS YOU...

- experiment with ways to make your wing rigid

KEY TERM

- diagonal

Exploration 2

ANGLES of TRIANGLES and QUADRILATERALS

SET UP *Work with a partner. You will need:*
- *scissors* • *ruler* • *tape* • *4 index cards (3 in. by 5 in.)*
- *wing from Exploration 1*

▶ **The nonvertical supports on the *Wright Flyer III* shown on page 422 provide a different type of support for the wings. In this exploration you will explore the effect of supports like these on wing design.**

13 **Use Labsheet 4A.** Create Wing 2 using nonvertical supports. Follow the directions on Labsheet 4A to make Base 1 and the four supports. Then tape one end of each support to Base 1.

Fold the tabs away from each other so they do not overlap.

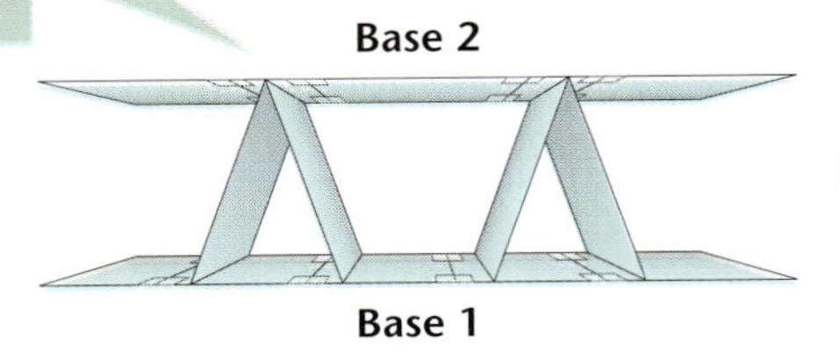

a. For Base 2, draw two support lines. Draw each support line $1\frac{1}{2}$ in. from an end.

b. Tape the free end of each support to a support line of Base 2. Two supports will be taped to each support line.

14 Is the wing you made in Exploration 1 stronger than the one in Question 13? Which wing is rigid?

▶ **You can use the angle relationships you discovered in Exploration 1 to help you find the sum of the measures of the angles of a triangle.**

15 **Try This as a Class** Use the diagram of Wing 2 below.

a. Find the sum: $m\angle 1 + m\angle 2 + m\angle 3 =$ __?__.

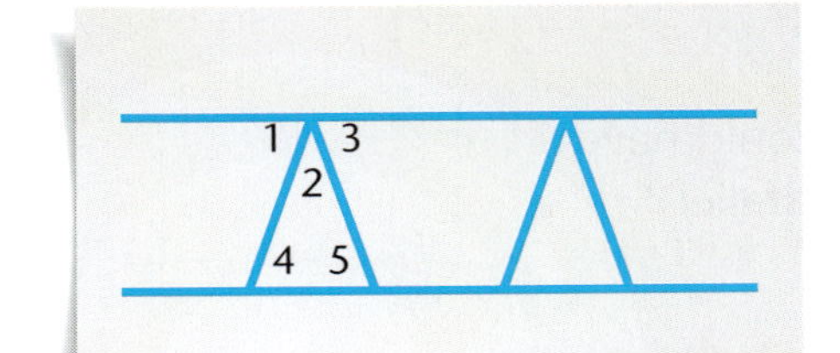

b. Which angle, $\angle 2$ or $\angle 4$, is congruent to $\angle 1$? Why?

c. Which angle, $\angle 2$ or $\angle 5$, is congruent to $\angle 3$? Why?

d. Rewrite the equation in part (a) by replacing $\angle 1$ and $\angle 3$ with the angles that are congruent to them.

e. What is the sum of the measures of the angles of a triangle?

▶ **You can use a different method to confirm your results in Question 15.**

16 **a.** Follow the directions below to find the sum of the measures of the angles of a triangle.

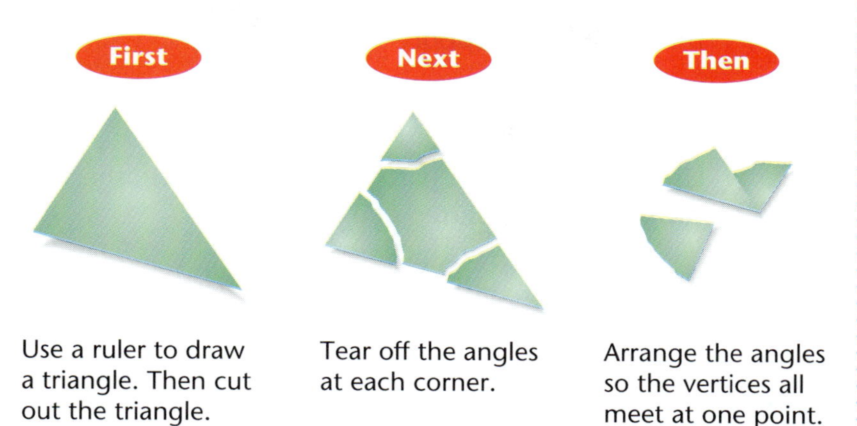

Use a ruler to draw a triangle. Then cut out the triangle.

Tear off the angles at each corner.

Arrange the angles so the vertices all meet at one point.

b. What do you notice about the arrangement of the three angles? What is the sum of their measures? Why?

▶ **One way to make Wing 1 rigid is to add a nonvertical support.**

17 **a.** Follow the directions below to add a nonvertical support.

Cut out a $1\frac{1}{2}$ in. by $2\frac{1}{4}$ in. nonvertical support from an index card. Fold $\frac{1}{4}$ in. tabs on each end of the support.

Slide the nonvertical support between two vertical supports in Wing 1 and tape it in place.

b. Discussion What do Wing 2 and the new Wing 1 have in common? What makes a structure rigid?

You can use what you know about triangles to find the sum of the measures of the angles of a rectangle.

18 **a.** Sketch the rectangle in Wing 1 that contains the nonvertical support. How many triangles is the rectangle divided into by the nonvertical support?

b. What is the sum of the measures of the angles in each of the triangles that make up the rectangle?

c. Use your answers in parts (a) and (b) to find the sum of the measures of the angles of a rectangle.

A rectangle is one type of quadrilateral. Now you'll find the sum of the measures of the angles of any quadrilateral.

19 **Try This as a Class** Use the quadrilaterals below.

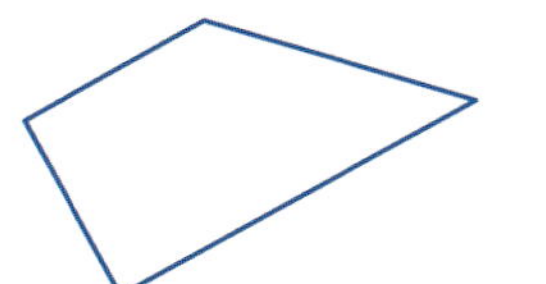

trapezoid

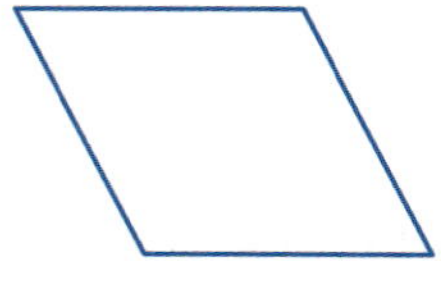

rhombus

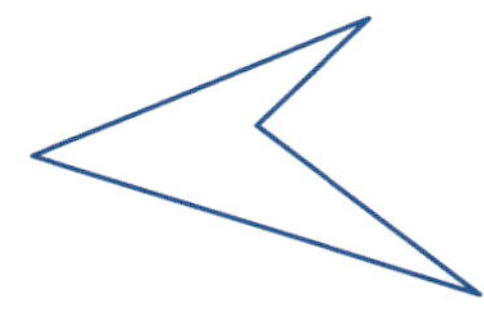

concave quadrilateral

a. What do you think is the sum of the measures of the angles of each figure?

b. A **diagonal** is a segment that connects two nonconsecutive vertices of a polygon. How can you use diagonals to find the sum of the measures of the angles of each figure?

20 Use the method shown in Question 16 to find the sum of the measures of the angles of a quadrilateral.

✓ QUESTION 21

...checks that you can find the sums of the measures of the angles of a triangle and a quadrilateral.

21 **✓ CHECKPOINT** Find the sum of the measures of the angles of each polygon highlighted in each wing design.

a.

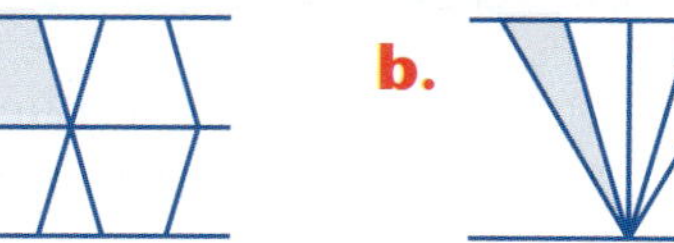

b.

c.

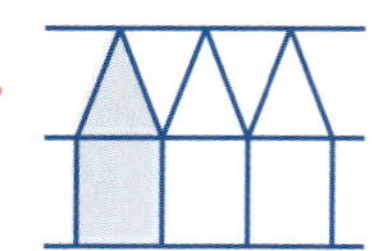

22 **Discussion** Which wing design in Question 21 is rigid? Which do you think would be strongest? Explain your choices.

HOMEWORK EXERCISES ► See Exs. 16–23 on p. 431.

Section 4

Key Concepts

Key Terms

Parallel Lines and Transversals (pp. 423–425)

A line that intersects two lines is a transversal. When a transversal intersects parallel lines, the measures of the eight angles formed are related.

transversal

interior angles

alternate interior angles

exterior angles

alternate exterior angles

corresponding angles

vertical angles

Example In the figure below, line *r* intersects parallel lines *p* and *q*.

$\angle 1 \cong \angle 8$, since alternate exterior angles are congruent.

$\angle 3 \cong \angle 6$, since alternate interior angles are congruent.

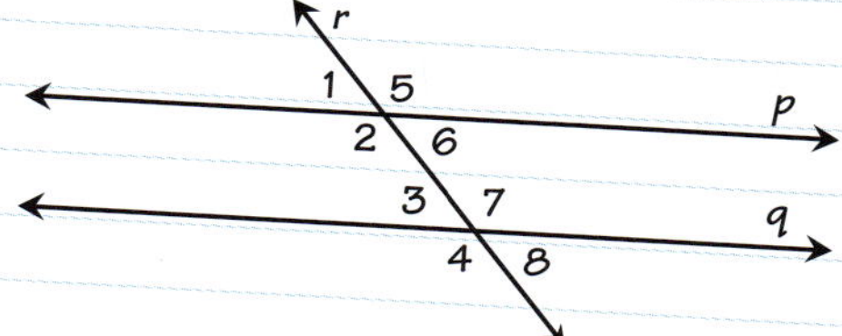

$\angle 2 \cong \angle 4$, since corresponding angles are congruent.

$\angle 3 \cong \angle 8$, since vertical angles are congruent.

Sums of the Measures of the Angles of a Triangle and of a Quadrilateral (pp. 426–428)

The sum of the measures of the angles of a triangle is 180°.
The sum of the measures of the angles of a quadrilateral is 360°.

Example

The sum of the measures of the angles of $\triangle ABF$ is 180°.

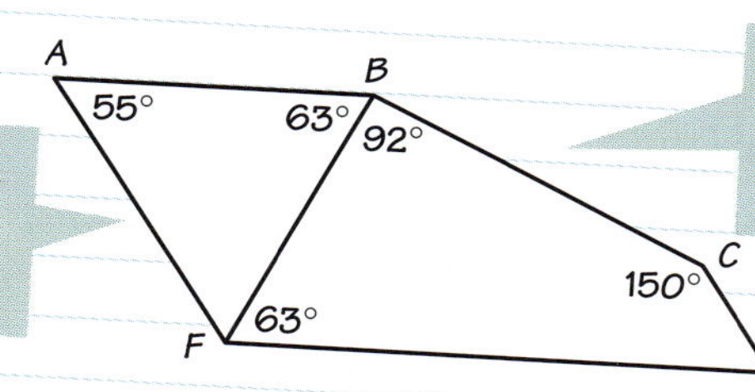

The sum of the measures of the angles of quadrilateral *BCDF* is 360°.

A diagonal is a segment whose endpoints are two nonconsecutive vertices of a polygon. In the Example, $\overline{FB}$ is a diagonal of *ABCDF*.

diagonal

Key Concepts Questions

23 Suppose that $m\angle 5$ is 130° in the first Example above. Find the measures of all the other angles shown.

24 Find each unknown angle measure in pentagon *ABCDF* in the second Example above.

Section 4 Practice & Application Exercises

In the photo of a staircase, two parallel lines *a* and *b* are cut by transversal *c*. Use the diagram for Exercises 1–7.

For Exercises 1–6, name an angle or a pair of angles that fits each description.

1. interior angle
2. exterior angle
3. pair of alternate interior angles
4. pair of alternate exterior angles
5. pair of corresponding angles
6. pair of vertical angles

7. The measure of $\angle 1$ is 55°. What is the measure of each angle you named in Exercises 1–6?

8. **Challenge** The two pairs of parallel lines below form a parallelogram.

   a. Explain why $\angle 1$ and $\angle 4$ are congruent.

   b. How do the measures of $\angle 2$ and $\angle 3$ compare?

   c. Do you think angles in other parallelograms are related in the same way? Explain.

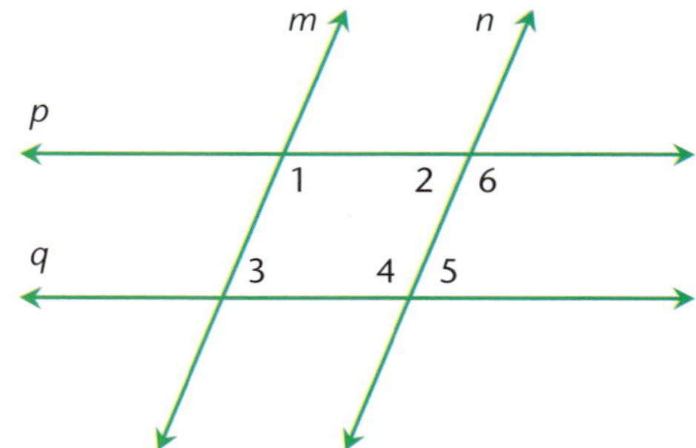

9. Use the parallelogram in Exercise 8.

   a. Explain how to use $\angle 5$ to show that $\angle 3$ and $\angle 4$ are supplementary.

   b. What other pairs of angles of the parallelogram are supplementary?

   c. Use pairs of supplementary angles to find the sum of the measures of the angles of the parallelogram without using a protractor.

Line u is parallel to line t in the figure below. Tell whether each statement is *True* or *False*. Explain your reasoning.

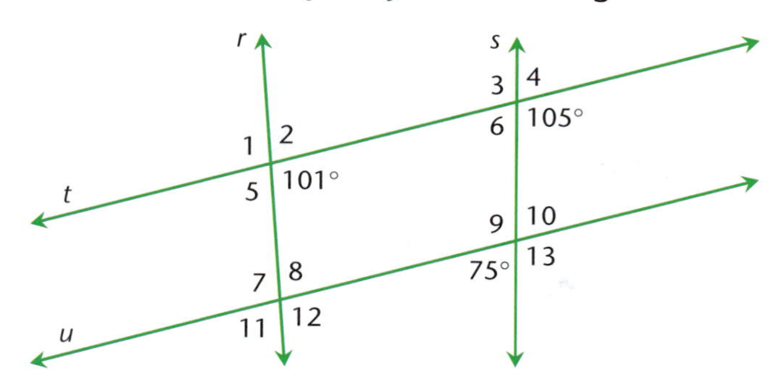

10. $m\angle 1 = 101°$

11. $m\angle 8 = 79°$

12. $m\angle 12 = 75°$

13. $m\angle 4 = 105°$

14. $m\angle 9 + m\angle 6 = 180°$

15. $m\angle 10 = m\angle 11$

Find the unknown angle measure in each triangle or quadrilateral.

16. 66° 41°

17. 55°

18. 141° 60° 92°

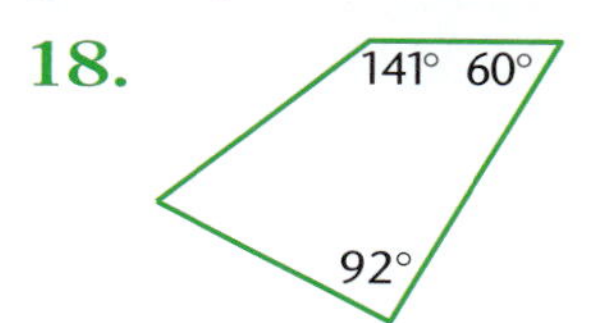

The measures of two of the angles of a triangle are given. Find the measure of the third angle of each triangle. Then tell whether the triangle is *acute, obtuse,* or *right.*

19. 10° and 75°

20. 33° and 57°

21. 61° and 64°

22. 123° and 31°

Reflecting on the Section

23. Suppose you draw both diagonals of a quadrilateral, as shown.

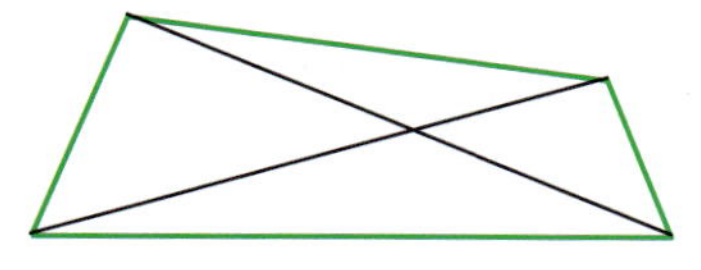

a. How many nonoverlapping triangles are formed?

b. What is the sum of the measures of the angles of the triangles?

c. What is the sum of the measures of the angles formed at the intersection of the diagonals?

d. Explain how you can use your answers to parts (b) and (c) to show that the sum of the measures of the angles of a quadrilateral is 360°.

Visual THINKING

Exercise 23 checks that you understand how to find the sum of the measures of the angles of a quadrilateral.

Spiral Review

Classify each triangle as *acute, obtuse,* or *right.* (Module 6, p. 417)

24. 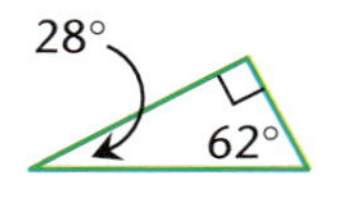

25. 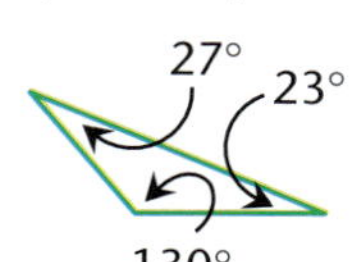

26. 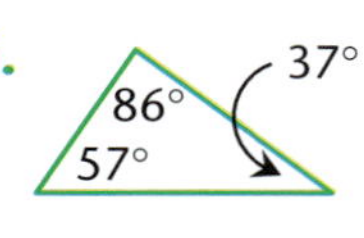

Solve each equation. Check each solution. (Module 4, p. 300)

27. $3 + 2x = 6$ **28.** $2n - 7 = 39$ **29.** $\frac{y}{2} - 10 = 5$

Find the volume of a cube with each side length. (Module 1, p. 21)

30. 3 cm **31.** 4 in. **32.** 1 ft **33.** 10 cm

Extension

The Sum of the Measures of the Angles of Any Polygon

The sum of the measures of the angles of any polygon can be determined using triangles.

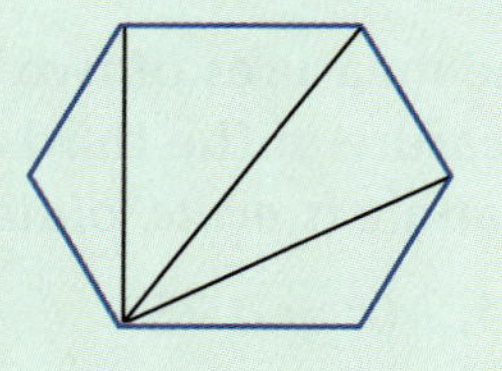

34. **a.** How many diagonals can be drawn from a vertex of a hexagon?
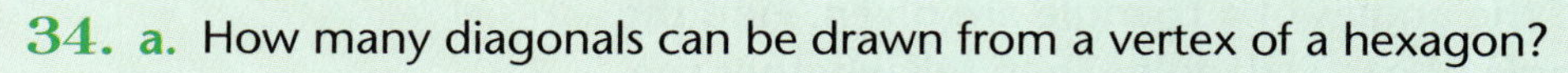

b. How many triangles are formed by the diagonals?
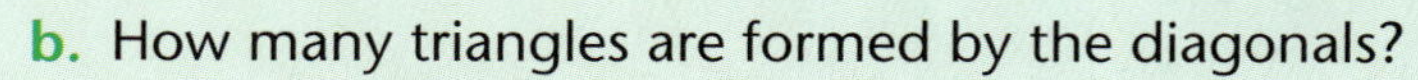

c. What is the sum of the measures of the angles of the hexagon?
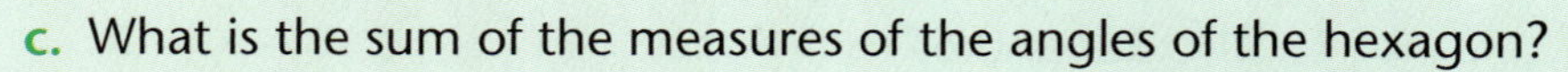

35. Copy and complete the table to find the sum of the angles of polygons with 3, 4, 5, 6, 7, and 8 sides.

Polygon	Name of polygon	Number of sides	Number of triangles formed by the diagonals from one vertex	Sum of the measures of the angles
	triangle	3	1	180°
	quadrilateral	4	2	360°

36. **a.** For each polygon, how is the number of triangles related to the number of sides?

b. How can you find the sum of the measures of the angles of any polygon?

c. What is the sum of the measures of the angles of a nonagon (a 9-sided polygon)?

d. The sum of the measures of the angles of a polygon is 1980°. How many sides does the polygon have?

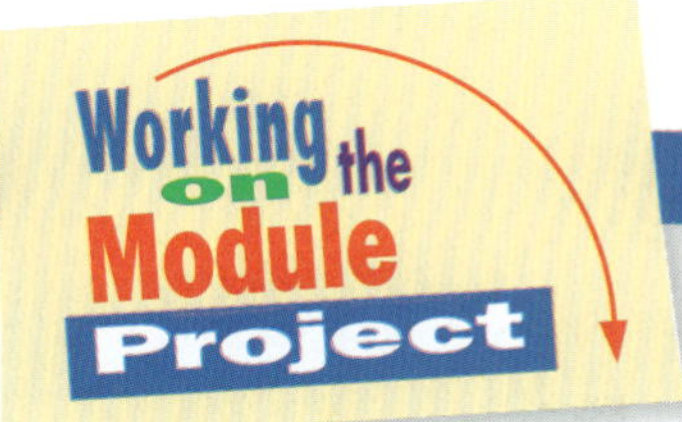

Wild Wings

Using Similar Figures Do you think a larger Wild Wing will fly as well as the one you made for Project Question 1 on page 408? To find out, you'll construct a Wild Wing on which every face is twice as long and twice as wide.

SET UP

You will need:
- *Project Labsheet A*
- *ruler*
- *tape*

Use Project Labsheet A. Tape four sheets of paper together to make a 17 in. by 22 in. sheet. Repeat the steps to *Create a Wild Wing,* but make the tail end 4 in. wide.

a. Try flying your new Wild Wing. Do you think it flies better than the first one you made? Explain why or why not.

b. Work with a partner to design a test to decide whether the larger Wild Wing flies better than the smaller one.

c. Conduct your test. Then write a report on your conclusions.

Section 4
Extra Skill Practice

The figure below shows two parallel lines, *x* and *y*, cut by transversal *z*. Use this diagram for Exercises 1–12.
Name the angles or pairs of angles that fit each description.

1. four interior angles
2. four exterior angles
3. two pairs of alternate interior angles
4. two pairs of alternate exterior angles
5. two pairs of vertical angles
6. two pairs of corresponding angles

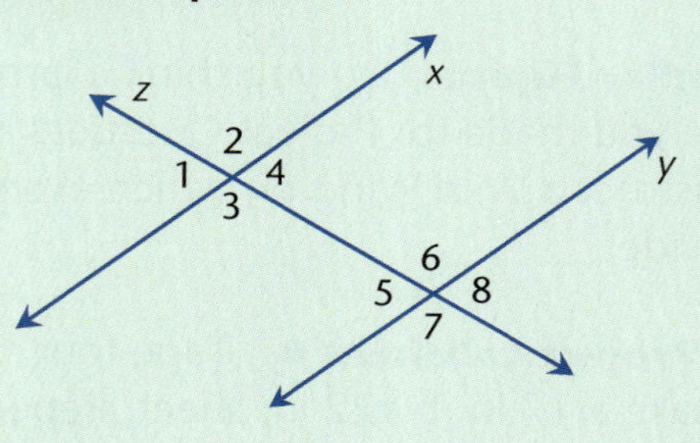

Find the measure of each angle if the measure of ∠1 is 67°.

7. ∠3
8. ∠4
9. ∠5
10. ∠6
11. ∠7
12. ∠8

Find the unknown angle measure in each triangle or quadrilateral. Label each triangle as *acute, obtuse,* or *right.*

13.

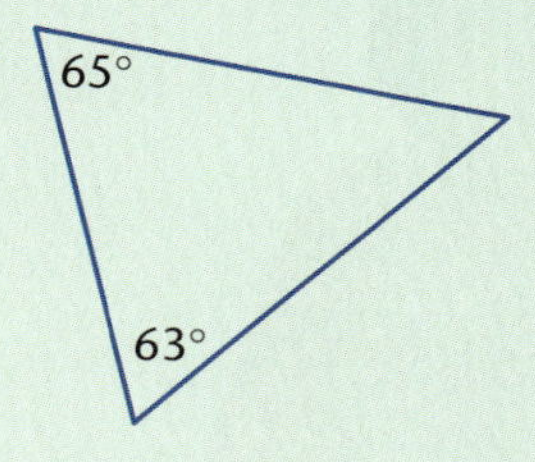

14.

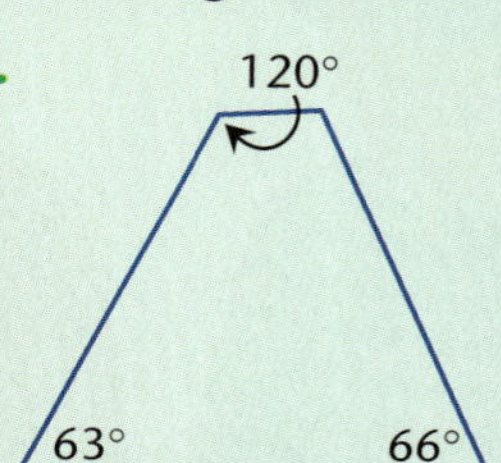

15.

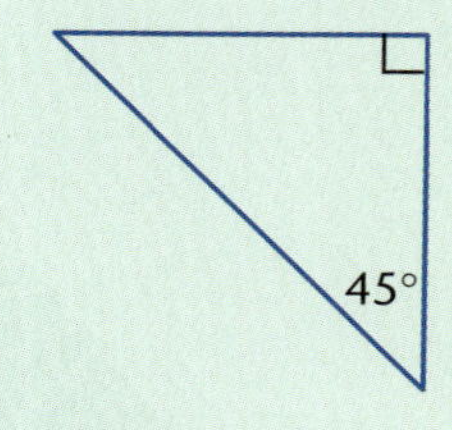

Standardized Testing ▶ Performance Task

$\overline{AB}$ and $\overline{DF}$ are parallel. Identify all pairs of congruent angles and explain how you know they are congruent.

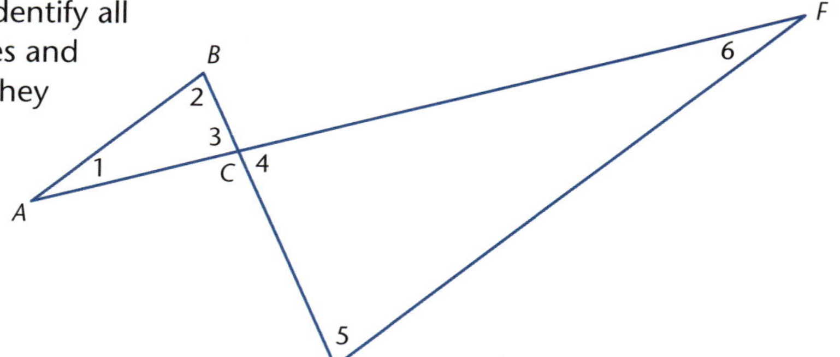

FOR ASSESSMENT AND PORTFOLIOS

EXTENDED E2 EXPLORATION

LOCATING THE HUB

SET UP *You will need:* • *Extended Exploration Labsheet* • *ruler*

The Situation

Many airlines plan their routes using a hub-and-spoke system. In this system, most flights land at or leave from a centrally located city, called a *hub.* Suppose a small airline flies to three major cities: Dallas, Texas; Omaha, Nebraska; and Cincinnati, Ohio.

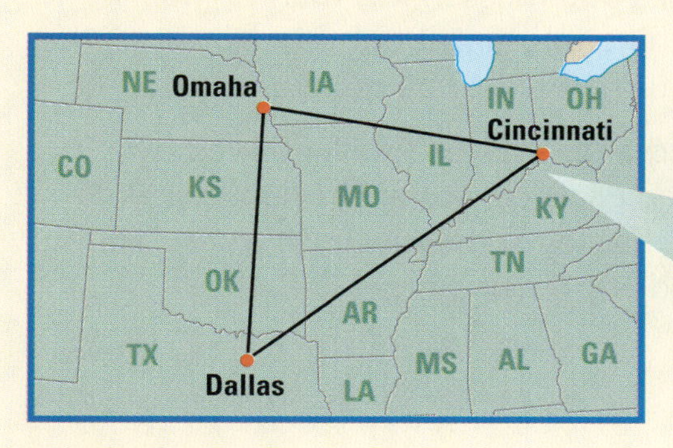

Draw a triangle like this on the *Map of the Central Region of the United States.*

The Problem

The airline wants to use a fourth city as a hub, and to keep the total air miles between the hub and each of the three major cities it serves as small as practical. Which city should the airline choose as its hub?

Something to Think About

- What information would help you choose a city to be the hub?
- Is the best hub *inside, outside,* or *on* the triangle that has the three major cities as its vertices?
- Would a city's population, weather, or geography affect the decision?

Present Your Results

Present your choice for a hub city in a written report. Include an explanation of how you reached your decision.

Volume of a Prism and Metric Relationships

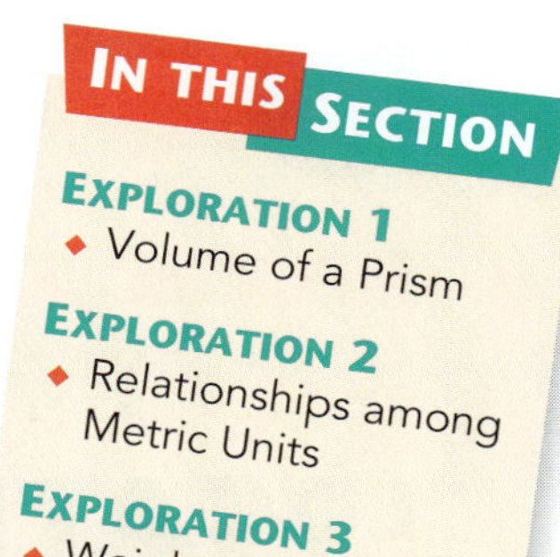

A WHALE OF A PROBLEM

Setting the Stage

Keiko is lowered into his new pool by a sling attached to a giant crane.

On January 7, 1996, Phyllis Bell, president of the Oregon Coast Aquarium, signed for a package that had flown over 2000 miles in less than 24 hours. There was nothing unusual about this. However, the package itself turned out to be quite unusual.

It was delivered atop a flatbed trailer towed by a truck. Inside the package was a 21 ft long whale named Keiko, the star of the movie *Free Willy*. He had just arrived at his new home!

Think About It

1 The shipping company that transported Keiko delivers about 12 million items each day. About 1.3 million of these items are shipped by airplane. What percent of the daily deliveries is this?

2 **a.** Keiko is an orca, a type of whale that is also called a killer whale. Orcas feed on large fish, squid, and smaller marine mammals. About how much do you think an orca weighs?

b. What factors, other than Keiko's weight, do you think were important to think about when planning how to ship him?

3 What was the advantage of shipping the whale by plane instead of by truck or by ship?

In this section you'll learn about Keiko's journey from Mexico City to his new home in Oregon.

Exploration 1

VOLUME of a PRISM

GOAL

LEARN HOW TO...
- find the volume of a prism

AS YOU...
- compare the sizes of Keiko's old and new pools

SET UP *Work with a partner. You will need 48 centimeter cubes.*

Keiko had grown too large for his 27.4 m × 13.1 m × 6.1 m pool at *Reino Aventura* (Adventure Kingdom) in Mexico City. The solution was to build a new 45.7 m × 22.9 m × 7.6 m pool for him at the Oregon Coast Aquarium.

▶ **To compare the sizes of two pools, you need to know their volumes.**

4 What is the volume of a centimeter cube?

For Questions 5–7, use the rectangular prism shown below.

5 **a.** Use centimeter cubes to build the rectangular prism shown. The prism has one layer of cubes.

b. What are the area of a base and the height of this prism?

c. What is the volume of the prism in cubic centimeters? How is the volume related to the area of a base?

6 **a.** Add a second layer to your prism. What are the area of a base and the height of the new prism?

b. Find the volume of the new prism in cubic centimeters. How is the volume related to the area of a base and the height?

c. Before adding more layers to your prism, predict what its volume would be if its height were 4 cm. Check your answer by adding extra layers and counting the centimeter cubes.

7 **Discussion** What would be the volume of a prism with the same base as the rectangular prism shown but with 20 layers? How did you find your answer?

FOR HELP with *the volume of a cube*, see **MODULE 1, p. 21**

8 **a.** Use 36 cubes to build a rectangular prism. Record the dimensions (length, width, and height), the area of a base, the volume, and the surface area of the prism in a table.

b. Make four more rectangular prisms with different dimensions. Use 36 cubes for each prism. Record the dimensions, the area of a base, the volume, and the surface area of each prism in your table.

c. What do you notice about the volumes of the prisms? the surface areas?

d. Does your method from Question 7 work for finding the volumes of these rectangular prisms? Explain.

9 **Try This as a Class** Think about the prisms in Question 8.

a. What is the least surface area that a prism made with 36 cubes can have? What is the greatest surface area?

b. Do you think there is a least surface area for rectangular prisms with a volume of 36 cm^3? a greatest surface area? Explain.

...checks that you can find the volume of a rectangular prism.

10 **CHECKPOINT** The area of the bottom of a shoe box is 50 $in.^2$ and it is 4 in. deep. What is the volume of the shoe box?

▶ **Not all prisms are rectangular. In Question 11 you'll compare the volumes of two different kinds of prisms.**

11 **a.** Use centimeter cubes to build the rectangular prism shown. What is the volume of the prism?

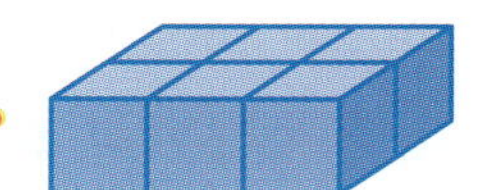

b. Suppose the prism were cut in half as shown. What kind of prisms are formed? What are the height and the area of a base of one of the prisms? How did you find the area of a base?

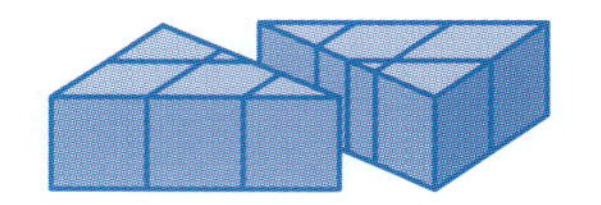

c. Find the volume of one of the prisms formed in part (b). Describe your method.

d. Record the height, the area of a base, and the volume of one of the prisms in a table.

e. Add 4 more layers to the rectangular prism you built in part (a). Each time you add a layer, record in your table the height, the area of a base, and the volume of one of the prisms formed by cutting the prism in half as in part (b).

12 **Try This as a Class** Look at the table you made in Question 11.

a. What patterns do you see in the data?

b. Find the volume of a triangular prism with 20 layers and the same base as the prisms in Question 11. Explain your method.

c. How is finding the volume of a triangular prism related to finding the volume of a rectangular prism?

d. Explain how you can find the volume of any prism without using cubes.

e. Use your method to find the volume of the prism shown. Build the prism with centimeter cubes to check your result.

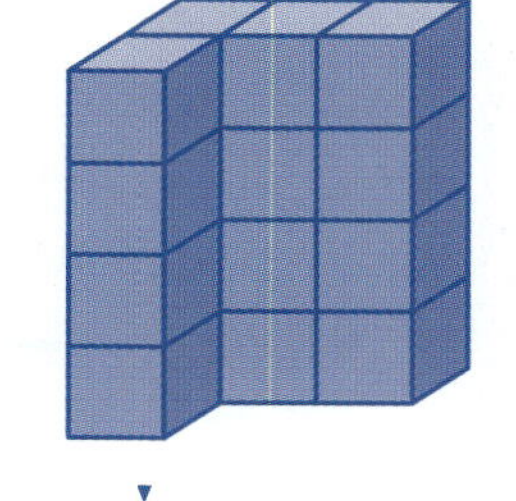

13 Suppose Keiko's old and new pools were rectangular prisms. Keiko's new pool is 45.7 m × 22.9 m × 7.6 m. His old pool is 27.4 m × 13.1 m × 6.1 m. About how many times larger would the volume of his new pool be compared with his old one?

HOMEWORK EXERCISES ▶ See Exs. 1–6 on pp. 446–447.

Exploration 2

RELATIONSHIPS AMONG METRIC UNITS

GOAL

LEARN HOW TO...
- use the relationship among metric units of volume, capacity, and mass

AS YOU...
- investigate how Keiko was shipped

KEY TERMS
- capacity
- milliliter (mL)
- mass
- gram (g)
- liter (L)
- kilogram (kg)

Building a new pool for Keiko solved one problem, but it created another—how to transport Keiko 2200 mi quickly and safely. A shipping company driver whose route included the Oregon Coast Aquarium came up with the solution.

The shipping company would use a cargo plane that could carry up to 22,600 kg of cargo, so carrying a 3200 kg whale would be no problem. But would the plane be able to carry the whale, the shipping container, and the water in the container?

14 Which do you think was greater, Keiko's mass or the mass of the water in his 8.23 m × 1.98 m × 2.13 m shipping container? Why?

▶ **The size of Keiko's shipping container can be measured using units of volume or *capacity*. A container's capacity is the amount of fluid it can hold. In the metric system, mass, capacity, and volume are related.**

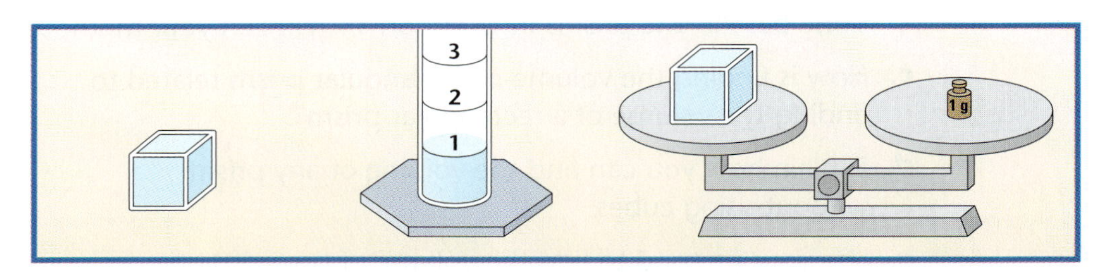

A volume of one cubic centimeter (cm^3) has … … a capacity of one **milliliter (mL)** and … … a **mass** of one **gram (g)** when filled with water.

15 **Try This as a Class** A container is shaped like a rectangular prism and measures 10 cm × 8 cm × 6 cm.

a. What is the volume of the container in cubic centimeters?

b. What is its capacity in milliliters?

c. Suppose the container is filled with water. What is the mass of the water?

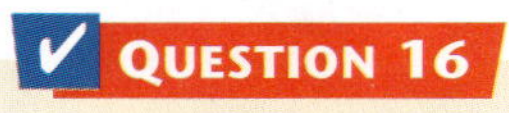

QUESTION 16

...checks that you can use the relationships among the volume, mass, and capacity of water in metric units.

16 **CHECKPOINT** A bottle holds 473 mL of water.

a. What is the volume of the water in cubic centimeters?

b. What is its mass in grams?

▶ **The relationship among volume, capacity, and mass was shown using cubic centimeters, milliliters, and grams. For larger amounts of fluid, such as the water in Keiko's shipping container, liters (L) are used to measure capacity and kilograms (kg) are used to measure mass.**

17 **Discussion** A liter of liquid will fill a cube measuring 10 cm on each edge.

a. What is the volume in cubic centimeters of a cube measuring 10 cm on each edge?

b. Use your answer from part (a) to find the number of milliliters in a liter.

c. What is the mass of a liter of water in grams?

d. A kilogram is 1000 grams. What is the mass of a liter of water in kilograms?

18 **a.** The prefix *milli* means one thousandth. Why is *milli* used in the word *milliliter*?

b. The prefix *kilo* means one thousand. Why is *kilo* used in the word *kilogram*?

19 **Discussion** Explain how to make the following conversions.

a. 3560 mL = __?__ L **b.** 6.5 L = __?__ mL

c. 250 g = __?__ kg **d.** 12 kg = __?__ g

20 ✓ **CHECKPOINT** Since whales breathe air just as humans do, it was not necessary to completely cover Keiko with water during his trip. Keiko's 8.23 m long by 1.98 m wide shipping container was filled to a depth of only about 90 cm.

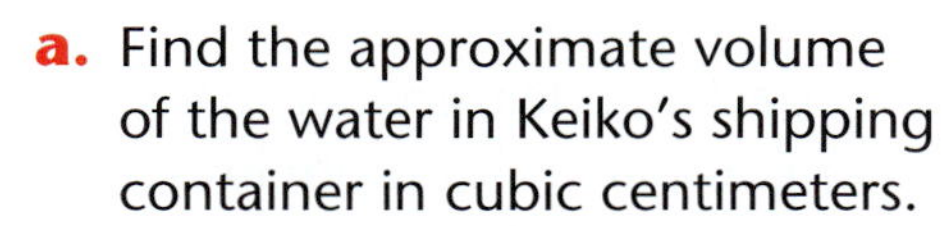

a. Find the approximate volume of the water in Keiko's shipping container in cubic centimeters.

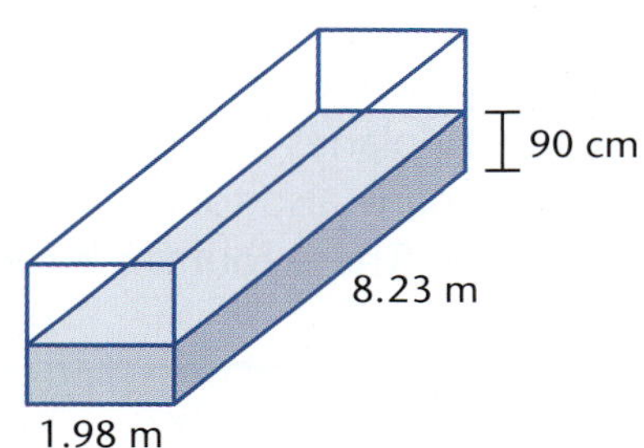

b. About how many milliliters of water were in the container? How many liters is this?

c. What was the mass of the water in the container in grams? How many kilograms is this?

✓ **QUESTION 20**

... checks that you can compute volume, mass, and capacity.

21 **a.** Which had a greater mass, Keiko or the water in his shipping container?

b. The shipping container had a mass of about 4500 kg. Find the approximate total mass of Keiko, the container, and the water.

22 According to one report, the water in Keiko's shipping container appeared to be about 150 cm deep.

a. What would the mass of the water in the shipping container have been if it were actually 150 cm deep?

b. Would the cargo plane have been able to carry Keiko, the water from part (a), and the shipping container? Explain.

c. How would you explain the statement that the water was 150 cm deep during shipping?

HOMEWORK EXERCISES ▶ **See Exs. 7–19 on p. 447.**

GOAL

LEARN HOW TO...

- use networks

AS YOU...

- analyze delivery routes

KEY TERMS

- network
- vertex of a network
- arc of a network
- weighted network

Exploration 3

WEIGHTED Networks

SET UP *You will need Labsheet 5A.*

Transporting a whale from Mexico City to Oregon in less than a day is amazing. But few people consider overnight delivery of smaller packages amazing. Fleets of airplanes and efficient routing help make overnight delivery possible.

In 1988 the world's largest express package delivery company acquired nearly 40 planes by buying another company. But more importantly, the company also took over the overseas delivery routes of the company it bought. These routes are represented in the diagram below the map.

23 Using the routes shown at the left, which cities might a package travel through when shipped from Columbus, Ohio, to Manila?

▶ **The figure above is a *network*. A network consists of points or vertices and arcs that connect the vertices. Arcs can be curves or segments.**

24 **Discussion** Use the network on page 442.

a. How does the network show that there was a direct delivery route from Singapore to Dubai but not from Singapore to Melbourne?

b. Melbourne is 3759 mi from Singapore. Dubai is 3615 mi from Singapore. Does the network show that Singapore is closer to Dubai than to Melbourne? Explain.

c. Suppose the arc connecting Singapore to Dubai had been drawn as a segment. Why would this have been confusing?

▶ **The network below shows the international routes before the purchase of the smaller company.**

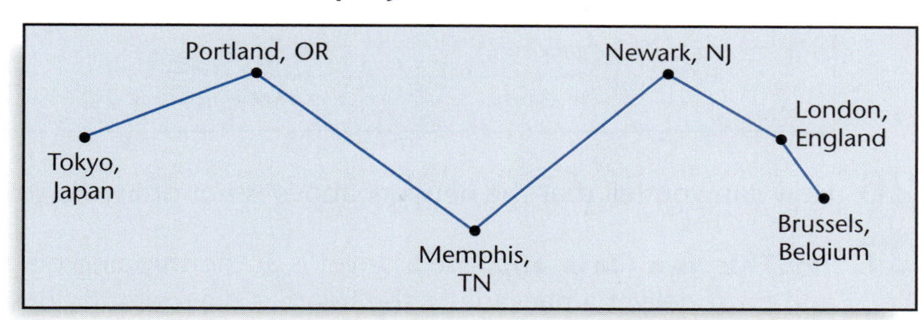

25 ✓ CHECKPOINT **Use Labsheet 5A.** The vertices of a network for the *Combined International Routes* are shown on the labsheet.

a. Connect the vertices with arcs to show the combined routes of the two companies. Use the network above and the one on page 442 to help you.

b. There are no arcs that directly connect Columbus, Ohio, and Sydney, Australia. What does this tell you?

c. How many arcs connect London directly to other vertices?

d. How many vertices are directly connected to Tokyo by arcs?

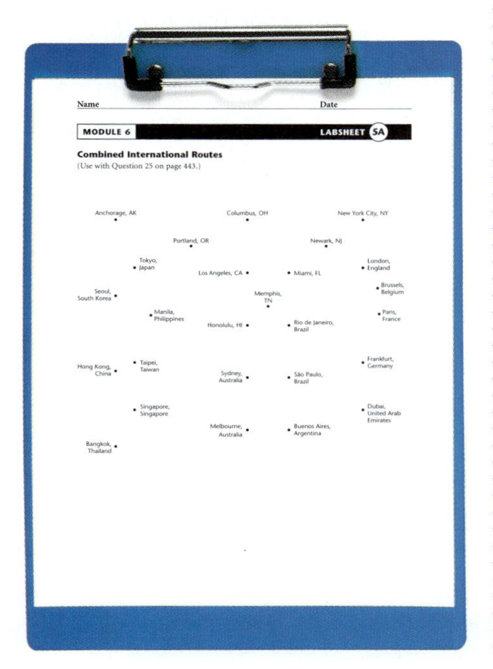
Name Date

MODULE 6 LABSHEET 5A

Combined International Routes
(Use with Question 25 on page 443.)

Anchorage, AK
Columbus, OH
New York City, NY
Portland, OR
Newark, NJ
Tokyo, Japan
Los Angeles, CA
Miami, FL
London, England
Seoul, South Korea
Memphis, TN
Brussels, Belgium
Manila, Philippines
Honolulu, HI
Rio de Janeiro, Brazil
Paris, France
Hong Kong, China
Taipei, Taiwan
Sydney, Australia
São Paulo, Brazil
Frankfurt, Germany
Singapore, Singapore
Dubai, United Arab Emirates
Melbourne, Australia
Buenos Aires, Argentina
Bangkok, Thailand

... checks that you can identify arcs and vertices and interpret a network.

▶ **A driver for a shipping company may deliver as many as 500 packages in a day, so drivers' routes must be efficiently planned. To route their trucks, a shipping company can use weighted networks like the one below, where the arcs are labeled with travel times in minutes between delivery points.**

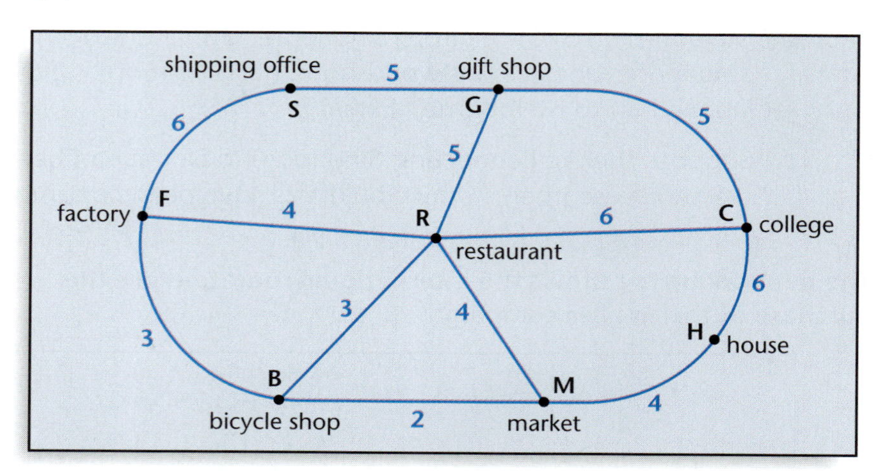

26 How can you tell that the network above is not drawn to scale?

27 **Try This as a Class** Suppose a driver is at the shipping office and must deliver a package to the house. One route the driver could use is to go from S to G to C to H. This route can be written as S–G–C–H.

a. What is the travel time for this route?

b. What is another route the driver can use? What is the travel time for this route?

✔ **QUESTION 28**

... checks that you can interpret a weighted network.

28 ✔ **CHECKPOINT** Suppose a driver must start at the shipping office, deliver packages to each delivery point, and return to the shipping office.

a. One route the driver can use is S–G–C–H–M–R–B–F–S. Find the travel time for this route.

b. What is another route the driver can use? What is the travel time for this route?

29 For the situation in Question 28, find the fastest route that starts at the shipping office, goes through each delivery point, and returns to the shipping office. What is its total travel time?

HOMEWORK EXERCISES ▶ See Exs. 20–25 on p. 448.

Section 5 Key Concepts

Key Terms

Volume of a Prism (pp. 437–439)

The volume V of a prism is the product of the area of the base B and the height h.

Example Find the volume of the rectangular prism below.

Area of base $= 2 \cdot 3$
$= 6$

Volume = Area of base × height
$V = Bh$
$= 6 \cdot 5$
$= 30$

5 cm
3 cm
2 cm

The volume is 30 cm^3.

Mass, Capacity, and Volume (pp. 439–441)

In the metric system, mass, capacity, and volume are related:

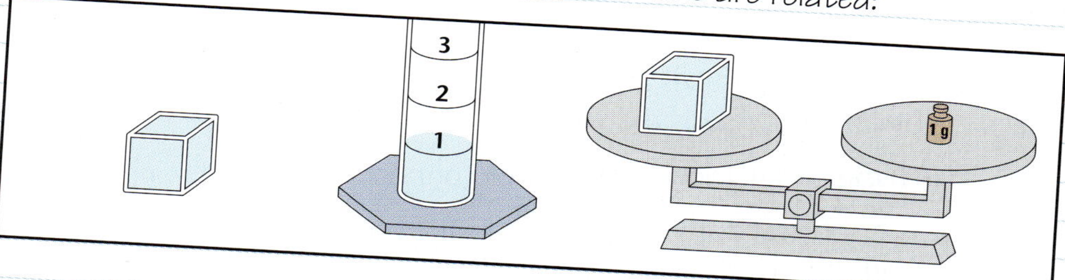

A volume of one cubic centimeter (1 cm^3) … … has a capacity of one milliliter (1 mL) and … … a mass of one gram (1 g) when filled with water.

1 L of liquid fills a cube with 10 cm edges. There are 1000 mL in a liter.

The mass of a liter of water is one kilogram. A kilogram is 1000 grams.

mass
- **gram (g)**
- **kilogram (kg)**

capacity
- **milliliter (mL)**
- **liter (L)**

Key Concepts Questions

30 **a.** What is the difference between volume and surface area?

b. What kind of units are used to measure each?

31 Give a possible length, width, and height for a container filled with 2.4 kg of water.

Continued on the next page

Section 5 Key Concepts

Key Terms

network

vertex

arc

weighted network

Networks (pp. 442–444)

A network is a figure made up of points called vertices that are connected by segments or curves called arcs. A network in which the arcs are labeled with numbers representing such things as distances or times is a weighted network.

Example One path from vertex E to vertex B is E–C–B. The length of this path is 5 + 3 = 8.

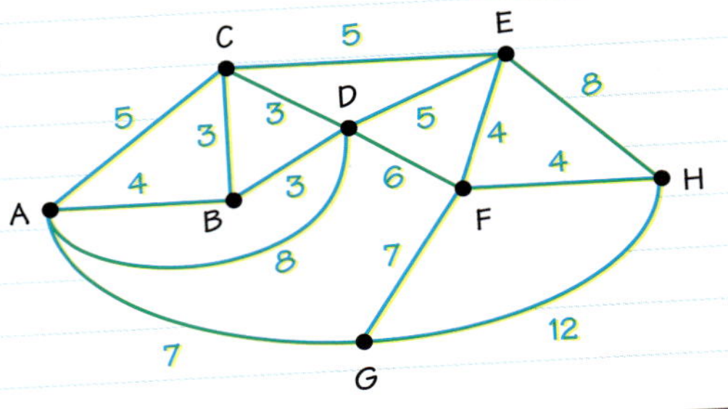

32 Key Concepts Question Use the network in the Example above.

a. Name two vertices in the network that are connected directly by an arc. What is the weight of the arc between them?

b. Name two vertices that are not connected directly by an arc.

c. The shortest path from A to H in the network is A–B–D–F–H. Find the length of this path.

Section 5 Practice & Application Exercises

YOU WILL NEED

For Ex. 36
- Labsheet 5B

Find the volume of each prism.

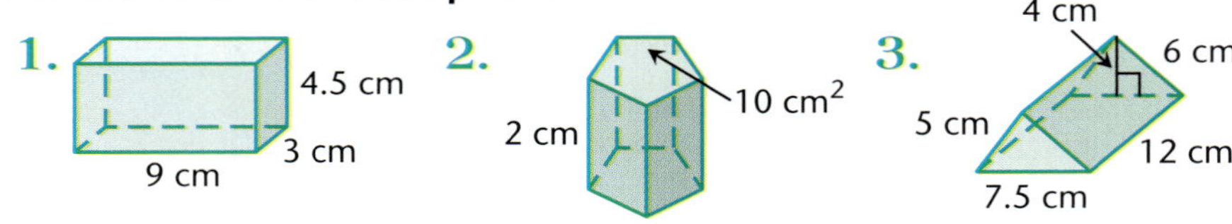

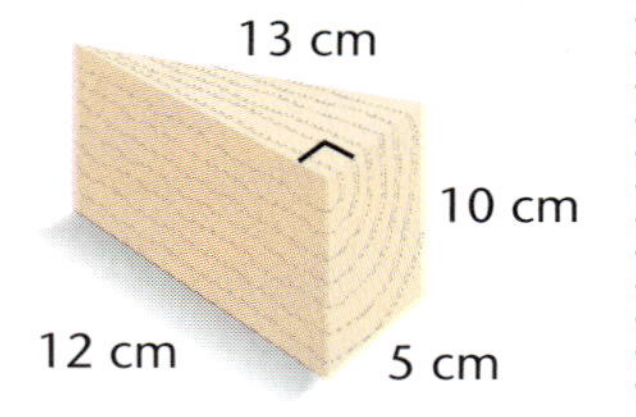

4. a. Suppose wedges like the one at the left are being manufactured for door stops. What is the volume of one wedge?

b. How many wedges can be cut out of a block of wood that is a rectangular prism 10 cm × 30 cm × 12 cm?

5. If the area of the base of a rectangular prism is 15 cm^2 and its volume is 75 cm^3, what is the height of the prism?

6. A cement block that has the shape and dimensions shown will be used as a parking curb. Find the volume of the block.

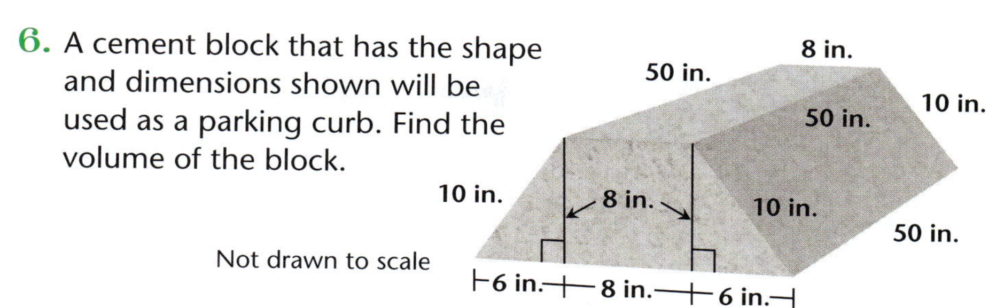

Marine Biology **Replace each ? with the number that makes the statement about orcas true.**

7. In one day, an orca can eat 91 kg or __?__ g of fish.

8. In one day, an orca can swim 121,000 m or __?__ km.

9. The average length of an adult male orca is 0.0075 km or __?__ m.

10. In one year, Keiko eats an average of about 27,000,000 g or __?__ kg of food.

Replace each ? with the number that makes the statement true.

11. 2700 L = __?__ kL

12. 1.5 kL = __?__ L

13. 172 mL = __?__ L

14. 3.75 L = __?__ mL

15. 215 cm^3 = __?__ mL

16. 0.7 L = __?__ cm^3

17. Keiko's new home at the Oregon Coast Aquarium is a tank that measures about 45.7 m × 22.9 m × 7.6 m.
    a. What is the volume of the tank in cubic centimeters?
    b. What is the capacity of the tank in liters?
    c. If the tank were completely filled with water, what would be the mass of the water in kilograms?

Keiko's new tank has underwater viewing windows.

18. The capacity of a soft drink can is 355 mL. The empty can has a mass of 15 g. If the can is filled with water, what is the combined mass of the water and the can in grams?

19. **Weather** The record for rainfall during a single day in the northern hemisphere occurred in Taiwan in 1963. In one 24-hour period, 125 cm of rain fell.
    a. Find the number of liters of rain that fell on 1 m^2 of land.
    b. Find the mass in kilograms of the rain that fell on 1 m^2 of land.

Aviation History Use the network below for Exercises 20–22. The network shows parts of existing or proposed transatlantic air routes in 1937. The lengths in miles of several of the routes are given.

The first nonstop transatlantic airmail service began in 1938. The flight from New York to Lisbon, Portugal, to Marseilles, France, took 29 h.

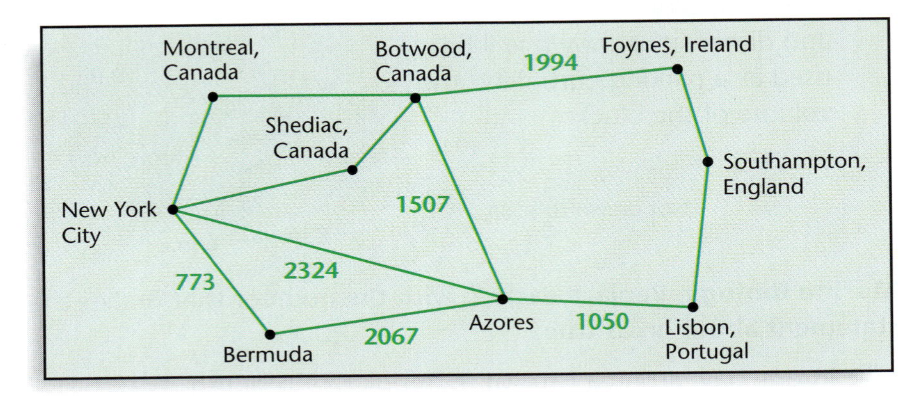

20. Find the length of the path New York City–Azores–Lisbon.

21. Find the length of the path New York City–Bermuda–Azores–Lisbon.

22. **Challenge** There are other paths from New York to Lisbon. List as many of them as you can.

Use the network below for Exercises 23 and 24. This network shows road mileage between selected United States cities.

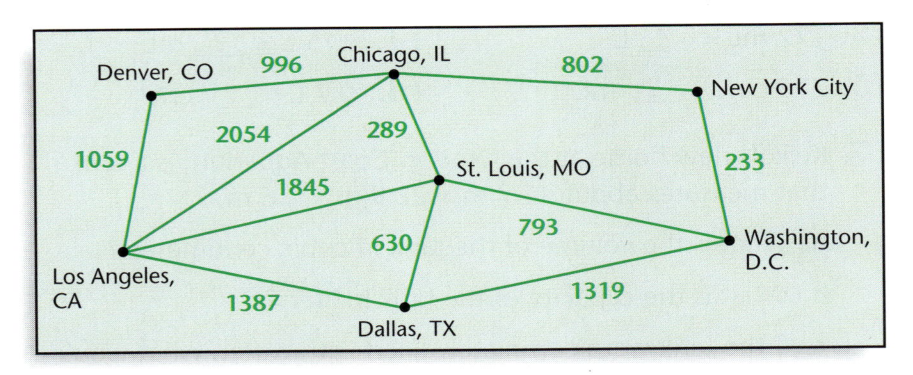

23. Find the shortest path from Los Angeles to New York.

24. Find the shortest path that starts in Los Angeles, visits all the other cities at least once, and returns to Los Angeles.

Reflecting on the Section

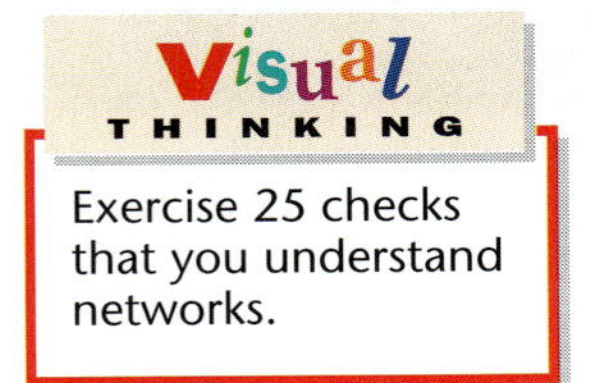

Exercise 25 checks that you understand networks.

25. Make a network where the vertices are important locations in your classroom or school. Connect the vertices with arcs representing possible paths between the locations. Then describe a path that you regularly follow during the school day.

Find each unknown angle measure. (Module 6, p. 429)

26. 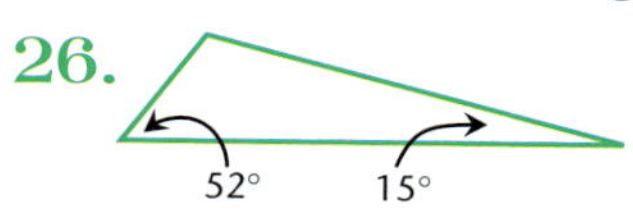

27. 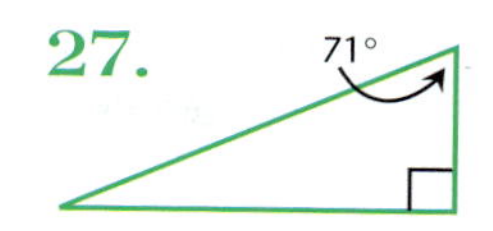

28. 

Use the box-and-whisker plots shown. (Module 5, p. 337)

Masses of Largest Types of Whales (1000 kg)

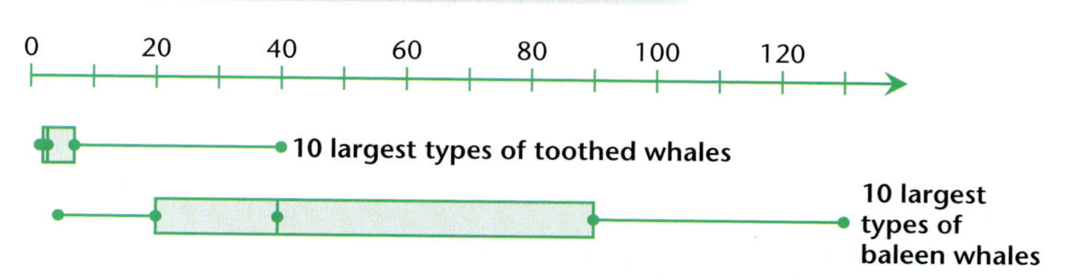

29. How is the largest type of toothed whale shown on the graph?

30. Estimate the range of each of the data sets.

Use 3.14 to find the area of a circle with each radius. (Module 6, p. 405)

31. 2.5 cm 32. 4 in. 33. 10 m 34. 1.38 cm

Extension ▶▶

Traversable Networks

A network is *traversable* if it can be drawn without lifting your pencil off the paper or drawing any arc more than once.

35. Sketch each network at the right and convince yourself that the upper one is traversable and the lower one is not.

This network is traversable.

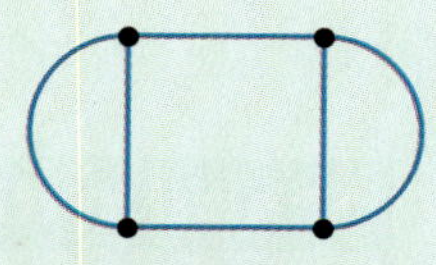

This network is not traversable.

36. **Use Labsheet 5B.** Follow the instructions for *Testing for Traversability* to discover when a network is traversable.

Each network in Exercises 37–39 is not traversable. Copy each network and add arcs to make it traversable.

37. 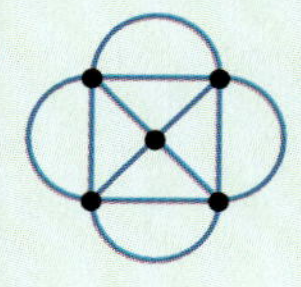

38. 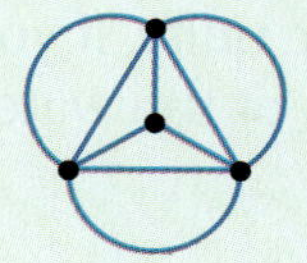

39. 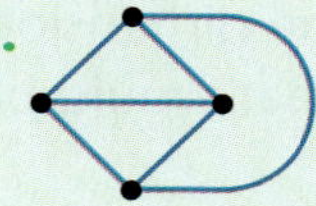

Find the volume of each prism.

1.

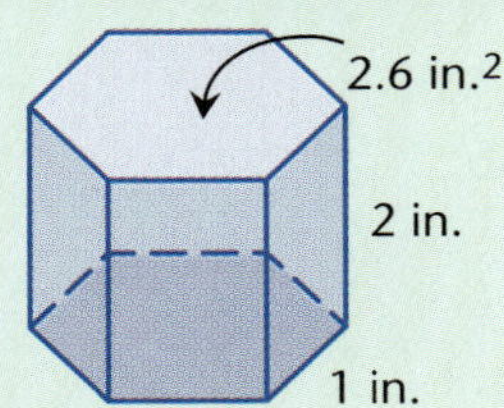

2.

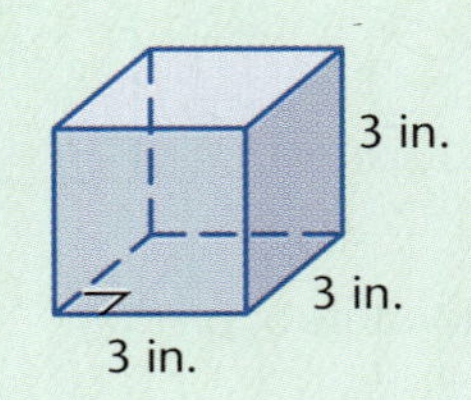

3.

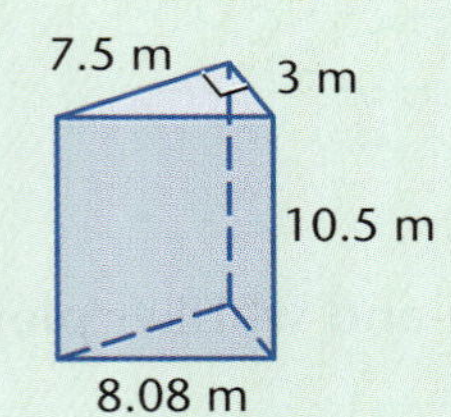

4.

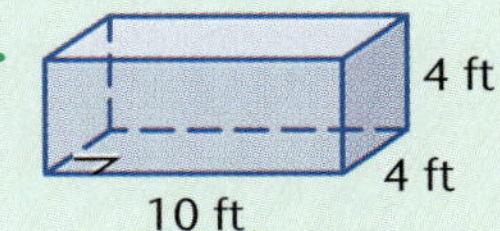

5.

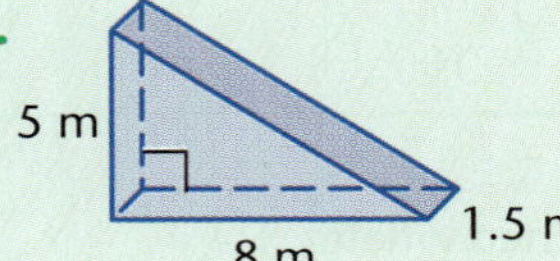

6.

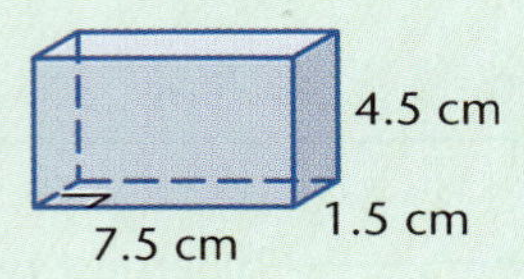

Replace each ? with the number that makes the statement true.

7. 12 kg = __?__ g

8. 3.5 kL = __?__ mL

9. 47 mL = __?__ cm^3

10. 14 L = __?__ mL

11. 77 g = __?__ kg

12. 94 L = __?__ kL

This network shows approximate road distances in kilometers between some cities in India.

13. Find the length of the route from Jodhpur to Calcutta that goes through Jaipur, Kanpur, and Patna.

14. Find the length of the route Ahmadabad–Jodhpur–Jaipur–New Delhi.

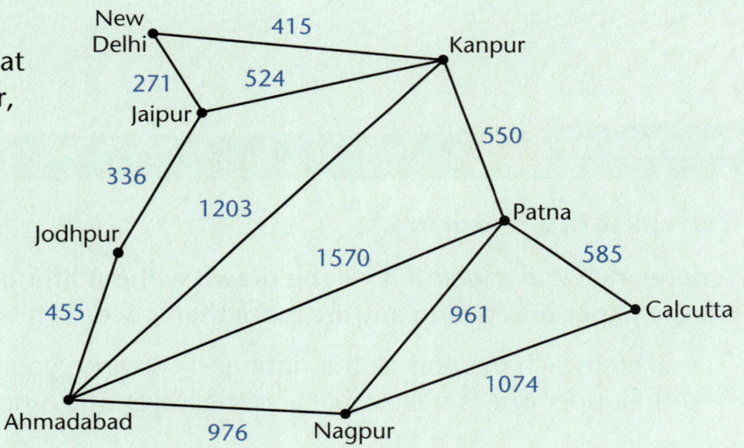

Standardized Testing ▸ Open-ended

Draw a prism and label the dimensions in metric units. If you filled your prism with water, what would be the mass of the water?

Wild Wings

You have constructed two gliders and developed a test to decide which flies better. Now you'll compare some of the physical traits of the gliders and make recommendations to build a better glider.

1. the exterior surface area
2. the weight
3. the sail loading

6 Make a table that displays the information on the notebook for each Wild Wing.

7 Suppose both Wild Wings had a top and a bottom base.

a. Place the small Wild Wing inside the large one. How many small Wild Wings can fit in the large one?

b. What is the volume of each Wild Wing? How many times larger is the large Wild Wing than the small one?

8 **Try This as a Class** In what ways is the larger Wild Wing like the small one? In what ways is it different?

9 Form a discussion group with three other students. Meet with them to discuss your findings and answer the following questions.

a. Which Wild Wing flew better? How did your test prove this?

b. If you wanted to create a better Wild Wing, how would you change the surface area or weight?

c. What other design changes would you make?

MODULE 6 Review and Assessment

You will need: • *metric ruler* (Ex. 13)

Write and graph inequalities to represent each situation. (Sec. 1, Explor. 1)

1. In a recent year, about 50% of airplane captains earned from \$7514 to \$11,267 each month.
2. In a recent year, about 44% of flight attendants worked at least 80 hours but less than 85 hours each month.

The dimensions of the parallelograms and triangles in the kite are in feet.

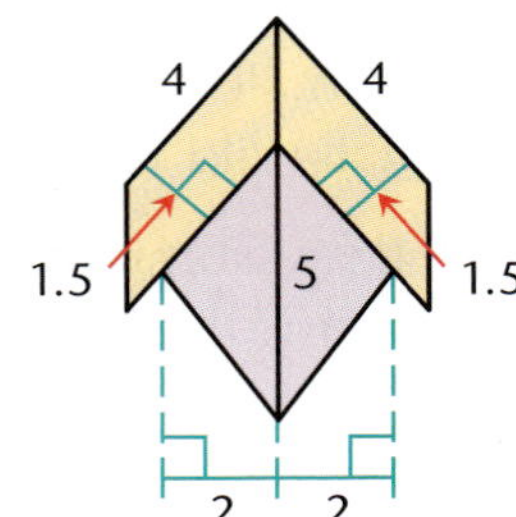

3. Find the area of the kite. (Sec. 1, Explor. 2)
4. Find the probability that a raindrop that falls on the kite hits one of the gold parallelogram regions. (Sec. 1, Explor. 3)

Find each square root. If the square root is not an integer, estimate it to the nearest tenth. (Sec. 2, Explor. 1)

5. $\sqrt{121}$
6. $\sqrt{20}$
7. $\sqrt{175}$

Use the triangular prism shown for Exercises 8 and 9. (Sec. 2, Explor. 2)

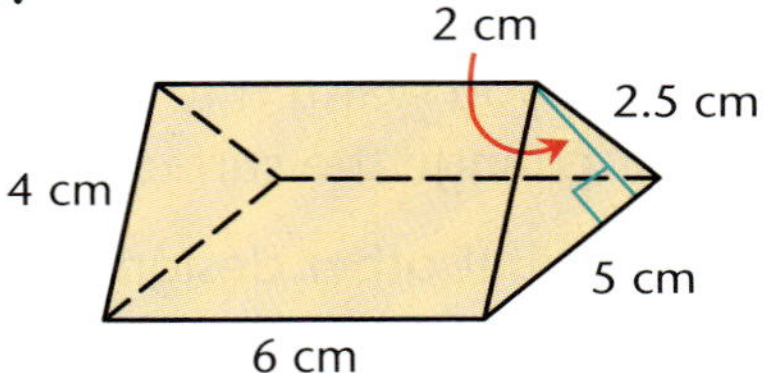

8. Sketch a net for the prism. Label the dimensions of each face.
9. Find the surface area of the triangular prism.

Find the exact area of each circle. Then use 3.14 for π to find the approximate area. (Sec. 2, Explor. 3)

10. 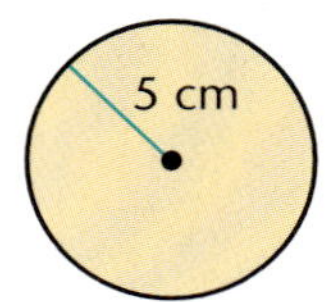

11. 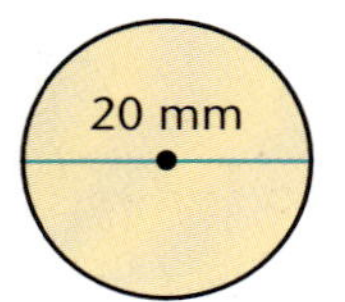

12. 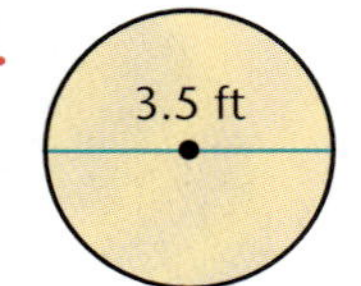

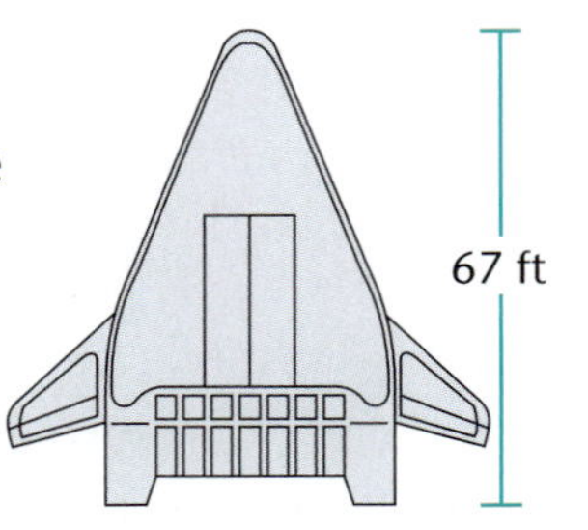

13. The figure at the right is a scale drawing of a prototype space shuttle. The actual height of the proposed shuttle is 67 ft. (Sec. 3, Explor. 1)
    a. Measure the height of the drawing in millimeters. What is the scale of the drawing?
    b. Estimate the wingspan of the proposed shuttle.

14. Quadrilateral *ABCD* is similar to quadrilateral *FEHG*. Find the measures of all the unlabeled segments and angles. (Sec. 3, Explor. 2)

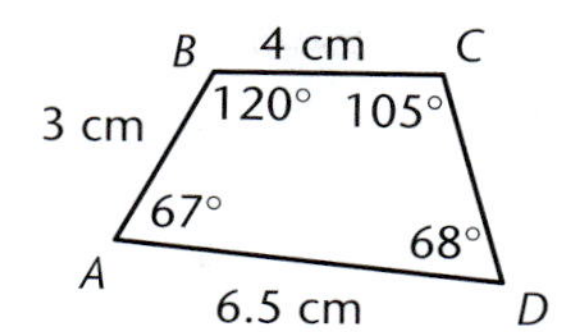

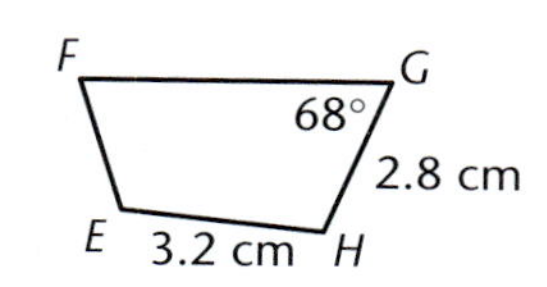

15. Lines *m* and *n* are parallel. Find the measures of angles 1, 2, 3, 4, 5, 6, and 7. (Sec. 4, Explor. 1)

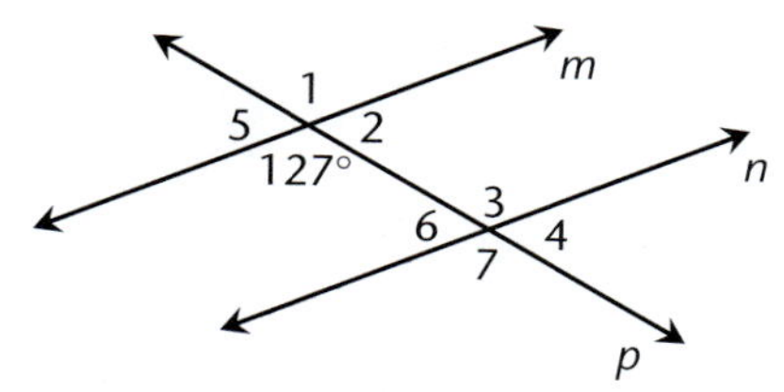

The measures of two of the angles of a triangle are given. Find the measure of the third angle of each triangle and tell whether the triangle is *acute, obtuse,* or *right.* (Sec. 4, Explor. 2)

16. 18° and 72°

17. 22° and 63°

18. 37° and 58°

Use the prism for Exercises 19 and 20. (Sec. 5, Explor. 1)

19. What is the volume of the prism in cubic centimeters?

20. What is the capacity of the prism in milliliters? in liters?

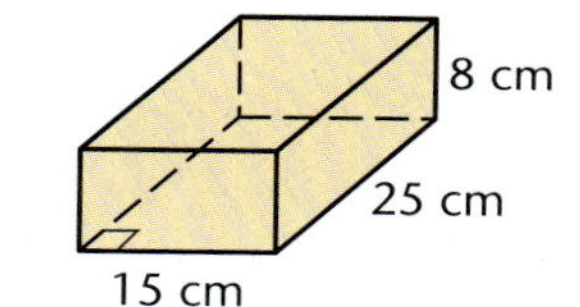

Replace each ? with the number that makes the statement true. (Sec. 5, Explor. 2)

21. 2345 mL = ? L

22. 0.75 L = ? mL

23. 4 g = ? kg

For Exercises 24–26, use the network below, which shows driving distances in miles between five cities. (Sec. 5, Explor. 3)

24. Which cities shown are connected directly to Portland?

25. How long is the Portland–Seattle–Spokane route?

26. Find a route from Portland to Spokane that is shorter than the route in Exercise 25.

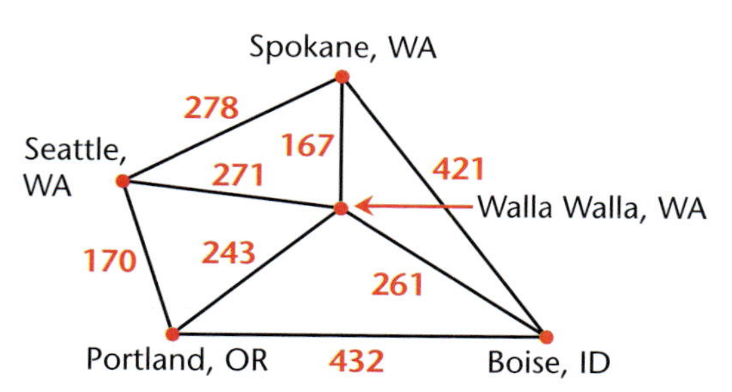

Reflecting on the Module

27. **Writing** Write a description of how you would find the surface area and volume of a piece of furniture in your classroom. Include a sketch of the piece of furniture.

HEALTH and FITNESS

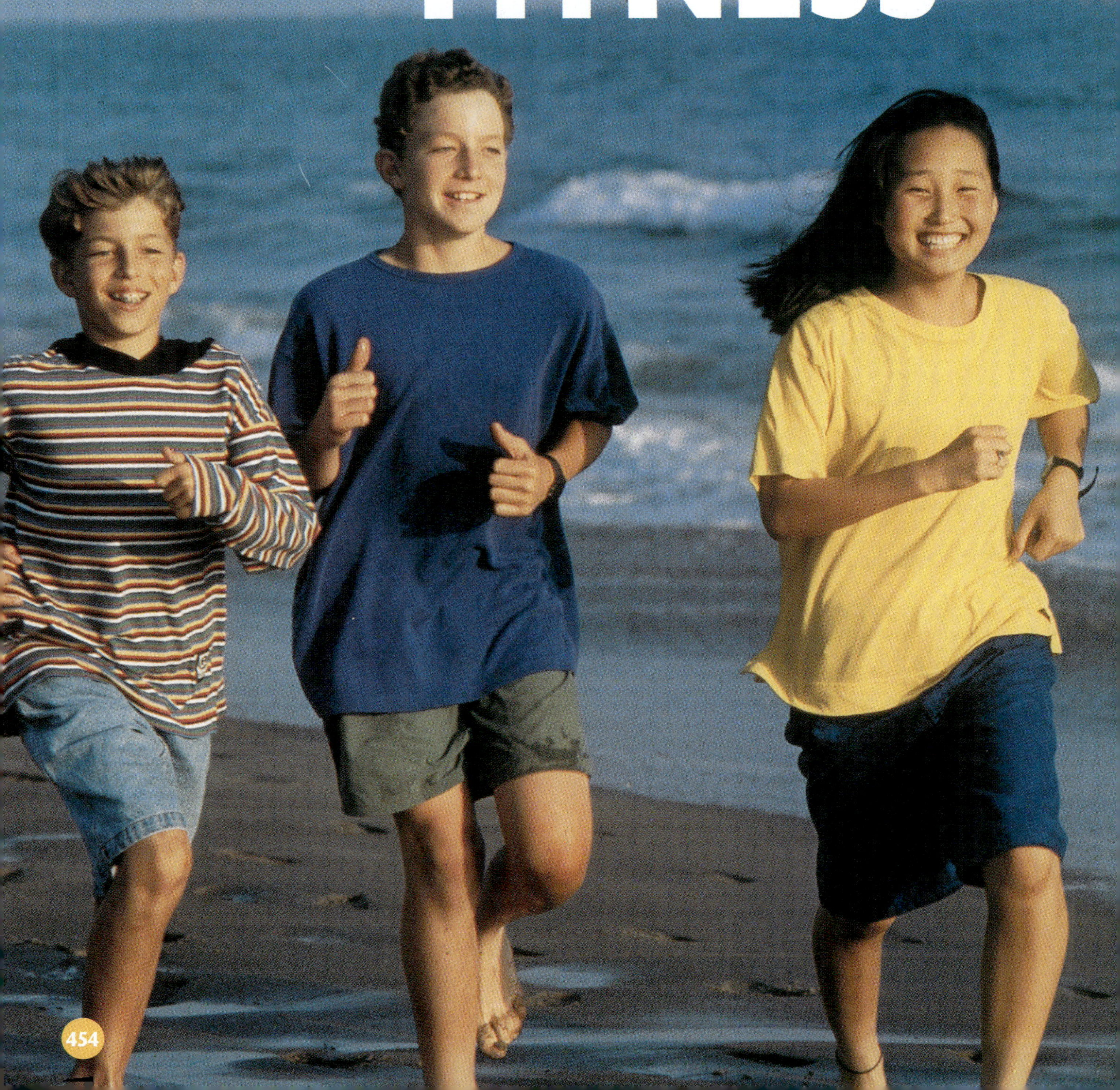

CONNECTING MATHEMATICS & The Theme

SECTION OVERVIEW

1 Cylinders and Graphs
As you investigate Calorie use:
- Find the volumes of cylinders
- Find slopes and graph formulas
- Recognize misleading graphs

2 Percent Equations
As you study heart rate data:
- Use percents greater than 100%
- Find percent of change

3 Customary Capacity and Inequalities
As you interpret nutrition labels on food products:
- Convert customary units of capacity
- Write and solve inequalities
- Make box-and-whisker plots

4 Circle Graphs, and Choosing a Graph
As you examine sleeping habits and the importance of rest:
- Make circle graphs
- Choose an appropriate graph to display data

5 Quadrilaterals
As you analyze the USDA Food Guide Pyramid:
- Classify quadrilaterals
- Find the areas of trapezoids

The Module Project

The Picture of Health

How can you inform people about a health issue that affects their lives? You'll research the statistics on a health or fitness issue and make colorful, eye-catching visual displays that get across your message.

More on the Module Project
See pp. 469, 510, and 523.

INTERNET
To learn more about the theme:
http://www.mlmath.com

Section 1 Cylinders and Graphs

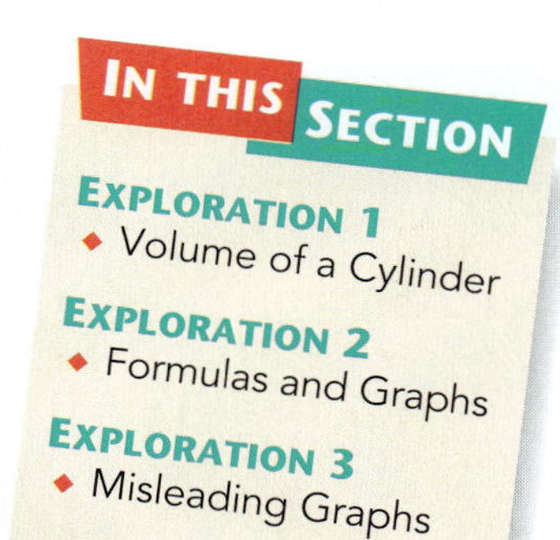

BURNING CALORIES

Setting the Stage

In this module, you'll learn about nutrition and other health- and fitness-related topics. The mathematics you learn will help you make the best choices for your own well-being.

Exercise is a great way to burn excess energy and to relieve stress. You may be surprised to learn that a 100 lb person burns 11.4 Calories while sitting and talking for 10 min. That same person would burn 45.5 Calories in 10 min of playing basketball.

Think About It

1. About how many times as many Calories does a person burn playing basketball instead of sitting and talking about it?

2. Which of the exercises shown do you think burns the most Calories?

SWIMMING

PLAYING BASKETBALL

WALKING UP STAIRS

WALKING DOWN STAIRS

▶ **In this section you'll explore what a Calorie is and determine which of the exercises above burn the most Calories.**

Exploration 1

VOLUME of a CYLINDER

GOAL

LEARN HOW TO...
- find the volume of a cylinder

AS YOU...
- explore the meaning of Calorie

KEY TERM
- cylinder

You have probably heard the word *Calorie* many times, but what is a Calorie? Technicians determine the number of Calories in a food by burning the food and measuring how much heat it generates. The experiment below may help you understand.

First water is placed in a pot and its temperature is recorded.

Then the water temperature is recorded again after the peanut has been burned.

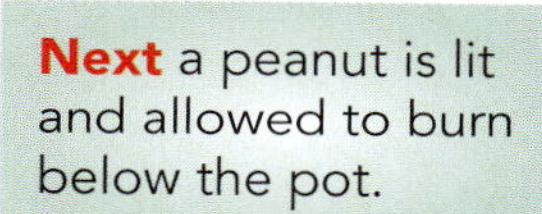

Next a peanut is lit and allowed to burn below the pot.

3 Discussion One Calorie (1 Cal) is the amount of heat required to raise the temperature of 1 L of water one degree Celsius (1°C).

a. How many Calories does it take to raise the temperature of 1 L of water 3°C**?** of 3 L of water 1°C**?**

b. Suppose your class burned a peanut as shown above, and the temperature of the water was recorded before and after the peanut was burned. What do you need to know to determine the number of Calories in the peanut**?**

▶ **The container used in the experiment is a circular *cylinder*. A circular cylinder is a space figure with two congruent parallel circular bases. In this book, all the cylinders are circular cylinders.**

To find the volume of a cylinder, you can use the same formula you use to find the volume of a prism.

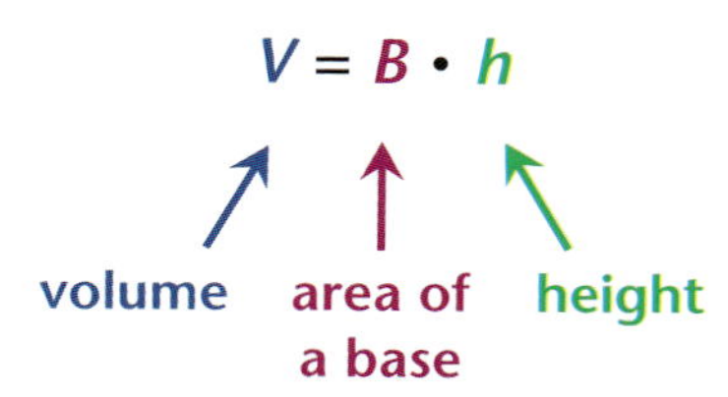

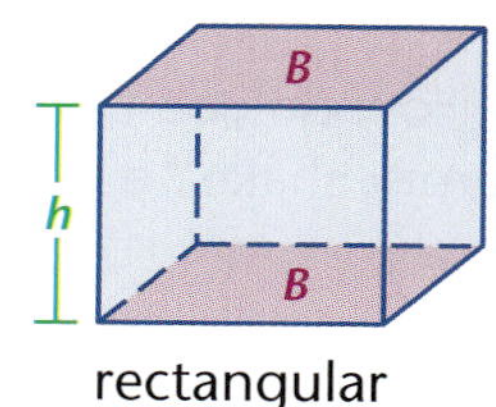

rectangular prism

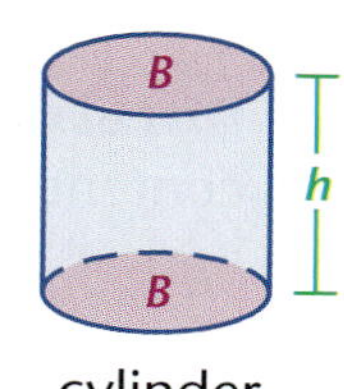

cylinder

▶ **To find the volume of a cylinder, you first need to find the area of its base.**

4

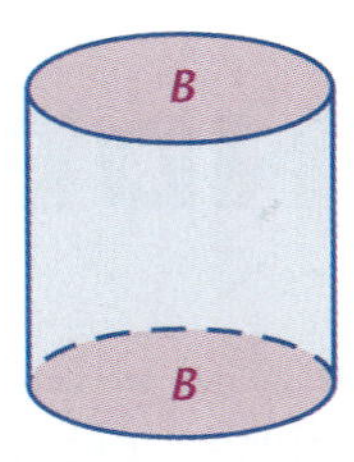

a. Write an equation you can use to find the **area of a base** of a cylinder.

b. Rewrite the equation for the volume of a cylinder, $V = Bh$, using your answer in part (a).

c. What measurements do you need to know before you can find the volume of a cylinder?

FOR◀HELP
with *metric units of volume and capacity*, see
MODULE 6, p. 445

5 Suppose a class used the cylinder shown to perform the Calorie experiment.

14 cm

6.5 cm

a. Find the volume of the water in the container to the nearest cubic centimeter (cm^3). Use 3.14 for π.

b. One cubic centimeter holds one milliliter of water. How many milliliters of water are in the container? How many liters?

c. Suppose that before the experiment was performed, the temperature of the water was 25°C. After the peanut was burned, the temperature of the water was 29.5°C. According to the definition of Calorie, how many Calories did the peanut contain?

...checks that you can find the volume of a cylinder.

6 ✓ **CHECKPOINT** Suppose a class planned to conduct the Calorie experiment. Choose the letter of each cylinder below that they could use to hold 1 L of water. Explain your choice.

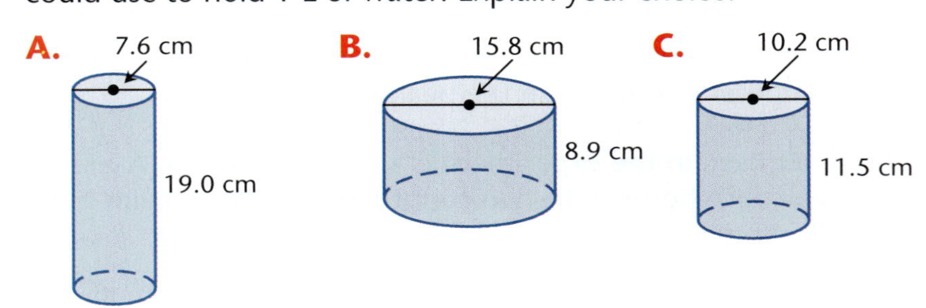

7 **Discussion** How do you think technicians determine the Calorie content of a milk shake? a celery stalk? a bowl of soup?

HOMEWORK EXERCISES ▶ See Exs. 1–8 on pp. 465–466.

Exploration 2

Formulas AND Graphs

SET UP *You will need graph paper.*

GOAL

LEARN HOW TO...
- choose a scale for a graph
- use formulas to find values and make graphs
- find the slope of a line

AS YOU...
- investigate the number of Calories burned during exercise

KEY TERMS
- scale
- rise
- run
- slope

▶ **In Exploration 1 you investigated the Calorie content of food. In this exploration you'll examine the number of Calories burned during exercise.**

For any exercise, the actual number of Calories burned depends on body weight. The formula below gives a good estimate of the number of Calories most people burn playing 10 min of basketball.

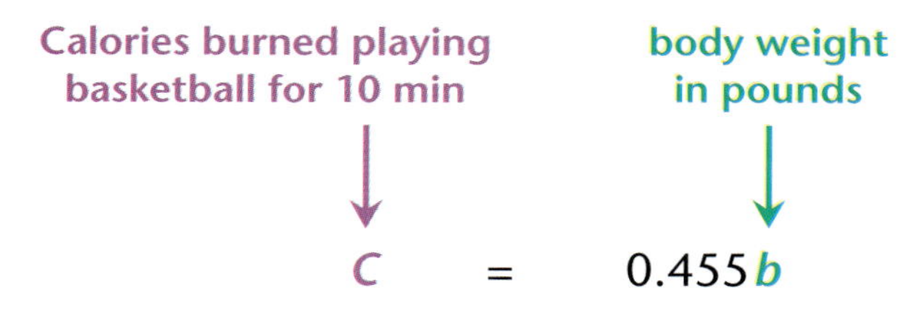

$$C = 0.455b$$

8 Copy and complete the table. For each body weight b in pounds, find the number of Calories C burned in 10 min of basketball playing.

b	C
100	?
150	?
175	?
200	?

▶ **The relationship between body weight and Calories burned can be shown with a graph.**

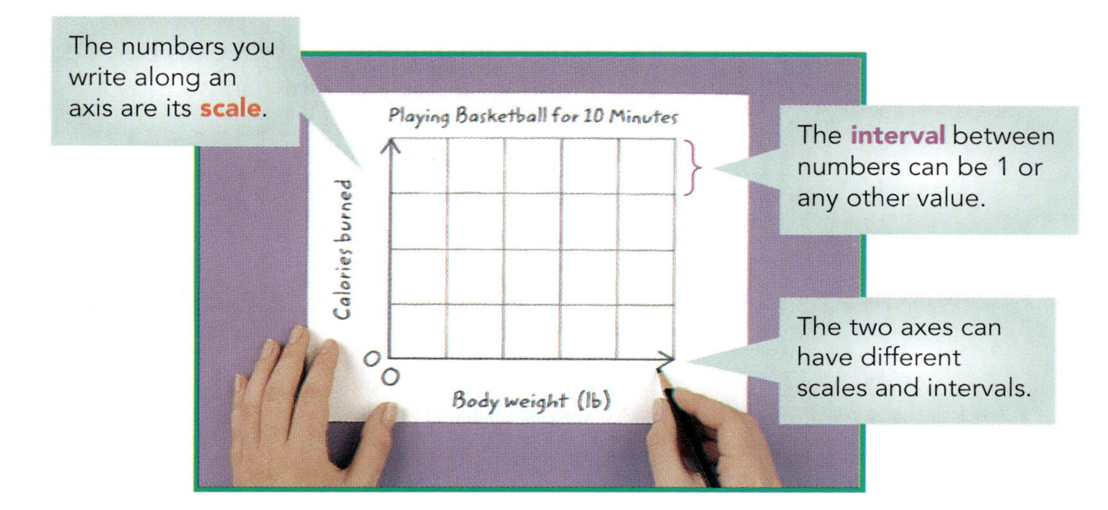

9 **Try This as a Class** Use the table of values you made in Question 8.

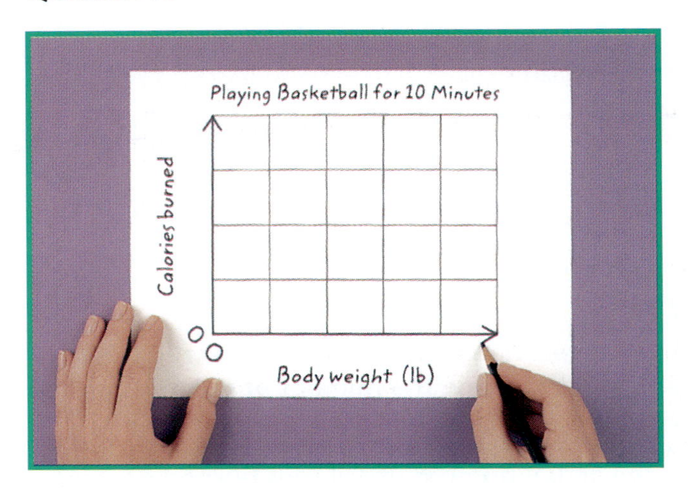

a. Look at the graph. What data will the horizontal axis show?

b. What are some reasonable values to include on the horizontal axis of your graph?

c. Look at the body weights in your data table. Use the maximum and minimum values and your answer to part (b) to decide what values should be on the horizontal axis.

d. What interval should you use on the horizontal axis?

e. Graph the data from your table on graph paper.

f. Connect the points on your graph. What do you notice?

▶ **You can use the coordinate plane from Question 9 to graph the formula for the Calories burned in 10 min of swimming.**

10 The formula $C = 0.606b$ gives the number C of Calories burned during 10 min of swimming for a body weight b in pounds.

a. Make a table of values for this equation.

b. Plot your points on the graph and connect them. Write a title above your graph that describes both sets of data.

11 **a.** How many Calories does an 80 lb person burn playing basketball for 10 min? swimming for 10 min?

b. How many Calories does a 220 lb person burn playing basketball for 10 min? swimming for 10 min?

12 The graph at the right shows the number of Calories burned by swimming for 10 min.

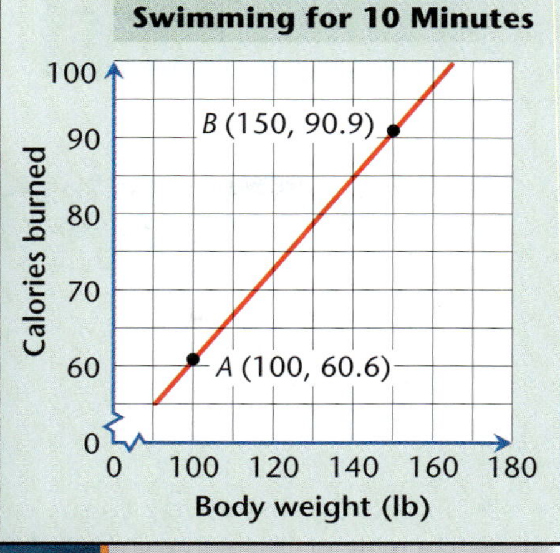

a. What is the number of Calories burned at point *A*? point *B*?

b. What is the change in the Calories burned between points *A* and *B*? This is the **rise**. Why do you think it is called the rise?

c. What is the weight at point *A*? at point *B*?

d. What is the change in weight between points *A* and *B*? This is the **run**.

e. The **slope** of the line is the ratio of the rise to the run. What is the slope of the line for swimming?

f. Why do you think points *A* and *B* were chosen rather than other points on the line?

13 ✓ **CHECKPOINT** Use the graph you made in Question 9 showing the number of Calories burned playing basketball. Find the slope of the line.

✓ **QUESTION 13**

...checks that you can find the slope of a line.

14 **Discussion** Use your answers to Questions 12 and 13.

a. How can the slopes of the swimming and basketball lines help you decide which exercise burns more Calories?

b. The slope of the line for watching TV for 10 min is 0.076. Is this slope *greater than* or *less than* the slope for swimming? for playing basketball?

c. What do you think the line for watching TV would look like on your graph?

HOMEWORK EXERCISES See Exs. 9–20 on pp. 466–467.

GOAL

LEARN HOW TO...
- determine how the scale affects the appearance of a graph

AS YOU...
- identify misleading graphs

Exploration 3

MISLEADING Graphs

SET UP *You will need:* • *Labsheet 1A* • *graph paper*

▶ **If you do not study them carefully, graphs can be misleading. For example, if you want to burn the most Calories, should you walk up stairs or down them? The graphs below seem to show that it does not make very much difference.**

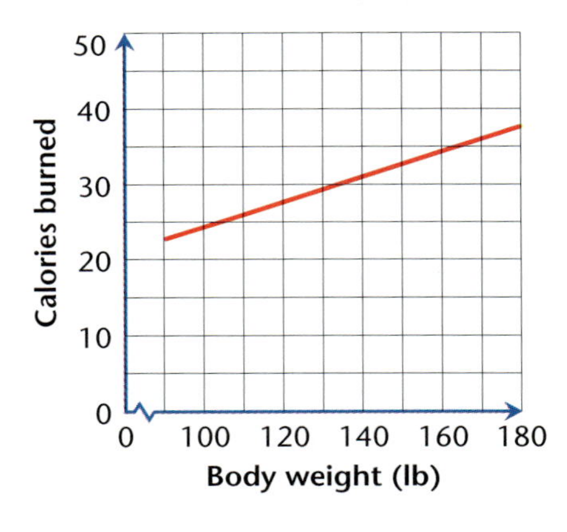

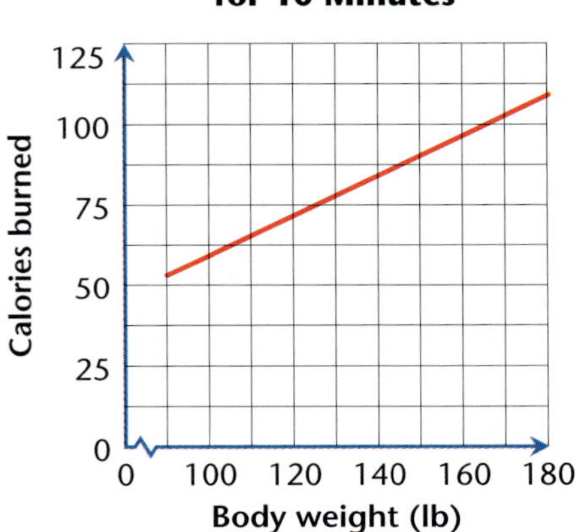

15 **a.** How many Calories does a 170 lb person burn walking up stairs for 10 min? down stairs for 10 min?

b. Does a 170 lb person burn more Calories walking up stairs or down stairs?

16 **Discussion** Look at the scale on the vertical axis of each graph.

a. How are the scales different?

b. How does the interval chosen affect the steepness of the line on a graph?

c. Estimate the slope of each line. Does the slope tell you which type of exercise burns more Calories? Explain.

▶ **Changes in the horizontal scale can also affect the look of a graph.**

17 The graph at the right shows the relationship between body weight and Calories burned while reading.

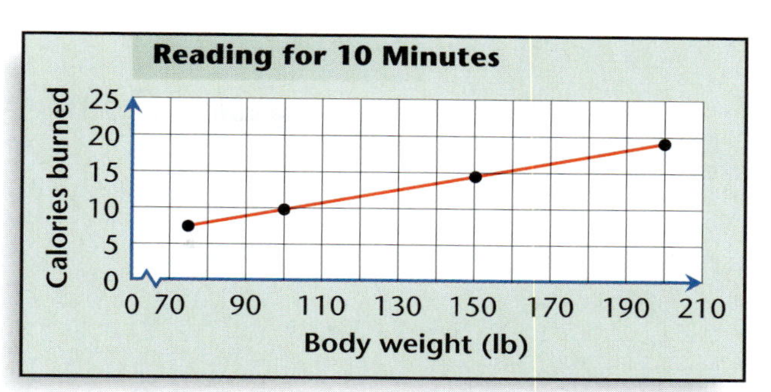

a. Suppose each interval on the horizontal scale were changed to represent 20 lb instead of 10 lb. About how much shorter would the horizontal axis be?

Predict how a scale change from 10 lb to 20 lb intervals would affect the line on the graph.

b. Suppose each interval on the horizontal scale were changed to represent 5 lb instead of 10 lb. Predict how that scale change would affect the line on the graph.

c. **Use Labsheet 1A.** Make two graphs of the data, *Changing the Horizontal Scale* to 20 lb and to 5 lb intervals. How accurate were the predictions you made in parts (a) and (b)?

▶ **You just saw how changing the scale on a graph can make the data look different, but there are other ways that graphs can be misleading. The graph below compares the numbers of Calories in different juices.**

18 Prune juice has about twice as many Calories as the same amount of grapefruit juice. Grapefruit juice has about 80% of the Calories as the same amount of apple juice.

a. How are the relationships among the Calorie contents of prune, grapefruit, and apple juice shown on the graph?

b. In the graph, each can is drawn 21 mm high. The widths of the drawings for prune, apple, and grapefruit are 32 mm, 20 mm, and 16 mm, respectively. Find the volume of each can in the graph.

c. **Discussion** Do you think this graph accurately shows how the Calorie contents of the juices compare? Explain.

HOMEWORK EXERCISES ▶ See Exs. 21–22 on p. 467.

Section 1 Key Concepts

Key Terms

cylinder

Volume of a Cylinder
(pp. 457–458)

To find the volume of a cylinder, multiply the area of the base by the height.

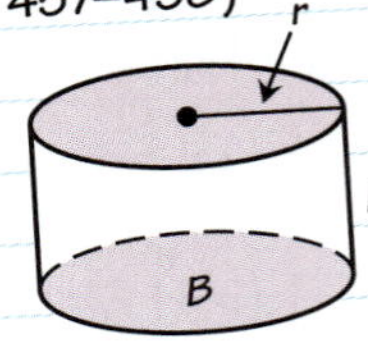

area of the base of a cylinder

$V = Bh = \pi r^2 h$

scale

Choosing a Scale for a Graph
(pp. 459–460)

The numbers written along an axis of a graph are its scale. Usually, the maximum and minimum data values determine the range of the scale. The size of the interval depends on how spread out the data are.

slope

rise

run

Finding the Slope of a Line
(p. 461)

The slope of a line is the ratio of the rise to the run.

Example

Find the slope of the line on the graph.

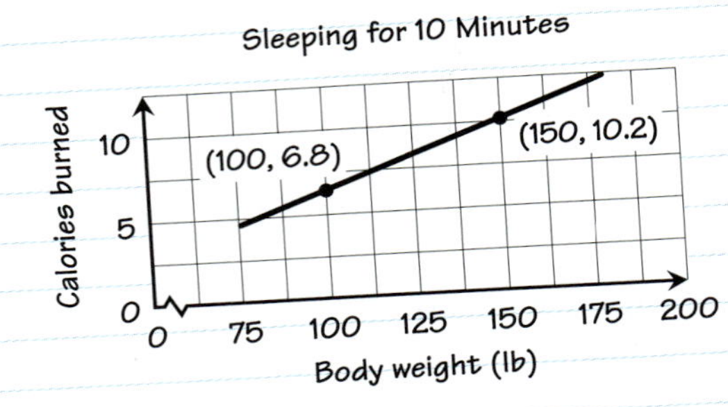

A 100 lb person burns 6.8 Cal while sleeping 10 min.
A 150 lb person burns 10.2 Cal while sleeping 10 min.

$$\text{slope} = \frac{\text{rise}}{\text{run}} = \frac{\text{change in the number of Calories}}{\text{change in body weight}} = \frac{10.2 - 6.8}{150 - 100} = \frac{3.4}{50} = 0.068$$

Key Concepts Questions

19 A cylinder has a radius of 4 cm and a volume of 402 cm^3. What is the height of the cylinder? Round your answer to the nearest centimeter.

20 Find the slope of a line with each rise and run.

a. rise 4
run 4

b. rise 6
run 2

c. rise 3
run 1

d. rise 1
run 3

Section 1 Key Concepts

Misleading Graphs (pp. 462–463)

The scales chosen for a graph will affect the way the data appear.

Example The graphs show the numbers of Calories from two nutrients.

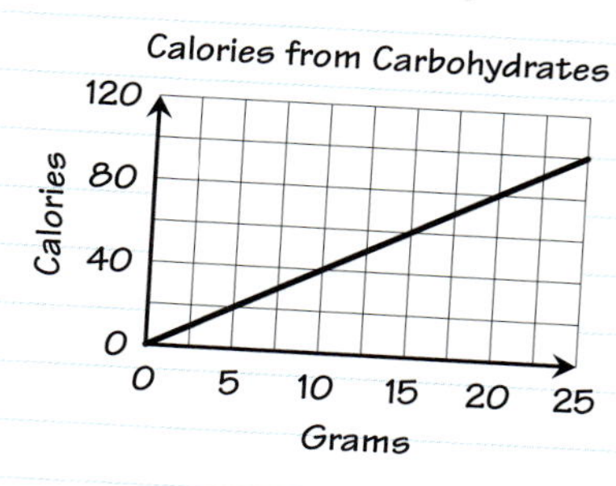

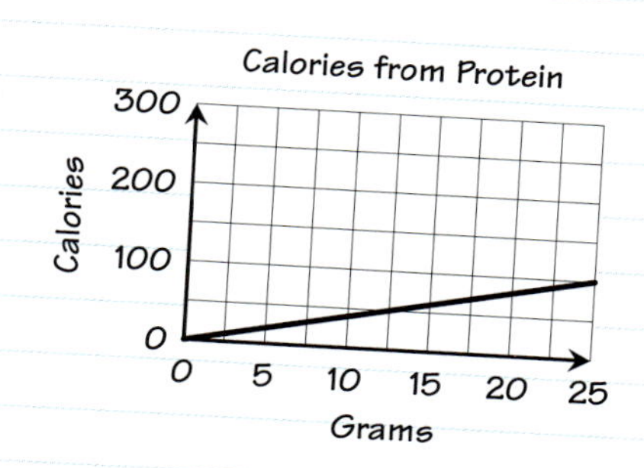

Key Concepts Question

21 **a.** Compare the graphs in the Example above. Why are the graphs misleading?

b. How should you change the scales on the graphs to better represent the data?

Section 1 Practice & Application Exercises

YOU WILL NEED

For Exs. 9–11, 20, 21:
- graph paper

For Exercises 1–8, use 3.14 or the π key on a calculator. Round each answer to the nearest hundredth.

Find the volume of each cylinder.

1. 3 ft, 4.5 ft

2. 28 m, Area of base = 154 m^2

3. 1 cm, 22 cm

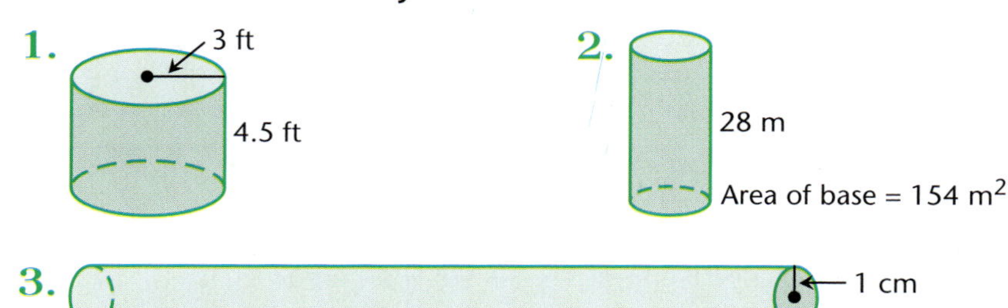

4. Suppose a 5 in. long section of pipe has an inside diameter of 1 in.

   a. What is the volume of the pipe section?

   b. **Challenge** Will a 2 in. diameter pipe section with the same length hold twice as much liquid? Explain.

Find the unknown measure for each cylinder.

5. $r = 2$ in., $h = 3$ in., $V \approx$ _?_ in.^{3}

6. $B = 5$ in.^{2}, $h =$ _?_ in., $V = 40$ in.^{3}

7. $B =$ _?_ ft^2, $h = 3$ ft, $V = 48$ ft^3

8. $r \approx$ _?_ cm, $h = 4$ cm, $V \approx 12.56$ cm^3

9. The number of Calories burned in 10 min of studying can be described by the formula $C = 0.136b$, where C is Calories and b is body weight in pounds.

   a. Make a table of values for the numbers of Calories burned by 75 lb, 100 lb, 150 lb, and 200 lb people in 10 min of studying.

   b. Plot the data points and connect them.

   c. Find the slope of the line in part (b).

   d. Estimate how many Calories you burn in 10 min of studying.

10. **Insects** A mosquito completes about 600 up-and-down wing beats in 1 s of flight.

    a. Suppose you make a graph with numbers of wing beats on the vertical axis and numbers of seconds on the horizontal axis. What scale would you use for each axis? Explain.

    b. Draw and label a graph of the data.

11. **Exercise** Use the table below.

Numbers of Calories Burned in 10 min Periods of Activity

Activity	Body Weight			
	75 lb	100 lb	150 lb	200 lb
	5.1 Cal	6.8 Cal	10.2 Cal	13.6 Cal
	14.2 Cal	18.9 Cal	28.4 Cal	37.8 Cal

    a. What scales would you use to make graphs relating body weights and Calories burned for each activity?

    b. Make a graph for each activity on a separate coordinate plane.

Find the slope of each line.

12.

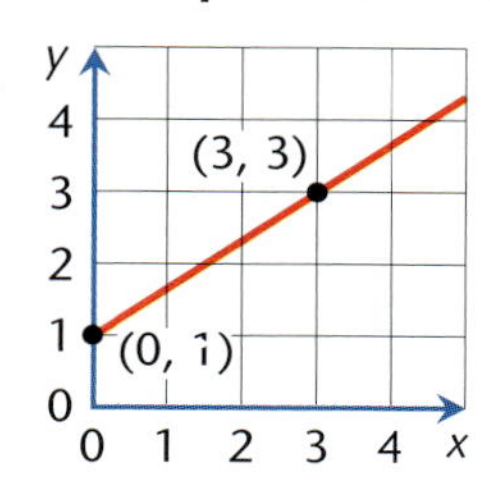

13.

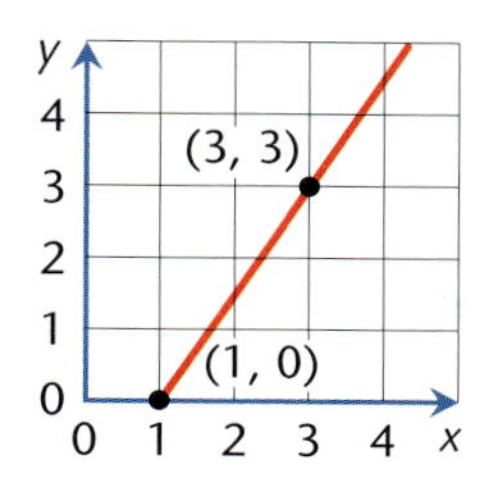

14.

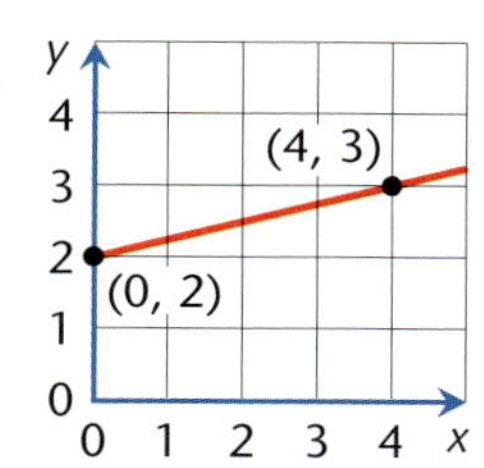

15.

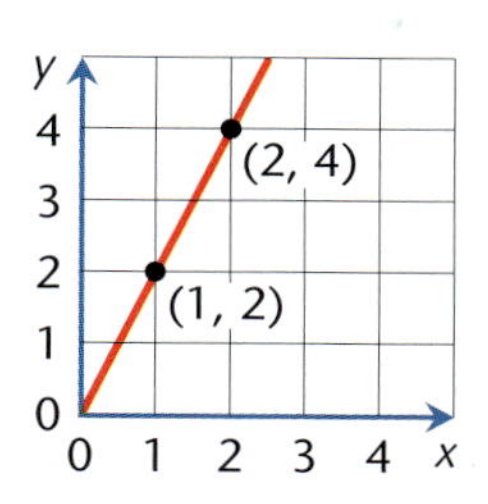

Find the slope of a line with each rise and run.

16. rise 9
run 3

17. rise 10
run 5

18. rise 5
run 10

19. rise 5
run 5

20. **Writing** On graph paper, sketch a line with each slope in Exercises 16–19. How does a line with a slope greater than 1 compare with a line with a slope less than 1?

21. The data in the table show the populations of people, cats, and dogs in the United States in 1996. The data were used to make the graph shown.

a. Does the graph use height or area to represent the populations?

b. Explain why the graph is misleading.

c. Make a different graph that is not misleading.

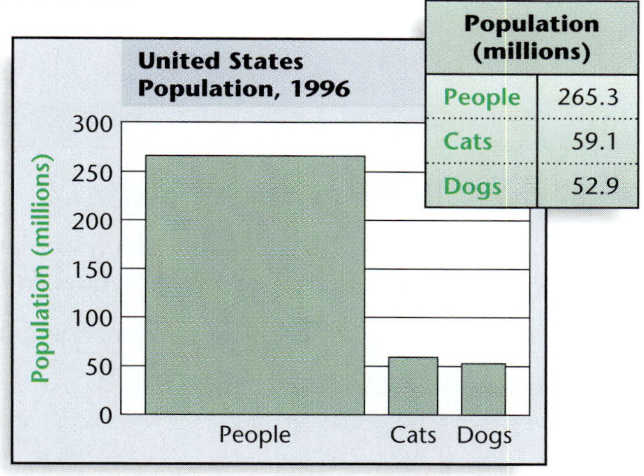

	Population (millions)
People	265.3
Cats	59.1
Dogs	52.9

Reflecting on the Section

22. Find a graph in a newspaper or magazine. Is the graph effective? Is it accurate? Could it be considered misleading? Explain your answers.

RESEARCH

Exercise 22 checks that you can evaluate the effectiveness of graphs.

Spiral Review

Find the volume of each prism. (Module 6, p. 445)

23. 3 cm, 4 cm, 4 cm

24. 8 in., 6 in., 9 in.

25. 18 cm, 13.5 cm, 18 cm

For each spinner, find the theoretical probability that the pointer will land on the number shown. (Module 1, p. 33)

26.

27.

28. Suppose each spinner above is spun 100 times. For each spinner, about how many times do you expect the outcome to be "2"?

Write each ratio in percent form. (Module 5, p. 366)

29. 4 : 100 **30.** 8 : 50 **31.** 13 : 20 **32.** 48 : 200

Extension

Negative, Zero, and Undefined Slopes

In this section, the slopes of the lines were always greater than 0. There are also lines with slopes that are less than 0, equal to 0, or undefined.

33. a. For each graph below, find the slope of the line.

Graph A

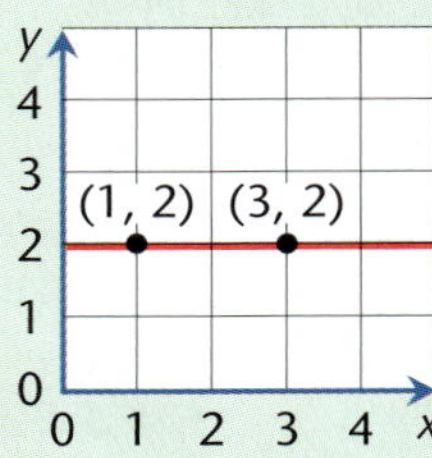

Graph B

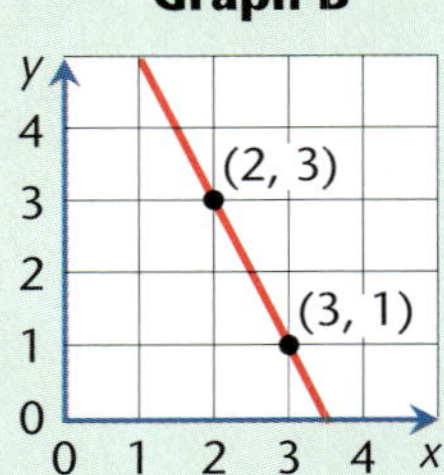

Graph C

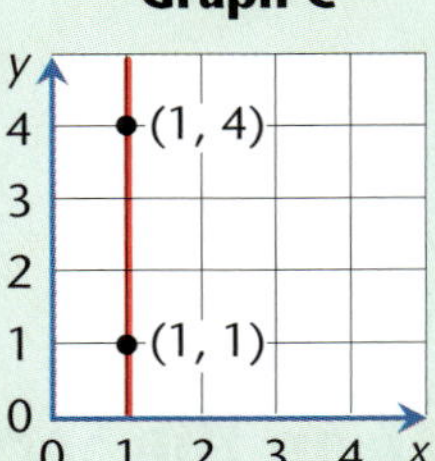

b. Explain why the slope of the line on Graph C is *undefined*.

c. Explain how a line with a negative slope looks different from a line with a positive slope.

The Picture of Health

SET UP *You will need Project Labsheet A.*

Visual displays help people understand and remember facts or data. In this module you'll learn new ways to graph data, when it is appropriate to use a graph, and how a graph can be misleading. At the end of the module, you'll make a graph to help people understand a health or fitness issue.

Choosing a Data Display Two important features of any data display are its visual appeal and how well it represents the data.

Use Project Labsheet A for Project Questions 1 and 2.

Look at the *Three Bicycle Riding Graphs*. Which graph gets your attention? Why?

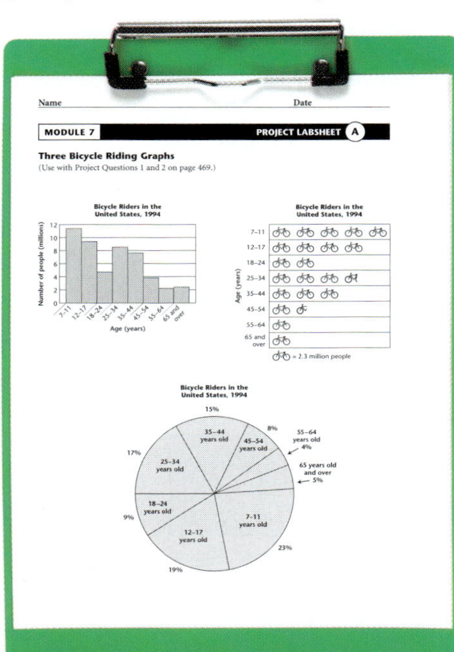

Name ____________ Date ____________

MODULE 7 **PROJECT LABSHEET A**

Three Bicycle Riding Graphs

(Use with Project Questions 1 and 2 on page 469.)

a. Which graph do you think best shows how the number of people who ride bicycles varies among different age groups?

b. Is the number of 12–17 year olds and 25–34 year olds who ride bicycles about the same? Which graph would you use to support your answer? Why?

At the end of this module, you'll make your own graph about a health or fitness issue. Think of a health or fitness issue that would be interesting to middle school students. Then begin looking for data for your graph.

Section 1 Extra Skill Practice

Find the unknown measure for each cylinder. Use 3.14 or the π key on a calculator.

1. $r = 3$ yd, $h = 2$ yd, $V \approx$ __?__ yd^3
2. $r \approx$ __?__ cm, $h = 5$ cm, $V \approx 62.8\ \text{cm}^3$

Find the slope of a line with each rise and run.

3. rise 2, run 2
4. rise 5, run 10
5. rise 3, run 4
6. rise 3, run 1
7. rise 12, run 6

Use the graphs for Exercises 8 and 9.

8. About how many Calories does a 100 lb person burn in 10 min while reading? while dancing?

9. Are these graphs misleading? If they are, explain why and redraw them so that they are not misleading.

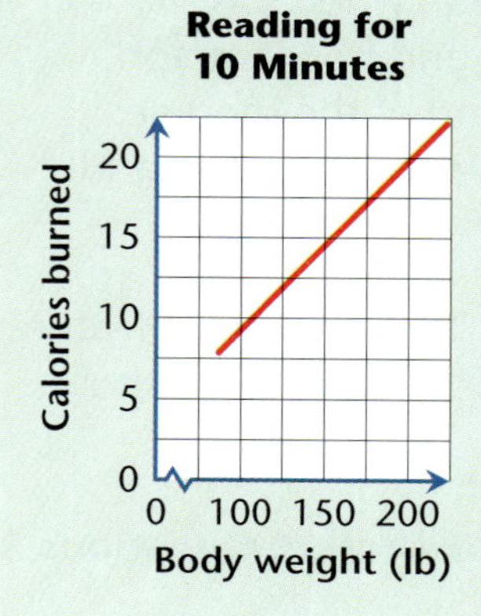

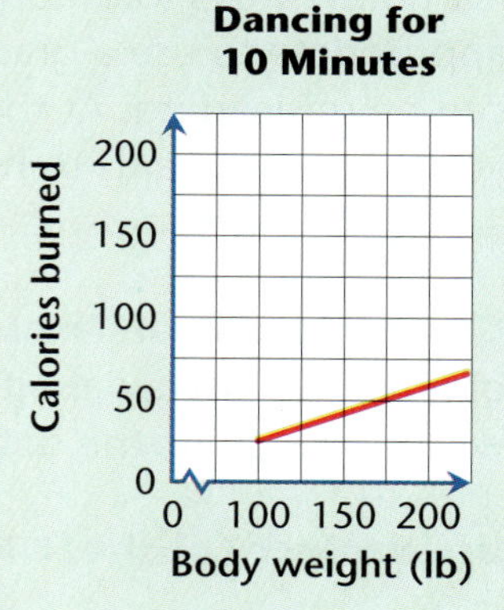

Study Skills ▸ Using Graphic Organizers

A *graphic organizer* is a visual display that can help you relate ideas and organize information. A flow chart illustrates a sequence of steps.

1. a. Describe the steps of the process shown in the flow chart below.
   b. Describe what happens when $x = 9$.

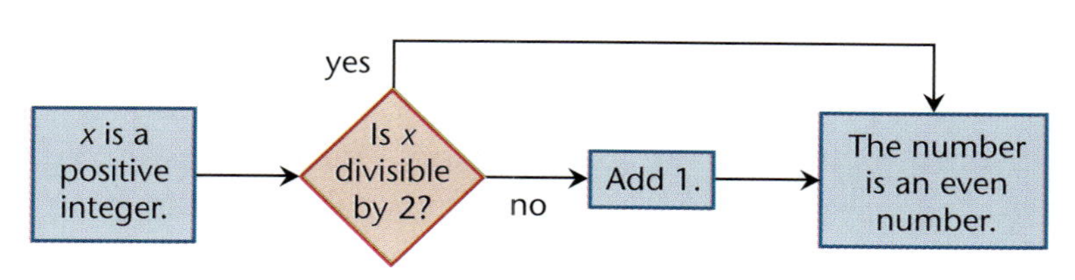

2. Think of a process that involves following steps in order. Draw a flow chart to illustrate this process.

Section 2 Percent Equations

IN THIS SECTION

EXPLORATION 1
- Percents Greater than 100%

EXPLORATION 2
- Percent of Change

HEART RATES

Setting the Stage

The reading below from James Ramsey Ullman's *Banner in the Sky* describes part of 16-year-old Rudi Matt's first climb as a member of a mountain climbing team in the Alps.

BANNER IN THE SKY *by James Ramsey Ullman*

He moved from the broad ledge to the narrow one. . . . He took a careful step—a second step—a third. One more would bring him to the jutting platform. But before he could take it there was a soft tremor beneath his feet. One moment, his footing was a seemingly solid band of mountain granite; in the next, it was a crumbling mass of loose fragments. With a violent leap he thrust himself clear, lunged forward and landed on the platform, and in the same instant, behind him, the whole ledge on which he had been standing disintegrated and plunged in spinning fragments into space below.

For perhaps a minute he stood motionless. Leaning in against the rock, he struggled to control the rasp of his breathing and the pounding of his heart. Then, when he had half succeeded, he turned and took stock of his position.

Think About It

1. What does it mean to have a pounding heart? Why do you think Rudi's heart was pounding?

2. Describe the changes in Rudi's heart rate during the time covered in the reading.

GOAL

LEARN HOW TO...
- find percents greater than 100%

AS YOU...
- compare your resting and active heart rates

Exploration 1

PERCENTS GREATER THAN 100%

SET UP *You will need:* • *Labsheet 2A* • *watch or clock with a second hand*

Have you ever wondered how much your heart rate increases when you climb stairs, run for the bus, or watch an exciting movie? Before you can calculate the change in your heart rate, you need to measure your resting heart rate while sitting still.

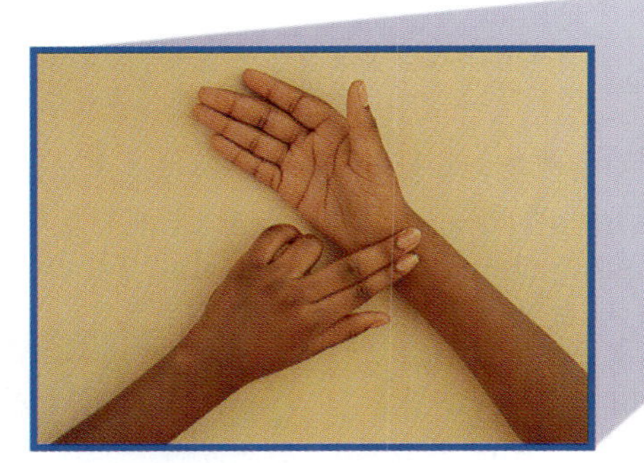

You can feel the action of your beating heart at pulse points where the arteries come close to the skin. This is why we use the pulse to measure heart rate.

3 Place the index and middle finger of one hand so that you can feel your pulse in your wrist. Count how many times your heart beats for each number of seconds. Record each count.

a. 6 s **b.** 10 s **c.** 20 s

4 Rewrite each count in Question 3 as a rate in beats per minute.

5 Do you think one time span is more accurate than the others for counting your pulse? Why?

▶ **In this section, your resting heart rate is your rate per minute based on your count for 20 s. Now you'll find your active heart rate.**

6 **a.** Following the directions of your teacher, do some physical activity for two minutes. Then immediately count your pulse for 20 s and record the number of beats.

b. Rewrite your count from part (a) as a rate in beats per minute. Use this rate as your active heart rate throughout this section.

7 **Use Labsheet 2A.** Gather the heart rate data from all class members. Record the data in the first two columns of the *Heart Rate Data* table.

▶ **Percents Greater than 100%** **Suppose Jane's resting heart rate is 60 beats per minute and her active heart rate is 96 beats per minute. One way to compare these two rates is to ask: "Jane's active heart rate is what percent of her resting heart rate?"**

One way to visualize the comparison between Jane's active heart rate and her resting rate is with a percent bar model like the one in the Example below.

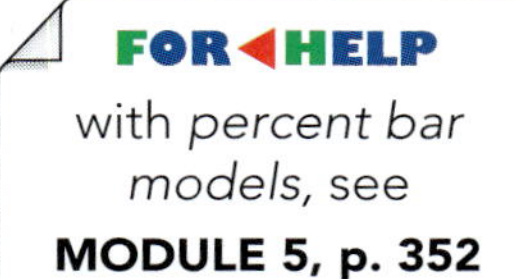

MODULE 5, p. 352

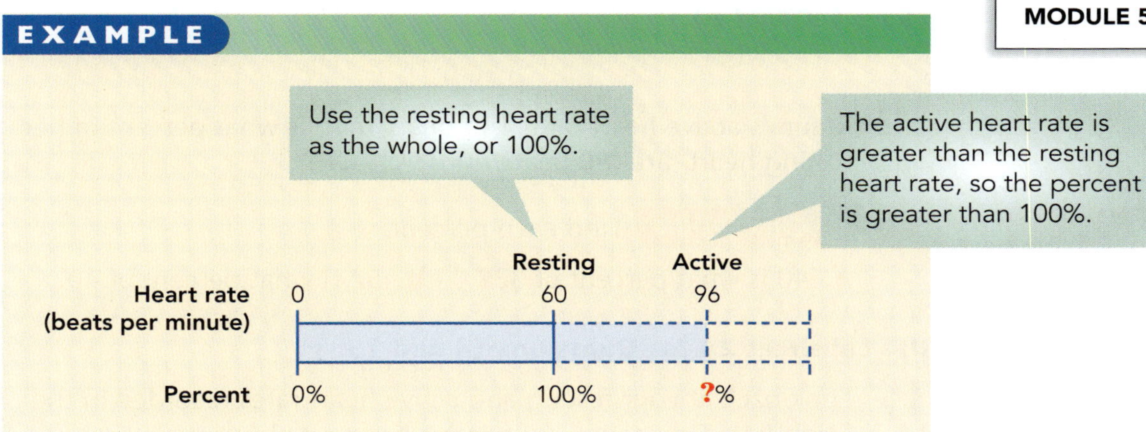

8 How many heart beats is 50% of 60? 100% of 60?

9 Since 150% = 100% + 50%, how many heartbeats is 150% of 60? How many heartbeats is 200% of 60?

10 Use the percent bar model above and your answers to Question 9 to estimate what percent Jane's active heart rate is of her resting heart rate.

11 ✓ CHECKPOINT Maura's resting heart rate is 80 beats per minute and her active heart rate is 140 beats per minute. Estimate what percent Maura's active heart rate is of her resting heart rate.

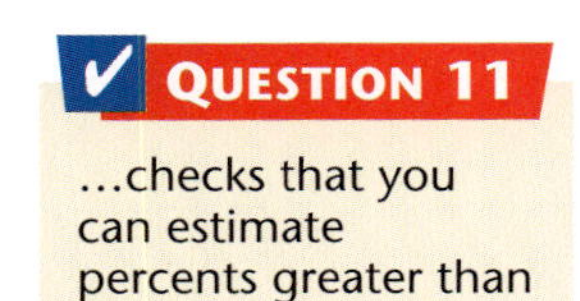

▶ Using an Equation to Find a Percent You can use an equation to find what percent Jane's active heart rate is of her resting heart rate.

EXAMPLE

96 is what percent of 60?

SAMPLE RESPONSE

Using an equation

96 is what percent of 60?

p is the unknown part of 100 percent.

$$96 = \frac{p}{100} \cdot 60$$
$$96 = \frac{60p}{100}$$
$$100 \cdot 96 = 60p$$
$$\frac{9600}{60} = p$$
$$160 = p$$

Using a proportion

$$\frac{96}{60} = \frac{p}{100}$$
$$60p = 100 \cdot 96$$
$$p = \frac{9600}{60}$$
$$p = 160$$

Use cross products.

96 is 160% of 60.

12 Maura's active heart rate (140 beats/min) is what percent of her resting heart rate (80 beats/min)?

...checks that you can find a percent greater than 100%.

13 ✓ **CHECKPOINT** Find each percent.

a. 40 is what percent of 32? **b.** 52 is what percent of 40?

Use Labsheet 2A for Questions 14 and 15.

14 Look back at your resting and active heart rates recorded in the *Heart Rate Data* table. Your active heart rate is what percent of your resting heart rate? Round to the nearest whole percent.

▶ Increasing your heart rate to reach a target rate between 60% and 85% of your maximum heart rate is important when you exercise. To find your maximum heart rate, subtract your age from 220.

15 **a.** What is your maximum heart rate?

b. What is your minimum target heart rate? What is your maximum target heart rate?

c. Was your active heart rate in the target heart rate interval?

HOMEWORK EXERCISES ▶ See Exs. 1–9 on p. 480.

Exploration 2

PERCENT of Change

SET UP *You will need Labsheet 2A.*

GOAL

LEARN HOW TO...
- find a percent of increase or decrease

AS YOU...
- examine resting and active heart rates

KEY TERM
- percent of change

▶ **Another way to compare resting and active heart rates is to look at the difference between these rates. You can then use percent to compare the difference with the original amount.**

16 **Use Labsheet 2A.** Use your heart rate data from the *Heart Rate Data* table.

a. Find the difference between your active heart rate and your resting heart rate.

b. Is the difference in part (a) *greater than* or *less than* your resting heart rate?

▶ **Percent of change is the percent by which an amount increases or decreases from its original amount.**

Camila's resting heart rate is 70 beats per minute when she is awake.

When she is sleeping, her heart rate slows to 63 beats per minute.

17 **a.** What is the difference between Camila's two heart rates?

b. The difference you found in part (a) is what percent of Camila's resting heart rate when she is awake?

c. Is the percent of change you found in part (b) a *percent of increase* or a *percent of decrease*? Explain.

Use the heart rate data in the table below for Questions 18–20.

Heart Rate Data				
Student	Resting heart rate	Active heart rate	Difference (active – resting)	Percent of increase
Nancy	57	102	45	?
Bruce	63	126	63	?
Mei	66	99	33	50%
Terry	72	180	108	?
Ella	78	117	39	?
Kamau	72	144	72	100%
Jerome	81	168	87	?

18 **a.** Mei's heart rate increased 50%. The difference between her active and resting heart rates is what fraction of her resting heart rate?

b. Find another student whose heart rate increased 50%.

19 **a.** Kamau's heart rate increased 100%. How does the difference between his active and resting heart rates compare with his resting heart rate?

b. Find another student whose heart rate increased 100%.

20 To find his active heart rate, Terry jogged in place.

a. The difference between Terry's active and resting heart rates is 108 beats per minute. This difference is how many times his resting heart rate?

b. If Terry's heart rate had increased 100%, what would the difference in the two rates be?

c. If Terry's heart rate had increased 50%, what would the difference in the two rates be?

d. Terry's heart rate increased 108 beats per minute. What is the percent of increase?

21 Nancy's heart rate increased from 57 to 102 beats per minute. This is a difference of 45 beats per minute. Will the percent of increase in Nancy's heart rate be *greater than 100%, less than 50%*, or *between 50% and 100%*?

▶ **Using an Equation** **You can write an equation to find a percent of change. First you need to know the amount of change.**

EXAMPLE

After exercising, Nancy's heart rate increased from 57 to 102 beats per minute. Find the percent of change in her heart rate.

SAMPLE RESPONSE

First find the difference in her heart rates: 102 – 57 = 45
Then ask:

The **difference** is what percent of the **original amount**?

45 is what percent of **57**?

$$45 = \frac{x}{100} \cdot 57$$

x is the unknown part of 100 percent.

$$45 = \frac{57x}{100}$$

$$4500 = 57x$$

$$79 \approx x$$

Round to the nearest whole number.

The symbol ≈ means "is approximately equal to."

45 is about 79% of 57, so Nancy's heart rate increased about 79%.

22 ✓ **CHECKPOINT** Jerome's heart rate increased from 81 beats per minute to 168 beats per minute. Find the percent of increase in Jerome's heart rate.

...checks that you can find a percent of change.

23 **Use Labsheet 2A.**

a. Find the percent of change in your heart rate from resting to active.

b. Complete the *Difference* and *Percent of increase* columns of the table.

c. Find an example where one student has a higher active heart rate but a lower percent of increase than another student. Explain how this happens.

d. Find two students whose heart rates increased by the same number of beats. Are their percents of increase the same? If not, explain how this happens.

HOMEWORK EXERCISES ▶ See Exs. 10–24 on pp. 480–482.

TECHNOLOGY Using Spreadsheet Software

You can use spreadsheet software to answer Question 23 on page 477. You can set up the spreadsheet to find the differences between resting heart rates and active heart rates, as well as the percents of increase.

Step 1 Set up your spreadsheet with the same headings as the table on Labsheet 2A. Enter the class data about heart rates.

File Edit Format Calculate Options View

RESTING AND ACTIVE HEART RATES

B4 | × | √ | 120

	A	B	C	D
1	Resting Heart Rate	Active Heart Rate	Difference (Active – Resting)	Percent of Increase
2	50	90		
3	70	140		
4	80	120		

Step 2 In cell C2 (the box in column C and row 2) enter a formula that will calculate the difference between resting and active heart rates. Every formula must begin with an equals sign.

The formula takes the number in cell B2 and subtracts the number in cell A2.

File Edit Format Calculate Options View

RESTING AND ACTIVE HEART RATES

C2 | × | √ | = B2 – A2

	A	B	C	D
1	Resting Heart Rate	Active Heart Rate	Difference (Active – Resting)	Percent of Increase
2	50	90	40	
3	70	140		
4	80	120		

The result appears in cell C2.

Step 3 In cell D2, enter the formula "= C2/A2*100" to find the percent of increase.

Step 4 Use the *fill down* command in columns C and D to apply the formulas to the data in the remaining rows.

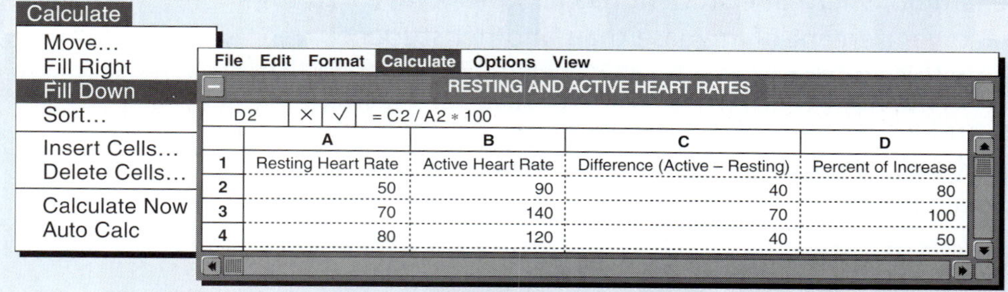

	A	B	C	D
1	Resting Heart Rate	Active Heart Rate	Difference (Active – Resting)	Percent of Increase
2	50	90	40	80
3	70	140	70	100
4	80	120	40	50

Section 2 Key Concepts

Key Term

Percents Greater than 100% (pp. 472–474)

You can write equations to solve percent problems. Some percent problems involve percents greater than 100%.

Example

45 is what percent of 40?

$$45 = \frac{x}{100} \cdot 40$$

$$45 = \frac{40x}{100}$$

$$4500 = 40x$$

$$112.5 = x$$

x is the unknown part of 100 percent.

45 is 112.5% of 40.

Think: 45 is greater than 40, so 45 is more than 100% of 40.

Percent of Change (pp. 475–477)

You can find the percent of change between two numbers by comparing the difference of the numbers with the original amount.

percent of change

Example

Kenyatta's heart rate changed from 70 to 91 beats per minute. What is the percent of change?

Find the difference.

$91 - 70 = 21$

Find the percent.

21 is what percent of 70?

24 **Key Concepts Question** Find the percent of change in Kenyatta's heart rate in the Example above. Is the change an *increase* or a *decrease*? How can you tell?

Section 2 Practice & Application Exercises

1. Muriel's resting heart rate is 65 beats per minute. After 2 min of exercise, her heart rate is 117 beats per minute. Muriel's active heart rate is what percent of her resting heart rate?

Find each percent.

2. 15 is what percent of 75?
3. 12 is what percent of 96?
4. 80 is what percent of 50?
5. 108 is what percent of 80?
6. 255 is what percent of 255?
7. 152 is what percent of 76?
8. Phil's active heart rate is 200% of his resting heart rate. If his resting heart rate is 64 beats per minute, what is his active heart rate?
9. Jerry's resting heart rate is 72 beats per minute. He wants to increase his heart rate 125%. What should his active heart rate be?
10. **Computers** In 1984, there were 12,284,000 students aged 3 to 17 years old using a computer at school in the United States. In 1993, the number had risen to 28,848,000. What is the percent of increase in computer use at school from 1984 to 1993? Round your answer to the nearest percent.
11. **Biology** Some mammals that spend time under water have lower heart rates (in beats per minute) when they dive. Copy and complete the table.

Animal	American beaver	Manatee	Bottle-nosed dolphin	Harbor seal
Surface heart rate	140	55	110	100
Diving heart rate	10	30	50	10
Difference (surface – diving)	?	?	?	?
Percent of decrease	?	?	?	?

Find each percent of change.

12. original value: 60
final value: 85

13. original value: 12
final value: 8

14. original value: 150
final value: 250

15. original value: 48
final value: 180

16. original value: 10
final value: 125

17. original value: 35
final value: 14

Use the table for Exercises 18–20.

Visits to Mexico by People Living in the United States

Year	Number of visitors
1987	13,074,000
1988	13,463,000
1989	14,163,000
1990	16,381,000
1991	15,042,000
1992	16,114,000
1993	15,285,000

18. **a.** Find the percent of change in the number of people visiting Mexico from 1988 to 1989. Is this a percent of *increase* or *decrease*?

b. Find the percent of change in the number of people visiting Mexico from 1992 to 1993. Is this a percent of *increase* or *decrease*?

19. Calculator Scientific calculators follow the order of operations. Choose the letter of the expression that you would enter to find the percent of increase in visitors from 1991 to 1992. Explain your choice.

A. 16114000 – 15042000 ÷ 15042000 • 100

B. (16114000 – 15042000) ÷ 15042000 • 100

C. 15042000 ÷ 16114000 • 100

20. Between which two years does the greatest percent of increase occur? How much is it?

21. **Sale Prices** Martina saw this sign in a store window: "Buy one sweater at the regular price and get a second sweater of equal or lesser value at half price." Suppose Martina bought two sweaters. The regular prices of the sweaters were $26.99 and $28.99.

a. How much did Martina pay for the two sweaters?

b. What percent of the total regular price for both sweaters was her discount (the amount of money she saved due to the sale)? Round your answer to the nearest whole percent.

22. **Writing** When an amount doubles, how much is the percent of change? Explain.

23. **Challenge** A store had an end-of-the-season sale. The first week of the sale, all seasonal items were marked 40% off the original price.

The store continued the sale a second week and marked down all seasonal items an additional 60% off the discounted price. Is the store offering 100% savings in the second week of the end-of-the-season sale? Explain.

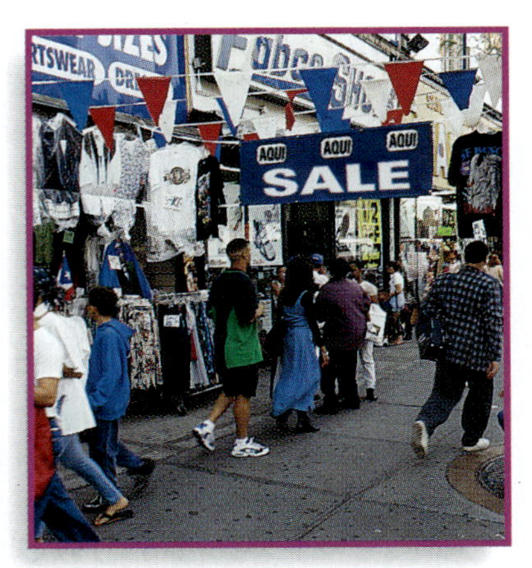

Journal

Exercise 24 checks that you understand percent of change and percents greater than 100%.

Reflecting on the Section

Write your response to Exercise 24 in your journal.

24. A student's heart rate increases from 60 beats per minute to 135 beats per minute. Without finding the percent of increase, explain how you know that the percent of change will be greater than 100%.

Spiral Review

Find the slope of a line with each rise and run. (Module 7, p. 464)

25. rise 3
run 3

26. rise 4.5
run 9

27. rise 6
run 4

28. rise 2
run 8

Find the product. Write each product in lowest terms. (Module 4, p. 241)

29. $\frac{5}{6} \cdot \frac{3}{4}$

30. $2\frac{1}{3} \cdot \frac{4}{5}$

31. $1\frac{5}{6} \cdot 3\frac{1}{4}$

32. Choose two animal heart-rate intervals from the table below. Write an inequality for each, then graph each inequality on a number line. (Module 6, p. 388)

Resting Heart Rates (beats per minute)			
canary	500 to 800	dog	70 to 120
mouse	300 to 500	person	60 to 80
chicken	300 to 350	lion	40 to 50
cat	120 to 140	elephant	25 to 50

Section 2
Extra Skill Practice

Find each percent.

1. 65 is what percent of 13?
2. 160 is what percent of 128?
3. 75 is what percent of 25?
4. 60 is what percent of 40?
5. 75 is what percent of 40?
6. 92 is what percent of 60?
7. 195 is what percent of 195?
8. 172 is what percent of 86?

Find each percent of change.

9. original value: 18
   final value: 32
10. original value: 8
    final value: 2
11. original value: 50
    final value: 150
12. original value: 10
    final value: 20
13. Lizette's active heart rate is 150% of her resting heart rate. If her resting heart rate is 68 beats per minute, what is her active heart rate?
14. Bryan's heart rate increased from 72 to 94 beats per minute. What is the percent of change in his heart rate?
15. Jena's heart rate decreased from 89 to 75 beats per minute. What is the percent of change in her heart rate?
16. Last year the school newspaper printed 650 copies of each issue. This year, 800 copies of each issue were printed. What is the percent of increase in the number of copies printed from last year to this year?
17. Elizabeth Martin owns a company. Last year, the company's profit was $250,000. This year, the company expects a profit of $300,000. What would be the percent of change in the company's profit? Is this a percent of *increase* or *decrease*?

Standardized Testing Open-ended

Sketch a cylinder and label its height and the radius of a base. Sketch and label the dimensions of a second cylinder that has the same height as your first cylinder but a larger base. Find the percent of change in the volume that occurs when you enlarge the base of the first cylinder to match the base of the second cylinder.

FOR ASSESSMENT AND PORTFOLIOS

The Situation

A health food company is planning a sales promotion to encourage people to try a new citrus drink. Under the bottle cap of each citrus drink, there is a number printed. A prize of $1000 will be given to anyone who collects bottle caps with numbers that total exactly 100. The company has already manufactured bottle caps that contain the following numbers: 3, 15, 18, 33, 45, 66, 75, 84, and 90.

The Problem

The company is going to manufacture bottle caps that contain one additional number. In order to advertise the promotion as a "$1 Million Giveaway," the company wants 1000 people to win, but also wants to be certain that there will not be more than 1000 winners. What additional number would you recommend the company use? How many bottle caps should the company manufacture that contain that number?

Something to Think About

- What do the numbers 3, 15, 18, 33, 45, 66, 75, 84, and 90 have in common?
- If these are the only numbers the company prints on the bottle caps, will there be any winners? How do you know?

Present Your Results

Write your recommendation to the company. Describe the strategies you used to make your decision.

Section 3 Customary Capacity and Inequalities

IN THIS SECTION

EXPLORATION 1
- Customary Units of Capacity

EXPLORATION 2
- Solving Inequalities

EXPLORATION 3
- Making Box-and-Whisker Plots

HEALTHY CHOICES

Setting the Stage

What should you have for lunch? The choice is yours, and it can be a healthy one if you take a moment to understand the nutrition facts for various foods. Does this sound like too much trouble? It's not—just look at the food label.

In this section, you'll find out how much fat is too much.

Spaghetti
IN TOMATO SAUCE WITH CHEESE

Nutrition Facts
Serving Size: 1 cup (252g)
Servings Per Container: about 2

Amount Per Serving	
Calories 210	Calories from Fat 20
	% Daily Value*
Total Fat 2g	**3%**
Saturated Fat 1g	**5%**
Cholesterol 5mg	**2%**
Sodium 1,020 mg	**43%**
Total Carbohydrate 41g	**14%**
Dietary Fiber 3g	**12%**
Sugars 14g	
Protein 7g	
Vitamin A 10%	Vitamin C 0%
Calcium 4%	Iron 10%

* Percent Daily Values are based on a 2,000 calorie diet. Your daily values may be higher or lower depending on your calorie needs.

"Daily value" is often the most you need each day.

Think About It

Look at the nutrition label at the right from a can of prepared spaghetti.

1 Do you think 1 cup is a realistic serving size? Explain.

2 What happens to the amounts of fat and other nutrients if you double the serving size?

3 One serving of canned spaghetti contains 2 g of fat. For most foods, each gram of fat contains 9 Calories. How many of the Calories in one serving of canned spaghetti are from fat? How does this compare with the Calorie information at the top of the label?

4 How much Vitamin C does a serving of canned spaghetti have?

When the amount of a vitamin or mineral in a food is less than 2% of the daily value, "0%" may be written on the nutrition label.

5 Nutritionists say people need at least 60 mg of Vitamin C each day.

a. Suppose one serving of canned spaghetti has 0.2 mg of Vitamin C. What percent of the daily value would you get in one serving? Round to the nearest tenth of a percent. Is this the same as 0%?

b. How much Vitamin C should a food contain to have at least 1% of the daily value? 2% of the daily value?

GOAL

LEARN HOW TO...
- convert customary units of capacity

AS YOU...
- interpret nutrition labels on food products

KEY TERMS
- tablespoon (tbsp)
- cup (c)
- fluid ounce (fl oz)
- pint (pt)
- quart (qt)
- gallon (gal)

Exploration 1

CUSTOMARY UNITS of CAPACITY

Besides nutritional information, food labels list the size of a serving and the number of servings in a container. For liquid foods, the serving size is listed in tablespoons (tbsp), cups (c), or fluid ounces (fl oz). If you read them carefully, the labels can tell you how these customary units of capacity are related.

6 The label at the right is from a jar of gravy. The container holds 12 fl oz. How many fluid ounces are in $\frac{1}{4}$ c? $\frac{1}{2}$ c? 1 c?

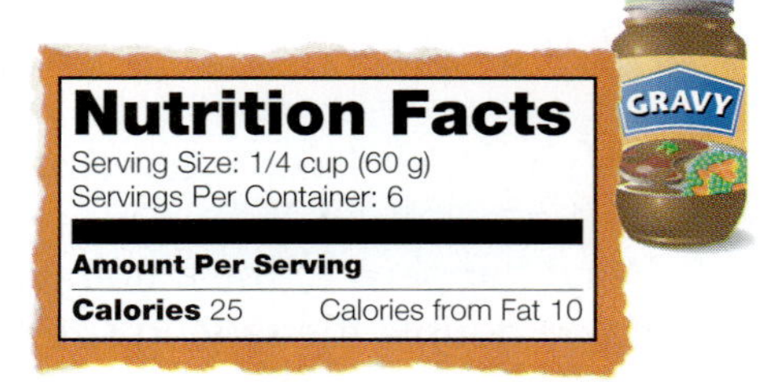

7 A recipe calls for $2\frac{1}{2}$ c of tomato sauce. How many 15 fl oz cans of tomato sauce will be enough to make the recipe? How much tomato sauce will be left?

8 **a.** What is the capacity, in fluid ounces, of the bottle of pancake syrup with the label shown?

b. The amount of syrup listed on the front of the bottle is 1 pt 8 fl oz. How many fluid ounces are in a **pint (pt)?**

c. How many cups are in a pint?

Nutrition Facts
Serving Size: 1/4 cup (60 mL)
Servings Per Container: about 12
Amount Per Serving
Calories 100 Calories from Fat 0
SYRUP

9 The label on a jar of mayonnaise lists the capacity of the jar as 32 fl oz or 1 qt.

a. How many tablespoons are in a fluid ounce?

b. How many cups are in a **quart (qt)?** How many pints are in a quart?

10 The nutrition label for low fat milk is shown at the right.

a. The container of low fat milk holds how many pints?

b. The capacity is listed on the container as $\frac{1}{2}$ gal. How many pints are in a **gallon (gal)?**

11 Copy the table below. Then look back at your work in Questions 6–10 to complete the table.

Unit of measure	Symbol	Relationship
tablespoon	tbsp	1 tbsp = __?__ fl oz
cup	c	1 c = __?__ fl oz
pint	pt	1 pt = __?__ c
quart	qt	1 qt = __?__ pt = __?__ c
gallon	gal	1 gal = __?__ qt = __?__ pt = __?__ c

12 ✓ **CHECKPOINT** A small teacup holds 4 fl oz of mint tea. How much mint tea does it contain in each indicated unit?

a. tablespoons **b.** cups **c.** quarts **d.** pints

✓ **QUESTION 12**

...checks that you can convert customary units of capacity.

HOMEWORK EXERCISES See Exs. 1–8 on pp. 494–495.

GOAL

LEARN HOW TO...
- solve inequalities

AS YOU...
- investigate daily nutritional requirements

Exploration 2

SOLVING INEQUALITIES

Nutritionists use your daily Calorie needs to decide how much protein, carbohydrate, and fat you need. Tony is a 13-year-old boy who needs about 2800 Cal per day. The table below shows how much protein, carbohydrate, and fat were in Tony's breakfast, lunch, and dinner one day.

Meal	Protein (g)	Carbohydrate (g)	Fat (g)	Calories
Breakfast	10.7	33.1	5.2	208
Lunch	21.9	117.6	29.8	797
Dinner	58.3	204.9	53.8	1525

13 **Discussion** Do you think Tony is close to achieving his goal of 2800 Cal per day?

▶ **Of all nutrients, only proteins, carbohydrates, and fats produce energy. This energy is measured in Calories. For most foods, each gram of protein or carbohydrate provides about 4 Cal. Each gram of fat provides about 9 Cal.**

14 Some nutritionists believe that to have a healthy diet, 12% of your daily Calorie intake should come from protein. Depending on your sex, age, and activity level, your daily Calorie needs may be as low as 1600 Cal or as high as 2800 Cal.

a. According to the guideline stated above, how many of the Calories in a 1600 Cal daily total should come from protein?

b. How many Calories should come from protein in a 2800 Cal daily total?

15 **a.** Use your answers to Question 14 to write an inequality that represents the number of Calories from protein p that a person should consume in one day based on the total numbers of Calories indicated.

b. Rewrite the inequality in part (a) to show the number of grams of protein a person should consume in one day.

c. Did Tony get enough protein?

▶ **Carbohydrates should account for 55% or more of your diet. For a daily intake of 2000 Cal, over 1100 Calories should come from carbohydrates. Because the amount is 55% *or more*, carbohydrate need is modeled with an inequality.**

16 **Discussion** The inequality below describes the minimum number c of grams of carbohydrates needed based on a daily Calorie need of d.

$$4c \geq 0.55d$$

a. What does $0.55d$ represent?

b. Why is c multiplied by 4?

▶ **If you know a person's Calorie needs, you can use the inequality $4c \geq 0.55d$ to find the minimum number of grams of carbohydrates needed.**

EXAMPLE

Suppose Rowena Thompson needs 1600 Cal each day. How many grams of carbohydrates does she need daily?

SAMPLE RESPONSE

$$4c \geq 0.55d$$

$$4c \geq 0.55 \cdot 1600$$

Substitute **1600** for ***d***.

$$4c \geq 880$$

$$\frac{4c}{4} \geq \frac{880}{4}$$

Divide both sides by **4**.

$$c \geq 220$$

Rowena Thompson should have at least 220 g of carbohydrates each day.

17 Tony needs 2800 Cal per day. Write an inequality to represent the number of grams of carbohydrates he should get each day.

18 **Try This as a Class** The inequality $4c + 4 \cdot 355.6 \geq 0.55 \cdot 2800$ can be used to find the *additional* grams of carbohydrates that Tony still needs after eating breakfast, lunch, and dinner.

a. Simplify the inequality by finding the products $4 \cdot 355.6$ and $0.55 \cdot 2800$. Then rewrite the inequality.

b. What should you do to solve for the variable c?

c. Finish solving the inequality. How many more grams of carbohydrates does Tony need to get to the 55% minimum?

✓ QUESTION 19

...checks that you can solve inequalities.

19 **✓ CHECKPOINT** Solve each inequality.

a. $8x \leq 28$ **b.** $37 \leq 5x$ **c.** $59.5 < x + 33.5$

d. $x - \frac{1}{4} \geq -\frac{3}{4}$ **e.** $7x + 4 \leq 50$ **f.** $3x - 2 < 14$

20 Many nutritionists believe that no more than 30% of your daily Calorie intake should come from fat.

a. Write an inequality to describe the maximum number of grams of fat a person should have each day. Use the variables d for daily Calorie need, and f for grams of fat.

b. Use your inequality to find Tony's *maximum fat gram goal,* or the maximum number of grams of fat he should have each day.

c. Was Tony within his maximum fat gram goal?

21 **Discussion** Which food(s) in the table could Tony snack on after dinner and still meet his Calorie, fat, protein, and carbohydrate goals for the day?

Snack	Protein (g)	Carbohydrate (g)	Fat (g)	Calories
apple	0.3	21.1	0.5	81
apple juice	0.3	27.6	0.3	111
banana	1.2	26.7	0.6	105
chocolate brownie	1.0	20.0	5.0	130
oatmeal cookies (2)	2.2	24.4	6.4	160
orange	1.4	16.3	0.1	65
pear	0.7	25.1	0.7	98
popcorn	1.8	10.7	0.7	54
vanilla ice cream	4.8	31.7	14.3	269

HOMEWORK EXERCISES ▶ See Exs. 9–19 on pp. 495–496.

Exploration 3

MAKING BOX-and-WHISKER PLOTS

SET UP *You will need Labsheets 3A and 3B.*

GOAL

LEARN HOW TO...
- make a box-and-whisker plot

AS YOU...
- examine the amounts of sugar in foods

KEY TERMS
- lower extreme
- upper extreme
- lower quartile
- upper quartile

Have you ever heard the warning, "Don't eat too many sweets!"? Are some foods especially high in sugars compared with others?

▶ **In this exploration, you'll look at the amounts of sugar in candy bars and desserts, and then answer the question, "Is there more sugar in a piece of pie or in a candy bar?" One way to find out is to make a box-and-whisker plot.**

A box-and-whisker plot shows how spread out the data values are.

22 Use the box-and-whisker plot to identify the minimum and maximum data values, and the median.

Amounts of Sugar in 20 Candy Bars (g)

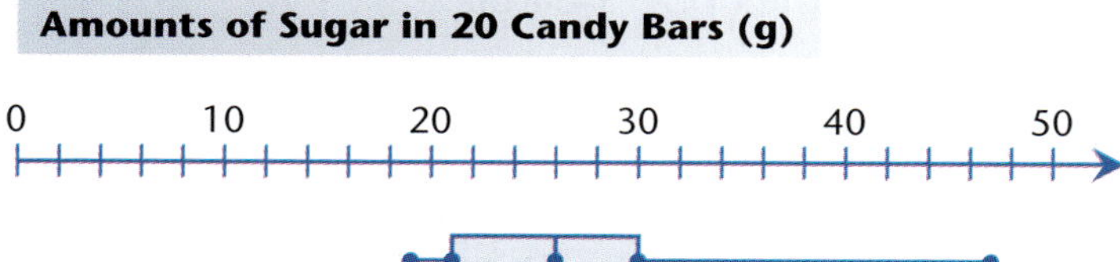

▶ **To find out how the amounts of sugar in these candy bars compare with the amounts in the desserts listed on Labsheet 3A, you'll make a box-and-whisker plot of the amounts of sugar in the desserts.**

Use Labsheet 3A for Questions 23–26.

23 **Step 1** **Order the data.**

Order the *Sugar Contents of 20 Desserts* from least to greatest.

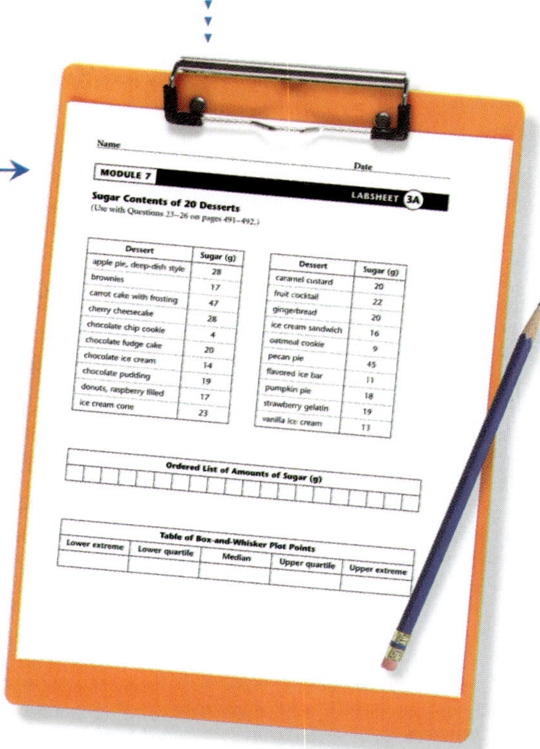

Name
Date

MODULE 7 LABSHEET 3A

Sugar Contents of 20 Desserts
(Use with Questions 23–26 on pages 491–492.)

Dessert	Sugar (g)
apple pie, deep-dish style	28
brownies	17
carrot cake with frosting	47
cherry cheesecake	28
chocolate chip cookie	4
chocolate fudge cake	20
chocolate ice cream	14
chocolate pudding	19
donuts, raspberry filled	17
ice cream cone	23

Dessert	Sugar (g)
caramel custard	20
fruit cocktail	22
gingerbread	20
ice cream sandwich	16
oatmeal cookie	9
pecan pie	45
flavored ice bar	11
pumpkin pie	18
strawberry gelatin	19
vanilla ice cream	13

Ordered List of Amounts of Sugar (g)

Table of Box-and-Whisker Plot Points

Lower extreme	Lower quartile	Median	Upper quartile	Upper extreme

24 **Step 2** **Find the *extremes* of the data.**

The **lower extreme** is the least value in the set of data. The **upper extreme** is the greatest data value.

a. Record the lower extreme of the grams of sugar in the *Table of Box-and-Whisker Plot Points*.

b. Record the upper extreme of the grams of sugar in the *Table of Box-and-Whisker Plot Points*.

25 **Step 3** **Find the median of the data.**

a. Find and record the median of the sugar data.

b. About what percent of the data values lie above the median? below the median?

26 **Step 4** **Find the *quartiles*.**

Draw a vertical segment through the middle data item or between the two middle items. Circle the data values in your ordered list that are to the left of the segment. The median of these values is the **lower quartile** of the data.

Circle the data values in your ordered list that are to the right of the segment. The median of these values is the **upper quartile**.

a. Find and record the lower quartile.

b. Find and record the upper quartile.

Use Labsheet 3B for Questions 27–29.

27 **Step 5** **Graph the median, the extremes, and the quartiles below a number line. Then draw the box and whiskers.**

Follow the directions for *Comparing Sugar Contents* to make a box-and-whisker plot for the numbers of grams of sugar in the desserts.

28 Compare the numbers of grams of sugar in candy bars with the numbers of grams of sugar in desserts by comparing the medians for the two data sets. Which appear to have more sugar, *candy bars* or *desserts*? Explain.

29 **Discussion** Which contains more sugar, a *slice of pie* or a *candy bar*? Explain.

HOMEWORK EXERCISES ▶ **See Exs. 20–22 on pp. 496–497.**

Section 3 Key Concepts

Customary Units of Capacity (pp. 486–487)

Customary units of capacity include fluid ounce (fl oz), tablespoon (tbsp), cup (c), pint (pt), quart (qt), and gallon (gal). The table shows the relationships among customary units of capacity.

Customary Units of Capacity
1 tbsp = 0.5 fl oz
1 c = 8 fl oz
1 pt = 2 c = 16 fl oz
1 qt = 2 pt = 4 c = 32 fl oz
1 gal = 4 qt = 16 c = 128 fl oz

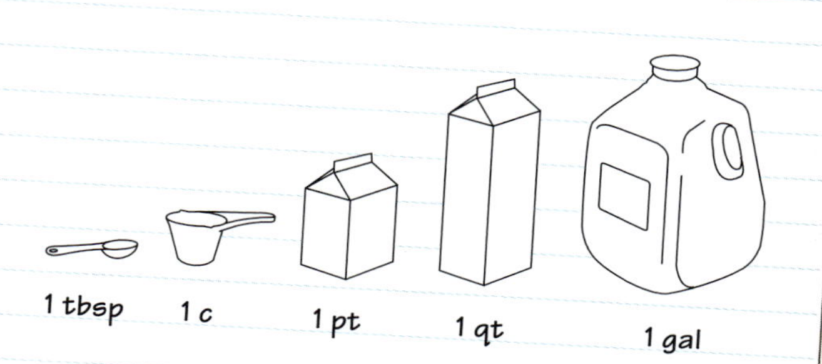

Solving Inequalities (pp. 488–490)

When you solve problems that ask for a minimum or maximum amount, you might want to use an inequality.

Example $12x + 4 \geq 10$

$12x + 4 - 4 \geq 10 - 4$ Subtract **4** from each side.

$12x \geq 6$

$\frac{12x}{12} \geq \frac{6}{12}$ Divide both sides of the inequality by **12**.

$x \geq \frac{1}{2}$

Key Terms

- fluid ounce (fl oz)
- tablespoon (tbsp)
- cup (c)
- pint (pt)
- quart (qt)
- gallon (gal)

Key Concepts Questions

30 The label on a full carton of buttermilk states that it contains $\frac{1}{2}$ pt. You pour out $\frac{3}{4}$ c and 2 tbsp of buttermilk. How much buttermilk remains in the carton?

31 Solve each inequality.

a. $3x > 18$ **b.** $x - 5 < 12$ **c.** $8 + x \leq 20$

Continued on the next page

Section 3

Key Concepts

Key Terms

lower extreme

upper extreme

lower quartile

upper quartile

Box-and-Whisker Plots (pp. 491–492)

Box-and-whisker plots show the median and how spread out the data values are. They are useful for comparing sets of data.

Example

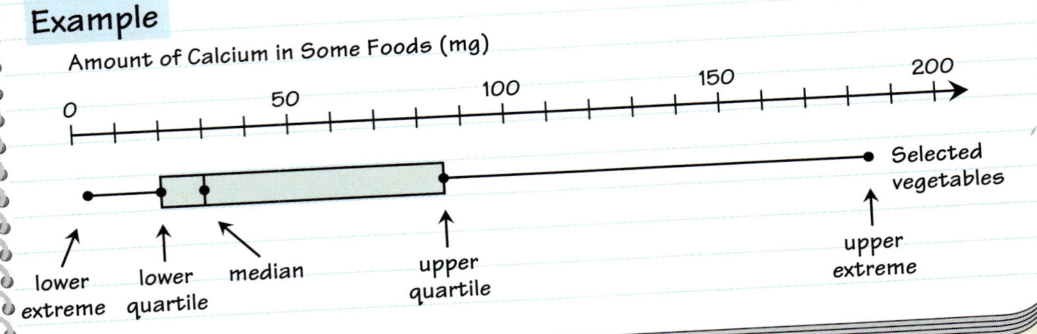

32 Key Concepts Question The amounts of calcium in 20 vegetables were included in the box-and-whisker plot in the Example above. How many vegetables are represented by each whisker? by the box?

Section 3

Practice & Application Exercises

YOU WILL NEED

For Exs. 20–21:
- graph paper

For Ex. 34
- Labsheet 3C

Replace each ? with the number that makes each a true statement.

1. 2 c = ___?___ tbsp
2. 12 fl oz = ___?___ pt
3. $\frac{1}{2}$ gal = ___?___ c
4. $\frac{3}{4}$ c = ___?___ fl oz
5. 1 qt = ___?___ fl oz
6. ___?___ pt = $1\frac{1}{2}$ gal
7. **Health** Many health experts recommend that everyone needs 8 to 10 glasses of water each day, or about $2\frac{1}{2}$ qt. Use these facts to find the capacity of a glass.

8. The directions on a 16 fl oz can of concentrated orange juice say to add 3 cans of cold water.

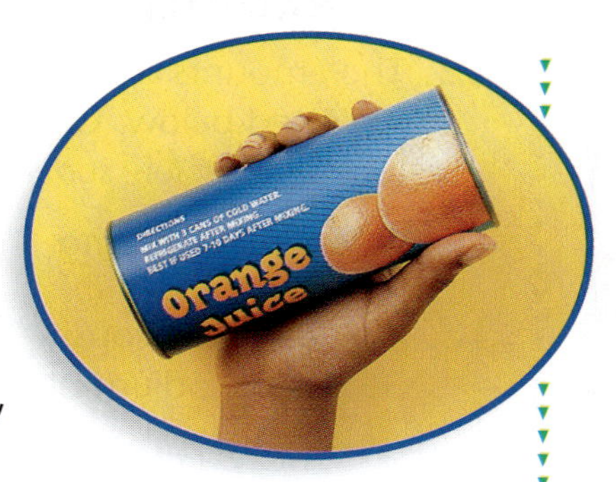

a. How many cups of water should be added?

b. About how many quarts of orange juice will one can make? About how many gallons?

9. Rachel has some crackers labeled "low fat" for an afternoon snack. One serving of the crackers has 2 g of fat and 60 Calories.

a. Each gram of fat contains 9 Cal. How many of the Calories in one serving of crackers come from fat?

b. What percent of the Calories in one serving of crackers comes from fat?

c. If less than 30% of the Calories from a food item come from fat, the food is considered to be *low fat*. Are Rachel's crackers actually *low fat*? Explain.

10. Look back at your work in Exercise 9.

a. Write an equation that can be used to find what percent of the Calories in a food item are from fat.

b. Write an inequality that must be true for an item to be considered *low fat*.

c. A cupcake provides 129 Cal and 4.5 g of fat. What percent of the Calories in the cupcake comes from fat? Is the cupcake *low fat*?

d. A container of fruit yogurt contains 225 Cal. About 10.4% of the Calories are from fat. About how many Calories are from fat? Round to the nearest Calorie.

11. Beverages are said to be *very low sodium* if there is less than 35 mg of sodium in 8 fl oz.

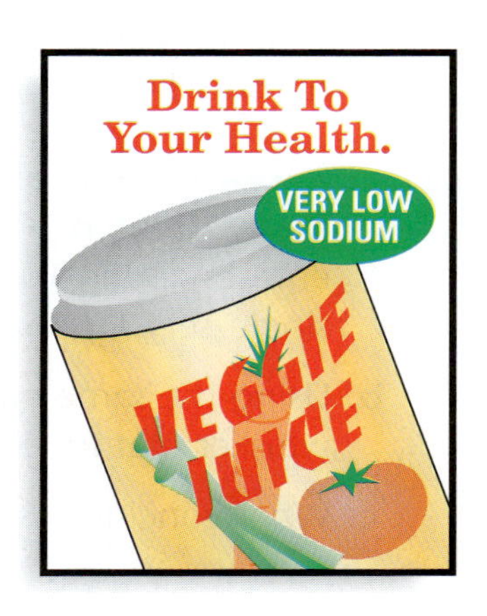

a. What is the most sodium that is allowed in a 12 fl oz can of *very low sodium* beverage?

b. Write an inequality to describe the amount of sodium allowed in a 12 fl oz can of *very low sodium* beverage.

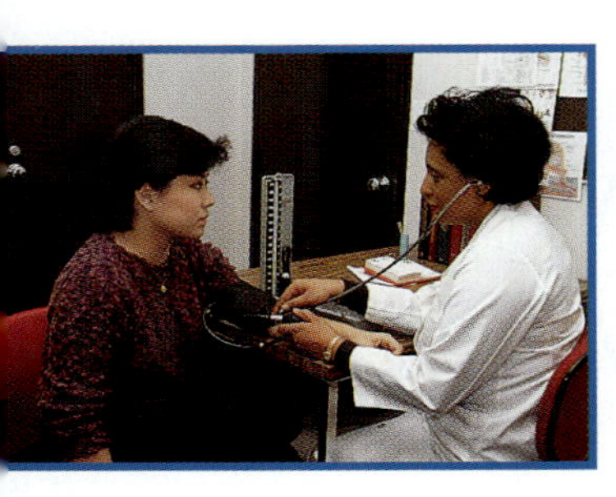

▲ People with high blood pressure need to limit their intake of sodium.

12. The amounts of sodium in 12 fl oz cans of three types of soft drinks are listed below. Choose the letters of the soft drinks that can be labeled *very low sodium* as defined in Exercise 11 on page 495.

A. orange—35 mg **B.** root beer—55 mg **C.** cola—50 mg

13. A beverage is considered *low sodium* if 8 fl oz contains more than 35 mg of sodium but less than 140 mg of sodium.

a. Write an inequality to show the amount of sodium allowed in 8 fl oz of a *low sodium* drink.

b. Tell whether each drink below is a *low sodium* beverage. Explain your reasoning.

- 16 fl oz of citrus punch containing 380 mg of sodium
- 15.5 fl oz of chocolate drink containing 329 mg of sodium
- 20 fl oz of citrus sports drink containing 275 mg of sodium

Solve each inequality.

14. $5x \leq 100$ **15.** $-2 + x \geq 6$ **16.** $4 < 7 + x$

17. $\frac{1}{2}x < 14$ **18.** $3x + 1 \geq 4$ **19.** $2 \geq -4 + 6x$

20. Use the data in the table to make a box-and-whisker plot.

Average March Water Temperature at Eight Beaches (°F)			
Newport, RI	37	Oceanside, CA	58
Ocean City, MD	42	Seattle, WA	46
Key West, FL	75	Honolulu, HI	76
Freeport, TX	62	Juneau, AK	37

a. Order the data. **b.** Find the extremes.

c. Find the median. **d.** Find the quartiles.

e. Graph the median, the extremes, and the quartiles below a number line. Then draw the box and the whiskers.

21. a. Research Find and record the numbers of grams of fat in 10 regular single-serving frozen entrees and in 10 reduced-Calorie or low-fat single-serving frozen entrees.

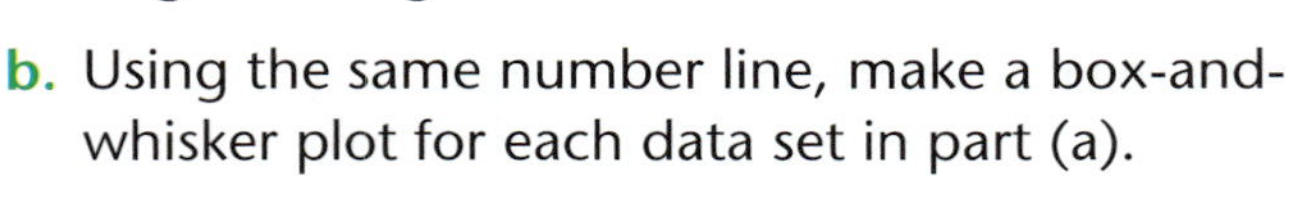

b. Using the same number line, make a box-and-whisker plot for each data set in part (a).

c. What conclusions can you draw from your graph? Explain.

Reflecting on the Section

Be prepared to report on the following topic in class.

22. Why do you think nutrition labels state the serving size in both customary and metric units, but the amounts of fat, protein, and carbohydrate in metric units only?

Oral Report

Exercise 22 checks that you understand customary units.

Spiral Review

Find each percent. (Module 7, p. 479)

23. 30 is what percent of 12?
24. 15 is what percent of 5?
25. 86 is what percent of 44?
26. 6 is what percent of 5?

Find each square root. (Module 6, p. 404)

27. $\sqrt{16}$
28. $\sqrt{36}$
29. $\sqrt{100}$

Find each amount. (Module 5, p. 352)

30. 15% of 28
31. 40% of 32
32. 80% of 155

Extension

Outliers

One candy bar in the box-and-whisker plot has 47 g of sugar. Another has 40 g of sugar.

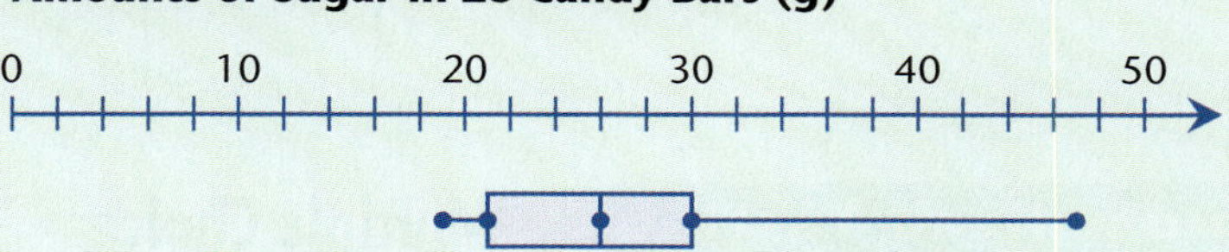

33. a. Where are these two candy bars located on the box-and-whisker plot?

    b. How do the numbers of grams of sugar in these two candy bars compare with those in the other candy bars?

Data values that are much greater or much smaller than the other data values are *outliers*.

34. **Use Labsheet 3C.** Follow the steps in *Determining Outliers* to decide if the candy bars with 40 g and 47 g of sugar are outliers.

Extra Skill Practice

Replace each ? with the number that makes each a true statement.

1. 3 fl oz = __?__ tbsp
2. 16 fl oz = __?__ pt
3. $\frac{3}{4}$ gal = __?__ qt
4. $\frac{1}{2}$ qt = __?__ fl oz
5. 2 pt = __?__ fl oz
6. $2\frac{3}{4}$ gal = __?__ pt

Solve each inequality.

7. $4x \leq 88$
8. $-3 + x \geq 9$
9. $3 < 8 + x$
10. $\frac{3}{4}x < 52$
11. $5x \geq 7$
12. $5 \geq 10 + x$

13. Make a box-and-whisker plot for the data in the table.

Food	Protein per serving (g)
bread	3
cereal	2
margarine	0
oatmeal	6
peanut butter	4
spaghetti	7
yogurt	8

Standardized Testing ▶ Multiple Choice

For each measure, choose the letter of the greater measure.

1. 16 pt

   A 2 gal B 10 qt C 30 c D 1 gal 2 qt

2. 1 pt 1 c

   A $1\frac{1}{2}$ pt B 3 c C 2 c 6 fl oz D 30 fl oz

Section 4 Circle Graphs, and Choosing a Graph

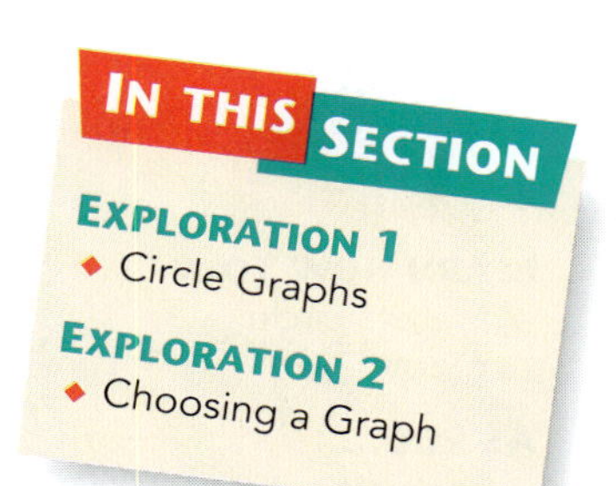

GETTING YOUR Zzzzz

Setting the Stage

Some studies show that many teens do not get enough sleep during the school week. In this section you'll examine how much sleep you and your classmates get. Then you'll compare this data with a survey of over 800,000 adults at least 29 years old.

The survey asked people how long they sleep each night. The results are shown in the graph at the right.

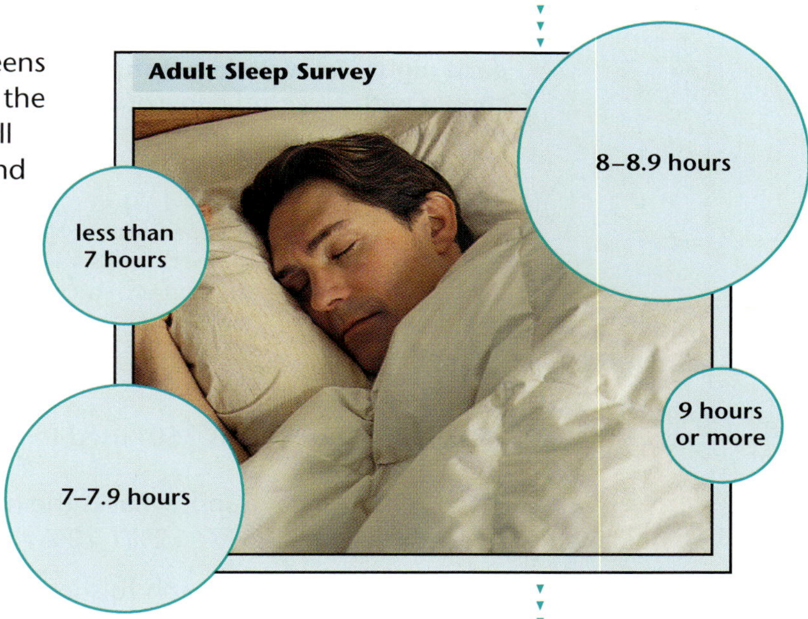

Think About It

1 Use the graph above. The percents of adults who fall into each sleep category are shown by the relative sizes of the circles.

a. The greatest percent of people sleep how many hours?

b. The least percent of people sleep how many hours?

2 **Try This as a Class** About 45% of the adults surveyed sleep between 8 h and 8.9 h each night. About what percent of the adults surveyed sleep less than 7 h? Was it difficult to estimate the percent? Explain.

GOAL

LEARN HOW TO...
- make a circle graph

AS YOU...
- conduct a survey on sleep habits

KEY TERMS
- circle graph
- central angle
- sector

Exploration 1

Circle GRAPHS

SET UP *You will need:* • *compass* • *protractor*

▶ **Different kinds of graphs can be used to describe the same data. A *circle graph* can be used to show the percent of adults in each sleep category of the survey discussed in the *Setting the Stage* on page 499. In a circle graph, the entire circle represents the whole, or 100%.**

About 45% of the adults surveyed said they sleep between 8 h and 8.9 h each night. On a circle graph this is shown with a *central angle* of 162°, since 45% of 360° is 162°.

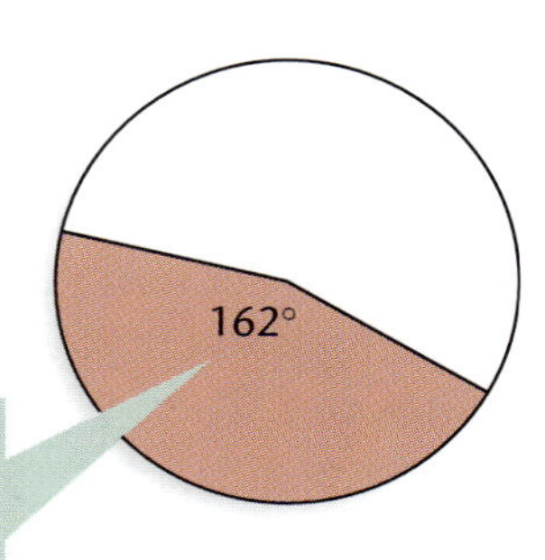

A **central angle** is an angle that has its vertex at the center of a circle.

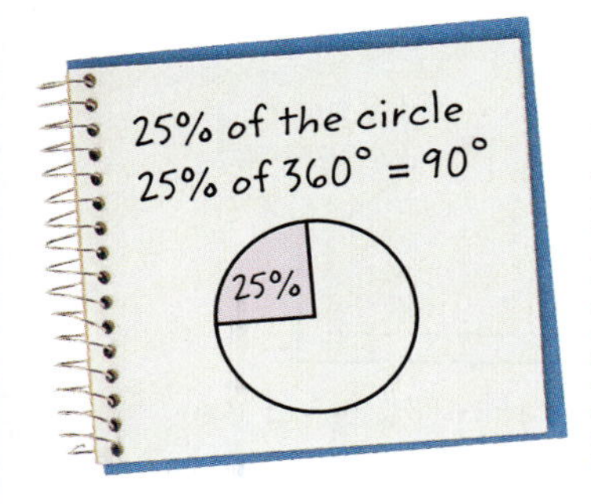

3 Discussion Why is 360° used to find the central angle?

4 a. On a circle graph, what is the measure of a central angle that represents 25%? 10%? 20%?

b. Sketch a circle graph to show each percent in part (a). Clearly label each percent.

▶ **The complete circle graph for the survey is shown at the right. Each *sector* represents the data in a different sleep category.**

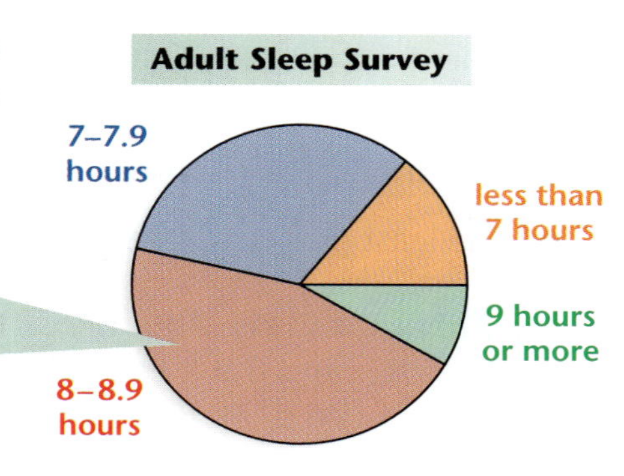

A **sector** is a wedge-shaped region bounded by two radii and an arc of a circle.

Use the completed circle graph on page 500 to answer Questions 5 and 6.

5 **a.** Estimate the percent of adults who sleep 7 h–7.9 h each night.

b. Use a protractor to find how many degrees represent the sleep category 7 h–7.9 h. What percent of 360° is this?

c. How does your estimate in part (a) compare with your answer in part (b)?

6 **Discussion** Compare the circle graph on page 500 with the graph on page 499. Which graph do you think shows the survey results more clearly? Explain.

▶ **You have seen how much adults sleep each night. How do you think your sleeping habits and those of your classmates compare with those of adults?**

7 **Try This as a Class** Your teacher will announce each sleep category aloud to the class. Raise your hand when the sleep category that describes your own sleeping habit is announced.

a. Record the number of students in each sleep category in a table like the one shown.

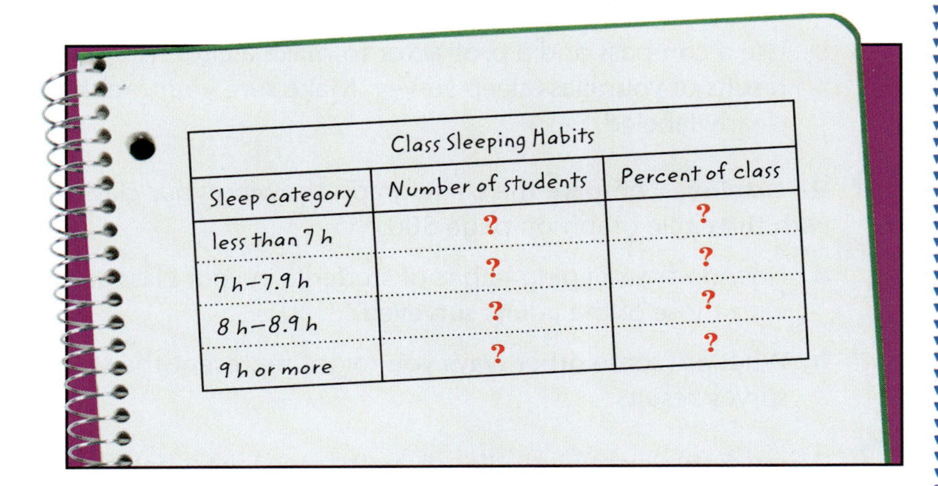

Class Sleeping Habits		
Sleep category	Number of students	Percent of class
less than 7 h	?	?
7 h–7.9 h	?	?
8 h–8.9 h	?	?
9 h or more	?	?

b. Find the percent of students in each sleep category. Round each answer to the nearest tenth of a percent.

▶ **To show your sleep data on a circle graph, you need to find the measure of the central angle that represents the percent in each sleep category.**

EXAMPLE

Suppose 58.1% of students said they slept 8 h–8.9 h each night. Find the measure of a central angle on a circle graph that represents this percent.

SAMPLE RESPONSE

Using a Proportion

$\frac{58.1}{100} = \frac{x}{360}$ ← part (x), ← whole (360)

$100x = 58.1 \cdot 360$

$x = 209.16$

Using an Equation

58.1% of 360 is what number?

$\frac{58.1}{100} \cdot 360 = x$

$209.16 = x$

Write the percent in fraction or decimal form.

Rounding to the nearest degree gives a central angle of 209°.

8 Suppose 22.4% of the students in one class said they slept 7 h–7.9 h every night. Find the measure of a central angle that represents 22.4%. Round your answer to the nearest degree.

✓ QUESTION 9

...checks that you can make a circle graph.

9 **✓ CHECKPOINT** Use your class data from Question 7.

a. Find the measure of a central angle for each sleep category.

b. Use a compass and a protractor to make a circle graph of the results of your class sleep survey. Make sure your graph is clearly labeled.

10 **Discussion** Compare the circle graph showing your class results with the circle graph on page 500.

a. How do the sleeping habits of students in your class compare with those of the adults surveyed?

b. What are some other ways you might represent the sleep survey results?

11 **Discussion** Scientific studies show that teenagers need more sleep than children or adults.

a. Why do you think teenagers need more sleep?

b. Many teenagers need more than 9 h of sleep each night. What percent of your class is getting this much sleep?

HOMEWORK EXERCISES ▶ See Exs. 1–11 on pp. 507–508.

Exploration 2

Choosing a GRAPH

GOAL

LEARN HOW TO...
- choose an effective visual representation

AS YOU...
- perform an experiment on rest

SET UP *Work with a partner. You will need:*
- *protractor* • *compass* • *ruler* • *stopwatch*

▶ **How important is getting enough rest? Can even small amounts of rest make a difference? You'll answer these questions after completing an activity. The class will be divided into two groups—students who rest between trials and those who do not.**

12 **Try This as a Class** With your partner, decide which of you will rest between trials. This person is in Group A. The other person is in Group B. Students in both groups should complete three trials of the experiment.

Students in Group A should rest 30 seconds between each trial. Students in Group B should not rest between trials.

First

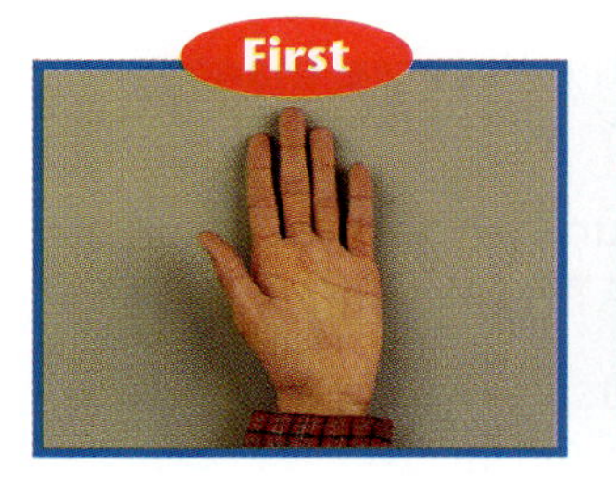

Place the arm you use for writing flat on your desk with your hand open, the palm up, and your fingers together.

Then

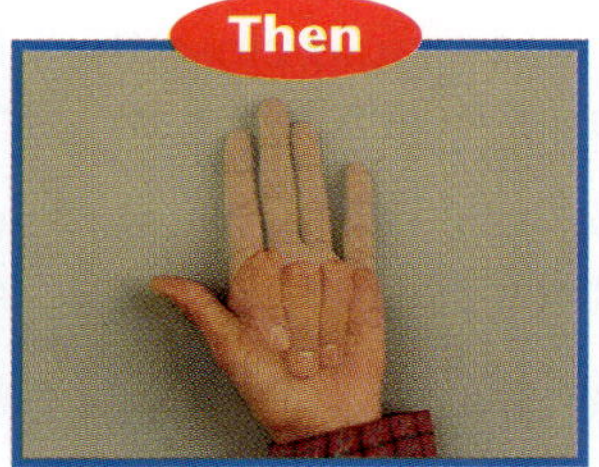

After your teacher gives a signal, close and open your hand as many times as you can in 30 seconds.

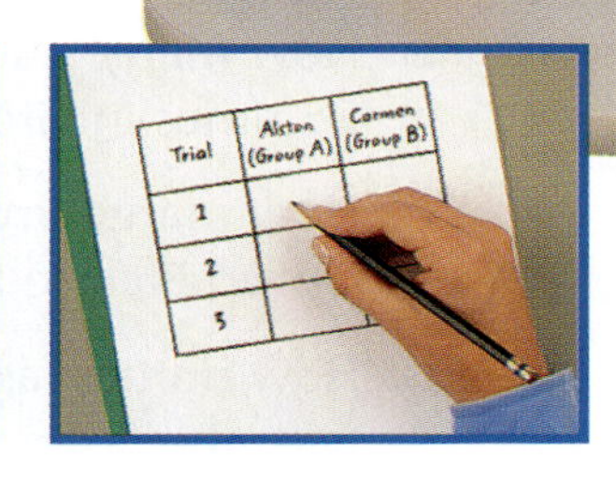

Have your partner count and record how many times your fingers hit the desk.

As you open and close your hand, be sure your fingertips touch the desk and your palm.

a. Record the results of each trial.

b. Record the class results of the third trial for Groups A and B in a table like the one shown.

c. How do the results for students who rested between trials compare with the results for those who did not?

Class Results of Third Trial

Group A	Group B
?	?
?	?
?	?

▶ **Comparing Representations** To compare data values or sets of data, you can display the data using a graph. You have already learned several ways to represent a set of data. Some of those include:

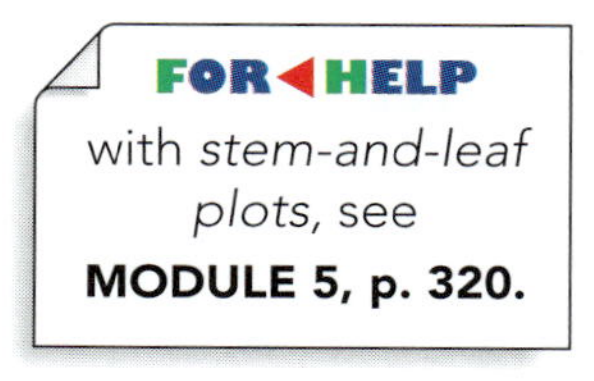

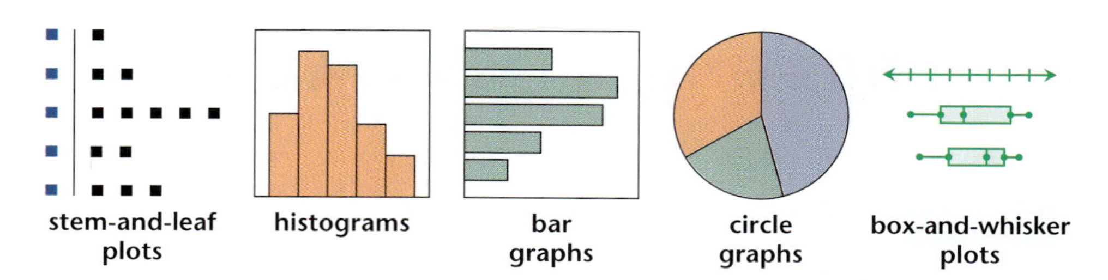

13 Use your class results from Question 12. With your partner, make each graph below to compare the results of Groups A and B.

a. Make two box-and-whisker plots comparing the results of Group A with those of Group B.

b. Make two circle graphs. You may need to divide each data set into intervals.

c. Display the class results in either a stem-and-leaf plot, a bar graph, or a line plot.

14 Work with your partner to answer each question in parts (a)–(e). Tell which graph from Question 13 you chose to find each answer, and explain your choices.

a. What was the range of data for Group A? for Group B?

b. How many students could close their hands more than 25 times in Group A? in Group B?

c. How many times could the greatest number of students in Group B close their hands? in Group A?

d. How do the fastest 25% of the students in Group A compare with the fastest 25% of the students in Group B?

e. Are there any gaps or clusters in the data for each group? If so, where?

15 **Discussion** Examine the graphs you made in Question 13.

a. Which graph do you think is most effective in showing the importance of rest? Explain.

b. Do you think small amounts of rest make a difference in performance? Explain.

HOMEWORK EXERCISES ▶ See Exs. 12–16 on pp. 508–509.

Section 4

Key Concepts

Key Terms

Circle Graphs (pp. 500–502)

A circle graph can be used to compare parts of a data set with the whole, or to display percent data.

circle graph

Example 1011 adults in the United States were surveyed about their sleeping habits. The circle graph below shows how they responded.

Question:
Do you think you get more or less sleep than you need?

Number of people	Response
167	more
541	less
282	just right
21	don't know

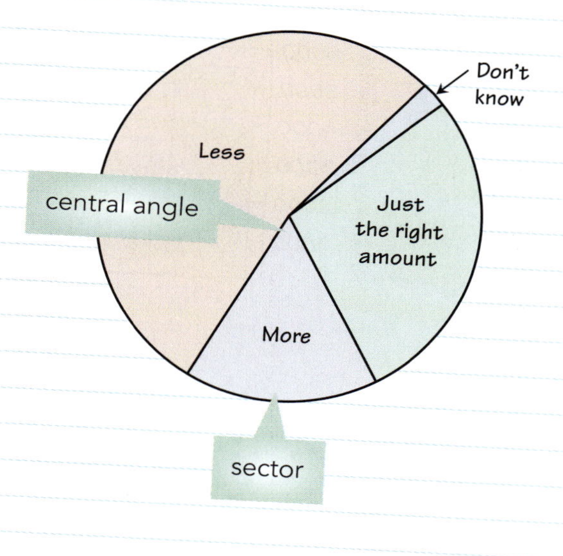

central angle

sector

16 Key Concepts Question Use the circle graph in the Example above.

a. Estimate the percent of adults who gave each response shown on the circle graph.

b. Measure the central angle for each sector to the nearest degree. Then find the actual percents. How close were your estimates?

Continued on the next page

Section 4 Key Concepts

Choosing a Graph (pp. 503–504)

The graph you choose to represent a data set depends on what message you want to communicate.

Box-and-whisker plots are good for comparing two sets of data.

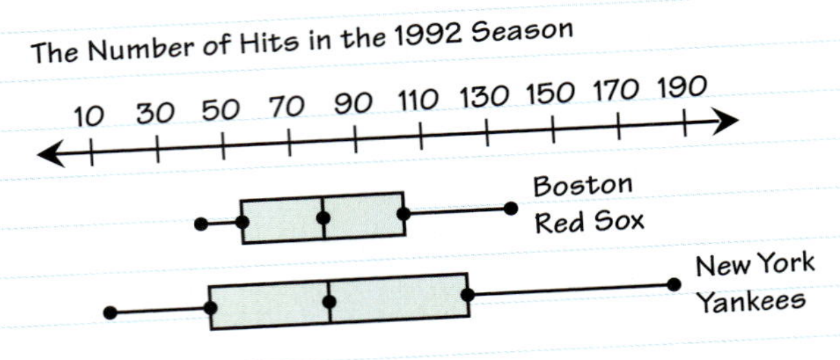

Bar graphs or **histograms** can be used to compare values in a data set.

Participation in Soccer, 1994	
Age in years	Number of participants
7–11	5494
12–17	3536
18–24	1394
25–34	1023

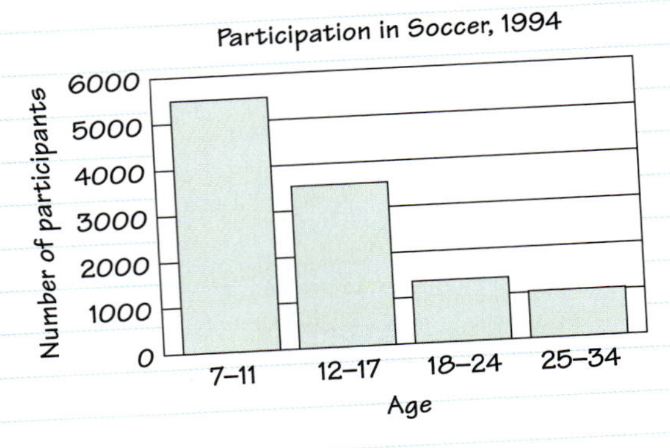

A frequency table is helpful when you have a large set of data to organize.

Stem-and-leaf plots display individual data values. These plots can help you organize data and see gaps and clusters in the data.

Number of Bushels of Wheat Harvested per Acre for Selected States (1990)

2	8
3	1 2 4 5
4	0 8 8
5	
6	1
7	3

6 | 1 represents 61 bushels.

17 **Key Concepts Question** Which types of graphs described above would *not* be appropriate to use to represent the results of your class sleep survey? Explain your choices.

Practice & Application Exercises

YOU WILL NEED
For Ex. 10:
◆ compass
◆ protractor
For Exs. 12–14:
◆ Labsheet 4A
◆ compass
◆ protractor

Estimation **For Exercises 1–3, use the circle graph to estimate each percent.**

1. the percent of 1994 sports and compact cars that were red, green, or white

2. the percent of 1994 sports and compact cars that were blue

3. the percent of 1994 sports and compact cars that were black

Colors of New Sports Cars and Compact Cars, 1994 Model Year

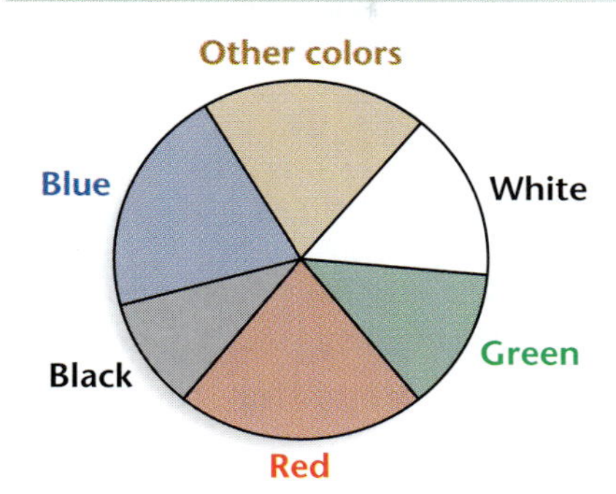

For Exercises 4–9, find the measure of the central angle for each sector of the circle. Round each measure to the nearest degree.

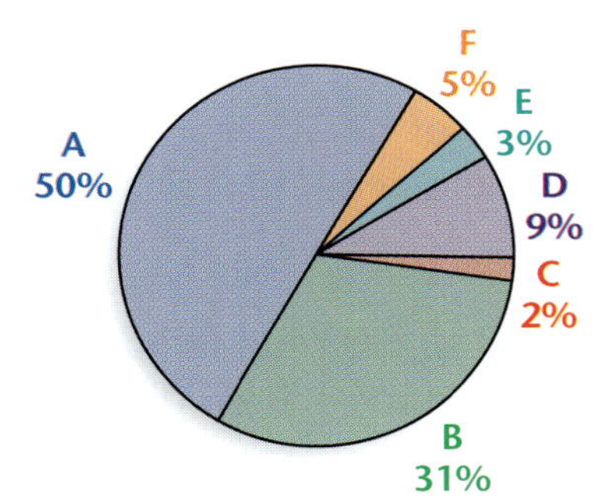

4. A
5. B
6. C
7. D
8. E
9. F

10. **Sleep Survey** A thousand people were asked to identify the main consequence of not getting enough sleep. Their responses are summarized in the table.

 a. Write each number as a percent.

 b. Find the measures of the central angles that represent the six responses on a circle graph.

 c. Make a circle graph to show the results of the survey. Make sure your graph is clearly labeled.

Main Consequence of Too Little Sleep

Response	Number of people
loss of energy	483
crankiness	200
less alert	103
less productive	76
other	48
do not know/ no response	90

11. Surveys People in France were asked how interesting they thought their lives were. Of those surveyed, 14% rated their lives as very interesting, 60% as fairly interesting, 22% as fairly dull, 3% as very dull, and 1% did not know. Choose the letter of the circle graph that shows these results. Explain your choice.

A.
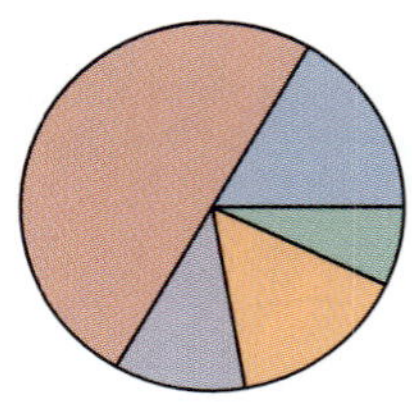

B.
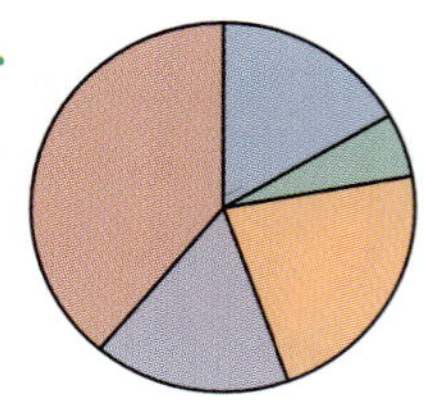

C.
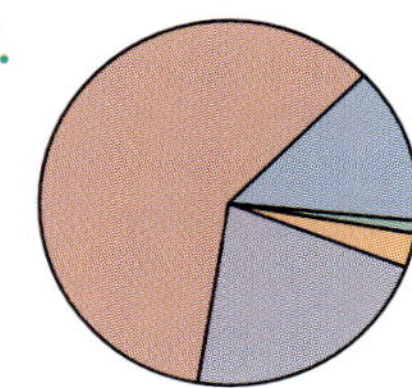

Use Labsheet 4A for Exercises 12–14.

12. Vacation Days *The Vacation Days Table* compares the number of vacation days per year for different jobs in various world cities. Make a graph that compares the vacation days for two of the jobs.

13. Write three conclusions you can draw based on the graph you made in Exercise 12.

14. Several surveys have been done to find out the average time people go to sleep and wake up each day. The *Sleep Time Survey* results show the bedtimes and wake-up times of 11–15 year old girls and boys. Do teenagers get less sleep as they get older? Make a graph to support your answer.

15. Radio Listening A radio station reports that of the total radio listening audience in the United States, 36% listen to the radio at work, 32% listen at home, and 30% listen in the car. Terri decides to show these results with a graph. Do you think her graph is accurate and effective? Explain.

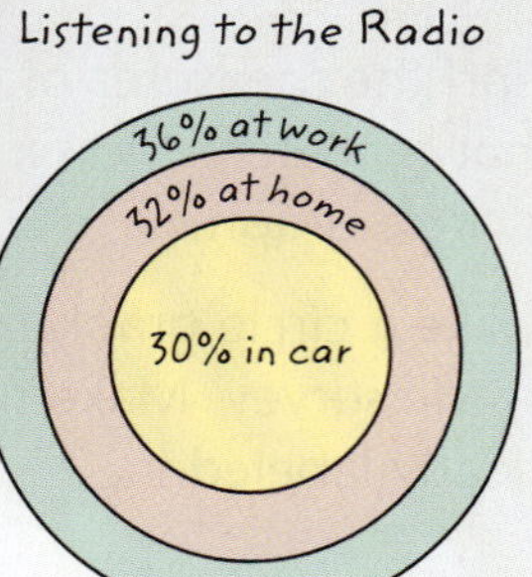

Reflecting on the Section

16. Sleep Research Scientists have divided sleep into stages. A group of sleepers were monitored to find out how much time they spent in each stage. The average percent of the total sleep period spent in each stage is shown in the graph. Each percent is represented by the height of a rectangular prism.

a. About what percent of sleep time is spent in Stage 2? Is it possible for someone to incorrectly read the graph? Explain.

b. Suppose you want to show that the total amount of time people spend in Stages 1, 3, and 4 is about the same as the time spent in REM sleep. Does this graph show this? Explain.

c. Explain how you could represent the same results with a different type of graph.

Sleep stages are defined by brain wave (EEG) patterns. There are two basic types of sleep—REM and non-REM, or NREM. The colorful, visual dreams that people are most likely to remember occur during REM, or rapid eye movement, sleep.

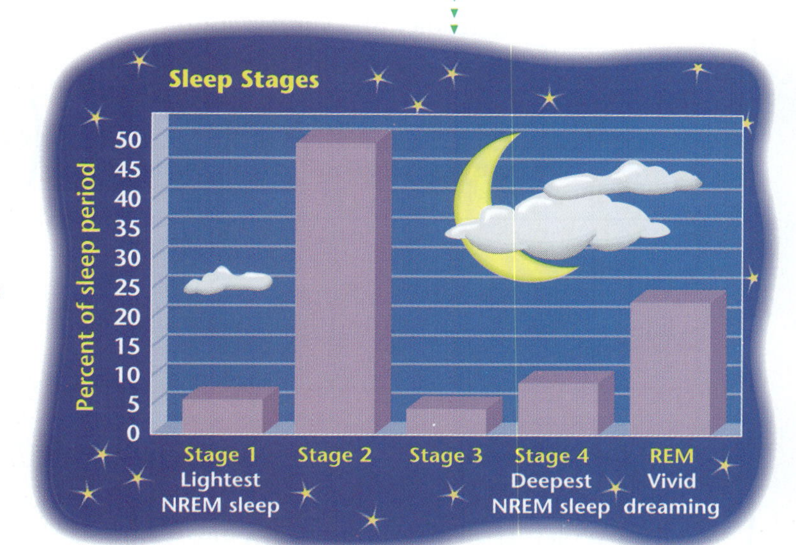

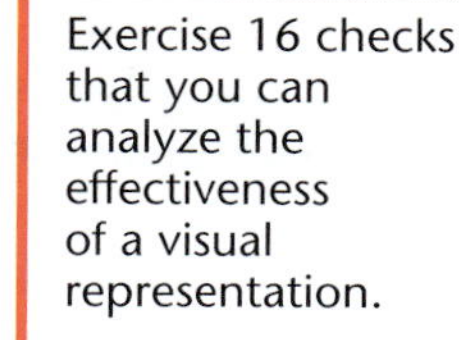

Exercise 16 checks that you can analyze the effectiveness of a visual representation.

Spiral Review

Replace each ? with the number that makes each a true statement. (Mod 7, p. 493)

17. 6 tbsp = __?__ fl oz

18. 12 fl oz = __?__ qt

19. $\frac{3}{4}$ qt = __?__ gal

20. $\frac{1}{2}$ gal = __?__ fl oz

Evaluate each expression. (Module 4, p. 284)

21. $\frac{1}{4}(-10) - 1$

22. $3.7 \div 2 + -8$

23. $-12 \cdot \frac{5}{8} + 7$

Find the area of each figure. (Module 6, p. 388)

24.

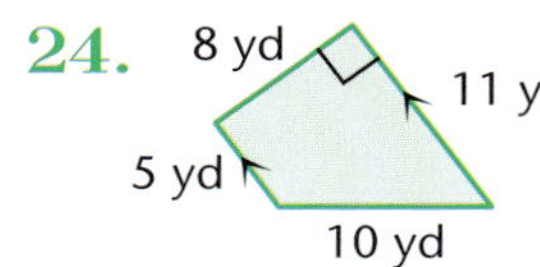

25.

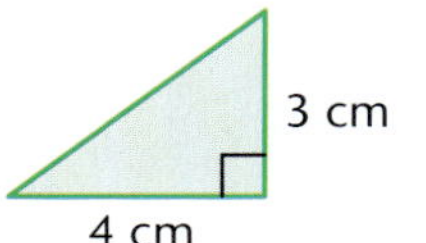

26.

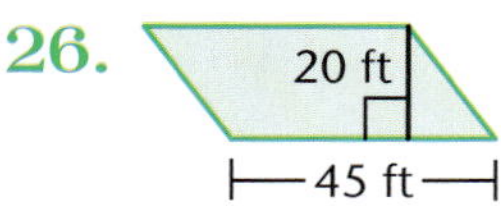

The Picture of Health

Analyzing Data Before making a graph, you should decide what message you want the graph to convey. Begin by looking at your data.

The table lists the results of a survey conducted in the United States in 1993.

Participation in Exercise Activities			
Grade	Vigorous exercise	Stretching exercises	Strengthening exercises
9th	74.5%	64.3%	60.9%
10th	69.5%	57.4%	55.0%
11th	62.5%	50.9%	48.5%
12th	57.8%	46.9%	44.6%

VIGOROUS EXERCISE

What message could you convey with this data? Here are some ideas to think about.

- Which type of exercise is the most popular?
- Is there a dramatic difference in participation among the different grade levels?
- Are there any surprising results in this data?
- Why is the total participation at each grade level greater than 100%?

Make a graph that illustrates your ideas about participation in exercise activities by students in grades 9–12.

STRENGTHENING EXERCISES

Section 4 Extra Skill Practice

For each sector of the circle graph, find the measure of the central angle. Round each measure to the nearest degree.

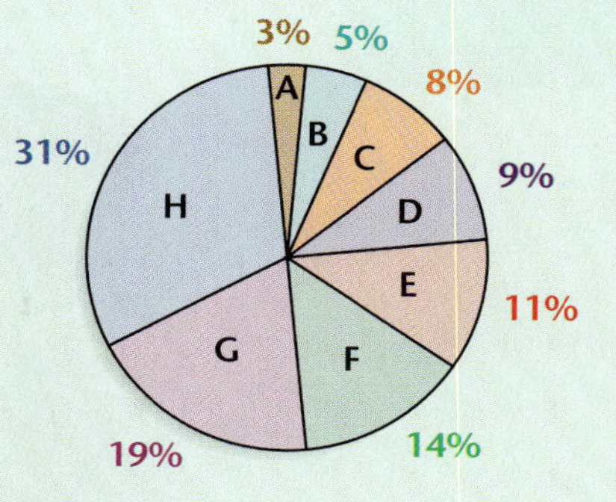

1. A
2. B
3. C
4. D
5. E
6. F
7. G
8. H

9. a. Choose the best kind of graph to compare the average daily household television viewing during the months of February and July for the years listed in the table.

   b. Draw the graph you have chosen.

   c. Write three conclusions you can draw based on your graph.

Average Daily Household Television Viewing (minutes)

Year	February	July
1988–1989	452	387
1989–1990	436	384
1990–1991	450	386
1991–1992	452	399
1992–1993	461	407

Standardized Testing ▶ Performance Task

Complete Exercises 1 and 2 for each type of graph named.

a. **bar graph** b. **stem-and-leaf-plot** c. **circle graph**
d. **box-and-whisker plot** e. **scatter plot** f. **histogram**

1. Tell what information about a data set can be read from each type of graph, and explain how each type of information is displayed.

2. Tell whether it is possible to make each type of graph misleading, and if it is possible, describe one way to do so.

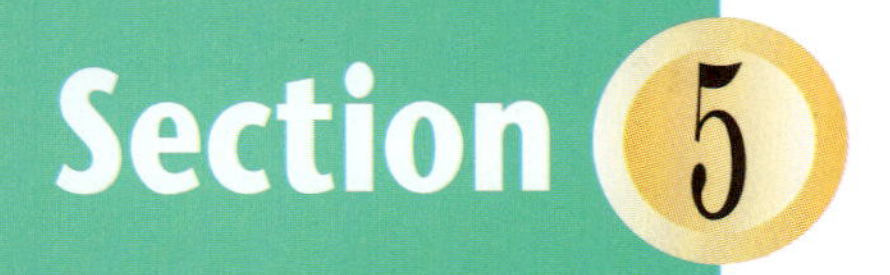

Quadrilaterals

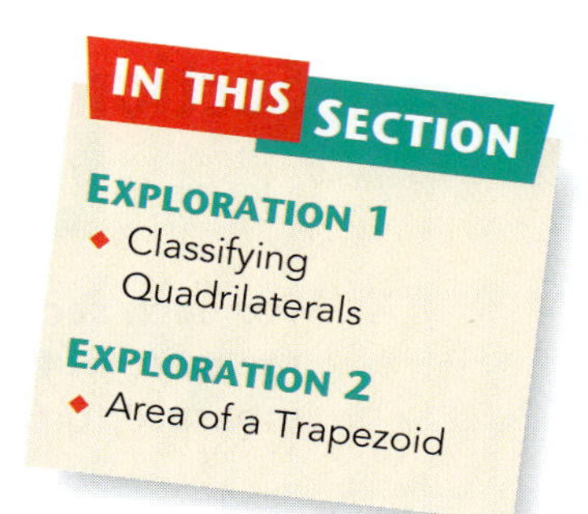

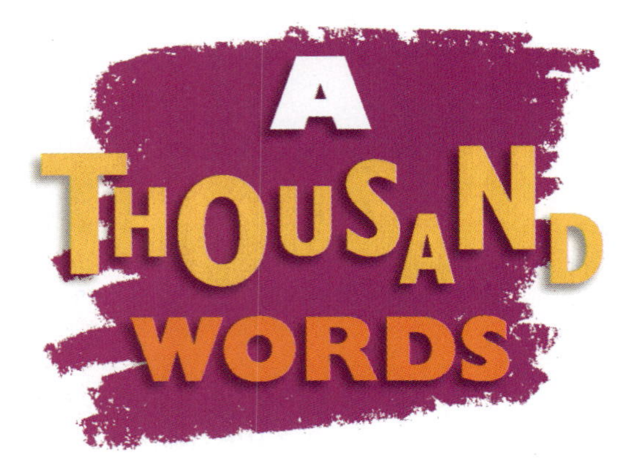

Setting the Stage

Have you ever heard the expression, "A picture is worth a thousand words"? Pictures and graphs have long been used to present ideas. The United States Department of Agriculture (USDA) uses graphs to educate people about the importance of nutrition. The graph below is the USDA's Food Guide Pyramid.

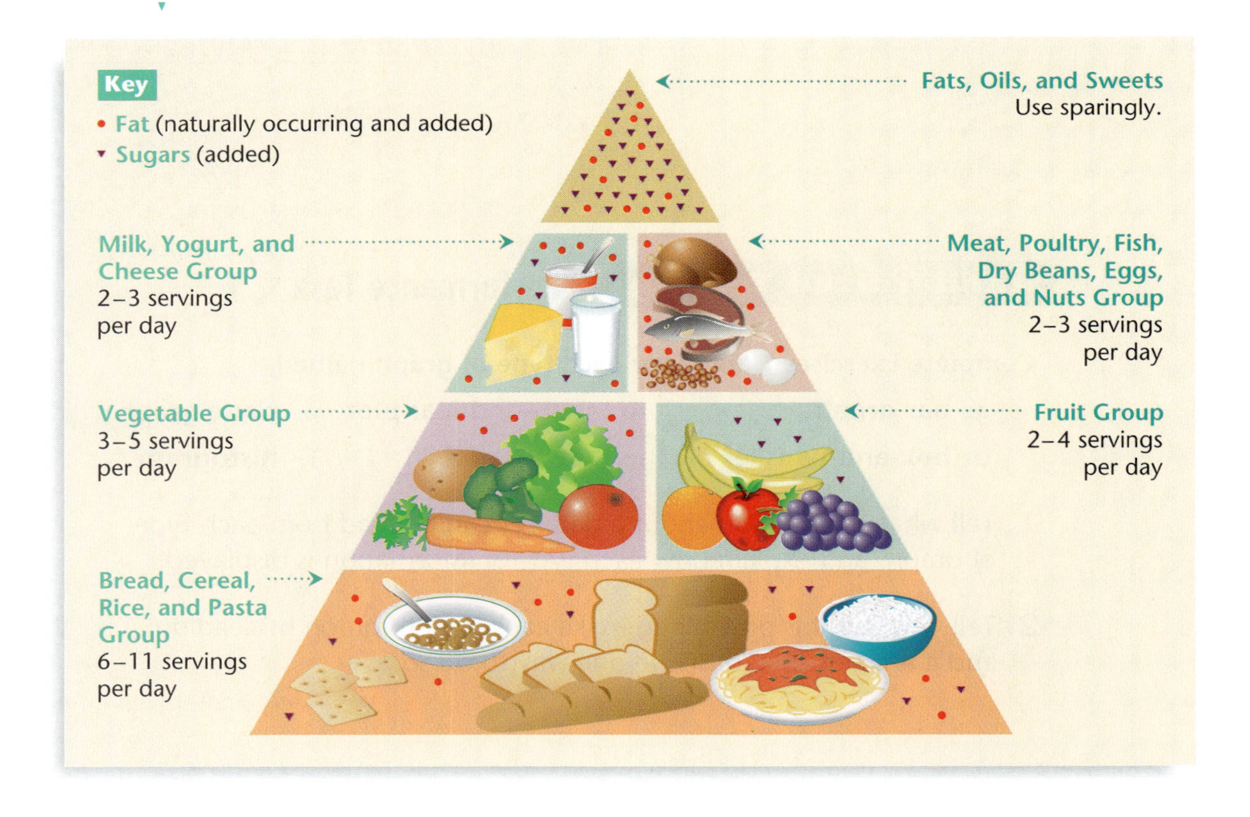

Think About It

1 The key for the Food Guide Pyramid shows symbols for fat and sugar. Where do these symbols appear in the pyramid?

2 Why do you think there are sugar symbols in the *Milk, Yogurt, and Cheese Group*?

3 Which food group of the pyramid shows no fats?

4 The USDA chose polygons to represent each food group of the pyramid. How many different types of polygons were used?

5 Are any of these polygons congruent? If so, which ones?

Exploration 1

CLASSIFYING Quadrilaterals

GOAL

LEARN HOW TO...
- identify trapezoids and rhombuses
- classify quadrilaterals

AS YOU...
- play the game *Quadrilateral Sets*

KEY TERMS
- trapezoid
- bases of a trapezoid
- rhombus

SET UP *Work in a group of three. You will need:*
- *Labsheets 5A–5C*
- *scissors*

The USDA surveyed people to determine the effectiveness of different graphs. Those surveyed generally felt that the pyramid was more visually appealing than other representations, such as a bar graph or a circle graph.

6 Look at the Food Guide Pyramid. Describe the shapes of the food group polygons.

▶ **Except for the *Fats, Oils, and Sweets Group*, the parts of the Food Guide Pyramid are all *trapezoids*.**

7 **Discussion** These polygons are all trapezoids. List two properties common to all the trapezoids.

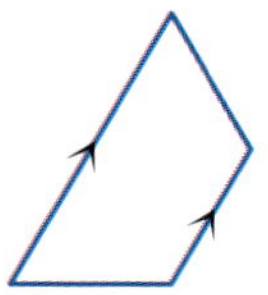

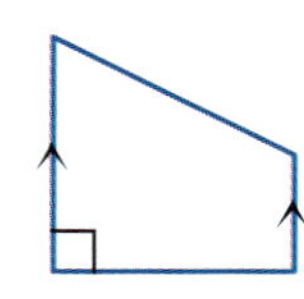

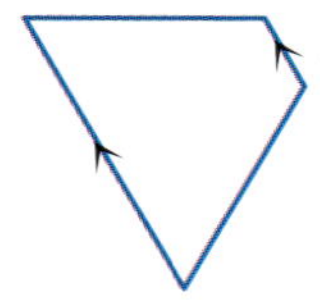

The arrowheads show that segments are parallel.

▶ A **trapezoid** is a quadrilateral that has only one pair of opposite sides which are parallel.

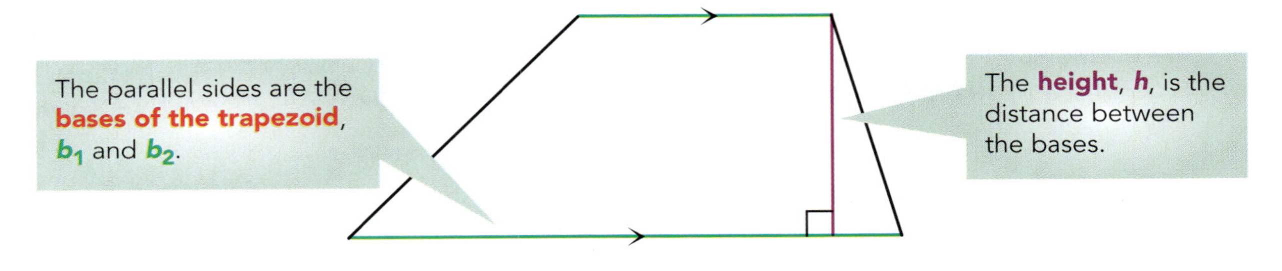

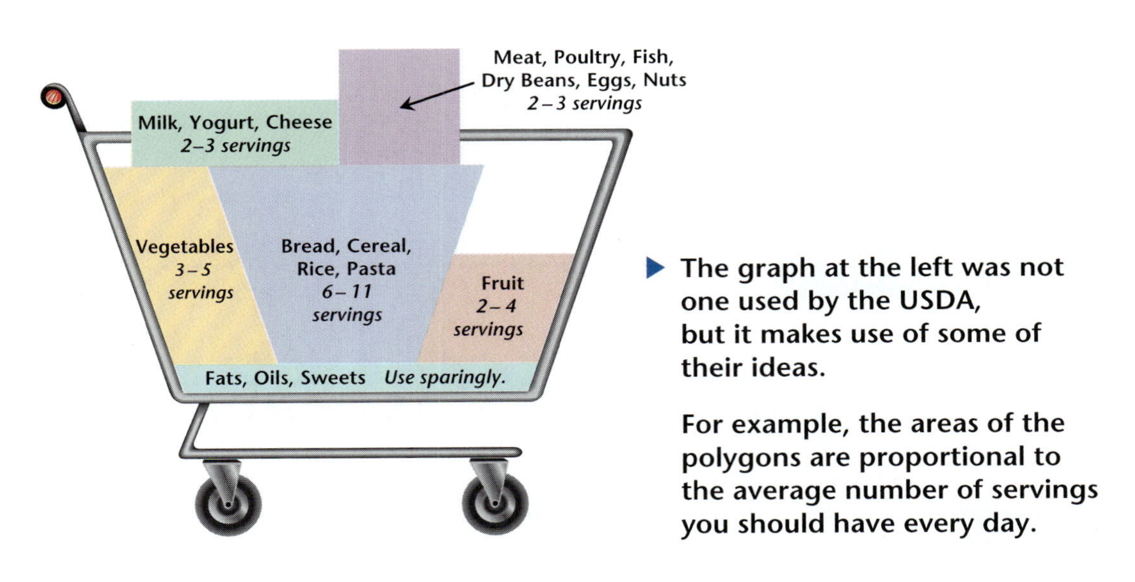

▶ The graph at the left was not one used by the USDA, but it makes use of some of their ideas.

For example, the areas of the polygons are proportional to the average number of servings you should have every day.

8 **Try This as a Class** Use the graph above.

a. Give as many names as you can for each polygon in the graph.

b. The polygon for the *Fruit Group* is a *rhombus*. A **rhombus** is a parallelogram that has four congruent sides. The quadrilaterals for which other food groups in the graph are rhombuses?

▶ In the game *Quadrilateral Sets*, you'll match a picture of a quadrilateral with the quadrilateral's name and one of its *attributes*, or properties.

Each set must contain one quadrilateral card, one name card, and one attribute card.

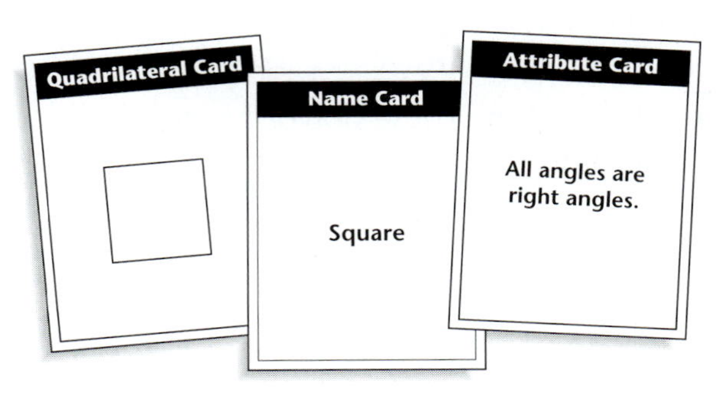

9 **Try This as a Class** Suppose you received the cards below in the game *Quadrilateral Sets*. Can you make two complete sets? Explain.

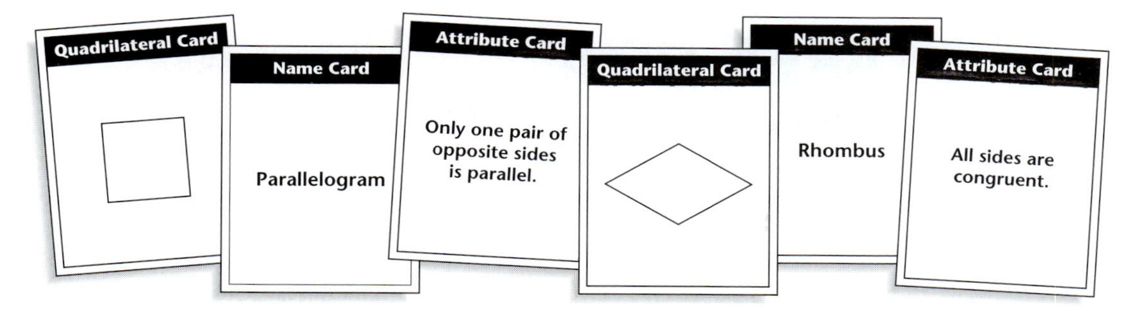

10 **Use Labsheets 5A–5C.** Cut out the *Quadrilateral Sets Game Cards*. Read the directions below and play the game twice.

Quadrilateral Sets

Set up

- Cut out the cards on Labsheets 5A–5C. Shuffle the cards and deal six cards face down to each of the three players. Any remaining cards should be placed face down in the middle of the table. This is the draw deck.
- Turn over the top card. This is the start of the discard pile.

Play

- Play begins with the player to the dealer's left and continues clockwise.
- On your turn, you may pick up the top card from either the discard pile or the draw deck. Use your cards to try to make two sets, each one containing one name, one attribute, and one quadrilateral card that go together.
- Then discard one card. Your turn is now over.

Winning

When you have two complete sets of cards, show them to the other players. If the sets are complete and correct, you win!

Challenge

You may challenge another player's set by showing that one of the cards does not belong. If the sets are not complete or accurate, the cards are picked up and the game continues.

11 **Discussion** What strategies did you use in the game? Were some cards better to keep than others? Why?

HOMEWORK EXERCISES See Exs. 1–9 on p. 519.

GOAL

LEARN HOW TO...
- find the area of a trapezoid

AS YOU...
- analyze the Food Guide Pyramid

Exploration 2

AREA OF A Trapezoid

SET UP *Work in a group. You will need:* • *Labsheet 5D* • *scissors* • *metric ruler* • *tracing paper*

In designing the Food Guide Pyramid, the USDA considered the relative sizes of the parts. For instance, the *Bread Group*, with 6–11 servings, should be larger than the *Milk Group*, with 2–3 servings. You can explore the relative sizes of the food groups by comparing their areas.

FOR HELP with *area of a parallelogram*, see **MODULE 6, p. 388**

▶ **You can use what you know about the area of a parallelogram to determine the area of a trapezoid.**

Parallelogram

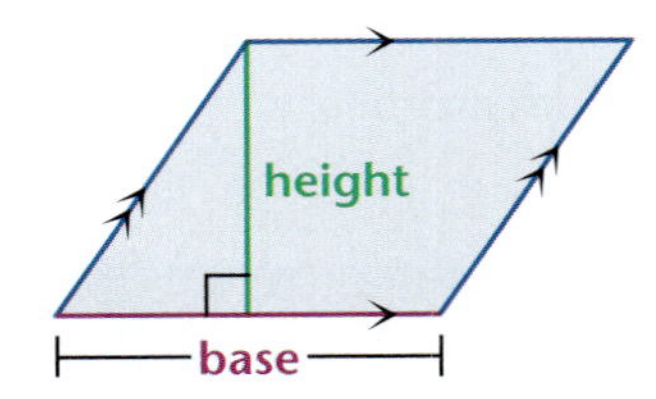

Area = base length • height

Trapezoid

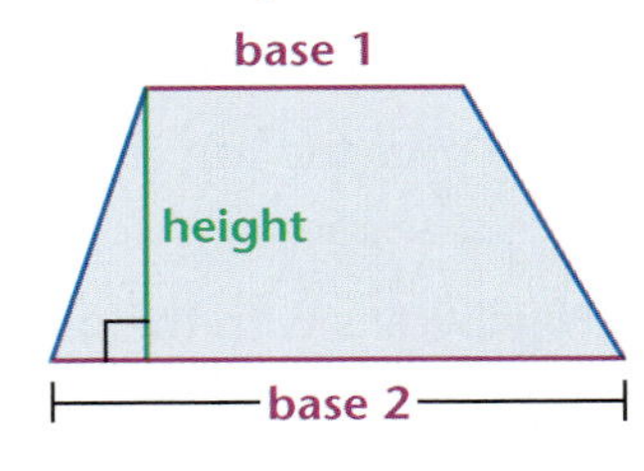

Area = ?

12 Use Labsheet 5D.

a. Cut out one of the *Trapezoids*. (Each member of your group should work with a different trapezoid.) Estimate the area of your trapezoid in square centimeters.

b. Trace your trapezoid from part (a) and cut it out. The two trapezoids are congruent. Form a parallelogram with the trapezoids.

c. Find the area of the parallelogram in square centimeters. Explain how you found the area.

d. What is the area of the original trapezoid? Explain how you found the area.

e. How close was your estimate in part (a) to your answer in part (d)?

13 **Try This as a Class** In Question 12, you used two trapezoids to form a parallelogram.

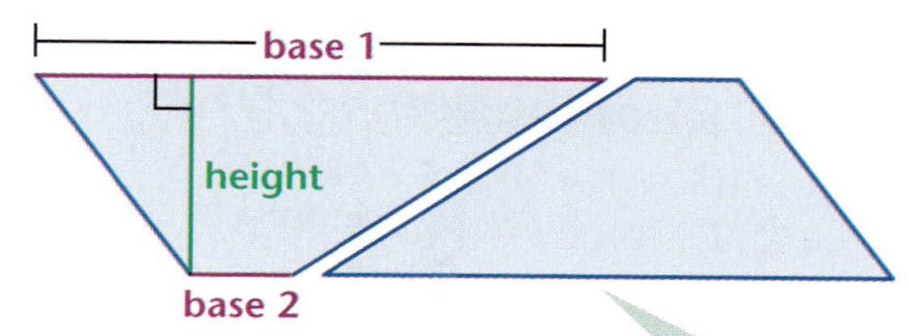

a. Use the diagram above to write an expression for the area of the parallelogram.

b. The area of one trapezoid is half the area of the parallelogram. Write a formula for the area of a trapezoid.

14 Use your trapezoid from Question 12.

a. Calculate the area of your trapezoid using your formula from Question 13(b).

b. Compare your answer in part (a) with your answer in Question 12(d).

15 ✓ **CHECKPOINT** Use the *Bread Group* and *Milk Group* polygons from the Food Guide Pyramid on page 512.

a. Find the area of each polygon.

b. About how many times as many servings should you have of the *Bread Group* as of the *Milk Group*? Do you think the relative areas of the parts of the Food Guide Pyramid show this? Explain.

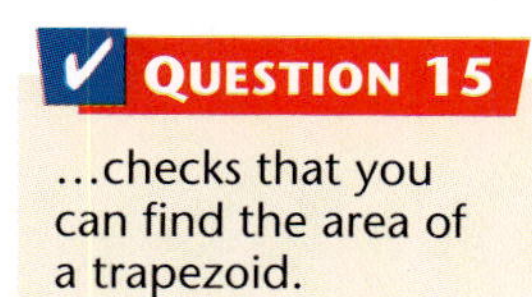

...checks that you can find the area of a trapezoid.

HOMEWORK EXERCISES ▶ See Exs. 10–20 on pp. 519–520.

Section 5 Key Concepts

Key Terms

trapezoid

bases of a trapezoid

rhombus

Trapezoids and Rhombuses (pp. 513–515)

A trapezoid is a quadrilateral that has exactly one pair of parallel sides. The sides that are parallel are the bases of the trapezoid.

A rhombus is a parallelogram that has four congruent sides (as indicated by the tick marks).

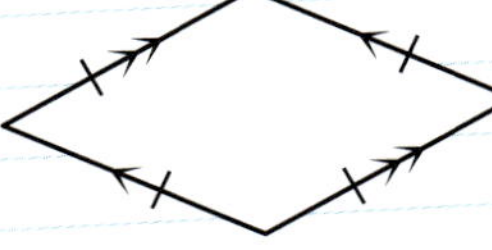

Area of a Trapezoid (pp. 516–517)

The area of a trapezoid can be calculated using the formula

$$A = \frac{1}{2}(b_1 + b_2)h$$

where A is the area, h is the height, and b_1 and b_2 are the base lengths.

Example Find the area of the trapezoid shown.

$$A = \frac{1}{2}(3 + 4.5)2 = \frac{1}{2}(7.5)2 = \left(\frac{7.5}{2}\right)2 = 7.5$$

The area is 7.5 m^2.

Key Concepts Questions

16 Copy the Venn diagram below and then fill in the missing quadrilateral names.

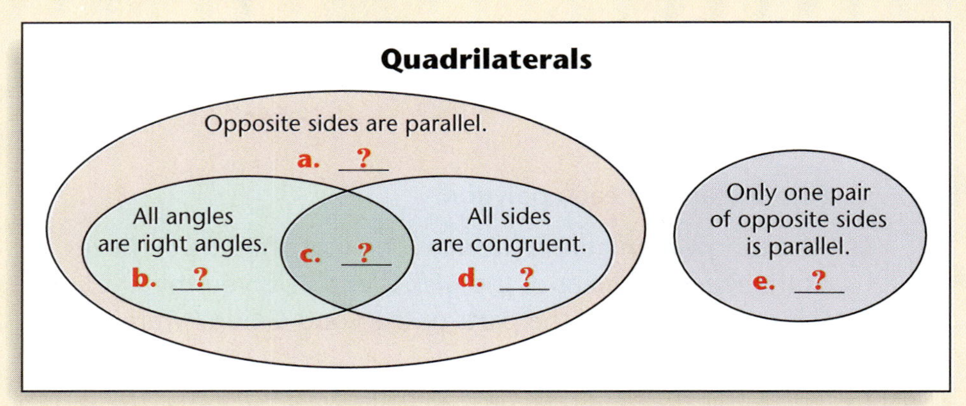

17 Find the area of a trapezoid with base lengths 3 cm and 5 cm and height 4 cm.

Section 5 Practice & Application Exercises

YOU WILL NEED

For Ex. 6:
- graph paper

For Exs. 18 and 19:
- Labsheet 5D
- metric ruler

Choose the letters of all the figures of each type.

1. trapezoid
2. parallelogram that is not a rhombus
3. rhombus

A.

B.

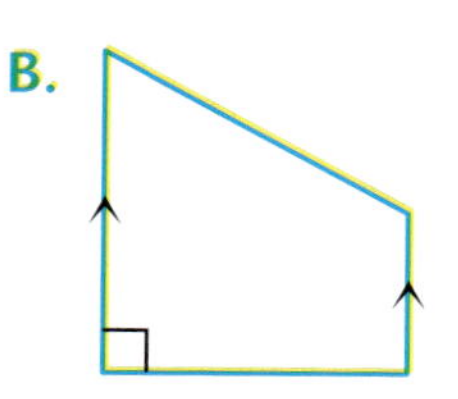

C.

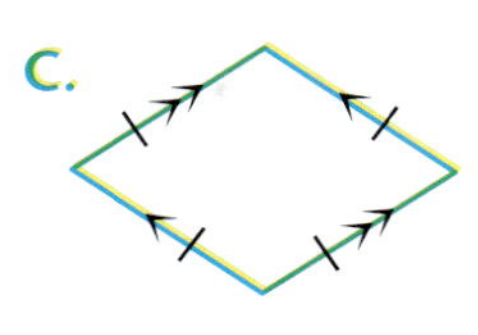

D.

E.

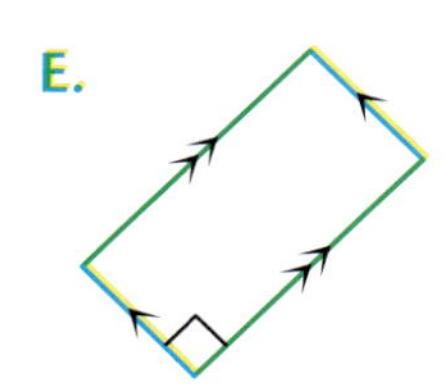

F.

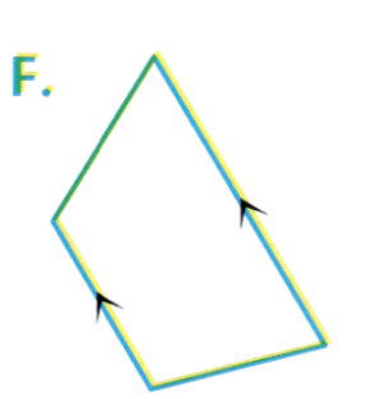

4. Suppose you have a parallelogram card in your hand during a game of *Quadrilateral Sets*. Which attribute cards can go with it?

5. Suppose you have the attribute card "All sides are congruent." in a game of *Quadrilateral Sets*. Which quadrilateral cards can go with it?

6. **Open-ended** Draw a trapezoid, a rhombus, a square, a parallelogram, and a rectangle on graph paper.

Find the area of each rhombus.

7.

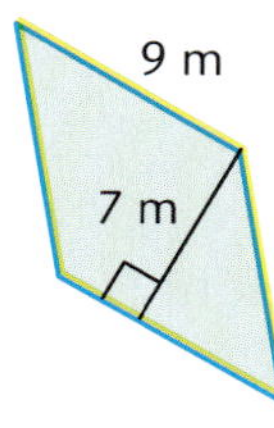

8.

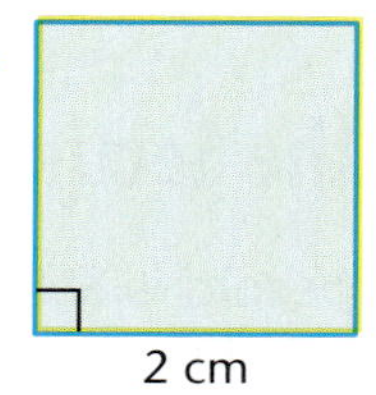

9.

4 in.

3 in.

10. **Urban Gardening** A corner plot of an urban garden is set aside for the Rodriguez family, as shown. What *percent* of the garden will be used by the Rodriguez family?

Find the area of each trapezoid with the given measurements.

11. $b_1 = 4$ in., $b_2 = 2$ in., $h = 6$ in.

12. $b_1 = 4.3$ m, $b_2 = 5.1$ m, $h = 2.7$ m

13. $b_1 = 4\frac{1}{4}$ in., $b_2 = 7\frac{1}{2}$ in., $h = 3\frac{1}{2}$ in.

14. $b_1 = 6.75$ cm, $b_2 = 5.64$ cm, $h = 3.2$ cm

For each trapezoid, find the unknown dimension or the area.

15. 2 cm, $A = ?$, 5 cm, 9 cm

16.

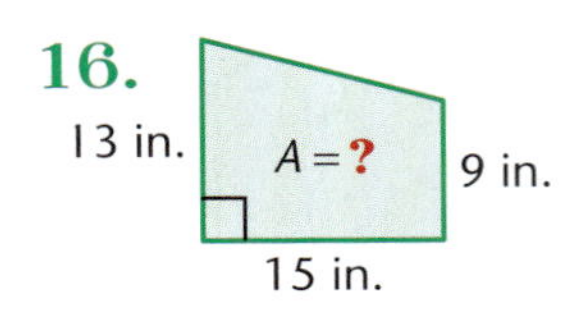

17.

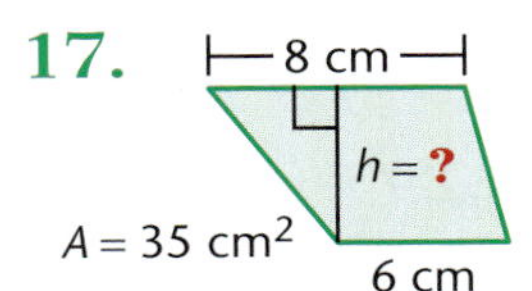

Use Labsheet 5D for Exercises 18 and 19.

18. In Exploration 2, you found the area of a trapezoid by forming a parallelogram from two congruent trapezoids. Another way to find the area is to think of the trapezoid as a *composite figure*—one made from a combination of other shapes.

   a. Draw segments to separate the *Trapezoid* into other shapes.

   b. Find the area of the *Trapezoid* by finding the area of these smaller shapes. Measure to the nearest tenth of a centimeter.

   c. Is this method easier to use than the other methods you learned in Exploration 2? Why or why not?

19. **Open-ended** Separate the *Polygon* into quadrilaterals and triangles. Find the area of the *Polygon* in square centimeters.

Reflecting on the Section

Visual THINKING

Exercise 20 checks that you understand what a trapezoid is and how to find its area.

20. Suppose the area of a trapezoid is 8 cm^2 and its height is 2 cm. Draw two trapezoids that fit this description.

Spiral Review

For each sector of the circle graph, find the measure of the central angle. Round to the nearest degree. (Module 7, p. 505)

21. A 22. B 23. C

24. D 25. E 26. F

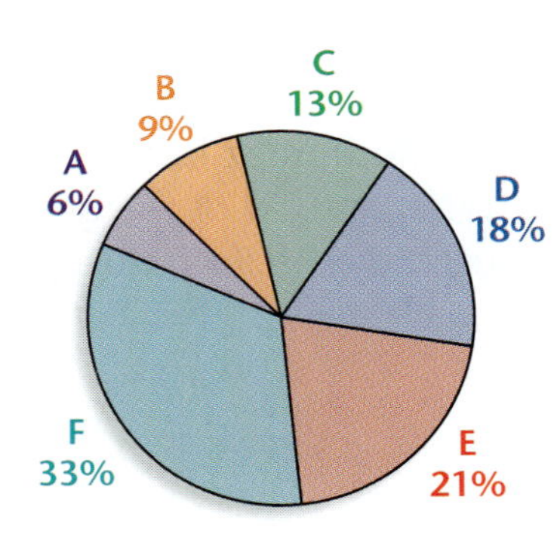

For Exercises 27 and 28, write an expression that models each situation. (Module 2, p. 124)

27. Danny's Aunt Judy is twice as old as Danny. Danny is x years old. How old is Danny's aunt?

28. Marisa studied 20 minutes more than Burt did. If Marisa studied for t min, how long did Burt study?

29. Draw a tree diagram to represent all the possible outcomes when you toss a coin twice. (*Hint:* The outcomes are *heads* (H) and *tails* (T).) How many outcomes are there? (Module 3, p. 171)

Career Connection

Research Geologist: Martha Withjack

Geology is the study of the earth and its rocks. Martha Withjack uses her knowledge of geology to help locate underground deposits of oil and natural gas. To find these deposits, she needs to understand how the rocks that hold the oil and natural gas have moved through time.

Rocks can be pulled apart, or *extended*. When the stressed rock layer breaks, part of it collapses, forming a hole. Since the rock layer has only changed shape and no rock has been removed or destroyed, the amount of rock that left the gap is the same as the amount of rock in the extended part of the layer.

Martha Withjack constructs scaled laboratory models to understand how rocks change through time.

30. a. Find the area of the side view of the hole in the rock layer.

b. Use your answer from part (a) to find HG, the amount of extension.

Area of trapezoid ***ABCD*** = Area of rectangle ***EFGH***

Original Rock Formation

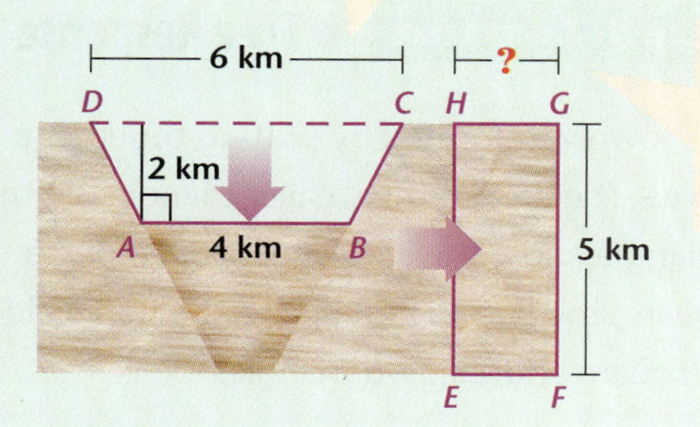

Extended Rock Formation

The amount of extension is the distance the rock has moved.

Section 5 Extra Skill Practice

Choose the letters of all the figures of each type.

1. trapezoid
2. parallelogram that is not a rhombus
3. rhombus

A. 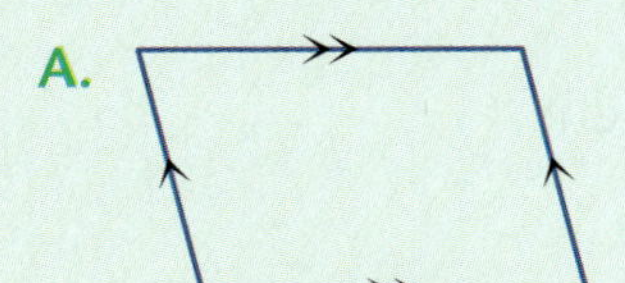

B. 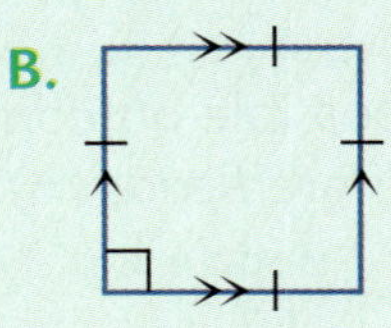

C. 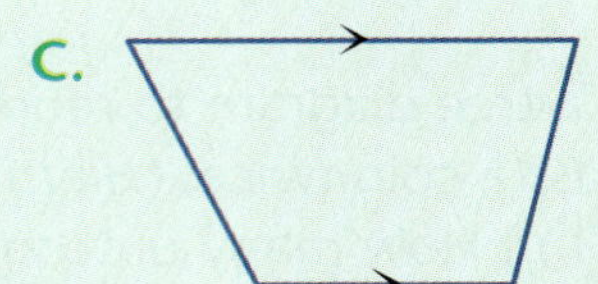

D. 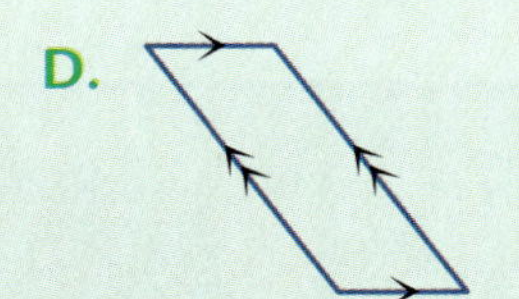

E. 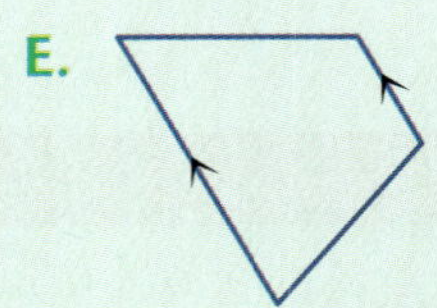

F. 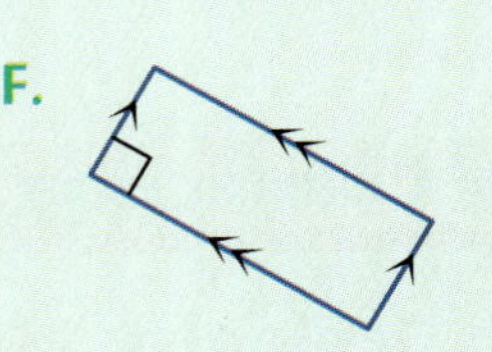

Find the area of each trapezoid.

4. 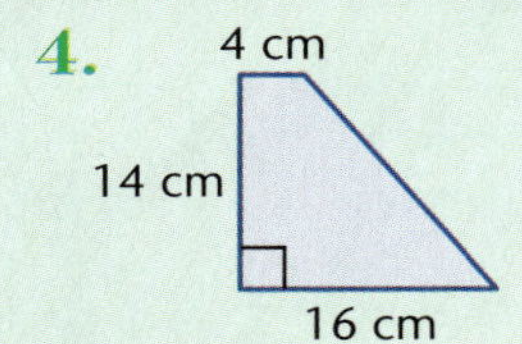

5. 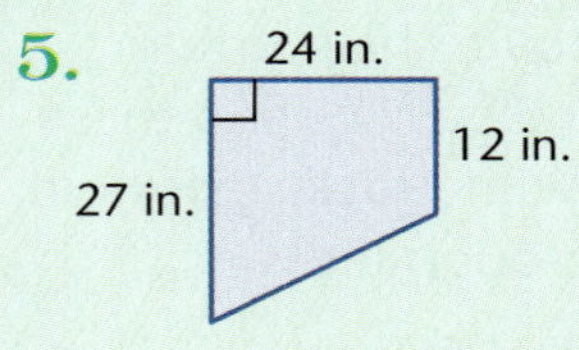

6. 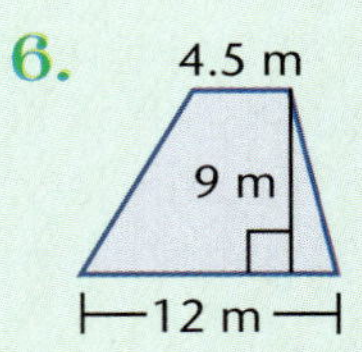

For each quadrilateral, find each unknown dimension or the area.

7. Trapezoid

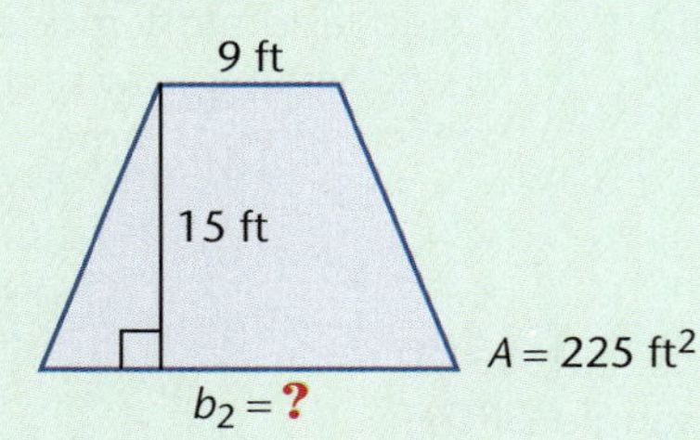

8. Parallelogram

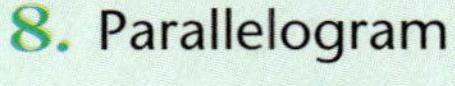
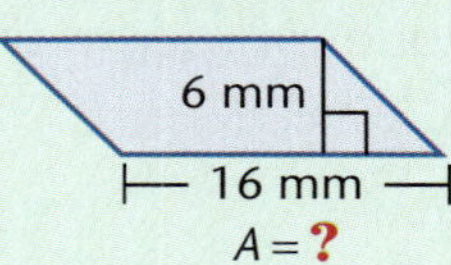

9. Trapezoid

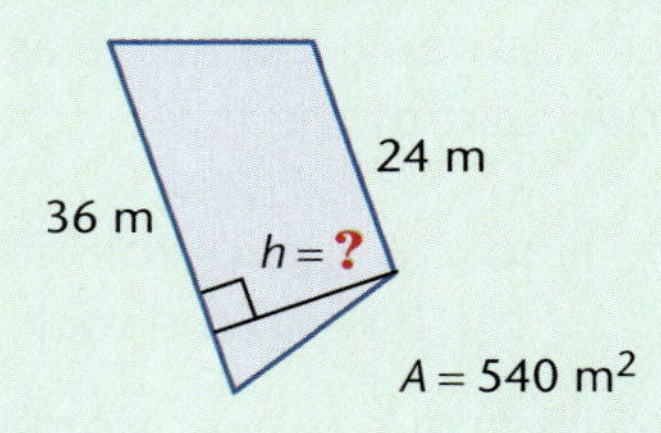

Standardized Testing ▶ Free Response

The trapezoid shown was formed by putting together a square and two triangles. The area of the smaller triangle is $\frac{1}{2}$ the area of the larger triangle and $\frac{1}{4}$ the area of the square. Find the areas of the square, the two triangles, and the trapezoid formed by the square and the two triangles.

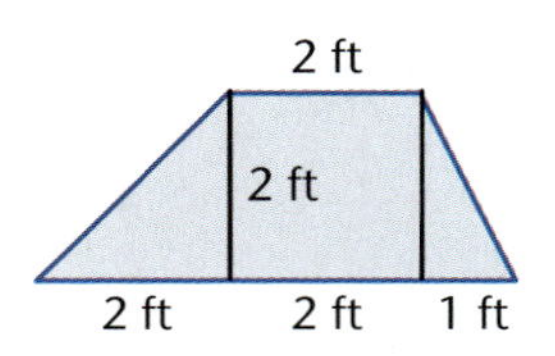

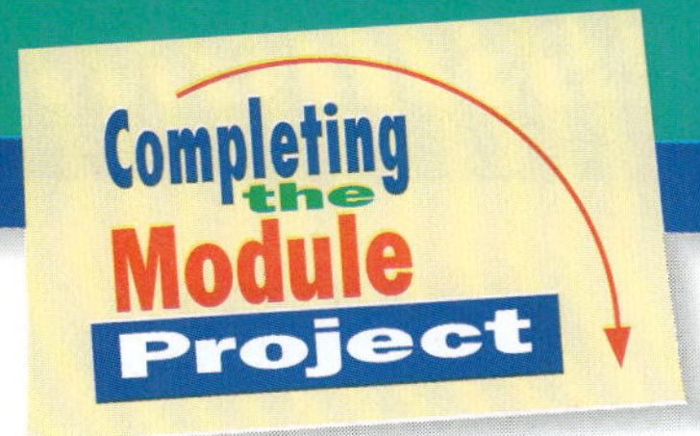

The Picture of Health

Choosing a Data Display In this module, you have seen several examples of how data can be presented, and you have made a graph using data that you were given. Now you are ready to make your own graph, using data you have selected. To convey information *and* get the reader's attention, you may want to use photos, drawings, and colors to make your graph stand out.

6 Examine the data you have selected for your project. What message would you like to convey with these data? Write a paragraph about the data that explains your conclusions.

7 **a.** What types of graphs could you use to display the data?

b. Decide which type of graph you think will best represent the data. Then make a graph of the data.

8 Does the graph tell your message clearly? Could it be considered misleading? Is it easy to understand? How could you change your graph to better represent the data?

9 Create an eye-catching poster or brochure that includes your graph and your paragraph from Project Question 6. Think of ways you might make your graphic design more interesting for the reader.

MODULE 7 Review and Assessment

You will need: • *compass* (Ex. 24) • *protractor* (Ex. 24)

Find the volume of each cylinder. Use 3.14 for π. (Sec. 1, Explor. 1)

1. 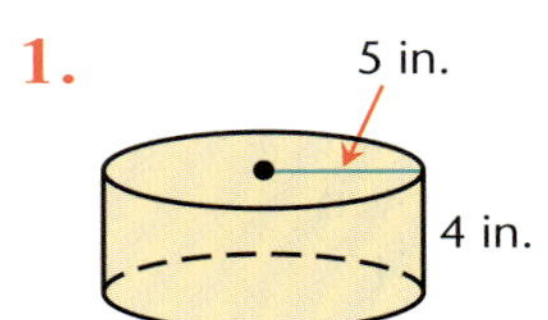

2. 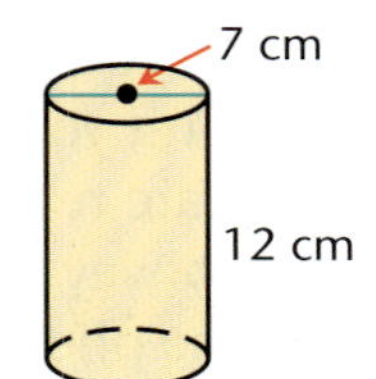

3. 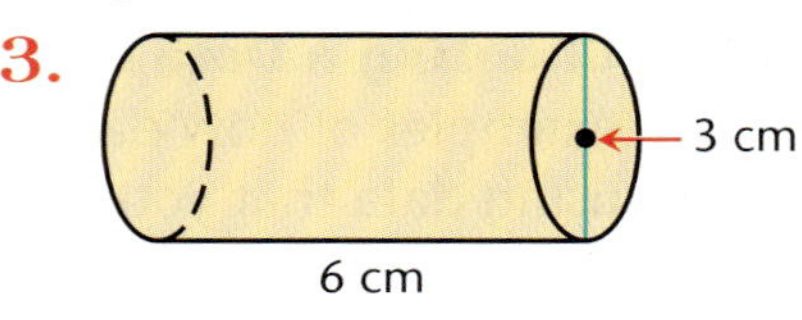

Find the slope of a line with each rise and run. (Sec. 1, Explor. 2)

4. rise 2
run 4

5. rise 9
run 9

6. rise 8
run 2

7. rise 0
run 3

For Exercises 8–11, use the bar graph.
(Sec. 1, Explor. 3)

8. Without looking at the scale, compare the data values visually.

9. Use the scale to estimate the data values.

10. Based on your estimates of the data values, were your visual comparisons in Exercise 8 accurate?

11. How can you redraw the graph so that it is less misleading?

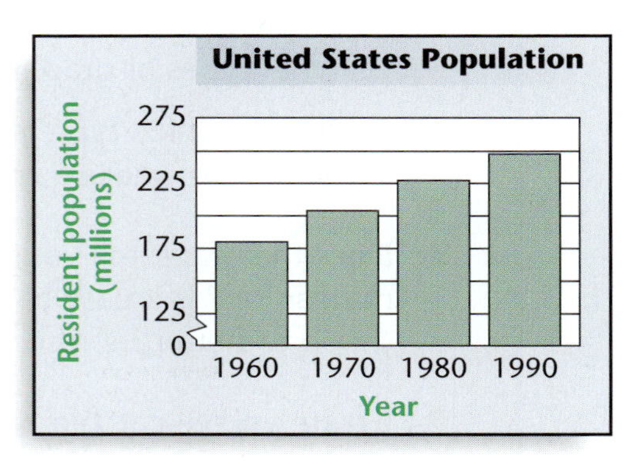

Find each percent. Round each answer to the nearest whole percent.
(Sec. 2, Explor. 1)

12. 72 is what percent of 45?

13. 126 is what percent of 84?

14. 175 is what percent of 20?

15. 83 is what percent of 17?

For Exercises 16–17, find each percent of change. (Sec. 2, Explor. 2)

16. Yesterday's price: $28.00
Today's price: $24.80

17. First-year enrollment: 180
Second-year enrollment: 240

18. The cost to send a child to a daycare center for a week increased by 10% from 1993 to 1996. The cost per week was $150 in 1993. What was the cost in 1996? (Sec. 2, Explor. 2)

Replace each ? with the number that makes each a true statement.
(Sec. 3, Explor. 1)

19. 5 pt = ? c

20. 7 c = ? qt

21. $\frac{1}{2}$ gal = ? fl oz

22. Suppose a test has two types of questions: multiple-choice, worth 3 points each, and short-answer, worth 5 points each. A student gets *m* multiple-choice questions and *n* short-answer questions correct. Write an inequality that models the relationship among *m*, *n*, and the maximum score of 100. **(Sec. 3, Explor. 2)**

23. Estimate the median, the upper and lower extremes, and the upper and lower quartiles in the box-and-whisker plot. **(Sec. 3, Explor. 3)**

Amount of Vitamin C in Some Foods (mg)

0 10 20 30 40 50 60 70 80

Some common fruits

24. Make a circle graph for the data in the table below. **(Sec. 4, Explor. 1)**

Public School Enrollment in the U.S., October 1992 (thousands)				
Grade	pre-school	1–8	9–12	college
Enrollment	4605	27,054	12,158	11,065

25. **Choosing a Data Display** To display the ages of all the members of the U.S. Congress, would you draw a *box-and-whisker plot*, a *stem-and-leaf plot*, or a *histogram*? Explain. **(Sec. 4, Explor. 2)**

26. **Writing** Suppose in a phone call to a friend you have to explain what a parallelogram is. How would you describe the relationship between opposite sides? opposite angles? **(Sec. 5, Explor. 1)**

Find the area of each trapezoid. (Sec. 5, Explor. 2)

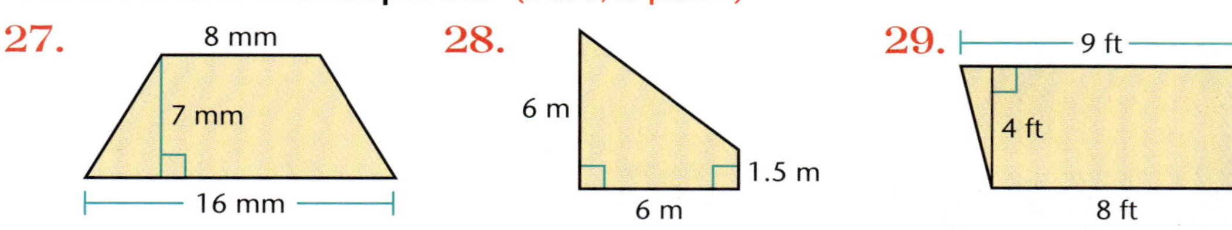

Reflecting on the Module

30. **Research** Find a variety of graphs in newspapers or magazines. Analyze them based on what you have learned in this module.

MODULE 8

HEART OF THE CITY

CONNECTING MATHEMATICS & The Theme

SECTION OVERVIEW

1 Counting Problems

As you find travel routes between and within cities:

- Find all the different ways to order a group of items
- Use tree diagrams and the counting principle

2 Drawing Views and Finding Volumes

As you build models of skyscrapers:

- Draw front, back, and side views of space figures
- Find volumes of pyramids

3 Permutations and Combinations

As you find the shortest paths through a grid of city streets:

- Find permutations with repeated items
- Select items to create combinations when order is not important

4 Tessellations and Volumes of Cones

As you explore how art is used to brighten up the urban landscape:

- Create tessellations with triangles and quadrilaterals
- Find volumes of cones

The Module Project

Traffic Flow

Have you ever been caught in a traffic jam? You'll use your problem solving, measurement, and estimation skills to analyze and develop a plan to improve the movement of foot traffic through a busy hallway in your school.

More on the Module Project

See pp. 538, 561, and 577.

INTERNET
To learn more about the theme:
http://www.mlmath.com

Section 1 Counting Problems

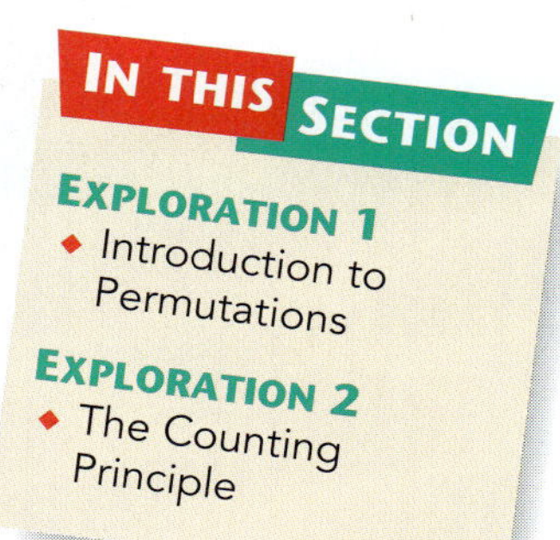

Setting the Stage

In *City in All Directions*, urban poet Arnold Adoff describes the constant motion of life in New York City.

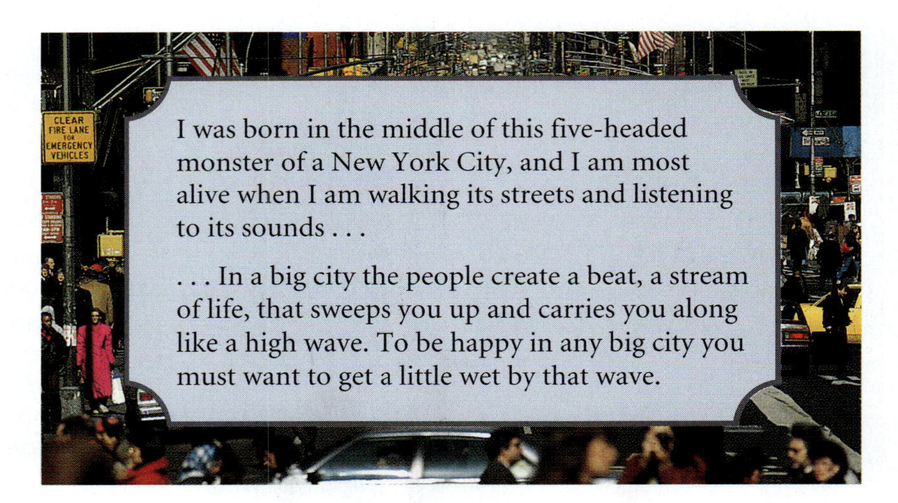

I was born in the middle of this five-headed monster of a New York City, and I am most alive when I am walking its streets and listening to its sounds . . .

. . . In a big city the people create a beat, a stream of life, that sweeps you up and carries you along like a high wave. To be happy in any big city you must want to get a little wet by that wave.

Think About It

1. What do you think the poet means when he says that people in a city create a "beat" and a "stream of life"?
2. Name some things that make a city interesting or exciting for you.

Perhaps you have had the chance to experience the rhythm and energy of a big city yourself. Did you know that mathematics plays a very important role in making this "stream of life" flow smoothly?

Managing traffic, planning routes, constructing skyscrapers, and designing plazas all depend on mathematics. In this module, you'll see how many aspects of city life are organized using mathematics.

Exploration 1

INTRODUCTION TO Permutations

GOAL

LEARN HOW TO...
- find all possible arrangements of items

AS YOU...
- plan routes for a trip

KEY TERM
- permutation

SET UP *Work in a group of five.*

There are many guidebooks that rank cities in the United States according to aspects such as weather and recreation. Suppose it is up to you to rank the ten United States cities shown below.

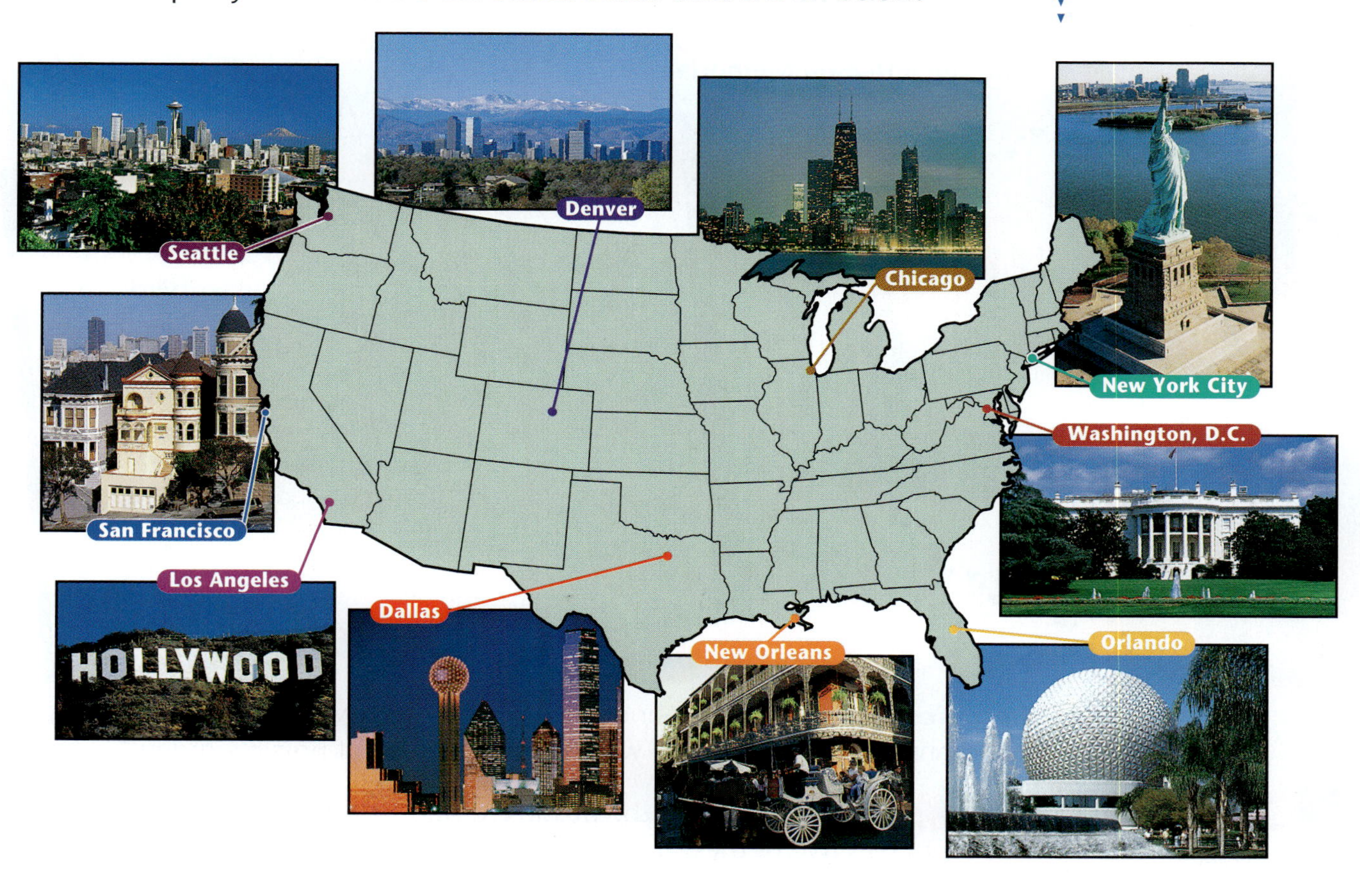

3 **a.** Work independently. Rank the cities in order from the one you most want to visit (1) to the one you least want to visit (10).

b. Give some reasons why you ranked the cities the way you did.

4 **Discussion** Suppose your group is going on a tour together and can visit only five of the cities on page 529.

a. How can your group use each person's individual rankings to decide on the five cities your group would most like to visit?

b. Together choose the top five cities for your group to visit.

c. Is the order in which your group selected or listed the cities in part (b) important? Why or why not?

5 **a.** List the five cities your group selected in the order you would prefer to visit them. Why did you choose this order?

b. **Discussion** Compare your list with those of the other members in your group. How many different orders did your group find?

▶ **Permutations** **An arrangement of a group of items in which the order is important is called a permutation. The notebook below shows the six possible orders in which a group visiting Washington, D.C., can visit the Washington Monument, the Lincoln Memorial, and the Jefferson Memorial.**

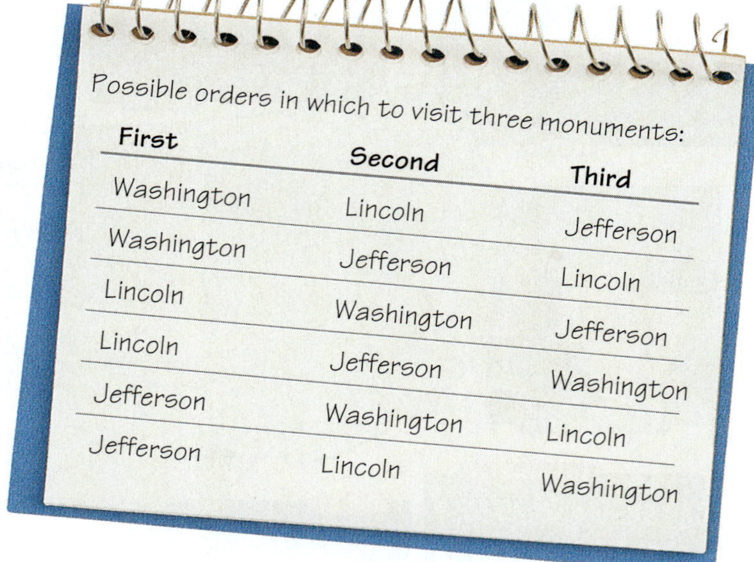
Possible orders in which to visit three monuments:

First	Second	Third
Washington	Lincoln	Jefferson
Washington	Jefferson	Lincoln
Lincoln	Washington	Jefferson
Lincoln	Jefferson	Washington
Jefferson	Washington	Lincoln
Jefferson	Lincoln	Washington

6 **Discussion** Suppose your group will visit only two of the monuments shown. How will this affect the list of possible orders?

✔ QUESTION 7

...checks that you can use an organized list to find permutations.

7 **✔ CHECKPOINT** List all the possible orders in which your group could visit two of these four monuments: the Washington Monument, the Lincoln Memorial, the Jefferson Memorial, and the FDR Memorial.

HOMEWORK EXERCISES ▶ See Exs. 1–6 on p. 535.

Exploration 2

GOAL

LEARN HOW TO...
- apply tree diagrams to counting problems
- use the counting principle

AS YOU...
- find the number of routes between cities

KEY TERM
- counting principle

SET UP *You will need Labsheet 1A.*

To find the best routes between cities, travel agents and managers of shipping or trucking companies may need to identify and compare all the possible orders of travel. One way to solve this type of problem is to start by solving a simpler one.

Use the *Table of Orders* on Labsheet 1A to record the results of Questions 8 and 9.

8 To find all the possible orders to travel among five cities, begin with the top two cities that your group chose in Question 4.

a. In how many orders can you visit the two cities? Use the abbreviations to record the orders in the *Table of Orders*. For example, write the order New York City to Orlando as NY-O.

b. With two cities, how many cities can you choose from to visit first?

c. After you have chosen the city to visit first, how many cities are left to choose from for the next city on the trip?

9 Now consider the top three cities your group chose in Question 4.

a. In how many orders can you visit the three cities? Use the abbreviations to record the orders. For example, write the order Los Angeles to Denver to New York City as LA-De-NY.

b. With three cities, how many cities can you choose from to visit first?

c. After you have chosen the city to visit first, how many cities are left to choose from to visit second?

d. After you have chosen the first two cities to visit, how many cities are left to choose from for the third city?

Using Tree Diagrams A tree diagram is a useful tool for finding permutations. This tree diagram shows all the possible orders for traveling among Los Angeles, New York City, and New Orleans.

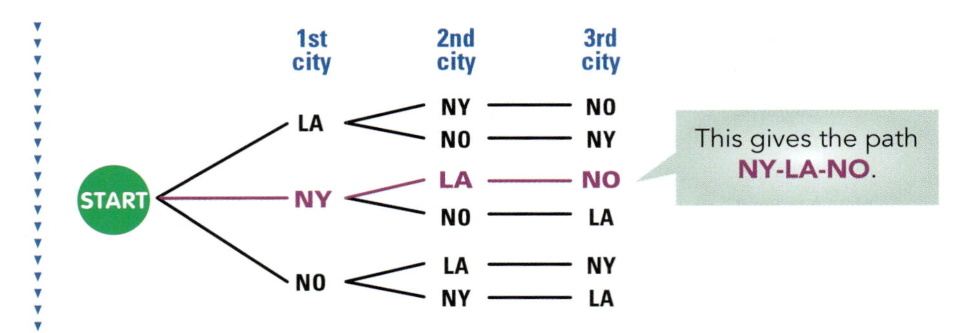

Here is part of another tree diagram. It shows all the possible orders for traveling among Los Angeles, New York City, New Orleans, and Chicago when Los Angeles is the first city you visit.

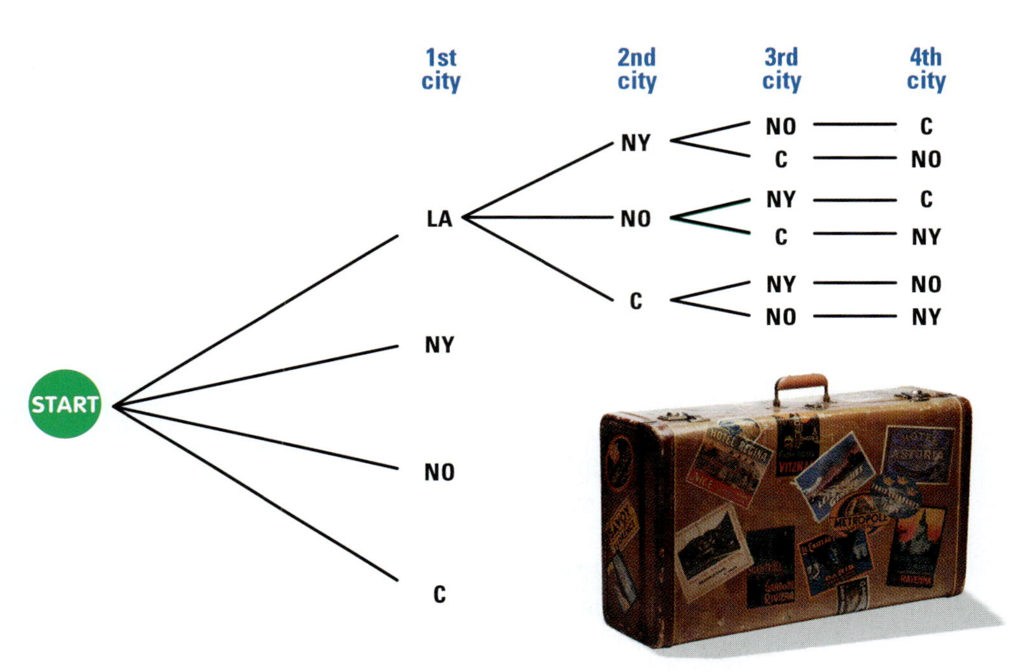

10 Refer to the tree diagram above. In how many different orders can you visit the four cities if you visit Los Angeles first and New York City second? if you visit Los Angeles first and either New Orleans or Chicago second?

Use Labsheet 1A for Questions 11–13.

11 Use the top four cities chosen by your group in Question 4. Make a *Tree Diagram for Four Cities* on Labsheet 1A to show all the possible orders in which you can visit the four cities.

12 Use your *Tree Diagram for Four Cities* to complete the last row of the *Table of Orders* with your answers to these questions.

a. How many choices are there for the first city you would visit**?**

b. After leaving the first city, how many choices are there for the second city you would visit**?**

c. After leaving the second city, how many choices are there for the third city you would visit**?**

d. After leaving the third city, how many choices are there for the fourth city you would visit**?**

e. In how many different orders can you visit the four cities**?**

13 **Try This as a Class** Look for a pattern in your *Table of Orders*. Explain how the total number of orders in which you can visit the cities is related to the number of choices for each stop on the trip.

▶ **The pattern you explored in Question 13 is called the counting principle. The example below shows how to apply this principle to find the total number of permutations.**

EXAMPLE

You can use the counting principle to find the number of possible orders in which a group can visit the Washington Monument, the Lincoln Memorial, and the Jefferson Memorial.

Number of choices for the 1st monument		Number of choices remaining for the 2nd monument		Number of choices remaining for the 3rd monument		Total possible orders for visiting all three monuments
3	•	2	•	1	=	6

Multiply the number of choices at each stop on the tour.

There are six possible orders in which to visit the monuments.

14 **✓ CHECKPOINT** Use the counting principle to calculate the number of different orders in which you can visit the five cities your group chose in Question 4.

...checks that you can calculate the total number of permutations.

HOMEWORK EXERCISES ▶ **See Exs. 7–18 on p. 536.**

Section 1 Key Concepts

Key Terms

permutation

Permutations (pp. 529–530)

The possible arrangements of a group of items in which order is important are called permutations. An organized list can help you find permutations.

Example Reta, Amy, Trinja, and Jennifer are being considered for the lead role and a supporting role in a play. Here are the possible ways in which the roles can be assigned.

Lead role	Supporting role	Lead role	Supporting role
Reta	Amy	Trinja	Reta
Reta	Trinja	Trinja	Amy
Reta	Jennifer	Trinja	Jennifer
Amy	Reta	Jennifer	Reta
Amy	Trinja	Jennifer	Amy
Amy	Jennifer	Jennifer	Trinja

counting principle

Tree Diagrams and the Counting Principle (pp. 531–533)

A tree diagram can also be used to list permutations. However, if you want to know only the *number* of permutations, you can simply multiply together the number of options at each point where you make a choice. This fact is called the counting principle.

Example You can use the counting principle to find the number of ways in which the roles can be assigned.

Number of choices for the lead		Number of choices remaining for the supporting role		Total possible ways in which the roles can be assigned
4	•	3	=	12

15 **Key Concepts Question** Suppose there is a fifth person named Julie in the Examples above. Use the counting principle to find the number of ways in which the roles can be assigned. Check the result by making a tree diagram.

Practice & Application Exercises

YOU WILL NEED

For Ex. 12–15:
- calculator

List all the permutations for each situation.

1. Two out of four plants, an azalea, an ivy, a fern, and a cactus, must be arranged side by side.

2. A person marks his or her first and second choices out of five movies labeled A, B, C, D, and E.

3. The High School marching band, Boy Scouts, Girl Scouts, and Fire Department will all march in the Memorial Day parade.

4. **Sports** The Ironman Triathlon is held annually on the Saturday in October closest to the full moon, in Kailua-Kona, Hawaii. The men and women who compete in this triathalon do a 2.4 mile ocean swim, followed by a 112 mile bicycle race, followed by a 26.2 mile run. List all the *other* possible orders for these three events.

5. **Area Codes** The first three digits of a long distance telephone number are called the *area code*. In the United States, every state has a different area code and some states with large urban areas have more than one area code.
   a. Suppose you remember that the numbers in the Montana area code are 6, 4, and 0, but you have forgotten the order of these digits. List all the possible orders of these three digits.
   b. If the number 0 (used to call the operator) cannot be used as the first digit, how many orders are possible?

6. Beth, Carol, and Danielle are finalists in a figure skating competition. The order of their performances in the final event will be determined by a random drawing.

   a. List all possible orders in which they might skate in the final event.
   b. **Probability Connection** What is the probability that Beth will skate first? that Danielle will not skate last?
   c. **Writing** Do you think the order in which skaters skate in a competition matters? Why or why not?

Find how many permutations are possible for each situation.

7. four runners on a relay team
8. nine batters in a batting order
9. the first three finishers in an eight-swimmer race
10. the top 2 candidates out of 100 applicants for a job

11. A school cafeteria has organized its serving line so that students can choose chicken or roast beef at the first station, rice, potatoes, or bread at the second station, and soup or salad at the third station.

    a. Suppose one item is chosen at each station. Draw a tree diagram to show all the possible meals that could be chosen.

    b. How many different meals are possible?

    c. Suppose a fourth station is added that serves milk or juice. How does this affect the number of possible meals?

Calculator **The value of 6!, read "six factorial," is the product $6 \cdot 5 \cdot 4 \cdot 3 \cdot 2 \cdot 1 = 720$. Use the factorial key x! on a calculator to find the total number of permutations for each set of items. Tell whether your answer is approximate or exact. Explain.**

12. 4 musical notes
13. 13 songs on a CD
14. 20 poems in a book
15. 52 cards in a deck

16. **ZIP Codes** In 1963, the United States Postal Service first introduced the ZIP Code to reorganize the routing of mail to different cities and also to different areas within a city.

    a. How many different 5-digit ZIP Codes can the Postal Service create using the digits 1, 2, 3, 4, and 5, if each digit is used only once?

    b. How many different 5-digit ZIP Codes can be created using the digits 0 through 9, if each digit can be repeated?

17. **Challenge** Suppose you are designing a door lock. To open the door, you have to press each of a set of colored buttons in a particular order. For better security, you want to have at least 5000 possible orders. How many buttons must the lock have?

Oral Report

Exercise 18 checks that you recognize applications of permutations and tree diagrams.

Reflecting on the Section

Be prepared to report on the following topic in class.

18. Permutations and tree diagrams are mathematical ideas that can be applied in many situations. Describe how each of these two ideas can be applied to situations related to a city.

Spiral Review

Find the area of each trapezoid. (Module 7, p. 518)

19.

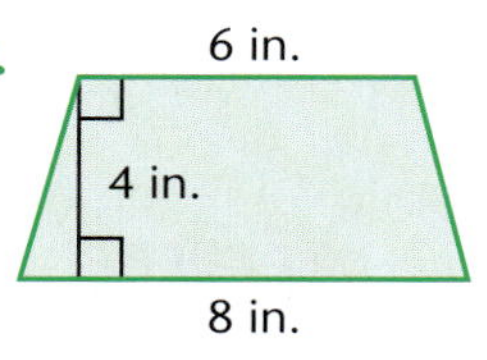

20.

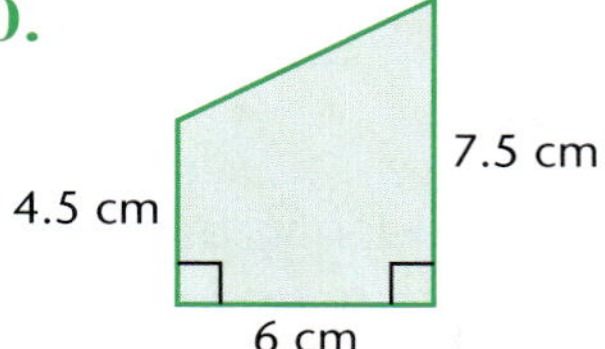

Solve each equation. Check each solution. (Module 4, p. 300)

21. $5 - 2n = 9$

22. $2x + 4 = 20$

23. $11 = 3c - 4$

24. $-6y + 7 = -5$

25. $\frac{b}{2} + 3 = 5$

26. $a - \frac{2}{3} = \frac{4}{3}$

Find the surface area of a right rectangular prism with the given dimensions. (Module 6, p. 404)

27. 4 ft, 5 ft, 7 ft

28. 3.5 m, 2.5 m, 6 m

29. $2\frac{1}{2}$ yd, $2\frac{1}{2}$ yd, 8 yd

30. 3 cm, 6 mm, 2 mm

Career Connection

Computer Hardware Engineer: Omar Green

At Xionics, Omar Green helps to design computer chips to perform certain tasks. When he tests the computer chips, he creates permutation charts to list the possible orders in which the tasks can be performed.

Suppose the following tasks can be performed in any order: rotate an image 90°, make a color image black and white, and change the size of an image.

31. In how many orders can these three tasks be performed? List all the possibilities.

32. In how many orders can any two of these three tasks be performed? List all the possibilities.

Traffic Flow

SET UP

Work in a group. You will need:

- *tape measure*

Imagine walking to the lunchroom. Suddenly, the student in front of you stops. You swerve and bump into someone else. Looking for a clear path, you slow your pace. There seem to be hundreds of students ahead of you, all heading in the same direction!

For this project, you'll work in a group. Using the techniques of traffic engineers, your group will develop a plan to improve the traffic flow in your school.

Estimating and Measuring Lengths You'll estimate and measure the length and width of a section of hallway where there is a traffic problem.

1 Identify a hallway in your school that has a traffic problem.

2 **a.** Use estimation to mark off a 25 ft long section of the hallway. Measure to check your estimate.

b. Estimate the width of the hallway. Measure to check your estimate.

3 Describe any places where students gather and any obstacles, such as drinking fountains, that could interfere with traffic flow.

Scale Drawings In order to study the section of hallway you selected, you'll make a scale drawing of it.

4 **a.** Make a scale drawing of the section of hallway that you measured. Be sure to label the width and the length, and include the scale. Label all obstacles and gathering places.

b. Find the area of the chosen section of the hallway.

5 One way to solve the traffic problem is to widen the hallway.

a. If the width of the chosen section of the hallway were doubled, what would happen to the area of that section?

b. If the width *and* length were doubled, what would happen to the area?

Section 1 Extra Skill Practice

For Exercises 1 and 2, list all the permutations for each situation.

1. Four singers, Alma, Mei, Dyani, and Luz, must line up for a photo.

2. Two out of three instruments, a trumpet, a saxophone, and a flute, must be hung side by side in a display case.

3. Your seven-digit phone number consists of an *exchange* (the first three digits) and your individual number (the last four digits).
   a. Suppose only the digits 1, 2, 3, and 4 can be used for the individual number and no digit can be repeated. Use a tree diagram to list all the possible phone numbers with the exchange 555. How many phone numbers are possible?
   b. Suppose any digits can be used for the individual number and the digits can be repeated. Use the counting principle to determine how many phone numbers there can be with the exchange 555.

4. How many permutations are possible when 6 movies are to be shown in 6 different theaters?

5. How many permutations are possible when 4 out of 20 students are called on to give oral reports?

6. Suppose Norma has a seven-period school day. Her main subjects are mathematics, English, science, and social studies. She also has electives in French and art, and she plays trumpet in the band. In how many different orders can Norma's classes meet? Explain.

Study Skills Teaching Another Person

Teaching another person requires that you know the material extremely well, so teaching can help you find out whether there are any ideas or topics that you do not fully understand.

1. Look back at the ideas presented in this section. Choose a topic that you feel you understand well. Teach it to another student.

2. Describe what happened when you taught another student. Could you explain the material clearly? Did the other student have difficulty understanding your explanations? Did you discover any ideas that were unclear to you?

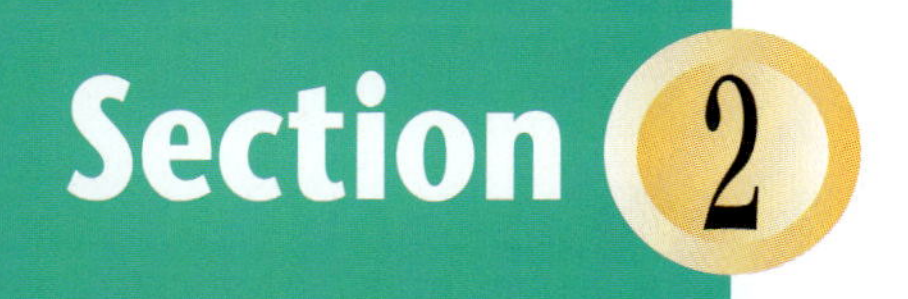

Drawing Views and Finding Volumes

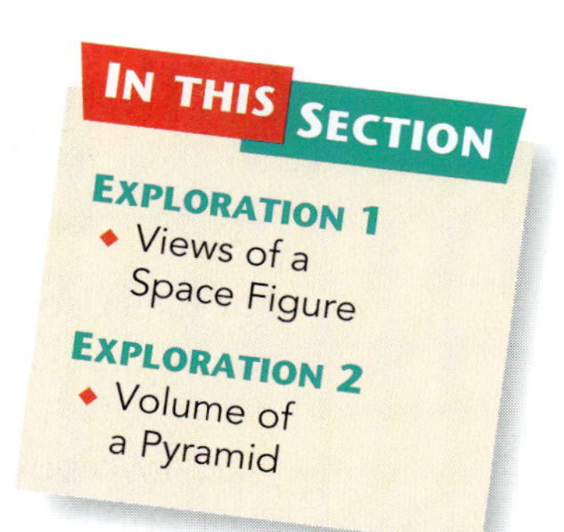

A Tower of Power

▲ Petronas Towers in Kuala Lumpur, Malaysia

Setting the Stage

SET UP *You will need 20 centimeter cubes.*

As cities have become more populated, and the land available for constructing new buildings has decreased, many have expanded in the only direction remaining—straight up! The tallest skyscraper, the Petronas Towers in Kuala Lumpur, Malaysia, now soars 1,483 ft into the air.

> "There's no limit to the height you can build if you have a place big enough to put it."
> Leslie Robertson, structural engineer

Think About It

1 **a.** What is the maximum height a skyscraper could reach, according to structural engineer Leslie Robertson?

b. Why do you think a taller building requires more ground space?

2 Use centimeter cubes for parts (a)–(d).

a. Explain why the volume of a single cube is 1 cubic centimeter.

b. Start with a single centimeter cube and stack as many cubes as possible above it to build the highest tower that you can. What is the volume of the tower you built?

c. What do you think causes the tower to topple when it becomes too high?

d. The space figure you built in part (b) is an example of a *rectangular prism*. Give dimensions for 3 different rectangular prisms that all have the same volume as one another.

Exploration 1

VIEWS OF A SPACE FIGURE

LEARN HOW TO...
- draw different views of a space figure

AS YOU...
- create model buildings with centimeter cubes

SET UP *You will need 20 centimeter cubes.*

▶ **In order to design and construct buildings, architects, engineers, and construction workers must be able to visualize shapes from various views. Several different views of a building are shown below.**

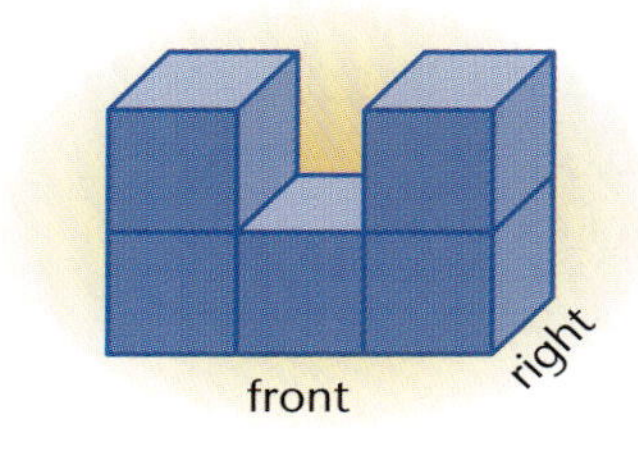

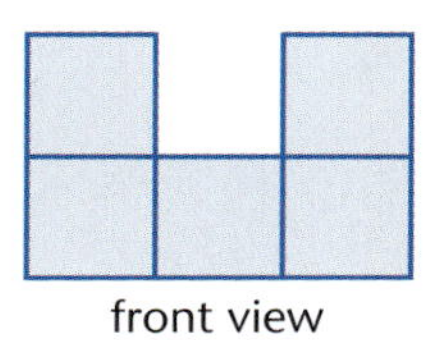
front view

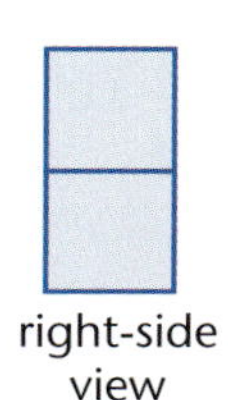
right-side view

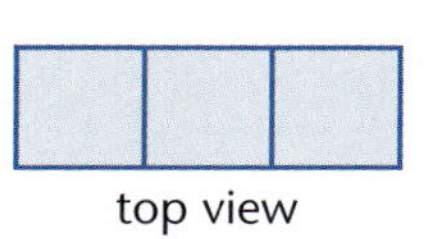
top view

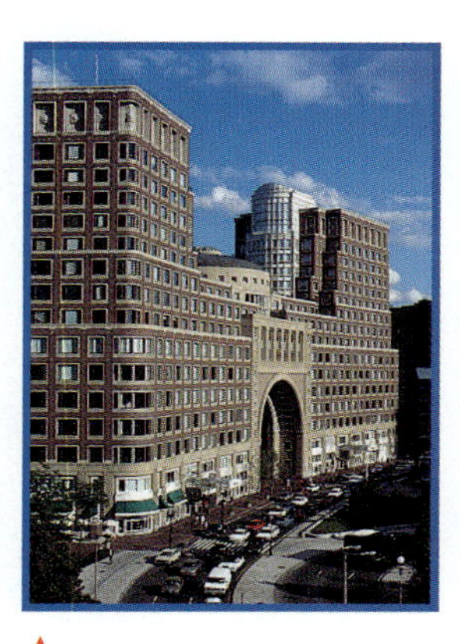

▲ Rowes Wharf, Boston, Massachusetts

▶ **A building plan includes a *base plan*. You can think of a base plan as a view looking directly down on a building, with the height of each section of the base indicated by numbers. A base plan for the building above is shown.**

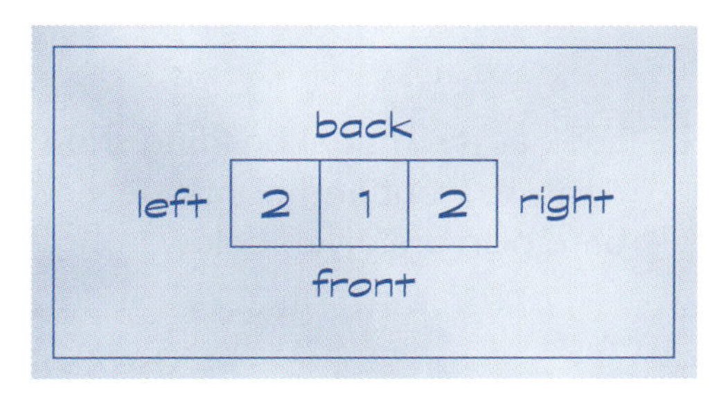

3 a. Use centimeter cubes to create a model of the building shown above.

b. Look at the building from the top, the front, and the right side to check each of the drawings above. Which view—the *top*, the *front*, or the *right-side*—is used in the base plan?

c. Draw the back and the left-side views of the building.

d. How do the front and the back views compare?

e. How do the right-side and the left-side views compare?

f. Do you think the answers to parts (d) and (e) are true for all buildings? Experiment by building other structures with your centimeter cubes.

...checks that you can draw different views of a space figure.

4 ✓ **CHECKPOINT** Use centimeter cubes.

a. Build the model building shown. Begin with the partial base plan.

b. Draw the front and right-side views of the model building.

c. Copy and complete the base plan for the model building.

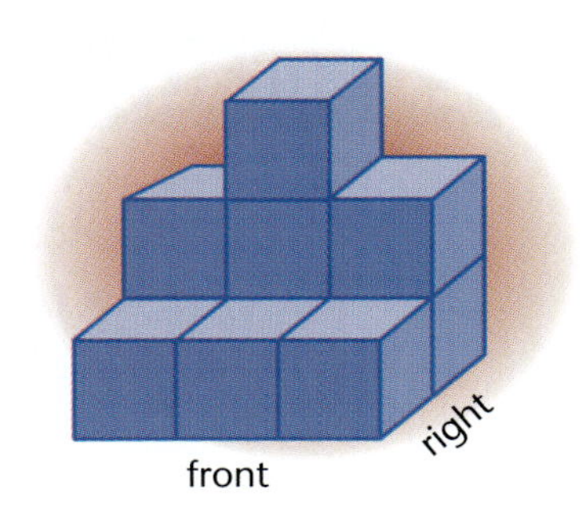

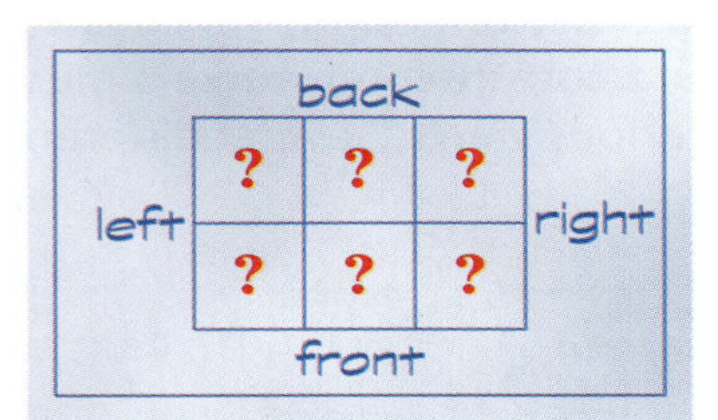

5 Look at the model building shown at the right. Its front and right-side views and its base plan are given below.

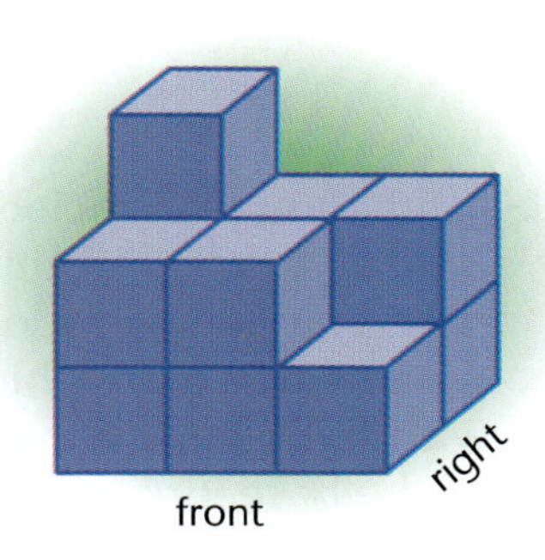

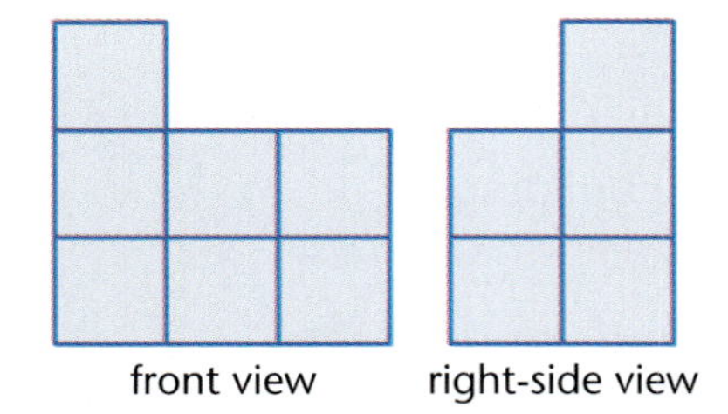

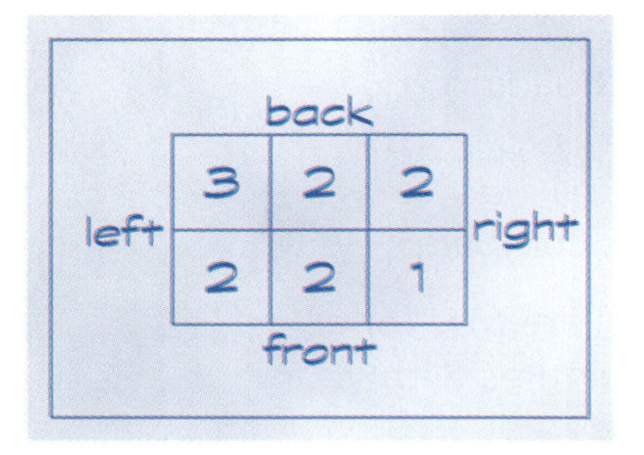

a. Use centimeter cubes to build the model building.

b. What is the volume of the model building?

c. By moving only one cube, change the building into a rectangular prism.

d. Draw the base plan for the rectangular prism you built in part (c).

e. How can you find the volume of the rectangular prism in part (c) without counting the cubes?

f. Does moving a cube to a different position in the building change the volume of the building? Why or why not?

6 **a.** Use centimeter cubes to build a model building with the base plan shown. Then find the volume.

b. Draw the front and right-side views of the model building.

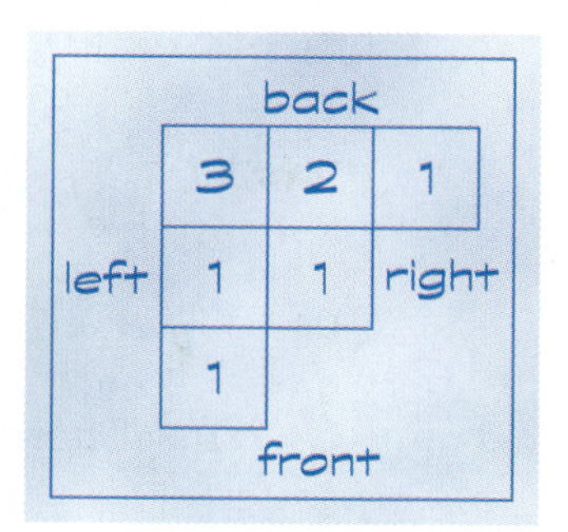

c. Suppose you want to paint the outside of your model building, including the base. How many cube faces will you need to paint? Recall that this number represents the *surface area* of the building in square centimeters.

d. By moving exactly 3 cubes, change the building into a rectangular prism. Then draw the base plan for the rectangular prism.

e. Find the volume and the surface area of the new rectangular prism. Compare them to the original volume and surface area.

FOR HELP with *surface area,* see **MODULE 6, p. 404**

7 Suppose the base plan for the model building shown is 3 units long by 2 units wide. Use 14 centimeter cubes to build the model building.

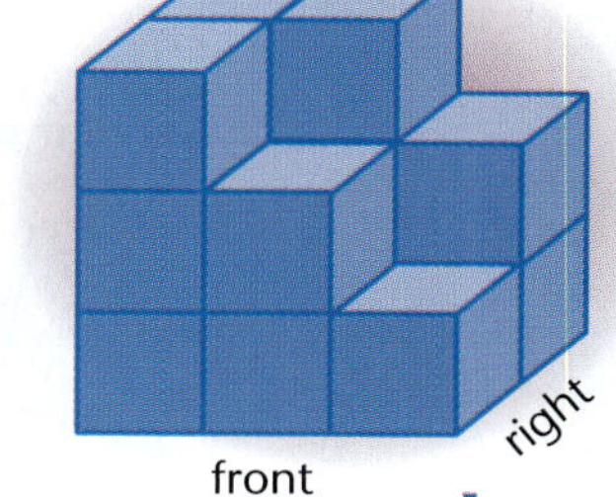

a. Rearrange the cubes to form a model building that has a larger surface area than the original model building but the same base. Then draw the base plan of the structure you built.

b. Rearrange the cubes to form a model building that has the largest possible surface area but the same base. Then draw the base plan of the structure you built.

c. Explain why you think the structure you built in part (b) has the largest possible surface area.

8 The front and right-side views of a building are shown below.

a. Copy and complete the base plan for the building, using the front and right-side views.

b. **Discussion** Is there a different base plan that would produce the same front and right-side views? Explain.

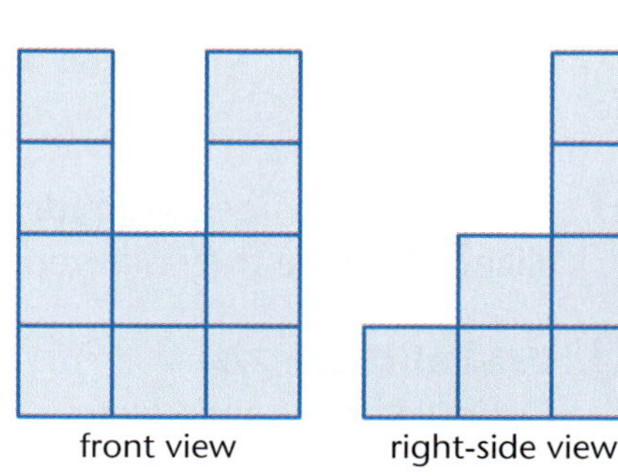

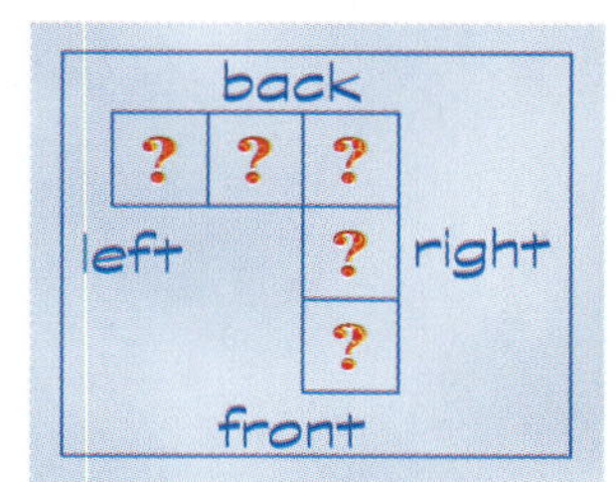

HOMEWORK EXERCISES ▶ See Exs. 1–6 on pp. 548–549.

GOAL

LEARN HOW TO...
- recognize a pyramid
- find the volume of a pyramid

AS YOU...
- build rectangular prisms using pyramid blocks

KEY TERM
- pyramid

Exploration 2

VOLUME OF A PYRAMID

SET UP *You will need:* • *Labsheet 2A* • *scissors* • *tape* • *metric ruler*

▶ **A city skyline usually contains many different types of space figures. To organize the space of a building efficiently, architects need to consider the amount of space or volume a building will enclose. In this exploration you'll see how the volume of a pyramid relates to the volume of a rectangular prism. Several types of pyramids are shown below.**

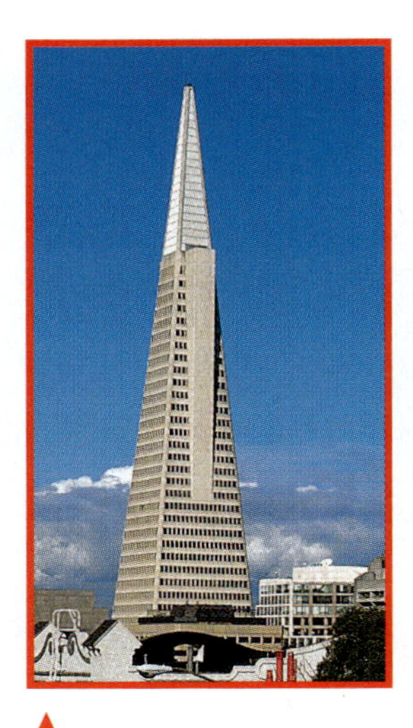

The Transamerica Building in San Francisco, California, incorporates a square pyramid.

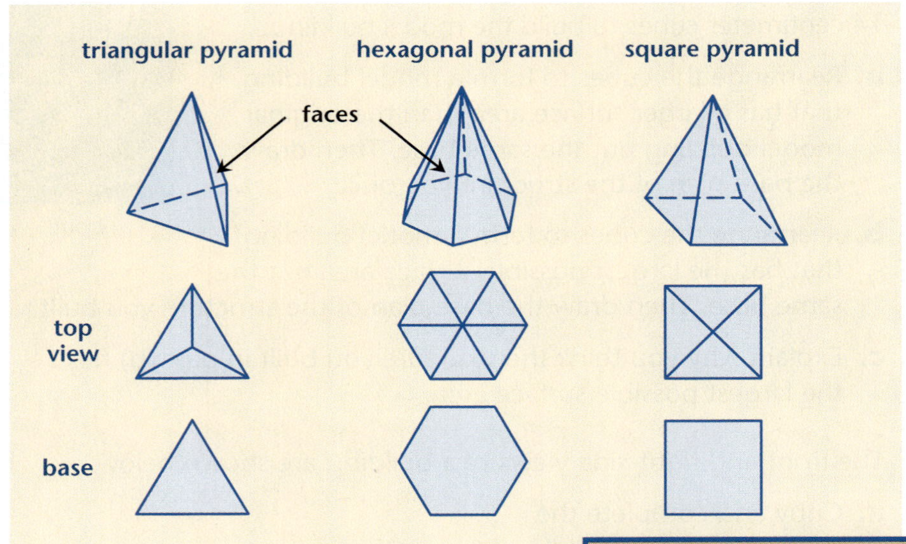

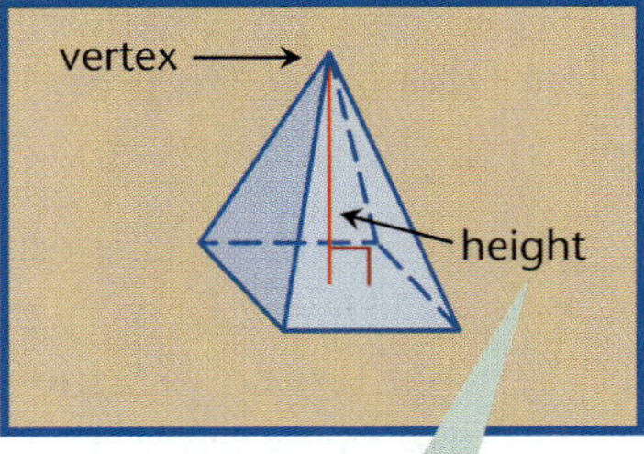

The *height* is the perpendicular distance from the base to the vertex opposite it.

9 How are the three pyramids above alike? How are they different?

10 **Use Labsheet 2A.** Cut out the *Pyramid Nets*. Crease each net along the dashed lines. Then fold each net and tape the edges together to form two pyramids.

For Questions 11–17, use the pyramids you made in Question 10.

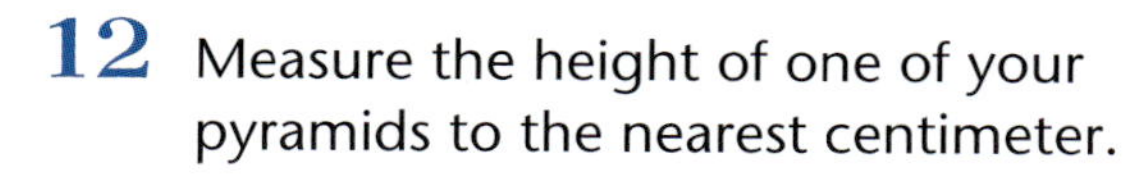

11 The two pyramids you made are identical. Look at one of the pyramids.

a. What type of pyramid did you form?

b. Not including the base, how many faces does the pyramid have?

c. Which faces of the pyramid are congruent? Explain.

12 Measure the height of one of your pyramids to the nearest centimeter.

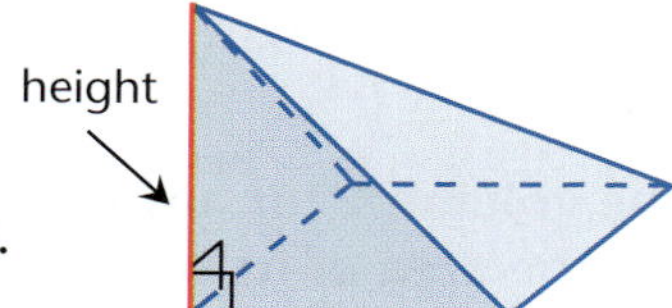

13 The dashed lines below represent folds.

a. Use your two pyramids to make a figure with the views shown.

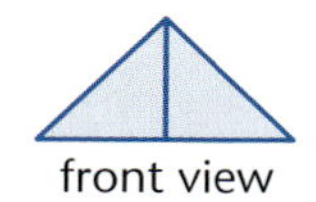
front view

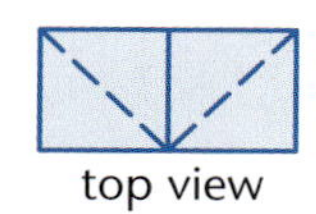
top view

right-side view

b. Use your two pyramids to make a figure with the front and back views shown. Then draw the top view of the figure.

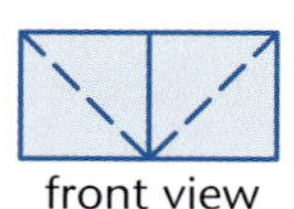
front view

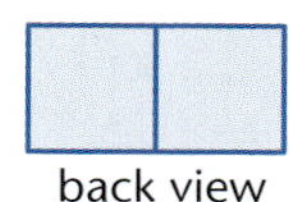
back view

14 Work with a partner.

a. Make a cube by putting three of your pyramids together.

b. Write an expression to represent the volume of the cube. Use B for the area of the base of the cube and h for the height of the cube.

c. Compare the area of the base and the height of a single pyramid with the area of the base and the height of the cube you formed.

d. Suppose you know the volume of a cube formed by putting together three identical pyramids as in part (a). How can you find the volume of each pyramid?

e. Use your answers to parts (b)–(d) to write an expression for the volume of a pyramid with height h and base area B.

15 Work as a group. Think of the pyramids you made in Question 10 as "pyramid blocks."

a. Build a square pyramid using four pyramid blocks.

b. Add pyramid blocks to the square pyramid you made in part (a) until it forms a rectangular prism with the same height and base as the square pyramid. How many pyramid blocks does it take to form the rectangular prism**?**

c. The volume of the rectangular prism you made in part (b) is given by $B \cdot h$ where B is the area of the prism's base and h is the height. Write an expression for the volume of the square pyramid you made in part (a).

▶ **The volume V for any pyramid is given by the formula $V = \frac{1}{3}Bh$ where B is the area of its base, and h is its height.**

EXAMPLE

Find the volume of a pyramid that has a base area of 12 cm^2 and a height of 4 cm.

$$V = \frac{1}{3}Bh$$
$$= \frac{1}{3}(12)(4)$$
$$= 16$$

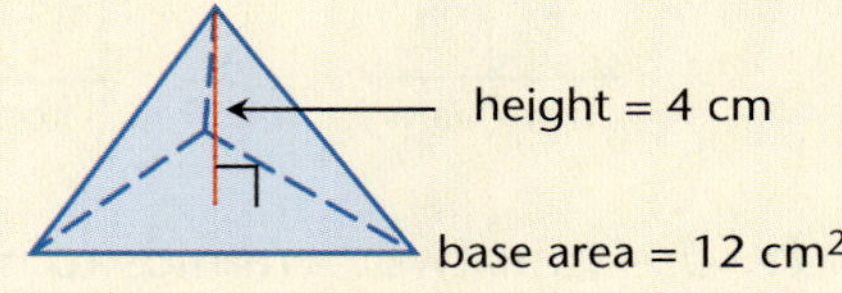

The pyramid has a volume of 16 cm^3.

16 Measure the height and the dimensions of the base of a single pyramid block from Question 10 to the nearest centimeter. Then find its volume to the nearest cubic centimeter.

17 **a.** Use your answer from Question 16 to find the volume of the square pyramid you constructed in Question 15(a).

b. Measure the height and a side of the base of the square pyramid to the nearest centimeter. Use the formula for the volume of a pyramid to find its volume to the nearest cubic centimeter. Compare this answer with the result in part (a).

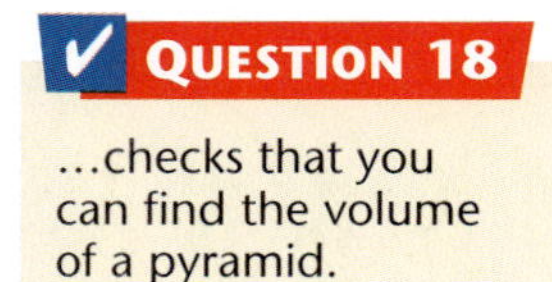

18 ✓ **CHECKPOINT** The Transamerica Pyramid shown on page 544 is 853 ft tall and has a base area of 21,025 ft^2. Find its volume. Round your answer to the nearest cubic foot.

HOMEWORK EXERCISES ▶ **See Exs. 7–17 on pp. 549–550.**

Section 2 Key Concepts

Key Term

Views of Space Figures (pp. 541–543)

Space figures with the same volume can have different surface areas.

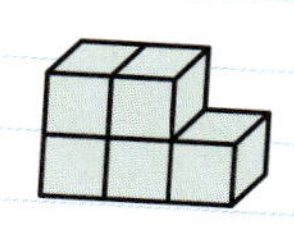

Volume = 5 cm^3

Surface area = 20 cm^2

Volume = 5 cm^3

Surface area = 22 cm^2

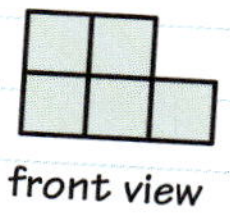

front view

right-side view

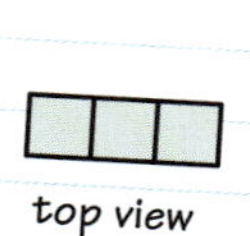

top view

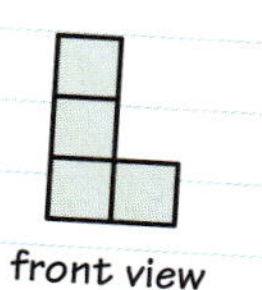

front view

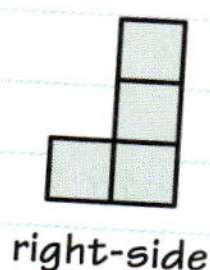

right-side view

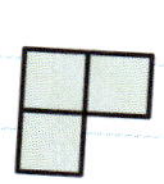

top view

Volume of a Pyramid (pp. 544–546)

pyramid

A pyramid is a space figure that has one base. All the other faces are triangles that meet at a single vertex. The height is the perpendicular distance from the base to the vertex opposite it.

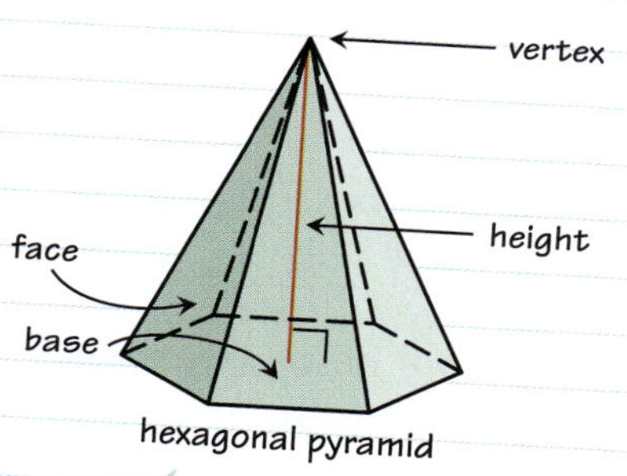

hexagonal pyramid

A pyramid is named for the shape of its base.

The volume V of a pyramid is given by the formula $V = \frac{1}{3}Bh$, where B is the area of its base, and h is its height.

Example Suppose a hexagonal pyramid has a base area of 36 cm^2 and a height of 7 cm. Find its volume.

$$V = \frac{1}{3}Bh = \frac{1}{3}(36)(7) = 84$$

The volume of the pyramid is 84 cm^3.

19 Key Concepts Question A pyramid has a height of 12 ft and a volume of 351 ft^3. What is the area of the base of the pyramid?

Section 2

Practice & Application Exercises

YOU WILL NEED

For Ex. 1:
- Labsheet 2B
- scissors
- tape

1. a. **Use Labsheet 2B.** Follow the directions on Labsheet 2B to make four cubes using the *Cube Nets*.

   b. Form three different buildings by putting together all the cubes.

   c. For each building in part (b), sketch front and right-side views, and a base plan.

   d. Does every building you made in part (b) have the same volume? the same surface area? Explain.

For Exercises 2 and 3, use the front and right-side views of a building that are shown below.

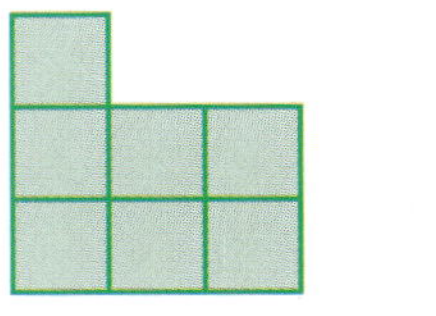

front view

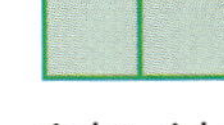

right-side view

2. Draw a base plan that will create a building with the greatest possible volume, using the given front and right-side views.

3. Draw a base plan that will create a building with the least possible volume, using the given front and right-side views. Each cube must share a face with at least one other cube.

4. **Challenge** The front of the Reception Building in the Olympic Port of Barcelona is shown in the photograph. Tell whether each view is the *right-side*, *left-side*, or *back view* of the building.

a.

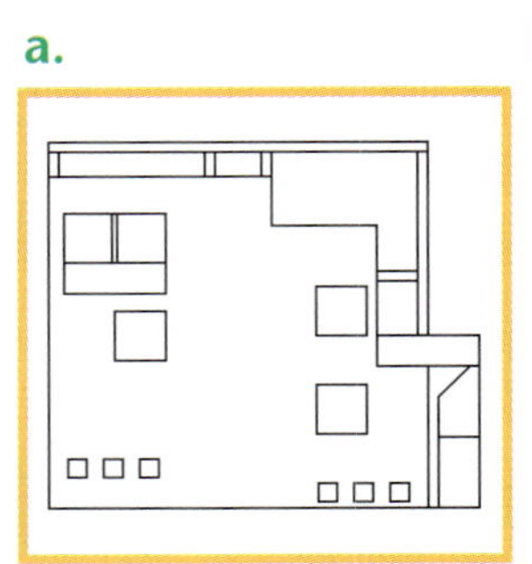

b.

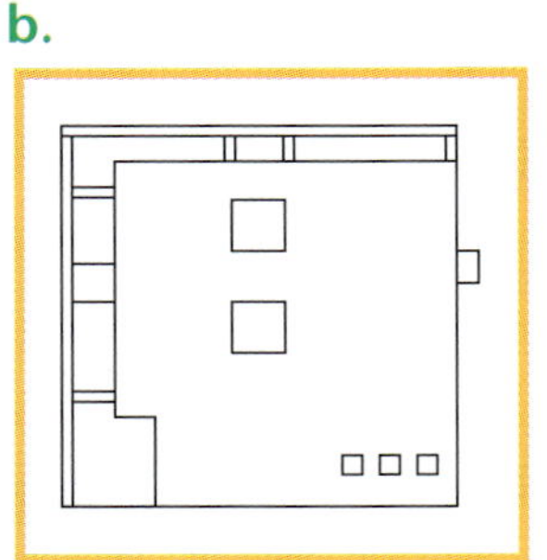

c.

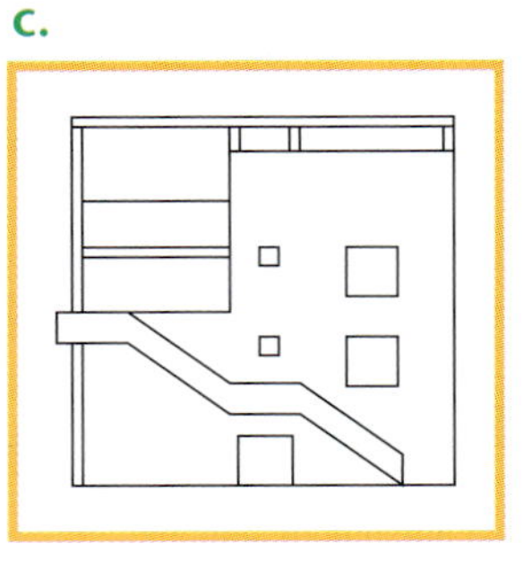

5. The cube-shaped Reception Building has edges that are 12.5 m long. What are the volume and the surface area of such a cube?

6. Industrial Design An industrial designer strives to design products that are easy to use and that can be produced at a reasonable cost. Industrial designers describe their designs with drawings of different views. For each view shown, tell whether it is the *front*, *top*, or *side view* of the product shown.

a.

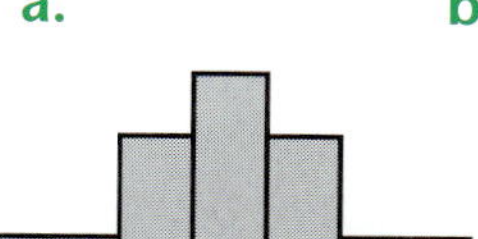

b.

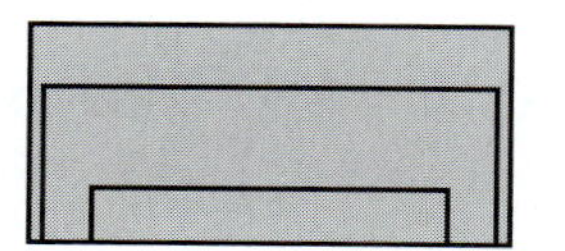

c.

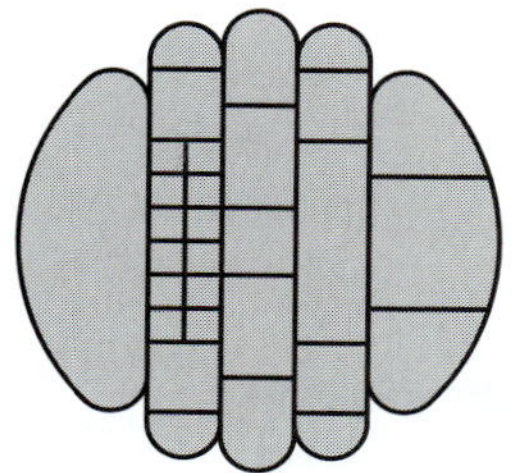

For Exercises 7–9, use the pyramid at the right. Use the letters of the vertices to name each of the following.

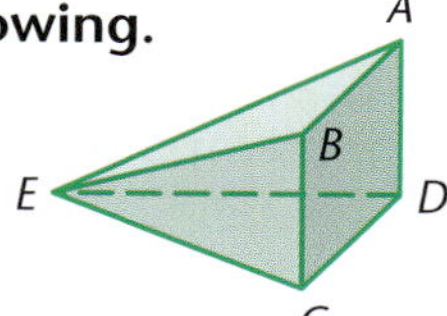

7. the base

8. the other faces

9. the vertex opposite the base

Mental Math **The base of each figure is a rectangle. Use mental math to estimate the volume of each figure. Then find each volume. Round decimal answers to the nearest tenth.**

10.

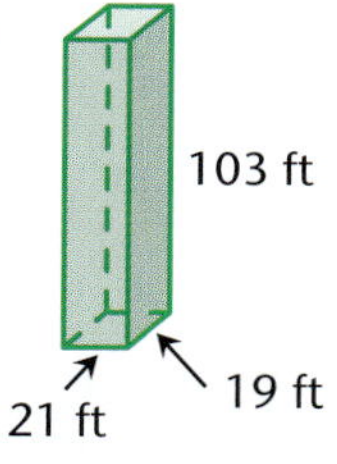

11.

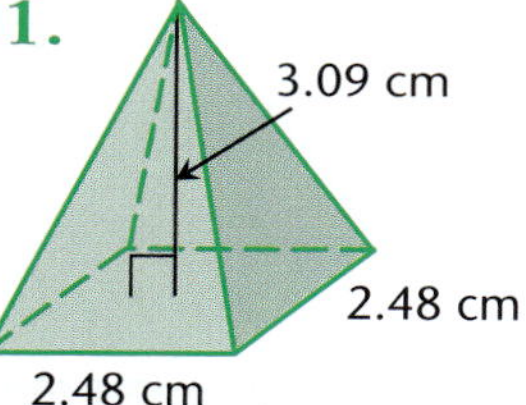

12.

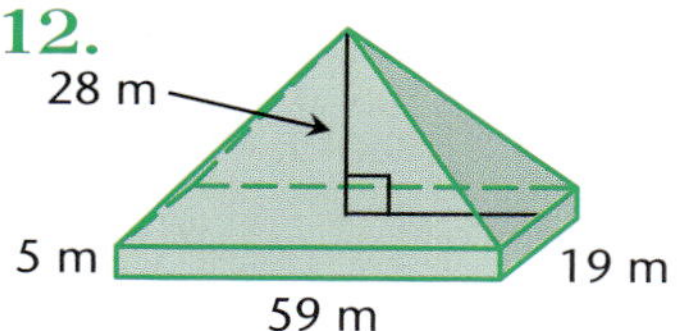

Determine whether each net can be folded to create a pyramid. If so, identify the type of pyramid it will form.

13.

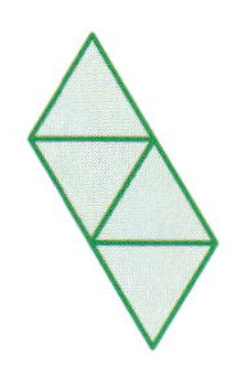

14.

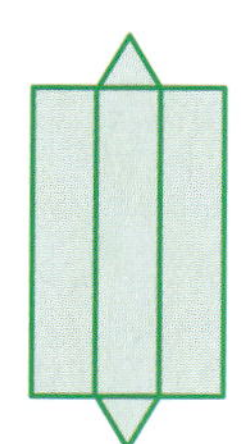

15.

16. Rainforest Pyramid The *Rainforest Pyramid* in Galveston Island, Texas, is 100 ft high. Its base is a square that is 200 ft on a side. What is the volume of the Rainforest Pyramid?

The Rainforest Pyramid is home to a wide variety of tropical plants and other wildlife, including over 2000 butterflies.

Journal

Exercise 17 checks that you can draw different views of space figures.

Reflecting on the Section

Write your response to Exercise 17 in your journal.

17. a. Draw sketches to show how the faces of prisms and pyramids can be different types of geometric figures.

b. Suppose you are sketching the top view of a pyramid or a prism that is sitting on its base. How many different geometric figures are possible? Explain your reasoning.

Spiral Review

Find how many permutations are possible for each situation. (Module 8, p. 534)

18. 7 charms on a bracelet

19. 11 hats on 11 heads

Tell whether each set of side lengths can or cannot form a triangle. If they can, tell whether the triangle is *isosceles, equilateral,* or *scalene.* (Module 3, p. 223)

20. 2 m, 3 m, 4 m

21. 4 in., 4 in., 7 in.

22. 3 cm, 5 cm, 8 cm

Sketch an example of each shape. Mark parallel sides. (Module 7, p. 518)

23. trapezoid

24. quadrilateral

25. rhombus

Extension 

Three-Dimensional Views

Three-dimensional views of model buildings made from centimeter cubes, like the ones shown in Exercises 1–3 at the top of page 551, show depth as well as length and width.

26. Draw a three-dimensional view of a model building that has the two-dimensional views shown.

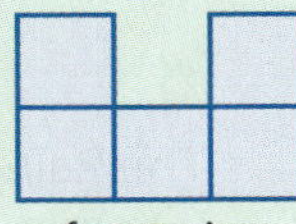
front view

right-side view

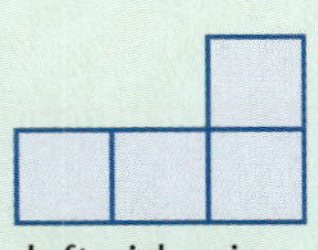
left-side view

27. Draw a three-dimensional view of another model building with the same front, right, and left views as in Exercise 26, but a different number of centimeter cubes.

Choose the letter from A to I of the front view and the right-side view for each model building.

1.

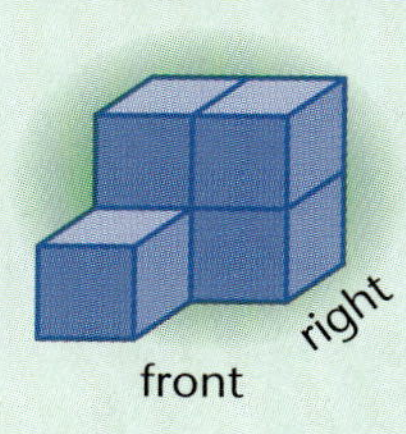

2.

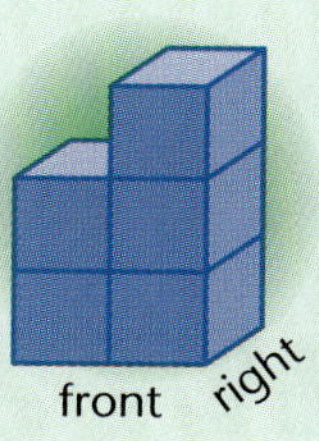

3.

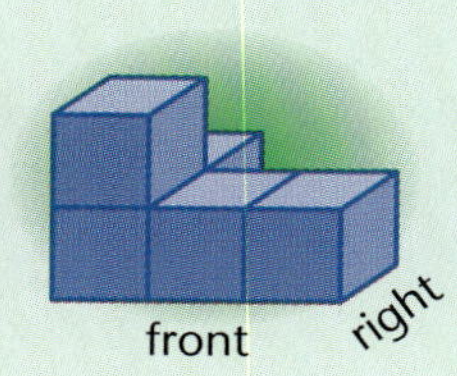

A. 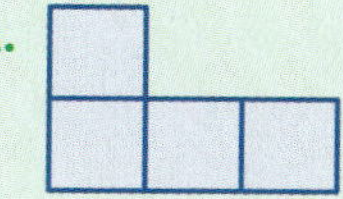

B. 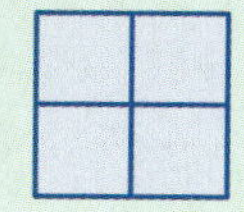

C. 

D. 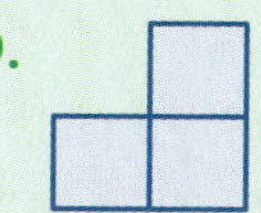

E. 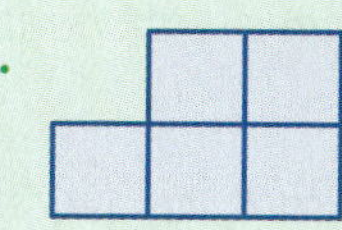

F. 

G. 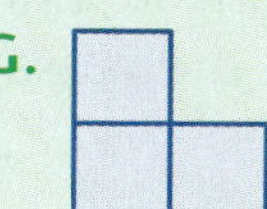

H. 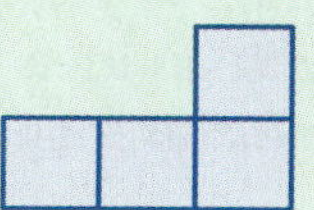

I. 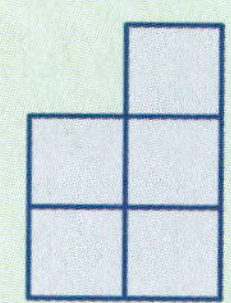

Find the volume of each pyramid with the given base area B and height h. Round decimal answers to the nearest tenth.

4. $B = 22\text{ cm}^2$
   $h = 6\text{ cm}$
5. $B = 48\text{ in.}^2$
   $h = 7\text{ in.}$
6. $B = 19\text{ ft}^2$
   $h = 12\text{ ft}$
7. $B = 32\text{ mm}^2$
   $h = 10\text{ mm}$

Standardized Testing ◆ Open-ended

Suppose you have eight centimeter cubes.

1. Draw a space figure consisting of eight cubes.
2. Draw the right, left, and front views of your space figure, and the base plan.
3. Find the volume and the surface area of your space figure.

Section 3 Permutations and Combinations

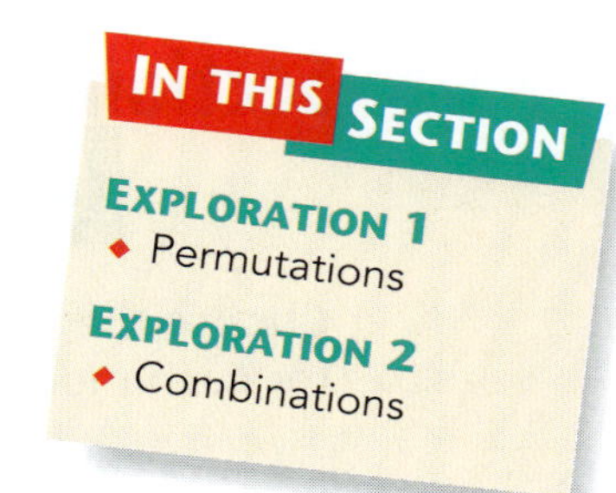

Escape to Central Park

Setting the Stage

SET UP *You will need Labsheet 3A.*

The Horses of Central Park, by Michael Slade, is the story of a boy named Wendell who communicates with horses. He learns that the horses that pull carriages in New York City's Central Park are unhappy. Wendell comes up with an idea to raise their spirits. In the passage below Wendell explains his idea to his friend Judith.

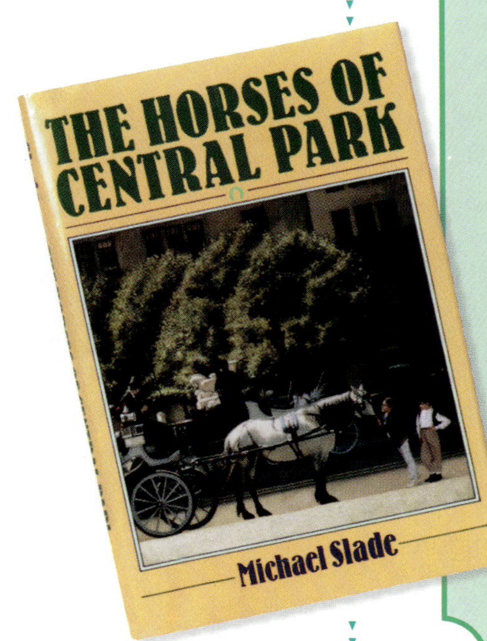

Wendell looked around to make sure no one was near. Then he looked Judith dead in the eye and very softly and sincerely said, "I'm going to set them free."

Judith could feel herself smiling on the inside as well as the outside. She might not be able to hear the horses, but Judith knew that she was very good at planning things. "Where are the stables?" she asked.

"West Forty-sixth Street," said Wendell, a little nervously. "Very West Forty-sixth Street. Almost to the river. Between Eleventh and Twelfth avenues."

The Hudson River was as west as you could go in Manhattan. It's what separates New York from New Jersey.

The smile vanished from Judith's face. Somehow, she had just assumed that the horses lived somewhere right by the park. West Forty-sixth Street between Eleventh and Twelfth avenues was quite a walk from the park. They were going to have to find a way to get the horses from Forty-sixth Street to Central Park without anybody seeing them. "Let's go have a look," said Judith, very seriously.

Think About It

Use Labsheet 3A for Questions 1 and 2.

1 **a.** Find the Hudson River on the *Map of New York City*.

b. Label the general location of the horse stables.

c. Label the location of the entrance to Central Park nearest the horse stables.

2 Judith's and Wendell's initial plan is to free the horses from the stable and lead them in ones and twos to the nearest Central Park entrance, by the shortest possible route. To avoid suspicion, they want to take each group of horses by a *different* route.

a. Explain how it is possible for two different routes to be the same distance.

b. Trace three different routes the horses could take, using the shortest distance possible.

c. **Discussion** Compare your answers in part (b) with those of other classmates. Estimate how many possible shortest routes the horses could take. Then discuss how you could find all the possible shortest routes.

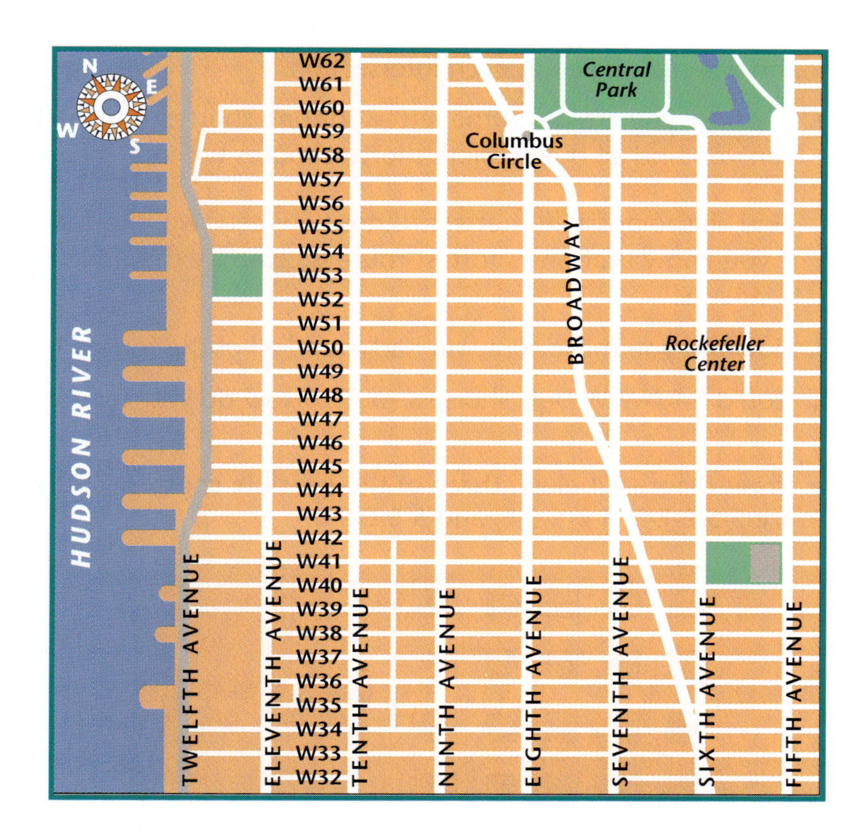

GOAL

LEARN HOW TO...
- list and find the number of permutations when items repeat

AS YOU...
- find the shortest paths between two points on a street grid

Exploration 1

PERMUTATIONS

SET UP *You will need Labsheet 3B.*

▶ **To find all the possible shortest routes that the horses could take on their journey from the stables to the entrance of Central Park, you could first solve a simpler problem. Think about the possible shortest routes from the intersection marked "X" to the intersection marked "Y."**

This route can be labeled S-E-E for "one block south then two blocks east."

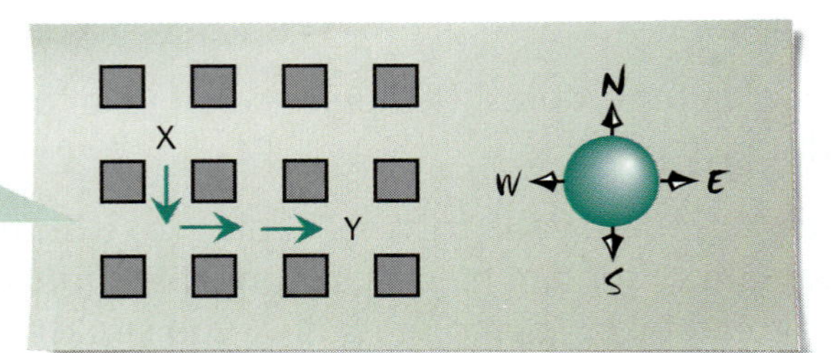

3 **a.** What are all the possible shortest routes from intersection X to intersection Y? Make a list of the routes using letters to show the direction taken at each intersection.

b. Suppose you are given the letters for one shortest route. How can you find all the possible shortest routes without the map?

4 **a.** Find all the possible shortest routes between two intersections if you know that one shortest route is given by the directions S-W-W-S.

b. How did you make sure you had found all of the routes?

c. Could S-W-W-W be a shortest route? How do you know?

▶ **In the street diagram below, three of the possible shortest paths from X to Y are S-S-E-E-E, S-E-S-E-E, and S-E-E-S-E.**

The route shown is written "S-E-S-E-E."

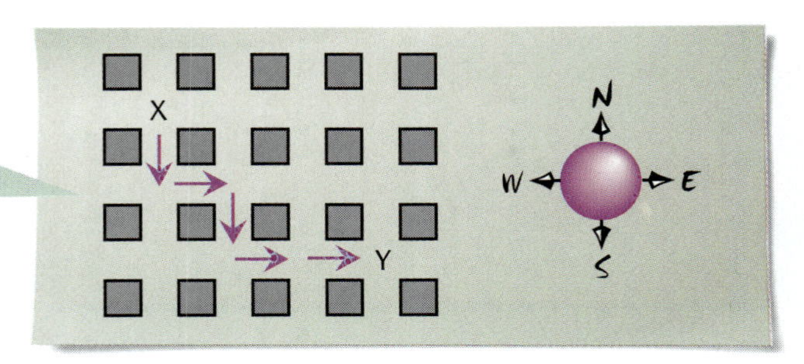

5 Use the street diagram at the bottom of page 554.

a. How many possible shortest paths from X to Y do you think there are?

b. Describe a strategy you can use to find all the possible shortest paths from X to Y. (*Hint:* Look for a pattern in the three given paths).

c. Find all the possible shortest paths from X to Y. How many are there?

d. **Discussion** Compare your answers in part (c) with those of other classmates. Compare the methods used to find all the routes. Decide which method you think worked best.

Use the *Street Diagram* on Labsheet 3B for Questions 6 and 7.

6 Follow the directions on Labsheet 3B to fill in the circles on the *Street Diagram*.

7 Suppose the variables p, s, and t represent the total number of shortest paths from intersection X on the street diagram below. Use your results from Question 6 to write an equation that shows the relationship between the variables p, s, and t.

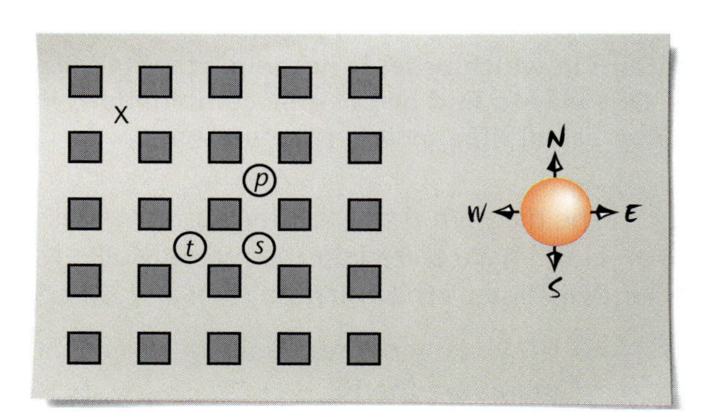

8 **CHECKPOINT** Use the *Escape Route Map* on Labsheet 3B.

a. Assume that all the horses must start at the intersection of 11th Avenue and West 46th Street. How many possible shortest routes are there to the Columbus Circle entrance of Central Park? Explain how you found your answer.

b. How does your answer in part (a) compare with your original estimate in Question 2?

...checks that you can find all the possible permutations when items repeat.

HOMEWORK EXERCISES See Exs. 1–7 on p. 559.

GOAL

LEARN HOW TO...
- list and find all the possible combinations
- distinguish a combination from a permutation

AS YOU...
- consider ways to group horses

KEY TERM
- combination

Exploration 2

Combinations

Wendell and Judith plan to free ten horses: Elmer, Winston, Molly, Archibald, Quentin, Angelina, Samantha, Cromwell, Chloe, and Old Barnaby. Each name can be represented by its first two letters: El, Wi, Mo, Ar, Qu, An, Sa, Cr, Ch, and Ol.

9 a. Which of the following selections represents the same group of ten horses listed above?

Selection 1:	Wi, Mo, Qu, An, Ol, Ch, Cr, Sa, El, Ar
Selection 2:	Mo, Qu, An, Sa, Cr, Ch, Ol, Ch, Mo, Ar
Selection 3:	Sa, Ch, Ol, Ar, Mo, El, Qu, Wi, Cr

b. Does changing the order of the horses change the group itself?

▶ **A selection of items in which order is not important is called a combination. One way to find all possible combinations in a situation is to first list all the possible permutations.**

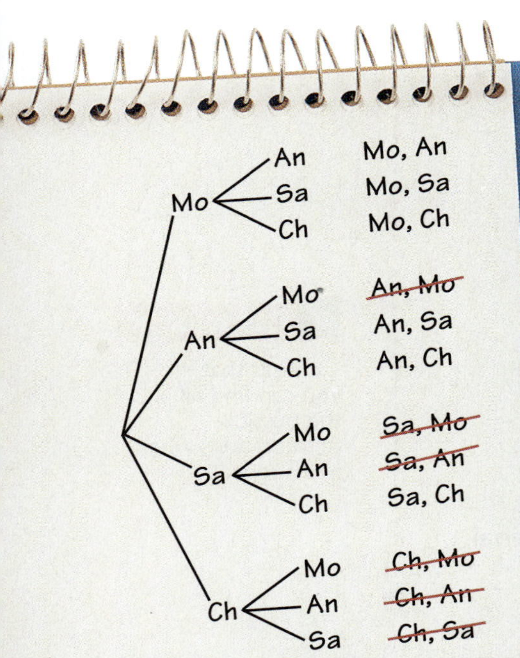

10 The diagram shows all the ways Wendell and Judith could have paired up the mares Molly (Mo), Angelina (An), Samantha (Sa), and Chloe (Ch).

a. How many permutations of two of these four mares are there?

b. **Discussion** Why are some of the permutations crossed out?

c. How many different combinations are possible in this situation?

11 **Try This as a Class** How is a combination different from a permutation?

▶ **Sometimes it is not practical to list all the possible permutations and then cross out repeats to find the combinations. Instead, you can make an organized list just of the combinations.**

12 Suppose Judith and Wendell want to divide all ten horses into groups of two and lead each group on a different route to the Park. Copy and extend the table as you answer the questions.

First horse picked	Possible second horses to pick	Combinations of two horses	Number of combinations
El	Wi Mo Ar Qu An Sa Cr Ch Ol	El, Wi El, Mo El, Ar El, Qu El, An El, Sa El, Cr El, Ch El, Ol	9
Wi	?	?	?

a. With which horse is Winston already grouped in the table?

b. Which horses remain to be grouped with Winston?

c. Use your answers to parts (a) and (b) to complete Winston's row of the table.

d. Extend the table to include all the possible combinations for this situation. What pattern do you notice?

e. How many different groups of two horses could Judith and Wendell form?

13 ✓ **CHECKPOINT** Suppose six horses are entered in a race. First, second, and third place results are recorded.

a. How many results are possible for the first three places?

b. Suppose the first three horses are recorded in no particular order. How many results are possible?

c. Which question in parts (a) and (b) is a permutation question? Which is a combination question? Explain your answers.

...checks that you understand the difference between a permutation and a combination.

HOMEWORK EXERCISES ▶ See Exs. 8–16 on pp. 559–560.

Section 3 Key Concepts

Key Term

Permutations with Repeated Items (pp. 554–555)

The number of permutations of 4 different items is $4 \cdot 3 \cdot 2 \cdot 1 = 24$. When items repeat, the number of permutations is reduced.

Example Suppose the letters N and E stand for the map directions north and east. The permutations of the letters N, E, E, and N give the 6 possible shortest routes from intersection A to intersection B below.

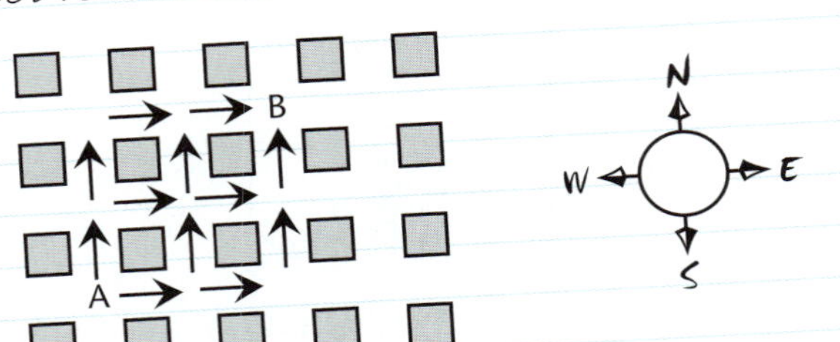

Route 1: N-E-E-N
Route 2: N-E-N-E
Route 3: N-N-E-E
Route 4: E-N-E-N
Route 5: E-N-N-E
Route 6: E-E-N-N

combination

Combinations (pp. 556–557)

A combination is a selection of objects in which order is not important.

Example An organized list can help you find combinations. This list shows the 10 possible groups of 3 out of the 5 options A, B, C, D, and E.

1st option picked	2nd option picked	Possible 3rd option	Combinations	Number of combinations
A	B	C D E	ABC ABD ABE	3
A	C	D E	ACD ACE	2
A	D	E	ADE	1
B	C	D E	BCD BCE	2
B	D	E	BDE	1
C	D	E	CDE	1

14 **Key Concepts Question** Is the following list a correct list for the situation in the second Example above?

EDC, EDB, EDA, ECB, ECA, EBA, DCB, DCA, DBA, CBA

Why or why not?

Practice & Application Exercises

List all the permutations of the letters in each word.

1. EAT **2.** FREE **3.** NOON **4.** PUPPY **5.** DEEDED

6. Find the number of permutations of four letters in each case.

a. All four letters are the same.

b. Three of the letters are the same.

c. Two of the letters are the same.

d. The four letters are different.

7. Challenge The numbers below have been arranged in a right triangle shape.

a. Explain the multiplication pattern in each column shown, as you move from the top to the bottom of the column.

b. Copy the triangle and use the pattern you found in part (a) to add three more columns to the triangle.

c. How are the numbers in the triangle related to your answers to Exercise 6?

d. Suppose you have eight letters and exactly three of them are the same. Use the triangle to find the number of possible permutations of the letters. Explain your method.

							?
						?	?
					?	?	?
				1	?	?	?
			1	5	?	?	?
		1	4	20	?	?	?
	1	3	12	60	?	?	?
1	2	6	24	120	?	?	?

8. Suppose there are seven police officers who patrol in a certain city precinct. They are assigned to work in groups of two per patrol car. How many different groups of two officers can be assigned to a patrol car? Explain how you solved the problem.

9. Geometry Connection Draw all possible segments connecting five different points on a circle. How many segments are there? (*Hint:* Only one segment can be drawn between two points.)

For Exercises 10–12, tell whether each is a *permutation* or a *combination*.

10. Ten planes are lining up to take off on a runway.

11. Two players from a team of twelve are chosen for an all-star team.

12. Three out of a group of eight paintings are hung in a row.

13. a. Suppose you are choosing four out of these five pieces of fruit: an apple, a banana, a kiwi, an orange, and a pear. List all of the possible combinations.

    b. Repeat part (a) for three out of five, two out of five, and one out of five pieces of fruit.

14. The triangle of numbers below is sometimes referred to as *Pascal's triangle.*

    a. Describe three number patterns you can see in the triangle.

    b. Copy the triangle and use the patterns you found in part (a) to add the next three rows.

    c. **Challenge** Explain how to use the triangle to find the number of possible combinations for a situation.

1
1 1
1 2 1
1 3 3 1
1 4 6 4 1
1 5 10 10 5 1
1 6 15 20 15 6 1

15. **Elections** In order to count the possible outcomes of an election, sometimes you need to use permutations and sometimes you need to use combinations.

    a. Suppose eight candidates are running for two openings on a school council. How many different pairs of candidates can be elected?

    b. Suppose an eight-member council chooses a chairperson and a secretary. How many results are possible?

    c. Which question in parts (a) and (b) is a permutation question? Which is a combination question? Explain your answers.

Exercise 16 checks that you recognize situations involving permutations and combinations.

Reflecting on the Section

Write your response to Exercise 16 in your journal.

16. Give an example of a situation that can be described using a combination. Then identify a situation that can be described using a permutation. How are the two concepts different?

Spiral Review

Find the volume of a pyramid with the given base area and height. (Module 8, p. 547)

17. Area of base = 30 cm^2
Height = 12.5 cm

18. Area of base = 12 ft^2
Height = 25 ft

Find each sum or difference. (Module 3, p. 183)

19. $3\frac{5}{6} - 1\frac{2}{3}$ **20.** $1\frac{3}{5} + 3\frac{1}{12}$ **21.** $6\frac{1}{2} - 4\frac{6}{7}$ **22.** $7\frac{3}{5} + 9\frac{3}{4}$

23. The measures of three angles in a quadrilateral are 45°, 85°, and 100°. Find the measure of the fourth angle. (Module 6, p. 429)

Traffic Flow

Estimation Traffic engineers need to estimate the amount of traffic during peak travel times.

6 Identify two peak travel times for the section of hallway you chose.

7 Suppose that for one instant during each peak travel time, you could magically stop everyone walking in the hallway. Brainstorm with your group to determine a method you could use to estimate the number of students in the chosen section of hallway at any instant during peak travel times.

8 **a.** During both peak travel times, estimate the number of students in that section of hallway at any instant.

b. Use your estimate in part (a) to determine the number of square feet of hallway per walker during each peak travel time.

c. Did your answers to part (b) vary greatly for the two peak travel times you identified in Project Question 6? Explain.

Section 3 Extra Skill Practice

List all the permutations of the letters in each word.

1. ERR
2. LULL
3. DADDY
4. LLAMA

5. Find the number of permutations of three letters in each case.
   a. All three letters are different.
   b. Two of the letters are the same.
   c. All three letters are the same.

For Exercises 6–8, tell whether each is a *permutation* or a *combination*.

6. Students in a class of 24 are organized into groups of 3.
7. Three photos out of a group of ten are chosen to be used in a magazine article.
8. Twenty people are forming a line to buy movie tickets.
9. List all the ways four tennis players, Sue, Flora, Hiroko, and Yuki, can be matched up for the semifinal round of a singles tennis tournament.
10. How many different groups of three students can be formed from a group of four students? Did you find the answer using the idea of a combination or a permutation? Explain.

Standardized Testing ▶ Free Response

Tell whether each situation is a *permutation*, a *combination*, *neither*, or *both*. Explain your answer.

1. Maria is catering a party. She will serve five appetizers. The host wants her to serve the stuffed mushrooms first and the shrimp last. In how many orders can Maria serve the appetizers?
2. Four people are in line for theater tickets. There are only five tickets left. If only one ticket is required to get into the theater, how many people can get into the theater?
3. Suppose you want to buy five different pens, but only have enough money for four pens. How many different groups of pens can you buy?

FOR ASSESSMENT AND PORTFOLIOS

EXTENDED E2 EXPLORATION

Wrap It Up

SET UP *You will need:* • *paper bag* • *scissors* • *tape or glue* • *ruler*

The Situation

Many of the products we buy in stores come in boxes. The shapes of boxes are chosen for various reasons, such as shelf size or ease of handling. Package designers must also think about the amount of material used to create them. Reducing the total area of the outside surface of the box is a major factor in any package design.

The Problem

What is the biggest box that can be wrapped using a paper bag?

Something to Think About

- What kind of space figure is a box?
- How can making a net help you solve the problem?
- What measure(s) do you need to maximize in order to produce the biggest box?
- Is there any other information you need to obtain before you can begin working on this problem? If so, what is it?

Present Your Results

Give an oral report describing how you created your box design. Include the volume and the surface area of the box. Be sure to display your net and the box it forms.

Tessellations and Volumes of Cones

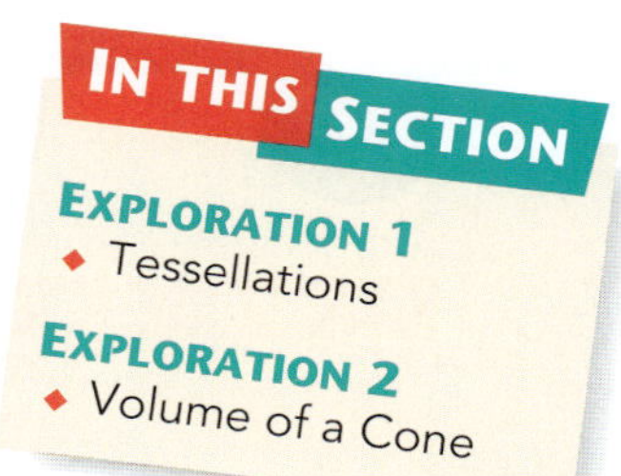

Setting the Stage

SET UP *Work with a partner. You will need $\frac{1}{2}$ bucket of pattern blocks.*

Plazas are one place in a city where people can gather for entertainment, food, and conversation while also enjoying the outdoors. Plazas like the one shown provide a place for festivals, street performers, and public forums.

The photo shows how Stockholm, Sweden, brought color and art to a plaza.

Think About It

1 Use your pattern blocks to create a colorful, artistic walkway for a plaza. Do not leave gaps between your pattern blocks or lay one pattern block on top of another. (Save your walkway tiling to use in Question 4.)

2 **a.** Which polygons did you use? Why?

b. What types of polygons do you think could be used to cover a walkway?

Exploration 1

Tessellations

SET UP *Work with a partner. You will need:* • *pattern blocks* • *protractor* • *index card* • *ruler* • *scissors* • *graph paper*

GOAL

LEARN HOW TO...
- create a tessellation

USING...
- triangles and quadrilaterals

KEY TERMS
- tessellation
- vertex of a tessellation

▶ **A tiling that uses congruent polygons in a repeating pattern to cover a plane with no gaps or overlaps is a tessellation. Designers often use tessellations to bring beauty and color to a plaza.**

3 The **vertices of a tessellation** are the points where the corners of the polygons touch. One **vertex** is marked in the tessellation shown.

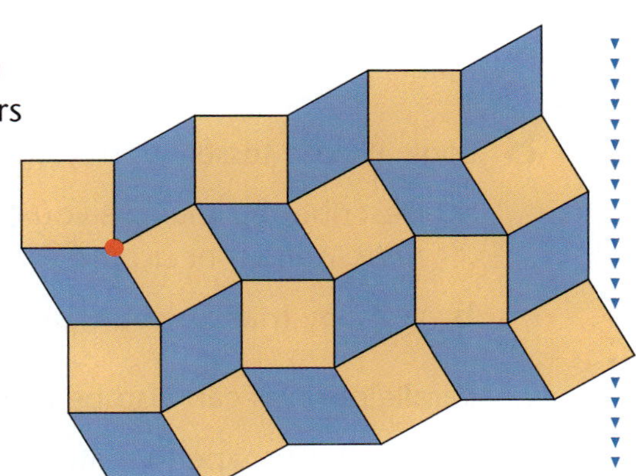

a. What polygons surround each vertex?

b. Use your pattern blocks to form one vertex of this tessellation.

c. Measure the angle of each pattern block that forms the vertex.

d. What is the sum of the angle measures at the vertex?

e. What group of polygons form the repeating pattern?

4 **Discussion** Look at your tiling from Question 1. Is there a group of polygons that repeat in a pattern? Did you cover a portion of the plane with no gaps or overlaps? Is your tiling a tessellation?

▶ **In Question 1 you had no restrictions on your tiling. You could have used one type of pattern block or many different ones. Many tessellations are created using a single shape repeatedly to form a pattern.**

5 **Discussion** Look at the pattern in the tiling shown on page 564.

a. What types of polygons were used to create the pattern?

b. Do you think there are other types of triangles that can be used to create a tessellation? Explain.

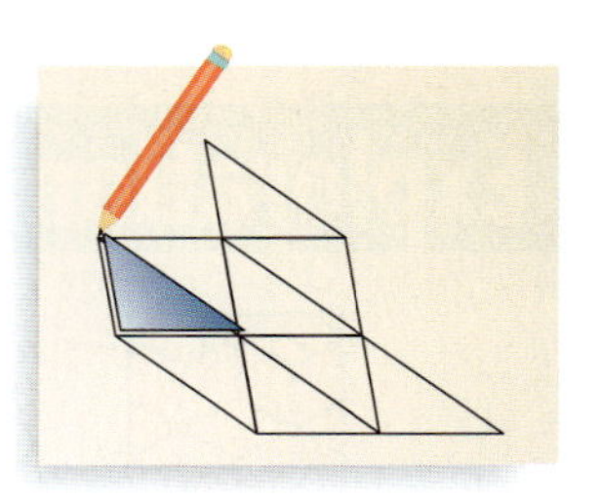

6 **a.** Use a ruler to draw a triangle on an index card and cut it out.

b. Trace around your triangle to create a tessellation. Be sure to line up the corresponding sides.

FOR ◀ HELP with the *sum of the angles of a triangle*, see **MODULE 6, p. 429**

7 **Discussion** The tessellation below was created by tracing around a triangle. Why are six triangles needed at the vertex rather than five or seven?

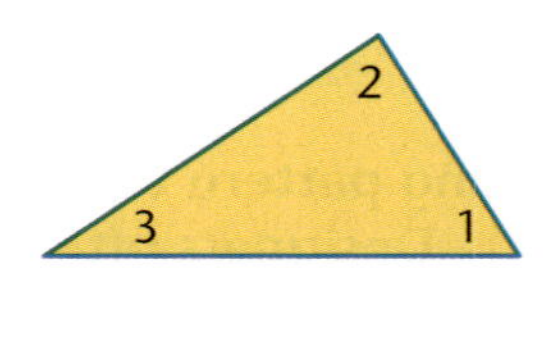

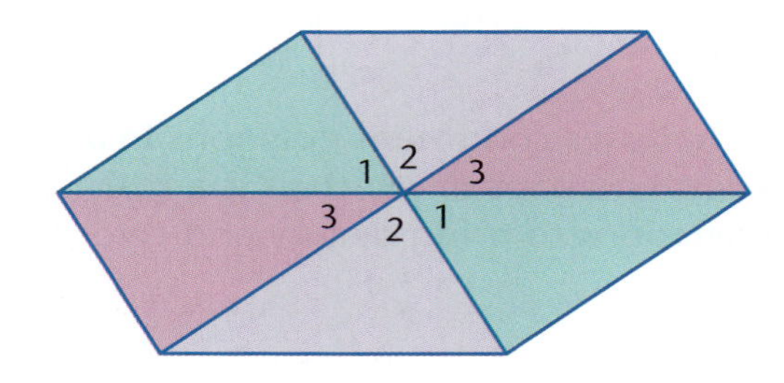

8 Look at your tessellation from Question 6.

a. Describe the triangle you used in your tessellation. Was it *right*, *obtuse*, or *acute*? Was it *scalene*, *isosceles*, or *equilateral*?

b. Will any triangle tessellate? Explain.

9 Parallelograms can also be used to create a tessellation.

a. On graph paper, create a tessellation using a parallelogram. Be sure every parallelogram is congruent to the first one you drew.

b. Is there a larger similar parallelogram in your tessellation? If so, outline it.

...checks that you can create a tessellation.

10 **CHECKPOINT** Use a ruler to draw a quadrilateral on an index card. Cut out your quadrilateral. Then trace around your quadrilateral to create a tessellation. Be sure to match up the corresponding sides.

FOR ◀ HELP with *concave and convex polygons*, see **MODULE 6, p. 388**

11 **Discussion** Look at your tessellation from Question 10.

a. Was your quadrilateral in Question 10 concave or convex?

b. Will any convex quadrilateral tessellate? Explain.

c. Will any concave quadrilateral tessellate? Explain.

HOMEWORK EXERCISES ▶ See Exs. 1–6 on pp. 572–573.

TECHNOLOGY Using Computer Drawing Software

You can also use computer drawing software to create a tessellation, as in Questions 6, 9, and 10 on page 566.

Step 1 Use the polygon tool to draw a triangle or another shape. Then duplicate the polygon a number of times.

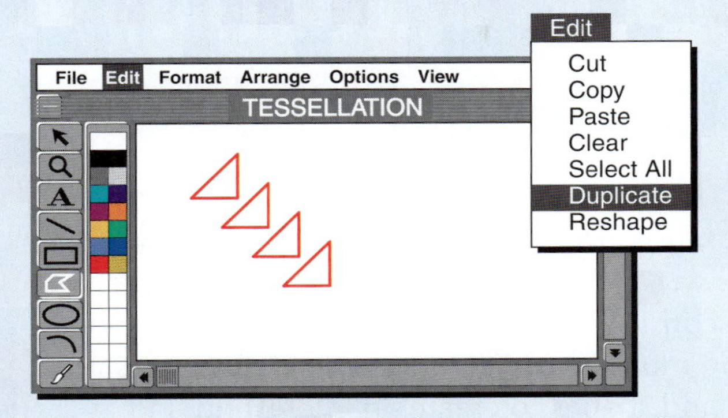

Step 2 Flip or rotate the copies and move them together to form a pattern.

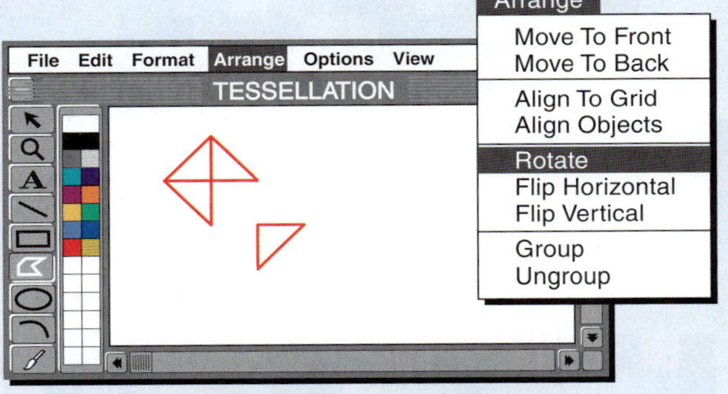

Step 3 Group the polygons in the pattern together to form one object. This new object can be duplicated and moved as one piece to create a tessellation.

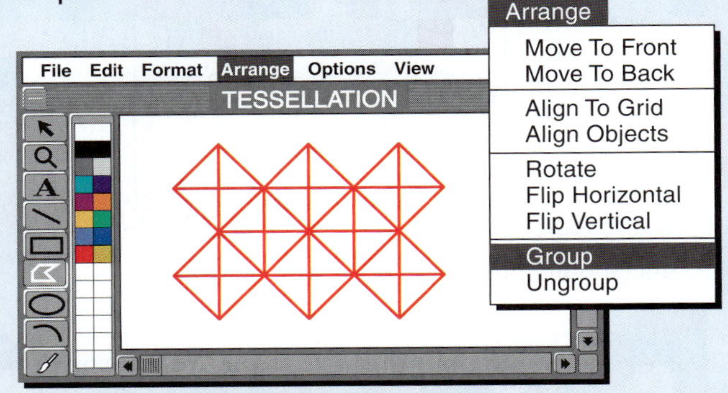

GOAL

LEARN HOW TO...
- find the volume of a cone

AS YOU...
- examine sculptures

KEY TERM
- cone

Exploration 2

Volume of a Cone

SET UP *Work with a partner. You will need:* • *Labsheets 4A and 4B* • *scissors* • *tape* • *rice*

Museums bring art to the city in different ways. Museums themselves are sometimes considered works of art. The Spiral Building, a museum in Tokyo, uses light, shadow, and shapes to create an interesting and complex exterior. What shapes and tessellations do you notice?

12 **Discussion** On the upper right side of the building is a steel circular *cone*. Why do you think the architects decided to use a circular cone instead of a circular cylinder or a rectangular prism?

▶ **All the cones and cylinders in this section have circular bases. You can refer to them as cones and cylinders rather than *circular cones* and *circular cylinders*.**

A space figure with a circular base and a vertex is a circular **cone**.

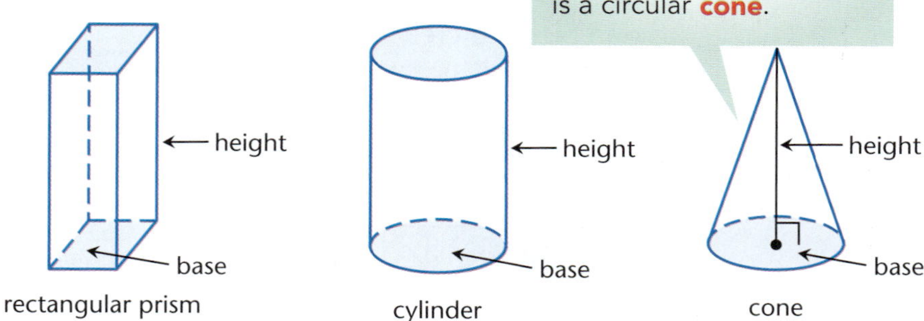

13 Suppose each figure above is the same height and the areas of the bases are equal. Which figure do you think has the least volume? Why?

▶ **When a cone and a cylinder have the same height and the areas of their bases are equal, their volumes are related.**

14 **Use Labsheet 4A.** Follow the directions on Labsheet 4A to investigate the relationship between the volumes of cones and cylinders using the *Cone and Cylinder Nets.*

15 **Try This as a Class** The graph shows the volumes of several cones that have a height of 1 m.

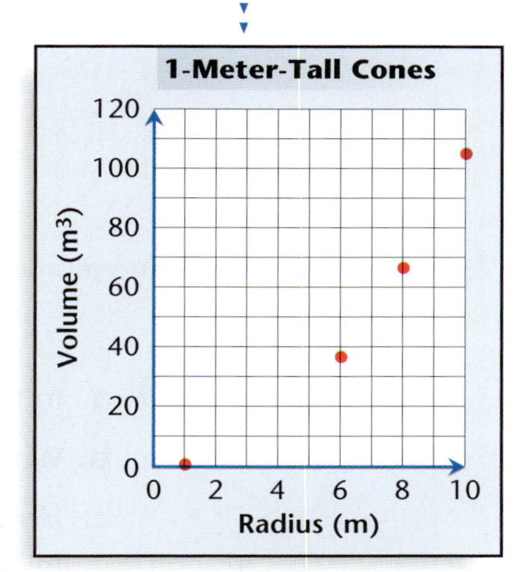

a. Suppose you want to estimate the volume of a cone with a radius of 3 m. How would you connect the points in the graph? Would you use segments or a curve?

b. Copy the graph. Use segments to estimate the volume of a cone with a radius of 3 m. Then use a curve to estimate the volume.

c. The volume of a cone with a radius of 3 m is about 9.5 m^3. Which method in part (b) gave the best estimate of the volume of the cone?

Use Labsheet 4B for Questions 16 and 17.

16 Follow the directions on Labsheet 4B to complete the *Comparing Volumes of Cones and Cylinders* table and graph.

FOR◀HELP with *volume of a cylinder*, see **MODULE 7, p. 464**

17 Look at your completed graph from Question 16.

a. A cylinder with a radius of 5 m and a height of 1 m has a volume of about 78.5 m^3. Estimate the volume of a cone with the same radius and height.

b. A cone with a radius of 7 m and a height of 1 m has a volume of about 51.3 m^3. Estimate the volume of a cylinder with the same radius and height.

c. How many times greater is the volume of a cylinder compared to the volume of a cone when both have the same radius and height? How does the graph show this?

18 **Discussion** The volume of a cylinder can be found using the equation $V = Bh$.

a. What do V, B, and h represent in the equation?

b. Based on your work in Questions 14, 16, and 17, what equation can you use to find the volume of a cone?

EXAMPLE

Find the volume of a cone with a radius of 1.5 m and a height of 0.7 m.

SAMPLE RESPONSE

$$V = \frac{1}{3}Bh$$

B = area of base

$$V = \frac{1}{3} \cdot \pi r^2 \cdot h$$

$$\approx \frac{1}{3} \cdot 3.14 \cdot (1.5)^2 \cdot 0.7$$

Remember, $\pi \approx 3.14$.

$$\approx 1.6485$$

The volume of the cone is about 1.6 m^3.

19 **a.** In the Example, what does r represent? What is the value of r?

b. What is the area of the base?

c. How can you use the diameter of the base instead of the radius to find the volume of a cone?

20 The diameter of a cone is 12 ft. The height is 3.5 ft. Find the volume.

✓ QUESTION 21

...checks that you can find the volume of a cone.

21 **✓ CHECKPOINT** The cone on the Spiral Building has a radius of 2.5 m and a height of 7.5 m. What is the volume of a cone with these dimensions?

22 The Spiral Building's cone is made of steel. Steel has a mass of 7860 kg for every cubic meter (m^3).

a. Find the mass of a steel cone with a radius of 2.5 m and a height of 7.5 m.

b. An African bull elephant has a mass between 5400 kg and 7200 kg. About how many elephants are equivalent to the mass of the steel cone in part (a)?

23 **Discussion** The floor under the steel cone on the Spiral Building can support no more than 5900 kg. How do you think the architects reduced the mass of the steel cone?

HOMEWORK EXERCISES ▶ See Exs. 7–13 on pp. 573–574.

Section 4 Key Concepts

Key Terms

tessellation

vertex of a tessellation

cone

Tessellations (pp. 565–566)

A tessellation is a tiling that uses congruent polygons in a repeating pattern to cover a plane with no gaps or overlaps. All triangles and quadrilaterals tessellate.

The sum of the angle measures around a vertex is 360°.

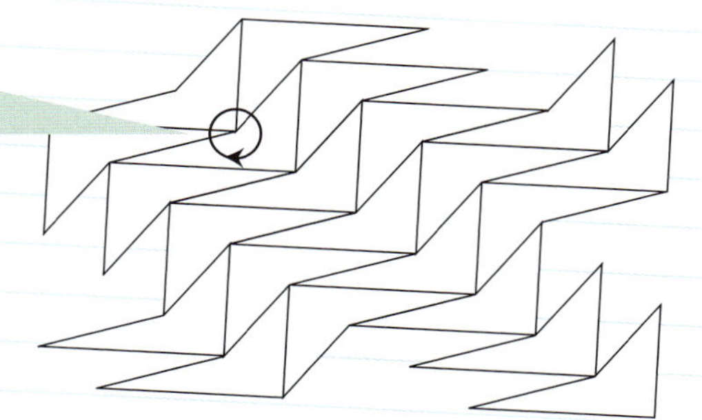

Volume of a Cone (pp. 568–570)

The volume of any cone is given by the formula $V = \frac{1}{3}Bh$ where B equals the area of its base and h equals its height.

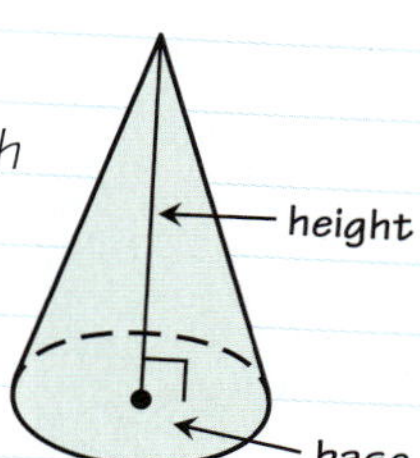

Example

The height of a cone is 4 ft and the base has an area of 12 ft^2. Find the volume.

$$V = \frac{1}{3}(12)(4) = 16$$

The volume of the cone is 16 ft^3.

Key Concepts Questions

24 In the tessellation above, three of the angles at a vertex have measures of 90°, 38°, and 18°. What is the measure of the fourth angle?

25 How would the volume of the cone in the Example change if it were twice as high? if the radius were doubled but the height did not change?

Section 4
Practice & Application Exercises

YOU WILL NEED

For Ex. 4:
- Labsheet 4C

For Ex. 5:
- index card
- scissors
- tape

For Ex. 16:
- graph paper

For Ex. 17:
- $\frac{1}{2}$ bucket of pattern blocks

Trace each polygon below and then create a tessellation with it. Be sure to match up the corresponding sides.

1. 

2. 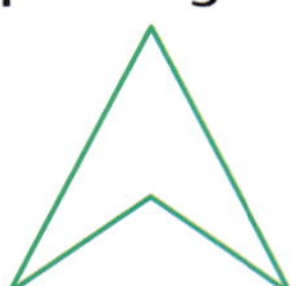

3. 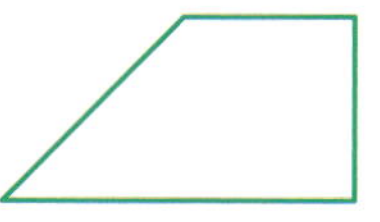

4. **Use Labsheet 4C.** A polygon is called a *repeated tile*, or *rep-tile*, if congruent polygons can be arranged to form a larger similar polygon. The equilateral triangle pattern block is a rep-tile. For each other pattern block that is a rep-tile, make a sketch to show how four of the blocks can be made into a larger similar polygon.

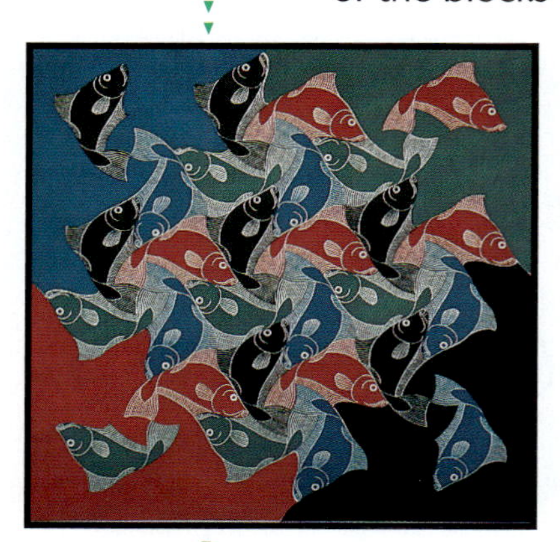

5. **Create Your Own** Maurits Cornelius Escher, the Dutch artist known as M. C. Escher, used tessellations, rotations, and translations to create many fascinating tilings like the one shown.

   a. Follow Steps 1–3 below to create your own tiling.

   b. **Research** Look up another of Escher's tilings. Describe the transformations he used.

Step 1

Draw a parallelogram on an index card and cut it out.

Step 2

Draw a design along one side of the parallelogram. Cut it out and translate it to the opposite side. Tape on the translated piece.

Step 3

Repeat the last step on the other sides, if you wish. Then use your shape to create a tiling. Personalize it by adding color and other details.

6. In a *regular tessellation*, one regular polygon is used to create the tessellation. Four regular polygons are shown.

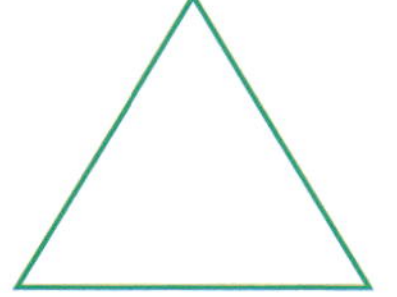
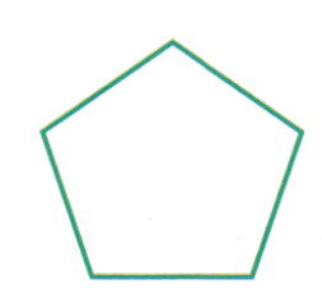
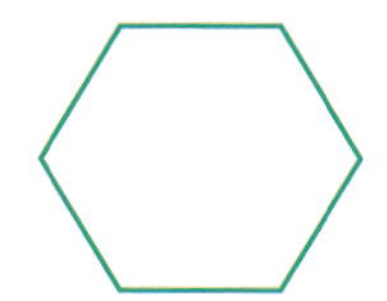

a. What is the measure of an interior angle of each polygon? (*Hint:* Draw diagonals to form triangles.)

b. How can you use the measure of the interior angle to determine if a regular polygon will tessellate?

c. Which of these four regular polygons will tessellate?

Use the approximate dimensions given to estimate the volume of each cone. Round decimal answers to the nearest tenth.

7. 

8. 

9. 

10. A cone and a cylinder both have volumes of 12π cm^3.

a. Give a set of possible dimensions for the cylinder. Then sketch a model.

b. If the cone and the cylinder have congruent bases, what is the relationship between their heights?

11. Suppose a cone and a cylinder have congruent bases and equal heights. A pyramid and a prism also have congruent bases and equal heights. Write a proportion to relate the volumes of all four solids.

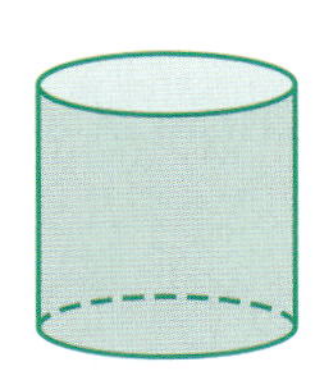
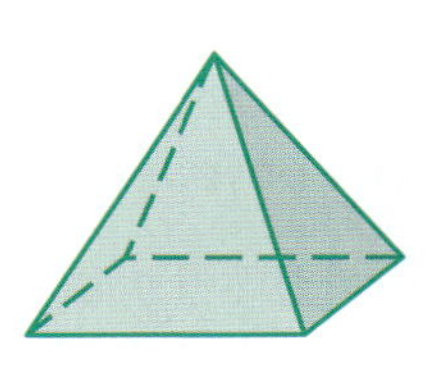
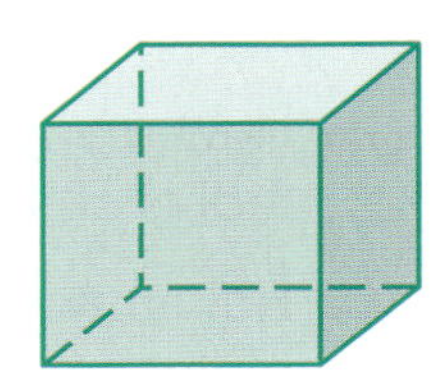

$$\frac{\text{volume of ?}}{\text{volume of ?}} = \frac{\text{volume of ?}}{\text{volume of ?}}$$

12. **Challenge** The cone on the Spiral Building is hollow and the walls are 6 mm thick. To find the volume of the walls of the hollow cone you can think of it as a cone inside a cone, as shown in the drawing below. Use the information below to find the volume of the walls of the hollow cone.

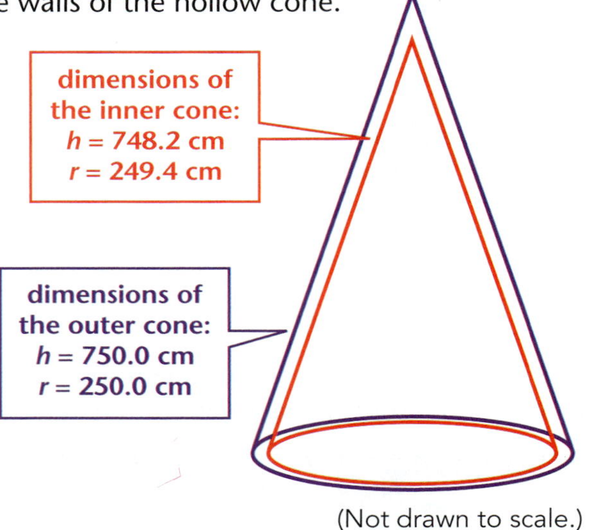

(Not drawn to scale.)

Reflecting on the Section

Discussion

Exercise 13 checks that you can find and compare volumes of cones.

Be prepared to discuss your response to Exercise 13 in class.

13. The table and graph show the volumes of cones that all have a height of 10 in.

10-Inch-Tall Cones

Radius (in.)	Volume (in.^{3})
0.5	2.62
1.5	23.55
2.5	65.42
3.5	128.22
4.5	211.95
5.5	316.62

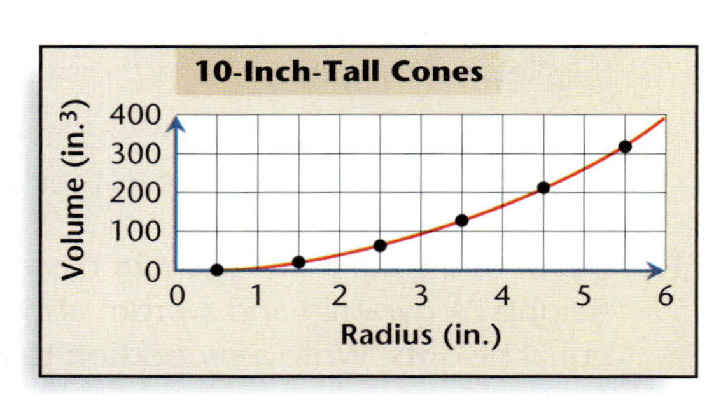

a. How many times greater is the volume of a cone with a radius of 4.5 in. compared to a cone with a radius of 1.5 in.?

b. How many times greater is the volume of a cone with a radius of 5 in. compared to a cone with a radius of 2.5 in.?

c. In general, how does a change in the radius change the volume? How does the graph show this?

Spiral Review

Tell whether each is a *permutation* or a *combination*. (Module 8, p. 558)

14. the number of ways to arrange 6 books on a shelf

15. the number of ways to select 3 books from a choice of 7 books

16. a. Plot and label each point in a coordinate plane. Then draw segments connecting A to B, B to C, and so on up to E to F. Finally, connect F to A. (Module 2, p. 95)

$A(1, 3)$ $\quad$ $B(2, 2)$ $\quad$ $C(-1, -1)$

$D(-3, 1)$ $\quad$ $E(-2, 2)$ $\quad$ $F(-1, 1)$

b. Use coordinates to describe a transformation that will result in an image similar to the polygon you plotted in part (a). Then draw the image after your transformation. (Module 4, p. 299)

Extension

Semi-Regular Tessellations

In Exercise 6 on page 573, you saw that one regular polygon can be used to create a tessellation. You can also create tessellations using more than one regular polygon. For example, an equilateral triangle and a regular hexagon were used to create the tessellation below.

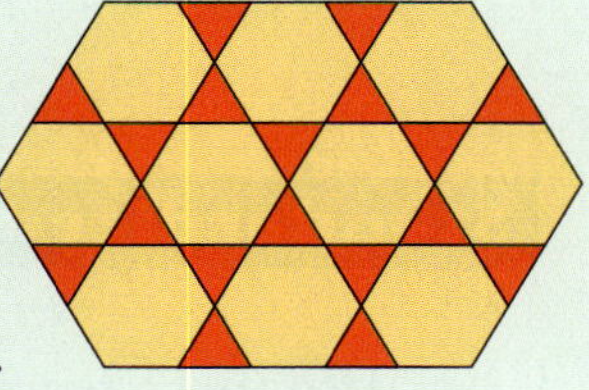

17. a. Which pattern blocks are regular polygons?

b. Create two or three different tessellations that include more than one type of the pattern blocks you identified in part (a).

A *semi-regular tessellation* uses more than one kind of regular polygon, and has the same arrangement of polygons at every vertex. The tessellation shown above is an example of a semi-regular tessellation.

18. Two different arrangements of regular polygons appear in the tessellation below, so it is not a semi-regular tessellation.

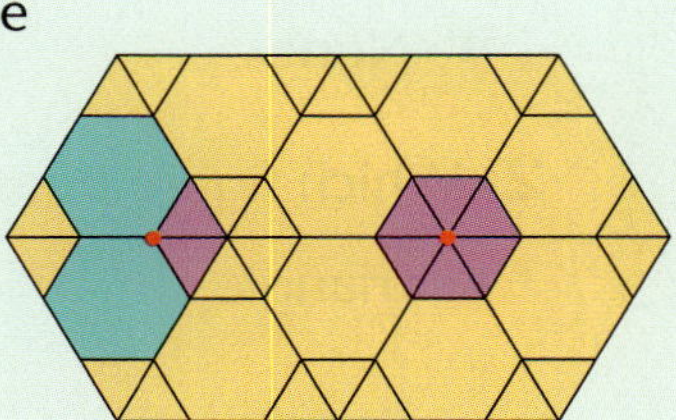

a. Identify which of your tessellations from Exercise 17(b) are semi-regular tessellations.

b. Is the tessellation shown on page 565 a semi-regular tessellation? Explain.

Section 4 Extra Skill Practice

Trace each polygon below and then create a tessellation with it. Be sure to match up the corresponding sides.

1. 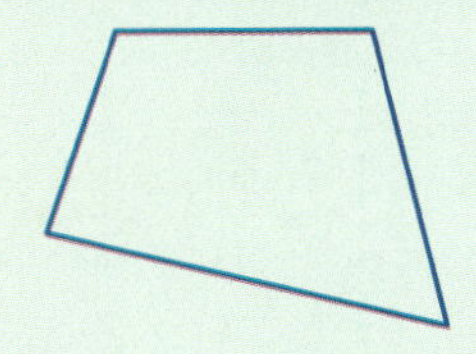

2. 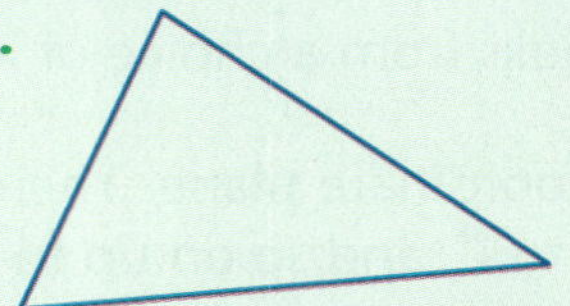

3. 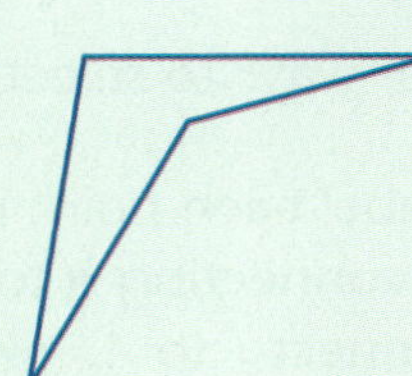

Use the figures below for Exercises 4 and 5.

A. 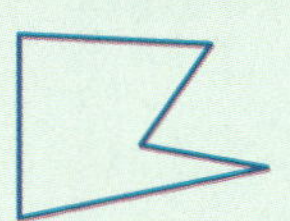

B. 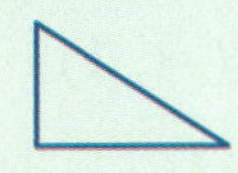

C. 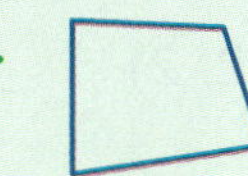

D. 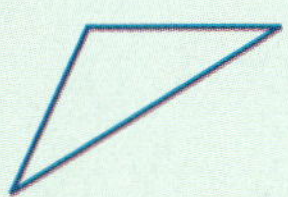

4. Which of the figures tessellate?

5. Which two figures can combine to tessellate?

Find the volume of each cone. Round decimal answers to the nearest tenth.

6. 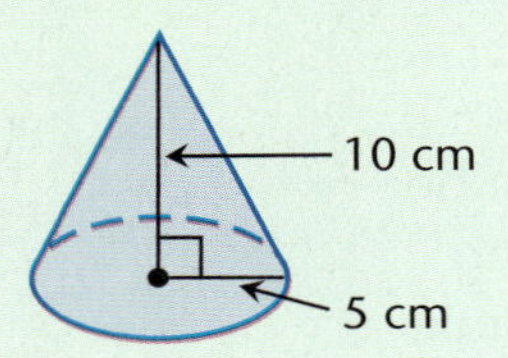

7. 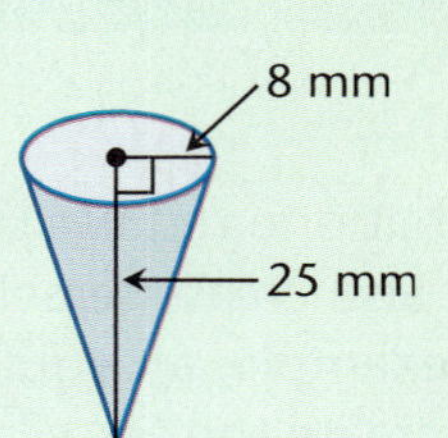

8. 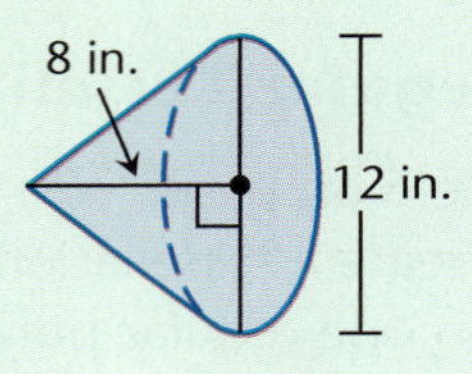

Standardized Testing ▶ Multiple Choice

1. Use these heights and base radii of cones to answer the question.

   I. $h = 9$ cm, $r = 2$ cm II. $h = 2$ cm, $r = 4$ cm III. $h = 1$ cm, $r = 6$ cm IV. $h = 4$ cm, $r = 3$ cm

   Which dimensions produce cones with the same volume? ($\pi \approx 3.14$)

   (A) None (B) I and III only (C) III and IV only (D) I, III, and IV only

2. Which figure does not always tessellate?

   (A) triangle (B) pentagon (C) convex quadrilateral (D) concave quadrilateral

Traffic Flow

You determined the traffic flow through a section of hallway in your school that has a traffic problem. Now you'll develop a plan for improving the flow of traffic through that section of hallway.

Traffic engineers have found that there are no limits on walking speed when each walker has at least 40 ft^2 of floorspace. Then, as a walkway becomes more crowded, it becomes harder to walk at certain speeds.

The engineers' findings are summarized in this table. *Maximum capacity flow* is the greatest number of walkers that a walkway can hold.

Effect of Overcrowding on Walking Speed				
No speeds restricted	Few speeds restricted	Some speeds restricted	All speeds restricted	Maximum capacity flow
40 ft^2/walker	24–40 ft^2/walker	15–24 ft^2/walker	6–15 ft^2/walker	6 ft^2/walker

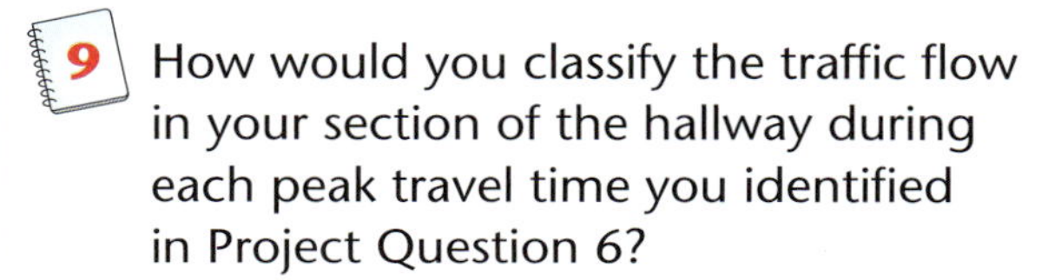

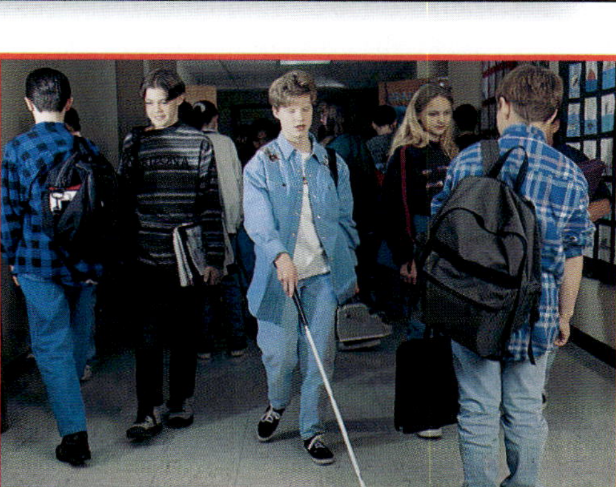

9 How would you classify the traffic flow in your section of the hallway during each peak travel time you identified in Project Question 6?

10 Is the traffic in your hallway over the maximum capacity? If not, how many more students can use the hallway?

11 Suppose you want to alter your section of hallway so students can walk at any speed. Give dimensions for the least width that would allow this during peak travel times. Would it be practical to build a hallway this wide?

12 Think about how obstacles or gathering places cause traffic jams in the hallway.

a. Describe any changes you think should be made.

b. If no changes are needed, estimate how much enrollment would have to increase to create a traffic problem.

13 Make a presentation of your findings and recommendations. Use graphs and traffic flow data to support your views.

MODULE 8

Review and Assessment

You will need: • *graph paper* **(Ex. 23)**

List all the permutations for each situation. **(Sec. 1, Explor. 1)**

1. A band and an orchestra will perform separately at a concert.

2. A family will visit three vacation sites: Sequoia National Park, Joshua Tree National Park, and Mono Lake.

3. A student will do homework for Spanish, art, and social studies.

4. Two out of four colored blankets will be layered on a bed. The colors are beige, pink, yellow, and green.

Find how many permutations are possible for each situation. **(Sec. 1, Explor. 2)**

5. five bicycles being put in a bicycle rack

6. eight songs to be sung in a concert

7. the first three batters on a softball team with ten players

8. the first two finishers in a race among 50 runners

For Exercises 9–12, use the base plan below. **(Sec. 2, Explor. 1)**

9. Draw the front and right-side views of the building.

10. What is the volume of the building?

11. What is the surface area of the building?

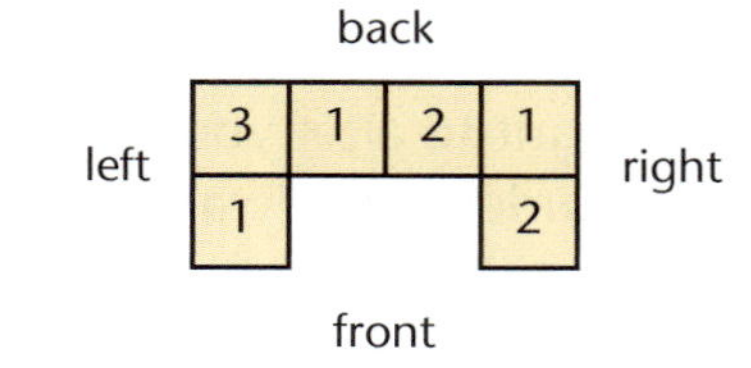

12. Suppose a building has the shape of a rectangular prism that is 5 cubes long, 2 cubes wide, and 1 cube high. Compare the volume and the surface area of this building to the volume and the surface area of the building in Exercises 9–11.

Find the volume of each pyramid with the given base area B and height h. **(Sec. 2, Explor. 2)**

13. $B = 15 \text{ cm}^2$, $h = 5 \text{ cm}$

14. $B = 21 \text{ ft}^2$, $h = 8 \text{ ft}$

15. $B = 40 \text{ m}^2$, $h = 12 \text{ m}$

Use the street diagram. Find all of the shortest routes between the given intersections. (Sec. 3, Explor. 1)

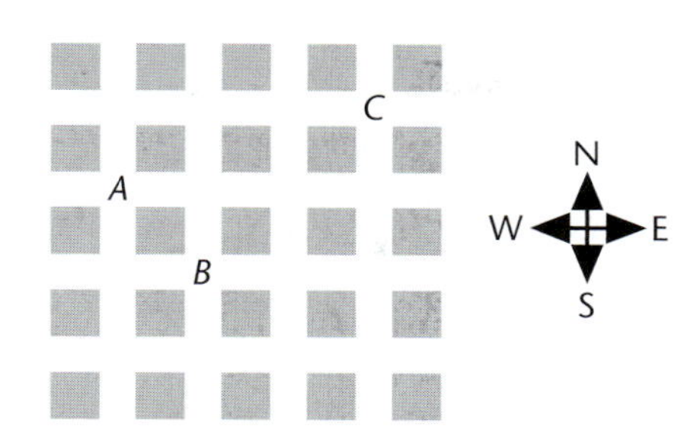

16. from A to B

17. from B to C

18. from C to A

List all the permutations of the letters in each word. (Sec. 3, Explor. 1)

19. BOOT

20. BELLE

21. NANNY

22. Freddi has five dogs: Bubba, Taffy, Radar, Dexter, and Lucky. Suppose she takes them for walks in groups of two or more. (Sec. 3, Explor. 2)

a. How many different groups of three dogs can she take?

b. How many different groups of two dogs can she take?

c. How are your answers to parts (a) and (b) related? Explain.

d. Is this situation a *permutation* or a *combination*? Explain.

23. Draw a trapezoid on graph paper. Then create a tessellation with it. Explain why any trapezoid will tessellate. (Sec. 4, Explor. 1)

Find the volume of each cone. Round decimal answers to the nearest tenth. (Sec. 4, Explor. 2)

24.

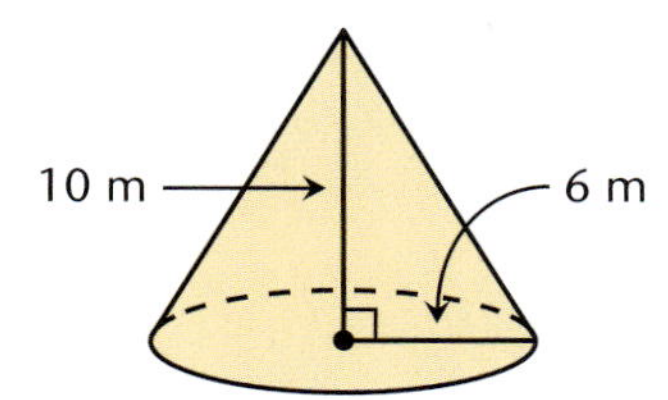

25.

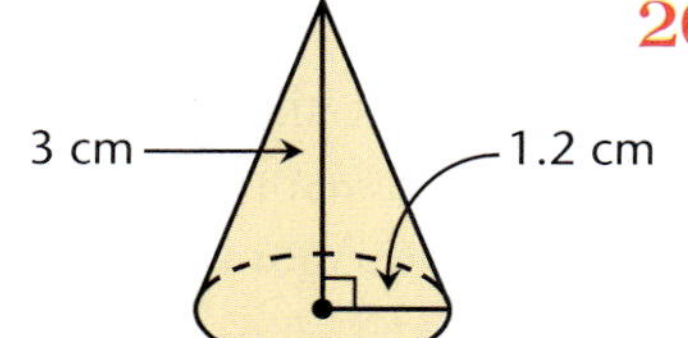

26.

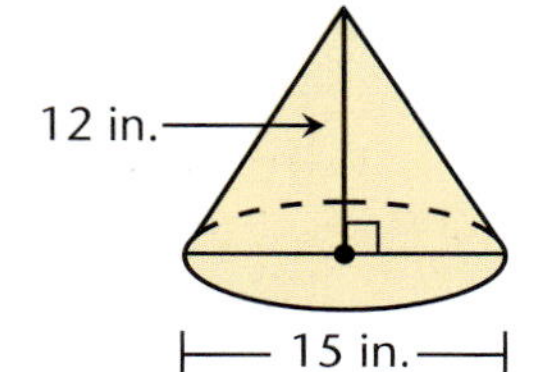

Reflecting on the Module

27. Suppose the following four measurements can be either the height or the radius of a cone: 2 m, 5 m, 6 m, and 12 m.

a. How many different cones can be formed with these measurements?

b. Which dimensions will make the cone with the least volume? the greatest volume? Explain.

CONTENTS

STUDENT RESOURCES

STUDENT RESOURCES

TOOLBOX

NUMBERS and OPERATIONS

Adding and Subtracting Decimals

When you add or subtract decimals, line up the decimal places and use the same rules as for adding and subtracting whole numbers.

EXAMPLE

$7.75 + 6.61 \rightarrow$

$$\begin{array}{r} \overset{1}{7}.75 \\ +\ 6.61 \\ \hline 14.36 \end{array}$$

$4.6 - 2.25 \rightarrow$

$$\begin{array}{r} 4.\overset{5\ 10}{\cancel{6}0} \\ -\ 2.25 \\ \hline 2.35 \end{array}$$

Write a zero so that both numbers have the same number of decimal places.

You may find it helpful to use mental math skills to add and subtract decimals.

EXAMPLE

Find 32 + 19.8.

Trade a whole number for 19.8: 19.8 + **0.2** = **20**

SOLUTION

32 + **20** = 52

52 – **0.2** = 51.8

32 + 19.8 = 51.8

Take off the extra **0.2** that you added.

EXAMPLE

Find 2.8 + 3.6 + 2.2 + 5.4.

SOLUTION Pair up numbers that are compatible and can be added easily.

2.8 + **3.6** + **2.2** + **5.4** = **5** + **9** = 14

Find each sum or difference. Use mental math when possible.

1. 7.2 + 14
2. 38.9 – 16
3. 5.25 + 8.75
4. 13.3 + 24.16
5. 8.5 – 3.1
6. 4.4 – 1.7
7. 6.75 – 3.5
8. 8.3 – 6.15
9. 0.42 + 3.7
10. 4.08 + 0.6
11. 9 – 5.1
12. 32.5 + 8.7
13. 14.9 – 6.03
14. 6.85 + 2.8
15. 20.97 + 3.58
16. 18.4 – 9.68
17. 11.7 + 9.3 + 4
18. 44.8 + 7.5 + 23.2
19. 48.5 + 2.4 + 3.6 + 11.5

Divisibility by 2, 5, and 10

A number is divisible by two if its last digit is 0, 2, 4, 6, or 8.

A number is divisible by five if its last digit is 0 or 5.

A number is divisible by ten if its last digit is 0.

EXAMPLE

376 is divisible by 2 because its last digit is 6.

12,040 is divisible by 2, 5, and 10 because its last digit is 0.

81 is not divisible by 2, 5, or 10 because its last digit is 1.

Tell whether each number is divisible by 2, 5, and 10.

1. 48
2. 26
3. 125
4. 10,273
5. 1065
6. 390
7. 862
8. 39,407
9. 3270
10. 76,195

Estimation

You can estimate an answer if you do not need it to be exact. One way to estimate a sum or difference is to round each number first.

EXAMPLE

Round each addend to the nearest hundred. Then use mental math to add.

$$\begin{array}{r} 1213 \\ 468 \\ +\ \ 96 \\ \hline \end{array} \longrightarrow \begin{array}{r} 1200 \\ 500 \\ +\ 100 \\ \hline 1800 \end{array}$$

Round each number to the nearest whole number. Then use mental math to subtract.

$43.45 - 8.7 \longrightarrow 43 - 9 = 34$

Use rounding to estimate each sum or difference.

1. 509 + 384
2. 176 – 93
3. 20.8 + 5.7
4. 87.2 – 49.6
5. 1226 – 479
6. 58.8 – 40.36
7. 64.6 + 35.4
8. 4841 + 7385
9. 3.85 + 11.2
10. 61,432 – 13,951
11. 9132 + 342 + 188
12. 18,970 + 1,304 + 978
13. $14.95 + $1.25 + $.99 + $2.05

Another way to estimate an answer is to first look at the front-end digits and then use the other digits to adjust.

EXAMPLE

```
  2372 }
+ 3027 } about 370 + 30, or 400
------
  5000 + 400
```

The sum is about 5400.

```
  1.21 }
  7.89 } about 1
  2.56 }
+ 8.44 } about 1
------
  18 + 2
```

The sum is about 20.

You can use rounding to multiply whole numbers. You can use compatible numbers to divide whole numbers. Compatible numbers have sums, products, or quotients that are easy to compute.

EXAMPLE

$602 \cdot 17 \rightarrow 600 \cdot 20 = 12{,}000$

Round each factor to the greatest decimal place.

The product $602 \cdot 17$ is about 12,000.

EXAMPLE

$382 \div 23 \rightarrow 400 \div 25 = 16$

Round the dividend to the greatest decimal place or places.

Change the divisor to the closest convenient factor of the new dividend.

The quotient $382 \div 23$ is about 16.

Estimate each sum by adjusting the sum of the front-end digits.

14. 595 + 308
15. 83.1 + 47.4
16. 3.126 + 5.283
17. 9783 + 10,215
18. 264.8 + 41.6
19. 14,898 + 875.2
20. 497 + 228 + 561
21. 38.15 + 11.25 + 9.65
22. 2520 + 3214 + 1387

Use rounding or compatible numbers to estimate each product or quotient.

23. $19 \cdot 69$
24. $24 \cdot 48$
25. $692 \div 12$
26. $783 \div 39$
27. $485 \cdot 18$
28. $9125 \div 307$
29. $586 \cdot 712$
30. $1621 \div 78$

Finding a Fraction

A fraction compares a part to a whole. The numerator represents the part, and the denominator represents the whole.

EXAMPLE

There are six circles in the whole set. Five of the six parts are shaded.

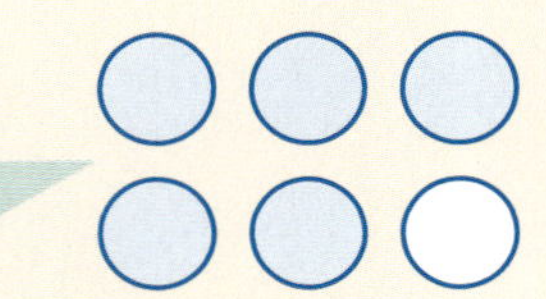

part → $\mathbf{\frac{5}{6}}$ ← numerator
whole → ← denominator

You can use a diagram or mental math to help you find a fraction of a number.

EXAMPLE

To find $\frac{3}{4}$ of 12, first find $\frac{1}{4}$ of 12.

The denominator tells you to divide the 12 dots into four groups with the same number of dots in each group.

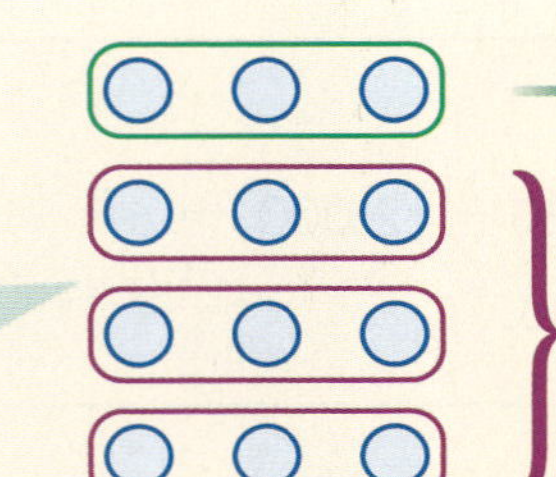

$\frac{1}{4}$ of 12 is **3**.

$\mathbf{\frac{3}{4}}$ **of 12 is 9.**

EXAMPLE

To find $\frac{2}{3}$ of 12, think: $\frac{1}{3}$ of 12 is 4, so $\frac{2}{3}$ of 12 is $\mathbf{2} \cdot 4 = 8$.

$\mathbf{\frac{2}{3}}$ **of 12 is 8.**

Write a fraction to represent each shaded region or part of a set.

1. 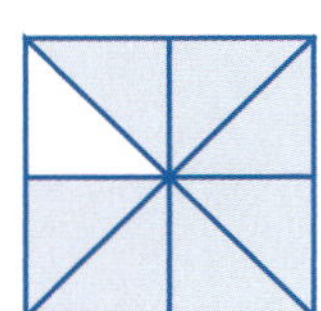

2. 

3. 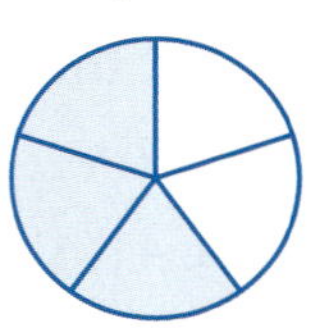

4. 

Find each value.

5. $\frac{1}{3}$ of 6

6. $\frac{1}{2}$ of 10

7. $\frac{2}{7}$ of 14

8. $\frac{4}{5}$ of 15

9. $\frac{3}{4}$ of 16

10. $\frac{5}{6}$ of 18

11. $\frac{2}{3}$ of 21

12. $\frac{7}{10}$ of 30

13. $\frac{7}{8}$ of 40

14. $\frac{5}{9}$ of 63

15. $\frac{15}{16}$ of 80

16. $\frac{11}{12}$ of 120

Finding Equivalent Fractions

Equivalent fractions are fractions that name the same part of a whole.

EXAMPLE

$\frac{1}{2}$ →

$\frac{4}{8}$ →

There are 4 times as many parts, but each part is one fourth of its original size.

$\frac{1}{2}$ and $\frac{4}{8}$ are equivalent fractions.

You can multiply or divide the numerator and the denominator of a fraction by the same whole number other than zero to find an equivalent fraction.

EXAMPLE

Find the missing number to complete each pair of equivalent fractions.

SOLUTION

$\frac{24}{30} = \frac{?}{5}$

What number do you divide 30 by to get 5?

$\frac{24}{30} = \frac{24 \div 6}{30 \div 6}$

$\mathbf{\frac{24}{30} = \frac{4}{5}}$

$\frac{1}{3} = \frac{?}{21}$

What number do you multiply 3 by to get 21?

$\frac{1}{3} = \frac{1 \cdot 7}{3 \cdot 7}$

$\mathbf{\frac{1}{3} = \frac{7}{21}}$

Complete each pair of equivalent fractions.

1. $\frac{8}{12} = \frac{?}{3}$
2. $\frac{1}{2} = \frac{?}{48}$
3. $\frac{4}{5} = \frac{?}{15}$
4. $\frac{15}{20} = \frac{3}{?}$
5. $\frac{12}{16} = \frac{3}{?}$
6. $\frac{15}{27} = \frac{?}{9}$
7. $\frac{2}{3} = \frac{14}{?}$
8. $\frac{5}{8} = \frac{30}{?}$

Write three equivalent fractions for each fraction.

9. $\frac{1}{3}$
10. $\frac{3}{4}$
11. $\frac{12}{60}$
12. $\frac{18}{54}$
13. $\frac{35}{140}$
14. $\frac{60}{150}$
15. $\frac{80}{96}$
16. $\frac{36}{63}$

Comparing Fractions

To find out if a fraction is greater or less than another fraction, you can use a diagram or equivalent fractions.

EXAMPLE

Compare $\frac{5}{12}$ and $\frac{1}{2}$.

SOLUTION Use fraction strips that are the same length.

Shade $\frac{5}{12}$ of one strip.

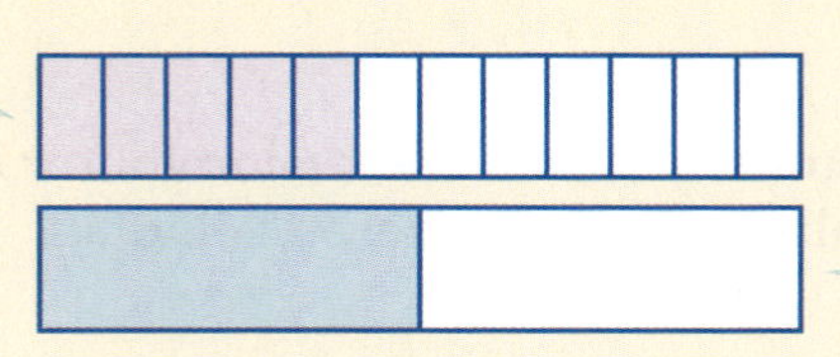

Shade $\frac{1}{2}$ of the other strip.

Compare the shaded parts. $\frac{5}{12} < \frac{1}{2}$

EXAMPLE

Replace the ? with >, <, or =: $\frac{1}{2}$? $\frac{7}{12}$

SOLUTION Write a fraction equivalent to $\frac{1}{2}$ with denominator 12.

$\frac{1}{2} = \frac{?}{12}$

$\frac{1}{2} = \frac{1 \cdot 6}{2 \cdot 6} = \frac{6}{12}$

$\frac{6}{12} < \frac{7}{12}$, so $\frac{1}{2} < \frac{7}{12}$

Replace each ? with >, <, or =.

1. $\frac{5}{7}$? $\frac{6}{7}$
2. $\frac{16}{24}$? $\frac{3}{4}$
3. $\frac{2}{3}$? $\frac{11}{15}$
4. $\frac{5}{6}$? $\frac{15}{18}$
5. $\frac{1}{2}$? $\frac{7}{16}$
6. $\frac{16}{48}$? $\frac{3}{8}$
7. $\frac{25}{35}$? $\frac{4}{5}$
8. $\frac{1}{4}$? $\frac{7}{28}$
9. $\frac{4}{9}$? $\frac{12}{36}$
10. $\frac{11}{33}$? $\frac{1}{3}$
11. $\frac{6}{40}$? $\frac{3}{20}$
12. $\frac{7}{20}$? $\frac{2}{5}$

Adding and Subtracting Fractions

To add or subtract fractions with the same denominator, add or subtract the numerators of the fractions.

EXAMPLE

$$\frac{2}{8} + \frac{3}{8} = \frac{2+3}{8}$$

Add the numerators.

$$= \frac{5}{8}$$

EXAMPLE

$$\frac{11}{12} - \frac{4}{12} = \frac{11-4}{12}$$

Subtract the numerators.

$$= \frac{7}{12}$$

You can use mental math skills to add and subtract mixed numbers.

EXAMPLE

Add the **whole numbers**.

Add the **fractions**.

$$\begin{array}{r} 6\frac{2}{5} \\ +\ 3\frac{1}{5} \\ \hline 9\frac{3}{5} \end{array}$$

$6\frac{2}{5} + 3\frac{1}{5} = 9\frac{3}{5}$

Subtract the **whole numbers**.

Subtract the **fractions**.

$$\begin{array}{r} 6\frac{2}{5} \\ -\ 3\frac{1}{5} \\ \hline 3\frac{1}{5} \end{array}$$

$6\frac{2}{5} - 3\frac{1}{5} = 3\frac{1}{5}$

Find each sum or difference.

1. $\frac{3}{10} + \frac{4}{10}$
2. $\frac{4}{5} - \frac{1}{5}$
3. $\frac{2}{7} + \frac{4}{7}$
4. $\frac{7}{9} - \frac{3}{9}$
5. $\frac{8}{15} - \frac{4}{15}$
6. $\frac{9}{11} - \frac{5}{11}$
7. $\frac{3}{14} + \frac{5}{14} + \frac{1}{14}$
8. $\frac{3}{10} + \frac{3}{10} + \frac{3}{10}$
9. $\frac{8}{12} + \frac{6}{12} - \frac{3}{12}$
10. $4\frac{1}{3} + 2\frac{1}{3}$
11. $5\frac{6}{7} - 2\frac{1}{7}$
12. $7\frac{3}{5} - 4\frac{2}{5}$
13. $3\frac{5}{9} + 8\frac{2}{9}$
14. $5\frac{1}{10} + 4\frac{1}{10} + 6\frac{7}{10}$
15. $\frac{6}{12} - \frac{2}{12} + \frac{1}{12}$

Modeling Percent

Percent means "per hundred" or "out of 100." You can use a 100-square grid to model a percent.

EXAMPLE

To model 39 percent shade 39 out of the 100 squares on the grid.

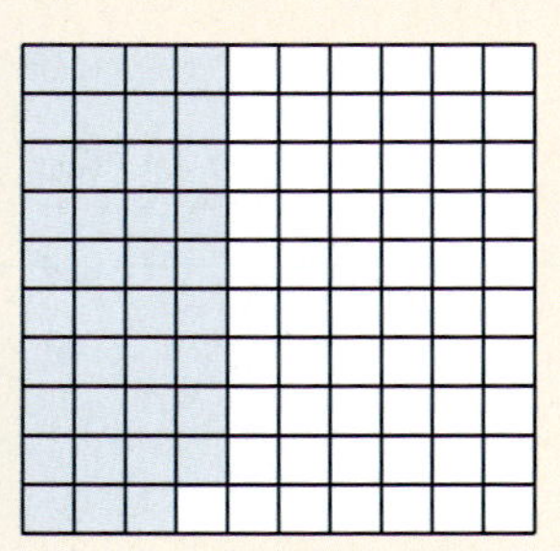

$\frac{39}{100}$ of the grid is shaded.

0.39 of the grid is shaded.

39% of the grid is shaded.

% is the symbol for percent.

Tell what percent each 100-square grid represents.

1. 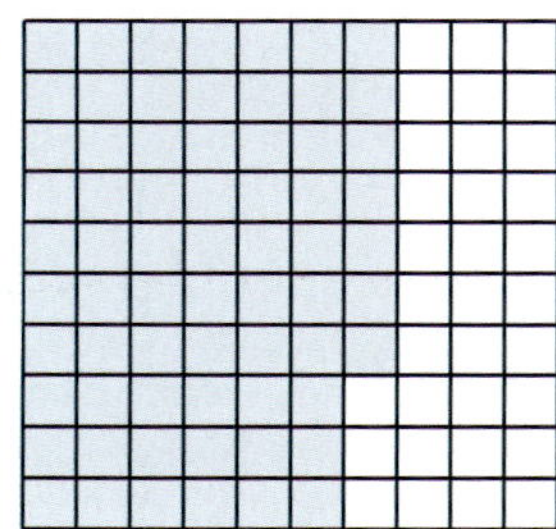

2. 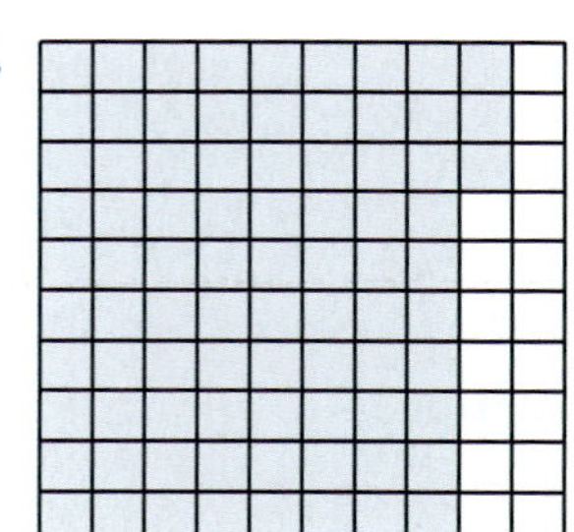

3. 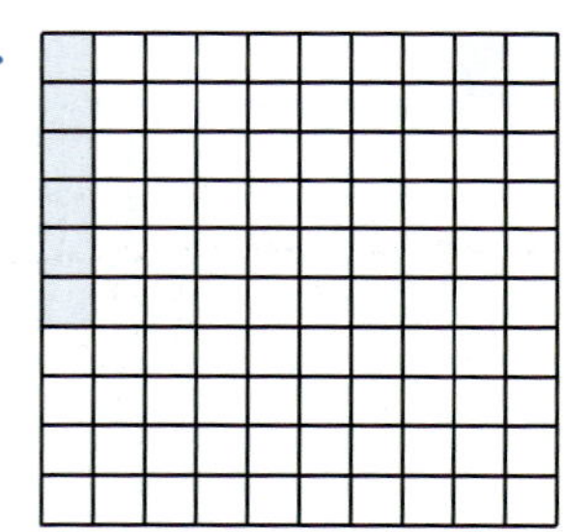

4. 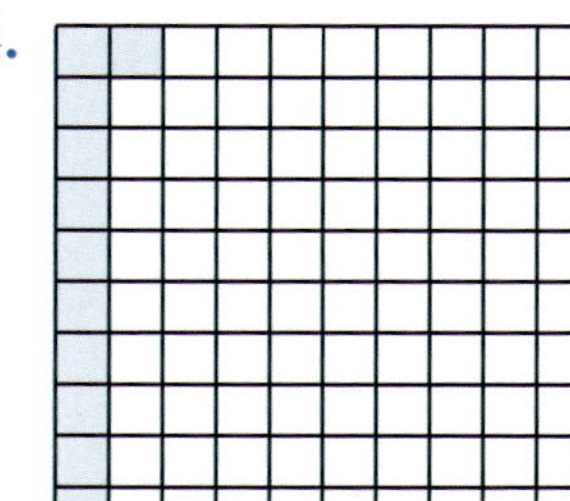

5. 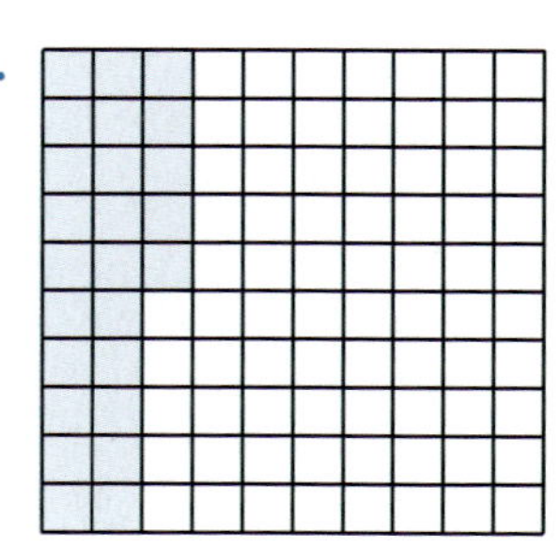

6. 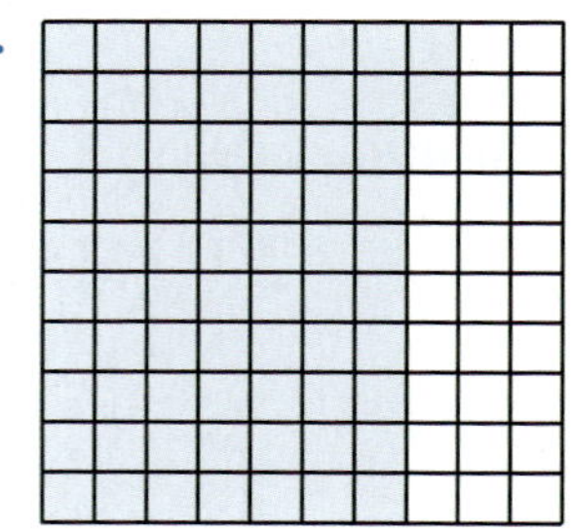

Sketch a 100-square grid to represent each percent.

7. 95%
8. 78%
9. 8%
10. 50%
11. 22%
12. 49%
13. 18%
14. 61%

Modeling Integers

The integers are the numbers ... –3, –2, –1, 0, 1, 2, 3, ... You can model integers with integer chips.

EXAMPLE

+	–	– –	– +	+ + + + / – – – –
1	–1	–2	0	0

You read this as "negative two."

These two chips form a zero pair.

To add with integer chips, model each number and count the total number of chips.

EXAMPLE

+ + + + + + +
3 + 4 = 7

– – – – –
–2 + (–3) = –5

EXAMPLE

+ + + + + – – – = + + + + + / – – –
5 + (–3) = 0 + 2 = 2

Tell what number each group of integer chips models.

1. + + +
2. – – –
3. + + + + + / – – – – –
4. – – – –
5. + + / – –
6. + + + + +

Find each sum.

7. 4 + (–2)
8. –3 + 1
9. 4 + (–3)
10. –5 + 5
11. –5 + 2
12. 2 + (–2)
13. 3 + (–1)
14. –4 + 4
15. 2 + (–7)
16. 2 + (–6)
17. –6 + 4
18. 3 + (–5)

To subtract with integer chips, model the first number, then remove the chips that represent the second number.

EXAMPLE

To find –5 – (–3):

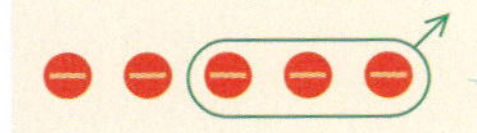

–5 – (–3) = –2

Remove three negative chips. Two negative chips remain.

EXAMPLE

To find –3 – 2:

Model the first number.  –3

To subtract two positive chips, add two zero pairs. –3 + 0

Remove two positive chips. –3 + 0 – 2 = –5

Five negative chips remain.

–3 – 2 = –5

EXAMPLE

To find –1 – (–4):

Model the first number.  –1

Add zero pairs until there are four negative chips to subtract.  –1 + 0

Remove four negative chips. 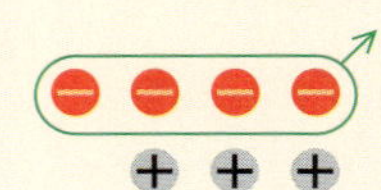 –1 + 0 – (–4) = 3

Three positive chips remain.

–1 – (–4) = 3

Find each sum or difference.

19. 4 + (–2)
20. 3 – 5
21. –3 – (–3)
22. 5 – 3
23. –3 + (–5)
24. –2 – 4
25. –1 + 6
26. 4 – (–3)
27. –2 – (–5)
28. 6 – (–6)
29. –1 + 4
30. 2 – 8
31. 5 + (–2)
32. –1 + 2
33. 6 – 7
34. 1 – (–4)
35. –7 + 7
36. –5 + (–1)

Perimeter and Using a Ruler

The perimeter, *P*, of a figure is the sum of the lengths of its sides.

EXAMPLE

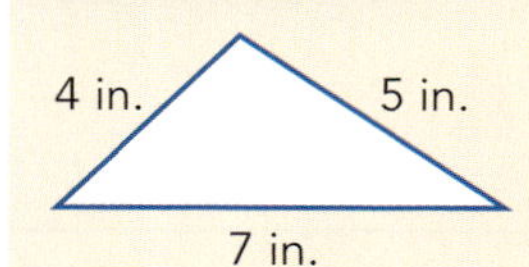

$4 + 5 + 7 = 16$

$P = 16$ **in.**

7 cm

3 cm | 3 cm

7 cm

$3 + 7 + 3 + 7 = 20$

$P = 20$ **cm**

You can use a ruler to measure the length of a segment. A United States customary ruler shows measurements in inches.

EXAMPLE

Measure the segment to the nearest $\frac{1}{16}$ of an inch.

Line up one end of the segment with the 0 mark on the ruler.

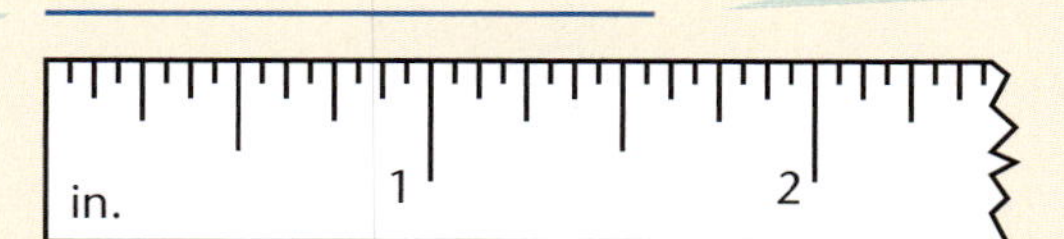

The other end of the segment is between $1\frac{9}{16}$ in. and $1\frac{5}{8}$ in., closer to $1\frac{9}{16}$ in.

The segment is about $1\frac{9}{16}$ in. long.

Find the perimeter of each figure.

1. 8 m, 8 m, 8 m, 8 m

2.

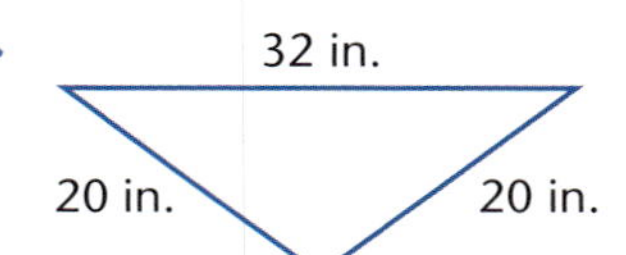

3.

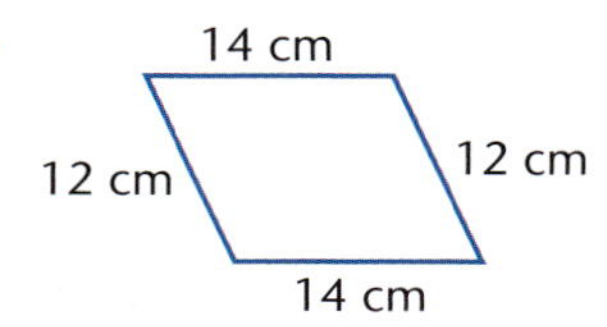

Measure the length of each segment to the nearest $\frac{1}{16}$ of an inch.

4. ______________________________

5. ____________

Use a ruler to find the perimeter of each figure. Measure to the nearest $\frac{1}{16}$ of an inch.

6.

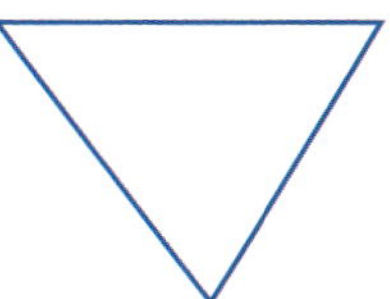

7.

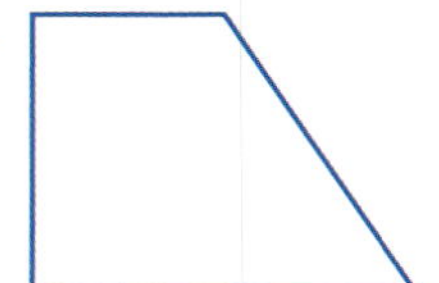

8.

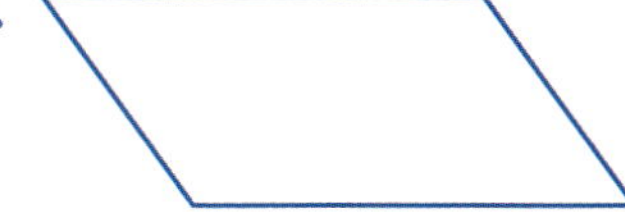

Converting Measurements

To change from a larger unit of measure to a smaller one, multiply. Use the Table of Measures on page 597.

EXAMPLE

There are **5280 ft** in 1 mi, so multiply by **5280**.

4 mi = ? ft

$4 \cdot 5280 = 21{,}120$

4 mi = 21,120 ft

EXAMPLE

There are 16 oz in 1 lb, so **3 lb = 3 · 16 oz = 48 oz**.

3 lb 8 oz = ? oz

48 + 8 = 56

3 lb 8 oz = 56 oz

To change from a smaller unit of measure to a larger one, divide.

EXAMPLE

There are **12 in.** in 1 ft, so divide by **12**.

67 in. = ? ft

$67 \div 12 = 5\frac{7}{12}$

67 in. = $5\frac{7}{12}$ ft, or 5 ft 7 in.

Replace each ? with the correct number. Use the Table of Measures on page 597.

1. 21 ft = ? in.
2. 83 oz = ? lb
3. 50 yd = ? ft
4. 6000 lb = ? tons
5. 2 mi = ? ft
6. 77 in. = ? yd
7. 3 lb = ? oz
8. 5280 yd = ? mi
9. 171 oz = ? lb
10. 5 yd = ? in.
11. 4 tons = ? lb
12. 95,040 ft = ? mi
13. 156 in. = ? ft
14. 28 ft = ? yd
15. 10 mi = ? yd
16. 10 ft 6 in. = ? in.
17. 8 tons 60 lb = ? lb
18. 22 lb 13 oz = ? oz
19. 26 mi 385 yd = ? yd
20. 75 in. = ? yd ? in.
21. 6000 ft = ? mi ? ft
22. 35 oz = ? lb ? oz
23. 4500 lb = ? tons ? lb
24. 65 in. = ? ft ? in.
25. 100 ft = ? yd ? ft

Perimeter and Area of a Rectangle

The perimeter, P, of a rectangle is the sum of the lengths of its sides. You can use the formula at the right, where l represents the length and w represents the width, to find the perimeter of a rectangle.

l

w w

l

$P = l + l + w + w$
$P = 2 \cdot l + 2 \cdot w$

EXAMPLE

3 in.

5 in.

$P = 2 \cdot l + 2 \cdot w$
$= 2 \cdot 5 + 2 \cdot 3$
$= 10 + 6$
$= 16$

The perimeter of the rectangle is 16 in.

The area, A, of a rectangle is the amount of surface that the rectangle covers. Area is measured in square units.

EXAMPLE

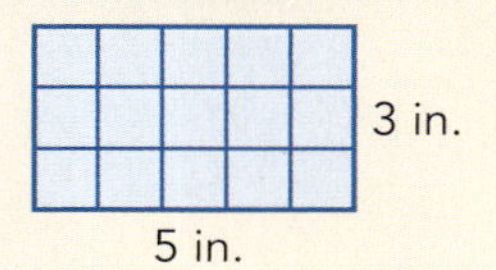

The rectangle can be divided into 3 rows with 5 square inches in each row.

$A = 3 \cdot 5$
$= 15$

The area of the rectangle is 15 square inches, or 15 in.^{2}.

Find the perimeter and the area of each rectangle.

1. 8 in.; 5 in.

2. 6 ft; 6 ft

3. 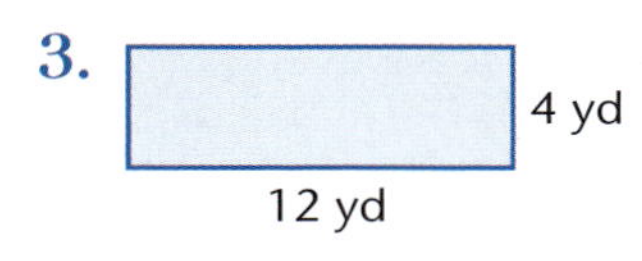

4. a rectangle with length 16 ft and width 8 ft
5. a square with sides of length 7 in.
6. a rectangle with length 3 yd and width 4 ft

Making a Bar Graph

You can use a bar graph to display data that are in categories, such as the national park data shown in this table.

National Park	Approximate area (mi^2)	Number of months open	Miles of hiking trails
Glacier (MT)	1580	5	700
Isle Royale (MI)	850	7	165
Mt. Rainier (WA)	378	6	240
Shenandoah (VA)	310	12	500

EXAMPLE

Follow the steps below to make a bar graph to display the hiking trail data for the national parks.

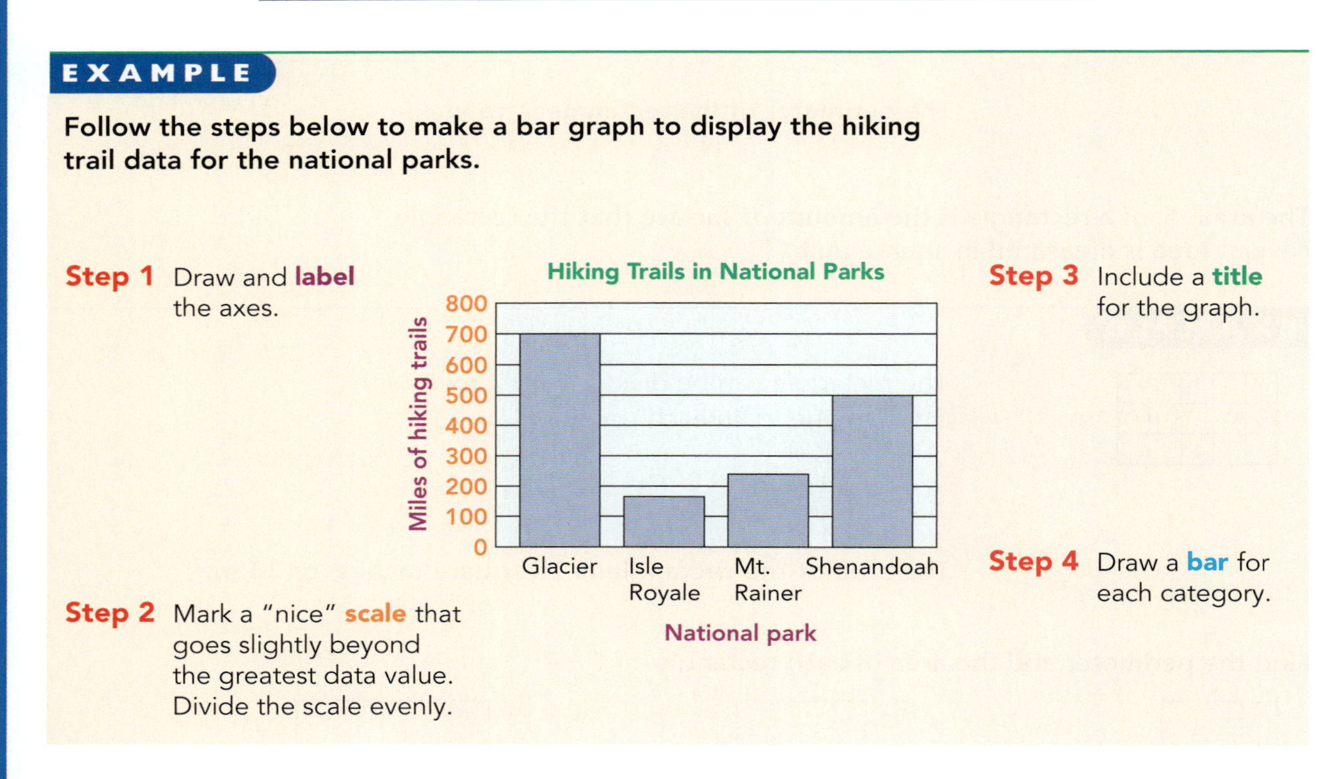

Use the data in the table above. Make a bar graph for each set of data.

1. the areas of the national parks
2. the number of months the national parks are open

Making a Line Graph

Use a line graph to show how data change over time.

Average temperature (°F)						
City	Jan/Feb	Mar/Apr	May/Jun	Jul/Aug	Sep/Oct	Nov/Dec
Indianapolis, IN	28	46	68	74	61	37
Duluth, MN	9	31	55	64	49	21
Phoenix, AZ	54	65	82	91	79	57

EXAMPLE

Follow the steps below to make a line graph to display the temperature data for Indianapolis.

Step 1 Draw and **label** the axes.

Step 2 Mark "nice" **scales**. Divide each scale evenly.

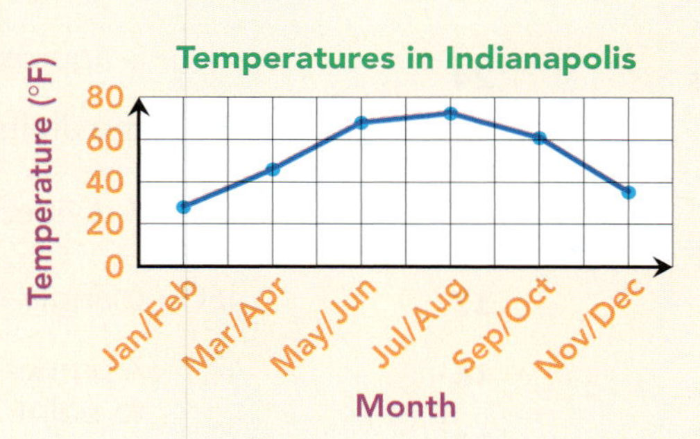

Step 3 Include a **title** for the graph.

Step 4 Graph each data item as a **point**. Connect the points.

Make a line graph for each set of data.

1. the temperature data for Duluth
2. the temperature data for Phoenix

Finding the Mean

To find the mean of a data set, find the sum of all the data items. Then divide the sum by the number of data items.

EXAMPLE

To find the mean of this data set, add the numbers and divide by 8:

6, 8, 5, 9, 7, 11, 4, 6

$$\text{mean} = \frac{6+8+5+9+7+11+4+6}{8} = \frac{56}{8} = 7$$

There are **8** data items.

The mean is 7.

Find the mean of each set of data.

1. 8, 4, 6, 10, 7
2. 24, 33, 27, 32, 24, 28
3. 120, 110, 110, 132, 160, 100

TABLE OF SYMBOLS

SYMBOL		Page
%	percent	**3**
$=$	equals	**11**
$\ldots$	and so on	**14**
$\cdot$	times	**15**
$-$	minus	**15**
3^4	3 to the 4th power	**17**
$\frac{1}{2}$	1 part of 2 equal parts	**24**
$P(A)$	probability of event *A*	**32**
$+$	plus	**37**
1.2	decimal point	**37**
$\overline{)}$	divided into	**46**
$\div$	divided by	**57**
( )	parentheses—grouping symbol	**61**
[ ]	brackets—grouping symbol	**61**
$\overrightarrow{AB}$	ray *AB*	**77**
$\angle A$	angle *A*	**78**
$^\circ$	degree(s)	**78**
$m\angle A$	measure of angle *A*	**78**
∟	right angle	**83**
-1	negative 1	**89**
$>$	is greater than	**90**
$<$	is less than	**90**
-3	the opposite of 3	**91**
$\lvert -4 \rvert$	the absolute value of -4	**91**
$(1, -2)$	ordered pair of numbers	**93**
10^{-2}	$\frac{1}{10^2}$	**195**
$\times$	times	**206**
$\overline{CD}$	segment *CD*	**218**
π	pi, a number approximately equal to 3.14	**234**
$\geq$	is greater than or equal to	**241**
$\approx$	is approximately equal to	**248**
$0.\overline{54}$	the digits 5 and 4 repeat	**253**
$\frac{6}{11}$	6 divided by 11	**253**
$\triangle ABC$	triangle *ABC*	**266**
A'	*A* prime—point *A* goes to point *A′* after a transformation	**267**
$1:2$	ratio of 1 to 2	**359**
$\leq$	is less than or equal to	**381**
$\sqrt{}$	positive square root	**396**
$\sim$	is similar to	**413**
$\cong$	is congruent to	**413**
AB	length of $\overline{AB}$	**415**
$\overleftrightarrow{AB}$	line *AB*	**425**
$6!$	6 factorial	**536**

TABLE OF MEASURES

Time

60 seconds (s)	=	1 minute (min)
60 minutes	=	1 hour (h)
24 hours	=	1 day
7 days	=	1 week
4 weeks (approx.)	=	1 month
365 days 52 weeks (approx.) 12 months	=	1 year
10 years	=	1 decade
100 years	=	1 century

METRIC

Length

10 millimeters (mm)	=	1 centimeter (cm)
100 cm 1000 mm	=	1 meter (m)
1000 m	=	1 kilometer (km)

Area

100 square millimeters (mm^2)	=	1 square centimeter (cm^2)
10,000 cm^2	=	1 square meter (m^2)
10,000 m^2	=	1 hectare (ha)

Volume

1000 cubic millimeters (mm^3)	=	1 cubic centimeter (cm^3)
1,000,000 cm^3	=	1 cubic meter (m^3)

Liquid Capacity

1000 milliliters (mL)	=	1 liter (L)
1000 L	=	1 kiloliter (kL)

Mass

1000 milligrams (mg)	=	1 gram (g)
1000 g	=	1 kilogram (kg)
1000 kg	=	1 metric ton (t)

Temperature **Degrees Celsius (°C)**

0°C	=	freezing point of water
37°C	=	normal body temperature
100°C	=	boiling point of water

UNITED STATES CUSTOMARY

Length

12 inches (in.)	=	1 foot (ft)
36 in. 3 ft	=	1 yard (yd)
5280 ft 1760 yd	=	1 mile (mi)

Area

144 square inches ($in.^2$)	=	1 square foot (ft^2)
9 ft^2	=	1 square yard (yd^2)
43,560 ft^2 4840 yd^2	=	1 acre (A)

Volume

1728 cubic inches ($in.^3$)	=	1 cubic foot (ft^3)
27 ft^3	=	1 cubic yard (yd^3)

Liquid Capacity

8 fluid ounces (fl oz)	=	1 cup (c)
2 c	=	1 pint (pt)
2 pt	=	1 quart (qt)
4 qt	=	1 gallon (gal)

Weight

16 ounces (oz)	=	1 pound (lb)
2000 lb	=	1 ton (t)

Temperature **Degrees Fahrenheit (°F)**

32°F	=	freezing point of water
98.6°F	=	normal body temperature
212°F	=	boiling point of water

TABLE OF FORMULAS

RECTANGLE

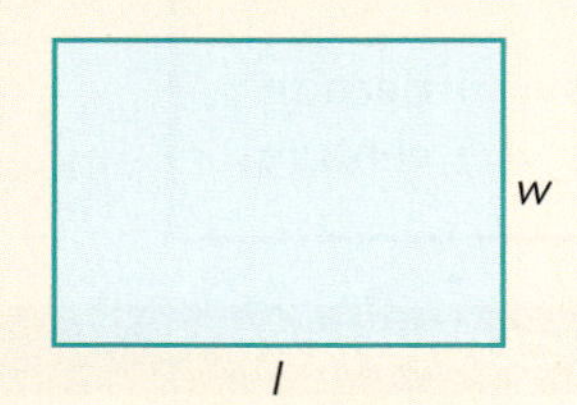

Area:
A = length × width
$A = lw$

Perimeter:
$P = 2l + 2w$

PARALLELOGRAM

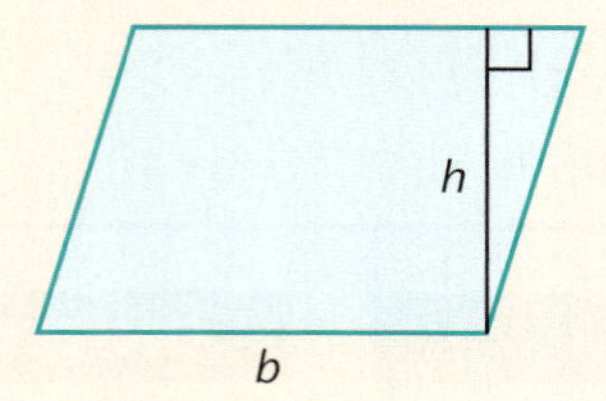

Area:
A = base × height
$A = bh$

TRIANGLE

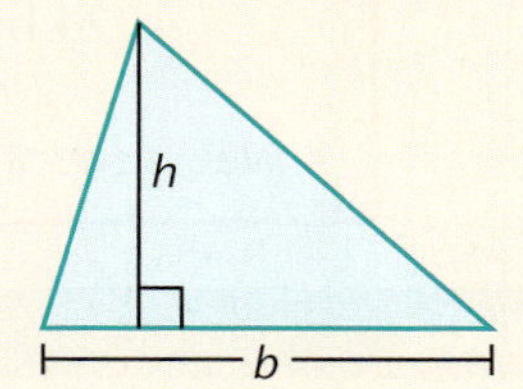

Area:
$A = \frac{1}{2}$ × base × height

$A = \frac{1}{2}bh$

CIRCLE

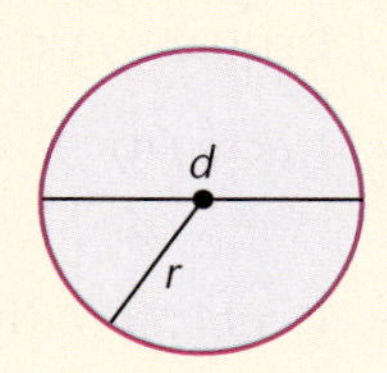

Area:
$A = \pi r^2$

Circumference:
$C = 2\pi r$ or $C = \pi d$

TRAPEZOID

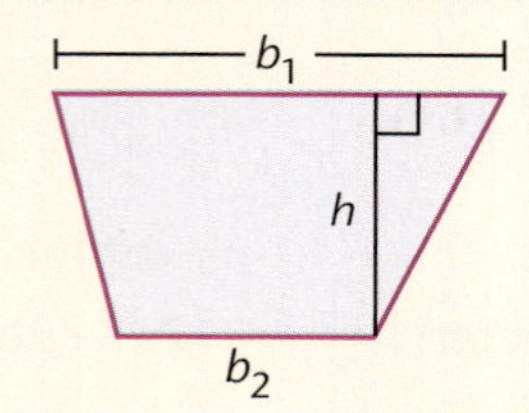

Area:
$A = \frac{1}{2}$ × (sum of bases) × height

$A = \frac{1}{2}(b_1 + b_2)h$

PRISM

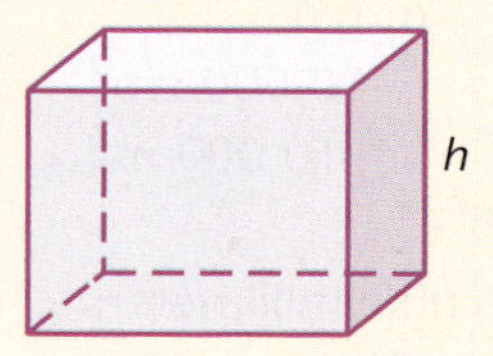

Volume:
V = (area of base) × height
$V = Bh$

Surface Area:
$S.A.$ = sum of areas of faces

CYLINDER

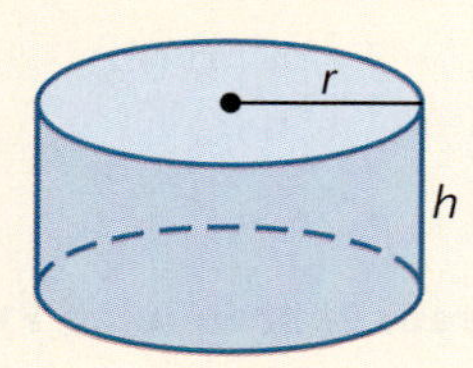

Volume:
V = (area of base) × height
$V = Bh = \pi r^2 h$

PYRAMID

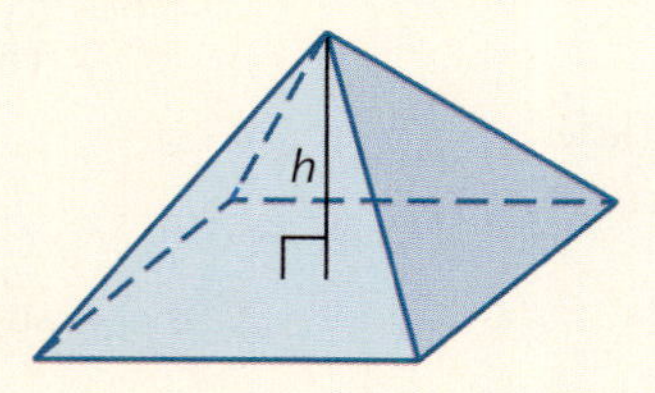

Volume:
$V = \frac{1}{3}$ × (area of base) × height

$V = \frac{1}{3}Bh$

CONE

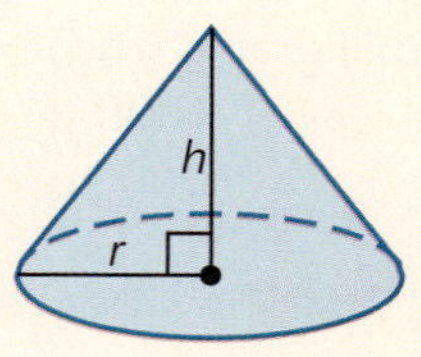

Volume:
$V = \frac{1}{3}$ × (area of base) × height

$V = \frac{1}{3}Bh = \frac{1}{3}\pi r^2 h$

PRE-COURSE TEST

NUMBERS AND OPERATIONS

Decimals and Whole Numbers (Toolbox, pp. 581–583)

Find each sum or difference. Use mental math when possible.

1. $3.8 + 4.2$
2. $12.09 + 7.98$
3. $15.75 - 2.25$
4. $20.06 - 18.78$

Tell whether each number is divisible by 2, 5, and 10.

5. 504
6. 67,995
7. 2550
8. 34,235

Estimate each sum, difference, product, or quotient.

9. $702 + 895$
10. $229 - 57$
11. $8120 \div 92$
12. 589×38
13. $25.6 - 17.9$
14. $15.83 + 65.16$

Fraction Concepts (Toolbox, pp. 584–587)

Find each value.

15. $\frac{4}{7}$ of 49
16. $\frac{2}{3}$ of 24
17. $\frac{5}{12}$ of 60

Replace each ? with >, <, or =.

18. $\frac{1}{3}$? $\frac{4}{15}$
19. $\frac{19}{36}$? $\frac{10}{18}$
20. $\frac{27}{42}$? $\frac{9}{14}$

Find each sum or difference.

21. $\frac{3}{6} + \frac{2}{6}$
22. $\frac{11}{12} - \frac{4}{12}$
23. $8\frac{1}{7} + 2\frac{3}{7}$

Modeling Percents and Integers (Toolbox, pp. 588–589)

Sketch a 100-square grid to represent each percent.

24. 26%
25. 83%
26. 12%

Find each sum or difference.

27. $5 + (-14)$
28. $8 - (-3)$
29. $-7 - 7$

GEOMETRY AND MEASUREMENT

Using and Converting Measurements (Toolbox, pp. 591–592)

Find the perimeter of each figure.

30.

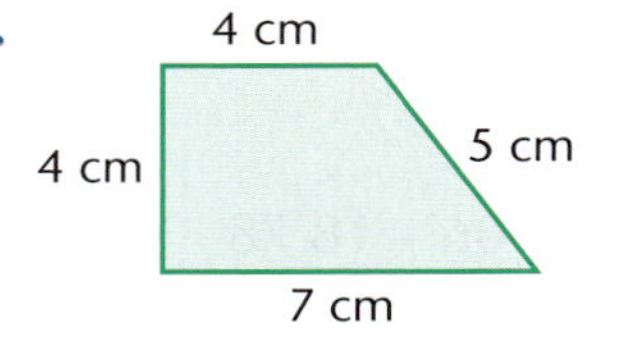

31.

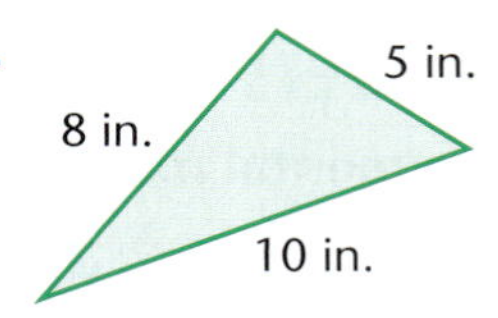

Replace each ? with the correct number. Use the Table of Measures on page 597.

32. 48 oz = _?_ lb 33. 5 ft = _?_ in. 34. 10,560 ft = _?_ mi 35. 18 yd = _?_ in.

Perimeter and Area of a Rectangle (Toolbox, p. 593)

Find the perimeter and the area of each rectangle.

36. a rectangle with length 9 in. and width 2 in.

37. a rectangle with length 7 m and width 5 m

DATA ANALYSIS AND DISPLAYS

Making Bar Graphs and Line Graphs (Toolbox, pp. 594–595)

38. Make a bar graph of the data below.

Day	Mon	Tues	Wed	Thurs	Fri
Minutes of exercise	30	50	45	20	30

39. Make a line graph of the data below.

Minutes of exercise	0	5	10	15
Heart rate (beats per minute)	72	90	124	130

Finding the Mean (Toolbox, p. 595)

Find the mean of the data.

40. 20, 24, 43, 32, 35, 16, 18, 36

41. 250, 175, 205, 270, 300, 180

TEST-TAKING SKILLS

READING AND SOLVING WORD PROBLEMS

Reading a Word Problem

Before you can solve a word problem, you have to understand the information being given and the question being asked.

- Read quickly through the problem once to get a general sense of what the problem is about.
- Read carefully through the problem a second time, focusing on those things that relate to solving the problem.

Problem

Maggie wants to tile the kitchen wall behind her stove with 2 rows of tiles. The portion of the wall behind the stove is 3 feet across. She has already tiled the first row with 6-in. by 6-in. tiles. She can use either 5-in. by 5-in. tiles or 4-in. by 4-in. tiles to do the second row. If Maggie does not want to cut any of the tiles, should she use the 5-in. by 5-in. or 4-in. by 4-in. tiles?

Solving a Word Problem

- Underline, jot down, and/or make a quick sketch of any information that can be used to solve the problem.

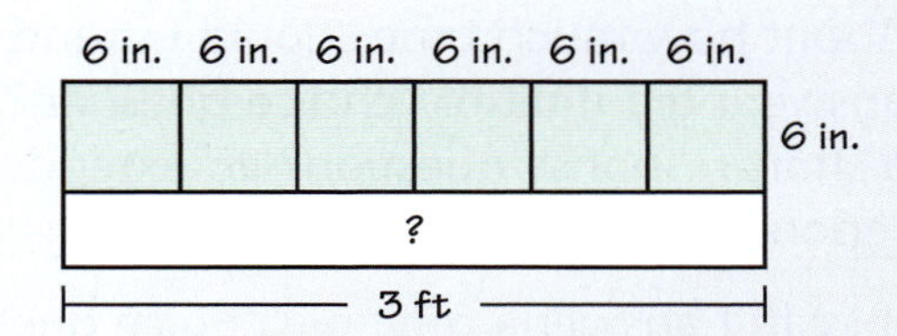

Tiles in the second row are 5 in. by 5 in. or 4 in. by 4 in.
Tiles cannot be cut.

- Decide which math topic(s) relate to the problem. Think of procedures, formulas, and definitions related to that topic that can be used to solve the problem.

Conversion: 1 foot = 12 inches

Divisibility: Does 5 or 4 divide the length evenly?

- Solve the problem, making sure that the question answered is the question asked.

Convert: 1 foot = 12 inches
3 feet = 36 inches

Divide: $36 \div 5 = 7$ R1
$36 \div 4 = 9$

Maggie should use 4 in. by 4 in. tiles.

- Check your work.

$6 \cdot 6$ in. = 36 in.

36 in. $\div$ 4 = 9 tiles

Keep up with the course.

Ask questions about things you don't understand. Take advantage of extra-help sessions. If you get a problem wrong on a test or on your homework, try to figure out why you got it wrong. If you are absent, find out what material you missed and make up the work.

Become familiar with the test.

Make sure you know the answers to the following questions before you take the test:

- How much time do I have to complete the test?
- How many points are assigned to each type of question?
- About how much time should I spend answering a multiple choice question? a short response question? an extended reponse question?
- If I can't answer a multiple choice question, is it better to guess, or to leave a blank?
- Am I better off answering the easy, or the more difficult questions first, or should I just answer the questions as they come?
- Is paper provided for scrap work, or should it be done in the white space of the test booklet?
- On which, if any, parts of the test may I use a calculator?

During the Test

- As soon as the test begins, jot down on scrap paper or in the white space of the test booklet any formulas or procedures you're afraid you'll forget.
- Quickly scan the entire test to get an idea of which problems will probably take you the most time to do. Some people prefer to do those problems first. Others do them last.
- Skip over any question you are stuck on. Make a mark next to the question in your test booklet so that you can go back to it later if you have time. Be sure to leave a blank on your answer sheet for the answer to the question.
- Read an entire problem carefully before you start to answer it. Don't assume you know the question that will be asked.
- When answering a multiple choice question, don't assume your answer is correct because it is one of the choices. Always double check your work.
- If you think you can't do a multiple choice question, try substituting each choice back into the problem to see if it is the correct choice.
- If you must guess on a multiple choice question, first try to eliminate any choices that are obviously wrong because they have the wrong units or sign, for example.
- As you write the answer to an extended or short response question, imagine that you are writing an explanation for a fellow student who doesn't know how to solve the problem.
- If you can do part, but not all, of an extended or short response question, write down what you can do. Something written may receive partial credit. Nothing written definitely receives no credit.

BUILDING TEST-TAKING SKILLS (For use after Module 2.)

Strategies for Answering

Multiple Choice Questions

You can use the 4-step approach to solving problems on page 44 to solve any problem. If you have difficulty solving a problem involving multiple choice, you may be able to use one of the strategies below to choose the correct answer. You may also be able to use these strategies and others to check whether your answer to a multiple choice question is reasonable.

Strategy: Estimate the Answer

Problem 1

At a bakery, bagels cost $.89 each and muffins cost $2.05. How much will it cost to buy 3 bagels and 2 muffins?

You need to add the cost of buying 3 bagels and the cost of buying 2 muffins.

A. $2.94

B. $5.17

C. $6.77

D. $8.24

Estimate: $3(0.89) + 2(2.05) \approx 3(1) + 2(2) = 7$, so the correct answer is C.

Strategy: Use Visual Clues

Problem 2

The line graph shows the amount of money in Jerome's bank account over several weeks. Between which two weeks did Jerome deposit the greatest amount of money?

Look for the steepest segment connecting two consecutive points.

F. week 0 and week 1

G. week 3 and week 4

H. week 5 and week 6

I. week 9 and week 10

The steepest segment occurs between week 5 and week 6, so the correct answer is H.

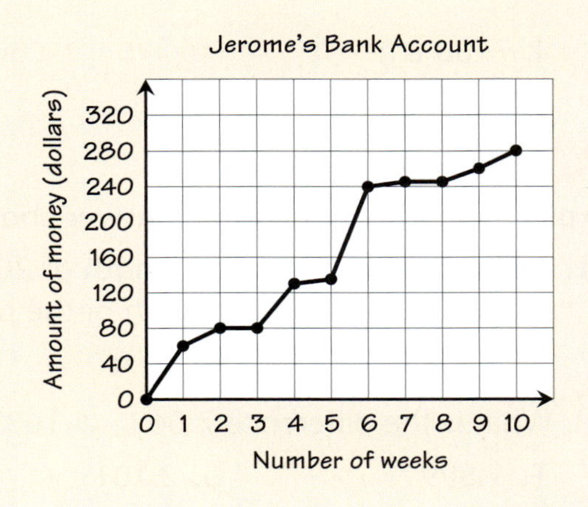

Strategy: Use Number Sense

Problem 3

What value of x would make the expression $6 \cdot (2 + x)$ equal to 0?

Use the fact that the product of 0 and any number is 0. Multiplying 6 by 0 would equal 0, so think of what value of x would make $2 + x$ equal to 0.

A. –2 — $2 + (-2) = 0$ and $6 \cdot 0 = 0$, so the correct answer is A.

B. 0

C. 1

D. 2

Eliminating Unreasonable Choices

The strategies used to find the correct answers for Problems 1–3 can also be used to eliminate answer choices that are unreasonable or obviously incorrect.

Strategy: Eliminate Choices

Problem 4

The length of a tablecloth is 110 centimeters. The width is 40 centimeters less than the length. What is the area?

Read the problem carefully. The width of the tablecloth is $110 - 40 = 70$ cm, not 40 cm. Use the formula $A = lw$ to find the area.

F. 4400 cm² — *Not* the correct answer: $110 \cdot 70 \approx 100 \cdot 70 = 7000$.

G. 6800 cm² — *Not* the correct answer: In the estimate above, 110 is rounded down, so the actual area should be greater than 7000 cm².

H. 7500 cm — *Not* the correct answer: area is measured in *square* units.

I. 7700 cm² — $110 \cdot 70 = 7700$, so I is the correct answer.

Watch Out!
Some answers may appear correct at first glance, but they may be incorrect answers you would find by making common errors.

TRY THIS

Explain why the highlighted answer choice is unreasonable.

1. An in-ground pool has a length of 20 feet and a perimeter of 64 feet. What is the width of the pool?

   A. 5 ft **B.** 10 ft² **C.** 12 ft **D.** 14 ft

2. What is the difference $7.062 - 5.163$?

   F. 1.899 **G.** 2.101 **H.** 2.899 **I.** 12.225

3. The data below show the number of minutes Beth spent talking on the phone each day for 2 weeks. What is the mean number of minutes?

   24, 30, 10, 0, 52, 12, 35, 4, 20, 7, 14, 5, 0, 25

   A. 15 **B.** 17 **C.** 25 **D.** 60

Practicing Test-Taking Skills

Multiple Choice

1. Predict the 10th term in the following sequence.

   3, 7, 11, 15, ...

   A. 11 **B.** 19 **C.** 35 **D.** 39

2. What is the value of the expression $5x - y$ when $x = 7$ and $y = 4$?

   F. 13 **G.** 31 **H.** 35 **I.** 39

3. The dimensions of a family room are shown below. If carpeting costs $2.90 per square foot, how much will it cost to carpet the family room?

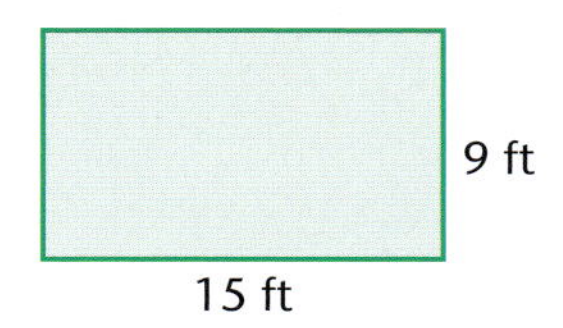

   A. $47.93 **B.** $69.60
   C. $135.00 **D.** $391.50

4. What is the value of $5.17 + 0.94 + 2.08$?

   F. 3.19 **G.** 8.19
   H. 12.74 **I.** 16.65

5. The table gives the number of yards gained or lost during each of the first 5 plays of a football game. What was the total number of yards gained or lost?

Play	Yards gained or lost
1	5
2	–3
3	7
4	2
5	–6

   A. –5 **B.** 0 **C.** 5 **D.** 10

6. The bar graph shows the prices of different passes to a theme park. About how many times more does a child's one-week pass cost than a child's one-day pass?

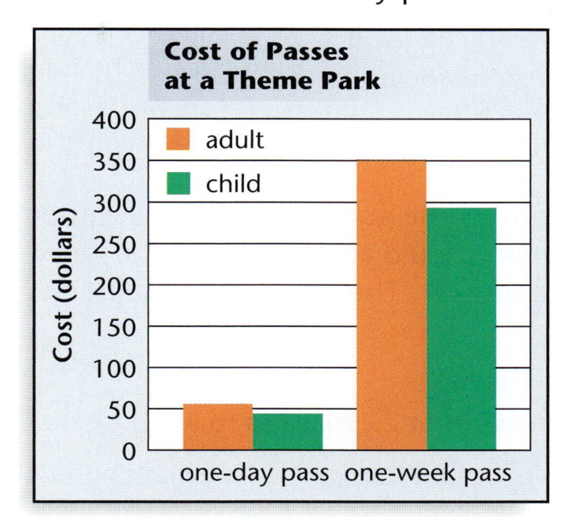

   F. 2 times more **G.** 3 times more
   H. 4 times more **I.** 6 times more

7. The ages of 8 people in a family are listed below. What is the median age?

   77, 52, 22, 10, 75, 50, 16, 20

   A. 36 **B.** 38 **C.** 50 **D.** 70

8. Which of the following statements is *not* true about the angles shown below?

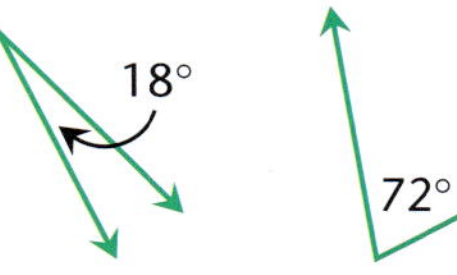

   F. The angles are complementary.
   G. The angles are supplementary.
   H. The sum of the angle measures is 90°.
   I. Both angles are acute.

BUILDING TEST-TAKING SKILLS (For use after Module 4.)

Strategies for Answering Short Response Questions

Scoring Rubric

FULL CREDIT
- answer is correct, *and*
- work or reasoning is included

PARTIAL CREDIT
- answer is correct, but reasoning is incorrect, *or*
- answer is incorrect, but reasoning is correct

NO CREDIT
- no answer is given, *or*
- answer makes no sense

A *short response* question should take about five minutes to answer. A solution should always include the work or reasoning that leads to a correct answer. The three ways a solution can be scored are listed above.

Problem

It takes about $2\frac{1}{2}$ minutes to wash a car and about $4\frac{1}{4}$ minutes to wax it. How many can can be washed and waxed in $5\frac{1}{2}$ hours?

FULL CREDIT SOLUTION

The number of cars equals the total number of minutes for the car wash, 330, divided by the sum of the time it takes to wash a car and the time it takes to wax a car. — This reasoning is the key to choosing the operations you need.

Cars = Total time ÷ (Wash time + Wax time) — The steps of the solution are clearly written.

$$= 330 \div \left(2\frac{1}{2} + 4\frac{1}{4}\right) = 330 \div 6\frac{3}{4} = 330 \times \frac{4}{27} = \frac{440}{9} = 48\frac{8}{9}$$

Because there is not enough time for 49 cars, the team can wash and wax 48 cars. — The question asked is answered correctly.

PARTIAL CREDIT SOLUTION

Divide the total amount of time, 330 minutes, by the time needed for each car, $6\frac{3}{4}$ minutes. — The reasoning and calculations are correct.

$$\text{Cars} = 330 \div \frac{27}{4} = 330 \times \frac{4}{27} = \frac{440}{9} = 48\frac{8}{9}$$

The team can wash $48\frac{8}{9}$ cars. — The answer makes no sense. You cannot have a fractional number of cars.

PARTIAL CREDIT SOLUTION

The total amount time it takes to wash and wax each car is about 7 minutes. — The problem does not call for an estimated answer.

The team can wash 48 cars. — The answer is correct, but there is no evidence of work or calculations.

NO CREDIT SOLUTION

$5\frac{1}{2} \div (2\frac{1}{2} + 4\frac{1}{4}) = 5\frac{1}{2} \div 6\frac{3}{4}$ — The units are not equivalent. Hours should be converted to minutes.

$= \frac{11}{2} \times \frac{27}{4} = \frac{297}{8} = 37\frac{1}{8}$ — The student did not multiply by the reciprocal.

The team can wash 37 cars. — The answer is incorrect.

TRY THIS

Score each solution to the short response question below as *full credit, partial credit,* or *no credit.* Explain your reasoning.

Watch Out!
Remember to think about positive and negative numbers when working with depth.

Problem

A submarine containing 3 marine biologists dives 1250 feet below the surface of the water. The submarine rises 720 feet to observe some marine life, and then dives 300 feet. How many feet below the surface of the water is the submarine?

1. $-1250 - 720 + 300 = -1670$. The submarine is 1670 feet below the surface of the water.

2. $-1250 + 720 = -530$; $-530 - 300 = -830$. After rising 720 feet, the submarine was 530 feet below the surface of the water. Diving another 300 feet makes the submarine 830 feet below the surface of the water.

3. The submarine started at 300 feet below the surface of the water and then went another 1250 feet, putting it at 1550 feet below the surface. Rising 720 feet brought the submarine to 830 feet below the surface of the water.

Short Response

1. Your school is holding a talent competition. Each talent act is allowed $2\frac{1}{2}$ minutes to perform. The judges are given $1\frac{1}{4}$ minutes to score each talent act. How many acts can perform if the talent competition is $1\frac{1}{3}$ hours long? Show your work.

2. Darcy is packaging bath products to sell at a fair. She has 64 small bottles of shampoo and 96 small bars of soap. If the packages are identical and there are no leftovers, what is the greatest number of packages that Darcy can put together? How many bottles of shampoo and bars of soap would be in each package?

3. The tables below show the wins and losses for the basketball teams at Valley Middle School. (There were no ties.) Did the girls' team or the boys' team win the greater fraction of the games? Explain.

Girls' Team	
Won	Lost
6	4

Boys' Team	
Won	Lost
7	5

4. Darren is starting an exercise program. His goal is to run a total of 8 miles in four days. In the next four days Darren runs 1 mile, $1\frac{3}{4}$ miles, $2\frac{1}{4}$ miles, and $2\frac{1}{2}$ miles. Did Darren meet his goal? Explain your reasoning.

5. On Saturday, 18 volunteers showed up to work at the senior center. Of these volunteers, $\frac{1}{3}$ painted the walls of the recreation room. Of the remaining volunteers, $\frac{3}{4}$ raked leaves. The remaining volunteers served lunch. How many volunteers served lunch? Explain your reasoning.

6. The integers 5, 9, –10, 13, –18, and –7 are temperature readings in degrees Celsius. Graph the integers on a number line and find the median temperature.

7. A bowling alley's pricing information is shown below. Let x = the number of games bowled. Write an equation for the total cost of bowling for a person who needs to rent shoes. Hanna rented shoes and bowled several games. If Hanna paid a total of \$22.25, how many games did she bowl? Show your work.

Shoe rental	**\$2.25**
Cost per game bowled	**\$4.00**

8. An embroidery hoop has a diameter of 23 inches. Another embroidery hoop has a diameter of 18 inches. What is the difference in the circumferences of the hoops? Show your work.

9. Can a triangle be formed by the three segments shown below? Explain why or why not.

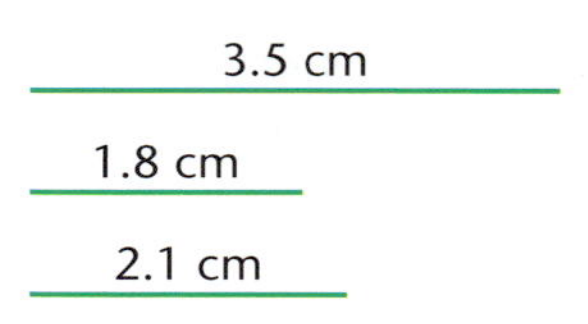

BUILDING TEST-TAKING SKILLS (For use after Module 6.)

Strategies for Answering

Context-Based Multiple Choice Questions

Some of the information you need to solve a context-based multiple choice question may appear in a table, a diagram, or a graph.

Problem 1

A canoe rental company charges by the hour. How much would it cost to rent a canoe from 9 A.M. to 4 P.M.?

A. $27.50 **B.** $33.00

C. $38.50 **D.** $44.00

Hours	Cost
1	$5.50
2	$11.00
3	$16.50
4	$22.00

Solution

1) Look for a pattern in the table. You can use the pattern to write a function that models the cost of renting a canoe.

Compare the rental cost to the number of hours for each row of the table.

$\frac{\$5.50}{1 \text{ hour}}$ $\frac{\$11.00}{2 \text{ hours}} = \frac{\$5.50}{1}$ $\frac{\$16.50}{3 \text{ hours}} = \frac{\$5.50}{1}$ $\frac{\$22.00}{4 \text{ hours}} = \frac{\$5.50}{1}$

In each case, you get the same unit rate, $5.50 per hour.

Read the problem carefully. Decide what information you are given and how you can use it to solve the problem.

2) The cost y of renting a canoe for x hours is given by the function $y = 5.5x$.

Write the function.

3) The cost of renting a canoe from 9 a.m. to 4 p.m. is the value of the function when $x = 7$. Substitute 7 for x in the function rule.

$$y = 5.5x = 5.5(7) = 38.50$$

The cost is $38.50. The correct answer is C.

There are 7 hours between 9 A.M. to 4 P.M.

4) As a check, extend the table. For each additional hour, the cost increases by $5.50. The cost for 7 hours is $38.50. The correct answer is C .

Hours	Cost
5	$27.50
6	$33.00
7	$38.50

Check to see that your answer is reasonable.

Problem 2

An object is randomly dropped and lands in the square shown. What is the probability that the object lands in the shaded target?

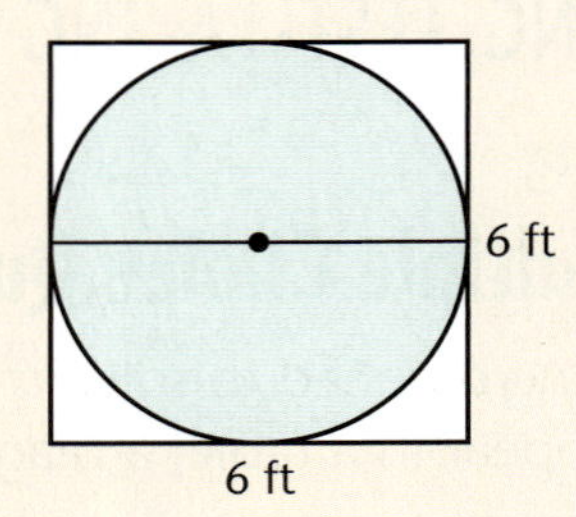

F. 7.85% **G.** 28.26%

H. 36% **I.** 78.5%

Solution

1) The area of the circular target = $\pi(3)^2 = 9\pi \approx 28.26$ ft². --- Use the formula for the area of a circle, $A = \pi r^2$.

2) The area of the square landing area = $6^2 = 36$ ft². --- Use the formula for the area of a square $A = s^2$.

3) Find the probability that the object lands in the target area by finding the ratio of the target area to the total landing area: --- Write the ratio as a percent, since that is the form in which the answer choices are given.

$$\text{Probability} = \frac{28.26 \text{ ft}^2}{36 \text{ ft}^2} = 0.785 = 78.5\%$$

The probability that the object lands in the target area is 78.5%, so the correct answer is I.

TRY THIS

1. In Problem 2, what is the probability that the object does not land in the shaded circle?

   A. 11.5% **B.** 21.5% **C.** 36% **D.** 78.5%

2. What is the unknown angle measure in the triangle?

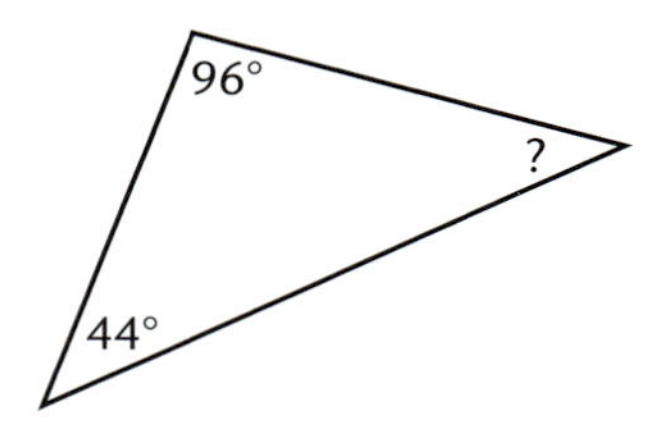

   F. 40° **G.** 44°

   H. 50° **I.** 54°

3. A scale drawing of a rug is shown at the right. The actual rug is 4.5 meters long. How wide is the actual rug?

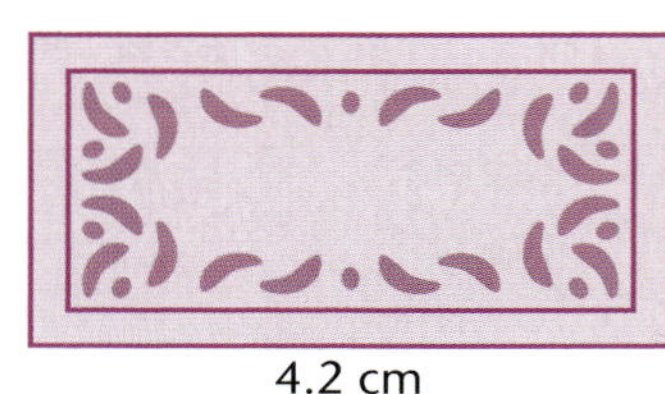

   A. 2.25 cm **B.** 2.25 m

   C. 9 cm **D.** 9 m

Context-Based Multiple Choice

1. A scale drawing of a school banner is shown. If the width of the actual banner is 3 feet, what is the length of the actual banner?

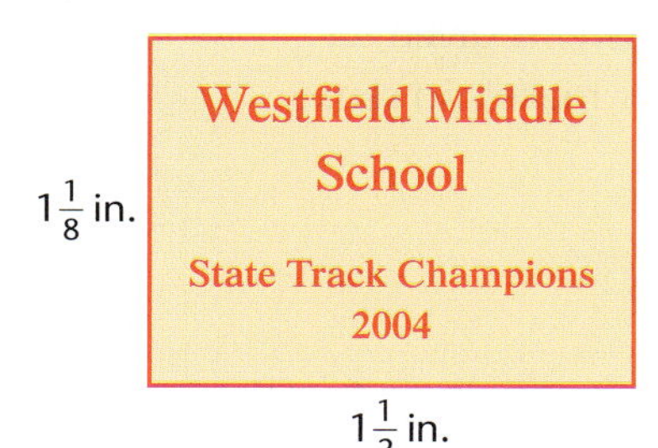

A. $2\frac{1}{4}$ ft **B.** $3\frac{3}{8}$ ft

C. $3\frac{1}{2}$ ft **D.** 4 ft

2. A personal trainer charges $50 for one training session. The discounts the trainer offers for buying more than one training session are listed in the table. How many training sessions can you buy for $500?

Sessions	2	3	4	5
Discount	$5	$10	$15	$20

F. 10 **G.** 11 **H.** 12 **I.** 13

3. The stem-and-leaf plot shows the ages (in months) of children at a daycare center. What is the median age of the children?

0	5 7 7
1	1 4
2	2 2 5 6 6 9
3	1 2 3 3 7 8 8
4	0 0 3

Key: 3 | 1 represents 31 months

A. 26.6 months **B.** 29 months

C. 30 months **D.** 31 months

4. In the diagram below, lines m and n are parallel. What is the measure of $\angle 1$?

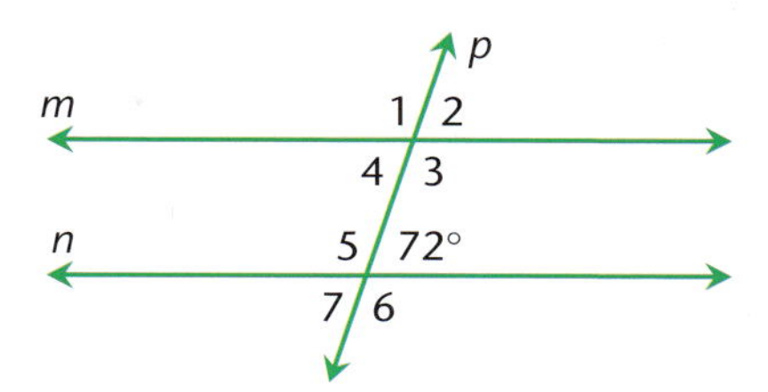

F. 5° **G.** 18° **H.** 28° **I.** 108°

5. What is the unknown angle measure in the quadrilateral?

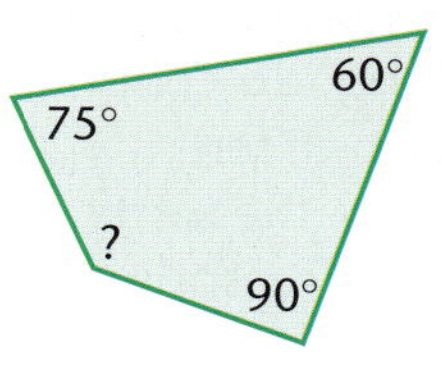

A. 55° **B.** 75°

C. 135° **D.** 145°

6. The table shows how Carey used the $300 she earned last summer. How much more did Carey spend on clothing than on movies?

Summer Spending	
Savings	40%
Clothing	30%
Movies	15%
Food	10%
Other	5%

F. $15 **G.** $45 **H.** $90 **I.** $135

7. The volume of the prism at the right is 2500 cm^3. Which measurements are not possible for the length and width?

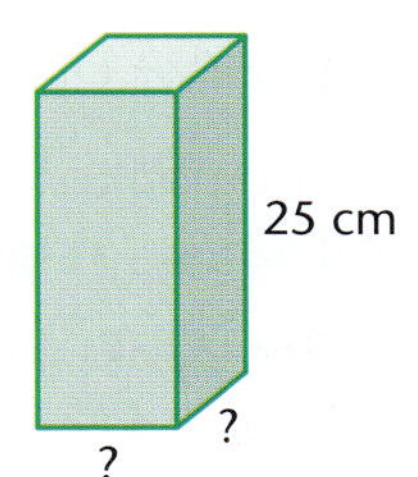

A. 25 cm and 4 cm

B. 10 cm and 10 cm

C. 20 cm and 5 cm

D. 15 cm and 6 cm

Building Test-Taking Skills (For use after Module 8.)

Strategies for Answering

Extended Response Questions

Scoring Rubric

Full Credit
- answer is correct, *and*
- work or reasoning is included

Partial Credit
- answer is correct, but reasoning is incorrect, *or*
- answer is incorrect, but reasoning is correct

No Credit
- no answer is given, *or*
- answer makes no sense

Problem

A company packs cans of tuna in a box that is 34 centimeters long, 26 centimeters wide, and 17 centimeters high. Describe two different ways to pack the cans in the box, so that the cans have the same orientation. Which way fits more cans? Explain your reasoning.

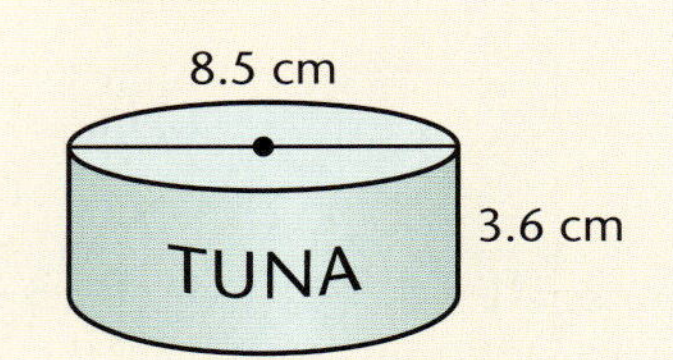

Full Credit Solution

The cans could be flat or on their sides. I found the number of cans that fit in one layer of the box by dividing the length and width of the box by the dimension of the can.

The method for finding the number of cans that fit in one layer of the box is explained.

Cans packed flat

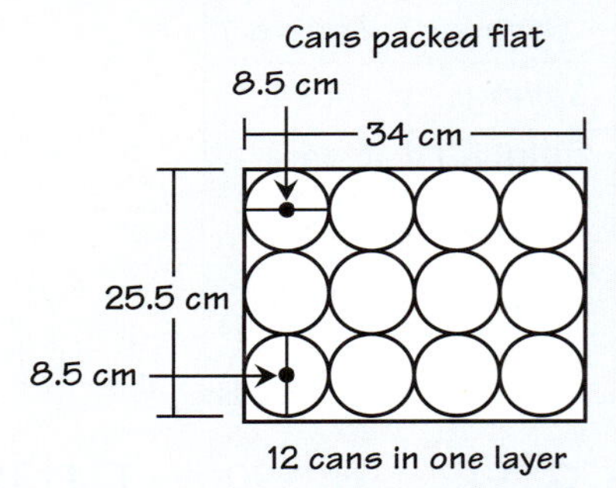

12 cans in one layer

Cans packed on sides

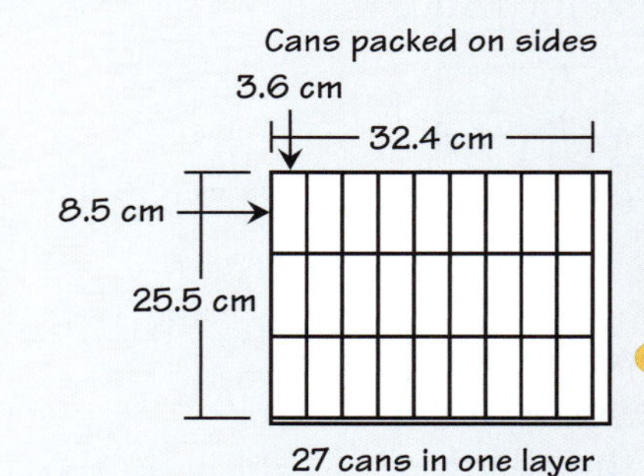

27 cans in one layer

The diagrams support the answer.

To find the number of layers that could fit in the box, I divided the height of the box by the appropriate dimension of the can.

Cans packed flat: $17 \text{ cm} \div 3.6 \text{ cm} \approx 4.7$, so 4 layers can fit in the box.
$12 \text{ cans} \times 4 \text{ layers} = 48 \text{ cans}$.

Cans packed on sides: $17 \text{ cm} \div 8.5 \text{ cm} = 2$, so 2 layers can fit in the box.
$27 \text{ cans} \times 2 \text{ layers} = 54 \text{ cans}$.

More tuna cans fit in the box when the cans are packed on their sides. Packed this way, 54 tuna cans fit in the box.

The answer is correct. The explanation is clear, complete, and reflects correct mathematical thinking.

Partial Credit Solution

I calculated the number of tuna cans that could fit on their sides in one layer of the box by dividing the box's length by 8.5 centimeters and dividing the box's width by 3.6 centimeters.

The reasoning is correct.

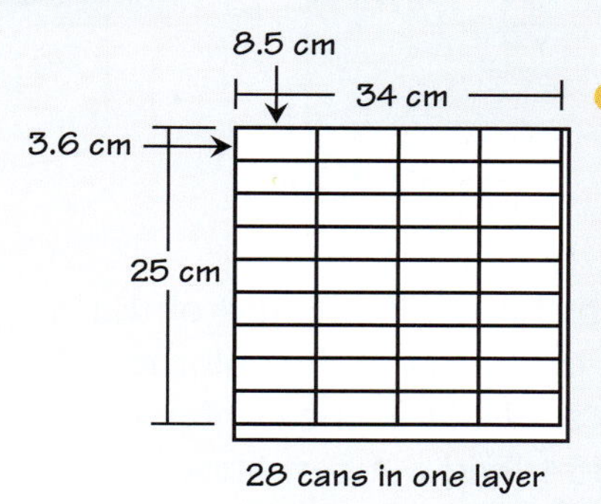

28 cans in one layer

It is correctly determined that 28 cans fit in one layer. The diagram supports this calculation.

A total of 28 cans fit in the first layer of the box. To find the number of layers that fit in the box, divide the height of the box by 8.5 centimeters.

17 cm ÷ 8.5 = 2, so 2 layers can fit in the box.

28 cans × 2 layers = 56 cans.

The number of cans that can be packed in the box is 56.

The solution is correct, but the problem asks for two different solutions. The answer is incomplete.

Try This

1. A student's answer to the problem on page 612 is given below. Score the solution as *full credit, partial credit,* or *no credit*. Explain your choice. If you choose *partial credit* or *no credit,* explain how you would change the answer to earn a score of *full credit*.

Watch Out!
Scoring is often based on how clearly you explain your reasoning.

Because 34 ÷ 8.5 = 4, 4 cans fit along the length of the box.

Because 26 ÷ 8.5 ≈ 3.1, 3 cans fit along the width of the box.

Because 17 ÷ 3.6 ≈ 4.7, 4 cans can fit stacked along the height of the box.

Since 4 × 3 × 4 = 48, the number of cans that can be packed in the box is 48.

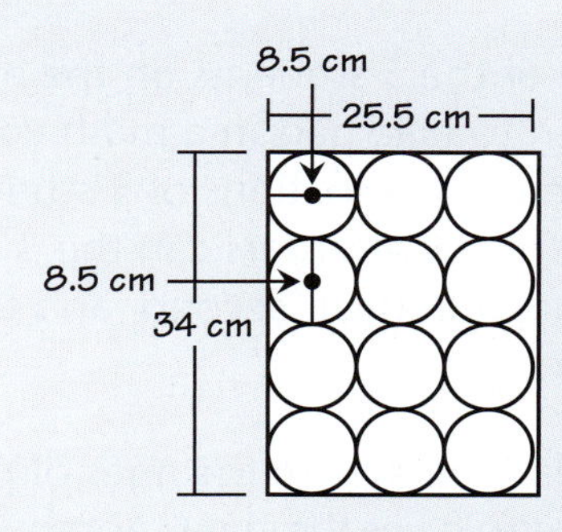

Extended Response

1. At a movie theater, you can buy a small box of popcorn for $3.75 or a large cylindrical tub of popcorn for $5.25. Which size of popcorn is the better buy? Explain.

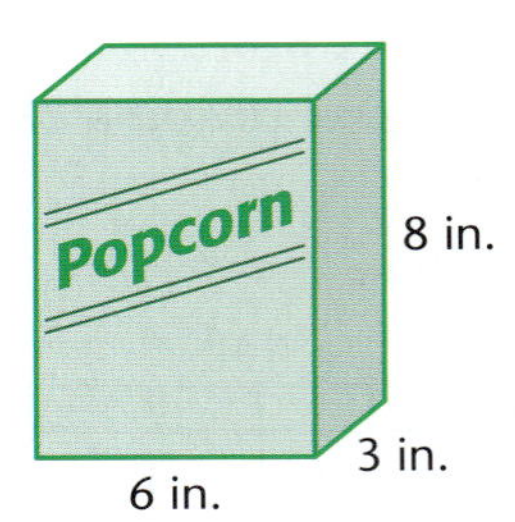

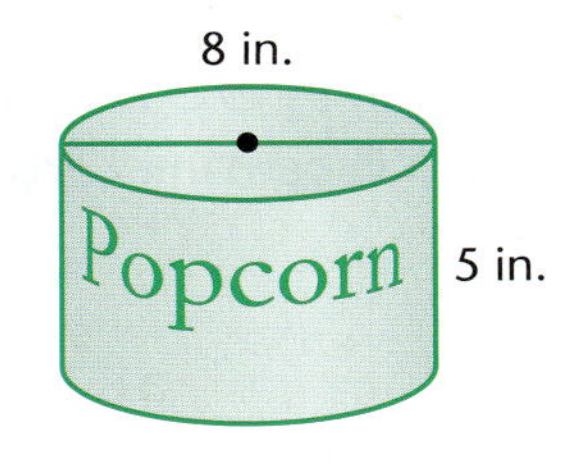

2. An insulated beverage container is cylindrical in shape. The height of the container is 8.9 inches and the diameter is 2.9 inches. Find the volume of the container. About how many cups of water will fit in the container? Use the fact that 1 cubic inch equals about 0.554 fluid ounces. Show your work.

3. A clothing store is having a clearance sale and displays the sign below. Which item is marked down by the greatest percent? Show your work.

Item	Original price	Sale price
T-shirts	$15	$8.50
Sweatshirts	$29	$15
Slippers	$19.99	$8.99

Item	Original price	Sale price
Jeans	$42.50	$29.99
Sweaters	$49.95	$24
Sweatpants	$21.50	$12.50

4. The circle graph at the right shows the results of a survey in which 350 students were asked to name the European country they want to visit. Find the percent of students who gave each of the responses shown. The "Other" sector includes 35 students who named Spain as the European country they want to visit. Explain how you could redraw the circle graph to include a sector for Spain.

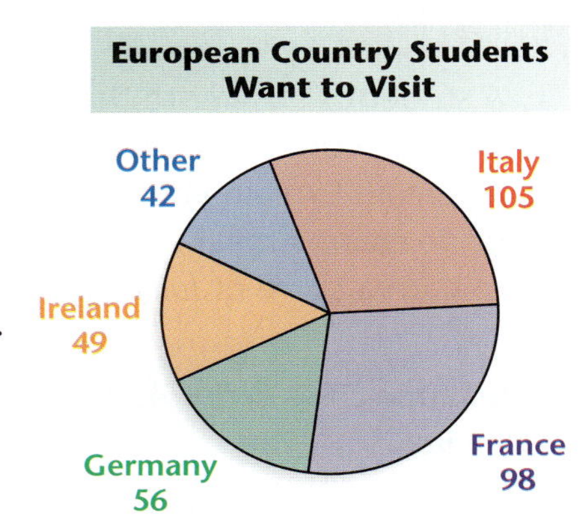

5. Three of the 5 students on the math team are being chosen to take part in a math competition. How many different combinations of 3 students are possible? In how many different orders can the 3 students finish the competition (first, second, and third)? Explain your method.

6. The data below are the ages of people at a family reunion. Make a box-and-whisker plot of the data. About what percent of the people are between the ages of 11 and 58? Explain how you can tell from the box-and-whisker plot.

7, 10, 12, 32, 65, 70, 41, 35, 2, 56, 23, 60, 18

GLOSSARY

A

absolute value (p. 91) The distance from a number to zero on a number line.

acute angle (p. 83) An angle whose measure is greater than 0° but less than 90°. *See also* angle.

acute triangle (p. 415) A triangle with three acute angles.

alternate exterior angles (p. 425) A pair of angles outside two lines intersected by a transversal and on different sides of the transversal.

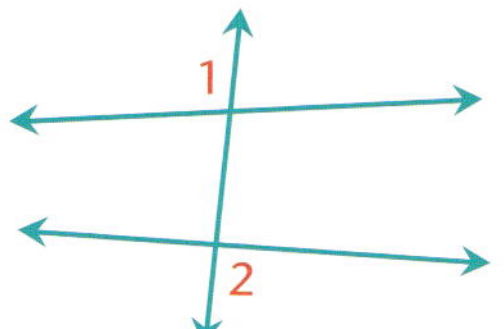

Angles 1 and 2 are alternate exterior angles.

alternate interior angles (p. 424) A pair of angles between two lines intersected by a transversal and on different sides of the transversal.

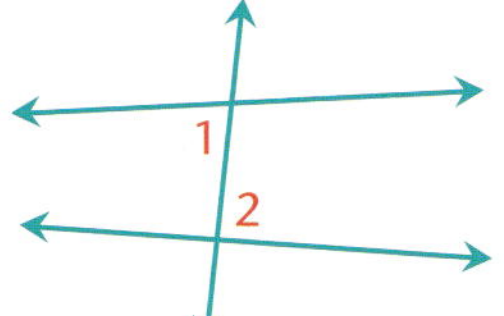

Angles 1 and 2 are alternate interior angles.

angle (p. 78) A figure formed by two rays with a common endpoint, called the *vertex*.

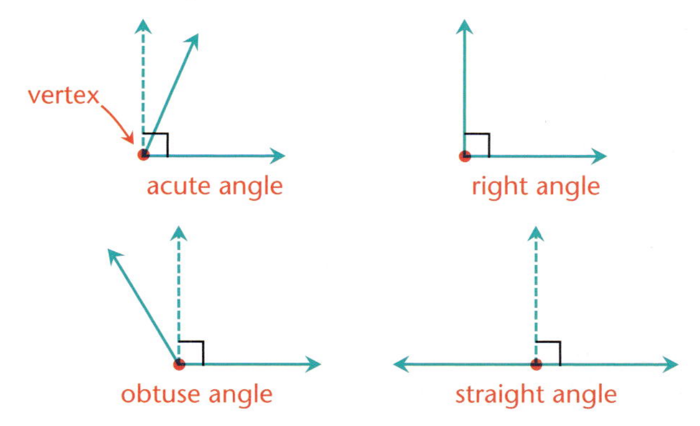

arc (p. 218) A part of a circle.

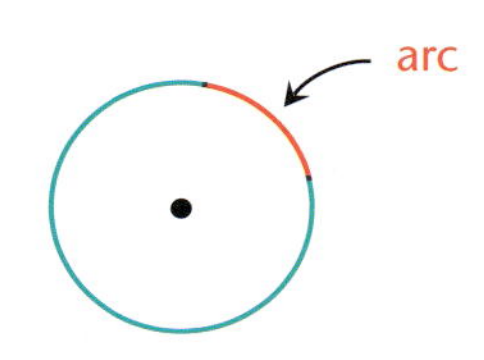

arc of a network (p. 442) A curve or segment connecting vertices of a network. *See also* network.

associative property of addition (p. 105) Changing the grouping of numbers in an addition problem does not affect the sum.

associative property of multiplication (p. 281) Changing the grouping of factors in a multiplication problem does not affect the product.

axis (plural: axes) (p. 3) *See* coordinate plane.

B

bar graph (p. 3) A visual display of data that fall into distinct categories.

base (p. 17) *See* exponential form.

base of a polygon (pp. 383, 388, 514) *See* parallelogram *and* trapezoid.

base of a space figure (pp. 398, 457, 547, 568) *See* prism, cylinder, pyramid, *and* cone.

benchmark (p. 208) An item whose measure you know that can be used to estimate other measures.

box-and-whisker plot (pp. 334, 492) A diagram that shows the median, the other quartiles, and the extremes for a numerical set of data. The *box* contains about 50% of the data values. The two *whiskers* each contain about 25% of the data values.

Average January Temperature in 50 U.S. Cities

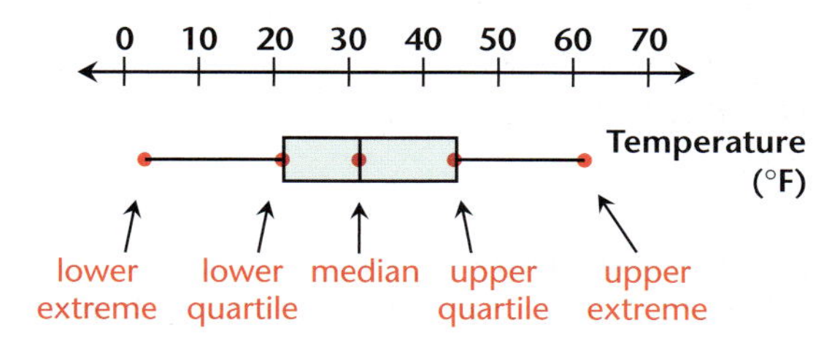

C

capacity (p. 440) The amount of fluid a container can hold.

center (p. 218) *See* circle.

central angle (p. 500) An angle with its vertex at the center of a circle.

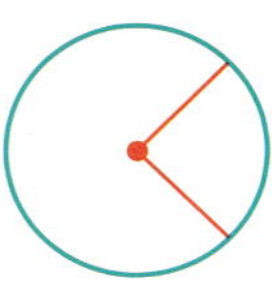

certain event (p. 33) An event that has a probability of 1.

chord (p. 218) A segment whose endpoints are both on a given circle. *See also* circle.

circle (p. 218) The set of all points in a plane that are the same distance from a given point.

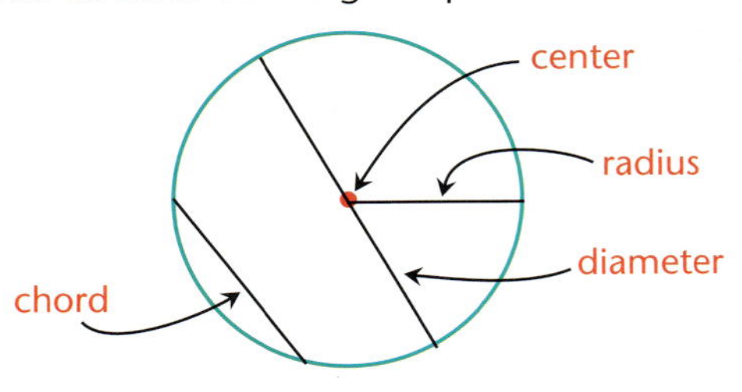

circle graph (p. 500) A graph in which the entire circle represents the whole, or 100%.

circumference (p. 233) The distance around a circle.

combination (p. 556) A selection of items in which order is not important.

commutative property of addition (p. 105) Changing the order of numbers in an addition problem does not affect the sum.

commutative property of multiplication (p. 281) Changing the order of the factors in a multiplication problem does not affect the product.

compatible numbers (p. 583) Numbers which have sums, differences, products, or quotients that are easy to compute.

complementary angles (p. 82) Two angles whose measures have a sum of 90°.

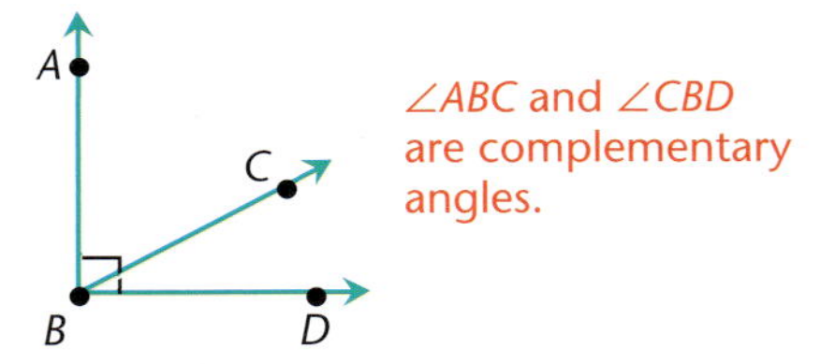

complementary events (p. 386) Two events where one or the other must occur, but they cannot both happen at the same time.

composite number (p. 150) A whole number greater than 1 that has more than two factors.

concave (p. 382) A polygon that is not convex is concave. *See also* polygon.

cone (p. 568) A space figure with one curved base and a vertex.

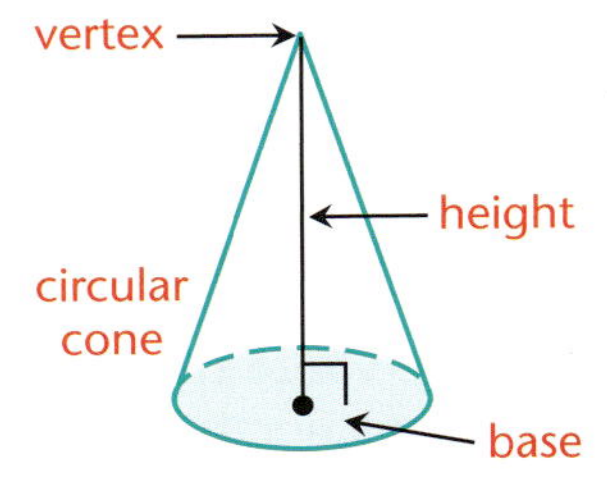

congruent (pp. 217, 267) Two figures that have the same shape and the same size are congruent.

construction (p. 219) A figure drawn using only a straightedge and compass.

convex (p. 382) A polygon is convex when all of its diagonals lie in the interior of the polygon. *See also* polygon.

coordinate (p. 93) A number in an ordered pair that gives a point's location left or right of zero, or up or down from zero. *See also* coordinate plane.

coordinate plane (p. 93) A grid with a horizontal axis and a vertical axis that intersect at a point.

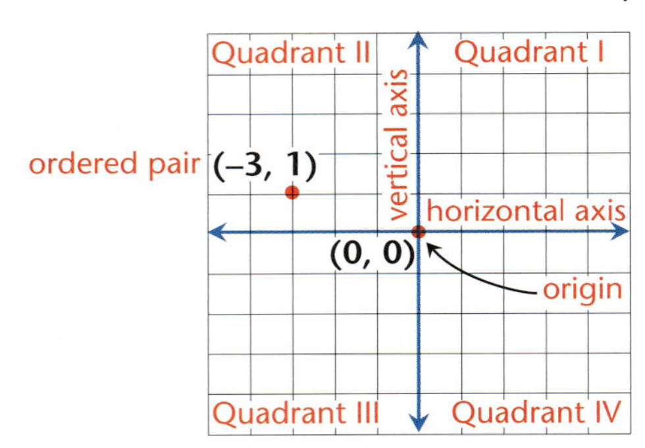

corresponding angles (p. 424) Angles in the same position with respect to two lines and a transversal.

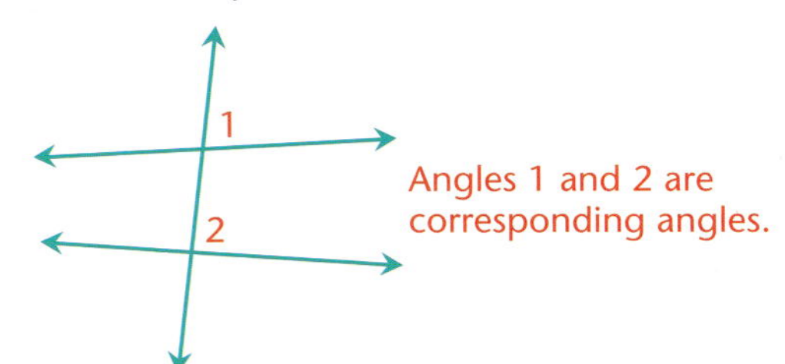

corresponding parts (p. 412) When two figures are similar, for each angle or side of one figure there is a similar angle or side on the other figure.

counting principle (p. 533) To find the number of permutations, you can multiply together the number of options at each point where you make a choice.

cross products (p. 329) Products formed from a pair of ratios by multiplying the numerator of each fraction by the denominator of the other fraction.

cube (p. 18) A closed space figure with six square surfaces.

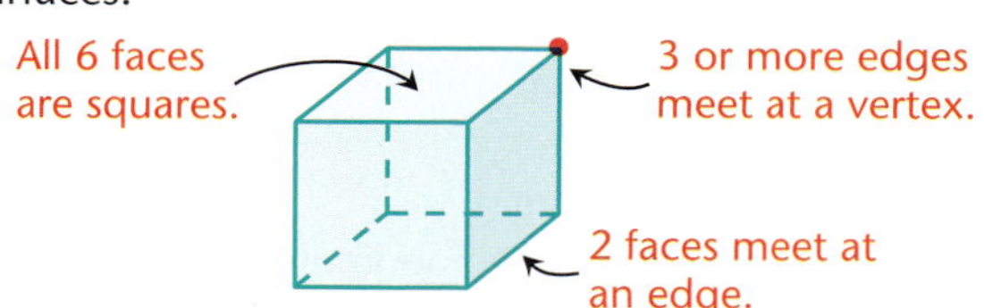

cylinder (p. 457) A space figure that has a curved surface and two parallel, congruent bases.

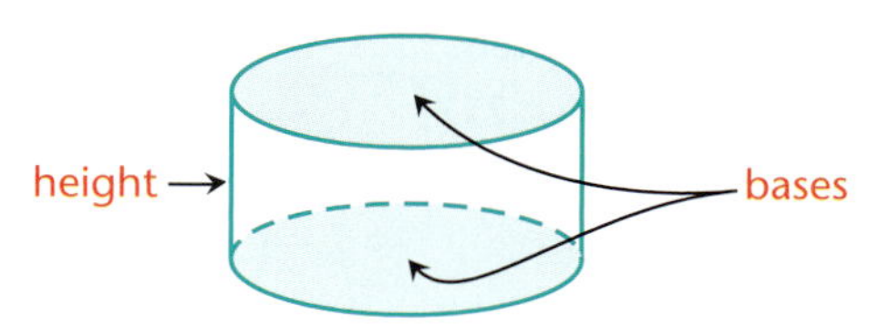

D

decimal places (p. 191) The positions of the digits in a number which determine their values.

degree (p. 78) A unit of measurement of an angle that is $\frac{1}{360}$ of a complete turn.

diagonal (p. 428) A segment that connects two nonconsecutive vertices of a polygon.

diameter (p. 218) Any chord that passes through the center of a circle. The length of a diameter is called *the* diameter. *See also* circle.

distributive property (p. 237) Each addend inside a set of parentheses can be multiplied by a factor outside the parentheses. For example, $5\left(2 + \frac{3}{5}\right) = (5 \cdot 2) + \left(5 \cdot \frac{3}{5}\right)$.

divisible (p. 150) When a number can be divided evenly by another number, it is divisible by that number.

E

edge (pp. 19, 398) A segment where two faces of a space figure are joined. *See also* cube *and* prism.

equally likely (p. 30) When the probability of two or more outcomes is the same, the outcomes are equally likely.

equation (p. 16) A mathematical sentence stating that two quantities or expressions are equal.

equilateral triangle (p. 217) A triangle with three congruent sides.

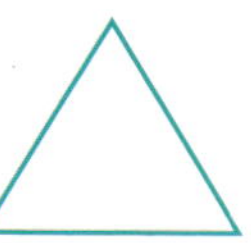

equivalent fractions (p. 163) Fractions that represent the same amount.

evaluate (pp. 61, 119) To carry out mathematical operations in the correct order or to substitute a value for a variable and perform the operations in the correct order. *See also* order of operations.

event (p. 28) A set of outcomes of an experiment.

experiment (p. 28) An activity whose results can be observed and recorded.

experimental probability (p. 28) A probability determined by repeating an experiment a number of times and observing the results. To calculate an experimental probability, you can divide the number of times an outcome occurs by the number of times the experiment is done.

exponent (pp. 17, 20) A raised number that tells the power of the base. *See also* exponential form.

exponential form (p. 17) A way of writing a number using exponents. A number that can be written using an exponent and a base is a power of the base.

8 is a power of 2.

standard form $8 = 2 \cdot 2 \cdot 2 = 2^3$ exponential form (exponent: 3; base: 2)

expression (p. 60) A mathematical phrase that can be formed using numbers, variables, and operation symbols.

exterior angle (p. 424) An angle that is outside two lines intersected by a transversal.

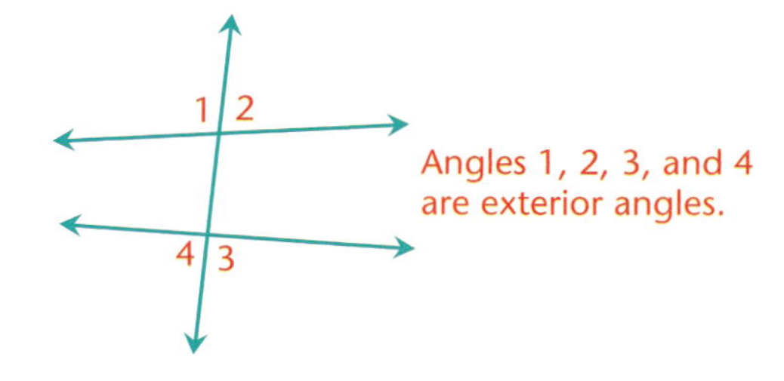

F

face (pp. 19, 398) A flat surface of a space figure. *See also* cube *and* prism.

factor (p. 150) When one whole number divides another whole number with no remainder, the first number is a factor of the second.

fitted line (p. 332) A line drawn on a scatter plot to identify the trend in the data. Roughly half the points fall above the line and half the points fall below it. *See also* scatter plot.

frequency (p. 5) The number of times a data item occurs.

frequency table (pp. 5, 7) A table which shows how often each data item occurs.

function (p. 119) A relationship between input and output. For each input there is exactly one output. Output depends on input.

G

geometric probability (p. 387) A probability that is based on length, area, or volume.

greatest common factor (p. 154) The greatest number that is a factor of each of two or more numbers.

H

height of a polygon (pp. 383, 388, 514) *See* parallelogram *and* trapezoid.

height of a space figure (pp. 398, 457, 547, 568) *See* prism, cylinder, pyramid, and cone.

histogram (p. 318) A special type of bar graph that displays the frequencies of data in given intervals of equal width. Each bar touches the next.

horizontal axis (p. 3) A horizontal line on a graph that is labeled with the categories or with the scale. *See also* coordinate plane.

I

image (p. 264) The figure resulting from a transformation.

impossible event (p. 33) An event that has a probability of 0.

inequality (pp. 90, 380) A mathematical sentence stating that one quantity or expression is greater than or less than another.

integer (p. 89) A whole number or the opposite of a whole number, which is any number in the set of numbers ..., –3, –2, –1, 0, 1, 2, 3, ...

interior angle (p. 424) An angle that is between two lines intersected by a transversal.

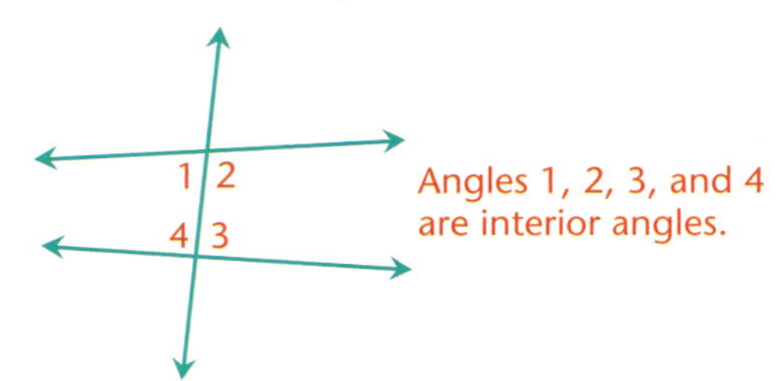

intersect (p. 92) When two geometric figures share at least one point, they intersect.

interval (p. 4) The step between grid lines on a scale.

inverse operations (p. 135) Operations which "undo" each other like addition and subtraction or multiplication and division.

isosceles triangle (p. 217) A triangle with at least two congruent sides.

L

least common denominator (p. 165) The least common multiple of the denominators of two or more fractions.

least common multiple (p. 155) The least number that is a multiple of each of two or more numbers.

line graph (p. 4) A graph on which plotted points are connected with line segments. It can be used to show change in data over time.

line symmetry (p. 268) If one half of a figure is a reflection of the other half, the figure has line symmetry.

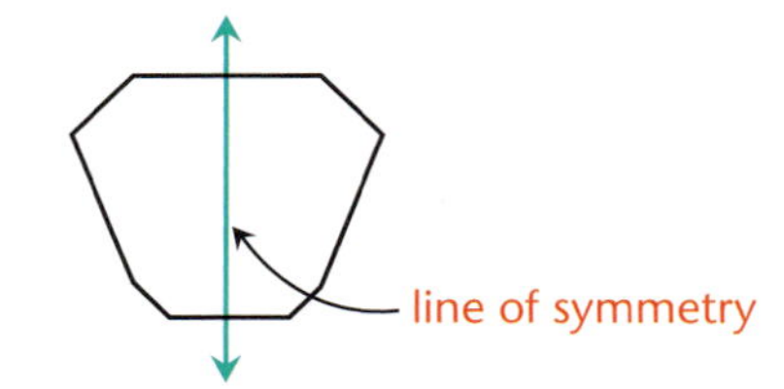

lower extreme (p. 492) The least data value in a set of data. *See also* box-and-whisker plot.

lower quartile (p. 492) The median of the data values that are less than the median of the total data set. *See also* box-and-whisker plot.

lowest terms (p. 163) A fraction is in lowest terms when the greatest common factor of the numerator and denominator is 1.

M

mass (p. 440) The amount of matter in an object.

mean (p. 595) In a numerical data set, the sum of all the data divided by the number of data items.

median (p. 315) The middle item in a data set ordered from least to greatest. If there is no single middle item, the number halfway between the two data items closest to the middle.

mixed number (p. 178) The sum of a nonzero whole number and a fraction between 0 and 1.

mode (p. 315) The item or items that appear most often in a data set. There can be no mode.

multiple (p. 154) The multiple of a whole number is the product of that number and any nonzero whole number.

multistage experiment (p. 365) A situation that involves two or more events happening one after another.

N

negative (p. 89) Less than zero.

net (p. 399) A flat pattern that can be cut out and folded to form a space figure without any gaps or overlaps.

network (p. 442) Vertices connected by arcs.

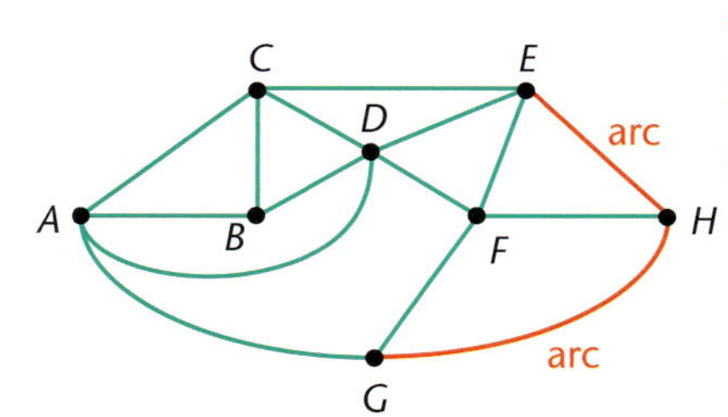

One path from vertex *E* to vertex *G* is *E-H-G*.

numerator (p. 584) The top number in a fraction that tells how many parts of the whole to consider.

O

obtuse angle (p. 83) An angle whose measure is greater than 90°. *See also* angle.

obtuse triangle (p. 415) A triangle with one obtuse angle.

opposites (p. 91) Two numbers that are the same distance from 0 but on opposite sides of 0 on a number line. The opposite of 3 is −3.

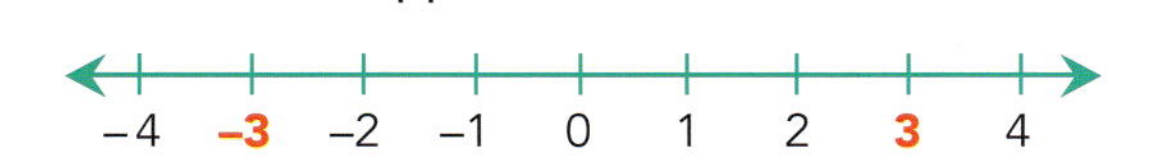

order of operations (p. 61) The correct order in which to perform the mathematical operations in an expression: operations inside grouping symbols first, exponents next, then multiplication and division in order from left to right, and finally addition and subtraction in order from left to right.

ordered pair (p. 93) A pair of numbers used to identify and plot points in a coordinate plane. *See also* coordinate plane.

origin (p. 93) *See* coordinate plane.

outcome (p. 28) The result of an experiment.

P

parallel (p. 92) In a plane, two lines that do not intersect are parallel.

parallelogram (p. 383) A four-sided polygon in which both pairs of opposite sides are parallel.

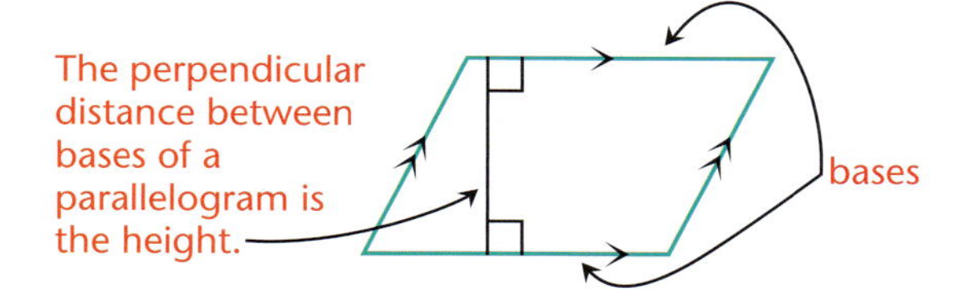

percent (p. 3) Percent means "per hundred" or "out of 100."

percent of change (p. 475) The percent by which an amount increases or decreases from its original amount.

permutation (p. 530) A possible arrangement of a group of items in which order is important.

perpendicular (p. 92) Two lines that intersect at 90° angles are perpendicular.

plane (p. 92) A flat surface that goes on forever.

polygon (p. 382) A closed figure made from segments that are drawn on a flat surface and do not cross.

convex polygons

concave polygons

A polygon can have 3 or more sides. Some types of polygons are:

pentagon (5 sides)
hexagon (6 sides)
octagon (8 sides)
decagon (10 sides)

positive (p. 89) Greater than zero.

power (p. 17) *See* exponential form.

prime factorization (p. 151) The expression of a number written as the product of prime factors.

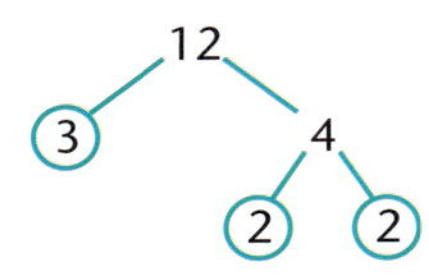

The prime factorization of 12 is 2 • 2 • 3.

prime number (p. 150) A whole number greater than 1 that has exactly two factors, 1 and itself.

principal square root (p. 396) The positive square root. The symbol for it is $\sqrt{}$.

prism (p. 398) A space figure with faces shaped like polygons. Two of the faces, the bases, are parallel and congruent. The other faces are parallelograms. In a *right* prism, the other faces are rectangles.

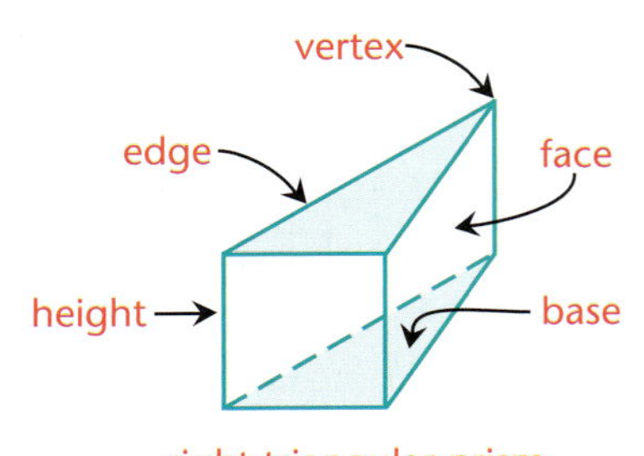

right triangular prism

probability (p. 28) A number from 0 to 1 that tells how likely an event is to happen.

proportion (p. 314) An equation stating that two ratios are equivalent.

pyramid (p. 547) A space figure that has one polygon-shaped base. All the other faces are triangles that meet at a single vertex.

square pyramid

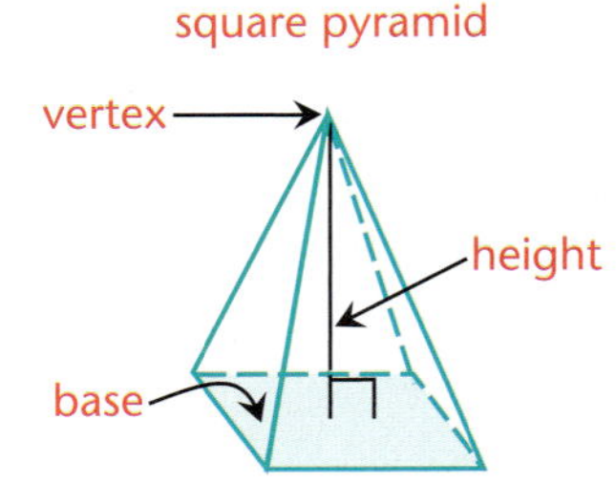

Q

quadrilateral (p. 383) A four-sided polygon.

R

radius (plural: radii) (p. 218) A segment whose endpoints are the center and any point on a given circle. The length of a radius is called *the* radius. *See also* circle.

range (p. 316) The difference between the greatest data value and the least data value in a data set.

rate (p. 313) A ratio that compares quantities measured in different units.

ratio (p. 313) A comparison of two quantities by division. The ratio of 6 and 8 can be expressed as 6 to 8, 6:8, or $\frac{6}{8}$.

ray (p. 77) A part of a line that starts at an endpoint and goes on forever in one direction.

reciprocals (p. 238) Two numbers whose product is 1.

reflection (p. 267) A flip of a figure across a line.

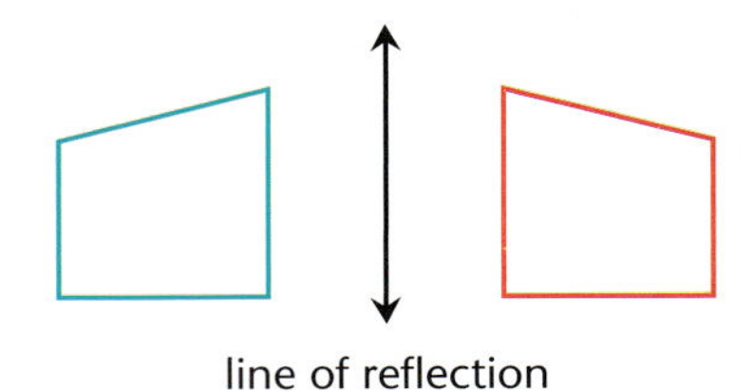

line of reflection

repeating decimal (p. 252) A decimal in which a digit or a sequence of digits keeps repeating.

rhombus (p. 514) A parallelogram that has four congruent sides.

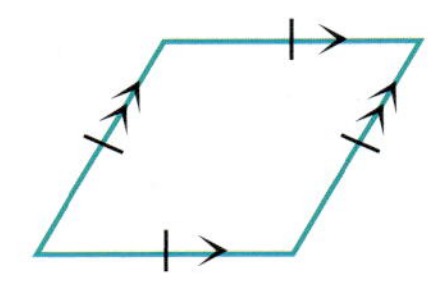

right angle (p. 83) An angle whose measure is 90°. *See also* angle.

right triangle (p. 415) A triangle with one right angle.

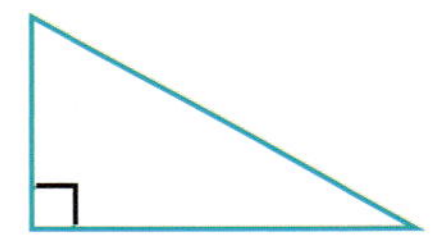

rise (p. 461) *See* slope.

rotation (p. 264) A turn of a figure about a fixed point, the center of rotation, a certain number of degrees either clockwise or counterclockwise.

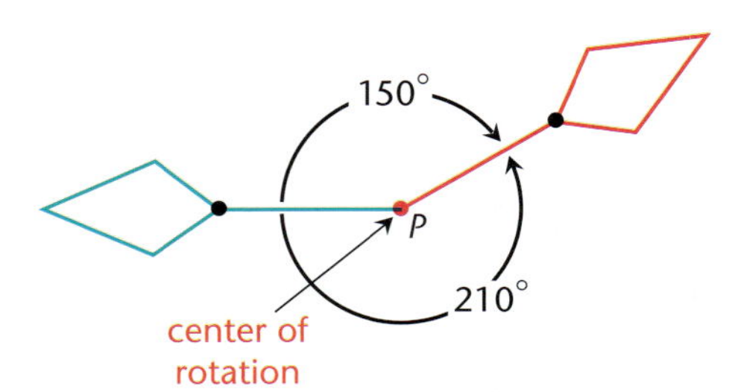

rotational symmetries (p. 265) The numbers of degrees less than 360° that a figure can be rotated and fit exactly on itself.

rotational symmetry (p. 265) When a figure can be rotated less than 360° about its center and fit exactly on itself, the figure has rotational symmetry.

run (p. 461) *See* slope.

S

scale of a drawing (p. 413) The ratio of a length measurement on a drawing to the measurement of the corresponding part on the object represented.

scale on a graph (p. 4) The numbers written along an axis of a graph.

scalene triangle (p. 217) A triangle with no congruent sides.

scatter plot (p. 332) A graph of a set of data points in a coordinate plane that represents a relationship between two quantities.

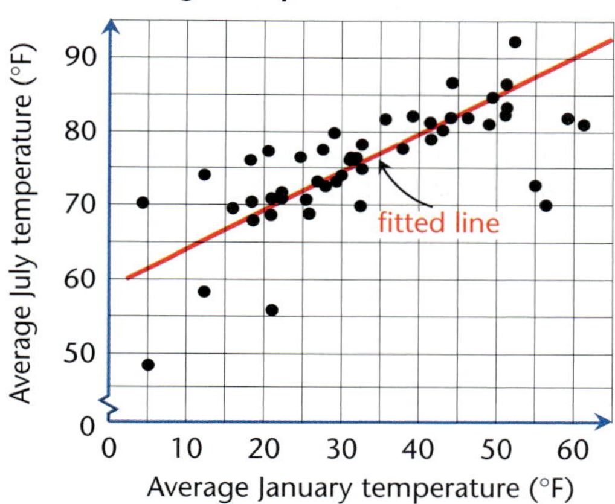

scientific notation (p. 197) A number is in scientific notation when it is written as the product of a decimal greater than or equal to 1 and less than 10 and a power of 10. For example:

standard form → $5261 = 5.261 \cdot 10^3$ ← scientific notation

sector (p. 500) A wedge-shaped region in a circle bounded by two radii and an arc.

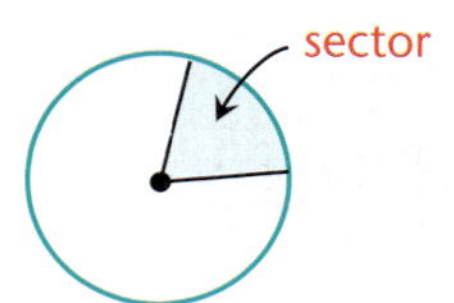

sequence (p. 14) An ordered list of numbers or objects.

similar (pp. 295, 417) Figures are similar if they have the same shape, but not necessarily the same size. In similar polygons, the measures of the corresponding angles are equal, and the ratios of the lengths of the corresponding sides are equal.

slope (p. 461) The ratio of the vertical change to the horizontal change along a line.

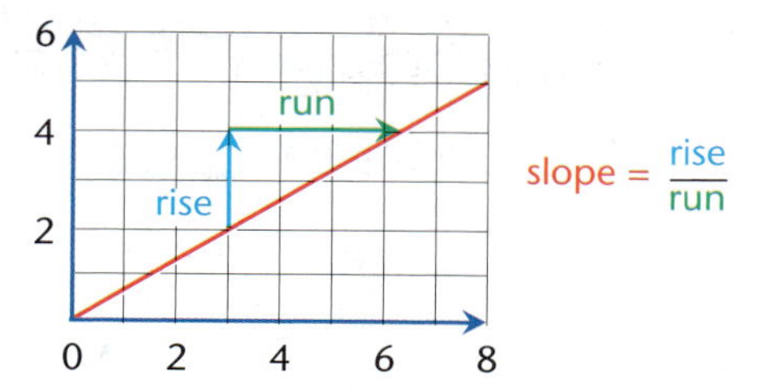

solution of an equation (p. 134) A value of a variable that makes an equation true.

solving an equation (p. 134) The process of finding a solution.

square root (p. 396) If $A = s^2$, then s is a square root of A. For example, 5 and –5 are square roots of 25. The symbol for a positive square root is $\sqrt{}$. The symbol for a negative square root is $-\sqrt{}$.

standard form (p. 17) *See* exponential form.

stem-and-leaf plot (p. 316) A display of data where each number is represented by a *stem* (the left-most digits) and a *leaf* (the right-most digits).

straight angle (p. 83) An angle whose measure is 180°. *See also* angle.

supplementary angles (p. 81) Two angles whose measures have a sum of 180°.

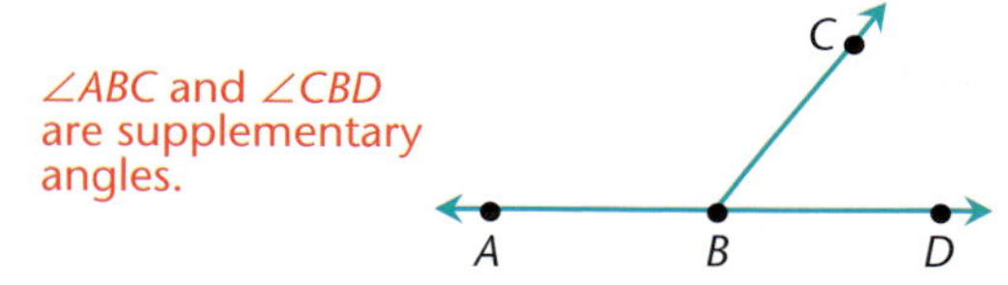

surface area of a prism (p. 399) The sum of the areas of a prism's faces.

T

term number (p. 14) A number indicating the position of a term in a sequence.

term of a sequence (p. 14) A number or object in a sequence.

terminating decimal (p. 253) A decimal in which the digits stop, or *terminate*.

tessellation (p. 565) A tiling that uses congruent polygons in a repeating pattern to cover a plane with no gaps or overlaps.

theoretical probability (p. 30) A probability that can be determined without actually doing an experiment. If the outcomes of an experiment are equally likely, you can calculate the theoretical probability by dividing the number of favorable outcomes by the number of possible outcomes.

transformation (p. 291) A change made to the shape, size, or position of a figure.

translation (p. 291) A transformation that slides each point of a figure the same distance in the same direction.

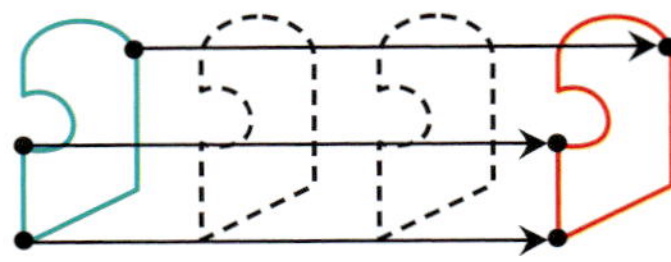

transversal (p. 423) A line that intersects two lines in a plane at separate points.

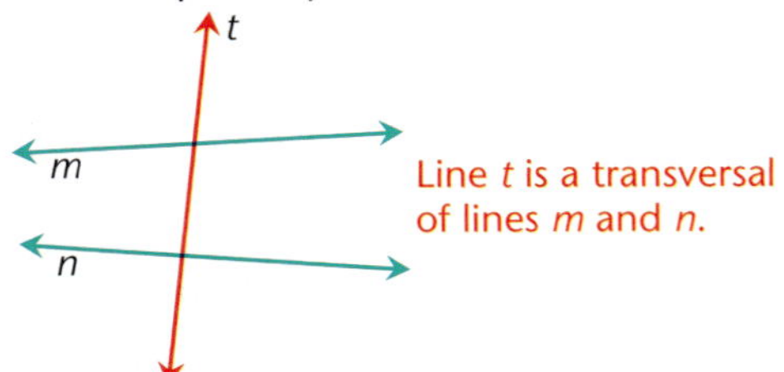

trapezoid (p. 514) A quadrilateral that has only one pair of opposite sides that are parallel.

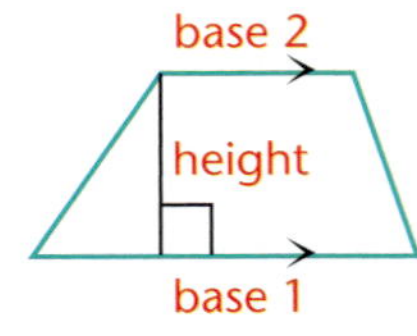

traversable (p. 449) When a network can be drawn without lifting your pencil off the paper or drawing any arc more than once, the network is traversable.

tree diagram (p. 168) A display of the possible outcomes of an experiment.

triangle (p. 58) A three-sided polygon.

U

unit rate (p. 313) A ratio that compares a quantity to one unit of another quantity.

upper extreme (p. 492) The greatest data value in a set of data. *See also* box-and-whisker plot.

upper quartile (p. 492) The median of the data values that are greater than the median of the total data set. *See also* box-and-whisker plot.

V

variable (p. 16) A quantity, usually represented by a letter, that is unknown or that changes.

vertex of an angle (p. 78) The common endpoint of two rays that form an angle. *See also* angle.

vertex of a cube (plural: vertices) (p. 19) A point where three or more edges of a cube meet. *See also* cube.

vertex of a network (p. 442) A point in a network. *See also* network.

vertex of a prism (p. 398) A point where three or more edges of a prism meet. *See also* prism.

vertex of a tessellation (p. 565) A point where the corners of the polygons in a tessellation touch.

vertical angles (p. 424) Two angles whose sides form two pairs of opposite rays.

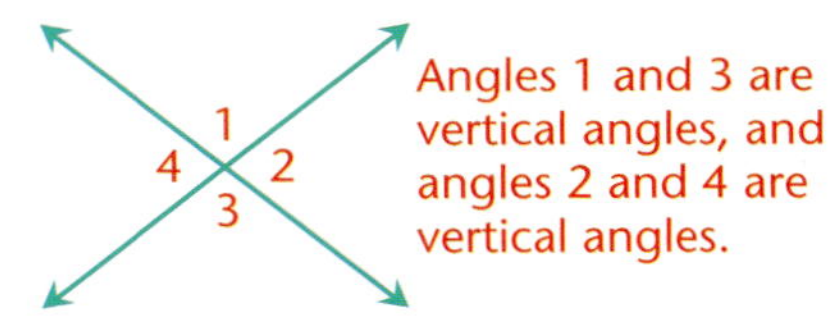

vertical axis (p. 3) A vertical line on a graph that is labeled with the categories or with the scale. *See also* coordinate plane.

volume (p. 18) The amount of space inside a space figure. Volume is measured in cubic units.

W

weighted network (p. 444) A network in which the arcs are labeled with numbers representing such things as distances and times.

X

***x*-axis** (p. 292) The horizontal number line in a coordinate plane. *See also* coordinate plane.

Y

***y*-axis** (p. 292) The vertical number line in a coordinate plane. *See also* coordinate plane.

INDEX

A

B

C

D

L

M

N

Q

R

U

V

W

Z

CREDITS

ACKNOWLEDGMENTS

13 *"Smart"* poem from *Where the Sidewalk Ends* by Shel Silverstein. Copyright © 1974 by Evil Eye Music, Inc. **35** Excerpt from "There's a Moral Here, Cougar Fans" by Jerry Kirshenbaum. Copyright © 1983, Time Inc. Reprinted courtesy of *Sports Illustrated*, September 5, 1983. All rights reserved. **50** "Wed., August 13, 1980," from *Alesia* by Eloise Greenfield and Alesia Revis. Copyright © 1981 by Eloise Greenfield and Alesia Revis. Reprinted by permission of Scott Treimel, New York, for the author. **162** Diagrams from *Mathematisches Arbeitsbuch* by Walter Traeger and Karl-Heinz Unger. By permission of Verlag Moritz Diesterweg. **164** Diagram from *Matematnka 5. KAAC.* By permission of Prosveta Publishers. **166** Diagram from *Maths 8 2E* by Lynch, Parr, Picking, Keating. Reprinted by permission of Addison Wesley Longman Australia. **166** Diagram from *Hightop Shougaku 3-nen Suugaku* mathematics textbook. By permission of Obunsha Co., Ltd., Tokyo, Japan. **411** Excerpt from *Epic of Flight: Barnstormers & Speed Kings* by Paul O'Neil and the Editors of Time-Life Books, © 1981 Time-Life Books, Inc.

COVER PHOTOGRAPHY

Front (*clockwise*) Joe McBride/Tony Stone Images; Holway & Lobel Globus/The Stock Market; Fred Chase/Impact Visuals; Doug Milner/Uniphoto Picture Agency; RMIP/Richard Haynes; Per Eide/The Image Bank; Corbis (2002 ed.), Gianfranco Gorgoni/Contact Press Images (1999 ed.); David Young Wolff/Tony Stone Images. **Back** Photo of STEM pilot students: Sal Skog

PHOTOGRAPHY

iii RMIP/Richard Haynes; **iv** David Young Wolff/Tony Stone Images; **v** Per Eide/The Image Bank; **vi** Fred Chase/Impact Visuals; **vii** Holway & Lobel Globus/The Stock Market; **viii** Doug Milner/Uniphoto Picture Agency; **vix** Joe McBride/Tony Stone Images; **x** David Young Wolff/Tony Stone Images; **xi** Corbis (2002 ed.), Gianfranco Gorgoni/Contact Press Images (1999 ed.); **1** RMIP/Richard Haynes; **2** Nancie Battaglia; **5** Ian Shaw/Tony Stone Images; **8** National Baseball Hall of Fame; **9** Courtesy of the Vermont Youth Corps; **11** Jeff Greenberg/The Picture Cube; **15** RMIP/Richard Haynes; **24** Lawrence Migdale; **26** RMIP/Richard Haynes; **27** School Division, Houghton Mifflin Company; **28** School Division, Houghton Mifflin Company; **32** School Division, Houghton Mifflin Company; **34** Uniphoto (tl); Bachmann/Image Works (tr); David Wientraub/Stock Boston (bl); B.W. Hoffman/ Unicorn Stock Photo (br); **36** RMIP/Richard Haynes; **38** RMIP/Richard Haynes; **41** Randy Ory/The Stock Market; **43** RMIP/Richard Haynes; **45** Inga Spence/The Picture Cube; **46** School Division, Houghton Mifflin Company; **51** School Division, Houghton Mifflin Company; **56** RMIP/Richard Haynes; **57** RMIP/Richard Haynes; **59** Watterson/Universal Press Syndicate; **62** RMIP/Richard Haynes; **66** School Division, Houghton Mifflin Company; **68** Stanley Rowin/The Picture Cube; **69** RMIP/Richard Haynes; **71** RMIP/Richard Haynes; **74-75** Per Eide/The Image Bank; **76** David Lissy/The Picture Cube; **79** RMIP/Richard Haynes; **80** PhotoDisc, Inc.; **82** David Lissy/The Picture Cube; **85** PhotoDisc, Inc.; **88** Gayna Hoffman; **92** Emory Kristof/National Geographic Image Collection; **99** RMIP/Richard Haynes; **101** RMIP/Richard Haynes; **111** Sue McCartney/Photo Researchers; **112** Fred Hirschman/Tony Stone Images (tl); Art Wolfe/Tony Stone Images (tr); Larry Urlich/Tony Stone Images (bl); **114** RMIP/Richard Haynes; **116** RMIP/Richard Haynes; **117** Michael J. Howell/Stock Boston (l); Alese & Mort Pechter/The Stock Market (r); **121** Mug Shots/The Stock Market; **122** Jack Van Antwerp/The Stock Market; **125** Courtsey of the Institute of Texan Cultures; **126** Brown Brothers; **127** Julian Calverly/Uniphoto (t); Ken Lax/Photo Researchers (b); **128** Amy Etra; **130** RMIP/Richard Haynes; **134** RMIP/Richard Haynes; **138** UPI/Corbis-Bettman (tl); Dennis Brack/Black Star (r); Archive Photos (b); **139** Superstock; **143** RMIP/Richard Haynes; **146-147** Fred Chase/Impact Visuals; **148** Mark E. Gibson (t); Lawrence Migdale/Stock Boston (b); **151** School Division, Houghton Mifflin Company; **153** School Division, Houghton Mifflin Company; **155** Jose Azel/AURORA; **157** Michael Newman/ PhotoEdit; **160** Corbis-Bettmann; **162** School Division, Houghton Mifflin Company; **163** RMIP/Richard Haynes; **165** RMIP/Richard Haynes; **172** National Geographic Image Collection; **173** Lawrence Migdale/Stock Boston; **174** RMIP/Richard Haynes; **177** Courtesy of the Museum of the American Numismatic Assoication; **180** The Granger Collection; **184** James P. Rowan/DRK Photo (tr); Jeff Foott/Tom Stack & Associates (cl); Barbara Gerlach/DRK Photo (cr); Stephen J. Krasemann/ DRK Photo (bl); **185** Johnny Johnson/DRK Photo; **186** PhotoDisc, Inc.; **187** Donn Carl Harper; **189** Eric P. Newman Numismatic Education Society (t); RMIP/ Richard Haynes (b); **190** The Granger Collection; **193** RMIP/Richard Haynes; **196** School Division, Houghton Mifflin Company; **200** Red Morgan; **201** Ken Edward/Photo Researchers, Inc.; **204** RMIP/Richard Haynes; **206** Mark E. Gibson; **207** RMIP/Richard Haynes; **208** RMIP/Richard Haynes; **209** RMIP/Richard Haynes; **211** Mitsuaki Iwago/Minden Pictures; **218** RMIP/Richard Haynes; **225** RMIP/Richard Haynes; **227** RMIP/Richard Haynes; **230-231** Holway & Lobel Globus/The Stock Market; **232** School Division, Houghton Mifflin Company; **233** RMIP/Richard Haynes; **242** Gayna

Hoffman/Stock Boston; **243** Edward S. Curtis/San Diego Museum of Man (t); David Ball/The Stock Market (b); **245** A. Adducci; **247** S. Dalton/Animals Animals; **248** S. Dalton/Animals Animals; **250** The Harold E. Edgerton 1992 Trust, Courtesy of Palm Press, Inc.; **252** The Harold E. Edgerton 1992 Trust, Courtesy of Palm Press, Inc.; **260** RMIP/Richard Haynes; **263** RMIP/Richard Haynes; **265** Dr. E. R. Degginger/Color-Pic, Inc. (l); Index Stock Photography, Inc. (r); **266** RMIP/Richard Haynes; **268** David Scharf/Peter Arnold, Inc.; **272** James Solliday/Biological Photo Service; **273** Addison Doty; **275** RMIP/Richard Haynes; **277** RMIP/Richard Haynes; **279** RMIP/Richard Haynes; **282** RMIP/Richard Haynes; **285** Novastock/PhotoEdit; **305** Courtesy of Karen Kiser; **307** RMIP/Richard Haynes; **308** Index Stock Photography, Inc.; **310-311** Doug Milner/Uniphoto Picture Agency; **312** PhotoDisc, Inc.; **313** Spencer Grant/The Picture Cube; **318** Douglas Landrum; **321** Dan Campbell (t); Robert Houser (b); **322** Lee Snider; **327** Alan Baldwin (b); Courtesy of Ashrita Furman; **328** Dennis Kitchen/Tony Stone Images; **329** Library of Congress, Negative No. USZ62-063370; **331** RMIP/Richard Haynes; **332** RMIP/Richard Haynes; **334** Courtesy of John Kolar; **338** M.C. Chamberlain/DRK Photo; **342** Michelle Bridwell/PhotoEdit; **344** David Young-Wolff/PhotoEdit; **350** Antonio Balducci/FPG International; **353** Laima Druskis/Stock Boston; **355** David Young-Wolff/Tony Stone Images; **356** RMIP/Richard Haynes; **358** David Madison/Duomo (l); PhotoDisc, Inc. (r); **359** PhotoDisc, Inc.; **360** RMIP/Richard Haynes; **361** Jim Cummins/FPG International (t); David Madison/Duomo (b); **365** David Madison/Duomo; **368** Reuters/Gary A. Cameron/Archive Photos; **369** Steve Maines/Stock Boston; **371** Courtesy of the Mayo Clinic; **373** RMIP/Richard Haynes; **376-377** Joe McBride/Tony Stone Images; **378** The Smithsonian Institution; **379** RMIP/Richard Haynes; **381** Stephen Dalton/Animals Animals; **382** Johnny Johnson/Animals Animals; **383** RMIP/Richard Haynes; **385** Jean-Francois Causse/Tony Stone Images (r); RMIP/Richard Haynes (l); **386** RMIP/Richard Haynes; **390** UPI/Corbis-Bettmann (t); The Smithsonian Institution (b); **394** Glenn Randall (l); UPI/Corbis-Bettmann (r); **397** Chris Luneski/Image Cascade; **399** RMIP/Richard Haynes (t); School Division, Houghton Mifflin Company (b); **401** UPI/Corbis-Bettmann (r); Bob Harris (l); **407** Peter Essick/Aurora; **408** RMIP/Richard Haynes (l, c); School Division, Houghton Mifflin Company (r); **410** Digging It Up/University of North Florida (r); Culver Pictures (l); **411** RMIP/Richard Haynes; **414** RMIP/Richard Haynes; **418** Courtesy of the Boeing Company; **420** Anson Seale (t); *La Raspa* by Jesse Trevino, Collection of Elaine DeganBela and Richard Bela (b); **422** Brown Brothers; **425** RMIP/Richard Haynes; **427** RMIP/Richard Haynes; **430** Emmanuel Faure/Superstock; **433** RMIP/Richard Haynes; **436** Courtesy of United Parcel Service; **437** Aaron Strong/Liaison; **438** RMIP/Richard Haynes; **447** Courtesy of United Parcel Service; **451** RMIP/Richard Haynes; **454-455** David Young Wolff/Tony Stone Images; **456** Tony Freeman/PhotoEdit (l); Dennis MacDonald/Unicorn Stock Photo (cl); Gayna Hoffmann (cr); Nancy Sheehan/The Picture Cube (r); **459** RMIP/Richard Haynes; **460** RMIP/Richard Haynes; **461** Tony Freeman/PhotoEdit; **466** David Young-Wolff/PhotoEdit; **469** RMIP/Richard Haynes (r); School Division, Houghton Mifflin Company (l); **471** Don Mason/The Stock Market; **472** RMIP/Richard Haynes; **475** RMIP/Richard Haynes; **476** RMIP/Richard Haynes; **480** Wayne Lynch/DRK Photo (tl); Doug Perrine/DRK Photo (bl); **480** Francois Gohier/Photo Researchers (tr); **480** Joe McDonald/ Animals, Animals (br); **482** Robert Brenner/PhotoEdit; **485** Mary Kate Denny/PhotoEdit; **488** RMIP/Richard Haynes; **490** RMIP/Richard Haynes; **491** School Division, Houghton Mifflin Company; **495** RMIP/Richard Haynes; **496** Capece/Monkmeyer; **499** Roy Morsch/The Stock Market; **503** RMIP/Richard Haynes; **507** Corbis-Bettmann **508** RMIP/Richard Haynes; **510** Brooks Dodge/New England Stock Photo (t); Kindra Clineff/The Picture Cube (c); Richard Hutchings/PhotoEdit (b); **515** RMIP/Richard Haynes; **516** RMIP/Richard Haynes; **519** Joseph Schuyler/Stock Boston; **521** Don Tremain; **523** RMIP/Richard Haynes; **526-527** Corbis;
528 Ken Ross/FPG International; **529** *(clockwise)* Mark Segal/Tony Stone Images; Jerry Driendl/FPG International; Vladimir Pcholkin/FPG International; A & L Sinibaldi/Tony Stone Images; Tony Stone Images; Age Fotostock/FPG International; Andre Jenny/Photo 20-20; Wes Thompson/The Stock Market; Chromosohm/Sohm/Photo Researchers, Inc.; Travelpix/FPG International; **530** Joachim Messerschmidt/FPG International (t); Jerry Driendl/FPG International (c); Telegraph Colour Library/FPG International (b); **532** PhotoDisc, Inc.; **535** Lawrence Migdale/Tony Stone Images (t); PhotoEdit (b); **537** Donna Wright; **538** RMIP/Richard Haynes; **540** J. Apicella/CP&A; **541** M. Dwyer/Stock Boston; **542** RMIP/Richard Haynes; **544** Richard Bryant/Arcaid; **545** RMIP/Richard Haynes; **548** Luis Casals/Fotografia; **549** Courtesy of The Pyramids of Moody Gardens (b); School Division, Houghton Mifflin Company (t); **556** School Division, Houghton Mifflin Company; **557** Richard Laird/FPG International; **561** PhotoDisc, Inc.; **563** PhotoDisc, Inc. (background); RMIP/Richard Haynes (b); **564** PhotoDisc, Inc. (t); Ulf Sjostedt/FPG International (r); **568** Richard Bryant/Arcaid; **570** Richard Bryant/Arcaid; **572** "Fish" (woodcut on textile) by M.C. Escher. © 1997 Cordon Art-Baarn-Holland. All rights reserved. (t); RMIP/Richard Haynes (b); **573** Elizabeth Simpson/FPG International (l); Michael Dwyer/Stock Boston (c); JPL/NASA (r); **574** Richard Bryant/Arcaid; **577** PhotoDisc, Inc. (t); Robin L. Sachs (b).

ILLUSTRATIONS
50 George Ford; **82, 84, 86, 88, 92, 99, 114** John Sanderson; **121, 122, 126** Ellen Kuzdro; **138** Dave Ballard; **194, 195, 395** Jeremy Spiegel;
All other illustrations by School Division, Houghton Mifflin Company, or by McDougal Littell Design Group;
Electronic Technical Art Network Graphics.

SELECTED ANSWERS

MODULE 1

Section 1, Practice and Application (p. 8)

1. about \$1300 **3.** about \$4500; I extended the graph. **7.** less than **9.** more than **11.** less than **13.** Japan

17.

Pieces of mail received each day for a month	Tally	Frequency
5	卌 I	6
6	卌 II	7
7	卌	5
8	卌	5
9	III	3
10	I	1

19.

Sizes of sweatshirts for a softball team	Tally	Frequency
small	III	3
medium	卌	5
large	卌 I	6
extra large	I	1

Spiral Review

22. 40 in.^{2} **23.** 54 yd^2 **24.** 20 ft^2 **25.** $\frac{3}{5}$ **26.** $\frac{4}{6}$ or $\frac{2}{3}$ **27.** $\frac{6}{8}$ or $\frac{3}{4}$ **28.** Sample Response:

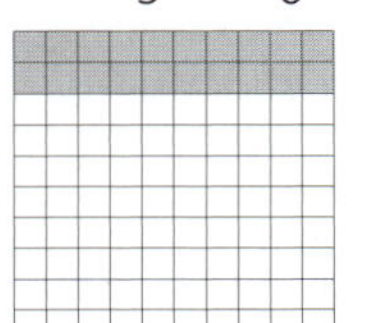

29. Sample Response:

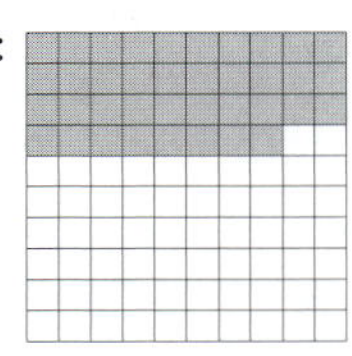

30. Sample Response:

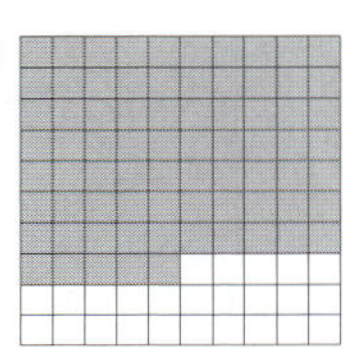

Extra Skill Practice

1. about 2,200,000 **3.** Yes; The graph is of data that changes over time. **5.** less than **7.** more than

9.

Ages of students cleaning up a neighborhood playground	Tally	Frequency
10	II	2
11	III	3
12	卌 I	6
13	III	3
14	卌	5
15	卌	5

Study Skills, Taking Notes

1. a. Sample Response: ideas about the differences between line and bar graphs **b.** Sample Response: Use fewer words and more diagrams.

Section 2, Practice and Application (p. 21)

1. \$1.88 **5.** $t = 6n$ **7.** $t = n + 5$

9.

Term number	1	2	3	4
Term	7	14	21	28

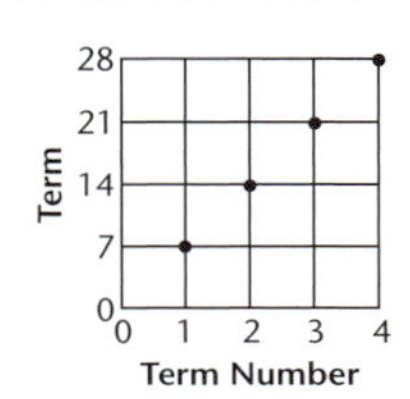

If t = the term and n = the term number, then $t = 7n$; 700

11. a. 1859 **b.** 153 **13.** 3^2 **15.** 25 **17.** 14,641 **19.** 1,000,000 **21.** 1 **23.** 200^3 **25.** 1331 ft^3 **27.** 15,625 in.^{3} **29.** 9

Spiral Review

33. about $\frac{150}{750}$ or $\frac{1}{5}$ **34.** Jordan **35.** Sample Response: $\frac{4}{8}$ **36.** Sample Response: $\frac{60}{75}$ **37.** Sample Response: $\frac{30}{70}$

Career Connection

39. after 22 m^3

Extra Skill Practice

1. $t = 8n$ **3.** $t = n - 5$

5.

Term number	1	2	3	4
Term	4	8	12	16

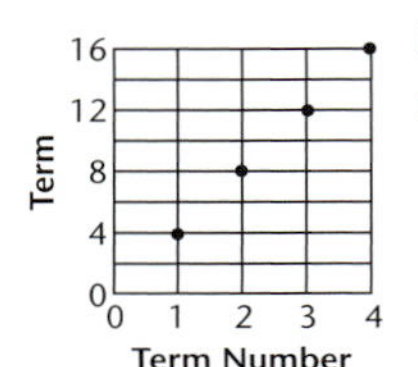

If t = the term and n = the term number, then $t = 4n$; 400

7.

Term number	1	2	3	4
Term	12	13	14	15

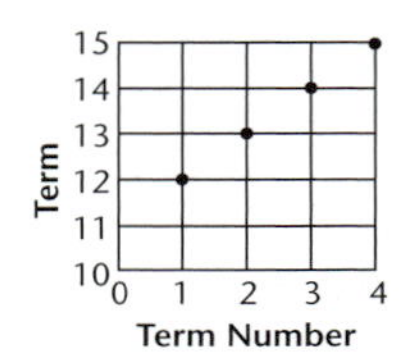

If t = the term and n = the term number, then $t = n + 11$; 111

9.

Term number	1	2	3	4
Term	$\frac{1}{2}$	1	$\frac{3}{2}$	2

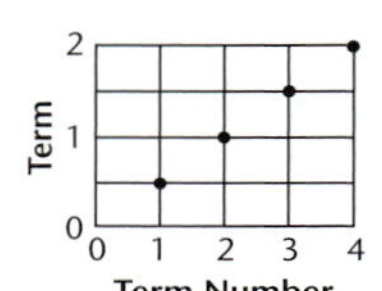

If t = the term and n = the term number, then $t = \frac{1}{2}n$; 50

11. 5^2 **13.** 3^6 **15.** $3 \cdot 7^2$ **17.** 81 **19.** 32 **21.** 10,000 **23.** 0 **25.** 8 in.^{3} **27.** 3375 m^3 **29.** 1728 in.^{3} **31.** 140,608 cm^3

Standardized Testing, Open-ended

1. Sample Response: 1, 4, 9, 16,...
2. Sample Response: $t = n^2$

Section 3, Practice and Application (p. 34)

1–3. Answers will vary from 0 to 1. **5. a.** $\frac{10}{26}$ or $\frac{5}{13}$ **b.** Sample Response: The spinner stops on a number less than 9; The spinner stops on a number greater than 10.
7. Sample Response: 6 and 3, 5 and 2, 4 and 1
9. Sample Response: 5 and 1, 4 and 2, 3 and 3
11. Sample Response: 6 and 1, 6 and 2, 6 and 3
13. a. $\frac{1}{2}, \frac{1}{2}$ **b.** They are about the same. **15.** 7, 8, 9, 10, 12; 6, 7, 8, 9, 10, 11; 6, 7, 8, 9, 10; 4, 5, 6, 7, 8, 9; 3, 4, 5, 6, 7, 8; 2, 3, 4, 5, 6, 7 **17.** $\frac{5}{36}$ **19.** $\frac{5}{36}$ **21.** $\frac{6}{36}$ or $\frac{1}{6}$ **23.** $\frac{18}{36}$ or $\frac{1}{2}$ **25. a.** 2, 4, 6, 8, 10, 12, 14, 16, 18, 20, 22, 24; 1, 3, 5, 7, 9, 11, 13, 15, 17, 19, 21, 23 **b.** $\frac{1}{2}$
27. a. green, blue **b.** No; Blue covers a larger area. **c.** $\frac{1}{4}, \frac{3}{4}$; The area covered by blue is 3 times that covered by green.

Spiral Review

31.

Term number	1	2	3	4
Term	10	20	30	40

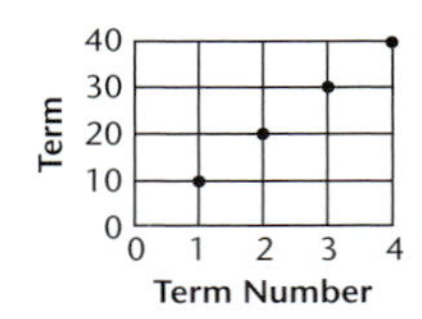

If t = the term and n = the term number, then $t = 10n$; 1000

32.

Term number	1	2	3	4
Term	16	17	18	19

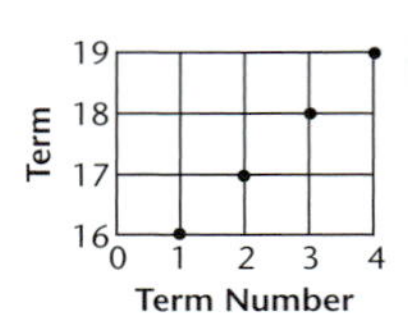

If t = the term and n = the term number, then $t = n + 15$; 115

33. 37.63 **34.** 14.55 **35.** 5.017 **36.** 25 min

Extension

37. a. $P(\text{red}) = \frac{3}{6} = \frac{1}{2}$, $P(\text{green}) = \frac{2}{6} = \frac{1}{3}$, $P(\text{yellow}) = \frac{1}{6}$ **b.** 1 **c.** 4; Since 5 out of 10 cubes would be yellow, $P(\text{yellow}) = \frac{5}{10} = \frac{1}{2}$.

Extra Skill Practice

1. $\frac{40}{100} = \frac{2}{5}$ **3.** $\frac{28}{100} = \frac{7}{25}$ **5.** $\frac{60}{100} = \frac{3}{5}$ **7.** $\frac{88}{100} = \frac{22}{25}$ **9.** $\frac{80}{100} = \frac{4}{5}$ **11.** $\frac{2}{8} = \frac{1}{4}$ **13.** $\frac{2}{8} = \frac{1}{4}$ **15.** $\frac{4}{8} = \frac{1}{2}$ **17.** $\frac{0}{8} = 0$
19. 125; Sample Response: theoretical; Experimental probability can vary greatly for a small number of trials. As the number of trials increases, the experimental probabilities should begin to approach the theoretical probabilities. So when they can be calculated, it is better to use theoretical probabilities to make predictions.

Standardized Testing, Performance Task

1. $\frac{1}{8}$; One quarter out of 8 is dated 1975. **2.** $\frac{3}{7}$; There are 7 quarters left and 3 are dated 1985. **3.** 1; All the coins in the bank are quarters.

Section 4, Practice and Application (p. 45)

1. a. 12 min **b.** 240 min **c.** 561,600 min **d.** No; It takes almost 6 times as long to burn 2000 Cal jogging as it does stair-stepping. **3.** 3 dogs **5.** No; She would have to get a 120 on the next quiz.

Spiral Review

8. a. R, B, W **b.** $P(R) = \frac{3}{6}$ or $\frac{1}{2}$, $P(B) = \frac{2}{6}$ or $\frac{1}{3}$, $P(W) = \frac{1}{6}$ **c.** about 15 **9.** about 5 **10.** about 2 **11.** about 4

Extra Skill Practice

1. 5 h **3.** 36

Standardized Testing, Free Response

48 different orders

Section 5, Practice and Application (p. 56)

1. B, Sample Response:

Spiral Review

8. Eliminate 5, 19, and 47 because the sum of 6 odd integers is an even integer. Eliminate 56 because the highest possible score is 54 (9 • 6). A score of 32 is possible because 5 • 5 + 7 = 32. **9.** 540 **10.** 144 **11.** 3 **12.** 20 **13.** 80 **14.** 1 **15.** about 4800; 240 • 20 = 4800 **16.** about 30; 2700 ÷ 90 = 30 **17.** about 1070; 240 + 480 + 350 = 1090 **18.** about 1500; 1900 – 400 = 1500 **19.** about 6000; 50 • 120 = 6000 **20.** about 300; 100 + 90 + 110 = 300

Extra Skill Practice

1. a. 4 pennies, 4 dimes, and 3 quarters or 4 pennies, 9 dimes, and 1 quarter **b.** If there were one more of any of the coins, the change could be made. If, for example, there were 5 pennies, 4 dimes, and 3 quarters, the change would be 5 pennies, 3 quarters, and 2 dimes. If there were 4 pennies, 5 dimes, and 3 quarters, the change would be 5 dimes and 2 quarters. **2. a.** 37 **3. a.** Yes; If the average movie is 2.5 h long, this is about 436 movies or about 7 per year from age 12 on.

Standardized Testing, Free Response

a. Make an organized list of the 8 possible combinations and find the cost of each. Then use estimation or mental math to find the combination that would feed a whole number of friends at a total cost that comes closest to $12 without going over. Deluxe sandwich, apple, and water costs $3, so he can feed 4 people for exactly $12. **b.** Yes; Look at the table to see whether any meal costs exactly $3 or $4. **c.** Yes; Take the price of the combination he chooses and multiply by 4 or 5.

Section 6, Practice and Application (p. 66)

1. 6 **3.** 64 **5.** 81 **7.** 3 **9.** 2.25 **11.** (28 – 9) • 2 = 38 **13.** (6 + 6) ÷ 2 • (6 – 1) = 30 **17. a.** Draw a square. **b.** Both sets of instructions are correct. One is appropriate for someone who doesn't know what a square is and the other is not. **19.** 4000 **21.** Sample Response: There was a sharp increase in the number of Hispanic public officials between 1991 and 1992. Overall, the number of Hispanic public officials has increased over the years 1985–1994. **23.** Sample Response: 3; The first diagram would be clearer if brackets were used to show the top row is composed of 3 squares plus 4 squares.

Spiral Review

27. $\frac{20}{60}$ or $\frac{1}{3}$ **28.** $\frac{33}{60}$ or $\frac{11}{20}$ **29.** $\frac{7}{60}$ **30.** 2 red, 3 white, 1 blue; Using the experimental probabilities, 1 out of 3 or 2 out of 6 faces are red, about 1 out of 2 or 3 out of 6 are white, and the remaining face is blue.

Extra Skill Practice

1. 12 **3.** 12 **5.** 22 **7.** 2 **9.** 2 **11.** 38 **13.** (3 + 12) • 6 = 90 **15.** $(3^2 + 5^2) \div 2 = 17$

Standardized Testing, Multiple Choice

1. B **2.** B

Review and Assessment

1. $15 **2.** March 1 and June 1 **3.** March and April **4.** May **5.** about $47.50; The value of the stock is increasing at a rate of about $2.50/month.

6.

Amount of Money Withdrawn	Tally	Frequency
$10	I	1
$20	II	2
$30	III	3
$40	I	1
$50	II	2
$100	I	1

7. a. The number corresponds to the number of small triangles in the shape.

b.

Term number	1	2	3	4
Term	1	4	9	16

c.

Term number	1	2	3	4
Term	1	4	9	16
Exponential form of term	1^2	2^2	3^2	4^2

;

Each term is the term number squared. If t = the term and n = the term number, then $t = n^2$. **d.** 25, 5^2, 25 **e.** 2500

8.

Term number	1	2	3	4
Term	6	12	18	24

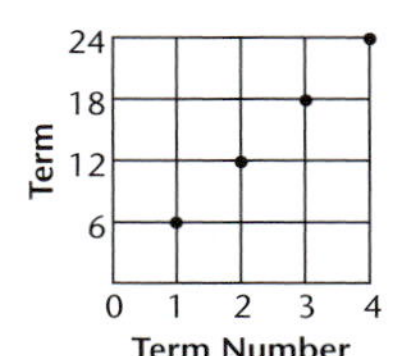

If t = the term and n = the term number, then $t = 6n$; 600

9. 729 cm^3 **10.** $P(\text{red}) = \frac{14}{50}$ or $\frac{7}{25}$, $P(\text{blue}) = \frac{10}{50}$ or $\frac{1}{5}$, $P(\text{green}) = \frac{26}{50}$ or $\frac{13}{25}$ **11.** red, blue, green **12.** $P(\text{red}) = \frac{1}{4}$, $P(\text{blue}) = \frac{1}{4}$, $P(\text{green}) = \frac{1}{2}$ **13.** about 15 **14.** 26; There are 16 triangles which are 1 triangle high, 6 which are 2 triangles high, 3 which are 3 triangles high, and 1 which is 4 triangles high. **16.** 0 **17.** 162 **18.** 6 **19.** 10

MODULE 2

Section 1, Practice and Application (p. 84)

1. $\overrightarrow{CH}$ **3.** $\angle BCH$, $\angle HCG$, $\angle HCF$ **5.** Possible answers: $\angle BCH$, 40°; $\angle GCF$, 45° **7.** 90° right angle **9.** 138° obtuse angle

11. 53° acute angle **13.** 100° obtuse angle **15.** About 135° **19.** $\angle CBK$ and $\angle KBH$; $\angle GBF$ and $\angle FBD$ **21. a.** 165° **b.** 75°

23. a. 135° **b.** 45° **25. a.** 93° **b.** 3° **27. a.** 85° **b.** not possible

Spiral Review

31. 44 **32.** 15 **33.** 22 **34.**
35. 14 ft **36.** 46 in.

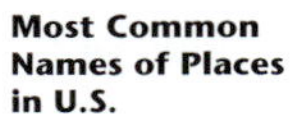

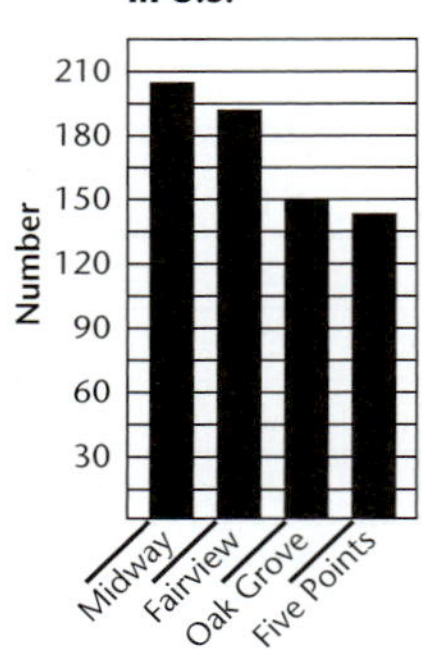

Extra Skill Practice

1. Sample Response: $\overrightarrow{TW}$, $\overrightarrow{VW}$ **3.** $\angle VTQ$, $\angle STQ$
5. 180° straight angle **7.** 65° acute angle **9.** $\angle WTP$, $\angle PTS$

11. a. 17° **b.** not possible **13. a.** 124° **b.** 34°

Section 2, Practice and Application (p. 95)

1. $25 **3.** –5 points **7.** > **9.** < **11.** > **13.** Sample Response: 60°F or 16°C **15.** –40°F **17.** 0°C **19.** 5°C **21.** 0, –2, –4 **23.** –50, 0, 50 **25.** –6 **27.** 9 **29.** 24 **31.** 0 **33.** –4 **35.** 100 **37.** 8 **39.** 0 **41.** 62 **43.** 514 **45.** > **47.** > **49.** > **51.** Sample Response: Calle 13 and Calle 14 **53.** Sample Response: Calle Rufino Barrios and Calle 15 **55. a.** $V(-2, 4)$, $W(1, 3)$, $X(4, 0)$, $Y(2, -2)$, $Z(-3, -4)$ **b.** V and Y, V and Z

Spiral Review

60. 47° **61.** 8° **62.** 64°

63.

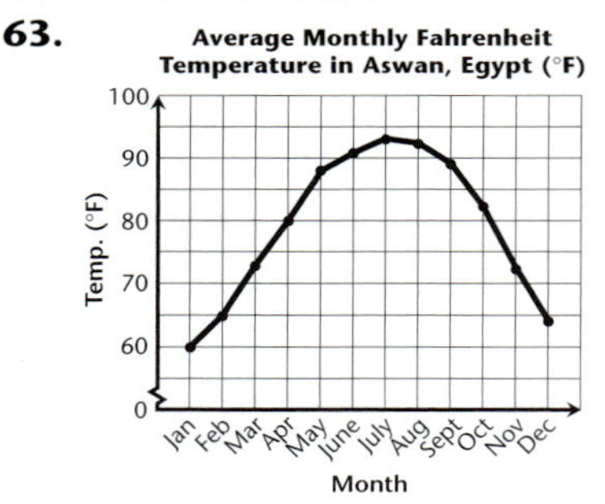

64. $\frac{3}{5}$ **65.** $\frac{3}{4}$ **66.** $\frac{5}{9}$ **67.** $\frac{1}{6}$

Extra Skill Practice

1. –85 ft **3.** < **5.** > **7.** < **9.** < **11.** < **13.** > **15.** –8, 8 **17.** 16, 16 **19.** 2001, 2001 **21.** 93, 93 **23.** 72, 72 **25.** d, a **27.** a and b intersect at (–4, 1), b and c at (4, 3), c and a at (–1, –2), and d and a at (1, –4).

Standardized Testing, Open-ended

1. Sample Response: A man weighed 160 lb. He lost 5 lb and then gained 18 lb. How much did he then weigh? **2.** Sample Response: At the beginning of 1989, the population of a town was 5557. During the year, 206 people moved out of the town and 157 people moved in. What was the population of the town at the end of 1989? **3.** People would probably be wearing shorts or other summer clothing. They might be swimming or just sitting outside to stay cool. **4.** People would be wearing winter coats or jackets. They might be skiing or making a snowman. **5.** People would be wearing layers and layers of clothing trying to stay warm. The only people who would be involved in outdoor activities would be those who had to work outdoors (like a police officer directing traffic).

Section 3, Practice and Application (p. 110)

1. –6; –4 + (–2) = –6 **3.** –8; 0 – 8 = –8 **5. a.** –1 **b.** Start at 2. Face the positive direction. Move backward 3 units. **c.** Sample Response: Start at 2. Face the positive direction. Move forward 0 units. **7.** –17 **9.** –21 **11.** –11 **13.** –9 **15.** 300 **17.** Mike; Danessa's score is 0, Jonah's is –900, and Mike's is 100. **19.** –30,000 + 43,000 = 13,000; $13,000 gain **21.** –15 **23.** 8 **25.** –10 + 2 **27.** 9 + 17 **29.** About –17°F **31.** –17 **33.** 6 **35.** 19 **37.** 1493 ft **39.** 25 **41.** 11 **43.** 13 **45.** No.

Spiral Review

48. (coordinate grid with points A, B, C, D; axes x, y; O; 2)

49. 3.34
50. 67.46
51. 6.57
52. 15, 11, 7
53. 81, 100, 121

Extension

55. –2, –1, 0, 1, 2, 3, 4, 5

Extra Skill Practice

1. –2 + 5 = 3 **3.** –1 – 3 = –4 **5.** –9 **7.** –3 **9.** 5 **11.** –100 **13.** –10 **15.** 0 **17.** 40 **19.** 0 **21.** –20 **23.** 6 **25.** 21 **27.** 16 **29.** –10 **31.** –30 **33.** 6 **35.** –9

Standardized Testing, Multiple Choice

1. B **2.** C

Section 4, Practice and Application (p. 125)

1. C **3.** $p + 3$ **5.** 120 **7.** 24 **9.** 21 **11.** 7 **13.** –12 **15.** 8 **17.** –4 **19.** 36 **21.** 12 **23.** 24

25. a.

Travel time (hours)	Distance covered by Covered Wagon (miles)	Distance covered by Stage Coach (miles)
0	0	0
1	2	5
2	4	10
3	6	15
4	8	20
5	10	25
6	12	30

Travel time (hours)	Distance covered by Pony Express (miles)	Distance covered by Railroad (miles)
0	0	0
1	10	22
2	20	44
3	30	66
4	40	88
5	50	110
6	60	132

b. Possible answers: for the covered wagon, $d = 2t$; for the stage coach, $d = 5t$; for the pony express, $d = 10t$; for the railroad, $d = 22t$

c–d. Possible answers:

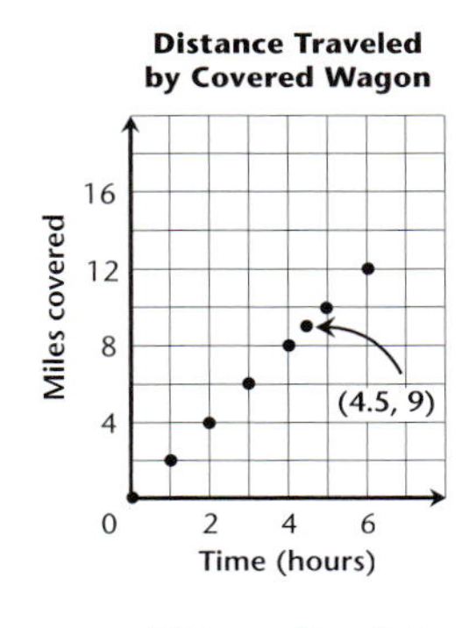

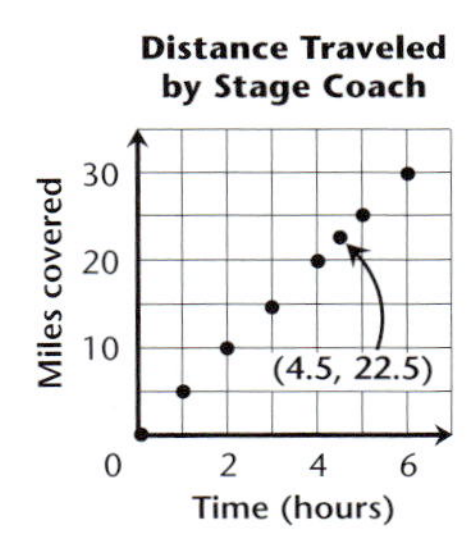

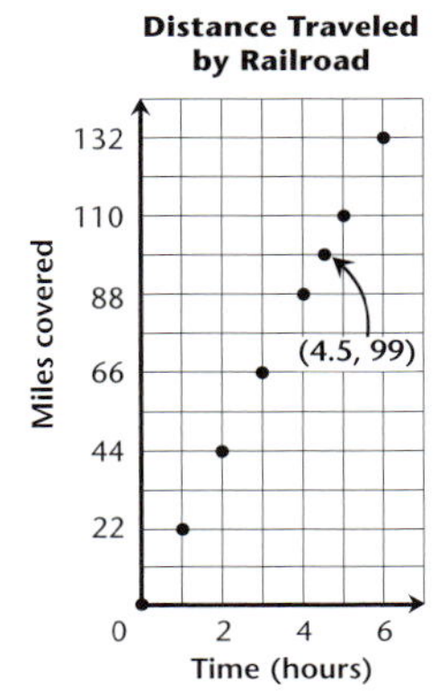

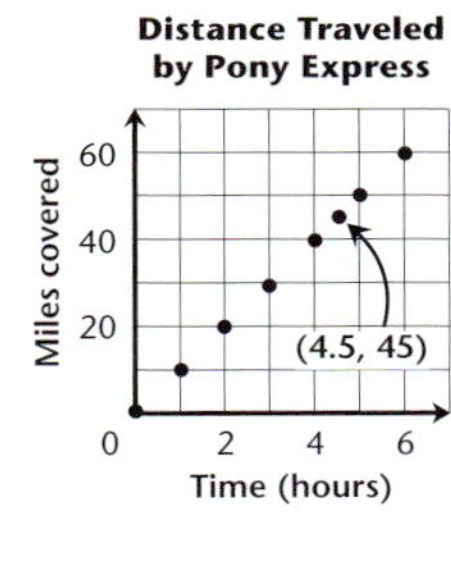

27.

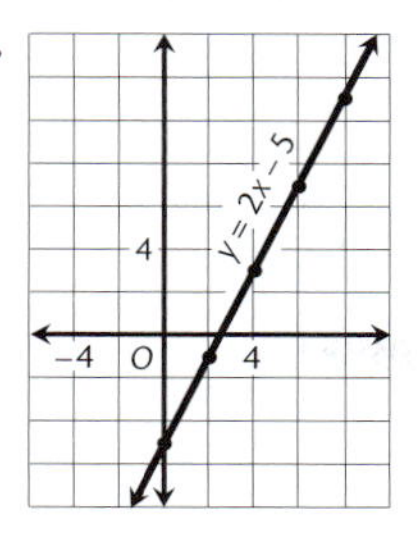

x	−10	−5	0	5	10
y	−25	−15	−5	5	15

29.

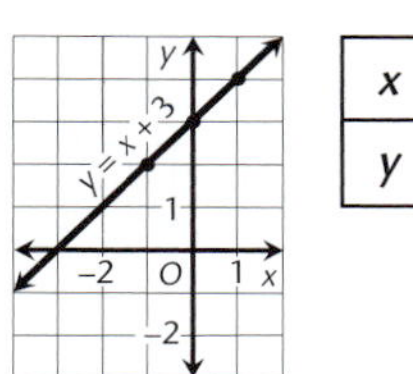

x	−1	0	1
y	2	3	4

31.

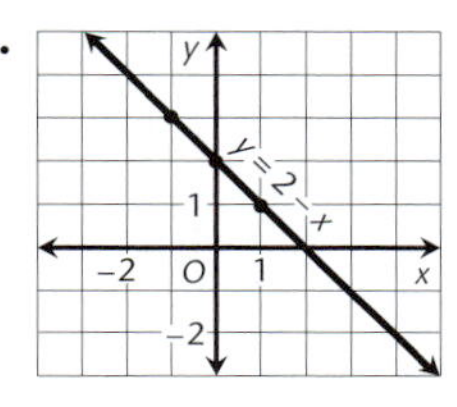

x	−1	0	1
y	3	2	1

35. a. Bowling Alley A: $y = 17x + 4$; Bowling Alley B: $y = 18.50x + 2$

b.

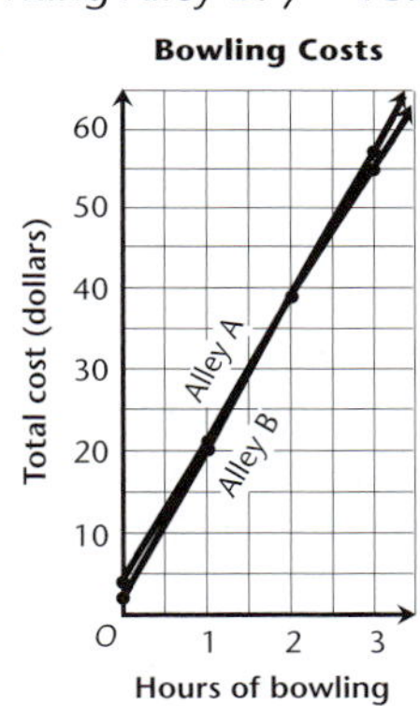

c. when the bowling time is more than 1 h 20 min

d. when the bowling time is 1 h 20 min

Spiral Review

37. −60 **38.** 7 **39.** −17 **40.** $\frac{1}{8}$ **41.** 0 **42.** $\frac{4}{8}$ or $\frac{1}{2}$

43.

Place in sequence p	1	2	3	4
Value v	6	7	8	9

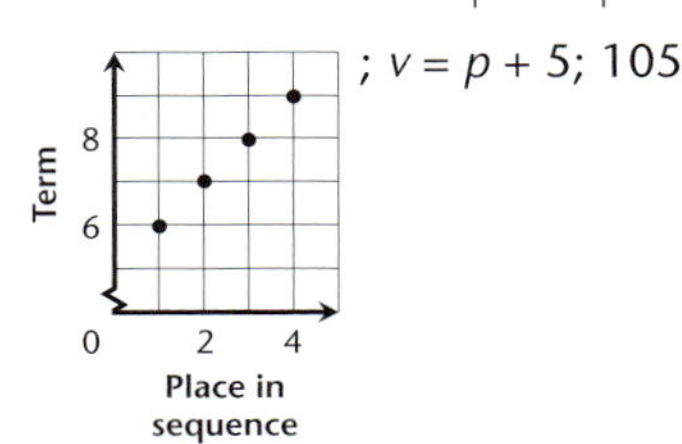

; $v = p + 5$; 105

Extra Skill Practice

1. $n + 5$ (cm) **3.** 50 **5.** 0 **7.** 2 **9.** 36 **11.** 13 **13.** –11

15. Sample Response:

Nearby house number x	4	6	10
House number y	2	4	8

$y = x - 2$

17. Sample Response:

Number x	1	2	3
Number y	8	10	12

$y = 2x + 6$

19.

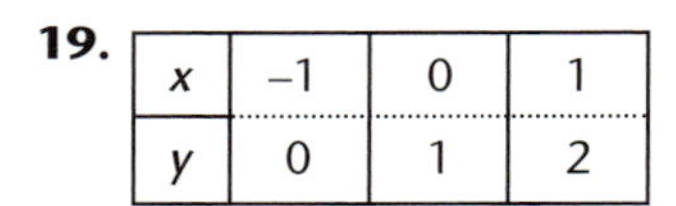

x	–1	0	1
y	0	1	2

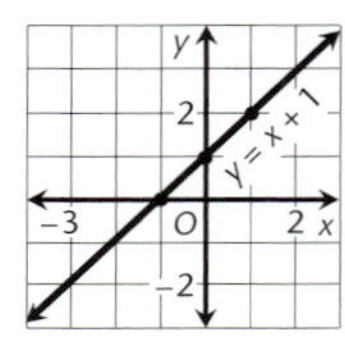

21.

x	–1	0	1
y	3	4	5

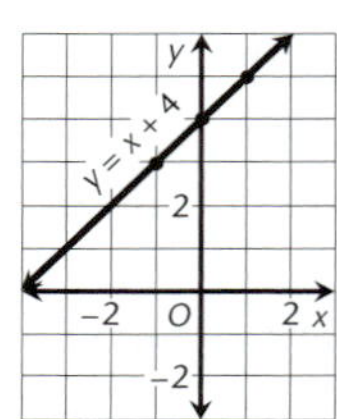

Standardized Testing, Free Response

Sample Response: Because the road from Praitis to Mt. Boris was undergoing construction, the Kartanels had to travel slowly, at an average rate of 50 km/h. The ascent up Mt. Boris, which took them about half an hour, slowed them up even more. Their progress was further delayed when, between 1:30 P.M. and 2:00 P.M., they decided to have lunch at a restaurant they had passed about 10 km back. After lunch, they cautiously descended Mt. Boris on a narrow, twisting road at an average rate of 50 km/h. Once they hit the Flat Lands, they picked up speed and were able to cover the last 125 km of their journey in about 1 h.

Section 5, Practice and Application (p. 138)

1. $x + 4 = 8$ **5.** $x = 2$ **7.** $x = 8$ **9.** $y + 1973 = 1979$ **11. a.** $x + 150 = 180$ **b.** $180 - x = 150$ **13.** Let n represent the number of people in the dash who did not set a personal best. So, $n + 5 = 12$. **15.** Let n represent the number of prints Anna originally had. So, $n - 70 = 8$. **17.** Let p represent the number of original subscribers. So, $p - 4 = 28$. **19.** 102 **21.** 72 **23.** 23 **25.** 40 **27.** 82 **29.** 0 **33.** Let d represent Darius's deposit. So, $1271.63 + d = 1453.95$; \$182.32. **37–43.** Sample methods are given. **37.** mental math; 15 **39.** mental math; –10 **41.** mental math; 20.1 **43.** mental math; 5 **45. a.** $a + 37 = 90$ **b.** 53

Spiral Review

47. 1 **48.** –9 **49.** –59 **50.** 23 **51.** –26 **52.** –48 **53.** 12 h; Strategies will vary. **54.** 75 is divisible by 5. **55.** 215 is divisible by 5. **56.** 253 is not divisible by 2, 5, or 10. **57.** 630 is divisible by 2, 5, and 10.

Extension

59. Remove one rectangular tile from each side of the equation and then remove two square tiles from each side. (The two steps can be reversed.) **61.** Remove three square tiles from each side of the equation and then remove one rectangular tile from each side. (The two steps can be reversed.) **63. a.** No; adding 35 to a number will never give the same result as adding 13 to the same number. **b.** Yes; any number increased by 4 is the same as 4 increased by the number. Every number is a solution.

Extra Skill Practice

1. $x + 5 = 6$ **3.** $6 = 1 + m$ **5.** Sample Response: Let b represent the number of apples Jill's brother picked. So, the equations are $53 + b = 85$ and $85 - b = 53$. **7.** Sample Response: Let s represent the number of points Jenn has before she takes her last turn. So, the equations are $8 + s = 121$ and $121 - s = 8$. **9.** 50 **11.** –43 **13.** 56 **15.** –55 **17.** 72 **19.** 0 **21.** –5 **23.** 18

Standardized Testing, Performance Task

Sample Response: I don't agree with Sue. Heidi's goals to shots ratio was $\frac{3}{15}$, or $\frac{1}{5}$, Jen's was $\frac{4}{12}$, or $\frac{1}{3}$, and Sheila's was $\frac{3}{9}$, or $\frac{1}{3}$. Sue's reasoning seems to be that the person who had the highest goals to shots ratio during practice will be the person most likely to score during the game. Since Sheila and Jen had the same ratio, they are equally likely to be that person.

Review and Assessment

1. Possible answers: $\angle FCB$, $\angle BCE$, $\angle ACD$
2. Possible answers: $\angle ACB$, $\angle DCF$, $\angle DCE$
3. $\angle ACE$, $\angle DCB$ **4. a.** 45° **b.** $\angle BCF$ or $\angle ACD$, 45°; $\angle ACB$ or $\angle DCE$, 135° **5.** If 0 represents ground level, then negative integers represent meters below ground level, and positive integers represent meters above ground level. So, the stadium was built at –50 m.
6. –10, –5, –2, 0, 6, 8, 14 **7.** –5; 5 **8.** 1; 1 **9.** –72; 72 **10.** 303; 303 **11. a.** If a line were drawn through the jumper's upper body and another through the skis, the lines would not intersect. **b.** The skier would be standing up straight. **12–15.**

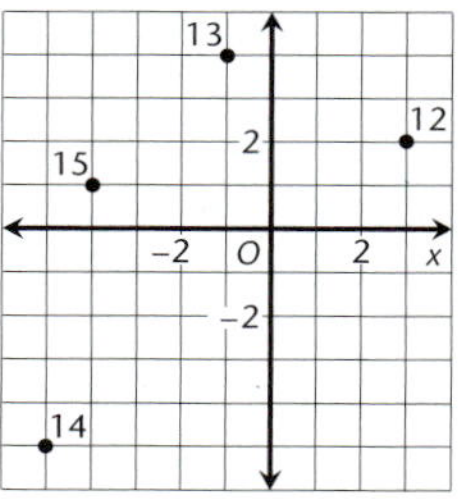

16. –4 **17.** –12
18. –4 **19.** –11
20. –3 **21.** 7
22. 3 **23.** –19
24. 30 **25.** 9
26. 3 **27.** –17
28. 15 **29.** 14

30. a.

Time (seconds)	Distance traveled (feet)	
	Recreational skier	Speed skier
10	220	2040
20	440	4080
30	660	6120
40	880	8160

b. Recreational skier, $d = 22t$; Speed skier, $d = 204t$.

c.

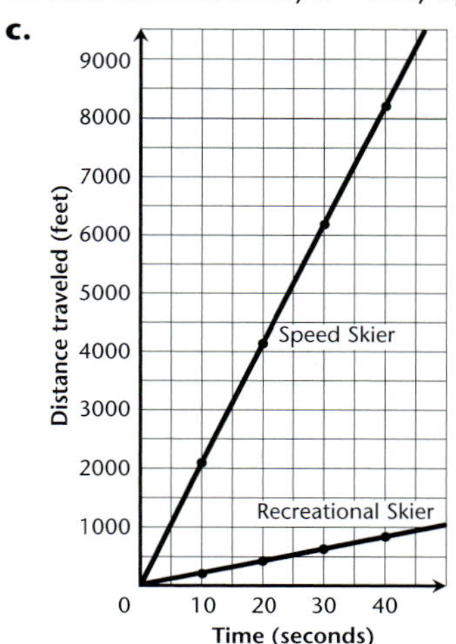

d. the speed skier; about 8000 ft **31.** Let b represent the original number of baseball cards. So, $b + 45 = 315$. **32.** 51 **33.** –8 **34.** –5 **35.** 6 **36.** –7 **37.** 21

MODULE 3

Section 1, Practice and Application (p. 157)

1. 1, 2, 3, 4, 6, 12 **3.** 1, 3, 5, 9, 15, 45 **5.** 1, 2, 4, 8, 16, 32, 64 **7.** 1, 2, 4, 5, 10, 20, 25, 50, 100 **9.** 1, 11, 121 **11.** 1, 2, 3, 5, 6, 10, 15, 25, 30, 50, 75, 150 **13.** Sample Response: 36, 49, 64, 81, 100; Perfect squares have an odd number of factors. **15.** composite **17.** prime **19.** prime **21.** prime **23.** 2 • 2 • 7 **25.** 2 • 2 • 3 • 3 **27.** 2 • 5 • 5 **29.** 2 • 5 • 17 **33. a.** 30 m^2, 26 m **b.** 5 m by 6 m **c.** 2 m by 15 m, or 1 m by 30 m **35.** none **37.** 2, 4 **39.** 2, 3, 4, 5, 6, 10 **41.** 2, 3, 4, 5, 6, 10. **43.** If the number formed by the last 3 digits of the number is divisible by 8, the entire number is divisible by 8. Example: 9416 ÷ 8 = 1177 **45.** 3 **47.** 15 **49.** 1 **51.** 15 **53.** 13 **57.** 12 **59.** 40 **61.** 100 **63.** 36 **65.** Since the numbers listed are all multiples of 63, start with the lowest number and see if it is divisible by both 14 and 36. If it is, that is the LCM. If it isn't, repeat the process with the next larger number in the list. Continue until the LCM (252) is found. **67. a.** No; If x is any common multiple of a set of numbers, then 2 • x is also a common multiple, and it is greater than x. So there is always a greater common multiple. **b.** Yes; Every whole number is divisible by 1, and 1 is the smallest whole number that can be a divisor, so 1 is the least common divisor of any set of whole numbers.

Spiral Review

69. 52 **70.** 851 **71.** –55 **72.** 90°, right **73.** 30°, acute **74.** 120°, obtuse **75.** $\frac{3}{5}$ **76.** $\frac{2}{8}$ **77.** $\frac{3}{23}$ **78.** $\frac{20}{35}$

Extra Skill Practice

1. 1, 2, 3, 6, 9, 18 **3.** 1, 3, 17, 51 **5.** 1, 2, 3, 4, 6, 8, 9, 12, 18, 24, 36, 72 **7.** 1, 2, 3, 4, 6, 7, 12, 14, 21, 28, 42, 84 **9.** 1, 2, 3, 4, 6, 9, 12, 18, 27, 36, 54, 108 **11.** 1, 7, 13, 91 **13.** 2 • 2 • 2 • 3 **15.** 3 • 3 • 3 • 3 **17.** 2 • 3 • 3 • 5 **19.** 2 • 2 • 2 • 3 • 5 **21.** 2 • 3 • 3 • 3 **23.** 2 • 2 • 2 • 2 • 3 **25.** 2, 3, 6 **27.** 3 **29.** 2, 4 **31.** 2, 3, 4, 5, 6, 9, 10 **33.** 9 **35.** 5 **37.** 16 **39.** 7 **41.** 18 **43.** 45 **45.** 40 **47.** 60

Section 2, Practice and Application (p. 171)

1. $\frac{1}{5}$ **3.** $\frac{3}{4}$ **5.** $\frac{3}{7}$ **7.** $\frac{5}{13}$ **11.** $\frac{1}{4}$ **13. a.** Since $\frac{1}{14}$ of something is larger than $\frac{1}{16}$ of the same thing, $\frac{3}{14} > \frac{3}{16}$. **b.** The fraction with the smaller denominator is greater. **c.** Sample Response: $\frac{5}{21}$ **15. a.** greater than, less than, greater than **b.** Sample Response: Divide the denominator of the fraction by 2. If the numerator is less than the quotient, the fraction is less than $\frac{1}{2}$. If the numerator is more than the quotient, the fraction is more than $\frac{1}{2}$. **17.** $\frac{1}{2}$ **19.** $\frac{1}{2}$ **21–27.** Sample methods are given. **21.** mental math; > **23.** mental math; = **25.** estimation or paper and pencil; > **27.** mental math; <

29.

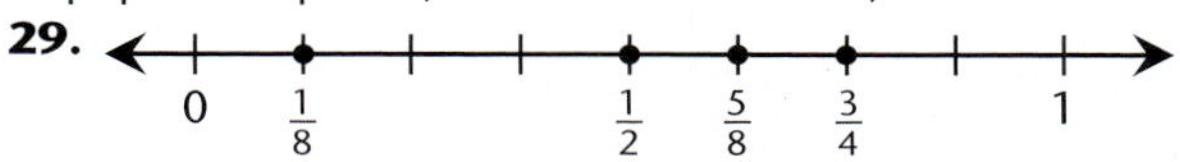

31. $\frac{11}{24}$ **33.** $\frac{1}{20}$ **35.** $\frac{7}{9}$ **37.** $\frac{1}{36}$ **39.** 2 **43.** Yes; $\frac{3}{4} + \frac{1}{20} + \frac{1}{5} = \frac{20}{20}$ **45. a.** The tree diagram shown uses an egg as the fourth item.

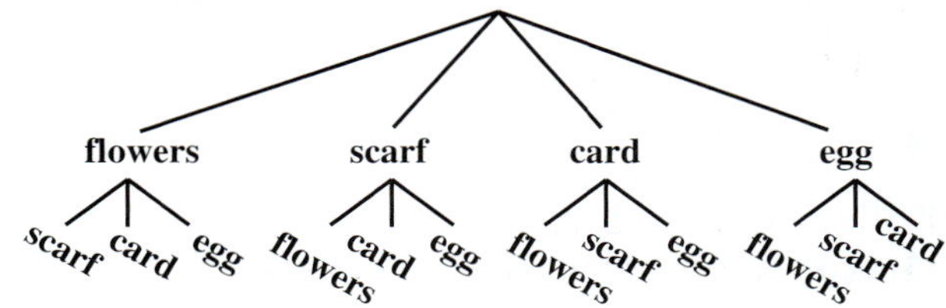

There are 12 possible outcomes. **b.** Sample Response: P(flowers, scarf) = $\frac{1}{12}$. P(flowers, not scarf) = $\frac{2}{12}$ or $\frac{1}{6}$. **47. a.** $\frac{1}{12}$ **b.** $\frac{1}{12}$ **c.** $\frac{1}{6}$

Spiral Review

49. 2 **50.** 18 **51.** 1 **52.** 100 **53.** 32 **54.** 1 **55.** $12\frac{2}{3}$ **56.** $10\frac{4}{7}$ **57.** $3\frac{3}{5}$

Extra Skill Practice

1. $\frac{3}{4}$ **3.** $\frac{2}{3}$ **5.** $\frac{1}{9}$ **7.** $\frac{15}{31}$ **9.** $\frac{9}{13}$ **11.** > **13.** > **15.** < **17.** >

19. $\frac{15}{16}$ **21.** $\frac{5}{18}$ **23.** $\frac{2}{3}$ **25.** $\frac{23}{30}$ **27. a.** No; Each number represents a position on the relay team and is to be used only once. **b.**

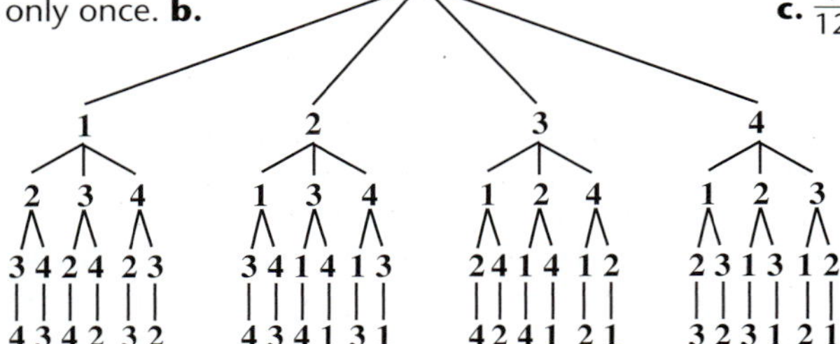

c. $\frac{1}{12}$

Standardized Testing, Performance Task

1. the yellow cake; the pineapple cake; Sample Response: I wrote each fraction as a decimal and compared the decimals. **2.** The first row represents the choices for server 1, the second row represents the choices for server 2, and so on, for the four servers. Let Y = yellow cake, C = chocolate cake, S = strawberry cake, and P = pineapple cake.

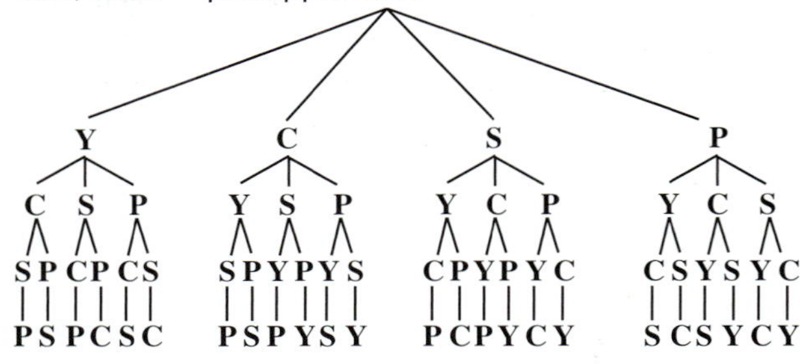

Sample Response: There would be more choices for each server to choose from, so the number of possible ways that they could share the cake would increase.

Section 3, Practice and Application (p. 184)

1. $4\frac{3}{5}$ **3.** $4\frac{1}{5}$ **5.** The fraction is not between 0 and 1; $2\frac{2}{3}$ **7.** The remainder was ignored; $15\frac{1}{2}$ **9.** $\frac{9}{8}$ **11.** $\frac{40}{9}$ **13.** $\frac{47}{5}$ **15.** $\frac{29}{2}$ **17.** $5\frac{1}{2}$ **19.** $\frac{27}{200}$ **21–25.** Sample methods are given. **21.** mental math; > **23.** mental math; < **25.** paper and pencil; < **27.** $2\frac{3}{4}$ **29.** $1\frac{5}{8}$ **31.** $10\frac{2}{3}$ **33.** $3\frac{1}{12}$ **35.** $23\frac{1}{22}$ **37.** $8 = x + 5\frac{1}{3}$; $2\frac{2}{3}$ **39.** $18\frac{1}{2} = x + 15\frac{1}{2}$; 3 **41. a.** $11\frac{9}{16}$ in. **b.** $2\frac{1}{16}$ in. **c.** so you know exactly how much wood is left

Spiral Review

44. $\frac{11}{12}$ **45.** $\frac{7}{18}$ **46.** $\frac{2}{3}$ **47.** $1\frac{7}{36}$ **48.** 2.055 **49.** 0.65 **50.** 2.9122 **51.** 90°; 45°

Extra Skill Practice

1. $1\frac{3}{5}$ **3.** $1\frac{3}{4}$ **5.** $7\frac{2}{3}$ **7.** $13\frac{1}{5}$ **9.** $4\frac{2}{7}$ **11.** $10\frac{1}{5}$ **13.** $\frac{14}{5}$ **15.** $\frac{66}{7}$ **17.** $\frac{33}{4}$ **19.** $\frac{121}{6}$ **21.** $\frac{154}{5}$ **23.** $\frac{193}{3}$ **25.** $4\frac{1}{12}$ **27.** $\frac{1}{4}$ **29.** $1\frac{8}{9}$ **31.** $11\frac{1}{5}$ **33.** $\frac{29}{35}$ **35.** $23\frac{1}{24}$

Standardized Testing, Multiple Choice

1. D **2.** A, D

Section 4, Practice and Application (p. 199)

1. two thousand five hundred twenty-three and twelve hundredths **3.** forty-three and sixty-five thousandths **5.** $\frac{98}{100}$ or $\frac{49}{50}$ **7.** $\frac{208}{1000}$ or $\frac{26}{125}$ **9.** $1\frac{19}{10,000}$ **11.** $10\frac{85421}{1,000,000}$ **13.** easier to read; 6,400,000; 13,200,000 **15.** < **17.** > **19.** < **21.** C **23.** F **25.** H **27.** G **29.** tenths, hundredths, thousandths **31.** 100 **33.** 10 **35.** 0.1 **37.** 0.0001 **39.** $\frac{1}{16}$ **41.** $\frac{1}{216}$ **43.** $\frac{1}{625}$ **45.** $\frac{1}{144}$ **47.** 10^6 **49.** 10^1 **51.** 10^{-6} **53.** 10^{-8} cm **55.** 1,000,000,000,000,000,000,000 **57.** 0.01225 **59.** 130,240 **61.** 0.0000139 **63.** 0.0436 **65.** 5.437 **67.** 0.01205 **69.** $1.20684 \cdot 10^5$ **71.** $2.290098 \cdot 10^2$ **73.** $7.5 \cdot 10^{-5}$ **75.** 0.54 **77.** 2,000,000,000,000,000; 10,800,000,000,000,000; 19,100,000,000,000,000; 5,680,000,000,000,000; 38,200,000,000,000,000

Spiral Review

80. $2\frac{3}{8}$ **81.** $2\frac{5}{9}$ **82.** $1\frac{21}{40}$ **83.** $2\frac{7}{15}$ **84.** 125 in.^{3} **85.** 1000 ft^3 **86.** 1 m^3 **87.** 125 cm^3 **88.** about 6 ft **89.** about 75 in. **90.** about 25 yd

Extension

91. a. 10,000; 10^4 **b.** 256; 2^8 **c.** 64; 4^3 **d.** $\frac{1}{256}$; 2^{-8} **e.** 0.001; 10^{-3} **f.** 9; 9^1 **g.** 100; 10^2 **h.** 4; 2^2 **i.** $\frac{1}{5}$; 5^{-1} **j.** $\frac{1}{64}$; 4^{-3} **k.** $\frac{1}{10,000,000}$; 10^{-7} **l.** 59,049; 9^5 **93.** To multiply, add the exponents. To divide, subtract the exponents.

Extra Skill Practice

1. $\frac{1}{200}$ **3.** $12\frac{4}{5}$ **5.** < **7.** > **9.** > **11.** 1000 **13.** 1 **15.** 1,000,000 **17.** 100,000 **19.** 100,000,000 **21.** $\frac{1}{8}$ **23.** $\frac{1}{32}$ **25.** $\frac{1}{4096}$ **27.** $\frac{1}{81}$ **29.** $\frac{1}{1}$ **31.** 0.00245 **33.** 1.29723 **35.** 1.046 **37.** 305,908 **39.** 0.00312 **41.** $6.1 \cdot 10^{-3}$ **43.** $1.84536 \cdot 10^5$ **45.** $1.0177 \cdot 10^3$ **47.** $9.0533 \cdot 10^2$

Standardized Testing, Multiple Choice

1. D **2.** B

Section 5, Practice and Application (p. 211)

1. a. 3000 m; 5000 m; 10,000 m **b.** about 6000; about 10,000; about 20,000 **3.** 1800 **5.** 0.4 **7.** 0.06804 **9.** 600,000,000 **11.** = **13.** < **15.** < **17.** Sample Response: Change mm to m. **19.** Sample Response: Change mm to m. **31.** 90 mm **33.** 1.25 m **35.** unreasonable; Sample Response: A doorknob comes about to my waist and the distance from the floor to my waist is about 1 m. **37.** unreasonable; Sample

Response: The length of our classroom is about 7 m, so the length of a room in a house would be about 5 m. **39.** reasonable; Sample Response: Since two of my classrooms could probably fit along the edge of a pool and my classroom is about 7 m long, 15 m is reasonable. **40. a.** the meter stick; yes, but the longer the measurement, the greater the error. **b.** kilometers to meters; Multiplying 8×1000 is easier than multiplying 5×1760.

Spiral Review

41. 10^3 **42.** 10^{-3} **43.** 10^1 **44.** 10^0 **45.** about 5 h, about 2 h **46.** about 7.5 mi, about 17.5 mi **47.** 25 **48.** 27 **49.** 46 **50.** 30 **51.** –12 **52.** 149

Extra Skill Practice

1. 48,200 **3.** 5,000,000 **5.** 0.032 **7.** 3,960,000 **9.** 0.5008 **11.** $<$ **13.** $=$ **15.** $>$ **17.** $<$ **19.** $>$ **21.** 60.0 **23.** 14.5 **25.** 80

Section 6, Practice and Application (p. 224)

5. cannot **7.** can; scalene **9.** can; scalene **11.** 9 **13.** 18 **15.** 20 **17.** 400 **19.** $n = 3l$, where n = the number of volunteers this year and l = the number of volunteers last year; 36 volunteers **21.** $c = 5p$, where c = the number of chickens and p = the number of pigs; 30 chickens **23. a.** $t = 4l$, where t = the number of pens sold this year and l = the number of pens sold last year **b.** $l = \frac{t}{4}$, where l = the number of pens sold last year and t = the number of pens sold this year **c.** 19 pens

Spiral Review

25. 3 **26.** 4600 **27.** 97.5 **28.** 0.0001084 **29. a.** $-43 + x = -34$ **b.** 9 **30.** 20 cm **31.** 40 in. **32.** 70 m **33.** 11 ft

Extra Skill Practice

1. can; scalene **3.** cannot **5.** can; isosceles and equilateral **7.** can; scalene **9.** cannot **11.** 36 **13.** 10 **15.** 99 **17.** 15 **19.** 75 **21.** 14 **23.** $t = 2l$, where t = the number of students in chorus this year and l = the number of students in chorus last year; 78 students

Standardized Testing, Free Response

2. $f = 3s$, where f = the length of the first banner and s = the length of the second banner; $2\frac{5}{6}$ ft

Review and Assessment

1. $2 \cdot 2 \cdot 3$ **2.** $3 \cdot 7$ **3.** $2 \cdot 2 \cdot 2 \cdot 3$ **4.** $2 \cdot 3 \cdot 7$ **5.** $2 \cdot 2 \cdot 17$ **6.** 2, 24 **7.** 18; 180 **8.** 5; 150 **9.** 2; 840 **10.** $<$ **11.** $<$ **12.** $>$ **13.** $=$ **14. a.**

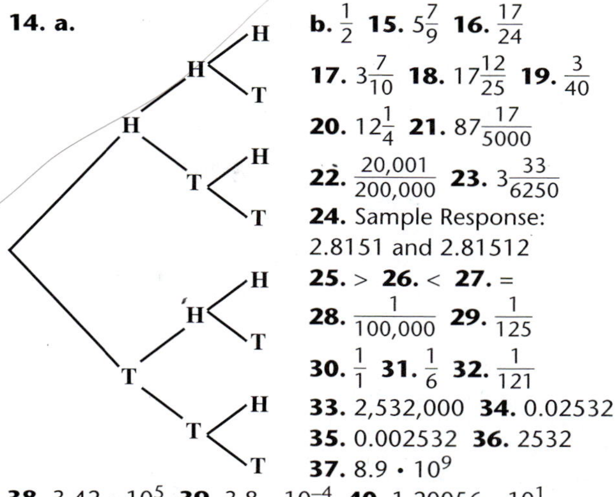

b. $\frac{1}{2}$ **15.** $5\frac{7}{9}$ **16.** $\frac{17}{24}$ **17.** $3\frac{7}{10}$ **18.** $17\frac{12}{25}$ **19.** $\frac{3}{40}$ **20.** $12\frac{1}{4}$ **21.** $87\frac{17}{5000}$ **22.** $\frac{20{,}001}{200{,}000}$ **23.** $3\frac{33}{6250}$ **24.** Sample Response: 2.8151 and 2.81512 **25.** $>$ **26.** $<$ **27.** $=$ **28.** $\frac{1}{100{,}000}$ **29.** $\frac{1}{125}$ **30.** $\frac{1}{1}$ **31.** $\frac{1}{6}$ **32.** $\frac{1}{121}$ **33.** 2,532,000 **34.** 0.02532 **35.** 0.002532 **36.** 2532 **37.** $8.9 \cdot 10^9$ **38.** $3.42 \cdot 10^5$ **39.** $3.8 \cdot 10^{-4}$ **40.** $1.20056 \cdot 10^1$ **41.** 350 **42.** 300 **43.** 0.440 **44.** unreasonable; My waist is about 100 cm above the floor and the top of a desk is about 30 cm below my waist. **45.** reasonable; The length of a jump rope is about 2 m, or 0.002 km. **46.** can; scalene **47.** cannot **48.** can; isosceles and equilateral **49.** 36 **50.** 28 **51.** 17 **52.** 132 **53. a.** Let b = total area of black squares. Let f = area of flag. $b = \frac{1}{2}f$ **b.** 30 in.^{2} **c.** 48 in.^{2}

MODULE 4

Section 1, Practice and Application (p. 242)

1. 59.66 ft or 59.69 ft **3.** 3.14 in. **5.** Sample Response: about 16 ft **7.** $3\frac{1}{2}$ **9.** $9\frac{1}{2}$ **11.** $2\frac{5}{8}$ **13.** $18\frac{3}{8}$ **15.** Rewrite the mixed numeral in the problem as the sum of a whole number and a fraction. Multiply each part of the sum by the other factor in the problem; 9, 10, 13 **17.** a little more than 4 **19.** a little more than 6 **21. a.** $2\frac{1}{4}$ **b.** 360 **c.** 400, 600 **23.** $\frac{7}{3}$ **25.** $\frac{8}{25}$ **29.** $3\frac{1}{2}$ **31.** $3\frac{1}{3}$ **33.** 48 **35.** $\frac{3}{22}$ **37.** $1\frac{1}{5}$ **39.** $2\frac{1}{4}$

Spiral Review

44. cannot **45.** can **46.** 9 **47.** 32 **48.** 40 **49.** 10^2 **50.** 10^{-2} **51.** 10^{-2} **52.** 10^{-3}

Extra Skill Practice

For 1–5, the first answer is found by using 3.14. The second is found by using π. **1.** 15.7 or 15.71 m **3.** 75.36 or 75.40 ft **5.** 32.97 or 32.99 cm **7.** $\frac{3}{22}$ **9.** 20 **11.** 14 **13.** 6 **15.** 76 **17.** $8\frac{4}{7}$ **19.** $\frac{11}{8}$ **21.** $\frac{3}{13}$ **23.** 10 **25.** $1\frac{1}{2}$ **27.** 14 **29.** $3\frac{3}{7}$ **31.** $1\frac{14}{19}$ **33.** $2\frac{1}{7}$

Section 2, Practice and Application (p. 257)

1. 0.648 **3.** 3.11656 **5.** 253.302 **7.** 71.47 **9.** 0.819 **11.** Yes; Sample Response: 3 • \$1.60 = \$4.80; less than; 2.7 < 3 and \$1.59 < \$1.60 **13.** 292.5 **15.** 12.5 **17.** Problems 2 and 5 are incorrect; Since the divisors in both problems are less than 1, the quotients should be greater than the dividend. **19.** 8.5 **21.** 5.8 **23.** 0.725 **25. a.** smaller **b.** 4.16 cm **c.** 45 mm **27.** $0.\overline{315}315$ **29.** $0.02\overline{7}777$ **31.** $0.78\overline{3}$ **33.** $0.\overline{518}$ **35.** undefined **37.** 0.63 **39.** 0.58 **41.** less than; The divisor is greater than 1. **43.** less than; The divisor is greater than 1.

Spiral Review

47. $\frac{3}{22}$ **48.** 10 **49.** 18 **50.** 4 **51.** $\frac{11}{12}$ **52.** 18 **53.** 7 blocks due west

54. **55.** **56.** **57.**

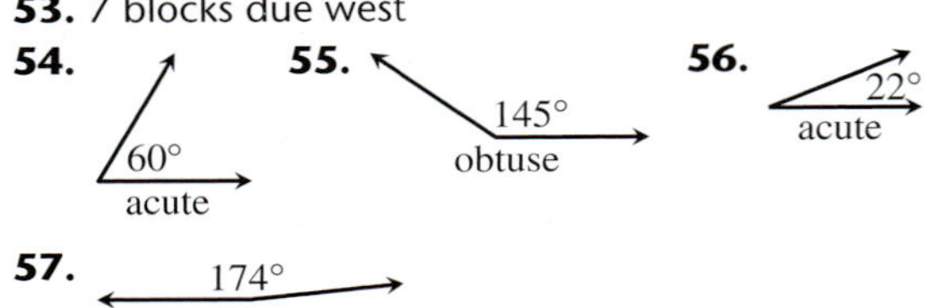

Extra Skill Practice

1. 13.78 **3.** 5.4984 **5.** 0.15572 **7.** 2.6064 **9.** 4599.74 **11.** 1214.88 **13.** less than; 0 < 0.23 < 1 **15.** equal to; Any number multiplied by 1 is the number itself. **17.** 0.003; 0.210 ÷ 70 = 0.003 **19.** 6.49; 10 ÷ 2 = 5 **21.** 6; 2 ÷ 0.5 = 4 **23.** $0.\overline{1}$; 2 ÷ 20 = 0.1 **25.** 230; 17 ÷ 0.1 = 170 **27.** 0.98; 49 ÷ 49 = 1 **29.** greater than; 0 < 0.38 < 1 **31.** equal to; The divisor is 1. **33.** less than; 3488 > 1 **35.** greater than; 0 < 0.8 < 1

Standardized Testing, Multiple Choice

1. A **2.** D

Section 3, Practice and Application (p. 271)

1. a. Sample Response: about 100° clockwise **b.** 105° clockwise **c.** 255° counterclockwise **3.** 30°; 72° **5.** 180° **7.** 60°, 120°, 180°, 240°, and 300° **9.** 180° **11.** 120° and 240° **15.** No; The figures are not the same size. **17.** Yes **19.** No **21.** Yes **23.** Yes; 180°.

Spiral Review

32. 2.128 **33.** 325.2 **34.** 119.14 **35.** $0.4\overline{36}$ **36.** 0.00534 **37.** 96.5 **38. a.** $\frac{12}{40}$, or $\frac{3}{10}$; $\frac{15}{40}$, or $\frac{3}{8}$ **b.** 36, 45 **39.** –9 **40.** 39 **41.** 0 **42.** –33 **43.** –28 **44.** –46

Extension

45. a. Sample Response: about $\frac{1}{2}$ in. below the base of the shaded figure along a vertical line through the dot on the figure; about 120° **d.** The angles are right angles. **e.** The distances are about the same. **g.** It is a little bit closer to the base of the shaded figure. **h.** about 135°; It is a little greater than the estimate.

Extra Skill Practice

1. Sample Response:

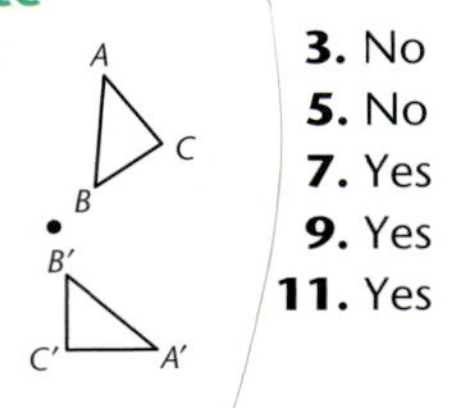

3. No **5.** No **7.** Yes **9.** Yes **11.** Yes

Standardized Testing, Free Response

1–3. Sample responses are given. **1.** a 90° rotation counterclockwise followed by a reflection **2.** a 180° rotation **3.** a 180° rotation followed by a reflection

Section 4, Practice and Application (p. 285)

1. –30 **3.** –42 **5.** 36 **7.** –36 **9.** –4 **11.** 5 **13.** 11 **15.** –50 **17.** –48 **19.** –72 **21.** 168 **23.** when all the factors are positive or when there are an even number of negative factors; when there are an odd number of negative factors **25. a.** –70 **b.** 9 **c.** –1 **27.** 19.5 **29.** –35 **31.** 4 **33.** –38 **35.** –32 **37.** 1.44 **39.** 4.88 **41.** 17 **43.** –7 **45.** $3\frac{3}{4}$ **47.** $7\frac{1}{2}$ **51.** about 23°C

Spiral Review

53. both **54.** line symmetry **55.** rotational symmetry **56.** 7 **57.** 144 **58.** 9 **59.** 676

60. a–b.

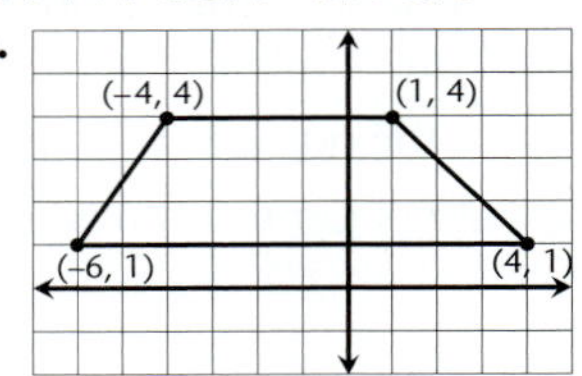

a trapezoid

Extension

61. $5x + 1$ **63.** $3x + 9$ **65.** $7x + 6$

Extra Skill Practice

1. –28 **3.** 9 **5.** 48 **7.** 5 **9.** –14 **11.** –64 **13.** –71 **15.** 7.6 **17.** 15.5 **19.** $5\frac{1}{4}$ **21.** $7\frac{1}{2}$ **23.** 2.1 **25.** 13.6 **27.** 32 **29.** 24

Standardized Testing, Performance Task

Sample Response: Roger Jones incorrectly stated the discount as (23 – 2) • 16 = 336, or \$3.36. This is his cost, and the discount is 2 • 16 = 32¢. The cashier incorrectly calculated the discount as (2 – 23) • 16 = –336, or –\$3.36, which would mean Roger Jones owed him that amount. The cashier subtracted incorrectly by subtracting the cost from the discount instead of the discount from the cost.

Section 5, Practice and Application (p. 300)

1. No; The figure has been rotated. **3.** Yes **5.** $(x, y - 5)$ **7.** $(x + 3, y)$ **9.** $(x - 2, y - 4)$ **13.** The image of the rectangle should be 2 units to the left and 5 units below the original. **15.** A and C **17.** C **19.** B

21. a. $A(4, 5)$, $B(6, -1)$, $C(0, 2)$; $A'(-4, 5)$, $B'(-6, -1)$, $C'(0, 2)$ **b.** Multiply the y-coordinate by -1; Multiply the x-coordinate by -1. **c.** $(-3, 7)$, $(-4, 0)$, $(5, -8)$, $(-4, -9)$
23. 30 **25.** 2.3 **27.** $-1\frac{2}{3}$ **29.** $2\frac{1}{4}$ **31.** $2n + 7 = 31$; 12
33. $4 + 6n = 18$; $2\frac{1}{3}$

37. [5] [+] [1] [2] [=] [×] [7] [=]; 119

Spiral Review

40. 59 **41.** −13 **42.** $-2\frac{1}{3}$ **43.** $31\frac{1}{4}$ **44.** 0.48 **45.** −88
46. 180 **47.** 1500 **48.** $1\frac{1}{2}$ **49.** $<$ **50.** $<$ **51.** $>$

Extra Skill Practice

1. No; The figure has been rotated or reflected.
3. No; The figure has been rotated or reflected.
5. $(x - 1, y + 5)$ **7.** The image of the rectangle will be 2 units to the left and 3 units above the original. **9.** No; There is only horizontal stretching. **11.** The sketch should be the same horizontal length and $\frac{1}{4}$ of the vertical length. **13.** 4 **15.** 2 **17.** 96 **19.** 135

Standardized Testing, Open-ended

The transformation is a horizontal stretch by a factor of 2 followed by a horizontal translation 2 units right, and a vertical squash by a factor of $\frac{3}{4}$.

Review and Assessment

1. 37.70 cm **2.** 25.13 ft **3.** 72.26 ft **4.** 1 **5.** $\frac{8}{5}$ **6.** $\frac{3}{4}$
7. $\frac{1}{9}$ **8.** $\frac{5}{18}$ **9.** $\frac{3}{4}$ **10.** $22\frac{1}{2}$ **11.** $1\frac{1}{3}$ **12.** $3\frac{3}{5}$ **13.** $12\frac{7}{15}$
14. $25\frac{5}{7}$ **15.** 2 **16.** 0.32, greater than, 0.288
17. 4, greater than, $3.\overline{5}$ **18.** $0.\overline{4}$, less than, 0.412
19. 4700, greater than, $4272.\overline{72}$ **20.** 0.3, less than, 0.3125 **21.** 10, greater than, 9.875 **22.** 2.8, greater than, $2.\overline{66}$ **23.** 100, less than, $120.\overline{6}$ **24.** 0.375
25. $0.8\overline{3}$ **26.** $0.\overline{2}$ **27.** 1.6 **28.** $\frac{3}{8}$ and $\frac{8}{5}$; $\frac{5}{6}$ and $\frac{2}{9}$
29. Yes; 20°; 40°; 60°; 80°; 100°; 120°; 140°; 160°; 180°; 200°; 220°; 240°; 260°; 280°; 300°; 320°; 340°
30. No; The distance from A to the line of symmetry is not the same as the distance from A' to the line of symmetry. **31.** −63 **32.** −7 **33.** 72 **34.** −6 **35.** 13
36. −26 **37.** −4 **38.** 420 **39.** 29.4 **40.** $\frac{15}{16}$ **41.** −4
42. a. $(x - 3, y - 1)$ **b.** Vertices are at $A'(-1, -2)$, $B'(1, 1)$, $C'(3,-2)$. **43. a.** I: The image will be twice as wide and half as high; II: The image will be twice as wide and twice as high; III: The image will be half as wide, but the same height. **b.** Vertices are: I: $A'\left(4, -\frac{1}{2}\right)$, $B'(8, 1)$, $C'\left(12, -\frac{1}{2}\right)$; II: $A'(4, -2)$, $B'(8, 4)$, $C'(12, -2)$; III: $A'(1, -1)$, $B'(2, 2)$, $C'(3, -1)$; Only transformation II results in a similar triangle. **44.** 12 **45.** 12 **46.** 8

MODULE 5

Section 1, Practice and Application (p. 321)

1. 6.5 min/mi **3.** \$5.50/lb **5.** 6¢/min **7.** 31.5
9. 4.8 mi/h **11. a.** 6, 60, 2400; 10 **b.** 40 h
13. a. 125 ft **c.** 125 ft; It is the same. **15. a.** 63 years **b.** 28 years; 18 years and 25 years **c.** The median changes to 29. The mode is unaffected. **17. a.** 5 ages **b.** 6 women **c.** From the histogram, we know only that the woman was between 55 and 59 years old.

Spiral Review

19. $8\frac{1}{4}$ **20.** 264 **21.** −48 **22.** about \$2.00 **23.** about \$7.50 **24.** about \$2.00 **25.** $\frac{1}{3}$ **26.** $\frac{1}{5}$ **27.** $\frac{1}{2}$ **28.** $\frac{1}{5}$
29. $\frac{2}{5}$ **30.** $\frac{5}{6}$

Extra Skill Practice

1. \$10.75/h **3.** 224 noodles/box **5.** 1.5 questions/min
7. greater than

Study Skills, Creating a Test

1. a. Sample Response: writing and simplifying ratios, rates, and proportions; interpreting and creating stem-and-leaf plots, frequency tables, and histograms; finding the mean, mode, median, and range of a set of data values

Section 2, Practice and Application (p. 337)

1. 20 lb **3.** 144 g **5.** 900 lb **7.** 4 **9.** 7 **11. a.** Yes **b.** Ang simplified the left side of the proportion and then multiplied both sides by 5. **c.** Sample Response: $5 \times 4.8 \div 2$ **13. a.** about 90 stories
15. a–b.

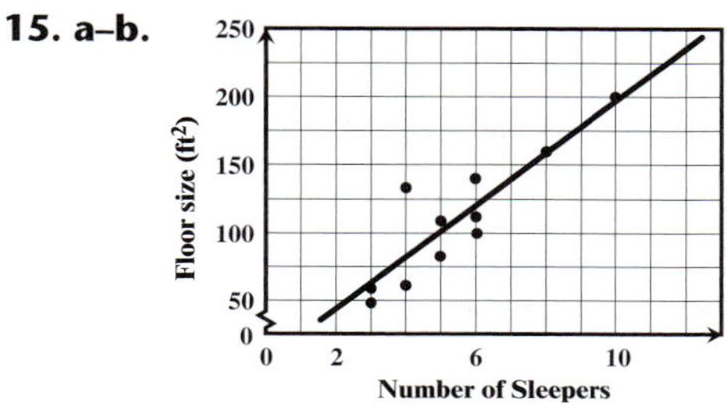

c. Sample Response: about \$400 **17.** C; The lowest data value, 12, and the highest data value, 63, are shown at the end of the whiskers in the stem-and-leaf plot in C.

Spiral Review

19. \$7.25/h **20.** 9 min/mi **21.** \$6.50/lb **22.** 5^2
23. 4^4 **24.** 3^5 **25.** 0.4 **26.** $0.\overline{3}$ **27.** 0.2

Extra Skill Practice

1. 18 **3.** 45

5.

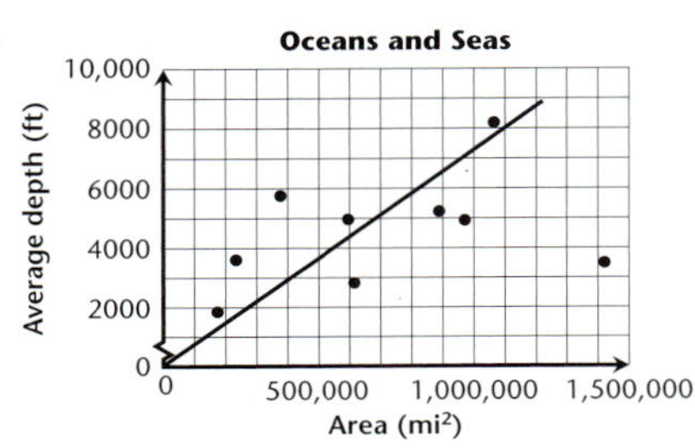

7. about 3800 ft **9.** about 8

Section 3, Practice and Application (p. 353)

1.

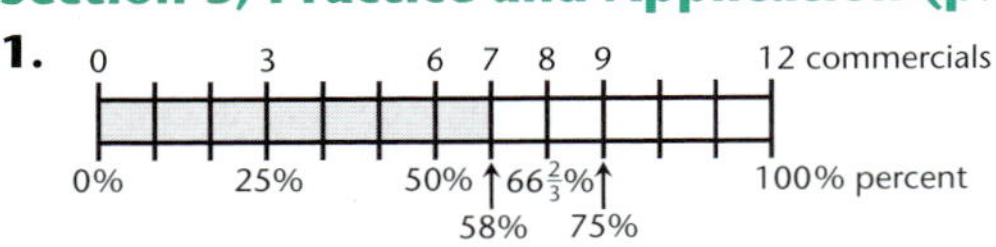

3. a. Sample Response: $\frac{1}{3}$ **b.** Sample Response: $33\frac{1}{3}$% **5.** Sample Response: about 80% **7.** Sample Response: about 75% **9.** 33.3% **11.** 75% **13.** about 41% **15. a.** about 175 million Americans **b.** about 83 million Americans **17.** 550 students; $\frac{68}{100} = \frac{374}{x}$ **19.** 40 **21.** 15.5 **23.** $16.00 **25. a.** Yes; The ratios Jo has set up are not equivalent. **b.** $\frac{34}{100} = \frac{x}{350}$; 119

Spiral Review

27. 9 **28.** 1 **29.** 10 **30.** 121 **31.** 43 **32.** 1 **33.** $\frac{5}{6}$ **34.** $\frac{2}{7}$ **35.** $\frac{1}{3}$

Extension

37. $504 **39. a.** $559.44 **b.** Answer to part (a) is greater.

Extra Skill Practice

1. about 55% **3.** about 22% **5.** 28% **7.** about 80% **9.** 25% **11.** 66.7% **13.** 61.1% **15.** 70% **19.** 700 **21.** 10.8 **23.** 600

Standardized Testing, Performance Task

75; 6; 1
59.3; 25.9; 14.8
8; 13;16
25;12.5; 15; 62.5
20; 10; 14; 70

Sample conclusion: Students liked the lunches better on Mon. through Wed. than on Thurs. and Fri.

Section 4, Practice and Application (p. 368)

1. Holdsclaw: $\frac{6}{16}$, 0.375, 37.5%; Conklin: $\frac{5}{8}$, 0.625, 62.5%; Marciniak: $\frac{5}{13}$, 0.385, 38.5%; T. Johnson: $\frac{7}{10}$, 0.7, 70% **3.** 0.304 **5.** Kruk; Sample Response: Round the decimal forms of the ratios of *number of hits* to *times at bat* to the nearest ten-thousandth and compare the decimal numbers. **7.** 18% **9.** 10% **11.** 62.5% **13.** 1.5 oz **17.** about 5 million **19.** $\frac{3}{16}$ or 18.75% **21.** $\frac{3}{8}$ or 37.5%

23. a.

Color of First Marble | Color of Second Marble | Color of Third Marble

0.4 R
- 0.4 R
  - 0.4 R
  - 0.6 B
- 0.6 B
  - 0.4 R
  - 0.6 B

0.6 B
- 0.4 R
  - 0.4 R
  - 0.6 B
- 0.6 B
  - 0.4 R
  - 0.6 B

b. 0.064, 0.216, 0.144, 0.096, 0.288, 0.784

Spiral Review

26. 16 **27.** 75 **28.** 80 **29.** 50

Career Connection

31. a. 50 mg/mL **b.** $\frac{50 \text{ mg}}{1 \text{ mL}} = \frac{900 \text{ mg}}{x \text{ mL}}$; 18 mL

Extra Skill Practice

1. $\frac{1}{3}$, 0.33$\overline{3}$, $33\frac{1}{3}$% **3.** $\frac{4}{5}$, 0.8, 80% **5.** $\frac{2}{3}$, 0.66$\overline{7}$, $66\frac{2}{3}$% **7.** $\frac{9}{20}$, 0.45, 45% **9.** $\frac{7}{32}$, about 0.22, about 22% **11.** 52% **13.** Sample Response: about 22% **15.** Sample Response: about 75% **17.** about 19% **19. a.** $\frac{2}{7}$ **b.** R = rain, N = no rain **c.** $\frac{25}{49} \approx 50\%$ **d.** $\frac{10}{49} \approx 20\%$

Standardized Testing, Multiple Choice

1. B, D **2.** D

Review and Assessment

1. about 8.6 min/mi **2.** $3.75/lb **3.** about 28.7 mi/gal **4.** 15.625 km/L

5.

Areas of State Parks in 9 States

Stem	Leaves
0	9
1	
2	5
3	
4	1 2 7
5	0 7
6	6
7	5

7 | 5 represents 75,000 acres

6. range: 66 thousand; mean: about 45.8 thousand; median: 47 thousand; mode: none **7.** I would have to add 27 more stems (8–34) and one more leaf. **8.** about 95 skaters **9.** No; Individual times are not indicated. **10.** 4:00–4:59 and 8:00–8:59 **11.** 34 **12.** 13.5 **13.** 18 **14. a.** about 5.5 **b.** 2.5 mi **15. a.** about 150 m **b.** about 3.3 ft **16.** about 2:23; about 2:44 **17.** about 20% **18.** about 80% **19.** about 67% **20.** 40% **21.** 50%, about 55%; $\frac{32}{58}$ **22.** 77.$\overline{7}$%, about 81%; $\frac{63}{78}$

23. 135.54 **24.** $1166.\overline{6}$

25. a. First marble Second marble

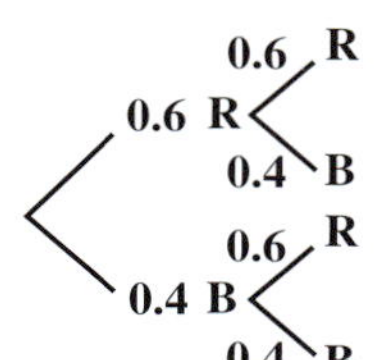

$\frac{9}{25}$, 0.36, 36% **b.** about 108 times

MODULE 6

Section 1, Practice and Application (p. 389)

1. $x < 8$

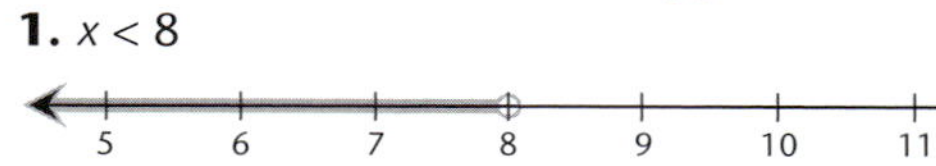

3. $5 < h \leq 11$

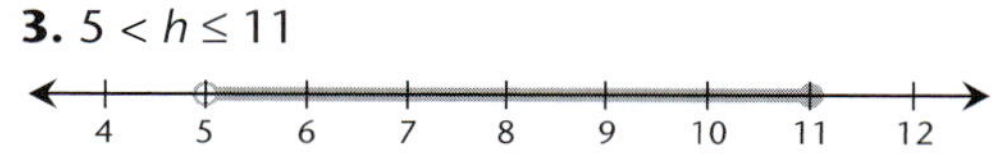

5. If l = the hours of logged flight time, then $l \geq 500$.

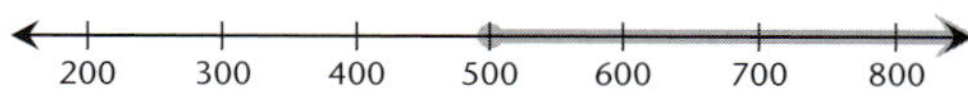

7. from about 2.25 in. to about 8.5 in. **9.** If p = the percent of a hummingbird's body weight that is flight muscle, then $22 \leq p \leq 34$. **11.** Find which parts of the graphs overlap. **13.** square, rhombus, and rectangle; The kite has no pairs of opposite parallel sides and the trapezoid has only 1 such pair. A parallelogram has 2 pairs of opposite parallel sides. **17. a.** $\overline{EY}$; Neither of the others are segments perpendicular to $\overline{EF}$ and $\overline{HG}$. **b.** 12 cm^2 **19.** $\frac{2}{5}$ **21.** $\frac{1}{2}$ **23.** 60 m^2 **25.** Board B; The probability of landing in the shaded area is greater for Board B (about 57%), than for Board A (about 42%) or Board C (50%).

Spiral Review

27. about 50% **28.** about $33\frac{1}{3}$% **29.** about 25% **30.** about 20% **31.** 2 • 2 • 3 **32.** 5 • 5 **33.** 2 • 2 • 2 • 2 • 3 **34.** 2 • 2 • 5 • 5 **35.** 4 **36.** 25 **37.** 81 **38.** 100

Extra Skill Practice

1. $a > 8$

3. $4 < r < 7$

5. $6 < t \leq 13$

7. No; The quadrilateral has only 1 pair of opposite parallel sides and a parallelogram has 2 such pairs. **9.** Yes **11.** concave **13.** concave **15.** $\frac{1}{3}$, or $33\frac{1}{3}$% **17.** $\frac{5}{9}$, or $55\frac{5}{9}$%

Section 2, Practice and Application (p. 405)

1. 9 ft × 9 ft **3.** –15 **5.** 1 and 2 **7.** about 14.3 **9.** about 23.4 **11. a.** 6 cm^2, 10 cm^2, 14 cm^2, 18 cm^2 **b.** 42 cm^2; Each time a cube is added, one face is lost and 5 are added for a total increase in area of 4 cm^2. Surface area = $6 + 4n$, where n is the number of added cubes.
13. a. Sample Response:

b. 150 cm^2, 150 cm^2, 40 cm^2, 40 cm^2, 60 cm^2, 60 cm^2 **c.** 500 cm^2 **17.** 3660.25π m^2; Possible answers: 11,493.19 m^2 or 11,499.02 m^2 **19.** about 8.46 ft **21.** about 2.31 yd

Spiral Review

24. $t > 11$ **25.** $p \leq 6$ **26.** 0.125 **27.** 0.400 **28.** about 0.609 **29.** about 0.677 **30.** $\frac{1}{2}$ **31.** $\frac{1}{4}$ **32.** $\frac{3}{5}$ **33.** $\frac{3}{8}$

Extra Skill Practice

1. 8 **3.** 7 **5.** about 8.9 **7.** about 5.5
9. a hexagonal prism
11. a. Sample Response:

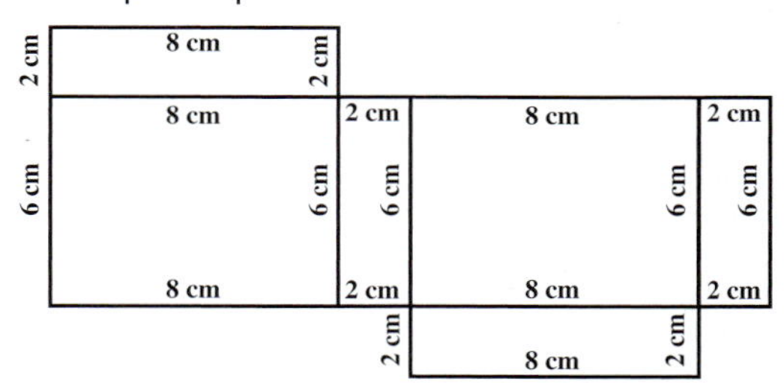

b. 152 cm^2 **13.** 5.76π cm^2; Possible answers: 18.09 cm^2 or 18.10 cm^2

Standardized Testing, Multiple Choice

1. B **2.** C

Section 3, Practice and Application (p. 418)

1. congruent and similar ; $ABCD \cong PSRQ$ **3.** similar; $FGHKL \sim EABCD$ or $FGHKL \sim AEDCB$ **5.** about 70.8 m **7.** about 64.8 m **9.** 180 mm **11.** acute **13.** acute **15.** obtuse **17.** 120°, 23°, 127° **19.** 18 ft, 6 ft

Spiral Review

22. 920 in.^{2} **23.** 17.18 cm^2 **24.** $\frac{7}{8}$ **25.** 1 **26.** 3 **27.** 108° **28.** 90° **29.** 68° **30.** 25°

Career Connection

31. a. about 87 ft 5 in. **b.** about 39 ft 7 in. high and 54 ft 5 in. across

Extra Skill Practice

1. $\overline{VT}$, $\overline{UV}$ **3.** 5 in., 2 in. **5.** acute **7.** obtuse **9.** right **11.** 125°, 55°, 65°

Standardized Testing, Free Response

1. No; The ratios of corresponding sides may not be equal. For example, two house-shaped pentagons could have corresponding angles congruent, but one could have all side lengths equal and one could have vertical sides twice as long as the other sides. **2.** No; The measures of corresponding angles may not be equal. For example, a house-shaped pentagon and a regular pentagon could have congruent sides but would have different angle measures.

Section 4, Practice and Application (p. 430)

1. $\angle 2$, $\angle 3$, $\angle 6$, $\angle 7$ **3.** $\angle 2$ and $\angle 7$, $\angle 3$ and $\angle 6$ **5.** $\angle 1$ and $\angle 3$, $\angle 2$ and $\angle 4$, $\angle 5$ and $\angle 7$, $\angle 6$ and $\angle 8$ **7.** $m\angle 6 = m\angle 3 = m\angle 8 = 55°$, $m\angle 2 = m\angle 5 = m\angle 4 = m\angle 7 = 125°$

9. a. Sample Response: Since they form a straight angle, $m\angle 4 + m\angle 5 = 180°$. Since $\angle 3$ and $\angle 5$ are corresponding angles formed by 2 parallel lines and a transversal, $m\angle 3 = m\angle 5$. Substituting $m\angle 3$ for $m\angle 5$ in the first equation, $m\angle 4 + m\angle 3 = 180°$. So, $\angle 3$ and $\angle 4$ are supplementary. **b.** $\angle 1$ and $\angle 2$, $\angle 1$ and $\angle 3$, $\angle 1$ and $\angle 5$, $\angle 2$ and $\angle 4$, $\angle 2$ and $\angle 6$, $\angle 3$ and $\angle 6$, $\angle 4$ and $\angle 5$, $\angle 5$ and $\angle 6$ **c.** 360° **11.** True; $\angle 7$ and the 101° angle have the same measure since they are alternate interior angles, and $\angle 7$ and $\angle 8$ are supplementary angles, so $m\angle 8 = 180° - 101° = 79°$. **13.** False; $\angle 4$ and the 105° angle are supplementary angles, so $m\angle 4 = 75°$. **15.** False; $\angle 10$ and the 75° angle are vertical angles, so $m\angle 10 = 75°$. $\angle 11$ and $\angle 12$ are supplementary and $m\angle 12 = 101°$ since it is a corresponding angle to a 101° angle. Therefore, $m\angle 11 = 180° - 101° = 79°$ and $m\angle 10 \neq m\angle 11$. **17.** 35° **19.** 95°, obtuse **21.** 55°, acute

Spiral Review

24. right **25.** obtuse **26.** acute **27.** $\frac{3}{2}$ **28.** 23 **29.** 30 **30.** 27 cm^3 **31.** 64 in.^{3} **32.** 1 ft^3 **29.** 1000 cm^3

Extension

35.

Polygon	Name of polygon	Number of sides	Number of triangles formed by the diagonals from 1 vertex	Sum of the measures of the angles
	triangle	3	1	180°
	quadrilateral	4	2	360°
	pentagon	5	3	540°
	hexagon	6	4	720°
	heptagon	7	5	900°
	octagon	8	6	1080°

Extra Skill Practice

1. $\angle 3, \angle 4, \angle 5, \angle 6$ **3.** $\angle 3$ and $\angle 6$, $\angle 4$ and $\angle 5$ **5.** Possible answers: $\angle 1$ and $\angle 4$, $\angle 2$ and $\angle 3$, $\angle 5$ and $\angle 8$, $\angle 6$ and $\angle 7$ **7.** 113° **9.** 67° **11.** 113° **13.** 52°; acute **15.** 45°; right

Standardized Testing, Performance Task

Since $\overline{AF}$ and $\overline{BD}$ are transversals that intersect parallel lines $\overleftrightarrow{AB}$ and $\overleftrightarrow{DF}$, $\angle 1$ and $\angle 6$ are alternate interior angles and are congruent and $\angle 2$ and $\angle 5$ are alternate interior angles and are congruent. $\angle 3$ and $\angle 4$ are vertical angles and are also congruent.

Section 5, Practice and Application (p. 446)

1. 121.5 cm^3 **3.** 180 cm^3 **5.** 5 cm **7.** 91,000 **9.** 7.5 **11.** 2.7 **13.** 0.172 **17. a.** 7,953,628,000 cm^3 **b.** 7,953,628 L **c.** 7,953,628 kg **19. a.** 1250 L **b.** 1250 kg **21.** 3890 mi **23.** Los Angeles–Chicago–New York

Spiral Review

26. 113° **27.** 19° **28.** 105° **29.** by the endpoint of the right-hand whisker in the upper box plot **30.** toothed whales: about 40,000 kg; baleen whales: about 125,000 kg **31.** 19.625 cm^2 **32.** 50.24 $in.^2$ **33.** 314 m^2 **34.** about 5.98 cm^2

Extension

Sample responses are given. **37.**

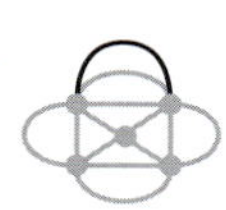

39.

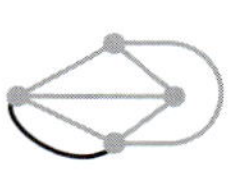

Extra Skill Practice

1. 5.2 $in.^3$ **3.** 118.125 m^3 **5.** 30 m^3 **7.** 12,000 **9.** 47 **11.** 0.077 **13.** 1995 km

Review and Assessment

1. If s = salary in dollars, then $7514 \le s \le 11{,}627$.
2. If t = the hours worked each month, then $80 \le t < 85$.
3. 22 ft^2 **4.** $\frac{12}{22}$, or $\frac{6}{11}$ **5.** 11 **6.** 4.5 **7.** 13.2
8. Sample Response:
9. 79 cm^2

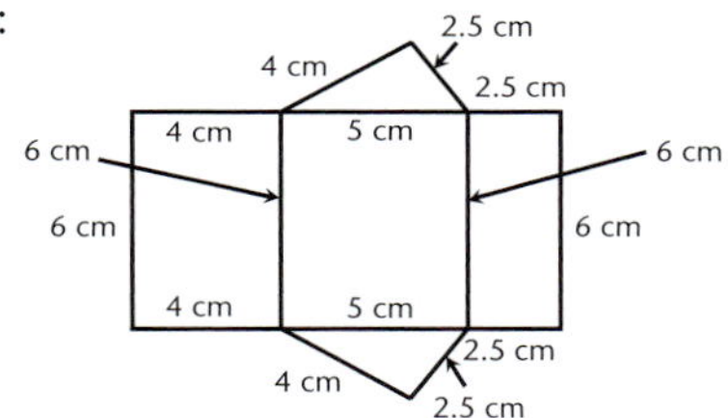

10. 25π cm^2; 78.5 cm^2 **11.** 100π mm^2; 314 mm^2 **12.** 3.0625π ft^2; about 9.6 ft^2 **13. a.** 1 mm : 2 ft **b.** about 64 ft **14.** $CD = 3.5$ cm, $EF = 2.4$ cm, $FG = 5.2$ cm; $m\angle ABC = 120°$, $m\angle FEH = 120°$, $m\angle EHG = 105°$, $m\angle GFE = 67°$ **15.** $m\angle 1 = m\angle 3 = m\angle 7 = 127°$, $m\angle 2 = m\angle 5 = m\angle 6 = m\angle 4 = 53°$ **16.** 90°, right **17.** 95°, obtuse **18.** 85°, acute **19.** 3000 cm^3 **20.** 3000 mL; 3 L **21.** 2.345 **22.** 750 **23.** 0.004 **24.** Seattle, Walla Walla, Boise **25.** 448 mi **26.** Portland-Walla Walla-Spokane

MODULE 7

Section 1, Practice and Application (p. 465)

1. 127.23 ft^3 **3.** 69.12 cm^3 **5.** 37.7 **7.** 16

9. a.

b	C
75	10.2
100	13.6
150	20.4
200	27.2

b.

Calories Burned During 10 min of Studying

Calories burned: 0, 5, 10, 15, 20, 25, 30
Body Weight (lb): 0, 75, 100, 125, 150, 175, 200

c. 0.136

11. a. Sample Response: a horizontal scale from 75–200 lb for both graphs; vertical scales of 5–14 Cal for sleeping, and 14–38 Cal for preparing food.
b. Sample Responses:

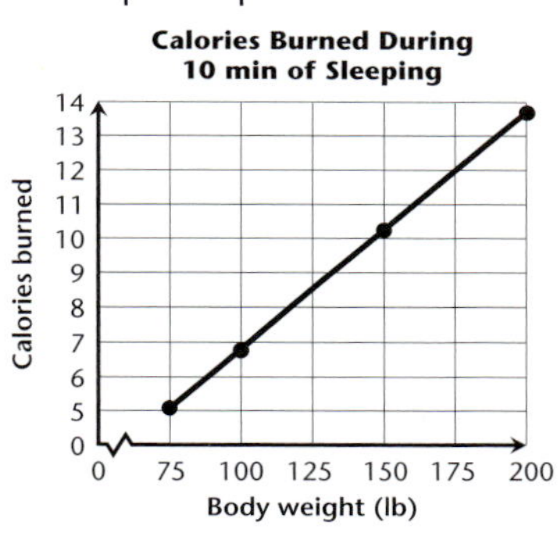

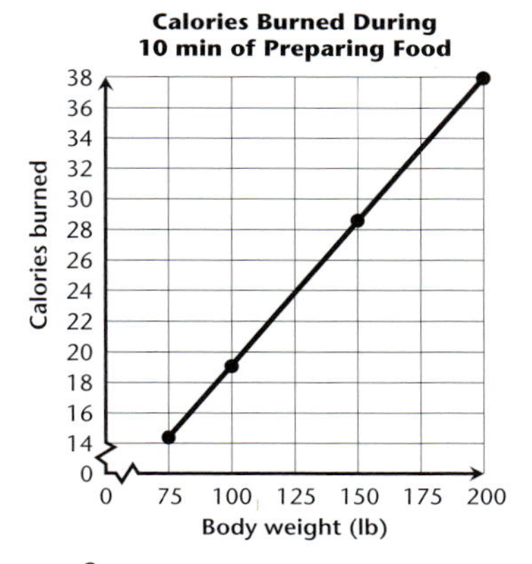

13. $\frac{3}{2}$, or 1.5 **15.** 2 **17.** 2 **19.** 1 **21. a.** height **b.** The heights of the graphs are in the same proportion as the populations, but the areas are not.

c. Sample Response:

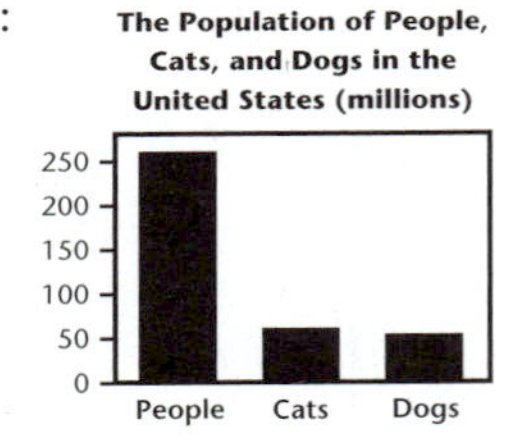

Spiral Review

23. 48 cm^3 **24.** 216 in.^{3} **25.** 2187 cm^3 **26.** $\frac{4}{8}$, or $\frac{1}{2}$ **27.** $\frac{2}{9}$ **28.** about 50 times, about 22 times **29.** 4% **30.** 16% **31.** 65% **32.** 24%

Extension

33. a. 0, –2, undefined **b.** Since the slope = $\frac{\text{rise}}{\text{run}} = \frac{3}{0}$ and division by 0 is undefined, the slope is undefined.
c. A line with a negative slope slants downward from left to right, while one with a positive slope slants upward from left to right.

Extra Skill Practice

1. 56.5 **3.** 1 **5.** $\frac{3}{4}$, or 0.75 **7.** 2 **9.** Yes; Different scales are used on the vertical axes. Sample Response:

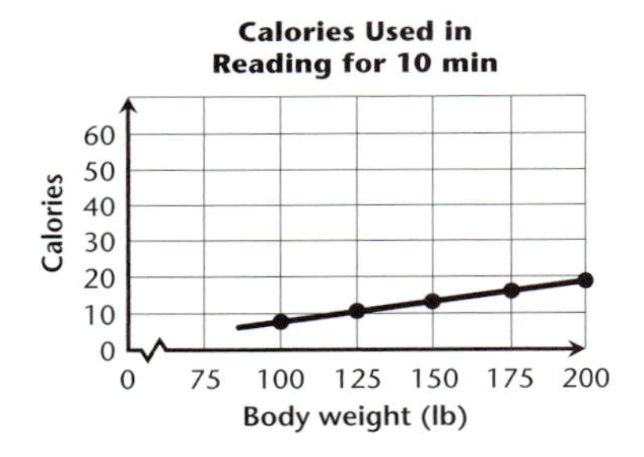

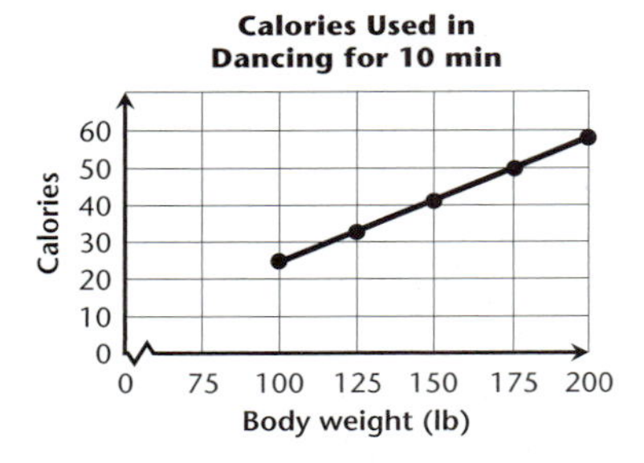

Study Skills, Using Graphic Organizers

1. a. If the starting number is not divisible by 2, you add 1 to make it an even number. **b.** Since 9 is not divisible by 2, you add 1 to generate 10.

Section 2, Practice and Application (p. 480)

1. 180% **3.** 12.5% **5.** 135% **7.** 200% **9.** 162 beats per min **11.** 130, 25, 60, 90; 93%, 45%, 55%, 90% **13.** $33\frac{1}{3}$% decrease **15.** 275% increase **17.** 60% decrease **19.** B; Since there are no parentheses in A, the original amount, rather than the change in the original amount, is divided by the original amount; The expression in C has nothing to do with percent of change. **21. a.** \$42.49 **b.** 24%

Spiral Review

25. 1 **26.** $\frac{1}{2}$, or 0.5 **27.** $\frac{3}{2}$, or 1.5 **28.** $\frac{1}{4}$, or 0.25 **29.** $\frac{5}{8}$ **30.** $1\frac{13}{15}$ **31.** $5\frac{23}{24}$ **32.** Possible Answers: Let r = the resting heart rate in beats per minute.

Canary: $500 \le r \le 800$

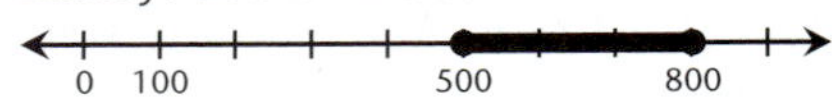

Mouse: $300 \le r \le 500$

Chicken: $300 \le r \le 350$

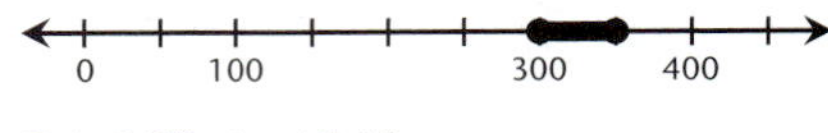

Cat: $120 \le r \le 140$

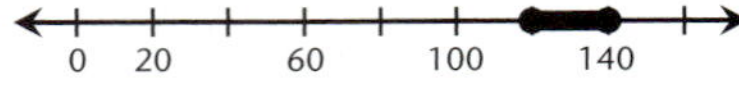

Dog: $70 \le r \le 120$

0 20 60 100 140

Person: $60 \le r \le 80$

Lion: $40 \le r \le 50$

0 20 60 100

Elephant: $25 \le r \le 50$

Extra Skill Practice

1. 500% **3.** 300% **5.** 187.5% **7.** 100% **9.** $77.\overline{7}$% increase **11.** 200% increase **13.** 102 beats/min **15.** about a 16% decrease **17.** 20%; increase

Standardized Testing, Open-ended

Sample Response: If the base radii of the first and second cylinders are 5 cm and 10 cm respectively, and the height of both cylinders is 10 cm, then the percent increase in the volume is $\frac{\text{Vol. of cyl. 2} - \text{Vol. of cyl. 1}}{\text{Vol. of cyl. 1}} \cdot 100 = \frac{1000\pi - 250\pi}{250\pi} \cdot 100 = 300\%$

Section 3, Practice and Application (p. 494)

1. 32 **3.** 8 **5.** 32 **7.** 8 to 10 oz **9. a.** 18 Calories **b.** 30% **c.** No; Exactly 30%, not less than 30% of the Calories come from fat. **11. a.** 52.5 mg **b.** Let s = the mg of sodium in 12 fl oz. Then, $s < 52.5$.
13. a. Let s = the mg of sodium in 8 fl oz. Then, $35 < s < 140$. **b.** No, 16 fl oz has to contain less than 280 mg; No, 15.5 oz has to contain less than 271 mg; Yes, 20 fl oz has to contain less than 350 mg and more than 87.5 mg. **15.** $x \ge 8$ **17.** $x < 28$ **19.** $x \le 1$

Spiral Review

23. 250% **24.** 300% **25.** $195.\overline{45}\%$ **26.** 120% **27.** 4 **28.** 6 **29.** 10 **30.** 4.2 **31.** 12.8 **32.** 124

Extension

33. a. They are within the right whisker. **b.** They have more sugar than at least 75% of the other candy bars.

Extra Skill Practice

1. 6 **3.** 3 **5.** 32 **7.** $x \le 22$ **9.** $x > -5$ **11.** $x \ge 1\frac{2}{5}$

13.

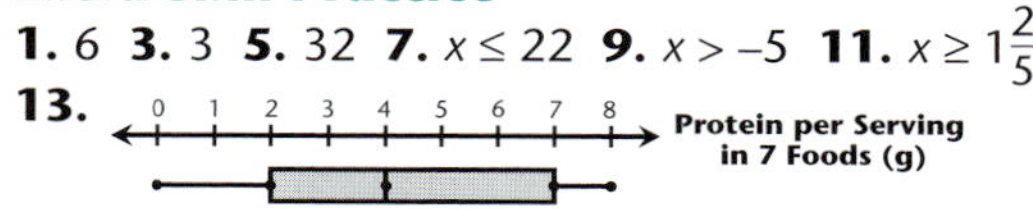

Standardized Testing, Multiple Choice

1. B **2.** D

Section 4, Practice and Application (p. 507)

1. about 50% **3.** about 10% **5.** 112° **7.** 32° **9.** 18° **11.** C; Graph C is the only graph that shows a section greater than $\frac{1}{2}$ the circle to represent 60% and that has other fractional parts that correspond to the data.

13. Sample Response: The median number of days off is highest for plant managers. About 25% of the bus drivers, 75% of the auto mechanics, and 50% of the secretaries have 20 or fewer days off. **15.** Sample Response: No; The greatest percent appears to occupy the least area.

Spiral Review

17. 3 **18.** $\frac{3}{8}$ **19.** $\frac{3}{16}$ **20.** 64 **21.** $-3\frac{1}{2}$ **22.** -6.15 **23.** -0.5 **24.** 64 yd^3 **25.** 6 cm^2 **26.** 900 ft^2

Extra Skill Practice

1. 11° **3.** 29° **5.** 40° **7.** 68°

9. a. Sample Response: a histogram

b.

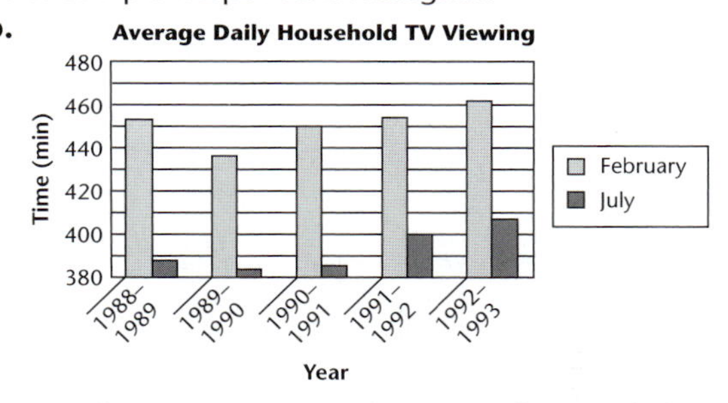

c. Sample Response: Over the years, the trends for February and July were the same. The time spent watching TV in February was greater than that in July for all years. The time spent watching TV in February and in July declined in 1989–1990.

Standardized Testing, Performance Task

1. Sample responses are given. **a:** How different categories of values compare; data values are represented by height of bars in the graph. **b:** Extreme values, median, how the data values cluster; stem values are listed vertically and leaves are listed horizontally beside the corresponding stem. **c:** The percent of the total that the data value represents; the values are drawn as areas in a circle. **d:** The minimum, lower quartile, median, upper quartile, maximum, any extreme values. The five values are calculated from the data and plotted above a number line. Then the box and whiskers are drawn. **e:** Specific data values and how they increase or decrease from one to the next; Data points are plotted on a two-dimensional grid. **f:** How different categories of values compare; Data intervals are made on the horizontal axis and the corresponding data values are shown as the heights of the bars. **2.** Sample responses are given. **a:** Yes; different vertical scales could be used and the bars could be made different widths.
b: Yes; the stems chosen could be of various intervals.
c: No. **d:** No. **e:** Yes; different horizontal and vertical scales could be used to display the data.
f: Yes; different horizontal and vertical scales could be used and the bars could be made different widths.

Section 5, Practice and Application (p. 519)

1. B, F **3.** C, D **5.** rhombus, square **7.** 63 m^2 **9.** 12 in.^{2} **11.** 18 in.^{2} **13.** $20\frac{9}{16}$, or 20.5625 in.^{2} **15.** 27.5 cm^2 **17.** 5 cm

Spiral Review

21. 22° **22.** 32° **23.** 47° **24.** 65° **25.** 76° **26.** 119° **27.** $2x$ **28.** $t - 20$ **29.**

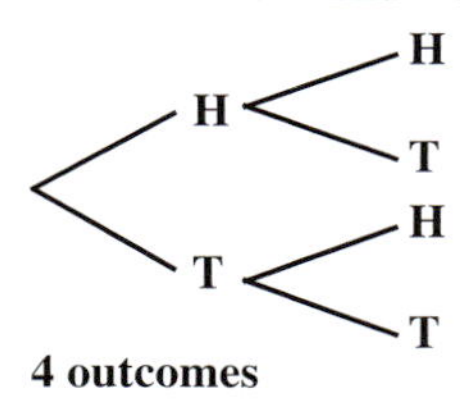

Extra Skill Practice

1. C, E **3.** B **5.** 468 in.^{2} **7.** 21 ft **9.** 18 m

Standardized Testing, Free Response

area of square = 4 ft^2; area of small △ = 1 ft^2
area of large △ = 2 ft^2; area of trapezoid = 7 ft^2

Review and Assessment

1. 314 in.^{3} **2.** 461.58 cm^3 **3.** 42.39 cm^3 **4.** $\frac{1}{2}$ **5.** 1 **6.** 4 **7.** 0 **8.** Sample Response: The values appear to increase rapidly with the greatest value about twice the least value. **9.** about 175 million, about 200 million, about 225 million, about 250 million **10.** No.
11. Eliminate the gap in the vertical scale. **12.** 160% **13.** 150% **14.** 875% **15.** 488% **16.** about an 11.4% decrease **17.** $33\frac{1}{3}\%$ increase **18.** \$165 **19.** 10 **20.** $1\frac{3}{4}$ **21.** 64 **22.** $3m + 5n \le 100$ **23.** lower extreme: about 1, lower quartile: about 9, median: about 15, upper quartile: about 31, upper extreme: about 80

24. School enrollments

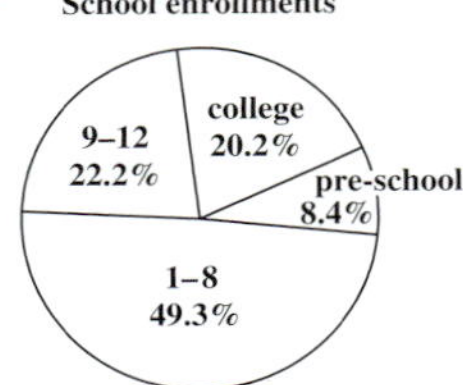

25. a histogram; the number of people with a given age can be read from the height of the bars. You wouldn't use a stem-and-leaf plot because there are over 500 data points. A box-and-whisker plot does not show individual data points. **26.** Both pairs of opposite sides are congruent; Both pairs of opposite angles are congruent. **27.** 84 mm^2 **28.** 22.5 m^2 **29.** 34 ft^2

MODULE 8

Section 1, Practice and Application (p. 535)

1. azalea-ivy, azalea-fern, azalea-cactus, ivy-azalea, ivy-fern, ivy-cactus, fern-azalea, fern-ivy, fern-cactus, cactus-azalea, cactus-ivy, cactus-fern
3. band–BS–GS–FD, band–BS–FD–GS, band–GS–BS–FD, band–GS–FD–BS, band–FD–BS–GS, band–FD–GS–BS, BS–band–GS–FD, BS–band–FD–GS, BS–GS–band–FD, BS–GS–FD–band, BS–FD–band–GS, BS–FD–GS–band, GS–band–BS–FD, GS–band–FD–BS, GS–BS–band–FD, GS–BS–FD–band, GS–FD–band–BS, GS–FD–BS–band, FD–band–BS–GS, FD–band–GS–BS, FD–BS–band–GS, FD–BS–GS–band, FD–GS–band–BS, FD–GS–BS–band
5. a. 640; 604; 460; 406; 064; 046 **b.** 4 **7.** 24 **9.** 336
11. a.

1st Station 2nd 3rd
Chicken — Rice — Soup / Salad
Chicken — Potatoes — Soup / Salad
Chicken — Bread — Soup / Salad

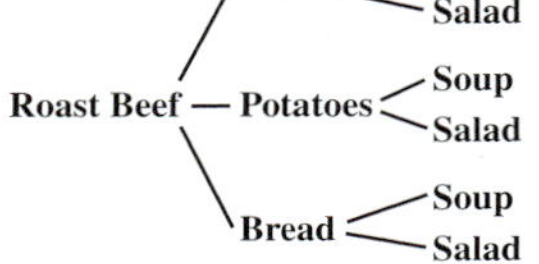

b. 12 **c.** The number of possible meals is doubled. **13.** 6,227,020,800; exact **15.** 8.07×10^{67}; approximate

Spiral Review

19. 28 $in.^2$ **20.** 36 cm^2 **21.** –2 **22.** 8 **23.** 5 **24.** 2 **25.** 4 **26.** 2 **27.** 166 ft^2 **28.** 89.5 m^2 **29.** $92\frac{1}{2}$ yd^2 **30.** 504 mm^2

Career Connection

31. 6; rotate–color/bw–size, rotate–size–color/bw, color/bw–rotate–size, color/bw–size–rotate, size–rotate–color/bw, size–color/bw–rotate

Extra Skill Practice

1. Alma, Mei, Dyani, Luz; Alma, Mei, Luz, Dyani; Alma, Dyani, Mei, Luz; Alma, Dyani, Luz, Mei; Alma, Luz, Mei, Dyani; Alma, Luz, Dyani, Mei; Mei, Alma, Dyani, Luz; Mei, Alma, Luz, Dyani; Mei, Dyani, Alma, Luz; Mei, Dyani, Luz, Alma; Mei, Luz, Alma, Dyani; Mei, Luz, Dyani, Alma; Dyani, Alma, Mei, Luz; Dyani, Alma, Luz, Mei; Dyani, Mei, Alma, Luz; Dyani, Mei, Luz, Alma; Dyani, Luz, Alma, Mei; Dyani, Luz, Mei, Alma; Luz, Alma, Mei, Dyani; Luz, Alma, Dyani, Mei; Luz, Mei, Alma, Dyani; Luz, Mei, Dyani, Alma; Luz, Dyani, Alma, Mei; Luz, Dyani, Mei, Alma **3. a.** Answers will vary; 24 numbers **b.** 10,000 phone numbers **5.** 116,280

Section 2, Practice and Application (p. 548)

1. d. Yes, No; The same number of cubes is used; the number of exposed cube faces is not the same.
3. Sample Response:

1	2	2
3		
1		

5. V = 1953.125 m^3; SA = 937.5 m^2 **7.** *ABCD* **9.** *E*
11. about 6 cm^3; 6.3 cm^3
13. Yes; triangular pyramid
15. Yes; hexagonal pyramid

Spiral Review

18. 5040 **19.** 39,916,800 **20.** can; scalene **21.** can; isosceles **22.** cannot **23.**

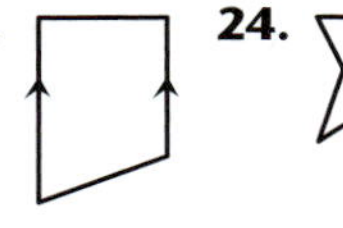

24.

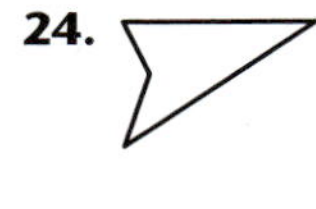

25.

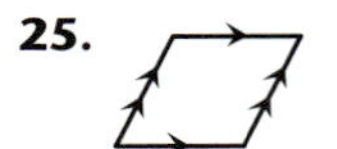

Extension

27. Sample Response:

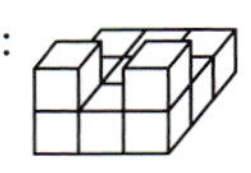

Extra Skill Practice

1. B, D **3.** A, G **5.** 112 $in.^3$ **7.** 106.7 mm^3

Standardized Testing, Open-ended

1–3. Sample Responses are given.
1.

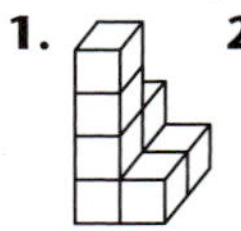

2.

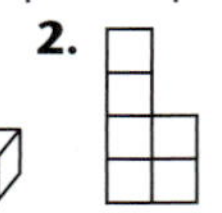

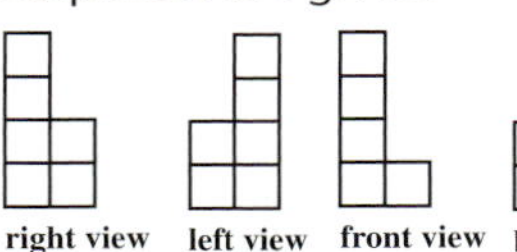

3. 8 cm^3; 30 cm^2

Section 3, Practice and Application (p. 559)

1. EAT, ETA, AET, ATE, TEA, TAE **3.** NOON, ONON, OONN, ONNO, NNOO, NONO **5.** DEEDED, DEEDDE, DEDEDE, DEDEED, DEDDEE, DEEEDD, DDEEED, DDEEDE, DDEDEE, DDDEEE, EDEDED, EDEDDE, EDEEDD, EDDEED, EDDEDE, EDDDEE, EEDDDE, EEDEDD, EEDDED, EEEDDD
9.

; 10 **11.** combination
13. a. apple-banana-kiwi-orange; apple-banana-kiwi-pear; apple-banana-orange-pear; apple-kiwi-orange-pear; banana-kiwi-orange-pear

b. 3 out of five: apple-banana-kiwi, apple-banana-orange, apple-banana-pear, apple-kiwi-orange, apple-kiwi-pear, apple-orange-pear, banana-kiwi-orange, banana-kiwi-pear, banana-orange-pear, kiwi-orange-pear; 2 out of five: apple-banana, apple-kiwi, apple-orange, apple-pear, banana-kiwi, banana-orange, banana-pear, kiwi-orange, kiwi-pear, orange-pear; 1 out of five: apple, banana, kiwi, orange, pear **15. a.** 28 **b.** 56 **c.** b, a; Order is important; Order is not important.

Spiral Review

17. 125 cm^3 **18.** 100 ft^3 **19.** $2\frac{1}{6}$ **20.** $4\frac{41}{60}$ **21.** $1\frac{9}{14}$ **22.** $17\frac{7}{20}$ **23.** 130°

Extra Skill Practice

1. ERR, RER, RRE **3.** DADDY, DADYD, DAYDD, DYDAD, DYDDA, DYADD, DDAYD, DDADY, DDYAD, DDYDA, DDDAY, DDDYA, ADDDY, ADYDD, ADDYD, AYDDD, YADDD, YDADD, YDDAD, YDDDA **5. a.** 6 **b.** 3 **c.** 1 **7.** combination **9.** Sue–Flora and Hiroko–Yuki, Sue–Hiroko and Flora–Yuki, Sue–Yuki and Flora–Hiroko

Standardized Testing, Free Response

1. permutation; Order is important. **2.** neither **3.** combination; Order is not important.

Section 4, Practice and Application (p.572)

7. about 3.7 in.^{3} **9.** 689,007.0 cm^3 **11.** Sample Response: $\frac{\text{volume of cone}}{\text{volume of cylinder}} = \frac{\text{volume of pyramid}}{\text{volume of prism}}$

Spiral Review

14. permutation **15.** combination

16. a. **b.** Sample Response: $(x + 2, y - 1)$

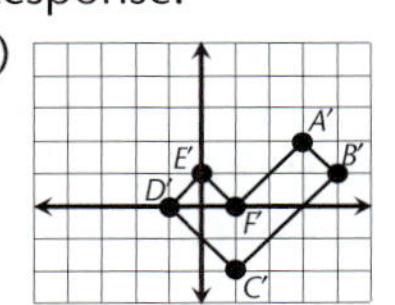

Extension

17. a. triangles, squares, hexagons **b.** Answers will vary.

Extra Skill Practice

5. B and D **7.** 1674.7 mm^3

Standardized Testing, Multiple Choice

1. D **2.** B

Review and Assessment

1. band–orchestra, orchestra–band **2.** Mono Lake–Joshua Tree–Sequoia, Mono Lake–Sequoia–Joshua Tree, Joshua Tree–Mono Lake–Sequoia, Joshua Tree–Sequoia–Mono Lake, Sequoia–Joshua Tree–Mono Lake, Sequoia–Mono Lake–Joshua Tree **3.** Spanish–art–social studies, Spanish–social studies–art, social studies–art–Spanish, social studies–Spanish–art, art–Spanish–social studies, art–social studies–Spanish **4.** beige-pink, beige-yellow, beige-green, pink-beige, pink-yellow, pink-green, yellow-beige, yellow-pink, yellow-green, green-beige, green-pink, green-yellow **5.** 120 **6.** 40,320 **7.** 720 **8.** 2450 **9.**

front view

right-side view

10. 10 cubic units **11.** 42 square units **12.** The volumes are the same; the surface area is less because fewer faces are exposed. **13.** 25 cm^3 **14.** 56 ft^3 **15.** 160 m^3 **16.** E-S, S-E **17.** N–N–E–E, E–E–N–N, N-E-N-E, E–N–E–N, N-E-E-N, E-N-N-E **18.** W–W–W–S, W-W-S-W, W–S–W–W, S-W-W-W **19.** BOOT, BOTO, BTOO, TBOO, TOBO, TOOB, OOTB, OOBT, OTBO, OBTO, OTOB, OBOT **20.** BELLE, BEELL, BELEL, BLLEE, BLELE, BLEEL, LLEBE, LLBEE, LLEEB, LEBEL, LEBLE, LELBE, LELEB, LEEBL, LEELB, LBLEE, LBEEL, LBELE, ELELB, ELEBL, ELBEL, ELLEB, ELLBE, ELBLE, EBELL, EBLEL, EBLLE, EELLB, EELBL, EEBLL **21.** NANNY, NANYN, NAYNN, NYANN, NYNAN, NYNNA, NNANY, NNAYN, NNYAN, NNYNA, NNNAY, NNNYA, ANNNY, AYNNN, ANYNN, ANNYN, YANNN, YNANN, YNNAN, YNNNA **22. a.** 10 groups **b.** 10 groups **c.** They are the same; To choose a group of 2 dogs from the 5 dogs, you can either choose the 2 that are in the group or you can choose the 2 that are not. So, the number of groups of 2 dogs is the same as the number of possible groups of 3 dogs. **d.** Combination; Order is not significant. **23.** Sample Response: Since the sum of the measures of the angles of a trapezoid is 360°, the angles will fill the space around a vertex without gaps or overlaps. **24.** 376.8 m^3 **25.** 4.5 cm^3 **26.** 706.5 in.^{3}

TOOLBOX ANSWERS

NUMBERS AND OPERATIONS

Adding and Subtracting Decimals

1. 21.2 **2.** 22.9 **3.** 14 **4.** 37.46 **5.** 5.4 **6.** 2.7 **7.** 3.25 **8.** 2.15 **9.** 4.12 **10.** 4.68 **11.** 3.9 **12.** 41.2 **13.** 8.87 **14.** 9.65 **15.** 24.55 **16.** 8.72 **17.** 25 **18.** 75.5 **19.** 66

Divisibility by 2, 5, and 10

1. 2 **2.** 2 **3.** 5 **4.** none **5.** 5 **6.** 2, 5, 10 **7.** 2 **8.** none **9.** 2, 5, 10 **10.** 5

Using Estimation

1–30. Answers may vary. Sample responses are given.
1. about 900 **2.** about 100 **3.** about 27 **4.** about 40 **5.** about 700 **6.** about 20 **7.** about 100 **8.** about 12,000 **9.** about 15 **10.** about 47,000 **11.** about 9,600 **12.** about 21,000 **13.** about \$19 **14.** about 900 **15.** about 130 **16.** about 8.4 **17.** about 20,000 **18.** about 300 **19.** about 16,000 **20.** about 1300 **21.** about 59 **22.** about 7000 **23.** about 1400 **24.** about 1250 **25.** about 70 **26.** about 20 **27.** about 10,000 **28.** about 30 **29.** about 420,000 **30.** about 20

Finding a Fraction

1. $\frac{7}{8}$ **2.** $\frac{3}{4}$ **3.** $\frac{3}{5}$ **4.** $\frac{4}{9}$ **5.** 2 **6.** 5 **7.** 4 **8.** 12 **9.** 12 **10.** 15 **11.** 14 **12.** 21 **13.** 35 **14.** 35 **15.** 75 **16.** 110

Finding Equivalent Fractions

1. 2 **2.** 24 **3.** 12 **4.** 4 **5.** 4 **6.** 5 **7.** 21 **8.** 48
9–16. Answers will vary. Sample responses are given.
9. $\frac{2}{6}, \frac{3}{9}, \frac{4}{12}$ **10.** $\frac{6}{8}, \frac{9}{12}, \frac{12}{16}$ **11.** $\frac{6}{30}, \frac{3}{15}, \frac{4}{20}$ **12.** $\frac{9}{27}, \frac{3}{9}, \frac{1}{3}$ **13.** $\frac{7}{28}, \frac{1}{4}, \frac{2}{8}$ **14.** $\frac{30}{75}, \frac{6}{15}, \frac{12}{30}$ **15.** $\frac{40}{48}, \frac{20}{24}, \frac{10}{12}$ **16.** $\frac{4}{7}, \frac{8}{14}, \frac{12}{21}$

Comparing Fractions

1. $<$ **2.** $<$ **3.** $<$ **4.** $=$ **5.** $>$ **6.** $<$ **7.** $<$ **8.** $=$ **9.** $>$ **10.** $=$ **11.** $=$ **12.** $<$

Adding and Subtracting Fractions

1. $\frac{7}{10}$ **2.** $\frac{3}{5}$ **3.** $\frac{6}{7}$ **4.** $\frac{4}{9}$ **5.** $\frac{4}{15}$ **6.** $\frac{4}{11}$ **7.** $\frac{9}{14}$ **8.** $\frac{9}{10}$ **9.** $\frac{11}{12}$ **10.** $6\frac{2}{3}$ **11.** $3\frac{5}{7}$ **12.** $3\frac{1}{5}$ **13.** $11\frac{7}{9}$ **14.** $15\frac{9}{10}$ **15.** $\frac{5}{12}$

Modeling Percent

1. 67% **2.** 83% **3.** 6% **4.** 11% **5.** 25% **6.** 72%

7.
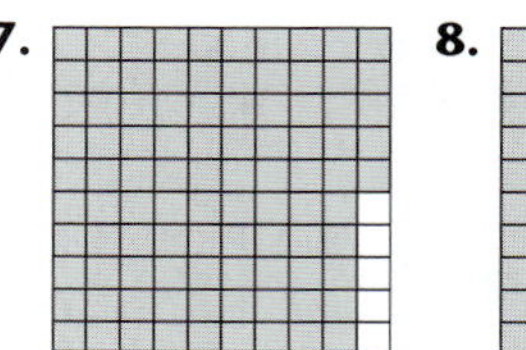
8.
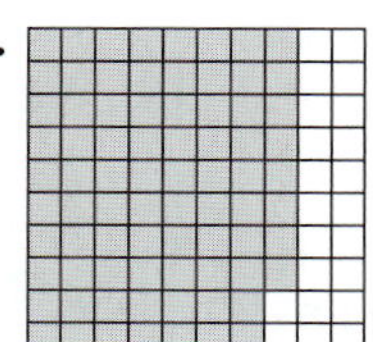
9.
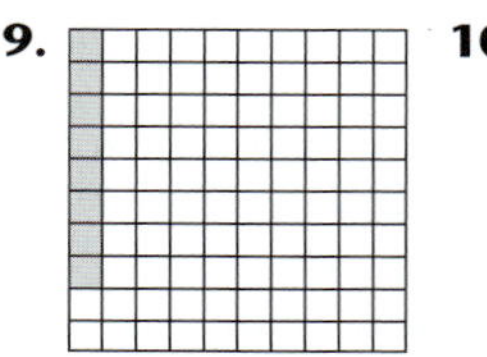
10.
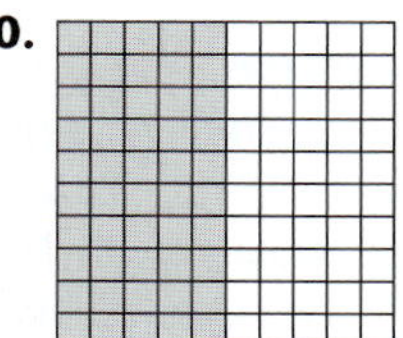
11.
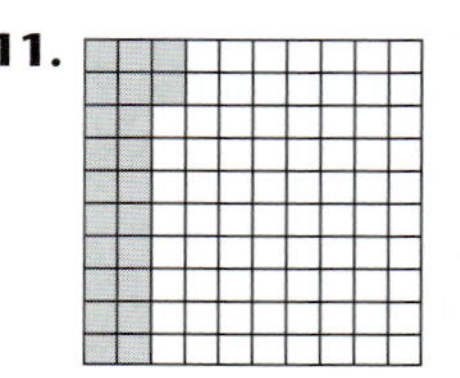
12.
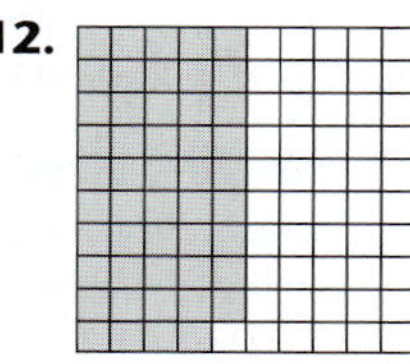
13.
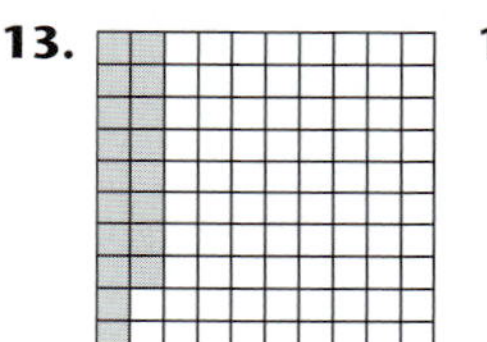
14.
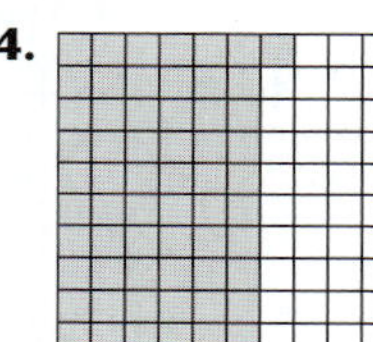

Modeling Integers

1. 3 **2.** –3 **3.** 0 **4.** –4 **5.** 0 **6.** 5 **7.** 2 **8.** –2 **9.** 1 **10.** 0 **11.** –3 **12.** 0 **13.** 2 **14.** 0 **15.** –5 **16.** –4 **17.** –2 **18.** –2 **19.** 2 **20.** –2 **21.** 0 **22.** 2 **23.** –8 **24.** –6 **25.** 5 **26.** 7 **27.** 3 **28.** 12 **29.** 3 **30.** –6 **31.** 3 **32.** 1 **33.** –1 **34.** 5 **35.** 0 **36.** –6

GEOMETRY AND MEASUREMENT

Perimeter and Using a Ruler

1. 32 m **2.** 72 in. **3.** 52 cm **4.** about $2\frac{7}{16}$ in. **5.** about $\frac{15}{16}$ in. **6.** about $2\frac{13}{16}$ in. **7.** about $3\frac{3}{16}$ in. **8.** about $3\frac{3}{4}$ in.

Converting Measurements

1. 252 **2.** $5\frac{3}{16}$ **3.** 150 **4.** 3 **5.** 10,560 **6.** $2\frac{5}{36}$ **7.** 48 **8.** 3 **9.** $10\frac{11}{16}$ **10.** 180 **11.** 8,000 **12.** 18 **13.** 13 **14.** $9\frac{1}{3}$ **15.** 17,600 **16.** 126 **17.** 16,060 **18.** 365 **19.** 46,145 **20.** 2; 3 **21.** 1; 720 **22.** 2; 3 **23.** 2; 500

24. 5; 5 **25.** 33; 1

Perimeter and Area of a Rectangle

1. $P = 26$ in.; $A = 40$ in.^{2} **2.** $P = 24$ ft; $A = 36$ ft^2
3. $P = 32$ yd; $A = 48$ yd^2 **4.** $P = 48$ ft; $A = 128$ ft^2
5. $P = 28$ in.; $A = 49$ in.^{2} **6.** $P = 26$ ft; $A = 36$ ft^2

DATA ANALYSIS AND DISPLAYS

Making a Bar Graph

1.

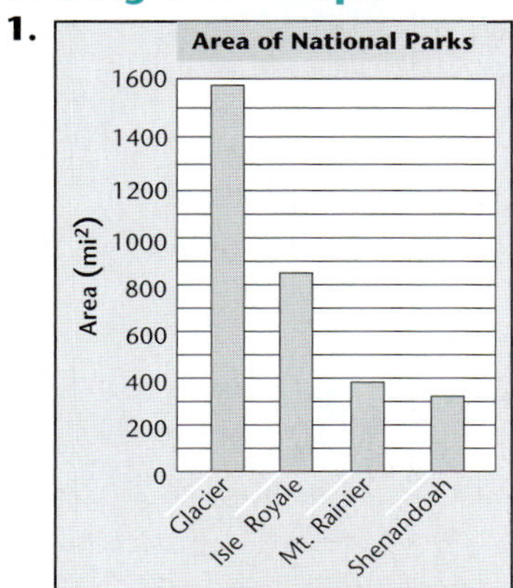

2.

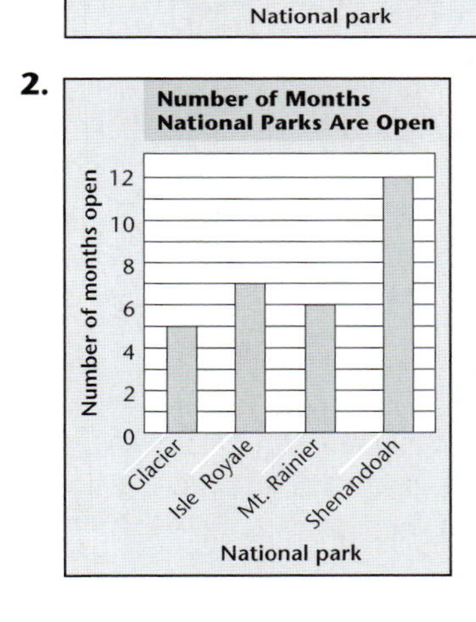

Making a Line Graph

1.

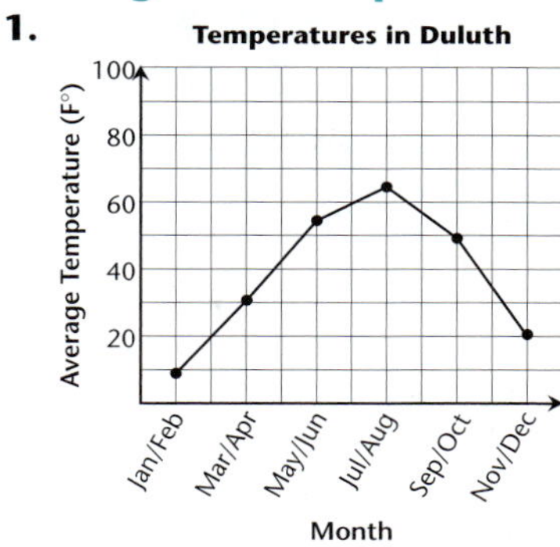

2.

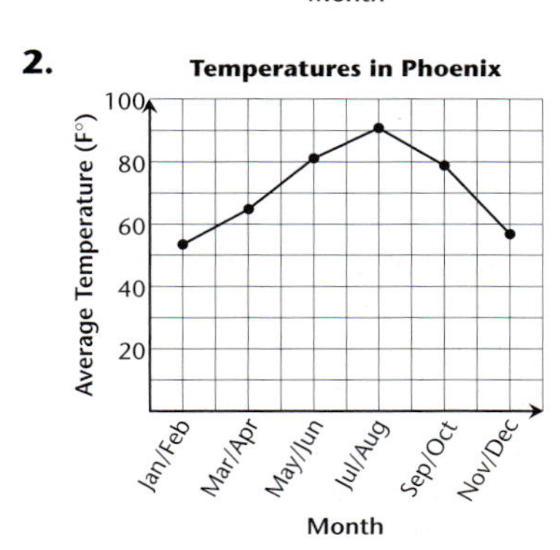

Finding the Mean

1. 7 **2.** 28 **3.** 122

TEST-TAKING SKILLS SELECTED ANSWERS

Building Test-Taking Skills (p. 604)

1. Sample Response: Width is not measured in square units. **3.** Sample Response: 60 is greater than every number in the data set, so it cannot be the mean.

Practicing Test-Taking Skills (p. 605)

1. D **3.** D **5.** C **7.** A

Building Test-Taking Skills (p. 607)

1. No credit; the answer is incorrect, nothing is explained and the incorrect operations were performed. **3.** Partial credit; the solution is correct, but the explanation is mixed up as to the order of the depths of the submarine.

Practicing Test-Taking Skills (p. 608)

1. 21 acts; $80 \div (2\frac{1}{2} + 1\frac{1}{4}) = 80 \div 3\frac{3}{4} = 80 \cdot \frac{4}{15} = \frac{64}{3} = 21\frac{1}{3}$ **3.** the girls' team; You need to find the fraction of games that each team won. For each team, divide the number of games won by the total number of games played. Girls' team: $6 \div (6 + 4) = \frac{6}{10} = \frac{3}{5}$. Boys' team: $7 \div (7 + 5) = \frac{7}{12}$; $\frac{3}{5} = \frac{3 \cdot 12}{5 \cdot 12} = \frac{36}{60}$, $\frac{7 \cdot 5}{12 \cdot 5} = \frac{35}{60}$, so $\frac{3}{5} > \frac{7}{12}$. **5.** 3 volunteers; $\frac{1}{3}$ of 18 volunteers, or 6, painted. That leaves $18 - 6 = 12$ volunteers. $\frac{3}{4}$ of 12 volunteers, or 9, raked leaves. That leaves $12 - 9 = 3$ volunteers who served lunch. **7.** Let c = the total cost. $c = 4x + 2.25$; 5 games; Substitute 22.25 for c. $22.25 = 4x + 2.25$, $22.25 - 2.25 = 4x$, $20 = 4x$, and $x = 5$. Hanna bowled 5 games. **9.** Yes; the sum of the lengths of the two shortest segments, 3.9 cm, is greater than the length of the longest segment, 3.5 cm.

Building Test-Taking Skills (p. 610)

1. B **3.** B

Practicing Test-Taking Skills (p. 611)

1. D **3.** B **5.** C **7.** D

Building Test-Taking Skills (p. 613)

1. Partial credit; the calculations for the number of cans that can be packed flat in the box are correct, but no reasoning is given. A second orientation was not considered. To earn full credit, explain the reasoning behind the calculations. Do the calculations for the number of cans that can be packed on their sides, which makes packing 54 cans or 56 cans possible.

Practicing Test-Taking Skills (p. 614)

1. the large tub of popcorn; volume of box $= 6 \cdot 3 \cdot 8 = 144$ in.^{3}; price per cubic inch of popcorn $= 3.75 \div 144 \approx$ \$.026; volume of tub $= \pi(4)^2(5) \approx 251$ in.^{3}; price per cubic inch of popcorn $= 5.25 \div 251 \approx$ \$.021; Since \$.021 < \$.026, the large tub of popcorn is the better buy. **3.** slippers; Find the percent of change for each item. T-shirts: $(15 - 8.5) \div 15 \approx 43\%$, sweatshirts: $(29 - 15) \div 29 \approx 48\%$, slippers: $(19.99 - 8.99) \div 19.99 \approx 55\%$, jeans: $(42.5 - 29.99) \div 42.5 \approx 29\%$, sweaters: $(49.95 - 24) \div 49.95 \approx 52\%$, sweatpants: $(21.5 - 12.5) \div 21.5 \approx 42\%$ **5.** 10 combinations; 6 orders; Sample Response: Number the students on the math team from 1 through 5 and make a list of the possible combinations of 3 students: 123, 124, 125, 134, 135, 145, 234, 235, 245, and 345; there are 3 choices for first, 2 choices for second, and 1 choice for third, so there are $3 \cdot 2 \cdot 1 = 6$ ways the students could finish.